Building a Foundation with Microsoft® Office 2013

ALEC FEHL
Asheville-Buncombe Technical Community College

JILL MURPHY
Custom Performance Solutions

RUSSEL STOLINS
Institute of American Indian Arts

ERIC A. WEINSTEIN
Suffolk County Community College

FLOYD JAY WINTERS & JULIE T. MANCHESTER
State College of Florida

Linebreak = shift enter

LABYRINTH
LEARNING™

Berkeley, CA

Building a Foundation with Microsoft Office 2013

Copyright © 2014 by Labyrinth Learning

Labyrinth Learning
2560 9th Street, Suite 320
Berkeley, California 94710
800.522.9746
On the web at lablearning.com

President:
Brian Favro

Product Development Manager:
Jason Favro

Managing Editor:
Laura Popelka

Production Editor:
Margaret Young

Production Manager:
Rad Proctor

eLearning Production Manager:
Arl S. Nadel

eLearning Development:
Judy Mardar and Andrew Vaughnley

Developmental Editors:
Trisha Conlon and Sandra Rittman

Indexing:
Joanne Sprott

Cover Design:
Mick Koller, SuperLab Design

Interior Design:
Mark Ong, Side-by-Side Studio

ITEM: 1-59136-486-8
ISBN-13: 978-1-59136-486-3

Manufactured in the United States of America.

10 9 8 7 6 5 4 3 2 1

Contents in Brief

Table of Contents

UNIT 3: MICROSOFT POWERPOINT

UNIT 4: MICROSOFT ACCESS

Quick Reference Tables

POWERPOINT

ACCESS

Preface

In today's digital world, knowing how to use the most popular suite of desktop software applications is critical. Our goal is to teach new users how to take advantage of this technology and to help experienced users understand how the applications have changed from previous versions. We begin with fundamental concepts and take learners through a systematic progression of exercises, resulting in skill mastery.

An online student resource center accompanies this book. It contains Concepts Review quizzes, student exercise files, and other learning tools. The URL for the student resource center is printed on the inside front cover of this textbook.

Supplemental Options

Video Tutorials: Our easy-to-follow instructional design is complemented with hundreds of videos that demonstrate the concepts and skills covered in this textbook. All videos can be accessed online with a single license key. Videos are an option for all learners. Keys can be purchased at http://lablearning.com/Store/Shop-Videos.

eLab Course Management System: eLab is a web-based learning systems that integrates seamlessly with this textbook. eLab is an option for students enrolled in instructor-led courses that have adopted eLab as part of their course curriculum.

Visual Conventions

This book uses visual and typographic cues to guide students through the lessons. Some of these cues are described below.

`Type this text`	Text you type at the keyboard is printed in this typeface.
Action words	The important action words in exercise steps are presented in boldface.
Ribbon	Glossary terms are presented in black text with a blue background.
⚠ TIP	Tips, notes, and warnings are called out with special icons.
Command→ Command→ Command→ Command	Commands to execute from the Ribbon are presented like this: Ribbon Tab→Command Group→Command→Subcommand.
FROM THE KEYBOARD Ctrl + S to save	These margin notes present shortcut keys for executing certain tasks.
FROM THE RIBBON File→Save	These margin notes show Ribbon paths for executing certain tasks.

Acknowledgements

This textbook has benefited greatly from the reviews and suggestions of the following instructors.

Anthony Adams, *Savannah Technical College*

Lori Allemand, *Pearl River Community College*

Richard Baugh Jr., *Jefferson Adult School*

Illaina Baylor-Johnson, *College of Lake County*

Marcia Bercot, *SkillSource*

Kim Bolden, *EHOVE Career Center*

Lawrence Bosek, *Macomb Community College*

Eric Bothur, *Midlands Technical College*

Odette Bradshaw-Sheeley, *Mid-Del Technology*

David Briggs, *Upper Valley Career Center*

Charlene Brooks, *PGCC*

Dawn Brown, *Habersham Central High School*

Marcus Brown, *EnVision Communication Concepts*

Pam Brunclik, *Osceola High School*

Melisa Bryant, *Forsyth Technical Community College*

Joy Bukowy, *Robeson Community College*

Dr. Pauline Camara, *Bristol Community College*

Ilda Casanova, *Alamo College and Palo Alto College*

Isabel Chan, *Langara College*

Laura Cinquini, *Napa Valley Adult Education*

Susan Clancy-Kelly, *College of Lake County*

Hyekyung Clark, *Central New Mexico Community College*

Dr. Frank T. Clements, Jr., *State College of Florida*

Stephanie Clymens, *Crook County Open Campus*

Lisa Cogley, *Rhodes State College*

Catherine Combs, *Tennessee Technology Center at Morristown*

Ioana Constantin, *Globe Education Network*

Rushia Cooper, *Lanier Technical College*

Lorie Costello, *Saint Paul College*

Becky Curtin, *William Rainey Harper College*

Roberta Czaplewski, *Riverland Community College*

Elaine Davis, *Carroll Community College*

Rhonda Davis, *Isothermal Community College*

Mike Deese, *University of New Mexico*

Candace Dejmal, *Decatur Community Jr./Sr. High School*

Anthony Dillon, *SC Department of Education*

Robert Doyle, *Doña Ana Community College*

Debbie Drake, *Southwest Applied Technology College*

Cindy Durkee, *Wahconah Regional High School*

Susan Fell-Johnson, *Alexandria Technical and Community College*

Jean Finley, *ABTCC*

Joseph Fischer, *JTF Training*

Suzette Fletcher, *Billings Adult Education*

Miriam Foronda, *University of New Mexico-Taos*

Brian Fox, *Santa Fe College*

Roger Fulk, *Wright State University – Lake Campus*

Marie Gabbard, *Volunteer State Community College and Nashville State Community College*

Alan Gandy, *Lone Star College, University Park*

Kay Gcrken, *College of DuPage*

Debby Godwin, *Lake Sumter Community College*

Bryna Gonzalez, *Norwalk Adult School*

Elizabeth Gonzales-Hughes, *Central New Mexico Community College*

Stephanie Gordon, *Washtenaw Community College*

Barbara Grane, *Orange Coast College*

Ara Greeny, *Visalia Adult School*

Betty Haar, *Kirkwood Community College*

Norma Hall, *Manor College*

Robyn Hart, *Fresno City College*

Amanda Hayman, *TCL*

Mary Jo Heiberger, *Visitation Catholic School*

Michael Held, *Portage Lakes Career Center*

Donna Hendricks, *South Arkansas Community College*

Laura Henige, *Macomb Community College*

Anita Herndon, *Tarrant County College*

Sandi Highfill, *High Plains Technology Center*

Taheshia Hobbs, *James Sprunt Community College*

Ira Hogan, Ivy Tech *Community College – Indianapolis*

Ron Houle, *Central Lakes College*

Lisa Hubbard, *Anoka Technical College*

Lisa Hunke, *Northeast Community College*

Laura Hunt, *Tulsa Community College*

Stephen Hustedde, *South Mountain Community College*

John Hutson, *Aims Community College*

Dale Jaedike, *Madison Area Technical College*

Christie Jahn Hovey, *Lincoln Land Community College*

Loretta Jarrell, *CATC Baton Rouge*

YIming Ji, *University of South Caroline Beaufort*

Guadalupe Jimenez, *Coachella Valley Adult School*

Kathy Johnson, *Glenn Hills High School*

Kerrie Johnson, *McHenry County Shah Center*

Marisa Johnson, *NCKTC*

Wendy Kauffman, *Sandhills Community College*

Vardeep Kaur, *Calmat*

Vickie Keitz, *Grayson College*

Donna Kilburn, *Tennessee Technology Center at Ripley – Bells Campus*

Jill Knight, *Plemons-Stinnett-Phillips CISD*

Ruby Kowaney, *West Los Angeles College*

Karon Kraft, *Moraine Park Technical College*

Cheryl Krider, *Wattsburg Area School District – Seneca High School*

Lisa Kropp, *Miami Dade College*

Ida Lambert, *North Tech High School*

Katharine Langille, *Red River College*

Gayle Larson, *Highline Community College and Green River Community College*

Sherry Lockman, *Kilgore High School, Kilgore Independent School District*

Teresa Loftis, *San Bernardino Adult School*

Sandi Lyman, *Rocky Mountain Business Academy*

Eileen Malin, *Nassau Boces*

Leslie Martin, *Gaston College*

John Martinez, *Clovis Adult Education*

Cheryl Martucci, *Diablo Valley College*

Alex Matthews, *Austin Community College*

Cindie Mayfield, *Ozark's Technical Community College*

Joe McCreery, *Elizabethtown Community and Technical College*

Donna McGill-Cameron, *Woodland Community College*

Joshua McMillan, *Muskogee High School*

Pam Meeks, *Northeast MS Community College*

Blanca Michaels, *Career College Consultants, Inc.*

Corena Miller, *Computer Services Plus Online*

Mary Miranda, *Clovis Adult Education*

Louis Mitchell, *Edgecombe Community College*

Susan Morrow, *AIB College of Business*

Janet Moulton, *Nova Scotia Community College*

Sheila Mullaney, *Lincoln Technical Institute*

Stephen Munsinger, *Wyoming State Penitentiary*

Michael Murphy, *Meriden Adult Education*

Diane Murray, *Highlands College of Montana Tech*

Christine Naylor, *Kent State University Ashtabula*

Kay Nelson, *The Lifelong Learning Center*

Linda Nestor, *Carroll Community College*

Cora Newcomb, *Technical College of the Lowcountry*

Jean Newman, *Charles A. Jones Career and Education Center*

Tami Norris, *Northwest State Community College*

Stephanie Novak, *Wisconsin Indianhead Technical College*

Sandy O'Neil, *Chase County Schools*

Monika Olsen, *Acalanes Adult Education*

Arleen Orland, *Santa Clarita Technology & Career Dev. Center*

Guillermo Ortiz-Caceres, *Bossier Parish Community College, Bossier City, LA*

Larry Overstreet, *College Of DuPage*

Morena Pacheco, *Riverside Adult School*

Christine Parrish, *Southwest Georgia Technical College*

Rex Parr, *Aims Community College*

Deloris Patterson, *Chattahoochee Technical College*

Betty Pearman, *Los Medanos College*

Rebecca Pein, *Western Technical College*

Mary Ester Perez, *Palo Alto College*

Joseph Perret, *LA Pierce College*

Felicia Peters, *Delta College*

Jason Peterson, *College of Redwoods*

Nancy Peterson, *Central Catholic High School*

Kari Phillips, *Davis Applied Technology College*

Gildga Pollard, *LAUSD-Harbor Occupational Center*

Jack Porter, *El Centro College*

Edna Prigmore, *Palomar College*

Marsha Ragen, *Southwestern Illinois College*

Tommie Redwine, *Clatsop Community College*

Brenda Rhodes-Martinez, *Northeastern Jr. College*

Sarah Rhoton, *Savannah Early College High School/Savannah Technical College*

Melinda Ricci, *Sandusky Career Center*

Patricia Richey, *Jacksonville College*

Carol Ricke, *Pratt Community College*

Sandra Roberts, *Snead State Community College*

Marsha Robison, *Simi Valley Adult School*

Valerie Romanczyk, *Macomb Community College*

Stephen Ross, *Mississippi Delta Community College*

David Rudnick, *Lane Community College*

Sonya Sample, *Greenville Technical College*

Joann Santillo, *Mahoning County Career and Technical Center*

Kellie Sartor, *Lee College*

Anita M. Schaffer, *Tacoma Community College*

Tina Schank, *EHOVE Career Center*

Don Schoesler, *North Idaho College*

Julie Sharrow, *Kent State University at Trumbull*

Susanne Silk, *Western Technology Center*

Sherri Silvian, *Macomb Community College*

Mary Sina, *Fox Valley Technical College*

Amy Sirott, *Pierce College*

Kathy Smith, *Kaskaskia College*

LaToya Smith, *Piedmont Community College*

Monica Smith, *Irwin County High School*

Randy Smith, *Monterey Peninsula College*

Sabrina Snider, *Forsyth Technical Community College*

Sheila Sokolinsky, *Isaac Bear Early College*

Debra Stafford-Gray, *Kansas City Kansas Community College, University of Phoenix, and Colorado Technical University*

Diane Stark, *Phoenix College*

Raymond Steinbart, *Maranatha Baptist Bible College*

Sheryl Stroud-Jones, *Savannah Technical College*

Cathy Struntz, *ATN*

Gary Sullivan, *Weatherford College*

Cynthia Sweeney, *J. M. Alexander Middle School*

Barbara Tietsort, *University of Cincinnati Blue Ash College*

Catherine Thomas, *J. Sargeant Reynolds Community College*

Pamela Toliver, *Soft-Spec*

Diana Tourney, *Delta-Montrose Tech College*

Tricia Troyer, *Waubonsee Community College*

Karen Ann Tuecke, *Tuecke Consulting*

Mona Valore, *Kingsborough Community College*

Garrett Wadkins, *Duval County Schools*

Jacqueline Wall, *Chaffey College*

Craig Watson, *Bristol Community College*

Miranda Watson, *Colorado Mountain College*

Laura Way, *Fortis Collge – Ravenna*

Sandra Webb, *Central Louisiana Technical Community College – Alexandria Campus*

Melinda White, *Seminole State College*

Amy Williams, *Abraham Baldwin Agricultural College*

Deborah Willwerth, *Crittenton Women's Union*

MaryLou Wilson, *Piedmont Technical College*

Leza Wood, *SUNY Adirondack*

Wanda Woods, *Jireh Mobile Computer Training*

Toni Wright, *OUSD*

Kevin Wyzkiewicz, *Delta College*

Peter Young, *San Jose State University*

Matt Zdybel, *Macomb County College*

Violet Zhang, *George Brown College*

Introducing Word Basics

LEARNING OBJECTIVES

After studying this lesson, you will be able to:

- Use the Word Start screen and window
- Work with the Ribbon and Quick Access toolbar
- Open, close, and navigate in documents
- Type a new document
- Use Word Help

Microsoft Word 2013 is a dynamic word-processing program that lets you easily create and modify a variety of documents. In this lesson, you will start Word, and then you'll work with the Word interface. You will open and navigate through a multipage document, and create and save a document. Finally, you will work with Word Help, and then exit Word.

Using My Virtual Campus

My Virtual Campus is a social networking technology company.
They sell their web application to colleges and universities,
allowing students, alumni, faculty, and staff to use this social networking website that is closed to the
public and branded for their institution. The marketing manager has asked you to create a brief summary
to describe their best-selling website and how it is used. This will provide you a good opportunity to see
just how easy Word 2013 is to use. And if you run into any problems along the way, you will appreciate
how much help is at your fingertips.

My Virtual Campus

Our best-selling website, a social networking Intranet established specifically for college communities worldwide, has been gaining popularity at an extraordinary rate.

The website is useful for all types of networking opportunities; for example, social events and career prospects can be publicized, prospective students can check out the campus, and professors and students can participate in extended training occasions and collaborate on special projects. It also proves useful when looking for a roommate or offering items for sale. Alumni can post job opportunities for current students and other noteworthy news, and so forth.

In general, here's how it works. You join and create a profile about yourself, choosing how much personal information to enter. Then, you can invite other people to join also. You can chat in real-time with other members, post photos to share, and most importantly, you control what information others can see about you.

Security is taken very seriously by My Virtual Campus and every step has been taken to ensure your privacy and protect your confidential information.

Presenting Word 2013

Video Library   http://labyrinthelab.com/videos   Video Number: WD13-V0101

Word provides tools to assist you in virtually every aspect of document creation. From desktop to web publishing, Word has the right tool. For these and many other reasons, Word is the most widely used word-processing program in homes and businesses.

Starting Word

The method you use to start Word and other Office 2013 applications depends on whether you are using the Windows 7 or Windows 8 operating system.

- **Windows 7:** Click Start 🪟, choose Microsoft Office from the All Programs menu, and then choose Microsoft Word 2013.
- **Windows 8:** Locate the Word 2013 tile on the Windows Start screen; click the tile to start Word.

Viewing the Word Start Screen

The Word Start screen is the first screen you see. It offers several ways to begin working. Don't be concerned if your Start screen is arranged differently from this example. You can rearrange the templates on the right, and the appearance also depends on your screen's resolution.

You can begin by working on a recent document or by opening another document you saved earlier.

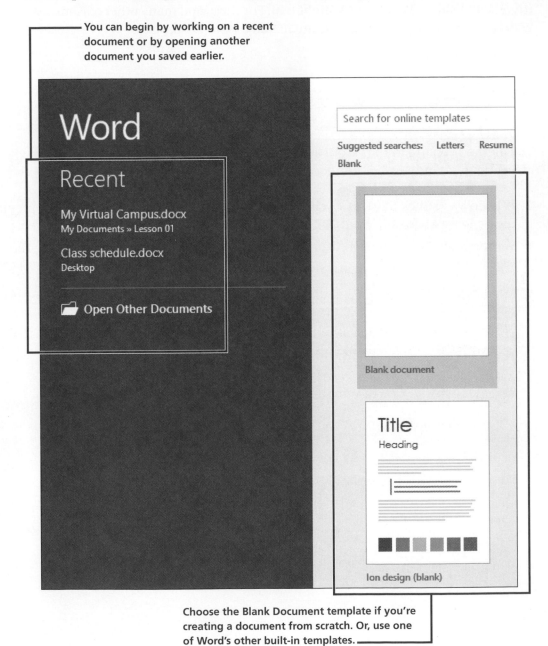

Choose the Blank Document template if you're creating a document from scratch. Or, use one of Word's other built-in templates.

DEVELOP YOUR SKILLS WD01-D01A

Start Word (Windows 8)

Windows 7 Users: Skip to the next exercise.

In this exercise, you will start the Word program.

1. If necessary, start your computer.
   The Windows Start screen appears.

2. Locate the **Word 2013 tile**.

3. Click the tile to start Word.
   The Word program loads and the Word Start screen appears.

4. Make sure the Word window is **maximized** 🗖.

5. Click the **Blank Document** template to open the Word window.

DEVELOP YOUR SKILLS WD01-D01B

Start Word (Windows 7)

Windows 8 Users: Skip this exercise.

In this exercise, you will start the Word program.

1. If necessary, start your computer.
   The Windows Desktop appears.

2. Click **Start** ⊞ at the left edge of the taskbar and choose **All Programs**.

3. Choose **Microsoft Office**, and then choose **Microsoft Word 2013** from the menu.
   The Word program loads and the Word Start screen appears.

4. Make sure the Word window is **maximized** 🗖.

5. Click the **Blank Document template** to open the Word window.

Viewing the Word 2013 Window

Video Library   http://labyrinthelab.com/videos   Video Number: WD13-V0102

The following illustration describes the main elements of the Word window. Don't be concerned if your document window looks somewhat different from this example. The Word screen is customizable.

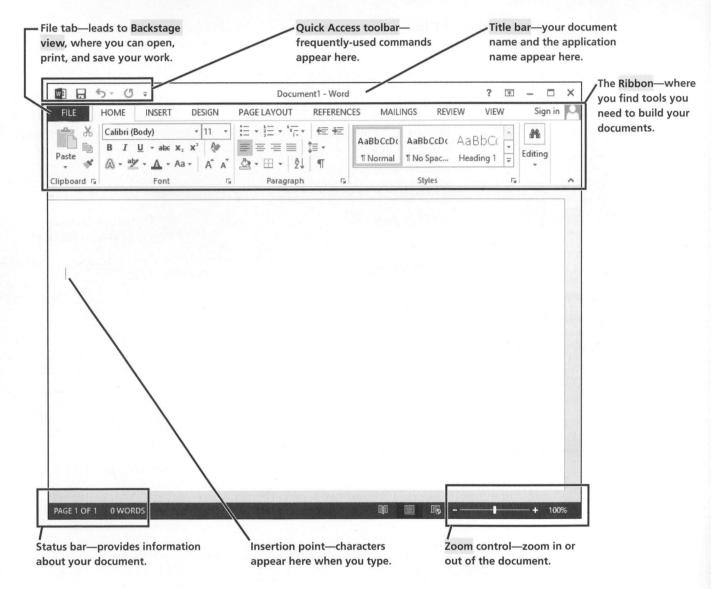

File tab—leads to **Backstage view**, where you can open, print, and save your work.

Quick Access toolbar—frequently-used commands appear here.

Title bar—your document name and the application name appear here.

The **Ribbon**—where you find tools you need to build your documents.

Status bar—provides information about your document.

Insertion point—characters appear here when you type.

Zoom control—zoom in or out of the document.

Opening Documents

Video Library   http://labyrinthelab.com/videos   Video Number: WD13-V0103

FROM THE RIBBON
File→Open

In Word and other Office 2013 applications, the Open screen is where you navigate to a storage place and open previously saved documents. Once a document is open, you can edit or print it.

FROM THE KEYBOARD
Ctrl+O to open a document

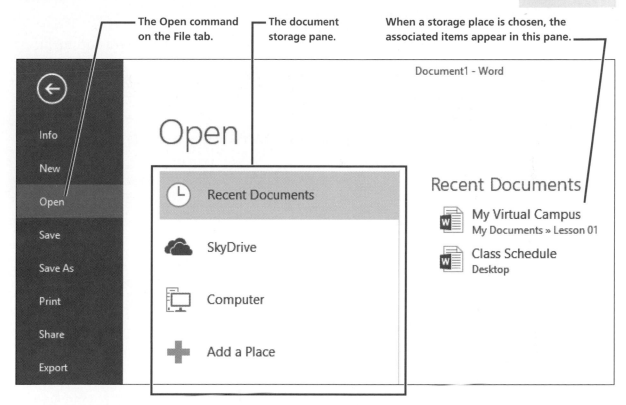

The Open command on the File tab. — The document storage pane. — When a storage place is chosen, the associated items appear in this pane.

Opening Older Word Documents

If you open a document created in a previous version of an Office 2013 application (2010 and earlier), it opens in Compatibility Mode. The term appears in the Title bar. Older documents do not understand the new features in Office 2013 applications, so those features are limited or disabled.

When an older document is open, a Convert command is available in Backstage view. Use it to upgrade the file and make the new features of Office 2013 applications available. The convert process overwrites the original file.

Open a Document

In this exercise, you will open an existing document through the Open screen in Backstage view.

Before You Begin: Navigate to the student resource center to download the student exercise files for this book.

1. Choose **File→Open** to display the Open screen in Backstage view.

2. Double-click the **Computer** icon.

3. When the Open dialog box appears, follow these steps to open a document:

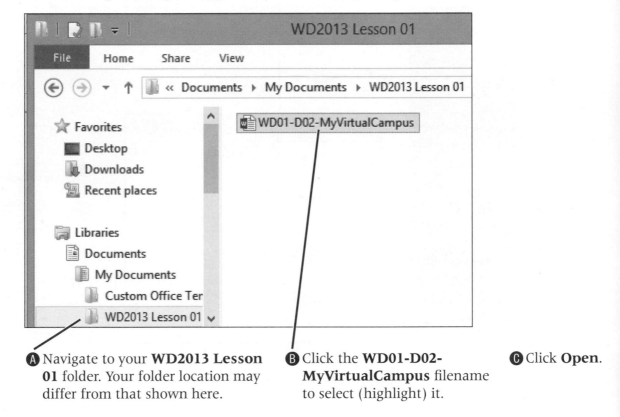

Ⓐ Navigate to your **WD2013 Lesson 01** folder. Your folder location may differ from that shown here.

Ⓑ Click the **WD01-D02-MyVirtualCampus** filename to select (highlight) it.

Ⓒ Click **Open**.

You can also double-click a filename to open the file.

4. Make sure the Word window is **maximized** ☐.

Working with the Word 2013 Interface

Video Library   http://labyrinthelab.com/videos   Video Number: WD13-V0104

The band running across the top of the screen is the Ribbon. This is where you find the tools for building, formatting, and editing your documents. It consists of three primary areas: tabs, groups, and commands. The tabs include Home, Insert, Design, and so on. A group houses related commands. Groups on the Home tab, for instance, include Clipboard, Font, and Paragraph.

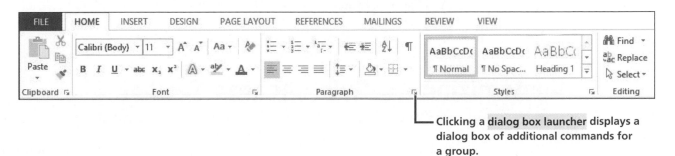

Clicking a **dialog box launcher** displays a dialog box of additional commands for a group.

The arrangement of buttons on the Ribbon can vary, depending on your screen resolution and how the Word window is sized.

Collapsing the Ribbon

If you want more room to work, you can collapse the Ribbon so only the tabs are visible. Clicking a tab expands the Ribbon temporarily, and then it collapses again when you work in the document.

FROM THE RIBBON

Right-click a
tab→Collapse the
Ribbon

Double-click the active
tab to display the
Ribbon again

FROM THE KEYBOARD

Ctrl + F1 to collapse/
display the Ribbon

DEVELOP YOUR SKILLS WD01-D03
Work with the Ribbon

In this exercise, you will explore various aspects of the Ribbon, including tabs, the dialog box launcher, and collapsing and expanding the Ribbon.

1. Click the **Insert** tab on the Ribbon to display the available commands.

2. Take a moment to investigate some other tabs; return to the **Home** tab.

3. Choose **Home→Font→dialog box launcher** 🗔 to open the Font dialog box.
   This dialog box provides additional tools for formatting text.

4. Click **Cancel** to close the dialog box.

Collapse and Expand the Ribbon

5. Follow these steps to collapse and expand the Ribbon:

Ⓐ Right-click a tab.　　Ⓑ Choose **Collapse the Ribbon**.　　　Ⓒ To display the Ribbon, right-click a tab and choose **Collapse the Ribbon** to turn the feature off.

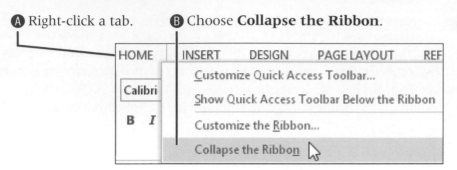

Customizing the Quick Access Toolbar

Video Library　http://labyrinthelab.com/videos　Video Number: WD13-V0105

The Quick Access toolbar in the upper-left corner of the Word window contains frequently used commands. You can add or remove buttons to suit your needs, and you can move the toolbar below the Ribbon if you like. If you're using a touch-mode screen, you can add a touch-mode button, which spaces buttons wider apart, making them easier to tap.

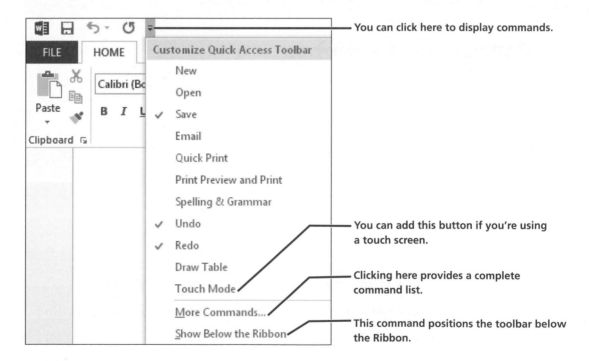

QUICK REFERENCE	WORKING WITH THE QUICK ACCESS TOOLBAR
Task	**Procedure**
Add a button	■ Click the Customize Quick Access toolbar button, and then choose a command or choose More Commands. Or, right-click a button on the Ribbon and choose Add to Quick Access Toolbar.
Remove a button	■ Right-click the button on the Quick Access toolbar you want to remove.
	■ Choose Remove from Quick Access Toolbar.
Change the toolbar location	■ Click the Customize Quick Access Toolbar button.
	■ Choose Show Below (or Above) the Ribbon.

DEVELOP YOUR SKILLS WD01-D04

Work with the Quick Access Toolbar

In this exercise, you will reposition the Quick Access toolbar, and then you will customize it by adding a button, and then you'll remove the button.

1. Follow these steps to move the Quick Access toolbar below the Ribbon:

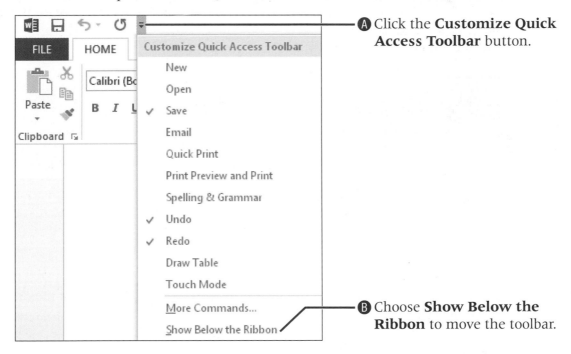

Ⓐ Click the **Customize Quick Access Toolbar** button.

Ⓑ Choose **Show Below the Ribbon** to move the toolbar.

The toolbar appears below the Ribbon. Now you will return it to its original position.

2. Click **Customize Quick Access Toolbar** again, and this time choose **Show Above the Ribbon**.

3. Make sure the **Home** tab is active.

4. Follow these steps to add the Bullets button to the toolbar:

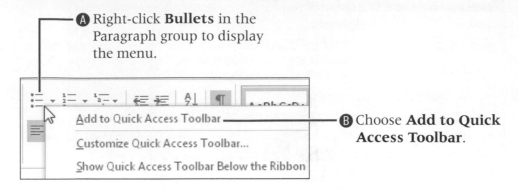

Ⓐ Right-click **Bullets** in the Paragraph group to display the menu.

Ⓑ Choose **Add to Quick Access Toolbar**.

5. Follow these steps to remove the Bullets button:

Ⓐ Right-click **Bullets** on the Quick Access toolbar.

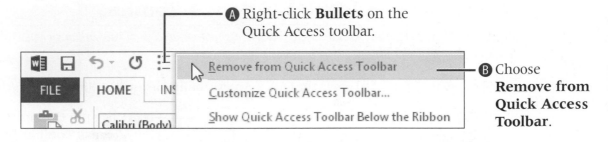

Ⓑ Choose **Remove from Quick Access Toolbar**.

Navigating in a Word Document

Video Library   http://labyrinthelab.com/videos   Video Number: WD13-V0106

If you are working in a multipage document, it is helpful to know about various techniques for moving through a document. You can navigate using the scroll bar located at the right side of the screen, or you can use keystrokes.

Navigating with the Scroll Bar

The scroll bar lets you browse through documents; however, it does not move the insertion point. After scrolling, you must click in the document where you want to reposition the insertion point.

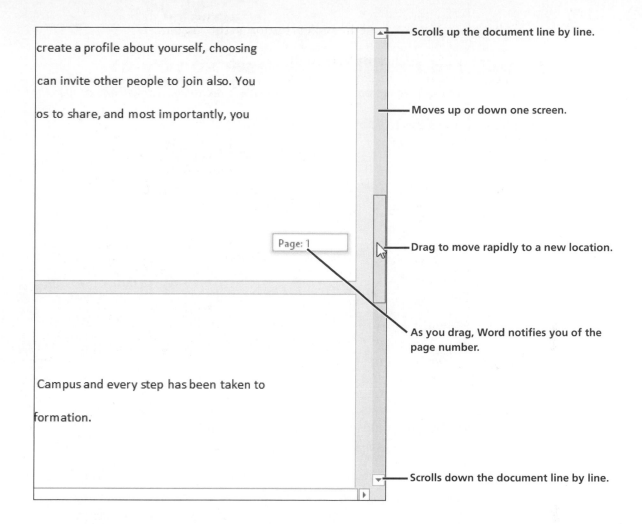

create a profile about yourself, choosing

can invite other people to join also. You

os to share, and most importantly, you

Page: 1

Campus and every step has been taken to

formation.

Scrolls up the document line by line.

Moves up or down one screen.

Drag to move rapidly to a new location.

As you drag, Word notifies you of the page number.

Scrolls down the document line by line.

Positioning the Insertion Point

When the mouse pointer is in a text area, it resembles an uppercase "I" and is referred to as an I-beam. The insertion point is positioned at the location where you click the I-beam and it begins flashing. Wherever the insertion point is flashing is where the action begins.

Scroll and Position the Insertion Point

In this exercise, you will use the scroll bar to move through a document. You will also position the insertion point.

1. Follow these steps to scroll in the document:

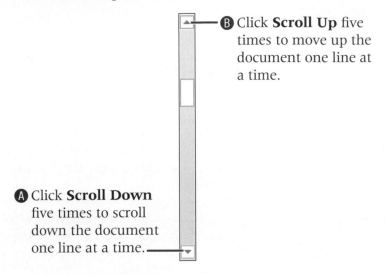

B Click **Scroll Up** five times to move up the document one line at a time.

A Click **Scroll Down** five times to scroll down the document one line at a time.

2. Place the **I-beam** I mouse pointer in the body of the document.

   Notice that the mouse pointer looks like an I-beam when it's inside the document.

3. Click the **I-beam** I anywhere in the document to position the blinking insertion point.

   The insertion point appears where you clicked. If the background is highlighted, you accidentally selected the text. Deselect by clicking the mouse pointer in the document background.

4. Move the mouse pointer into the left margin area.

   The white ⟲ selection arrow is now visible. You'll learn more about the selection arrow later in the course.

5. Follow these steps to use the scroll bar:

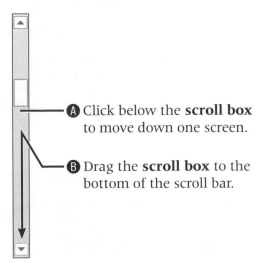

A Click below the **scroll box** to move down one screen.

B Drag the **scroll box** to the bottom of the scroll bar.

Notice that the insertion point is not blinking anywhere on the screen because all you have done is scroll through the document. You have not repositioned the insertion point yet.

6. Click the **scroll bar** above the scroll box, and then click the **I-beam** I at the end of the text to position the insertion point on the last page.

7. Drag the **scroll box** to the top of the scroll bar and click the **I-beam** I in front of the first word of the first paragraph.

Navigating with the Keyboard

Video Library   http://labyrinthelab.com/videos   Video Number: WD13-V0107

Whether you use the mouse or the keyboard to navigate through a document is up to you. Navigating with the keyboard always moves the insertion point, so it will be with you when you arrive at your destination. The following table provides keystrokes for moving quickly through a document.

KEYBOARD NAVIGATION			
Press	**To Move**	**Press**	**To Move**
→	One character to the right	Page Down	Down one screen
←	One character to the left	Page Up	Up one screen
Ctrl+→	One word to the right	Ctrl+End	To the end of the document
Ctrl+←	One word to the left	Ctrl+Home	To the beginning of the document
↓	Down one line	End	To the end of the line
↑	Up one line	Home	To the beginning of the line

DEVELOP YOUR SKILLS WD01-D06
Use the Keyboard to Navigate

In this exercise, you will use the keyboard to move through a document.

1. Click the **I-beam** I in the middle of the first line of the first paragraph.

2. Tap the right arrow → and left arrow ← three times each to move to the right and left, one character at a time.

3. Tap the down arrow ↓ and up arrow ↑ three times each to move down, and then up, one line at a time.

Use Additional Keys

4. Press Ctrl+Home to move the insertion point to the beginning of the document.

5. Use the arrow keys to position the insertion point in the middle of the first line of the first paragraph.

6. Press Ctrl+← three times to move to the left, one word at a time.

7. Press Ctrl+→ three times to move to the right, one word at a time.

8. Tap Home to move to the beginning of the line.

9. Tap End to move to the end of the line.

10. Spend a few moments navigating with the keyboard.

11. Press Ctrl + End to move the insertion point to the end of the document.

12. Move the insertion point back to the beginning of the document.

Closing Documents

Video Library http://labyrinthelab.com/videos Video Number: WD13-V0108

FROM THE RIBBON
File→Close

Word and other Office 2013 applications offer keyboard and Ribbon options for closing a document. If you haven't saved your document, Word will prompt you to do so.

FROM THE KEYBOARD
Ctrl + F4 to close

 You can also use Close ⊠ in the upper-right corner of the Word window to close a document.

DEVELOP YOUR SKILLS WD01-D07
Close the Document

In this exercise, you will close a file.

1. Choose **File→Close**.

2. If Word asks you if you want to save the changes, click **Don't Save**.

3. If a blank document is open on the screen, use the same technique to close it.

Starting a New Document

Video Library http://labyrinthelab.com/videos Video Number: WD13-V0109

FROM THE RIBBON
File→New

In Word and other Office 2013 applications, you can start a new document using a keyboard shortcut or the Ribbon. With the keyboard shortcut, the new document is based on the Blank Document template. Using the Ribbon command offers a choice of templates in Backstage view.

FROM THE KEYBOARD
Ctrl + N to open a new document

DEVELOP YOUR SKILLS WD01-D08
Start a New Document

In this exercise, you will open a new, blank document. There should not be any documents in the Word window at this time.

1. Press ⌈Ctrl⌉+⌈N⌉ to open a new document based on the Blank Document template.
   Now you will close the document and use the Ribbon command to start a new document.

2. Choose **File→Close**.

3. Choose **File→New**.
   Notice that when you use the File→New command, Word gives you choices other than the Blank Document template.

4. Click the **Blank Document template** to open a new document.

Typing and Editing in Word

Video Library   http://labyrinthelab.com/videos   Video Number: WD13-V0110

When you insert text in an existing document, you must position the insertion point before you begin typing. When you insert text in Word, existing text moves to the right as you type. When you type paragraphs, you should not tap ⌈Enter⌉ at the end of each line. Word will automatically wrap your text to the next line when you reach the right-hand margin. You use ⌈Enter⌉ when you want short lines to remain short, such as in an inside address.

Use ⌈Backspace⌉ and ⌈Delete⌉ to remove text. The ⌈Backspace⌉ key deletes characters to the left of the insertion point. The ⌈Delete⌉ key removes characters to the right of the insertion point.

Saving Your Work

It's important to save your documents! Power outages and accidents can result in lost data, so save frequently.

You can also use Save 💾 on the Quick Access toolbar.

FROM THE RIBBON
File→Save As
File→Save

FROM THE KEYBOARD
⌈Ctrl⌉+⌈S⌉ to save

Comparing Save and Save As

If the document was never saved, Word displays the Save As screen. If the document was previously saved, the Save command replaces the prior version with the edited one without displaying the Save As screen.

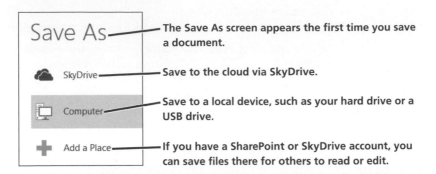

The Save As screen appears the first time you save a document.

Save to the cloud via SkyDrive.

Save to a local device, such as your hard drive or a USB drive.

If you have a SharePoint or SkyDrive account, you can save files there for others to read or edit.

Storing documents in SkyDrive is beyond the scope of this course. You will save your files on a local device.

After choosing a place in the Save As screen, the Save As dialog box opens where you will navigate to your storage location and name and save the file.

Word's DOCX File Format

Word 2003 and earlier versions saved documents in the *doc* file format. Word 2007 introduced the *docx* file format. Users of Word 2003 and prior versions may not be able to read Word files in the *docx* format. However, you can choose to save your document in the older *doc* format to maintain backward compatibility. Also, when you open a document created in earlier Word versions, the title bar displays *Compatibility Mode* next to the title. This means certain Word 2013 features not compatible with older versions are turned off while working in the document.

DEVELOP YOUR SKILLS WD01-D09
Create and Save a Document

In this exercise, you will begin by saving your document (in this case a blank document). This technique is used throughout this course so you can start each exercise with a fresh file.

1. Click **Save** 🖫 on the Quick Access toolbar.

   Since this is the first time you are saving this document, Word displays the Save As screen in Backstage view. Once you have saved the file, this button saves the current version of the file over the old version without displaying the Save As screen.

2. Double-click the **Computer** 🖵 icon to open the Save As dialog box.

3. Follow these steps to save your document:

Keep in mind that your dialog box may contain different files and folders than shown here.

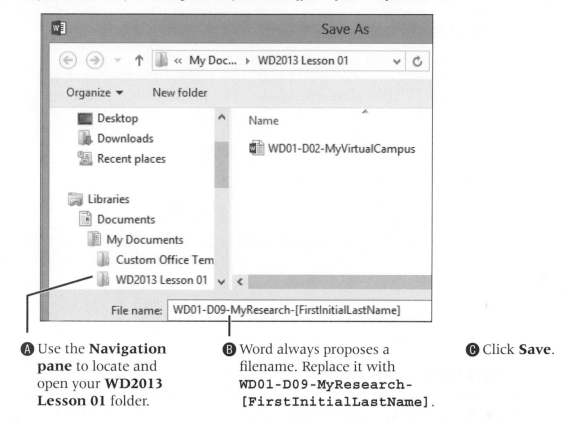

Ⓐ Use the **Navigation pane** to locate and open your **WD2013 Lesson 01** folder.

Ⓑ Word always proposes a filename. Replace it with `WD01-D09-MyResearch-[FirstInitialLastName]`.

Ⓒ Click **Save**.

In step B, replace the bracketed text with your first initial and last name. For example, if your name is Bethany Smith, your filename would look like this: WD01-D09-MyResearch-BSmith.

4. Type the following text and let Word Wrap do its thing.

If you make a typo, use Backspace *or* Delete *to remove it. Remember to position the insertion point next to the typo.*

In general, here's how it works. You join and create a profile about yourself, choosing how much personal information to enter. Then you can invite other people to join also. You can chat in real-time with other members, post photos to share, and most importantly, you control what information others can see about you.

5. Save the file and leave it open.

Getting Help in Word 2013

Video Library   http://labyrinthelab.com/videos   Video Number: WD13-V0111

The Microsoft Word Help button appears in the upper-right corner of the Word screen and other Office 2013 application screens. The Help window contains a search box, a list of popular searches, Getting Started aids, and online training options.

FROM THE KEYBOARD
F1 to open Help

DEVELOP YOUR SKILLS WD01-D10
Use Word Help

In this exercise, you will work with several Help techniques.

1. Click **Help** ? in the upper-right corner of the Word window.

2. Follow these steps for an overview of Word Help:

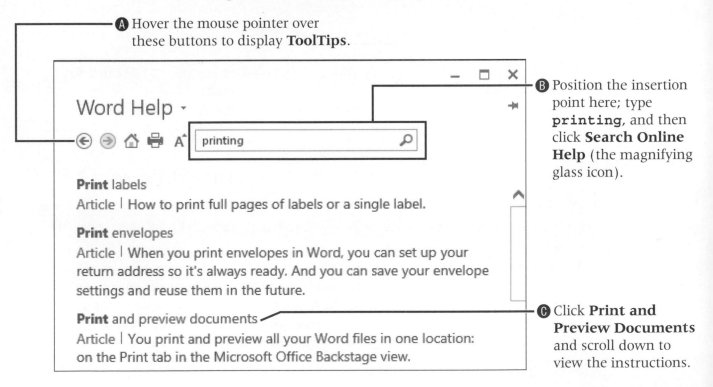

Ⓐ Hover the mouse pointer over these buttons to display **ToolTips**.

Ⓑ Position the insertion point here; type **printing**, and then click **Search Online Help** (the magnifying glass icon).

Ⓒ Click **Print and Preview Documents** and scroll down to view the instructions.

3. Take a few moments to experiment with Help. Try searching for **save** and **compatibility mode**. Feel free to explore any topics that interest you.

4. Click **Close** ✕ in the upper-right corner of the Help window.

Exiting from Word

Video Library   http://labyrinthelab.com/videos   Video Number: WD13-V0112

You exit Word and other Office 2013 applications by clicking the Close button in the upper-right corner of the window. If you have more than one document open, you need to close each document. It's important to exit your application in an orderly fashion. Turning off your computer before exiting could cause you to lose data.

DEVELOP YOUR SKILLS WD01-D11

Exit from Word

In this exercise, you will exit from Word. Since you haven't made any changes to your document, you won't bother saving it again.

1. Click **Close** |×| in the upper-right corner of the Word window.

2. If you are prompted to save your changes, click **Don't Save**.

3. If you have more than one document open, close any remaining documents without saving.
   Word closes and the Windows Desktop appears.

Concepts Review

To check your knowledge of the key concepts introduced in this lesson, complete the Concepts Review quiz by choosing the appropriate access option below.

If you are...	Then access the quiz by...
Using the Labyrinth Video Library	Going to http://labyrinthelab.com/videos
Using eLab	Logging in, choosing Content, and navigating to the Concepts Review quiz for this lesson
Not using the Labyrinth Video Library or eLab	Going to the student resource center for this book

Reinforce Your Skills

Work with the Word Interface

In this exercise, you will start Word and examine the Start screen and Word window. You will use correct terminology for the Word window, and you will collapse and expand the Ribbon. Finally, you will customize the Quick Access toolbar.

Start Word and Examine the Word Start Screen

1. Start **Word** and note how the Start screen helps you begin your work.

2. Open **WD01-R01-Worksheet** from your **WD2013 Lesson 01** folder and save it as
   `WD01-R01-Worksheet-[FirstInitialLastName]`.

3. Refer to your worksheet and list three ways the Start screen helps you begin your work.

Word Terminology

It's important to use the correct terms when talking about Word. If you need to discuss an issue with your IT department, the staff can help you more efficiently if they are clear on what you are referring to.

4. In your worksheet, enter the correct terms for items A–F in the following illustration.

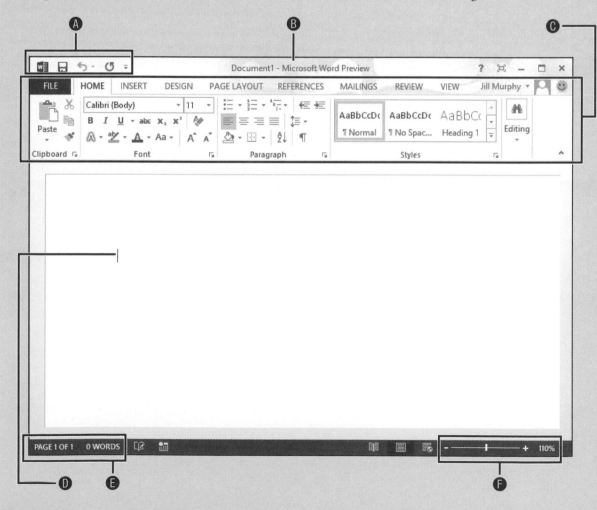

Open a Document

5. Refer to your worksheet and enter the phrase that appears in **Word's title bar** when you open a file that was created in an earlier version of Word.

6. Navigate to your **WD2013 Lesson 01** folder and open **WD01-R01-FarmersMarket**.

7. Refer to your worksheet and enter the name of the group that organized the field trip to the farmers' market.

Collapse the Ribbon

8. Collapse the **Ribbon**.

9. In your worksheet, list the steps you took to complete step 8.

10. Expand the **Ribbon**.

The Quick Access Toolbar

11. Move the **Quick Access toolbar** below the Ribbon.

12. In your worksheet, list the steps you took to complete step 11.

13. Choose **Page Layout→Page Setup** and add **Margins** ⊞ to the Quick Access toolbar.

14. In your worksheet, list the steps you took to complete step 13.

15. Move the **Quick Access** toolbar back above the Ribbon.

16. Remove **Margins** ⊞ from the toolbar.

17. Save your worksheet, close all files, and exit from **Word**. Submit your final file based on the guidelines provided by your instructor.

    To view examples of how your file or files should look at the end of this exercise, go to the student resource center.

Navigate in Word, Type a Document, and Use Help

In this exercise, you will use mouse and keyboard techniques to navigate in a multipage document. Then you will close the document, open and type in a new document, and then save your work. Finally, you will use Word's Help feature, and then exit from Word.

Navigate with the Scroll Bar and Keyboard

1. Start **Word**. Open **WD01-R02-Worksheet** from your **WD2013 Lesson 01** folder and save it as **WD01-R02-Worksheet-[FirstInitialLastName]**.

2. Open **WD01-R02-KidsNewsletter** from your **WD2013 Lesson 01** folder.

3. Follow these steps to scroll in the document:

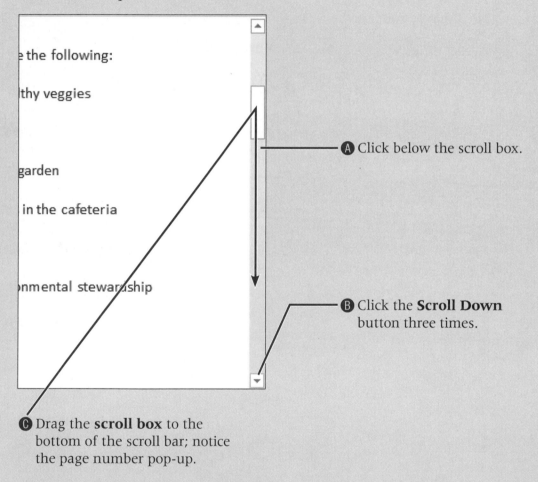

e the following:

lthy veggies

garden

in the cafeteria

onmental stewardship

Ⓐ Click below the scroll box.

Ⓑ Click the **Scroll Down** button three times.

Ⓒ Drag the **scroll box** to the bottom of the scroll bar; notice the page number pop-up.

4. Hover the mouse pointer over the body of the document and notice the pointer shape, and then hover the mouse pointer in the left margin and notice its shape.

5. Press [Ctrl]+[Home] and notice the position of the insertion point.

6. Position the insertion point in the middle of the first line of the first paragraph and press [Ctrl]+[→] three times.

7. Tap [Home] and notice the position of the insertion point.

8. Press [Ctrl]+[End] and notice the position of the insertion point.

9. Refer to your worksheet and answer the questions for steps 4–8.

Close the Document and Start a New Document

10. Choose **File→Close** to close **WD01-R02-KidsNewsletter**. If you are prompted to save changes, click **Don't Save**.

11. Choose **File→New** and open a new document using the **Blank Document template**.

12. Choose **File→Close** to close the new document, and then press [Ctrl]+[N] to start a new document.

    The new document is based on the Blank Document template.

13. Type the following text using [Backspace] or [Delete] to correct typos.

    `The Kids for Change "Think Globally, Act Locally" program is designed to help young people develop their understanding of an increasingly interrelated world. We have an exciting guest speaker for our next monthly meeting.`

14. Refer to your worksheet and answer the questions for steps 11–13.

Save Your Document

15. Choose **File→Save As** from the Ribbon and navigate to your **WD2013 Lesson 01** folder.

16. Save your document as `WD01-R02-GuestSpeaker-[FirstInitialLastName]`.

> The Kids for Change "Think Globally, Act Locally" program is designed to help young people develop their understanding of an increasingly interrelated world. We have an exciting guest speaker for our next monthly meeting.

17. Choose File→Close to close the document.

18. Refer to your worksheet and answer the question for step 16.

19. Choose **File→Open**, navigate to your **WD2013 Lesson 01** folder, and open **WD01-R02-FarmVisitLtr**.

    This document was created in Word 2003, which means it is a doc file rather than a Word 2013 docx file. Notice the phrase to the right of the file name in the title bar.

Explore Help and Exit from Word

20. Click **Help** ? in the upper-right corner of the Word window.

21. Use the **Search Box** to search for `Undo`, and then click the **Undo, Redo, or Repeat an Action** link.

    Make a note of the shortcut keystrokes for Undo.

22. Use the Help **Search Box** to search for `Clipboard` and click the **Use the Office Clipboard** link. Read the first paragraph of the Help text, and make a note of what is stored in the Clipboard.

23. **Close** × the **Help** window. Then, choose **File→Close** to close **WD01-R02-FarmVisitLtr.**

24. Refer to your worksheet and answer the questions for steps 20–22.

25. Save your worksheet, and exit from **Word**. Submit your final files based on the guidelines provided by your instructor.

    To view examples of how your file or files should look at the end of this exercise, go to the student resource center.

REINFORCE YOUR SKILLS WD01-R03

Use the Word Interface and Work with Documents

In this exercise, you will work with the Word interface, open and navigate in an existing document, and create and save a new document. Finally, you will work with Word Help, and then exit from Word.

Start Word and Examine the Word Start Screen

1. Start **Word**. Open **WD01-R03-Worksheet** from your **WD2013 Lesson 01** folder and save it as `WD01-R03-Worksheet-[FirstInitialLastName]`.

2. Refer to your worksheet and answer the step 2 question.

Word Window Terminology

3. Refer to your worksheet and answer the step 3 questions.

Open a Document and Collapse the Ribbon

4. Choose **File→Open** from the Ribbon and open **WD01-R03-OrgsPrtctEarth.**

5. Refer to your worksheet and answer the step 5 question.

The Quick Access Toolbar

6. In your worksheet, list the steps for removing a button from the Quick Access toolbar.

Navigate with the Scroll Bar and Keyboard

7. Refer to your worksheet and answer the step 7 questions.

Close a Document and Start a New Document

8. Choose **File→Close** to close WD01-R03-OrgsPrtctEarth.

9. Choose **File→New** and start a new document using the **Blank Document template**.

10. Type the following text:

    ```
    Organizations that are founded to protect our earth work in
    concert with nature through activities such as planting and
    caring for trees, protecting groundwater, and restoring wetlands.
    They work at the local, state, national, and international levels
    to improve policy for short- and long-term solutions. Their goal
    is to achieve a healthy planet. Kids for Change helps to connect
    kids to organizations such as these.
    ```

11. Refer to your worksheet and answer the step 11 questions.

Save Your Document in the Word DOCX File Format

12. Choose **File→Save**, navigate to your **WD2013 Lesson 01** folder, and save your document as `WD01-R03-HealthyPlanet-[FirstInitialLastName]`.

13. Refer to your worksheet and answer the step 13 question.

Get Help and Exit from Word

14. Click **Help** ? in the upper-right corner of the Word window.

15. Refer to step 15 in your worksheet, and use **ToolTips** to identify the buttons in the upper-left corner of the Help window.

16. **Close** × the **Help** window.

17. Click **Close** × in the upper-right corner of the Word window to close the document. Close any other open documents.

18. Save your worksheet, and exit from **Word**. Submit your final files based on the guidelines provided by your instructor.

Apply Your Skills

Open a Document and Work with the Word Interface

In this exercise, you will open a document and scroll through it to determine its length. You will examine the Ribbon in some detail, modify the Quick Access toolbar, and collapse the Ribbon. Finally you will return the Ribbon and the Quick Access toolbar to their default states.

Start Word and Open a Document

1. Start **Word**. Click the **Open Other Documents** link on the left side of the Word Start screen below the Recent list.

2. Navigate to your **WD213 Lesson 01** folder, open **WD01-A01-Worksheet**, and save it as `WD01-A01-Worksheet-[FirstInitialLastName]`.

3. Open **WD01-A01-CorpEvents** from your **WD2013 Lesson 01** folder.

4. Refer to your worksheet and answer the question for step 4.

Work with the Word 2013 Interface

5. Refer to your worksheet, and respond to step 5.

6. Choose **Insert→Illustrations** and add the **SmartArt** button to the **Quick Access** toolbar.

7. Position the **Quick Access toolbar** below the Ribbon; then collapse the **Ribbon**.

8. Tap Prt Screen on your keyboard to capture a picture of your screen.

9. Start a blank document and paste the screen capture into the document.

10. Save the file as `WD01-A01-ScreenShot-[FirstInitialLastName]` in your **WD2013 Lesson 01** folder.

11. Remove the **SmartArt** button from the **Quick Access** toolbar, expand the **Ribbon**, and move the **Quick Access** toolbar above the Ribbon.

12. Choose File→Close to close **WD01-A01-CorpEvents** and **WD01-A01-ScreenShot-[FirstInitialLastName]**.

13. Save your worksheet, and exit from **Word**. Submit your final files based on the guidelines provided by your instructor.

    To view examples of how your file or files should look at the end of this exercise, go to the student resource center.

APPLY YOUR SKILLS WD01-A02

Navigate in Word, Create a Document, and Use Help

In this exercise, you will open a document and scroll through it, and then you will create and save a document. Finally, you will use Help to learn about saving a Word file as a PDF file.

Navigate in Word

1. Start **Word**. Open **WD01-A02-Worksheet** from your **WD2013 Lesson 01** folder and save it as `WD01-A02-Worksheet-[FirstInitialLastName]`.

2. Open **WD01-A02-UniversalEvents** from your **WD2013 Lesson 01** folder.

3. Scroll to the bottom of the document, click the **scroll box**, and then, referring to your worksheet, respond to the question for step 3.

4. Choose File→Close to close **WD01-A02-UniversalEvents** and start a new blank document based on the **Blank Document template**.

Type and Save a New Document

5. Type the following:

    `Universal Corporate Events will manage every phase of your corporate travel needs. We work directly with travelers to provide the flights that meet their needs, and we arrange ground transportation to and from all events. We have staff available 24x7 to assist travelers if any unforeseen situations arise.`

6. Save the file as `WD01-A02-Travel-[FirstInitialLastName]` in your **WD2013 Lesson 01** folder, and then close it.

Use Help

7. Open **Help** [?], search for **Save**, and click the **Save as PDF** link.

8. Press [Alt] + [Prt Screen] to capture a picture of the Help screen.

9. Paste the screenshot in your worksheet where indicated, and save the worksheet.

10. Close **Help**, close any open documents, and then exit from **Word**.

11. Submit your final files based on the guidelines provided by your instructor.

    To view examples of how your file or files should look at the end of this exercise, go to the student resource center.

Use the Ribbon and Use Help to Research Word Features

In this exercise, you will use the dialog box launcher on the Ribbon to open dialog boxes, and you will research terms in Word Help. Finally, you will type a document showing the results of your research.

Start a New Document and Use a Dialog Box Launcher

1. Start **Word**. Start a new document based on the **Blank Document template**.

2. Choose **Home→Paragraph→dialog box launcher**.

3. Click the **Line and Page Breaks** tab and notice the term Widow/Orphan Control under the Pagination heading; close the dialog box.

4. Type **HELP RESEARCH** at the top of your document and tap ⏎Enter⏎.

Use Help

5. Open **Help** and search for **Widow/Orphan Control**.

6. Click the **Add a Page Break** link.

7. Scroll down and note what the **Widow/Orphan Control** feature accomplishes.

8. Minimize the **Help** window, and type a description of **Widow/Orphan Control** in your document.

   Minimize and restore the Help window as needed.

9. Click the **dialog box launcher** in the Font group, notice the term **Superscript** in the Effects section, and then close the dialog box.

10. Search for **Superscript** in Help and click the **"Superscript" is under "Home/Font"** link. Note the description of Superscript.

11. Type a description of superscript in your document, and then search in Help for **Save**.

12. Click the **Save Documents Online** link, and type a short description of how you save a document to the SkyDrive.

13. Save your file as **WD01-A03-HelpResearch-[FirstInitialLastName]** in the **WD2013 Lesson 01** folder.

14. Submit your final file based on the guidelines provided by your instructor.

Extend Your Skills

In the course of working through the Extend Your Skills exercises, you will think critically as you use the skills taught in the lesson to complete the assigned projects. To evaluate your mastery and completion of the exercises, your instructor may use a rubric, with which more points are allotted according to performance characteristics. (The more you do, the more you earn!) Ask your instructor how your work will be evaluated.

WD01-E01 That's the Way I See It

As an IT professional, you realize that many people need help adapting to Office 2013. You decide to start your own consulting business to fill this need. Your first client would like assistance with customizing the Quick Access toolbar in order to work more effectively. So, you will create a handout in Word that lists the steps for customizing the Quick Access toolbar.

Because your client uses a laptop, she would like to learn to collapse the Ribbon to free up space on the screen. Include instructions for collapsing the Ribbon in your handout. Finally, the client is interested in learning more about saving files "in the cloud." In the handout, include instructions for how to search Help for information on saving files in SkyDrive.

Save your handout as **WD01-E01-WordHandout-[FirstInitialLastName]** in your **WD2013 Lesson 01** folder. You will be evaluated based on the inclusion of all elements specified, your ability to follow directions, your ability to apply newly learned skills to a real-world situation, your creativity, and the relevance of your topic and/or data choice(s). Submit your final file based on the guidelines provided by your instructor.

WD01-E02 Be Your Own Boss

You are the owner of Blue Jean Landscaping and are also a bit of a "techie." You have decided to upgrade the company from Word 2010 to Word 2013. You want to provide online tutorials and reference materials to aid employees in the conversion. Start Word and use Help or online resources to locate three aids for this purpose (for example, opening older Word documents in Word 2013, Touch Mode, or how the Ribbon look has changed). Create a document named **WD01-E02-WordResources-[FirstInitialLastName]** and save it in the **WD2013 Lesson 01** folder. In the document, include the resource information and explain how each will help the employees (write three to five sentences per topic). Don't list resources without including an explanation.

You will be evaluated based on the inclusion of all elements specified, your ability to follow directions, your ability to apply newly learned skills to a real-world situation, your creativity, and your demonstration of an entrepreneurial spirit. Submit your final file based on the guidelines provided by your instructor.

Transfer Your Skills

In the course of working through the Transfer Your Skills exercises, you will use critical-thinking and creativity skills to complete the assigned projects using skills taught in the lesson. To evaluate your mastery and completion of the exercises, your instructor may use a rubric, with which more points are allotted according to performance characteristics. (The more you do, the more you earn!) Ask your instructor how your work will be evaluated.

WD01-T01 Use the Web as a Learning Tool

Throughout this book, you will be provided with an opportunity to use the Internet as a learning tool by completing WebQuests. According to the original creators of WebQuests, as described on their website (WebQuest.org), a WebQuest is "an inquiry-oriented activity in which most or all of the information used by learners is drawn from the web." To complete the WebQuest projects in this book, navigate to the student resource center and choose the WebQuest for the lesson on which you are currently working. The subject of each WebQuest will be relevant to the material found in the lesson.

WebQuest Subject: How Microsoft Word is used in business.

Submit your final file(s) based on the guidelines provided by your instructor.

WD01-T02 Demonstrate Proficiency

As the owner of Stormy BBQ, you have decided to customize the Word interface to help you work more effectively. In particular, you want to add buttons to the Quick Access toolbar that will help you in creating a brochure advertising your fresh, locally-grown vegetables and local, farm-raised pork and beef ribs.

Start Word and open a new, blank document. Examine the buttons on the Ribbon to determine which will be most useful for you. You may wish to use ToolTips or Help to determine the purpose of some of the buttons. Add five buttons to the Quick Access toolbar, and then list specific reasons for choosing each. Indicate if you prefer to have the Quick Access toolbar above or below the Ribbon and state the reason for your preference. Take a screen shot of your customized toolbar and paste it into your Word document. Reset the Quick Access toolbar to its default state when you are finished.

Save your file as **WD01-T02-CustomizeWord-[FirstInitialLastName]** in your **WD2013 Lesson 01** folder. Submit your final file based on the guidelines provided by your instructor.

WORD 2013

Creating and Editing Business Letters

LEARNING OBJECTIVES

After studying this lesson, you will be able to:

- Select and edit text and use AutoCorrect
- Set AutoFormat As You Type options
- Copy and move text
- Set page layout options
- Preview and print a document

In this lesson, you will create business letters while learning proper business letter formatting. You will learn techniques for entering and editing text, copying and moving text, and printing documents. In addition, you will learn to use Word's AutoComplete and AutoCorrect tools to insert frequently used text and to control automatic formatting that Word applies as you type.

Taking Care with Business Letters

You are a sales assistant at My Virtual Campus. A new prospect, Richmond University, has expressed interest in the networking website that My Virtual Campus sells. The sales manager has asked you to prepare a standard letter for potential new clients, thanking them for their interest and providing information about the website.

You start by referring to your business writing class textbook to ensure that you format the letter correctly for a good first impression and a professional appearance.

November 24, 2013

Ms. Paige Daniels
Richmond University
15751 Meadow Lane
Chester Allen, VA 23333

Dear Ms. Daniels:

Travis Mayfield referred you to us after he spoke with you about our extraordinary product. I want to take this opportunity to personally thank you for considering My Virtual Campus' social-networking website for your institution. As Travis may have mentioned, we pride ourselves in providing the latest in technology as well as excellent customer service with satisfaction guaranteed.

Enclosed you will find information to review regarding the features of the website. After reading the material, please contact our sales manager, Bruce Carter, at your earliest convenience to discuss your options. Thank you again for considering our amazing website.

Sincerely,

<your name>
Customer Service Representative
Sales Department

<typist's initials if other than sender>
Enclosures (2)
cc: Bruce Carter

Defining Typical Business Letter Styles

Video Library   http://labyrinthelab.com/videos   Video Number: WD13-V0201

There are several acceptable styles of business letters. The styles discussed in this text include block and modified block. All business letters contain similar elements but with varied formatting.

Block Style

The block style is the most common business-letter style. All elements are single spaced and left aligned, except for double spacing between paragraphs.

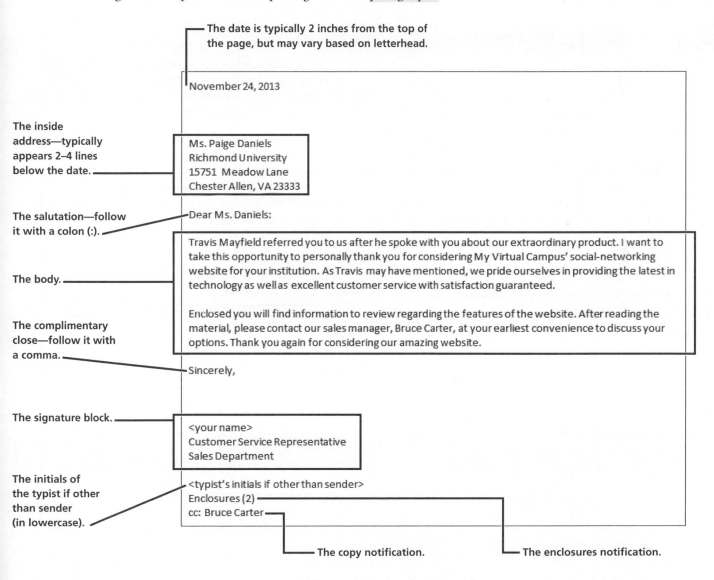

The date is typically 2 inches from the top of the page, but may vary based on letterhead.

November 24, 2013

The inside address—typically appears 2–4 lines below the date.

Ms. Paige Daniels
Richmond University
15751 Meadow Lane
Chester Allen, VA 23333

The salutation—follow it with a colon (:).

Dear Ms. Daniels:

The body.

Travis Mayfield referred you to us after he spoke with you about our extraordinary product. I want to take this opportunity to personally thank you for considering My Virtual Campus' social-networking website for your institution. As Travis may have mentioned, we pride ourselves in providing the latest in technology as well as excellent customer service with satisfaction guaranteed.

Enclosed you will find information to review regarding the features of the website. After reading the material, please contact our sales manager, Bruce Carter, at your earliest convenience to discuss your options. Thank you again for considering our amazing website.

The complimentary close—follow it with a comma.

Sincerely,

The signature block.

<your name>
Customer Service Representative
Sales Department

The initials of the typist if other than sender (in lowercase).

<typist's initials if other than sender>
Enclosures (2)
cc: Bruce Carter

The copy notification.

The enclosures notification.

Modified Block Style

Modified block is another commonly use letter format. The following illustration points out the differences in the modified block-style business letter compared to the block-style business letter.

The date line, complimentary close, and signature block begin at the center of the page. All other lines are left aligned.

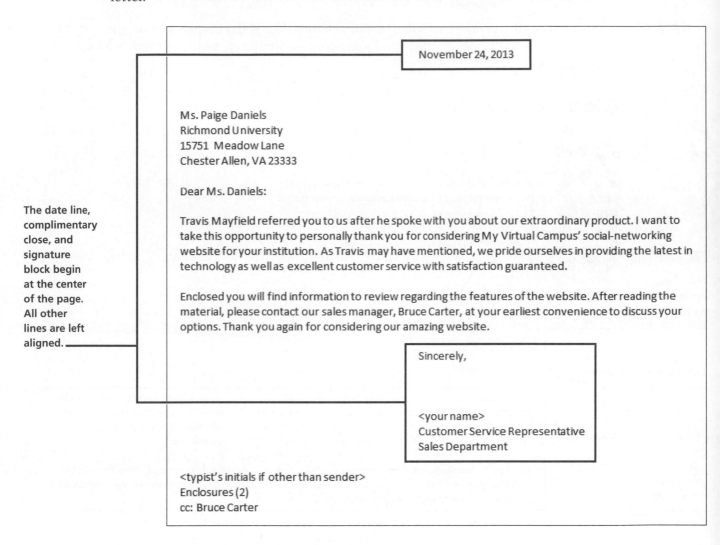

November 24, 2013

Ms. Paige Daniels
Richmond University
15751 Meadow Lane
Chester Allen, VA 23333

Dear Ms. Daniels:

Travis Mayfield referred you to us after he spoke with you about our extraordinary product. I want to take this opportunity to personally thank you for considering My Virtual Campus' social-networking website for your institution. As Travis may have mentioned, we pride ourselves in providing the latest in technology as well as excellent customer service with satisfaction guaranteed.

Enclosed you will find information to review regarding the features of the website. After reading the material, please contact our sales manager, Bruce Carter, at your earliest convenience to discuss your options. Thank you again for considering our amazing website.

Sincerely,

<your name>
Customer Service Representative
Sales Department

<typist's initials if other than sender>
Enclosures (2)
cc: Bruce Carter

Inserting Text

Video Library   http://labyrinthelab.com/videos   Video Number: WD13-V0202

You always insert text at the flashing insertion point. Therefore, you must position the insertion point at the desired location before typing.

Using AutoComplete

Word's AutoComplete feature does some of your typing for you. It recognizes certain words and phrases, such as names of months and days, and offers to complete them for you.

November (Press ENTER to Insert)
Nove

AutoComplete proposing the word November when *Nove* is typed.

You accept AutoComplete suggestions by tapping ⌷Enter⌷. If you choose to ignore the suggestion, just keep typing; the suggestion disappears.

AutoComplete does not offer to complete the months March through July, because the names are short.

Using the Enter Key

You use ⌷Enter⌷ to begin a new paragraph or to insert blank lines in a document. Word considers anything that ends by tapping ⌷Enter⌷ to be a paragraph. Thus, short lines such as a date line, an inside address, or even blank lines themselves are considered paragraphs.

Tapping ⌷Enter⌷ inserts a paragraph symbol in a document. These symbols are visible when you display formatting marks.

Showing Formatting Marks

Although formatting marks appear on the screen, you will not see them in the printed document. Viewing these characters can be important when editing a document. For example, you may need to see the formatting marks to determine whether the space between two words was created with the ⌷Spacebar⌷ or ⌷Tab⌷.

FROM THE RIBBON

Home→Paragraph→
Show/Hide ¶

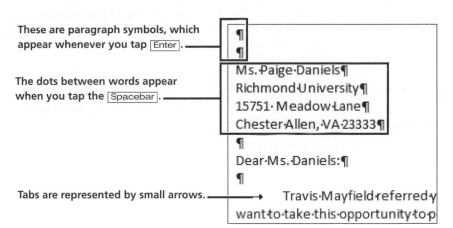

These are paragraph symbols, which appear whenever you tap ⌷Enter⌷.

The dots between words appear when you tap the ⌷Spacebar⌷.

Ms.·Paige·Daniels¶
Richmond·University¶
15751·Meadow·Lane¶
Chester·Allen,·VA·23333¶
¶
Dear·Ms.·Daniels:¶
¶
Tabs are represented by small arrows. → Travis·Mayfield·referred·y
want·to·take·this·opportunity·to·p

Spacing in Letters

The default spacing in Word 2013 is 1.08 rather than the traditional single spacing. It adds an extra 8 points (a little less than an eighth of an inch) at the end of paragraphs. Therefore, rather that tapping ⌷Enter⌷ twice at the end of a paragraph, you just tap ⌷Enter⌷ once, and Word adds the extra spacing.

FROM THE RIBBON

Home→Paragraph→
Line and Paragraph
Spacing

When you choose the Blank Document template on the Word Start screen or on the New screen, you are using the default 1.08 spacing. Some documents, however, typically require single spacing, such as business letters, reports, and proposals. Word offers these methods for applying single spacing:

- Single Spaced (Blank) template
- Line and Paragraph Spacing button

Applying Traditional Spacing Using the Single Spaced Template

Choosing the Single Spaced (Blank) template from the Word Start screen or from the New screen opens a single-spaced document. This is a good choice if the majority of your document will be single spaced. If you will use single spacing only in part of your document, the Line and Paragraph Spacing button is a good choice.

Changing Spacing Using the Line and Paragraph Spacing Button

If you start a new document using 1.08 spacing and then decide to apply single spacing to a portion of the document, you can choose the options indicated in the following figure. You must select (highlight) the text to be single spaced, or at a minimum, select the paragraph symbol at the end of the text before changing the spacing. Paragraph symbols carry formatting in them.

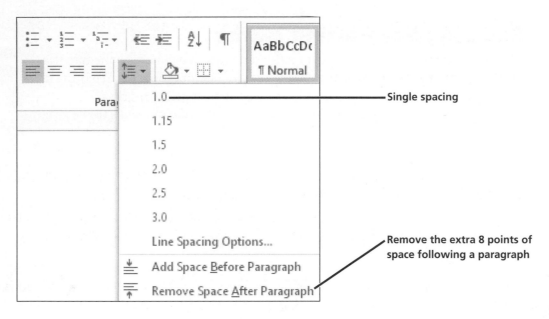

If you wish to use other spacing such as double- or triple-spacing, the Line and Paragraph Spacing button is the place to go.

QUICK REFERENCE	WORKING WITH LINE SPACING
Task	**Procedure**
Word Default Spacing	■ Choose the Blank Document template on the Word Start screen; choose File→New and choose Blank Document; or, press Ctrl + N
Single Spacing	■ Choose the Single Spaced (Blank) template on the Word Start screen; or, choose File→New and choose Single Spaced (Blank). ■ Click Create.
Other Line Spacing Options	■ Choose Home→Paragraph→Line and Paragraph Spacing.

DEVELOP YOUR SKILLS WD02-D01

Type a Business Letter

In this exercise, you will use the Single Spaced (Blank) template to create a business letter. You will also use AutoComplete and work with the Enter *key.*

1. Start **Word** and make sure the Word window is **maximized** ⬚.

2. Click the **Single Spaced (Blank)** template to start a new single-spaced letter.

   A window appears describing the template.

3. Click **Create** 🗋.

4. Choose **File→Save** and save the document in your **WD2013 Lesson 02** folder as **WD02-D01-DanielsLetter-[FirstInitialLastName]**.

   Replace the bracketed text with your first initial and last name. For example, if your name is Bethany Smith, your filename would look like this: WD02-D01-DanielsLetter-BSmith.

Throughout this book, you will usually save your working document with a new name in step 1 so you can start each exercise with a fresh document.

Begin the Letter and Use AutoComplete

5. Choose **Home→Paragraph→Show/Hide** ¶ to display formatting marks.

   New documents contain a paragraph symbol; you won't see it if you don't turn on the Show/Hide feature. Paragraph symbols carry formatting in them. In this example, the document formatting includes single spacing.

6. Choose **View→Show→Ruler** to display the ruler.

7. Tap Enter five times to place the insertion point 2 inches from the top of the page.

8. Type **Nove** but stop typing when AutoComplete displays a pop-up tip.

9. Tap Enter to automatically insert *November* in the letter.

10. Finish typing the date as **November 24, 2013**.

11. Continue typing the letter as shown, tapping ⎡Enter⎤ wherever you see a paragraph symbol.

If you catch a typo, you can tap ⎡Backspace⎤ *enough times to remove the error, and then continue typing.*

```
¶
¶
¶
¶
¶
November·24,·2013¶
¶
¶
¶
Ms.·Paige·Daniels¶
Richmond·University¶
15751·Meadow·Lane¶
Chester·Allen,·VA·23333¶
¶
Dear·Ms.·Daniels:¶
¶
¶
```

12. Type the body paragraph as shown. Let Word Wrap do its thing and tap ⎡Enter⎤ twice at the end of the paragraph.

```
Travis·Mayfield·referred·you·to·us·after·he·spoke·with·you·yesterday·about·our·extraordinary·product.·I·
want·to·take·this·opportunity·to·thank·you·for·considering·My·Virtual·Campus'·social-networking·website·
for·your·institution.·As·Travis·may·have·mentioned,·we·pride·ourselves·in·providing·the·latest·in·
technology·as·well·as·excellent·customer·service.¶
¶
¶
```

If you see a wavy red line, Word thinks the word *might* be misspelled. Wavy blue lines indicate possible grammatical errors. Ignore red and blue wavy lines for now.

13. Continue typing the letter as shown, tapping ⌈Enter⌉ where you see a paragraph symbol. Type your name where indicated.

I·have·enclosed·information·for·your·review·regarding·the·various·features·of·the·website.·After·reading· the·material,·please·contact·our·sales·manager,·ASAP,·to·discuss·your·options.·Thank·you·again·for· considering·our·amazing·website.¶
¶
Yours·truly,¶
¶
¶
¶
<your·name>¶
Customer·Service·Representative¶
Sales·Department¶
¶
¶

14. Choose **Home→Paragraph→Show/Hide** ¶ to turn off formatting marks.

15. Choose **View→Show→Ruler** to turn off the ruler.

Feel free to turn Show/Hide and the ruler on or off as you see fit throughout this course.

16. Click **Save** 🖫 on the Quick Access toolbar.
Always leave the file open at the end of an exercise unless instructed to close it.

Creating an Envelope

Video Library http://labyrinthelab.com/videos   Video Number: WD13-V0203

Microsoft Word is smart and versatile when it comes to creating envelopes. When you type a business letter with the recipient's name and address at the top, Word recognizes this as the delivery address. Word gives you two options: print the address directly on the envelope or insert the envelope at the top of the document.

FROM THE RIBBON
Mailings→Create→
Envelopes

The address from the letter is automatically inserted on the envelope.

You can type a return address or place a checkmark in the Omit box if a return address already exists.

You can print the envelope now or add it to your document.

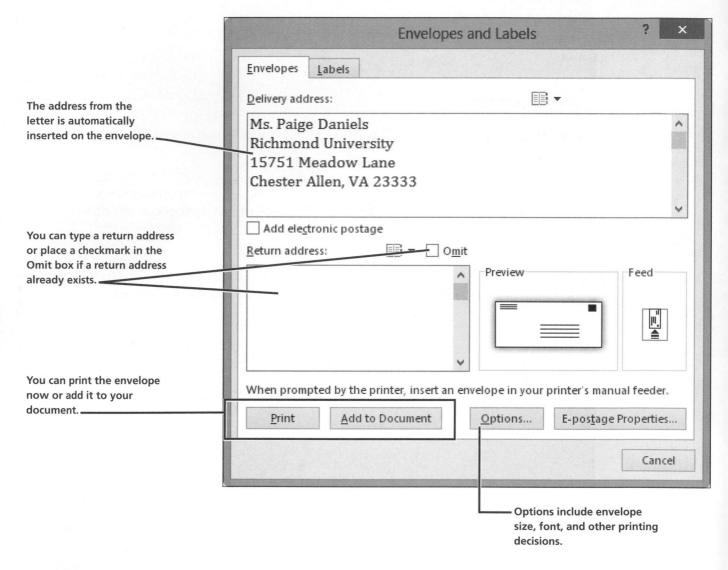

Options include envelope size, font, and other printing decisions.

When you enter a return address, you will be prompted to save it as the default so you don't have to type it each time.

Create an Envelope

In this exercise, you will create an envelope and add it to your letter.

1. Press [Ctrl]+[Home], and then choose **Mailings→Create→Envelopes** ⬜.

2. Follow these steps to add an envelope to the document:

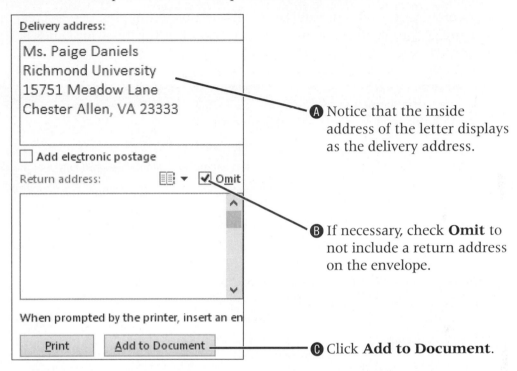

A Notice that the inside address of the letter displays as the delivery address.

B If necessary, check **Omit** to not include a return address on the envelope.

C Click **Add to Document**.

3. Observe the envelope, and then click **Undo** ↶ on the Quick Access toolbar to remove the envelope; you don't need it for this exercise.

You'll learn more about Undo later.

Word 2013

Selecting Text

Video Library   http://labyrinthelab.com/videos   Video Number: WD13-V0204

You must select (highlight) text if you wish to perform an action on it. Suppose you want to delete a line. You select the line first, and then tap [Delete].

Word provides many mouse and keyboard selection techniques. Deselect text by clicking in the text area of the document or by tapping an arrow key. The following Quick Reference table illustrates various selection techniques.

SELECTION TECHNIQUES

Item to Be Selected	Mouse Technique
One word	Double-click the word.
Continuous block of text	Hold down the left mouse button while dragging over the desired text.
A line	Place the mouse pointer selection arrow in the left margin, and click to select the line.
A sentence	Press [Ctrl] and click anywhere in the sentence.
One paragraph	Place the selection arrow in the left margin and double-click; or, triple-click the I-beam anywhere *within* the paragraph.
Multiple paragraphs	Place the selection arrow in the left margin and drag up or down; or, drag the I-beam over the desired paragraphs.
Entire document	Triple-click in the left margin; or, hold [Ctrl] and click in the left margin.
Nonadjacent areas	Select the first text block, and then hold [Ctrl] while dragging over additional blocks of text.
Item to Be Selected	**Keyboard Technique**
One word	Click at the beginning of the word, and then hold [Shift]+[Ctrl] while tapping [→].
Continuous block of text	Click at the beginning of the text, and then hold [Shift] while tapping an arrow key. Or, click at the beginning of the text block, hold [Shift], and then click at the end of the text block.
A line	Press [Shift]+[End] to select from the insertion point to the end of the line. Press [Shift]+[Home] to select from the insertion point to the beginning of the line.
Entire document	Press [Ctrl]+[A], or press [Ctrl] and click in the left margin.

The Mini toolbar appears when you select text. It contains frequently used commands. You can choose a command or ignore the toolbar and it will fade away.

Select Text

In this exercise, you will practice various selection techniques using the letter you just created. Selecting text causes the Mini toolbar to fade in. You can ignore it for now.

1. Follow these steps to select text using the left margin:

A Place the selection arrow in the margin to the left of the first line of the inside address; click to select the line.

B Use the selection arrow to select this line. (Notice that the previously selected line is no longer selected.)

Ms. Paige Daniels
Richmond University
15751 Meadow Lane
Chester Allen, VA 23333

Dear Ms. Daniels:

Travis Mayfield referred you to us after he spoke with you yesterday about our extraordinary product. I want to take this opportunity to thank you for considering My Virtual Campus' social-networking website for your institution. As Travis may have mentioned, we pride ourselves in providing the latest in technology as well as excellent customer service.

C Select this paragraph by double-clicking with the selection arrow.

2. Using the selection arrow, drag down the left margin to select text.

3. Click once anywhere in the body of the document to deselect.

4. Triple-click with the selection arrow anywhere in the left margin to select the entire document.

5. Click once anywhere in the body of the document to deselect.

Select Words

6. Double-click any word to select it.

7. Double-click a different word, and notice that the previous word is deselected.

Select Nonadjacent Selections

You can select multiple locations simultaneously.

8. Double-click to select one word.

9. Press and hold Ctrl as you double-click another word; release Ctrl.
   Both selections are active. You can select as many nonadjacent areas of a document as desired using the Ctrl key.

10. Follow these steps to drag and select a block of text:

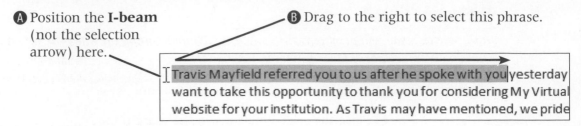

Ⓐ Position the **I-beam** (not the selection arrow) here.

Ⓑ Drag to the right to select this phrase.

Travis Mayfield referred you to us after he spoke with you yesterday want to take this opportunity to thank you for considering My Virtual website for your institution. As Travis may have mentioned, we pride

11. Click in the document to deselect.

Editing Text

Video Library   http://labyrinthelab.com/videos   Video Number: WD13-V0205

Word offers many tools for editing documents, allowing you to insert and delete text. You'll find Word's undo and redo features are very helpful.

Inserting and Deleting Text

Remember, you must position the insertion point before you begin typing. You can use Backspace and Delete to remove one character at a time. If you select a block of text, Backspace or Delete removes the entire block.

Using Undo and Redo

Word's Undo button on the Quick Access toolbar lets you reverse your last editing or formatting change(s). You can reverse simple actions such as accidental text deletions, or you can reverse more complex actions, such as margin changes.

FROM THE KEYBOARD
Ctrl+Z to undo the last action

Ctrl+Y to redo the last action

Clicking the menu button displays a list of recent changes.

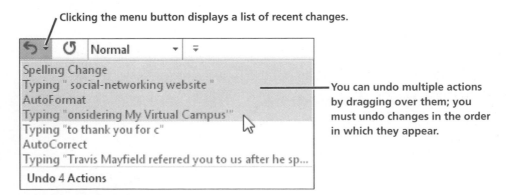

You can undo multiple actions by dragging over them; you must undo changes in the order in which they appear.

The Redo button reverses Undo. Use Redo when you undo an action and then change your mind.

Insert and Delete Text and Use Undo and Redo

In this exercise, you will insert and delete text. You will delete characters using both Backspace *and* Delete*, and you will select and delete blocks of text. You will also use the Undo and Redo buttons on the Quick Access toolbar. You will begin by saving your document. This technique is used throughout this course so you can start your exercise with a fresh file.*

1. Save your file in the **WD2013 Lesson 02** folder as `WD02-D04-DanielsLetter-[FirstInitialLastName]`.

2. In the first line of the first paragraph, double-click the word *yesterday* and tap Delete to remove it.

   > spoke with you yesterday about
   > for considering My Virtual Camp

3. Click with the **I-beam** I at the beginning of the word *thank* in the second line of the first paragraph, type **personally**, and tap Spacebar.

4. Position the insertion point at the end of the first paragraph between the word *service* and the final period.

5. Tap Spacebar and type **with satisfaction guaranteed**.

6. Drag to select the first three words of the second paragraph, and then type **Enclosed you will find** to replace the selected text.

7. In the same line, position the insertion point after the word *your* and tap Backspace until the words *for your* are deleted; then type **to**.

8. Double-click the word *various* in the same line and tap Delete.

9. In the next line, double-click *ASAP* and type **Bruce Carter, at your earliest convenience** in its place.

10. Delete the comma following *convenience*.

11. Place the selection arrow in the margin to the left of *Yours truly*.

12. Click once to select the line and type **Sincerely,** in its place.

Use Undo and Redo

13. You've decided that you prefer *Yours truly,* so click **Undo** ⤺ on the Quick Access toolbar enough times to remove *Sincerely.*

14. Well, maybe *Sincerely* is better after all. Click **Redo** ⤻ on the Quick Access toolbar enough times to insert *Sincerely.*

15. Save the document.

Working with AutoCorrect

Video Library   http://labyrinthelab.com/videos   Video Number: WD13-V0206

AutoCorrect is predefined text used for automatically correcting common spelling and capitalization errors. You may have noticed AutoCorrect changing the spelling of certain words while working through previous exercises.

The AutoCorrect feature corrects more than spelling errors. For example, you can set up an AutoCorrect entry to insert the phrase *as soon as possible* when you type *asap* and tap Spacebar or other characters, such as a Tab, Comma, or Period.

DEVELOP YOUR SKILLS WD02-D05
Use AutoCorrect

In this exercise, you will practice typing some terms that AutoCorrect will fix for you.

1. Press Ctrl + End to move the insertion point to the end of the document.

2. If necessary, tap Enter a few times to provide some space to practice.

3. Type **teh** and tap Tab.
   AutoCorrect capitalizes the word because AutoCorrect thinks it is the first word of a sentence.

4. Type **adn** and tap Spacebar; AutoCorrect fixes the error.

5. Now select and Delete the words you were just practicing with.

Using the AutoCorrect Options Smart Tag

Video Library   http://labyrinthelab.com/videos   Video Number: WD13-V0207

Word uses smart tags, small buttons that pop up automatically, to provide menus of options that are in context with what you are doing. One of those smart tags is AutoCorrect Options.

If Word automatically corrects something that you don't want corrected, a smart tag option allows you to undo the change. For example, when Word automatically capitalizes the first C in the cc: line, you can quickly undo the capitalization.

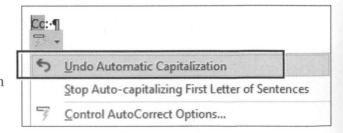

 You will see many smart tags as you work. If you do not want to use a smart tag, you can ignore it and it will disappear on its own.

Use the AutoCorrect Smart Tag

In this exercise, you will add typist initials to the letter and use the smart tag to undo capitalization when AutoCorrect incorrectly capitalizes the first initial.

1. Save your file as **WD02-D06-DanielsLetter-[FirstInitialLastName]**.

2. Choose **Home→Paragraph→Show/Hide ¶** to display formatting marks.
    The typist initials should appear on the second blank line following the signature block.

3. If necessary, tap Enter so there are at least two paragraph symbols.

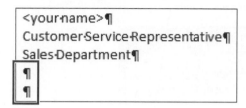

4. Follow these steps to add initials to the letter:

A Type **ss** as the typist's initials (lowercase) and tap Enter. Notice that AutoCorrect incorrectly capitalized the first initial.

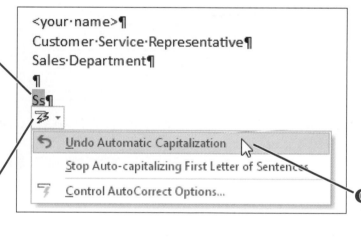

B Position the mouse pointer over the first initial until you see a small blue rectangle. Slide the mouse pointer down to display the AutoCorrect smart tag.

C Click the tag and choose **Undo Automatic Capitalization**.

Word marks the initials with a wavy red line, indicating that it's a possible spelling error. You can ignore it.

5. Make sure the insertion point is on the blank line below the initials.

6. Type **Enclosures (2)** and tap Enter.

7. Choose **Home→Paragraph→Show/Hide ¶** to turn off formatting marks.

8. Save the document.

Customizing AutoCorrect

Video Library   http://labyrinthelab.com/videos   Video Number: WD13-V0208

In addition to correcting errors, AutoCorrect lets you automatically insert customized text and special characters. It's also useful for replacing abbreviations with full phrases. For example, you could set up AutoCorrect to insert the name of your company whenever you type an abbreviation for it. And you can customize AutoCorrect by deleting entries that are installed with Word; however, please do not delete any in this classroom.

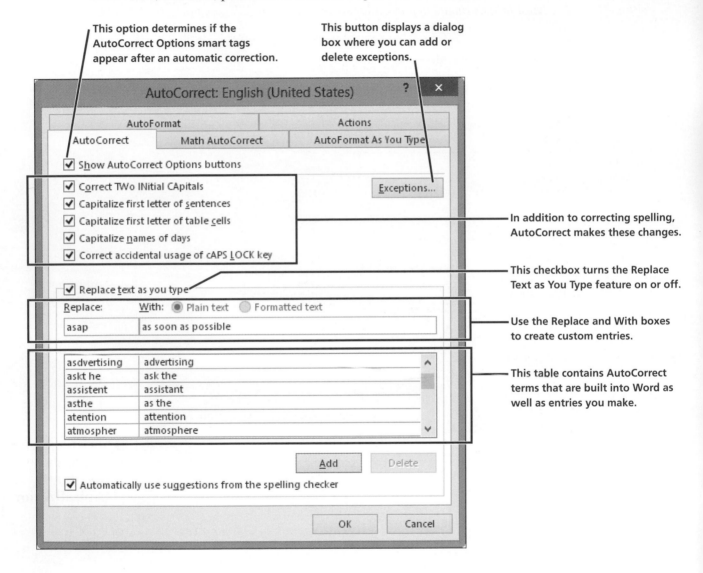

This option determines if the AutoCorrect Options smart tags appear after an automatic correction.

This button displays a dialog box where you can add or delete exceptions.

In addition to correcting spelling, AutoCorrect makes these changes.

This checkbox turns the Replace Text as You Type feature on or off.

Use the Replace and With boxes to create custom entries.

This table contains AutoCorrect terms that are built into Word as well as entries you make.

Using AutoCorrect Exceptions

You can designate exceptions to AutoCorrect when you don't want it to replace text that it normally would. For example, there is an option to capitalize the first letter of sentences. When word sees a period, it assumes that's the end of a sentence and it will capitalize the next word. However, you may not always want the capitalization to occur.

You can add capitalization exceptions here.

Some company names and products begin with two initial caps; you can add them as exceptions.

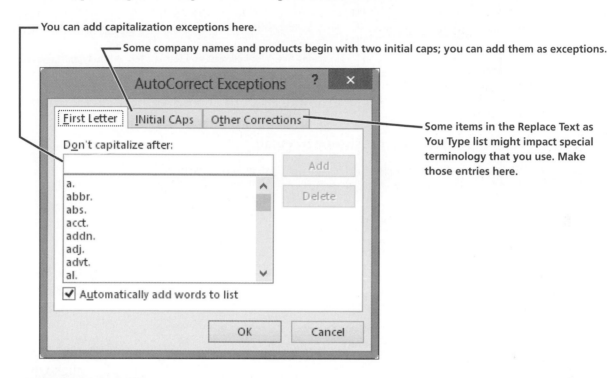

Some items in the Replace Text as You Type list might impact special terminology that you use. Make those entries here.

QUICK REFERENCE	USING AUTOCORRECT
Task	**Procedure**
Create a custom AutoCorrect entry	■ Choose File→Options. ■ Choose Proofing and click AutoCorrect Options. ■ Enter shortcut text in the Replace box and replacement text in the With box.
Create an AutoCorrect exception	■ Click Exceptions in the AutoCorrect dialog box. ■ Choose the appropriate tab and enter the exception.

DEVELOP YOUR SKILLS WD02-D07

Create a Custom AutoCorrect Entry

In this exercise, you will copy Bruce Carter on your memo. You need a courtesy copy notification. Since you work for him, you know you'll need to type his name frequently; therefore, it's a perfect candidate for a custom AutoCorrect entry.

1. Save your file as **WD02-D07-DanielsLetter-[FirstInitialLastName]**.

2. Choose **File→Options**.

3. Follow these steps to display the AutoCorrect dialog box:

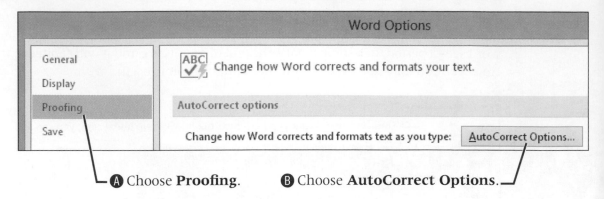

Ⓐ Choose **Proofing**. **Ⓑ** Choose **AutoCorrect Options**.

4. If necessary, click the **AutoCorrect** tab.

5. Follow these steps to add a custom AutoCorrect entry:

Ⓐ Type **bmc** in the Replace box.

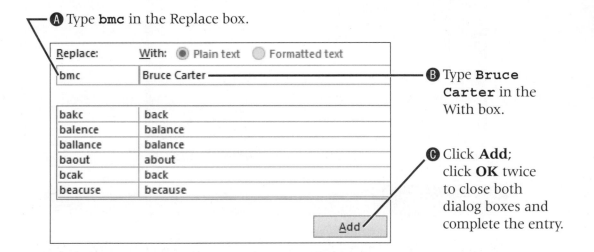

Ⓑ Type **Bruce Carter** in the With box.

Ⓒ Click **Add**; click **OK** twice to close both dialog boxes and complete the entry.

6. Make sure the insertion point is on the blank line following the Enclosures line. Add a blank line if necessary.

7. Follow these steps to add a courtesy copy notation:

Ⓐ Type **cc:** and tap ⎡Spacebar⎤. Use the **AutoCorrect Options** smart tag to undo the automatic capitalization.

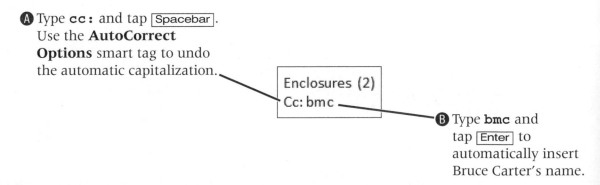

Ⓑ Type **bmc** and tap ⎡Enter⎤ to automatically insert Bruce Carter's name.

Delete the Custom AutoCorrect Entry

8. Choose **File→Options**.

9. Choose **Proofing** in the left panel, and then click **AutoCorrect Options**.

10. Follow these steps to remove the Bruce Carter entry:

Ⓐ Type **bmc** here and see that the list scrolls to Bruce Carter.

☑ Replace text as you type

Replace: With: ⦿ Plain text   ◯ Formatted text

bmc	

bmc	Bruce Carter
boxs	boxes
brodcast	broadcast
butthe	but the
bve	be
byt he	by the

Replace   Delete   Ⓑ Click **Delete**.

☑ Automatically use suggestions from the spelling checker

OK   Cancel   Ⓒ Click **OK** twice.

11. Save the document.

Setting AutoFormat As You Type Options

Video Library   http://labyrinthelab.com/videos   Video Number: WD13-V0209

One of the tabs in the AutoCorrect dialog box is AutoFormat As You Type. You may have noticed certain formatting taking place automatically; this is happening because certain options are already set for you. For example, AutoFormat will replace two typed hyphens (--) with a dash (—), an ordinal (1st) with superscript (1st), or a fraction (1/2) with a fraction character (½).

AutoFormat can also be set to create an automatic bulleted list when you start a line with an asterisk (*), a hyphen (-), or a greater than symbol (>) followed by a space or tab. Likewise, it can be set to create a numbered list when you start a line with a number followed by a period or tab.

Task	Procedure
Customize AutoCorrect	■ Choose File→Options, then choose Proofing in the left panel. ■ Click AutoCorrect Options, then click the AutoCorrect tab. ■ Type the misspelled word or an abbreviation in the Replace box and type the correct term in the With box. ■ Click OK twice.
Customize AutoFormat As You Type	■ Choose File→Options, then choose Proofing in the left panel. ■ Click the AutoFormat As You Type tab and add a checkmark where you want Word to AutoFormat. ■ Remove a checkmark for an item you don't want Word to AutoFormat. ■ Click OK twice.

DEVELOP YOUR SKILLS WD02-D08

Turn On Automatic Numbering

In this exercise, you will turn on the option that automatically creates a numbered list when you begin a sentence with a number.

1. Choose **File→Options**.

2. Click **Proofing** in the left panel, and then click **AutoCorrect Options**.

3. Follow these steps to turn on automatic numbering:

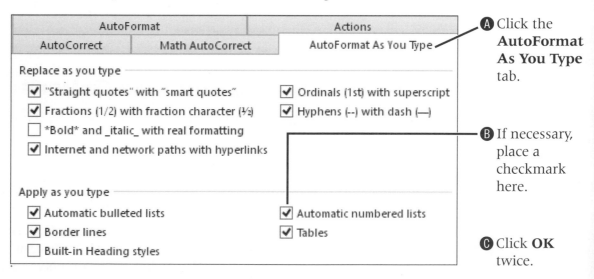

Ⓐ Click the **AutoFormat As You Type** tab.

Ⓑ If necessary, place a checkmark here.

Ⓒ Click **OK** twice.

4. Position the insertion point at the end of the document, tap [Enter], and then type **1.** (with a period) and tap [Spacebar].

5. Type **Item one** and tap [Enter].

   Word automatically generates the next number.

6. Select the numbered entries and tap [Delete].

Copying and Moving Text

Video Library http://labyrinthelab.com/videos   Video Number: WD13-V0210

Cut, Copy, and Paste allow you to copy and move text within a document or between documents. The Cut, Copy, and Paste commands are located on the Home tab in the Clipboard group.

FROM THE KEYBOARD

Ctrl + X to cut

Ctrl + C to copy

Ctrl + V to paste

Working with the Clipboard

The Clipboard lets you collect multiple items and paste them in another location in the current document or in a different document. The Clipboard task pane must be visible on the screen to collect the items; otherwise, only one item at a time is saved for pasting.

FROM THE RIBBON

Home→Clipboard→ dialog box launcher to display the Clipboard

The Clipboard holds up to 24 items. When the items you cut or copy exceed 24, the Clipboard automatically deletes the oldest item(s). By default, a pop-up appears near the right edge of the taskbar when you copy an item, notifying you of the number of items in the Clipboard.

5 of 24 – Clipboard Item collected.

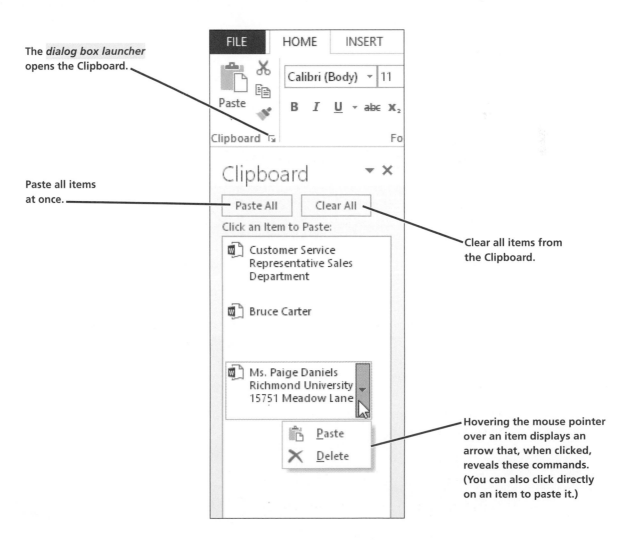

The *dialog box launcher* opens the Clipboard.

Paste all items at once.

Clear all items from the Clipboard.

Hovering the mouse pointer over an item displays an arrow that, when clicked, reveals these commands. (You can also click directly on an item to paste it.)

CUT, COPY, AND PASTE COMMANDS	
Command	**Description**
Cut	Removes text and places it on the Clipboard
Copy	Leaves text where it is and places a copy on the Clipboard
Paste	Inserts cut or copied text at the insertion point

Use Cut, Copy, and Paste

In this exercise, you will move and copy information and work with the Clipboard.

1. Save your file as **WD02-D09-DanielsLetter-[FirstInitialLastName]**.

2. If necessary, choose **Home→Paragraph→Show/Hide** ¶ to display the formatting marks.

3. Follow these steps to place the date on the Clipboard:

A Click here to open the Clipboard.

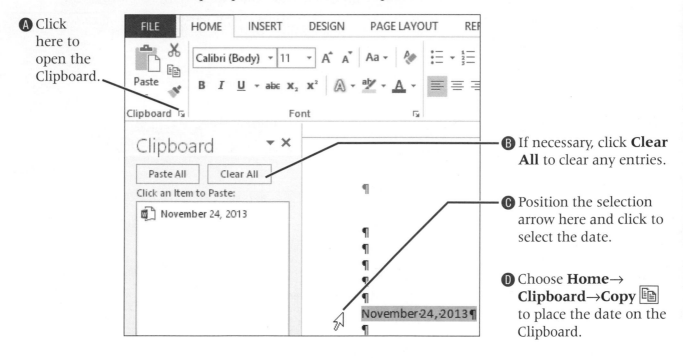

B If necessary, click **Clear All** to clear any entries.

C Position the selection arrow here and click to select the date.

D Choose **Home→Clipboard→Copy** to place the date on the Clipboard.

4. Press Ctrl + End to move the insertion point to the bottom of the document.

5. Follow these steps to paste the date at the bottom of the document:

Ⓐ If necessary, tap Enter to add some blank paragraphs at the bottom.

Ⓒ Choose **Paste** from the menu. (You can also click directly on the item to paste without using the menu.)

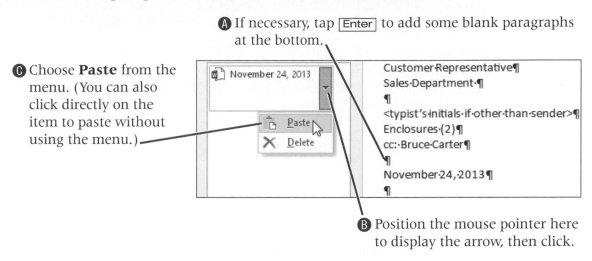

Ⓑ Position the mouse pointer here to display the arrow, then click.

Notice the Paste Options smart tag that appears when you paste the text.

6. Click the **smart tag** to view its menu, and then click in the document to close it.

7. Tap Esc to dismiss the smart tag.

If you don't tap Esc, the button will disappear on its own.

8. Click **Undo** ↻ to undo the paste.

Move the Inside Address

9. Scroll to the top of the letter, and use the selection arrow to drag and select all four lines of the inside address.

10. Press Ctrl + X to cut the text and place it on the Clipboard.

11. Press Ctrl + End to move to the bottom of the document.

12. Click the inside address on the **Clipboard** to paste it at the insertion point.

13. Click **Close** ✕ on the **Clipboard** task pane.

In the next exercise, you will return the inside address to its original position in the letter.

14. Save the document.

Editing with Drag and Drop

Video Library   http://labyrinthelab.com/videos   Video Number: WD13-V0211

The drag and drop feature produces the same result as cut, copy, and paste. It is efficient for moving or copying text a short distance within the same page. You select the text you wish to move, then drag it to the desired destination. If you press and hold Ctrl while dragging, the text is copied to the destination.

Drag and drop does not place the selection on the Clipboard task pane.

DEVELOP YOUR SKILLS WD02-D10
Use Drag and Drop

In this exercise, you will use drag and drop to move the inside address back to the top of the document.

1. If necessary, scroll so you can see both the inside address and the blank line above the salutation.

2. Save your file as **WD02-D10-DanielsLetter-[FirstInitialLastName]**.

3. Click and drag to select the inside address.

4. Position the mouse pointer over the highlighted text.
   The pointer now looks like a white arrow.

5. Follow these steps to move the selected text:

   A Press the mouse button, and drag the mouse pointer to the blank line above the salutation. A thick insertion point travels with the arrow. The rectangle on the arrow indicates you are in drag-and-drop mode.

   B Release the mouse button to complete the move; click to deselect.

6. Save the document.

Switching Between Documents

Video Library   http://labyrinthelab.com/videos   Video Number: WD13-V0212

There are several techniques for switching between documents. In the next exercise, you will use the taskbar at the bottom of the screen to do it. When several documents are open at the same time, they may share one taskbar button.

A small image of each open document displays when you hover the mouse pointer over the taskbar button. Below, the Daniels letter is the active document, and you can tell because it's lighter than the others. Clicking the image opens the document on the screen.

Open Word documents

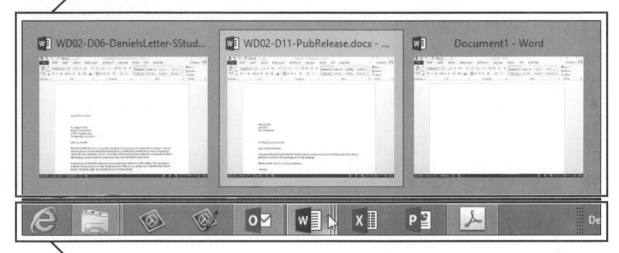

Taskbar buttons for open programs (Notice the Word button has three documents stacked on it.)

Your buttons may be different from the ones shown here, depending on which program buttons are displayed on your computer's taskbar.

Switch and Copy Between Documents

In this exercise, you will copy and paste between two documents using the taskbar buttons to switch from one document to another.

1. Open **WD02-D11-PubRelease** from the **WD2013 Lesson 02** folder and save it as `WD02-D11-PubRelease-[FirstInitialLastName]`.

2. Follow these steps to switch to your WD02-D10-DanielsLetter-[FirstInitialLastName] file:

Ⓐ Hover the mouse pointer over the **Word taskbar button** to display small images of the documents.

Ⓑ Click **WD02-D10-DanielsLetter-[FirstInitialLastName]**.

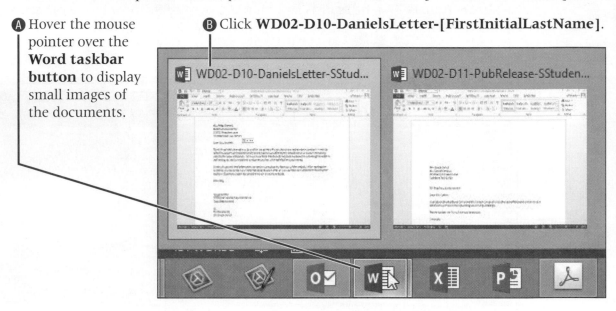

3. Select *Bruce Carter* in the second line of the second paragraph.

4. Press Ctrl + C to copy the name.

Switch Documents

5. Using the taskbar, switch to **WD02-D11-PubRelease-[FirstInitialLastName]**.

6. Select the *YOUR NAME* line in the inside address.

7. Press Ctrl + V to paste *Bruce Carter* over the selected text, and then, if necessary, tap Enter to move *ADDRESS* back to the second line.

8. Click the insertion point in front of *Bruce Carter*, type **Mr.**, and tap Spacebar.

9. Select the last two lines of the inside address and type the following:

```
My Virtual Campus
123 Cherry Blossom Lane
Salisbury, MD 21801
```

10. There should be two blank lines between the inside address and the RE: line. Add or delete blank lines as needed.

11. Select *SALES MANAGER* in the salutation and press Ctrl + V to paste *Bruce Carter* again.

12. Select *Bruce* and type **Mr.** in its place.

13. Select *SALES MANAGER* in the body paragraph and paste the name again.

14. Using the **taskbar**, switch back to the Daniels letter.

15. Select *Paige Daniels* in the inside address and press Ctrl + C to copy her name.

16. Switch back to the publicity release and paste her name over *YOUR NAME* at the bottom.

17. Save the changes you made in **WD02-D11-PubRelease-[FirstInitialLastName]**, and then close it.

Using Page Layout Options

Video Library http://labyrinthelab.com/videos   Video Number: WD13-V0213

The three most commonly used page layout options are margins, page orientation, and paper size. All of these are located in the Page Setup group on the Page Layout tab.

Setting Margins

Margins determine the amount of white space between the text and the edge of the paper. You can set margins for the entire document, a section, or selected text. The Margins gallery displays preset top, bottom, left, and right margins. The Custom Margins option at the bottom of the gallery opens a dialog box where you can set custom margins.

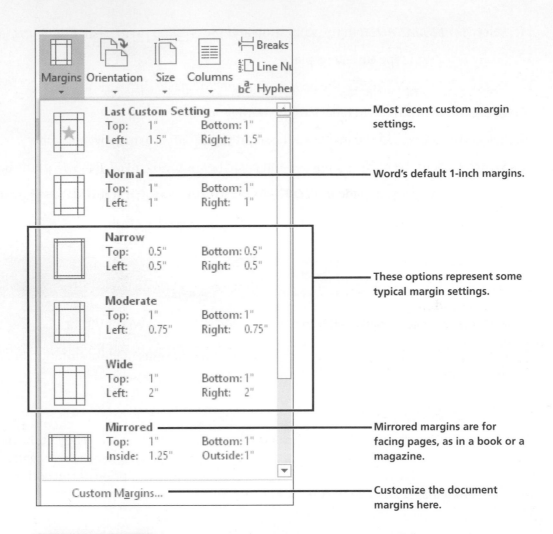

Most recent custom margin settings.

Word's default 1-inch margins.

These options represent some typical margin settings.

Mirrored margins are for facing pages, as in a book or a magazine.

Customize the document margins here.

QUICK REFERENCE	SETTING MARGINS
Task	**Procedure**
Change margins from the Margins gallery	■ Choose Page Layout→Page Setup→Margins and choose a predefined margin setting.
Set custom margins	■ Choose Page Layout→Page Setup→Margins and choose Custom Margins. ■ Enter settings for top, bottom, left, and right margins.

Set Margins

In this exercise, you will use the Margins gallery and the Page Setup dialog box to change the document's margins.

1. Choose **Page Layout→Page Setup→Margins** .

2. Choose **Narrow** from the gallery and observe the impact on your document.

3. Click **Margins** again and choose **Wide** to see how that affects the document.

4. Open the gallery again and change the margins back to **Normal**.

Set Custom Margins

5. Display the gallery and choose **Custom Margins** from the bottom of the menu to open the Page Setup dialog box.

Clicking the dialog box launcher at the bottom-right corner of the Page Setup group also opens the Page Setup dialog box.

Notice the options for changing the top, bottom, left, and right margins.

6. Set the left and right margins to **1.5 inches**.

7. Click **OK** and notice the change in your document's margins.

8. Click **Margins** and choose **Normal**.

Setting Page Orientation and Paper Size

Video Library   http://labyrinthelab.com/videos   Video Number: WD13-V0214

You can set page orientation and paper size using the Page Layout tab. The page orientation determines how the text is laid out on the paper. The options are Portrait (vertical) or Landscape (horizontal). The default orientation is Portrait. Some common uses for landscape orientation include brochures, flyers, wide tables, and so forth.

Most documents use the standard letter-size paper. However, Word supports the use of many other paper sizes, including legal, and also allows you to create custom sizes.

Working with Print and Print Preview

The Print command and Print Preview feature are available in Backstage view. The left pane includes printer and page layout options; the right pane is a preview of your document showing how it will look when printed. You can experiment with different options and see the results immediately.

Set number of copies to print, choose a different printer, and view printer properties.

Preview the document before printing.

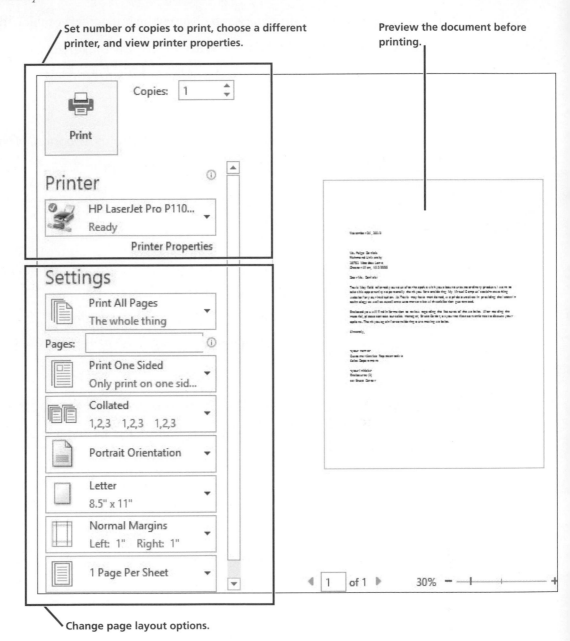

Change page layout options.

Task	Procedure
Change the page orientation	■ Choose Page Layout→Page Setup→Orientation. ■ Choose the desired orientation.
Change the paper size	■ Choose Page Layout→Page Setup→Size. ■ Choose the desired size; or, choose More Paper Sizes to create a custom paper size.
Print and Print Preview	■ Choose File→Print.

DEVELOP YOUR SKILLS WD02-D13

Change Page Layout and Print Options

In this exercise, you will experiment with the page orientation and paper size options. You will preview page orientation, and you will work with printing options.

Work with Page Orientation

1. Choose **File→Print**.

   The page is currently in the default Portrait orientation. Previewing the entire page allows you to see this clearly.

2. Click **Back** ⊙ in the upper-left corner to close Backstage view.

3. Choose **Page Layout→Page Setup→Orientation** ⧉ →**Landscape**.

4. Choose **File→Print** to preview landscape orientation.

5. Click **Back** ⊙.

6. Choose **Page Layout→Page Setup→Orientation** ⧉ again, and then choose **Portrait** to change the page back to a vertical layout.

View Paper Size Options

7. Choose **Page Layout→Page Setup→Size** ⧉ →**Legal**.

8. Scroll down to observe the legal paper.

9. Choose **Size** ⧉ again and choose **Letter**.

Explore Print Options

10. Choose **File→Print**.

11. Set the Copies box to **2**.

12. Click below the Settings heading and choose **Print Current Page**.

Observe Page Settings Options

13. Follow these steps to view other settings in the Print screen:

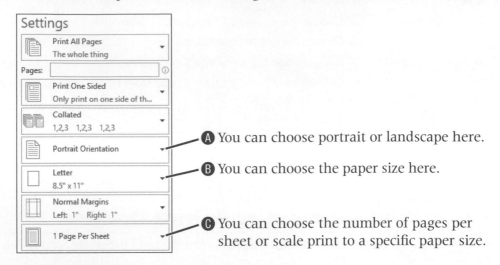

Ⓐ You can choose portrait or landscape here.

Ⓑ You can choose the paper size here.

Ⓒ You can choose the number of pages per sheet or scale print to a specific paper size.

14. You won't print at this time, so click **Back** .

15. Choose **Home→Paragraph→Show/Hide ¶** to turn off formatting marks.

16. Save and close the document, then exit from **Word**.

Concepts Review

To check your knowledge of the key concepts introduced in this lesson, complete the Concepts Review quiz by choosing the appropriate access option below.

If you are...	Then access the quiz by...
Using the Labyrinth Video Library	Going to http://labyrinthelab.com/videos
Using eLab	Logging in, choosing Content, and navigating to the Concepts Review quiz for this lesson
Not using the Labyrinth Video Library or eLab	Going to the student resource center for this book

Reinforce Your Skills

Create a Block-Style Letter with an Envelope

In this exercise, you will use traditional spacing in a block-style business letter and let Word Wrap and AutoComplete take effect. Then you will create an envelope for the letter.

Create a New Document and Insert Text

1. Start **Word** and create a new document based on the **Single Spaced (Blank)** template.

2. When the template description window appears, click **Create** .

3. Choose **Home→Paragraph→Show/Hide ¶** to display formatting marks.

4. Tap [Enter] five times to position the insertion point approximately **2 inches** from the top of the page.

5. Type **Nove** to begin the date, tap [Enter] when the AutoComplete prompt appears, and then finish typing the date as **November 19, 2013**.

6. Tap [Enter] four times.

7. Complete the block style letter as shown on the next page, tapping [Enter] wherever a paragraph symbol appears.

¶

¶
¶
¶
¶
¶
November·19,·2013¶
¶
¶
¶
Current·Resident·¶
123·Peach·Blossom·Lane¶
Atlanta,·GA·30313¶
¶
Dear·Neighbor:¶
¶
I·am·the·recycling·representative·for·Kids·for·Change,·and·our·motto·is·Think·Globally,·Act·Locally.·We·know·that·recycling·large·objects·takes·extra·effort·since·they·do·not·fit·in·your·city-provided·recycle·cans.·We·would·like·to·give·you·a·hand.·¶
¶
On·Tuesday,·November·26th,·we·will·collect·oversized·recyclable·objects·in·your·neighborhood.·Please·place·your·collectables··at·the·curb·in·front·of·your·house·before·9:00·a.m.·Please·visit· http://recycleatlanta.org/·to·ensure·you·are·following·the·city's·recycling·guidelines.··¶
¶
Thank·you·for·caring·about·our·planet.¶
¶
Yours·truly,¶
¶
¶
¶
Tania·Tulip¶
Recycling·Representative¶
Kids·for·Change¶
¶

Create an Envelope

8. Press Ctrl + Home .

9. Choose **Mailings→Create→Envelopes** ⌨ .

10. In the **Envelopes and Labels** dialog box, if necessary, check the **Omit** box to prevent a return address from being added to the envelope.

11. Click **Add to Document**.

12. Save the letter in your **WD2013 Lesson 02** folder as `WD02-R01-Recycle-[FirstInitialLastName]`. Close the file and exit **Word**.

13. Submit your final file based on the guidelines provided by your instructor.

    To view examples of how your file or files should look at the end of this exercise, go to the student resource center.

Edit a Document

In this exercise, you will edit a letter, create an AutoCorrect shortcut, and move a paragraph. You will then copy the letter into a new document, change margins and page orientation, and preview the letter.

Select and Edit Text

1. Start **Word**. Open **WD02-R02-CuyahogaCamp** from your **WD2013 Lesson 02** folder and save it as `WD02-R02-CuyahogaCamp-[FirstInitialLastName]`.

2. Make the following edits to the letter:

   - At the end of the first paragraph, replace the period with a comma and complete the sentence with the following, adding and deleting spaces as needed: `including hiking, bird watching, tree planting, and bug hunting.`

   - Double-click the word *sing* at the end of the third paragraph and tap `Delete`.

   - Position the insertion point at the end of the fourth paragraph, and tap `Delete` twice to combine the fourth and fifth paragraphs.

   - In the last paragraph, select the *8* in *28th* and replace it with **7**.

   - The date of the 28th was correct after all; click **Undo** ↺ on the Quick Access toolbar, and then click in the letter to deselect the text affected by the Undo command.

Work with AutoCorrect

Cuyahoga Camp is a term you will use frequently, so you will create an AutoCorrect shortcut.

3. Choose **File→Options** and choose **Proofing** from the left panel; then click **AutoCorrect Options**.

4. Type **cc** in the **Replace** box, tap `Tab`, type **Camp Cuyahoga** in the **With** box, and then click **OK** twice.

   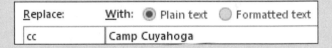

5. Position the insertion point to the right of *spend* in the first line of the first paragraph and tap `Spacebar`.

6. Type this text after the space: **a day with us at cc for**

   Word automatically corrects cc *to* Camp Cuyahoga.

7. At the end of the sentence, select *with us* and tap `Delete`.

8. Position the insertion point on the blank line following Olivia Pledger at the end of the letter, type **cc**, and tap `Enter`.

   AutoCorrect corrects cc *to be* Camp Cuyahoga. *Now you will delete your AutoCorrect shortcut.*

   Olivia Pledger
   Camp Cuyahoga

9. Choose **File→Options**, and then choose **Proofing** from the left panel.

10. Click **AutoCorrect Options**, and type **cc** in the **Replace** box.

    Your shortcut is now highlighted in the list.

11. Click **Delete**, and then click **OK** twice.

Move a Paragraph

12. Position the mouse pointer in the margin to the left of the second paragraph and drag down to select the paragraph and the blank line following it.

    The selected paragraph and blank line below it are highlighted.

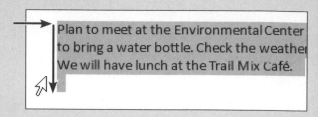

13. Press ⌨Ctrl+⌨X to cut the paragraph.

    When you issued the Cut command, everything that was selected (paragraph and following blank line) was deleted and placed on the Clipboard, ready for you to paste it elsewhere.

14. Position the insertion point to the left of *We* in the last paragraph, and press ⌨Ctrl+⌨V to paste the text.

Copy Text and Switch Between Documents

Since you will send this letter to other attendees, you will practice copying and pasting it into a blank document.

15. Choose **File→New**. Start a new document using the **Single Spaced (Blank)** template.

16. Click **Create** 🗋 to open the blank document.

17. Use the **Word** 🔳 taskbar button to switch back to **WD02-R02-CuyahogaCamp-[FirstInitialLastName]**.

18. Position the mouse pointer to the left of the word *Kids* in the first paragraph and drag down to the end of the letter.

19. Tap ⌨Ctrl+⌨C and use the **Word** 🔳 taskbar button to switch back to your new document.

20. Click in the document and press ⌨Ctrl+⌨V.

    That was just a test; you won't save the letter now.

21. Choose **File→Close**. Click **Don't Save** when the message appears.

Use Page Layout Options and Print Preview

22. Click in the **Cuyahoga Camp** document to deselect.

23. Choose **Page Layout→Page Setup→Margins** 🔲 and choose **Narrow**.

24. Choose **Page Layout→Page Setup→Orientation** and choose **Landscape**.

25. Choose **File→Print** to preview the document.

    The document looked better to begin with.

26. Click **Back** ⬅.

27. Click **Undo** ↩ twice to return the letter to its original margins and orientation.

28. Save and close the document and exit from **Word**.

29. Submit your final file based on the guidelines provided by your instructor.

    To view examples of how your file or files should look at the end of this exercise, go to the student resource center.

Create, Edit, and Print Preview a Letter

Word 2013

In this exercise, you will type a fundraising letter and an envelope and make some editing changes. You will create an AutoCorrect shortcut, and then add some text to the letter that you will copy from another document. Finally, you will preview the letter and modify the margins.

Insert Text and Use AutoComplete

You have been asked to draft a letter to send to Kids for Change members regarding the car wash fundraiser, which will be discussed at the next monthly meeting.

1. Start **Word**. Create a new document using the **Single Spaced (Blank)** template.

2. When the window appears describing the template, click **Create** 📄.

3. Save the letter as **WD02-R03-CarWash-[FirstInitialLastName]** in your **WD2013 Lesson 02** folder.

4. If necessary, choose **Home→Paragraph→Show/Hide** ¶ to display formatting marks.

5. Type this letter, tapping ⎡Enter⎤ wherever you see a paragraph symbol. Use **AutoComplete** to help with the dates.

¶
¶
¶
¶
¶
August·6,·2013¶
¶
¶
¶
MEMBER·NAME¶
STREET·ADDRESS¶
CITY,·STATE·ZIP¶
¶
Dear·MEMBER,·¶
¶
Our·local·chapter·of·Kids·for·Change·is·planning·to·hold·a·car·wash·fundraiser·to·collect·$300·in·order·to· adopt·a·seal·at·the·Center·for·Seals.··We're·aiming·for·August·31ˢᵗ·as·the·car·wash·date.·The·next·monthly· meeting·will·be·a·planning·session·for·the·car·wash.·Here·are·some·things·to·think·about·before·the· meeting:¶
¶

Create an Envelope

6. Position the insertion point at the top of the document.

7. Choose **Mailings→Create→Envelopes** 📧.

8. In the dialog box, if necessary, check the **Omit** box to prevent a return address, and then click **Add to Document**.

Select and Edit Text

Looking back over what you have typed, you see some changes you would like to make.

9. In the first line of the first paragraph, select *is planning* and replace it with **plans**.

10. Toward the end of the same line, select *in order* and tap Delete.

11. In the next line, select *August 31ˢᵗ as the car wash date* and replace it with **Saturday, September 7th**.

12. Tap Spacebar and the suffix following 7 changes to a superscript.

13. Tap Backspace to remove the extra space. Save your changes.

Work with AutoCorrect

Next you will check to see if an AutoFormat as You Type option caused th *to change to a superscript.*

14. Choose **File→Options**, and then choose **Proofing** from the left panel.

15. Click **AutoCorrect Options**. When the dialog box opens, click the **AutoFormat As You Type** tab.

The checkmark in the box next to Ordinals (1st) with Superscript is causing the superscripts. The checkmark in the box next to Automatic Numbered Lists will help you with the next part of the letter.

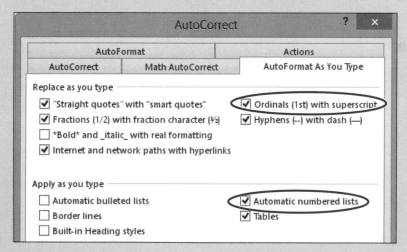

16. Click **OK** twice.

17. Hover the mouse pointer over the superscript in the September date, and drag down to display the **AutoCorrect Options smart tag**.

18. Click the tag and observe, but don't click, the Undo Superscript option.

19. Click away from the tag to close it.

20. Position the insertion point next to the paragraph symbol in the blank line following the main paragraph and tap Enter.

21. Type **1.** and tap Spacebar to begin automatic numbering.

    The AutoCorrect Options smart tag appears.

22. Click the **smart tag** to see the menu options; click away from the tag to close it.

23. Type the rest of the letter as shown, tapping Enter where you see a paragraph symbol.

    Hint: When you finish item 5, tap Enter three times: twice to turn off numbering and once to generate a blank line after the list.

> meeting·will·be·a·planning·session·for·the·car·wash.·Here·are·some·things·to·think·about·before·the·
> meeting:¶
> ¶
>   1.→ Choose·a·location.··Our·options·are·the·parking·lots·at·Jake's·Gas·Station,·Beulah's·Diner,·or·Dick's·
>   Grocery·Store.¶
>   2.→ What·hours·can·you·volunteer·on·September· 7th?¶
>   3.→ Can·you·supply·a·hose,·vacuum,·soap,·brushes,·sponges,·or·rags?¶
>   4.→ Should·we·set·a·price·or·request·a·donation?¶
>   5.→ Can·you·design·a·flyer·to·let·people·know·that·this·is·for·a·good·cause?¶
> ¶
> We·look·forward·to·a·great·planning·session.··See·you·at·the·meeting!¶
> ¶
> Sincerely,¶
> ¶
> ¶
> ¶
> Robert·Chan¶
> Kids·for·Change¶

Copy Text and Switch Between Documents

The supervisor wants to include information about the Center for Seals so the members will know the good work this organization does. You will copy the information from a document the supervisor provided.

24. Open **WD02-R03-Seals** from your **WD2013 Lesson 02** folder.

25. Press Ctrl + A to select all and then press Ctrl + C to copy all.

26. Close the **WD02-R03-Seals** document.

    Your car wash letter will be in the foreground.

27. Position the insertion point after the space following the first sentence in the first paragraph and tap Enter.

> Our·local·chapter·of·Kids·for·Change·plans·to·hold·a·car·wash·fundraiser·to·collect·$300·
> to·adopt·a·seal·at·the·Center·for·Seals.·¶
> We·are·aiming·for·Saturday,·September·7th·for·the·car·wash.·The·next·monthly·meeting·
> will·be·a·planning·session·for·the·car·wash.·Here·are·some·things·to·think·about·before·
> the·meeting:¶

28. Position the insertion point at the end of the first paragraph and press Ctrl + V.

    The Seals information is now part of the first paragraph.

Use Page Layout Options and Print Preview

Next you will preview the letter to see if it is well balanced on the page.

29. Choose **File→Print**, and preview the letter.

    You decide to widen the margins.

30. Click **Back** ⬅.

31. Choose **Page Layout→Page Setup→Margins** ⊞ and choose **Custom Margins** at the bottom of the gallery.

32. Use the spin boxes to change the Left and Right margins to 1.5", then click **OK**.

33. Choose **File→Print** to preview the letter.

    That looks better.

34. Click **Back** ⬅.

35. Save and close your letter, then exit from **Word**.

36. Submit your final file based on the guidelines provided by your instructor.

Apply Your Skills

Create a Letter and an Envelope

In this exercise, you will create a modified block-style letter, and you'll turn on the ruler to ensure the correct spacing for the date, complimentary close, and signature block. You will use AutoComplete to help you with the dates, and you will add an envelope to the letter.

Create a Block-Style Letter and Enter Text

1. Start **Word**. Create a new document using the **Single Spaced (Blank)** template.

2. Save the file in your **WD2013 Lesson 02** folder as `WD02-A01-BellLetter-[FirstInitialLastName]`.

3. Choose **View→Show→Ruler**.

4. Create the **modified block-style letter** shown in the following illustration.

Today's Date

Mrs. Suzanne Lee
8445 South Princeton Street
Chicago, IL 60628

Dear Mrs. Lee:

Congratulations on your outstanding sales achievement! Universal Corporate Events is organizing your Paris tour, which departs Saturday, October 6th and returns Wednesday, October 16th.

Please plan to attend the orientation meeting on Wednesday, September 18th in the Lake View conference room at 10:00 a.m.

We look forward to making your trip a memorable event!

Best regards,

Jack Bell
Universal Corporate Events

---

5. Follow these guidelines as you type your letter:
   - Space down the proper distance from the top of the page.
   - Use **AutoComplete** to help you with the dates.
   - Use ⌜Tab⌝ to align the date, closing, and signature block at **3 inches** on the ruler. (You'll need to tap ⌜Tab⌝ six times.)
   - Use correct spacing.

Create an Envelope

6. Create an envelope with no return address, and add it to the top of your letter.

7. Save and close the document; exit from **Word**.

8. Submit your final file based on the guidelines provided by your instructor.

    To view examples of how your file or files should look at the end of this exercise, go to the student resource center.

APPLY YOUR SKILLS WD02-A02

Edit a Document

In this exercise, you will make changes to a letter and copy text from another document into it. Then you will create an AutoCorrect entry, change margins, and preview your letter.

Edit Text and Work with AutoCorrect

1. Start **Word**. Open **WD02-A02-SFTours** from your **WD2013 Lesson 02** folder and save it as `WD02-A02-SFTours-[FirstInitialLastName]`.

2. Make the following editing changes, adjusting spacing as needed:
    - In the first line of the first paragraph, select *needs regarding planning your* and replace it with **annual**.
    - In the second line of the same paragraph, insert **San Francisco** to the left of *meeting*, and at the end of that sentence, ⌧Delete *in San Francisco*.
    - In the first line of the Sausalito paragraph, type **San Francisco** to the left of *skyline* and ⌧Delete *San Francisco* later in that sentence.
    - In the same sentence, type **the** to the left of *Bay*.
    - In the second sentence, type **waterfront** before *restaurant* and ⌧Delete *built over the water*. In the same sentence, ⌧Delete *the waterfront* and the comma that follows it.
    - In the second line of the Muir Woods paragraph, replace *wonderful* with **majestic**.

Switch Between Documents and Copy Text

Now you will copy some tour ideas from another document.

3. Open **WD02-A02-SiliconValley** from your **WD2013 Lesson 02** folder.

4. Select the entire document and copy it.

5. Switch back to the original letter, and position the insertion point on the second blank line following the Muir Woods paragraph.

6. Paste the copied text in the document; switch back to **WD02-A02-SiliconValley** and close it.

7. Type the current date at the top of the letter, positioning it approximately one inch from the top of the page.

8. Add the appropriate space after the date and type the following inside address:

```
Ms. Addison Alexander
Reukert Technology
123 Apple Blossom Lane
Detroit, MI 48217
```

9. If necessary, adjust the space between the address and the salutation.

Work with AutoCorrect, Margins, and Print Preview

10. Create an **AutoCorrect shortcut** for *Universal Corporate Events* using **uce** as the shortcut characters, but don't close the dialog box.

11. Press [Alt]+[Prt Screen] to take a screenshot of the dialog box showing your new entry; click **OK** twice to close the dialog boxes.

12. Paste the screenshot into a new, blank Word document and save it as **WD02-A02-ScnCap-[FirstInitialLastName]** in your **WD2013 Lesson 02** folder.

13. Close the file.

14. Change the margins in your letter to the **Narrow** setting in the Margins gallery.

15. Add the following complimentary close and signature block using your AutoCorrect shortcut for the company name, and ensure correct spacing.

```
Sincerely,
Geoff Simons
Universal Corporate Events
```

16. Open the **Word Options** window, and delete the **AutoCorrect entry** you just created.

17. Save and close your file; exit from **Word**.

18. Submit your final files based on the guidelines provided by your instructor.
    To view examples of how your file or files should look at the end of this exercise, go to the student resource center.

APPLY YOUR SKILLS WD02-A03

Type and Edit a Letter, Use AutoCorrect, and Copy Text

In this exercise, you will prepare a block-style letter and an envelope to send to a Universal Corporate Events employee, and you will make editing changes to the letter and work with AutoCorrect. You will copy text from another document, and you will preview the letter.

Insert Text and Add an Envelope

1. Start **Word**. Create a new document based on the **Single Spaced (Blank)** template.

2. Save your letter as **WD02-A03-WilliamsLtr-[FirstInitialLastName]** in your **WD2013 Lesson 02** folder.

3. Type this letter.

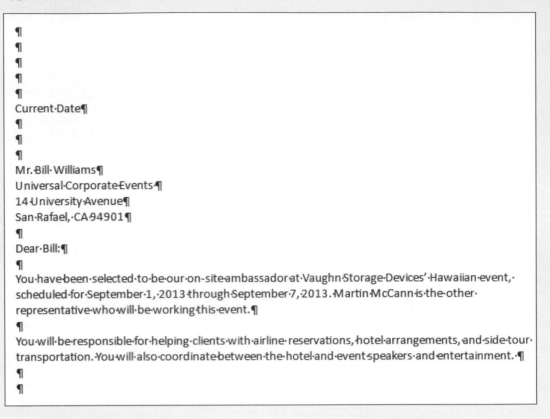

¶
¶
¶
¶
¶
Current·Date¶
¶
¶
¶
Mr.·Bill·Williams¶
Universal·Corporate·Events·¶
14·University·Avenue¶
San·Rafael,·CA·94901¶
¶
Dear·Bill:¶
¶
You·have·been·selected·to·be·our·on-site·ambassador·at·Vaughn·Storage·Devices'·Hawaiian·event,·scheduled·for·September·1,·2013·through·September·7,·2013.·Martin·McCann·is·the·other·representative·who·will·be·working·this·event.¶
¶
You·will·be·responsible·for·helping·clients·with·airline·reservations,·hotel·arrangements,·and·side·tour·transportation.·You·will·also·coordinate·between·the·hotel·and·event·speakers·and·entertainment.·¶
¶
¶

4. Create an envelope with no return address; add it to the top of your letter.

Edit Text

5. Make the following edits to the letter:
- In the first line of the first paragraph, change *ambassador* to **representative**.
- In the same line, change *Hawaiian* to **Kauai**.
- In the second line of the first paragraph, change the September dates to **8** through **14**.
- At the beginning of the second paragraph, position the insertion point after *You*, tap Spacebar, and type **and Martin**.
- Change *entertainment* at the end of the second paragraph to **entertainers**.

Work with AutoFormat
Next you will type ordinals (numbers that indicate order). Word's AutoFormat feature automatically changes the ordinal suffixes to superscripts. You will turn that feature off.

6. Open the **Word Options window**, choose **Proofing** from the left panel, and click **AutoCorrect Options**.

7. Click the **AutoFormat as You Type** tab, click in the box next to **Ordinals (1st) with Superscript** to remove the checkmark, and click **OK** twice.

AutoFormat As You Type
☐ Ordinals (1st) with superscript
☑ Hyphens (--) with dash (—)

8. Position the insertion point on the second blank line at the end of the document and type the following: **The side tours will take place on September 9th, 10th, 11th, and 12th.**

9. Reset the **Ordinals** checkbox back to its original state.

Switch Between Documents and Copy Text

10. Open **WD02-A03-SideTours** from the **WD2013 Lesson 02** folder.

11. Select and copy the text.

12. Switch back to the original letter and paste the text at the end of the sentence you just typed.

13. Switch back to **WD02-A03-SideTours** and close it.

14. Add the following closing and signature block to the end of the letter; be sure to use the correct spacing.

Sincerely,

Jose Ramirez
Universal Corporate Events

Use Page Layout Options

15. Choose **Page Layout→Page Setup→Size**, and choose **Executive** from the gallery.

16. Preview the document. You may need to adjust the zoom control in the bottom-right corner of the window to see the letter and the envelope at the same time.

    You realize that executive size paper doesn't work well with a standard business envelope.

17. Change the paper size back to **Letter**.

18. Save your letter and close it; exit from **Word**.

19. Submit your final file based on the guidelines provided by your instructor.

Extend Your Skills

In the course of working through the Extend Your Skills exercises, you will think critically as you use the skills taught in the lesson to complete the assigned projects. To evaluate your mastery and completion of the exercises, your instructor may use a rubric, with which more points are allotted according to performance characteristics. (The more you do, the more you earn!) Ask your instructor how your work will be evaluated.

WD02-E01 That's the Way I See It

You have decided to start your own landscaping business, and you are going to conduct some online research to see what's involved. Your friend is studying for his MBA, and you will send him a letter containing the results of your research and ask him what he thinks of your idea.

Create a block-style letter, including a list of five landscaping tools that your research shows you will need to purchase. Then research what is involved in becoming certified as a landscape professional, and explain to your friend how you plan to earn your certification. Finally, list three tips for running a successful landscaping business. The letter should include at least three paragraphs (one to give an overview of the business, one or more to discuss certification, and one for the conclusion) and a list of three tips. The spacing in the inside address and signature block should be 1.0. Proof your work and, as necessary, use Copy and Paste or drag and drop to make changes.

Set the orientation to Landscape, and then view your letter in Print Preview. Exit Backstage view and return the orientation to Portrait. Save the file in your **WD2013 Lesson 02** folder as **WD02-E01-NewBusiness-[FirstInitialLastName]**. You will be evaluated based on the inclusion of all elements specified, your ability to follow directions, your ability to apply newly learned skills to a real-world situation, your creativity, and the relevance of your topic and/or data choice(s). Submit your final file based on the guidelines provided by your instructor.

WD02-E02 Be Your Own Boss

Blue Jean Landscaping has a new client from outside of your region who learned about your services on the Internet. She would like you to landscape her front yard. Use your imagination to decide on the client's location and climate. Conduct online research to determine what shrubs and other plants work well for the climate you chose (for example, a home in Chicago would take different plants compared to a home in San Francisco). Send the client a modified block-style letter with indented paragraphs and traditional letter line spacing to propose four plant options that would work well for her. The letter should contain both an introductory and concluding paragraph, as well as a list of four plant options, and each option should be associated with two to three sentences that explain why it is a good choice for the client's front yard. Since you will, no doubt, type "Blue Jean Landscaping" multiple times, set up an AutoCorrect entry associated with BJL.

Save the letter as **WD02-E02-NewClient-[FirstInitialLastName]** in your **WD2013 Lesson 02** folder. Proof your work and, as necessary, use Copy and Paste and drag and drop to make edits. Remove the AutoCorrect entry. Then save and close the letter. You will be evaluated based on the inclusion of all elements specified, your ability to follow directions, your ability to apply newly learned skills to a real-world situation, your creativity, and your demonstration of an entrepreneurial spirit. Submit your final file based on the guidelines provided by your instructor.

Transfer Your Skills

In the course of working through the Transfer Your Skills exercises, you will use critical-thinking and creativity skills to complete the assigned projects using skills taught in the lesson. To evaluate your mastery and completion of the exercises, your instructor may use a rubric, with which more points are allotted according to performance characteristics. (The more you do, the more you earn!) Ask your instructor how your work will be evaluated.

WD02-T01 Use the Web as a Learning Tool

Throughout this book, you will be provided with an opportunity to use the Internet as a learning tool by completing WebQuests. According to the original creators of WebQuests, as described on their website (WebQuest.org), a WebQuest is "an inquiry-oriented activity in which most or all of the information used by learners is drawn from the web." To complete the WebQuest projects in this book, navigate to the student resource center and choose the WebQuest for the lesson on which you are currently working. The subject of each WebQuest will be relevant to the material found in the lesson.

WebQuest Subject: Proper business correspondence etiquette.

Submit your final file(s) based on the guidelines provided by your instructor.

WD02-T02 Demonstrate Proficiency

As the owner of Stormy BBQ, you've decided to hold a chili cook-off to attract new clients. Use online research to learn how to have a successful cook-off, and also research rules for the chefs to ensure that they are competing on a level playing field.

Create a letter using the style of your choice (making sure to properly format it) to send out to prospective chili chefs listing three important guidelines for a successful cook-off and three competition rules for your chefs. The letter should include both an introductory and a concluding paragraph, as well as the rules that have been established. Make up the name of the first chef you wish to invite and include the information in the inside address. Create an envelope addressed to the chef with no return address.

Proof your work and, as necessary, use Copy and Paste or drag and drop to make edits. Change all margins to 0.5" and view the effect in Print Preview.

Save your letter in the **WD2013 Lesson 02** folder as `WD02-T02-ChiliChef-[FirstInitialLastName]`. Submit your final file based on the guidelines provided by your instructor.

WORD 2013

Creating a Memorandum and a Press Release

LEARNING OBJECTIVES

After studying this lesson, you will be able to:

- Use Word's default tabs
- Insert dates, symbols, and page breaks
- Work with proofreading tools and the thesaurus
- Work with character formatting features
- Edit PDF files in Word

In this lesson, you will expand your basic Word skills. You will create a memo, apply character formatting, and use spelling and grammar checking. You will refine your word choice with the thesaurus, and you'll learn some efficient ways to navigate in documents. Finally, you will transform PDF files into fully editable Word documents.

Preparing a Memorandum

My Virtual Campus continues to grow and add the latest advances in technology. The public relations representative has asked you to create a memorandum and attach a press release announcing the launch of MyResume, which is being integrated into the website. You understand the importance of protecting proprietary information, so you use the appropriate trademark designations in your documents.

When the marketing department decides to change the product name, the Find and Replace feature makes changing the name throughout the document a snap.

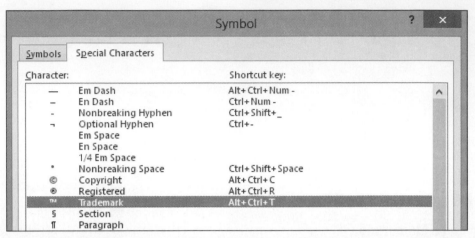

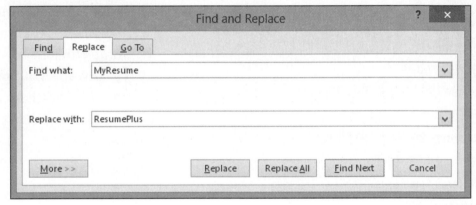

Typing a Memorandum

Video Library   http://labyrinthelab.com/videos   Video Number: WD13-V0301

There are a variety of acceptable memorandum styles in use today. They all contain the same elements, but with varied formatting. The style shown here is a traditional style with minimal formatting.

The introduction includes headings such as *Memo To* and *From*. ——

MEMO TO:	Galin Rodgers
FROM:	Suzanne Student
DATE:	December 10, 2013
SUBJECT:	My Virtual Campus Press Release

The body is next. —— I have attached a press release to announce the launch of the new MyResume service. Please review the press release and let me know if you have comments or suggestions. I will submit this press release to the media organization next week.

Extras, such as attachment notations, go here. —— Attachment

Introducing Default Tabs

The ⌈Tab⌋ key moves the insertion point to the nearest tab stop on the ruler. In Word, the default tab stops are set every one-half inch, thus the insertion point moves one-half inch when you tap ⌈Tab⌋. In this lesson, you will use Word's default tab settings.

FROM THE RIBBON
View→Show→Ruler

Inserting and Formatting the Date

Word lets you insert the current date in a variety of formats. For example, the date could be inserted as 12/10/13, December 10, 2013, or 10 December 2013.

FROM THE RIBBON
Insert→Text→Insert
Date and Time

FROM THE KEYBOARD
⌈Alt⌋+⌈Shift⌋ I ⌈D⌋ to
insert the date

Updating the Date Automatically

You can insert the date as text or as a field. Inserting the date as text has the same effect as manually typing the date. Fields, on the other hand, are updated whenever a document is saved or printed.

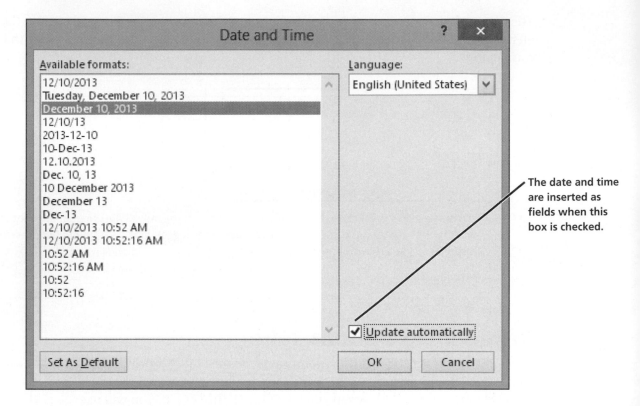

The date and time are inserted as fields when this box is checked.

Set Up a Memo and Insert the Date

In this exercise, you will create a memo using Word's default tab settings and automatically insert the date. You'll also use Word's Blank Document template, which applies 1.08 line spacing with extra space following paragraphs.

1. Start a new document using the **Blank Document template**. Make sure the Word window is **maximized** 🗖.

2. Save the file in your **WD2013 Lesson 03** folder as **WD03-D01-MartinMemo-[FirstInitialLastName]**.

   Replace the bracketed text with your first initial and last name. For example, if your name is Bethany Smith, your filename would look like this: WD03-D01-MartinMemo-BSmith.

3. If necessary, choose **Home→Paragraph→Show/Hide** ¶ to display formatting marks.

   Next you will turn on the ruler so you can observe that Word's default tabs are set at every one-half inch.

4. If necessary, choose **View→Show→Ruler**.

   The ruler opens below the Ribbon and on the left side of the screen.

5. Follow these steps to begin the memo:

A Tap Enter twice to position the insertion point approximately two inches from the top of the page. (Because this template uses after-paragraph spacing, you only need to tap Enter twice.)

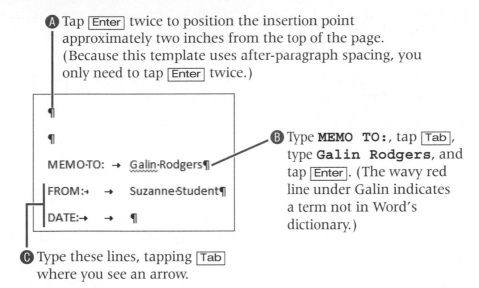

B Type **MEMO TO:**, tap Tab, type **Galin Rodgers**, and tap Enter. (The wavy red line under Galin indicates a term not in Word's dictionary.)

C Type these lines, tapping Tab where you see an arrow.

6. Choose **Insert→Text→Insert Date and Time** 📅.

7. Follow these steps to insert the date:

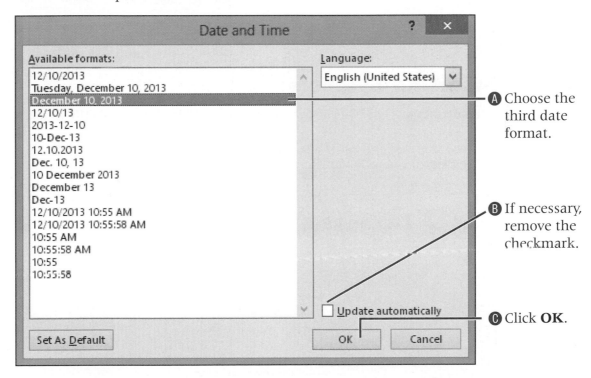

A Choose the third date format.

B If necessary, remove the checkmark.

C Click **OK**.

Leaving Update Automatically checked instructs Word to insert the date as a field, which means the original date would be lost if you opened and saved the document at a later date. In this instance, you do not want the date to change.

The date shown here may differ from the current date that you use.

8. Choose **Home→Paragraph→Show/Hide ¶** to turn off formatting marks.

9. Complete the rest of the memorandum as shown, using Tab to align the text in the Subject line. Bear in mind that you only need to tap Enter once between paragraphs due to this template's after-paragraph spacing.

MEMO TO: Galin Rodgers

FROM: Suzanne Student

DATE: December 10, 2013

SUBJECT: My Virtual Campus Press Release

I have attached a press release to announce the launch of the new MyResume service. Please review the press release and let me know if you have comments or suggestions. I will submit this press release to the media organization next week.

Attachment

---

10. Choose **View→Show→Ruler** to turn off the ruler.

11. Save the document and leave it open; you will modify it throughout this lesson.

Inserting Symbols

Video Library   http://labyrinthelab.com/videos   Video Number: WD13-V0302

Word lets you insert a variety of symbols and other characters not found on the keyboard. The following illustration shows the Symbol menu.

FROM THE RIBBON
Insert→Symbols
→Symbol

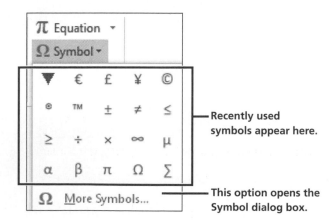

Recently used symbols appear here.

This option opens the Symbol dialog box.

The following figure points out the main features of the Symbol dialog box.

This tab displays commonly used special characters, such as copyright © and registered trademark ®.

You can choose characters from a variety of fonts.

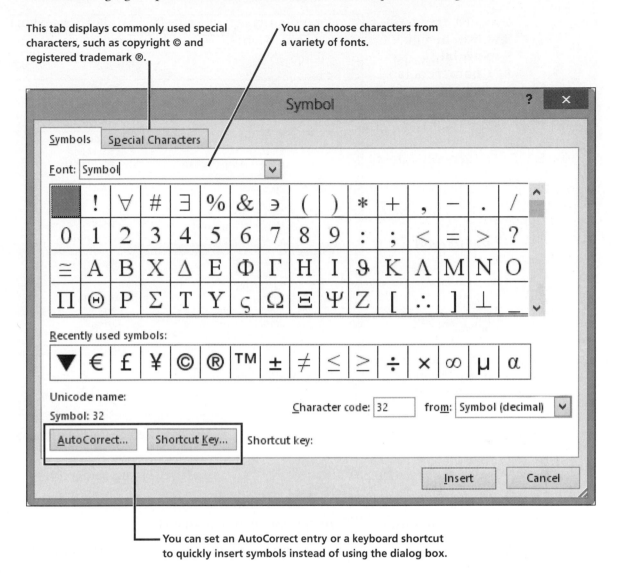

You can set an AutoCorrect entry or a keyboard shortcut to quickly insert symbols instead of using the dialog box.

DEVELOP YOUR SKILLS WD03-D02

Insert Symbols

In this exercise, you will add a trademark symbol and a registered trademark symbol to your document.

1. Save your file as **WD03-D02-MartinMemo-[FirstInitialLastName]**.

2. Position the insertion point to the right of My Virtual Campus in the **Subject** line.

3. Choose **Insert→Symbols→Symbol** Ω, and then choose **More Symbols** at the bottom of the menu.

4. Follow these steps to insert the registered trademark symbol:

Ⓐ Click the **Special Characters** tab.

Ⓑ Choose **Registered**.

Ⓒ Click **Insert**. (The dialog box remains open so you can insert additional symbols.)

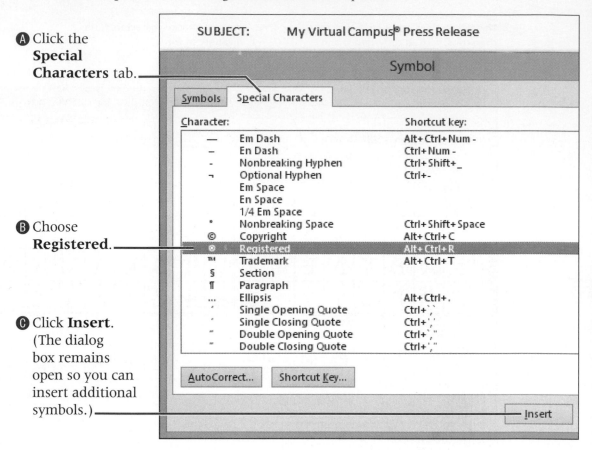

5. Position the insertion point to the right of *MyResume* in the main paragraph.
You may need to drag the dialog box out of the way.

6. Click the **Trademark** (™) symbol, and then click **Insert**.

7. Click the **Symbols** tab and choose different fonts from the **Font** list to see other sets of symbols.

8. When you finish experimenting, click **Close**.

9. Save the memo.

Working with Page Breaks

Word 2013

Video Library   http://labyrinthelab.com/videos   Video Number: WD13-V0303

If you are typing text and the insertion point reaches the bottom of a page, Word inserts an *automatic* page break. Automatic page breaks are convenient when working with long documents. For example, imagine you are writing a report and you decide to insert a new paragraph in the middle. Word automatically repaginates the report.

A manual page break remains in place unless you remove it. You insert manual page breaks whenever you want to control the starting point of a new page.

FROM THE RIBBON

Page Layout→Page Setup→Breaks→Page

FROM THE KEYBOARD

Ctrl + Enter to insert a manual page break

Removing Manual Page Breaks

If you turn on the Show/Hide feature, you can see the page break in Print Layout view. You delete a page break the same way you delete other content in a document.

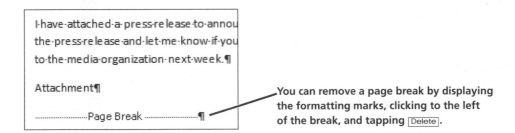

You can remove a page break by displaying the formatting marks, clicking to the left of the break, and tapping Delete.

DEVELOP YOUR SKILLS WD03-D03
Work with Page Breaks

In this exercise, you will insert a page break, thereby creating a new page, so you can copy and paste a press release into the new page.

1. Save your file as **WD03-D03-MartinMemo-[FirstInitialLastName]**.

   Next you will ensure you are in Print Layout view so you can see the page break. You can see a page break in other views, but you will use Print Layout view.

2. Choose **View→Views→Print Layout** ▤.

3. Press Ctrl + End to position the insertion point at the end of the document. If necessary, tap Enter to generate a blank line below the *Attachment* line.

4. Choose **Insert→Pages→Page Break** ⊟.

5. If necessary, scroll to the bottom of page 1 to see the new page 2.

6. Scroll up until the *Attachment* line is visible.

7. If necessary, choose **Home→Paragraph→Show/Hide** ¶ to display formatting marks.

8. Position the insertion point to the left of the page break and tap Delete.

9. Try scrolling down to the second page and you will see that it is gone.

10. Check to see that the insertion point is just below the *Attachment* line, and press Ctrl + Enter to reinsert the page break.

11. Choose **Home→Paragraph→Show/Hide** ¶ to hide the formatting marks.

Copy and Paste from Another Document

12. Open **WD03-D03-PressRelease** from your **WD2013 Lesson 03** folder.
    Notice that a number of terms are flagged by the spelling checker (red wavy underlines) and grammar checker (blue wavy underline). Ignore these notations for now.

13. In the press release document, press Ctrl + A to select the entire document.

14. Press Ctrl + C to copy the document.
    Now you will switch to your memo.

15. Follow these steps to switch to the memo:

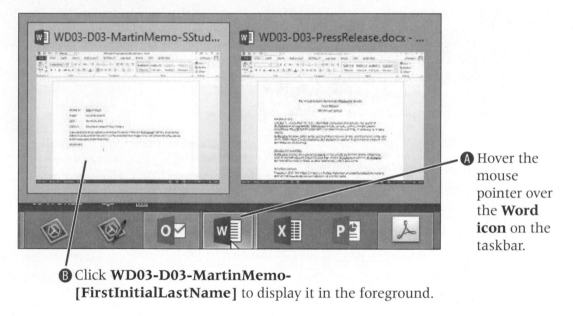

Ⓐ Hover the mouse pointer over the **Word icon** on the taskbar.

Ⓑ Click **WD03-D03-MartinMemo-[FirstInitialLastName]** to display it in the foreground.

16. Make sure the insertion point is at the top of **page 2**.

17. Choose **Home→Clipboard→Paste** 📋.
    Now you will switch back to the press release and close it.

18. Use the taskbar button to switch to the press release document.

19. Choose **File→Close**.
    The memo document should now be in the foreground.

20. Save the file.

Working with Proofreading Tools

Video Library   http://labyrinthelab.com/videos   Video Number: WD13-V0304

Word's spelling and grammar tools help you avoid errors. You can choose to use the default *on-the-fly* checking, where Word marks possible errors as you type, or you can save proofing until you've completed your document. Word provides many choices allowing you to set the level of grammar and style checking from strict to casual.

Proofing tools can help polish your writing; however, they are proofreading *aids*, not the final word. You still need human judgment in a final round of proofing.

FROM THE RIBBON
Review→Proofing
→Spelling & Grammar

FROM THE KEYBOARD
F7 for proofreading tools

Options can be turned on and off, including checking spelling and grammar as you type, which is the default.

You can have Word check your writing style by choosing this option and clicking the Settings button.

When correcting spelling and grammar in Word

- ☑ Check spelling as you type
- ☑ Mark grammar errors as you type
- ☑ Frequently confused words
- ☑ Check grammar with spelling
- ☐ Show readability statistics

Writing Style: Grammar Only ∨   Settings...

Recheck Doc

Grammar & Style
Grammar Only

Grammar Setting

Writing style:
Grammar & Style

Grammar and style options:
- ☑ Punctuation
- ☑ Questions
- ☑ Relative clauses
- ☐ Subject-verb agreement
- ☑ Verb phrases

Style:
- ☑ Clichés, Colloquialisms, and Jargon
- ☑ Contractions
- ☐ Fragment - stylistic suggestions
- ☑ Gender-specific words
- ☑ Hyphenated and compound words
- ☑ Misused words - stylistic suggestions
- ☑ Numbers
- ☑ Passive sentences

Choose options to suit your writing style.

Word 2013

Using the Spelling Checker

Word can automatically check your spelling as you type. It flags spelling errors with wavy red lines. You can address a flagged error by right-clicking it and choosing a suggested replacement word or other option from the pop-up menu.

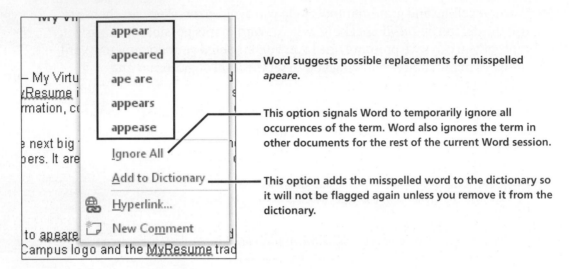

Word suggests possible replacements for misspelled *apeare*.

This option signals Word to temporarily ignore all occurrences of the term. Word also ignores the term in other documents for the rest of the current Word session.

This option adds the misspelled word to the dictionary so it will not be flagged again unless you remove it from the dictionary.

Working with Word's Dictionaries

The main Word dictionary contains thousands of common words, though it does not include all proper names, technical terms, and so forth. Word marks a term not found in the main dictionary as a possible error. If you use that term frequently, you can add it to a custom dictionary so it will not be marked as an error.

Using Dictionary Options

When Suggest from Main Dictionary Only is checked, Word only searches the main dictionary; if that option is unchecked, Word searches in custom dictionaries as well. Adding a word to the dictionary during spell checking adds it to a custom dictionary.

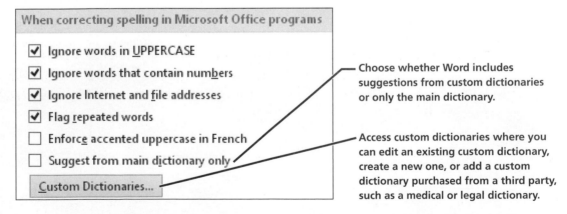

Choose whether Word includes suggestions from custom dictionaries or only the main dictionary.

Access custom dictionaries where you can edit an existing custom dictionary, create a new one, or add a custom dictionary purchased from a third party, such as a medical or legal dictionary.

The options you set for custom dictionaries in Word apply to all Office programs.

Adding or Deleting Words in a Custom Dictionary

In addition to adding words through the spelling checker, you can add words using the Custom Dictionaries dialog box. If you add a word to the dictionary by mistake, you can remove it.

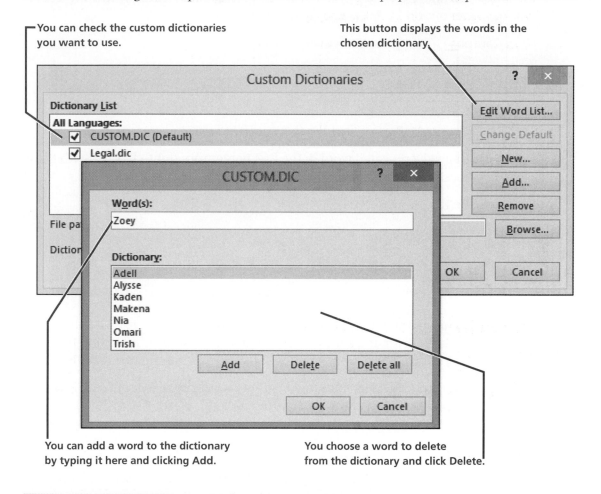

You can check the custom dictionaries you want to use.

This button displays the words in the chosen dictionary.

You can add a word to the dictionary by typing it here and clicking Add.

You choose a word to delete from the dictionary and click Delete.

Use the Automatic Spelling Checker

In this exercise, you will add a term to Word's dictionary. You will also delete a repeated word.

1. Save your file as **WD03-D04-MartinMemo-[FirstInitialLastName]**.

   Notice that the term MyResume in the first line of page 2 has a wavy red underline. MyResume is spelled correctly, but it does not appear in Word's dictionary. Thus, Word flags it as a possible spelling error.

2. Follow these steps to add *MyResume* to the dictionary:

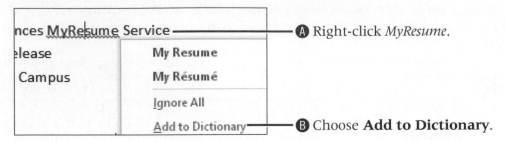

Ⓐ Right-click *MyResume*.

Ⓑ Choose **Add to Dictionary**.

You will delete MyResume from the dictionary a little later.

3. Word flagged a repeated word in the first paragraph; right-click *our* with the wavy red line and choose **Delete Repeated Word**.

4. Save the file.

Using the Grammar Checker

Video Library http://labyrinthelab.com/videos   Video Number: WD13-V0305

Word has a grammar checker that flags errors with wavy blue lines. Like the spelling checker, you right-click the error and choose a replacement phrase or other option from the menu. The grammar checker isn't perfect; there is no substitute for careful proofreading.

Like the spelling checker, the grammar checker also checks *on the fly*, and like the spelling checker, you can turn it off and save checking for later. Word uses the Spelling and Grammar task panes for making suggestions.

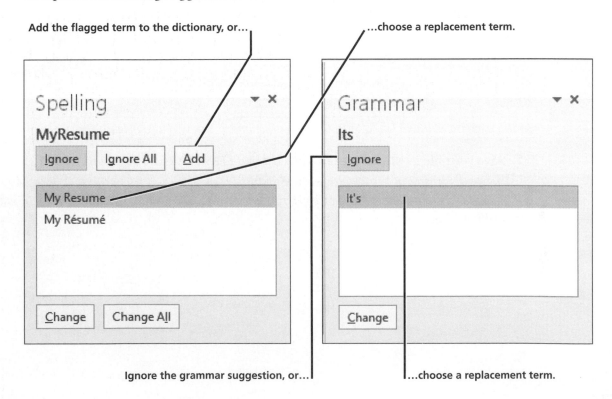

Add the flagged term to the dictionary, or...

...choose a replacement term.

Ignore the grammar suggestion, or...

...choose a replacement term.

QUICK REFERENCE	USING SPELLING AND GRAMMAR OPTIONS
Task	**Procedure**
Set level of grammar and style checking	■ Choose File→Options and choose the Proofing category. ■ Choose the Writing Style and click Settings.
Work with custom dictionaries	■ Choose File→Options and choose the Proofing category. ■ Click the Custom Dictionaries button.
Turn off spelling and grammar checking as you type	■ Choose File→Options and choose the Proofing category. ■ Uncheck the options for checking spelling and marking grammar as you type.

DEVELOP YOUR SKILLS WD03-D05

Use the Spelling and Grammar Checkers

In this exercise, you will make spelling and grammar corrections to the Martin Memo using the Spelling and Grammar task panes.

1. Save the file as **WD03-D05-MartinMemo-[FirstInitialLastName]**.

2. Position the insertion point at the beginning of the first line on **page 2**.

3. Choose **Review→Proofing→Spelling & Grammar** ✓.
   The Spelling task pane opens, and wiht *is noted as a possible spelling error.*

4. The error is a typo, and the suggestion *with* is correct, so click **Change**.
   Now Word points out Its *as a possible grammatical error.*

5. Click **Change** to accept the grammar suggestion.

6. The next error is a spelling error, and the suggestion *Delivery* is correct, so click **Change**.

7. Finish checking the rest of the document using your good judgment regarding what changes to make. When *Galin* is flagged, click **Ignore All**.

8. When the message appears indicating that the spelling and grammar check is complete, click **OK**.

Remove a Word from the Custom Dictionary

9. Choose **File→Options** and choose the **Proofing** category.

10. Follow these steps to delete MyResume:

Ⓐ Click **Custom Dictionaries**.　　　　　　　　Ⓑ Click **Edit Word List**.

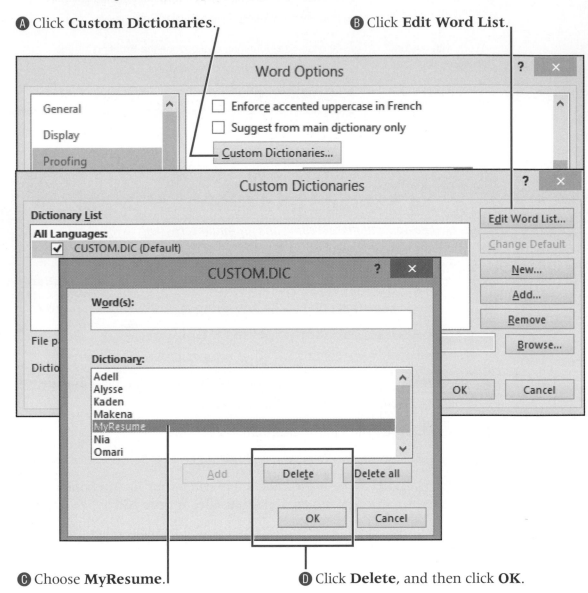

Ⓒ Choose **MyResume**.　　　　　　　　Ⓓ Click **Delete**, and then click **OK**.

11. Click **OK** two more times.

    MyResume is flagged again, because you removed it from the dictionary.

12. Right-click *MyResume* and choose **Ignore All**.

13. Save the file.

Using the Thesaurus to Find a Synonym

Video Library   http://labyrinthelab.com/videos   Video Number: WD13-V0306

You can view a list of synonyms by right-clicking a word and choosing Synonyms from the menu. For a more extensive list, choose Thesaurus from the bottom of the submenu to open the Thesaurus task pane.

The Thesaurus task pane goes beyond displaying a list of alternate words. As you know, a word can have different meanings depending upon the context in which it is used. For example, the word *launch* can be used to mean *presentation*, *takeoff*, *hurl*, or *open*. Using the task pane, you can look up those additional synonyms by clicking any word displayed in the results list.

FROM THE RIBBON
Review→Proofing
→Thesaurus

FROM THE KEYBOARD
Shift + F7 to open the
Thesaurus

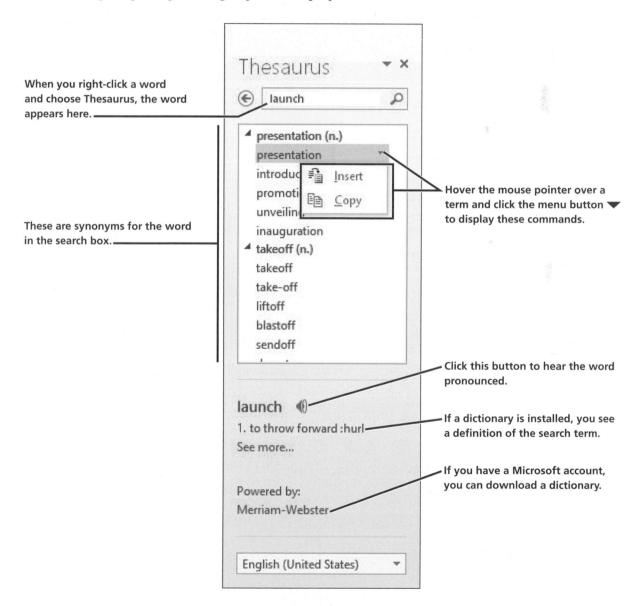

When you right-click a word and choose Thesaurus, the word appears here.

These are synonyms for the word in the search box.

Hover the mouse pointer over a term and click the menu button ▼ to display these commands.

Click this button to hear the word pronounced.

If a dictionary is installed, you see a definition of the search term.

If you have a Microsoft account, you can download a dictionary.

Use the Thesaurus

In this exercise, you will use the pop-up menu to locate a synonym. You will also use the Thesaurus task pane.

1. Save your file as **WD03-D06-MartinMemo-[FirstInitialLastName]**.

2. Scroll down to view the press release page.

3. Right-click the word *launch* in the first sentence of the *Announcement* paragraph.

4. Follow these steps to replace the word with a synonym:

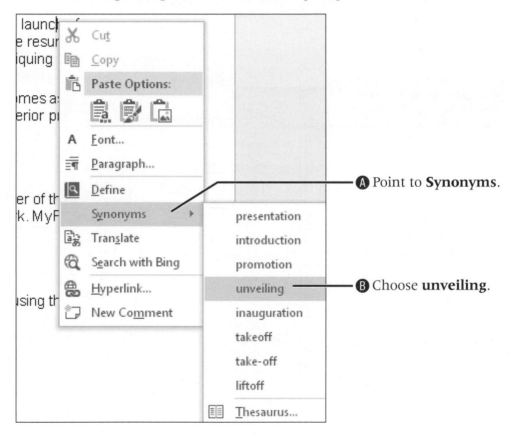

Ⓐ Point to **Synonyms**.

Ⓑ Choose **unveiling**.

Now you'll look up synonyms in the Thesaurus task pane.

5. Choose **Review→Proofing→Thesaurus** 📖.

6. Follow these steps to re-insert *launch* in place of *unveiling*.

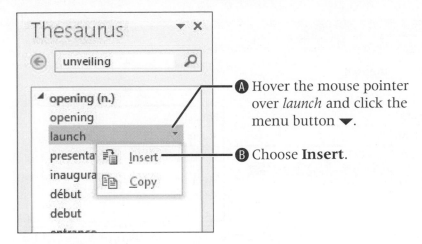

Ⓐ Hover the mouse pointer over *launch* and click the menu button ▼.

Ⓑ Choose **Insert**.

7. While the Thesaurus task pane is still open, click any word in the list to view synonyms for that word.

8. Click **Close** ☒ in the upper-right corner of the Thesaurus task pane.

9. Save the file.

Formatting Text

Video Library   http://labyrinthelab.com/videos   Video Number: WD13-V0307

You can format text using the Font group on the Home tab. Options include changing the font, size, and color and applying various enhancements, including bold, italics, and underline. You can also clear all added formatting from text, returning it to its default formats. You can change the text formatting before you start typing, or you can select existing text and then make the changes.

FROM THE KEYBOARD
Ctrl+B for bold
Ctrl+I for italics
Ctrl+U for underline

Additional options are available through the Font dialog box. The dialog box launcher in the bottom-right corner of the Font group opens the dialog box.

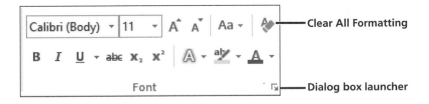

Clear All Formatting

Dialog box launcher

The following illustration describes the Font dialog box.

You can choose a font here.

You can choose a font color here.

Special effects are available here.

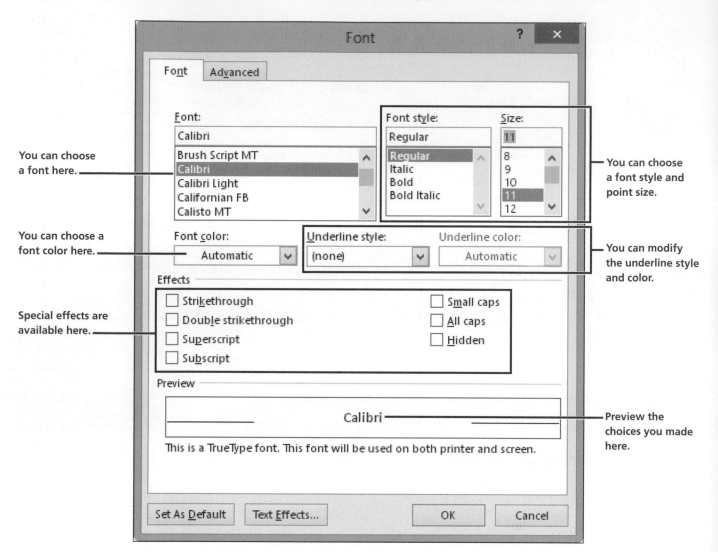

You can choose a font style and point size.

You can modify the underline style and color.

Preview the choices you made here.

Using Live Preview

Live Preview shows what a formatting change looks like without actually applying the format. Many formatting features provide a Live Preview. In the following example, selecting a block of text and then hovering the mouse pointer over a font name previews how the text would look.

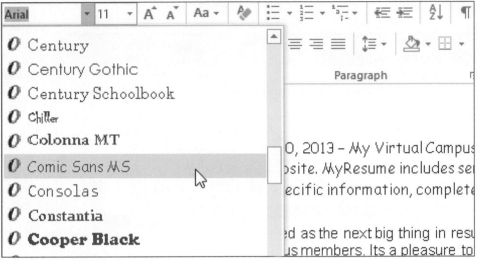

Live Preview of the Comic Sans MS font

Format Text

In this exercise, you will explore fonts using Live Preview. You will use both the Ribbon and the Font dialog box to format text.

1. Save your file as **WD03-D07-MartinMemo-[FirstInitialLastName]**.

2. Scroll to the top of the second page and select the three heading lines.

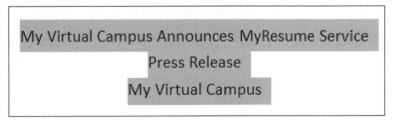

3. Choose **Home→Font** and click the drop-down arrow ▼ to the right of **Calibri (Body)**.

4. Slide the mouse pointer down the font list to see the effect of different fonts with Live Preview.

5. Click in the document to close the font list, and then make sure the first three lines on page 2 are still selected.

   Now you'll use the Font dialog box to change the font and font size.

6. Follow these steps to make the changes:

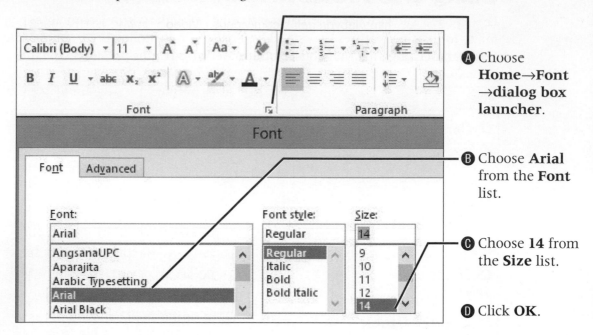

Ⓐ Choose **Home→Font →dialog box launcher**.

Ⓑ Choose **Arial** from the **Font** list.

Ⓒ Choose **14** from the **Size** list.

Ⓓ Click **OK**.

7. With the three lines still selected, press Ctrl+B and then Ctrl+U to apply bold and underline to the headings.

8. Choose **Home→Font→Underline** Ⓤ to remove the underline.

9. Follow these steps to apply bold formatting to multiple selections at the same time:

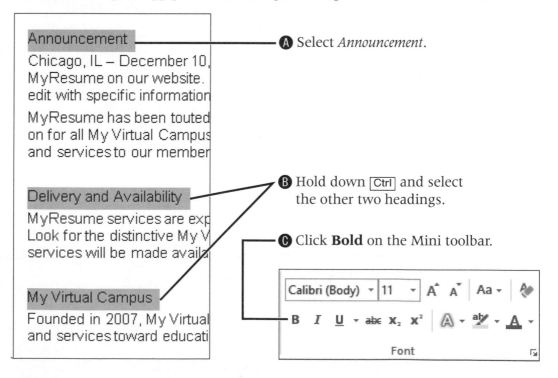

Ⓐ Select *Announcement*.

Ⓑ Hold down Ctrl and select the other two headings.

Ⓒ Click **Bold** on the Mini toolbar.

10. Save the file.

Working with the Format Painter

Video Library   http://labyrinthelab.com/videos   Video Number: WD13-V0308

FROM THE RIBBON

Home→Clipboard
→Format Painter

FROM THE KEYBOARD

Ctrl + Shift + C to
copy a format

Ctrl + Shift + V to
paste a format

The Format Painter lets you copy text formats, including font, font size, and color, from one location to another. This saves time and helps create consistent formatting throughout a document. The Format Painter command is on both the Ribbon and the Mini toolbar.

QUICK REFERENCE	COPYING TEXT FORMATS WITH THE FORMAT PAINTER
Task	**Procedure**
Copy text formats with the Format Painter	■ Select the text with the format(s) to copy.
	■ Choose Home→Clipboard→Format Painter once to copy formats to one location (double-click to copy to multiple locations).
	■ Select the text location(s) to format.
	■ If you double-clicked initially, click the Format Painter again to turn it off.

DEVELOP YOUR SKILLS WD03-D08
Use the Format Painter

In this exercise, you will use both the Mini toolbar and the Format Painter to apply and copy formats. You will also copy a format and apply it to multiple blocks of text.

1. Save your file as **WD03-D08-MartinMemo-[FirstInitialLastName]**.

2. Scroll to page 2, if necessary, and select the *Announcement* heading line.

3. When the Mini toolbar appears, follow these steps to apply color to the heading line. (If the toolbar fades away, right-click the selected term to redisplay it.)

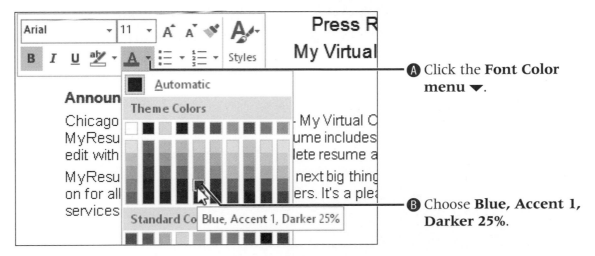

Ⓐ Click the **Font Color menu** ▼.

Ⓑ Choose **Blue, Accent 1, Darker 25%**.

4. Keep the text selected and the Mini toolbar active, and follow these steps to apply additional formats to the text:

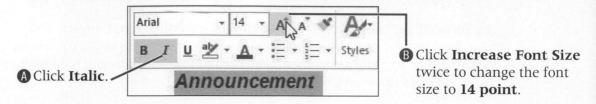

A Click **Italic**.

B Click **Increase Font Size** twice to change the font size to **14 point**.

Copy Formats to One Location

5. Make sure the *Announcement* heading line is selected.

6. Click the **Format Painter** on the Mini toolbar.
   A paintbrush icon is added to the mouse pointer once it is positioned over the document.

7. Drag the mouse pointer across the *Delivery and Availability* heading; release the mouse button.
   The 14 point italic blue formats should be copied to the heading.

8. Make sure the *Delivery and Availability* heading line is still selected.

9. Choose **Home→Clipboard→Format Painter** , and then select the last heading, *My Virtual Campus*, to copy the format again.

Copy Formats to More Than One Location

10. Scroll to the top of page 1 and select the heading *MEMO TO:* (include the colon).

11. Choose **Home→Font→Bold** Ⓑ.

12. Double-click the **Format Painter** and drag over *FROM:* to apply the formatting from *MEMO TO:*.

13. Drag over *DATE:* and *SUBJECT:* to format those headings.

14. Choose **Home→Clipboard→Format Painter** to turn it off.

15. Save the file.

Using Find and Replace

Video Library   http://labyrinthelab.com/videos   Video Number: WD13-V0309

The Find command lets you search a document for a word or phrase. You can also search for text formats, page breaks, and a variety of other items. Find is often the quickest way to locate a phrase, format, or other item. You can use Find and Replace to search for text and replace it with something else.

FROM THE RIBBON
Home→Editing→Find
Home→Editing
→Replace

FROM THE KEYBOARD
Ctrl+F for Find
Ctrl+H for Replace

Word 2013

Searching with the Navigation Pane

Clicking Find opens the Navigation task pane. When you search for an item, the results display in the task pane, giving you a quick view of everywhere the item appears.

The Search for More Things menu button ▼ displays a list of search options.

Results are also highlighted in the document.

You can enter the search term here.

These tabs control what displays in the task pane.

Found items appear here.

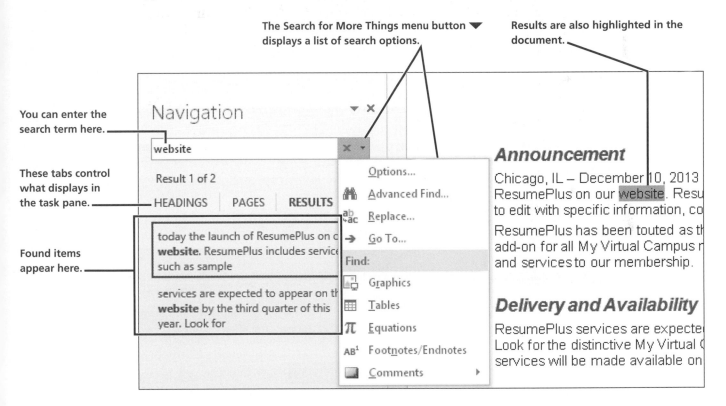

Using the Find and Replace Dialog Box

The Find and Replace dialog box includes the Find, Replace, and Go To tabs. The Find tab allows you to perform a more detailed search than the Navigation pane. The Replace tab allows you to enter a *Replace With* item to replace the *Find What* item. The Go To tab allows you to jump to a specific place in the document.

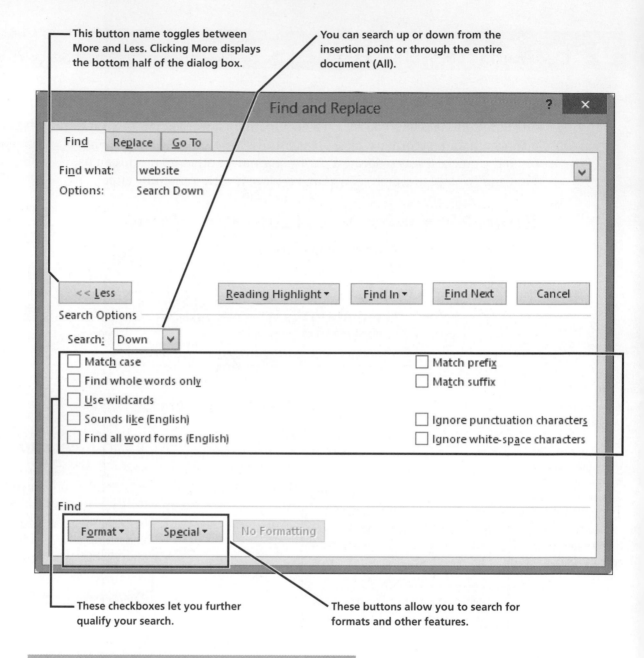

This button name toggles between More and Less. Clicking More displays the bottom half of the dialog box.

You can search up or down from the insertion point or through the entire document (All).

These checkboxes let you further qualify your search.

These buttons allow you to search for formats and other features.

Use Find

In this exercise, you will search with the Navigation pane and explore search options in the Find and Replace dialog box.

1. Save your file as **WD03-D09-MartinMemo-[FirstInitialLastName]**.

2. Position the insertion point at the top of page 2, and make sure no text is selected.

3. Choose **Home→Editing→Find** 🔍 to open the Navigation pane.

4. Type **website** in the search box to find all occurrences of the term.

   Notice that the search results appear in the Navigation pane, and they are highlighted in the document as well.

TIP If you don't see the search results, click the Results tab toward the top of the task pane.

5. Scroll to the top of the document and position the insertion point anywhere in the first line of the memo.

6. Click in the **Navigation pane** search box, delete *website*, and type **Announce** (with a capital A) in its place.

   Word located announce *in the first paragraph of the memo with a lowercase a, even though you typed it in uppercase.*

7. Click the second instance in the Navigation pane results list and notice that *Announces* is highlighted in the first line of the press release.

   Word found Announce, *even though it is part of* Announces. *By default, the search feature is not case sensitive and doesn't recognize the difference between a whole word and part of a word. You will change this, however, in the next few steps.*

Use the Match Case Option
Now you will use the Search for More Things menu to display the Find and Replace dialog box, and then you will use the Match Case option.

8. Place the insertion point in the first line of the first page.

9. Follow these steps to display the Find and Replace dialog box and activate Match Case:

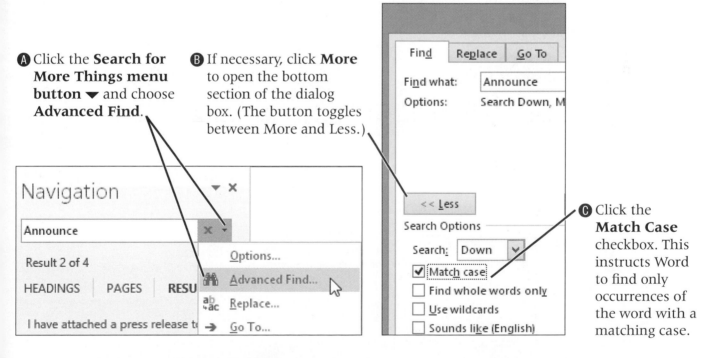

A Click the **Search for More Things menu button ▼** and choose **Advanced Find**.

B If necessary, click **More** to open the bottom section of the dialog box. (The button toggles between More and Less.)

C Click the **Match Case** checkbox. This instructs Word to find only occurrences of the word with a matching case.

10. Click **Find Next** and Word locates the capitalized *Announces*.

11. Click **Find Next** again and Word locates the capitalized *Announcement*.

12. Click **Find Next** again and Word indicates that the entire document has been searched.

   Word skipped over the lowercase forms of announce.

13. Click **OK** in the message box; then close the Find and Replace dialog box and the Navigation task pane.

14. Save the file.

Using Replace

Video Library   http://labyrinthelab.com/videos   Video Number: WD13-V0310

The Replace feature allows you to replace words, formats, and other elements in a document. As an example, you could search for a particular font and replace it with another.

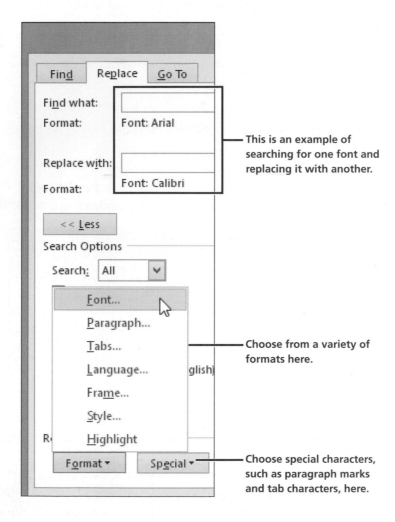

This is an example of searching for one font and replacing it with another.

Choose from a variety of formats here.

Choose special characters, such as paragraph marks and tab characters, here.

Use Replace

In this exercise, you will use the Replace feature. The Marketing Department decided to change the name MyResume to ResumePlus, so having Word automatically make the replacements for you is a real time saver.

1. Save your file as **WD03-D10-MartinMemo-[FirstInitialLastName]**.

2. Position the insertion point at the top of the document, and make sure no text is selected.

3. Press **Ctrl**+**H** to display the Find and Replace dialog box.
    Notice that the Replace tab is active in the dialog box.

4. If necessary, click **More** to expand the dialog box. (The button toggles between More and Less.)
    Match Case is still active from the previous exercise.

5. Uncheck **Match Case** to turn it off.

6. Click **Less** to collapse the More options section of the dialog box.

7. Follow these steps to replace MyResume with ResumePlus:

Ⓐ Replace the current text with **MyResume**. Ⓑ Type **ResumePlus** here. Ⓒ Click **Find Next**.

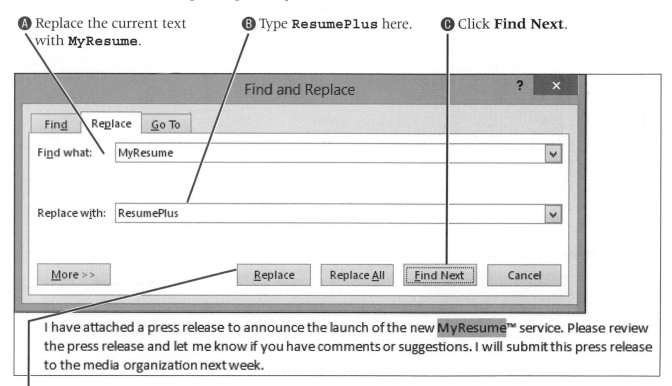

Ⓓ Click **Replace** to make the change, and Word moves to the next occurrence of MyResume.

8. Click **Replace All** to make all remaining changes at once.
    The message box informs you that Word made seven replacements.

Use Replace All with caution. You should be confident about the replacements Word will make before you use this feature. Using *Replace* allows you to monitor each replacement.

9. Click **OK** to dismiss the message, and then close the **Find and Replace** dialog box and observe the *ResumePlus* replacements. You can ignore the wavy red lines.

10. Save the file.

Navigating in Documents

Video Library   http://labyrinthelab.com/videos   Video Number: WD13-V0311

Two highly efficient navigation methods are bookmarks and hyperlinks. You can create bookmarks to move to specific locations in a document, and you can insert hyperlinks that function just like hyperlinks in web pages. A hyperlink in Word uses bookmarks or heading styles to jump to places that are within the same document.

Using Bookmarks

You can assign a bookmark name to text or other objects in a document. Once a bookmark is set up, you can easily navigate to it by choosing the desired bookmark name from the Bookmark dialog box or the Go To tab in the Find and Replace dialog box.

QUICK REFERENCE	USING BOOKMARKS
Task	**Procedure**
Create a bookmark	■ Select the text/object to use as a bookmark and choose Insert→Links→Bookmark. ■ Type the bookmark name (without spaces) and click Add.
Jump to a bookmark using the Bookmark dialog box	■ Choose Insert→Links→Bookmark, choose a bookmark name, and click Go To.
Jump to a bookmark using the Find and Replace dialog box	■ Choose Home→Editing→Find. ■ In the Navigation pane, click the Search for More Things menu ▼ button and choose Go To. ■ Choose Bookmark in the Go To What box, type or select the Bookmark name, and click Go To.

Create and Use Bookmarks

Word 2013

In this exercise, you will create bookmarks and use them to jump to different areas of the document. Then you will delete the bookmarks.

1. Save your file as **WD03-D11-MartinMemo-[FirstInitialLastName]**.

2. With page 2 displayed, select the word *Delivery* in the second heading.

3. Choose **Insert→Links→Bookmark** 🔖.

4. Follow these steps to create a Bookmark:

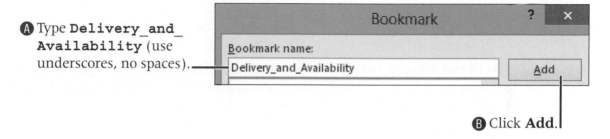

Ⓐ Type **Delivery_and_ Availability** (use underscores, no spaces).

Ⓑ Click **Add.**

5. Scroll, if necessary, and select the *Announcement* heading.

6. Choose **Insert→Links→Bookmark** 🔖.

7. In the **Bookmark Name** box, replace the current text with **Announcement** and click **Add**.

8. Press Ctrl + Home to move to the beginning of the document.

9. Choose **Insert→Links→Bookmark** 🔖.

10. Choose **Delivery_and_Availability** and click **Go To**.

11. Close the Bookmark dialog box, then choose **Insert→Links→Bookmark.**

12. Choose **Announcement** and click **Go To**.

Delete Bookmarks

13. With *Announcement* selected in the dialog box, click **Delete**.

14. Select **Delivery_and_Availability** and click **Delete**.

15. Close the dialog box and save the file.

Using Hyperlinks

Video Library   http://labyrinthelab.com/videos   Video Number: WD13-V0312

A hyperlink is text or a graphic that jumps you to another place when clicked. To use a hyperlink *within* a document, the location you link to must first be set up as a bookmark or be formatted with a heading style.

There are four primary types of hyperlinks.

- **Hyperlinks to other documents or files:** A hyperlink can open another Word document or even another program, such as Excel or PowerPoint.
- **Hyperlinks to web pages:** You can create a link to jump to a web page by entering a URL address for the hyperlink.
- **Hyperlinks to areas within the current document:** This works much like a Bookmark, jumping the reader to another location in the document.
- **Hyperlinks to email addresses:** You can create a hyperlink to an email address. When the hyperlink is clicked, a new message window opens with the email address already in the To: box.

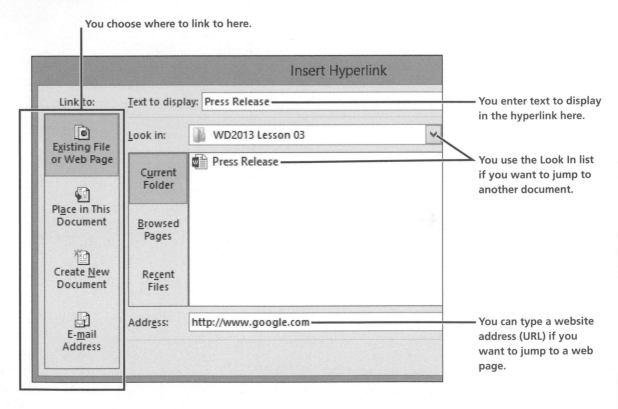

You choose where to link to here.

You enter text to display in the hyperlink here.

You use the Look In list if you want to jump to another document.

You can type a website address (URL) if you want to jump to a web page.

QUICK REFERENCE	CREATING HYPERLINKS
Task	**Procedure**
Create a hyperlink	■ Select the text/graphic to use as a hyperlink and choose Insert→Links→Hyperlink.
	■ Choose the item to link to in the left pane.
	■ In the center pane:
	◆ Choose the filename if linking to a file.
	◆ Type the URL in the Address box if linking to a web page.
	◆ Choose a heading or bookmark name if you chose Place in This Document in the Link To list.
	■ Click OK.
Remove a hyperlink	■ Click in the hyperlink, then choose Insert→Links→Hyperlink and click Remove Link; or, right-click the hyperlink and choose Remove Hyperlink.

DEVELOP YOUR SKILLS WD03-D12

Work with Hyperlinks

In this exercise, you will create a hyperlink and use it to jump to another document. Then, you will remove the hyperlink.

1. Save your file as **WD03-D12-MartinMemo-[FirstInitialLastName]**.

2. Move the insertion point to the beginning of the document.

3. Select the words *Press Release* in the **Subject** line.

4. Choose **Insert→Links→Hyperlink** 🌐.

5. Follow these steps to create a hyperlink to another document:

Ⓐ Choose **Existing File or Web Page**.

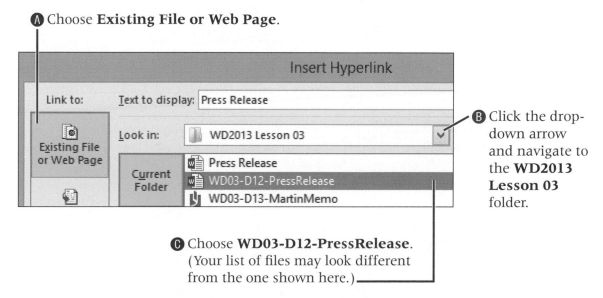

Ⓑ Click the drop-down arrow and navigate to the **WD2013 Lesson 03** folder.

Ⓒ Choose **WD03-D12-PressRelease**. (Your list of files may look different from the one shown here.)

6. Click **OK** to create the hyperlink.

   The text formatting changes once this hyperlink is created.

Use and Remove the Hyperlink

7. Press ⌈Ctrl⌉ and click the link to open Press Release.

8. Close **Press Release** but leave the Martin Memo open.
   Notice that the hyperlink changes color once it is used.

9. Click anywhere in the hyperlink.

10. Choose **Insert→Links→Hyperlink** 🌐.

11. Click **Remove Link** in the bottom-right corner of the dialog box.

12. Save the memo document, then choose **File→Close** to close the document.

Opening, Editing, and Saving a PDF File

Video Library   http://labyrinthelab.com/videos   Video Number: WD13-V0313

You can open, edit, and save a PDF file in Word 2013 without purchasing and learning separate, and often expensive, editing software. After editing the file, you can save it as a Word or PDF file. The file you open is considered a read-only file, so you must save it under a different name.

You can optimize a PDF file based on how your audience will likely read the file. And there are additional options, such as the range of pages you want to save and the ability to create bookmarks in the PDF file.

If your audience will be printing the PDF, leave the option at Standard. If the file will only be viewed online, you can choose the Minimize Size option.

Choose additional publishing options here.

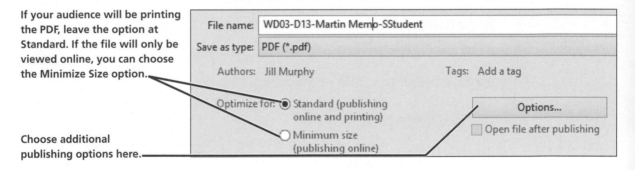

QUICK REFERENCE	OPENING PDF FILES AND SAVING AS PDF FILES
Task	**Procedure**
Open a PDF file in Word	■ Choose File→Open, navigate to the file location, and double-click the file.
	■ When the message appears, click OK.
Saving a Word document as a PDF file	■ Choose File→Save As and navigate to your file storage location.
	■ Choose PDF (*.pdf) from the Save as Type list and, if desired, choose optimization and publishing options.

DEVELOP YOUR SKILLS WD03-D13

Open and Edit a PDF File

In this exercise, you will open a PDF file in Word and make editing changes. You will then resave the file as a PDF.

1. Choose **File→Open**.

2. Navigate to your **WD2013 Lesson 03** folder and open **WD03-D13-MartinMemo.pdf**.

3. When the message box appears, click **OK**.

   The PDF file opens with all the Word editing and formatting tools available.

 When you open a PDF in Word, there may be formatting issues. Don't worry about that now. Concentrate on opening so in the future, you know how to open and edit a PDF for which you don't have the original Word file.

4. Scroll to the top of page 2 and select the three lines at the top of the page.

5. In the Mini toolbar, click the **Font Color** ![A icon] menu ▾ and choose **Blue, Accent 1, Darker 25%**.

   If the toolbar fades away, right-click the selected text to redisplay it.

6. Still using the Mini toolbar, change the Font Size to **16 point**.

7. Choose **File→Save As** and navigate to your **WD2013 Lesson 03** folder.

8. Append your first initial and last name to the filename: `WD03-D13-MartinMemo-[FirstInitialLastName]`.

9. Choose **PDF (*.pdf)** from the Save as Type list.

10. Click **Save** at the bottom of the dialog box. (If the PDF file opens in a PDF reader, close the PDF window.)

    Remember, the original file is read-only, so saving it under a different name saved the changes in a new file. Now you'll close the original file without saving.

11. The original file is still open in Word, so choose **File→Close**.

12. When prompted to save the file, click **Don't Save**. Exit **Word**.

Concepts Review

To check your knowledge of the key concepts introduced in this lesson, complete the Concepts Review quiz by choosing the appropriate access option below.

If you are...	Then access the quiz by...
Using the Labyrinth Video Library	Going to http://labyrinthelab.com/videos
Using eLab	Logging in, choosing Content, and navigating to the Concepts Review quiz for this lesson
Not using the Labyrinth Video Library or eLab	Going to the student resource center for this book

Reinforce Your Skills

Type a Memorandum

In this exercise, you will type a memorandum announcing a meeting, aligning the memo heading using the default tab grid. You will insert a page break and copy a document into page 2. Then you will use the proofreading tools to help ensure the accuracy of your memo.

Create a Memorandum Using Default Tabs

1. Start **Word** and create new a document using the **Blank Document template**.

2. Save the file as **WD03-R01-FoodDrive-[FirstInitialLastName]** in your **WD2013 Lesson 03** folder.

3. If necessary, choose **Home→Paragraph→Show/Hide** ¶ to display formatting marks.

4. Type the following memo, tapping [Enter] where you see paragraph symbols and [Tab] where you see arrows.

   Because you are using the default template, which has additional spacing, you only need to tap [Enter] once between paragraphs.

¶

¶

MEMO·TO: → Kids·for·Change¶

FROM:→ → Suzanne·Frost¶

DATE:→ → October·1,·2013¶

SUBJECT: → Combat·Hunger·Food·Drive¶

Think·globally,·act·locally!¶

Kids·for·Change·is·sponsoring·a·holiday·season·food·drive·in·coordination·with·our·local·community·food·bank.·The·drive·will·begin·on·November·1ˢᵗ,·and·we·have·lots·of·organizing·to·do·before·then.·¶

We·are·looking·for·volunteers·to·help·us·in·this·effort.·There·is·a·To·Do·list·on·the·next·page.·Look·it·over·and·see·what·you·would·like·to·volunteer·for.·We·will·discuss·the·list·and·assign·teams·during·our·October·meeting.·¶

We're·looking·forward·to·a·successful·drive·for·2013!¶

¶

¶

Work with Page Breaks and Insert a Symbol

5. Position the insertion point at the end of the memo.

6. Choose **Insert→Pages→Page Break** ⊟.
   Now you will copy a To Do list from another document into page 2.

7. Open **WD03-R01-ToDo** from the **WD2013 Lesson 03** folder.

8. Select the entire document and press Ctrl + C to copy it; close the file.

9. Make sure your insertion point is at the **top of page 2** and press Ctrl + V to paste the text.
   Now you will insert a symbol on the second page.

10. Position the insertion point after *heart* in the second line and tap Spacebar.

11. Choose **Insert→Symbols→Symbol** Ω and choose **More Symbols**.

12. Choose the **Webdings** font and the **heart-shaped symbol**; if necessary, use Character Code 89 to locate the symbol.

13. Click **Insert**, and then close the dialog box.

Use Proofreading Tools
There are some spelling errors in the To Do list; you will correct those now.

14. Right-click the red underlined word in the first bullet point and choose *create* from the menu.

15. Right-click the red underlined word in the third bullet point and choose *collect*.

16. Use your good judgment in making the next two spelling corrections.
    Now you will use the Thesaurus to find a synonym.

17. Select *goal* at the end of the second-to-last bullet point.

18. Choose **Review→Proofing→Thesaurus** 📖 to open the task pane.

19. Hover the mouse pointer over *objective* (the second one in the list), and then click the drop-down arrow to open the menu.

20. Click **Insert** to replace *goal* with *objective*.

21. Close the **Thesaurus task pane**.

22. Save and close your file, and exit from **Word**.

23. Submit your final file based on the guidelines provided by your instructor.
    To view examples of how your file or files should look at the end of this exercise, go to the student resource center.

Format a Document and Save It in PDF

In this exercise, you will format the headings in a document, use Find and Replace, and add bookmarks and hyperlinks. Finally, you will save it as a PDF file.

1. Start **Word**. Open **WD03-R02-Energy** from the **WD2013 Lesson 03** folder and save it as `WD03-R02-Energy-[FirstInitialLastName]`.

Format Text and Use the Format Painter

2. Select *Home Energy Inspector* at the top of the document.

3. Choose **Home→Font→dialog box launcher** ⌐.

4. Choose **Century Gothic, Bold, 14 point**, and then choose **Small Caps** in the Effects area.

5. Click **OK** to apply the formats.
   You've decided you'd like to try some more options, so you'll clear your formats.

6. Make sure the heading is still selected.

7. Choose **Home→Font→Clear All Formatting** ✎.

8. With the heading still selected, choose **Home→Font**. Then click the **menu button** ▼ next to Calibri (Body) and choose **Comic Sans MS**.

9. Choose **Home→Font→Font Size menu button** ▼ and choose **16 point**.

10. Choose **Home→Font→Bold** Ⓑ.

11. Choose **Home→Font→Font Color** Ⓐ **menu button** ▼ and choose a **blue** color.
    Now you're ready to format the other headings.

12. Select the *What About Energy Leaks?* heading.

13. Choose **Home→Font→Font menu button** ▼ and choose **Euphemia**.

14. Choose **Home→Font→Bold** Ⓑ.
    Next you'll use the Format Painter to copy the format to the other headings.

15. Make sure the heading is still selected.

16. Choose **Home→Clipboard** and double-click the **Format Painter** ✼.
    Remember, double-clicking the Format Painter keeps it turned on.

17. Use the **Format Painter** ✼ to format the rest of the headings:
    - What About Appliances?
    - What Are the Best Light Bulbs?
    - What are the Worst Offenders?
    - Who Is Responsible?

18. Choose **Home→Clipboard→Format Painter** ✼ to turn off the feature.

Find and Replace

You've noticed some words you would like to change, so you will use Find and Replace to make the changes.

19. Position the insertion point at the top of the document.

20. Choose **Home→Editing→Replace** 🔲 to open the Find and Replace dialog box.

21. Type **program** in the Find What box and **project** in the Replace With box.

22. Click **Find Next**, and then click **Replace**.

23. When the message appears, click **OK**.

24. Use the **Find and Replace** feature to change *offenders* to *wasters*.
    Hint: There are two occurrences of offenders.

25. When the message appears, click **OK**; close the dialog box.

Navigate with Bookmarks and Hyperlinks

Next you will create a bookmark for the last topic in the document and a hyperlink to another document.

26. Press ⎡Ctrl⎤+⎡End⎤ to move to the end of the document.

27. Select the last heading, *Who Is Responsible?*

28. Choose **Insert→Links→Bookmark** 🔲.

29. Type **WhoIsResponsible** (no spaces) in the **Bookmark Name** box; click **Add**.

30. Select the first heading at the top of the document.

31. Choose **Insert→Links→Hyperlink** 🔲 to open the Insert Hyperlink dialog box.

32. Make sure **Existing File or Web Page** is chosen in the Link To area.

33. In the Look In area, navigate to your **WD2013 Lesson 03** folder, choose **WD03-R02-EnergyHelp** from the file list, and click **OK**.

34. Click **OK** again to create the hyperlink.
    The formatting changes when the hyperlink is applied. Now you'll test your hyperlink and bookmark.

35. Press ⎡Ctrl⎤ and click the hyperlink to open the Energy Help document, and then close it.
    The appearance of the hyperlink changes after it is used.

36. Choose **Insert→Links→Bookmark** 🔲 from the menu.

37. Choose the bookmark and click **Go To**; close the dialog box.

Save the Document as a PDF

38. Choose **File→Save As** and navigate to your **WD2013 Lesson 03** folder.

39. Use the same file name and choose **PDF (*.pdf)** from the Save As Type menu.

40. Leave the optimization at **Standard**, and then click **Save**. (If the PDF file opens in a PDF reader, close the PDF window.)

41. Save and close the original document, and then exit from **Word**.

42. Submit your final file based on the guidelines provided by your instructor.
    To view examples of how your file or files should look at the end of this exercise, go to the student resource center.

Type and Format a Memorandum

In this exercise, you will create a memorandum, insert a page break, copy text, and use proofing tools. You will create a hyperlink to an external document and save your memo as a PDF file.

Type a Memo and Insert a Page Break

1. Start **Word**. Create new a document using the **Blank Document template** that is saved to the **WD2013 Lesson 03** folder as WD03-R03-Green-[FirstInitialLastName].

2. If necessary, choose **Home→Paragraph→Show/Hide ¶** to turn on formatting marks.

3. Type the following memo using these guidelines:
   - Use formatting marks as a guide for spacing.
   - Use the Insert Date and Time feature on the Insert tab to insert and format the current date, and choose not to update automatically.

¶

¶

MEMO·TO: → Kids·for·Change·Members¶

FROM:→ → Harvey·Rodrick¶

DATE:→ → Today's·Date¶

SUBJECT: → Green·Construction¶

An·extension·is·being·added·to·the·building·where·we·hold·our·meetings.·We·would·like·to·ensure·that·the·owner,·Mr.·Evans,·hires·a·company·that·specializes·in·green·construction.·See·page·2·to·learn·what's·involved·in·this·type·of·construction.·¶

Mr.·Evans·has·agreed·to·meet·with·us·to·consider·our·ideas.·Please·take·time·before·our·next·monthly·meeting·to·research·this·topic·so·we·can·prepare·a·winning·presentation.·¶

¶

¶

---

4. Make sure the insertion point is at the end of the document, and then press Ctrl + Enter to insert a page break.

5. Open **WD03-R03-Construction** from the **WD2013 Lesson 03** folder.

6. Select all of contents of the document, and then press Ctrl + C to copy it.

7. Close the **Construction** document, and then paste the copied material at the top of page 2 of the **Green** document.

Use Proofing Tools

8. Tap F7 to start proofing.

NOTE If F7 does not work as expected, you may need to tap F-Lock at the top of your keyboard so F7 behaves as a function key.

Fluoorescent is highlighted in the Spelling task pane.

9. Click **Change** to correct the spelling.

10. Click **Change** to correct *sustainable*.
    Daniel's last name is spelled correctly.

11. Click **Add** to add his name to the dictionary.
    The Grammar checker caught the incorrect use of a pronoun.

12. Click **Change** to make the correction, and then when the message appears, click **OK**.
    Now you will remove the name you added to the dictionary so the next student using your computer will have the same experience.

13. Choose **File→Options**, and then choose **Proofing** from the left panel.

14. Click **Custom Dictionaries**, and then in the Custom Dictionaries dialog box, click **Edit Word List**.

15. If necessary, scroll to locate *Datar* and click **Delete**, and then click **OK**.

16. Click **OK** two more times.
    Datar is flagged again because you removed it from the dictionary.

Format Text

17. Select the *Green Construction* heading at the top of page 2, format it with **Century Gothic**, **14 point**, **Bold**; deselect the heading.

18. Scroll to the bottom of page 2, and then apply **Bold** and **Italics** to *Daniel Datar*.

19. Scroll to the top of page 1, and then apply **Bold** to the memo heading elements: *MEMO TO:*, *FROM:*, *DATE:*, and *SUBJECT:*.

20. Select *Green Construction* in the subject line, format it with a shade of green of your choice, and then apply **Bold**.

21. In the last sentence of the first paragraph on page 1, italicize *See page 2*.

22. Underline the last two words on page 1, *winning presentation*.

Use Find and Replace

23. Position the insertion point at the top of the document.

24. Choose **Home→Editing→Replace** to open the Find and Replace dialog box.

25. Type **concepts** in the **Find What** box and **ideas** in the **Replace With** box.

26. Click **Find Next**, and then when *concepts* is highlighted, click **Replace**.

27. Click **OK** when the message appears, and then close the dialog box.

    You've located some additional information on solar heating, so you will create a hyperlink to that information.

Create and Test a Hyperlink to Use for Navigation

28. Select *Solar heating* on page 2.

29. Choose **Insert→Links→Hyperlink** .

30. Make sure **Existing File or Web Page** is chosen.

31. In the Look In area, navigate to your **WD2013 Lesson 03** folder, and then choose **WD03-R03-Solar** from the list.

32. Click **OK** twice to create the hyperlink.

33. Press Ctrl and click the hyperlink to open the **Solar** document, and then close it.

Save the Document as a PDF

34. Choose **File→Save As**, and then navigate to your **WD2013 Lesson 03** folder.

35. Use the same filename, and then choose **PDF (*.pdf)** from the Save As Type menu.

36. Leave the optimization at **Standard**, and then click **Save**. (If the PDF file opens in a PDF reader, close the PDF window.)

    Next you will open and edit a PDF file. This is so you can understand the mechanics of how to do it.

> **NOTE** When you open a PDF file in Word, there will be formatting issues. Don't worry about making the file look perfect. Concentrate more on how to open and edit, so you will be able to accomplish this task in the future when you need to edit a PDF file for which you don't have an original Word file.

Open and Edit the PDF

37. Open the **PDF** file you just saved.

38. When the message appears, click **OK**.

    The conversion to PDF misaligned the data in the FROM: and DATE: lines of the memo heading.

39. Add tabs to the *FROM:* and *DATE:* lines to realign them.

40. Change **Harvey Rodrick** in the FROM: line to `Miles Chung`.

41. Resave the file as a **PDF** in the **WD2013 Lesson 03** folder, named `WD03-R03-Green2-[FirstInitialLastName]`. (If the PDF file opens in in a PDF reader, close the PDF window.)

42. Close the original **PDF** without saving.

43. Save and close all documents; exit from **Word**.

44. Submit your final file based on the guidelines provided by your instructor.

Apply Your Skills

Create a Memorandum and a Press Release

In this exercise, you will type a memorandum, insert a page break, and copy text into page 2 of the memo. You will then insert a trademark symbol, correct spelling errors, and use the Thesaurus to find a synonym.

Type a Memorandum and Insert a Page Break

1. Start **Word**. Use the **Blank Document template** and save the file in your **WD2013 Lesson 03** folder as `WD03-A01-NewOffice-[FirstInitialLastName]`.

2. Type the following memo using proper spacing and tabs for aligning the memo head.

MEMO TO:	Malcolm Wesley
FROM:	Melissa Jones
DATE:	August 8, 2013
SUBJECT:	Bangalore Press Release

Malcolm I've attached the press release for our Bangalore announcement. Would you please look it over and let me now if you have any changes or suggestions? Thanks!

3. Insert a **page break** at the end of the memo.

4. Open **WD03-A01-BangalorePR** from your **WD2013 Lesson 03** folder and copy everything from the document and paste it into the second page of the memo. Close the Bangalore file.

Insert a Symbol and Use Proofing Tools

5. Insert the **trademark symbol** after *Universal Corporate Events* in the first line of the first body paragraph in the press release.

6. Correct the spelling errors, and then use the **Thesaurus** to replace *aspects*, in the second line of the second paragraph, with a synonym of your choice.

7. Save and close the file; exit from **Word**.

8. Submit your final file based on the guidelines provided by your instructor.
   To view examples of how your file or files should look at the end of this exercise, go to the student resource center.

Use Formatting, Find and Replace, and a Bookmark

In this exercise, you will format headings in a document, use Find and Replace to make some editing changes, and create a bookmark to use for navigation. Finally, you will save the file as a PDF file.

Make Formatting Changes and Use Find and Replace

1. Start **Word**. Open **WD03-A02-IndiaTips** from your **WD2013 Lesson 03** folder and save it as **WD03-A02-IndiaTips-[FirstInitialLastName]**.

2. Select the first two heading lines.

3. Choose **Home→Font→Font menu button ▼**, and then use **Live Preview** to test several different fonts, and then test the **Tahoma** font.

4. Choose **Tahoma** and also apply **14 point, Bold**.

5. Select the *What Not to Do* heading, and then apply **Tahoma**, **Bold**, and **Italic**.

6. Use the **Format Painter** [icon] to copy the formatting to the other headings.

7. Use the Replace feature to make the following changes:
   - Replace *conversing* with *talking*
   - Replace *irritation* with *frustration*
   - Replace *another's* with *another person's*
   - Replace *appropriate* with *proper* (3 occurrences)

Navigate with a Bookmark and Save the File as a PDF

8. Select the *Dining* heading at the end of the document, and then create a **bookmark** named **Dining**.

9. Scroll to the top of the document and test your bookmark.

10. Save your file as a **PDF** using the same filename.

11. Save your original Word file and close it; exit from **Word**.

12. Submit your final file based on the guidelines provided by your instructor.

    To view examples of how your file or files should look at the end of this exercise, go to the student resource center.

Create, Format, and Navigate in a Memo

In this exercise, you will type a memo, insert a page break, and copy text into the new page. You will use the proofing tools, and then format the headings. You will use Find and Replace, insert a hyperlink, and finally, you will save the memo as a PDF file.

Create a Memorandum

1. Start **Word**. Create a new document using the **Blank Document template** and save to your **WD2013 Lesson 03** folder as `WD03-A03-HenslowMemo-[FirstInitialLastName]`.

2. Type the following memo using the appropriate spacing, automatically insert the date using the third date format, and don't check the Update Automatically feature.

MEMO TO: Dennis Henslow

FROM: Jordan Miller

DATE: Today's Date

SUBJECT: Additions to the London Trip

Dennis, since you're a Londoner, would you please take a look at the additional tours we're thinking of making available to our clients. Let me know if you agree or if you have any suggestions.

Insert a Page Break and Use Proofing Tools

3. Insert a **page break** at the end of the memo, and then open **WD03-A03-LondonTours** from your **WD2013 Lesson 03** folder.

4. Copy the content of the document, and then close it.

5. Paste the content into page 2 of your memo, and then correct the spelling and grammar. *Hint:* Cotswolds *is spelled correctly. The grammar error is in the second line of the first paragraph.*

Format Text

6. Format the heading at the top of page 2 with **Verdana**, **14 point**, **Bold**.

7. Format the *Local Excursions* heading with **Verdana**, **Bold**, and **Underline**.

8. Use the **Format Painter** to copy the formatting to the *Day Trips* heading, and then deselect the heading.

Use Find and Replace and Insert a Hyperlink

9. Use the **Replace** feature to find *St. Paul's Cathedral* and replace it with *Westminster Abbey*.

10. Select *Stonehenge*, and then insert a hyperlink to **WD03-A03-Stonehenge** in your **WD2013 Lesson 03** folder.

11. Test the hyperlink, and then close the **Stonehenge** file.

Save the File in PDF

12. Save your memo as a PDF file using the same filename.

Next you will open and edit a PDF file. This is so you can understand the mechanics of how to do it.

When you open a PDF file in Word, there will be formatting issues. Don't worry about making the file look perfect; instead, concentrate more on how to open and edit so you will be able to accomplish this task in the future.

Open and Edit the PDF

13. Open your **WD03-A03-HenslowMemo.pdf** file. When the message appears, click **OK**.

The conversion to PDF misaligned the FROM: and DATE: lines in the memo heading.

14. Add tabs to the *FROM:* and *DATE*: lines to realign them.

15. Scroll to page 2 and remove the **underlines** from the *Local Excursions* and *Day Trip* headings.

16. Resave the file in **PDF** to the **WD2013 Lesson 03** folder. Name the file **WD03-A03-HenslowMemo2-[FirstInitialLastName]**. (If the PDF file opens in a PDF reader, close the PDF window.)

17. Save and close your Word version of the Henslow memo; exit from **Word**.

18. Submit your final file based on the guidelines provided by your instructor.

Extend Your Skills

In the course of working through the Extend Your Skills exercises, you will think critically as you use the skills taught in the lesson to complete the assigned projects. To evaluate your mastery and completion of the exercises, your instructor may use a rubric, with which more points are allotted according to performance characteristics. (The more you do, the more you earn!) Ask your instructor how your work will be evaluated.

WD03-E01 That's the Way I See It

Your friend has hired you to do marketing for her local small business. You need to research what is involved in producing a press release, because her company is planning to announce a new service soon. Conduct online research to determine:

- The purpose of a press release
- The main elements that typically appear in a press release
- How to create effective content for a press release
- Three suggestions for distributing a press release

Create a new Word document named **WD03-E01-PressRel-[FirstInitialLastName]** and saved to your **WD2013 Lesson 03** folder. Then, type the information you find into the document.

Create a page break, and then type a press release for the new service (make up the service you will be promoting) using the guidelines you have discovered and documented. Make sure to format the document so it is easy to read, using the Format Painter tool as needed. Preview how the file will appear when printed, and then save it as a PDF file named **WD03-E01-PressRelPDF-[FirstInitialLastName]** in your **WD2013 Lesson 03** folder.

You will be evaluated based on the inclusion of all elements specified, your ability to follow directions, your ability to apply newly learned skills to a real-world situation, your creativity, and the relevance of your topic and/or data choice(s). Submit your final files based on the guidelines provided by your instructor.

WD03-E02 Be Your Own Boss

You are the owner of Blue Jean Landscaping. Use your imagination to determine a new service that your company plans to offer and write a press release to announce the service. Be sure to include the primary elements of a press release and explain your service in an interesting way so a reporter reading your press release will be motivated to write a good story. Indicate how you will distribute your press release.

Use the formatting skills you have learned in this lesson to make the press release visually appealing. Save your finished press release as a PDF file as **WD03-E02-BJLPressRel-[FirstInitialLastName]** in your **WD2013 Lesson 03** folder.

You will be evaluated based on the inclusion of all elements specified, your ability to follow directions, your ability to apply newly learned skills to a real-world situation, your creativity, and your demonstration of an entrepreneurial spirit. Submit your final file based on the guidelines provided by your instructor.

Transfer Your Skills

In the course of working through the Transfer Your Skills exercises, you will use critical-thinking and creativity skills to complete the assigned projects using skills taught in the lesson. To evaluate your mastery and completion of the exercises, your instructor may use a rubric, with which more points are allotted according to performance characteristics. (The more you do, the more you earn!) Ask your instructor how your work will be evaluated.

WD03-T01 Use the Web as a Learning Tool

Throughout this book, you will be provided with an opportunity to use the Internet as a learning tool by completing WebQuests. According to the original creators of WebQuests, as described on their website (WebQuest.org), a WebQuest is "an inquiry-oriented activity in which most or all of the information used by learners is drawn from the web." To complete the WebQuest projects in this book, navigate to the student resource center and choose the WebQuest for the lesson on which you are currently working. The subject of each WebQuest will be relevant to the material found in the lesson.

WebQuest Subject: Why does a company need a press kit?

Submit your final file based on the guidelines provided by your instructor.

WD03-T02 Demonstrate Proficiency

As the owner of Stormy BBQ, create a memo to your employees about a new product you will be offering. (Use your imagination to come up with a new product.) In the memo, ask your employees to review the press release and offer any changes or suggestions they have. Create the press release on page 2 of the memo, advertising the new product. Conduct online research to determine the elements required for an effective press release, if necessary. Use Spell Check to make sure all words are spelled correctly, and then format the memo and press release using the tools you have learned in this lesson to make your document visually appealing.

Save your completed work as a PDF file named **WD03-T02-NewProdPDF-[FirstInitialLastName]** in your **WD2013 Lesson 03** folder. Submit your final file based on the guidelines provided by your instructor.

WORD 2013

Creating a Simple Report

LESSON OUTLINE

LEARNING OBJECTIVES

After studying this lesson, you will be able to:

- Use paragraph alignment settings
- Set custom tab stops
- Format lists
- Apply borders, shading, and styles
- Insert page numbers

In this lesson, you will create a simple report. Reports are important documents often used in business and education. You will format your report using various paragraph formatting techniques, including paragraph alignment, custom tab stops, and Word's indent feature. You will work with bulleted and numbered lists, and you will add interest to the report by applying borders, shading, and styles. You will be introduced to headers and footers, and you will use the Navigation pane to navigate by heading styles and to quickly reorganize your document.

Formatting a Research Report

A business analyst at My Virtual Campus has asked you to assist in researching the use of social media at universities. The report will be a useful tool for management to have as background information. It is important to understand how the "always connected" generation is using technology to pursue their education, to study, and to perform classroom activities. You will use paragraph formatting techniques such as indents, styles, and bullets and numbering to prepare an easy-to-read, properly formatted, and professional-looking document.

My Virtual Campus

SOCIAL MEDIA IN UNIVERSITIES

Universities today are engaging constantly-connected Millennials through social media. Use of Facebook, YouTube, Twitter, blogging, and podcasting have all experienced double-digit increases on campus in the last year. Students are checking out universities through student-run blogs, and recruiters are checking out students on Facebook and LinkedIn.

The Net Generation

In her article appearing in The Teaching Professor, August/September 2009, Dalton State College psychology professor Christy Price makes the following observations:

"...the ideal learning environment was Millennials' preference for a variety of teaching methods, as opposed to a "lecture only" format."

"Respondents thought professors who involved them in class with a variety of methods (not just lecture) as more connected to millennial culture."

Formatting Reports

Video Library http://labyrinthelab.com/videos   Video Number: WD13-V0401

There is a variety of acceptable report formats. Different formats can be used for marketing publications and other types of business and educational documents. The following example shows a traditional business report in unbound format.

The title is positioned at approximately 2 inches from the top of the page and centered.

The title is in uppercase and bold; you can also apply a distinctive font to the title.

SOCIAL MEDIA IN UNIVERSITIES

Universities today are engaging constantly-connected Millennials through social media. Use of Facebook, YouTube, Twitter, blogging, and podcasting have all experienced double-digit increases on campus in the last year. Students are checking out universities through student-run blogs, and recruiters are checking out students on Facebook and LinkedIn.

The Net Generation

In her article appearing in The Teaching Professor, August/September 2009, Dalton State College psychology professor Christy Price makes the following observations:

"...the ideal learning environment was Millennials' preference for a variety of teaching methods, as opposed to a "lecture only" format."

"Respondents thought professors who involved them in class with a variety of methods (not just lecture) as more connected to millennial culture."

The body is double-spaced with paragraphs indented to ½ inch.

Quotations and other text you want to emphasize are indented on the left and right.

Formatting Paragraphs

Paragraph formatting includes paragraph alignment, line spacing, and bullets and numbering, to mention a few. In Word, a paragraph is created anytime you tap Enter. In other words, a paragraph could consist of several lines that end with Enter or just one line, such as a heading, that ends with Enter. Tapping Enter to generate a blank line creates a paragraph, even though there is no text in it. What's more, Word stores formats in the paragraph symbol.

Each of these is a paragraph because each ends with a paragraph symbol (heading, blank lines, text paragraph).

Social·Media·Benefits·for·Students¶

¶

Technology·can·be·used·to·reach·the·Net°Generation·in·an·effective·way.·They·consider· technology·a·natural·way·to·pursue·their·education,·to·study,·and·to·perform·classroom·activities.·¶

¶

◆→ Search·for·classes·online¶
      ○→ Locate·desired·subjects,·dates,·and·times¶
      ○→ Review·syllabi¶

Each of these lines is a paragraph.

Comparing Paragraph Formatting to Character Formatting

Selecting paragraphs for formatting purposes is a little different from selecting characters. With character formatting, you typically select the entire block of text you want to format, which is necessary in the majority of cases. With paragraph formatting, you need only click in the paragraph to *select* it. On the other hand, if you want to apply formatting to more than one paragraph, you must select at least part of each paragraph.

Using Paragraph Alignment

Paragraph alignment determines how text aligns between the margins. Left alignment gives paragraphs a straight left margin and ragged right margin. Center alignment is usually applied to headings. Right alignment generates a straight right and ragged left margin. Justify provides straight left and right margins.

FROM THE RIBBON
Home→Paragraph→ Alignment Option

FROM THE KEYBOARD
Ctrl+L align left
Ctrl+E center
Ctrl+R align right
Ctrl+J justify

Here's how the different paragraph alignment settings look in Word.

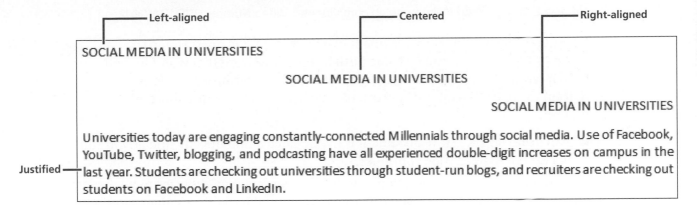

Align Text

In this exercise, you will use the alignment buttons in the Paragraph group of the Home tab to align your report heading.

1. Start **Word**. Create a new, blank document using the **Blank Document template** and make sure the Word window is **maximized**.

2. Save the file as **WD04-D01-SocMediaRprt-[FirstInitialLastName]** in your **WD2013 Lesson 04** folder.

   Replace the bracketed text with your first initial and last name. For example, if your name is Bethany Smith, your filename would look like this: WD04-D01-SocMediaRprt-BSmith.

3. Tap Enter twice to position the insertion point approximately **2 inches** from the top of the page.

4. Turn on Caps Lock, and then choose **Home→Font→Bold** B.

5. Type the report title, **SOCIAL MEDIA IN UNIVERSITIES**.

6. Choose **Home→Font→Bold** B and then tap Caps Lock to turn both off.

7. Tap Enter twice to provide blank lines before the body of the report, which you will add shortly.

8. Position the insertion point in the report heading.

Align the Heading

9. Choose **Home→Paragraph→Align Right** ▤.

10. Choose **Home→Paragraph→Align Left** ▤.

11. Choose **Home→Paragraph→Center** ▤.

12. Save the file and leave it open; you will modify it throughout the lesson.

Adding Hyphenation

Video Library   http://labyrinthelab.com/videos   Video Number: WD13-V0402

Typically, when you create a document, you let Word Wrap do its thing; that is, it adds all of the text it can on a line until it comes to a word that won't fit, and then it wraps down to the next line. Sometimes this can cause your right margin to appear too ragged. You can use hyphenation to create a more even margin.

FROM THE RIBBON

Page Layout→Page Setup→Hyphenation

- **Automatic:** The entire document is hyphenated automatically, and as you edit or revise the document hyphenation continues.
- **Manual:** Manual hyphenation searches for words you might want to hyphenate and provides a prompt where you can accept, modify, or reject the hyphenation.

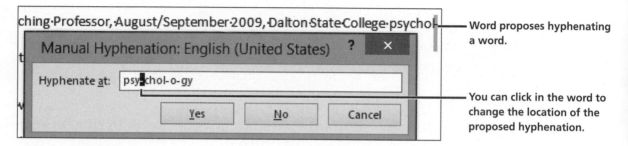

ching·Professor,·August/September·2009,·Dalton·State·College·psychol—   Word proposes hyphenating a word.

Manual Hyphenation: English (United States)   ?   ×

Hyphenate at: psy‖chol-o-gy

Yes   No   Cancel

You can click in the word to change the location of the proposed hyphenation.

DEVELOP YOUR SKILLS WD04-D02
Use Manual Hyphenation

In this exercise, you will copy the content for your report from another document, and then you will use manual hyphenation to smooth out the right-hand margin.

1. Save your file as **WD04-D02-SocMediaRprt-[FirstInitialLastName]**.

2. If necessary, choose **Home→Paragraph→Show/Hide ¶** to turn on formatting marks.

3. Open **WD04-D02-RprtContent** from your **WD2013 Lesson 04** folder.

4. Press Ctrl + A to select all content, and then press Ctrl + C to copy it.

5. Close **WD04-D02-RprtContent**.

   You will now paste the copied document in the Social Media Report document.

6. Follow these steps to paste the document into the report:

Ⓐ Position the insertion point next to the second paragraph symbol after the heading.

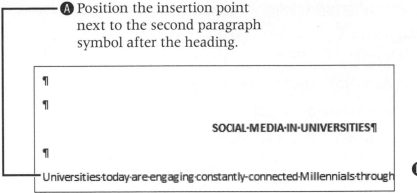

Ⓑ Press Ctrl + V to paste the content.

7. Choose **Home→Paragraph→Show/Hide ¶** to turn off formatting marks.

8. Press Ctrl + Home .

Hyphenate Words

9. Choose **Page Layout→Page Setup→Hyphenation** 🇧🇨 and choose **Manual** from the menu.

10. When Word proposes hyphenating *Facebook*, click **No**.

   In this example, we prefer to keep Facebook as one word even though it could be hyphenated.

11. When Word proposes hyphenating *psychology*, click **Yes** to accept the suggestion.

12. When Word proposes hyphenating *opposed*, click **Yes** to accept the suggestion.

13. When Word suggests hyphenating *increases*, click **Cancel** to end Manual hyphenation.

14. Save the report.

Inserting a Nonbreaking Hyphen or Space

Video Library   http://labyrinthelab.com/videos   Video Number: WD13-V0403

FROM THE KEYBOARD
Ctrl + Shift + Hyphen to add a nonbreaking hyphen

Ctrl + Shift + Spacebar to add a nonbreaking space

Word allows you to keep terms together that should remain together on one line, such as dates or hyphenated names. You use nonbreaking hyphens and nonbreaking spaces to accomplish this.

QUICK REFERENCE	USING NONBREAKING HYPHENS AND SPACES
Task	**Procedure**
Insert Nonbreaking Hyphens	■ Choose Insert→Symbols→Symbol, and then choose More Symbols. ■ Click the Special Characters tab, choose Nonbreaking Hyphen, and click Insert.
Insert Nonbreaking Spaces	■ Choose Insert→Symbols→Symbol, and then choose More Symbols. ■ Click the Special Characters tab, choose Nonbreaking Space, and click Insert.

Insert Nonbreaking Hyphens and Spaces

In this exercise, you will insert nonbreaking hyphens and spaces in your document. Then you will test to see if the words stay together as one term.

1. Save your file as **WD04-D03-SocMediaRprt-[FirstInitialLastName]**.

2. Scroll to the top of the document.

3. Follow these steps to insert a nonbreaking hyphen in double-digit:

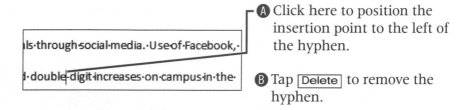

Ⓐ Click here to position the insertion point to the left of the hyphen.

Ⓑ Tap Delete to remove the hyphen.

4. Choose **Insert→Symbols→Symbol** Ω.

5. Choose **More Symbols** from the menu, and when the Symbol dialog box opens, click the **Special Characters** tab.

6. Choose **Nonbreaking Hyphen**, click **Insert**, and close the dialog box.

7. Position the insertion point to the left of *double-digit*.

8. Tap Spacebar several times to move double-digit to the right until it wraps to the next line as a single term.

   Notice the nonbreaking hyphen you inserted kept the hyphenated word together.

9. Click **Undo** 🔄 on the Quick Access toolbar to undo the spaces you inserted.

Insert and Test a Nonbreaking Space

10. Scroll to the end of the document.

11. Follow these steps to insert a nonbreaking space:

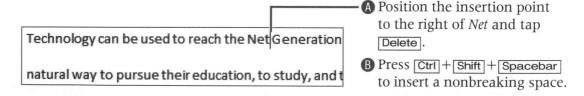

Ⓐ Position the insertion point to the right of *Net* and tap Delete.

Ⓑ Press Ctrl + Shift + Spacebar to insert a nonbreaking space.

12. Position the insertion point to the left of *Net* and tap Spacebar until *Net Generation* wraps to the next line as one term.

    The nonbreaking space kept the words together as one term.

13. Click **Undo** 🔄 on the Quick Access toolbar.

14. Save the report.

Indenting Text

Video Library   http://labyrinthelab.com/videos   Video Number: WD13-V0404

Indents offset text from the margins. You can set indents by using the buttons on the Ribbon or by dragging the indent markers on the ruler.

FROM THE RIBBON

Home→Paragraph→
Decrease/Increase
Indent

FROM THE KEYBOARD

Ctrl + Shift + M to
decrease the indent

Ctrl + M to increase
the indent

Adjusting Indents with the Ribbon

The Increase Indent and Decrease Indent buttons adjust the indent of an entire paragraph (or one or more selected paragraphs) and they affect the left indent only. They adjust the indent based on the default tab stops, which are set at every half inch.

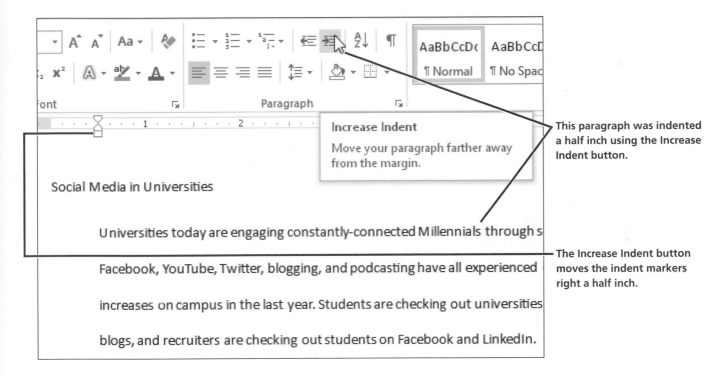

Increase Indent
Move your paragraph farther away from the margin.

Social Media in Universities

Universities today are engaging constantly-connected Millennials through s

Facebook, YouTube, Twitter, blogging, and podcasting have all experienced

increases on campus in the last year. Students are checking out universities

blogs, and recruiters are checking out students on Facebook and LinkedIn.

This paragraph was indented a half inch using the Increase Indent button.

The Increase Indent button moves the indent markers right a half inch.

DEVELOP YOUR SKILLS WD04-D04
Experiment with Left Indents

In this exercise, you will use the Increase Indent button to indent quotations to one inch. Then you will use the Decrease Indent button to return the quotations to the left margin.

1. Save your file as **WD04-D04-SocMediaRprt-[FirstInitialLastName]**.

2. If necessary, choose **View→Show→Ruler** to turn on the ruler.

3. Follow these steps to indent multiple paragraphs:

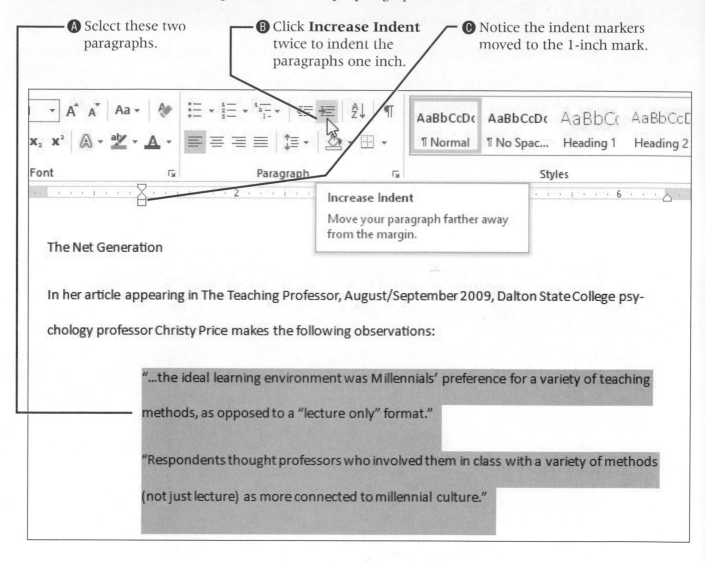

Ⓐ Select these two paragraphs.

Ⓑ Click **Increase Indent** twice to indent the paragraphs one inch.

Ⓒ Notice the indent markers moved to the 1-inch mark.

4. Make sure the paragraphs are still selected.

5. Choose **Home→Paragraph→Decrease Indent** twice to return the paragraphs to the left margin.

6. Save the report.

Setting Custom Indents on the Ruler

Video Library   http://labyrinthelab.com/videos   Video Number: WD13-V0405

You can set indents by dragging the indent markers on the horizontal ruler. The following illustration shows the ruler and the indent markers.

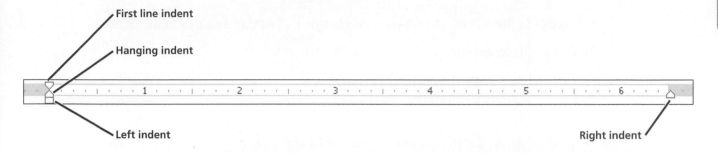

INDENT MARKERS	
Item	**Description**
First Line Indent	Indents the first line of the paragraph.
Hanging Indent	This triangle is *attached* to the Left Indent rectangle. Place the mouse pointer in the triangle and drag right to indent everything except the first line.
Left Indent	This rectangle is *attached* to the Hanging Indent triangle. Place the mouse pointer in the rectangle and drag left/right to position all lines simultaneously. Whether the triangles are aligned with each other or separated, dragging the rectangle positions both triangles simultaneously.
Right Indent	Drag to indent the entire paragraph from the right.

Using Hanging Indents

Hanging indents are not often used, thus many people are not familiar with the term. The following illustration shows an example of a hanging indent, where the first line is *outdented* and the remaining lines of the paragraph are *indented*.

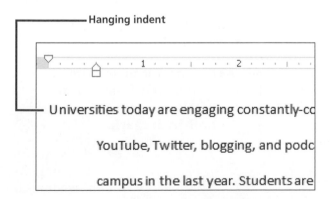

Use the Indent Markers to Indent Paragraphs

In this exercise, you will use the indent markers on the horizontal ruler to indent the quotations from both the left and right. You will also use the First Line Indent marker to indent the first line of the other paragraphs.

1. Save your file as **WD04-D05-SocMediaRprt-[FirstInitialLastName]**.

2. Follow these steps to adjust the left and right indents:

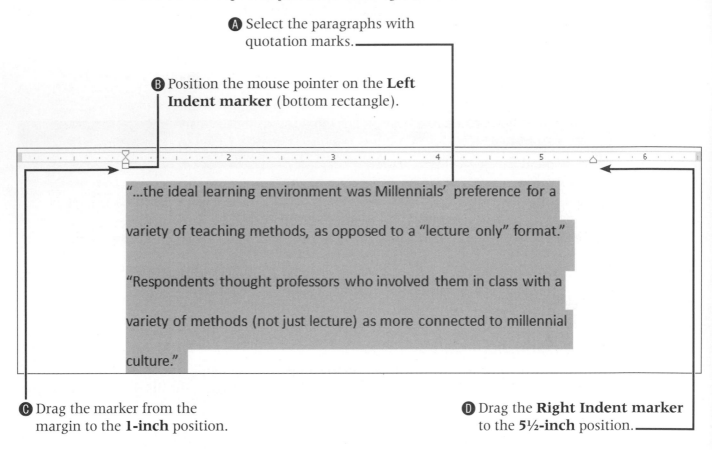

Ⓐ Select the paragraphs with quotation marks.

Ⓑ Position the mouse pointer on the **Left Indent marker** (bottom rectangle).

"...the ideal learning environment was Millennials' preference for a

variety of teaching methods, as opposed to a "lecture only" format."

"Respondents thought professors who involved them in class with a

variety of methods (not just lecture) as more connected to millennial

culture."

Ⓒ Drag the marker from the margin to the **1-inch** position.

Ⓓ Drag the **Right Indent marker** to the **5½-inch** position.

3. Follow these steps to indent the first line of paragraphs:

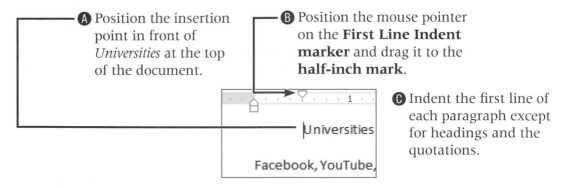

Ⓐ Position the insertion point in front of *Universities* at the top of the document.

Ⓑ Position the mouse pointer on the **First Line Indent marker** and drag it to the **half-inch mark**.

Universities

Facebook, YouTube,

Ⓒ Indent the first line of each paragraph except for headings and the quotations.

4. Save the report.

Using Custom Tab Stops

Video Library   http://labyrinthelab.com/videos   Video Number: WD13-V0406

Default tab stops are set every one-half inch, so the insertion point moves one-half inch whenever you tap Tab. You can customize tab stops if you want other settings, or if you want to use a special tab, such as one that center aligns.

Never use the spacebar to line up columns of text. Even if it looks right on the screen, it most likely will not print correctly.

Setting Custom Tab Stops with the Ruler

Word has four types of custom tab stops: left, right, center, and decimal. You can set all four types using the horizontal ruler. It is critical that you position the insertion point on the line where you plan to set tabs. Tab settings are carried inside the paragraph symbol to the next paragraph when you tap Enter.

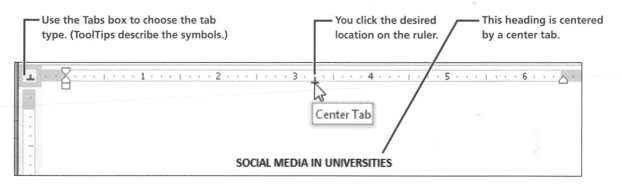

Use the Tabs box to choose the tab type. (ToolTips describe the symbols.)

You click the desired location on the ruler.

This heading is centered by a center tab.

Center Tab

SOCIAL MEDIA IN UNIVERSITIES

DEVELOP YOUR SKILLS WD04-D06
Set Tabs Using the Ruler

In this exercise, you will use custom tabs to set up text in a columnar format.

1. Save your file as **WD04-D06-SocMediaRprt-[FirstInitialLastName]**.

2. If necessary, choose **Home→Paragraph→Show/Hide ¶** to display formatting marks.

3. If necessary, choose **View→Show→Ruler** to turn on the ruler.

4. Follow these steps to set tabs for the heading line of your table:

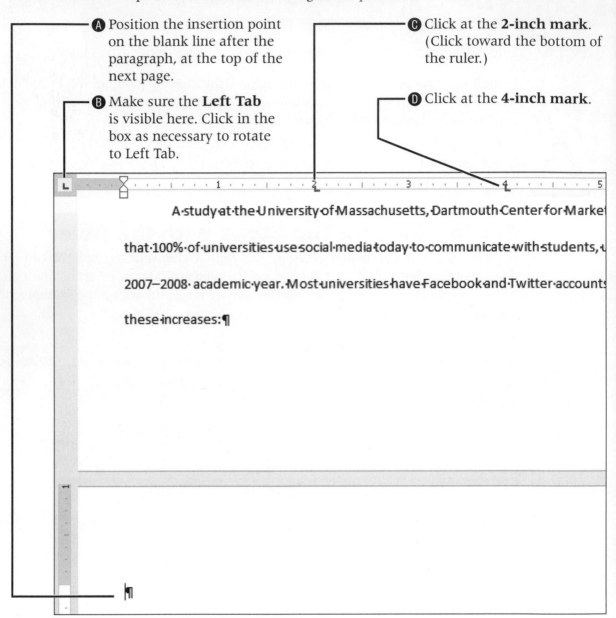

Ⓐ Position the insertion point on the blank line after the paragraph, at the top of the next page.

Ⓑ Make sure the **Left Tab** is visible here. Click in the box as necessary to rotate to Left Tab.

Ⓒ Click at the **2-inch mark**. (Click toward the bottom of the ruler.)

Ⓓ Click at the **4-inch mark**.

A·study·at·the·University·of·Massachusetts,·Dartmouth·Center·for·Marke

that·100%·of·universities·use·social·media·today·to·communicate·with·students,·

2007–2008·academic·year.·Most·universities·have·Facebook·and·Twitter·account

these·increases:¶

5. Type the following heading line, tapping ⌨Tab where you see small arrows.

Media   →   2009–2010   →   2010–2011¶

6. Tap ⌨Enter at the end of the line, and notice that the ruler still reflects the tabs you set in the previous line.

7. Save the report.

Working with the Tabs Dialog Box

Video Library   http://labyrinthelab.com/videos   Video Number: WD13-V0407

You can set custom tab stops in the Tabs dialog box. You can specify precise positions for custom tabs, choose the type of tab (alignment), clear custom tab stops, and set leader tabs.

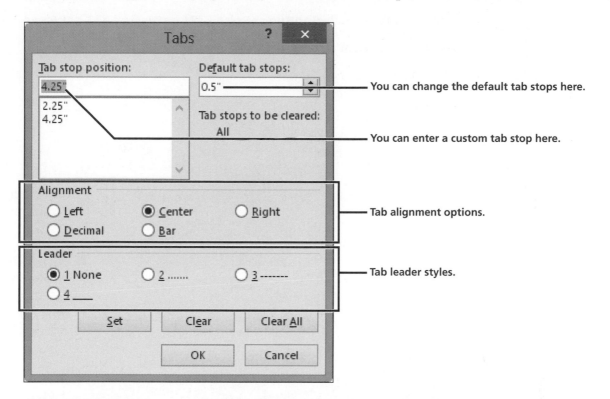

You can change the default tab stops here.

You can enter a custom tab stop here.

Tab alignment options.

Tab leader styles.

QUICK REFERENCE	USING THE INDENT MARKERS
Task	**Procedure**
Set tabs	■ Choose the desired tab in the Tabs box and click the desired location on the ruler; or, choose Home→Paragraph→dialog box launcher and click Tabs.
	■ Enter the settings in the Tab Stop Position field, choose the Alignment, and click Set.
Modify tab settings	■ Drag the tab(s) to a new location on the ruler; or, in the Tabs dialog box, clear the tab(s) you want to change, enter new settings in the Tab Stop Position field, and click Set.
Clear tabs	■ Drag the tab(s) off the ruler; or, use the Clear or Clear All button in the Tabs dialog box.

Use the Tabs Dialog Box

In this exercise, you will use the Tabs dialog box to clear tabs that were set for the table's heading line and to set custom tabs for the body of the table.

1. Save your file as **WD04-D07-SocMediaRprt-[FirstInitialLastName]**.

2. Follow these steps to clear all tabs:

Ⓐ The insertion point should be in the line below the heading line.

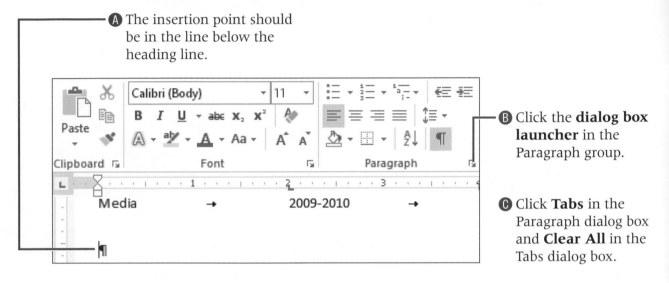

Ⓑ Click the **dialog box launcher** in the Paragraph group.

Ⓒ Click **Tabs** in the Paragraph dialog box and **Clear All** in the Tabs dialog box.

3. Follow these steps to set new tabs for the rest of the table:

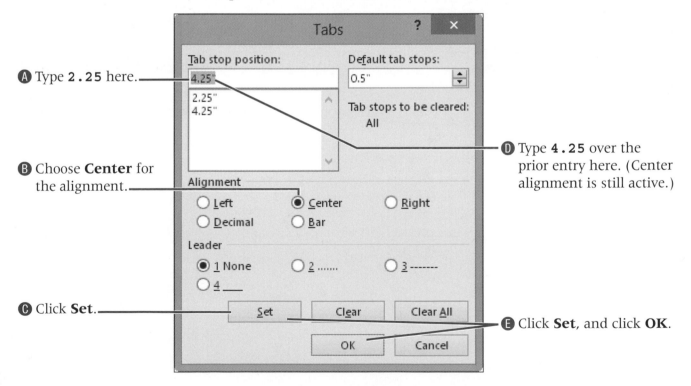

Ⓐ Type **2.25** here.

Ⓑ Choose **Center** for the alignment.

Ⓒ Click **Set**.

Ⓓ Type **4.25** over the prior entry here. (Center alignment is still active.)

Ⓔ Click **Set**, and click **OK**.

4. Type the rest of the table, tapping ⌷Tab⌷ wherever an arrow appears, and tapping ⌷Enter⌷ at the end of each line.

Media		2009–2010		2010–2011¶
Facebook	→	87%	→	98%¶
Twitter	→	59%	→	84%¶
Blogs	→	51%	→	66%¶
Podcasts	→	22%	→	41%¶

5. Select the first line in the table and choose **Home→Font→Bold** ⃞B⃞.

6. Save the file.

Modifying Tab Stops with the Ruler

Video Library   http://labyrinthelab.com/videos   Video Number: WD13-V0408

To adjust a tab setting on the ruler, you select the paragraphs containing the tab stops you want to change, and then drag the tab to the new location. Delete a tab by dragging it off the Ruler.

If you accidentally drag a tab stop off the ruler while trying to move it, just click Undo.

DEVELOP YOUR SKILLS WD04-D08

Modify and Delete Tab Stops from the Ruler

In this exercise, you decided the percentages could be better centered below the headings. You will use the ruler to modify the tab stops for the body of the table but not the heading line. Then you will delete a tab stop.

1. Save your file as **`WD04-D08-SocMediaRprt-[FirstInitialLastName]`**.
2. Follow these steps to adjust the tabs:

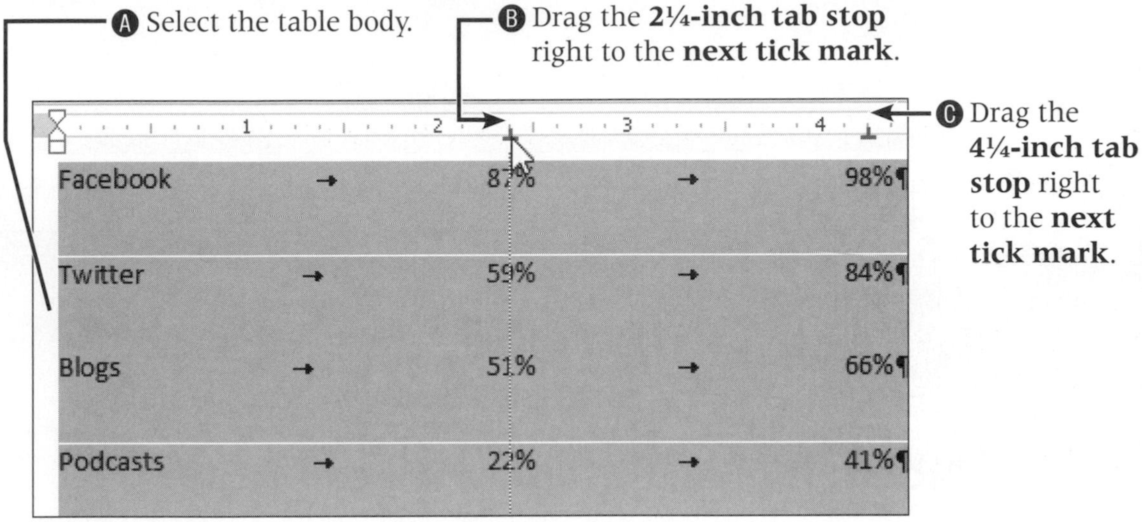

Ⓐ Select the table body.
Ⓑ Drag the **2¼-inch tab stop** right to the **next tick mark**.
Ⓒ Drag the **4¼-inch tab stop** right to the **next tick mark**.
Facebook 87% 98%
Twitter 59% 84%
Blogs 51% 66%
Podcasts 22% 41%

Now you will delete a tab stop.

3. Place the mouse pointer on the **4 3/8 inch tab** and drag it straight down off the ruler to remove the tab.
4. Click **Undo** on the Quick Access toolbar to replace the tab stop.
5. Save the report.

Using Numbered and Bulleted Lists

Video Library   http://labyrinthelab.com/videos   Video Number: WD13-V0409

Numbered and bulleted lists are effective in drawing your reader's attention to items of interest. You can turn them on before you begin typing or apply them after you type the list. Numbered lists are automatically renumbered if you insert or delete an item. A good example of when to use a numbered list is when sequence is important, as in a series of steps. Items in a bulleted list have no sequence.

FROM THE RIBBON

Home→Paragraph→
Bullets

Home→Paragraph→
Numbering

Promoting and Demoting List Items

Demoting an item increases the indent level by shifting it to the right. To promote an item decreases the indent level by moving it back to the left. When you demote items in a list, it creates an outline effect, indicating the level of importance of the items in the list.

FROM THE KEYBOARD

Shift + Tab to promote a list item

Tab to demote a list item

- Search for classes online
  - Locate desired subjects, dates, and times
  - Review syllabi
- Use course homepages

These two items were demoted by increasing the indent level.

QUICK REFERENCE	WORKING WITH LISTS
Task	**Procedure**
Convert text to a bulleted or numbered list	■ Select the text to be formatted, and choose Home→Paragraph→Bullets or Numbering.
Turn off bullets and numbering	■ Tap Enter twice at the end of the list; or, click the Bullets or the Numbering button.
Demote an item in a list	■ Select the item and choose Home→Paragraph→Increase Indent; or, tap Tab.
Promote an item in a list	■ Select the item and choose Home→Paragraph→Decrease Indent; or, press Shift + Tab.
Customize Bullets and Numbering	■ Choose Home→Paragraph→Bullets or Numbering menu button ▼ and choose Define New Bullet or Define New Number Format.
Remove a custom bullet or numbering from the gallery	■ Right-click the image and choose Remove.

Work with Bullets and Numbering

In this exercise, you will convert text to a numbered list, and then you'll create a bulleted list, promoting and demoting levels within the list.

1. Save your file as **WD04-D09-SocMediaRprt-[FirstInitialLastName]**.

2. Follow these steps to create a list:

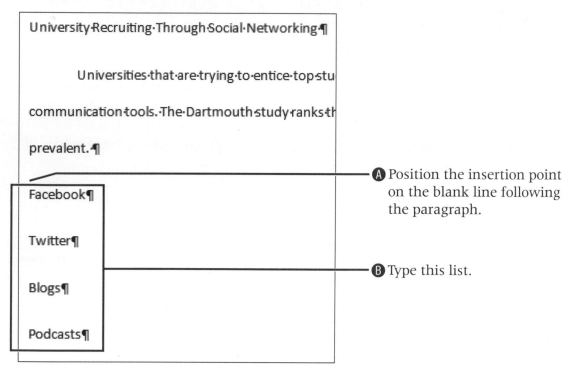

University·Recruiting·Through·Social·Networking.¶

Universities·that·are·trying·to·entice·top·stu

communication·tools.·The·Dartmouth·study·ranks·th

prevalent.·¶

Facebook¶

Twitter¶

Blogs¶

Podcasts¶

Ⓐ Position the insertion point on the blank line following the paragraph.

Ⓑ Type this list.

3. Select the list and choose **Home→Paragraph→Numbering** 📋.

4. Position the insertion point on the first blank line following the last paragraph.
   You will switch to single spacing before typing the bulleted list.

5. Choose **Home→Paragraph→Line and Paragraph Spacing menu button** ▼, and then choose **1.0** from the menu.

6. Follow these steps to create a bulleted list:

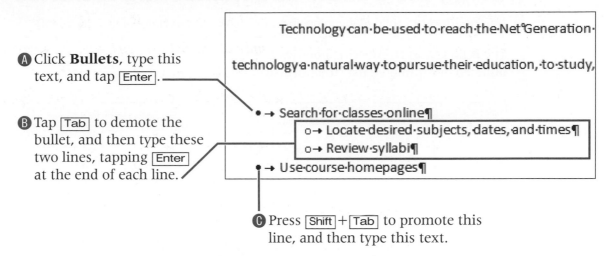

A Click **Bullets**, type this text, and tap Enter.

B Tap Tab to demote the bullet, and then type these two lines, tapping Enter at the end of each line.

C Press Shift + Tab to promote this line, and then type this text.

Technology·can·be·used·to·reach·the·Net°Generation·

technology·a·natural·way·to·pursue·their·education,·to·study,

• → Search·for·classes·online¶
  o→ Locate·desired·subjects,·dates,·and·times¶
  o→ Review·syllabi¶
• → Use·course·homepages¶

7. Type the rest of the list as shown, demoting and promoting the bullet levels as needed.

• → Use·course·homepages¶
    o→ Read·announcements¶
    o→ Get·student·handouts¶
    o→ Conduct·threaded·conversations·on·message·boards¶
    o→ Communicate·with·instructors·in·chat·rooms¶
• → View·faculty·office·hours·online¶
• → Review·academic·history·online¶

8. Save the report.

Using the Bullets and Numbering Libraries

Video Library   http://labyrinthelab.com/videos   Video Number: WD13-V0410

FROM THE RIBBON
Home→Paragraph→
Bullets menu button ▼

Home→Paragraph→
Numbering menu
button ▼

The Bullets and Numbering libraries enable you to choose a style for your bulleted or numbered list. You can also define your own custom formats.

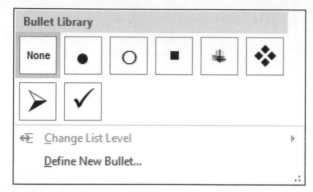

Bullet Library

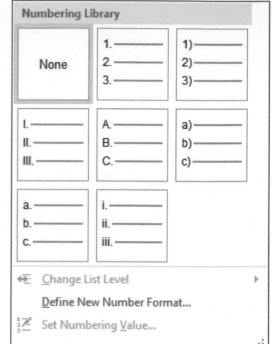

Numbering Library

DEVELOP YOUR SKILLS WD04-D10

Change the Bullet Style

In this exercise, you will choose a different bullet style for the first-level bullets from the Bullet Library.

1. Save your file as **WD04-D10-SocMediaRprt-[FirstInitialLastName]**.

2. Follow these steps to apply a different bullet:

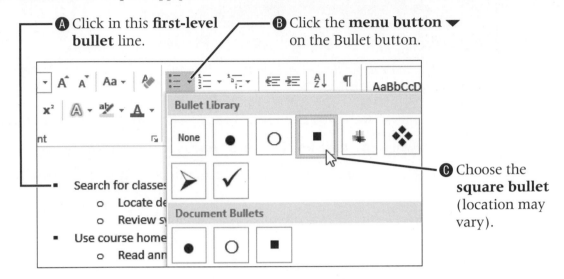

Ⓐ Click in this **first-level bullet** line.

Ⓑ Click the **menu button** ▼ on the Bullet button.

Ⓒ Choose the **square bullet** (location may vary).

Notice that the bullet shape changed for all first-level bullets.

3. Save the report.

Customizing Bullet and Number Styles

Video Library   http://labyrinthelab.com/videos   Video Number: WD13-V0411

You can customize bullet styles by defining a symbol, picture, font, or alignment. You can customize the numbering style, font, format, and alignment.

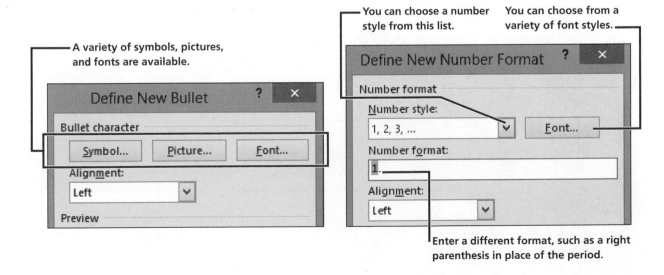

A variety of symbols, pictures, and fonts are available.

You can choose a number style from this list.

You can choose from a variety of font styles.

Enter a different format, such as a right parenthesis in place of the period.

Restarting or Continuing Numbering

Many documents have more than one numbered list. You may want the numbering to continue sequentially from one list to the next. For example, if one list ends with the number 4 you may want the next list to begin with 5. If you type text after the first list, when you begin the next list, Word assumes you want to restart numbering at 1. If you want to continue numbering, Word provides an AutoCorrect smart tag where you can choose Continue Numbering.

DEVELOP YOUR SKILLS WD04-D11
Experiment with Custom Bullets

In this exercise, you will use the Define New Bullet dialog box to create a custom bullet. You will use a symbol as the new bullet style.

1. Save your file as **WD04-D11-SocMediaRprt-[FirstInitialLastName]**.

2. Click anywhere in a **first-level bulleted line** (such as *Search for classes online*).

3. Choose **Home→Paragraph→Bullets** :≡ **menu button** ▼ and choose **Define New Bullet**.

4. Follow these steps to define a symbol as a new bullet:

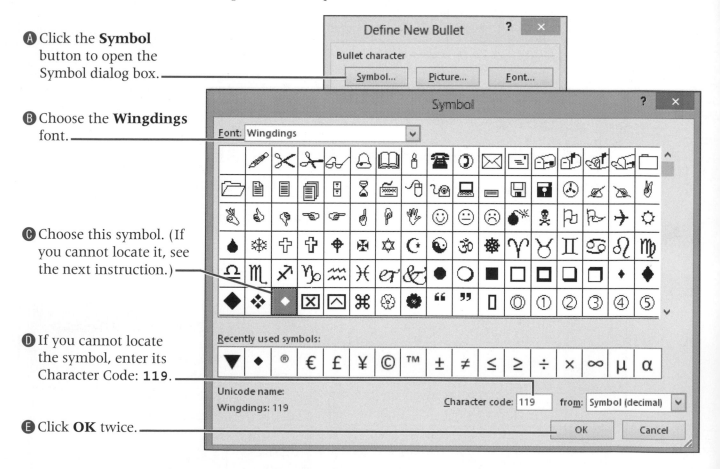

ⓐ Click the **Symbol** button to open the Symbol dialog box.

ⓑ Choose the **Wingdings** font.

ⓒ Choose this symbol. (If you cannot locate it, see the next instruction.)

ⓓ If you cannot locate the symbol, enter its Character Code: **119**.

ⓔ Click **OK** twice.

Notice that all the first-level bullets have changed to the custom bullet.

5. Choose **Home→Paragraph→Bullets** menu button ▼ to display the Bullet Library.

   The new bullet was added to the library. Now you'll remove the bullet so the next student who uses your computer will have the same experience.

6. Right-click the new bullet in the Bullet Library area, and choose **Remove**.

7. Display the **Bullet Library** again and notice that the new bullet was removed; close the menu.

8. Save the report.

Setting Line Breaks

| Video Library | http://labyrinthelab.com/videos | Video Number: WD13-V0412 |

FROM THE KEYBOARD
Shift+Enter to create a line break

When working with bullets and numbering, tapping Enter generates a new bullet or number. What if you want to type something relative to a bulleted or numbered item on the next line(s) without generating a new bullet or number? A manual line break starts a new line (without inserting a paragraph mark) and continues the text on the new line. Line breaks are inserted with the Shift + Enter keystroke combination.

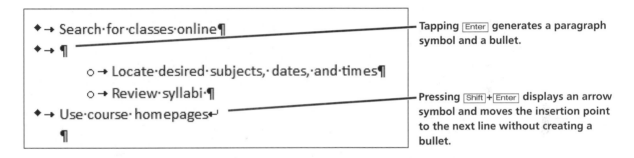

Tapping Enter generates a paragraph symbol and a bullet.

Pressing Shift+Enter displays an arrow symbol and moves the insertion point to the next line without creating a bullet.

DEVELOP YOUR SKILLS WD04-D12
Insert Line Breaks in a List

In this exercise, you will use line breaks to add descriptive information about Facebook and Twitter. The line breaks will allow you to type additional information without generating a new number.

1. Save your file as **WD04-D12-SocMediaRprt-[FirstInitialLastName]**.

2. If necessary, choose **Home→Paragraph→Show/Hide** ¶ to display formatting marks.

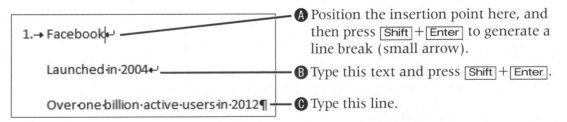

Ⓐ Position the insertion point here, and then press Shift + Enter to generate a line break (small arrow).

Ⓑ Type this text and press Shift + Enter.

Ⓒ Type this line.

3. Position the insertion point to the right of *Twitter* in your numbered list.

4. Press ⟨Shift⟩+⟨Enter⟩ to generate a line break.

5. Type **Launched in 2006** and press ⟨Shift⟩+⟨Enter⟩.

6. Type the following: **Over 500 million active users in 2012.**

7. Save the report.

Using Paragraph Space Settings

Video Library http://labyrinthelab.com/videos Video Number: WD13-V0413

The default spacing in Word 2013 is 1.08 rather than the traditional single spacing (1.0). Word adds 8 points (a little less than an eighth of an inch) of after-paragraph spacing when you use the Blank Document template. You can modify the amount of space that comes before or after a paragraph.

FROM THE RIBBON
Page Layout→
Paragraph→Before

Page Layout→
Paragraph→After

Indent		Spacing	
⊫ Left:	0"	↕≣ Before:	0 pt
≣ Right:	0"	↓≣ After:	8 pt
		Paragraph	⌐

→ Before and After paragraph spacing

72 points = 1 inch

DEVELOP YOUR SKILLS WD04-D13

Set Paragraph Spacing

In this exercise, you will change the paragraph spacing between the headings and their following paragraphs.

1. Save your file as **WD04-D13-SocMediaRprt-[FirstInitialLastName]**.

2. Click in the heading *The Net Generation* on page 1.

3. Choose **Page Layout→Paragraph**, click the **After** box, type **2**, and tap ⟨Enter⟩.
   Notice there is a little less space following the heading.

The spin box controls in the Spacing section use 6-point increments. If you want to use a different measurement, you must enter it manually.

4. Repeat the process for the remaining three headings.

5. Save the report.

Formatting with Borders and Shading

Video Library   http://labyrinthelab.com/videos   Video Number: WD13-V0414

You can apply borders and shading to selected text, paragraphs, and objects, such as tables. Page borders are also available to outline an entire page. In this lesson, you will apply borders to paragraphs. You can choose the style, color, and thickness of borders, and you can also select various shading colors and patterns.

Using Borders and Shading Buttons and the Dialog Box

The Borders and Shading buttons have memory. The button face displays the last choice you made. That way you can apply the same type of border or shading several times in a row without opening the menu.

FROM THE RIBBON
Home→Paragraph→
Borders menu button ▾
Home→Paragraph→
Shading menu button ▾

Default bottom border ⎯⎯⎯⎯⎯⎯⎯⎯⎯   ⎯⎯⎯ Button face where the last choice was Outside Borders

Choosing Borders and Shading from the Borders button menu displays the dialog box. The following illustrations show the features available in the Borders tab and Shading tab.

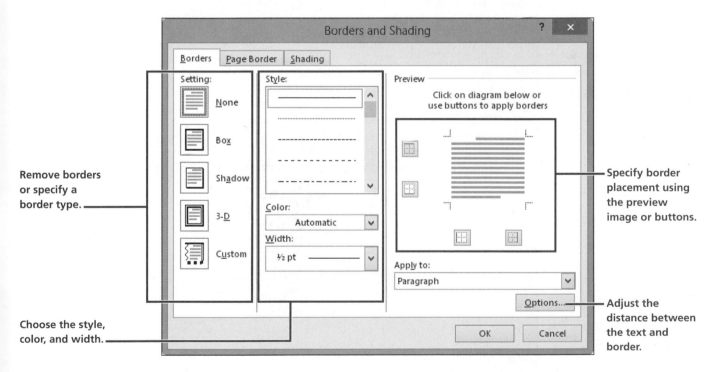

Remove borders or specify a border type.

Choose the style, color, and width.

Specify border placement using the preview image or buttons.

Adjust the distance between the text and border.

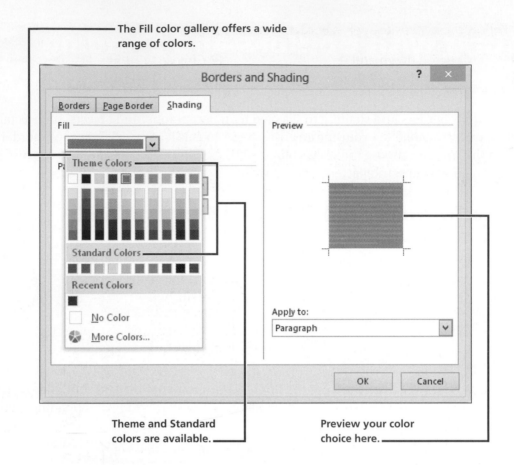

The Fill color gallery offers a wide range of colors.

Theme and Standard colors are available.

Preview your color choice here.

Apply Borders and Shading to Headings

In this exercise, you will apply borders and shading to the headings using the Borders and Shading dialog box.

1. Save your file as **WD04-D14-SocMediaRprt-[FirstInitialLastName]**.

2. Click anywhere in the heading **The Net Generation**.

3. Choose **Home→Paragraph→Borders** ⊞ **menu button ▼**.

4. Choose **Borders and Shading** at the bottom of the menu to open the dialog box.

5. If necessary, click the Borders tab to bring it to the front of the dialog box.

6. Follow these steps to apply a border to the heading:

Ⓐ Choose **Box** as the border setting.

Ⓑ Scroll down and choose the **double line** style.

Ⓒ Choose ¾ **pt** as the border width.

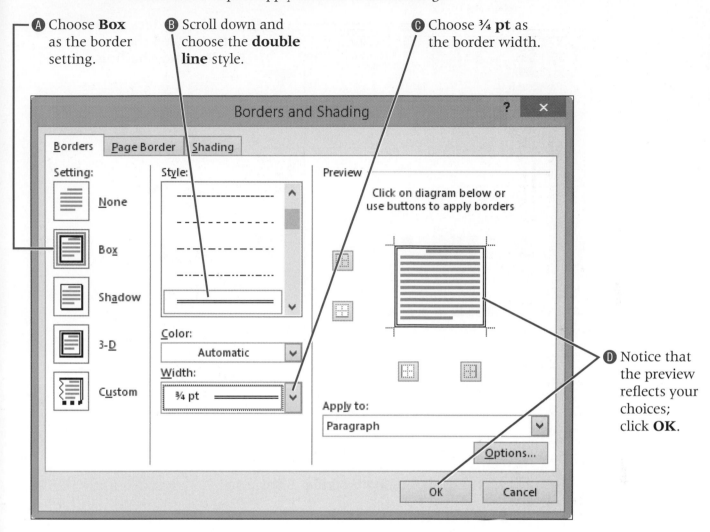

Ⓓ Notice that the preview reflects your choices; click **OK**.

The border extends between the margins. Paragraph borders fill the space between the margins, unless the paragraph(s) is indented or a specific amount of text is selected.

7. Follow these steps to apply shading:

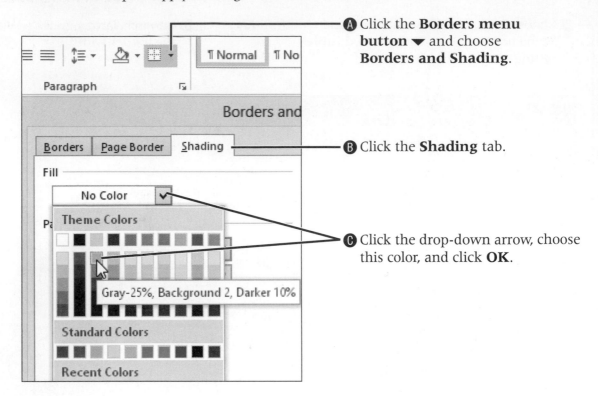

Ⓐ Click the **Borders menu button** ▼ and choose **Borders and Shading**.

Ⓑ Click the **Shading** tab.

Ⓒ Click the drop-down arrow, choose this color, and click **OK**.

The text appears too close to the top border. Next you will adjust the spacing between the text and the top border.

8. Choose **Home→Paragraph→Borders** 🔲 **menu button** ▼.

9. Choose **Borders and Shading** at the bottom of the menu.

10. Click **Options** in the Borders tab.

11. Enter **8** in the **Top** box, and then click **OK** twice.
    Eight points of space were added between the text and the border.

Use the Format Painter to Copy the Heading Formats

12. Make sure your insertion point is still positioned in *The Net Generation* heading.

13. Double-click the **Format Painter** 🖌 in the Clipboard group of the Home tab.
    Remember, double-clicking keeps the Format Painter turned on.

14. Select the following headings to format them:
    - Rapid Increase in the Use of Social Media
    - University Recruiting Through Social Networking
    - Social Media Benefits for Students

15. Click the **Format Painter** 🖌 to turn it off.

16. Save the report.

Formatting Text with Styles

Video Library   http://labyrinthelab.com/videos   Video Number: WD13-V0415

A style is one of the most powerful formatting tools in Word. It is a *group of formats* enabling you to apply multiple formats to a block of text all at once. Styles are based on the current template's theme, which is a set of colors, fonts, and graphic effects. Word contains styles for document elements, such as headings, titles, and special character formats, providing consistent formatting throughout a document.

Understanding Types of Styles

Word has many built-in styles, and you are always working within a style in Word. There are two basic types of styles: character and paragraph.

- Character styles: Character styles are applied to the word the insertion point is in or a selected group of words. Character styles only contain character formats, not paragraph formats. You can apply character styles to text *within* a paragraph that is formatted with a paragraph style.

- Paragraph styles: Paragraph styles are applied to all text in selected paragraphs or to the paragraph containing the insertion point. You can use any character or paragraph formats in a paragraph style. For example, you may want to format a heading with a large, bold font (character formatting) and apply paragraph spacing before and after the heading (paragraph formatting).

Using the Styles Gallery and the Styles Task Pane

Styles are located in the Styles gallery on the Ribbon and in the Styles task pane. Live Preview makes it easy to test a variety of styles in the gallery, while the Styles task pane provides style descriptions in ToolTips.

The gallery is limited to frequently used styles and is always at hand on the Ribbon. The Styles task pane is where you go if you need a more in-depth approach to styles.

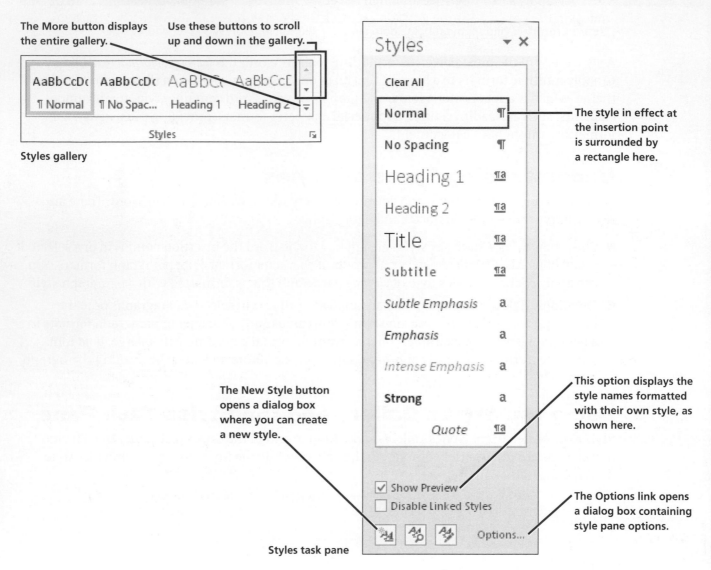

The More button displays the entire gallery.

Use these buttons to scroll up and down in the gallery.

Styles gallery

The style in effect at the insertion point is surrounded by a rectangle here.

The New Style button opens a dialog box where you can create a new style.

This option displays the style names formatted with their own style, as shown here.

The Options link opens a dialog box containing style pane options.

Styles task pane

Collapsing Heading Topics

When you apply a heading style and then hover the mouse pointer over the heading, a small triangle marker appears at the left. You can click the marker to collapse and expand the text below it. This allows you to focus on certain portions of the document.

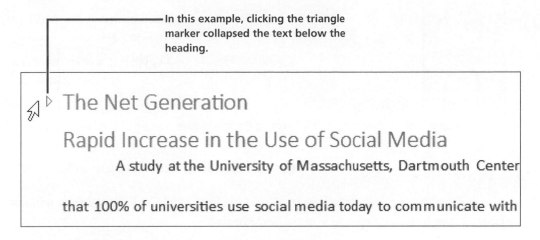

In this example, clicking the triangle marker collapsed the text below the heading.

DEVELOP YOUR SKILLS WD04-D15
Apply Styles

In this exercise, you will use Live Preview in the Styles gallery to find styles that will give your report a professional, polished look. You will apply the Title style to the report's main heading and you will apply the Heading 1 style to the other headings.

1. Save your file as **WD04-D15-SocMediaRprt-[FirstInitialLastName]**.

2. Click anywhere in the report's main heading, **Social Media in Universities**.

3. Follow these steps to view and apply the Title style to the main heading.

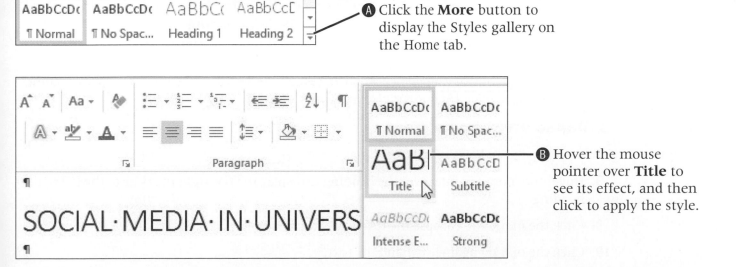

Ⓐ Click the **More** button to display the Styles gallery on the Home tab.

Ⓑ Hover the mouse pointer over **Title** to see its effect, and then click to apply the style.

4. Follow these steps to apply the Heading 1 style to the next heading:

Ⓐ Click to place the insertion point here.

Ⓑ Click **More** ⌄ in the bottom-right corner of the Styles gallery.

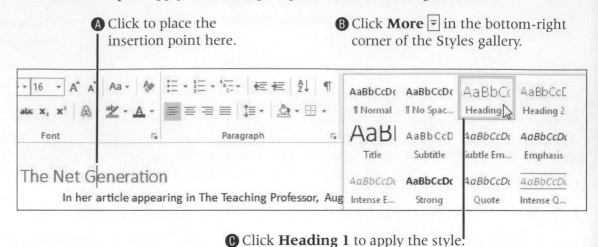

Ⓒ Click **Heading 1** to apply the style.

The Styles task pane includes all the styles that are in the Styles gallery. Now you will use the task pane to apply the Heading 1 style to the next heading.

5. Follow these steps to apply the Heading 1 style from the Styles task pane:

Ⓐ Click the Styles group **dialog box launcher**.

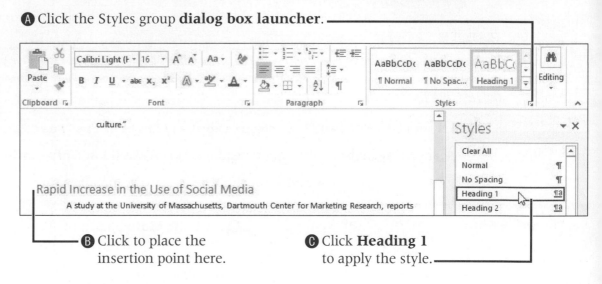

Ⓑ Click to place the insertion point here.

Ⓒ Click **Heading 1** to apply the style.

6. Using the method of your choice, apply the **Heading 1** style to the remaining two headings: *University Recruiting Through Social Networking* and *Social Media Benefits for Students*.

Collapse and Expand Text

7. Scroll up to *The Net Generation* heading.

8. Hover the mouse pointer over the heading to display the **triangle marker** to the left of the heading.

9. Click the marker to collapse the text below the heading.

10. Click the marker again to expand the text.

11. Save the report.

Creating a New Custom Style

Video Library http://labyrinthelab.com/videos Video Number: WD13-V0416

Thus far, you have applied built-in styles. However, there may be situations where the built-in styles do not meet your needs. For example, you may have corporate formatting standards set for different types of documents. You can create custom styles to meet those standards.

There are two approaches you can take to create custom styles. The method you choose is a matter of personal preference; both are equally effective.

- **Style by definition:** Choose all formats in the Create New Style from Formatting dialog box.
- **Style by example:** Format a block of text with the formats you wish to include in your style. The Create New Style from Formatting dialog box is able to copy the formats in your formatted text.

The following illustration points out the important elements in the Create New Style from Formatting dialog box.

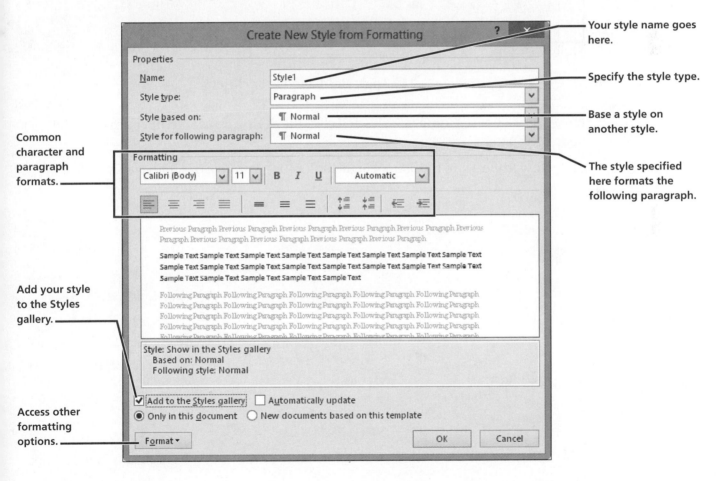

Create a New Style

In this exercise, you will create a new "style by example." It will be a character style, and you will apply the style to selected blocks of text.

1. Save your file as **WD04-D16-SocMediaRprt-[FirstInitialLastName]**.

2. Follow these steps to format the "style by example" text:

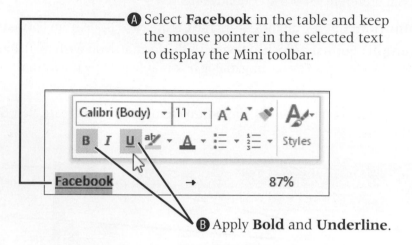

A Select **Facebook** in the table and keep the mouse pointer in the selected text to display the Mini toolbar.

B Apply **Bold** and **Underline**.

3. If necessary, choose **Home→Styles** and click the **dialog box launcher** ⌐ to open the Styles task pane.

4. Click **New Style** 🔏 in the bottom of the task pane. (Use ToolTips if necessary.)

5. Follow these steps to complete the new style:

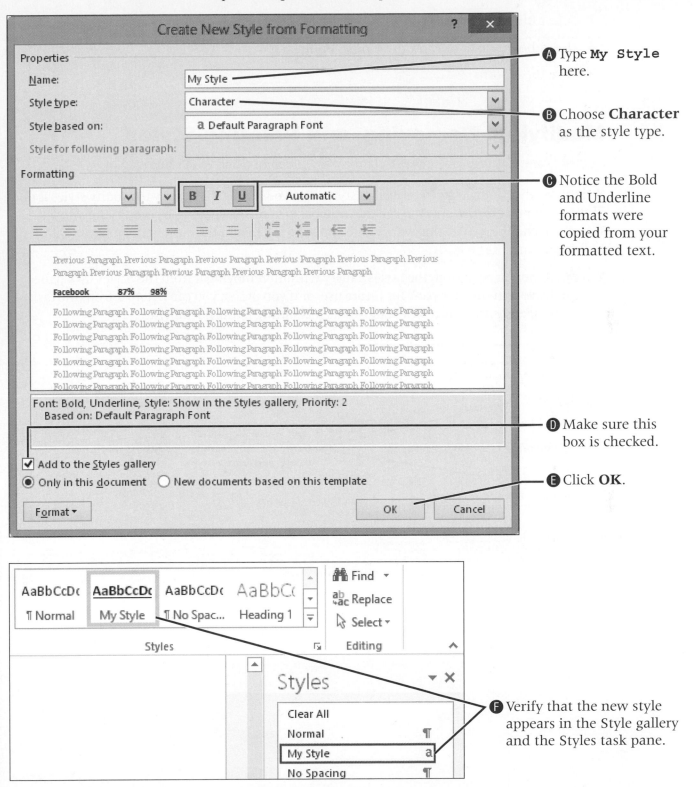

A Type **My Style** here.

B Choose **Character** as the style type.

C Notice the Bold and Underline formats were copied from your formatted text.

D Make sure this box is checked.

E Click **OK**.

F Verify that the new style appears in the Style gallery and the Styles task pane.

Now you will apply the style to the rest of the row headings.

6. Select **Twitter** and choose **Home→Styles→My Style**.

7. Select **Blogs** and click **My Style** in the Styles task pane.

8. Use either method to apply the style to **Podcasts**.

9. Save the report.

Modifying, Removing, and Deleting Styles

Video Library   http://labyrinthelab.com/videos   Video Number: WD13-V0417

You can modify built-in styles as well as styles that you create. The ability to modify styles is one of the great powers of Word. You can make global formatting changes by modifying a style. When you change a style, the changes are applied to all text in the current document that is formatted with the style.

You can remove a style from the Styles gallery without removing it from the Styles task pane. You can leave it in the task pane for future use, or if you prefer, you can delete it from the task pane. Completely deleting a style removes its formatting in the document.

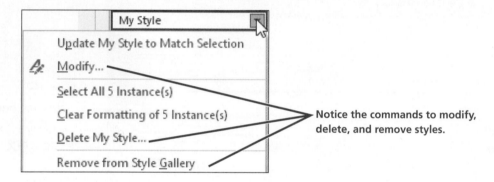

Notice the commands to modify, delete, and remove styles.

QUICK REFERENCE	USING WORD STYLES
Task	**Procedure**
Apply a style	■ **Character Style:** Select the text and choose a style from the Styles gallery or the Styles task pane. ■ **Paragraph Style:** Click in the paragraph and choose a style from the Styles gallery or the Styles task pane. To apply a style to more than one paragraph, select at least part of each paragraph.
Create a new style by definition	■ Click the New Style button, choose all desired formats from within the dialog box, and then click OK.
Create a new style by example	■ Format a block of text and click the New Styles button. ■ Name the style and click OK.
Modify a style	■ Choose Modify from the style's menu, make the desired changes, and then click OK.
Add a style to the Styles gallery	■ Choose Add to Style Gallery from the style's menu.
Remove a style from the Styles gallery	■ Choose Remove from Style Gallery from the style's menu, or right-click the style in the gallery and choose Remove from Style Gallery.
Delete a custom style	■ Choose Delete [style name] from the style's menu.

DEVELOP YOUR SKILLS WD04-D17
Modify and Remove a Style

In this exercise, you will modify a style to see how it impacts all text formatted with that style. Then you will remove the style from the Styles gallery and the Styles task pane.

1. Save your file as **WD04-D17-SocMediaRprt-[FirstInitialLastName]**.

2. Hover the mouse pointer over **My Style** in the Styles task pane and click the **menu button▼**.

3. Choose **Modify** from the menu to open the Modify Style dialog box.

   This dialog box contains the same elements as the Create New Style from Formatting dialog box.

4. Click **Italic** $\boxed{I}$ to add that format, and click **OK**.

   The row headings are italicized. Now you will remove the style from the Styles gallery and the Styles task pane.

5. Hover the mouse pointer over **My Style** in the Styles task pane and click the **menu button ▼**.

6. Choose **Remove from Style Gallery**.

   My Style no longer appears in the gallery.

7. Open the menu for **My Style** in the task pane, and choose **Delete My Style**.

8. When the message appears verifying the deletion, click **Yes**.

   The style is removed from the task pane and the style formatting is removed from the row headings in the document.

9. **Close** ☒ the Styles task pane, and save your report.

Navigating with the Navigation Pane

Video Library   http://labyrinthelab.com/videos   Video Number: WD13-V0418

The Navigation pane provides a great way to navigate through your document using heading styles. This gives you a bird's-eye view of your document so you can easily see the overall flow of topics.

FROM THE RIBBON
View→Show→
Navigation Pane

FROM THE KEYBOARD
Ctrl+F to open the
Navigation pane

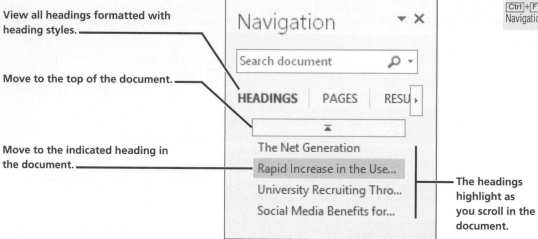

View all headings formatted with heading styles.

Move to the top of the document.

Move to the indicated heading in the document.

The headings highlight as you scroll in the document.

Rearranging Topics

Rearranging parts of your document is one of the most powerful uses of the Navigation pane. When you drag a heading to a new location, all of its lower-level headings and associated text move with it.

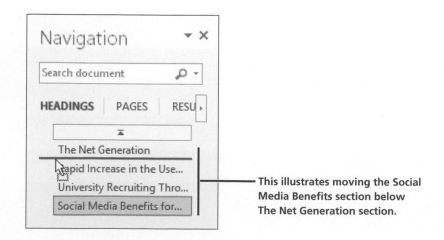

This illustrates moving the Social Media Benefits section below The Net Generation section.

QUICK REFERENCE	REARRANGING A DOCUMENT USING THE NAVIGATION PANE
Task	**Procedure**
Display headings in the Navigation pane	■ Choose View→Show→Navigation Pane and click the Headings button at the top of the pane.
Rearrange a section	■ Click and drag a heading up or down to a new location.

DEVELOP YOUR SKILLS WD04-D18

Navigating and Rearranging Topics

In this exercise, you will use the Navigation pane to move through the report using heading styles. Then, you will use the Navigation pane to move a topic.

1. Save your file as **WD04-D18-SocMediaRprt-[FirstInitialLastName]**.

2. Choose **View→Show→Navigation Pane**, and click **Headings** at the top of the pane.

3. Click the **Social Media Benefits for Students** link in the pane to jump to that topic.

4. Scroll to the top of the report and notice that the highlighting in the pane changes as you scroll to show you where you are in the document.

5. In the Navigation pane, drag the **Social Media Benefits** topic below **The Net Generation** topic.

6. Scroll in the document to see how the topics were rearranged.

7. Delete the extra blank line below The Net Generation topic and, if necessary, below Social Media Benefits for Students topic to tighten up the text.

8. Close ⊠ the **Navigation pane** and save the document.

Introducing Headers and Footers

Video Library http://labyrinthelab.com/videos   Video Number: WD13-V0419

Headers and footers appear at the top and bottom of every page in a document, respectively, above and below the margins. You can place text, page numbers, dates, and other items in the header and footer areas. When you enter information in these areas, it is repeated on every page of the document.

Word offers a variety of header and footer formatting styles, or you can create your own.

FROM THE RIBBON

Insert→Header & Footer→Header/Footer

Insert→Header & Footer→Page Number

Rapid Increase in the Use of Social Media

   A study at the University of Massachusetts, Dartmouth Center for Marketing Research, reports

that 100% of universities use social media today to communicate with students, up from 61% in the

2007–2008 academic year. Most universities have Facebook and Twitter accounts. The study reports

these increases:

1

One of Word's built-in page number designs.

QUICK REFERENCE	WORKING WITH HEADERS, FOOTERS, AND PAGE NUMBERS
Task	**Procedure**
Insert a built-in header/footer/page number	■ Choose Insert→Header & Footer→Header/Footer/Page Number and choose a built-in style.
Create or modify header/footer	■ Choose Insert→Header & Footer→Header/Footer and choose Edit Header/Footer.
Format page numbers	■ Choose Insert→Header & Footer→Page Number and choose Format Page Numbers.
Delete a header/footer/page number	■ Choose Insert→Header & Footer→Header/Footer/Page Number and choose Remove Header/Footer/Page Numbers.
Open/close header/footer	■ Double-click the header/footer areas to open them. ■ Double-click the main document to close the header/footer.

Add a Header and Page Numbers to the Report

In this exercise, you will add headers and page numbers to the report. You will use Word's built-in formats.

1. Save your file as **WD04-D19-SocMediaRprt-[FirstInitialLastName]**.

2. Choose **Insert→Header & Footer→Header** and choose the **Sideline** format from the gallery.

3. Click **Document Title** and type **My Virtual Campus** in its place.

4. Double-click in the document to close the header.

5. Choose **Insert→Header & Footer→Page Number** and slide the mouse pointer down the menu to **Bottom of Page**.

6. Scroll down in the gallery and choose **Large Color 3**.

7. Double-click in the document to close the page-number footer.
   You can open the header/footer area by double-clicking anywhere in the header/footer area.

8. Double-click in the footer area to open it, and then double-click in the document again to close the footer area.

9. Scroll through the report and observe the headers and page numbers.

10. Save the report.

Using the Resume Reading Bookmark

Video Library   http://labyrinthelab.com/videos   Video Number: WD13-V0420

When you close a document and then reopen it, Word remembers your last editing point and presents a pop-up bookmark offering to let you pick up where you left off. This Resume Reading feature provides a fast startup if you don't recall exactly where you were when you last worked in the document.

Welcome back!
Pick up where you left off:

Social Media Benefits for Students
A few seconds ago

Word 2013

Use the Resume Reading Bookmark

In this exercise, you will make an editing change to your report, and then save and close it. When you reopen the report, the Resume Reading Bookmark will let you quickly jump to where you left off.

1. Save your file as **WD04-D20-SocMediaRprt-[FirstInitialLastName]**.

2. Scroll to the **University Recruiting Through Social Networking** heading.

3. In the first line below the heading, change *top* to **the best**.

4. Save and close the report.

5. Follow these steps to display the Resume Reading Bookmark:

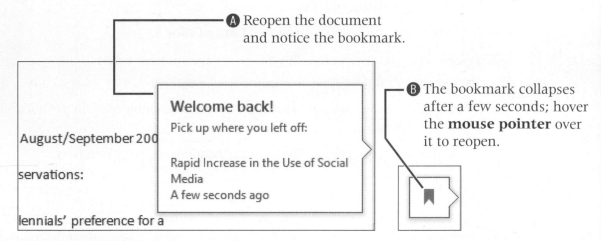

Ⓐ Reopen the document and notice the bookmark.

Ⓑ The bookmark collapses after a few seconds; hover the **mouse pointer** over it to reopen.

Welcome back!
Pick up where you left off:

Rapid Increase in the Use of Social Media
A few seconds ago

6. Click the **bookmark** to jump to your last editing location.

7. Save and close the report. Exit **Word**.

Concepts Review

To check your knowledge of the key concepts introduced in this lesson, complete the Concepts Review quiz by choosing the appropriate access option below.

If you are...	Then access the quiz by...
Using the Labyrinth Video Library	Going to http://labyrinthelab.com/videos
Using eLab	Logging in, choosing Content, and navigating to the Concepts Review quiz for this lesson
Not using the Labyrinth Video Library or eLab	Going to the student resource center for this book

Reinforce Your Skills

Format a Recycling Report

In this exercise, you will polish a report that Kids for Change members researched. You will use paragraph alignment, hyphenation, and indents. You will set custom tabs on the ruler to use in a tabular table, and finally, you will add after-paragraph spacing to several paragraphs.

Format Reports and Paragraphs

1. Start **Word**. Open **WD04-R01-ElecRecyc** from your **WD2013 Lesson 04** folder and save it as **WD04-R01-ElecRecyc-[FirstInitialLastName]**.

2. Position the insertion point in the heading at the top of the document.

3. Choose **Home→Paragraph→Center** ☰.

4. Keep the insertion point at the top of the document.

5. **Choose Page Layout→Page Setup→Hyphenation** 🔤, and choose **Manual** from the menu.

6. When the message appears to hyphenate *following*, click **Yes**.

7. Click **Yes** to hyphenate *replaced*.

8. When the Hyphenation Is Complete message appears, click **OK**.
   Now you will insert a nonbreaking hyphen and nonbreaking space so terms will stay together if future editing repositions them.

9. Position the insertion point after *earth* in the first paragraph and tap ⌷Delete⌷ to remove the hyphen.

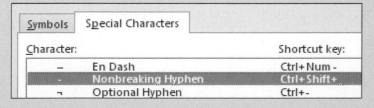

10. Choose **Insert→Symbols→Symbol** Ω and choose **More Symbols**.

11. Click the **Special Characters** tab and choose **Nonbreaking Hyphen**.

Symbols	Special Characters	
Character:		Shortcut key:
–	En Dash	Ctrl+Num -
-	Nonbreaking Hyphen	Ctrl+Shift+
¬	Optional Hyphen	Ctrl+-

12. Click **Insert**, then **Close**.

13. Position the insertion point after *Agency* in the second paragraph and tap Delete.

The United States Environmental Protection Agency (EPA) points out the following recycling benefits on their website:

14. Choose **Insert→Symbols→Symbol** Ω and choose **More Symbols**.

15. When the Symbol dialog box opens, click the **Special Characters tab** and choose **Nonbreaking Space**.

16. Click **Insert**, then **Close**.

Indent Text

17. If necessary, choose **View→Show→Ruler** to turn on the ruler.

18. Position the insertion point in the third paragraph.

19. Place the mouse pointer on the **Left Indent marker** (the rectangle) and drag it to the **half-inch mark**, and then place the mouse pointer on the **Right Indent marker** and drag it to the **6-inch mark**.

"Electronic products are made from valuable resources and materials, including metals, plastics, and glass, all of which require energy to mine and manufacture. Donating or recycling consumer electronics conserves our natural resources and avoids air and water pollution, as well as greenhouse gas emissions that are caused by manufacturing virgin materials."

Notice where the indent markers are now positioned.

Work with Tab Stops

20. Position the insertion point at the bottom of the document.

21. Type the following heading line using the default tab grid, tapping Tab where you see small arrows, and then tap Enter at the end of the line.

Ellsworth·Electronics →　　→　　　→　　Arlington·Electronics →　　→　　　→　　Wilson·Appliances¶
¶

22. Select the heading line and choose **Home→Font→Bold** B.

23. Position the insertion point in the blank line below the heading line where you will set custom tabs.

24. Click the tabs box to display the **Center Tab**. (It looks like an upside down T.)

25. Perform these actions to set the following tab stops:

- Click the ruler one tick mark to the right of a ½-inch.
- Click one tick mark to the right of the 3-inch mark.
- Click at the 5½-inch mark.

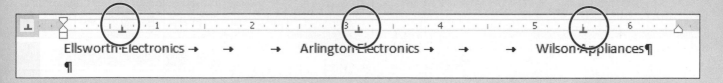

26. Type the following table, tapping Tab where you see a small arrow.

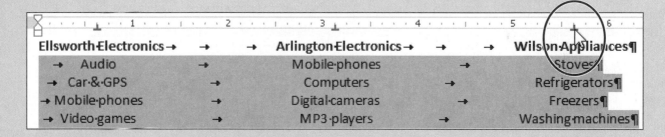

Now you will adjust the last tab stop so it is better centered.

27. Select all lines to which the tab stop applies and drag the tab one tick mark to the right of 5½ inches.

Ellsworth·Electronics →	→	→	Arlington·Electronics →	→	→	Wilson·Appliances¶
→ Audio	→		Mobile·phones		→	Stoves¶
→ Car·&·GPS	→		Computers		→	Refrigerators¶
→ Mobile·phones	→		Digital·cameras		→	Freezers¶
→ Video·games	→		MP3·players		→	Washing·machines¶

Apply Bullets and Numbers

28. Select the lines highlighted below and choose **Home→Paragraph→Bullets** ▤.

The EPA provides the following examples of energy saved and metals retrieved:

- Recycling one million laptops saves the energy equivalent to the electricity used by more than 3,500 US homes in a year.
- For every million cell phones we recycle, 35 thousand pounds of copper, 772 pounds of silver, 75 pounds of gold, and 33 pounds of palladium can be recovered.

29. Make sure the text is still selected; choose **Home→Paragraph→Bullets menu button** ▼, then **Define New Bullet**.

30. Click **Symbol** in the Define New Bullet dialog box.

31. Choose **Webdings** in the Font list, and then choose the symbol shown here. (If you cannot locate it, type **52** in the Code field at the bottom of the dialog box.)

32. Click **OK** twice to set the new bullet symbol.

33. Select the lines shown below in the fifth paragraph.

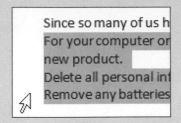

34. Choose **Home→Paragraph→Numbering** ⊞.

Apply Paragraph Space Settings

35. Position the insertion point in the second paragraph.

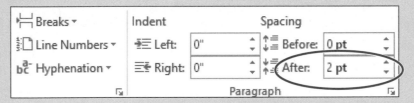

36. Choose **Page Layout→Paragraph**, type **2** in the Spacing After field, and tap ⌷Enter⌷.

Breaks ▾	Indent		Spacing	
Line Numbers ▾	Left:	0"	Before:	0 pt
bc Hyphenation ▾	Right:	0"	After:	2 pt
			Paragraph	

37. Use the same process to apply additional space to both the paragraph starting with *The EPA provides* and the paragraph starting with *Since so many*.

38. Save and close the file; exit from **Word**.

39. Submit your final file based on the guidelines provided by your instructor.
    To view examples of how your file or files should look at the end of this exercise, go to the student resource center.

Format a Composting Report

In this exercise, you will format a composting research document, transforming it into a professional-looking report.

Format with Borders and Shading

1. Start **Word**. Open **WD04-R02-ActLocally** from your **WD2013 Lesson 04** folder and save it as `WD04-R02-ActLocally-[FirstInitialLastName]`.

2. Position the insertion point in the heading at the top of the document.

3. Choose **Home→Paragraph→Borders menu ▼**, and then choose **Borders and Shading**.

4. Choose **Shadow** as the border Setting, choose the sixth color in the last column (a dark green), and then set the Width to **2 ¼ pt**.

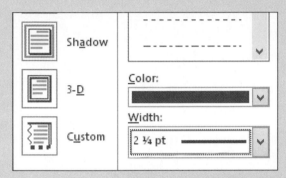

You will now apply shading to the area within the border.

5. Click the **Shading tab**.

6. Click the **Fill drop-down arrow**, choose the **second color** in the **last column**, and click **OK**.

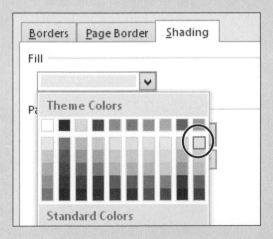

Use and Modify a Style and Collapse Headings

7. Select the *Obtain a Composting Bin* heading and choose **Home→Styles→Heading 2**.

8. Apply the **Heading 2** style to the rest of the headings in the document.
   Now you will modify the style so it will blend with the heading at the top of the document.

9. Click in one of the headings formatted with the **Heading 2** style.

10. Right-click the **Heading 2** style in the Styles group and choose **Modify** from the menu.

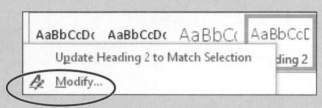

11. Click the **Bold** button, and then click the drop-down arrow and choose the darkest green theme color.

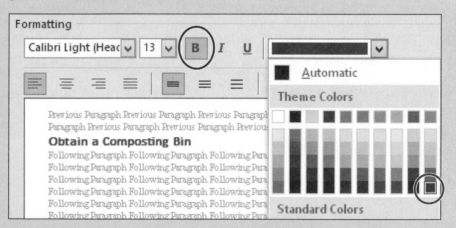

12. Click **OK** to save the changes to the heading style.
    Notice that all headings formatted with Heading 2 are now green and bold. Now you will collapse some of the headings.

13. Hover the mouse pointer over the *What Materials Can You Compost?* heading and notice the little triangle to the left of the heading.

14. Click the triangle to collapse the text below the heading, and then click it again to expand the text.

15. Try expanding and collapsing some other headings, and then expand all headings.

Use the Navigation Pane to Rearrange Topics

16. Choose **View→Show→Navigation Pane**.

17. If necessary, click the **Headings tab** toward the top of the task pane.

18. Select the *Become a Composting…* topic, drag it to just above *Summary*, and drop it.

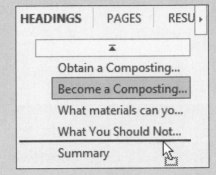

19. Close the **Navigation pane**.

Insert a Page Number Footer

20. Choose **Insert→Header & Footer→Page Number menu ▼**.

21. Choose **Bottom of Page→Plain Number 1**.

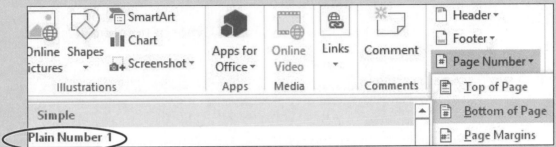

The chosen page number style appears in the footer of the document.

22. Double-click the body of the document to close the footer area.

Use the Resume Reading Bookmark

Now you'll save and close the file so when you open it again, the bookmark will appear. First, however, you will make an editing change so you can see how the bookmark guides you to your last location.

23. Go to page 2 and position the insertion point to the right of *ratio* in the *Carbon-nitrogen ratio* bullet point.

24. Tap ⌷Enter⌷ to generate another bullet and type **Inocula**.

25. Save and close the document; reopen it.

26. Click the **bookmark** and notice how it jumps you to the area where you were last working. (If the bookmark collapses, hover the mouse pointer over it to open it.)

27. Close the file and exit from **Word**.

28. Submit your file based on guidelines provided by your instructor.

To view examples of how your file or files should look at the end of this exercise, go to the student resource center.

Format a Groundwater Report

In this exercise, you will work with paragraph formats, indents, and custom tab stops. You will create a numbered list and add after-paragraph spacing to headings. You'll work with borders and styles, and add a header, and then you'll use the Resume Reading bookmark.

Align Paragraphs and Hyphenate Text

1. Start **Word**. Open **WD04-R03-Groundwater** from your **WD2013 Lesson 04** folder and save it as **WD04-R03-Groundwater-[FirstInitialLastName]**.

2. Position the insertion point in the heading at the top of the document.

3. Choose **Home→Paragraph→Center** 📄.
   Next you will hyphenate the document.

4. Choose **Page Layout→Page Setup→Hyphenation**, and then choose **Manual**.

5. Click **Yes** when Word prompts you to hyphenate *atmosphere*.

6. Click **Yes** to hyphenate *below*.

7. Click **No** when prompted to hyphenate *hazardous*.

8. Click **OK** when the Hyphenation Is Complete message appears.

Indent Text

9. Select the lines at the bottom of the document starting with *Reduce Household chemical* through the last line of text.

10. Choose **Home→Paragraph→Increase Indent** 📄.

Work with Tab Stops

The kids have decided to conduct further research into groundwater contamination. You will create a table listing the kids and the topics each is assigned to.

11. If necessary, choose **Home→Paragraph→Show/Hide** ¶ to turn on formatting marks.

12. Position the insertion point on the last paragraph symbol at the bottom of the document.

13. Type the following heading line, tapping ⌈Tab⌉ wherever you see a small arrow, and tap ⌈Enter⌉ at the end of the line.

14. Select the heading line and choose **Home→Font→Bold** Ⓑ.

15. Position the insertion point on the line below the heading line.

16. Choose **Home→Paragraph→dialog box launcher** 📄.

17. Click **Tabs** in the bottom-left corner of the dialog box.

18. Type **2** in the **Tab Stop Position** box, click the **Center** option in the Alignment area, and then click **Set**.

19. Type **4.5** in the **Tab Stop Position** box, click **Set**, and then click **OK** to accept both of the new tabs.

20. If necessary, choose **View→Show→Ruler** to turn on the ruler, and then observe your custom tabs.

21. Type the following table, tapping [Tab] wherever you see a small arrow. Tap [Enter] at the end of the table.

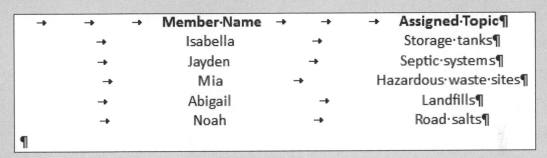

Next you will remove the tabs from the ruler. It's good practice to confine custom tabs to the area where they are used.

22. Position the mouse pointer on the **tab at the 2**" mark and drag it down off the ruler.

23. Use the same process to remove the **tab at the 4.5**" mark.

Create a Numbered List

24. Select the lines that you indented earlier, starting with *Reduce household* and continuing through *water education*.

25. Choose **Home→Paragraph→Numbering** [icon].

The first item might look better if it didn't extend so far to the right. If you use [Enter] to shorten it, you will create a new number. So instead, you'll use a line break, which will shorten the line without generating a number.

26. Scroll up, position the insertion point to the left of *chemicals* in item 1, and press [Shift] + [Enter].

Use Paragraph Space Settings

27. Position the insertion point in the *What is Groundwater?* heading.

28. Choose the **Page Layout** tab, type **2** in the Spacing After field, and then tap [Enter].

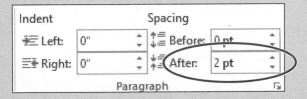

29. Repeat the process in steps 27 and 28 to add **2** points below the *How Can We Help?* heading.

Apply Borders and Styles

30. Position the insertion point in the heading at the top of the page and choose the **Home→Styles→dialog box launcher** 🔲.

31. In the Styles task pane, click the **Title** style to apply it to the heading.

32. Keep the insertion point in the heading, and choose **Home→Paragraph→Borders menu button** ▼.

33. Choose **Bottom Border**.

34. Position the insertion point in the *What is Groundwater?* heading.

35. Click **Heading 2** in the Styles task pane.

36. Choose **Page Layout→Paragraph**.

    Notice that the 2 points after-paragraph spacing is back to 0. The Heading 2 style overrode your formatting. Leave the spacing as it is.

37. Click in the *How Can We Help?* heading and apply the **Heading 2** style.

38. Keep the insertion point in the heading, hover the mouse pointer over **Heading 2** in the task pane, click the **drop-down arrow**, and choose **Modify**.

    You will now change the font color for the Heading 2 style.

39. Click the **drop-down arrow** to open the color gallery, choose the **Black, text 1** theme color, and then click **OK**.

    The color changes for both Heading 2 items.

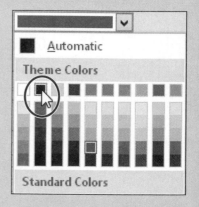

40. Close the **Styles** task pane, and choose **View→Show→Ruler** to turn off the ruler.

Use the Navigation Pane

41. Position the insertion point at the top of the document.

42. Choose **View→Show→Navigation Pane**.

43. Click **Headings** to display the document's heading list, if necessary.

44. Click *How Can We Help?* in the Headings list.

    Word jumps down to the heading selected.

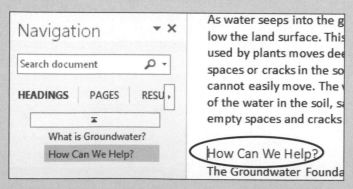

45. Close the **Navigation pane**.

Add a Header

46. Choose **Insert→Header & Footer→Header** 🗋 and choose **Blank** at the top of the list.

47. Type `Groundwater` and double–click in the document to close the header area.

    Next you will make an editing change, and then close and reopen the document. Then you will use the Resume Reading bookmark to go to the last location where you were working in the document.

48. Click to the left of the left-most tab symbol in the first line of your table.

49. Press Ctrl + Enter to insert a page break and move the entire table to the next page.

Use the Resume Reading Bookmark

50. Save and close the document, and then reopen it to display the Resume Reading bookmark.

51. Click the **bookmark** and Word jumps to the area where you last worked in the document.

52. Choose **Home→Paragraph→Show/Hide** ¶ to turn off formatting marks.

53. Save and close the document; exit from **Word**.

54. Submit your final file based on guidelines provided by your instructor.

Apply Your Skills

Format a Trip Report

In this exercise, you will create a report using paragraph alignment, hyphenation, and indents. You will then set custom tabs, apply bullets, and add after-paragraph spacing.

Format Paragraphs

1. Start **Word**. Open **WD04-A01-Belize** from your **WD2013 Lesson 04** folder and save it as **WD04-A01-Belize-[FirstInitialLastName]**.

2. Center-align the heading at the top of the document.

3. Choose **Page Layout→Page Setup→Hyphenation**, and then choose **Manual**.

4. When prompted to hyphenate *ambergriscaye* in the URL, click **No**.

5. Click **No** when prompted to hyphenate *Caribbean*.

6. Click **Yes** for all of the remaining hyphenation prompts.

7. Click **OK** when the Hyphenation Is Complete message appears.

8. Insert a **nonbreaking space** in all occurrences of *San Pedro*.
   Hint: There are four occurrences; you might want to use the Find feature to locate all of them.

Indent Text and Set Custom Tabs

9. Turn on the ruler, if necessary.

10. Click in the paragraph below the *Overview* heading.

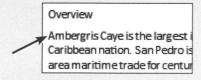

11. Use the **indent markers** on the ruler to indent the paragraph ¼ **inch**.

12. Use the same process to indent the *Diving and Snorkeling* paragraph, the *Ruins* paragraphs, and the *Artists* paragraph.

13. If necessary, turn on the **Show/Hide** ¶ feature.

14. Position the insertion point at the second paragraph symbol at the end of the document.

15. Type the following heading row, using the formatting marks as a guide. Be sure to tap Enter at the end of the heading line.

16. Apply **Bold** **B** to the heading line.

17. Position the insertion point in the line below the heading and set custom **Center tabs** at **1.75"** and **3.75"**.

18. Type the rest of the table as shown, using the formatting marks as a guide.

Use Bullets and Paragraph Spacing

19. Scroll to the top of the document and select the four lines shown here.

20. Apply bullets to the selected lines and customize the bullets using a symbol of your choice.

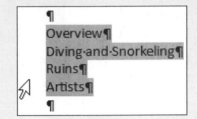

21. Apply **6 points of after-paragraph** spacing to the headings *Overview, Diving and Snorkeling, Ruins,* and *Artists.*

22. Save and close the file; exit from **Word**.

23. Submit your final file based on guidelines provided by your instructor.

    To view examples of how your file or files should look at the end of this exercise, go to the student resource center.

APPLY YOUR SKILLS WD04-A02

Format an Itinerary

In this exercise, you will create a document using borders and styles. You will use the Navigation pane to rearrange topics, and you will add headers and footers to the document. Finally, you will use the Resume Reading bookmark.

Use Borders and Styles

1. Start **Word**. Open **WD04-A02-Tahiti** from your **WD2013 Lesson 04** folder and save it as **WD04-A02-Tahiti-[FirstInitialLastName]**.

2. Open the **Styles task pane** and format the heading at the top of the document with the **Title** style.

3. Apply a **Bottom Border** from the **Borders** menu button ▼.

4. Format the headings for each day (Day One – Tahiti, Day Two – Tahiti, and so on) with the **Heading 2** style.

    Now you will use the small gray triangle to the left of a Heading 2 style to collapse and expand the text under it.

5. Hover the mouse pointer over the *Day One – Tahiti* heading and click the **triangle** to collapse the text below it.

6. Click the **triangle** again to expand the text.

   Now you will create a "style by example" to use on the subheadings for each day's schedule.

7. Select the subheading *Discover the Real Papeete* and format it with **10 point Verdana** font.

8. Apply the font color shown.

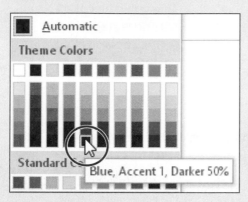

9. Click **New Style** at the bottom of the Styles task pane.

10. Name the style **My Style** and click **OK**.

11. Apply the style to all the subheadings in the itinerary.

    Next you will modify the style and all of the subheadings will automatically update.

12. In the Styles task pane, click the **My Style drop-down arrow** and choose **Modify**.

13. Click **Italic** *I* in the dialog box, and then click **OK**.

    All of the subheadings are italicized.

14. Close the **Styles task pane**.

Use the Navigation Pane and Add a Header and Footer

15. Choose **View→Show→Navigation Pane** to open it, and if necessary, click **Headings** at the top of the pane.

16. Drag and drop the **Day Two** heading above **Day One**; close the **Navigation pane**.

17. Rename the first heading **Day One – Tahiti** and rename the second heading **Day Two – Tahiti**.

18. Choose **Insert→Header & Footer→Header**, and then scroll down the gallery and choose **Sideline**.

19. Click in **Document Title**, type **Universal Corporate Events**, and close the header area.

20. Choose **Insert→Header & Footer→Footer**, scroll down the gallery, choose **Sideline**, and then close the footer area.

Use the Resume Reading Bookmark

Now you'll make an editing change so when you reopen the document, Word will provide a bookmark to return you to the area where you were last working in the document.

21. Scroll down to **Day Seven**. In the subtitle, replace *a Perfect* with **an Ideal**.

22. Save and close the document; reopen it.

23. Click the **bookmark** to jump to the location where you were last working in the document.

24. Close the file and exit **Word**.

25. Submit your final file based on guidelines provided by your instructor.

    To view examples of how your file or files should look at the end of this exercise, go to the student resource center.

APPLY YOUR SKILLS WD04-A03

Format a Sales Report

In this exercise, you will align text, use indents, and type a table using custom tab stops. You will customize bullets, insert a line break, and add after-paragraph spacing. After using the Navigation pane to reorganize text, you will add header text, and then you will use the Resume Reading bookmark.

Format Paragraphs and Indent Text

1. Start Word. Open **WD04-A03-SalesRpt** from the **WD2013 Lesson 04** folder and save it as **WD04-A03-SalesRpt-[FirstInitialLastName]**.

2. Center the *Sales Report* heading.

3. Use **Increase Indent** 📑 to indent the paragraph that begins with *The following table*.

4. Use manual hyphenation and accept any proposed hyphenations.

5. Click at the end of the paragraph you just indented and tap [Enter] twice.

6. Click **Decrease Indent** 📑 to position the insertion point at the left margin.

Apply Bullets and Set Custom Tab Stops

7. Type **Pending Deals** and tap [Enter].

   Next you will set tabs for your Pending Deals table.

8. Use the Tabs dialog box to set **Left tabs** at **2.5"** and **4.5"**.

9. Type this table.

Pending·Deals¶				
Company	→	Destination	→	Dates¶
Rogers·Electronics	→	Hawaii	→	Sept·2·through·7¶
Wilson·Construction	→	Miami	→	Sept·11·through·17¶
Milltown·Mortgage	→	New·York·City	→	October·11·through·17¶

10. **Bold** 🅑 the heading row.

11. Select the entire table, and use the ruler to move the 2½" tab to **2¾"** and the 4½" tab to **4¾"**.

12. Select the six lines below *Mega Storage Devices* and apply **bullets**.

13. Add bullets to the lines below the other companies: **Springer Business College**, **Martin Medical Supplies**, and **Citizens Bank**.

14. Customize all of the bullets using a symbol of your choice. (Use the same symbol for all bullets.)

15. Click at the end of the *Accommodations* line below *Springer Business College* and insert a line break.

16. Type this text: **The owner's cousin works for a hotel chain.**

17. Select the heading line in your table and add **4 points of after-paragraph spacing**.

Apply Borders and Styles

18. Format the *Sales Report* heading with the **Heading 1** style.

19. The style overrode your centering, so center the heading again.

20. Choose **Home→Paragraph→Borders** ⊞ and apply a **Bottom Border**.

21. Format the *Pending Deals* and *Bookings* headings with the **Heading 2** style.

22. Modify the **Heading 2** style by adding **Bold**.
    Notice that both headings update.

23. Format the company names (such as Mega Storage Devices) in the Bookings section with the **Heading 3** style.

Use the Navigation Pane and Insert a Header

24. Use the Navigation pane to move *Martin Medical Supplies* above *Springer Business College*.
    You may need to click the triangle to the left of Bookings to expand the text below it.

25. Insert a header using the **Blank style**, and type **Universal Corporate Events** as the header.

Make Use of the Resume Reading Bookmark

26. Position the insertion point at the end of the last bullet point below the Citizens Bank heading.

27. Tap [Enter] and type **Fuentes Imports** and apply the **Heading 3** style to that line.

28. Save and close the document, and then reopen it and use the **Resume Reading bookmark** to navigate to the area where you were last working in the document.

29. Close the file and exit **Word**.

30. Submit your final file based on guidelines provided by your instructor.

Extend Your Skills

In the course of working through the Extend Your Skills exercises, you will think critically as you use the skills taught in the lesson to complete the assigned projects. To evaluate your mastery and completion of the exercises, your instructor may use a rubric, with which more points are allotted according to performance characteristics. (The more you do, the more you earn!) Ask your instructor how your work will be evaluated.

WD04-E01 That's the Way I See It

As the owner of a small business in your community, you want to improve your business acumen so you can grow your business further. Therefore, you are taking night classes at your local community college. Your professor assigned the following research project.

- List three types of business reports. Format the names of the reports with a built-in heading style. Customize the style with borders and shading.
- Type a brief paragraph describing each type of report below each of the headings; use the indent feature to indent the paragraphs below the headings.
- List three elements included in each type of report, making them bulleted items. Then customize the bullets using a symbol or picture of your choice. Add after-paragraph spacing to the bulleted items.

Save your findings in a Word document named **WD04-E01-BizReports-[FirstInitialLastName]** and saved to your **WD2013 Lesson 04** folder. You will be evaluated based on the inclusion of all elements specified, your ability to follow directions, your ability to apply newly learned skills to a real-world situation, your creativity, and the relevance of your topic and/or data choice(s). Submit your final file based on the guidelines provided by your instructor.

WD04-E02 Be Your Own Boss

You belong to a small business breakfast club that meets monthly. Members support each other by sharing knowledge and experiences. Your business, Blue Jean Landscaping, has been very successful, and you've been asked to present a report detailing your success.

Provide a heading for the report and format it with a built-in heading style. Customize the heading style with formatting of your preference. Write a brief introductory paragraph, and then use the First Line Indent marker to indent the first line of the paragraph. Use a numbered list to point out the top five elements that are most responsible for your success. Add several points of after-paragraph spacing to the numbered items.

As a result of your success, you are planning to expand your business to three new locations. Create a tabular table using custom tab stops to list the names of the locations, the number of employees for each location, and the opening dates. Provide a heading above the table using a built-in heading style. Include a page-number footer for the report.

Compose a report in Word and save it as **WD04-E02-BizSuccess-[FirstInitialLastName]** in your **WD2013 Lesson 04** folder.

You will be evaluated based on the inclusion of all elements specified, your ability to follow directions, your ability to apply newly learned skills to a real-world situation, your creativity, and your demonstration of an entrepreneurial spirit. Submit your final file based on the guidelines provided by your instructor.

Transfer Your Skills

In the course of working through the Transfer Your Skills exercises, you will use critical-thinking and creativity skills to complete the assigned projects using skills taught in the lesson. To evaluate your mastery and completion of the exercises, your instructor may use a rubric, with which more points are allotted according to performance characteristics. (The more you do, the more you earn!) Ask your instructor how your work will be evaluated.

WD04-T01 Use the Web as a Learning Tool

Throughout this book, you will be provided with an opportunity to use the Internet as a learning tool by completing WebQuests. According to the original creators of WebQuests, as described on their website (WebQuest.org), a WebQuest is "an inquiry-oriented activity in which most or all of the information used by learners is drawn from the web." To complete the WebQuest projects in this book, navigate to the student resource center and choose the WebQuest for the lesson on which you are currently working. The subject of each WebQuest will be relevant to the material found in the lesson.

WebQuest Subject: Design elements of a well-formatted report.

Submit your file(s) based on the guidelines provided by your instructor.

WD04-T02 Demonstrate Proficiency

Stormy BBQ has been losing business lately. There is a new restaurant in town, and you suspect your customers are migrating to the competition. Create a report, which you will share with your employees, researching the competition.

Provide a heading for the report and format it with a border and shading. Add after-paragraph spacing to the heading.

Include three reasons you believe the competition is attracting your customers. Each of the reasons should be a heading formatted with a built-in heading style, customized with the heading formatting style of your choice. Write a short paragraph below each of the headings describing your reasons in more detail. Use the indent markers on the ruler to indent the paragraphs ¼".

Using the Numbering feature, list three steps you intend to take to win back your customers. Add your company name as a header and provide a page number in the footer area.

Save the report as **WD04-T02-Competition-[FirstInitialLastName]** in your **WD2013 Lesson 04** folder. Submit your file based on the guidelines provided by your instructor.

Working with Tables

LEARNING OBJECTIVES

After studying this lesson, you will be able to:

- Insert a table in a document
- Modify, sort, and format tables
- Apply built-in table styles
- Perform calculations in tables
- Insert and size columns and rows

A table is one of Word's most useful tools for organizing and formatting text and numbers. Tables are flexible and easy to use. Word provides a variety of features that let you set up, modify, and format tables. In this lesson, you will merge and split table cells, sort rows, quickly apply table styles, and perform calculations within tables.

Creating Tables for My Virtual Campus

You are an administrative assistant for the product development team at My Virtual Campus. The team is always looking for new ideas to enhance the websites. You have a few ideas of your own that may be useful for students: a list of typical expenses with totals, and a simple layout for viewing class schedules. You decide to create tables to present your ideas at the next product development meeting.

Personal Expenses	Estimate	Actual	Difference
Food	425	435	$ 10.00
Entertainment	100	150	$ 50.00
Transportation/Gas	50	55	$ 5.00
Cell Phone	75	85	$ 10.00
Totals	650	725	$ 75.00

You can insert formulas in tables.

The Table Styles gallery makes it easy to format a table.

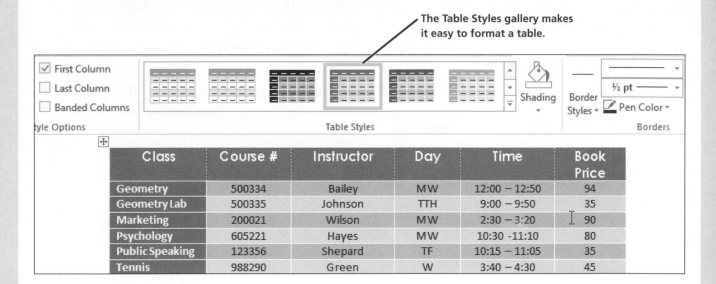

Class	Course #	Instructor	Day	Time	Book Price
Geometry	500334	Bailey	MW	12:00 – 12:50	94
Geometry Lab	500335	Johnson	TTH	9:00 – 9:50	35
Marketing	200021	Wilson	MW	2:30 – 3:20	90
Psychology	605221	Hayes	MW	10:30 -11:10	80
Public Speaking	123356	Shepard	TF	10:15 – 11:05	35
Tennis	988290	Green	W	3:40 – 4:30	45

Introducing Tables

Video Library   http://labyrinthelab.com/videos   Video Number: WD13-V0501

Tables provide a convenient method of organizing and aligning data in an easy-to-read format, and they are a nice way to break up a text-heavy document. Using Word's table styles adds flair to your documents, and tables draw your reader's attention to key items.

Tables are organized in columns and rows. Where columns and rows intersect, they form a rectangle known as a cell. You can type text or numbers in cells, and you can even perform simple calculations.

Personal Expenses	Estimate	Actual	Difference
Food	425	435	$ 10.00
Entertainment	100	150	$ 50.00
Transportation/Gas	50	55	$ 5.00
Cell Phone	75	85	$ 10.00
Totals	650	725	$ 75.00

Contextual Tabs

Contextual tabs appear in context with the task you are performing. The Tables feature, as well as other Word features, uses contextual tabs. They appear on the Ribbon when the insertion point is in a table. The following illustration shows the Table Tools' Design and Layout tabs, where you can format tables.

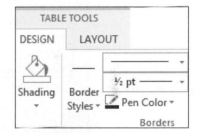

Navigating in a Table

You can move the insertion point by clicking in a cell, or you can use a variety of keystrokes for navigating.

TABLE NAVIGATION KEYSTROKES	
Move To	**Keystroke**
Next cell	Tab
Previous cell	Shift + Tab
Next row	↓
Previous row	↑
Beginning of row	Alt + Home
End of row	Alt + End
Top of column	Alt + Page Up
End of column	Alt + Page Down

Navigate and Enter Data

In this exercise, you will navigate in a table and enter data.

1. Open **WD05-D01-StdntTables** from your **WD2013 Lesson 05** folder and save it as **WD05-D01-StdntTables-[FirstInitialLastName]**.

   Replace the bracketed text with your first initial and last name. For example, if your name is Bethany Smith, your filename would look like this: WD05-D01-StdntTables-BSmith.

2. Position the insertion point in the first cell of the **Expense Table** on the first page.

3. Tap Tab twice to move to the end of the first row.

4. Tap Tab again to move the beginning of the second row.

5. Press Shift + Tab three times to move back one cell at a time.

6. Press Alt + End to move to the end of the row.

7. Press Alt + Home to move to the beginning of the row.

8. Test some other keystrokes.

   Refer to the preceding table as necessary for navigation keystrokes.

9. Enter the following data in your table.

Personal Expenses	Estimate	Actual
Food	425	435
Entertainment	100	150
Transportation/Gas	50	55
Cell Phone	75	85

10. Save the file and leave it open; you will modify it throughout the lesson.

Inserting Tables

Video Library   http://labyrinthelab.com/videos   Video Number: WD13-V0502

You can insert a table using the Table button, the Insert Table dialog box, and the Quick Tables gallery. You can even draw a table with the mouse pointer.

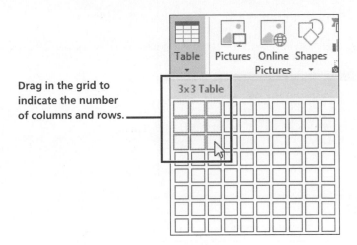

Drag in the grid to indicate the number of columns and rows.

Using the Insert Table dialog box, you can choose various options for the table.

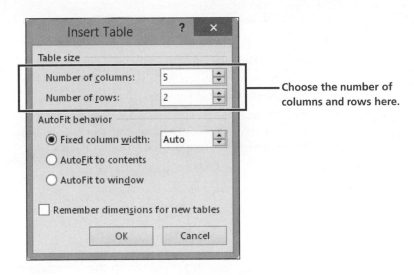

Choose the number of columns and rows here.

The Quick Table gallery lets you choose predesigned tables, such as calendars and various table layouts.

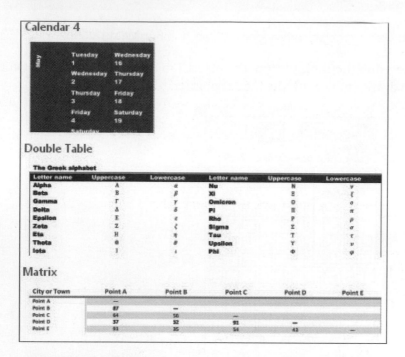

QUICK REFERENCE	INSERTING A TABLE
Task	**Procedure**
Insert a table	■ Choose Insert→Tables→Table and drag in the grid to select the number of columns and rows.
Insert a table using the Insert Table dialog box	■ Choose Insert→Tables→Table and choose Insert Table. ■ Set the number of rows and columns.
Insert a Quick Table	■ Choose Insert→Tables→Table and choose a Quick Tables style.
Draw a table	■ Choose Insert→Tables→Table and choose Draw Table. ■ Click and drag to draw a rectangle for the table. ■ Drag to draw the row and column lines inside the rectangle.

You can add a row to the bottom of a table by tapping Tab when the insertion point is in the last table cell.

Insert Tables

In this exercise, you will create a 3x3 table and enter data. You will also add rows to the bottom of the table. Then you will insert a Quick Table.

1. Save your file as **WD05-D02-StdntTables-[FirstInitialLastName]**.

2. If necessary, choose **Home→Paragraph→Show/Hide** ¶ to display formatting marks.

3. Position the insertion point on the blank row below the *Schedule Planning* heading on page 2.

4. Follow these steps to insert a table:

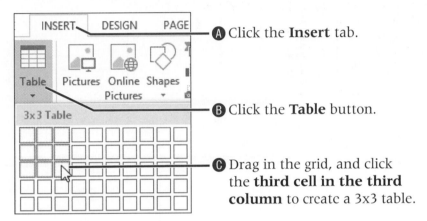

Ⓐ Click the **Insert** tab.

Ⓑ Click the **Table** button.

Ⓒ Drag in the grid, and click the **third cell in the third column** to create a 3x3 table.

5. Enter the text shown, tapping Tab when you need to add a new row.

Course	Days	Units
Math	MWF	3
Science	MWF	3
International Tourism	TTH	2
Biology	TH	3
Biology Lab	W	1

Insert a Quick Table

Because you are hoping to join a fraternity/sorority, you will insert the Greek Alphabet table to help you learn the characters. You can use this table for any purpose by deleting the text and replacing it with your own data.

6. Navigate to the top of page 4, and choose **Insert→Tables→Table** ⊞.

7. Follow these steps to insert the table:

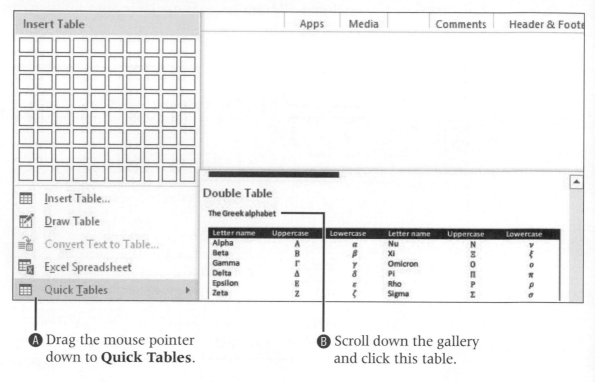

Ⓐ Drag the mouse pointer down to **Quick Tables**.

Ⓑ Scroll down the gallery and click this table.

The Quick Table is added to your document.

8. Save your file.

Converting Tables

Video Library   http://labyrinthelab.com/videos   Video Number: WD13-V0503

Sometimes data is best set in tabular columns and sometimes it's best in a table. When you first begin laying out your data, you may not know which options to choose. Word's ability to convert from one to the other prevents you from having to start over.

Converting Text to a Table

Tabs are commonly used as separators in columnar tables. Note that there must only be one tab between columns for the conversion to work properly. When you convert, you are telling Word to replace each tab with a new table column.

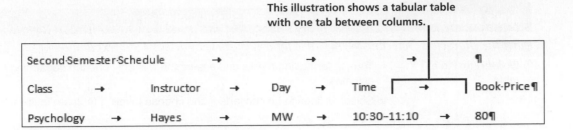

This illustration shows a tabular table
with one tab between columns.

Second·Semester·Schedule	→		→		→		¶
Class	→	Instructor	→	Day	→	Time	→	Book·Price¶
Psychology	→	Hayes	→	MW	→	10:30–11:10	→	80¶

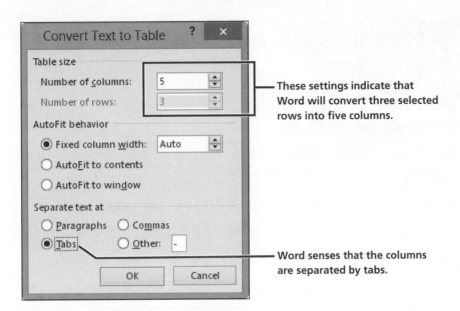

These settings indicate that
Word will convert three selected
rows into five columns.

Word senses that the columns
are separated by tabs.

Converting a Table to Text

You can specify whether the converted text should be separated by paragraph marks, tabs, commas, or another character that you specify.

Choose the text separator here.

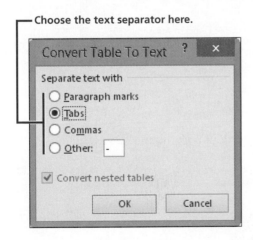

Word 2013

Task	Procedure
Convert text to a table	■ Turn on formatting marks and ensure there is only one tab separating the columns.
	■ Select all lines to be converted, and choose Insert→Tables→Table→Convert Text to Table.
	■ Choose the text separator and the number of columns.
Convert a table to text	■ Click in any table cell and choose Table Tools→Layout→Data→Convert to Text.
	■ Choose the desired text separator.

DEVELOP YOUR SKILLS WD05-D03

Convert Text to a Table

In this exercise, you will convert text currently in tabular columns into a table. Then you will convert the table back to regular text.

1. Save your file as **WD05-D03-StdntTables-[FirstInitialLastName]**.

2. Scroll to page 3 and select all the rows, including the *Second Semester Schedule* heading.

3. Choose **Insert→Tables→Table** 📋, and choose **Convert Text to Table**.

4. Follow these steps to create a table from the selected text:

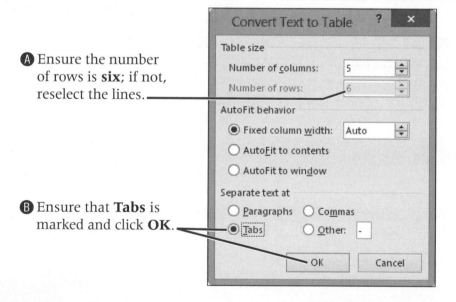

🅐 Ensure the number of rows is **six**; if not, reselect the lines.

🅑 Ensure that **Tabs** is marked and click **OK**.

The text is now in a five-column table. Don't worry about the heading being in one cell. You'll fix that a little later.

Convert a Table to Text

5. Click in any table **cell**.

NOTE Notice the two new Table Tools tabs, Design and Layout, have been added to the Ribbon. These are contextual tabs, meaning they appear in context with what you are working on, in this case, when the insertion point is in a table.

6. Choose **Table Tools→Layout→Data→Convert to Text**. When the dialog box appears, verify that **Tabs** is chosen and click **OK**.
   The table is converted back to a tabular table.
7. Click **Undo** to return the text to table format.
8. Save the file.

Selecting Data in a Table

Video Library http://labyrinthelab.com/videos Video Number: WD13-V0504

The mouse pointer changes shape depending on whether you're selecting a cell, row, column, or the entire table. The following illustrations display the various pointer shapes when selecting in a table.

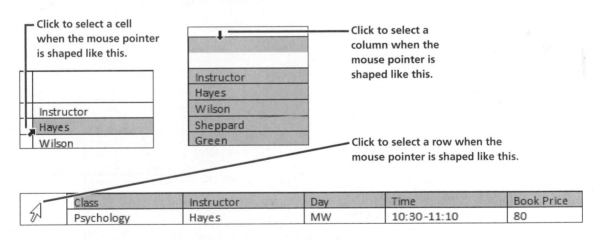

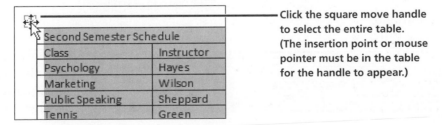

Customizing Alignment, Direction, and Cell Margins

Data can be aligned horizontally or vertically, and you can change the direction of text. You can also modify the cell margins. These commands are found in the Alignment group on the contextual Layout tab that appears when the insertion point is positioned in a table.

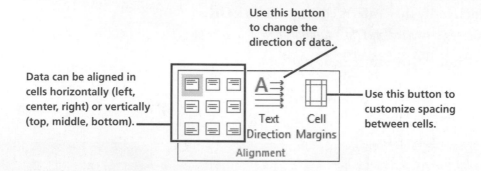

Data can be aligned in cells horizontally (left, center, right) or vertically (top, middle, bottom).

Use this button to change the direction of data.

Use this button to customize spacing between cells.

Select and Align Data, and Modify Cell Margins

In this exercise, you will center-align data, change text direction, and increase cell margins.

1. Save your file as **WD05-D04-StdntTables-[FirstInitialLastName]**.

2. Follow these steps to center the heading row data:

   A Position the mouse pointer in the margin left of the second row and click when the mouse pointer looks like this.

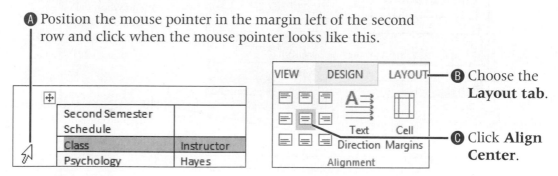

   B Choose the **Layout tab**.

   C Click **Align Center**.

3. Follow these steps to center the data in a range of cells:

   A Click and drag to select these cells.

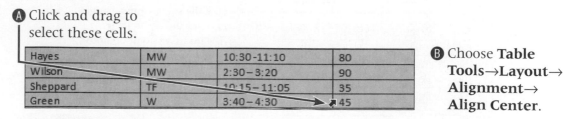

   B Choose **Table Tools→Layout→ Alignment→ Align Center**.

Change Text Direction

4. Select the **second row**.

5. Choose **Table Tools→Layout→Alignment→Text Direction** ⊞ twice to change to vertical with the text facing to the right.

6. Click **Undo** ↶ twice to change back to horizontal alignment.

Change Cell Margins

7. Follow these steps to increase the distance between the text and cell borders:

Ⓐ Click the **Move** handle to select the entire table.

Ⓑ Choose **Table Tools→Layout→Alignment→Cell Margins**.

Ⓒ Enter **0.08** for the Top and Bottom margins and click **OK**.

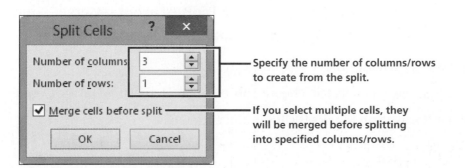

8. Save your file.

Merging and Splitting Cells

Video Library   http://labyrinthelab.com/videos   Video Number: WD13-V0505

You can merge two or more adjacent cells in the same row or column into a single cell. The merge option is often used to center a heading across the top of a table. You can also split a single cell into multiple cells.

A dialog box, shown in the following illustration, appears when you click the Split Cells button so you can determine the specifics of your split.

The contextual Layout tab containing the Merge Cells and Split Cells commands appears when the insertion point is in a table.

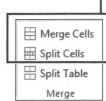

Specify the number of columns/rows to create from the split.

If you select multiple cells, they will be merged before splitting into specified columns/rows.

Task	Procedure
Merge cells	■ Select the cells to merge, and choose Table Tools→Layout→Merge→Merge Cells.
Split cells	■ Select the cell to split, and choose Table Tools→Layout→Merge→Split Cells. ■ Choose the number of rows and/or columns.

DEVELOP YOUR SKILLS WD05-D05

Merge and Split Cells in a Table

In this exercise, you will merge the cells in the first row to create one cell, where you will center the title across the width of the table. You will practice splitting cells, and then you will convert the title to regular text.

1. Save your file as **WD05-D05-StdntTables-[FirstInitialLastName]**.

2. Follow these steps to merge the table row and center the title:

Ⓐ Select the first row.　　Ⓑ Click the **Layout** tab and click **Merge Cells**.　　Ⓒ Click **Align Center**.

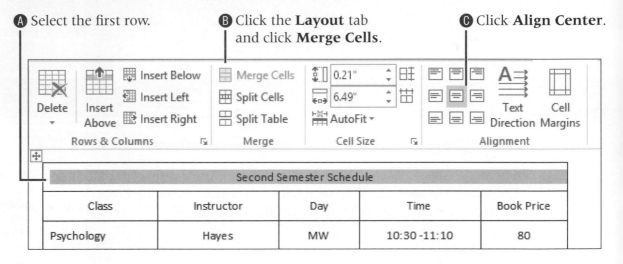

3. With the first row still selected, choose **Table Tools→Layout→Merge→Split Cells** ⊞.

4. When the dialog box opens, choose **three columns** and **one row**; click **OK**.

5. Click **Undo** ↶ to merge the cells again.

6. With the first row still selected, choose **Table Tools→Layout→Data→Convert to Text**.

7. Verify that **Paragraph Marks** is chosen and click **OK**.

8. Save the file.

Formatting with Borders, Shading, and Styles

Word 2013

Video Library http://labyrinthelab.com/videos Video Number: WD13-V0506

Borders, shading, and styles can enhance the readability of a table, and they add pizzazz. These tools are conveniently located on the contextual Design tab that appears when the insertion point is in a table. The Borders and Shading buttons have memory, meaning they reflect the last option chosen in the current session. This is convenient if you want to apply the same effect multiple times. Newly created tables have borders by default.

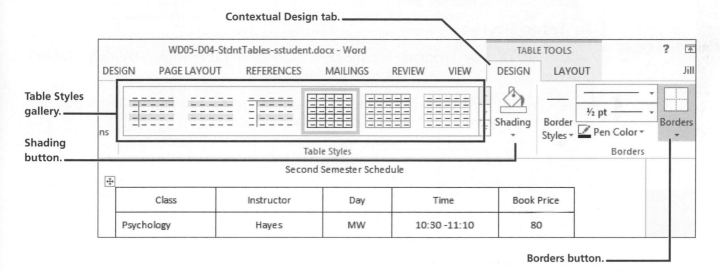

Modifying Formats

Just like regular text, you can easily modify table formats using the formatting tools on the Home tab. Or use the *Mini toolbar*, which provides convenient formatting tools right at your mouse pointer when you select data.

DEVELOP YOUR SKILLS WD05-D06
Use Borders, Shading, and Styles

In this exercise, you will remove all borders from your table, and then apply borders and shading to the first row. Then you will choose a table style to format your table.

1. Save your file as **WD05-D06-StdntTables-[FirstInitialLastName]**.

2. Click the **move handle** in the upper-left corner of the Second Semester Schedule table to select it.

   Remember, the insertion point has to be in the table or you have to hover the mouse pointer over the table for the move handle to appear.

3. Choose **Table Tools→Design→Borders→Borders** 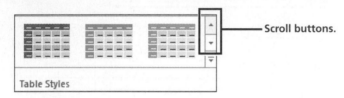 menu button ▼ and choose **No Border**.

You may see gridlines within the table, but they won't print; they are just there to guide you. The Borders button menu on the Design tab provides the option to turn gridlines on or off.

4. Select the **first table row**, choose **Table Tools→Design→Borders→Borders** menu button ▼, and choose **Outside Borders**.

5. Keep the first row selected and choose **Table Tools→Design→Table Styles→Shading** menu button ▼.

6. Choose the third color in the third column, **Tan, Background 2, Darker 25%**.

Use Table Styles

7. Make sure the insertion point is in the table, and choose **Table Tools→Design→Table Styles**.

8. Click the **scroll buttons** to look through the gallery, and then hover the **mouse pointer** over several styles to see a **Live Preview** of the styles.

Scroll buttons.

9. Click the **More** button below the scroll buttons to open the gallery and choose **Grid Table 5 Dark – Accent 1** (toward the bottom of the gallery).

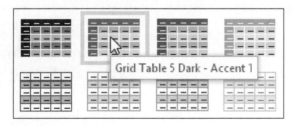

The style overrides your cell margin spacing and borders and shading. In turn, you can override Table Styles formatting.

10. Select the first row of the table; choose **Home→Font→Font menu button** ▼ and choose **Century Gothic**.

11. With the first row still selected, choose **Home→Font→Font Size menu button** ▼ and choose **12 points**.

12. Save the file.

Sorting Data in a Table

Video Library   http://labyrinthelab.com/videos   Video Number: WD13-V0507

The Sort button in the Data group on the contextual Layout tab opens the Sort dialog box, which provides options to sort one or more columns in ascending or descending order, and choose whether the first row of the table contains column headings.

You can choose to sort a table by up to three levels. For example, say you have a table containing column headings for city, state, and zip. You can have Word sort the table first by state, then by city within state, and then by zip code within city for a three-level sort.

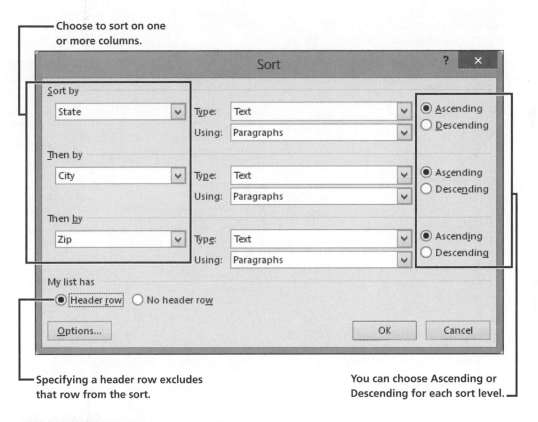

Choose to sort on one or more columns.

Specifying a header row excludes that row from the sort.

You can choose Ascending or Descending for each sort level.

QUICK REFERENCE	SORTING TABLES
Task	**Procedure**
Sort a table	■ Click in the table and choose Table Tools→Layout→Data→Sort.
	■ Choose Header Row or No Header Row, and select the columns to sort by.
	■ Choose the Type of data and choose Ascending or Descending for each sort level.

Sort Table Rows

In this exercise, you will practice sorting the Second Semester Schedule table.

1. Save your file as **WD05-D07-StdntTables-[FirstInitialLastName]**.

2. Position the insertion point in any cell in the **Second Semester Schedule** table.

3. Choose **Table Tools→Layout→Data→Sort** 🔤.
   Word displays the Sort dialog box.

4. Follow these steps to sort the table:

Ⓐ If necessary, choose **Header Row**.   **Ⓑ** Choose **Book Price** here.   **Ⓒ** Word automatically sensed the data Type as **Number**.

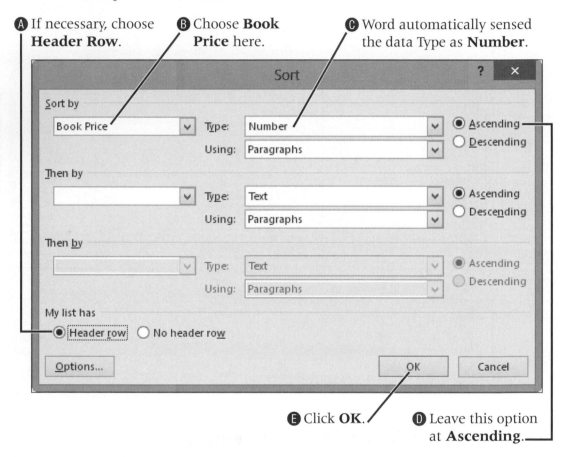

Ⓔ Click **OK**.   **Ⓓ** Leave this option at **Ascending**.

Word sorts the table numerically by book price.

5. Choose **Table Tools→Layout→Data→Sort** 🔤 again.

6. In the Sort dialog box, make sure **Header Row** is chosen, choose **Class** from the Sort By list, and click **OK**.
   The table is now sorted in ascending order by Class.

7. Save your file.

Inserting Rows and Columns

Video Library   http://labyrinthelab.com/videos   Video Number: WD13-V0508

You can insert columns and rows in an existing table. If you wish to insert multiple columns or rows, you must first select the same number of existing columns or rows as you wish to insert. For example, to insert two new rows, select two existing rows.

You can use the buttons in the Rows & Columns group on the Layout tab to insert columns and rows, or you can use the drop-down menu that appears when you right-click a selected column or row.

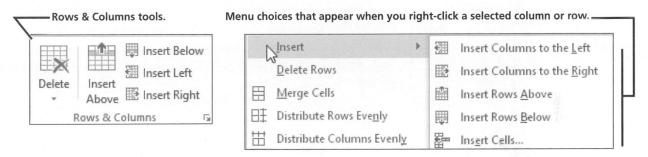

Rows & Columns tools.

Menu choices that appear when you right-click a selected column or row.

A quick and easy way to insert a column or row is with the Insert Control that appears when the insertion point is in the table and you move the mouse pointer between two columns or rows, as shown here.

Click the Insert Control to insert a column.

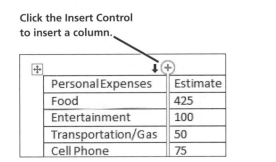

Click the Insert Control to insert a row.

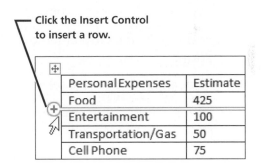

Moving Rows and Columns

You can move a row or column by using the Cut and Paste commands or by using the mouse to drag and drop. When you select the entire row or column and move it to another location, Word automatically makes room for the selection by moving the other rows down or the other columns to the right.

If you select an individual cell within a row or column, when you paste, Word replaces any existing data in the cell. You can prevent data loss by inserting a blank row or column prior to moving.

DEVELOP YOUR SKILLS WD05-D08

Insert Rows and a Column

In this exercise, you will insert multiple rows and a new column in the table.

1. Save your file as **WD05-D08-StdntTables-[FirstInitialLastName]**.

2. Position the mouse pointer to the left of the **Marketing** row until it becomes the white arrow.

3. Click and drag down to select the **Marketing and Psychology** rows.

4. Choose **Table Tools→Layout→Rows & Columns→Insert Above** ▦ to insert two new rows above the Marketing row.

5. Add the following data to the new blank rows:

Geometry	Bailey	MW	12:00 − 12:50	94
Geometry Lab	Johnson	TTH	9:00 − 9:50	35

6. Follow these steps to insert a new column:

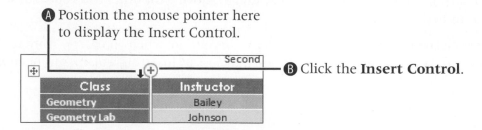

ⓐ Position the mouse pointer here to display the Insert Control.

ⓑ Click the **Insert Control**.

A new column is inserted to the right of the Class column.

7. Type **Course #** as the new column heading.

8. Enter the following data in the column.

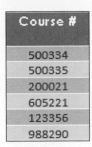

Course #
500334
500335
200021
605221
123356
988290

9. Scroll back up to the *Expense Table* on page 1 and position the insertion point in the **Actual** column.

10. Choose **Table Tools→Layout→Rows & Columns→Insert Right** ▦.

11. Type **Difference** as the new column heading; save the file.

Performing Calculations in Tables

Video Library   http://labyrinthelab.com/videos   Video Number: WD13-V0509

When the Formula dialog box opens, it displays the Sum function. The Sum function recognizes whether there are numbers in the cells above or to the left of the formula cell and indicates that in the formula automatically. However, sometimes you may need a formula for something other than addition. In that case, you use cell addresses in the formula. Although the columns and rows are not lettered or numbered as they are in Excel, which is the Microsoft application designed to "crunch numbers," you must use cell addresses for certain calculations in a table. The first cell in a table is considered to be cell A1 (first column, first row).

Word's formulas are not nearly as sophisticated as Excel's; however, they are adequate for simple calculations.

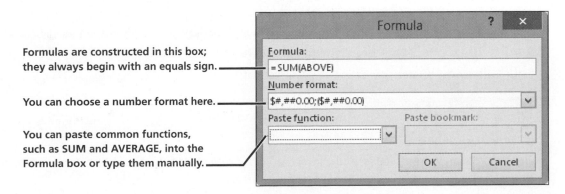

Formulas are constructed in this box; they always begin with an equals sign.

You can choose a number format here.

You can paste common functions, such as SUM and AVERAGE, into the Formula box or type them manually.

Formula

Formula:
= SUM(ABOVE)

Number format:
$#,##0.00;($#,##0.00)

Paste function:

Paste bookmark:

OK   Cancel

Constructing Formulas

You construct formulas by typing directly into the Formula dialog box. In Word, formulas can contain a combination of the following elements.

- **Arithmetic operators:** The most common arithmetic operators are + (addition), – (subtraction), / (division), and * (multiplication). For more complex formulas, use Microsoft Excel and copy and paste into Word.

- **Cell addresses:** In Word tables, columns are labeled A, B, C, etc., and rows are numbered 1, 2, 3, etc. Each cell has an address formed by the column letter and row number. For example, cell A1 refers to the cell in column A and row 1. You can use cell references in formulas. For example, the formula =D2–C2 subtracts the number in cell C2 from the number in cell D2.

- **Functions:** Functions are predefined formulas that perform calculations on cells. The most common functions are SUM, AVERAGE, MIN, and MAX.

  A function is followed by a set of parentheses in which you enter arguments. Arguments include numbers, cell addresses, a range of cells, or direction references (see next bullet).

  A range of cells is separated by a colon. For example, to include cells C2, C3, and C4 only in a formula, you would type C2:C4.

- **Direction references:** In Word, functions can use direction references to indicate cell ranges. The direction references are ABOVE, BELOW, LEFT, and RIGHT. As an example, the formula =SUM(ABOVE) would sum all numbers above the cell containing the formula.

If a number relating to a formula changes, right-click the cell containing the formula and choose Update Field to recalculate the formula.

QUICK REFERENCE	CONSTRUCTING FORMULAS
Task	**Procedure**
Create a formula	■ Choose Table Tools→Layout→Data→Formula and delete the formula in the formula box. ■ Type an equals (=) sign and construct the formula using cell addresses. ■ Use the appropriate operator: + (add), – (subtract), * (multiply), / (divide).
Calculate with a function	■ Choose Table Tools→Layout→Data→Formula and delete the formula in the formula box. ■ Type an equals (=) sign and choose a function from the Paste Function list. ■ Enter the arguments within the parentheses.

DEVELOP YOUR SKILLS WD05-D09
Construct Formulas

In this exercise, you will use formulas to calculate the difference for each expense item and calculate the totals for the Estimate, Actual, and Difference columns.

1. Save your file as **WD05-D09-StdntTables-[FirstInitialLastName]**.

2. Click in the **second row** of the *Difference* column.

   This cell is named D2 because it is the fourth column (D) in the second row (2).

3. Choose **Table Tools→Layout→Data→Formula** fx.

4. Follow these steps to create a formula to subtract the *Estimate* from the *Actual* expense:

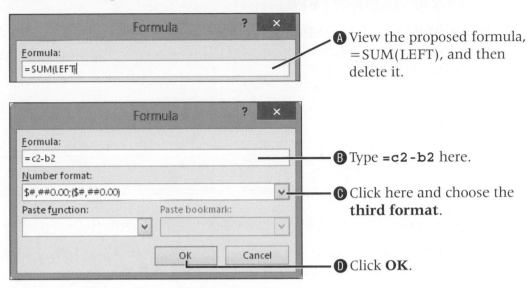

Ⓐ View the proposed formula, =SUM(LEFT), and then delete it.

Ⓑ Type **=c2-b2** here.

Ⓒ Click here and choose the **third format**.

Ⓓ Click **OK**.

This formula subtracts the estimated food expense (column b, row 2) from the actual food expense (column c, row 2). Notice that the result, $10.00, displays with a dollar sign and two decimal places because of the dollar format chosen.

If you wish to display the dollar format without the two decimal places, you must delete them manually from each cell.

5. Click in the cell beneath the formula.

6. Choose **Table Tools→Layout→Data→Formula** fx.

7. Remove the proposed formula and type **=c3-b3**.

8. Click the **Number Format** menu arrow, choose the **third format**, and click **OK**.

9. Enter formulas in the remaining rows in the *Difference* column choosing the same format as before.

Create a Formula to Total the Columns

10. Position the insertion point in the last table cell and tap ⎯Tab⎯ to create a new row.

Personal Expenses	Estimate	Actual	Difference
Food	425	435	$ 10.00
Entertainment	100	150	$ 50.00
Transportation/Gas	50	55	$ 5.00
Cell Phone	75	85	$ 10.00

11. Type **Totals** in the first cell and tap ⎯Tab⎯ to move to the next cell.

12. Choose **Table Tools→Layout→Data→Formula** fx.

Word assumes you want to add the numbers above the formula cell.

13. Click **OK**.

The result should be 650. Notice that the total does not have the dollar sign or decimals, since you did not specify any special formatting.

14. Calculate the total for *Actual* column with no formatting.

15. Calculate the total for the *Difference* column and add the same formatting as the other numbers in the column.

16. Save the file.

Sizing Rows and Columns

Video Library   http://labyrinthelab.com/videos   Video Number: WD13-V0510

You can easily resize columns and rows in a table. Word offers a variety of techniques for this. The adjust pointer, a double-headed arrow, appears whenever you position the mouse pointer on a row or column gridline. You can adjust the column width and row height by dragging the gridline.

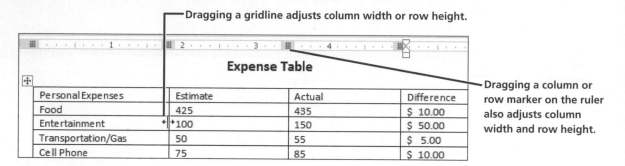

The Cell Size group in the contextual Layout tab provides handy tools for working with column and row sizes.

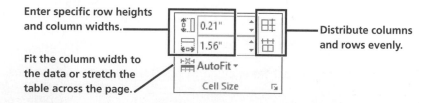

DEVELOP YOUR SKILLS WD05-D10
Adjust Column Widths

In this exercise, you will adjust column widths using the adjust pointer and the tools in the Cell Size group on the Layout tab.

1. Save your file as `WD05-D10-StdntTables-[FirstInitialLastName]`.

2. Follow these steps to change the width of the first column:

Ⓐ Position the mouse pointer here, and it changes to the adjust pointer (a double-headed arrow).

Ⓑ Drag to the right about a half inch and release the mouse button.

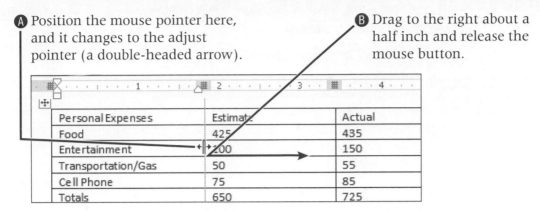

Personal Expenses	Estimate	Actual
Food	425	435
Entertainment	200	150
Transportation/Gas	50	55
Cell Phone	75	85
Totals	650	725

3. Follow these steps to distribute the last three columns evenly:

Ⓑ Drag right to select all three columns.

Ⓐ Position the mouse pointer at the top of this column. (It should appear as a small black arrow.)

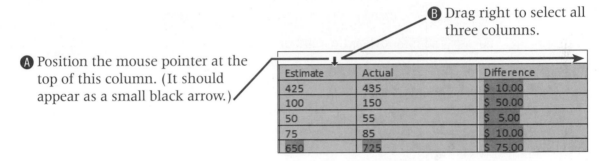

Estimate	Actual	Difference
425	435	$ 10.00
100	150	$ 50.00
50	55	$ 5.00
75	85	$ 10.00
650	725	$ 75.00

4. Choose **Table Tools→Layout→Cell Size→Distribute Columns** ⊞ to make the selected columns the same size.

AutoFit Columns

5. Scroll to the **Schedule Planning table** on **page 2** and select the **entire table**.

6. Choose **Table Tools→Layout→Cell Size→AutoFit** 🔲, and choose **AutoFit Contents**.
All columns are now as wide as they need to be based on the width of their contents.

7. Save and close the file. Exit **Word**.

Concepts Review

To check your knowledge of the key concepts introduced in this lesson, complete the Concepts Review quiz by choosing the appropriate access option below.

If you are...	Then access the quiz by...
Using the Labyrinth Video Library	Going to http://labyrinthelab.com/videos
Using eLab	Logging in, choosing Content, and navigating to the Concepts Review quiz for this lesson
Not using the Labyrinth Video Library or eLab	Going to the student resource center for this book

Reinforce Your Skills

Insert Tables and Align Data

Kids for Change are partnering with the local Center for Environmental Health to identify products in the home that present a risk to babies. In this exercise, you will create, enter data in, and navigate a table. You will convert a tabular document to a table and format alignment, text direction, and cell margins. Finally, you will merge and split cells.

Navigate in a Table

1. Start **Word**. Open **WD05-R01-RiskTeam** from your **WD2013 Lesson 05** folder and save it as **WD05-R01-RiskTeam-[FirstInitialLastName]**.

2. Position the insertion point in the first table cell and tap ⬇.

3. Tap Tab to move to the right one cell.

4. Press Shift + Tab to move to the left one cell.

5. Press Shift + Tab again to move to the end of the previous row.

6. Press Alt + Home to move to the beginning of the row.

7. Press Alt + End to move to the end of the row.

8. Press Alt + Page Down to move to the bottom of the column.

9. Press Alt + Page Up to move to the top of the column.

Insert Tables

10. If necessary, choose **Home→Paragraph→Show/Hide** to display formatting marks.

11. Position the insertion point on the second blank line below the table.

12. Insert a **3x6 table** and enter the data shown here.

Remember, you can add rows to the bottom of a table by tapping Tab when you reach the last table cell.

Product	Risk factor	Risk
Foam products	Chlorinated Tris	Gene mutations
Drop-side cribs	Side can drop	Suffocate or strangle
Sleep positioners	Face against positioner	Suffocate or strangle
Blankets	Baby becomes entangled	Suffocate
Crib tents	Baby becomes entangled	Strangle
Changing tables	Baby can fall	Injury
Bath seats	Can tip	Drown

Next you will insert a calendar quick table so you can keep track of meetings with the Center for Environmental Health.

13. Position the insertion point at the end of the document and tap ⌗Enter⌗.

14. Choose **Insert→Tables→Table** ⊞ and slide the mouse pointer down to **Quick Tables**.

15. Insert **Calendar 2**.

16. Position the insertion point at the end of the document and tap ⌗Enter⌗.
    Now you will copy a tabular table from another file and paste it into your document.

17. Open **WD05-R01-FoodRisk** from your **WD2013 Lesson 05** folder.

18. Copy the contents of the document and paste it at the end of your **Risk Team** document.

19. Close the **Food Risk** file.

Convert Text to a Table

20. Select the entire tabular table.

21. Choose **Insert→Tables→Table→Convert Text to Table**.

22. Accept the defaults in the dialog box and click **OK**.

Select Table Data

23. Click in the **food risk** table to deselect.

24. Position the mouse pointer at the top of the middle column, and when the mouse pointer appears as a black down-pointing arrow, click to select the column.

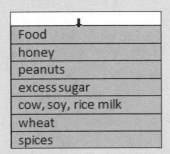

25. Position the insertion point just inside the left edge of the **Walker** cell, and when the mouse pointer appears as a black-tilted arrow, click to select the cell.

26. Position the mouse pointer in the margin to the left of the **Parker** row, and when the mouse pointer appears as a white-tilted arrow, click to select the row.

27. Click the insertion point in the table to display the move handle, then position the mouse pointer over the move handle. When the mouse pointer appears, click to select the entire table.

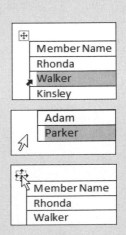

Align Data, Change Text Direction, and Modify Cell Margins

28. Select the **Food and Risk Factor columns**.

29. Choose **Table Tools→Layout→Alignment→Align Center** ⊟.

30. Select the first column and choose **Layout→Alignment→Align Center Right** ⊟.
    The first column should still be selected.

31. Choose **Table Tools→Layout→Alignment→Align Center Left** ⊟.

32. Select the first row and choose **Table Tools→Layout→Alignment→Text Direction** Ⓐ.

33. Click **Text Direction** ⒶΞ again.

34. Click **Undo** ↺ twice to return to horizontal alignment.

35. Select the entire table and choose **Table Tools→Layout→Alignment→Cell Margins** ⊞.

36. In the Table Options dialog box, change the **top and bottom margins** to 0.04 and click **OK**.

Merge and Split Cells

37. Click in the first table row.

38. Choose **Table Tools→Layout→Rows & Columns→Insert Above** ⊞.
    The new row should be selected.

39. Choose **Table Tools→Layout→Merge→Merge Cells** ⊟.

40. Click in the new row and type **Food Risk**.

41. Choose **Table Tools→Layout→Merge→Split Cells** ⊞.

42. Accept the default number of columns and rows and click **OK**.

43. Click **Undo** ↺ to merge the cells again.

44. Save and close the file; exit from **Word**.

45. Submit your final file based on the guidelines provided by your instructor.
    To view examples of how your file or files should look at the end of this exercise, go to the student resource center.

REINFORCE YOUR SKILLS WD05-R02

Format, Organize, and Calculate Tables

In this exercise, you will use borders, shading, table styles, and font formatting. You will sort a table, work with columns and rows, and perform calculations. Finally, you will adjust column widths.

Format with Borders, Shading, and Styles
The Kids for Change members are planning a demonstration of safe cleaning products at the Community Center. They need to figure out how much salt, lemon, vinegar, and baking soda they will need.

1. Start **Word**. Open **WD05-R02-SafeClean** from your **WD2013 Lesson 05** folder and save it as WD05-R02-SafeClean-[FirstInitialLastName].

2. Position the insertion point in the table on page 1 and choose **Table Tools→Design→Table Styles**.

3. Open the gallery and choose **Grid Table 4 – Accent 6**.

   Hint: It's a green style.

4. Select the table, choose **Table Tools→Design→Borders→Borders** menu button ▼, and then choose **Outside Borders**.

5. Select the first row, choose **Table Tools→Design→Borders→Borders** menu button ▼, and then choose **Bottom Border**.

6. With the first row still selected, choose **Table Tools→Design→Table Styles→Shading** menu button ▼.

7. Choose the last green color in the right-hand column, **Green, Accent 6, Darker 50%**.

8. Select the entire table, choose **Home→Font→Font menu button** ▼, and then choose **Comic Sans MS**.

9. Select in the first column starting at *Clean coffee pot* through the end of the column.

10. Choose **Home→Font→Italic** *I*.

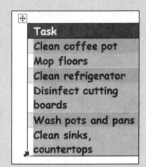

Sort Table Data

Dylan, a Kids for Change member, volunteers at a green cleaning supplies company so he can become familiar with safe cleaning products. He has been asked to complete the Order Tracking Sheet.

11. Go to page 2 of the **Safe Clean** file and select the entire table.

12. Choose **Table Tools→Layout→Data→Sort** and, if necessary, choose the **Header Row** option in the Sort dialog box.

13. Click the **Sort By field drop-down arrow** and choose **Item #**; click **OK**.

    The Item # column is now in ascending numeric order.

14. Use the same process to sort by the **Customer ID column** in ascending order.

Insert a Column and Row

15. Position the insertion point in the **Price column**.

16. Choose **Table Tools→Layout→Rows & Columns→Insert Right**.

17. Position the insertion point in the last cell of the new column and tap Tab to add a row.

18. Type **Total** in the first cell of the new row, and then type **Total** at the top of the new column.

Perform Calculations in a Table

19. Position the insertion point in the second cell of the last column.

20. Choose **Table Tools→Layout→Data→Formula** *fx*.

    You will multiply Quantity by Price to calculate the total price for the first customer.

21. Delete the contents of the **Formula box** and type **=d2*e2** in the box.

    Remember, the asterisk (*) is the multiply sign.

22. Choose the **dollar** format (third format) from the Number Format drop-down list, and then click **OK**.

23. Repeat the process to calculate the total and apply the currency format for the rest of the customers.

    Now you will total the last column.

24. Position the insertion point in the last cell of the Total column.

25. Choose **Table Tools→Layout→Data→Formula** fx

    The formula defaults to =SUM(ABOVE), which is what you want.

26. Choose the **dollar** format, and then click **OK**.

Size Columns

27. Select the entire table.

28. Choose **Table Tools→Layout→Cell Size→AutoFit** ⊞ and choose **AutoFit Contents**.

    The width of the columns is adjusted based on the widest entry in each column.

29. Save and close the file; exit from **Word**.

30. Submit your final file based on the guidelines provided by your instructor.

    To view examples of how your file or files should look at the end of this exercise, go to the student resource center.

REINFORCE YOUR SKILLS WD05-R03

Insert and Format Tables

This holiday season, Kids for Change members are working with the local fire department to collect toys for needy kids. The members will be assigned to different neighborhoods for collecting. In this exercise, you will format a table that tracks how many toys each member collects.

Navigate in a Table

1. Start **Word**. Open **WD05-R03-Toys** from your **WD2013 Lesson 05** folder and save it as `WD05-R03-Toys-[FirstInitialLastName]`.

2. Position the insertion point in the first table cell (page 1) and press Alt + End to move to the end of the row.

3. Press Alt + Page Down to move to the bottom of the column.

4. Press Alt + Home to move to the beginning of the row.

5. Tap Tab twice to move two cells to the right.

6. Press Shift + Tab to move to the left one cell.

7. Tap ↑ to move up one row.

Insert a Table

Kids for Change members decided to take up a collection from friends and family to purchase additional toys. You will insert a Quick Table to track the donations.

8. Scroll to the end of the document and press Ctrl + Enter to insert a page break.

9. Choose **Insert→Tables→Table** 🔳 and slide the mouse pointer down to **Quick Tables**.

10. In the submenu, scroll down and choose **Tabular List**.

11. Select the *ITEM* heading and type **MEMBER** in its place.

12. Select the *NEEDED* heading and type **AMOUNT** in its place.

13. Select the remaining rows and tap Delete.

14. Enter the new data as shown.

MEMBER	AMOUNT
Ella	$20
Tom	$17
Roger	$32
Stella	$15
Jennifer	$22
Max	$29
Jose	$35
Albert	$40

Convert Text to a Table

15. Scroll to page 2 and select the rows in the tabular table from *Exposure* through *Lacerations*.

16. Choose **Insert→Tables→Table** 🔳 and choose **Convert Text to Table**.

17. When the Convert Text to Table dialog box appears, click **OK**.

Select Table Data

18. Position the mouse pointer in the margin to the left of the third row and click to select the row.

19. Position the mouse pointer at the top of the Danger column, and when the mouse pointer appears as a black down-pointing arrow, click to select the column.

20. Position the mouse pointer in the bottom-left corner of the Pull toys cell, and when the mouse pointer appears as a tilted black arrow, click to select the cell.

21. Click the move handle in the upper-left corner of the table to select the entire table.

Align Data, Change Text Direction, and Modify Cell Margins

22. Scroll to the table on page 1.

23. Select the second and third columns.

24. Choose **Table Tools→Layout→Alignment→Align Center Right** 🔳.

25. Choose **Table Tools→Layout→Alignment→Align Center** 🔳.

26. Select the first table row.

27. Choose **Table Tools→Layout→Alignment→Text Direction** 🔲.

28. Click **Undo** 🔲 to return to horizontal alignment.

29. Select the entire table.

30. Choose **Table Tools→Layout→Alignment→Cell Margins** 🔲.

31. Change the **top and bottom margins** to 0.06, then click **OK**.

Merge Cells

32. Select the four Sycamore cells in the third column.

33. Choose **Table Tools→Layout→Merge→Merge Cells** 🔲.

34. Delete three of the Sycamore entries.

35. Use the same technique to merge the Homestead Valley and Middle Ridge cells, and then delete three Homestead Valley and three Middle Ridge entries.

Use Borders, Shading, and Table Styles

36. Select the entire table.

37. Choose **Table Tools→Design→Borders→Borders** 🔲 **menu button** ▼, and then choose **No Border**.

38. Choose **Table Tools→Design→Table Styles**, click the More 🔲 button on the Styles gallery, and then choose the **Grid Table 4 – Accent 5** style.

    Hint: It's a blue style.

Sort Data

Several Kids for Change regional directors plan to meet following the toy collection to discuss plans for next year's collection. They compiled a mailing list of directors who will be notified of the meeting.

39. Scroll to the table on page 3 and position the insertion point in the table.

40. Choose **Table Tools→Layout→Data→Sort** 🔲.

41. If necessary, choose **Header Row** in the Sort dialog box, then choose sort by **State**, then by **City**, then by **Zip**, and then click **OK**.

    The California cities sorted in ascending alphabetic order within State, and the Dallas zip codes sorted in ascending numeric order within City.

Insert Rows and Resize Columns

42. Scroll to the table on page 4.

Region 5 was accidentally omitted.

43. Position the mouse pointer to the left of the last two rows until the **Insert Control** appears.

Region¤
1¤
2¤
3¤
4¤
6¤

44. Click the control to insert a blank row between the last two rows, and then enter the following data in the new row.

5	1,951	2,543

45. Select the entire table, choose **Table Tools→Layout→Cell Size→AutoFit**, and choose **AutoFit Contents**.

Perform Calculations

46. Position the insertion point in the last table cell and tap Tab to insert a new row at the bottom of the table.

47. Type **Totals** in the first cell of the new row and tap Tab to move to the next cell.

Now you will calculate the totals for all regions for both years.

48. Choose **Table Tools→Layout→Data→Formula** fx.

49. Accept the default Sum function in the Formula box and click **OK**.

50. Use the same process to calculate this year's total.

51. Save and close the file and exit from **Word**.

52. Submit your final file based on the guidelines provided by your instructor.

Apply Your Skills

Insert Tables, and Align and Merge Cells

In this exercise, you will navigate in a table, insert a new table, and convert a table to tabular text. You will select and align data and use cell margins. Then you will merge cells to create a table heading.

Navigate in and Insert a Table

1. Start **Word**. Open **WD05-A01-CorpEvents** from your **WD2013 Lesson 05** folder and save it as **WD05-A01-CorpEvents-[FirstInitialLastName]**.

2. Navigate in the table on page 1 using the keystrokes shown in the *Navigating in a Table* section of the main lesson.

3. If necessary, choose **Home→Paragraph→Show/Hide** ¶ to display formatting marks.

4. Scroll to page 2 and position the insertion point on the first blank line below *Oceanic Cruise Lines*.

5. Insert a **4x5 table** and enter the data shown.

Date	Itinerary	Ship	From
03/18/2013	4-night Bahamas Cruise from Miami	Oceanic Star	$279
03/22/2013	3-night Bahamas Cruise from Miami	Oceanic Jewel	$289
03/24/2013	7-night Bahamas Cruise from New York	Oceanic Star	$1159
03/25/2013	7-night Bahamas Cruise from New York	Oceanic Jewel	$599

Convert a Table to Text, Select Data, and Customize Alignment

6. Scroll to page 3 and select the table.

7. Choose **Table Tools→Layout→Data→Convert to Text** ⊞.

8. Make sure **Tabs** is chosen in the Convert Table to Text dialog box and click **OK**.

9. Scroll to page 1 and select data using the selection techniques described in this lesson.

10. Select the second and third columns and click **Align Center** ≡ on the Layout tab.

11. Select the second row and click **Text Direction** ⊞ on the Layout tab.

12. Click **Undo** ↶ to return to horizontal alignment.

Use Cell Margins and Merge Cells

13. Select the page 1 table and use the **Cell Margins** ⊞ on the Layout tab to set the top and bottom margins at **0.08"**.

14. Merge the first row and type **Travel Special** as the table heading.

15. Save and close the file; exit from **Word**.

16. Submit your final file based on the guidelines provided by your instructor.

    To view examples of how your file or files should look at the end of this exercise, go to the student resource center.

APPLY YOUR SKILLS WD05-A02

Format, Organize, and Calculate Tables

In this exercise, you will format with borders, shading, and table styles, and then you will sort data. You will insert columns and rows, and finally, you will perform calculations and size columns.

Apply Borders, Shading, and a Table Style

1. Start **Word**. Open **WD05-A02-Universal** from your **WD2013 Lesson 05** folder and save the file as **WD05-A02-Universal-[FirstInitialLastName]**.

2. Select the table on page 1; choose **Table Tools→Design→Borders→Borders** ⊞ **menu button** ▼ and choose **No Border**.

3. Select the first row, and use **Borders** ⊞ to apply a **bottom border**.

4. Apply a bottom border to the last row of the table.

5. Select the first row, then choose **Table Tools→Design→Table Styles→Shading** ▨ **menu button** ▼ and choose **Gold, Accent 4, Darker 25%**.

6. Select the third row and apply **Gold, Accent 4, Lighter 60%**.

7. Apply the same color you used in the third row to the **fifth row**.

8. Scroll to page 2, position the insertion point in the table, choose **Table Tools→Design→Table Styles**, and open the Table Styles gallery.

9. Choose the **Grid Table 6 Colorful – Accent 4** style; it's a yellow style.

Sort Data and Insert a Row and Column

10. Using the page 2 table, sort by the **Travel Package column** in ascending order, specifying that the table has a header row.

11. Scroll to the page 1 table and sort by the **Group Travel column** in descending order, specifying that the table has a header row.

12. Using the same table, sort by the **Visa/Passport column** in ascending order, specifying that the table has a header row.

13. Using the page 1 table, insert a **blank row at the top** of the table, **merge** the cells in the **first row**, and type **Universal Corporate Events**.

14. Use **Align Center** 🔲 to center the heading.

15. Scroll to page 3 and add a **column** at the end of the table and a row at the bottom of the table.

Perform Calculations and Size Columns

16. Type **Totals** in the blank cell at the bottom of the first column.

17. Insert a formula using the **Sum function** and **dollar** format to total columns two through four.

18. Delete the **decimal point and zeros** at the end of each total.
    Hint: Position the insertion point to the left of the decimal point before deleting.

19. Type **Totals** in the first cell of the last column and insert a formula using the **Sum function** and **dollar** format to total the rows for the three plans. Be sure to check that the formula is correct before clicking OK.

20. Delete the **decimal point and zeros** at the end of each total.

21. Scroll to page 2 and use the **AutoFit** feature to autofit the contents of the table.

22. Save and close the file; exit from **Word**.

23. Submit your final file based on the guidelines provided by your instructor.
    To view examples of how your file or files should look at the end of this exercise, go to the student resource center.

APPLY YOUR SKILLS WD05-A03

Create and Format Tables

In this exercise, you will navigate in a table, insert a new table, and convert a table to text. You will change cell margins, merge cells, and apply borders and shading. You will also sort data, delete and add columns/rows, perform calculations, and resize cells.

Navigate in and Insert a Table; Convert a Table to Text

1. Start **Word**. Open **WD05-A03-Travel** from your **WD2013 Lesson 05** folder and save the file as **WD05-A03-Travel-[FirstInitialLastName]**.

2. If necessary, position the insertion point in the first table cell on page 1.

3. Tap ⬇ twice to move to the third row.

4. Press ⎙Shift⎙+⎙Tab⎙ to move to the end of the second row.

5. Press ⎙Alt⎙+⎙Home⎙ to move to the beginning of the row.

6. Press ⎙Alt⎙+⎙Page Down⎙ to move to the bottom of the column.

7. Press ⎙Alt⎙+⎙Page Up⎙ to move to the top of the column.

8. If necessary, choose **Home→Paragraph→Show Hide** ¶ to display formatting marks.

9. Scroll to page 2 and position the insertion point next to the first paragraph symbol at the top of the page.

10. Insert a **4x5 table** and enter the data shown.

Day Tours	From	When	Duration
Versailles	$70	Daily except Mon	4 hrs.
Eiffel Tower	$75	Daily	3 hrs.
Louvre Museum	$65	Daily except Tue	2.5 hrs.
Moulin Rouge Show	$153	Daily	4.5 hrs.

11. Scroll to page 3 and select the table.

12. Convert the table to text; ensure that **Tabs** are chosen to separate text.

Select Data, Customize Alignment, and Modify Cell Margins

13. Scroll to page 1 and use the **move handle** to select the table.

14. Select the **Bangkok** row.

15. Select the **Thailand** and **Vietnam** cells.

16. Select columns two through five and click **Align Center** ☰ on the Layout tab.

17. Select the table and change all cell margins to `0.04`.

18. Select the table and change the top and bottom cell margins to `0.06`.

Merge Cells, and Use Borders and Shading

19. Scroll to page 2 and insert a blank row at the top of the table.

20. Merge all cells in the first row, type **Universal Corporate Events** in the row, and center align the row.

21. Select the table, remove all borders, and select the **first row**.

22. Apply **outside borders** to the row, and apply a **blue shading** color of your choice.

Sort a Table, and Work with Columns and Rows

23. Scroll to page 1, sort by the **price column** in ascending order, and indicate that the table has a Header Row.

24. Sort the **Dates column** in ascending order indicating a Header Row.

25. Delete the **Duration column**.

26. Add a row to the bottom of the table and enter the data shown.

Hong Kong	6/9/2013	2438	10%

27. Add a **column** at the end of the table and type **Discount Amount** as the column header.

Perform Calculations and Size Columns

28. In the **second cell** in that column, enter the formula, `=c2*d2`, choosing the **second format** in the Number Format field.

29. Enter **formulas** to calculate the discount amount for the remaining rows using the second number format.

30. Add a **new row** to the bottom of the table and type `Maximum Price` in the first cell.

31. Position the **insertion point** at the bottom of the **Price column**, enter the formula, `=MAX(c2:c7)`, and do not use any special number formatting.

The formula determines the highest tour price in the column.

32. Select **columns two through five** and position the **adjust pointer** (double-headed) arrow between two of the selected columns.

33. Double-click to autofit the columns to the width of the longest entry in each column.

34. Save and close the file; exit from **Word**.

35. Submit your final file based on the guidelines provided by your instructor.

Extend Your Skills

In the course of working through the Extend Your Skills exercises, you will think critically as you use the skills taught in the lesson to complete the assigned projects. To evaluate your mastery and completion of the exercises, your instructor may use a rubric, with which more points are allotted according to performance characteristics. (The more you do, the more you earn!) Ask your instructor how your work will be evaluated.

WD05-E01 That's the Way I See It

You are the owner of a small store. You have a few corporate customers who order from you in large quantities and you plan to keep track of their orders in a table. Start a new Word document named **WD05-E01-CorpCustomers-[FirstInitialLastName]** and saved to your **WD2013 Lesson 05** folder. Create a 5x6 table with the following column headings: Order Date, Item, Units, Cost, and Total.

Enter five rows of order data for the first four columns. In the Total column, enter formulas for all five rows to multiply Units by Cost. Add a row at the end of the table and use the Sum function to add the Cost and Total columns to determine total costs and sales to date. Add another row to the bottom of the table and enter formulas at the bottom of the Cost and Total columns to determine the maximum cost and maximum total. Enter labels in the last two rows to appropriately describe the data.

Add a row to the top of the table, merge the cells, and enter your company name. Apply a table style of your choice to the table and, if necessary, center-align your company name and right-align the last three columns. AutoFit the last three columns.

You will be evaluated based on the inclusion of all elements specified, your ability to follow directions, your ability to apply newly learned skills to a real-world situation, your creativity, and the relevance of your topic and/or data choice(s). Submit your final file based on the guidelines provided by your instructor.

WD05-E02 Be Your Own Boss

Your company, Blue Jean Landscaping, is offering a spring flower planting special. Start a new Word document named **WD05-E02-SpringFlowers-[FirstInitialLastName]** and saved to your **WD2013 Lesson 05** folder. Create a 3x8 table with the following column headings: Flower Name, Price, and Discount Percent.

Enter data that you decide on in the rows below the heading row. Add a column at the end of the table and enter formulas to calculate the discount amount for each row. Use the dollar format for the numbers. Supply an appropriate column heading for the new column. Sort the table in ascending, alphabetic order by the Flower Name column. Add a row at the bottom of the table and enter a formula in the Price column that determines the highest priced flower and add a suitable label to the row. Apply borders and shading to the table to enhance its readability and make it attractive.

You will be evaluated based on the inclusion of all elements specified, your ability to follow directions, your ability to apply newly learned skills to a real-world situation, your creativity, and your demonstration of an entrepreneurial spirit. Submit your final file based on the guidelines provided by your instructor.

Transfer Your Skills

In the course of working through the Transfer Your Skills exercises, you will use critical-thinking and creativity skills to complete the assigned projects using skills taught in the lesson. To evaluate your mastery and completion of the exercises, your instructor may use a rubric, with which more points are allotted according to performance characteristics. (The more you do, the more you earn!) Ask your instructor how your work will be evaluated.

WD05-T01 Use the Web as a Learning Tool

Throughout this book, you will be provided with an opportunity to use the Internet as a learning tool by completing WebQuests. According to the original creators of WebQuests, as described on their website (WebQuest.org), a WebQuest is "an inquiry-oriented activity in which most or all of the information used by learners is drawn from the web." To complete the WebQuest projects in this book, navigate to the student resource center and choose the WebQuest for the lesson on which you are currently working. The subject of each WebQuest will be relevant to the material found in the lesson.

WebQuest Subject: How tables are used in business.

Submit your final file(s) based on the guidelines provided by your instructor.

WD05-T02 Demonstrate Proficiency

A new chef has just been hired at Stormy BBQ. He is placing the weekly food order for the first time, and the owner has asked you to work with him to be sure his order makes sense. Start a new Word document named **WD05-T02-ChefOrder-[FirstInitialLastName]** and saved to your **WD2013 Lesson 05** folder. Set up a table for the order that includes elements such as the name of the food item, the price, the quantity, and total costs, and then insert the formulas to calculate the total costs.

Assume that it is summer and order fruits and vegetables that are in season and in quantities that guarantee freshness for the week. Sort the table in an order that you think will make sense for the food seller. Add a row at the top of the table, merge the cells, and enter Stormy BBQ, centered, as the heading. Size the table in a way that ensures that it is easy to read, and apply a table style of your choice that also enhances readability.

Submit your final file based on the guidelines provided by your instructor.

Creating a Research Paper

LEARNING OBJECTIVES

After studying this lesson, you will be able to:

- Insert footnotes, endnotes, and citations
- Generate a bibliography
- Insert captions and a table of figures
- Create templates

In this lesson, you will learn about research papers, a requirement for nearly every undergraduate and graduate student, and for many professionally employed individuals. You will use Word to develop a research paper using widely accepted style conventions. Your paper will include footnotes, citations, and a table of figures. Then you will create a research paper template to simplify writing future research papers.

Researching Internet Commerce

Green Clean is a successful environmentally conscious janitorial service company. You are the administrative assistant at Green Clean while continuing with your undergraduate work in marketing. You were assigned the task of writing a research paper. The main topic must be on Internet commerce, and since you are also interested in the environment, you put your own spin on the paper to include what effect ecommerce has had on the environment.

You use Word to set up the research paper. Following Modern Language Association (MLA) guidelines, you use footnotes, citations, and captions. You find that the Bibliography and Table of Figures features make it easy to organize reference information in your paper.

Simpson 2

Brian Simpson

Professor Williams

Marketing 222

May 10, 2013

Internet Commerce and Its Effect on the Environment

The Internet had its origins in the 1960s when the Department of Defense developed a communications network to connect the computers of various military installations. The Department of Defense removed its computers from this network in the 1980s and turned over the control to the National Science Foundation (NSF). In 1992, the U.S. government withdrew funding from the NSF and encouraged private companies to administer and control the "Internet." It was at this point that Internet commerce was born. Companies both large and small suddenly realized the enormous marketing potential of this global computer network. In fact, by 2007 the Internet had no doubt become the largest global marketplace.[1]

The commercial potential of the Internet stems from the fact that it is a global network with inexpensive access.[2] The Internet is also available 24x7. The multimedia capability to the Internet is important for marketing and advertising. Quick product delivery, automated order-taking, and low overhead are several more factors that are driving Internet commerce.[3]

---

[1] This is the opinion of many business leaders and economists.

[2] This is true in the United States, but some nations still have high rates due to limited competition among Internet service providers.

[3] These factors depend upon the capabilities of individual companies.

Using Research Paper Styles

Video Library   http://labyrinthelab.com/videos   Video Number: WD13-V0601

There are several documentation styles, each with their own specific formatting requirements. The MLA style has been the standard for undergraduate and graduate research papers for many years.

Understanding the MLA Documentation Style

The MLA publishes the *Modern Language Association Handbook for Writers of Research Papers*. The MLA style has very specific formatting requirements, *some* of which are already defaults within Microsoft Word. For example, Word's default margins are one inch, which complies with the MLA requirement. However, Word does not comply with *all* MLA guidelines by default.

 This lesson does not presume to be a resource for MLA guidelines. Refer to the MLA handbook or MLA website (http://mla.org) for guidance in complying with MLA requirements.

Following is an overview of *some* of the MLA style guidelines.

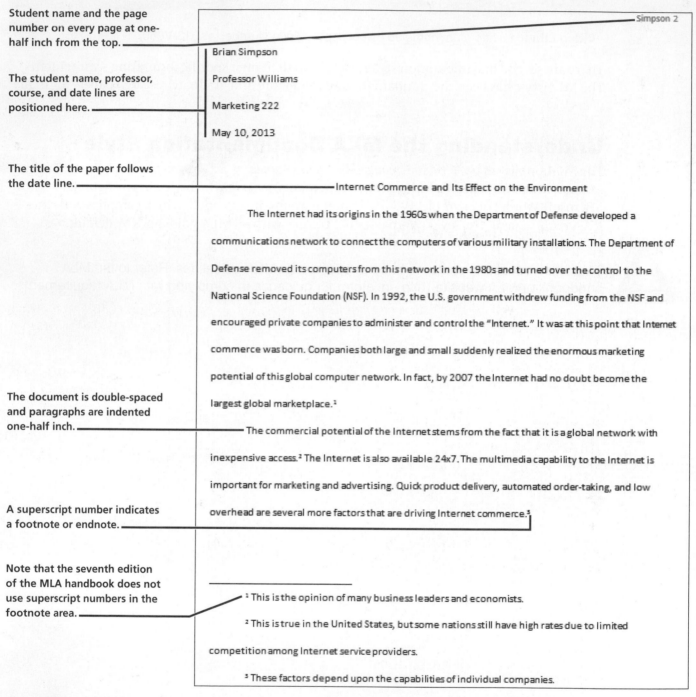

Student name and the page number on every page at one-half inch from the top.

The student name, professor, course, and date lines are positioned here.

The title of the paper follows the date line.

The document is double-spaced and paragraphs are indented one-half inch.

A superscript number indicates a footnote or endnote.

Note that the seventh edition of the MLA handbook does not use superscript numbers in the footnote area.

Simpson 2

Brian Simpson

Professor Williams

Marketing 222

May 10, 2013

Internet Commerce and Its Effect on the Environment

The Internet had its origins in the 1960s when the Department of Defense developed a communications network to connect the computers of various military installations. The Department of Defense removed its computers from this network in the 1980s and turned over the control to the National Science Foundation (NSF). In 1992, the U.S. government withdrew funding from the NSF and encouraged private companies to administer and control the "Internet." It was at this point that Internet commerce was born. Companies both large and small suddenly realized the enormous marketing potential of this global computer network. In fact, by 2007 the Internet had no doubt become the largest global marketplace.[1]

The commercial potential of the Internet stems from the fact that it is a global network with inexpensive access.[2] The Internet is also available 24x7. The multimedia capability to the Internet is important for marketing and advertising. Quick product delivery, automated order-taking, and low overhead are several more factors that are driving Internet commerce.[3]

[1] This is the opinion of many business leaders and economists.

[2] This is true in the United States, but some nations still have high rates due to limited competition among Internet service providers.

[3] These factors depend upon the capabilities of individual companies.

You can select the superscripted number in the footnote area and remove the checkmark from the superscript checkbox in the Font dialog box, if necessary.

Working with Footnotes, Endnotes, and Citations

Video Library   http://labyrinthelab.com/videos   Video Number: WD13-V0602

Footnotes, endnotes, and citations are important parts of most research papers. You use them to comment on, or cite a reference to, a designated part of the text. Footnotes appear at the bottom of pages; endnotes, as the name implies, appear at the end of a document or section; and citations appear on a separate Works Cited page at the end of the document. The Works Cited page is another name for a bibliography.

For simplicity, the following topics use the term *footnote* only. All details described for footnotes apply equally to endnotes.

Inserting Footnotes

When you insert a footnote, Word inserts a footnote reference mark in the document and a corresponding mark at the bottom of the page. Word automatically numbers footnotes and renumbers them if you add or delete one. The Footnote and Endnote dialog box offers features for formatting and controlling various aspects of notes.

FROM THE RIBBON
References→Footnotes →Insert Footnote

FROM THE KEYBOARD
Alt + Ctrl + F to insert a footnote

Indicate if you are dealing with footnotes or endnotes.

Indicate the footnote location: Bottom of Page or Below Text.

You can convert footnotes to endnotes and vice versa.

You can choose a number format or create a custom mark.

You can specify a starting number for each section or page.

Specify if numbering should be continuous or restarted at each section or page.

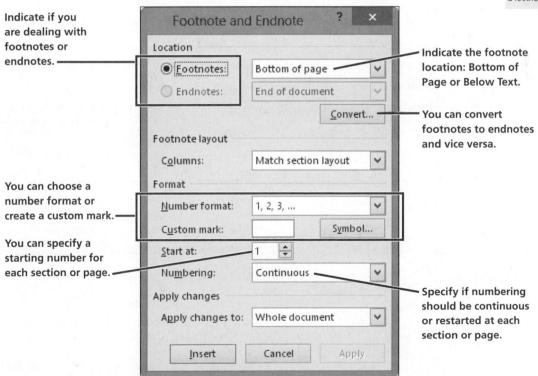

Inserting Citations

You use a citation to refer to material you obtained from an outside source that you are using in the paper. You can enter the source information when you create the citation or insert a placeholder and add the source data later. The citation appears inside parentheses at the end of the cited material; this notation takes the place of the superscript number that is placed for a footnote.

FROM THE RIBBON

References→
Citations &
Bibliography→Insert
Citation

There are a number of citation systems in addition to the MLA documentation style. Examples include the American Psychological Association (APA) style and the *Chicago Manual of Style* (CMS). The source information relating to the citation appears in a bibliography (or Works Cited page, depending on the citation system), usually at the end of the document. You choose the documentation style when you create the citation. The Create Source dialog box contains different fields depending on the documentation style you select.

Choose the type of source
(book, website, etc.).

The source information goes here.

Create Source

? ✕

Type of Source | Web site ▾

Bibliography Fields for MLA

Author		Edit
	☐ Corporate Author	
Name of Web Page	
Year	
Month	
Day	
Year Accessed	
Month Accessed	
Day Accessed	
Medium	

☐ Show All Bibliography Fields

Tag name

Placeholder1

OK | Cancel

If you need additional
fields, check this box.

Word uses tags internally to reference
bibliography entries.

Insert Footnotes and Citations

In this exercise, you will create a research paper and insert footnotes and citations, and you will convert footnotes to endnotes.

1. Start **Word**. Open **WD06-D01-Internet** from your **WD2013 Lesson 06** folder and save it as **WD06-D01-Internet-[FirstInitialLastName]**.

   Replace the bracketed text with your first initial and last name. For example, if your name is Bethany Smith, your filename would look like this: WD06-D01-Internet-BSmith.

2. If necessary, choose **View→Views→Print Layout** ▤.

   Footnotes may differ in appearance depending on the view you are using.

3. Position the insertion point at the top of the document and type the four lines of text above the title, tapping ⎶Enter⎶ once after each line, except the last line.

Simpson·1¶

¶

Brian·Simpson¶

Professor·Williams¶

Marketing·222¶

May·10,·2013¶

Internet·Commerce·and·Its·Effect·on·the·Environment¶

The·Internet·had·its·origins·in·the·1960s·when·the·Department·of·Defense·developed·a·

communications·network·to·connect·the·computers·of·various·military·installations.·The·Department·of·

Notice that the paragraph text is double-spaced and the extra space after the paragraphs has been removed per MLA requirements.

Insert Footnotes

4. Position the insertion point to the right of the period at the end of the first paragraph.

5. Choose **References→Footnotes→Insert Footnote** AB[1].

   Word places the footnote reference mark at the insertion point location, and a corresponding footnote appears at the bottom of the page.

6. Follow these steps to complete the footnote:

Ⓐ Note that Word inserts both a separator line and the correct number.

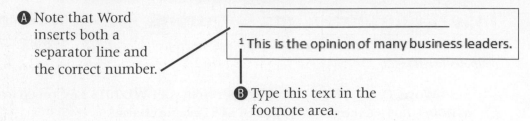

Ⓑ Type this text in the footnote area.

7. Use the same process to insert the footnote reference marks and associated footnotes shown here.

The commercial potential of the Internet stems from the fact that it is a global network with inexpensive access.[2] The Internet is also available 24x7. The multimedia capability to the Internet is important for marketing and advertising. Quick product delivery, automated order-taking, and low overhead are several more factors that are driving Internet commerce.[3]

Internet commerce will be a driving force in the global economy of the twenty-first century. There are still obstacles to overcome, but technology and market forces will propel this new commercial medium forward at a rapid pace.

---
[1] This is the opinion of many business leaders.
[2] This is true in the United States, but some nations still have high rates due to limited competition among Internet service providers.
[3] These factors depend upon the capabilities of individual companies.

The formatting of the footnotes does not adhere to MLA requirements. The text should use the same formatting as the body of the document (double-spaced, first line indented). You will format the footnotes later.

8. Type these paragraphs after the last paragraph.

> The environmental outlook is indeed bright: According to the latest study by Carnegie Mellon University, more than half (about 65%) of total emissions was produced by consumers driving to and from retail stores as opposed to buying online.
>
> Geoffrey Fowler, in his March 3, 2009 article on the Wall Street Journal website cited the following environmental benefits to e-commerce shopping:
>
> - Uses about one-third less energy than conventional retail shopping
>
> - Uses a one-third smaller carbon footprint than a standard building
>
> - A truck delivering numerous packages along its way is the largest environmental savings, as it uses less energy per package than if the consumers had driven to the shops themselves.

Convert Footnotes to Endnotes

9. Choose **References→Footnotes→dialog box launcher** ⌐ and click **Convert**.

10. When the Convert Notes box opens, click **OK** and then close the **Footnote and Endnote** dialog box.

11. Scroll through the document and notice that the footnotes are no longer at the bottom of page 1; they now appear as endnotes on the last page.

12. Click **Undo** ↺ to reinstate the footnotes at the bottom of page 1.

Select the MLA Style and Insert a Citation

13. Choose **References→Citations & Bibliography→Style menu** ▼**→MLA Seventh Edition**.

14. Position the insertion point between the word *online* and the period at the end of the first paragraph on page 2; tap Spacebar .

15. Choose **References→Citations & Bibliography→Insert Citation** ⬇, and then choose **Add New Source**.

16. Follow these steps to create the new source to insert as the citation:

Ⓐ If necessary, choose **Web Site** here.

Ⓑ Type the author's name as shown. Example text appears at the bottom of the window for each field.

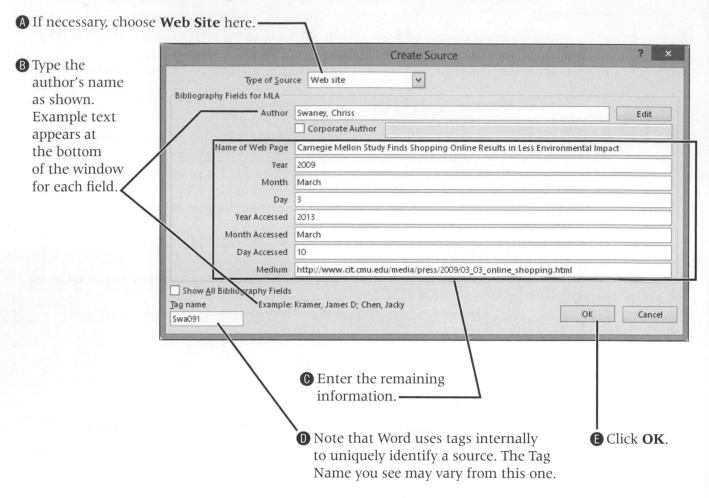

Ⓒ Enter the remaining information.

Ⓓ Note that Word uses tags internally to uniquely identify a source. The Tag Name you see may vary from this one.

Ⓔ Click **OK**.

Notice the author's last name is inserted as the name of the citation.

Remember, Word does not follow all MLA guidelines. Refer to the MLA handbook or website when writing academic papers.

Insert a Citation Placeholder

17. Position the insertion point at the end of the document between *themselves* and the period and tap Spacebar.

18. Choose **Reference→Citations & Bibliography→Insert Citation**, and then choose **Add New Placeholder**.

19. Follow these steps to create a placeholder for a citation named Fowler:

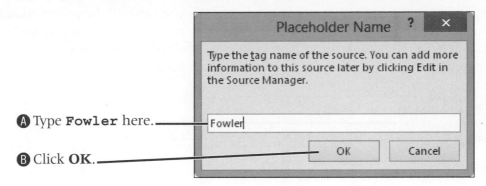

Ⓐ Type **Fowler** here.

Ⓑ Click **OK**.

20. Save the file.

Editing and Formatting Footnotes

Video Library http://labyrinthelab.com/videos   Video Number: WD13-V0603

You can edit footnote text directly in the footnote area. In addition to editing the text of a footnote, you can also:

- **Reposition:** You can change the position of a footnote reference mark by dragging it to another location in the document.
- **Format:** You can change various formatting features of footnotes using the Footnote and Endnote dialog box. For example, you can change the numbering scheme, change the starting number, or even replace a footnote number with a special symbol.

In this example, uppercase letters replace the normal numbering for footnotes.

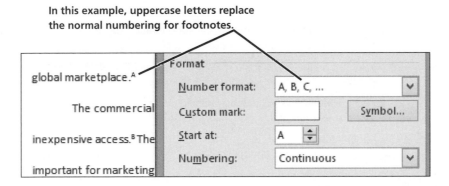

Editing a Footnote

Word's default style for footnote text does not meet MLA documentation style requirements. You must change the formatting if you want to be in compliance with MLA. MLA requirements state the text should be the same formatting as the text in the document; that is, double-spaced with the first line indented. You make those types of formatting changes, as well as editing changes, directly in the footnote area of the document.

Editing a Citation

Once you insert a citation or a citation placeholder you can edit the information in the Edit Source dialog box, which contains the same fields as the Create Source dialog box. The default citation in the body of the document is the author's last name; however, you can choose to suppress it and instead show the name of the web page.

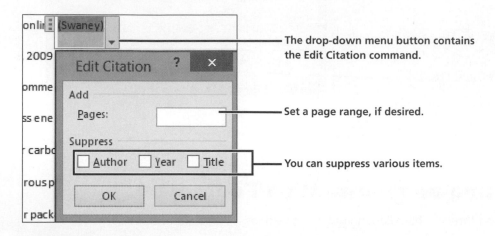

The drop-down menu button contains the Edit Citation command.

Set a page range, if desired.

You can suppress various items.

QUICK REFERENCE	WORKING WITH FOOTNOTES AND CITATIONS
Task	**Procedure**
Insert a footnote	Choose References→Footnotes→Insert Footnote.
Navigate to footnotes	Choose References→Footnotes→Next/Previous Footnote.
Edit/format footnotes in Print Layout view	Edit in the footnote area at the bottom of the page.
Format a footnote	Choose References→Footnotes, click the dialog box launcher, and then make the desired changes.
Delete a footnote	Select the footnote reference mark and tap Delete to delete the reference mark and the note.
Insert a citation	Choose References→Citations & Bibliography→Insert Citation, choose Add New Source, and enter data in the dialog box.
Edit a citation source	Click the citation in the document, click the arrow on the right, choose Edit Source, and make the desired changes.
Edit a citation	Click the citation in the document, click the arrow on the right, choose Edit Citation, and make the desired changes.
Delete a citation	Click the citation in the document, click the handle on the left to select the citation, and tap Delete.

DEVELOP YOUR SKILLS WD06-D02

Work with Footnotes and Citations

In this exercise, you will format, edit, and delete footnotes and edit a citation placeholder and source.

1. Save your file as **WD06-D02-Internet-[FirstInitialLastName]**.

2. Position the insertion point at the beginning of the second paragraph on page 1 and scroll, if necessary, to see the three footnote reference marks and the footnotes at the bottom of the page.

3. Choose **References→Footnotes→dialog box launcher** ⌐ to display the Footnote and Endnote dialog box.

4. Follow these steps to change the numbering format:

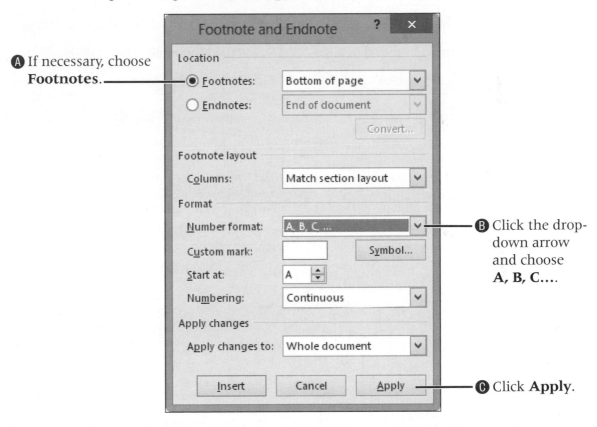

Ⓐ If necessary, choose **Footnotes**.

Ⓑ Click the drop-down arrow and choose **A, B, C…**.

Ⓒ Click **Apply**.

The footnote numbers change to alphabetic characters. You use the same technique to change the format of endnotes.

5. Click **Undo** ↺ to return to number formatting.

6. If necessary, choose **View→Show→Ruler** to display the ruler.

7. Select the three footnotes, and then follow these steps to format the footnotes:

   ■ Change line spacing to **double-space**.

   ■ Change the font size to **11 points**.

   ■ On the ruler, drag the **First Line Indent** marker (top triangle) to the **half-inch** mark.

Delete and Edit Footnotes

8. Follow these steps to delete a footnote:

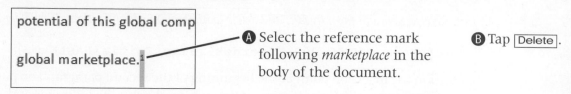

Ⓐ Select the reference mark following *marketplace* in the body of the document.

Ⓑ Tap Delete .

The reference mark and the footnote are removed, and the remaining footnotes renumber.

9. Click **Undo** ↶ to replace the footnote.

10. Position the insertion point between the last word and the period of the first footnote, tap Spacebar , and type **and economists**.

Edit a Citation Placeholder

11. Scroll to the end of page 2 and locate the **Fowler** citation.

12. Follow these steps to open the Edit Source dialog box:

Ⓐ Click the **Fowler** citation placeholder.

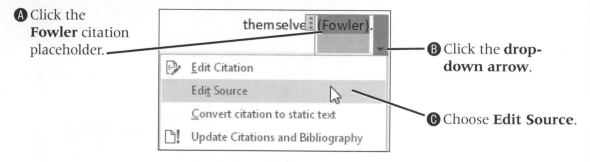

Ⓑ Click the **drop-down arrow**.

Ⓒ Choose **Edit Source**.

13. Follow these steps to add the source information to the Fowler citation:

Ⓐ If necessary, choose **Web Site**.

Ⓑ Enter the author's name as shown.

Ⓒ Enter the remaining data.

Ⓓ Click **OK**.

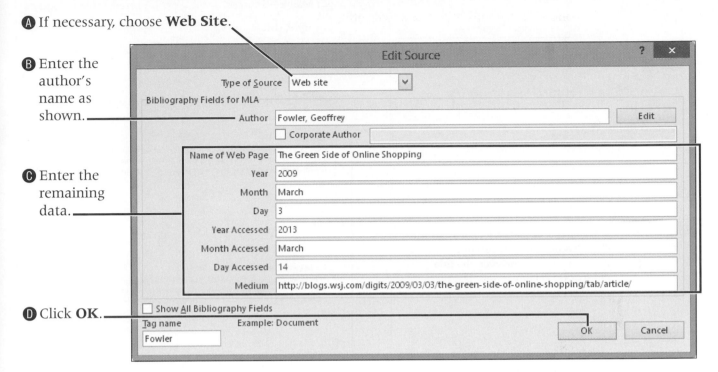

14. Click **Yes** if a message appears asking if you want to update the master list and current document.

The citation may have picked up the name of the web page (title).

15. If necessary, click the drop-down arrow to the right of the Fowler citation and choose **Edit Citation**, check the **Title** box, and click **OK**.

16. Save the file.

Working with Bibliographies

Video Library   http://labyrinthelab.com/videos   Video Number: WD13-V0604

A bibliography is a list of the sources cited in the preparation of the document. Word automatically generates a bibliography based on the source information that you provide in the Create Source dialog box. The bibliography picks up the correct punctuation; however, certain formatting requirements are not Microsoft defaults and must be addressed separately.

The Bibliography button in the Citations & Bibliography group on the References tab contains three built-in options: Bibliography, References, and Works Cited. You can choose any of these; however, the formatting may or may not meet the requirements of the document style you chose. For example, the Works Cited option for the MLA style does not format the title, the paragraph spacing, or the line spacing correctly.

The Bibliography options may not format references as needed. Use the Insert Bibliography command to create citations more precisely.

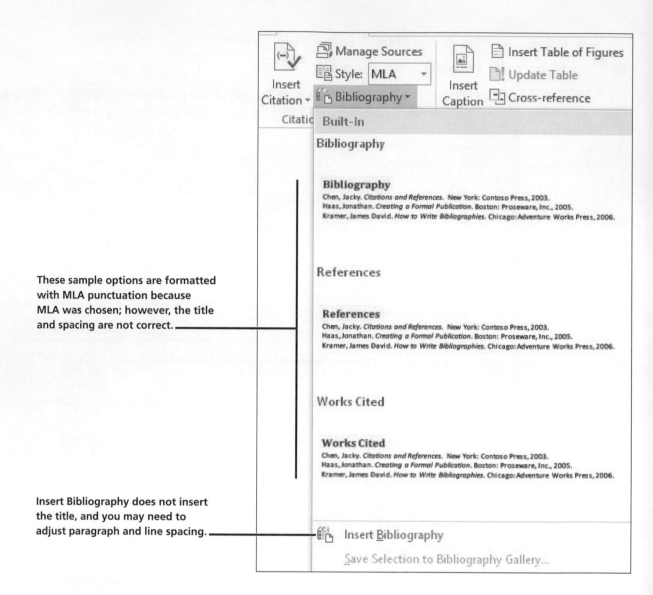

These sample options are formatted with MLA punctuation because MLA was chosen; however, the title and spacing are not correct.

Insert Bibliography does not insert the title, and you may need to adjust paragraph and line spacing.

Updating a Bibliography

When you edit the citation source or add a new one, you can easily update the bibliography list using the Update Field command on the menu when you right-click on the list. The Update Field command reformats the list to single-spacing again; thus, you must remember to change back to double-spacing.

Create a Bibliography

In this exercise, you will create a bibliography for the citations in the document. You will title the page as Works Cited, since the lesson is following the MLA documentation style. Finally, you will edit an existing citation, update the bibliography, and format the paragraphs with double-spacing.

1. Save your file as **WD06-D03-Internet-[FirstInitialLastName]**.

2. Position the insertion point at the end of the document.

3. Tap Enter twice; then, press Ctrl + Enter to insert a new page for the bibliography.

4. Choose **Home→Paragraph→Center** ☰, and then type **Works Cited** and tap Enter.

Insert and Update the Bibliography

5. Choose **References→Citations & Bibliography→Bibliography** 📖.

6. Choose **Insert Bibliography** at the bottom of the menu.

7. Scroll up to the bottom of the second page and click the **Fowler** citation, and then click the arrow on the right.

8. Choose **Edit Source** to open the dialog box.

9. Change the **Day Accessed** to **10** and click **OK**.

10. If the citation picked up the name of the web page, click the drop-down arrow, choose **Edit Citation**, check the **Title** box, and click **OK**.

11. Scroll down the **Works Cited page** and notice nothing has changed yet in the list.

12. Follow these steps to update the bibliography:

Ⓐ Right-click anywhere in the list.

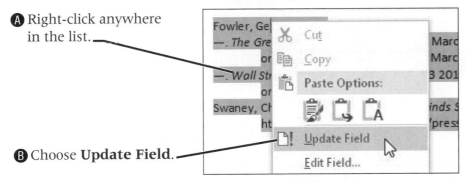

Ⓑ Choose **Update Field**.

Notice the date accessed for the Fowler citation changed to 10 March 2013.

Format the List

13. Select the bibliography list, but not the Works Cited title.

If you click the list, it highlights in light gray. You must *drag* to select the list, which then highlights in a darker gray.

14. Choose **Home→Paragraph→Line and Paragraph Spacing** ↕≣, and then choose **2.0**.

15. Save the file.

Inserting Captions and a Table of Figures

Video Library   http://labyrinthelab.com/videos   Video Number: WD13-V0605

You use captions to insert text associated with figures in a paper. Word then uses the captions as entries in the table of figures. Later, if you alter some of the captions, Word updates these when you regenerate the table of figures.

Inserting Captions

Word can automate the creation of captions for certain types of objects. Click AutoCaption and choose the file types you want Word to automatically assign captions to.

The caption text is entered here.

The default label is Figure; Equation and Table are the other options.

Check this box to prevent a word before the number.

You can create a custom label.

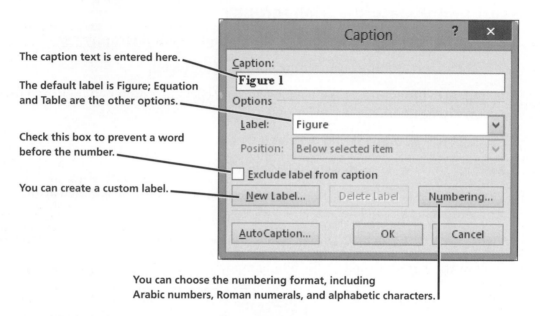

You can choose the numbering format, including Arabic numbers, Roman numerals, and alphabetic characters.

DEVELOP YOUR SKILLS WD06-D04
Add Captions to Figures

In this exercise, you will insert a file between pages 1 and 2 that contains five PowerPoint slides from a presentation. You will add captions to the slides in preparation for creating a table of figures.

1. Save your file as **WD06-D04-Internet-[FirstInitialLastName]**.

2. Position the insertion point after the third footnote reference mark in the body of the document (not the footnote area) at the bottom of the first page.

3. Press [Ctrl] + [Enter] to insert a page break.

4. Choose **Insert→Text→Object** 🔲 menu ▼→**Text from File**.

5. In the Insert File dialog box, navigate to your **WD2013 Lesson 06** folder, choose **WD06-D04-Slides**, and click **Insert**.

Add and Edit Captions

6. If necessary, choose **Home→Paragraph→Show/Hide ¶** to display formatting marks.

7. Position the insertion point on the first blank line below the first slide.

8. Choose **References→Captions→Insert Caption** 📄.

9. The Caption dialog box should match the following illustration. If *Figure 1* does not appear in the Caption text box, follow these steps. Otherwise, go to step 10.

Ⓐ Click the **Label menu** button and choose **Figure**.

Ⓑ Click **Numbering** to open the **Caption Numbering** dialog box.

Ⓒ Click the **Format menu** button, and then choose the **1, 2, 3, ...** format.

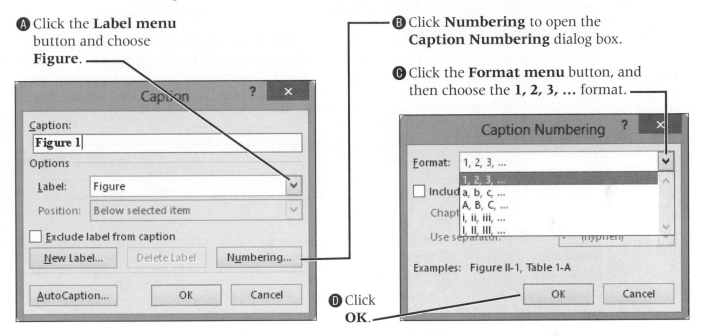

Ⓓ Click **OK**.

10. If necessary, position the insertion point to the right of *Figure 1* in the Caption text box.

11. Tap the [Spacebar], type **DOD and ARPANET**, and click **OK** to insert the caption.
    The caption is placed at the left margin.

12. Choose **Home→Paragraph→Center** ≡.

13. Position the insertion point in the first blank line below the second slide.

14. Choose **References→Captions→Insert Caption** 📄.

15. Tap the [Spacebar], type **NSF**, and click **OK**.

16. **Center** ≡ the caption.

17. Add these captions and center them:

Slide Number	Caption Text
3	MILNET and TCP/IP
4	First Graphical Browser
5	Netscape

Edit a Caption

18. Return to slide 2, select *NSF*, and type `National Science Foundation` in its place.

19. Save the file.

Inserting a Table of Figures

Video Library   http://labyrinthelab.com/videos   Video Number: WD13-V0606

Academic papers often include a table of figures at the front, which guides the reader to illustrations, charts, tables, and other figures. This is particularly helpful in long documents. The table entries conveniently function as hyperlinks if you are reading the document online.

QUICK REFERENCE	CREATING CAPTIONS AND TABLES OF FIGURES
Task	**Procedure**
Insert a caption	■ Choose References→Captions→Insert Caption, and then type the caption text.
Insert a table of figures	■ Choose References→Captions→Insert Table of Figures, and then make the formatting choices.
Update a table of figures	■ Right-click the table and choose Update Field.

DEVELOP YOUR SKILLS WD06-D05
Generate a Table of Figures

In this exercise, you will generate a table of figures from the captions you inserted earlier. You will change the numbering format of your captions, and then you will update the table to reflect the change.

Insert the Table of Figures

1. Save your file as `WWD06-D05-Internet-[FirstInitialLastName]`.

2. Move the insertion point to the top of the document and insert a page break.

3. Press `Ctrl`+`Home` to position the insertion point at the top of the new page, and then type `Table of Figures` and tap `Enter` twice.

4. Format the heading you just typed with **center, bold 16 point**.

5. Place the insertion point in the blank line below the heading.

6. Choose **References→Captions→Insert Table of Figures** 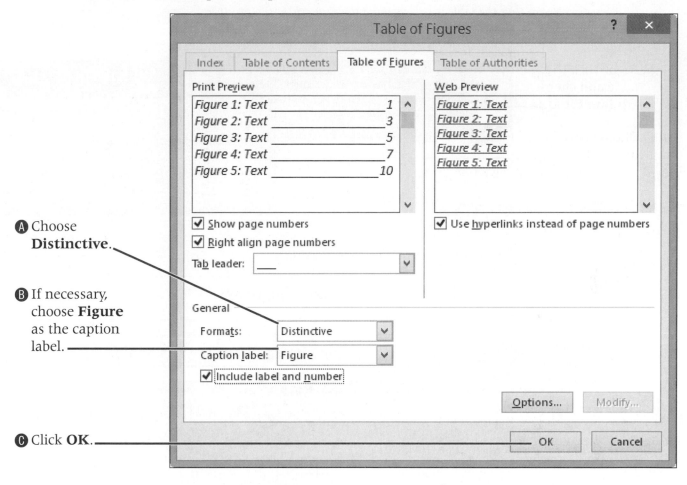.

7. Follow these steps to set up the table:

A Choose **Distinctive**.

B If necessary, choose **Figure** as the caption label.

C Click **OK**.

8. Position the insertion point on page 3 so you will be able to see the effect of the next change.

Change the Numbering Format of the Captions

9. Choose **References→Captions→Insert Caption** .

10. Click **Numbering** to display the Caption Numbering dialog box.

11. Choose the **A, B, C, ...** format and click **OK**.

12. Click **Close** in the Caption dialog box, and then scroll through the slides.

   Notice that the figure numbers changed to alphabetic characters.

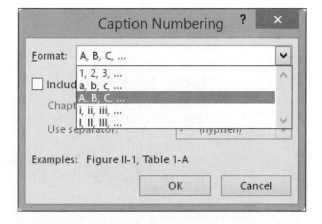

Update the Table of Figures

13. Scroll up to view the **Table of Figures** on page 1.

Notice that the table is still showing the numeric figure numbers.

14. Follow these steps to update the Table of Figures:

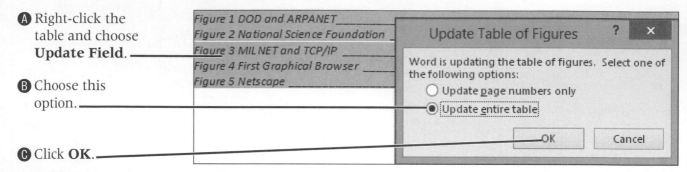

Ⓐ Right-click the table and choose **Update Field**.

Ⓑ Choose this option.

Ⓒ Click **OK**.

The table should match the following illustration.

Table of Figures

Figure A DOD and ARPANET _____		3
Figure B National Science Foundation _____		3
Figure C MILNET and TCP/IP _____		3
Figure D First Graphical Browser _____		4
Figure E Netscape _____		4

The text switched from Figures 1–5 to Figures A–E.

15. Save and then close the file.

Working with Templates

Video Library   http://labyrinthelab.com/videos   Video Number: WD13-V0607

All Word documents are based on templates, which can include text, formatting, graphics, and any other objects or formats available in Word. The default Word template is Blank Document. The benefit of templates is that they do not change when documents *based on them* change. When you start a new document, Word opens a *copy* of the template. This lets you use templates repeatedly as the basis for new documents. Word provides a variety of ready-to-use templates, or you can also create your own personal templates.

Creating a Document from a Template

Templates are located in the Word Start screen or in Backstage view when you choose the New screen. Basing a new document on a template can save you a lot of time since much of the formatting is already included in the template for you.

If you don't find a template you want in the Featured templates, you can search online by entering your own search term or by choosing a suggested search.

If you create personal templates, click here to view them.

Clicking a template displays a window that describes the template; double-clicking a template immediately opens it in the Word window.

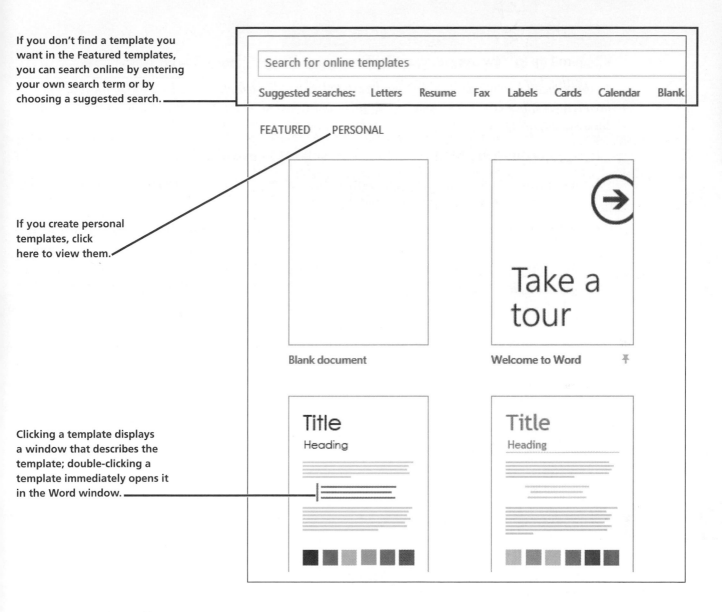

Saving Personal Templates

When you create a document containing specific formatting, you can save it to use later as a template. You should save the template in the Custom Office Templates folder unless instructed to do otherwise. The Custom Office Templates folder is the default in the Save As window when a template is chosen in the Save As Type field. This is what causes your templates to appear when you click the Personal link on the templates screen. You can save a template as a Word Template or as a Word Macro-Enabled Template. A macro-enabled template is one that contains a special series of instructions called a macro.

Choose the template type from the Save As Type list in the Save As window.

Create a Template from an Existing Document

In this exercise, you will open a copy of a report and save it as a template. The body text of the report has been removed; however, other elements are still in place, including the cover page, the table of figures, and the double-spacing. You will then save time by starting a new report based on the template.

1. Open **WD06-D06-MyReport** from your **WD2013 Lesson 06** folder.

2. Scroll through the document and notice the elements that are still in place and that will be useful when you create a new report.

3. Choose **File→Save As**, navigate to any file storage location, and choose **Word Template** from the **Save As Type** list at the bottom of the dialog box.

   Notice the file path that appears at the top of the Save As dialog box. Word defaults to the Custom Office Templates folder in the My Documents folder as the file storage location.

4. Save the file as **WD06-D06-MyReport-[FirstInitialLastName]**.

5. Choose **File→Close** to close the template file.

6. Choose **File→New**.

7. Follow these steps to open a copy of your template:

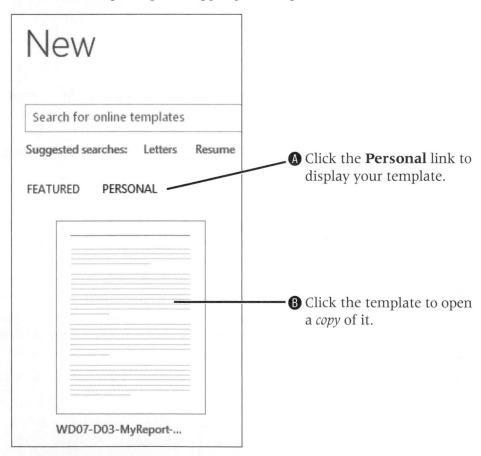

Ⓐ Click the **Personal** link to display your template.

Ⓑ Click the template to open a *copy* of it.

Notice the generic Documentx filename in the title bar at the top of the Word window. This indicates you are working on a copy of the template rather than the template itself.

8. Scroll to page 3 and replace *[DOCUMENT TITLE]* with **Green Life**.

9. Save the document as **WD06-D06-GreenLife-[FirstInitialLastName]** in your **WD2013 Lesson 06** folder.

10. Close the file and exit **Word**.

Deleting a Template

Video Library   http://labyrinthelab.com/videos   Video Number: WD13-V0608

When a template is no longer useful, you may wish to delete it. Templates are easily removed from the Custom Office Templates folder.

QUICK REFERENCE	CREATING AND DELETING TEMPLATES
Task	**Procedure**
Save an existing document as a template	■ Choose File→Save As and navigate to the desired file storage location. ■ Choose Word Template from the Save as Type list, enter the template name, and click Save.
Delete a template	■ Click File Explorer on the taskbar, navigate to the Documents folder, and double-click the Custom Office Templates folder. ■ Choose the desired template and tap ⌜Delete⌟.

Delete a Template

In this exercise, you will delete the template you created.

1. Click **File Explorer** 🖳 on the taskbar at the bottom of the screen.

2. Follow these steps to delete the My Report template:

Ⓐ Navigate to the **Documents** folder.

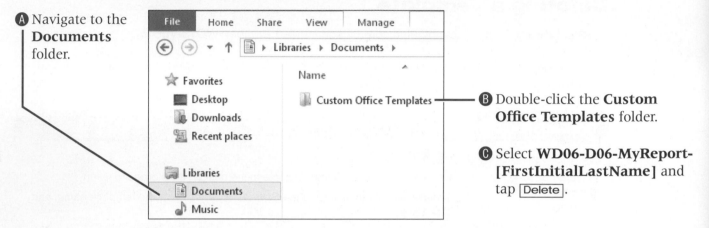

Ⓑ Double-click the **Custom Office Templates** folder.

Ⓒ Select **WD06-D06-MyReport-[FirstInitialLastName]** and tap ⟨Delete⟩.

3. Close the **File Explorer** window.

Concepts Review

To check your knowledge of the key concepts introduced in this lesson, complete the Concepts Review quiz by choosing the appropriate access option below.

If you are...	Then access the quiz by...
Using the Labyrinth Video Library	Going to http://labyrinthelab.com/videos
Using eLab	Logging in, choosing Content, and navigating to the Concepts Review quiz for this lesson
Not using the Labyrinth Video Library or eLab	Going to the student resource center for this book

Reinforce Your Skills

Create Footnotes, Endnotes, Citations, and a Bibliography

In this exercise, you will work with endnotes, footnotes, and citations. Then you will generate a bibliography. Although you will select the MLA style in the Citations & Bibliography group, because this research paper is not for academic purposes, you will not follow strict MLA formatting guidelines.

Work with Footnotes and Endnotes

1. Start **Word**. Open **WD06-R01-GlobalLocal** from your **WD2013 Lesson 06** folder and save it as `WD06-R01-GlobalLocal-[FirstInitialLastName]`.

2. Position the insertion point after the period following *sales* in the second paragraph.

> Kids for Change is a non-profit organization that helps minors in their
>
> social/community service within the mindset of "Think Globally, Act Locally."
>
> fundraisers, such as car washes, bake sales, and rain barrel sales. The kids are

3. Choose **References→Footnotes→Insert Endnote** .

4. Type this endnote text.

> ——————————
> i Proceeds go to organizations, such as the local pantry.

5. Position the insertion point after the comma following *construction* in the second to last line of the second paragraph.

> fundraisers, such as car washes, bake sales, and rain barrel sales.
>
> community recycling drives, researching green construction, and
>
> garden program.

6. Choose **References→Footnotes→Insert Endnote** .

7. Type the endnote text as shown in the following illustration.

> ⁱⁱ Kids for Change successfully encouraged a local businessman to use green construction in a building addition.

You noticed a word is missing in the first endnote, so you will make that change now.

8. In the first endnote, position the insertion point to the left of *pantry*, type **food**, and tap Spacebar.

You've decided to convert the endnotes to footnotes so they will appear on the same page as the text they refer to.

9. Choose **References→Footnotes→dialog box launcher** ▣.

10. Click **Convert**.

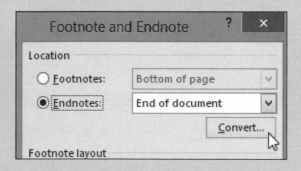

11. When the Convert Notes message appears, click **OK**; close the **Footnote and Endnote** dialog box.

Insert Citations

12. Choose **References→Citations & Bibliography**, and then choose **MLA Seventh Edition** from the Styles drop-down list.

13. Position the insertion point at the end of the fourth bullet point in the **Juniper Russo** citation.

> • Supporting local businesses and agriculture|

14. Tap Spacebar.

15. Choose **References→Citations & Bibliography→Insert Citation** ▣, and then choose **Add New Source**.

16. If necessary, choose **Web Site** in the Type of Source drop-down list.

17. Enter the following information in the Create Source dialog box:

- Author: **Russo, Juniper**
- Name of Web Page: **What Does "Think Globally, Act Locally" Mean?**
- Year: **2011**
- Month: **August**
- Day: **3**
- Year Accesses: **2013**
- Month Accessed: **December**
- Day Accessed: **15**
- Medium: **http://voices.yahoo.com/what-does-think-globally-act-locally-mean-8908513.html?cat=57**

18. Click **OK**.

19. Position the insertion point following *Fluids* at the end of the fourth bullet point in the **Jennifer King** citation.

20. Tap Spacebar.

21. Choose **References→Citations & Bibliography→Insert Citation**, and then choose **Add New Source**.

22. Make sure **Web Site** is chosen as the Type of Source.

23. Enter the following information in the Create Source dialog box:

- Author: **King, Jennifer**
- Name of Web Page: **How Does Car Pollution Affect the Environment & Ozone Layer?**
- Year Accessed: **2011**
- Month Accessed: **December**
- Day Accessed: **15**
- Medium: **http://greenliving.nationalgeographic.com/car-pollution-affect-environment-ozone-layer-20133.html**

24. Click **OK**.

25. Position the insertion point at the end of the document between the period and *Nations*.

26. Tap Spacebar.

27. Choose **References→Citations & Bibliography→Insert Citation**, and then choose **Add New Source**.

28. Make sure **Web Site** is chosen as the Type of Source.

29. Enter the following information in the Create Source dialog box:
   - Author: **Trex, Ethan**
   - Name of Web Page: **Whatever Happened to the Hole in the Ozone Layer?**
   - Year: **2012**
   - Month: **May**
   - Day: **23**
   - Year Accessed: **2013**
   - Month Accessed: **December**
   - Day Accessed: **15**
   - Medium: **http://www.mentalfloss.com/blogs/archives/127568**

30. Click **OK**.

Generate and Update a Bibliography

31. Position the insertion point at the end of the document, tap [Enter] twice, and press [Ctrl] + [Enter] to insert a new page for the bibliography.

32. Choose **Home→Paragraph→Center** ☰, type **Works Cited**, and tap [Enter].

33. Choose **References→Citations & Bibliography→Bibliography** ▣.

34. Choose **Insert Bibliography** at the bottom of the menu.
   Now you'll make a change to a citation.

35. Scroll to and click the **King** citation at the bottom of page 1.

36. Click the arrow on the right and choose **Edit Source**.

37. Change the **Year Accessed** to **2013** and click **OK**.

38. If you are prompted to update the master list, click **Yes**.

39. Scroll to the **Works Cited** page, right-click the list, and choose **Update Field**.
   The year accessed changes to 2013.

40. Save and close the file; exit from **Word**.

41. Submit your final file based on the guidelines provided by your instructor.
   To view examples of how your file or files should look at the end of this exercise, go to the student resource center.

Insert Captions and a Table of Figures, and Create a Template

In this exercise, you will add captions to figures and create a table of figures. Then you will create a letter template.

Insert Captions

1. Start **Word**. Open **WD06-R02-Sustainable** from your **WD2013 Lesson 06** folder and save it as WD06-R02-Sustainable-[FirstInitialLastName].

2. If necessary, choose **Home→Paragraph→Show/Hide ¶** to turn on formatting marks.

3. Position the insertion point on the first blank line following the **Healthy, Safe Home** slide.

4. Choose **References→Captions→Insert Caption**.

5. If necessary, change the Label field to **Figure**, click the Numbering button, and change the format to **1, 2, 3, …**; click **OK**.

6. Choose **Home→Paragraph→Center**.

7. Tap [Spacebar] and type Healthy, Safe Home.

8. Use the same procedure to type the following captions for the remaining slides:
   - Transportation
   - Reduce and Reuse
   - Recycle

Insert a Table of Figures

9. Position the insertion point at the top of the document and press [Ctrl]+[Enter] to insert a page break.

10. Press [Ctrl]+[Home] to position the insertion point at the top of the document.

11. Type Table of Figures and tap [Enter] twice.

12. **Center** the heading you just typed, and then position the insertion point on the blank line below the heading.

13. Choose **References→Captions→Insert Table of Figures**.

14. If necessary, choose **Formal** as the format and make sure the caption label is **Figure**; click **OK**.

15. Save and then close the file.

Create a Template from an Existing Document

16. Open **WD06-R02-Letter** from your **WD2013 Lesson 06** folder.

    Notice that the letter is already set up with placeholders for the variables.

17. Choose **File→Save As**, navigate to any file storage location, and choose **Word Template** from the Save As Type list.

    The Custom Office Templates folder appears at the top of the Save As dialog box.

18. Save the file as `WD06-R02-Letter-[FirstInitialLastName]`.

19. Choose **File→Close** to close the **Template file**.

20. Choose **File→New**, and then click the **Personal** link toward the top of the New screen.

21. Click your template thumbnail to open a copy of it.

22. Enter the current date, and then replace the inside address and greeting placeholders with information of your choice.

23. Save the file as `WD06-R02-FormLtr-[FirstInitialLastName]` in the **WD2013 Lesson 06** folder; close the file.

Delete a Template

24. Click **File Explorer** 🖳 on the taskbar at the bottom of the screen.

25. Navigate to the **Documents folder** in the left panel.

26. Double-click the **Custom Office Templates** folder on the right.

27. Select **WD06-R02-Letter-[FirstInitialLastName]** and tap Delete.

28. Close **File Explorer**, and then, if necessary, exit from **Word**.

29. Submit your final file based on the guidelines provided by your instructor.

    To view examples of how your file or files should look at the end of this exercise, go to the student resource center.

Format and Distribute a Research Paper

In this exercise, you will insert a footnote and citations in an organic food research paper. You will choose the MLA style; however, since this is not an academic paper, you will not follow strict MLA formatting guidelines. Then you will insert captions, generate a table of figures, and create a template.

Work with Footnotes and Citations

1. Start **Word**. Open **WD06-R03-OrganicFood** from your **WD2013 Lesson 06** folder, and save it as `WD06-R03-OrganicFood-[FirstInitialLastName]`.

2. If necessary, choose **Home→Paragraph→Show/Hide** ¶ to turn on formatting marks.

3. Position the insertion point to the right of the period at the end of the first paragraph.

4. Choose **References→Footnotes→Insert Footnote** AB¹.

5. Type this text in the footnote area.

---

¹ See Sustainable Animal Agriculture for details on raising animals with care.

Now you will choose the style for citations.

6. Choose **Reference→Citations & Bibliography**, click the **Style menu button ▼**, and choose **MLA Seventh Edition**.

7. Position the insertion point between the period and the word *bay* at the end of the second paragraph below the *Plant Production* heading, and tap `Spacebar`.

8. Choose **References→Citations & Bibliography→Insert Citation** ⬇, and then choose **Add New Source**.

9. Make sure **Web Site** is chosen as the Type of Source.

10. Enter the following information:
    - Author: **Mayo Clinic, Staff**
    - Name of Web Page: **Nutrition and healthy eating**
    - Year Accessed: **2013**
    - Month Accessed: **December**
    - Day Accessed: **15**
    - Medium: **http://www.mayoclinic.com/health/organic-food/NU00255**

11. Click **OK**.

The citation may have picked up the name of the web page (title).

12. If necessary, click the drop-down arrow to the right of the citation and choose **Edit Citation**, check the **Title** box, and click **OK**.

13. Position the insertion point at the end of the fourth bullet point below the *Benefits of Organic Food* heading and tap `Spacebar`.

14. Choose **References→Citations & Bibliography→Insert Citation** ⬇, and then choose **Add New Source**.

15. Ensure that **Web Site** is the Type of Source.

16. Enter the following information:
    - Author: **Blake, Daniel**
    - Name of Web Page: **13 Benefits of Organic Food**
    - Year: **2012**
    - Month: **December**
    - Day: **10**
    - Year Accessed: **2013**
    - Month Accessed: **December**
    - Day Accessed: **13**
    - Medium: **http://ecoscraps.com/13-benefits-organic-food/**

17. Click **OK**.

Work with a Bibliography

18. Position the insertion point at the end of the document and press [Ctrl] + [Enter] to insert a page break.

19. Choose **Home→Paragraph→Center** ≣, and then type **Works Cited** and tap [Enter].

20. Choose **References→Citations & Bibliography→Bibliography** 📑, and then choose **Insert Bibliography** at the bottom of the menu.

    Next you will edit the footnote and a citation, and update the bibliography.

21. Click the **Blake** citation on page one, click the arrow, and choose **Edit Source**.

22. Change the Month Accessed to **November** and click **OK**.

23. Click **Yes** if you are prompted to update both lists.

24. Scroll to the bibliography, right-click the list, and choose **Update Field**.

    The month accessed changes to November.

Inserting Captions and a Table of Figures

25. Position the insertion point on the first blank line below the first picture.

26. Choose **References→Captions→Insert Caption** 📄.

27. If necessary, choose **Figure** in the Label field and make sure the numbering format is **1, 2, 3, …**.

28. If necessary, position the insertion point to the right of **Figure 1** in the Caption text box.

29. Tap [Spacebar], type **Better for the Soil**, and click **OK**.

30. Position the insertion point in the first blank line below the second picture.

31. Choose **References→Captions→Insert Caption** 📄.

32. Tap [Spacebar], type **Better for the Water**, and click **OK**.

33. Follow the same process to place a caption titled **Increases Consumer Choices** below the third picture and **Fresher, Better Tasting** below the fourth picture.

34. Press [Ctrl] + [Home] to position the insertion point at the top of the document.

35. Press [Ctrl] + [Enter] to insert a page break; position the insertion point at the top of the first page.

36. Type **Table of Figures** and tap [Enter] twice.

37. Select the heading and apply **center, bold 16 points** formatting.

38. Position the insertion point on the blank line below the heading.

39. Choose **References→Captions→Insert Table of Figures** 📄.

40. In the dialog box, choose **Distinctive** as the format style, ensure that the caption label is **Figure**, and click **OK**.

    Now you'll change the number format style for the captions and update the Table of Figures.

41. Choose **References→Captions→Insert Caption** 📄 **→Numbering**.

42. Choose the **i, ii, iii, …** format and click **OK**.

43. Close the **Caption** dialog box, and then scroll through the pictures and notice the change to lowercase Roman numerals.

44. Scroll to the **Table of Figures** on page 1, right-click the table, and choose **Update Field**.

45. If necessary, choose **Update Entire Table** and click **OK**.

   Notice the figure numbers updated in the table.

46. Save and then close the file.

Create and Delete a Template

Kids for Change will use this document as a handout when giving organic food presentations at community schools. They will send a letter, along with the document, to the school principals for their approval. They will create a template they can use repeatedly for this task.

47. Open the **WD06-R03-PrincipalLtr** from your **WD2013 Lesson 06** folder.

48. Choose **File→Save As**, navigate to any file storage location, and choose **Word Template** from the Save As Type list.

   Notice that Word switches to the Custom Office Templates folder as the file storage location.

49. Save the file as `WD06-R03-PrincipalLtr-[FirstInitialLastName]`, and then choose **File→Close** to close the template file.

   Now you'll open a copy of the template.

50. Choose **File→New**, and then click the **Personal** link to display your template.

51. Click the template thumbnail to open a copy of the template.

52. Save the file as `WD06-R03-PrinLtrFinal-[FirstInitialLastName]` in the **WD2013 Lesson 06** folder.

53. Delete the placeholder text for the date; enter the current date.

54. Replace the placeholder text for the inside address with the following inside address:

   ```
   Ms. Eleanor Roberts
   Bascom High School
   951 Elm Street
   Annapolis, MD 21405
   ```

55. Replace the salutation placeholder name with `Ms. Roberts`.

56. Replace the member name with your name.

57. Save and then close the file.

   Now you will delete the template.

58. Click **File Explorer** on the taskbar at the bottom of the screen.

59. Navigate to the **Documents** folder in the left-hand panel.

60. Double-click the **Custom Office Templates** folder on the right.

61. Select the **WD06-R03-PrincipalLtr-[FirstInitialLastName]** file and tap Delete.

62. Close **File Explorer**; exit from **Word**.

63. Submit your final files based on the guidelines provided by your instructor.

Apply Your Skills

Work with Footnotes, Citations, and a Bibliography

In this exercise, you will create a report detailing some Italian tourist sites and providing tips on train travel in Italy. You will insert footnotes and citations, generate a bibliography, edit a citation, and update the bibliography. Since this is not an academic report, you will not hold to strict MLA guidelines.

Insert Footnotes

1. Start **Word**. Open **WD06-A01-Italy** from your **WD2013 Lesson 06** folder and save it as `WD06-A01-Italy-[FirstInitialLastName]`.

2. Position the insertion point at the end of the first paragraph in the document.

3. Insert this footnote: `Other major attractions are listed on this website.`

4. Position the insertion point after the period following the word *choices* in the paragraph beginning, *In the article, "Italy Train Travel....*

5. Insert this footnote: `This article also offers advice on train schedules, buying tickets, and boarding your train.`

Enter Citations and Create a Bibliography

6. Choose **MLA Seventh Edition** as the style in the Citations & Bibliography group on the References tab.

7. Position the insertion point after the **Colosseum** bullet point near the top of the document.

8. Tap `Spacebar`, ensure that **Web Site** is the Type of Source, and enter the following citation information:

   - Author: `Rome Travel, Guide`
   - Name of Web Page: `Rome travel guide`
   - Year Accessed: `2013`
   - Month Accessed: `May`
   - Day Accessed: `23`
   - Medium: `http://www.rome.info/`

9. Click **OK**.

10. Position the insertion point after *Trastevere* at the end of the third bullet point below the *Off the Beaten Path* heading.

11. Tap ⌷Spacebar⌷, ensure that **Web Site** is the Type of Source, and enter the following information:

   - ■ Author: `Casura, Lily`
   - ■ Name of Web Page: `Rome off the beaten path`
   - ■ Year Accessed: `2013`
   - ■ Month Accessed: `May`
   - ■ Day Accessed: `23`
   - ■ Medium: `http://www.tripadvisor.com/Guide-g187791-1295-Rome_Lazio.html`

12. Click **OK**.

13. Position the insertion point between *more* and the period at the end of the last paragraph.

14. Tap ⌷Spacebar⌷, ensure that **Web Site** is the Type of Source, and enter the following information:

   - ■ Author: `Bakerjian, Martha`
   - ■ Name of Web Page: `Italy Train Travel - Tips on Riding Italian Trains`
   - ■ Year Accessed: `2013`
   - ■ Month Accessed: `May`
   - ■ Day Accessed: `23`
   - ■ Medium: `http://goitaly.about.com/od/italytransportation/a/trains.htm`

15. Click **OK**.

16. Position the insertion point at the end of the document, tap ⌷Enter⌷ twice, and insert a page break.

17. Type `Works Cited` as the heading and tap ⌷Enter⌷.

18. **Center** ⌷☰⌷ the heading; position the insertion point on the blank line below the heading.

19. Insert a bibliography on the new page using the **Insert Bibliography** command.
   Now you will edit a citation and then update the bibliography.

20. Edit the **Casura** citation source on page 1 by changing the month accessed to `September`. If you are prompted to update the source, click Yes.

21. Update the bibliography and check that the change to the Casura citation is there.

22. Save and then close the file; exit from **Word**.

23. Submit your final file based on the guidelines provided by your instructor.
   To view examples of how your file or files should look at the end of this exercise, go to the student resource center.

Insert Captions and a Table of Figures, and Create a Template

One of Universal Corporate Events' clients plans to send their high sales achievers on an African safari as a reward for their hard work. They are preparing a handout to use in conjunction with their presentation. In this exercise, you will add captions to pictures and generate a table of figures. Then you will create a template from an existing letter.

Insert Captions and Create a Table of Figures

1. Start **Word**. Open **WD06-A02-Safari** from your **WD2013 Lesson 06** folder and save it as **WD06-A02-Safari-[FirstInitialLastName]**.

2. Insert and **center** ☰ the following captions for the pictures in your Safari document; use the **1, 2, 3, …** number format and the **Figure** label.
   - Picture 1 caption: **Wildebeest**
   - Picture 2 caption: **Elephants**
   - Picture 3 caption: **Rhinos**
   - Picture 4 caption: **Leopard**
   - Picture 5 caption: **Lion**
   - Picture 6 caption: **Buffalo**

3. Position the insertion point at the top of the document and insert a page break.

4. Position the insertion point at the top of the new page, type **Table of Figures**, and tap ⌷Enter⌷ twice.

5. Format your heading with **center, bold 16 points**.

6. Position the insertion point on the blank line below the heading and generate the table of figures using the **Distinctive** format and **Figure** as the caption label.

   Next you will edit two captions and then regenerate the table of figures.

7. The Leopard and Lion captions should be plural, so add an **s** to the end of each of the captions.

8. Update the entire table of figures and check to make sure the changes took place.

9. Save and then close the file.

Work with a Template

Universal Corporate Events needs to send travel information to the people going on safari, so they will create a template letter that they can use for all the participants.

10. Open **WD06-A02-SafariLtr** from your **WD2013 Lesson 06** folder.

    Notice the variables in uppercase.

11. Save the file as a **Word Template** in the default **Custom Office Templates** folder; choose **File→Close** to close the template.

12. Choose **File→New** and access your **personal templates**.

13. Open a copy of the template, replace the variable text with the current date, inside address, and salutation of your choice. Enter you own name as the travel agent.

14. Save the file as **WD06-A02-SafariLtrFinal-[FirstInitialLastName]** in your **WD2013 Lesson 06** folder; close the file and exit from **Word**.

    Now you will delete the template.

15. Open **File Explorer** from the taskbar, navigate to the **Documents** folder, open the **Custom Office Templates** folder, and delete your template.

16. Close **File Explorer**.

17. Submit your final files based on the guidelines provided by your instructor.

    To view examples of how your file or files should look at the end of this exercise, go to the student resource center.

Work with Footnotes, Citations, Captions, and Templates

The intern at Universal Corporate Events has been asked to research travel in Thailand for one of the corporate clients. In this exercise, you will use some of your report-writing skills to help her create her report. Since this is not academic research, you will not conform to strict MLA guidelines.

Work with Footnotes

1. Start **Word**. Open **WD06-A03-Bangkok** from your **WD2013 Lesson 06** folder and save it as **WD06-A03-Bangkok-[FirstInitialLastName]**.

2. Position the insertion point to the right of *markets* in the first line and insert this footnote.

   ---

   [1] Floating markets piled high with tropical fruits and vegetables provide an easy day trip from Bangkok.

3. Position the insertion point to the right of *temples* in the first line and insert this footnote.

   [2] Don't miss Wat Traimit's Golden Buddha or Wat Pho's famous Reclining Buddha.

   Now you will edit the second footnote.

4. Insert the word **renowned** before *Golden*.

Use Citations and Generate a Bibliography

5. Choose the **MLA Seventh Edition** style for citations.

   Now you will insert a citation at the end of the first bullet point.

6. Ensure that **Web Site** is the Type of Source and enter the following information:
   - Author: **Thyberg, David**
   - Name of Web Page: **Bangkok Travel Tips**
   - Year Accessed: **2013**
   - Month Accessed: **September**
   - Day Accessed: **22**
   - Medium: **http://getawaytips.azcentral.com/bangkok-travel-tips-1945.html**

   Now you will insert a citation at the end of the last bullet point on page 1.

7. Ensure that **Web Site** is the Type of Source and enter the following information:
   - Author: **Doman, Gaby**
   - Name of Web Page: **Off the Beaten Track**
   - Year Accessed: **2013**
   - Month Accessed: **September**
   - Day Accessed: **22**
   - Medium: **http://www.tripadvisor.com/Guide-g293916-1104-Bangkok.html**

   Next you will insert a citation at the end of the last bullet point on page 2.

8. Ensure that **Web Site** is the Type of Source and enter the following information:
   - Author: **Rowthorn, Chris**
   - Name of Web Page: **Take the boat out of Bangkok**
   - Year: **2012**
   - Month: **April**
   - Day: **13**
   - Year Accessed: **2013**
   - Month Accessed: **September**
   - Day Accessed: **22**
   - Medium: **http://www.lonelyplanet.com/thailand/bangkok/travel-tips-and-articles/77110**

9. Add a new page at the end of the document for the bibliography, title the page **Works Cited**, and tap Enter.

10. **Center** ☰ the heading; generate the bibliography on a blank line below the title using the **Insert Bibliography** command.

   Now you'll modify a citation and regenerate the bibliography.

11. Change the date accessed for the **Doman** citation to **August 27**.

12. If a message appears asking if you want to update both lists, click **Yes**.

13. Regenerate the bibliography and check that the change was made.

14. Save and close the **Bangkok** file.

Insert Captions and Create a Table of Figures

The Universal Corporate Events art department has created several logo images for the company to use in its pre-travel seminar announcements. The head of the department is asking for input from the stakeholders.

15. Open **WD06-A03-Logo** from your **WD2013 Lesson 06** folder and save it as `WD06-A03-Logo-[FirstInitialLastName]`.

16. If necessary, display formatting marks.

17. Position the insertion point on the first blank line below the first logo image.

18. Open the **Caption dialog box** and ensure that the label is **Figure** and the numbering choice is **1, 2, 3, …**.

19. Enter and **Center** ≡ the following captions for all of the logos in the order indicated here.
- Picture 1 caption: `Option 1`
- Picture 2 caption: `Option 2`
- Picture 3 caption: `Option 3`
- Picture 4 caption: `Option 4`
- Picture 5 caption: `Option 5`

20. Position the insertion point at the end of the document and insert a **page break**.

21. Type `Table of Figures` at the top of the new page and tap Enter.

22. If necessary, **center** ≡ the heading; apply **bold** B.

23. Generate the table on the blank line below the heading using the **Formal** format and **Figure** as the caption label.

24. Save and close the file.

Create a Template

Universal Corporate Events wants to standardize the branding for their pre-travel seminar announcements and save it as a template they can use repeatedly.

25. Open **WD06-A03-Seminar** from your **WD2013 Lesson 06** folder.

    Notice the elements of the announcement that will work for any travel seminar.

26. Save the file as a template in the **Custom Office Templates** folder, naming it `WD06-A03-Seminar-[FirstInitialLastName]`.

27. Close the template.

28. Open a copy of the template and replace the *[DESTINATION]* placeholder with `Central America`.

29. Save the file as `WD06-A03-SeminarFinal-[FirstInitialLastName]` in your **WD2013 Lesson 06** folder; close the file.

    Next you will delete the template.

30. Open **File Explorer**; navigate to the **Documents** folder and then to the **Custom Office Template** folder.

31. Delete **WD06-A03-Seminar-[FirstInitialLastName]**.

32. Close **File Explorer**; if necessary, exit from **Word**.

33. Submit your final files based on the guidelines provided by your instructor.

Extend Your Skills

In the course of working through the Extend Your Skills exercises, you will think critically as you use the skills taught in the lesson to complete the assigned projects. To evaluate your mastery and completion of the exercises, your instructor may use a rubric, with which more points are allotted according to performance characteristics. (The more you do, the more you earn!) Ask your instructor how your work will be evaluated.

WD06-E01 That's the Way I See It

You are an intern working for a major grocery store chain. Your manager has asked you to research the pros and cons of reusable shopping bags compared to plastic bags. You have decided to follow MLA conventions in your research paper. Start a new Word document named **WD06-E01-ShopBags-[FirstInitialLastName]** and saved to your **WD2013 Lesson 06** folder.

Type an original introductory paragraph for the paper, and include two footnote comments in the paragraph.

Using the search engine of your choice, find two sources who favor reusable shopping bags and two sources who do not. Pull information from these sources into your research paper, compare the two sides of the issue, and present your opinion. Insert citations at the end of each source and generate a bibliography for the citations.

Open **WD06-E01-ShopBags** from your **WD2013 Lesson 06** folder. Copy and paste the pictures into your research paper, add creative captions to the figures, and create a table of figures.

You will be evaluated based on the inclusion of all elements specified, your ability to follow directions, your ability to apply newly learned skills to a real-world situation, your creativity, and the relevance of your topic and/or data choice(s). Submit your final file based on the guidelines provided by your instructor.

WD06-E02 Be Your Own Boss

As the owner of Blue Jean Landscaping, you plan to hold a rose-pruning seminar for your customers. You will research correct pruning techniques and create a report of your research results to hand out to customers at the event. Write an original introductory paragraph of at least five sentences, and cite three different sources in your report using the MLA Seventh Edition style. Then generate a bibliography of your citations. Because this is not an academic paper, you will not follow strict MLA guidelines. Save your file as **WD06-E02-RoseSeminar-[FirstInitialLastName]** in your **WD2013 Lesson 06** folder.

Create a letter template with variable placeholders that will be used to notify customers of the seminar. Save the template as **WD06-E02-Template-[FirstInitialLastName]**. Use a copy of the template to generate a sample customer letter named **WD06-E02-SampleLetter-[FirstInitialLastName]**. Store the files in your **WD2013 Lesson 06** folder.

You will be evaluated based on the inclusion of all elements specified, your ability to follow directions, your ability to apply newly learned skills to a real-world situation, your creativity, and your demonstration of an entrepreneurial spirit. Submit your final files based on the guidelines provided by your instructor.

Transfer Your Skills

In the course of working through the Transfer Your Skills exercises, you will use critical-thinking and creativity skills to complete the assigned projects using skills taught in the lesson. To evaluate your mastery and completion of the exercises, your instructor may use a rubric, with which more points are allotted according to performance characteristics. (The more you do, the more you earn!) Ask your instructor how your work will be evaluated.

WD06-T01 WebQuest: Use the Web as a Learning Tool

Throughout this book, you will be provided with an opportunity to use the Internet as a learning tool by completing WebQuests. According to the original creators of WebQuests, as described on their website (WebQuest.org), a WebQuest is "an inquiry-oriented activity in which most or all of the information used by learners is drawn from the web." To complete the WebQuest projects in this book, navigate to the student resource center and choose the WebQuest for the lesson on which you are currently working. The subject of each WebQuest will be relevant to the material found in the lesson.

WebQuest Subject: Elements of a research paper based on the MLA Seventh Edition documentation style.

Submit your final file(s) based on the guidelines provided by your instructor.

WD06-T02 Demonstrate Proficiency

The owner of Stormy BBQ is proud to use free-range cattle. He wants his employees to understand the benefits of using natural, grass-fed beef so they can discuss the idea with customers. He has asked you to prepare a report that he can distribute to all employees. Start a new Word document named **WD06-T02-GrassFed-[FirstInitialLastName]** and saved to your **WD2013 Lesson 06** folder. Conduct online research on the benefits of using free-range, natural beef. Write an original introductory paragraph of at least five sentences that includes two commentary footnotes. Cite three sources who favor free-range beef. Generate a bibliography for the citations using the MLA Seventh Edition style, but because this is not an academic paper, you don't need to follow strict MLA guidelines.

Open **WD06-T02-Cattle** from your **WD2013 Lesson 06** folder. Copy and paste the pictures into your report, insert creative captions for the pictures, and generate a table of figures.

Submit your final file based on the guidelines provided by your instructor.

Using Mail Merge

In this lesson, you will manage mail using Word 2013's Mail Merge feature. You will set up data sources where you store name and address information, and you will set up form letters. Then you'll merge your form letters with a data source to produce personalized letters. You'll also generate personalized envelopes and labels. Because you only type the main document once, you only have to proof it once—versus proofing many individually typed letters. When you've validated a data source, you can use it repeatedly without having to check the variable information each time.

LESSON OUTLINE

LEARNING OBJECTIVES

After studying this lesson, you will be able to:

- Work with data sources
- Create main documents
- Perform a mail merge
- Work with merge problems
- Generate envelopes and labels

Generating a Marketing Mass Mailing

You are the administrative assistant for Green Clean. The company wants to expand their business, and the marketing manager has chosen mass mailings as a good way to generate new prospects. You have been tasked with creating the mailing for the upcoming sales campaign. Mail Merge will save you many hours that would have otherwise been spent addressing each letter individually.

719 Coronado Drive
San Diego, California 92102

Today's Date

Mr. Andre Adams
Mills Insurance
2224 Culver Drive
San Diego, CA 92102

Dear Andre:

Green Clean is a locally owned and operated commercial janitorial service. Our employees are highly trained, and our supervisors check on every job every night to ensure the best quality work.

We follow all EPA guidelines and comply with OSHA standards. We use only environmentally safe cleaning products, providing you with a healthy, nontoxic, clean place of business.

Good customer service is our number one priority. Our proactive account managers stay in touch with our clients and follow through on all requests. We have been in business over twenty years and we have scores of long-term clients.

Andre, one of our account managers will contact you in the near future to discuss you janitorial needs.

Sincerely,

Ahn Tran
President

Variable codes in the form letter merge with the data source to generate personalized letters.

Introducing Mail Merge

Video Library　http://labyrinthelab.com/videos　Video Number: WD13-V0701

Word's Mail Merge feature is most often used for generating personalized form letters, mailing labels, and envelopes. However, Mail Merge is a versatile tool that can be used with any type of document that combines boilerplate text with variable information, such as standard contracts and legal verbiage. Mail Merge can be a big time-saver and is valuable for managing large mailings.

Components of Mail Merge

Merging creates a merged document by combining information from two files. They are known as the main document and the data source.

- **Main document:** This document controls the merge. It contains the fixed information into which the variable information is merged. A typical form letter, for instance, has a different inside address and greeting line in each letter, while the rest of the text is the same for everyone receiving the letter.

- **Data source:** The data source can be another Word document, a spreadsheet, a database file, or a contacts list in Outlook.

- **Merged document:** This document is the result of the merge. It contains all of the letters addressed to each individual in your data source.

You can merge an existing main document with an existing data source, or you can create the main document and data source while stepping through the merge process.

719 Coronado Drive
San Diego, California 92102

Today's Date

Last N... ▼	First... ▼	Title ▼	Company Name ▼	Address Line 1 ▼	City ▼	State ▼	ZIP Code ▼
Adams	Andre	Mr.	Mills Insurance	2224 Culver Drive	San Diego	CA	92102
Bouras	Talos	Mr.	Conrad Corporation	854 Whitmore Drive	San Diego	CA	92101
Chowdery	Michael	Mr.	Seligman Enterprises	146 Meadow Lane	La Jolla	CA	92103
Novarro	Derek	Mr.	Gourmet Warehouse	3300 Maple Drive	La Jolla	CA	92103
Romero	Nicole	Ms.	Harris Health Services	132 Lake Street	San Diego	CA	92101
Wright	Mary	Ms.	Rogers Electric Company	1240 Potrero Avenue	San Diego	CA	92101

«AddressBlock»

«GreetingLine»

The data source can be a Mail Merge recipient list, a Word table, an Excel database, or an Access table.

Green Clean is a locally owned and operated commercial janitorial service. Our employees are highly trained, and our supervisors check on every job every night to ensure the best quality work.

We follow all EPA guidelines and comply with OSHA standards. We use only environmentally safe cleaning products, providing you with a healthy, nontoxic, clean place of business.

Good customer service is our number one priority. Our proactive account managers stay in touch with our clients and follow through on all requests. We have been in business over twenty years and we have scores of long-term clients.

«First_Name», one of our account managers will contact you in the near future to discuss you janitorial needs.

Sincerely,

Ahn Tran
President

The main document contains standard text and merge codes where variables from the data source will be merged.

719 Coronado Drive
San Diego, California 92102

Today's Date

Mr. Andre Adams
Mills Insurance
2224 Culver Drive
San Diego, CA 92102

Dear Andre:

Green Clean is a locally owned and operated commercial janitorial service. Our employees are highly trained, and our supervisors check on every job every night to ensure the best quality work.

We follow all EPA guidelines and comply with OSHA standards. We use only environmentally safe cleaning products, providing you with a healthy, nontoxic, clean place of business.

Good customer service is our number one priority. Our proactive account managers stay in touch with our clients and follow through on all requests. We have been in business over twenty years and we have scores of long-term clients.

Andre, one of our account managers will contact you in the near future to discuss you janitorial needs.

Sincerely,

Ahn Tran
President

The completed merge document with variables from the data source.

The Benefits of Using Mail Merge

Mail Merge saves a lot of time. For example, imagine you want to send a letter to 100 customers. Without Mail Merge, you would have to type the same text in all 100 letters (or copy and paste 100 times). However, with Mail Merge, you create one main document with the standard text and one data source containing customer names and addresses.

You will also really appreciate Mail Merge when you later decide you want to make a change. Using Mail Merge, you can edit the main document once and remerge it with the data source to produce a new merged document. Without Mail Merge, you would need to edit each letter individually.

The Mailings Tab

The Mailings tab provides guidance in setting up both the main document and data source, and it helps you conduct the merge. The Start Mail Merge group is the beginning point. Alternatively, you can choose Step-by-Step Mail Merge Wizard from the Start Mail Merge menu to walk you through the process.

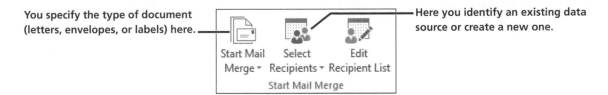

You specify the type of document (letters, envelopes, or labels) here.

Here you identify an existing data source or create a new one.

Working with the Data Source

Data sources typically contain names, addresses, telephone numbers, and other contact information. However, you can include any information in a data source. For example, you could include part numbers and prices to create a parts catalog. You can create a data source in Word, or you can use an external data source, such as an Access or Excel database. Once a data source is created, it can be merged with many different main documents.

Designing Effective Data Sources

It is important to design effective data sources. The most important consideration is the number of fields—the more fields, the more flexibility. You cannot merge a portion of a field. If a field contains both a first and last name, for example, you would not be able to merge the last name without the first name into a greeting line such as *Dear Ms. Alvarez*. In this example, you would need to use one field for the first name and a separate field for the last name. You would also need to use a field for titles (Mr., Ms., and Mrs.). This guideline is not critical if you know you will not use the data source again and the main document does not require this flexibility.

Creating a New Address List

You can use the New Address List dialog box to set up address lists (data sources) for mail merges. This tool stores the addresses in a table in a Microsoft Access database. Each row in the table is referred to as a record. This table, which becomes the data source for the merge, is connected to the mail merge main document.

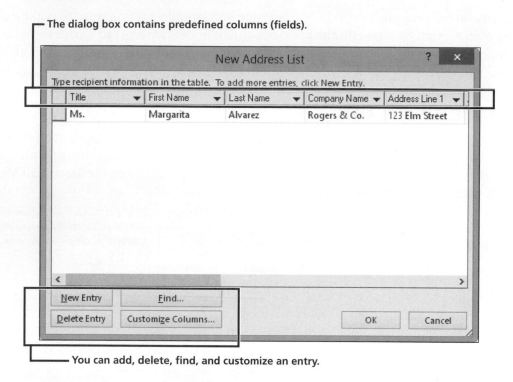

The dialog box contains predefined columns (fields).

You can add, delete, find, and customize an entry.

Customizing an Address List

The Customize Address List dialog box allows you to modify the predefined columns. It's easy to set up the mailing list just as you want it.

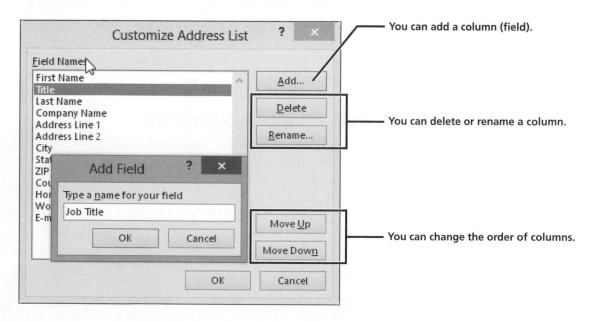

You can add a column (field).

You can delete or rename a column.

You can change the order of columns.

Specify the Main Document and Create a Data Source

In this exercise, you will use the Start Mail Merge group to specify a letter as your main document, to customize the data source, and to enter data.

1. Start **Word**. Open **WD07-D01-SalesLetter** from your **WD2013 Lesson 07** folder and save it as `WD07-D01-SalesLetter-[FirstInitialLastName]`.

   Replace the bracketed text with your first initial and last name. For example, if your name is Bethany Smith, your filename would look like this: WD07-D01-SalesLetter-BSmith.

2. Choose **Mailings**→**Start Mail Merge**→**Start Mail Merge** 📄 →**Letters**.

   You are indicating that the letter you just opened will be the main document. Now you will create your mailing list.

3. Choose **Mailings**→**Start Mail Merge**→**Select Recipients** 📇 →**Type a New List**.

   The New Address List dialog box opens. Now you will remove unnecessary fields and add a new field.

4. Click **Customize Columns** to open the Customize Address List dialog box.

5. Choose **Address Line 2** and click **Delete**; click **Yes** to verify the deletion.

6. Delete **Country or Region**, **Home Phone**, **Work Phone**, and **E-mail Address**, and then click **Title** at the top of the list.

7. Follow these steps to add a field:

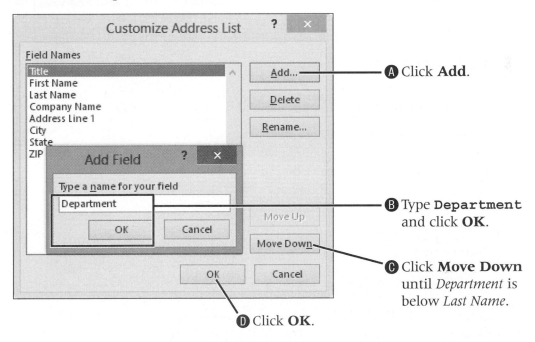

Ⓐ Click **Add**.

Ⓑ Type **Department** and click **OK**.

Ⓒ Click **Move Down** until *Department* is below *Last Name*.

Ⓓ Click **OK**.

Enter Records
The insertion point should be in the Title field.

8. Follow these steps to begin the first record:

Ⓐ Type **Mr.** here.

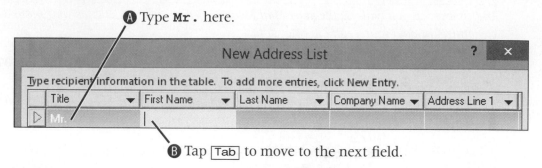

Ⓑ Tap [Tab] to move to the next field.

Do not type spaces after entering information in a field. Word takes care of adding the necessary spaces. You can click a field and make editing changes if necessary.

9. Type **Talos** and tap [Tab] to move to the next field.

10. Finish entering the Talos Bouras data shown here, tapping [Tab] between fields. The list of fields will scroll as you [Tab] and type.

11. When you complete the first record, click **New Entry** or tap [Tab] to generate a new row for the next record; then, enter the two remaining records shown.

Mr. Talos Bouras	Ms. Nicole Romero	Mr. Michael Chowdrey
Administration	Maintenance	Operations
Conrad Corporation	Harris Health Services	Seligman Enterprises
854 Whitmore Drive	132 Lake Street	900 C Street
San Diego CA 92101	San Diego CA 92101	La Jolla CA 92103

If you accidentally tap [Tab] after the last record, just click Delete Entry to remove the blank record.

12. Leave the **New Address List** dialog box open.

Reviewing Your Records

Video Library http://labyrinthelab.com/videos Video Number: WD13-V0703

It's a good idea to review your records for accuracy before saving the data source. However, if you miss an error, you can always edit it later.

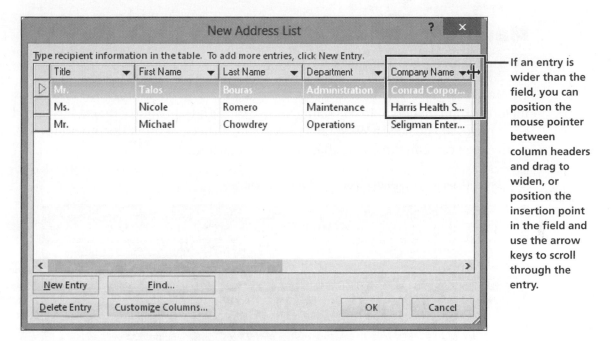

If an entry is wider than the field, you can position the mouse pointer between column headers and drag to widen, or position the insertion point in the field and use the arrow keys to scroll through the entry.

DEVELOP YOUR SKILLS WD07-D02
Review and Save Your Work

In this exercise, you will examine your records for accuracy and save your data source.

1. Position the mouse pointer on the scroll bar at the bottom of the dialog box, and drag left and right to view all the fields.

2. Follow these steps to review your records:

A Position the insertion point here and use the arrow keys to move through the entry.

	Department	Company Name	Address Line 1	City
	Administration	Conrad Corpor...	854 Whitmore Drive	San Diego

B Position the mouse pointer here and drag to the right to display the entire entry.

3. Correct any typos.

4. When you finish reviewing your records, click **OK** to open the Save Address List dialog box.

5. Save the data source file as `WD07-D02-SalesLtrData-[FirstInitialLastName]` in the **WD2013 Lesson 07** folder.

Your data source is now connected to the main document.

Managing the Address List

Video Library   http://labyrinthelab.com/videos   Video Number: WD13-V0704

The Mail Merge Recipients dialog box lets you sort and filter address lists and choose records to include in a mail merge. To edit data, you use the Edit Data Source dialog box to add, delete, and edit entries. If you used a Word table, Excel spreadsheet, or other document for your data source, you can edit directly in that data source document.

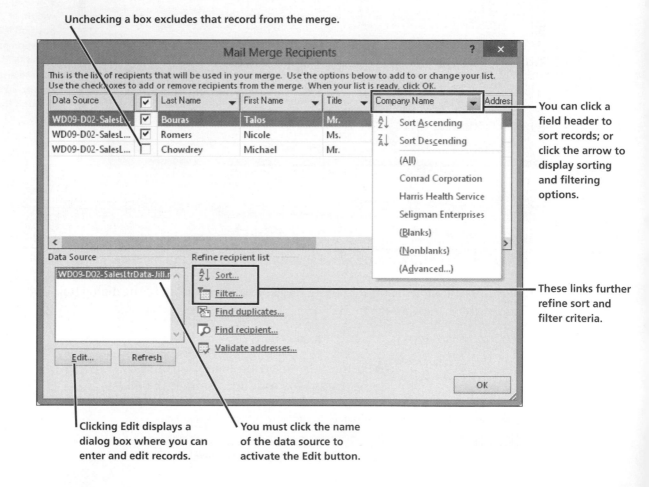

Unchecking a box excludes that record from the merge.

You can click a field header to sort records; or click the arrow to display sorting and filtering options.

These links further refine sort and filter criteria.

Clicking Edit displays a dialog box where you can enter and edit records.

You must click the name of the data source to activate the Edit button.

Use Recipient Options and Edit Records

In this exercise, you will work with the Mail Merge Recipients dialog box, where you can sort, filter, and edit your mailing list.

1. Choose **Mailings→Start Mail Merge→Edit Recipient List** 📝.

2. Follow these steps to sort and filter the list and open the Edit Data Source dialog box:

Ⓐ Click this field header to sort the list in ascending order by last name.

Ⓑ Click the drop-down arrow and choose **Chowdery** to filter out other entries. Click the arrow again and choose **(All)** to redisplay all records.

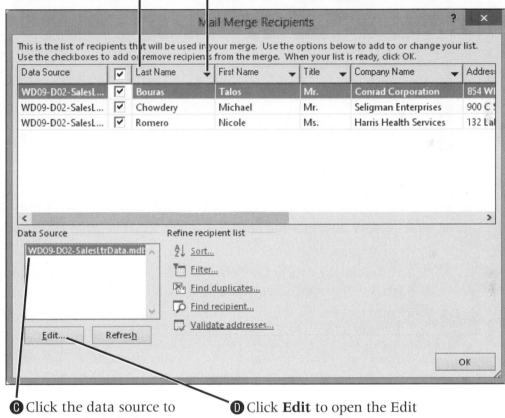

Ⓒ Click the data source to activate the Edit button.

Ⓓ Click **Edit** to open the Edit Data Source dialog box.

Edit a Record

The Edit Data Source dialog box looks and operates like the New Address List dialog box.

3. Follow these steps to edit a record:

A. Scroll right to display the **Address Line 1** field.

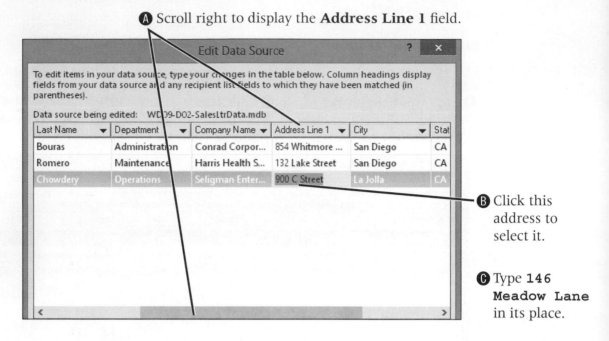

B. Click this address to select it.

C. Type **146 Meadow Lane** in its place.

4. Follow these guidelines to enter the three records in the following illustration:

   ■ Use the **New Entry** button or tap Tab at the end of each row for each new record.

   ■ Tap Tab to move from one field to the next.

   ■ Notice that the third record does not include a department name. Tap Tab to pass through the Department field and leave it empty.

   ■ Make sure to enter the data in the correct fields.

Ms. Mary Wright	Mr. Derek Navarro	Mr. Andre Adams
Administration	Operations	Mills Insurance
Rogers Electric Company	Gourmet Warehouse	2224 Culver Drive
1240 Potrero Avenue	3300 Maple Drive	San Diego CA 92102
San Diego CA 92101	La Jolla CA 92103	

5. Click **OK** to close the dialog box.

6. Click **Yes** when the message appears verifying your update.

   Notice your changes in the Mail Merge Recipients dialog box.

7. Click **OK** to close the Mail Merge Recipients dialog box.

Video Library   http://labyrinthelab.com/videos   Video Number: WD13-V0705

You accomplish a merge by combining a main document with a data source. A main document is attached to a data source that includes one or more merge fields. Merge fields in a main document correspond to fields in the data source. Some merge codes, such as the Address Block code, are composite fields consisting of a number of grouped fields. For example, Title, First Name, Last Name, Address, City, State, and Zip would be included in the Address Block code.

When you conduct a merge, a customized letter, envelope, or label is created for each record in the data source. The following figure shows the command buttons in the Write & Insert Fields group that you use to insert merge fields into your document.

This command allows you to insert an Address Block code for the inside address.

This command lets you insert a Greeting Line code.

This command allows you to insert individual fields from your data source.

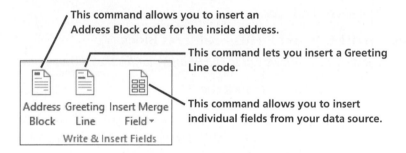

719 Coronado Drive
San Diego, California 92102

Today's Date

«AddressBlock»

«GreetingLine»

Green Clean is a locally owned and operated commercial janitorial service. Our employees are highly trained, and our supervisors check on every job every night to ensure the best quality work.

We follow all EPA guidelines and comply with OSHA standards. We use only environmentally safe cleaning products, providing you with a healthy, nontoxic, clean place of business.

Good customer service is our number one priority. Our proactive account managers stay in touch with our clients and follow through on all requests. We have been in business over twenty years and we have scores of long-term clients.

«First_Name», one of our account managers will contact you in the near future to discuss you janitorial needs.

Sincerely,

Ahn Tran
President

Here is a form letter with the merge fields inserted. When you execute the merge, the Address Block, Greeting Line, and First Name codes are replaced with information from the data source.

Use MailMerge Wizard instead

Set Up a Form Letter

In this exercise, you will set up a form letter. The sales letter main document should still be open.

1. If necessary, choose **Home→Paragraph→Show/Hide** ¶ to display formatting characters.

2. Select the **Today's Date** line and tap Delete.

3. Choose **Insert→Text→Insert Date and Time** 📅.

4. Choose the third date format, check **Update Automatically**, and click **OK**.

   Checking the Update Automatically option means the date in your letter will always be the current date, which is a convenient option for form letters that you want to use again.

5. Tap Enter four times after inserting the date.

   Now you will insert the Address Block code.

6. Choose **Mailings→Write & Insert Fields→Address Block** 📄.

   The Insert Address Block dialog box allows you to choose a format for the address block.

7. Follow these steps to insert an Address Block code:

   Ⓐ Choose different formats and view the preview on the right; then choose **Mr. Joshua Randall Jr.**

   Insert Address Block ? ✕

   Specify address elements

   ☑ Insert recipient's name in this format:

   > Joshua
   > Joshua Randall Jr.
   > Joshua Q. Randall Jr.
   > Mr. Josh Randall Jr.
   > Mr. Josh Q. Randall Jr.
   > **Mr. Joshua Randall Jr.**

   ☑ Insert company name

   ☑ Insert postal address:
   - ○ Never include the country/region in the address
   - ○ Always include the country/region in the address
   - ● Only include the country/region if different than:

     United States

   ☑ Format address according to the destination country/region

   Preview

   Here is a preview from your recipient list:

   |◁ ◁ 1 ▷ ▷|

   > Mr. Andre Adams
   > Mills Insurance
   > 2224 Culver Drive
   > San Diego, CA 92102

   Correct Problems

   If items in your address block are missing or out of order, use Match Fields to identify the correct address elements from your mailing list.

   Match Fields...

   OK   Cancel

   Ⓑ Leave the remaining options as shown and click **OK**.

   The <<AddressBlock>> code appears in the letter. During the merge, Word will insert inside address information from the data source at the Address Block code location.

8. Tap `Enter` twice.

Now you will insert the Greeting Line code.

9. Choose **Mailings→Write & Insert Fields→Greeting Line** 📄.

10. Follow these steps to modify and insert the Greeting Line code:

Ⓐ Change this option to a **colon (:)**.

Ⓑ This style greeting will be used for data records if they are missing last names.

Ⓒ Choose **Joshua** from the list.

Ⓓ Click **OK**.

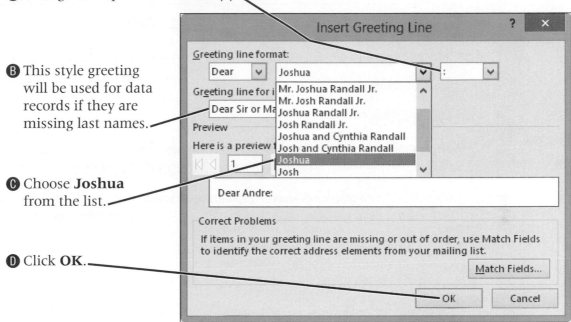

11. Tap `Enter` twice.

12. Follow these steps to insert the First Name code into the letter:

Ⓑ Click the **Insert Merge Field** menu button ▼.

Ⓐ Position the insertion point to the left of One.

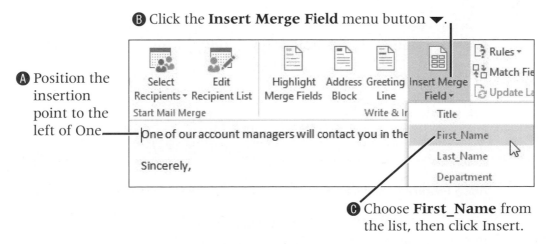

Ⓒ Choose **First_Name** from the list, then click Insert.

13. Close the Insert Merge Field dialog box.

14. Type a comma and tap `Spacebar`; then delete the **uppercase O** and replace it with a **lowercase o**.

15. Take a few moments to review your letter, making sure the merge fields match this example. In particular, make sure you used the proper punctuation and spacing between fields and the text.

The merge fields are highlighted in the following illustration to help you locate them; your merge fields do not need to be highlighted. (The Highlight Merge Fields button is in the Write & Insert Fields group.)

Any punctuation or spacing errors that occur in your main document will appear in every merged letter.

16. Choose **Home→Paragraph→Show/Hide** ¶ to turn off formatting marks.

17. Save your file.

Conducting a Merge

> **Video Library**   http://labyrinthelab.com/videos   Video Number: WD13-V0706

Merging combines a main document with a data source document. If you are merging a form letter with a data source, Word produces a personalized copy of the form letter for each record in the data source.

Previewing the Results

It's always a good idea to preview the merge results before you complete the merge so you can make corrections if needed. If you notice an error that needs to be fixed in the main document, simply click the Preview Results button again to return to the main document.

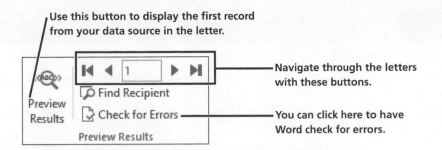

Use this button to display the first record from your data source in the letter.

Navigate through the letters with these buttons.

You can click here to have Word check for errors.

Using "Check for Errors"

When you have many records to preview, rather than previewing each one individually, you can use Check for Errors. Word goes through the document checking for common errors, such as an invalid field code. In the Checking and Reporting Errors dialog box, you have three options for viewing errors.

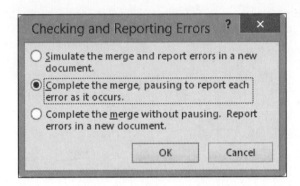

Finishing the Merge

When you feel confident that your letter and data source are accurate, you use the Finish & Merge command.

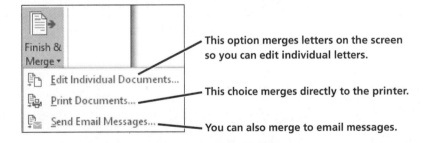

This option merges letters on the screen so you can edit individual letters.

This choice merges directly to the printer.

You can also merge to email messages.

To Save or Not to Save

Merged documents are rarely saved because they can easily be reconstructed by merging the main document with the data source. Instead, merged documents are usually previewed, printed, and closed without saving. But you can certainly save the merged document if you wish to have a record of it. If a merged document contains errors, you can close it without saving, edit the main document or data source, and conduct the merge again.

Task	Procedure
Specify the main document	■ Choose Mailings→Start Mail Merge→Start Mail Merge; specify the main document type.
Create data source	■ Choose Mailings→Start Mail Merge→Select Recipients; choose the data source option.
Customize data source	■ Choose Mailings→Start Mail Merge→Select Recipients, choose Type a New List, and click Customize Columns.
Sort and filter data source	■ Choose Mailings→Start Mail Merge→Edit Recipient List. ■ Click the drop-down arrow in the column header; choose the sort option or filter item.
Edit data source	■ Choose Mailings→Start Mail Merge→Edit Recipient List, click the data source, and click Edit.
Insert merge codes in main document	■ Position the insertion point where the merge code should appear. ■ Choose Mailings→Write & Insert Fields, and then choose Address Block, Greeting Line, or Insert Merge Field.
Preview results	■ Choose Mailings→Preview Results→Preview Results.
Conduct a merge	■ Choose Mailings→Finish→Finish & Merge; choose the result.

DEVELOP YOUR SKILLS WD07-D05

Conduct a Merge

In this exercise, you will use the Preview Results commands to review your letters. Then you will complete the merge on the screen.

1. Follow these steps to preview the merge:

Ⓐ Click **Preview Results** to display the first inside address.

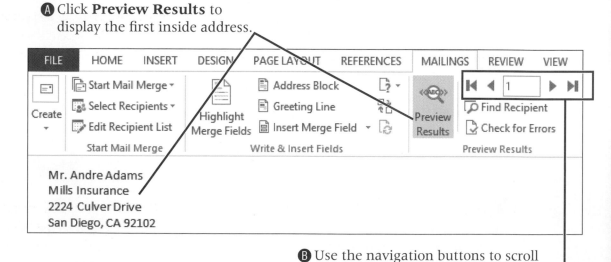

Ⓑ Use the navigation buttons to scroll through all of your merged documents.

2. Choose **Mailings→Finish→Finish & Merge** 📑 →**Edit Individual Documents** to merge the letters on the screen.

3. Click **OK** to merge all records.

4. Scroll through the letters and scan their contents.

   Notice that there is one letter for each record in the data source.

5. Close the merged document without saving.

6. Choose **Mailings→Preview Results→Preview Results** again to display the main document instead of the preview.

Working with Merge Problems

Video Library | http://labyrinthelab.com/videos | Video Number: WD13-V0707

Several common errors can cause a merge to produce incorrect results. The merged document (or preview) will usually provide clues as to why a merge fails to produce the intended results. Once you identify an error in the merged document, such as leaving out a comma or space before or after a merge field, you can make changes to the main document. You can also edit the data source. You can then conduct the merge again to determine if the error was fixed. Repeat this process until the merge works as intended.

Solving Common Merge Problems

Several problems are common in merges. These problems and their solutions are described in the following Quick Reference table.

COMMON MERGE PROBLEMS	
Problem	**Solution**
The same error appears in *every* merge letter.	The problem is in the main document. Correct the error and perform the merge again.
Some letters are missing data.	Some records in the data source are missing data. Add data and perform the merge again.
Some letters have incorrect data.	Some records in the data source are incorrect. Correct the errors, and perform the merge again.

DEVELOP YOUR SKILLS WD07-D06

Fix Merge Problems

In this exercise, you will examine your document for merge problems. This exercise does not address all possible merge problems; it does, however, address one specific error that you will make intentionally. You will insert a colon after the Greeting Line code.

1. Position the insertion point after **<<GreetingLine>>** and type a colon.

2. Choose **Mailings→Finish→Finish & Merge→Edit Individual Documents**.

3. Click **OK** to merge all records.

4. Browse through the merged document and notice that there are two colons following the greeting line in *every* letter.

   Because the error occurs in every letter, you know the error is in the main document.

5. Locate any other errors and notice how often the errors occur (in every merged letter or just one).

   Next you will correct the double colon error and any other errors you discovered that occurred in all letters.

6. Close the merged document without saving; then, edit and save the main document.

7. Follow these guidelines if you find a data error in *just one letter*.
   - Choose **Mailings→Start Mail Merge→Edit Recipient List** .
   - In the Mail Merge Recipients dialog box, highlight the **Data Source** in the bottom-left corner, and click **Edit**.
   - Fix any errors and click **OK**; click **Yes** to update the data.
   - Click **OK** to close the dialog box.

8. When you have corrected any errors, execute the merge again.

9. Close the merged document without saving it.

10. Save and close the sales letter main document.

Merging Envelopes and Labels

Video Library   http://labyrinthelab.com/videos   Video Number: WD13-V0708

When you begin a mail merge, Word presents you with options for the type of main document you can create. In addition to form letters, you can choose envelopes, labels, and other types of documents. You can use the same data source for various main documents. For example, you can use the same data source for envelopes and mailing labels that you used for the form letter.

Generating Envelopes with Mail Merge

Mail Merge lets you choose the envelope size and formats. The standard business (Size 10) envelope is the default. Check your printer manual for instructions on loading envelopes.

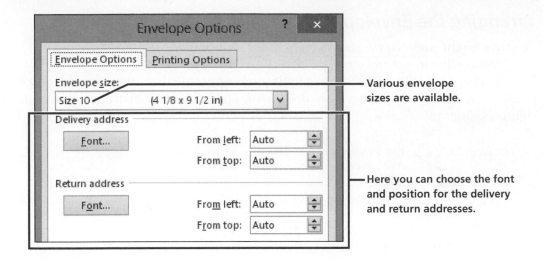

Various envelope sizes are available.

Here you can choose the font and position for the delivery and return addresses.

Choose an Envelope Size and Attach a Data Source

In this exercise, you will choose an envelope as the main document and connect the sales letter data file to the envelope.

1. Start a new blank document.

2. Choose **Mailings→Start Mail Merge→Start Mail Merge** →**Envelopes**.

3. In the Envelope Options dialog box, if necessary, choose **Size 10** as the Envelope Size and click **OK**.

   Now you will attach the data source that you used for your letter.

4. Choose **Mailings→Start Mail Merge→Select Recipients** →**Use an Existing List**.

5. In the Select Data Source dialog box, navigate to your **WD2013 Lesson 07** folder and open **WD07-D02-SalesLtrData-[FirstInitialLastName]**.

Arranging the Envelope

Video Library   http://labyrinthelab.com/videos   Video Number: WD13-V0709

You can insert an Address Block code in the envelope main document. You save an envelope main document like any other main document. The following illustration shows an envelope main document.

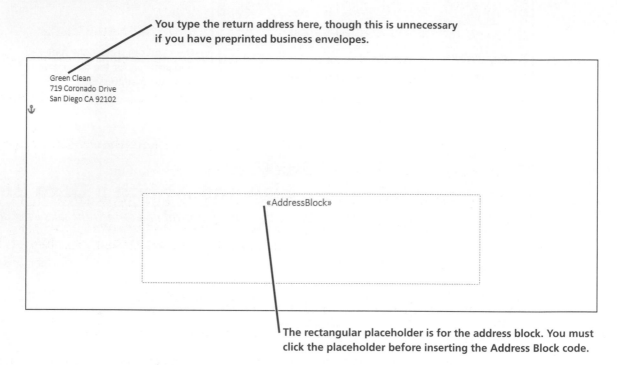

You type the return address here, though this is unnecessary if you have preprinted business envelopes.

Green Clean
719 Coronado Drive
San Diego CA 92102

«AddressBlock»

The rectangular placeholder is for the address block. You must click the placeholder before inserting the Address Block code.

DEVELOP·YOUR SKILLS WD07-D08
Merge to Envelopes

In this exercise, you will place the return address and the address block code on the envelope. You will also merge the envelope main document with the data source.

1. If necessary, choose **Home→Paragraph→Show/Hide** ¶ to turn on formatting marks.

2. Type the following return address starting at the first paragraph symbol in the upper-left corner of the envelope.

   Green Clean
   719 Coronado Drive
   San Diego CA 92102

3. Position the insertion point next to the paragraph symbol toward the center of the envelope.

4. Choose **Mailings→Write & Insert Fields→Address Block** 📄 .

5. Click **OK** to accept the default address block settings.

   Word will merge the address information from the data source into this location when you perform the merge. First, you will preview the merge.

6. Choose **Mailings→Preview Results→Preview Results** 🔍 to display a record from the data source in the envelope.

7. Use the navigation buttons in the Preview Results group to scroll through all of your merged envelopes.

8. Choose **Mailings→Finish→Finish & Merge** 📄 **→Edit Individual Documents** and click **OK** to merge all records.

9. Choose **Home→Paragraph→Show/Hide** ¶ to turn off formatting marks.

10. Scroll through the envelopes, and notice that there is one envelope for each record in the data source.

    You could use the envelopes for mailing the letters created in the previous exercises, because they are generated from the same data source.

11. If necessary, fix any problems with the mail merge and merge the envelopes again.

12. When you finish, close the merged document without saving it.

13. Choose **Mailings→Preview Results→Preview Results** 🔍 to turn off the preview.

14. Save the main document envelope as `WD07-D08-SalesLtrEnv-[FirstInitialLastName]` in your **WD2013 Lesson 07** folder; close the document.

Generating Labels with Mail Merge

Video Library   http://labyrinthelab.com/videos   Video Number: WD13-V0710

You can use Mail Merge to generate mailing labels for each record in a data source. Mail Merge lets you choose the label format, sheet size, and other specifications. It also lets you insert an Address Block code and other codes in the main document. Like other main documents, a labels main document can be saved for future use. The following illustration shows a portion of the labels main document that you will set up.

«AddressBlock»	«Next Record»«AddressBlock»	«Next Record»«AddressBlock»
«Next Record»«AddressBlock»	«Next Record»«AddressBlock»	«Next Record»«AddressBlock»
«Next Record»«AddressBlock»	«Next Record»«AddressBlock»	«Next Record»«AddressBlock»

Using Label Options

The Label Options dialog box allows you to choose printer options and the type of label you will use. You will find a number on the package of labels you purchase that may correspond to the Product Number in the Label Options dialog box. If you buy a brand name not included in the Label Vendors list, you can match your label size with the label size in the Label Information section.

You choose the appropriate printer information in this area. ——

You choose the label vendor here. ——

You choose the label type here. ——

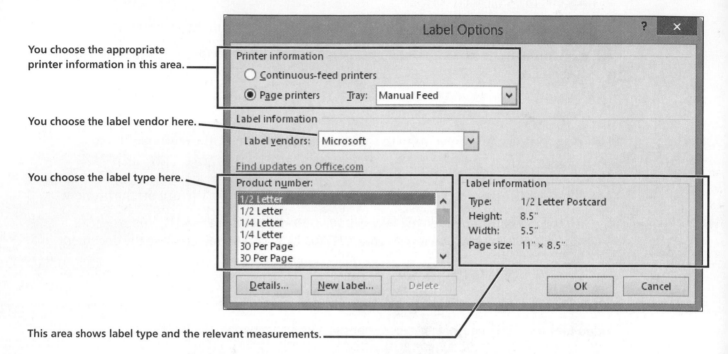

This area shows label type and the relevant measurements. ——

Use Mail Merge to Generate Mailing Labels

In this exercise, you will set up a labels main document and merge it with the data source used in the previous exercises.

1. Start a new blank document.

2. If necessary, choose **Home→Paragraph→Show/Hide ¶** to display formatting marks.

3. Choose **Mailings→Start Mail Merge→Start Mail Merge ▤ →Labels**.

4. Follow these steps to choose a printer option and a label:

Ⓐ Choose **Default Tray**.　　　　　　　Ⓑ Choose **Avery US Letter**.

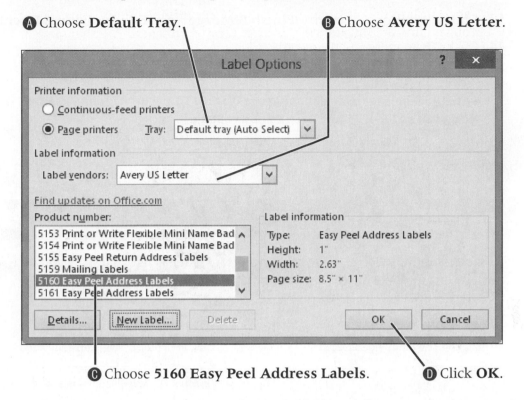

Ⓒ Choose **5160 Easy Peel Address Labels**.　　　Ⓓ Click **OK**.

The labels main document appears in the Word window. Labels are contained in a Word table, but don't worry, you don't have to be a table expert to create labels.

Connect the Data Source

5. Choose **Mailings→Start Mail Merge→Select Recipients** ▦ **→Use an Existing List**.

6. In the Select Data Source dialog box, navigate to your **WD2013 Lesson 07** folder and open **WD07-D02-SalesLtrData-[FirstInitialLastName]**.

7. Make sure the insertion point is next to the paragraph symbol in the first address label.
Notice that the space for the first label is blank and all the rest have a Next Record code in them. Now you will add the Address Block code.

8. Choose **Mailings→Write & Insert Fields→Address Block** 📄 and click **OK**.

9. Choose **Mailings→Write & Insert Fields→Update Labels** 🔁 to place the Address Block code in all labels.
Your addresses will fit the labels better if you remove Word's additional spacing.

10. Select the table.

11. Choose **Page Layout→Paragraph**, type **0** in the **Before Spacing** field, and tap [Enter].

12. Choose **Mailings→Preview Results→Preview Results** 🔍 to see how the labels will look when you print them. Turn off Preview Results when you are finished.

Conduct the Merge

13. Choose **Mailings→Finish→Finish & Merge** ▣→**Edit Individual Documents**.

14. Click **OK** to merge all the records.

15. Close your merged document without saving it.

16. Save the labels main document in the **WD2013 Lesson 07** folder as `WD07-D09-MergeLabels-[FirstInitialLastName]`.

17. Close the document, then exit from **Word**.

Concepts Review

To check your knowledge of the key concepts introduced in this lesson, complete the Concepts Review quiz by choosing the appropriate access option below.

If you are...	Then access the quiz by...
Using the Labyrinth Video Library	Going to http://labyrinthelab.com/videos
Using eLab	Logging in, choosing Content, and navigating to the Concepts Review quiz for this lesson
Not using the Labyrinth Video Library or eLab	Going to the student resource center for this book

Reinforce Your Skills

Create a Data Source and Main Document

In this exercise, you will create a data source and main document for a Kids for Change mailing. The kids are holding a fundraiser for a micro-lending project that focuses on poor people in India. They will conduct a mailing to announce the upcoming project and canvass their neighborhoods for donations.

Work with a Data Source

1. Start **Word**. Open **WD07-R01-Fundraiser** from your **WD2013 Lesson 07** folder and save it as `WD07-R01-FundRaiser-[FirstInitialLastName]`.

2. Choose **Mailings→Start Mail Merge→Start Mail Merge→Letters** to identify the fund raising letter as the main document.

3. Choose **Mailings→Start Mail Merge→Select Recipients** ▦ **→Type a New List**.
    Now you will customize the list of fields.

4. Click **Customize Columns**.

5. Click **Address Line 2** and click **Delete**.

6. Click **Yes** to confirm the deletion.

7. Also delete the following fields:
    - Country or Region
    - Home Phone
    - Work Phone
    - E-mail Address

    Now you will rename a field.

8. Click **Address Line 1** and click **Rename**.

9. Delete everything except *Address* and click **OK**.

Now you will add two fields.

10. Click **Zip Code** and click **Add**.

11. Type **Member Last Name** in the Add Field dialog box and click **OK**.

12. Also add a field called **Member First Name**.

    Next you will move a field.

13. Click **Member Last Name**, click **Move Down** once, and click **OK** to position Member First Name above Member Last Name.

14. Make sure the insertion point is in the **Title** field, type **Ms.**, and tap Tab.

15. Type **Loretta** in the First Name field and tap Tab.

16. Continue typing and tabbing to complete the first record shown here. Be sure to include the member first name, Eric, and last name, Speck, in the first record.

Ms. Loretta Morales Morales Super Market 311 Ocean Street Miami FL 33130	Mr. Tony D'Agusto Tony's Trattoria 675 Miller Ave. Miami FL 33129	Mr. Allan Morgan 951 4th Street Miami FL 33136	Ms. Margarita Elizondo Elan Fashions 307 Dolphin Way Miami FL 33136
Member: Eric Speck	**Member:** Wendy Chang	**Member:** Stella Hopkins	**Member:** Diego Cantero

17. Tap Tab to begin a new record.

18. Continue typing and tabbing to enter the next three records shown in step 16.

19. Be sure to skip the **Company** field for the third record.

20. Review your records for accuracy; click **OK** when you are satisfied with your work.

21. Save the data source in your **WD2013 Lesson 07** folder as **WD07-R01-FundraiserData-[FirstInitialLastName]**.

    Your fundraiser letter should be on the screen.

Set Up the Main Document

22. If necessary, choose **Home→Paragraph→Show/Hide** ¶ to display formatting marks.

23. In the fundraiser letter, select **[Inside Address]** but not the paragraph symbol at the end of the line and tap Delete.

24. Choose **Mailings→Write & Insert Fields→Address Block** 📄, and then click **OK** to accept the default address block settings.

25. Delete **[Name]** in the greeting line, but not the paragraph symbol at the end of the line.

26. Choose **Mailings→Write & Insert Fields→Greeting Line** 📄.

27. Choose **Joshua** and colon in the Greeting Line Format area as shown and click **OK**.

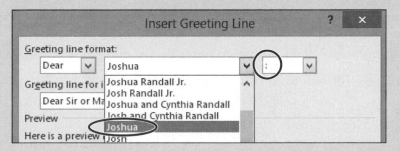

28. In the last sentence of the first paragraph, delete **[Member Name]**.

29. Choose **Mailings→Write & Insert Fields→Insert Merge Field** 🖹 **menu button ▼→Member_First_Name**.

30. Tap Spacebar and insert the Member_Last_Name field, then close the dialog box.

31. Save and close the letter; exit from **Word**.

32. Submit your final files based on the guidelines provided by your instructor.

To view examples of how your file or files should look at the end of this exercise, go to the student resource center.

REINFORCE YOUR SKILLS WD07-R02

Merge a Letter, Envelopes, and Labels

In this exercise, you will merge a data source with a letter and work with a merge problem. You will also merge the data source with envelopes and labels.

Conduct a Merge and Preview Results

1. Start **Word**. Open **WD07-R02-ParentLtr** from your **WD2013 Lesson 07** folder and save it as `WD07-R02-ParentLtr-[FirstInitialLastName]`.

2. Choose **Mailings→Start Mail Merge→Start Mail Merge→Letters**.

3. Choose **Mailings→Start Mail Merge→Select Recipients** 🖼️ **→Use an Existing List**.

4. Navigate to your **WD2013 Lesson 07** folder and open **WD07-R02-ParentData**.

5. Choose **Mailings→Preview Results→Preview Results** 🔍 to preview the first record.

Notice that the greeting line is incorrect.

6. Preview all three records, and notice that the greeting line is incorrect in all.

This indicates that the error is in the main document.

7. Choose **Mailings→Preview Results→Preview Results** 🔍 to turn off the preview.

Fix Merge Problems and Complete the Merge

8. In the greeting line, delete *Dear* and the space that follows it; then delete the colon at the end of the greeting line.

   Dear and the punctuation at the end of the greeting line are included in the Greeting Line code.

9. Choose **Mailings→Preview Results→Preview Results** 🔍.

   Notice that the greeting line is now correctly formatted.

   Notice the child's name (Aiden, in the first record) has no spaces around it.

10. Choose **Mailings→Preview Results→Preview Results** 🔍 to return to the main document, and then insert a space before and after the **Child Name** code.

11. Preview the letter again and notice that the **Child Name** variable is correctly spaced.

12. Make sure the spacing between the address block and the greeting line and between the greeting line and the first paragraph are correct.

13. Turn off **Preview Results** 🔍, and make any changes necessary.

14. Choose **Mailings→Finish→Finish & Merge** 📄→**Edit Individual Documents**, and then click **OK** to merge all records.

15. Scroll through the merged letters; close the file without saving it.

16. Save and close the parent letter main document.

Generate an Envelope

17. Start a new blank document.

18. Choose **Mailings→Start Mail Merge→Start Mail Merge** 📄→**Envelopes**.

19. Click **OK** to accept the envelope options defaults.

20. Choose **Mailings→Start Mail Merge→Select Recipients** 📇→**Use an Existing List**.

21. Navigate to your **WD2013 Lesson 07** folder and open **WD07-R02-ParentData** to attach the data source to the envelope.

22. If necessary, choose **Home→Paragraph→Show/Hide** ¶ to display formatting marks.

23. Type the following return address at the first paragraph symbol in the upper-left corner of the envelope.

    ```
    Kids for Change
    726 Throckmorton Ave.
    Sacramento CA 95612
    ```

24. Click the insertion point next to the paragraph symbol toward the center of the envelope.

25. Choose **Mailings→Write & Insert Fields→Address Block** 📄.

26. Click **OK** to accept the address block default formats.

27. Choose **Mailings→Preview Results→Preview Results** 🔍.

28. Navigate through all three records to ensure they appear correctly on the envelope.

29. Turn off **Preview Results** 🔍 .

30. Save the envelope as `WD07-R02-ParentEnv-[FirstInitialLastName]` in your **WD2013 Lesson 07** folder; close the envelope file.

Generate Mailing Labels

31. Start a new blank document.

32. Choose **Mailings→Start Mail Merge→Start Mail Merge→** 📄**Labels**.

33. Choose **Avery US Letter** as the Label Vendor, choose **5160 Easy Peel Address Labels** as the Product Number, and click **OK**.

34. If necessary, choose **Home→Paragraph→Show/Hide** ¶ to display formatting marks.

35. Choose **Mailings→Start Mail Merge→Select Recipients** 📇**→Use an Existing List**.

36. Navigate to your **WD2013 Lesson 07** folder and open **WD07-R02-ParentData**.

37. Make sure the insertion point is next to the paragraph symbol in the first label.

38. Choose **Mailings→Write & Insert Fields→Address Block** 📄 .

39. Click **OK** to accept the address block defaults.

40. Choose **Mailings→Write & Insert Fields→Update Labels** 📄 to insert the Address Block code on all labels.

41. Choose **Mailings→Preview Results→Preview Results** 🔍 to verify that the labels will print correctly.

    Because these addresses are three-line addresses, they fit on the Avery 5160 labels without removing Word's extra spacing.

42. Turn off **Preview Results** 🔍 to return to the labels main document.

43. Save the labels file as `WD07-R02-ParentLabels-[FirstInitialLastName]` in your **WD2013 Lesson 07** folder. Close the file and exit from **Word**.

44. Submit your final files based on the guidelines provided by your instructor.

    To view examples of how your file or files should look at the end of this exercise, go to the student resource center.

REINFORCE YOUR SKILLS WD07-R03

Merge a Letter, Envelopes, and Labels

In this exercise, you will create a data source and a main document. Then you will preview the results and correct any merge problems before conducting the merge. Finally, you will generate envelopes and mailing labels.

Create a Data Source

1. Start **Word**. Open **WD07-R03-Walkers** from your **WD2013 Lesson 07** folder and save it as `WD07-R03-Walkers-[FirstInitialLastName]`.

2. Choose **Mailings→Start Mail Merge→Start Mail Merge** 📄**→Letters** to designate the Walkers letter as the main document.

3. Choose **Mailings→Start Mail Merge→Select Recipients** 🖼→**Type a New List**.
   Now you will customize the data source columns.

4. Click **Customize Columns** to display the Customize Address List dialog box.

5. Click **Company Name** and click **Delete**; click **Yes** to confirm the deletion.

6. Delete the following fields:
   - Address Line 2
   - Country or Region
   - Work Phone
   - E-mail Address

7. Click **Address Line 1** and click **Rename**.

8. Delete everything except the word *Address* and click **OK** twice.

9. Ensure the insertion point is in the **Title** field, type **Mr.**, and tap ⌨Tab to move to the next field.

10. Type **Sean** in the **First Name** field, tap ⌨Tab, and type **Corn** in the **Last Name** field.

11. Continue tabbing and typing to complete the Sean Corn record as shown.

Mr. Sean Corn 308 Alhambra Avenue Monterey CA 93940 831-555-1234	Mr. Craig Dostie 31200 Erwin Street Monterey CA 93940 831-555-4567	Ms. Alexia Lopez 2134 Harbor Blvd. Monterey CA 93942 831-555-9632
Ms. Margaret Wong 1308 West Ramona Blvd. Monterey CA 93940 831-555-1598	Ms. Phyllis Coen 4745 Buffin Avenue Monterey CA 93943 831-555-3578	Mr. Winston Boey 263 East Howard Street Monterey CA 93944 831-555-7896

12. Either tap ⌨Tab or click **New Entry** to begin the next record, and finish entering the remaining records in the table.

13. Review your records for accuracy.
    Now you will sort your list by Last Name.

14. Click the **Last Name** column header to sort the list alphabetically in ascending order.

15. Click **OK**; then, navigate to your **WD2013 Lesson 07** and save the file as **WD07-R03-WalkerData-[FirstInitialLastName]**.

Title ▼	First Name ▼	Last Name ▼
Mr.	Winston	Boey
Ms	Phyllis	Coen
Mr.	Sean	Corn
Mr.	Craig	Dostie
Ms.	Alexia	Lopez
Ms.	Margaret	Wong

Set Up the Main Document

16. Replace *INSIDE ADDRESS* with the **Address Block** code using the default formats.

17. Replace *GREETING LINE* with the **Greeting Line** code, changing the Greeting Line Format name to **Joshua**.

18. In the last paragraph, replace *HOME PHONE* with the **Home Phone** code.

Conduct the Merge and Preview Results

19. Preview your letters and correct any errors in the main document, paying particular attention to spacing.

- There should be a blank line between the inside address and the greeting line, and between the greeting line and the body of the letter.
- There should be a space before the home phone.

Work with Merge Problems

20. Turn off **Preview Results** and make any changes necessary to the main document.
Phyllis Cohen's name is misspelled. You will make that correction now.

21. Choose **Mailings→Start Mail Merge→Edit Recipient List**.

22. Click the data source in the bottom-left corner and click **Edit**.

23. Change the spelling from *Coen* to **Cohen**.

24. Click **OK**; click **Yes** to verify the update and then click **OK** again.

25. Preview the results again to verify the change to the data source and any changes you made to the main document, and then turn off the preview.

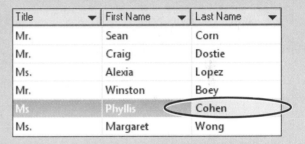

Title	First Name	Last Name
Mr.	Sean	Corn
Mr.	Craig	Dostie
Ms.	Alexia	Lopez
Mr.	Winston	Boey
Ms	Phyllis	Cohen
Ms.	Margaret	Wong

26. Choose **Mailings→Finish→Finish & Merge →Edit Individual Documents**, and then click **OK** to merge all records.

27. Scroll through your letters, and then close the merged document without saving it.

28. Save and close the main document letter.

Merge Envelopes

29. Start a new blank document.

30. Choose **Mailings→Start Mail Merge→Start Mail Merge →Envelopes**.

31. Make sure the envelope is **Size 10** and click **OK**.
Now you will attach the data source to your envelope.

32. Choose **Mailings→Start Mail Merge→Select Recipients →Use an Existing List**.

33. Navigate to your file storage location and open **WD07-R03-WalkerData-[FirstInitialLastName]**.

34. If necessary choose **Home→Paragraph→Show/Hide** to turn on formatting marks.

35. Type the following return address at the top paragraph symbol in the upper-left corner of the envelope:

```
Kids for Change
456 Bayside Road
Monterey CA 93943
```

36. Position the insertion point next to the paragraph symbol toward the middle of the envelope.

37. Choose **Mailings→Write & Insert Fields→Address Block** 📄, and then click **OK** to accept the default settings.

38. Choose **Mailings→Preview Results→Preview Results** 🔍. Use the navigation buttons to view all envelopes then turn off the preview.

39. Choose **Mailings→Finish→Finish & Merge** 📄→**Edit Individual Documents**, and then click **OK** to merge all records.

40. Scroll through the envelopes then close the file without saving it.

41. Save the envelope main document as `WD07-R03-WalkersEnv-[FirstInitialLastName]` in your **WD2013 Lesson 07** folder; close the document.

    Now you will merge the labels.

Generate Labels with Mail Merge

42. Start a new blank document.

43. Choose **Mailings→Start Mail Merge→Start Mail Merge**→📄 **Labels**.

44. Choose **Avery US Letter** as the Label Vendor and **5160 Easy Peel Address Labels** as the Product Number; click **OK**.

45. Choose **Mailings→Start Mail Merge→Select Recipients** 📇→**Use an Existing List**.

46. Navigate to your **WD2013 Lesson 07** folder and open **WD07-R03-WalkerData-[FirstInitialLastName]**.

47. Ensure the insertion point is in the first label.

48. Choose **Mailings→Write & Insert Fields→Address Block** 📄 and click **OK**.

49. Choose **Mailings→Write & Insert Fields→Update Labels** 🔄 to insert the Address Block code on all labels.

50. Choose **Mailings→Preview Results→Preview Results** 🔍 to see how the labels will look when they print, and then turn off the preview.

    Because the addresses are all three-line addresses, they fit on the label without removing Word's extra spacing.

51. Choose **Mailings→Finish→Finish & Merge** 📄→**Edit Individual Documents**.

52. Click **OK** to merge all records, and then close the merged document without saving it.

53. Save the labels main document in your **WD2013 Lesson 07** folder as `WD07-R03-WalkerLabels-[FirstInitialLastName]`. Close the document and exit from **Word**.

54. Submit your final files based on the guidelines provided by your instructor.

Apply Your Skills

Create a Data Source and Main Document

In this exercise, you will create a data source, and then you will review the records and sort the list. Then you will specify a letter as a main document and insert merge fields in the letter.

Work with a Data Source

1. Start **Word**. Open **WD07-A01-SmallBiz** from your **WD2013 Lesson 07** folder and save it as WD07-A01-SmallBiz-[FirstInitialLastName].

2. Specify the **SmallBiz letter** as the main document.

   Next you will customize the columns for your new data source.

3. Delete, add, and rename columns as needed to create the following fields in your data source:
   - Title
   - First Name
   - Last Name
   - Company Name
   - Address
   - City
   - State
   - Zip Code
   - Agent Name

4. Add the following records to your data source:

Mr. Tony Simpson	Mr. Jason Jones	Ms. Debbie Thomas
Bigger Time Video Distributors	Move It Distribution	Barker Books
312 York Lane	2233 Crystal Street	497 Tennessee Street
Richmond CA 94804	San Mateo CA 94403	Richmond CA 94804
Agent Name: David Roth	**Agent Name:** Tammy Nelson	**Agent Name:** Jacob Williams

5. Sort the data source in ascending alphabetic order by **Company Name**.

6. Save the data source as WD07-A01-SmallBizData-[FirstInitialLastName] in your **WD2013 Lesson 07** folder.

Work with the Main Document

7. In the main document, replace *INSIDE ADDRESS* with the **Address Block** code using the default formats.

8. Replace *GREETING LINE* with the **Greeting Line** code and change the ending punctuation to a colon.

9. In the last paragraph, replace *AGENT NAME* with the **Agent Name** code.

10. Preview the letters and check to be sure the spacing is correct.

11. Turn off the preview, and then make any needed changes to the main document.

12. Save and close the document; exit from **Word**.

13. Submit your final files based on the guidelines provided by your instructor.

    To view examples of how your file or files should look at the end of this exercise, go to the student resource center.

APPLY YOUR SKILLS WD07-A02

Merge Documents and Work with Merge Problems

In this exercise, you will merge letters, envelopes, and labels. You will also correct merge problems.

Conduct a Merge and Work with Merge Problems

1. Start **Word**. Open **WD07-A02-VisaLtr** from your **WD2013 Lesson 07** folder and save it as **WD07-A02-VisaLtr-[FirstInitialLastName]**.

2. Designate the letter as the main document.

3. Specify **WD07-A02-VisaData** in your **WD2013 Lesson 07** folder as the data source for this letter.

4. Preview the merge and notice that there are two errors in the greeting line.

5. Close the preview; edit the main document and preview the letters again, checking that the greeting line is correct.

6. Close the preview; save and close the main document.

Merge Envelopes and Labels

7. Start a new blank document and create a **Size 10** envelope as a main document with the following return address:

   Suzanne Frost
   Sales Manager
   Universal Corporate Events
   Middlefield CT 06455

8. Attach **WD07-A02-VisaData** as the data source for the envelope.

9. Insert an address block, using the default formats, in the middle of the envelope.

10. Preview the envelopes then close the preview.

11. Save the envelope main document as **WD07-A02-VisaEnv-[FirstInitialLastName]** in your **WD2013 Lesson 07** folder. Close the document.

12. Start a new blank document and create a labels main document using **Avery US Letter** as the Label Vendor and **5160 Easy Peel Address Labels** as the Product Number.

13. Attach **WD07-A02-VisaData** as the data source.

14. Insert the **Address Block** code in the first label using the default formats.

15. Use the **Update Labels** 🔁 command to replicate the Address Block code on all labels.

16. Preview the results and notice that the addresses don't fit well on the labels.

17. Close the preview, select the labels table, and remove Word's extra spacing in the Paragraph group on the Page Layout tab. Enter 0 in the Before field.

18. Preview the results again to ensure that the labels fit correctly.

19. Close the preview, and save the labels main document as **WD07-A02-VisaLabels-[FirstInitialLastName]** in your **WD2013 Lesson 07** folder.

20. Close the labels main document; exit from **Word**.

21. Submit your final files based on the guidelines provided by your instructor.

    To view examples of how your file or files should look at the end of this exercise, go to the student resource center.

APPLY YOUR SKILLS WD07-A03

Merge a Data Source and Main Documents, and Work with Merge Problems

In this exercise, you will create a data source using customized columns. You will add merge codes to main documents. You will preview and merge the main documents with the data source, make an editing change to a record, and sort the data source.

Work with a Data Source and Main Document

1. Start **Word**. Open **WD07-A03-TokyoLtr** from your **WD2013 Lesson 07** folder and save it as **WD07-A03-TokyoLtr-[FirstInitialLastName]**.

2. Specify the letter as the main document.

3. Start a new data source list.

4. Customize the columns by deleting and renaming fields. The final columns should be those shown here.
   - Title
   - First Name
   - Last Name
   - Company Name
   - Address
   - City
   - State
   - Zip Code

5. Create the data source shown here and save it as `WD07-A03-TokyoData-[FirstInitialLastName]` in your **WD2013 Lesson 07** folder.

Ms. Jasleen Mahal	Mr. George Iverson	Mr. Anthony Waldek
Superior Storage Devices	Superior Storage Devices	Superior Storage Devices
951 Industrial Way	951 Industrial Way	951 Industrial Way
Trenton NJ 08601	Trenton NJ 08601	Trenton NJ 08601

6. In the main document, replace *INSIDE ADDRESS* with the **Address Block** code using the default formats.

7. Replace *GREETING LINE* with the **Greeting Line** code using the default formats.

8. In the first paragraph, replace *COMPANY NAME* with the **Company Name** code.

9. In the last paragraph, replace *FIRST NAME* with the **First Name** code.

Preview the Results and Fix Merge Problems

10. Preview the merge and make sure the spacing is correct; close the preview.

11. Modify spacing in the main document if necessary.
    You've realized that the greeting line should be less formal, so you want to change the format to the recipient's first name.

12. Right-click the **Greeting Line** code, and choose **Edit Greeting Line** from the menu.

13. In the Greeting Line Format, click the drop-down arrow next to Mr. Randall, choose **Joshua** from the list, and click **OK**.

14. Preview the letters again to ensure the change was made.

15. Edit the recipient list, and change *Waldek* to **Waldecker**.

16. Sort the list in ascending alphabetic order by the **Last Name** column.

17. Merge the letter with the data source, choosing **Edit Individual Letters**, and then scroll through the letters.

18. Close the merged document without saving it; save and close the main document.

Merge Envelopes and Labels

19. Start a new blank document, designate it as a mail merge envelope, and use a **Size 10** envelope.

20. Insert the following return address on the envelope:

    ```
    Ms. Tasha Reynolds
    Universal Corporate Events
    456 Riverview Road
    Trenton NJ 08601
    ```

21. Attach the Tokyo data source to the envelope and insert the **Address Block** code.

22. Merge the envelopes and check them for accuracy.

23. If necessary, correct any errors and conduct the merge again.

24. Close the merged document without saving it; make any necessary changes.

25. Save the envelope main document as `WD07-A03-TokyoEnv-[FirstInitialLastName]` in your **WD2013 Lesson 07** folder. Close the document.

26. Start a new blank document and designate it as mail merge labels.

27. Choose **Avery US Letter** as the Label Vendor and **5160** as the Product Number.

28. Attach the Tokyo data source, insert the **Address Block** code in the first label, and update the labels to replicate the Address Block code in all.

29. Preview the labels and notice that the addresses don't fit well due to Word's extra spacing.

30. Close the preview, select the labels table, and remove the extra spacing.

31. Preview the labels again to verify the change in spacing; close the preview.

32. Save the labels main document as `WD07-A03-TokyoLabels-[FirstInitialLastName]` in your **WD2013 Lesson 07** folder. Close the document and exit from **Word**.

33. Submit your final files based on the guidelines provided by your instructor.

Extend Your Skills

In the course of working through the Extend Your Skills exercises, you will think critically as you use the skills taught in the lesson to complete the assigned projects. To evaluate your mastery and completion of the exercises, your instructor may use a rubric, with which more points are allotted according to performance characteristics. (The more you do, the more you earn!) Ask your instructor how your work will be evaluated.

WD07-E01 That's the Way I See It

You are planning a field trip for the fifth-grade class you teach. Create a two- to three-page permission letter informing parents of the trip and how it relates to students' school work (e.g., going to an aquarium after studying about ocean life). Ask parents to sign and then return the letter. Save the letter in your **WD2013 Lesson 07** folder as **WD07-E01-ParentLtr-[FirstInitialLastName]**.

Create a three-record data source of parent names and addresses and any other variables you choose. Customize the data source with only the column headings you need in the letter. Save the data source as **WD07-E01-ParentData-[FirstInitialLastName]**. Insert the merge field codes in the form letter and merge the main document and data source. Save the merged document as **WD07-E01-ParentLtrMerge-[FirstInitialLastName]**. Create an envelope main document with your return address, saved as **WD07-E01-ParentEnv-[FirstInitialLastName]**. Merge it with the data source. Save the merged document as **WD07-E01-ParentEnvMerge-[FirstInitialLastName]**.

You will be evaluated based on the inclusion of all elements specified, your ability to follow directions, your ability to apply newly learned skills to a real-world situation, your creativity, and the relevance of your topic and/or data choice(s). Submit your final files based on the guidelines provided by your instructor.

WD07-E02 Be Your Own Boss

You have created a rewards program for Blue Jean Landscaping customers. Create a form letter of two to three paragraphs describing how customers can accumulate points toward purchases. Mention three other benefits (make them up) for program members. Save the letter in your **WD2013 Lesson 07** folder as **WD07-E02-RewardsLtr-[FirstInitialLastName]**.

Create a data source of three customer's names and addresses and any other needed fields. Customize the data source for only those columns needed for the letter. Save the file as **WD07-E02-RewardsData-[FirstInitialLastName]**. Insert the merge field codes in the letter and conduct the merge, saving the merged document as **WD07-E02-RewardsMerge-[FirstInitialLastName]**.

You will include a brochure in the mailing, so use mailing labels for the oversized envelopes. Create a labels document named **WD07-E02-RewardsLabels-[FirstInitialLastName]** and merge it with your data source. Save the merged labels as **WD07-E02-MergeLabels-[FirstInitialLastName]**.

You will be evaluated based on the inclusion of all elements specified, your ability to follow directions, your ability to apply newly learned skills to a real-world situation, your creativity, and your demonstration of an entrepreneurial spirit. Submit your final files based on the guidelines provided by your instructor.

Transfer Your Skills

In the course of working through the Transfer Your Skills exercises, you will use critical-thinking and creativity skills to complete the assigned projects using skills taught in the lesson. To evaluate your mastery and completion of the exercises, your instructor may use a rubric, with which more points are allotted according to performance characteristics. (The more you do, the more you earn!) Ask your instructor how your work will be evaluated.

WD07-T01 Use the Web as a Learning Tool

Throughout this book, you will be provided with an opportunity to use the Internet as a learning tool by completing WebQuests. According to the original creators of WebQuests, as described on their website (WebQuest.org), a WebQuest is "an inquiry-oriented activity in which most or all of the information used by learners is drawn from the web." To complete the WebQuest projects in this book, navigate to the student resource center and choose the WebQuest for the lesson on which you are currently working. The subject of each WebQuest will be relevant to the material found in the lesson.

WebQuest Subject: How mail merge is used in business.

Submit your final file(s) based on the guidelines provided by your instructor.

WD07-T02 Demonstrate Proficiency

Stormy BBQ has added brisket of beef to its menu! They offered a free brisket of beef meal and a $20 gift certificate to the first five customers who visited their restaurant on New Year's Day. They plan to mail the certificates to the qualifying customers. As a Stormy BBQ employee, you have been asked to compose a congratulatory letter to go with the certificates. Since the letter will go to five people, it makes sense to use Word's Mail Merge feature.

Compose an appropriate letter with two or three paragraphs and save it as **WD07-T02-CertLtr-[FirstInitialLastName]** in your **WD2013 Lesson 07** folder. Create a name and address data source for the five winners. Customize the data source by adding any fields you want to use in your letter; delete any fields you don't intend to use. Save the data source as **WD07-T02-CertData-[FirstInitialLastName]**. Merge the letter and the data source and save the merged document as **WD07-T02-CertLtrMerge-[FirstInitialLastName]**.

Create an envelope main document to go with the mailing and include Stormy BBQ's return address and the Address Block code on a Size 10 envelope. Save the envelope main document as **WD07-T02-CertEnv-[FirstInitialLastName]**. Preview the envelopes and verify that they will print correctly.

Submit your final files based on the guidelines provided by your instructor.

EXCEL 2013

Exploring Excel 2013

LEARNING OBJECTIVES

After studying this lesson, you will be able to:

- Explain how Excel can help your productivity
- Navigate the Excel window and issue commands
- Enter text and numbers in cells
- Distinguish between a text and a number entry in a cell
- Save, "save as," and close workbooks

In this lesson, you will develop fundamental Excel skills. This lesson will provide you with a solid understanding of Excel so you are prepared to master advanced features later. You will learn how to navigate around a worksheet, enter various types of data, select cells, and save your work.

In selected area, tab & enter to move ⟷ & ↕

Building a Basic Worksheet

Welcome to Green Clean, a janitorial product supplier and cleaning service contractor to small businesses, shopping plazas, and office buildings. Green Clean uses environmentally friendly cleaning products and incorporates sustainability practices wherever possible, including efficient energy and water use, recycling and waste reduction, and reduced petroleum use in vehicles. In addition to providing green cleaning services, the company also sells its eco-friendly products directly to customers.

You need to create a list of hours that cleaning service employees worked during the weekend (Friday through Sunday). Your manager has asked you to compile the data from employee time sheets and report hours on a daily basis. Your worksheet is shown in the following illustration.

	A	B	C	D	E
1	Service Employees Weekend Hours Worked				
2					
3	Alton Mall		Friday	Saturday	Sunday
4		Barnes	6	6	6
5		Chau	8	8	8
6		Lee	4	0	4
7		Olsen	4	3	0
8		Total Hrs			
9	Century Bank				
10		Garcia	3	5	0
11		Kimura	3	4	0
12		Tan	3	5	0
13		Total Hrs			
14	Newport Medical				
15		Kowalski	8	6	8
16		Silva	6	6	0
17		Wilson	5	2	5
18		Total Hrs			

Excel makes it easy for you to organize your data in columns and rows.

Presenting Excel 2013

Video Library   http://labyrinthelab.com/videos   Video Number: EX13-V0101

Microsoft Office Excel is an electronic worksheet program that allows you to work with numbers and data much more efficiently than the pen-and-paper method. Excel is used in virtually all industries and many households for a variety of tasks such as:

- Creating and maintaining detailed budgets
- Performing "what-if" scenarios and break-even analyses
- Producing detailed charts to graphically display information
- Creating invoices or purchase orders
- Working with reports exported from small business accounting software programs such as Intuit's QuickBooks®

As you can see, Excel is a powerful program that is used not only to work with numbers but also to maintain databases. In fact, if you have started a database in Excel, you can even import it into Microsoft Access (the Microsoft Office Suite database program). Many people use Excel to track their databases rather than Access because of its ease of use and because Access is not included in all of the Microsoft Office editions.

Starting Excel

The method you use to start Excel and other Office 2013 applications depends on whether you are using the Windows 7 or Windows 8 operating system.

Windows 7

- Click the Start ⊕ button, choose Microsoft Office 2013 from the All Programs menu, and then choose Excel 2013 or another Office 2013 application.

Windows 8

- Locate the tile labeled Excel 2013 on the Windows Start screen, and then click the tile to start Excel.

Start Excel

In this exercise, you will start your computer and open Microsoft Excel. If you are using Windows 7, follow the steps below the Windows 7 heading. If you are using Windows 8, follow the steps below the Windows 8 heading.

1. If necessary, start your computer.

   The Windows Desktop (Windows 7) or Start screen (Windows 8) appears. Now, follow the steps for your version of Windows.

Windows 7

2. Click the Start button at the left edge of the taskbar and choose **All Programs**.

3. Choose **Microsoft Office 2013**, and then choose **Excel 2013** from the menu.

4. Make sure the Excel window is **maximized**.

5. Click the **Blank Workbook** template to open the Excel window.

Windows 8

6. Locate, and then click the **Excel 2013 tile**.

7. Make sure the Excel window is **maximized**.

   The program loads and the Excel Start screen appears.

8. Click the **Blank Workbook** template to open the Excel window.

Exploring the Excel Program Window

Video Library   http://labyrinthelab.com/videos   Video Number: EX13-V0102

When you start Excel, you will see a blank workbook displayed. The following illustration describes important objects in the Excel program window.

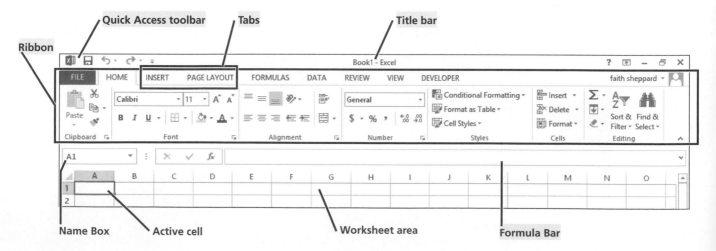

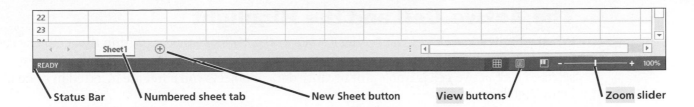

Status Bar   Numbered sheet tab   New Sheet button   View buttons   Zoom slider

Using Worksheets and Workbooks

Video Library   http://labyrinthelab.com/videos   Video Number: EX13-V0103

FROM THE RIBBON
File→New→ Blank Workbook

A workbook is a file containing one or more worksheets. Excel displays a blank workbook with a single worksheet when you start the program. Worksheets are represented by tabs at the bottom of the screen. One tab will be shown for each worksheet within the workbook. New sheets can be added by clicking the New Sheet button. You can enter text, numbers, formulas, charts, and other objects within these worksheets.

FROM THE KEYBOARD
`Ctrl`+`N` to open a new workbook

Excel 2013

| **Annual** | Winter | Spring | Summer | Fall | ⊕ |

Here, worksheet tabs organize annual and seasonal data.

The terms *spreadsheet* and *worksheet* can be used interchangeably.

A worksheet has a grid structure with 1,048,576 horizontal rows and 16,384 vertical columns, though only a small number of rows and columns are visible at one time. The intersection of each row and column is referred to as a cell. A cell reference is composed of a column letter and row number. For example, A1 is the reference for the cell in the top-left corner of the worksheet, at the intersection of column A and row 1.

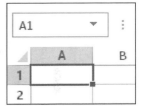

The cell reference A1 is displayed in the Name Box.

Mousing Around in Excel

The shape of the mouse pointer will change as you move it around the Excel window. The pointer shape determines what happens when you click or drag on a cell or object.

Mouse Pointer Shape	**Function**
⊹	Click to select a cell; drag to select multiple cells.
✛	Drag the fill handle (bottom-right corner of a cell) to fill adjacent cells with a series of numbers, dates, etc.
⌖	Click to perform many tasks including issuing a command from the Ribbon or selecting a new tab.
⬈	Drag selected cell contents to another location.
↕ ⟷ ⤡	Drag the resize pointers to change the height and/or width of objects such as pictures, shapes, or charts.
⬇ ⬇	Select a row or column.
I	Click the I-beam pointer to enter text in locations such as the Formula Bar.

The Active Cell and the Highlight

When you click in a cell a thick border known as the *highlight* appears within that cell. The cell containing the highlight is known as the *active cell* and we often refer to that cell as being selected. The active cell is important because data or objects you enter are inserted in or near the active cell.

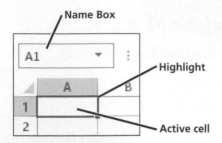

Scrolling Along in a Worksheet

The Excel window contains both vertical and horizontal scroll bars. They allow you to view other areas of the worksheet without changing the active cell. There are three ways to use the scroll bars to view other areas of your worksheet.

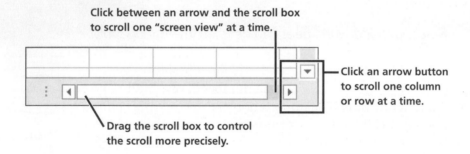

Navigating in a Worksheet

You can change the active cell by clicking in another cell, using the keyboard, or entering a cell reference in the Name Box. The vertical and horizontal scroll bars let you scroll through a worksheet; however, scrolling does not change the active cell. After scrolling, you need to change the active cell before you can enter data into that cell. The following table lists keystrokes that can be used to change the active cell.

You may type a cell reference in the Name Box and then tap ⌈Enter⌉ to navigate to that cell.

Keystroke(s)	How the Active Cell Changes
→ ← ↑ ↓	One cell right, left, up, or down
Home	Beginning (column A) of current row
Ctrl+Home	Home cell, usually cell A1
Ctrl+End	Last cell in active part of worksheet
Page Down	Down one visible screen
Page Up	Up one visible screen
Alt+Page Down	One visible screen right
Alt+Page Up	One visible screen left
Ctrl+G	Displays Go To dialog box; enter cell reference and click OK

Customizing the Ribbon

The Customize Ribbon category in Excel Options allows you to rearrange the tab order, create a new tab, add a new group to an existing tab, add or remove commands, and export all customizations for use on other computers. The built-in tabs cannot be removed, but they may be hidden. An individual tab or all tabs and the Quick Access toolbar may be reset to their original default items.

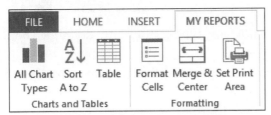

A custom tab named My Reports added to the Ribbon with commands grouped according to the user's preference and workflow.

DEVELOP YOUR SKILLS EX01-D02
Navigate and Explore the Excel Window

In this exercise, you will navigate in a worksheet by scrolling, using the keyboard, and using the Name Box.

1. Slide the mouse pointer and notice the thick **cross shape** ✛ when it is in the worksheet area.

   If you click with this pointer shape, you will change the active cell.

2. Click any cell and notice that the highlight appears around that cell.

   This is now the active cell.

3. Change the active cell five times by clicking in various cells.

   Now you will learn how to use the keyboard to move around a worksheet.

4. Use the →, ←, ↑, and ↓ keys to position the highlight in **cell F10**.

5. Tap ⌷Home⌷ and see that the highlight moves to **cell A10**.

   The ⌷Home⌷ key always makes active the cell in column A of the current row.

6. Press ⌷Ctrl⌷+⌷Home⌷ to move the highlight to **cell A1**.

7. Tap ⌷Page Down⌷ three times.

   Notice that Excel displays the next 25 or so rows (one "visible" screen's worth) each time you tap ⌷Page Down⌷.

8. Press and hold ⌷↑⌷ until **cell A1** is the active cell.

Use the Scroll Bars

The scroll bars allow you to see other portions of the Excel worksheet area without changing the active cell.

9. Click the **Scroll Right** ⌷▶⌷ button on the horizontal scroll bar until columns AA and AB are visible.

   Excel labels the first 26 columns A–Z and the next 26 columns AA–AZ. A similar labeling scheme is used for the remaining columns out to the final column, XFD.

10. Click the **Scroll Down** ⌷▼⌷ button on the vertical scroll bar until row 100 is visible.

    Notice that cell A1 remains displayed in the Name Box, as the highlight has not moved. To move the highlight, you must click in a cell or use the keyboard.

Use the Go To Command

11. Press ⌷Ctrl⌷+⌷G⌷ to display the Go To dialog box, type **g250** in the Reference box, and click **OK**.

    Keep in mind that cell references are not case sensitive so you can enter the letters in either upper or lower case.

12. Use the **Go To** command to move to three different cells.

13. Press ⌷Ctrl⌷+⌷Home⌷ to return to **cell A1**.

14. Follow these steps to navigate with the Name Box:

    Ⓐ Click in the **Name Box** at the left end of the Formula Bar.

    Ⓑ Type **ab9** and tap ⌷Enter⌷.

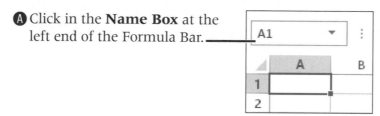

    The highlight should now be in cell AB9.

15. Press ⌷Ctrl⌷+⌷Home⌷ to return to **cell A1**.

16. Follow these steps to explore the Excel window:

Ⓐ Click the **New Sheet** button.

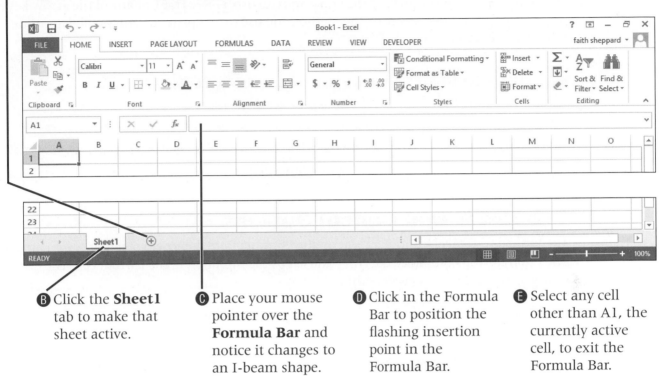

Ⓑ Click the **Sheet1** tab to make that sheet active.

Ⓒ Place your mouse pointer over the **Formula Bar** and notice it changes to an I-beam shape.

Ⓓ Click in the Formula Bar to position the flashing insertion point in the Formula Bar.

Ⓔ Select any cell other than A1, the currently active cell, to exit the Formula Bar.

17. Select **cell A1**.

Leave the Excel window open.

Entering Data in Excel

Video Library   http://labyrinthelab.com/videos   Video Number: EX13-V0104

Within Excel, data is entered into the active cell. Text is used for descriptive headings, and entries that require alphabetic characters. Numbers can be entered directly or can be calculated using formulas. Excel recognizes the data you enter and decides whether the entry is text, a number, or a formula that performs a calculation.

Data Types

Entries are defined as one of two main classifications: constant values or formulas. Constant values can be text, numeric, or a combination of both, and they do not change when other worksheet information changes. Conversely, formula entries display the results of calculations, and a result can change when a value in another cell changes.

| f_x | 1263 | **A constant value** |

| f_x | =SUM(C5:C8) | **A formula** |

Excel 2013

Completing Cell Entries

Text and numbers are entered by positioning the highlight in the desired cell, typing the desired text or number, and completing the entry. You can use Enter, Tab, or any of the arrow keys (→, ←, ↑, ↓) to complete an entry. The method you use to complete the entry will determine where the active cell moves.

Entry Completion Method	Where the Active Cell Will Appear
Enter	It will move down to the next cell.
Tab	It will move to the next cell to the right.
→ ↑ ↓ ←	It will move to the next cell in the direction of the arrow key.
Esc	The entry will be deleted and the current cell will remain active.

The Enter and Cancel Buttons

The Enter and Cancel buttons appear on the Formula Bar whenever you enter or edit an entry. The Enter button completes the entry and keeps the highlight in the current cell. The Cancel button cancels the entry, as does the Esc key.

The Cancel and Enter buttons appear when an entry is being entered or edited.

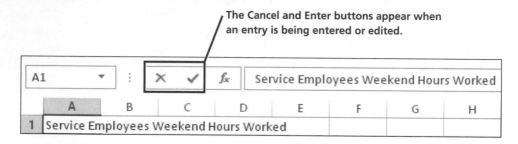

Deleting and Replacing Entries

You can delete an entire entry after it has been completed by clicking in the cell and tapping Delete. Likewise, you can replace an entry by clicking in the cell and typing a new entry.

Long Text Entries

Text entries often do not fit in a cell. These entries are known as long entries. Excel will either display the long entry over the adjacent cell (if the cell to the right of the long entry is empty), or Excel will shorten, or truncate, the display of the long entry (if the cell to the right of the long entry is in use.) In this latter instance, the entire long entry remains within the cell, but it is not fully visible. You can widen a column to accommodate a long entry.

	A	B	C	D	E
1	Service Employees Weekend Hours Worked				
2					

This is a long entry. The entire phrase is entered in cell A1, although it displays over the range A1:E1.

Enter Text

In this exercise, you will enter text, including long entries, and will use various keystrokes to complete entries.

1. Make **cell A1** active by clicking the **mouse pointer** ✛ in it.

2. Type **Service Employees Weekend Hours Worked**, and then tap ⌑Enter⌑.

   The text is entered in the cell and the highlight moves down to cell A2. Notice that the entry displays over cells B1, C1, D1, and E1, although the entire entry still belongs to cell A1.

3. Click **cell A1** and note the appearance of the Formula Bar.

   Notice that the Formula Bar displays the name of the active cell (A1) as well as its content.

4. Tap →| to make cell B1 active.

5. Look at the **Formula Bar** and notice that cell B1 is empty.

   The long entry belongs to cell A1 even though it is displayed over the range A1:E1.

Type Additional Text Entries

6. Click in **cell C3**.

7. Type **Friday** and tap →| once.

   Notice that the entry is completed and the highlight moves to cell D3.

8. Type **Wednesday** in **cell D3** and tap →|.

9. Type **Sunday** in **cell E3** and tap ←|.

   Notice that the display of Wednesday *is shortened, or truncated.*

Friday	Wednesd	Sunday

10. Type **Saturday** in **cell D3** and tap ⌑Enter⌑.

    The new entry in cell D3 replaces the previous entry.

11. Enter the remaining text entries shown here.

If Excel proposes any entries for you as you type, simply continue typing.

	A	B	C	D	E
1	Service Employees Weekend Hours Worked				
2					
3	Alton Mall		Friday	Saturday	Sunday
4		Barnes			
5		Chau			
6		Lee			
7		Olsen			
8		Total Hrs			
9	Century Bank				
10		Garcia			
11		Kimura			
12		Tan			
13		Total Hrs			
14	Newport Medical				
15		Kowalski			
16		Silva			
17		Wilson			
18		Total Hrs			

Working with Numbers

Video Library   http://labyrinthelab.com/videos   Video Number: EX13-V0105

Number entries can contain only the digits 0–9 and a few other characters. Excel initially right-aligns numbers in cells, although you can change this alignment. The following table lists characters that Excel accepts as part of a number entry.

Valid Characters in Number Entries
The digits 0-9
The following characters: + - ( ) , / $ % . *

Entering numbers using the numeric keypad is more efficient than using the number keys at the top of the keyboard.

Number Formats

It isn't necessary to type commas, dollar signs, and other number formats when entering numbers. Instead, you can use Excel's formatting commands to add the desired number formats.

Decimals and Negative Numbers

You should always type a decimal point if the number you are entering requires one. Likewise, you should precede a negative number entry with a minus (–) sign or enclose it in parentheses ( ).

Enter Numbers

In this exercise, you will practice entering numbers and canceling entries before completion.

1. Position the highlight in **cell C4** and type **6**, but don't complete the entry.

2. Look at the Formula Bar and notice the **Cancel** ☒ and **Enter** ☑ buttons.
   These buttons appear whenever you begin entering or editing data in a cell.

3. Click **Enter** ☑ to complete the entry.
   Notice that the highlight remains in cell C4.

Use the Cancel Button and the ⌴Esc⌴ Key

◢	A	B	C	D	E
1	Service Employees Weekend Hours Worked				
2					
3	Alton Mall		Friday	Saturday	Sunday
4		Barnes	6	6	6
5		Chau	8	8	8
6		Lee	4	0	4
7		Olsen	4	3	0
8		Total Hrs			
9	Century Bank				
10		Garcia	3	5	0
11		Kimura	3	4	0
12		Tan	3	5	0
13		Total Hrs			
14	Newport Medical				
15		Kowalski	8	6	8
16		Silva	6	6	0
17		Wilson	5	2	5
18		Total Hrs			

4. Position the highlight in **cell C5** and type **8**, but don't complete the entry.

5. Click **Cancel** ☒ on the Formula Bar.

6. Type **8** again, and this time tap ⌴Esc⌴.
   The ⌴Esc⌴ key has the same effect as the Cancel button.

7. Type **8** once again, and this time tap ⬇.

   Notice that Excel right-aligns the number in the cell.

8. Enter the remaining numbers shown on the prior page.

To use the numeric keypad to enter numbers, the Number Lock light, which is included on most keyboards, must be on. If it's not, press the Num Lock key on the keypad.

Understanding Save Concepts

Video Library   http://labyrinthelab.com/videos   Video Number: EX13-V0106

One important lesson to learn is to save your workbooks every 10–15 minutes, in order to avoid losing data as a result of power outages and careless accidents. Workbooks are saved to file storage locations such as a USB drive, the Documents folder, a shared network drive, and websites on the Internet. When a worksheet is first saved, the Save As dialog box appears so that you can assign a name, and location on the computer, to your file. If the worksheet has already been saved and you choose the Save command, Excel replaces the previous version with the new edited version.

FROM THE RIBBON
File→Save

FROM THE KEYBOARD
Ctrl+S to save

FROM THE RIBBON
File→Save As

FROM THE KEYBOARD
Alt, F, A or F12 to save as

Issuing Commands from the Keyboard

While commands are always available on the ribbon, it can be more efficient to issue them from the keyboard. Try to use both the keyboard shortcuts that are highlighted throughout this text and the key tips that display when the Alt key is tapped.

QUICK REFERENCE	SAVING A WORKBOOK AND MANAGING WORKBOOK FILE VERSIONS
Task	**Procedure**
Save for the first time	■ Click Save 💾 on the Quick Access toolbar, choose Computer, and choose Browse. ■ Name the workbook, choose the save location, and click Save.
Save changes in the workbook	■ Click Save 💾 on the Quick Access toolbar.
Save in a new location or with a new name	■ Choose File→Save As, choose Computer, and choose Browse. ■ Change the name of the workbook, the file storage location, or both, and click Save.
Save the workbook in the Excel 97-2003 Format	■ Choose File→Save As, choose Computer, choose Browse, enter the filename, and navigate to the desired file storage location. ■ Choose Excel 97-2003 from the Save as Type list, and click Save.
Use key tips to choose a command	■ Tap the Alt key to display key tips. ■ Tap the letter or number key that corresponds to the desired tab on the Ribbon or Quick Access toolbar button, and tap the letter(s) in the key tip for the desired command on the Ribbon.

Save the Workbook

In this exercise, you will save the workbook you have been working on. You will also use key tips to select a command on the Ribbon and view Excel's options for saving workbooks.

Before You Begin: Navigate to the student resource center to download the student exercise files for this book.

1. Click the **Save** 💾 button on the Quick Access toolbar, choose **Computer**, and choose **Browse**.

   The Save As dialog box appears because this is the first time you are saving the workbook.

2. Navigate to your file storage location.

   Notice that the proposed name Book1 (something similar, such as Book 2, may be displayed on your screen) appears in the File Name Box.

3. Type **EX01-D05-WeekendHours-[FirstInitialLastName]** to replace the proposed name.

   Replace the bracketed text with your first initial and last name. For example, if your name is Bethany Smith, your filename would look like this: EX01-D05-WeekendHours-BSmith.

4. Click **Save** or tap Enter.

   Notice that the filename appears in the Title Bar of the window to indicate that the workbook is saved.

EX01-D05-WeekendHours-BSmith - Excel

Use Key Tips to Save As

5. Tap Alt.

   Key tips display on the Quick Access toolbar and Ribbon.

6. Tap F.

   The File tab displays with the Info tab selected.

7. Tap A.

   The Save As tab displays.

8. Tap B.

   The Save As dialog box displays.

9. Tap Esc to cancel the dialog box without saving.

10. Tap ESC again to return to the active worksheet.

    Leave the workbook open for the next exercise.

Excel 2013

Closing Workbooks

Video Library   http://labyrinthelab.com/videos   Video Number: EX13-V0107

The Close command is used to close an open workbook. When you close a workbook that has not been saved, Excel prompts you to save the changes. If you choose to save at the prompt and the workbook has previously been saved, Excel simply saves the changes and closes the workbook. If the workbook is new, Excel displays the Save As dialog box, allowing you to assign a name and file storage location to the workbook. Any other workbooks that are being used will remain open until you close them or exit Excel.

DEVELOP YOUR SKILLS EX01-D06
Close the Workbook and Start a New Workbook

In this exercise, you will close the workbook that you have been working on throughout this lesson.

1. Choose **File→Close**.

2. Click the **Save** or **Yes** button if Excel asks you if you want to save the changes.
   Notice that no workbook appears in the Excel window. The Excel window always has this appearance when all workbooks have been closed.

3. Click **Close** ⊠. Exit **Excel**.
   The Excel window has now closed as well.

Concepts Review

To check your knowledge of the key concepts introduced in this lesson, complete the Concepts Review quiz by choosing the appropriate access option below.

If you are...	Then access the quiz by...
Using the Labyrinth Video Library	Going to http://labyrinthelab.com/videos
Using eLab	Logging in, choosing Content, and navigating to the Concepts Review quiz for this lesson
Not using the Labyrinth Video Library or eLab	Going to the student resource center for this book

Reinforce Your Skills

Use Excel 2013

In this exercise, you will start Excel and examine various elements of the program.

Present and Start Excel

1. Consider the different tasks that you perform when completing classwork. Think about ways your work could be minimized through the use of Excel.

   As you complete the remaining steps for this exercise, keep in mind these potential benefits.

2. Follow your step for the version of Windows you are running:

   - **Windows 7:** Choose **Start→All Programs→Microsoft Office 2013→Excel 2013→Blank Workbook**.
   - **Windows 8:** Choose **Excel 2013 tile→Blank Workbook**.

   Notice that in either case a blank workbook is displayed when you open Excel.

Explore the Excel Window

3. Ensure that **cell A1** is selected.

   Notice that the name bar displays the name of the active cell.

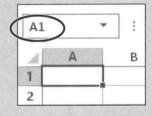

4. Click **Scroll Down** ▼ to scroll down to row 100

5. Click **cell B100**.

   The Name Box now displays the name of the new active cell.

6. Press Ctrl + Home to return to cell A1.

Work with Tabs and Ribbons

7. Click the **Data** tab on the Ribbon.

   Look at the types of commands available. Many of them will be covered in later lessons of this book.

8. Click the **View** tab.

9. Click the **Collapse the Ribbon** ▲ button at the upper-right corner of the window.

10. Click the **Home** tab to display the Ribbon once again.

The Home tab is displayed because you chose it to redisplay the Ribbon.

11. Click the **Pin the Ribbon** button to permanently display the Ribbon once again.

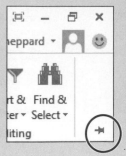

12. Click the **Customize Quick Access Toolbar** button.

13. Add the **Quick Print** button to the toolbar by selecting it from the menu that appears.

14. Use the Print Screen key on your keyboard, and paste the screen into a Microsoft Word document.

The Print Screen key makes a copy of the entire screen (although no indication of this can be seen within Excel), which can then be pasted in a variety of programs.

15. Save the Word document as **EX01-R01-ScreenShot-[FirstInitialLastName]** in the **EX2013 Lesson 01** folder. Exit **Word** and **Excel**.

16. Submit your final file based on the guidelines provided by your instructor.

To view examples of how your file or files should look at the end of this exercise, go to the student resource center.

REINFORCE YOUR SKILLS EX01-R02

Enter and Save Data

In this exercise, you will create and save a simple spreadsheet.

Enter Data

1. Start **Excel**. Open a blank workbook.

2. Enter text in **rows 1 through 10** as shown.

Use Tab and Enter as necessary to enter the data. Type the customer's name and address in cells B6, B7, and B8.

	A	B	C	D	E
1	Kids for Change				
2	Order Tracking Worksheet				
3					
4	Order No.	1552			
5					
6	Sold to:	Empire Dry Cleaning			
7		1833 Franklin Highway			
8		Huntington, WV 25716			
9					
10	Item	In Stock?	Quantity	Price	Discount

Work with Numbers

3. In **cells A11–E15**, enter the data shown here.

   Type a decimal point (.) in the Price and Discount columns, where displayed. Type a minus (–) sign before the numbers in the Discount column.

	A	B	C	D	E
10	Item	In Stock?	Quantity	Price	Discount
11	A423	Y	2	63.95	-3.15
12	A321	Y	4	28.95	0
13	D928	N	16	5.85	-0.59
14	S251	N	8	3.09	-0.31
15	B444	Y	20	8.77	-0.88

Employ Save Concepts

4. Choose **Save** 🖫 on the Quick Access toolbar, and then choose **Computer→Browse**.

5. Type **EX01-R02-OrderTracking-[FirstInitialLastName]** and navigate to your **EX2013 Lesson 01** folder.

6. Click **Save** or tap ⌷Enter⌷.

   The workbook is saved in the location that you specified.

Close and Start a New Workbook

7. Select **File→Close**.

8. Select **File→New→Blank workbook**.

Exit from Excel

9. Click **Close** ⌷×⌷ to close Excel.

   As you haven't yet entered data into this workbook, Excel closes without asking you to save.

10. Submit your final file based on the guidelines provided by your instructor.

    To view examples of how your file or files should look at the end of this exercise, go to the student resource center.

REINFORCE YOUR SKILLS EX01-R03

Explore Excel 2013

In this exercise, you will enter data into a new workbook.

Present and Start Excel

1. Think back to spreadsheets you have used in the past that likely originated from Excel.

   As you focus on this in the future, you will be surprised to see how many uses there are for Excel.

2. Follow your step for the version of Windows you are running:

   ■ **Windows 7:** Choose **Start→All Programs→Microsoft Office 2013→Excel 2013→Blank workbook**.

   ■ **Windows 8:** Choose **Excel 2013 tile→Blank workbook**.

   In both instances you are presented with a blank Excel worksheet.

Explore the Excel Window

3. Select **cell B3**.

   The Name Box displays the name of the active cell.

4. Use the **Scroll Right** ▶ button to scroll to **column Z**.

   Notice that the next column is named "AA." You will get accustomed to the order of the column names as you use them more frequently.

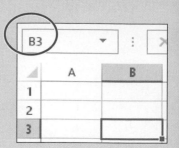

5. Click **cell Z1**.

   The name bar now displays the name of the new active cell.

6. Click ⌐Home⌐ to return to **cell A1**.

   Remember that ⌐Home⌐ brings you to column A within your current row.

Work with Tabs and Ribbons

7. Click the **Page Layout** tab on the Ribbon.

   Look at the types of commands available. Many of them will be covered in later lessons of this book.

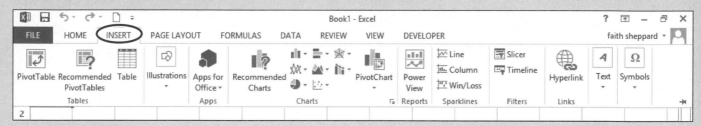

8. Click the **Review** tab.

9. Click the **Customize Quick Access Toolbar** button.

10. Add the **New** button to the toolbar by selecting it from the menu that appears.

11. Click **Collapse the Ribbon** ⌃ at the upper-right corner of the window.

12. Click the **Insert** tab to display the Ribbon once again.

Notice that the Insert tab is displayed because you chose it to redisplay the Ribbon.

13. Click **Pin the Ribbon** to permanently display the Ribbon once again.

Enter Data

14. Enter text in **rows 1–8** as shown.

	A	B	C	D
1	Kids for Change			
2	Expense Listing			
3				
4		January	February	March
5	Rent			
6	Utilities			
7	Supplies			
8	Cable			

Use Tab *and* Enter *as necessary to enter the data. Type the months in cells B4, C4, and D4.*

Work with Numbers

15. In the **range B5:D8**, enter the data shown.

4		January	February	March
5	Rent	$350	$350	$350
6	Utilities	$120	$110	$145
7	Supplies	$60	$95	$75
8	Cable	$100	$100	$100

Employ Save Concepts

16. Click **Save** 🖫 on the Quick Access toolbar, and then choose **Computer→Browse**.

17. Type **EX01-R03-ExpenseTracking-[FirstInitialLastName]** then navigate to your **EX2013 Lesson 01** folder.

18. Click **Save** or tap Enter.

The workbook is saved in the location that you specified.

Close and Start a New Workbook

19. Select **File→Close**.

20. Select **File→New→Blank workbook**.

Exit from Excel

21. Click **Close** ☒ to close Excel.

22. Submit your final file based on the guidelines provided by your instructor.

Apply Your Skills

Examine Excel Features

In this exercise, you will navigate through a variety of features within a blank Excel workbook.

Open and Explore a Blank Worksheet

1. Start **Excel** and open a **Blank Workbook**.

2. Select **cell V87** by scrolling through the worksheet.

Utilize and Alter the Ribbon

3. Select the **Formulas** tab on the Ribbon.

4. Collapse the Ribbon.

5. Add the **Spelling** button to the Quick Access toolbar.

6. Use the **Print Screen** key on your keyboard, and then paste the screen into a Microsoft Word document.

7. Save the Word document as **EX01-A01-RibbonWork-[FirstInitialLastName]** in your **EX2013 Lesson 01** folder.

8. Submit your file based on the guidelines provided by your instructor.

   To view examples of how your file or files should look at the end of this exercise, go to the student resource center.

Create a New Workbook

In this exercise, you will create a new worksheet, enter data, and then save and close the worksheet.

Enter Data and Numbers

1. Open a **Blank Worksheet**.

2. Create the worksheet shown here.

	A	B	C	D	E
1	Universal Corporate Events			Q1 Expenses	
2					
3	Item		January	February	March
4	Building	Lease	3000	3000	3000
5		Utilities	1689	1572	1646
6		Phone	250	242	329
7		Insurance	8696	0	0
8		Total			
9					
10	Equipment		1211	506	4890
11					
12	Salaries	Mgmt	4500	4500	4500
13		Full Time	20658	19777	21422
14		Part Time	24656	25980	25316
15		Total			
16					
17	Supplies	Office	1963	2432	1784
18		Vehicle	872	944	903
19		Total			
20					
21	Other	Fuel			
22		Adver.	500	300	200
23		Uniforms	63	101	83
24		Misc	162	471	65
25		Total			

Proofread all data. You will not create formulas to calculate totals in this exercise.

Close the Workbook and Exit Excel

3. Save the workbook as **EX01-A02-Q1Expenses-[FirstInitialLastName]** in your **EX2013 Lesson 01** folder.

4. Close **Excel**.

5. Submit your final file based on the guidelines provided by your instructor.

   To view examples of how your file or files should look at the end of this exercise, go to the student resource center.

APPLY YOUR SKILLS EX01-A03

Adjust the Ribbon and Build a Worksheet

In this exercise, you will create and save a new workbook.

Open and Explore a Blank Worksheet

1. Open a **Blank Worksheet**.
2. Use a single keystroke to scroll down one visible screen.

Utilize and Alter the Ribbon

3. Click the **Data** tab on the Ribbon.
4. Add the **Print Preview and Print** button to the Quick Access toolbar.
5. Collapse the Ribbon.

Enter Data and Numbers

6. Create the worksheet shown in the following illustration.

	A	B	C	D	E
1	Universal Corporate Events			Q2 Revenues	
2					
3	Type		April	May	June
4	Consult	Dept. A	5500	7500	6000
5		Dept. B	3000	2500	2500
6		Dept. C	9000	12000	4500
7		Dept. D	1500	300	3200
8		Total			
9					
10	Sales	Branch A	7000	8000	8000
11		Branch B	4200	3700	4000
12		Total			

7. Save the workbook as **`EX01-A03-Q2Revenues-[FirstInitialLastName]`** in your **EX2013 Lesson 01** folder.
8. Close **Excel**.
9. Submit your final file based on the guidelines provided by your instructor.

Extend Your Skills

In the course of working through the Extend Your Skills exercises, you will think critically as you use the skills taught in the lesson to complete the assigned projects. To evaluate your mastery and completion of the exercises, your instructor may use a rubric, with which more points are allotted according to performance characteristics. (The more you do, the more you earn!) Ask your instructor how your work will be evaluated.

EX01-E01 That's the Way I See It

You are known as the neighborhood Excel expert for small businesses! By request, you have created the first draft of a worksheet containing employee timesheet hours for the community's most popular bakery. The worksheet contains all necessary data, as the employees have already entered their hours. Before presenting the worksheet to the bakery, you want to review it with an eye toward layout and, of course, you want to check the spelling throughout.

Start Excel, and then open **EX01-E01-Bakery** from the **EX2013 Lesson 01** folder and save it as **EX01-E01-Bakery-[FirstInitialLastName]**.

Enter the name of your local bakery at the top, and then review the data included. Using your own literacy skills, manually make changes to the worksheet in order to correct spelling errors.

You will be evaluated based on the inclusion of all elements specified, your ability to follow directions, your ability to apply newly learned skills to a real-world situation, your creativity, and the relevance of your topic and/or data choice(s). Submit your final file based on the guidelines provided by your instructor.

EX01-E02 Be Your Own Boss

In this exercise, you will create a telephone listing for your new company, Blue Jean Landscaping. This unique business saves its customers money by allowing them to "get their hands dirty" with the physical landscaping work. As you are starting your business, this listing will allow all employees to stay in contact with one another.

Open a blank worksheet and save it as **EX01-E02-Telephone-[FirstInitialLastName]** in the **EX2013 Lesson 01** folder.

(206) 555-7164,	Stephen Samuels
(425) 555-9138,	Billy Mitchell
(206) 555-6180,	Warren Kennedy
(206) 555-1148,	Abraham Sorenson
(253) 555-0346,	Peter Smith
(425) 555-2315,	Stanley Bogart

To the right is the contact information that you will need to create the telephone listing. Make sure to structure the telephone listing in a logical manner, consistent with the skills you have learned in this lesson. At a minimum it should contain appropriate headers for each column.

Expand your telephone listing to include each employee's birthday and nickname (make them up) to make the file a more robust and useful reference.

You will be evaluated based on the inclusion of all elements specified, your ability to follow directions, your ability to apply newly learned skills to a real-world situation, your creativity, and your demonstration of an entrepreneurial spirit. Submit your final file based on the guidelines provided by your instructor.

Transfer Your Skills

In the course of working through the Transfer Your Skills exercises, you will use critical-thinking and creativity skills to complete the assigned projects using skills taught in the lesson. To evaluate your mastery and completion of the exercises, your instructor may use a rubric, with which more points are allotted according to performance characteristics. (The more you do, the more you earn!) Ask your instructor how your work will be evaluated.

EX01-T01 Use the Web as a Learning Tool

Throughout this book, you will be provided with an opportunity to use the Internet as a learning tool by completing WebQuests. According to the original creators of WebQuests, as described on their website (WebQuest.org), a WebQuest is "an inquiry-oriented activity in which most or all of the information used by learners is drawn from the web." To complete the WebQuest projects in this book, navigate to the student resource center and choose the WebQuest for the lesson on which you are currently working. The subject of each WebQuest will be relevant to the material found in the lesson.

WebQuest Subject: Design elements of a high-quality Excel worksheet

Submit your final file based on the guidelines provided by your instructor.

EX01-T02 Demonstrate Proficiency

During its first month of operations, Stormy BBQ has begun working with a number of corporate clients. These clients place multiple catering orders each month. The contact person for each client, and the revenue received from each, are as follows: Max Kenton, $5,000; Katy Super, $7,000; Chandra Shuff, $2,000; Sofia Burgoyne, $14,000; and Kenya Polasek, $6,500. In order to track the monthly revenue you will create a worksheet containing these figures, listing the clients from greatest to least revenue generated.

Open a blank worksheet and save it as **EX01-T02-StormyRevenue-[FirstInitialLastName]** in the **EX2013 Lesson 01** folder. Use the worksheet techniques learned in this lesson to track the monthly revenue, listing the clients from greatest to least revenue generated. Make sure that the worksheet is well-structured and easily readable.

Submit your final file based on the guidelines provided by your instructor.

EXCEL 2013

Editing Worksheets

In this lesson, you will expand your basic skills in Excel. You will learn various methods of editing worksheets, including replacing entries, deleting entries, and using Undo and Redo. You will also work with AutoComplete, AutoFill, and AutoCorrect. When you have finished this lesson, you will have developed the skills necessary to produce carefully edited and proofed worksheets.

LEARNING OBJECTIVES

After studying this lesson, you will be able to:

■ Select, move, and copy cells and ranges

■ Use Undo and Redo

■ Clear cell contents, including formatting

■ Complete cell entries automatically

■ Use AutoCorrect effectively

Creating a Basic List in Excel

You are employed at Green Clean, a janitorial product supplier and cleaning service contractor that employs environmentally friendly practices. As the business grows, you find that organization is becoming more and more important. You decide to use Excel to create, manage, and maintain a list of employees.

green clean

	A	B	C	D	E
1	Green Clean				
2	Management and Support Roster				
3					
4	Name	Phone	Position	Employment Date	On Call
5	Tommy Choi	619-555-3224	President		
6	Mary Wright	858-555-3098	VP, Sales and Marketing	5/22/2007	Monday
7	Derek Navarro	619-555-3309	VP, Operations	3/30/2009	Tuesday
8	Isabella Riso-Neff	858-555-0211	Risk Management Director	4/13/2009	Wednesday
9	Kenneth Hazell	619-555-3224	Human Resources Director	7/17/2006	Thursday
10	D'Andre Adams	760-555-3876	Facilities Services Manager	12/7/2005	Friday
11	Talos Bouras	858-555-1002	Sales Manager	5/10/2004	Saturday
12	Michael Chowdery	858-555-0021	Purchasing Manager	10/26/2009	Sunday
13	Ahn Tran	760-555-0728	Office Manager	6/26/2006	
14	Jenna Mann	951-555-0826	Administrative Assistant	3/15/2010	
15	Nicole Romero	858-555-4987	Payroll Assistant	5/25/2009	
16	Amy Wyatt	619-555-4016	Customer Service Rep	8/17/2009	
17	Brian Simpson	858-555-3718	Customer Service Rep	12/1/2013	
18	Leisa Malimali	619-555-4017	Sales Assistant	12/1/2013	

You will use this worksheet to organize the management of key employee data.

Opening Workbooks

Video Library   http://labyrinthelab.com/videos   Video Number: EX13-V0201

The Open menu lets you navigate to any file storage location and open previously saved workbooks. Once a workbook is open, you can browse it, print it, and make editing changes. The organization and layout of the Open menu are similar to those of the Save As menu.

FROM THE RIBBON
File→Open

FROM THE KEYBOARD
Ctrl+O to open a new workbook

Excel 2013

DEVELOP YOUR SKILLS EX02-D01
Open the Workbook

In this exercise, you will open a workbook that lists various employees.

1. Start **Excel** and choose **Open Other Workbooks** to display the Open menu.

2. Click **Computer**, and then click the **Browse** button to display the Open dialog box.

3. Navigate to your file storage location (such as a USB flash drive) and double-click the **EX2013 Lesson 02** folder to open it.

4. Select **EX02-D01-Roster** and click **Open**.

To open a document, you can also double-click its filename in the Open dialog box.

Editing Entries

Video Library   http://labyrinthelab.com/videos   Video Number: EX13-V0202

You can edit the active cell by clicking in the Formula Bar and making the desired changes. You can also double-click a cell and edit the contents right there. This technique is known as in-cell editing.

Replacing Entries

Editing an entry is efficient both for long entries and for complex formulas. If the entry requires little typing, however, it is usually easier to simply retype it. If you retype an entry, the new entry will replace the previous entry.

Deleting Characters

Use the Delete and Backspace keys to edit entries in the Formula Bar and within a cell. The Delete key removes the character to the right of the insertion point, while the Backspace key removes the character to the left of the insertion point.

This is the flashing insertion point.

Tapping Backspace **will remove the "A."**

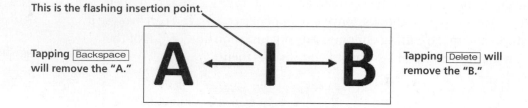

Tapping Delete **will remove the "B."**

Edit Entries

In this exercise, you will use the Formula Bar to revise the contents of cell A2, replace the contents of cell D4, and edit cell A8 directly in the cell.

1. Save your file as **EX02-D02-Roster-[FirstInitialLastName]**.

   Replace the bracketed text with your first initial and last name. For example, if your name is Bethany Smith, your filename would look like this: EX02-D02-Roster-BSmith.

2. Click **cell A2** to select it.

3. Follow these steps to edit cell A2 using the Formula Bar:

   Ⓐ Click in the **Formula Bar** just to the right of the word *List*.

   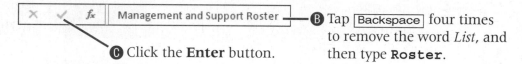

   Ⓑ Tap Backspace four times to remove the word *List*, and then type **Roster**.

   Ⓒ Click the **Enter** button.

Replace an Entry

4. Click **cell D4**.

5. Type **Employment Date** and tap Enter.

   The entry Employment Date *replaces the entry* Starting Date. *Notice that the cell formatting (underlining) has been applied to the new entry.*

Use In-Cell Editing

6. Double-click **cell A8** (the cell with the name Isabella Riso).

7. Use the mouse or right arrow key → to position the flashing insertion point to the right of the last name, *Riso*.

8. Type **–Neff** and tap Enter to complete the change.

   The entry should now read Isabella Riso-Neff.

9. Click the **Save** 🖫 button to update the changes. Keep the file open.

   Clicking Save automatically saves changes to a workbook that has previously been saved.

Selecting Cells and Ranges

Video Library http://labyrinthelab.com/videos   Video Number: EX13-V0203

To edit a worksheet (move, copy, delete, or format) you must first select the cell(s). The most efficient way to select cells is with the mouse, although you can also use the keyboard. A group of adjacent cells is called a range.

Entire columns or rows may be selected by clicking or dragging the column headings (such as A, B, C) or row headings (such as 1, 2, 3).

FROM THE KEYBOARD
Ctrl + A to select all
Ctrl + Spacebar to select a column
Shift + Spacebar to select a row

Excel 2013

Excel Ranges

Each cell has a reference. For example, A1 refers to the first cell in a worksheet, which is at the intersection of column A and row 1. Likewise, a range reference specifies the cells included within a range. The range reference includes the first and last cells in the range, separated by a colon (:). For example, the range A4:E4 includes cells A4, B4, C4, D4 and E4.

	A	B	C	D	E
A6		fx	Mary Wright		
1	Green Clean				
2	Management and Support Roster				
3					
4	Name	Phone	Position	Employment Date	On Call
5	Tommy Choi	619-555-3224	President		
6	Mary Wright	858-555-3098	VP, Sales and Marketing	5/22/2007	
7	Derek Navarro	619-555-3309	VP, Operations	3/30/2009	
8	Isabella Riso-Neff	858-555-0211	Risk Management Director	4/13/2009	
9	Kenneth Hazell	619-555-3224	Human Resources Director	7/17/2006	
10	D'Andre Adams	760-555-3876	Facilities Services Manager	12/7/2005	
11	Talos Bouras	858-555-1002	Sales Manager	5/10/2004	
12	Michael Chowdery	858-555-0021	Purchasing Manager	10/26/2009	
13	Ahn Tran	760-555-0728	Office Manager	6/26/2006	
14	Jenna Mann	951-555-0826	Administrative Assistant	3/15/2010	

Range A1:A2 — (rows 1–2, column A)
Range A4:E4 — (row 4)
Range A6:D10 — (rows 6–10)

The selected ranges are shaded. Cell A6 is the active cell, as it is not shaded, has an outline around it, and is displayed in both the Name Box and Formula Bar.

DEVELOP YOUR SKILLS EX02-D03

Make Selections

In this exercise, you will select multiple ranges and entire rows and columns using the mouse. You will also use Shift *and* Ctrl *to practice selecting cell ranges.*

1. Save your file as **EX02-D03-Roster-[FirstInitialLastName]**.

2. Position the **mouse pointer ✛** over **cell A4**.

3. Press and hold down the left mouse button while dragging the mouse to the right until the **range A4:E4** is selected; release the mouse button.

   Notice that for each range that is selected, the corresponding row and column headings are displayed in gray.

4. Click once anywhere in the worksheet to deselect the cells.

5. Follow these steps to select two ranges:

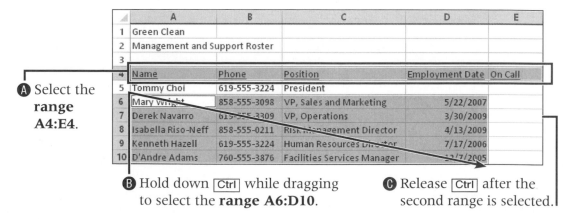

Ⓐ Select the **range A4:E4**.

Ⓑ Hold down Ctrl while dragging to select the **range A6:D10**.

Ⓒ Release Ctrl after the second range is selected.

The ranges A4:E4 and A6:D10 are selected. The Ctrl *key lets you select more than one range at the same time.*

6. Hold down ⌈Ctrl⌉ while you select any other range, and then release ⌈Ctrl⌉.
You should now have three ranges selected.

7. Make sure you have released ⌈Ctrl⌉, and then click once anywhere on the worksheet to deselect the ranges.
The highlighting of the previous selections disappears.

8. Follow these steps to select various rows and columns:

Ⓐ Click the **column A** heading to select the entire column.

Ⓑ Position the mouse pointer on the **column C** heading and drag right until **columns C–E** are selected.

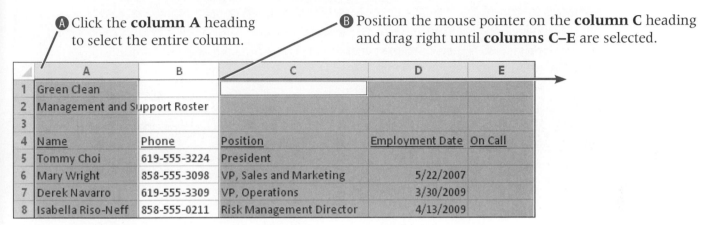

Column A will be deselected because you did not hold down ⌈Ctrl⌉.

Ⓒ Click the **Select All** button to select the entire worksheet.

Ⓓ Click the **row 1** heading to select the entire row.

Ⓔ Drag the mouse pointer down over the **row 6–10** headings.

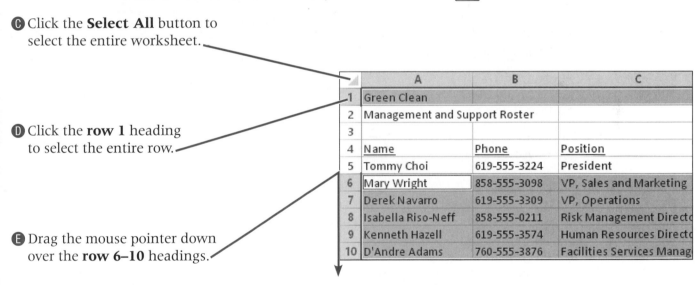

Row 1 will be deselected because you did not hold down ⌈Ctrl⌉.

9. Follow these steps to select cells using keystrokes:

Ⓐ Click **cell A4**.

Ⓑ Hold down ⎇Shift⎈ and click **cell E16** to select the range A4:E16.

	A	B	C	D	E
4	Name	Phone	Position	Employment Date	On Call
5	Tommy Choi	619-555-3224	President		
6	Mary Wright	858-555-3098	VP, Sales and Marketing	5/22/2007	
7	Derek Navarro	619-555-3309	VP, Operations	3/30/2009	
8	Isabella Riso-Neff	858-555-0211	Risk Management Director	4/13/2009	
9	Kenneth Hazell	619-555-3224	Human Resources Director	7/17/2006	
10	D'Andre Adams	760-555-3876	Facilities Services Manager	12/7/2005	
11	Talos Bouras	858-555-1002	Sales Manager	5/10/2004	
12	Michael Chowdery	858-555-0021	Purchasing Manager	10/26/2009	
13	Ahn Tran	760-555-0728	Office Manager	6/26/2006	
14	Jenna Mann	951-555-0826	Administrative Assistant	3/15/2010	
15	Nicole Romero	858-555-4987	Payroll Assistant	5/25/2009	
16	Amy Wyatt	619-555-4016	Customer Service Rep	8/17/2009	

	A	B	C	D
12	Michael Chowdery	858-555-0021	Purchasing Manager	10/26/2009
13	Ahn Tran	760-555-0728	Office Manager	6/26/2006
14	Jenna Mann	951-555-0826	Administrative Assistant	3/15/2010
15	Nicole Romero	858-555-4987	Payroll Assistant	5/25/2009
16	Amy Wyatt	619-555-4016	Customer Service Rep	8/17/2009

Ⓒ Click **cell A12**.

Ⓓ Hold down ⎇Shift⎈ then tap → three times and ↓ four times.

The range A12:D16 is selected. Notice that the ⎇Shift⎈ *key techniques give you precise control when selecting. You should use the* ⎇Shift⎈ *key techniques if you find selecting with the mouse difficult or if you have a large range to select that is not entirely visible on your screen.*

10. Take a few moments to practice different selection techniques; then, **Save** 💾 the file.

Using Cut, Copy, and Paste

Video Library http://labyrinthelab.com/videos Video Number: EX13-V0204

You use the Cut, Copy, and Paste commands to move and copy cells. For example, use the Copy command to copy a range and the Paste command to paste it somewhere else on the same worksheet, another worksheet, or even another program. Similarly, use Cut to remove (delete) a range from one area and move it to another.

When an item is copied or cut, it is placed on the Office Clipboard. These items can then be pasted from the Clipboard, which can be opened by clicking the dialog box launcher on the Clipboard group of the Home tab.

FROM THE RIBBON

Home→Clipboard →Copy

Home→Clipboard →Cut

Home→Clipboard →Paste

FROM THE KEYBOARD

Ctrl + C to copy

Ctrl + X to cut

Ctrl + V to paste

Excel 2013

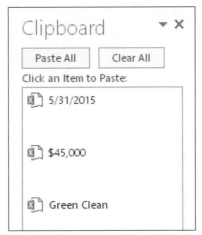

A dialog box launcher

The Office Clipboard with several items available to paste.

Paste Options

The Paste Options button displays at the lower-right corner of the destination cell(s) after a paste action. Its drop-down list provides options that let you modify the effect of the Paste command. The button disappears upon the next action you take.

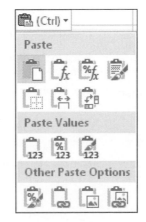

The Paste Options menu.

The Shortcut menu that appears when you right-click a cell.

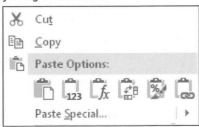

Moving and Copying Cells via Drag and Drop

Drag and drop produces the same results as Cut, Copy, and Paste. However, Drag and drop is preferable if the original location and new destination are both visible onscreen. When using drag and drop, the mouse pointer changes to a four-headed arrow as you point at the highlighted box surrounding the selected cell or range.

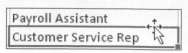

Moving and Copying Cells via Right-Dragging

Move Here
Copy Here
Copy Here as Values Only
Copy Here as Formats Only
Link Here
Create Hyperlink Here
Shift Down and Copy
Shift Right and Copy
Shift Down and Move
Shift Right and Move
Cancel

Right-dragging is a variation of the drag-and-drop technique. With the right-drag method, the right mouse button is used to drag the selected cell or range. When the right mouse button is released, you can choose to move, copy, or link from the resulting menu (as shown here). This approach provides more control because there is no need to use Ctrl when copying. In addition, it's easy to cancel the command if you change your mind.

QUICK REFERENCE	USING CUT, COPY, AND PASTE
Task	**Procedure**
Cut a cell	Select Home→Clipboard→Cut, or right-click the cell and select Cut.
Copy a cell	Select Home→Clipboard→Copy, or right-click the cell and select Copy.
Paste a cell	Select Home→Clipboard→Paste, or right-click the cell and select Paste.
Move cells with drag and drop	Point to the dark line surrounding the selected range and drag to the desired location.
Copy cells with drag and drop	Hold Ctrl, point to the dark line surrounding the selected range, and drag to the desired location.
Move cells with right-drag and drop	Point to the dark line surrounding the selected range, right-click, and drag to the desired location.
Display the Office Clipboard	Choose Home→Clipboard→dialog box launcher.

Move and Copy Selections

In this exercise, you will use the Cut, Copy, and Paste commands as well as drag and drop to move and copy selections.

1. Save your file as **EX02-D04-Roster-[FirstInitialLastName]**.

2. Follow these steps to copy and paste a cell's contents:

Ⓐ Click **cell A1**, which is the cell you wish to copy.

Ⓑ Choose **Home→Clipboard→Copy**. Notice the flashing marquee that appears.

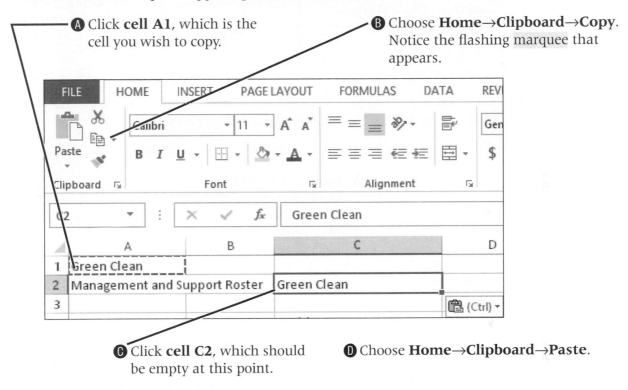

Ⓒ Click **cell C2**, which should be empty at this point.

Ⓓ Choose **Home→Clipboard→Paste**.

Notice that the contents of cell A1 remain, while they now also appear in cell C2.

3. Follow these steps to cut and paste a cell's contents:

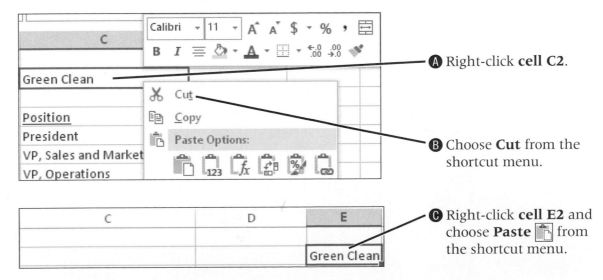

Ⓐ Right-click **cell C2**.

Ⓑ Choose **Cut** from the shortcut menu.

Ⓒ Right-click **cell E2** and choose **Paste** from the shortcut menu.

Cell C2 will now be empty because the contents were moved to cell E2.

Excel 2013

4. Follow these steps to move the contents of cell E2 via the drag-and-drop method:

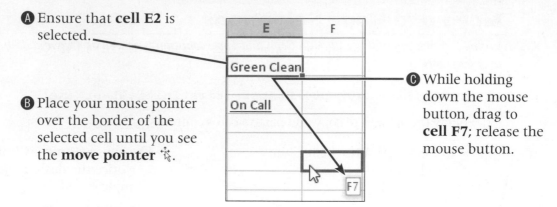

Ⓐ Ensure that **cell E2** is selected.

Ⓑ Place your mouse pointer over the border of the selected cell until you see the **move pointer** ⁀.

Ⓒ While holding down the mouse button, drag to **cell F7**; release the mouse button.

When you drag a cell with this method, Excel shows what cell the selection will be dropped into by displaying it on a ScreenTip, and by placing a highlight around the cell.

5. Follow these steps to copy a cell using the right-drag method:

Ⓐ Click **cell E4** and place your mouse pointer over the border of the **cell E4** until you see the **move pointer** ⁀.

Ⓑ Start dragging with the *right* mouse button. Keep the right mouse button held down.

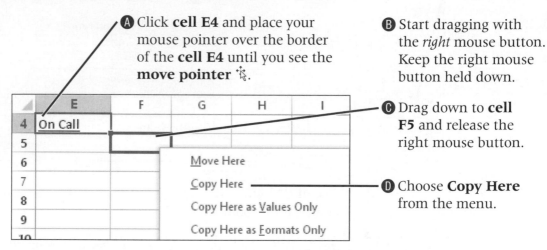

Ⓒ Drag down to **cell F5** and release the right mouse button.

Ⓓ Choose **Copy Here** from the menu.

The contents of cell E4 remain in the cell and are copied to the destination cell, F5.

6. Save 🖫 the workbook.

Using Undo and Redo

Video Library   http://labyrinthelab.com/videos   Video Number: EX13-V0205

The Undo button lets you reverse actions taken within a worksheet. Most actions can be undone, but those that cannot include printing and saving workbooks.

The Redo button reverses an Undo command. The Redo button will be visible on the Quick Access toolbar only after you have undone an action.

Undoing Multiple Actions

Clicking the arrow on the Undo button displays a list of actions that can be undone. You can undo multiple actions by dragging the mouse over the desired actions. You must undo actions in the order in which they appear on the drop-down list.

FROM THE KEYBOARD
Ctrl+Z to undo
Ctrl+Y to redo

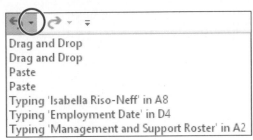

When you click the arrow on the Undo button, you will see a list of previous actions, with the most recent at the top.

Limitations to Undoing

In Excel, there are times when the Undo command will not work, such as when you select any command from the File tab. When an action cannot be undone, Excel will change the Undo ScreenTip to "Can't Undo."

QUICK REFERENCE	UNDOING AND REDOING ACTIONS
Task	**Procedure**
Undo the last action	■ Click Undo 🔄 on the Quick Access toolbar, or tap Ctrl+Z.
Undo a series of actions	■ Click the drop-down arrow 🔄▾ on the Undo button and choose the desired actions.
Redo an undone action	■ Click Redo ↪ on the Quick Access toolbar.

Excel 2013

Undo Actions

In this exercise, you will delete the contents of a column and use Undo to reverse the deletion. You will then use Redo to reverse an Undo command.

1. Save your file as **EX02-D05-Roster-[FirstInitialLastName]**.

2. Replace the contents of **cell C5** with **CEO**.

3. Click the **row 4** heading to select the entire row.

4. Tap [Delete].

   All of the contents in row 4 are deleted.

5. Repeat **steps 3–4** for **rows 8, 12, and 14**.

Use Undo and Redo

6. Follow these steps to undo the last five commands:

   A Click the **Undo menu** ▼ button to display a list of recent actions.

   B Slide the mouse pointer down and choose this item.

   Excel undoes your last five commands.

7. Click **Redo** ⟳ once to restore the *CEO* title in cell C5, and then click **Undo** ↺ to revert back to *President*.

8. Save the workbook.

Clearing Cell Contents and Formats

Video Library   http://labyrinthelab.com/videos   Video Number: EX13-V0206

In Excel, you can format cells by changing font style, size, and/or color. You can also add enhancements such as bold, italics, and underline. In this lesson, you will learn how to clear existing formatting. Clicking the Clear button displays a menu (shown here) that lets you clear content, formats, and comments from cells.

FROM THE RIBBON
Home→Editing→
Clear→Clear All

FROM THE KEYBOARD
Delete to clear cell contents

Excel 2013

QUICK REFERENCE	CLEARING CELL CONTENTS AND FORMATTING
Task	**Procedure**
Delete cell or range contents but retain formatting	Choose Home→Editing→Clear 🖌 ▾ →Clear Contents.
Delete all formatting	Choose Home→Editing→Clear 🖌 ▾ →Clear Formats.
Delete comments within a cell or range of cells	Choose Home→Editing→Clear 🖌 ▾ →Clear Comments.
Delete all links within a cell or range of cells	Choose Home→Editing→Clear 🖌 ▾ →Clear Hyperlinks.
Delete everything	Choose Home→Editing→Clear 🖌 ▾ →Clear All.

Clear Cell Contents and Formatting

In this exercise, you will use the Clear command to delete cell contents and cell formats.

1. Save your file as **EX02-D06-Roster-[FirstInitialLastName]**.

2. Click **cell F5**.

3. Choose **Home→Editing→Clear** and then choose **Clear Formats** from the menu.

   The contents of the cell were underlined. When you choose to clear only the formats, the contents remain and the underline is removed.

4. Click **Undo** on the Quick Access toolbar.

5. Ensure that **cell F5** is selected; then click **Clear** and choose **Clear All**.

6. Type your name and tap Enter.

   Notice that the contents are no longer underlined in cell F5 because you cleared "all" (formatting and contents) from it.

7. Use Ctrl + Z to undo the typing of your name.

8. Click **cell F7** and tap Delete.

   The entry Green Clean is deleted and the formatting remains in the cell.

9. Save the workbook.

Using Auto Features

Video Library   http://labyrinthelab.com/videos   Video Number: EX13-V0207

Excel offers "auto" features that help you work more efficiently. AutoFill allows you to quickly fill a range of cells. AutoComplete makes it easy to enter long entries by typing an acronym or a series of characters, which are converted to the desired entry. AutoCorrect can also assist in correcting commonly misspelled words.

Working with AutoFill

AutoFill allows you to quickly extend a series, copy data, or copy a formula into adjacent cells by selecting cells and dragging the fill handle, which is the small black square that appears at the bottom-right corner of a selected cell or range. If the selected cell does not contain data that AutoFill recognizes as a series, the data will be copied into the adjacent cells. A black cross appears when you position the mouse pointer on the fill handle. You can drag the fill handle to fill adjacent cells to accomplish the following tasks.

- **Copy an entry:** If the entry in the active cell is a number, formula, or text entry, the fill handle copies the entry to adjacent cells.

- **Expand a repeating series of numbers:** If you select two or more cells containing numbers, Excel assumes you want to expand a repeating series. For example, if you select two cells containing the numbers 5 and 10 and drag the fill handle, Excel will fill the adjacent cells with the pattern that you have established: 15, 20, 25, etc.

- **AutoFill of date entries:** If the active cell contains any type of date entry, Excel will determine the increment of the date value and fill in the adjacent cells. For example, if the current cell contains the entry May and you drag the fill handle, AutoFill will insert the entries June, July, August, etc. in the adjacent cells.

The following table and illustrations provide examples of series that AutoFill can extend.

Selected Cells	Extended Series
Mon	Tue, Wed, Thu
Monday	Tuesday, Wednesday, Thursday
Jan	Feb, Mar, Apr
January	February, March, April
Jan, Apr	Jul, Oct, Jan
1, 2	3, 4, 5, 6
100, 125	150, 175, 200
1/10/11	1/11/11, 1/12/11, 1/13/11
1/15/11, 2/15/11	3/15/11, 4/15/11, 5/15/11
1st Qtr	2nd Qtr, 3rd Qtr, 4th Qtr

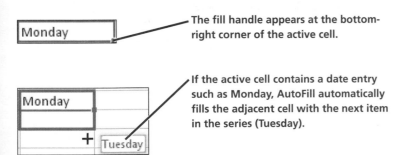

The fill handle appears at the bottom-right corner of the active cell.

If the active cell contains a date entry such as Monday, AutoFill automatically fills the adjacent cell with the next item in the series (Tuesday).

The completed series with the AutoFill Options button displayed.

AutoComplete vs. AutoFill

AutoComplete is useful when you want the same entry repeated more than once in a column. AutoFill allows you to select a cell and fill in entries by completing a series or copying the source cell, whereas AutoComplete works within a cell as you type. If the first few characters you type match another entry in the column, AutoComplete will offer to complete the entry for you. You accept the offer by tapping Tab or Enter; reject it by typing the remainder of the entry yourself.

| 16 | Amy Wyatt | 619-555-4016 | Customer Service Rep |
| 17 | Brian Simpson | 858-555-3718 | customer Service Rep |

Here, a "c" was typed and AutoComplete suggested completing the entry as *Customer Service Rep*. To accept this entry and move to the next cell, tap Tab.

AutoComplete will complete the entry "case sensitive" to match the existing entry.

DEVELOP YOUR SKILLS EX02-D07
Use AutoComplete and AutoFill

In this exercise, you will enter two new employees and use AutoComplete to speed up your work. In addition, you use AutoFill to complete a series of the days of the week.

1. Save your file as **EX02-D07-Roster-[FirstInitialLastName]**.

2. Click **cell A17**, type **Brian Simpson**, and tap Tab to move to the next cell.

3. Type **858-555-3718** and tap Tab.

4. Type **c** and notice that Excel suggests *Customer Service Rep* as the entry. Tap Tab to accept the suggestion and move one cell to the right.

   The entry is capitalized.

5. Type today's date and tap Enter.

   Notice that when you tap Enter, the highlight moves to cell A18, where you can begin typing the next list entry.

6. Type **Leisa Malimali** and tap Tab.

7. Type **619-555-4017** and tap Tab.

8. Type **S** in **cell C18**.

   Excel suggests Sales Manager *from a previous row. Leisa, however, is a sales assistant, so you need to continue typing your entry. Make sure you have typed a capital S, as that will not pull from the previous entries.*

9. Continue typing **ales Assistant** and tap Tab.

   Excel replaces the AutoComplete suggestion with the entry you typed, Sales Assistant.

10. Hold Ctrl and tap ', then tap Enter to display today's date.

    Ctrl + ' *copies the contents of the cell one row above the active cell.*

Use AutoFill to Expand a Series

Now you will fill in the column showing the manager responsible for being on emergency call each evening.

11. Click **cell E6**.

12. Type **Monday** and click the **Enter** ☑ button.

13. Follow these steps to fill the adjacent cells:

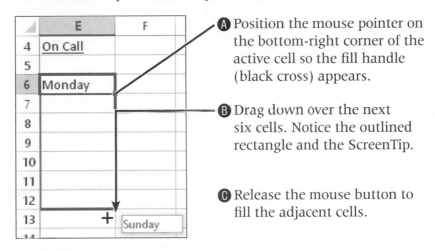

ⓐ Position the mouse pointer on the bottom-right corner of the active cell so the fill handle (black cross) appears.

ⓑ Drag down over the next six cells. Notice the outlined rectangle and the ScreenTip.

ⓒ Release the mouse button to fill the adjacent cells.

14. Select **cell A1** and then save your changes.

The Auto Fill Options Button

Video Library   http://labyrinthelab.com/videos   Video Number: EX13-V0208

The Auto Fill Options button appears after you fill cells in a worksheet. A menu of fill options appears when you click the Auto Fill Options button.

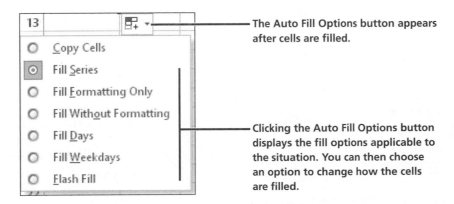

The Auto Fill Options button appears after cells are filled.

Clicking the Auto Fill Options button displays the fill options applicable to the situation. You can then choose an option to change how the cells are filled.

If you choose Fill Without Formatting, you can fill cells without copying the formatting from the original cell. Fill Formatting Only copies the formatting but not the contents from the source cells.

Use the Auto Fill Options Button

In this exercise, you will use the Auto Fill Options button to fill a data series without applying the source cell's formatting. You also will fill by applying only the formatting so that you may enter different data in cells.

1. Save your file as **EX02-D08-Roster-[FirstInitialLastName]**.

2. Choose the **Sheet2** tab at the bottom of the window, and select **cell A1**.

3. Follow these steps to AutoFill cell contents:

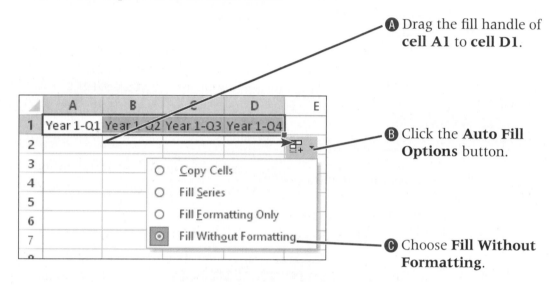

Ⓐ Drag the fill handle of **cell A1** to **cell D1**.

Ⓑ Click the **Auto Fill Options** button.

Ⓒ Choose **Fill Without Formatting**.

The formatting is removed from B1:D1.

4. Follow these steps to AutoFill formatting:

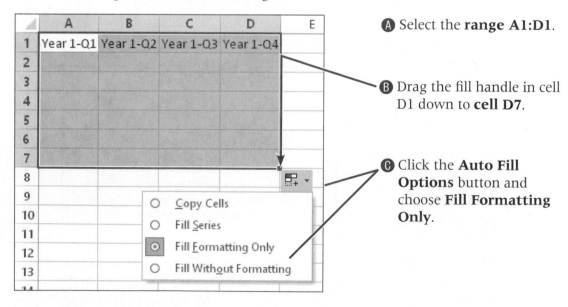

Ⓐ Select the **range A1:D1**.

Ⓑ Drag the fill handle in cell D1 down to **cell D7**.

Ⓒ Click the **Auto Fill Options** button and choose **Fill Formatting Only**.

The contents are removed from the range A2:D7, but the formatting is still applied.

5. Enter numbers shown here in the **range A2:D2**. *Notice that the formatting matches that of the range A1:D1.*

6. Select the **Sheet1** tab of the workbook; save the file.

▲	A	B	C	D
1	Year 1-Q1	Year 1-Q2	Year 1-Q3	Year 1-Q4
2	**222**	333	444	555

Using AutoCorrect

Video Library   http://labyrinthelab.com/videos   Video Number: EX13-V0209

AutoCorrect can improve the speed and accuracy of entering text. AutoCorrect is most useful for replacing abbreviations with full phrases. For example, you could set up AutoCorrect to substitute *Major League Baseball* whenever you type *mlb*. Other benefits of AutoCorrect include that it will automatically correct common misspellings (replacing "teh" with "the"), capitalize the first letter of a day (capitalizing the "s" in "sunday"), and correct words that are typed with two initial capital letters (changing the "R" to lowercase in "ORange").

AutoCorrect entries are shared by all programs in the Microsoft Office Suite, so if you've already added some in Word, they are available for you to use in Excel as well.

Expanding AutoCorrect Entries

AutoCorrect goes into action when you type a word in a text entry and tap ⎵Spacebar⎵, or when you complete a text entry. The word or entry is compared with all entries in the AutoCorrect table. The AutoCorrect table contains a list of words and their replacement phrases. If the word you type matches an entry in the AutoCorrect table, a phrase from the table is substituted for the word. This is known as expanding the AutoCorrect entry.

Undoing AutoCorrect Entries

There may be times that AutoCorrect replaces an entry against your wishes. AutoCorrect is treated as a single character, meaning that it is viewed by the Undo feature the same as if you typed an "a" or tapped ⎵Delete⎵. Therefore, you can use Undo to reverse an AutoCorrect entry before you confirm a cell entry.

Excel 2013

Creating and Editing AutoCorrect Entries

The AutoCorrect dialog box allows you to add entries to the AutoCorrect table, delete entries from the table, and set other AutoCorrect options. To add an entry, type the desired abbreviation in the Replace box and the desired expansion for the abbreviation in the With box.

If you create the abbreviation using uppercase letters, it will not work if you type it in lowercase letters later.

QUICK REFERENCE	USING AUTOCORRECT
Task	**Procedure**
Modify AutoCorrect options	▪ Choose File→Options→Proofing→AutoCorrect Options.
	▪ Make desired changes; click OK twice.

Use AutoCorrect

In this exercise, you will train AutoCorrect to replace an abbreviation with a phrase and learn how to override AutoCorrect.

1. Save your file as **EX02-D09-Roster-[FirstInitialLastName]**.

2. Select **cell A1**.

3. Type **teh cat adn dog ran fast** and tap Enter.
   Notice that both of the spelling errors have been corrected by AutoCorrect.

Override an AutoCorrect Command

4. Click **cell A1**; then type **adn** and tap Spacebar.
   AutoCorrect has corrected the misspelling.

5. Use Ctrl + Z to undo the last action.
   Undo will reverse the last command, in this case AutoCorrect.

6. Tap Esc to cancel the entry.

Create an AutoCorrect Entry

7. Choose **File→Options**.

8. Follow these steps to create an AutoCorrect entry:

Ⓐ Display the **Proofing** options.   Ⓑ Choose **AutoCorrect Options**.

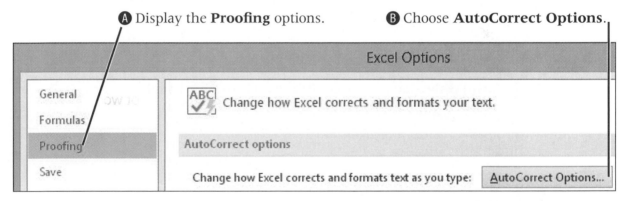

Ⓒ Type **gc** in the **Replace** box.

Ⓓ Tap Tab then type **Green Clean** in the **With** box.

Ⓔ Click **Add**.

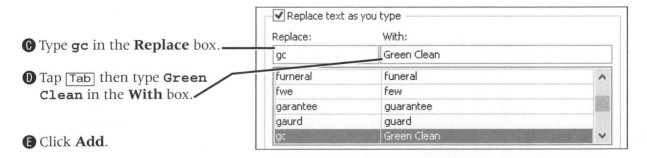

Your entry will be added to the list.

9. Click **OK** in the AutoCorrect dialog box.

10. Click **OK** in the Excel Options dialog box.

Use and Delete an AutoCorrect Entry

It is important to delete the AutoCorrect entry you just created. Otherwise it will still be there when the next student uses the computer.

11. Ensure that **cell A1** is still selected; then type **gc** and tap Enter.

    The AutoCorrect entry that you created is entered into the cell.

12. Choose **File→Options** and display the **Proofing** options.

13. Choose **AutoCorrect Options**.

14. Follow these steps to delete your AutoCorrect entry:

Ⓐ Type **gc** in the **Replace** box.

Ⓑ Click **Delete** and tap Enter.

15. Click **OK** in the Excel Options dialog box.

16. **Save** 💾 the changes and close the workbook. Exit **Excel**.

Concepts Review

To check your knowledge of the key concepts introduced in this lesson, complete the Concepts Review quiz by choosing the appropriate access option below.

If you are...	Then access the quiz by...
Using the Labyrinth Video Library	Going to http://labyrinthelab.com/videos
Using eLab	Logging in, choosing Content, and navigating to the Concepts Review quiz for this lesson
Not using the Labyrinth Video Library or eLab	Going to the student resource center for this book

Reinforce Your Skills

Edit a Worksheet

In this exercise, you will edit a worksheet using techniques such as cut, copy, and paste.

Edit Entries

1. Start **Excel**. Open **EX02-R01-Customers** from the **EX2013 Lesson 02** folder and save it as **EX02-R01-Customers-[FirstInitialLastName]**.

2. Select **cell B5**.

3. Type **Ralph** and tap Enter.

4. Replace the name *Calvin* in **cell B7** with the name **Stephen**.

Select Cells and Ranges

5. Select **cell D3**, drag the mouse to **cell D7**, and release the mouse button.

6. Select **cell B3**, drag the mouse to **cell F3**, and release the mouse button.
   The range D3:D7 is now deselected because you have highlighted a different range.

7. Hold Ctrl and highlight the **range B7:F7**.
   The range B3:F3 remains selected because you held down Ctrl.

8. Click the **column B** heading.
   All of column B is selected.

Work with Cut, Copy, and Paste

9. Select **cell E3**.

10. Choose **Home→Clipboard→Cut** ✂.

11. Select **cell E11** and choose **Home→Clipboard→Paste** 📋.

12. Select the **range A7:F7**; copy it using Ctrl+C.

13. Select **cell A8** and paste the **range A7:F7** using Ctrl+V.
    This approach can come in handy if you have a new entry that is very similar to an existing one!

14. Clear the contents in the **range A8:F8**.

15. Select **cell E11**.

16. Taking care to avoid the fill handle, point at the dark line surrounding the cell, press the right mouse button, and drag up to **cell E3**.
    The context menu appears when you release the mouse button.

132nd Street, Los Angeles, CA 95544

17. Choose **Move Here** from the context menu.

18. Edit the last four digits of the phone number in **cell D7** to **3535**, and confirm the change.

19. Use ⎡Ctrl⎤+⎡Home⎤ to return to **cell A1**.

20. Save your file then close it; exit **Excel**.

21. Submit your final file based on the guidelines provided by your instructor.

    To view examples of how your file or files should look at the end of this exercise, go to the student resource center.

REINFORCE YOUR SKILLS EX02-R02
Manage Cell Contents

In this exercise, you will alter the contents of a worksheet and use multiple auto features.

Use Undo and Redo

1. Start **Excel**. Open **EX02-R02-Customers2** from the **EX2013 Lesson 02** folder and save it as **EX02-R02-Customers2-[FirstInitialLastName]**.

2. Click **cell B6** and tap ⎡Delete⎤ to remove the cell contents.

   You realize that this data is necessary for the listing; it should not have been deleted.

3. Click **Undo** ⟲ on the Quick Access toolbar.

   Notice that the cell contents have returned to cell B6. Also notice that the Redo ⟳ *button is now active on the Quick Access toolbar.*

4. Click **Redo** ⟳ to remove the cell contents once again.

   If you realized that the cell contents were incorrect, you could choose this action to remove them.

5. Type **Brenda** in **cell B6**.

Clear Cell Contents and Formats

6. Click **cell C3**.

7. Choose **Home→Editing→Clear→Clear All**.

   Both the contents and the formatting have been removed from cell C3.

8. Type **Holmes** in **cell C3**.

   Notice that the blue fill color has not returned when the new entry is typed.

Use Auto Features

9. Select **cell F7** and type **oh**.

   Notice that AutoComplete does not suggest an entry when you type "o," as there are two "o" entries in the column.

10. Tap ⎡Tab⎤ to accept the suggested entry of *Ohio*.

11. Select **cell A3**.

    Before using AutoFill, you must select the cell that you will be using as the basis for the fill information.

12. Place your mouse pointer over the fill handle at the bottom-right corner of the selected cell and drag down through **cell A7**. Release the mouse button when the ScreenTip shows C535.

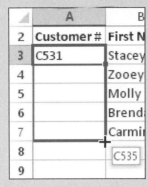

Notice that Excel recognizes C531 as the beginning of a series (C532, C533, etc.).

Use AutoCorrect

13. Choose **File→Options**.

14. Click the **Proofing** option along the left-side panel, and then click **AutoCorrect Options**.

15. In the **Replace** box, type **nc** and tap Tab.
    Remember to type the abbreviation in lowercase.

16. In the **With** box, type **North Carolina**.

17. Click the **Add** button; click **OK** twice.
    You have now added the abbreviation for North Carolina as an AutoCorrect entry.

18. Select **cell F6**.

19. Type **nc** and tap Spacebar.
    The state name appears in the cell.

20. Tap Enter to confirm the entry.

21. Save your file then close it; exit **Excel**.

22. Submit your final file based on the guidelines provided by your instructor.
    To view examples of how your file or files should look at the end of this exercise, go to the student resource center.

Create and Adjust a Worksheet

In this exercise, you will use various techniques to edit the contents and formatting of a worksheet.

Edit Entries

1. Start **Excel**. Open **EX02-R03-Customers3** from the **EX2013 Lesson 02** folder and save it as **EX02-R03-Customers3-[FirstInitialLastName]**.

2. Select **cell C7**.

3. Type **George** and tap Enter.

4. Replace *Ross* in **cell D5** with **Taft**.

Select Cells and Ranges

5. Select **cell B3**, drag the mouse to **cell F3**, and release the mouse button.

6. Select **cell B4**, drag the mouse to **cell F4**, and release the mouse button.
    The range B3:F3 is now deselected because you have highlighted a different range.

7. Hold Ctrl and highlight the **range B6:F6**.
    The range B4:F4 remains selected because you held down Ctrl.

8. Click the **row 2** heading.
    The entire row is now highlighted.

Work with Cut, Copy, and Paste

9. Select **cell F6**.

10. Choose **Home→Clipboard→Cut** ✂.

11. Select **cell F4** and choose **Home→Clipboard→Paste** .

12. Use Ctrl+C to copy the **range B7:E7**.

13. Select **cell B8** and use Ctrl+V to paste the range.

14. Select the **range B8:E8**.

15. Taking care to avoid the fill handle, point at the dark line surrounding the range, press the right mouse button, and drag up to the **range B7:E7**.
    The context menu appears when you release the mouse button.

16. Choose **Move Here** from the context menu.

17. Edit the entry in **cell F3** to the correct spelling of **Minnesota** and tap Enter.

18. Use Ctrl+Home to return to **cell A1**.

Use Undo and Redo

19. Click **cell E4** and tap Delete to remove the cell contents.

You realize that this data is necessary for the listing; it should not have been deleted.

20. Click **Undo** ⤺ on the Quick Access toolbar.

Notice that the cell contents have returned to cell E4. Also notice that the Redo ⤼ button now appears on the Quick Access toolbar.

21. Click **Redo** ⤼ to remove the cell contents once again.

If you realized that the cell contents were incorrect, you could choose this action to remove them.

22. Type **Mesa** in **cell E4**.

Clear Cell Contents and Formats

23. Click **cell D3** and choose **Home→Editing→Clear→Clear Formats**.

The contents remain while the formatting has been removed.

Use Auto Features

24. Select **cell F7** and type **ma**.

Notice that AutoComplete does not suggest an entry when you only type an "m," as there are two "m" entries in the column.

25. Tap Tab to accept the suggested entry of *Maine*.

26. Select **cell A3**.

Before using AutoFill, you must select the cell that you will be using as the basis for the fill information.

27. Place your mouse pointer over the fill handle at the bottom-right corner of the selected cell and drag down through **cell A7**. Release the mouse button when the ScreenTip shows R005.

Notice that Excel recognizes R001 as the beginning of a series (R002, R003, etc.).

Use AutoCorrect

28. Choose **File→Options**.

29. Click the **Proofing** option along the left-side menu, and then click **AutoCorrect Options**.

30. In the **Replace** box, type **wv** and tap Tab.

Remember to type the abbreviation in lowercase.

31. In the **With** box, type **West Virginia**.

32. Click the **Add** button; click **OK** twice.

You have now added the abbreviation for West Virginia as an AutoCorrect entry.

33. Select **cell F6**, type **wv**, and tap Spacebar.

The state name appears in the cell.

34. Tap Enter to confirm the entry.

35. Save your file, and then close it; exit **Excel**.

36. Submit your final file based on the guidelines provided by your instructor.

Apply Your Skills

APPLY YOUR SKILLS EX02-A01

Alter Worksheet Components

In this exercise, you will use multiple techniques to edit worksheet entries and move and copy data.

Select Cells and Ranges and Edit Entries

1. Start **Excel**. Open **EX02-A01-CarpetProd** from the **EX2013 Lesson 02** folder and save it as **EX02-A01-CarpetProd-[FirstInitialLastName]**.

2. Edit the label in **cell E3** to **Price**.

3. In **cell C11**, change the entry *Granular* to **Powder**.

4. Change the entry in **cell E17** to **$4.65**.

5. Select the **range A6:E18**.

6. Drag and drop the selection so the top of it is in **row 4**.
   The selection will now be contained in the range A4:E16.

Work With Cut, Copy, and Paste

7. Select the **range B3:E3** and issue the **Cut** command.

8. Click **cell B4** and issue the **Paste** command.

9. Copy the contents of the **range B4:E4** into the **range B12:E12**.

10. Save your file, and then close it; exit **Excel**.

11. Submit your final file based on the guidelines provided by your instructor.
    To view examples of how your file or files should look at the end of this exercise, go to the student resource center.

Adjust Cell Contents

In this exercise, you will use the Undo button. You will also clear cell contents and use various auto features.

Use Undo and Redo, and Clear Cell Contents and Formats

1. Start **Excel**. Open **EX02-A02-Training** from the **EX2013 Lesson 02** folder and save it as **EX02-A02-Training-[FirstInitialLastName]**.

2. Delete the contents of **cell C4**.

3. Click the **Undo** button to bring back the cell contents.

4. Select **column C** by clicking the column header.

5. Choose **Home→Editing→Clear→Clear Formats**.

   Notice that the Medium entries remain in column C, but they are no longer formatted with borders.

Use Auto Features

6. AutoFill the ID numbers in **column B**.

7. Use **AutoComplete** to enter **print**, **audio**, and **video** in **cells C8, C9, and C10**, respectively.

8. Create an **AutoCorrect** entry of **mmm** for **Middle Management Manual**.

9. Use your **AutoCorrect** entry to quickly place **Middle Management Manual** in **cell A16**.

10. Save your file, and then close it; exit **Excel**.

11. Submit your final file based on the guidelines provided by your instructor.

    To view examples of how your file or files should look at the end of this exercise, go to the student resource center.

Make Changes to a Worksheet

In this exercise, you will use the skills you have learned in this lesson to correct an income statement.

Select Cells and Ranges and Edit Entries

1. Start **Excel**. Open **EX02-A03-IncomeState** from the **EX2013 Lesson 02** folder and save it as **EX02-A03-IncomeState-[FirstInitialLastName]**.

2. Use the Formula Bar to change the entry in **cell A12** to **Auto Expense**.

3. Replace the entry in **cell A6** with **Sales Revenue**.

4. Select the **range A16:E16**.

5. Right-drag and drop the selection so it appears in **row 15**.

Work With Cut, Copy, and Paste

6. Select the **range C5:C6** and issue the **Cut** command.

7. Click **cell D5** and issue the **Paste** command.

Use Undo and Redo and Clear Cell Contents and Formats

8. Delete the contents of **cell E4**.

9. Click the **Undo** button to bring back the cell contents.

10. Click the **Redo** button to once again delete the contents of **cell E4**.

11. Select **rows 1–3** by clicking the row headers.

12. Choose **Home→Editing→Clear→Clear Formats**.
    All formatting from the header has now been removed.

Use Auto Features

13. AutoFill the account types in **cell G6** and in the **range G10:G13**.

14. Click the **row G** header and tap ⌷Delete⌷.

15. Create an **AutoCorrect** entry of **uce** for **Universal Corporate Events**.

16. Use your **AutoCorrect** entry to quickly place **Universal Corporate Events** in **cell A2**.

17. Save your file, and then close it; exit **Excel**.

18. Submit your final file based on the guidelines provided by your instructor.

Extend Your Skills

In the course of working through the Extend Your Skills exercises, you will think critically as you use the skills taught in the lesson to complete the assigned projects. To evaluate your mastery and completion of the exercises, your instructor may use a rubric, with which more points are allotted according to performance characteristics. (The more you do, the more you earn!) Ask your instructor how your work will be evaluated.

EX02-E01 **That's the Way I See It**

You are known as the neighborhood Excel expert for small businesses! You are creating a worksheet for the local bank that contains information about all employees. It contains most of the necessary data, but you know that certain items were entered incorrectly by your assistant. You are now reviewing the worksheet for any incomplete entries, spelling mistakes, and formatting issues.

Open **EX02-E01-BankListing** from the **EX2013 Lesson 02** folder and save it as **EX02-E01-BankListing-[FirstInitialLastName]**.

Create an AutoComplete entry for the name of your local bank and use it to enter the name in the merged cell at the top. Review the entire worksheet. Use AutoFill to complete the missing data, use Cut and Paste where appropriate, and clear out unnecessary formatting.

You will be evaluated based on the inclusion of all elements specified, your ability to follow directions, your ability to apply newly learned skills to a real-world situation, your creativity, and the relevance of your topic and/or data choice(s). Submit your final file based on the guidelines provided by your instructor.

EX02-E02 **Be Your Own Boss**

Your new company Blue Jean Landscaping is doing well, and you already need a customer listing. During the first week of your business, six new customers have utilized your service.

Open **EX02-E02-BlueJeanCust** from the **EX2013 Lesson 02** folder and save it as **EX02-E02-BlueJeanCust-[FirstInitialLastName]**.

On the Data tab you will find customer information that you will need to create the listing. Using the Customer Listing tab, create the worksheet in an efficient manner, consistent with the skills you have learned in this lesson (using Copy and Paste, for one).

You will be evaluated based on inclusion of all elements specified, your ability to follow directions, your ability to apply newly learned skills to a real-world situation, your creativity, and your demonstration of an entrepreneurial spirit. Submit your final file based on the guidelines provided by your instructor.

Transfer Your Skills

In the course of working through the Transfer Your Skills exercises, you will use critical-thinking and creativity skills to complete the assigned projects using skills taught in the lesson. To evaluate your mastery and completion of the exercises, your instructor may use a rubric, with which more points are allotted according to performance characteristics. (The more you do, the more you earn!) Ask your instructor how your work will be evaluated.

EX02-T01 Use the Web as a Learning Tool

Throughout this book, you will be provided with an opportunity to use the Internet as a learning tool by completing WebQuests. According to the original creators of WebQuests, as described on their website (WebQuest.org), a WebQuest is "an inquiry-oriented activity in which most or all of the information used by learners is drawn from the web." To complete the WebQuest projects in this book, navigate to the student resource center and choose the WebQuest for the lesson on which you are currently working. The subject of each WebQuest will be relevant to the material found in the lesson.

WebQuest Subject: Altering a spreadsheet to correct formatting issues

Submit your final file(s) based on the guidelines provided by your instructor.

EX02-T02 Demonstrate Proficiency

You have decided that, based on its overwhelming popularity, you will begin to sell the Stormy BBQ secret recipe BBQ sauce across the United States. To do so, you will hire five sales representatives and will assign each to ten states. To track the new sales representatives, you will assign each a unique five-digit employee ID#, and a listing should be created that shows the employee name, employee ID#, hire date (all employees were hired on 2/1/2013), and state assignments (ensure that each representative is assigned ten states close to one another). Use the names of five of your friends for the sales representatives.

Open a blank workbook and save it as **EX02-T02-SalesReps-[FirstInitialLastName]** in your **EX2013 Lesson 02** folder. Use the concepts you have learned in this lesson to efficiently create the worksheet described above in an easily understandable format.

Submit your final file based on the guidelines provided by your instructor.

Changing the Appearance of Worksheets

LEARNING OBJECTIVES

After this lesson, you will be able to:

- Print worksheets and change workbook properties
- Insert, delete, move, copy, and rename worksheets
- Modify column width and row height
- Insert, delete, hide, and unhide columns and rows
- Set the vertical alignment and rotate text

Proper organization within an Excel workbook is, in many ways, as important as the content itself. Workbooks to be shared must be organized in a manner that allows users to quickly identify and understand the data. In this lesson, you will organize worksheet data by adjusting tab order, rows, columns, and cell alignment. You will also print worksheets and edit worksheet properties. These topics will improve your ability to organize worksheets effectively.

Changing Workbook Tabs, Columns, and Rows

Safety is a chief concern at Green Clean, a janitorial product supplier and cleaning service. You are working with the Risk Management Department to prepare company policies and procedures for legal compliance, contracts, insurance, Worker's Compensation, and workplace safety.

You will organize the structure of a workbook containing multiple worksheets. A worksheet will contain a list of learning objectives for the training topic. Test questions will be created for each objective to assess an employee's knowledge and performance regarding the objective. The worksheet will show the number of test questions in each category as well as the total and percentage score. You will work with entire rows and columns to organize the worksheet, vertically align and rotate headings, and print worksheets.

	A	B	C	D	E	F
1		Green Clean				
2		Safety Training - Chemicals				
3			Exam Categories			
4		Performance Objectives	Knowledge	Comprehension	Performance	Analysis
5			(# of Items)			
6	1.	Identify and mix hazardous materials safely.				
7	a.	Understand and follow steps on material safety data sheets (MSDS) correctly.	2	1	2	
8	b.	Identify hazardous materials		2	2	1

Column widths and row heights are adjusted to display cell contents.

24	a.	Show first aid procedures for various given incidents.		2	2	2
25	b.	Show the use of an emergency wash station.		2	2	2
26						
27						

‹ › **Chemicals** | Lifting | Garbage | **Floors** | Notes | ⊕

Worksheet tabs are copied, rearranged, and colored to clearly identify the workbook structure.

Exploring the Many Views of Excel

Video Library   http://labyrinthelab.com/videos   Video Number: EX13-V0301

Changing the view in Excel does not change how the worksheet will print. When first opened, a blank worksheet displays in Normal view. Page Layout view allows you to see how your worksheet will appear when you print it, page by page. In this view you can add headers and footers, number pages, and edit other items that print at the top and bottom of every page. In the Page Break Preview you can see blue lines representing the location of the page breaks. These lines can be dragged to any desired location. You may use either the View tab or the View buttons in the lower-right corner of the worksheet window to switch among the different worksheet views.

Zooming the View

The Zoom control lets you change the size of the onscreen worksheet but has no effect on the printed worksheet. You can zoom from 10 to 400 percent. Zooming the view can make worksheet data easier to see, and therefore facilitates worksheet editing.

The Zoom box lets you control zoom percentages.

This button returns the zoom to 100 percent.

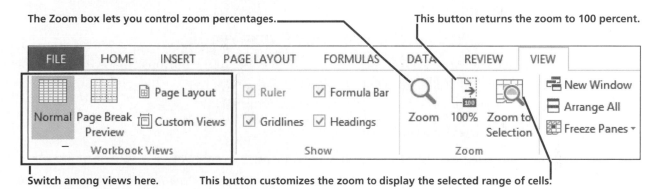

Switch among views here.

This button customizes the zoom to display the selected range of cells.

The View buttons are also available next to the Zoom controls.

Use the Zoom slider to rapidly change the zoom percentage.

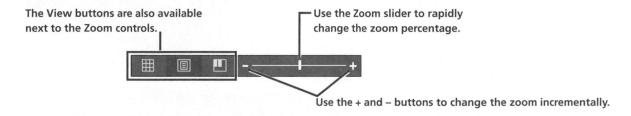

Use the + and – buttons to change the zoom incrementally.

DEVELOP YOUR SKILLS EX03-D01
Change Views and Use the Zoom Control

In this exercise, you will change the zoom and switch between Page Layout and Normal views.

1. Start **Excel**. Open **EX03-D01-SafetyTraining** from the **EX2013 Lesson 03** folder and save it as **EX03-D01-SafetyTraining-[FirstInitialLastName]**.

   Replace the bracketed text with your first initial and last name. For example, if your name is Bethany Smith, your filename would look like this: EX03-D01-SafetyTraining-BSmith.

2. Follow these steps to adjust the zoom percentage:

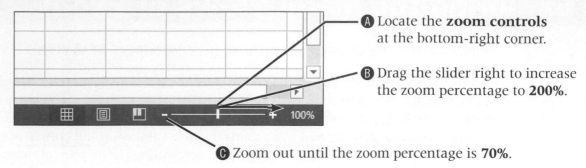

Ⓐ Locate the **zoom controls** at the bottom-right corner.

Ⓑ Drag the slider right to increase the zoom percentage to **200%**.

Ⓒ Zoom out until the zoom percentage is **70%**.

3. Select the **range A1:F5** and choose **View→Zoom→Zoom to Selection** 🔍.

   The Zoom to Selection option provides a close-up view of a selection.

4. Choose **View→Zoom→100%** 🗗.

Switch between Views

5. Choose **View→Workbook Views→Page Layout View** 📄.

   This view displays the worksheet as if printed on paper so you can check how many pages will print before printing.

6. Choose **View→Workbook Views→Normal View** ▦.

7. Click the **Page Layout** 📄 button, which is one of the buttons adjacent to the zoom bar at the bottom-right corner of the screen.

   The View buttons allow you to quickly toggle between views.

Check That Data Fit on One Page

8. Scroll down and to the right to view the entire worksheet.

   The gray areas will not print. They indicate which rows and columns would extend to additional printed pages if data were in them. All data in range A1:F24 fit on two pages.

9. Scroll up and to the left so **cell A1** is in view.

Edit in Page Layout View

10. Delete the contents of **cell A1**.

    You may edit the worksheet in Page Layout view just as you would in Normal view.

11. **Undo** ↶ the change.

12. Save the file and leave it open; you will modify it throughout this lesson.

    The current workbook view is saved and would reappear the next time the workbook is opened. Leave the workbook open for the next exercise.

Printing Worksheets

Video Library   http://labyrinthelab.com/videos   Video Number: EX13-V0302

Excel gives you several ways to print your work. These different options provide flexibility so that printing can be adapted to accommodate all workbooks.

 The light gridlines displayed around cells in Normal and Page Layout views do not print.

Print Preview

Print Preview shows how a worksheet will look when printed. It's always wise to preview a large or complex worksheet before sending it to the printer. The Print tab in Backstage view displays a preview along with print options. You cannot edit worksheets in Backstage view.

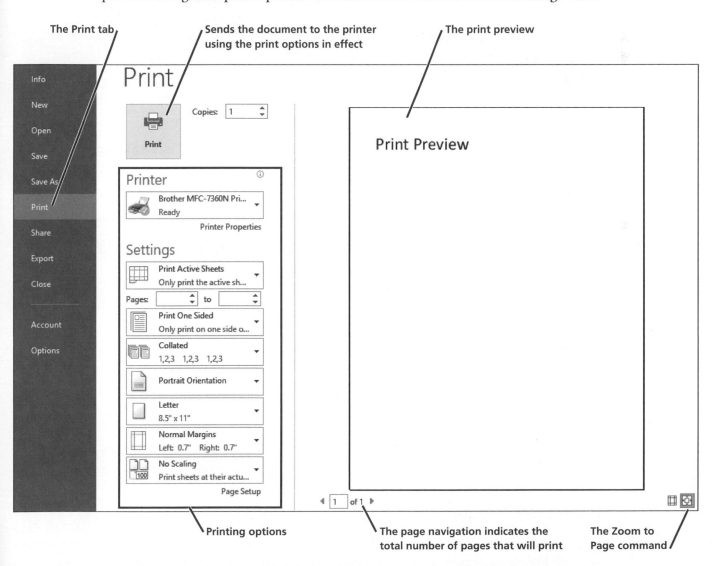

Print the Worksheet

You can customize the Quick Access toolbar to include the Quick Print button, which sends the entire worksheet to the current printer using those print options currently in effect. You must use the Print tab in Backstage view to change printers, adjust the number of copies to be printed, print only selected cells, and more.

FROM THE RIBBON
File→Print

FROM THE KEYBOARD
Ctrl+P to print

Printing Selections

You may want to print only a single range of cells or multiple nonadjacent ranges within a worksheet. To print a selection, you must first select the desired cells. You then choose the Print Selection option in Backstage view before executing the Print command. Nonadjacent selections print on separate pages.

To print a selection, you must select the cell range before issuing the Print command.

DEVELOP YOUR SKILLS EX03-D02

Preview and Print a Worksheet

In this exercise, you will preview your worksheet in the Print tab of Backstage view, and then send it to the printer.

1. Save your file as **EX03-D02-SafetyTraining-[FirstInitialLastName]**.

2. Click the **Sheet2** tab to make that sheet active.

3. Choose **File→Print**.

   The Print tab of Backstage view opens, and a preview of page 1 displays on the right. The page navigation option at the bottom-left corner of the preview indicates that you are viewing page 1 of 1.

4. Click the **Zoom to Page** button at the lower-right corner of the preview.

5. Use the scroll bar to view the zoomed-in view.

6. Click the **Zoom to Page** button again to zoom out.

7. Review the options available at the left of the Print tab of Backstage view, and then click **Print** at the top-left corner.

8. Save the file.

Editing Workbook Properties

Video Library   http://labyrinthelab.com/videos   Video Number: EX13-V0303

Certain information about a workbook is saved along with the workbook contents. You can view these workbook properties while a workbook is open. The Windows operating system also displays document properties for a selected file.

Standard Properties

The Info tab in Backstage view displays a group of standard properties associated with Microsoft Office files. The default author name is the User Name, although you may change this if you wish. You may also enter a title, subject, categories, and comments about the workbook.

Advanced Properties

In Backstage view, you can use the Show All Properties link to display an expanded properties list. You can access two other views by displaying the Properties menu in Backstage view. Custom properties do not display in Backstage view. If you know how to use a computer programming language such as Visual Basic for Applications (VBA), you can create code using custom properties to perform additional tasks in workbooks.

Properties ▾	
Size	Not saved yet
Title	Add a title
Tags	Add a tag
Categories	Add a category
Related Dates	
Last Modified	
Created	Today, 7:37 AM
Last Printed	Today, 7:41 AM
Related People	
Author	Add an author
Last Modified By	Not saved yet
Show All Properties	

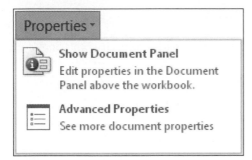

The Properties menu

QUICK REFERENCE	EDITING WORKBOOK PROPERTIES
Task	**Procedure**
Set the username	■ Choose File→Options.
	■ Enter the desired name in the User Name box.
Edit standard properties	■ Choose File→Info.
	■ Add or change the desired properties in Backstage view, or choose Properties menu ▼ →Show Document Panel to work with properties in the active worksheet.
Expand the Properties List	■ Choose File→Info.
	■ Select the Show All Properties link.
Edit standard, advanced, and custom properties	■ Choose File→Info.
	■ Choose Properties menu ▼ →Advanced Properties.
	■ Click the appropriate tab in the Properties dialog box and edit the desired items.

Edit Workbook Properties

In this exercise, you will verify the Microsoft Office username, display document properties in various ways, and set several properties.

1. Save your file as **EX03-D03-SafetyTraining-[FirstInitialLastName]**.

2. Choose **File→Options**.

   The General options category is selected by default.

3. Read the existing User Name at the bottom of the options window. (Your User Name will differ from the illustration.)

   This is the username set for all Microsoft Office documents. Do not change it unless your instructor directs you to do so.

4. Click **Cancel** to exit Excel Options.

Enter Standard Properties

5. Follow these steps to enter tags, a category, and an additional author for the workbook file:

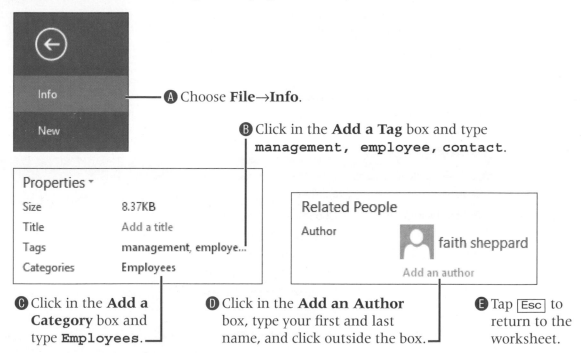

   Ⓐ Choose **File→Info**.

   Ⓑ Click in the **Add a Tag** box and type **management, employee, contact**.

   Ⓒ Click in the **Add a Category** box and type **Employees**.

   Ⓓ Click in the **Add an Author** box, type your first and last name, and click outside the box.

   Ⓔ Tap ⎇Esc⎇ to return to the worksheet.

Expand the Properties

6. If necessary, choose **File→Info**.

7. Choose **Show All Properties** at the bottom-right corner of Backstage view. (Scroll down to locate the command, if necessary.)

8. Review the expanded list of properties, which include Comments, Status, and Manager.

Explore Advanced and Custom Properties

9. Click the **Properties menu** ▼ button located above the Properties list and choose **Show Document Panel**.

After a few moments, the panel displays above the active worksheet with the properties you entered. You can also edit properties in the panel.

10. Follow these steps to explore advanced document properties:

Ⓐ Click the **Document Properties menu** ▼ button and choose **Advanced Properties**.

Ⓑ Explore the various tabs, ending with **Custom**. Click **Cancel** when you're finished.

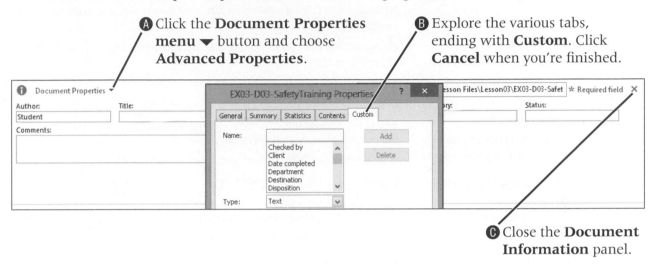

Ⓒ Close the **Document Information** panel.

A custom property may be selected or a name entered to create a new property. After the property's type and value are specified, the Add button is enabled.

11. Save the file.

Managing Worksheets

| Video Library | http://labyrinthelab.com/videos | Video Number: EX13-V0304 |

FROM THE RIBBON

Home→Cells→Insert
menu ▼→Insert Sheet

FROM THE KEYBOARD

Shift + F11 to insert a
worksheet

As you work with more complex workbooks, you will need to be comfortable with workbook management and worksheet navigation. You can organize a workbook by inserting, deleting, and rearranging worksheets. You also can rename worksheet tabs and apply colors to them. These options can be accessed via the Ribbon, by right-clicking, and by using keyboard controls.

The navigation buttons

The New Sheet button inserts a new sheet to the right of the active sheet tab.

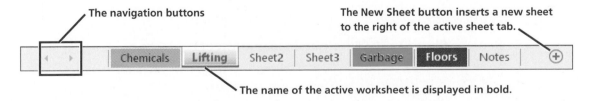

The name of the active worksheet is displayed in bold.

You cannot undo the Delete worksheet command. If you issue the command by mistake, you can close the workbook without saving and then reopen it to recover the lost worksheet.

Task	Procedure
Rename a worksheet	▪ Double-click the desired worksheet tab, type a new name, and tap Enter.
Select multiple worksheets	▪ **Adjacent:** Click the first tab in the range, hold down Shift, and click the last tab in the range. ▪ **Nonadjacent:** Click a worksheet tab, hold down Ctrl, and click additional worksheet tabs.
Change the worksheet tab color	▪ Right-click the desired sheet tab, choose Tab Color, and choose a color.
Insert a worksheet	▪ **To the right of active tab(s):** Click New Sheet. ▪ **Before the active tab:** Choose Home→Cells→Insert menu ▼→Insert Sheet.
Insert multiple worksheets before the active sheet tab	▪ Select the desired tab, hold down Shift, and click a sheet tab at the right equal to the number of worksheets to insert. ▪ Choose Home→Cells→Insert menu ▼→Insert Sheet.
Delete a worksheet	▪ Right-click the tab of the worksheet to delete and choose Delete.
Delete multiple worksheets	▪ Select the first worksheet tab to be deleted, hold down Ctrl, and click the other desired tab(s), or hold down Shift and select the last in a range of tabs. ▪ Choose Home→Cells→Delete menu ▼→Delete Sheet.
Move a worksheet	▪ Drag the worksheet tab to the desired location.

DEVELOP YOUR SKILLS EX03-D04

Modify Workbook Sheet Order

In this exercise, you will insert and move a new worksheet, and delete a worksheet.

1. Save your file as **EX03-D04-SafetyTraining-[FirstInitialLastName]**.

2. Follow these steps to rename Sheet1:

   Ⓐ Double-click the **Sheet1** tab at the bottom of the worksheet to select its name.

   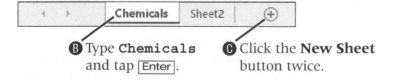

   Ⓑ Type **Chemicals** and tap Enter. **Ⓒ** Click the **New Sheet** button twice.

   Two new sheets appear to the right of the Chemicals sheet.

3. Rename **Sheet2** as **Lifting** and rename **Sheet1** as **Notes**.

Move and Delete Sheets

4. Drag the **Lifting** sheet to the left of **Notes**.

Notice that the mouse pointer displays an empty sheet icon as you drag to the desired position, indicated by the small triangle ▼.

5. Right-click **Sheet3** and choose **Delete**.

Excel does not ask you to confirm this deletion because the worksheet is empty.

6. Click the **Lifting** sheet tab to select the sheet.

7. Hold down [Shift] and select the **Notes** tab.

Both tabs are now selected.

8. Choose **Home→Cells→Insert menu ▼→Insert Sheet**.

Two new sheets were inserted before the Lifting sheet. Your sheet numbers may be different.

9. Drag the **Lifting** sheet to the left of Sheet5.

10. Select the **Sheet4** tab, hold down [Ctrl] and select the **Sheet5** tab.

The [Ctrl] key allows you to select nonadjacent sheets for deletion, while the [Shift] key selects all sheets between the active sheet tab and the next tab you select.

11. Choose **Home→Cells→Delete menu ▼ →Delete Sheet**.

The two sheets are deleted.

12. Save the file.

Copying and Hiding Worksheets

Video Library   http://labyrinthelab.com/videos   Video Number: EX13-V0305

At times it can be useful to copy a worksheet. You may want to save original data while updating the worksheet copy, or you may create a worksheet structure that can be utilized repeatedly.

Hiding and unhiding worksheets can also be useful, particularly when the end user will review only some of the worksheets. In this instance there is no benefit to showing all worksheets, and therefore hiding the unnecessary ones can create a more user-friendly workbook.

Excel 2013

Task	Procedure
Copy a worksheet	■ Select the desired sheet and hold down Ctrl while dragging its tab. ■ When the new tab is in the desired position, release the mouse button and Ctrl.
Hide a worksheet	■ Select the desired tab and choose Home→Cells→Format→Hide & Unhide→Hide Sheet, or right-click the sheet tab and choose Hide.
Unhide a worksheet	■ Choose Home→Cells→Format→Hide & Unhide→Unhide Sheet (or right-click any sheet tab and choose Unhide); then choose the desired sheet and click OK.

DEVELOP YOUR SKILLS EX03-D05
Modify Workbook Sheet Tabs

In this exercise, you will copy a sheet, rename worksheet tabs, and change tab colors. You will also hide and unhide a worksheet.

Copy a Sheet

1. Save your file as **EX03-D05-SafetyTraining-[FirstInitialLastName]**.

2. Click the **Lifting** sheet tab to select the sheet.

3. Hold down Ctrl, drag the **Lifting** tab to the right to position it between Lifting and Notes, release the mouse button, and release Ctrl.

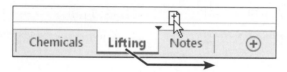

Notice that the mouse pointer displays a sheet icon containing a plus sign (+) as you drag, indicating that you are copying the sheet. The duplicated sheet is named Lifting (2).

4. Rename **Lifting (2)** to **Garbage**.

5. Repeat **steps 2–4** to copy the **Garbage** sheet and rename it as **Floors**.

6. In **cell A2** of the Floors sheet, edit *Lifting and Motion* to read **Floors**.

7. Select the **Garbage** sheet.

8. In **cell A2**, edit *Lifting and Motion* to read **Garbage**.

Change the Sheet Tab Color

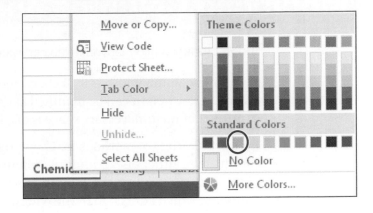

9. Right-click the Chemicals sheet, point to Tab Color in the context menu, and choose the orange theme color from the palette, as shown.

10. Repeat the above step to apply a blue theme shade to the **Lifting** sheet tab, a green theme shade to the **Garbage** sheet tab, and a purple theme shade to the **Floors** sheet tab.

    Leave the Notes tab in its original gray shade.

11. Select the **Chemicals** tab.

    Notice that the text of the currently selected tab turns bold and its color reduces to a subtle band below the text.

Hide and Unhide a Worksheet

12. Right-click the **Notes** sheet tab and choose **Hide**.

    The worksheet and its tab disappear.

13. Choose **Home→Cells→Format**.

14. Trace down to **Visibility**, point to **Hide & Unhide**, and choose **Unhide Sheet**.

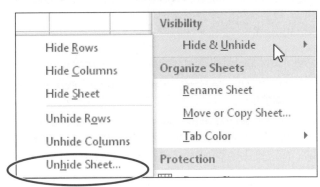

    The Unhide dialog box displays. The Notes sheet already is selected because it is the only one available to be unhidden.

15. Click **OK**.

16. Save the file.

Modifying Columns and Rows

Video Library   http://labyrinthelab.com/videos   Video Number: EX13-V0306

The default column width is 8.43 characters and the default row height is 15 points. Column width and row height can be modified as desired. Strive to make data fully visible while ensuring that no unnecessary space is displayed.

There are a variety of methods for changing column width and row height. They can be performed on either one or multiple columns or rows. One efficient way to adjust widths and heights is to simply drag the column or row headings. Another method employs the AutoFit command, which adjusts to fit the widest (column) or tallest (row) entry.

◢	A	↔	B
1	Safety Training - Chemicals		
2	Performance Objectives		
3			

When you point to the border between columns or rows, a double-pointed arrow appears.

QUICK REFERENCE	CHANGING COLUMN WIDTHS AND ROW HEIGHTS
Task	**Procedure**
Set a precise column width	■ Select the column, choose Home→Cells→Format→Column Width, and type the desired width.
Set column widths using AutoFit	■ **From the Ribbon:** Select the desired column(s) and choose Home→Cells→Format→AutoFit Column Width.
	■ **By double-clicking:** Select the desired column(s). Position the mouse pointer between any two selected headings (or to the right of the selected single column heading) and double-click when the double arrow mouse pointer appears.
Set a precise row height	■ Select the row, choose Home→Cells→Format→Row Height, and type the desired height.
Set row heights using AutoFit	■ Select the desired row and choose Home→Cells→Format→AutoFit Row Height. Or, select multiple rows and double-click between any two selected headings.
Manually adjust column widths and row heights	■ Select the desired column(s) or row(s) and drag (do not double-click) the heading line.

DEVELOP YOUR SKILLS EX03-D06
Change Column Width and Row Height

In this exercise, you will change the column width and row height to ensure that the cell entries fit properly.

1. Save your file as **EX03-D06-SafetyTraining-[FirstInitialLastName]**.

2. Display the **Chemicals** worksheet in **Normal** view.

3. Follow these steps to resize column A:

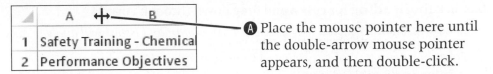

A Place the mouse pointer here until the double-arrow mouse pointer appears, and then double-click.

Notice that the column is resized to fit the widest entry, which is in row 1. You will be merging and centering the title in row 1, so this column is too wide for your use.

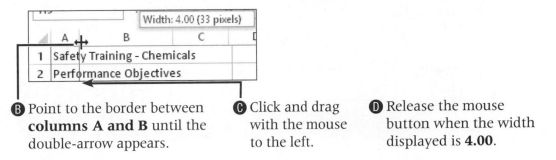

B Point to the border between **columns A and B** until the double-arrow appears.

C Click and drag with the mouse to the left.

D Release the mouse button when the width displayed is **4.00**.

4. Click the **column B heading** to select the entire column.

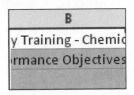

5. Follow these steps to precisely set the column width:

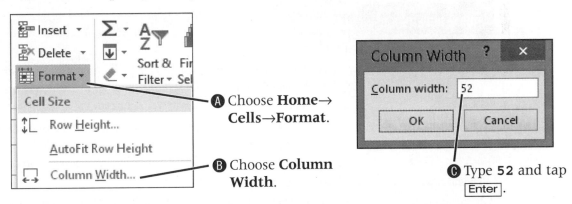

A Choose **Home→ Cells→Format**.

B Choose **Column Width**.

C Type **52** and tap Enter.

The column now accommodates the larger cell entries, which have "spread out" because the cells are formatted to wrap text.

Excel 2013

Use AutoFit to Adjust the Row Height

6. Click the **heading** for **row 4** and drag down through **row 24**.

Rows 4 through 24 should now be selected. Any command issued will apply to all selected rows.

7. Point between two of the selected rows to display the double-arrow pointer and double-click.

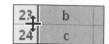

All of the selected rows shrink to fit the tallest entry. Alternatively, you can choose Home→Cells→Format→AutoFit Row Height.

8. Save the file.

Inserting and Deleting Columns, Rows, and Cells

Video Library   http://labyrinthelab.com/videos   Video Number: EX13-V0307

You can insert and delete columns, rows, and cells in your worksheets. If you want to insert or delete only cells, not entire rows or columns, you will issue a command that will prompt you to tell Excel how to shift the surrounding cells to either make room for the addition or fill the space. Depending on the format of your worksheet, this command could alter the overall structure, and should therefore be used cautiously.

QUICK REFERENCE	INSERTING AND DELETING ROWS, COLUMNS, AND CELLS
Task	**Procedure**
Insert rows	■ Select the number of rows you wish to insert (the same number of new rows will be inserted above the selected rows). ■ Choose Home→Cells→Insert 📋 or right-click the selection and choose Insert.
Insert columns	■ Select the number of columns you wish to insert (the same number of new columns will be inserted to the left of the selected columns). ■ Choose Home→Cells→Insert 📋 or right-click the selection and choose Insert.
Delete rows	■ Select the rows you wish to delete. ■ Choose Home→Cells→Delete 📋 or right-click the selection and choose Delete.
Delete columns	■ Select the columns you wish to delete. ■ Choose Home→Cells→Delete 📋 or right-click the selection and choose Delete.
Insert cells	■ Select the cells in the worksheet where you want the inserted cells to appear. ■ Choose Home→Cells→Insert 📋 or right-click the selection, choose Insert, and then choose the desired Shift Cells option.
Delete cells	■ Select the cells you wish to delete. ■ Choose Home→Cells→Delete 📋 or right-click the selection, choose Delete, and then choose the desired Shift Cells option.

Add and Remove Rows, Columns, and Cells

In this exercise, you will insert and delete rows, as well as insert cells into the worksheet.

1. Save your file as **EX03-D07-SafetyTraining-[FirstInitialLastName]**.

2. On the **Chemicals** worksheet, use the Ctrl key to select **rows 15 and 24**.

   The rows in which there are no objectives listed are now selected.

3. With both rows still selected, right-click **row 24** and choose **Delete**.

   The data below a deleted row moves up.

Add Another Row to the Sheet

4. Select **row 6**.

   When you choose to insert a row, the new row will be placed above the row you have selected.

5. Click the **Insert** button (not the menu ▼ button) and enter the text shown in the appropriate cells.

⬚	A	B	C	D	E	F
6	b.	Identify hazardous materials.		2	2	1

Insert Cells into the Worksheet

To merge and center the contents of cell A1 over the entire worksheet, you need to "bump" everything in columns C through F down one row.

6. Select the **range C1:F1**.

7. Follow these steps to insert the cells and shift your existing data down:

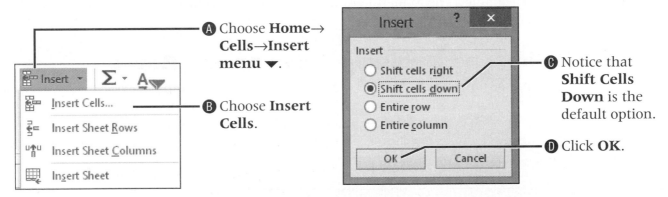

- **A** Choose **Home→Cells→Insert menu ▼**.
- **B** Choose **Insert Cells**.
- **C** Notice that **Shift Cells Down** is the default option.
- **D** Click **OK**.

8. Select the **range A3:B3** and choose **Home→Cells→Insert**.

   Everything in columns A and B, below cells A3 and B3, is shifted down one cell.

9. Select **row 1** and choose **Home→Cells→Insert** again.

   Because you selected an entire row first, a new row is inserted. You will now apply some formatting to make the worksheet more presentable.

10. Follow these steps to merge and center a range:

- Select the **range A1:F1**.
- Choose **Home→Alignment→Merge & Center** 🔲.
- While the merged range is still selected, choose Home→Font→Font Size→**16**.
- Type **Green Clean** in the merged cell.

The font size was applied to Green Clean *even though this formatting was changed before you typed the title.*

11. **Merge & Center** 🔲 the **range A2:F2** and change the font size to **14**.

12. **Merge & Center** 🔲 the **range A3:B5** and change the font size to **14**.

Notice that the Merge & Center command works to merge both columns and rows at once.

13. **Merge & Center** 🔲 the **range C3:F3** and choose Home→Font→Bottom Border.

14. **Merge & Center** 🔲 the **range C5:F5**.

15. Save the file.

Formatting and Hiding Columns and Rows

Video Library http://labyrinthelab.com/videos   Video Number: EX13-V0308

You can format, hide, and unhide columns and rows by first selecting the desired columns or rows. You can make your selection in several ways: clicking a single column or row heading, dragging to select adjacent headings, or holding ⌨Ctrl while you click each nonadjacent heading. Once you have selected the desired rows or columns, apply formatting just as you would to a single cell or range. The formatting is applied to every cell across the row or down the column to the end of the worksheet.

Hiding and Unhiding Columns and Rows

There may be times when you wish to hide certain rows or columns from view (such as when you distribute a worksheet to a user who is not interested in certain worksheet details). The hidden rows and columns will not be visible, nor will they print, but they will remain part of the worksheet. After rows or columns have been hidden, you can use Unhide to make them visible again.

	A	B	C	E
2		Safety Training - Chemicals		

Notice that column D and row 1 are not visible once the Hide command is issued.

QUICK REFERENCE	HIDING AND UNHIDING COLUMNS AND ROWS
Task	**Procedure**
Hide columns or rows	■ Select the desired column(s) or row(s) and choose Home→Cells→Format→Hide & Unhide→Hide Columns or Hide Rows. Or, right-click the column heading and choose Hide.
Unhide columns or rows	■ Select the columns to the left/right or rows above/below the column(s)/row(s) you wish to unhide. Drag up from row 2 or left from column B if unhiding row 1 or column A.
	■ Choose Home→Cells→Format→Hide & Unhide→Unhide Columns or Unhide Rows. Or, right-click the column heading and choose Unhide.

Hide and Unhide Columns and Rows

In this exercise, you will hide and unhide rows and columns.

1. Save your file as **EX03-D08-SafetyTraining-[FirstInitialLastName]**.

2. If necessary, select the **Chemicals** worksheet.

3. Follow these steps to hide columns C–D:

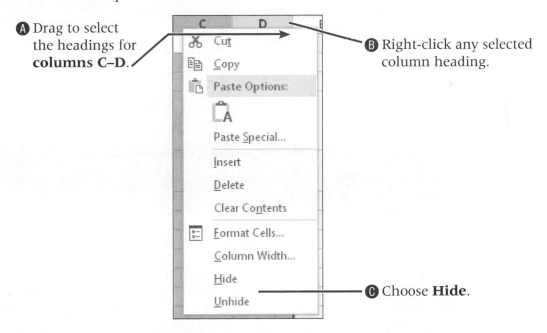

Ⓐ Drag to select the headings for **columns C–D**.

Ⓑ Right-click any selected column heading.

Ⓒ Choose **Hide**.

Columns C and D are no longer visible.

4. Right-click the **row 1** heading and choose **Hide**.

5. Follow these steps to unhide columns C–D:

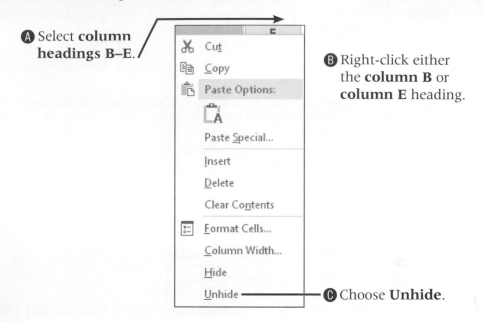

Ⓐ Select **column headings B–E**.

Ⓑ Right-click either the **column B** or **column E** heading.

Ⓒ Choose **Unhide**.

6. Follow these steps to unhide row 1:

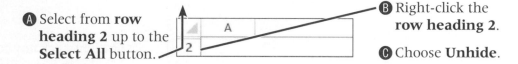

Ⓐ Select from **row heading 2** up to the **Select All** button.

Ⓑ Right-click the **row heading 2**.

Ⓒ Choose **Unhide**.

7. Save the file.

Changing Vertical Alignment and Rotating Text

Video Library   http://labyrinthelab.com/videos   Video Number: EX13-V0309

Vertical alignment positions cell contents between the top and bottom of the cell. Options include top, bottom, center, and justify; the default alignment is bottom. Justified alignment evenly distributes unused space between lines in a multiple-line entry so text fills the cell from the top edge to the bottom edge. Justify can only be selected via the Alignment dialog box launcher button.

Rotating Text

The Orientation option has several rotation options that you can apply to text in a cell. Excel increases the row height to accommodate the rotated text. While rotating text can make titles more aesthetically pleasing, be certain that the rotation does not increase row height such that worksheet data becomes difficult to view.

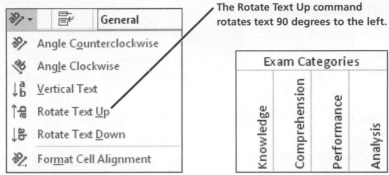

The Rotate Text Up command rotates text 90 degrees to the left.

Orienting the column headings vertically makes the column widths narrower.

QUICK REFERENCE	SETTING VERTICAL ALIGNMENT AND TEXT ROTATION
Task	**Procedure**
Set cell content to align vertically	▪ Select the desired cell(s) and choose Home→Alignment→Top Align, Middle Align, or Bottom Align.
Set cell content to justify vertically within a cell	▪ Select the desired cell(s), choose Home→Alignment dialog box launcher, click the Vertical drop-down arrow under Text Alignment, and choose Justify.
Rotate text within a cell using a preset option	▪ Select the desired cell(s), choose Home→Alignment→Orientation, and select the desired preset.
Rotate text within a cell using a precise number of degrees	▪ Select the desired cell(s), choose Home→Alignment dialog box launcher, and choose the desired text rotation.

DEVELOP YOUR SKILLS EX03-D09

Rotate Text and Change Its Vertical Alignment

In this exercise, you will rotate the categories at the top of the worksheet as well as change the vertical alignment in cells.

1. Save your file as **EX03-D09-SafetyTraining-[FirstInitialLastName]**.

2. Select the **range C4:F4** and choose **Home→Alignment→Orientation** ▧▾ →**Rotate Text Up**.

   The headings are rotated in their cells. Normally, the row height would increase automatically to AutoFit the headings. In this case, the merged text in row 3 prevented that from happening.

3. Point at the bottom of the **row 4 header** until the double-arrow pointer displays, and then double-click.

   The row height increases so that all rotated text is visible.

4. Follow these steps to AutoFit columns C–F:

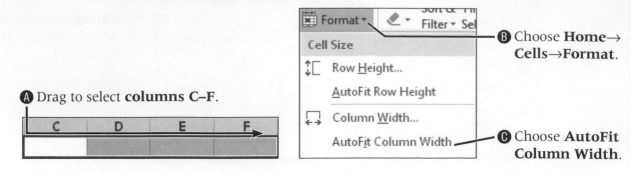

A Drag to select **columns C–F**.

B Choose **Home→ Cells→Format**.

C Choose **AutoFit Column Width**.

Change Vertical Alignment

5. Select **cell A3** and choose **Home→Alignment→Middle Align** ≣.

6. Select the **range A6:F25** and choose **Home→Alignment→Top Align** ≣.

   The data now aligns at the top of cells. You have decided that the alphabet letters in column A should be aligned at the right of their cells.

7. Select the **range A7:A10**, and choose **Home→Alignment→Align Right** ≣.

8. Choose **Home→Clipboard→Format Painter**, and select the range A12:A14 to copy the formatting from the range A7:A10. Repeat this process for the ranges A16:A17, A19:A22, and A24:A25.

9. Save and then close the file; exit **Excel**.

Concepts Review

To check your knowledge of the key concepts introduced in this lesson, complete the Concepts Review quiz by choosing the appropriate access option below.

If you are...	Then access the quiz by...
Using the Labyrinth Video Library	Going to http://labyrinthelab.com/videos
Using eLab	Logging in, choosing Content, and navigating to the Concepts Review quiz for this lesson
Not using the Labyrinth Video Library or eLab	Going to the student resource center for this book

Reinforce Your Skills

Preview, Print, and Manage a Worksheet

In this exercise, you will preview and then print a selection from a workbook. You will also alter workbook tags and insert a new worksheet.

Explore the Many Views of Excel

1. Start **Excel**. Open **EX3-R01-Birthdays** from the **EX2013 Lesson 03** folder and save it as **EX03-R01-Birthdays-[FirstInitialLastName]**.

2. Click the **Page Layout** button on the status bar at the left of the zoom slider.

   The worksheet contents fit on a single page.

3. Check the overall look of data on the page.

   Here you confirm that the printed page will have a logical appearance.

Print Worksheets

4. Choose **File→Print**.

   A preview displays at the right of the Print tab in Backstage view.

5. Take a moment to look at the print options but do not change them.

6. Tap Esc to cancel printing and return to Page Layout view.

7. Click the **Normal View** ⊞ button on the status bar.

   You will print just the birthdays for the first half of the year in the next steps. You could have selected the range in Page Layout view.

8. Select the **range A1:B7**.

9. Use Ctrl + P to display the Print tab in Backstage view.

10. Review the selected printer and ensure that it is correct.

    If directed by your instructor, print to a PDF file in this step.

11. Click **Print Active Sheets**, choose **Print Selection**, and click **Print**.

    Only the selected range prints.

12. Use Ctrl + Home to go to **cell A1**.

Edit a Workbook Property

13. Choose **File→Info** to enter Backstage view.

14. Enter the keywords **employees, birthday** in the Tags box.

15. Click the **Back** arrow to exit Backstage view.

Manage Worksheets

16. Double-click the **Sheet1** tab and rename it **Finance**.

17. Click the **New Sheet** button to create **Sheet1**.

18. Double-click the **Sheet1** tab and rename it **Marketing**.

   The tabs now represent individual departments within Kids for Change.

19. Right-click the **Marketing** tab and select a **Blue** tab color.

20. Save the file and then close it; exit **Excel**.

21. Submit your final file based on the guidelines provided by your instructor.

   To view examples of how your file or files should look at the end of this exercise, go to the student resource center.

REINFORCE YOUR SKILLS EX03-R02

Adjust Columns and Rows, and Align Text

In this exercise, you will modify a donation worksheet by removing, inserting, and modifying line items. You will also hide a column and alter text alignment.

Modify Columns and Rows

1. Start **Excel**. Open **EX03-R02-DonationForm** from the **EX2013 Lesson 03** folder and save it as **EX03-R02-DonationForm-[FirstInitialLastName]**.

2. Point at the border to the right of the **column A heading** until the pointer displays a two-headed arrow and then double-click.

   You have now AutoFit Column A, and can read the names of each donating corporation.

3. Select **column B** by clicking the column heading.

4. Choose **Home→Cells→Format→Column Width**, enter a width of **10**, and click **OK**.

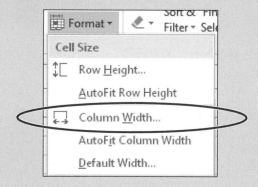

Insert and Delete Columns, Rows, and Cells

5. Select **row 3** by clicking the row heading.

6. Choose **Home→Cells→Delete** ▣ (taking care not to click the menu ▼ button).

7. Select **row 7** by clicking the row heading.

8. Choose **Home→Cells→Insert**.

9. Choose **Home→Cells→Format→Row Height**, enter a height of **6**, and click OK.

   These row adjustments have created more logical spacing throughout the worksheet.

Hide Columns and Rows

10. Select **row 15**.

11. Choose **Home→Cells→Format→Hide & Unhide→Hide Rows**.

    The thank-you message in row 15 is now hidden from view.

12. Select **rows 14 and 16**.

    The header for both rows must be selected in order to unhide row 15.

13. Choose **Home→Cells→Format→Hide & Unhide→Unhide Rows**.

Change Vertical Alignment and Rotate Text

14. Highlight **cells A6:B6**.

15. Choose **Home→Alignment→Orientation** ▣▾ **→Angle Counterclockwise**.

    The column titles within the cells now stand out from the text below.

16. Save the file and then close it; exit **Excel**.

17. Submit your final file based on the guidelines provided by your instructor.

    To view examples of how your file or files should look at the end of this exercise, go to the student resource center.

REINFORCE YOUR SKILLS EX03-R03

Change the Overall Worksheet Appearance

In this exercise, you will preview and then print the workbook. You will also alter workbook tags, insert a new worksheet, and adjust rows and columns.

Explore the Many Views of Excel

1. Start **Excel**. Open **EX03-R03-Partners** from the **EX2013 Lesson 03** folder and save it as **EX03-R03-Partners-[FirstInitialLastName]**.

2. Click the **Page Break Preview** ▣ button on the status bar at the left of the zoom slider.

   The blue line, representing a page break, is shown below row 9.

3. Drag the page break between **rows 15 and 16**.

   Because the print area ends at row 15, dragging the page break here will make it disappear.

Print Worksheets

4. Choose **File→Print**.

   A preview displays at the right of the Print tab in Backstage view.

5. Take a moment to look at the print options but do not change them.

6. Tap ⎡Esc⎤ to cancel the print and return to Page Break Preview.

7. Click the **Normal View** ⊞ button on the status bar.

   You will print the worksheet now so you can compare it with the completed worksheet that is produced at the end of the exercise.

8. Use ⎡Ctrl⎤+⎡P⎤ to display the Print tab of Backstage view.

9. Make certain that the selected printer is correct, and then click the **Print** button.

   If directed by your instructor, print to a PDF file in this step.

10. Use ⎡Ctrl⎤+⎡Home⎤ to go to cell A1.

Edit a Workbook Property

11. Choose **File→Info** to enter Backstage view.

12. Enter the keywords `partnership, cleanup` in the Tags box under **Properties** at the right of Backstage view.

13. Enter the Title `Partnership Organizations` in the Title box under **Properties** at the right of Backstage view.

14. Click the **Back** arrow to exit Backstage view.

Manage Worksheets

15. Hold down ⎡Ctrl⎤ and drag the **Sheet1** tab to the right.

    A copy of the Sheet1 tab has been created. This copy can be used to create a Partnership Form for a different program.

16. Double-click the **Sheet1** tab and rename it `Environmental`.

17. Double-click the **Sheet1 (2)** tab and rename it `Tutoring`.

    The tabs now represent two different programs within Kids for Change. You will modify only the Environmental tab in order to improve the appearance.

Modify Columns and Rows

18. With the Environmental worksheet selected, point at the border to the right of the **column A heading** until the pointer displays a two-headed arrow and double-click.

    You have now AutoFit Column A, however the width of the title in cell A2 causes the column to be too wide.

19. Point at the border to the right of the **column A heading**, and drag to the left so that the width equals 26 characters.

20. Select **column B** by clicking the column heading.

21. Choose **Home→Cells→Format→Column Width**, enter a width of 14, and click OK.

22. Select **row 1** by clicking the row heading.

23. Double-click the border between the headers for **row 1 and 2**.

    You have now AutoFit Row 1, and can read the company name.

Insert and Delete Columns, Rows, and Cells

24. Right-click the **row 3 heading** and choose **Delete**.

25. Right-click the **row 7 heading** and choose **Insert**.

    The new spacing gives the worksheet a better overall appearance.

Hide Columns and Rows

26. Right-click the **row 15 heading** and choose **Hide**.

    The note in row 15 is now hidden from view.

27. Select **rows 14 and 16**.

    The header for both rows must be selected in order to unhide row 15.

28. Right-click either of the selected rows, and choose **Unhide**.

    You decide that the worksheet looked better with the note hidden.

29. Click the **Undo** ⏎ button to again hide row 15.

Change Vertical Alignment and Rotate Text

30. Highlight **cells A6:C6** and choose **Home→Alignment→Orientation** 🖋 **→Angle Counterclockwise**.

    The column titles within the cells now stand out from the text below.

31. Save the file and then close it; exit **Excel**.

32. Submit your final file based on the guidelines provided by your instructor.

Apply Your Skills

Use Page Layout View; Edit and Manage a Workbook

In this exercise, you will adjust elements of a workbook and will review the print preview.

Explore the Many Views of Excel and Print Worksheets

1. Start **Excel**. Open **EX03-A01-Bonuses** from the **EX2013 Lesson 03** folder and save it as `EX03-A01-Bonuses-[FirstInitialLastName]`.

2. View the worksheet in **Page Layout** 🗔 view.

3. Edit the label in **cell A2** to read `Site Safety Bonuses`.

4. Enter **Backstage view** for the worksheet.

5. Check the preview on the **Print** tab to make certain the worksheet will print on one page.

6. Exit **Backstage view** without printing.

Edit Workbook Properties and Manage Worksheets

7. Add a **Category** workbook property that is appropriate for this worksheet.

8. Change the **Title** workbook property to `Bonuses`.

9. View the worksheet in **Normal** ▦ view.

10. Change the names of the worksheet tabs to indicate which half of the year is contained within each.

11. Hide the worksheet tab for the first half of the year.
    As this is not the current tab, hiding it will reduce clutter within the workbook.

12. Save the file and then close it; exit **Excel**.

13. Submit your final file based on the guidelines provided by your instructor.
    To view examples of how your file or files should look at the end of this exercise, go to the student resource center.

Restructure a Report

In this exercise, you will alter column and row widths, adjust and hide rows, and change the vertical alignment of the header.

Modify Columns and Rows

1. Start **Excel**. Open **EX03-A02-AcctsRec** from the **EX2013 Lesson 03** folder and save it as **EX03-A02-AcctsRec-[FirstInitialLastName]**.

2. Increase the row height of **rows 7–13** to add some extra space among the entries.
   For a more consistent presentation, ensure that these rows all have the same row height.

3. Increase the row height of **row 1** to 36.

4. AutoFit **column C** and widen **column A** to ensure that all entries can be read and that no column is unnecessarily wide.

Insert, Delete, and Hide Columns, Rows, and Cells

5. Delete the empty cells in **rows 5 and 8**.

6. Insert a new column after **column A**, and reduce the width to **2**.

7. Hide **rows 2 and 4** so the report name and date are not shown.
   After doing so, you realize that the report name should remain within the worksheet.

8. Unhide **row 2** so that the report name reappears.

Change Vertical Alignment and Rotate Text

9. **Middle Align** ☰ the title in **cell A1**.

10. **Top Align** ☰ the contents of **rows 6–11**.

11. Save the file and then close it; exit **Excel**.

12. Submit your final file based on the guidelines provided by your instructor.
    To view examples of how your file or files should look at the end of this exercise, go to the student resource center.

View, Print, and Restructure a Report

In this exercise, you will correct the structure of an accounts payable report.

Explore the Many Views of Excel and Print Worksheets

1. Start **Excel**. Open **EX03-A03-AcctsPay** from the **EX2013 Lesson 03** folder and save it as **EX03-A03-AcctsPay-[FirstInitialLastName]**.

2. View the worksheet in **Page Break Preview** 🔳.

3. Adjust the page break so all contents fit within one page.

Excel 2013

4. Enter **Backstage view** for the worksheet.

5. Check the Print Preview on the **Print** tab to confirm that the page break has been removed.

6. Exit **Backstage view** without printing.

Edit Workbook Properties and Manage Worksheets

7. Add an **Author** workbook property in the **Related People** section of the Info tab in Backstage view. Use your first and last name for the new author name.

8. Change the **Tags** workbook property to `Payables`.

9. View the worksheet in **Normal** ▦ view.

10. Change the name of the worksheet tab to indicate the content of the worksheet.

Modify, Insert, Delete, and Hide Columns, Rows, and Cells

11. Set the row height of **rows 7–13** to **18**.

12. Increase the row height of **row 1** to **36**.

13. AutoFit **column C** and widen **column A** to ensure that all entries can be read and that no column is unnecessarily wide.

14. Delete the empty cells in **rows 4 and 10**.

15. Insert a new column before **column B**, and reduce the width to **2**.

16. Hide **rows 1 and 4** so the company name and date are not shown.

    After doing so, you realize that the company name should remain within the worksheet.

17. Unhide **row 1** so that the company name reappears.

18. Delete the contents of **cell C3**.

Change Vertical Alignment and Rotate Text

19. **Top Align** ▤ the title in cell A1.

20. **Middle Align** ▤ the contents within rows 6:11.

21. Save the file and then close it; exit **Excel**.

22. Submit your final file based on the guidelines provided by your instructor.

Extend Your Skills

In the course of working through the Extend Your Skills exercises, you will think critically as you use the skills taught in the lesson to complete the assigned projects. To evaluate your mastery and completion of the exercises, your instructor may use a rubric, with which more points are allotted according to performance characteristics. (The more you do, the more you earn!) Ask your instructor how your work will be evaluated.

EX03-E01   That's the Way I See It

You are known as the neighborhood Excel expert for small businesses! In this exercise, you will create a worksheet that includes three different lists of your favorite local restaurants, retail stores, and movie theaters for inclusion in the local online newspaper.

For each list include five locations (you may want to use the Internet to identify suitable entries), as well as the associated address and phone number. Remember to include a heading at the top of the worksheet, properly name the worksheet tab, and include appropriate spacing throughout. Also ensure that the spreadsheet's appearance, when printed, will be logically structured and easy to understand. Save your file as **EX03-E01-FavoritesList-[FirstInitialLastName]** in the **EX2013 Lesson 03** folder.

You will be evaluated based on the inclusion of all elements specified, your ability to follow directions, your ability to apply newly learned skills to a real-world situation, your creativity, and the relevance of your topic and/or data choice(s). Submit your final file based on the guidelines provided by your instructor.

EX03-E02   Be Your Own Boss

In this exercise, you will create and format a pair of pricing sheets for your company, Blue Jean Landscaping. These pricing sheets will be used to estimate the total cost of a job based on the services that are requested. Create a new workbook named **EX03-E02-PricingSheets-[FirstInitialLastName]** in the **EX2013 Lesson 03** folder.

Create two worksheets, one listing the price of five different landscaping services that can be provided and another listing the price of five different types of greenery that can be planted. Within the greenery listing, create columns to allow for at least two different sizes of each plant. Be sure to appropriately name each tab, include a proper heading within each worksheet, and ensure that the printed sheet will have a logical appearance by both modifying columns and rows and by using vertical alignment and text rotation.

You will be evaluated based on the inclusion of all elements specified, your ability to follow directions, your ability to apply newly learned skills to a real-world situation, your creativity, and your demonstration of an entrepreneurial spirit. Submit your final file based on the guidelines provided by your instructor.

Transfer Your Skills

In the course of working through the Transfer Your Skills exercises, you will use critical-thinking and creativity skills to complete the assigned projects using skills taught in the lesson. To evaluate your mastery and completion of the exercises, your instructor may use a rubric, with which more points are allotted according to performance characteristics. (The more you do, the more you earn!) Ask your instructor how your work will be evaluated.

EX03-T01 Use the Web as a Learning Tool

Throughout this book, you will be provided with an opportunity to use the Internet as a learning tool by completing WebQuests. According to the original creators of WebQuests, as described on their website (WebQuest.org), a WebQuest is "an inquiry-oriented activity in which most or all of the information used by learners is drawn from the web." To complete the WebQuest projects in this book, navigate to the student resource center and choose the WebQuest for the lesson on which you are currently working. The subject of each WebQuest will be relevant to the material found in the lesson.

WebQuest Subject: Researching restaurant suppliers and creating a corresponding supplier listing

Submit your final file(s) based on the guidelines provided by your instructor.

EX03-T02 Demonstrate Proficiency

You have been maintaining a workbook listing ingredients used in the dishes served at Stormy BBQ. Within the workbook you have one worksheet for lunch ingredients and one worksheet for dinner ingredients. As you have been busy running the restaurant, you have not yet taken the time to modify the columns and rows in the worksheet so that it is structured in a logical manner.

Open **EX03-T02-Ingredients** from the **EX2013 Lesson 03** folder and save it as **EX03-T02-Ingredients-[FirstInitialLastName]**. Using the techniques you have learned in this lesson, include titles and proper spacing throughout both worksheets, utilize different vertical alignment and rotation settings, and name each worksheet appropriately. Ensure that the file will be easy to read when printed, and then print a file for your instructor or create a PDF file.

Submit your final file based on the guidelines provided by your instructor.

EXCEL 2013

Working with Formulas and Functions

LEARNING OBJECTIVES

After studying this lesson, you will be able to:

- Create formulas to calculate values
- Use functions such as sum, average, maximum, minimum, and IF
- Use relative, absolute, and mixed cell references in formulas
- Modify and copy formulas
- Display formulas rather than resulting values in cells

In this lesson, you will create and modify basic formulas and functions in Excel. Formulas are one of Excel's most powerful features, as they can save you time and increase the accuracy of your spreadsheets. You will reference cells in formulas and use AutoSum. Lastly, you will use IF functions, which can flag a cell with a text label, display a value, or perform a calculation when specific criteria are satisfied.

Creating a Spreadsheet with Formulas

Green Clean earns revenue by selling janitorial products and contracts for cleaning services. You want to set up a workbook with two worksheets, one to track commissions and the other to report how the projected profit would change based on costs and an increase or decrease in sales.

	A	B	C	D	E	F	G
1	**Sales Department**						
2	*First Quarter Commissions*						
3							
4	*Sales Team Member*	*January*	*February*	*March*	*Qtr 1 Total*	*Sales*	*Met Goal?*
5	Talos Bouras	250	486	415	1151	28775	
6	Leisa Malimali	74	88	101	263	6575	
7	Brian Simpson	389	303	422	1114	27850	
8	Amy Wyatt	346	381	502	1229	30725	Yes
9	**Monthly Total**	**1059**	**1258**	**1440**	**3757**		
10							
11	Average	264.75	314.5	360	939.25		
12	Maximum	389	486	502	1229		
13	Minimum	74	88	101	263		
14	Count	4	4	4	4		
15	Goal					30000	

This worksheet sums the monthly totals for all team members as well as the quarterly sales for each.

	A	B	C	D	E
1	**Sales Department**				
2	*Projected Net Profit*				
3		*Base*	*2%*	*5%*	*-5%*
4	Product Sales	$ 53,200	54,264	55,860	50,540
5	Contracts	241,000	245,820	253,050	228,950
6	**Total Revenue**	$ 294,200	$ 300,084	$ 308,910	$ 279,490
7					
8	Fixed Operating Cost	101,400	101,400	101,400	101,400
9	Marketing Expense	15,000	15,000	15,000	15,000
10	Commissions	27,824	28,380	29,215	26,433
11	**Total Costs**	$ 144,224	$ 144,780	$ 145,615	$ 142,833
12					
13	**Gross Profit**	$ 149,976	$ 155,304	$ 163,295	$ 136,657
14	**Net Profit**	$ 138,353	$ 143,267	$ 150,639	$ 126,066
15	**Gross Profit vs. Revenue**	51.0%	51.8%	52.9%	48.9%
16					
17	Contracts	482			
18	Average Contract	$ 500	Marketing	$ 15,000	
19	Product Commission Rate	7%	Fixed Cost	$ 101,400	
20	Contract Commission Rate	10%	Tax Rate	7.75%	

This worksheet reports the effect of various sales projections and costs on net profit.

Working with Formulas and Functions

Video Library   http://labyrinthelab.com/videos   Video Number: EX13-V0401

A formula is a math problem done in Excel. You can add, subtract, multiply, divide, and group cell contents to make your data work for you. A function is a prewritten formula that can simplify complex procedures for numbers and text. For instance, a function can be used to sum a group of numbers, to determine the payment amount on a loan, and to convert a number to text.

Using AutoSum to Create a SUM Formula

The AutoSum button automatically sums a column or row of numbers. When you click AutoSum, Excel starts the formula for you by entering =SUM( ) and proposes a range of adjacent cells within the parentheses. Excel first looks upward for a range to sum. If a range is not found there, it next looks left. You can accept the proposed range, which can be viewed in the Formula Bar, or drag in the worksheet to select a different range.

FROM THE RIBBON

Home→Editing
→AutoSum Σ

FROM THE KEYBOARD

Alt + =

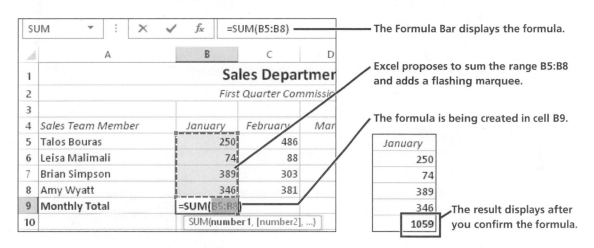

The Formula Bar displays the formula.

Excel proposes to sum the range B5:B8 and adds a flashing marquee.

The formula is being created in cell B9.

The result displays after you confirm the formula.

Average, Count, CountA, Max, and Min Functions

In addition to summing a group of numbers, the AutoSum button can perform a number of other calculations.

AutoSum and/or Status Bar Function	How Function Appears in Formula	Description
Sum	SUM	Adds the values in the cells
Average	AVERAGE	Averages the values in the cells
Count Numbers or Numerical Count	COUNT	Counts the number of values in the cells; cells containing text and blank cells are ignored
Count	COUNTA	Counts the number of nonblank cells
Max or Maximum	MAX	Returns the highest value in the cells
Min or Minimum	MIN	Returns the lowest value in the cells

Once you have entered a formula in a cell, you can use AutoFill to copy it to adjacent cells.

Status Bar Functions

The Status Bar, which is displayed at the bottom of the Excel window, can be customized to display a variety of functions including Average, Count, Numerical Count, Minimum, Maximum, and Sum. To customize the Status Bar, right-click anywhere on it and click to add or remove features. You can also customize additional features of the Status Bar, such as Zoom, Signatures, Overtype Mode, and Macro Recording.

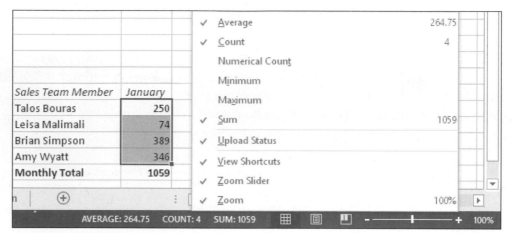

By default, Excel displays in the Status Bar the average, count of values, and sum of the selected range.

QUICK REFERENCE	USING AUTOSUM AND THE STATUS BAR FUNCTIONS
Task	**Procedure**
AutoSum a range of cells	■ Click in the desired cell and choose Home→Editing→AutoSum Σ. ■ Tap Enter to confirm the proposed range, or drag to select the correct range and tap Enter.
AutoSum across columns or down rows	■ Select the cell in the row directly below or column directly to the right of the data where you want the sums to appear and choose Home→Editing→AutoSum Σ.
Use Status Bar functions	■ Right-click the Status Bar and add or remove the desired functions. ■ Select the desired range, and view the results of the desired functions within the Status Bar.

Use AutoSum and Status Bar Functions

In this exercise, you will use AutoSum to calculate the monthly commission total for the sales team as well as the quarterly total for each sales team member.

1. Open **EX04-D01-Commissions** from the **Excel 2013 Lesson 04** folder, and save it as **EX04-D01-Commissions-FirstInitialLastName**.

   Replace the bracketed text with your first initial and last name. For example, if your name is Bethany Smith, your filename would look like this: EX04-D01-Commissions-BSmith. Notice the two tabs at the bottom of the window: Qtr 1 Commissions and Profit Projection.

2. With the **Qtr 1 Commissions** worksheet displayed, select **cell B9**.

3. Choose **Home→Editing→AutoSum** Σ.

   Excel displays a marquee around the part of the spreadsheet where it thinks the formula should be applied. You can change this selection as necessary.

4. Follow these steps to complete the Sum formula:

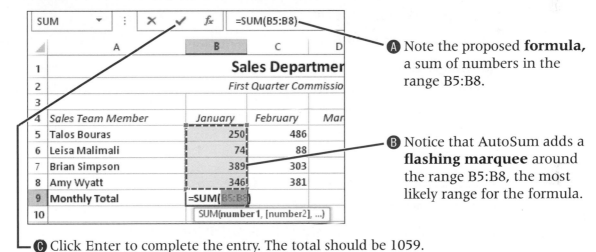

Ⓐ Note the proposed **formula,** a sum of numbers in the range B5:B8.

Ⓑ Notice that AutoSum adds a **flashing marquee** around the range B5:B8, the most likely range for the formula.

Ⓒ Click Enter to complete the entry. The total should be 1059.

5. Select **cell E7** and choose **Home→Editing→AutoSum** Σ.

   Notice that, as there are no values above cell E7, Excel looked to the left to find a range to sum, B7:D7. Now, assume that you wanted only cells B7:C7 to be summed.

6. Follow these steps to override the proposed range:

   Ⓐ Select the **range B7:C7.**

   Ⓑ Notice that the new range, B7:C7, appears in the formula.

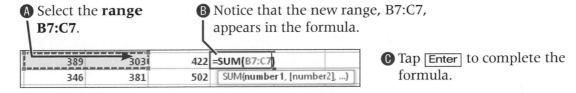

   Ⓒ Tap Enter to complete the formula.

7. **Undo** ↶ the formula.

Excel 2013

Use AutoFill to Extend a Formula

8. Follow these steps to AutoFill the formula in cell B9 into the cells to its right:

▲	A	B	C	D	E
1		**Sales Department**			
2		*First Quarter Commissions*			
3					
4	*Sales Team Member*	*January*	*February*	*March*	*Qtr 1 Total*
5	Talos Bouras	250	486	415	
6	Leisa Malimali	74	88	101	
7	Brian Simpson	389	303	422	
8	Amy Wyatt	346	381	502	
9	Monthly Total	1059			+

C Release the mouse button to fill the formula into the cells.

A Select **cell B9**.

B Position the mouse pointer over the **fill handle** at the bottom-right corner of the cell and drag to **cell E9**.

Cell E9 displays 0 because the cells above it are empty. You can create formulas that include empty cells and then enter data later.

9. Select the **range E5:E8**.

10. Choose **Home→Editing→AutoSum Σ** to calculate the quarterly totals.
   Excel created a formula in each cell of the selected range without requiring you to complete the formulas.

Qtr 1 Total
1151
263
1114
1229
3757

11. Delete the formulas in **range B9:E9** and **range E5:E8**.
   The data are returned to their original state.

12. Select the **range B5:E9** and click **AutoSum Σ**.
   The formula results appear in B9:E9 and E5:E8.

Explore Statistical Functions with AutoSum

13. Select **cell B11**.

14. Choose **Home→Editing→AutoSum ▼ menu button**.

15. Choose **Average** from the drop-down menu.
   Excel proposes the range B5:B10, which is incorrect.

16. Select the correct **range B5:B8** and tap Enter to complete the entry.
   The result should equal 264.75.

17. With **cell B12** selected, choose **Home→Editing→AutoSum Σ ▾ menu button→Max**.

18. Select the correct **range B5:B8** and tap Enter to display the highest value in the range.
   The result should equal 389.

19. Select **cell B13** and choose **Home→Editing→AutoSum ▼ menu button→Min**.
   Min represents Minimum, or the lowest value.

20. Correct the range to **B5:B8** and then click **Enter** ✓ on the Formula Bar to display the lowest value in the range.

 The result should equal 74.

21. Select **cell B14** and choose **Home→Editing→AutoSum ▼ menu button**.

22. Choose **Count Numbers**, correct the range to **B5:B8**, and click **Enter** ✓.

23. Select **cell B6** and delete the contents.

 The formula recalculates the count as 3, and both the average and minimum formulas recalculate as well.

24. **Undo** ↺ the deletion.

Use Status Bar Functions

25. Select the **range B5:B8**.

26. Look at the Status Bar in the lower-right corner of the window to see that the sum value displayed equals the result in cell B9. **Save** the workbook and leave it open.

AVERAGE: 264.75   COUNT: 4   SUM: 1059

Creating Formulas

Video Library   http://labyrinthelab.com/videos   Video Number: EX13-V0402

As you saw with AutoSum, functions begin with an equals (=) sign. Formulas begin with an equals sign as well, although Excel will automatically insert the equals sign if you first type a plus (+) or a minus (–) sign.

Cell and Range References

Formulas derive their power from the use of cell and range references. Using references in formulas ensures that formulas can be copied to other cells and that results are automatically recalculated when the data is changed in the referenced cell(s).

Do not type the results of calculations directly into cells. Always use formulas.

The Language of Excel Formulas

Formulas can include the standard arithmetic operators shown in the following table. Keep in mind that each formula you create will be entered into the same cell that displays the resulting calculation.

ARITHMETIC OPERATORS IN FORMULAS		
Operator	**Example**	**Comments**
+ (addition)	= B7+B11	Adds the values in B7 and B11
- (subtraction)	= B7–B11	Subtracts the value in B11 from the value in B7
* (multiplication)	= B7*B11	Multiplies the values in B7 and B11
/ (division)	= B7/B11	Divides the value in B7 by the value in B11
^ (exponentiation)	=B7^3	Raises the value in B7 to the third power (B7*B7*B7)
% (percent)	=B7*10%	Multiplies the value in B7 by 10% (0.10)
( ) (grouping)	=B7/(C4-C2)	Subtracts the value in C2 from the value in C4 and then divides B7 by the subtraction result

When typing a cell reference in a formula, you can type the column letter in lowercase and Excel will capitalize it for you.

"Please Excuse My Dear Aunt Sally"

Excel formulas follow the standard algebraic hierarchy. This means that the formula completes operations in the following order: parentheses, exponents, multiplication, division, addition, subtraction. The first letter of each of these is used in the mnemonic "Please Excuse My Dear Aunt Sally," which can be used to memorize this order.

To control the order of operations, you can use parentheses to cause Excel to add or subtract before multiplying or dividing. Review these examples to see how the order of operations works with and without parentheses.

$=53+ 7*5 = 53+35 = 88$ Multiplication and then addition

$=(53+7)*5 = (60)*5 = 300$ Parentheses and then multiplication

Excel includes two additional items in the order of operations between parentheses and exponents. At the beginning of a formula, a minus (-) sign is interpreted as a negative. A percent sign is also considered as an operator.

Use the Keyboard to Create Formulas

In this exercise, you will use the keyboard to enter formulas into the spreadsheet.

1. Save your file as **EX04-D02-Commissions-FirstInitialLastName.**

2. Click the **Profit Projection** sheet tab at the bottom of the Excel window.

3. Select **cell B5** and view its formula in the Formula Bar.

   This formula multiplies the number of contracts (B17) by the average contract revenue (B18).

4. Select **cell B6** and use **AutoSum** to sum the sales in the **range B4:B5**.

5. In **cell B11**, sum the costs in the **range B8:B10**.

   The total costs result is not correct, but you will enter data in cells B9 and B10 in the next exercise.

6. Select **cell B13**, the Gross Profit for the Base column.

7. Type **=B6-B11** in the cell, and then tap ⟨Enter⟩ to complete the formula.

   In order to calculate the gross profit, you need to subtract the total costs (B11) from total revenue (B6).

8. Select **cell B15**, which is within the Gross Profit vs. Revenue row.

9. Type **=b13/b6** in the cell, tap ⟨Enter⟩, and **save** the workbook.

   In this worksheet, the cell has been formatted to display a percentage for you.

Using Cell References in Formulas

Video Library   http://labyrinthelab.com/videos   Video Number: EX13-V0403

A cell reference can be used to represent a cell or range of cells containing the values used in a formula. Cell references are one of three types: relative, absolute, or mixed.

Relative Cell References

A relative cell reference is one where the location is *relative* to the cell that contains the formula. For example, when you enter the formula *=A3-B3* in cell C3, Excel notes that cell A3 is two cells to the left of the formula and that cell B3 is one cell to the left of the formula. When you copy the formula, the cell references update automatically. So, if the formula were copied to cell C4, the new formula would be *=A4-B4*. Excel updates the cell references so they are the same distance from cell C4 as were the cell references in the original formula in cell C3.

Absolute Cell References

In some situations, you may not want references updated when a formula is moved or copied. You must use either absolute or mixed references in these situations. Absolute references within a formula always refer to the same cell, even when the formula is copied to another location. You create absolute references by placing dollar signs in front of the column and row components of the reference. For example, if the formula = *$A$3-$B$3* were entered in cell C3, and then copied to cell C4, the formula within cell C4 would still read = *$A$3-$B$3*.

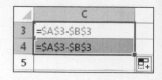

Mixed References

You can mix relative and absolute references. For example, the reference $C1 is a combination of an absolute reference to column C and a relative reference to row 1. This can be useful when copying a formula both across a row and down a column.

Using the [F4] Function Key

The [F4] function key can be used to insert the dollar signs within a cell reference. When [F4] is first tapped, dollar signs are placed in front of the column and row components of the cell reference. A second tap of [F4] places a dollar sign in front of only the row component, a third tap places one sign in front of only the column component, and a fourth tap removes all dollar signs.

The following table indicates what happens to different types of cell references when their formulas are copied to other locations.

Cell Reference	Type	Copy and Paste Action	Result When Pasted
B6	Relative	One column to the right	C6
B6	Relative	One row down	B7
$B$6	Absolute	One column to the right	$B$6
$B$6	Absolute	One row down	$B$6
$B6	Mixed	One column to the right	$B6
$B6	Mixed	One row down	$B7
B$6	Mixed	One column to the right	C$6
B$6	Mixed	One row down	B$6

Create Formulas Using Cell References

In this exercise, you will use absolute cell references to create formulas that can be copied to other cells.

1. Save your file as **EX04-D03-Commissions-FirstInitialLastName.**

2. Select **cell B9** and type **=** to begin a formula.

3. Select **cell D18** and tap F4.

If you have a keyboard that uses function keys for other purposes, you may have to tap F Lock to be able to utilize F4.

> *Notice $D$18 in the Formula Bar. In this case, you want the marketing expense to always reflect the value in cell D18.*

4. Tap Enter to complete the formula.

Calculate the Commissions Using Order of Operations

You will now enter a more complex formula to calculate the total commissions for product sales and contract sales.

5. Select **cell B10** and type **=** to begin a formula.

6. Select **cell B4** and type *****.
   Notice that when you click on cell B4, its cell reference is automatically placed within the formula. This is referred to as Point Mode, and it can help to minimize typing errors.

7. Select **cell B19** and tap F4.

8. Type **+** to continue the formula.

9. Select **cell B5** and type *****.

10. Select **cell B20** and tap F4.

11. Click **Enter** ✓.
    The result should be 27,824.

Calculate the Net Profit Using Parentheses

You will now create the formula =B13 * (1 - $D$20) to calculate the net profit.

12. Select **cell B14** and type **=**.

13. Select **cell B13** and type *** (1-** to continue the formula.

14. Select **cell D20** and tap F4.

15. Type **)** and tap Enter.
    The result should be $138,353.

Project a Sales Increase

*You will now create the formula =$B$4 * (1 + C$3) to project a 2 percent increase over the base product sales.*

16. Select **cell C4** and type an equals sign (=).

17. Select **cell B4** and tap F4.

18. Type ***(1+** to continue the formula.

19. Select **cell C3** and tap F4 two times to create the C$3 mixed cell reference.

20. Type **)** and tap Enter.
    The result should equal 54,264.

21. With **cell C5** selected, repeat **steps 16–20** (but using different cell references) to project a **2 percent increase** for base contract sales.
    The result should equal 245,820.

22. Save the workbook.

Modifying and Copying Formulas

Video Library   http://labyrinthelab.com/videos   Video Number: EX13-V0404

You can modify and copy formulas just like you edit and copy cells.

Modifying Formulas

You can edit a formula either in the Formula Bar or by double-clicking the formula cell. If you click or select a cell and enter a new formula, it replaces the previous contents.

When you select a formula to edit it, you will see colored lines around all cells referenced by the formula. This feature can help you track the formula elements.

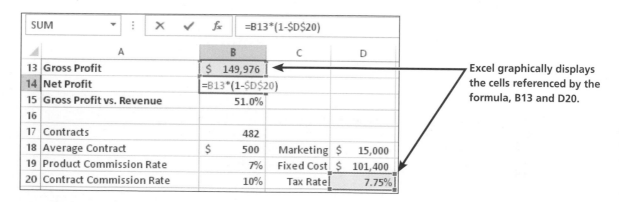

Excel graphically displays the cells referenced by the formula, B13 and D20.

Circular References

A circular reference occurs when the formula refers to its own cell or to another formula that refers to that cell. For example, the formula in cell C6 is =B6*C6. Excel cannot complete the calculation because cell C6 is the formula cell, not a reference to a value. Excel displays an error message if you create a circular reference.

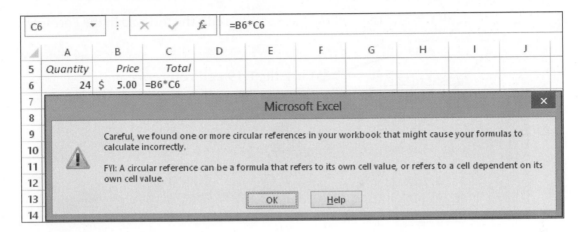

You must correct the formula manually after you close Help or the Circular Reference Warning message.

Copying Formulas

You can use either the Copy and Paste commands or AutoFill with formulas to copy them to new cells. If you use Auto Fill, the Auto Fill Options button will appear after you release the mouse button. Clicking this button allows you to customize your fill. The Fill Series option appears within the resulting list when you AutoFill values, but not when you AutoFill formulas.

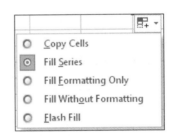

You can change what was copied in the cells through AutoFill with the Auto Fill Options button.

Modify and Copy Formulas

In this exercise, you will modify and copy formulas to complete your profit projection.

1. Save your file as **EX04-D04-Commissions-FirstInitialLastName.**

2. Select **cell B8**, and then follow these steps to edit the formula in the Formula Bar:

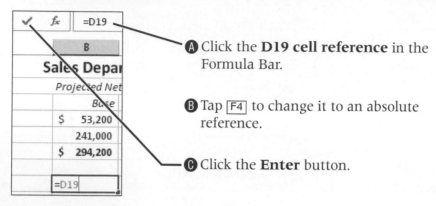

Ⓐ Click the **D19 cell reference** in the Formula Bar.

Ⓑ Tap F4 to change it to an absolute reference.

Ⓒ Click the **Enter** button.

3. Double-click **cell C6** to begin an in-cell edit.

4. Follow these steps to complete an in-cell edit:

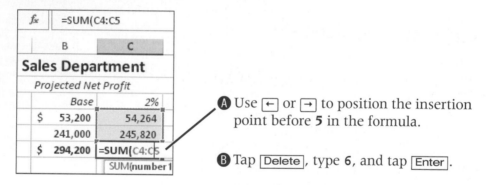

Ⓐ Use ← or → to position the insertion point before **5** in the formula.

Ⓑ Tap Delete, type **6**, and tap Enter.

Excel displays a Circular Reference Warning message because you referred to C6, the formula cell itself.

5. Choose **OK** in the Circular Reference Warning message.

6. **Undo** 🔄 the change.

Use Copy and Paste Commands to Copy a Formula

7. Select **cell B14** and then use Ctrl + C to **copy** the formula.

8. Select **cell C14** and then use Ctrl + V to **paste** the formula in the new cell.
   This method works great if you need to copy a formula to just one cell. You can use these commands to copy a formula to a range of cells as well.

9. Select the **range D14:E14** and then use Ctrl + V.
   The formula that you copied in step 6 is now pasted to the range of cells selected.

10. Tap Esc to cancel the marquee around cell B14.

11. Select **cell D14** and look at the formula in the Formula Bar.

The relative cell reference now indicates cell D13, whereas the absolute cell reference is still looking to cell D20.

12. Follow these steps to use AutoFill to copy the formula:

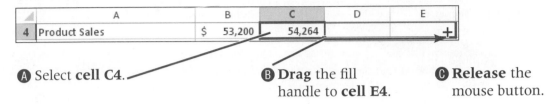

	A	B	C	D	E
4	Product Sales	$ 53,200	54,264		

A Select **cell C4.**

B Drag the fill handle to **cell E4.**

C Release the mouse button.

13. Use **AutoFill** to copy the formula from **cell C5** to the **range D5:E5**.

14. Select the **range B8:B15**.

15. Place your mouse pointer over the **fill handle** at the bottom right of the selected range.

16. When you see the thin cross ✚, **drag right** until the highlight includes the cells in **column E** and then release the mouse.

	A	B	C	D	E
8	Fixed Operating Cost	101,400	101,400	101,400	101,400
9	Marketing Expense	15,000	15,000	15,000	15,000
10	Commissions	27,824	28,380	29,215	26,433
11	Total Costs	$ 144,224	$ 144,780	$ 145,615	$ 142,833
12					
13	Gross Profit	$ 149,976	$ 155,304	$ 163,295	$ 136,657
14	Net Profit	$ 138,353	$ 143,267	$ 150,639	$ 126,066
15	Gross Profit vs. Revenue	51.0%	51.8%	52.9%	48.9%
16					

17. Deselect the filled range, and **save** the workbook.

Always deselect highlighted cells after performing an action to help avoid unintended changes.

Displaying and Printing Formulas

Video Library   http://labyrinthelab.com/videos   Video Number: EX13-V0405

Excel normally displays the results of formulas in worksheet cells, though you can choose to display the actual formulas. While formulas are displayed, Excel automatically widens columns to show more of the cell contents. Also, you can edit the formulas and print the worksheet with formulas displayed. When printing formulas, you may want to display the worksheet in Landscape orientation, due to the wider columns.

FROM THE RIBBON
Formulas→Formula Auditing→Show Formulas

FROM THE KEYBOARD
Ctrl+`

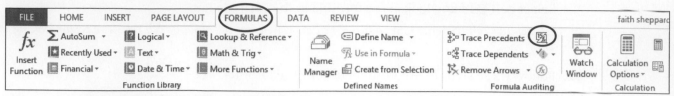

While formulas are shown, contents will be visible for those cells in which no formulas are used.

QUICK REFERENCE	VIEWING AND PRINTING FORMULAS
Task	**Procedure**
Display or hide formulas in a workbook	■ Choose Formulas→Formula Auditing→Show Formulas 📝.
Change page orientation	■ Choose Page Layout→Page Setup→Orientation→Landscape.
Print displayed formulas	■ Choose File→Print. ■ Choose any desired options in the Print tab and click Print.

DEVELOP YOUR SKILLS EX04-D05

Display Formulas in a Worksheet

In this exercise, you will display the formulas in the profit projection worksheet to see how it is constructed and to be able to troubleshoot any potentially inaccurate formulas.

1. Save your file as **EX04-D05-Commissions-FirstInitialLastName**.

2. Choose **Formulas→Formula Auditing→Show Formulas** 📝.
   You can use this feature to examine your formulas more closely.

3. Choose **Formulas→Formula Auditing→Show Formulas** 📝 again.
   The values are displayed once again.

Using Formula AutoComplete

Video Library   http://labyrinthelab.com/videos   Video Number: EX13-V0406

Formula AutoComplete assists you in creating and editing formulas. Once you type an equals (=) sign and any letter(s), Excel will display a list of functions beginning with the typed letter(s) below the active cell.

Functions Defined

A function is a predefined formula that performs calculations or returns a desired result. Most functions are constructed using similar basic rules, or syntax. This syntax also applies to the Min, Max, Average, Count, and CountA functions.

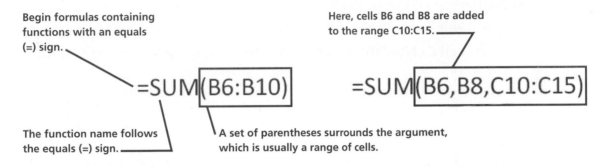

Begin formulas containing functions with an equals (=) sign.

Here, cells B6 and B8 are added to the range C10:C15.

=SUM(B6:B10)   =SUM(B6,B8,C10:C15)

The function name follows the equals (=) sign.

A set of parentheses surrounds the argument, which is usually a range of cells.

QUICK REFERENCE	USING FORMULA AUTOCOMPLETE TO ENTER A FORMULA INTO A CELL
Task	**Procedure**
Use Formula AutoComplete	■ Type an equals (=) sign and begin typing the formula.
	■ Double-click the formula in the list.
	■ Select the range where you will apply the formula.
	■ Type a closed parenthesis [)] to finish the formula.

DEVELOP YOUR SKILLS EX04-D06

Use Formula AutoComplete

In this exercise, you will use the Formula AutoComplete feature to create a formula.

1. Save your file as **EX04-D06-Commissions-FirstInitialLastName**.

2. Click the **Qtr 1 Commissions** worksheet tab.

3. Select **cell C11**.

4. Type **=ave** and observe the list that results.

   If you click on a function in the list, a ScreenTip will describe the function.

5. Double-click **AVERAGE**.

Excel fills in the function name for you, but you must select the range.

=ave							
fx AVEDEV	Returns the average (arithmetic mean) of its arguments, which can be numbers or names, arrays, or references that contain numbers					
fx AVERAGE						
fx AVERAGEA						
fx AVERAGEIF						
fx AVERAGEIFS						

6. Drag to select **cells C5:C8** as the formula range.

You do not include total rows or columns when completing most functions.

7. Tap Enter to complete the function.

Excel added the parenthesis at the end of the formula for you. The result should be 314.5.

8. Select **cell C11**, use the fill handle to **copy** the function to the **range D11:E11**, and **save** the workbook.

You now have the average commission for each month and the entire quarter.

Using Insert Function

Video Library http://labyrinthelab.com/videos Video Number: EX13-V0407

The Insert Function f_x button displays the Insert Function dialog box. It allows you to locate a function by typing a description or searching by category. When you locate the desired function and click OK, Excel displays the Function Arguments box, which helps you enter function arguments.

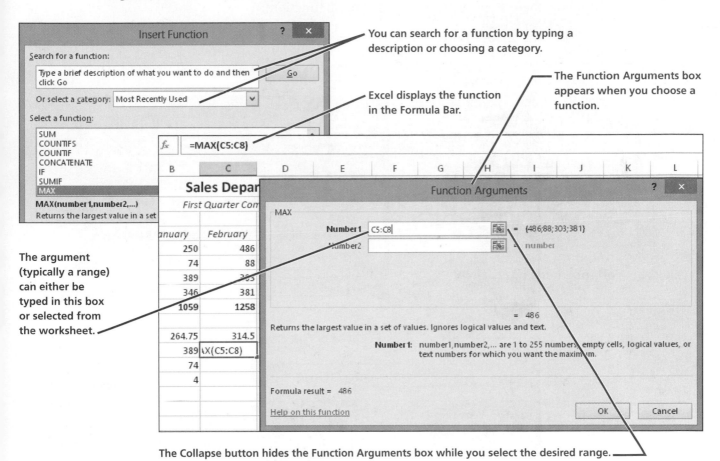

You can search for a function by typing a description or choosing a category.

Excel displays the function in the Formula Bar.

The Function Arguments box appears when you choose a function.

The argument (typically a range) can either be typed in this box or selected from the worksheet.

The Collapse button hides the Function Arguments box while you select the desired range.

TIP The Function Arguments dialog box can be moved by dragging its title bar to view the desired range on the worksheet.

QUICK REFERENCE	USING INSERT FUNCTION TO ENTER A FUNCTION IN A CELL
Task	**Procedure**
Create a function using Insert Function	▪ Select the cell in which you wish to enter a function.
	▪ Click the Insert Function f_x button.
	▪ Choose the desired function; click OK.
	▪ Select the ranges to include in each function argument; click OK.

Use Insert Function

In this exercise, you will complete the Commissions worksheet by using the Insert Function command to create maximum and minimum functions.

1. Save your file as **EX04-D07-Commissions-FirstInitialLastName**.

2. Select **cell C12**.

3. Follow these steps to create the Maximum function:

Ⓐ Click the **Insert Function** button.

Ⓑ Click the **drop-down arrow** and select **Statistical**.

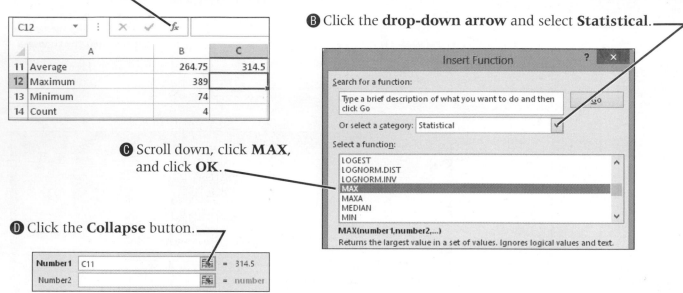

Ⓒ Scroll down, click **MAX**, and click **OK**.

Ⓓ Click the **Collapse** button.

Ⓔ Select the **range C5:C8**.

Ⓕ Click the **Expand** button to redisplay the dialog box, and click **OK**.

4. Using the procedure from **step 3**, create the **Minimum** function in **cell C13**.

5. Create the **Count** function in **cell C14**.

6. Select the **range C12:C14**, copy the formulas to the **range D12:E14**, and save the workbook.

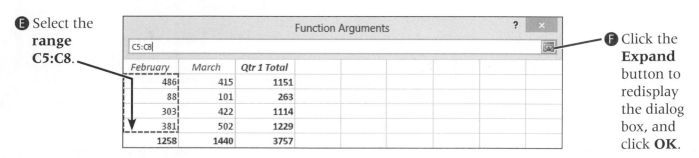

	A	B	C	D	E
11	Average	264.75	314.5	360	939.25
12	Maximum	389	486	502	1229
13	Minimum	74	88	101	263
14	Count	4	4	4	4

Creating Formulas with the IF Function

Video Library   http://labyrinthelab.com/videos   Video Number: EX13-V0408

Excel's IF function displays a value or text based on a logical test. It displays one of two results, depending on the outcome of your logical test. For example, if you offer customers a discount for purchases of $200 or more, an IF function could be used to display either the correct discount amount or $0. For purchases greater than $200, the IF function would calculate the discount; for purchases less than $200, the formula would insert $0.

IF Function Syntax

If you type the IF formula directly in its cell, you must add quotation (") marks around text arguments. If you use the Insert Function command, Excel adds the quotation marks for you.

The generic parts of the IF function are shown in the following table.

Function	Syntax
IF	IF(logical_test, value_if_true, value_if_false)

The following table outlines the arguments of the IF function.

Argument	Description
logical_test	The condition being checked using a comparison operator, such as =, >, <, >=, <=, or <> (not equal to)
value_if_true	The value, text in quotation (") marks, or calculation returned if the logical test result is found to be true
value_if_false	The value, text in quotation (") marks, or calculation returned if the logical test result is found to be false

How the IF Function Works

The formula =IF(C6>=200,C6*D6,0) is used as an example to explain the function result. Excel performs the logical test to determine whether the value in C6 is greater than or equal to 200. A value of 200 or more would evaluate as true. Any of the following would evaluate as false: a value less than 200, a blank cell, or text entered in cell C6. If the logical test proves true, the calculation C6*D6 is performed and the result displays in the formula cell. If the calculation proves false, the value 0 (zero) displays.

You may also use the IF function to display a text message or leave the cell blank. You may create complex calculations and even use other functions in arguments within an IF function, called nesting. Two examples that display text are shown in the following table.

Formula	Action if True	Action if False
IF(F3>150000, "Over Budget", "Within Budget")	The text *Over Budget* displays	The text *Within Budget* displays
IF(D6<=30, "", "Late")	The cell displays blank	The text *Late* displays

If you type "" (quotation marks without a space between) as the value_if_true or value_if_false argument, Excel leaves the cell blank.

Use the IF Function

In this exercise, you will use the IF function to display a text message when a salesperson achieves at least $30,000 in quarterly sales.

1. Save your file as **EX04-D08-Commissions-FirstInitialLastName.**

2. Type the column heading **Sales** in **cell F4** and **Met Goal?** in **cell G4**.

3. Enter values in the **range F5:F8** as shown.

4. Type **Goal** in **cell A15** and **30000** in **cell F15**.

    You will create a formula that compares the value in the Sales cell with the goal of $30,000. If sales are equal or greater, the message Yes displays. Otherwise, the cell displays No.

	F	G
4	*Sales*	*Met Goal?*
5	28775	
6	6575	
7	27850	
8	30725	

5. Select **cell G5** and click the **Insert Function** f_x button in the Formula Bar.

6. Follow these steps to find the IF function:

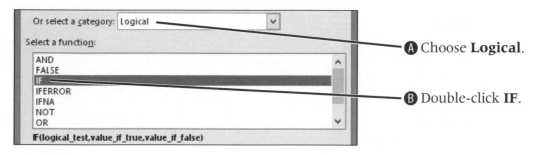

Ⓐ Choose **Logical**.

Ⓑ Double-click **IF**.

The Function Arguments dialog box appears for the IF function.

7. If necessary, move the Function Arguments dialog box out of the way by dragging its title bar until you can see **column G**.

8. Follow these steps to specify the IF function arguments:

Ⓐ Select **cell F5** in the worksheet, tap $\boxed{\text{Shift}}+\boxed{>}$, and then tap $\boxed{=}$ (for greater than or equal to).

Ⓑ Select **cell F15** (the $30,000 goal amount) and tap $\boxed{\text{F4}}$.

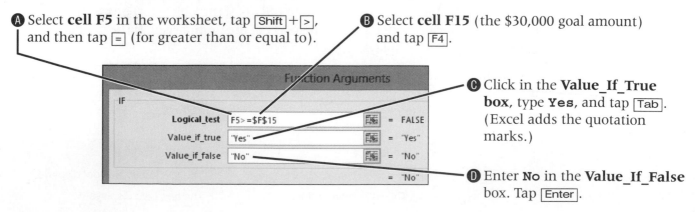

Ⓒ Click in the **Value_If_True box**, type **Yes**, and tap $\boxed{\text{Tab}}$. (Excel adds the quotation marks.)

Ⓓ Enter **No** in the **Value_If_False** box. Tap $\boxed{\text{Enter}}$.

9. Review the completed formula in the Formula Bar.

   The formula is =IF(F5>=$F$15,"Yes","No"). The message No appears in cell G5 because Talos Bouras' sales are not at least $30,000, the value in cell F15. The value_if_false argument applies.

10. Use **AutoFill** to copy the formula in **cell G5** down to the **range G6:G8**.

    The cell for Amy Wyatt displays Yes as specified by your value_if_true argument. The cells for all other salespeople display No.

Edit the IF Function

11. Select **cell G5**.

12. In the Formula Bar, click between the quotation (") mark and the N, and tap ⌦Delete twice to delete *No*.

    f_x | =IF(F5>=$F$15,"Yes","")

13. Click **Enter** ☑ in the Formula Bar.

    Cell G5 does not display a message because the value_if_false argument contains no text.

14. Use **AutoFill** to copy the formula in **cell G5** down to the **range G6:G8**, and **save** the workbook. Exit **Excel**.

    Notice that the cells that previously displayed No in column G now display no message, as shown in the illustration below. The salespeople who met goal are easier to identify.

	A	B	C	D	E	F	G
4	Sales Team Member	January	February	March	Qtr 1 Total	Sales	Met Goal?
5	Talos Bouras	250	486	415	1151	28775	
6	Leisa Malimali	74	88	101	263	6575	
7	Brian Simpson	389	303	422	1114	27850	
8	Amy Wyatt	346	381	502	1229	30725	Yes
9	Monthly Total	1059	1258	1440	3757		
10							
11	Average	264.75	314.5	360	939.25		
12	Maximum	389	486	502	1229		
13	Minimum	74	88	101	263		
14	Count	4	4	4	4		
15	Goal					30000	

Concepts Review

To check your knowledge of the key concepts introduced in this lesson, complete the Concepts Review quiz by choosing the appropriate access option below.

If you are...	Then access the quiz by...
Using the Labyrinth Video Library	Going to http://labyrinthelab.com/videos
Using eLab	Logging in, choosing Content, and navigating to the Concepts Review quiz for this lesson
Not using the Labyrinth Video Library or eLab	Going to the student resource center for this book

Reinforce Your Skills

Create Simple Formulas

In this exercise, you will create and modify formulas using AutoSum, the keyboard, and Point Mode.

Work with Formulas and Functions

1. Start **Excel**. Open **EX04-R01-OrdersReturns** from the **Excel 2013 Lesson 04** folder and save it as **EX04-R01-OrdersReturns-[FirstInitialLastName]**.

2. Select **cell E4**.

3. Choose **Home→Editing→AutoSum Σ**, and confirm the formula.

4. Use **AutoFill** to copy the formula to **cells E5** and **E6**.
   Note that the Status Bar shows the sum of the range E4:E6.

Create Formulas

5. Select **cell B18**.

6. Type **=B4+B9+B14**, and tap Enter.

7. Use **AutoFill** to copy the formula to **cells C18** and **D18**.

Use Cell References in Formulas

8. Select **cell B19**.

9. Type **=** , select **cell B5**, and type **+**.

10. Select **cell B10** and type **+**.

11. Select **cell B15** and tap Enter.

12. Use **AutoFill** to copy the formula to **cells C19** and **D19**.
    The relative cell references update as you AutoFill the formula.

13. With the range **B19:D19** still highlighted, **AutoFill** to copy the formulas to **B20:D20**.
    Again, relative cell references allow you to AutoFill here and arrive at the correct formulas.

Modify and Copy Formulas

14. Highlight the range **E4:E6**.

15. Click **Copy** 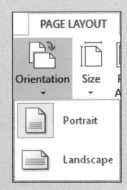.

16. Highlight the range **E9:E11**.

17. Click **Paste** from the Ribbon.

18. Highlight the range **E14:E16**.

19. Click **Paste**.

    Note that the marquee continued to surround E4:E6 after you pasted in step 17, so there was no need to click Copy prior to pasting in E14:E16.

20. Examine the formulas in the Formula Bar; then save and close the workbook. Exit **Excel**.

21. Submit your final file based on the guidelines provided by your instructor.

    To view examples of how your file or files should look at the end of this exercise, go to the student resource center.

REINFORCE YOUR SKILLS EX04-R02

Display Formulas and Use Functions

In this exercise, you will view formulas, use AutoComplete and Insert Function to create formulas, and use the IF Function.

Display and Print Formulas

1. Start **Excel**. Open **EX04-R02-Contracts** from the **Excel 2013 Lesson 04** folder and save it as **EX04-R02-Contracts-[FirstInitialLastName]**.

2. Tap ⎇Ctrl+⎘ to display the worksheet formulas.
   The grave accent key ⎘ is above the ⎈Tab *key.*

3. Choose **View→Workbook Views→Page Layout View** 🖺.

4. Take a few minutes to look at how the data and formulas display.
   Notice that Excel widened the columns so that most of the cell contents display. In this view, the worksheet fits on two pages.

5. Choose **Page Layout→Page Setup→Change Page Orientation→Landscape**.
   Landscape orientation prints across the wide edge of the paper, which can be useful for printing the formula view.

6. Choose **Page Layout→Page Setup→Change Page Orientation→Portrait**.
   Portrait orientation prints across the narrow edge of the paper, which is acceptable for printing this worksheet while formulas are hidden.

7. Click the **Normal View** button in the Status Bar at the bottom-right corner of the window.

8. Tap ⎇Ctrl+⎘ to hide the formulas.

Use Formula AutoComplete

9. Select **cell A10** and edit the label to `Kids for Change Contracts - Prior Year`.

10. Select **cell B2** and use **AutoFill** to copy the series Qtr 2, Qtr 3, and Qtr 4 into the **range C2:E2**.

11. Select **cell B8**.

12. Begin typing the formula `=aver`, and then tap Tab to choose **AVERAGE** as the function.

13. Drag to select **B3:B6** and then tap Enter.

    The result should equal 33.

14. Use the **fill handle** to copy the formula across **row 8**.

    The average for each quarter of the current year is now displayed.

Use Insert Function

15. Select **cell B17**.

16. Click **Insert Function** from the Formula Bar.

17. Click the drop-down arrow and select **Statistical**.

18. Click the **Average** function from the list, and click **OK**.

19. Modify the range to **B12:B15** and confirm the formula.

    The result should equal 23.5.

20. Use the **fill handle** to copy the formula across **row 17**.

21. Select **cell B20**.

22. Use **point mode** to enter the formula =B7-B16, and complete the entry.

    The result should equal 38.

23. Use the **fill handle** to copy the formula across **row 20**.

    The number of contracts decreased for the third quarter from 76 to 72.

Create Formulas with the IF Function

24. Select **cell B21** and click **Insert Function** from the Formula Bar.

25. Select the **IF** function from the Logical category and click **OK**.

    The Function Arguments dialog box displays.

26. For the Logical Test entry, select **cell B20** in the worksheet, tap Shift + > for the greater-than symbol, and type **0**.

27. Tap Tab to complete the entry.

28. Type `Increase` in the Value If True box and tap Tab.

29. Type `Decrease` in the Value If False box and tap Enter.

    The result displays as Increase.

30. Use the **fill handle** to copy the formula across **row 21**; save and close the workbook. Exit **Excel**.

31. Submit your final files based on the guidelines provided by your instructor.

    To view examples of how your file or files should look at the end of this exercise, go to the student resource center.

Use Formulas to Complete a Worksheet

In this exercise, you will utilize multiple techniques to create appropriate formulas throughout a worksheet.

Work with Formulas and Functions

1. Start **Excel**. Open **EX04-R03-BenefitPlan** from the **Excel 2013 Lesson 04** folder and save it as **EX04-R03-BenefitPlan-[FirstInitialLastName]**.

2. Select **cell C12**, and choose **Home→Editing→AutoSum menu ▼→Min**.

3. Change the range within the formula to **C5:C9**.

4. Use the AutoSum menu to insert the **Maximum** for this range in **cell C13**.

Create Formulas

5. Select **cell J5**.

6. Type **=C5+E5+G5+I5** and tap Enter.

7. Use **AutoFill** to copy the formula to **J6:J10**.

Use Cell References in Formulas

8. Select **cell C10**.

9. Type **=sum (**, select the **range C5:C9**, and confirm the formula.

10. With **cell C10** selected, choose **Home→Clipboard→Copy**.

11. Select cell **E10**, hold down Ctrl, and select **cells G10 and I10**.
    You can highlight nonadjacent cells by holding down the Ctrl key.

12. Choose **Home→Clipboard→Paste**.

13. Select **cell C15**.

14. Type **=** and select **cell C10**.

15. Type *****, select **cell J1**, and tap F4; confirm the formula.
    Absolute formatting is needed for cell J1 so that the Match Percentage cell reference does not change when the formula is copied.

Modify and Copy Formulas

16. Highlight the **range C12:C13**.

17. Click **Copy** 📋.

18. Highlight the **range E12:E13**, hold down Ctrl, highlight **G12:G13** and **I12:I13**.

19. Click **Paste** .

20. Repeat the prior four steps to replicate the formula in **cell C15** to **cells E15, G15,** and **I15**.
    Take a few minutes to examine the formulas in the Formula Bar.

Display and Print Formulas

21. Choose **Formulas→Formula Auditing→Show Formulas** 🔢.

22. Choose **View→Workbook Views→Page Layout View** 🖼️.

    Take a few minutes to look at the way the data and formulas display.

    Notice that Excel widened the columns so that most of the cell contents display.

23. Choose **Page Layout→Page Setup→ Change Page Orientation→Landscape**.

    Landscape orientation prints across the wide edge of the paper, which is useful for printing the formula view.

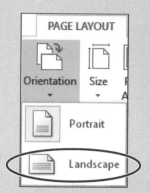

24. Click the **Normal View** button in the Status Bar.

25. Tap [Ctrl]+[`] to hide the formulas.

Use Formulas AutoComplete

26. Select **cell C17**.

27. Begin typing the formula **=aver**, and tap [Tab] to choose **AVERAGE**.

28. Hold [Ctrl] to select **cells C15, E15, G15, and I15**, and then tap [Enter].

Using Insert Function

29. Select **cell C14**.

30. Click **Insert Function** from the Formula Bar.

31. Click the drop-down arrow and select **Statistical**.

32. Click the **Count** function from the list, and click **OK**.

33. Modify the range to **C5:C9** and confirm the formula.

34. Copy the formula to cells **E14, G14, and I14**.

    Note that there were more contributions made in the second quarter than during any other quarter.

Create Formulas with the IF Function

35. Select **cell L5** and click **Insert Function** from the Formula Bar.

36. Select **IF** from the Logical category and click **OK**.

37. For the Logical Test entry, select **cell J5** in the worksheet, tap [Shift]+[>], and select **cell K5**.

38. Tap [Tab] to complete the entry.

39. Type **Yes** in the Value If True box and tap [Tab].

40. Type **No** in the Value If False box and tap [Enter].

    The result displays as No *because cells J5 and K5 contain equal values.*

41. Use the **fill handle** to copy the formula down **column L**; save and close the workbook. Exit **Excel**.

42. Submit your final file based on the guidelines provided by your instructor.

Apply Your Skills

Create Formulas, and Use Absolute References

In the exercise, you will create a price sheet with formulas that use absolute references.

Work with Formulas and Functions

1. Start **Excel**. Open **EX04-A01-PriceChange** from the **Excel 2013 Lesson 04** folder and save it as **EX04-A01-PriceChange-[FirstInitialLastName]**.

2. Use **AutoSum** to add the original prices in **cell B13**.

Create Formulas

3. Sum the discounted prices for the **range C6:C11** in **cell C13**.

   This formula will yield results when the discounted prices are entered in the worksheet.

Use Cell References in Formulas

4. Calculate the discounted price in **cell C6** as **Original Price * (1 - Discount Rate)**. Use an **absolute reference** when referring to the discount rate in **cell B3**.

5. Copy the formula in **cell C6** down the column.

   Cell C6 was formatted for you so it displays the price with two decimal places.

6. Change the percentage in **cell B3** to **10%**, and watch the worksheet recalculate.

7. Change the percentage in **cell B3** back to **15%**, and watch the worksheet recalculate.

   You use cell references within formulas so that when changes are made, such as to the discount rate here, the formulas will recalculate properly.

Modify and Copy Formulas

8. Type **Cutlery Upgrade** in **cell A12**, and type **90** in **cell B12**.

   Notice that the discounted price in cell C12 has automatically displayed.

9. Ensure that the discounted price in cell C12 is calculated properly; save and close the workbook. Exit **Excel**.

10. Submit your final file based on the guidelines provided by your instructor.

    To view examples of how your file or files should look at the end of this exercise, go to the student resource center.

Use the AVERAGE and IF Functions

In this exercise, you will create an IF function to indicate whether a department met the safety goal each month. You will create formulas to total the safety incidents in a six-month period, and calculate the average number of incidents per month.

Display and Print Formulas

1. Start **Excel**. Open **EX04-A02-SafetyGoal** from the **Excel 2013 Lesson 04** folder and save it as **EX04-A02-SafetyGoal-[FirstInitialLastName]**.

2. Enter **January** in **cell A6**. **AutoFill** down **column A** to display the months January through June.

3. Display the worksheet formulas.

   Because you have not yet entered any formulas, nothing changes.

4. Hide the worksheet formulas.

   This ensures that you will see the results of any formulas entered in upcoming steps.

Use Formula AutoComplete

5. Use **AutoComplete** to enter the sum function in **cell B12**. Add all incidents in column B within this formula.

Use Insert Function

6. Use **Insert Function** to enter the **Average** function in **cell B14** to find the average number of safety incidents per month from January through June.

   Your formula should return an average of one incident per month.

Create Formulas with the IF Function

7. Use the **IF** function to create a formula in **cell C6** that indicates whether the department met its goal of no safety incidents during the month. Excel should display *Met Goal* if the incidents are equal to zero (0) and *Not Met* if the incidents are more than 0.

8. Copy the formula down the column for the months February through June; save and close the workbook. Exit **Excel**.

9. Submit your final file based on the guidelines provided by your instructor.

   To view examples of how your file or files should look at the end of this exercise, go to the student resource center.

Create a Financial Report

In this exercise, you will create a worksheet by entering data, creating formulas, and using absolute references. You will also save, print a section of, and close the workbook.

Work with Formulas and Functions

1. Start **Excel**. Open **EX04-A03-NetProfit** from the **Excel 2013 Lesson 04** folder and save it as **EX04-A03-NetProfit-[FirstInitialLastName]**.

2. Use **AutoSum** to add the revenue in **cell F4**.

Create Formulas

3. Type a formula in **cell B10** to sum the costs for Q1 in **column B**.
   Practice typing the cell references here. You will use Point Mode later.

4. **AutoFill** the quarter headings in **row 3** and the Total Costs formula in **row 10**.
   Ensure that you AutoFill the total costs through column F.

Use Cell References in Formulas

5. Use a formula to calculate employee costs in **cell B6**. The formula should multiply the revenue (**cell B4**) by the percentage (**cell B15**). Use a **mixed reference** to refer to the revenue and an **absolute reference** to refer to the cost percentage.

6. Copy the titles in the range **A6:A9** to the range **A15:A18.**

7. Use formulas to calculate the other costs in the range **B7:B9**. Each formula should multiply the revenue in **row 4** by the related cost percentage in **rows 16–18**.

8. Calculate the net profit in **cell B13** as `Gross Profit * (1 - Tax Rate)`. Once again, use an absolute reference when referring to the tax rate in **cell B19**.
   Your Net Profit should equal 169,740.

Modify and Copy Formulas

9. Modify the formula in **cell B12** to calculate Gross Profit as Revenue minus Total Costs.

10. Copy the range **B12:B13** to the range **C12:F13.**

11. Copy the formulas in the range **B6:B9** to the range **C6:E9.**

Display and Print Formulas

12. Display the worksheet formulas.
    Review the formulas to ensure that they have been entered correctly.

13. Hide the worksheet formulas.

Use Formula AutoComplete

14. Use **AutoComplete** to calculate Total Employee Costs in **cell F6**.

15. Copy the formula from **cell F6** to **cell F7**.

    The Total Capital Expenditures in cell F7 should equal 377,300.

Use Insert Function

16. Use the **Insert Function Dialog Box** to sum the Total Materials Costs in **cell F8**.

17. Copy the formula from **cell F8** to **cell F9**.

Create Formulas with the IF Function

18. Create an IF Function in **cell H12** to determine if the Annual Gross Profit Goal in cell H4 has been met. Excel should display *Met Goal* if it has been met and *Missed Goal* if it has not been met. Save and close the workbook. Exit **Excel**.

    Since the Gross Profit of 463,050 is less than the 500,000 goal in cell H4, Missed Goal *is displayed in cell H12.*

19. Submit your final file based on the guidelines provided by your instructor.

Extend Your Skills

In the course of working through the Extend Your Skills exercises, you will think critically as you use the skills taught in the lesson to complete the assigned projects. To evaluate your mastery and completion of the exercises, your instructor may use a rubric, with which more points are allotted according to performance characteristics. (The more you do, the more you earn!) Ask your instructor how your work will be evaluated.

EX04-E01 That's the Way I See It

You are known as the neighborhood Excel expert for small businesses! The chamber of commerce has asked you to create a worksheet analyzing three different retail businesses in your area so they can determine the profitability of the businesses in order to help develop marketing plans for the individual chamber members as well as the community at large. You will evaluate the local competition for each business, and create a formula that shows how well positioned the three companies are in the marketplace.

Open **EX04-E01-Competition** from the **Excel 2013 Lesson 04** folder and save it as **EX04-E01-Competition-[FirstInitialLastName]**.

Enter three companies and their industries at the top of the worksheet. Be sure to select companies from three different industries (electronics, women's clothing, etc.). Enter the direct competitors for each company within the spreadsheet, and create formulas that will display the number of competitors for each. Lastly, include a formula that designates companies with three or more competitors as having "High" competition, and companies with fewer than three competitors as having "Low" competition.

You will be evaluated based on the inclusion of all elements specified, your ability to follow directions, your ability to apply newly learned skills to a real-world situation, your creativity, and the relevance of your topic and/or data choice(s). Submit your final file based on the guidelines provided by your instructor.

EX04-E02 Be Your Own Boss

In this exercise, you will create a customer listing that shows the number of jobs performed for each customer of Blue Jean Landscaping, and the billings associated with each.

Open **EX04-E02-CustomerBase** from the **Excel 2013 Lesson 04** folder and save it as **EX04-E02-CustomerBase-[FirstInitialLastName]**.

Create formulas in the designated cells within column B to determine the total number of jobs for each company type and to count the number of companies of each type. For the Billings Increase columns, first place the increase percentages in a suitable location within the spreadsheet, and then use absolute formatting to create formulas for each company referencing these percentages. Format the worksheet using your knowledge of Excel, ensuring that all numbers are displayed properly. Since this is your company, write a paragraph with at least five sentences that summarizes the data you have calculated. Type the paragraph below the data. In it, explain what you have learned from the calculations and how you might change how you do business as a result.

You will be evaluated based on the inclusion of all elements specified, your ability to follow directions, your ability to apply newly learned skills to a real-world situation, your creativity, and your demonstration of an entrepreneurial spirit. Submit your final file based on the guidelines provided by your instructor.

Transfer Your Skills

In the course of working through the Transfer Your Skills exercises, you will use critical-thinking and creativity skills to complete the assigned projects using skills taught in the lesson. To evaluate your mastery and completion of the exercises, your instructor may use a rubric, with which more points are allotted according to performance characteristics. (The more you do, the more you earn!) Ask your instructor how your work will be evaluated.

EX04-T01 Use the Web as a Learning Tool

Throughout this book, you will be provided with an opportunity to use the Internet as a learning tool by completing WebQuests. According to the original creators of WebQuests, as described on their website (WebQuest.org), a WebQuest is "an inquiry-oriented activity in which most or all of the information used by learners is drawn from the web." To complete the WebQuest projects in this book, navigate to the student resource center and choose the WebQuest for the lesson on which you are currently working. The subject of each WebQuest will be relevant to the material found in the lesson.

WebQuest Subject: Utilizing the IF function when classifying restaurant chains as successful or unsuccessful

Submit your final file(s) based on the guidelines provided by your instructor.

EX04-T02 Demonstrate Proficiency

You have decided to recreate the Product Markup Worksheet for Stormy BBQ to make it more user-friendly. Specifically, you would like to remove the markup percentages from individual formulas. You want to replace them with a cell reference from the worksheet that contains the markup percentage.

Open **EX04-T02-ProductMarkup** from the **Excel 2013 Lesson 04** folder and save it as **EX04-T02-ProductMarkup-[FirstInitialLastName]**. Use the formula writing and absolute formatting skills that you have learned in this lesson to create the markup formulas described above and produce a more user-friendly worksheet. Format the worksheet as desired, ensuring that all numbers are properly formatted and will appear in a logical manner when printed.

Submit your final file based on the guidelines provided by your instructor.

EXCEL 2013

Formatting Cell Contents, Basic Skills

LEARNING OBJECTIVES

After studying this lesson, you will be able to:

- Format worksheets using a variety of methods
- Control text to align and fit within cells
- Alter the appearance of numbers through a variety of methods
- Format cells with borders and fill colors
- Find and replace data and formatting

In this lesson, you will use Excel's formatting features to enhance your worksheets. You will also gain experience with Excel's Find and Replace commands, which allow you to quickly locate and change entries within worksheets. By the end of this lesson, you will have developed the skills necessary to create professional worksheets.

Formatting with Excel

The accountant for Green Clean, a janitorial product supplier and cleaning service contractor, has drafted an income statement, which you intend to use to examine quarterly revenue and expense figures. You will use many of Excel's formatting features to make the spreadsheet easier to read and understand. You will also create a workbook theme so uniform formatting may be applied to Green Clean's other worksheets.

	A	B	C	D	E
1	Green Clean				
2	Income Statement				
3	3rd Quarter [Current Year]				
4		*July*	*August*	*September*	*Quarter Total*
5	REVENUES				
6	Sales	254723	261378	188684	704785
7	Finance Charge Revenue	4702	3982	3370	12054
8	Total Revenues	259425	265360	192054	716839

	A	B	C	D	E
1			Green Clean		
2			Income Statement		
3			3rd Quarter [Current Year]		
4		*July*	*August*	*September*	*Quarter Total*
5	REVENUES				
6	Sales	$ 254,723	$ 261,378	$ 188,684	$ 704,785
7	Finance Charge Revenue	4,702	3,982	3,370	12,054
8	Total Revenues	$ 259,425	$ 265,360	$ 192,054	$ 716,839

The income statement is shown here before (top) and after (bottom) formatting changes have been made.

Formatting Worksheets

Video Library   http://labyrinthelab.com/videos   Video Number: EX13-V0501

Formatting deals with changing how the data in your worksheet looks, not with changing the data itself. In Excel and other Microsoft Office programs, you can format text by changing the font type, size, and color. You can also apply various font enhancements, including bold, italic, and underline. Excel's Live Preview feature allows you to preview many formatting changes by holding the mouse pointer over the option, so that you can see the formatting in action.

Formatting Entries

Formatting commands can be applied either through the Ribbon or by using the Mini toolbar. The Mini toolbar offers many of the same options as the Font group on the Home tab, but conveniently places them adjacent to the active cell. Different versions of the Mini toolbar will appear when you right-click a cell, and when you highlight a cell's contents.

FROM THE KEYBOARD
Ctrl+B for bold
Ctrl+I for italicize
Ctrl+U for underline

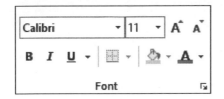

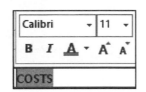

Formatting options can be selected from both the Ribbon and the Mini toolbar.

DEVELOP YOUR SKILLS EX05-D01
Format Cells with the Ribbon and Mini Toolbar

In this exercise, you will begin to format a worksheet by using both the Ribbon and the Mini toolbar.

1. Open **EX05-D01-IncomeStatement** file from the **EX2013 Lesson 05** folder and save it as **EX05-D01-IncomeStatement-[FirstInitialLastName]**.

   Replace the bracketed text with your first initial and last name. For example, if your name is Bethany Smith, your filename would look like this: EX05-D01-IncomeStatement-BSmith.

2. Follow these steps to change the font size of the entire worksheet:

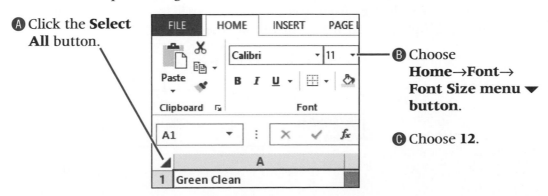

Ⓐ Click the **Select All** button.

Ⓑ Choose **Home→Font→ Font Size menu ▾ button**.

Ⓒ Choose **12**.

As you move the mouse pointer over the font size list, Excel shows how the worksheet would appear if each font size were selected.

Excel 2013

Use the Mini Toolbar

3. Follow these steps to apply Bold formatting to cell A5:

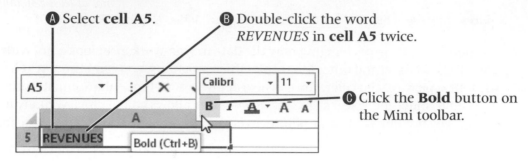

Ⓐ Select **cell A5**.

Ⓑ Double-click the word *REVENUES* in **cell A5** twice.

Ⓒ Click the **Bold** button on the Mini toolbar.

4. Right-click **cell A10** to display the Mini toolbar.

5. Click the **Bold** Ⓑ button on the Mini toolbar.

6. Save the file and leave it open; you will modify it throughout this lesson.

Using Excel's Alignment and Indent Features

Video Library   http://labyrinthelab.com/videos   Video Number: EX13-V0502

Excel allows you to alter how text is aligned within cells. In addition to the standard left, center, and right horizontal alignments, you can indent cells contents within a cell from either edge.

Aligning Entries

The Align Left, Center, and Align Right buttons let you align entries within cells. By default, text entries are left aligned and number entries are right aligned.

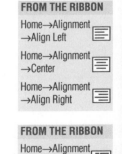

FROM THE RIBBON

Home→Alignment →Align Left

Home→Alignment →Center

Home→Alignment →Align Right

Indenting Cell Entries

The Increase Indent and Decrease Indent buttons let you offset entries from the edges of cells. If a cell entry is left aligned, it will indent from the left edge, and if it is right aligned, it will indent from the right edge.

FROM THE RIBBON

Home→Alignment →Increase Indent

Home→Alignment →Decrease Indent

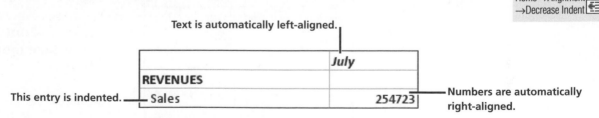

Text is automatically left-aligned.

This entry is indented. — Sales

Numbers are automatically right-aligned.

Work with Alignment and Indent

In this exercise, you will set the alignment in cells as well as indent entries.

1. Save your file as **EX05-D02-IncomeStatement-[FirstInitialLastName]**.

2. Select the **range B4:E4**.

3. Choose **Home→Alignment→Align Right** ▤.

4. Select the **range A6:A7**.

5. Choose **Home→Alignment→Increase Indent** ▤.

6. Select the **range A11:A22**.

7. Choose **Home→Alignment→Increase Indent** ▤.

8. Save the file and leave it open.

Excel 2013

Using Excel's Text Control Options

Video Library   http://labyrinthelab.com/videos   Video Number: EX13-V0503

The Alignment group on the Home tab provides options that allow you to merge cells and wrap lengthy text within a cell. Additionally, you can shrink text to fit within a cell.

Merging and Splitting Cells

The Merge Cells option allows you to combine cells. You can merge cells both vertically and horizontally, and merged cells behave as one large cell. The merged cell takes on the name of the top-left cell in the merged range. For example, if you merge cells A1:E1, the resulting merged cell will be named A1.

> **FROM THE RIBBON**
> Home→ Alignment→
> Merge & Center ▤

The Merge & Center button merges selected cells and changes the alignment of the merged cell to center. This technique can be used to center a heading across columns, but it can only be used on one row at a time. You can split a merged and centered cell by clicking the Merge & Center button again.

◢	A	B	C	D	E
1			Green Clean		

Here, the original contents of cell A1 are merged and centered over the range A1:E1

If you merge two or more cells, each containing data, some of the data will be lost.

Merge Across

Unlike the Merge & Center, the Merge Across command is used to merge the contents of multiple rows simultaneously. For example, if you used Merge & Center on the range A1:D2, the result would be one large merged cell over this range. However, if you used Merge Across on this same range, the result would be two merged cells (neither of which is centered) within the ranges A1:D1 and A2:D2.

Wrapping Text

The Wrap Text option forces text to wrap within a cell, ensuring that no text will be cut off. The row height increases to accommodate the additional lines of wrapped text.

FROM THE RIBBON
Home→ Alignment
→Wrap Text

Entering a Line Break

To display text on a second line within a single cell, you can insert a line break.

FROM THE KEYBOARD
Alt + Enter to insert
a line break

	Quarter
September	Total
188684	704785

The line break that forces "Total" to a second line can be removed by clicking here and tapping Delete .

Shrinking Text to Fit Within a Cell

There may be times when changing the width of a column or wrapping text is not appropriate, yet you still want all of the text within the cell to be displayed. The Shrink to Fit option allows you to reduce the text size of the cell entry to the exact size that fits the existing cell width.

QUICK REFERENCE	MERGING CELLS AND WRAPPING TEXT
Task	**Procedure**
Merge and center a range, one row	■ Select the desired cells and choose Home→Alignment→Merge & Center.
Merge and center a range, multiple adjacent rows	■ Select the desired cells. ■ Choose Home→Alignment→Merge & Center menu ▼→Merge Across. ■ Choose Home→Alignment→Center.
Unmerge cells	■ Select the desired cells and choose Home→Alignment→Merge & Center.
Wrap text within a cell	■ Select the desired cells and choose Home→Alignment→Wrap Text.
Shrink text to fit the column width	■ Right-click the desired cells and choose Format Cells. ■ On the Alignment tab, add a checkmark next to Shrink to Fit and click OK.

Control Text in Cells

In this exercise, you will merge and center cells as well as wrap text within a cell.

1. Save your file as **EX05-D03-IncomeStatement-[FirstInitialLastName]**.

2. Follow these steps to merge and center a range of cells:

A Select the range **A1:E1**.   **B** Choose **Home→Alignment→Merge & Center**.

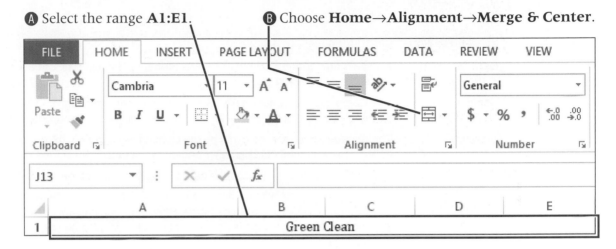

When you click in the merged cell, the Name Box displays A1 for the range.

Merge and Center on Multiple Adjacent Rows

3. Select the **range A2:E3**.

4. Choose **Home→Alignment→Merge & Center menu ▼→Merge Across**.

5. Choose **Home→Alignment→Center**.
   This method is more efficient when merging multiple rows.

Wrap Text within a Cell

6. Select **cell A29**.

7. Choose **Home→Alignment→Wrap Text**.
   The text will continue to wrap within the cell as it is edited and/or the column width is altered.

8. Follow these steps to manually enter a line break in a cell:

A Select **cell E4**.   **B** Click to the left of **Total** and tap [Backspace] to remove the space between words.

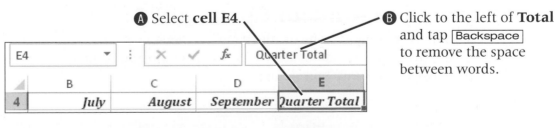

C Hold down [Alt] and tap [Enter].

The line break will remain when text is edited and column widths are altered.

9. Tap [Enter] to complete the entry; save your file and leave it open.

Excel 2013

Formatting Numbers

Video Library http://labyrinthelab.com/videos Video Number: EX13-V0504

Number formats change the way numbers are displayed, although they do not change the actual numbers. Once a number format has been applied to a cell, it remains with the cell—even if the contents are deleted.

Number Format	Description
General	Numbers are formatted with the General format by default. This format does not apply any special formats to the numbers.
Comma Style	The Comma Style format inserts a comma after every third digit in the number. This format also inserts a decimal point and two decimal places, and indents the entry.
Currency	The Currency format is the same as the Comma Style format, except that it adds a dollar ($) sign in front of the number and does not indent the entry.
Accounting	The Accounting format is the same as Comma Style format, except that a dollar sign is placed at the left edge of the cell.
Percent Style	The Percent Style, also known as Percentage, inserts a percent (%) sign to the right of the number. The percentage is calculated by multiplying the number by 100.

If you begin an entry with a dollar sign, the Currency format will automatically be applied.

The following table provides several examples of formatted numbers.

Number Entered	Format	How the Number Is Displayed
5347.82	General	5347.82
5347.82	Comma with 0 decimal places	5,348
5347.82	Comma with 2 decimal places	5,347.82
5347.82	Currency with 0 decimal places	$5,348
5347.82	Currency with 2 decimal places	$5,347.82
.5347	Percentage with 0 decimal places	53%
.5347	Percentage with 2 decimal places	53.47%

Using the Number Command Group

The Number command group on the Home tab allows you to format numbers in many ways. If you click the dialog box launcher in the Number group, the Format Cells dialog box will appear, providing further formatting options.

The number style of the selected cell

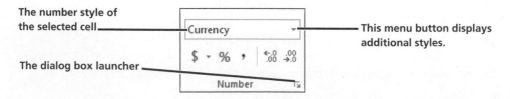

This menu button displays additional styles.

The dialog box launcher

Applying the Percent Style

The Percent Style, also called Percentage in Excel, adds a percent sign (%) after a number. To properly apply this style you must either apply the formatting before you type the number, or enter the value with two decimal places prior to applying the formatting.

How Numbers Display in Cells

Unlike text, numbers will not spill over into adjacent cells when they are too long. If the entry contains decimals, they will be rounded to as many decimal places as will fit within the cell. If the entry is formatted such that it cannot appear fully within the cell, number signs (###) will appear. In this instance you will widen the column to make the entry visible.

These formatted numbers are too wide to be visible.

⊿	A	B	C	D	E
25	Net Income (Loss)	##########	##########	##########	##########
26					
27	Net Income to Total Revenues	0.271361665	0.311508894	-0.03845273	0.203218575

Decimals in these entries are rounded.

Adjusting Decimal Places

Most number formats display two decimal places by default. You can adjust the number of decimal places displayed by using the Increase Decimal and Decrease Decimal buttons. Decimals within your entry will automatically round as you add or remove decimal places.

FROM THE RIBBON

Home→Number→
Increase Decimal

Home→Number→
Decrease Decimal

Displaying Negative Numbers

Negative number displays can be either preceded by a minus sign or surrounded by parentheses. You can also display negative numbers in red. The Currency and Number options in the Format Cells dialog box allow you to choose the format for negative numbers.

This negative entry is displayed with a negative sign.

⊿	A	B	C	D	E
25	Net Income (Loss)	70398	82662	-7385	145675
26					
27	Net Income to Total Revenues	0.271361665	0.311508894	(0.03845273)	0.203218575

This negative entry is displayed in red with parentheses.

Format Numbers

In this exercise, you will apply various number formatting options to the worksheet.

1. Save your file as **EX05-D04-IncomeStatement-[FirstInitialLastName]**.

2. Follow these steps to apply the Accounting format to a range of cells:

   Ⓐ Select the **range B6:E6**.   **Ⓑ** Choose **Home→Number→ Accounting Number Format**.

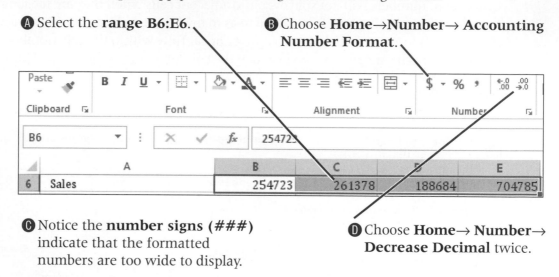

   Ⓒ Notice the **number signs (###)** indicate that the formatted numbers are too wide to display.   **Ⓓ** Choose **Home→ Number→ Decrease Decimal** twice.

   "Custom" is displayed as the number format on the Ribbon because you changed the number of decimal places of the Accounting format.

3. Select the **range B7:E7**.

4. Choose **Home→Number→Comma Style ▸**.

5. Choose **Home→ Number→Decrease Decimal** ⯆ twice.

6. Select the **range B8:E8**, hold down ⏎Ctrl, and select the **range B11:E11**.

   Remember that by using ⏎Ctrl, you can select multiple ranges to which you can apply formatting.

7. Choose **Home→Number→Accounting Number Format $**.

8. Choose **Home→Number→Decrease Decimal** ⯆ twice.

9. Repeat **steps 7–8** to apply **Accounting Number Format** with no decimals to the **ranges B23:E23** and **B25:E25**.

   Alternatively, after highlighting these two ranges, tapping the ⎔F4 key would have replicated the formatting applied above. Using the ⎔F4 key to repeat the most recent command (or most recent set of formatting changes) can save a significant amount of time.

Use Comma Style

10. Select the **range B12:E22**.

11. Apply **Comma Style** formatting with no decimals to the selection.

    Notice that the 0 entry in cell C16 now displays as a hyphen (–) because Comma Style formatting has been applied.

12. Follow these steps to apply the Percent Style to a range of cells:

Ⓐ Select the **range B27:E27**.

Ⓑ Choose **Home→Number→ Percent Style**.

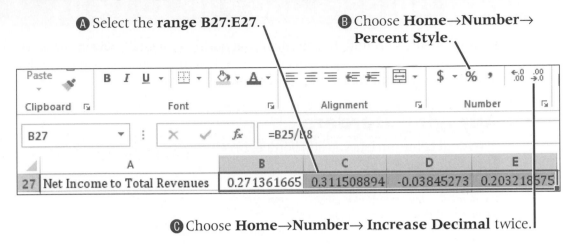

A	B	C	D	E
27 Net Income to Total Revenues	0.271361665	0.311508894	-0.03845273	0.203218575

Ⓒ Choose **Home→Number→ Increase Decimal** twice.

13. Save your file and leave it open.

Using the Format Cells Dialog Box

Video Library http://labyrinthelab.com/videos Video Number: EX13-V0505

The Format Cells dialog box contains six tabs that allow you to format your worksheet. Some options in this dialog box are not available on the Ribbon; you must use these tabs to access them.

These dialog box launchers allow you to access the Format Cells dialog box.

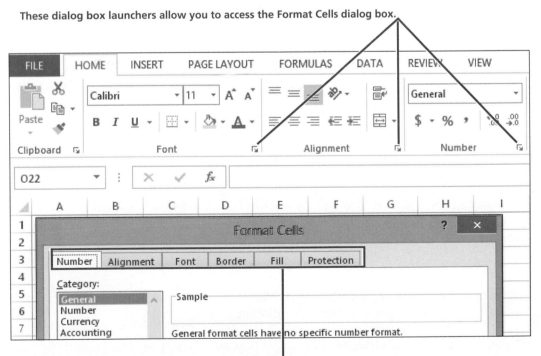

These tabs contain useful formatting options.

Excel 2013

Applying Borders and Fills to Cells

Borders are lines around the cell edges that both print and display in the worksheet. Fills are background shading and pattern effects that fill entire cells. Keep in mind that "less is more" when applying colors and other formatting.

Applying Borders

The Borders button lets you add borders to cell edges. When you click the Borders menu ▼ button, a list of options appears.

FROM THE RIBBON

Home→Font→ Borders

The Borders menu ▼ button displays the image of the last border applied.

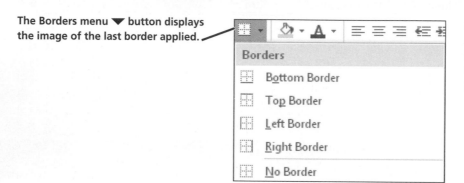

Aside from the All Borders option, each border must be applied one edge at a time to all cells in a selected range.

Applying Fill Colors and Patterns

The Fill Color button lets you fill the background of selected cells with color. When you click the Fill Color menu button, a palette of colors appears. You can apply a color to all selected cells by choosing it from the palette, and can remove a color by selecting the No Fill option.

FROM THE RIBBON

Home→Font→ Fill Color

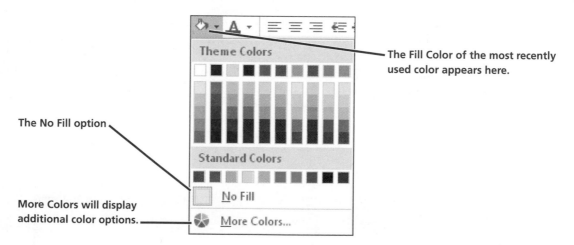

The Fill Color of the most recently used color appears here.

The No Fill option

More Colors will display additional color options.

Printing a test version of a worksheet allows you to see how your color choices will print. This is especially important for grayscale printers.

Format with the Format Cells Dialog Box

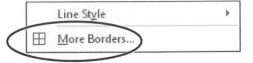

In this exercise, you will apply borders and fill colors to the worksheet.

1. Save your file as **EX05-D05-IncomeStatement-[FirstInitialLastName]**.

2. Select the **range A1:E27**.

3. Choose **Home→Font→Borders menu ▼→More Borders**.

4. Follow these steps to apply the border formatting:

   Ⓐ Click this line style.   **Ⓑ** Click the **Outline** option.

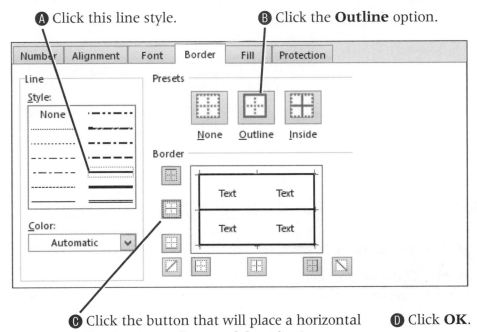

   Ⓒ Click the button that will place a horizontal line between all rows of the selection.   **Ⓓ** Click **OK**.

   The Borders button now displays this icon ⊞, which represents the More Borders option—the last option chosen from the Ribbon.

5. Use [Ctrl] + [Z] to undo the borders.

6. Select the **range B7:E7**, hold down [Ctrl], and select the **range B22:E22**. Release [Ctrl].

7. Click the **Borders menu ▼** button.

8. Choose **Bottom Border** to place a border along the bottom of the selected cells.
   A border will appear along the bottom of both of the selected ranges.

9. Select the **range B25:E25**.

10. Click the **Borders menu ▼ button** and choose **Top and Double Bottom Border**.

Apply Fill Color to a Range

11. Select the **range A5:E5**, hold down Ctrl, and select the **range A10:E10**. Release Ctrl.

12. Follow these steps to apply a fill color to the selected ranges:

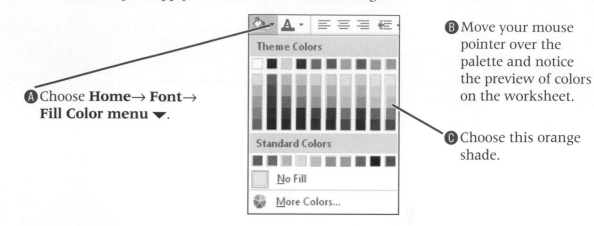

Ⓐ Choose **Home→ Font→ Fill Color menu ▼**.

Ⓑ Move your mouse pointer over the palette and notice the preview of colors on the worksheet.

Ⓒ Choose this orange shade.

13. Click away from the selection to view the color in the selected ranges. Save your file and leave it open.

Using Excel's Find and Replace Commands

Video Library   http://labyrinthelab.com/videos   Video Number: EX13-V0506

Excel's Find command can perform searches for a particular word, number, cell reference, formula, or format within a worksheet or an entire workbook. The Replace feature helps you to find an item and replace it with a specified item. While using these features you should keep in mind that Excel searches for text without regard for upper- or lowercase, but will replace text only with the exact case you type.

FROM THE KEYBOARD
Ctrl+F to find
Ctrl+H to replace

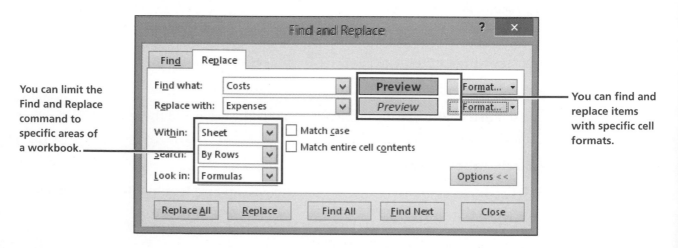

You can limit the Find and Replace command to specific areas of a workbook.

You can find and replace items with specific cell formats.

Task	Procedure
Find text or formatting	■ Choose Home→Editing→Find & Select→Find. ■ Indicate your search parameters and click Find Next or Find All.
Find and replace text or formatting	■ Choose Home→Editing→Find & Select→Replace. ■ Indicate your search parameters and desired replacements. ■ Click Replace (All) or Find (All), as appropriate.
Clear all find and replace options	■ Choose Home→Editing→Find & Select→Replace, clear all typed entries, and click Options. ■ Select the top Format menu ▼ button and choose Clear Find Format. ■ Select the bottom Format menu ▼ button and choose Clear Replace Format.

Excel 2013

DEVELOP YOUR SKILLS EX05-D06
Find and Replace Entries

In this exercise, you will find and replace text as well as formatting.

1. Save your file as **EX05-D06-IncomeStatement-[FirstInitialLastName]**.

2. Choose **Home→Editing→Find & Select 🔍→Replace**.
   The Find and Replace dialog box opens.

3. Follow these steps to prepare to replace all instances of *Costs* with *Expenses*.

Ⓐ Type **Costs** in the Find What field.

Ⓑ Tap [Tab] and type **Expenses** in the Replace With field.

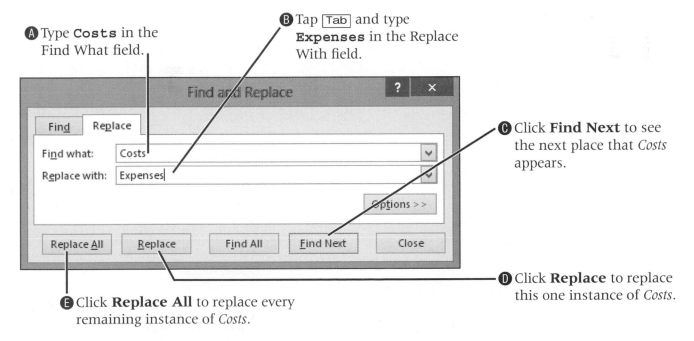

Ⓒ Click **Find Next** to see the next place that *Costs* appears.

Ⓓ Click **Replace** to replace this one instance of *Costs*.

Ⓔ Click **Replace All** to replace every remaining instance of *Costs*.

4. Click **OK** to acknowledge the total number of replacements.
   Leave the Find and Replace dialog box open.

Find and Replace Formatting

5. Click the **Options** button in the Find and Replace dialog box.

6. Follow these steps to begin setting the formatting to be found:

Ⓐ Delete the contents of the **Find What** and **Replace With** boxes.

Ⓑ Click the top **Format menu** ▼ **button** and select **Choose Format From Cell.**

Ⓒ Select **cell B4**.

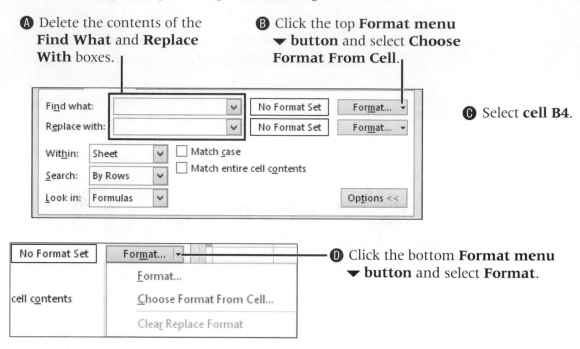

Ⓓ Click the bottom **Format menu** ▼ **button** and select **Format**.

7. Follow these steps to continue defining the format:

Ⓐ Select the **Font** tab.

Ⓑ Choose **Bold** and **11** for the font style and size.

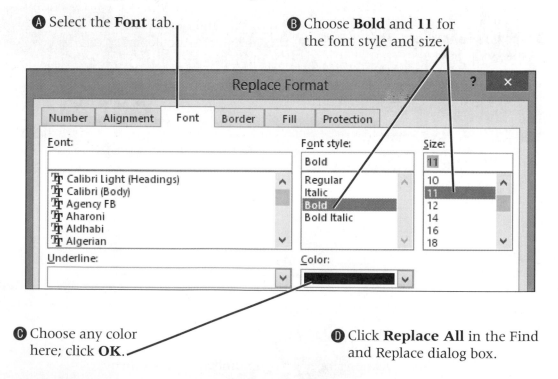

Ⓒ Choose any color here; click **OK**.

Ⓓ Click **Replace All** in the Find and Replace dialog box.

8. Click **OK** in the dialog box that appears.

All instances of formatting that are the same as that in cell B4 are replaced with the new formatting you chose. Because the formatting in cell E4 is not identical to B4, cell E4 does not change.

Clear Find and Replace Criteria

The Find and Replace criteria remain set even after the dialog box is closed. You must clear the criteria before performing another Find or Replace operation. (Exiting Excel also clears the dialog box.)

9. Click the top **Format menu** ▼ **button** and choose **Clear Find Format**.

10. Click the bottom **Format menu** ▼ **button** and choose **Clear Replace Format**.

11. Click **Close** to exit the Find and Replace dialog box.

12. Select **cell E4**.

13. Choose **Home→Font→Font Color menu** ▼ **button** and choose the same fill color applied to the **range B4:D4**.

    All entries within row 4 now appear uniform.

14. Save and then close your file. Exit **Excel**.

Concepts Review

To check your knowledge of the key concepts introduced in this lesson, complete the Concepts Review quiz by choosing the appropriate access option below.

If you are...	Then access the quiz by...
Using the Labyrinth Video Library	Going to http://labyrinthelab.com/videos
Using eLab	Logging in, choosing Content, and navigating to the Concepts Review quiz for this lesson
Not using the Labyrinth Video Library or eLab	Going to the student resource center for this book

Reinforce Your Skills

Format a Worksheet

In this exercise, you will format a worksheet using commands available on the Ribbon and on the Mini toolbar.

Format Worksheets

1. Start **Excel**. Open **EX05-R01-Budget** from the **EX2013 Lesson 05** folder and save it as **EX05-R01-Budget-[FirstInitialLastName]**.

2. Change the font for the entire worksheet to **Calibri**.

   Only those entries originally displayed in a font other than Calibri will change.

3. Select **cells A1, A7, and A15** using the Ctrl key.

4. Choose **Home→Font→Bold B**.

5. Right-click **cell A25** and choose **Bold B** from the Mini toolbar.

Use Excel's Alignment and Indent Features

6. Select the **range A8:A12**.

7. Choose **Home→Alignment→Increase Indent**.

   This indentation distinguishes the revenue items from the header and total rows.

8. Select the **range A16:A23**.

9. Choose **Home→Alignment→Increase Indent**.

10. Select **cell A4**.

11. Choose **Home→Alignment→Align Right**.

Use Excel's Text Control Options

12. Select the **range A1:C2**.

13. Choose **Home→Alignment→Merge & Center menu ▼→Merge Across**.

    The Merge Across command allows you to merge multiple rows at once.

14. Double-click **cell B6** to begin in-cell editing.

15. Move the insertion point just to the left of the *A* in *Actual*, and tap Backspace to remove the space between words.

16. Press Alt + Enter to insert a line break, and tap Enter to confirm the entry.

17. Repeat **steps 15–16** to insert a line break in the text of **cell C6**.

18. Align the text in the **range B6:C6** with the numbers in the columns.

Format Numbers

19. Select the **ranges B8:C8**, **B13:C13**, and **B16:C16** using `Ctrl`.

20. Choose **Home→Number→Accounting Number Format** `$`.

    Leave the default two decimal places as is.

21. Select the **range B24:C25**.

22. Right-click a selected cell and choose **Accounting Number Format** `$` from the Mini toolbar.

23. Select the **range B9:C12**.

24. Using the method of your choice, apply **Comma Style** with two decimal places to the selection.

    This ensures that no dollar sign is displayed for those amounts that are not located on the top or bottom row within the revenue section.

25. Select the **range B17:C23**.

26. Press `Ctrl` + `Y` to repeat the most recent action.

    Comma Style is applied to the selection.

27. Select **cell C4**.

28. Choose **Home→Number→Number Format menu** ▼ button and choose **Currency**.

    Notice that the dollar sign ($) displays next to the number. Compare this to the dollar sign placement in cell C8, to which you applied Accounting Number Format.

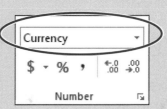

29. Save and then close the file; exit from **Excel**.

30. Submit your file based on guidelines provided by your instructor.

    To view examples of how your file or files should look at the end of this exercise, go to the student resource center.

REINFORCE YOUR SKILLS EX05-R02
Design a Budget Worksheet

In this exercise, you will format a budget worksheet using the Format Cells dialog box and the Ribbon.

Use the Format Cells Dialog Box

1. Start **Excel**. Open **EX05-R02-WebsiteBudget** from the **EX2013 Lesson 05** folder and save it as **EX05-R02-WebsiteBudget-[FirstInitialLastName]**.

2. Select **cell A6**.

3. Choose **Home→Font→dialog box launcher** to display the Format Cells dialog box.

    The Format Cells dialog box can be used to easily apply a wide variety of formatting.

4. Select the **Bold** font style and click **OK**.

Apply Borders and Fills to Cells

5. Select **cell A1**.

   Notice that the Merged Cell A1:B1 is highlighted.

6. Choose **Home→Font→Fill Color menu** ▼ button and select **Olive Green, Accent 3, Lighter 40%**.

7. Select the **range A3:B3**.

8. Choose **Home→Font→Borders menu** ▼**→Top and Bottom Border**.

   Borders offer another formatting option that can distinguish cells within a worksheet.

Use Excel's Find and Replace Command

9. Click **cell A1** and choose **Home→Editing→Find & Select→Replace**.

10. Enter **spending plan** in the **Find What** box and **Budget** in the **Replace With** box.

    You do not have to use a capital "S" or "P" in the Find What box. If you want the replacement text to be capitalized though, you must type it that way in the Replace With box.

11. Click **Replace All**, click **OK** in the dialog box that appears, and click **Close**.

12. Save and then close the file; exit from **Excel**.

13. Submit your final file based on the guidelines provided by your instructor.

    To view examples of how your file or files should look at the end of this exercise, go to the student resource center.

REINFORCE YOUR SKILLS EX05-R03
Format a Balance Sheet

In this exercise, you will format a balance sheet using a variety of commands and techniques.

Format Worksheets

1. Start **Excel**. Open **EX05-R03-BalanceSheet** from the **EX2013 Lesson 05** folder and save it as **EX05-R03-BalanceSheet-[FirstInitialLastName]**.

2. Change the font for the entire worksheet to **Calibri**.

   Regardless of which font you apply, in order to maintain consistency it should be applied throughout the entire worksheet.

3. Select **cells A5, A12, and A17** using the Ctrl key.

4. Choose **Home→Font→Bold** B.

   These headings should be distinguished from the rest of the worksheet in some manner, and although you used bold here, other formatting options would also have been effective.

5. Right-click **cell B4** and choose **Bold** B from the Mini toolbar.

Use Excel's Alignment and Indent Features

6. Select the **range A6:A9**.

7. Choose **Home→Alignment→Increase Indent** 📑.

8. Select the **range A13:A14,** and **cell A18** using `Ctrl`.

9. Choose **Home→Alignment→Increase Indent** 📑.

10. Select **cell B4**.

11. Choose **Home→Alignment→Center** ▤.

Use Excel's Text Control Options

12. Select the **range A1:B1**.

13. Choose **Home→Alignment→Merge & Center** ▣.

14. Select the **range A2:B3**.

15. Choose **Home→Alignment→Merge & Center menu** ▼**→Merge Across**.

    The Merge Across command allows you to merge multiple rows at once, but does not center the cell contents.

16. With the **range A2:B3** still selected, choose **Home→Alignment→Center**.

17. Double-click **cell A19** to begin in-cell editing.

18. Move the insertion point just to the left of the *O* in *Owners'* and tap `Backspace` to remove the space between words.

19. Use `Alt`+`Enter` to insert a line break.

    You can reduce column widths throughout a worksheet by using this technique to force text to wrap where you choose within a cell.

20. Right-click **cell A13**.

21. Choose **Format Cells**, insert a checkmark beside **Shrink to Fit** under the Alignment tab, and click **OK**.

Format Numbers

22. Select **cells B6, B10, and B13** using `Ctrl`.

23. Choose **Home→Number→Accounting Number Format** $.

    Leave the default two decimal places as is.

24. Select the **range B18:B19** and **cell B15** using `Ctrl`.

25. Right-click a selected cell and choose **Accounting Number Format** $ from the Mini toolbar.

26. Select the **range B7:B9** and **cell B14** using `Ctrl`.

27. Using the method of your choice, apply **Comma Style** with two decimal places.

Use the Format Cells Dialog Box

28. Select the **range A1:A3**.

29. Choose **Home→Font→dialog box launcher** to display the Format Cells dialog box.

The Format Cells dialog box can be used to easily apply a wide variety of formatting.

30. Select the **Bold** font style and click **OK**.

Apply Borders and Fills to Cells

31. Ensure that the **range A1:A3** is still selected.

Notice that the Merged Cells within the first three rows are highlighted.

32. Choose **Home→Font→Fill Color menu ▼** button and select **Standard Light Green**.

This fill color results in the selected cells standing out from the surrounding data.

33. Select **cells B10 and B19** using ⌈Ctrl⌉.

34. Choose **Home→Font→Borders menu ▼→Top and Double Bottom Border**.

Use Excel's Find and Replace Command

35. Click **cell A1** then choose **Home→Editing→Find & Select→Replace**.

36. Enter `resources` in the **Find What** box and `Assets` in the **Replace With** box.

You do not have to use a capital "R" in the Find What box. If you want the replacement text to be capitalized though, you must type it that way in the Replace With box.

37. Click **Replace All**, click **OK** in the dialog box that appears, and click **Close**.

38. Save and then close the file; exit from **Excel**.

39. Submit your final file based on the guidelines provided by your instructor.

Apply Your Skills

Format Text and Numbers

In this exercise, you will format text and numbers.

Format Worksheets and Use Excel's Alignment and Indent Features

1. Start **Excel**. Open **EX05-A01-Inventory** from the **EX2013 Lesson 05** folder and save it as **EX05-A01-Inventory-[FirstInitialLastName]**.

2. Apply **bold** formatting to the entries in **rows 4 and 12**.
   Bold formatting makes these column headers stand out from the other worksheet entries.

3. Format the title in **cell A1** with **bold**, and change the font size to **14**.

4. Right-align the entries in the **ranges D4:E4** and **D12:E12**.
   These headers are now aligned with the numbers listed below.

5. Indent the entries in the **ranges A5:A9** and **A13:A16**.

Use Excel's Text Control Options and Format Numbers

6. Merge and center the titles in **cells A1 and A2** across **columns A–E**.

7. Change **cell D4** to `Retail Price` and insert a **line break** so each word is on a separate line.

8. Insert a **line break** in **cell D12** so each word is on a separate line.

9. Format **cells D5 and D13** in **Currency Style** with two decimals.

10. Format the **ranges D6:D9** and **D14:D16** in **Number** style.

11. Format the **ranges E5:E10** and **E13:E17** in **Comma Style** with zero decimals.

12. Save and then close the file; exit from **Excel**.

13. Submit your final file based on the guidelines provided by your instructor.
    To view examples of how your file or files should look at the end of this exercise, go to the student resource center.

Add Borders and Fill Color, and Use Find and Replace

In this exercise, you will finalize the appearance of a worksheet by applying borders and fill colors, and replacing text.

Use the Format Cells Dialog Box and Apply Borders and Fills to Cells

1. Start **Excel**. Open **EX05-A02-CustomerBase** from the **EX2013 Lesson 05** folder and save it as **EX05-A02-CustomerBase-[FirstInitialLastName]**.

2. Use the Format Cells dialog box to format **cell E19** with **Bold** and **Italic** font style.

3. Place a **single border** along the bottom of the **range A2:F2** and a **double border** along the bottom of **cell E19**.

   A bottom double border is often used to denote the final figure on a worksheet.

4. Apply a Standard Orange fill color to the merged **range A1:F1**.

Use Excel's Find and Replace Commands

5. Find all instances of **projects** and replace with **Jobs**.

6. Find all instances of **project** and replace with **Job**.

7. Find all instances of **Currency** number formatting and replace with **Accounting** number formatting.

   This is an efficient way to make the same formatting change to multiple cells.

8. Save and then close the file; exit from **Excel**.

9. Submit your final file based on the guidelines provided by your instructor.

   To view examples of how your file or files should look at the end of this exercise, go to the student resource center.

Format an Event Listing

In this exercise, you will format both text and numbers within an event listing.

Format Worksheets and Use Excel's Alignment and Indent Features

1. Start **Excel**. Open **EX05-A03-EventListing** from the **EX2013 Lesson 05** folder and save it as **EX05-A03-EventListing-[FirstInitialLastName]**.

2. Apply **bold** formatting to the entries in **rows 5 and 15**.

3. Format the title in **cell A1** with **bold**, and change the font size to **14**.

4. Right-align the entries in the **range B5:D5**.

5. Indent the entry in **cell A15**.

Use Excel's Text Control Options and Format Numbers

6. Merge and center the title in **cell A1** across **columns A–D**.

7. **Merge Across** the titles in the **range A2:A3**; center the contents so they appear consistent with the title in row 1.

8. Insert a **line break** in **cell A11** so *Southwestern* is on a separate line.
   This line break was necessary, since the cell contents extended into column B.

9. Format the **range B6:D15** in **Currency Style** with **two decimals**.

10. Format **cell B17** in **Number** style with **zero decimals**.

Use the Format Cells Dialog Box and Apply Borders and Fills to Cells

11. Use the Format Cells dialog box to format **cell B17** with **Bold** and **Standard Red** font.

12. Place a **single border** along the bottom of the **range B5:D5** and a **top and double bottom border** on the **range B15:D15**.

13. Apply a Standard Yellow fill color to the merged cells in the **range A1:D3**.
    Fill color should be used sparingly in a worksheet, as too much color can give a scattered appearance.

Use Excel's Find and Replace Commands

14. Find all instances of **job** and replace with **Event**.

15. Find all instances of **Currency** number formatting and replace with **Accounting** number formatting.
    30 replacements are made here, as every cell in the range B6:D15, regardless of whether it contained data, previously had Currency formatting.

16. Save and then close the file; exit from **Excel**.

17. Submit your final file based on the guidelines provided by your instructor.

Extend Your Skills

In the course of working through the Extend Your Skills exercises, you will think critically as you use the skills taught in the lesson to complete the assigned projects. To evaluate your mastery and completion of the exercises, your instructor may use a rubric, with which more points are allotted according to performance characteristics. (The more you do, the more you earn!) Ask your instructor how your work will be evaluated.

EX05-E01 That's the Way I See It

You are making a list of the five charities to which you are most likely to donate a little extra cash in your pocket. The list will include the charity name, the cause that it supports, and the total donations that the charity received last year.

Create a new file in the **EX2013 Lesson 05** folder named **EX05-E01-Charity-[FirstInitialLastName]**.

Enter a header at the top of the worksheet and headers for each column that you create. Use text and number formats to improve the appearance of the worksheet, and place a fill color in the cell of the charity that you would be most likely to support. Conduct an Internet search to determine the information for each charity in order to complete the worksheet (you may enter a "best guess" estimate for any donation totals you are unable to locate).

You will be evaluated based on the inclusion of all elements specified, your ability to follow directions, your ability to apply newly learned skills to a real-world situation, your creativity, and the relevance of your topic and/or data choice(s). Submit your final file based on the guidelines provided by your instructor.

EX05-E02 Be Your Own Boss

You are working on the income statement for your company, Blue Jean Landscaping, for the month of July 2013.

Open **EX05-E02-IncomeStatement** from the **EX2013 Lesson 05** folder and save it as **EX05-E02-IncomeStatement-[FirstInitialLastName]**.

The file contains all necessary data to complete the income statement. Using the techniques you learned in this lesson, apply all borders, indents, and number formats required to properly format an income statement. If necessary, refer to the Develop Your Skills exercise within the main part of the lesson to identify the proper formatting. Use the Find and Replace dialog box to change all instances of *Costs* within the worksheet to *Expenses*.

You will be evaluated based on the inclusion of all elements specified, your ability to follow directions, your ability to apply newly learned skills to a real-world situation, your creativity, and your demonstration of an entrepreneurial spirit. Submit your final file based on the guidelines provided by your instructor.

Transfer Your Skills

In the course of working through the Transfer Your Skills exercises, you will use critical-thinking and creativity skills to complete the assigned projects using skills taught in the lesson. To evaluate your mastery and completion of the exercises, your instructor may use a rubric, with which more points are allotted according to performance characteristics. (The more you do, the more you earn!) Ask your instructor how your work will be evaluated.

EX05-T01 Use the Web as a Learning Tool

Throughout this book, you will be provided with an opportunity to use the Internet as a learning tool by completing WebQuests. According to the original creators of WebQuests, as described on their website (WebQuest.org), a WebQuest is "an inquiry-oriented activity in which most or all of the information used by learners is drawn from the web." To complete the WebQuest projects in this book, navigate to the student resource center and choose the WebQuest for the lesson on which you are currently working. The subject of each WebQuest will be relevant to the material found in the lesson.

WebQuest Subject: Create an ingredient spreadsheet to facilitate weekly orders

Submit your final file(s) based on the guidelines provided by your instructor.

EX05-T02 Demonstrate Proficiency

You have determined that to maximize revenue for Stormy BBQ you will need to fully examine local competing restaurants. Your evaluation will help you determine which local restaurants appeal to your customers and what dishes on their menus are most similar to yours.

Open **EX05-T02-Restaurants** from the **EX2013 Lesson 05** folder and save it as **EX05-T02-Restaurants-[FirstInitialLastName]**. Format your worksheet using techniques such as Merge & Center, Wrap Text, indentations, bold text, and borders. Also, determine which dishes are most like those at Stormy BBQ and apply green fill to the corresponding cells. Write a paragraph with at least five sentences in the cell below your data that explains what you see in the data—which restaurant is your biggest competitor, what dishes are the most similar to your own, and what action you might take based on this data. Merge and center the paragraph to extend across your entire data set.

Submit your final file based on the guidelines provided by your instructor.

Charting Worksheet Data

LEARNING OBJECTIVES

After studying this lesson, you will be able to:

- Create different types of charts
- Move and size embedded charts
- Modify and format chart elements
- Create trendlines and sparklines
- Preview and print worksheets

Charting is an important skill to have when using worksheets because comparisons, trends, and other relationships are often conveyed more effectively with charts than by displaying only data. In this lesson, you will use Excel to create column charts, line charts, and pie charts. You will edit and format legends, data labels, and other chart objects. You will also add trendlines and sparklines to worksheets.

Charting Sales Performance

green clean

You have been asked to prepare several charts for Green Clean, which sells janitorial products and contracts for cleaning services. You will prepare charts that compare sales in the various quarters, display the growth trend throughout the year, and illustrate the contributions of each sales team member to the company sales as a whole. You will use Excel's charting features to produce accurate and easy-to-understand visuals that meet Green Clean's high standards.

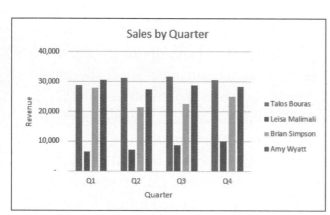

A column chart

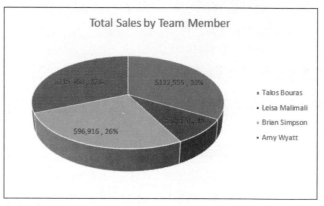

A pie chart

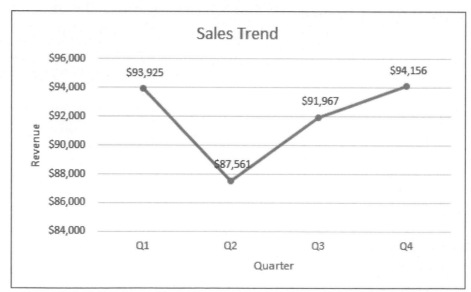

A line chart

Creating Charts in Excel

Video Library   http://labyrinthelab.com/videos   Video Number: EX13-V0601

Many people are "visual learners" and find that numerical data is easier to interpret when presented in a chart. Charts are linked to the data from which they are created, thus charts are automatically updated when worksheet data changes. You can apply options and enhancements to each chart element, such as the title, legend, plot area, value axis, category axis, and data series.

Chart Placement

You have the option of either embedding a new chart into the worksheet where the data resides or placing it on a separate sheet. This can be done when the chart is first created, or at any time thereafter.

Embedded charts can be created by choosing the chart type from the Insert tab. To avoid covering the worksheet data, you can move and resize an embedded chart.

FROM THE KEYBOARD
F11 to create a chart on its own sheet

You can use the F11 key to place a full-size chart on its own sheet. When you do, the chart on the new sheet will be based on the default chart type. You can easily change the type after creating the chart with the Change Chart Type option.

Choosing the Proper Data Source

It is important to select both the appropriate data, and the proper row and column headings for your column and bar charts to make sure the data are accurate. Usually, you will not include both individual category data and totals because the individual data would appear distorted.

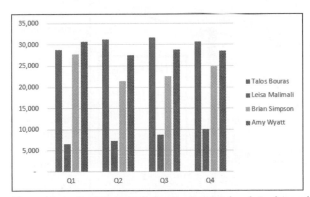
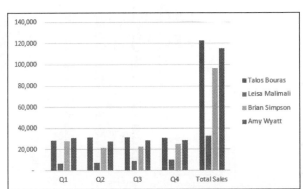

The column chart that excludes the Total Sales data does a better job of displaying the differences between each data series.

Chart Types

Excel provides 10 major chart types, as well as several subtypes for each. Each chart type represents data in a different manner, and you can also create a customized chart (which can be used as a template) to meet your exact needs.

FROM THE RIBBON

Insert→Charts→
Recommended Charts

Chart and Axis Titles

Excel allows you to create titles for your charts as well as for the value and category axes. If you choose a range of information that includes what appears to Excel to be a title, Excel will include it in the new chart.

	A	B	C	D	E	F
2	Quarterly and Total Sales - Fiscal Year					
3						
4		Q1	Q2	Q3	Q4	Total Sales
5	Talos Bouras	28,775	31,342	31,763	30,675	$ 122,555
6	Leisa Malimali	6,575	7,304	8,768	10,023	$ 32,670
7	Brian Simpson	27,850	21,471	22,634	24,961	$ 96,916
8	Amy Wyatt	30,725	27,444	28,802	28,497	$ 115,468
10	Quarter Total	$ 93,925	$ 87,561	$ 91,967	$ 94,156	$ 367,609

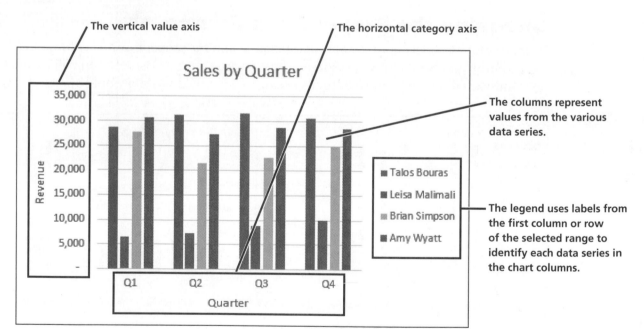

This column chart compares values using vertical bars. It was created using the highlighted worksheet data.

Chart Formatting Control

To quickly preview and select different chart elements, styles, and filters, you can use the chart formatting buttons that appear when a chart is selected. When you scroll over an option within any of the three buttons, its appearance will be previewed within your chart.

Chart Elements button

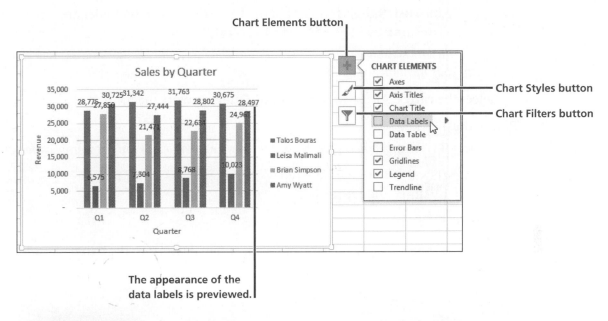

Chart Styles button

Chart Filters button

The appearance of the data labels is previewed.

QUICK REFERENCE	CREATING AND PLACING A CHART
Task	**Procedure**
Create a chart	■ Select the desired data range and choose the chart type from Insert→Charts.
Move an existing chart to its own sheet	■ Right-click a blank area of the chart and choose Move Chart. ■ Choose New Sheet, rename the sheet, and click OK.
Move a chart from its own sheet to another sheet as an embedded object	■ Right-click a blank area of the chart and choose Move Chart. ■ Choose Object In, select the desired worksheet, and click OK.
Add a title to a chart	■ Select the desired chart. ■ Choose Chart Tools→Design→Chart Layouts→Add Chart Element ▐▐▄ →Chart Title and select a chart title option. ■ Select the default title "Chart Title" and type in your title.
Add axis titles to a chart	■ Select the desired chart. ■ Choose Chart Tools→Design→Chart Layouts→Add Chart Element ▐▐▄ →Axis Titles and select an axis title option. ■ Select the default title "Axis Title" and type your title.
Add a legend to a chart	■ Select the desired chart. ■ Choose Chart Tools→Design→Chart Layouts→Add Chart Element ▐▐▄ →Legend and select a legend option.

Create a Chart

In this exercise, you will create an embedded clustered bar chart.

1. Open **EX06-D01-SalesCharts** from the **EX2013 Lesson 06** folder and save it as **EX06-D01-SalesCharts-[FirstInitialLastName]**.

   Replace the bracketed text with your first initial and last name. For example, if your name is Bethany Smith, your filename would look like this: EX06-D01-SalesChart-BSmith.

2. Select the **range A4:E8** in the **Sales by Quarter** worksheet.

3. Tap the F11 key.

   Tapping F11 creates a new sheet before the Sales by Quarter sheet in the workbook tab order.

4. Double-click the new chart tab, type **Sales by Rep**, and tap Enter.

Create a Clustered Bar Chart

5. Display the **Sales by Quarter** worksheet and make certain the **range A4:E8** is still selected.

6. Follow these steps to create a clustered bar chart:

Ⓐ Click the **Insert** tab.

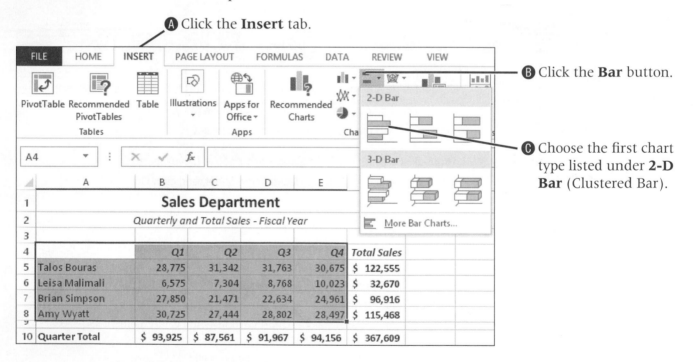

Ⓑ Click the **Bar** button.

Ⓒ Choose the first chart type listed under **2-D Bar** (Clustered Bar).

The chart will appear embedded in the Sales by Quarter worksheet with the default properties for the clustered bar chart type displayed.

7. Look at the Ribbon to see that the **Chart Tools** are now displayed and the **Design** tab is active.

   The additional Ribbon tabs under Chart Tools, which appear when a chart is selected, are referred to as contextual tabs.

Edit the Chart and Axis Titles

8. Follow these steps to title the chart:

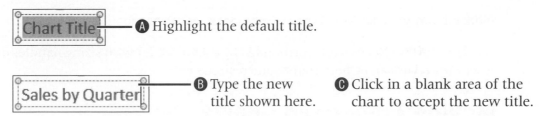

Ⓐ Highlight the default title.

Ⓑ Type the new title shown here.

Ⓒ Click in a blank area of the chart to accept the new title.

Instead of highlighting the title, you could have clicked the default title. However, the new title would have only displayed on the formula bar as you typed.

9. Remaining within the chart, follow these steps to add a vertical axis title:

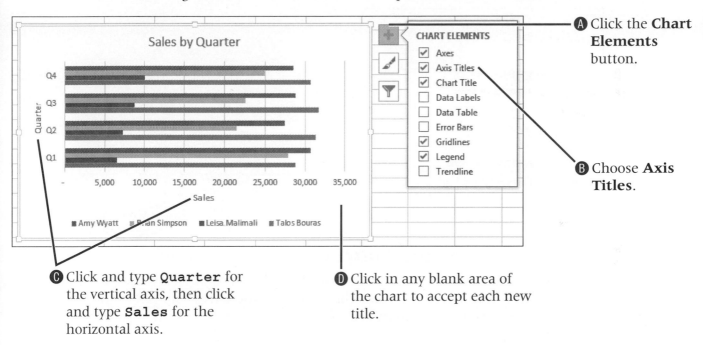

Ⓐ Click the **Chart Elements** button.

Ⓑ Choose **Axis Titles**.

Ⓒ Click and type **Quarter** for the vertical axis, then click and type **Sales** for the horizontal axis.

Ⓓ Click in any blank area of the chart to accept each new title.

10. Save the file and leave it open; you will modify it throughout this lesson.

Moving and Sizing Embedded Charts

Video Library   http://labyrinthelab.com/videos   Video Number: EX13-V0602

When a chart is selected, it is surrounded by a light border with sizing handles displayed. A selected chart can be both moved and resized.

Moving Embedded Charts

Charts that are embedded in a worksheet can easily be moved to a new location. A chart can be moved by a simple drag, but you need to ensure that you click the chart area and not a separate element.

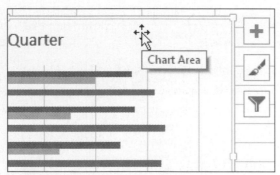

A four-pointed arrow (along with the "Chart Area" ScreenTip) indicates that you can drag to move this selected chart.

Sizing Embedded Charts

To size a chart, it must first be selected. You can drag a sizing handle when the double-arrow mouse pointer is displayed. To change a chart size proportionately, hold $\boxed{\text{Shift}}$ while dragging a corner handle. If you wanted to only change the height or width of a chart you would not hold $\boxed{\text{Shift}}$.

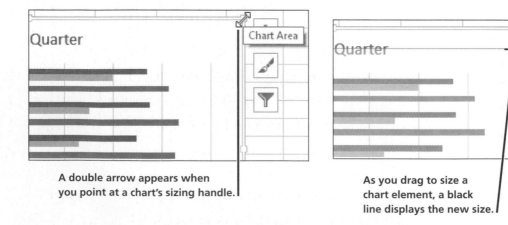

A double arrow appears when you point at a chart's sizing handle.

As you drag to size a chart element, a black line displays the new size.

Deleting Charts

Deleting an embedded chart is simple—just select the chart area and tap ⌷Delete⌷. You can delete a chart that is on its own tab by deleting the worksheet.

DEVELOP YOUR SKILLS EX06-D02
Size and Move an Embedded Chart

In this exercise, you will move and resize your chart. You will also copy a sheet containing an embedded chart and then delete the chart.

1. Save your file as **EX06-D02-SalesCharts-[FirstInitialLastName]**.

2. Click once on the chart area of the embedded chart in the **Sales by Quarter** sheet to select the chart.

   Sizing handles appear around the border of the chart.

3. Follow these steps to resize the chart to be smaller:

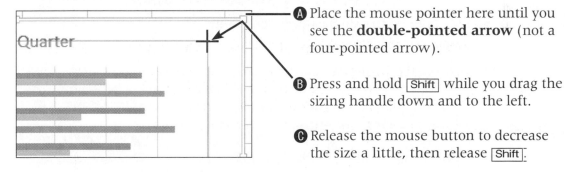

Ⓐ Place the mouse pointer here until you see the **double-pointed arrow** (not a four-pointed arrow).

Ⓑ Press and hold ⌷Shift⌷ while you drag the sizing handle down and to the left.

Ⓒ Release the mouse button to decrease the size a little, then release ⌷Shift⌷.

Excel resized the width and height proportionately because you held down the ⌷Shift⌷ key as you resized the chart.

4. Follow these steps to move the chart and center it below the worksheet data:

Ⓐ Place the mouse pointer over a blank area of the chart so that a **four-pointed arrow** appears.

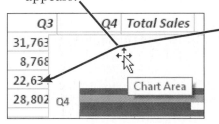

Ⓑ Drag the chart down and to the left until it is just below **row 11** and centered within **columns A–F.**

Ⓒ Release the mouse button.

5. Hold down Ctrl, drag the **Sales by Quarter** sheet tab to the right, and then release the mouse and Ctrl.

The downward-pointing arrow that indicates the location of the new sheet may not appear if the chart is positioned over it. The duplicate sheet is named Sales by Quarter (2).

6. Rename the **Sales by Quarter (2)** sheet to `Team Totals`.

Delete an Embedded Chart

7. Click once to select the chart in the **Team Totals** sheet and tap Delete.
   Excel deletes the chart.

8. Use Ctrl+Z to undo the Delete command.
   The chart reappears. You can restore an embedded chart right after it is deleted.

9. Use Ctrl+Y to redo the Delete command.
   The chart is once again deleted.

10. Save the file and leave it open.

Exploring Other Chart Types

Video Library   http://labyrinthelab.com/videos   Video Number: EX13-V0603

Here you will explore line and pie charts and how they can make your data work for you. Pie charts are suitable when you are examining data that represent portions of a whole (just as pieces of an apple pie, when combined, represent the whole pie).

Line Charts

Line charts are most useful for comparing trends over a period of time. Like column charts, line charts have category and value axes. Line charts also use the same or similar objects as column charts.

	A	B	C	D	E	F
1	Sales Department					
2	Quarterly and Total Sales - Fiscal Year					
3						
4		Q1	Q2	Q3	Q4	Total Sales
5	Talos Bouras	28,775	31,342	31,763	30,675	$ 122,555
6	Leisa Malimali	6,575	7,304	8,768	10,023	$ 32,670
7	Brian Simpson	27,850	21,471	22,634	24,961	$ 96,916
8	Amy Wyatt	30,725	27,444	28,802	28,497	$ 115,468
10	Quarter Total	$ 93,925	$ 87,561	$ 91,967	$ 94,156	$ 367,609

The chart was created using the selected data.

Data labels show the precise value of the various data points.

Pie Charts

You typically select only two sets of data when creating pie charts: the values to be represented by the pie slices and the labels to identify the slices.

	A	B	C	D	E	F
4		Q1	Q2	Q3	Q4	Total Sales
5	Talos Bouras	28,775	31,342	31,763	30,675	$ 122,555
6	Leisa Malimali	6,575	7,304	8,768	10,023	$ 32,670
7	Brian Simpson	27,850	21,471	22,634	24,961	$ 96,916
8	Amy Wyatt	30,725	27,444	28,802	28,497	$ 115,468
10	Quarter Total	$ 93,925	$ 87,561	$ 91,967	$ 94,156	$ 367,609

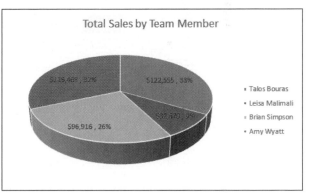

This pie chart is based on the selected data.

Exploding Pie Slices

There will be times when you want to draw attention to a particular slice of a pie chart. You can make one slice explode from the chart simply by dragging it away from the other slices.

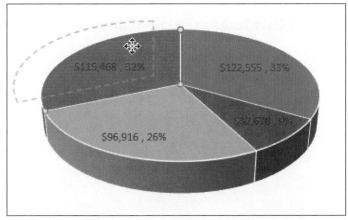

As you drag a slice out to give it an exploded effect, Excel will show with a dashed line where it will land.

Rotating and Elevating Pie Charts

You can change the rotation and perspective (also known as elevation) of pie charts to display data in a different position or change the angle at which it is viewed.

FROM THE RIBBON

Format→Shape
Styles→Shape
Effects→3-D
Rotation→3-D Rotation
Options

You can rotate other types of 3-D charts as well, but 2-D charts cannot be rotated.

DEVELOP YOUR SKILLS EX06-D03
Create a Line Chart

In this exercise, you will use the same data to create a line chart and a pie chart.

1. Save your file as **EX06-D03-SalesCharts-[FirstInitialLastName]**.

2. Select the **Sales by Quarter** worksheet.

3. Follow these steps to select the data for the line chart:

Ⓐ Select the **range A4:E4**.

Ⓑ Press and hold Ctrl while selecting the **range A10:E10**.

Ⓒ Choose **Insert→ Charts→ Insert Line Chart ▼ →Line with Markers**.

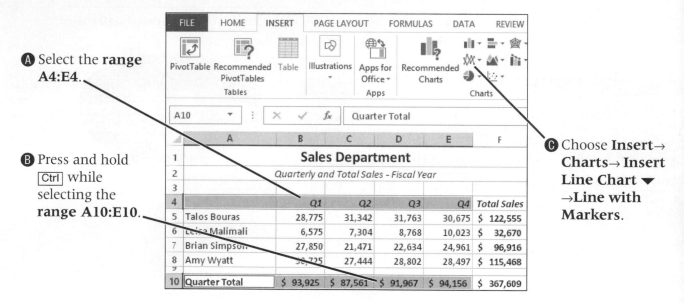

Excel creates an embedded line chart in the current worksheet.

4. With the chart selected, choose **Chart Tools→Design→Location→Move Chart** 🔳.

5. Follow these steps to move the chart to its own sheet:

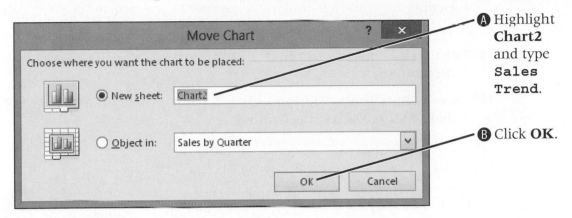

Ⓐ Highlight **Chart2** and type **Sales Trend**.

Ⓑ Click **OK**.

The chart now appears on its own worksheet.

Edit the Chart

6. Click the **Title** text box, type **Sales Trend**, and tap Enter.

7. Choose **Chart Tools→Design→Chart Layouts→Add Chart Element**▐▐→**Axis Titles→Primary Horizontal**.

A text box appears below the horizontal axis with the default name Axis Title.

8. Type **Quarter** and tap Enter to replace the default horizontal axis title.

9. Choose **Chart Tools→Design→Chart Layouts→Add Chart Element**▐▐→**Axis Titles→Primary Vertical**, type **Revenue**, and tap Enter.

10. Choose **Chart Tools→Design→Chart Layouts→Add Chart Element**▐▐→**Data Labels→Above**.

Excel displays the values above the data points on the chart.

Insert a Pie Chart

11. Select the **Team Totals** worksheet.

12. Follow these steps to select the range for the pie chart:

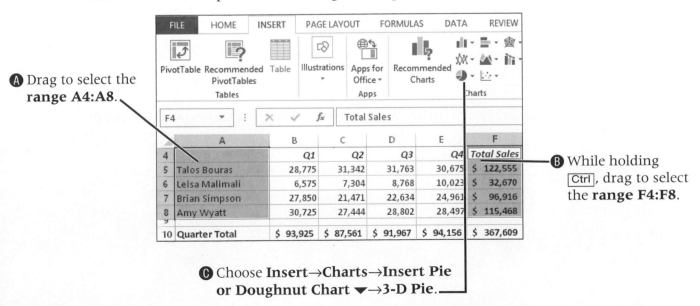

Ⓐ Drag to select the **range A4:A8**.

Ⓑ While holding Ctrl, drag to select the **range F4:F8**.

Ⓒ Choose **Insert→Charts→Insert Pie or Doughnut Chart** ▼→**3-D Pie**.

13. Place the mouse pointer over the chart area so that the **four-pointed arrow** appears, and then drag down and left until it is below **row 11** and centered between **columns A–F**.

Notice that the cell F4 entry, Total Sales, is used as the chart title.

14. Edit the chart title to read **Total Sales by Team Member**. Click outside of the Title box to accept the new title.

15. Choose **Chart Tools→Design→Chart Layouts→Add Chart Element ▮▮→Data Labels→More Data Label Options**.

The Format Data Labels task pane appears.

16. Follow these steps to format the data labels:

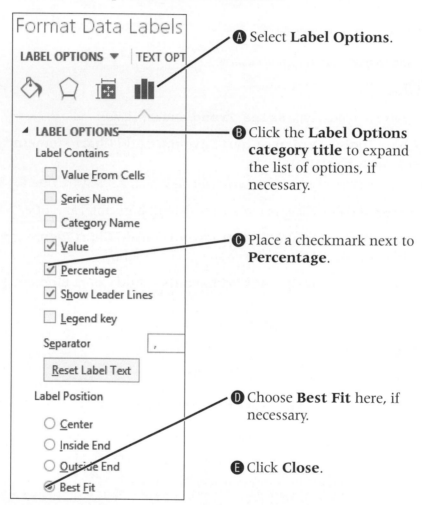

Ⓐ Select **Label Options**.

Ⓑ Click the **Label Options category title** to expand the list of options, if necessary.

Ⓒ Place a checkmark next to **Percentage**.

Ⓓ Choose **Best Fit** here, if necessary.

Ⓔ Click **Close**.

Excel displays both the value and the percentage in each pie slice wherever they "best fit."

Explode a Pie Slice

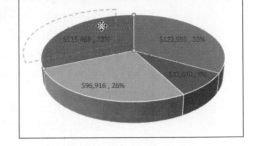

17. Click the slice representing **Amy Wyatt's sales**, and then pause and click it again.

The first click will select all slices, and the second click will select just the slice for Amy Wyatt.

18. Place the mouse pointer over the **Amy Wyatt** slice until you see a move pointer, and then drag away from the pie chart slightly and release.

Notice that as you drag the pie slice away from the main chart, a dashed line appears where the slice will land if you release the mouse button.

19. Save the file and leave it open.

Modifying Existing Charts

| **Video Library** | http://labyrinthelab.com/videos   Video Number: EX13-V0604 |

You can modify any chart object after the chart has been created. The following table describes the various Chart Tools available to modify your charts.

CHART TOOLS ON THE RIBBON	
Contextual Tab	**Command Groups on the Tab**
Design	■ *Chart Layouts:* Change the overall layout of the chart and add chart elements.
	■ *Chart Styles:* Choose a preset style for your chart.
	■ *Data:* Switch the data displayed on rows and columns, and reselect the data for the chart.
	■ *Type:* Change the type of chart, set the default chart type, and save a chart as a template.
	■ *Location:* Switch a chart from being embedded to being placed on its own sheet and vice versa.
Format	■ *Current Selection:* Select a specific chart element, apply formatting, and reset formatting.
	■ *Insert Shapes:* Insert and change shapes.
	■ *Shape Styles:* Visually make changes to the selected chart element.
	■ *WordArt Styles:* Apply WordArt to text labels in your chart.
	■ *Arrange:* Change how your chart is arranged in relation to other objects in your worksheet.
	■ *Size:* Change the size of your chart.

Changing the Chart Type and Source Data

It's easy to change an existing chart to a different type using the Change Chart Type dialog box. You can also change the source data from within the Select Data Source dialog box. You may find it easier to edit the existing data range by using the collapse button. Aside from editing the data range, you can also alter individual data series, add additional data series, and alter the horizontal axis. Note that the Switch Row/Column option swaps the data in the vertical and horizontal axes.

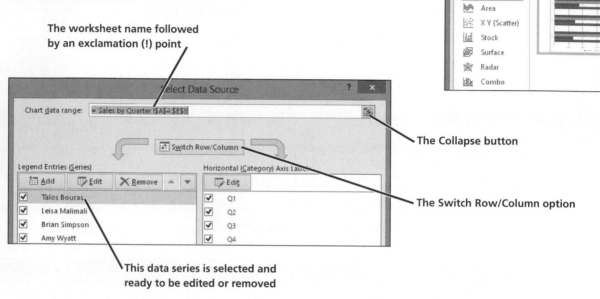

The worksheet name followed by an exclamation (!) point

The Collapse button

The Switch Row/Column option

This data series is selected and ready to be edited or removed

Using the arrow keys to edit a data range in a text box will result in unwanted characters. For best results, reselect a data range by dragging in the worksheet.

Modifying and Formatting Chart Elements

The legend, titles, and columns are chart elements. Once selected, you can delete, move, size, and format different elements. You can move a selected element by dragging it with the mouse when you see the move pointer, or change its size by dragging a sizing handle.

You can modify any chart element after the chart has been created by double-clicking the chart element to display a Format task pane with many options for that element. For example, options in the Format Chart Title dialog box allow you to adjust the vertical alignment, adjust the text direction, and apply a fill, border, or other visual effects.

Previewing Formatting Before Applying

The Chart Formatting buttons allow you to preview a variety of formatting changes. If you place the mouse pointer over an option accessed through these buttons, a preview displays how the change will look in your chart.

Task	Procedure
Change the chart type	■ Select the chart, choose Chart Tools→Design→Type→Change Chart Type, and double-click the desired type.
Select a new data range for an entire chart	■ Select the chart and choose Chart Tools→Design→Data→Select Data. ■ Click the Collapse 📷 button and select the new data range. ■ Click the Expand 📷 button and click OK.
Select a new range for a data series	■ Select the chart and choose Chart Tools→Design→Data→Select Data. ■ Select the desired item under the Legend Entries (Series) and click Edit. ■ Highlight the Series Values entry, select the new range, and click OK twice.
Add additional data series	■ Select the chart and choose Chart Tools→Design ›Data→Select Data. ■ Click Add under Legend Entries, enter the desired cell(s) for Series Name and Series Values, and click OK twice.
Delete a chart element	■ Select the desired chart element and tap ⌷Delete⌷.
Format an element on an existing chart	■ Select the chart element and choose the desired formatting command.

Modify a Chart

In this exercise, you will change a chart type and then apply various formatting features to the new chart.

1. Save the file as **EX06-D04-SalesCharts-[FirstInitialLastName]**.

2. Select the **Sales by Rep** worksheet, click anywhere within the column chart, and choose **Chart Tools→Design→Type→Change Chart Type**.

    The Change Chart Type dialog box appears.

3. Follow these steps to change the chart type:

Ⓐ Display the **Bar** category.

Ⓑ Choose **Clustered Bar**.

Ⓒ Click **OK**.

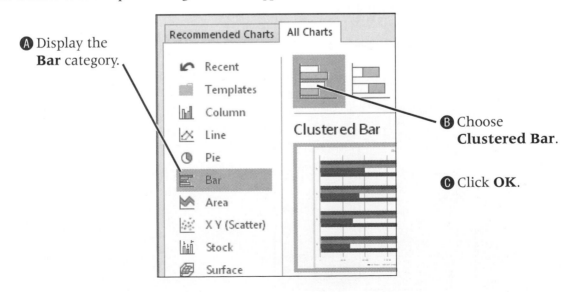

Excel 2013

4. Choose **Chart Tools→Design→Data→Select Data** 📊.

You will now exclude the sales performance of Talos Bouras from the data range.

5. Follow these steps to reselect the chart data range:

Ⓐ Click the **Collapse** button to view the worksheet data.

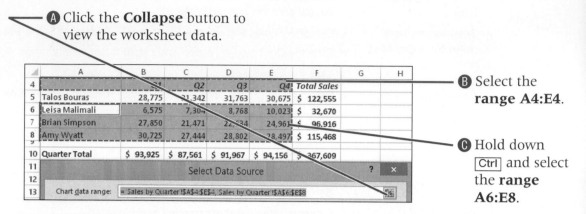

Ⓑ Select the **range A4:E4**.

Ⓒ Hold down ⌨Ctrl and select the **range A6:E8**.

Ⓓ Click the **Expand** 📊 button and click **OK**.

The Legend Entries (Series) now list Amy Wyatt, Brian Simpson, and Leisa Malimali.

6. Select one of the column bars for **Leisa Malimali** and tap ⌨Delete.

Now two data series display in the chart.

Format a Chart Using the Ribbon

7. Click anywhere within the top bar in the chart.

8. Follow these steps to apply formatting to the Amy Wyatt data series:

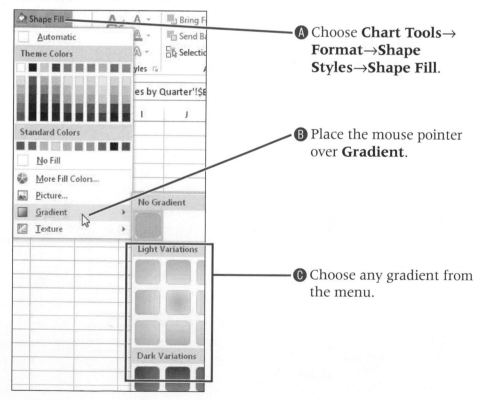

Ⓐ Choose **Chart Tools→ Format→Shape Styles→Shape Fill**.

Ⓑ Place the mouse pointer over **Gradient**.

Ⓒ Choose any gradient from the menu.

9. Click anywhere within the chart area to select it.

Remember that any formatting you choose will apply only to the chart element selected.

10. Choose **Chart Tools→Format→Shape Styles→Shape Outline ⬚→Weight** and select **3 pt**.

11. Choose **Chart Tools→Format→Shape Styles→Shape Outline ⬚** and apply any color; then, click away from the chart to review your formatting changes.

Format Axis Numbers

12. Double-click any of the values in the **horizontal axis**.

Be certain that the Format Axis task pane displays.

13. Follow these steps to format the axis numbers as Currency:

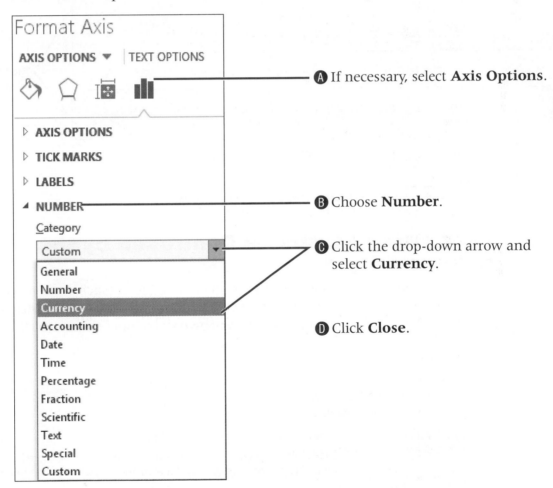

Ⓐ If necessary, select **Axis Options**.

Ⓑ Choose **Number**.

Ⓒ Click the drop-down arrow and select **Currency**.

Ⓓ Click **Close**.

14. Change the default chart title to `Sales by Rep`.

15. Save the file and leave it open.

Applying Layouts and Styles to Charts

Video Library   http://labyrinthelab.com/videos   Video Number: EX13-V0605

Chart layouts, also known as quick layouts, are designs that contain various preset chart elements. Choosing a chart layout saves time versus adding and formatting chart elements one at a time. Chart styles are based on the theme applied to your workbook. You can apply many preset styles to each chart type.

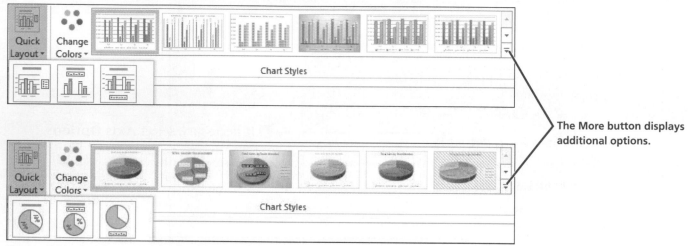

The More button displays additional options.

The available chart layouts and styles change based on the type of chart selected.

Formatting Attributes Controlled by the Selected Style

When you choose a style for your chart, the colors and effects (such as fill effects) change to match the style selected. Data in worksheet cells are not affected by any styles you apply to charts. Excel does not allow you to create your own styles, but you can save the formatting from a selected chart as a template to use as the basis for future charts.

QUICK REFERENCE	APPLYING A LAYOUT AND STYLE TO A CHART
Task	**Procedure**
Apply a layout or style to a chart	▪ Select the chart and click the Design tab. ▪ Click Quick Layouts in the Chart Layouts group, or the More ⬛ button in the Chart Styles group, to display the available choices and make your selection.

Apply a Layout and a Style to a Chart

In this exercise, you will apply a quick layout and Chart Style to your bar chart.

1. Save your file as **EX06-D05-SalesCharts-[FirstInitialLastName]**.

2. Select the **Sales by Rep** sheet and choose **Page Layout→Themes→Themes** 🅰 **→Organic**.

   A uniform color scheme, font set, and graphic effect are applied to the chart. If the worksheet contained additional data, it would have taken the new styles as well.

Change the Chart Layout

3. Click in the chart area of the **Sales by Rep** chart to select the chart, if necessary.

4. Choose **Chart Tools→Design→Chart Layouts→Quick Layout** 📊.

   Excel displays all of the chart layout choices for this type of chart.

5. Choose **Layout 2** in the list.

   A ScreenTip displays the layout name as you point at each layout. When selecting a chart layout, you may need to reenter any title that is not within the data range specified for the chart.

Change the Chart Style

6. Choose **Chart Tools→Design→Chart Styles→ More** ⏷.

7. Choose **Style 4** in the list.

8. Save the file and leave it open.

Excel 2013

Creating Trendlines

Video Library   http://labyrinthelab.com/videos   Video Number: EX13-V0606

Trendlines are used on charts for data analysis and prediction. A trendline displays the trend (increasing or decreasing) of one data series in a chart. There are several types of trendlines available, each suited to the display of particular data types. For example, a linear trendline works well with data that follow a fairly straight path. A moving average trendline will smooth out fluctuations in data by averaging two or more adjacent data points for each trendline data point.

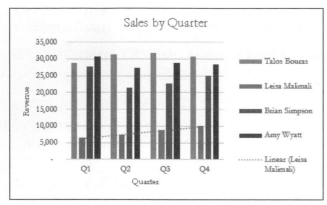

This linear trendline depicts the upward trend for Leisa Malimali's sales.

You cannot add a trendline to stacked, 3-D, or pie charts.

QUICK REFERENCE	CREATING TRENDLINES
Task	**Procedure**
Add a trendline to a chart	■ Display the chart and choose Chart Tools→Design→Chart Layouts→Add Chart Element ▐▟→Trendline. ■ Choose a trendline type and select a data series to base it on (if necessary).
Change the trendline type	■ Select the trendline. ■ Choose Chart Tools→Design→Chart Layouts→Add Chart Element ▐▟ →Trendline and select a trendline type.
Format the trendline	■ Double-click the trendline and choose the desired option.

Add a Trendline

In this exercise, you will add a trendline to an existing chart.

1. Save your file as **EX06-D06-SalesCharts-[FirstInitialLastName]**.

2. Follow these steps to add a trendline to the Amy Wyatt data series:

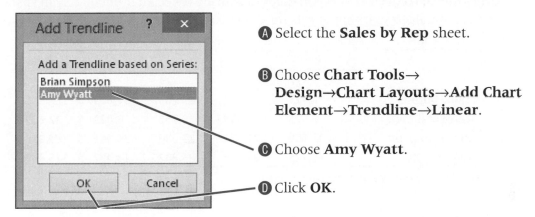

Ⓐ Select the **Sales by Rep** sheet.

Ⓑ Choose **Chart Tools→ Design→Chart Layouts→Add Chart Element→Trendline→Linear**.

Ⓒ Choose **Amy Wyatt**.

Ⓓ Click **OK**.

The trendline that appears shows the trend for Amy Wyatt only.

3. Position the tip of the pointer arrow against the trendline and click to select the trendline.

   Handles will display at the endpoints of the trendline.

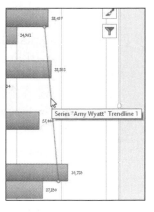

4. Choose **Chart Tools→Design→Chart Layouts→Add Chart Element**  **→Trendline→Linear Forecast**.

   The trendline lengthens to forecast sales in the next two quarters.

5. If necessary, double-click the trendline to open the **Format Trendline** task pane.

6. In the **Forecast** area of Trendline Options, change **Forward** from 2.0 periods to **1**; tap Enter.

   The trendline now forecasts only one quarter in the future.

7. With the trendline still selected, select **Moving Average** in the Format Trendline task pane; click **Close**.

   The trendline shortens to begin at the second quarter, omits the previously displayed forecast, and now displays an angle.

8. Save the file and leave it open.

Creating Sparklines in Cells

Video Library   http://labyrinthelab.com/videos   Video Number: EX13-V0607

Sparklines appear as miniature charts in worksheet cells. They allow you to show data graphically without creating a larger chart. You may select a cell range and create sparklines for every row or column at once. Changes to data are reflected immediately in sparklines adjacent to the data. Each sparkline charts the data in one row or column.

◢	A	B	C	D	E	F	G
4		Q1	Q2	Q3	Q4	Total Sales	
5	Talos Bouras	28,775	31,342	31,763	30,675	$ 122,555	
6	Leisa Malimali	6,575	7,304	8,768	10,023	$ 32,670	
7	Brian Simpson	27,850	21,471	22,634	24,961	$ 96,916	
8	Amy Wyatt	30,725	27,444	28,802	28,497	$ 115,468	

Sparklines show trends in data within a single cell.

Formatting Sparklines

You may format a sparkline as a line, column, or win-loss. The win-loss format shows whether figures are positive or negative. You may format sparklines with different styles and choose to display data points in various ways. Note that the same formatting must be applied to sparklines that were created all at once.

QUICK REFERENCE	CREATING SPARKLINES
Task	**Procedure**
Create a sparkline	▪ Select the cell or cell range that will display the sparkline.
	▪ Choose Insert→Sparklines and select the desired sparkline.
	▪ Select the data range containing the source values and click OK.
Format a sparkline	▪ Select the cell or range of cells containing the sparkline(s) and choose the desired option.

DEVELOP YOUR SKILLS EX06-D07
Create Sparklines

In this exercise, you will create sparklines to show upward and downward trends in data.

1. Save your file as **EX06-D07-SalesCharts-[FirstInitialLastName]**.

2. Display the **Team Totals** sheet and select the **range G5:G8**.
   These cells will contain the sparklines.

3. Choose **Insert→Sparklines →Line** 📉.

4. Follow these steps to create the sparkline:

Ⓐ Move the dialog box, if necessary, to view **column B** in the worksheet.

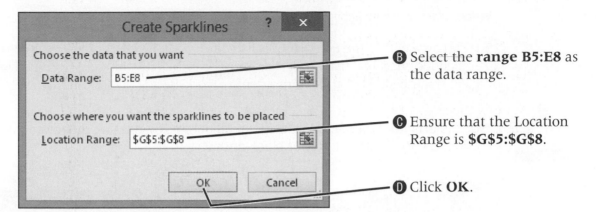

Ⓑ Select the **range B5:E8** as the data range.

Ⓒ Ensure that the Location Range is **$G$5:$G$8**.

Ⓓ Click **OK**.

5. Choose **Sparkline Tools→Design→Show→Markers** to place a checkmark next to **Markers**.

The sparklines display a dot marker for each quarter, thus making the upward and downward trends easier to understand.

6. Select **cell G10** and then choose **Insert→Sparklines→Column** 📊.

7. In the **Create Sparklines** dialog box, set the Data Range to **B10:E10**, verify that the Location Range is **$G$10**, and click **OK**.

This time you created a single sparkline.

Format Sparklines

8. If necessary, select **cell G10**.

9. follow these steps to change the sparkline style:

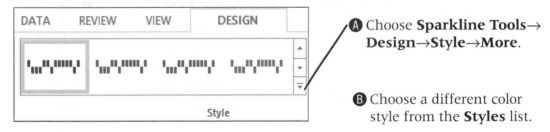

Ⓐ Choose **Sparkline Tools→ Design→Style→More**.

Ⓑ Choose a different color style from the **Styles** list.

10. Select **cell G5**.

The range G5:G8 is surrounded by an outline to indicate that the four sparklines are selected. You previously created these sparklines all at once.

11. Choose **Sparkline Tools→Design→Style→More** ⊡ button and choose a different style.

12. Save the file and leave it open.

Previewing and Printing Charts

Video Library   http://labyrinthelab.com/videos   Video Number: EX13-V0608

The print area within the File tab of Backstage view shows chart previews. Keep in mind that if an embedded chart is active when you choose to print, only the chart itself will print. You must deselect an embedded chart to print its entire worksheet.

Color fills and borders may not provide good contrast in charts printed on grayscale printers. Consider using shades of gray or black-and-white pattern fills.

QUICK REFERENCE	PRINTING CHARTS
Task	**Procedure**
Preview a chart	■ Select the embedded chart or display the chart sheet.
	■ Choose File→Print to see the preview in Backstage view.
Print a chart	■ Select the embedded chart or display the chart sheet.
	■ Choose File→Print, select printing options, and click print.

DEVELOP YOUR SKILLS EX06-D08
Preview and Print a Chart

In this exercise, you will preview the pie chart and print the line chart.

1. Save the file as **EX06-D08-SalesCharts-[FirstInitialLastName]**.

2. Select the **Team Totals** worksheet; then click once to select the pie chart.

3. Choose **File→Print**.

   The pie chart appears in the preview of the Print tab in Backstage view.

4. Tap Esc to exit Backstage view without printing.

5. Click in a cell away from the pie chart to deselect the chart.

6. Choose **File→Print**.

   Notice that when the chart is not selected, Excel will print the worksheet along with the embedded chart.

7. Tap Esc to exit Backstage view without printing.

8. Display the **Sales Trend** worksheet and, if desired, choose **File→Print** to print the worksheet.

9. Save then close the file. Exit **Excel**.

Concepts Review

To check your knowledge of the key concepts introduced in this lesson, complete the Concepts Review quiz by choosing the appropriate access option below.

If you are...	Then access the quiz by...
Using the Labyrinth Video Library	Going to http://labyrinthelab.com/videos
Using eLab	Logging in, choosing Content, and navigating to the Concepts Review quiz for this lesson
Not using the Labyrinth Video Library or eLab	Going to the student resource center for this book

Excel 2013

Reinforce Your Skills

Create and Modify a Column Chart

In this exercise, you will create, move, and modify a column chart that compares total new customers by time period.

Create Charts in Excel

1. Start **Excel**. Open **EX06-R01-Comparison** from the **EX2013 Lesson 06** folder and save it as **EX06-R01-Comparison-[FirstInitialLastName]**.

2. Select the **range A3:E7**.

3. Choose **Insert→Charts→Column→2-D Column→Stacked Column**.

   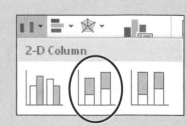

   The chart shows a column for each quarter with the four customer source categories stacked in each.

Move and Size Embedded Charts

4. Point at the chart area, and then drag the chart down and left until the upper-left corner is at **cell A11**.

5. Choose **Chart Tools→Design→Chart Layouts→Quick Layout→Layout 3**.

   ScreenTips help you locate Layout 3 in the list. The legend is moved below the horizontal axis and a title text box is added above the chart.

Explore Other Chart Types

6. Choose **Chart Tools→Design→Type→Change Chart Type→Line→Stacked Line**.

   After reviewing the stacked line chart, you decide that you prefer the stacked column chart.

7. Click **Undo**.

Modify Existing Charts

8. Select the chart title text box, type **=**, select **cell A3**, and tap Enter.

   As you type the formula, =Contracts!$A$3 appears within the Formula Bar.

9. Choose **Chart Tools→Design→Data→Switch Row/Column**.

   The data reverse so the horizontal category axis displays the customer source categories. Each column represents the total new customers in a customer source category.

10. Save and then close the file. Exit **Excel**.

11. Submit your final file based on the guidelines provided by your instructor.

    To view examples of how your file or files should look at the end of this exercise, go to the student resource center.

Finalize and Preview a Chart

In this exercise, you will add a trendline to an existing chart and add sparklines to existing data. You will also apply a chart layout and preview a chart's appearance prior to printing.

Apply Layouts and Styles to Charts

1. Start **Excel**. Open **EX06-R02-PayrollExpenses** from the **EX2013 Lesson 06** folder and save it as **EX06-R02-PayrollExpenses-[FirstInitialLastName]**.

2. Select the chart then choose **Chart Tools→Design→Chart Styles→Style #9**.

3. Choose **Chart Tools→Design→Chart Layouts→Quick Layout→Layout #1**.

4. Change the default chart title text to **Payroll Expenses Chart** and click elsewhere on the worksheet to confirm the new title.

5. Using the [Ctrl] key, select the **range B3:E3** and the **range B9:E9**.

6. Choose **Insert→Charts→Insert Pie or Doughnut Chart→2-D Pie→Pie**.

7. Move the chart to **row 11** below the worksheet data.

8. Click the **Chart Elements** button for the pie chart and hold your mouse pointer over **Data Labels**. Click the arrow that appears and choose **More Options**.

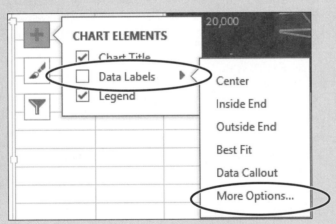

9. Under **Label Options**, place a checkmark next to **Category Name** and **Percentage**, remove the checkmark from **Value**, and click **Close**.

   If you had removed the checkmark from Value first, you would have immediately removed all data labels, which would have made the Label Options menu disappear.

10. Click the **Chart Elements** button for the pie chart, hold your mouse pointer over **Data Labels**, click the arrow, and choose **Inside End**.

11. Click in the legend for the pie chart and tap [Delete].

    The legend is unnecessary because the department names are displayed in the data labels.

12. Change the default chart title text for the pie chart to read **Payroll Expenses by Department**. Click elsewhere on the worksheet to confirm the new title.

Create Trendlines

13. Select the **Payroll Expenses Chart** and choose **Chart Tools→Design→Chart Layouts→Add Chart Element→Trendline→More Trendline Options**.

14. Choose to apply the trendline to the **Wages** data series and then close the Format Trendline task pane.

    Notice how the trendline has smoothed out the fluctuations in the Wages data series.

Create Sparklines in Cells

15. Select the **range G4:G8**.

16. Choose **Insert→Sparklines→Line** 〔�...〕, select the **range B4:E8,** and click **OK**.

    The Sparkline Tools Design tab appears when the sparklines are inserted.

17. Choose **Sparkline Tools→Design→Show** and click to place checkmarks beside **Markers** and **Low Point**.

    The markers indicate each department.

18. Choose **Sparkline Tools→Design→Style→Marker Color→Low Point** and choose a different theme color.

Preview and Print Charts

19. With the pie chart selected, choose **File→Print**.

    Only the chart is previewed in Backstage view because the pie chart is selected.

20. Tap ⎡Esc⎤ to exit Backstage view without printing.

21. Save and then close the file. Exit **Excel**.

22. Submit your final file based on the guidelines provided by your instructor.

    To view examples of how your file or files should look at the end of this exercise, go to the student resource center.

REINFORCE YOUR SKILLS EX06-R03

Create and Finalize a Chart

In this exercise, you will create, move, and modify a bar chart. You will also add trendlines and sparklines, and preview the worksheet.

Create Charts in Excel

1. Start **Excel**. Open **EX06-R03-Donations** from the **EX2013 Lesson 06** folder and save it as `EX06-R03-Donations-[FirstInitialLastName]`.

2. Select the **range A3:E7**.

3. Choose **Insert→Charts→Insert Bar Chart→2-D Bar→Clustered Bar**.

    The chart shows a cluster of four bars for each quarter. The bars represent the source of each donation.

Move and Size Embedded Charts

4. Point at the chart area and drag the chart down and to the left until the upper-left corner is at **cell A10**.

5. Hold [Shift], point at the bottom-right corner of the chart, and drag to reduce the chart size so it does not extend beyond **column F.**

   Holding the [Shift] key ensures that the chart will resize proportionally.

Explore Other Chart Types

6. Choose **Chart Tools→Design→Type→Change Chart Type→Line→Line with Markers**; click **OK**.

   After reviewing the line chart, you decide that you prefer the clustered bar chart.

7. Click **Undo** 🔄 .

Modify Existing Charts

8. Click in the chart title text box and type `Donation Source`. Click elsewhere in the worksheet to confirm the new title.

9. With the chart selected, choose **Chart Tools→Design→Chart Layouts→Add Chart Element→Legend→Top.**

10. Choose **Chart Tools→Design→Chart Layouts→Add Chart Element→Gridlines→Primary Minor Vertical.**

    Gridlines make it easier to determine the precise value of each bar within the chart.

Apply Layouts and Styles to Charts

11. Choose **Chart Tools→Design→Chart Styles→Style 2.**

12. Choose **Chart Tools→Design→Chart Layouts→Quick Layout** and review the available layouts.

    If you had not already modified various chart elements, you could choose a layout here to alter multiple aspects at once.

Create Trendlines

13. Choose **Chart Tools→Design→Chart Layouts→Add Chart Element→Trendline→Linear.**

14. Choose to apply the trendline to the **Web Orders** data series and click **OK**.

Create Sparklines in Cells

15. Select the **range G4:G7**.

16. Choose **Insert→Sparklines→Column** 📊 , select the **range B4:E7** as the data range, and click **OK**.

    The Sparkline Tools Design tab becomes accessible when the sparklines are inserted.

17. On the Design tab, change the style to **Sparkline Style Colorful #4.**

Preview and Print Charts

18. Choose **File→Print** to preview the worksheet.

19. Tap [Esc] to exit Backstage view without printing.

20. Save and then close the file. Exit **Excel**.

21. Submit your final file based on the guidelines provided by your instructor.

Apply Your Skills

Create a Line Chart

In this exercise, you will create a line chart on a separate sheet, rename the sheet tabs, and modify a chart.

Create Charts and Move and Size Embedded Charts in Excel

1. Start **Excel**. Start a new workbook and save it as **EX06-A01-WebOrders-[FirstInitialLastName]** in the **EX2013 Lesson 06** folder.

2. Create this worksheet using the following parameters:
   - Use **AutoFill** to expand the date series.
   - Resize the column widths as necessary.

	A	B
1	Universal Corporate Events	
2	Web Orders	
3		
4	Date	Web Orders
5	3/15/2014	92
6	4/15/2014	146
7	5/15/2014	122
8	6/15/2014	154
9	7/15/2014	128
10	8/15/2014	140
11	9/15/2014	231
12	10/15/2014	245
13	11/15/2014	258
14	12/15/2014	244
15	1/15/2015	231
16	2/15/2015	176
17	Total	2,167

3. Format the dates so they are displayed as Mar-14 (without the day).

4. Use the worksheet data to create the chart shown:
   - Set up the axis labels and title as shown.
   - Do not include a legend.

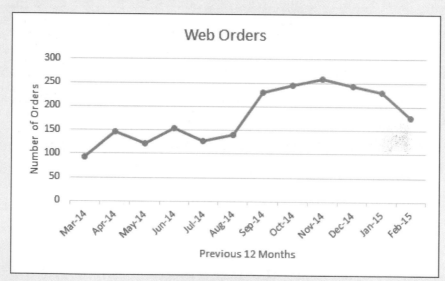

5. Place the chart on a separate sheet named **Web Orders Trend**.
   The dates will not appear slanted after the chart is moved.

6. Rename the **Sheet1** tab **Supporting Data**.

Explore Other Chart Types and Modify Existing Charts

7. Change chart type to a **3-D pie** chart.

   Since the data in this worksheet is not conveyed well in a pie chart, it's a good idea to change it once more.

8. Change chart type to a **3-D line** chart.

9. Remove the chart title and the **Depth (Series)** axis, which is displayed at the bottom-right of the chart.

10. Add a **legend** at the bottom of the chart.

    You can see that the legend lists only one data series, and therefore is not useful.

11. Click **Undo** to remove the legend.

12. Save and then close the file. Exit **Excel**.

13. Submit your final file based on the guidelines provided by your instructor.

    To view examples of how your file or files should look at the end of this exercise, go to the student resource center.

APPLY YOUR SKILLS EX06-A02

Present Data Using Multiple Methods

In this exercise, you will add sparklines, trendlines, and a column chart to a worksheet. You will also preview and print the worksheet.

Create Trendlines and Sparklines

1. Start **Excel**. Open **EX06-A02-ProjRev** from the **EX2013 Lesson 06** folder and save it as **EX06-A02-ProjRev-[FirstInitialLastName]**.

2. Use the data in the **range A6:F9** to create a **clustered column chart**.

3. Add a **linear trendline** to the **Revenue** data series.

4. Change the trendline to a **linear forecast trendline**.

5. Create **line sparklines** in **column G** to present the projected yearly changes in revenue, gross profit, and net profit.

6. Format the sparklines with **markers**.

Apply Layouts and Styles to Charts and Preview and Print Charts

7. Change the style of the chart to **Style 8**.

8. Change the layout of the chart to **Layout 10**.

   The layout change has deleted the trendline. Since you want to display the trendline, you need to undo the applied layout.

9. Click **Undo**.

10. Include the chart title **Financial Projections** and position the chart appropriately below the worksheet data.

11. Preview the worksheet and make any needed adjustments to the chart location.

12. Print the worksheet.

13. Save and then close the file. Exit **Excel**.

14. Submit your final file based on the guidelines provided by your instructor.

    To view examples of how your file or files should look at the end of this exercise, go to the student resource center.

APPLY YOUR SKILLS EX06-A03

Create a Column Chart and Edit Worksheets

In this exercise, you will create a column chart embedded in a worksheet. You will also move and print the chart and add sparklines to the worksheet.

Create Charts and Move and Size Embedded Charts in Excel

1. Start **Excel**. Start a new workbook and save it as **EX06-A03-NetIncome-[FirstInitialLastName]** in the **EX2013 Lesson 06** folder.

2. Create the worksheet and embedded column chart shown. Choose an appropriate chart layout so the negative numbers dip below the category axis in the chart.

The differences in row 6 are the revenues minus the expenses.

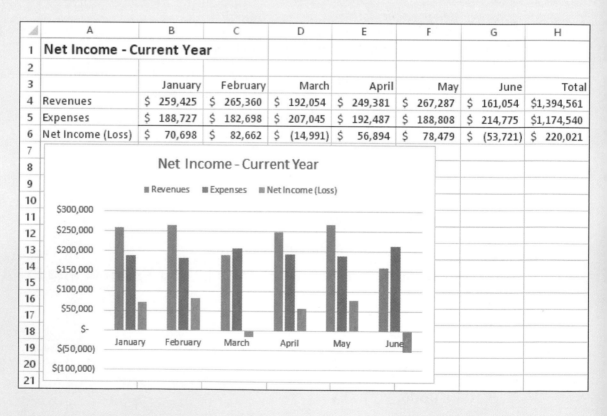

3. Move the chart to a separate sheet, and rename the sheet tab **Net Income Chart**.

4. Rename the worksheet tab `Net Income Analysis`.

5. Add the color of your choice to the **Net Income Analysis** tab.

Explore Other Chart Types and Modify Existing Charts

6. Create a **pie chart** on a separate sheet, showing revenues for the first six months of the year. Name the sheet `Revenue Chart`.

7. Explode the largest pie slice.

8. Change the chart colors of both charts to shades of gray, suitable for printing on a grayscale printer.

9. Italicize the chart titles of both charts.

Create Trendlines and Sparklines

10. Include a **linear trendline** within the column chart for **Net Income (Loss)**.

    Notice that the negative Net Income figures in March and June "drag" the trendline lower than it would be otherwise.

11. Within the Net Income Analysis tab, include **column sparklines** in column I for revenue, expenses, and net income.

12. Modify each sparkline to highlight the highest data point.

Apply Layouts and Styles to Charts and Preview and Print Charts

13. For the column chart, apply **Chart Style 5**.

14. For the pie chart, apply **Layout 6**.

15. Preview all three sheets within the workbook.

16. Print all three sheets in one step.

17. Save and close the file. Exit **Excel**.

18. Submit your final file based on the guidelines provided by your instructor.

Extend Your Skills

In the course of working through the Extend Your Skills exercises, you will think critically as you use the skills taught in the lesson to complete the assigned projects. To evaluate your mastery and completion of the exercises, your instructor may use a rubric, with which more points are allotted according to performance characteristics. (The more you do, the more you earn!) Ask your instructor how your work will be evaluated.

EX06-E01 That's the Way I See It

In this exercise, you will create a pie chart showing the box office receipts for the top five grossing movies from this past weekend. You can use the Internet to search for these figures, which should be readily available.

Create a new file named **EX06-E01-MovieGrosses-[FirstInitialLastName]** in the **EX2013 Lesson 06** folder.

Enter the box office data within your worksheet, making certain to include appropriate headers throughout. Create a pie chart based on the data and format the chart using the skills learned in this lesson. Explode the slice that represents your favorite movie of the weekend, apply an appropriate chart style, and move the chart to its own worksheet.

You will be evaluated based on the inclusion of all elements specified, your ability to follow directions, your ability to apply newly learned skills to a real-world situation, your creativity, and the relevance of your topic and/or data choice(s). Submit your final files based on the guidelines provided by your instructor.

EX06-E02 Be Your Own Boss

In this exercise, you will create and format sparklines for the equipment repair costs of your company, Blue Jean Landscaping.

Open **EX06-E02-RepairCost** from the **EX2013 Lesson 06** folder and save it as **EX06-E02-RepairCost-[FirstInitialLastName]**.

Use sparklines to show the cost trend for repairs on each of the three pieces of equipment. Apply a style and appropriate formatting to the sparklines. Then, type a paragraph (minimum of five sentences) in the row below your data to:

- Describe the purpose of the sparklines.
- Explain how sparklines can be used to evaluate your business's data.
- Detail what you have learned about Blue Jean Landscaping's equipment repair costs as a result of the sparklines.

Once you have completed the paragraph, print the data, including the sparklines and the paragraph, as a PDF, saving it as **EX06-E02-Sparklines-[FirstInitialLastName]**.

You will be evaluated based on the inclusion of all elements specified, your ability to follow directions, your ability to apply newly learned skills to a real-world situation, your creativity, and your demonstration of an entrepreneurial spirit. Submit your final files based on the guidelines provided by your instructor.

Transfer Your Skills

In the course of working through the Transfer Your Skills exercises, you will use critical-thinking and creativity skills to complete the assigned projects using skills taught in the lesson. To evaluate your mastery and completion of the exercises, your instructor may use a rubric, with which more points are allotted according to performance characteristics. (The more you do, the more you earn!) Ask your instructor how your work will be evaluated.

EX06-T01 Use the Web as a Learning Tool

Throughout this book, you will be provided with an opportunity to use the Internet as a learning tool by completing WebQuests. According to the original creators of WebQuests, as described on their website (WebQuest.org), a WebQuest is "an inquiry-oriented activity in which most or all of the information used by learners is drawn from the web." To complete the WebQuest projects in this book, navigate to the student resource center and choose the WebQuest for the lesson on which you are currently working. The subject of each WebQuest will be relevant to the material found in the lesson.

WebQuest Subject: Creating an appropriate chart based on worksheet data

Submit your final file(s) based on the guidelines provided by your instructor.

EX06-T02 Demonstrate Proficiency

Stormy BBQ's sales results are in! Your job is to chart the sales data so your manager can discuss the performance of each location in an upcoming team meeting.

Open **EX06-T02-SalesResults** from the **EX2013 Lesson 06** folder and save it as **EX06-T02-SalesResults-[FirstInitialLastName]**. Calculate the totals within the worksheet and consider the significant trends in sales performance. Create an embedded line chart with appropriate labeling for one of these trends. Show other worksheet results in a column chart on a separate sheet. Include a trendline within your column chart. Keep in mind the data relationships that each chart type can best display. When you have completed the charts, choose one of them and write a paragraph (minimum of 5 sentences) that summarizes the results for the team meeting. The summary should include how you plan to use the data to inform future decisions for the company and should be included on a separate worksheet.

Submit your final file based on the guidelines provided by your instructor.

Formatting Cell Contents, Advanced Skills

LEARNING OBJECTIVES

After studying this lesson, you will be able to:

- Format worksheets using preset themes
- Work with dynamic and static date functions
- Create custom number formats
- Apply conditional formatting to flag positive and negative trends
- Create cell names for navigation and formulas

In this lesson, you will build on the formatting techniques you have learned with techniques such as the Format Painter, which allows you to efficiently apply consistent formatting. Moreover, you will use Excel's Conditional Formatting tool, which can format values that fall within an acceptable range, thus drawing attention to those values. Lastly, you will name cells and ranges so they are easier to locate within the worksheet and can be more easily utilized within formulas.

Formatting with Excel

Having completed the third quarter income statement for Green Clean, a janitorial product supplier and cleaning service contractor, you want to determine how well the company has performed compared to the prior year. With your spreadsheet modified to include prior year data, you format the income statement to highlight important information. You also name cells and ranges within the spreadsheet so they may be more easily located.

Green Clean			
Income Statement Comparison			
3rd Quarter			
	Current Year	Prior Year	Dollar Change
REVENUES			
Sales	$ 704,785	$ 687,525	$ 17,260
Finance Charge Revenue	12,054	12,578	(524)
Total Revenues	$ 716,839	$ 700,103	$ 16,736
Vehicle Costs	63,226	67,498	(4,272)
Wages	373,937	362,495	11,442
Total Costs	$ 571,164	$ 559,957	$ 11,207
Net Income (Loss)	$ 145,675	$ 140,146	$ 5,529
Net Income to Total Revenues	20.3%	20.0%	33.0%
Date Created	11-Nov-2013		Check Figure
Date Reviewed	15-Nov-2013		$ 16,734
Elapsed Days	4		
Date Printed	11/15/2013 10:23 AM		

Formatting can make important spreadsheet data more easily understandable.

Working with the Format Painter and Quick Styles

Video Library   http://labyrinthelab.com/videos   Video Number: EX13-V0701

The Format Painter applies formatting from existing worksheet cells, while Quick Styles apply predefined formats to cells. Both of these tools can greatly simplify the formatting of a worksheet.

The Format Painter

The Format Painter lets you copy text and number formats from one cell to another. This can be extremely helpful if you have a cell to which many formatting options have been applied and you do not wish to go through the process of applying each option individually to another cell or range of cells.

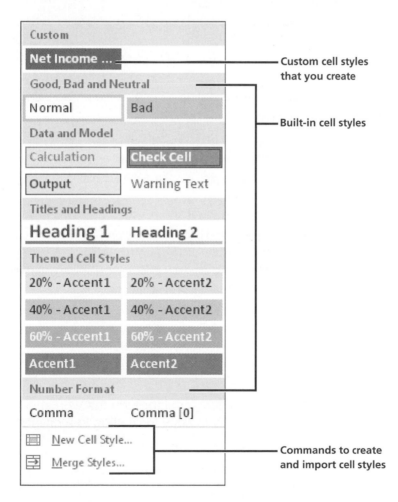

- Custom cell styles that you create
- Built-in cell styles
- Commands to create and import cell styles

Applying Quick Styles to Cells

You can apply Excel's built-in cell styles, also called Quick Styles, or create your own styles for a uniform worksheet design. A cell style's formatting may include the font, number format, borders, or fill.

New cell styles that you create appear in the Custom section of the styles list. They are based on the workbook theme, so the colors change automatically to match any new theme applied. Among the built-in styles, only the Themed Cell Styles change colors. Any styles you create or edit apply only to the currently open workbook. The Merge Styles command in the Styles list allows you to import styles created in a different workbook into the current workbook.

QUICK REFERENCE	WORKING WITH THE FORMAT PAINTER AND CELL STYLES
Task	**Procedure**
Copy formats to one other cell or range	■ Click the cell with the desired formatting and choose Home→Clipboard→Format Painter. ■ Select the destination cell or range.
Copy formats to multiple locations	■ Click the cell with the desired formatting and double-click Home→Clipboard→Format Painter. ■ Select the destination cells or ranges; when finished, click Format Painter or tap Esc.
Apply a Quick Style to a cell or range	■ Select the destination cells and choose Home→Styles→Cell Styles. ■ Select the desired style from the list.
Create a cell style	■ Choose Home→Styles→Cell Styles→New Cell Style. ■ Click the Format button, select the desired formatting options, and click OK. ■ Name the style in the Style dialog box, select the formatting categories to be included, and click OK.
Modify a cell style	■ Choose Home→Styles→Cell Styles. ■ Right-click the desired style and choose Modify (or Duplicate to create a new style based on the existing style). ■ Click the Format button, select the desired formatting options, and click OK. ■ Select the formatting categories to be included; click OK.
Import cell styles from a different workbook	■ Open the workbook from which you wish to import styles. ■ In the destination workbook, choose Home→Styles→Cell Styles→Merge Styles, choose the source workbook name, and click OK.

When you double-click the Format Painter, you can scroll through the worksheet to reach the desired location(s). You can also click a sheet tab to copy formatting to a different worksheet.

Change Formatting

In this exercise, you will copy the formatting from one cell to a range of cells. You also will apply cell styles and create a custom style.

1. Open **EX07-D01-ISComp** from the **EX2013 Lesson 07** folder and save it as **EX07-D01-ISComp-[FirstInitialLastName]**.

   Replace the bracketed text with your first initial and last name. For example, if your name is Bethany Smith, your filename would look like this: EX07-D01-ISComp-BSmith.

2. Follow these steps to apply consistent formats to the column headers using the Format Painter:

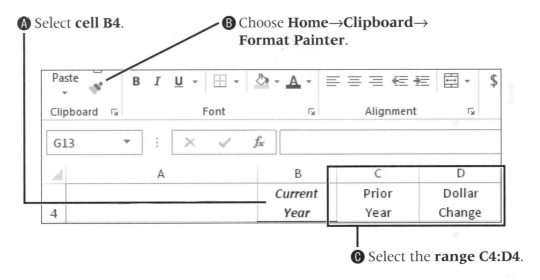

Ⓐ Select **cell B4**.

Ⓑ Choose **Home→Clipboard→ Format Painter**.

Ⓒ Select the **range C4:D4**.

The formatting from cell B4 is applied to the range C4:D4. Because you only clicked it once, the Format Painter button is no longer active. If you had double-clicked it, it would still be active.

Excel 2013

Apply Cell Styles

3. Select the **range A1:A3**.

4. Follow these steps to apply a built-in cell style:

Ⓐ Choose **Home→ Styles→Cell Styles**.

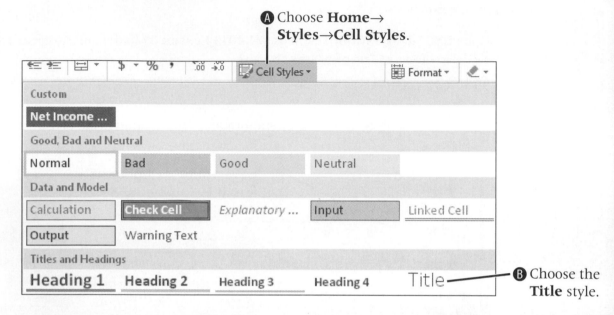

Ⓑ Choose the **Title** style.

Your styles may differ from those shown.

5. Select the **range B25:D25**.

6. Choose **Home→Styles→Cell Styles** and select **Total** from within the Titles and Headings group.

7. Deselect the range.

Because of the cell style selected, the range displays bold formatting with a top and double bottom border.

Create a Custom Cell Style

8. Choose **Home→Styles→Cell Styles**.

9. Choose **New Cell Style** at the bottom of the list.

10. Follow these steps to begin creating a cell style:

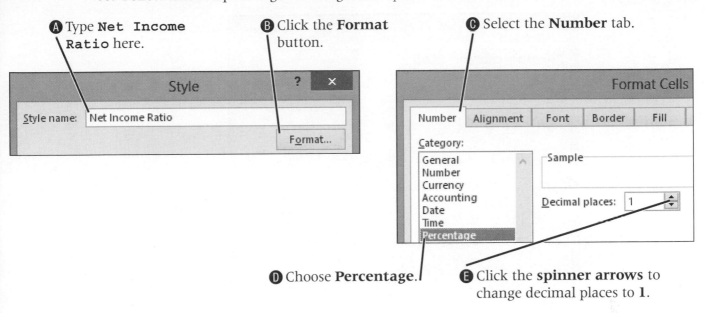

A Type **Net Income Ratio** here.

B Click the **Format** button.

C Select the **Number** tab.

D Choose **Percentage.**

E Click the **spinner arrows** to change decimal places to **1**.

11. With the Format Cells dialog box still displayed, select the **Fill** tab.

12. Choose a dark fill color, such as the fourth color in the sixth column of the Theme Colors palette.

13. Follow these steps to set the text characteristics for the cell style:

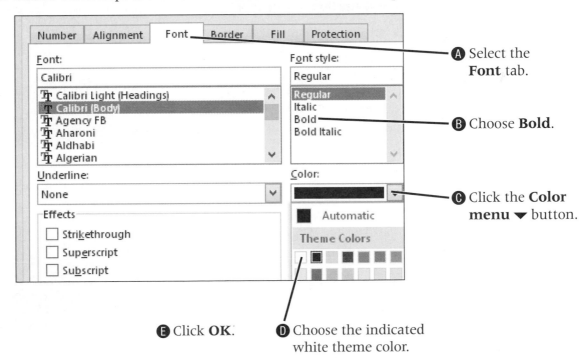

A Select the **Font** tab.

B Choose **Bold**.

C Click the **Color menu ▼** button.

D Choose the indicated white theme color.

E Click **OK**.

Notice that your changes are shown in the Style dialog box.

All the categories with a checkmark will be applied to the style. You can remove the checkmark from any formatting you don't want to use.

14. Click **OK** to close the Style dialog box.

Apply the Custom Cell Style

15. Select the **range A27:D27**.

16. Choose **Home→Styles→Cell Styles**  and select your **Net Income Ratio** style from the **Custom** group at the top of the list.

The range now displays your custom cell style, including bold, white font, and a dark fill color.

17. Deselect the range.

18. Save the file and leave it open; you will modify it throughout this lesson.

Formatting with Themes

Video Library   http://labyrinthelab.com/videos   Video Number: EX13-V0702

Themes allow you to easily apply formatting to entire workbooks. You can modify a theme by changing the font set, color palette, or graphic effect design. And, you can save the modifications as a custom theme that can be reused with other workbooks.

Themes allow you to choose a set of compatible fonts, one for headings and one for body text, which are identified at the top of the Font list. Likewise, the ten theme colors display at the top of the list when you are applying colors (such as fill color or font color).

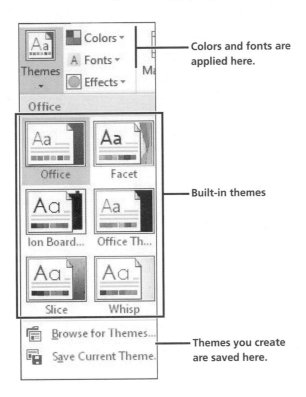

Colors and fonts are applied here.

Built-in themes

Themes you create are saved here.

Excel 2013

QUICK REFERENCE	APPLYING, MODIFYING, AND SAVING THEMES
Task	**Procedure**
Apply a theme to a workbook	■ Choose Page Layout →Themes→Themes 🔲 and choose the desired theme.
Modify and save a theme	■ Choose Page Layout→Themes→Themes 🔲 and choose the desired theme.
	■ Change the colors, fonts, and effects as desired.
	■ Choose Page Layout→Themes→Themes 🔲 →Save Current Theme, enter a theme name, and click Save.

Use Themes in a Workbook

In this exercise, you will apply a theme to the workbook. You also will modify a theme and explore how it would be saved.

1. Save your file as **EX07-D02-ISComp-[FirstInitialLastName]**.

2. Click the **Page Layout view** button in the Status Bar.

   The view buttons are located to the left of the zoom slider.

3. Choose **Page Layout→Themes→Themes**.

   Office is the default theme applied to new workbooks.

4. Point at various themes and observe the different effects shown in Live Preview.

   Note that you may be able to scroll down to display additional themes.

5. Choose the **Integral** theme and click anywhere within the worksheet data.

   The colors and font in the workbook now correspond to those indicated in the theme.

6. Locate the **Status Bar** at the bottom-left corner of the Excel window to see that this theme displays the worksheet on one page.

   If this worksheet contained more data, and therefore extended beyond one page, you could quickly determine this by looking here.

Modify and Explore Saving a Theme

7. Choose **Page Layout→Themes→Theme Fonts**.

8. Point at various font families and observe the different effects in Live Preview.

9. Choose the **Arial** theme fonts.

10. Choose **Page Layout→Themes→Themes→Save Current Theme**.

    The Save Current Theme dialog box displays. Notice the default folder for saving themes on your system. You could enter a filename to save the modified theme.

11. Click **Cancel** so that you *do not* save the theme.

12. Save the file and leave it open.

Inserting Date Functions and Formatting

Video Library   http://labyrinthelab.com/videos   Video Number: EX13-V0703

The date functions, which utilize a similar syntax to that of statistical functions like SUM and AVERAGE, display either today's date or a date of your choice. Excel determines the current date according to your computer's clock feature.

Working with Dates

Dates are used in workbooks in two ways. First, you can simply type and display dates in cells using various formats such as 11/20/14; November 20, 2014; or 20-Nov-14. Second, you can use dates in formulas. For example, you may want to compute the number of days an invoice is past due. You calculate this as the difference between the current date and the due date of the invoice.

Date Serial Numbers

When you enter a date in a cell, Excel converts the date to a serial number between 1 and 2,958,525. These numbers correspond to the period from January 1, 1900, through December 31, 9999. The date January 1, 1900, is assigned the serial number 1; January 2, 1900, is assigned the serial number 2; etc. Serial numbers extend all the way to December 31, 9999. When dates are converted to numbers, you can use the numbers/dates in calculations.

Excel recognizes an entry as a date as long as you enter it using a standard date format.

Function	Description
TODAY()	Displays the current system date and calculates the serial number. The date updates automatically when the worksheet is recalculated or reopened.
NOW()	Displays the current system date and time and calculates the serial number. The date and time update automatically when the worksheet is recalculated or reopened.
DATE(year, month, day)	Returns a specific date displayed in the default date format and calculates the serial number. The date does not update when the worksheet is recalculated or reopened.

Do not type anything within the parentheses of the TODAY and NOW functions.

QUICK REFERENCE	CREATING DATE AND TIME FUNCTIONS
Task	**Procedure**
Insert a date or time function	■ Click the cell in which you wish to place the function result.
	■ Click Insert Function f_x and choose Date & Time.
	■ Select the function you wish to create; click OK.
	■ Enter the appropriate function arguments (if necessary); click OK.

Use the TODAY Function and Format a Date

In this exercise, you will create formulas to calculate the current date, and you will format dates.

1. Save your file as **EX07-D03-ISComp-[FirstInitialLastName]**.

2. Select **cell B30**.

3. Type **9/1/14** and then click **Enter** ✓.

4. Display the **Home** tab and locate the **Number** group.

   Notice the number format style displayed is Date, which Excel formatted for you when you typed the number in the date format.

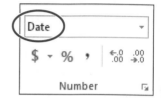

5. Choose **Home→Number→dialog box launcher** 🔲.

   The Format Cells dialog box opens with the Number tab displayed.

6. Follow these steps to change the date format:

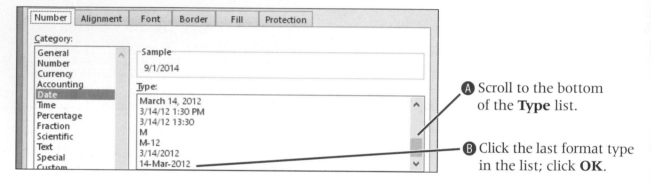

    Ⓐ Scroll to the bottom of the **Type** list.

    Ⓑ Click the last format type in the list; click **OK**.

7. Ensure that **cell B30** is still selected, and then tap ⌦ Delete .

   Look at the Number group on the Home tab and notice that even when you remove the contents of the cell (the date), the number format for the cell will remain as Date.

Use the TODAY Function and Calculate Dates

8. Follow these steps to enter the TODAY function in cell B30:

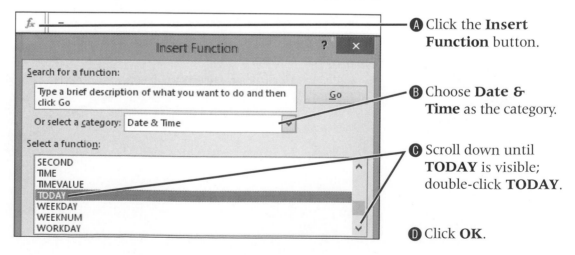

    Ⓐ Click the **Insert Function** button.

    Ⓑ Choose **Date & Time** as the category.

    Ⓒ Scroll down until **TODAY** is visible; double-click **TODAY**.

    Ⓓ Click **OK**.

The date will appear with the number formatting you set for the cell.

Working with Conditional Formatting

Video Library http://labyrinthelab.com/videos Video Number: EX13-V0705

The Conditional Formatting command applies formatting to cells that meet criteria that you set. Conditional formats are activated only when the criteria are met. For example, you may assign a yellow fill to a cell when its value is greater than 12. You may apply conditional formatting to cells containing values, text, dates, blanks, or errors. While conditional formatting can refer to a cell in a different sheet of the workbook, it cannot refer to cells in a different workbook.

Using Presets and Multiple Conditions

You can choose from conditional formatting presets on the Conditional Formatting menu for frequently used criteria, such as Greater Than, Equal To, Above Average, and Top 10 Items. You may set any number of conditional formats and create multiple rules to check for more than one condition in a cell. Conditional formatting rules are applied in the priority order you set. The Stop If True option, when selected in any rule, prevents further formatting by the remaining rules after a criterion is evaluated as True.

Creating a Conditional Formatting Rule

If no preset item on the Conditional Formatting menu has your desired criteria or formatting, you may create a new conditional formatting rule. The following illustration defines the parts of the New Formatting Rule dialog box. The options vary in the lower half of the dialog box depending on the rule type you select.

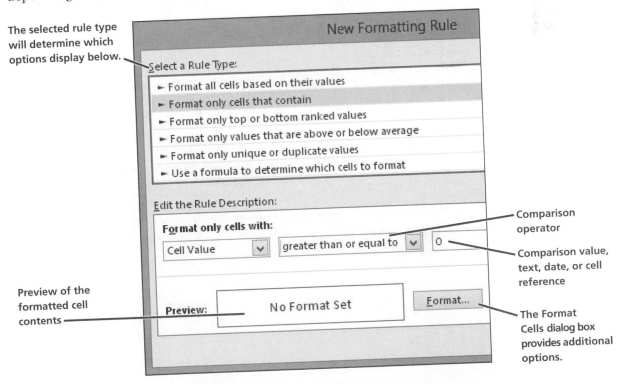

The selected rule type will determine which options display below.

New Formatting Rule

Select a Rule Type:
- Format all cells based on their values
- Format only cells that contain
- Format only top or bottom ranked values
- Format only values that are above or below average
- Format only unique or duplicate values
- Use a formula to determine which cells to format

Edit the Rule Description:

Format only cells with:

Cell Value | greater than or equal to | 0

Comparison operator

Comparison value, text, date, or cell reference

Preview of the formatted cell contents

Preview: No Format Set | Format...

The Format Cells dialog box provides additional options.

---

9. Select **cell B29** and enter the date that is four days prior to today.

10. Use the **Format Painter** to apply the date format from **cell B30** to **cell B29**.

11. Select **cell B31** and enter the formula **=B30-B29**.

   The result should equal 4. By subtracting dates in this manner, Excel can calculate the number of days between any two dates.

Use the NOW Function

12. Select **cell B32**, then type **=now(** and tap [Enter].

   Excel automatically adds the closing parenthesis for the formula. Number signs (###) display across the cell width, which means that the date is too long to fit.

13. AutoFit **column B** by double-clicking the right edge of the header.

   The NOW function displays the current date and time, which will be updated the next time you open the worksheet.

14. Save the file and leave it open.

Creating Custom Formats

Video Library http://labyrinthelab.com/videos Video Number: EX13-V0704

Excel's predefined number format options are usually sufficient, but you may also need a modified format. For example, you may want a date to display the year as two digits instead of four. Or, an identification or account number may need to be displayed with preceding zeros, such as 0004842. The Number tab of the Format Cells dialog box includes a Type box in which you can edit an existing number format or create a new one.

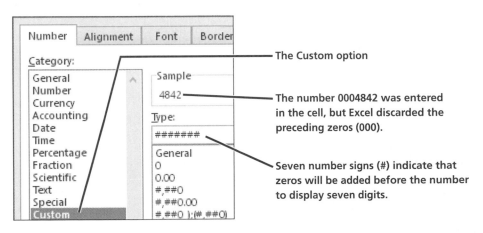

The Custom option

The number 0004842 was entered in the cell, but Excel discarded the preceding zeros (000).

Seven number signs (#) indicate that zeros will be added before the number to display seven digits.

Task	Procedure
Modify an existing number format to create a custom format	▪ Select the cell/range to which you wish to apply a custom number format. ▪ Choose Home→Number→dialog box launcher 🔲. ▪ Select the Custom category and choose the format closest to the desired format. ▪ Edit the formatting in the Type box and view the sample; click OK.

DEVELOP YOUR SKILLS EX07-D04

Modify a Date Format

In this exercise, you will edit the date format currently applied to the NOW function formula.

1. Save your file as **EX07-D04-ISComp-[FirstInitialLastName]**.

2. Select **cell B32**.

3. Follow these steps to modify the date format applied to the NOW function formula:

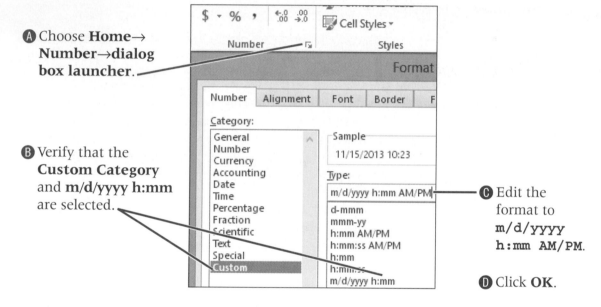

Ⓐ Choose **Home→ Number→dialog box launcher**.

Ⓑ Verify that the **Custom Category** and **m/d/yyyy h:mm** are selected.

Ⓒ Edit the format to **m/d/yyyy h:mm AM/PM**.

Ⓓ Click **OK**.

The time now displays either AM or PM.

4. Save the file and leave it open.

Formatting with Graphics

You can choose to conditionally format cells with data bars, a color scale, or an icon set. These graphics identify values that are average, above average, and below average in the selected cell range. You may select a menu preset or create a custom rule using any of these visual aids.

Equipment Lease	7,844	8,200	✖	(356)
Insurance	18,230	17,500	✔	730
Rent	25,000	25,000	✖	-

Conditional formatting with data bars, a color scale, or icon sets helps to highlight data.

 TIP Use consistent formatting and limit the use of data bars, color scales, and icon sets on one worksheet. Using multiple styles could confuse the reader.

The Conditional Formatting Rules Manager

Conditional formatting rules can be created, edited, rearranged, and deleted within the Conditional Formatting Rules Manager dialog box. The following illustration displays the rules set within an entire worksheet.

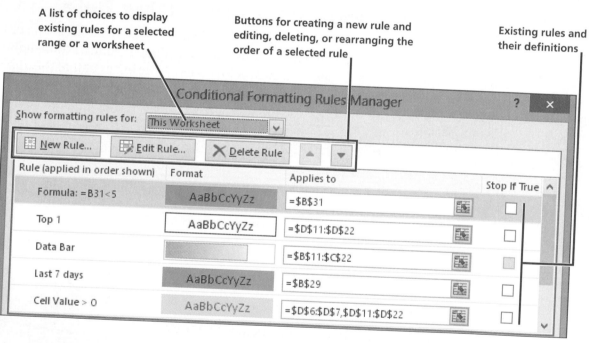

QUICK REFERENCE | APPLYING CONDITIONAL FORMATTING

Task	Procedure
Apply preset conditional formatting	■ Select the cells to receive formatting. ■ Choose Home→Styles→Conditional Formatting 📑, display a preset menu, and choose a command. ■ Edit options in the preset rule dialog box and click OK, if necessary.
Create a conditional formatting rule	■ Select the cells to receive formatting. ■ Choose Home→Styles→ Conditional Formatting 📑→New Rule. ■ Choose a rule type and formatting options in the New Formatting Rule dialog box; click OK.
Apply conditional formatting with data bars, a color scale, or an icon set	■ Select the cells to receive formatting. ■ Choose Home→Styles→ Conditional Formatting 📑→Data Bars, Color Scales, or Icon Sets. ■ Choose a preset item on the command's submenu or More Rules to create a custom rule.
Clear conditional formatting from specific cells	■ Select specific cells from which to remove formatting. ■ Choose Home→Styles→Conditional Formatting 📑→Clear Rules→Clear Rules from Selected Cells.
Clear all conditional formatting from a worksheet	■ Display the desired worksheet. ■ Choose Home→Styles→Conditional Formatting 📑→Clear Rules→Clear Rules from Entire Sheet.
Manage conditional formatting rules	■ Choose Home→Styles→Conditional Formatting 📑→Manage Rules. ■ Choose Current Selection or a worksheet from the Show Formatting Rules For list. ■ Use buttons in the dialog box to create a new rule or select an existing rule and edit, delete, or change its order.

DEVELOP YOUR SKILLS EX07-D05

Apply Conditional Formatting

In this exercise, you will apply various types of conditional formatting to cell ranges. You will also create a conditional formatting rule and remove conditional formatting from a range.

1. Save your file as **EX07-D05-ISComp-[FirstInitialLastName]**.

2. Select the **ranges D6:D7** and the **range D11:D22**.

3. Choose **Home→Styles→Conditional Formatting→Highlight Cells Rules→Less Than**.

   Next you will create a highlighting rule to identify those line items that have decreased from the prior year.

4. Follow these steps to apply conditional formatting:

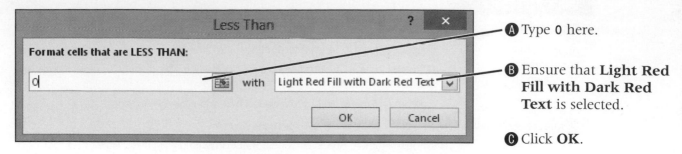

Ⓐ Type **0** here.

Ⓑ Ensure that **Light Red Fill with Dark Red Text** is selected.

Ⓒ Click **OK**.

5. With the prior ranges still selected, choose **Home→Styles→Conditional Formatting→Highlight Cells Rules→Greater Than**.

6. Repeat **step 4**, changing the format to **Green Fill with Dark Green Text**.

All revenues and expenses that changed now show either a red or green background.

Create a Conditional Formatting Rule

7. Highlight **cell B29** and choose **Home→Styles→Conditional Formatting→Highlight Cells Rules→More Rules**.

The New Formatting Rule dialog box appears.

8. Follow these steps to create a custom conditional formatting rule:

Ⓐ Select **Dates Occurring** here.

Ⓑ Select **In the Last 7 Days** here.

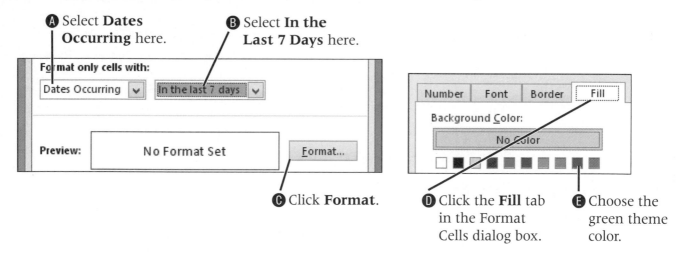

Ⓒ Click **Format**.

Ⓓ Click the **Fill** tab in the Format Cells dialog box.

Ⓔ Choose the green theme color.

9. Click **OK** to exit the Format Cells dialog box.

Notice the green fill in the Preview box of the New Formatting Rule dialog box.

10. Click **OK** to exit the New Formatting Rule dialog box.

The conditional formatting is applied to cell B29 to denote that the worksheet was created within the past week.

Format with Data Bars and a Top Rule

11. Select the **range B6:C7**.

12. Choose **Home→Styles→Conditional Formatting→Data Bars→Blue Data Bar**.

The data bars display the relative size of each revenue item. You may choose either gradient or solid data bars.

13. Select the **range B11:C22** and choose **Home→Styles→Conditional Formatting→Data Bars→Orange Data Bar**.

Data bars for revenues and expenses must be created separately, otherwise they will appear relative to one another (so the larger revenues would have big data bars and the smaller expenses would have small data bars).

14. Select the **range D11:D22** and choose **Home→Styles→Conditional Formatting→Top/Bottom Rules→Top 10 Items**.

15. Change 10 to **1** in the Top 10 Items dialog box.

16. Choose **Red Border** from the **With** list and click **OK**.

The highest expense item is now highlighted with a red border.

Format Using a Formula

In the next few steps, you will enter a formula that compares the date created to another date. If the result of this logical test is true, the cell's text will change to green.

17. Select **cell B30** and choose **Home→Styles→Conditional Formatting→New Rule**.

The New Formatting Rule dialog box displays.

18. Follow these steps to create a conditional formatting rule using a formula:

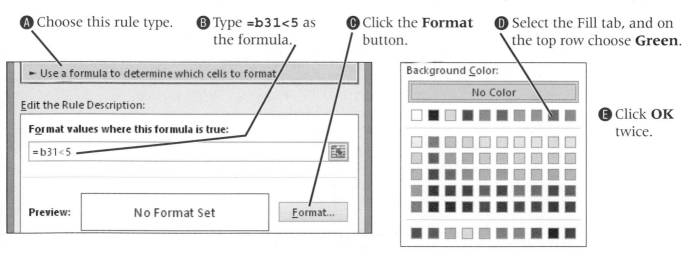

Ⓐ Choose this rule type.   **Ⓑ** Type **=b31<5** as the formula.   **Ⓒ** Click the **Format** button.   **Ⓓ** Select the Fill tab, and on the top row choose **Green**.

Ⓔ Click **OK** twice.

If Green Clean's goal of having schedules reviewed within fewer than five days has been met, cell B30 will display with green fill.

19. Select the **range B6:C7** and choose **Home→Styles→Conditional Formatting→Clear Rules→Clear Rules from Selected Cells**.

The data bars disappear from the cells containing revenue figures.

20. Save the file and leave it open.

Naming Cells and Ranges

Video Library   http://labyrinthelab.com/videos   Video Number: EX13-V0706

You may use a descriptive name instead of cell references in formulas and for worksheet navigation. Range names are easier to type, recognize, and remember. Excel refers to these as defined names. You may create a name for one cell or a range of cells.

Naming Rules

Excel has a few rules for naming cells. Defined names:

- Must begin with a letter.
- Cannot resemble a cell reference, as in A3 or BC14.
- Cannot consist of the single letters C or R, which Excel interprets as column or row.
- Cannot contain spaces, hyphens, or symbols.
- May contain an underscore, period, or capital letter to connect words.

Creating Defined Names

Defined names are available throughout a workbook by default. You may define a name in one worksheet and use the name to navigate to its cell reference(s) from within any other worksheet.

You may create a name using a few different methods, the easiest of which is to type a name in the Name Box of the Formula Bar.

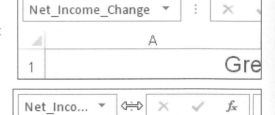

 The Name Box may be widened by dragging the three dots between the Name Box and the Formula Bar.

QUICK REFERENCE	ASSIGNING DEFINED NAMES
Task	**Procedures**
Assign cell and range names	Use any of these three methods: ■ Select the desired cell(s), click in the Name Box, type the new name, and tap Enter. ■ Select the desired cell(s), choose Formulas→Defined Names→Define Name, type the new name, and click OK. ■ Select the desired cell(s) (including the column or row titles), choose Formulas→ Defined Names→Create from Selection, select the location of the associated title, and click OK.

Using Defined Names

Defined names are mainly used to navigate workbooks and create linking formulas or calculation formulas.

Using Names to Navigate

Create defined names to move quickly to areas of the worksheet that you view or update frequently. To navigate to a named cell or range, you select its name from the Name list on the Formula Bar.

Using Names in Formulas

Formulas containing defined names help others to understand what the formulas are calculating. For example, the formula =AdvertisingTotal+MileageTotal is easier to understand than =AC10+AD10. Workbook users might prefer the linking formula =AdvertisingTotal, which uses a defined name, rather than =Advertising!B16. You may substitute a defined name for cell references in any formula. You may type the defined name or select it from the Use in Formula list on the Ribbon.

TIP

If the error message #NAME? displays in a cell, ensure that the spelling of the name is the same in the formula and Name list and that the name was not deleted from the list.

FROM THE RIBBON

Formulas→Defined Names→Name Manager

FROM THE KEYBOARD

Ctrl + F3

Modifying and Deleting Defined Names

Use the Name Manager dialog box to view all defined names and edit their properties. You may add and delete names in Name Manager. Formula cells, however, display the error message #NAME?# after names have been deleted. You will need to edit the cell references in formulas that used any deleted name.

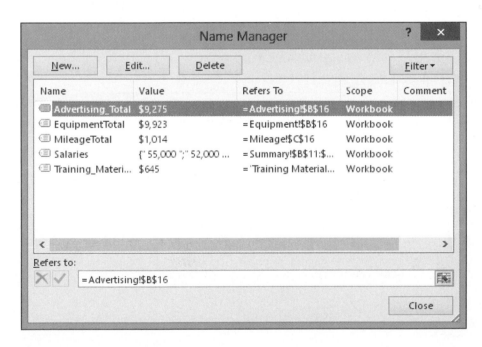

WARNING

To change the Refers To entry, use the Collapse button and point mode to select cells. Do not use arrow keys to edit the entry, as Excel would insert cell references rather than move the insertion point.

Task	Procedures
Name Cells	■ Select the range of cells, type a name in the Name Box, and tap Enter.
Create names from existing row or column titles	■ Select the labels and the cells to which they refer, and choose Formulas→Defined Names→Create from Selection. ■ Place a checkmark to indicate the location of the labels, and click OK.
Change a defined name	■ Choose Formulas→Defined Names→Name Manager, choose an existing name, click Edit, edit the name, click OK, and click Close.
Change the range to which a name refers	■ Choose Formulas→Defined Names→Name Manager, and choose an existing name. ■ Click the Collapse button next to Refers To, select the new range, and click the Expand button. ■ Click Close, and click Yes to confirm the change.
Delete a defined name	■ Choose Formulas→Defined Names→Name Manager, choose an existing name, click Delete, click OK, and click Close.
Navigate to a defined range	■ Choose the name from the Name list in the Formula Bar.
Use a defined name in a linking formula	■ Select the cell to contain the summary formula, choose Formulas→Defined Names→Use in Formula, choose the defined name, and tap Enter.
Use one or more defined names in a calculation formula	■ Select the cell to contain the formula, and type the function beginning, such as =SUM(■ Choose Formulas→Defined Names→Use in Formula, choose the defined name, continue typing the formula and choose defined names as necessary, and tap Enter.

DEVELOP YOUR SKILLS EX07-D06

Create and Use Defined Names

In this exercise, you will create names for single cells and then navigate to important areas of the workbook. You also will use defined names to create linking formulas.

1. Save your file as **EX07-D06-ISComp-[FirstInitialLastName]**.

2. Select **cell D25**.

3. Follow these steps to name the cell:

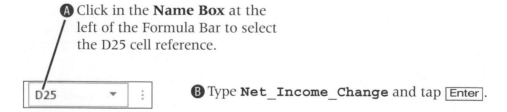

Ⓐ Click in the **Name Box** at the left of the Formula Bar to select the D25 cell reference.

Ⓑ Type **Net_Income_Change** and tap Enter.

You must tap Enter *after typing the name. If you simply click outside the Name Box, the name will not be created.*

4. Select any cell other than D25, and then select **cell D25** again.

   The Name Box displays Net_Income_Change.

5. To view the entire name, drag the three dots between the Name Box and Formula Bar, if necessary.

6. Select **cell D27** and choose **Formulas→Defined Names→Define Name** .

7. In the New Name dialog box, type **Profit_Margin_Percentage** and click **OK**.

   Notice that the Scope option is set to Workbook. If you had multiple worksheets within this workbook, you could select the defined name from within any worksheet.

Use Names to Navigate and Create Formulas

You will now use defined names to create a "check" formula to confirm that the formulas in cells D25 and D27 are calculated properly.

8. Choose **Net_Income_Change** from the Name list in the Formula Bar to navigate to cell D25.

9. Navigate to **Profit_Margin_Percentage**.

10. Select **cell D30**, choose **Formulas→Defined Names→Use in Formula** , and choose the defined name **Net_Income_Change**.

11. Continue the formula by typing **/**.

12. Choose **Formulas→Defined Names→Use in Formula** .

13. Choose the defined name **Profit_Margin_Percentage** and confirm the formula.

    Since this "check" formula result is the same as the value in cell D8, you have confirmed that the formulas in cells D25 & D27 were calculated properly.

14. Save and then close the file. Exit **Excel**.

Concepts Review

To check your knowledge of the key concepts introduced in this lesson, complete the Concepts Review quiz by choosing the appropriate access option below.

If you are...	Then access the quiz by...
Using the Labyrinth Video Library	Going to http://labyrinthelab.com/videos
Using eLab	Logging in, choosing Content, and navigating to the Concepts Review quiz for this lesson
Not using the Labyrinth Video Library or eLab	Going to the student resource center for this book

Reinforce Your Skills

Work with Dates, Cell Styles, and Themes

In this exercise, you will enter a date function that will calculate the current date for you. You will apply cell styles to worksheet cells and change the fonts in the workbook theme.

Work with the Format Painter and Quick Styles

1. Start **Excel**. Open **EX07-R01-BudgetDate** from the **EX2013 Lesson 07** folder and save it as **EX07-R01-BudgetDate-[FirstInitialLastName]**.

2. Select **cell B24**.

3. Choose **Home→Clipboard→Format Painter** and highlight the **range B25:C25** to apply consistent formatting to it.

4. Select **cell C4** and choose **Home→Styles→Cell Styles**.

5. Choose an appropriate **Quick Style** from the list to draw attention to the balance.

6. Select **cells A7, A15, and A25** using the Ctrl key.

7. Choose **Home→Styles→Cell Styles** and choose an appropriate themed cell style.

Format with Themes

8. Choose **Page Layout→Themes→Theme Fonts** A Fonts ▾.

9. Point at various font themes to preview the workbook; choose a font theme.
   Remember that you can scroll to view all the font themes.

10. Evaluate how the data appear and change the font theme, if necessary, until you are satisfied.
    Your goal is to identify a font theme that is suitable for the worksheet data and easily comprehensible by the user.

11. Add any formatting that you think enhances the workbook design.

Insert Date Functions and Formatting

12. Select **cell B4**.

13. Click the **Insert Function** *fx* button.

14. Choose the **Date & Time** category if you do not see the TODAY function in the Most Recently Used category.

15. Scroll down, select the **TODAY** function, and click **OK**.

16. Click **OK** in the Function Arguments window.
    The date will be returned in the default format.

17. Choose **Home→Number→dialog box launcher** ⬜.

18. Display the **Number** tab in the Format Cells dialog box. Scroll down if necessary, and choose the format that will display the date like 1-Jan-15.

Excel uses March 14, 2012, as its example date; however, the date that appears within the worksheet will be the one you have created.

19. Save and then close the file. Exit **Excel**.

20. Submit your final file based on the guidelines provided by your instructor.

To view examples of how your file or files should look at the end of this exercise, go to the student resource center.

REINFORCE YOUR SKILLS EX07-R02
Apply Conditional Formatting and Cell Names

In this exercise, you will apply conditional formatting to cell ranges to analyze trends. You will also create a custom number format and name cells.

Create Custom Formats

1. Start **Excel**. Open **EX07-R02-ShippingFee** from the **EX2013 Lesson 07** folder and save it as **EX07-R02-ShippingFee-[FirstInitialLastName]**.

2. Select **cell C21** and choose **Home→Number→dialog box launcher** ⬚.

   Notice that the contents of the range C21:D21 has been merged and centered.

3. Select the **Custom** category and choose **m/d/yyyy h:mm** as the format.

4. In the type box, edit the format to **m/d/yy h:mm AM/PM**; click **OK**.

   In addition to the date, cell C21 now shows the time and AM or PM as well.

Work with Conditional Formatting

5. Select the **range B4:B18**.

6. Choose **Home→Styles→ Conditional Formatting→ Highlight Cells Rules→A Date Occurring**.

   The A Date Occurring dialog box appears with the Yesterday option displayed.

7. Choose in **In the Last 7 Days** from the date list and choose **Green Fill with Dark Green Text** from the **With** list; click **OK**.

   The last four dates are highlighted in column B of the worksheet.

8. Select the **range E4:E18**.

9. Choose **Home→Styles→ Conditional Formatting→Color Scales→Green-White Color Scale**.

   The darkest green highlights the highest value, while the shades become lighter as the values decrease.

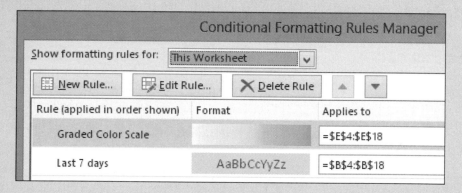

10. Select the **range C4:C18**.

11. Choose **Home→Styles→Conditional Formatting→Highlight Cells Rules→Text that Contains**.

12. Type **11** in the **Format Cells that Contain the Text** box and choose **Yellow Fill with Dark Yellow Text** from the **With** list; click **OK**.

    Next you will delete a conditional formatting rule.

13. Choose **Home→Styles→Conditional Formatting→Manage Rules**.

14. Choose to show formatting rules for **This Worksheet** and select the rule that displays yellow fill.

15. Click the **Delete Rule** button and click **OK**.

Now only these two conditional formatting rules remain in effect for the worksheet.

Name Cells and Ranges

16. Select **cell D19**.

17. Highlight **cell D19** in the Name Box, type **EstimatedTotal**, and tap Enter.

18. Follow the same steps to name **cell E19 ActualTotal**.

19. Select **cell F19**, type **=EstimatedTotal-ActualTotal**; confirm the formula.

    You have now calculated the total difference for all orders by using cell names within the formula.

20. Save and then close the file. Exit **Excel**.

21. Submit your final file based on the guidelines provided by your instructor.

    To view examples of how your file or files should look at the end of this exercise, go to the student resource center.

Apply Appropriate Formats

In this exercise, you will enter a date function that will calculate the current date. You will also apply cell styles to worksheet cells and change the fonts in the workbook theme.

Work with the Format Painter and Quick Styles

1. Start **Excel**. Open **EX07-R03-NonProfit** from the **EX2013 Lesson 07** folder and save it as **EX07-R03-NonProfit-[FirstInitialLastName]**.

2. Select **cell A4** and choose **Home→Clipboard→Format Painter** 🖌.

3. Select the **range B4:C4**, to which you will apply the formatting.

4. Select **cell A1**, choose **Home→Styles→Cell Styles**, and choose **Heading 1**.

Format with Themes

5. Choose **Page Layout→Themes→Theme Fonts** [A Fonts ▾].

6. Select the **Arial** theme.

Insert Date Functions and Formatting

7. Select **cell A12**, type **=NOW()**, and confirm your formula.

8. With **cell A12** selected, choose **Home→Number→Number Format ▼ menu→Long Date**.

   You decide that you do not like the appearance of the Long Date, so you will now create a custom date format.

Create Custom Formats

9. With **cell A12** highlighted, choose **Home→Number→dialog box launcher** 🗗.

10. Select the **Custom** category and choose **d-mmm** as the format.

11. In the Type box, edit the format to **d-mmm h:mm** and click **OK**.

Work with Conditional Formatting

12. Select the **range C5:C9**.

13. Choose **Home→Styles→Conditional Formatting→Color Scales→Red – White Color Scale**.

   This formatting applies the darkest shade of red to the highest rating, with progressively lighter shades applying to the ratings as they decrease.

14. With the **range C5:C9** selected, choose **Home→Styles→Conditional Formatting→Icon Sets > Three Traffic Lights (Unrimmed)**.

   Just like the color bars, the traffic light icons help to identify the magnitude of each rating.

15. With the **range C5:C9** selected, choose **Home→Styles→Conditional Formatting→Manage Rules**.

16. Select the **Icon Set** rule, choose **Delete Rule**, and click **OK**.

   Since the two rules accomplish the same goal, there is no need to display both.

Name Cells and Ranges

17. Select **cell C5**.

18. Highlight **cell C5** in the Name Box, type **FamilySupporters**, and tap [Enter].

19. Repeat **steps 17–18** to similarly name each cell in the **range C6:C9**.

    Remember that the apostrophe in Children's Assist *cannot be used within a defined name.*

20. Right-click the **row 10** heading and choose **Insert**.

21. Type **Average Rating** in **cell A10** and **=Average (** in **cell C10**.

22. Select **cell C5**.

    The defined name for cell C5 is entered into the formula.

23. Complete the formula by selecting each cell in the **range C6:C9**, using a comma to separate each cell reference.

    The defined names continue to display, making it easier to identify the components of the formula.

24. Save and then close the file. Exit **Excel**.

25. Submit your final file based on the guidelines provided by your instructor.

Apply Your Skills

Use the Format Painter, Themes, and Date Functions

In this exercise, you will use the Format Painter, apply themes to a worksheet, and insert the date using a date function.

Work with the Format Painter, Quick Styles, and Themes

1. Start **Excel**. Open **EX07-A01-RetailInventory** from the **EX2013 Lesson 07** folder and save it as **EX07-A01-RetailInventory-[FirstInitialLastName]**.

2. Select **cell B4** and apply the **Currency** cell style.

3. Use the **Format Painter** to apply the formatting from **cell A3** to the **range B3:C3**, and from **cell B4** to the **range B5:B8**.

4. Apply the **Mesh** theme to the workbook.
   Apply a theme of your choice if Mesh is not available.

5. Modify the workbook's theme font to **Corbel**.

Insert Date Functions and Formatting

6. Use a function to enter the current date in **cell A12**.

7. Format the entry in **cell A12** to display the current time in addition to the date.

8. Save and then close the file. Exit **Excel**.

9. Submit your final file based on the guidelines provided by your instructor.
   To view examples of how your file or files should look at the end of this exercise, go to the student resource center.

Add Conditional Formatting and Navigate with Cell Names

In this exercise, you will apply a conditional formatting rule to highlight low quantities of products in inventory. You will also navigate the worksheet using cell names.

Create Custom Formats and Work with Conditional Formatting

1. Start **Excel**. Open **EX07-A02-InternetInv** from the **EX2013 Lesson 07** folder and save it as **EX07-A02-InternetInv-[FirstInitialLastName]**.

2. Create a custom format for the date in **cell A12** so the time includes seconds.
   Within the type box, seconds are represented by ss.

3. Create a conditional formatting rule that highlights values below 200 in **column C**.
   Be sure not to apply the conditional formatting to the total row.

4. Create a conditional formatting rule that highlights values above 200 in **column C**.
   Be careful to apply a different highlight color. The second conditional format is not informative, so you decide to remove it.

5. Remove the conditional formatting rule you created in **step 4**.

Name Cells and Ranges

6. Ensure that the **range C4:C8** is still highlighted.
   Note in the name box that this range has already been named InternetQuantity.

7. Sum the product quantities in **cell C9** using this range name.

8. Create an appropriate defined name for **cell C9**.

9. Save and then close the file. Exit **Excel**.

10. Submit your final file based on the guidelines provided by your instructor.
    To view examples of how your file or files should look at the end of this exercise, go to the student resource center.

Format a Worksheet

In this exercise, you will use a variety of techniques to format a customer ratings worksheet.

Work with the Format Painter, Quick Styles, and Themes

1. Start **Excel**. Open **EX07-A03-CustomerRatings** from the **EX2013 Lesson 07** folder and save it as **EX07-A03-CustomerRatings-[FirstInitialLastName]**.

2. Use the **Format Painter** to apply formatting from **cell A4** to the **range B4:E4**.

3. Apply the **Title** cell style to **cell A1**.

4. Apply the **Facet** theme to the workbook.

5. Modify the theme color of the workbook to **Red Violet**.

Insert Date Functions and Formatting, and Create Custom Formats

6. Use the **Now** function to enter the date and time in **cell A12**.

7. Create a custom format for the dates in the **range B5:B9** to be consistent with Jan-01-2014.

Work with Conditional Formatting, and Name Cells and Ranges

8. Insert red data bars for all staff ratings.

9. Create a conditional formatting rule that highlights overall ratings greater than 3 with **Green Fill with Dark Green Text**.

10. Name the **range D5:D9** as **Staff_Ratings** and the **range E5:E9** as **Overall_Ratings**.

11. Write formulas in **cells D12 and E12**, using the range names you created, to show the average ratings.

12. Save and then close the file. Exit **Excel**.

13. Submit your final file based on the guidelines provided by your instructor.

Excel 2013

Extend Your Skills

In the course of working through the Extend Your Skills exercises, you will think critically as you use the skills taught in the lesson to complete the assigned projects. To evaluate your mastery and completion of the exercises, your instructor may use a rubric, with which more points are allotted according to performance characteristics. (The more you do, the more you earn!) Ask your instructor how your work will be evaluated.

EX07-E01 That's the Way I See It

In this exercise, you will create a worksheet listing your ten favorite musical artists. For each artist, list their musical genre, your favorite song by the artist, the most recent album, and the number of songs of each that you own. You can use the Internet to search for information as necessary.

Save your file as **EX07-E01-MusicalArtists-[FirstInitialLastName]** in the **EX2013 Lesson 07** folder.

Create appropriate headers and column titles within the worksheet. Use the Format Painter to apply formats throughout, enter the necessary data, and use conditional formatting to identify the three artists whose songs appear most in your music library. Apply the theme of your choice. Use a function to display the current date at the top of the worksheet, and for each artist use a function to display the date on which their most recent album was released. Then, create formulas that calculate the number of days since the release of each artist's most recent album.

You will be evaluated based on the inclusion of all elements specified, your ability to follow directions, your ability to apply newly learned skills to a real-world situation, your creativity, and the relevance of your topic and/or data choice(s). Submit your final file based on the guidelines provided by your instructor.

EX07-E02 Be Your Own Boss

In this exercise, you will format a worksheet listing all landscape architects used by your company, Blue Jean Landscaping, and their associated customer ratings.

Open **EX07-E02-Landscape** from the **EX2013 Lesson 07** folder and it save as **EX07-E02-Landscape-[FirstInitialLastName]**.

Apply appropriate formatting within the worksheet and use the Format Painter to copy it throughout. Use conditional formatting to highlight the contractor with the highest customer ratings and apply cell names to each cell containing a rating. Lastly, use a function to insert a custom date below all worksheet data that displays the date and time of worksheet completion, along with either "AM" or "PM."

You will be evaluated based on the inclusion of all elements specified, your ability to follow directions, your ability to apply newly learned skills to a real-world situation, your creativity, and your demonstration of an entrepreneurial spirit. Submit your final file based on the guidelines provided by your instructor.

Transfer Your Skills

In the course of working through the Transfer Your Skills exercises, you will use critical-thinking and creativity skills to complete the assigned projects using skills taught in the lesson. To evaluate your mastery and completion of the exercises, your instructor may use a rubric, with which more points are allotted according to performance characteristics. (The more you do, the more you earn!) Ask your instructor how your work will be evaluated.

EX07-T01 Use the Web as a Learning Tool

Throughout this book, you will be provided with an opportunity to use the Internet as a learning tool by completing WebQuests. According to the original creators of WebQuests, as described on their website (WebQuest.org), a WebQuest is "an inquiry-oriented activity in which most or all of the information used by learners is drawn from the web." To complete the WebQuest projects in this book, navigate to the student resource center and choose the WebQuest for the lesson on which you are currently working. The subject of each WebQuest will be relevant to the material found in the lesson.

WebQuest Subject: Effective application of conditional formatting

Submit your file(s) based on the guidelines provided by your instructor.

EX07-T02 Demonstrate Proficiency

You have created an information card that will be given to all customers at Stormy BBQ. You will be collecting customer information so you can maintain a customer list and use it to contact customers with promotional offers.

Open **EX07-T02-CustInfo** from the **EX2013 Lesson 07** folder and save it as **EX07-T02-CustInfo-[FirstInitialLastName]**.

Use the Format Painter to apply the existing formats throughout the worksheet. Ensure that the headers in rows 1 and 2 are consistent, and that the titles in row 4 are consistent. Enter the information for five of your friends in rows 5–9 and apply the formatting from row 5 throughout. Apply a theme of your choice to the worksheet and create a defined name for the range of data in rows 5–9. Lastly, insert a "created on" date (with appropriate label) that displays both the date and time of completion below all worksheet data. Write a paragraph (minimum of three sentences) below the data that details a new promotional offer that you plan to initiate utilizing the customer data collected.

Submit your final file based on the guidelines provided by your instructor.

Managing Multiple-Sheet Workbooks

LESSON OUTLINE

LEARNING OBJECTIVES

After studying this lesson, you will be able to:

- Sort worksheet rows in alphabetic and numeric order
- View nonadjacent areas of large worksheets and view multiple worksheets simultaneously
- Create formulas that summarize data from multiple worksheets
- Copy worksheets and their formats
- Print multiple worksheets of a workbook

In this lesson, you will learn several techniques for working with multiple-sheet workbooks. You will sort worksheet rows, freeze headings, and adjust print options. You will split the worksheet window to compare data from separate areas of a worksheet. You will organize workbooks by copying worksheets, moving worksheets, and linking formulas. Lastly, you will print selected worksheets by issuing a single command.

Tracking Project Expenses

Green Clean, a janitorial product supplier and cleaning service contractor, has developed a project budget. Your job is to create a workbook that tracks the year-to-date expenditures and consolidates the information on a summary worksheet. The summary worksheet will give you an instant overview of the amounts spent compared to the budget allocations. Formulas in the summary worksheet will be linked to cells in the detail sheets, where all the necessary detail information is stored.

	A	B
1	Advertising Tracking Sheet	
2		
3		Amount Spent
4	September	-
5	October	2,000
6	November	6,075
7	December	1,200
8	January	
9	February	
10	March	
11	April	
12	May	
13	June	
14	July	
15	August	
16	Total	$9,275

	A	B
1	Equipment Tracking Sheet	
2		
3		Amount Spent
4	September	8,547
5	October	3,640
6	November	5,072
7	December	1,211
8	January	
9	February	
10	March	
11	April	
12	May	
13	June	
14	July	
15	August	
16	Total	$9,923

	A	B	C
1	Mileage Tracking Sheet		
2			
3			Amount
		Mileage	Spent
4	September	720	317
5	October	885	389
6	November	280	123
7	December	420	185
8	January		-
9	February		-
10	March		-
11	April		-
12	May		-
13	June		-
14	July		-
15	August		-
16	Total	2,305	$1,014

	A	B	C
1	Training Materials Tracking Sheet		
2			
3		Amount Spent	
4	September	145	
5	October	1,620	
6	November	(1,705)	
7	December	730	
8	January		
9	February		
10	March		
11	April		
12	May		
13	June		
14	July		
15	August		
16	Total	$645	

	A	B	C
1	**Green Clean**		
2	**Budget and Expenses**		
3			
4	**General and Capital Expenses**	**Budget Allocation**	**Year-to-Date Spent**
5	Advertising	40,000	9,275
6	Equipment	25,000	9,923
7	Mileage	8,000	1,014
8	Training Materials	7,000	645

The summary worksheet tracks the totals from the detail sheets.

Sorting Worksheet Data

Video Library http://labyrinthelab.com/videos   Video Number: EX13-V0801

Excel can easily sort lists organized in alphabetic or numeric order. For example, you may sort by name, date, item number, or dollar amount. A sort is performed on all adjacent rows. You may, however, decide to select only certain rows to sort.

If a sorting problem arises and Undo is unavailable, close the workbook without saving it. Reopen the workbook to restore its original appearance.

Sorting by a Single Column

The Sort A to Z and Sort Z to A buttons let you sort quickly by one column. Sort A to Z sorts records in ascending order from lowest to highest, and Sort Z to A sorts in descending order from highest to lowest. Excel sorts all rows in the adjacent list unless it determines that the list has a header row.

Sorting Selected Rows

If the list contains rows you do not want included in the sort, you must select the rows you *do* want sorted before clicking one of the sort buttons. Excel will use column A as the sort key by default.

To keep data together for each record, always select *one cell* or *entire rows* before sorting. Do not highlight several cells in one column and then sort, as this sorts the selected cells only. The other cells belonging to each record will not move.

Sorting by Multiple Columns

The Sort dialog box is used to specify multiple sort keys for multiple-column sorts. For example, a worksheet displays last names in column A and first names in column B. Using the Sort dialog box, you may instruct Excel to sort the rows by last name and then by first name. You may also sort by more than two columns.

Last Name	First Name
Duran	Timothy
Alejo	Carmen
Martin	Michael
Carter	Aaron
Wintz	Siobhan
Carter	Adam

An unsorted list

Last Name	First Name
Alejo	Carmen
Carter	Aaron
Carter	Adam
Duran	Timothy
Martin	Michael
Wintz	Siobhan

A list sorted by last name and then first name

Task	Procedure
Sort by a single column	■ Select one cell in the desired column on or under the header row. ■ Choose Data→Sort & Filter→Sort A to Z [A↓Z] or Sort Z to A [Z↓A]
Sort selected rows by a single column	■ Select a cell in the sort key column, and select the rows to be sorted. ■ Choose Data→Sort & Filter→Sort A to Z [A↓Z] or Sort Z to A [Z↓A]
Sort by multiple columns	■ Select any cell within the data to be sorted and choose Data→Sort & Filter→Sort. ■ Choose the first column to be sorted from the Sort By list; change the Sort On and Order settings, if necessary. ■ Click Add Level to add additional sort categories and change their settings, if necessary. ■ If the list to be sorted has a header row, place a checkmark next to My Data Has Headers; click OK.

DEVELOP YOUR SKILLS EX08-D01

Sort Worksheet Columns

In this exercise, you will use the sort buttons and Sort dialog box to sort lists in a workbook.

1. Open **EX08-D01-ProjectBudget** from the **EX2013 Lesson 08** folder and save it as **EX08-D01-ProjectBudget-[FirstInitialLastName]**.

   Replace the bracketed text with your first initial and last name. For example, if your name is Bethany Smith, your filename would look like this: EX08-D01-ProjectBudget-BSmith.

2. Click the **Prior Year** sheet tab.

3. Follow these steps to sort the General and Capital Expenses by amount:

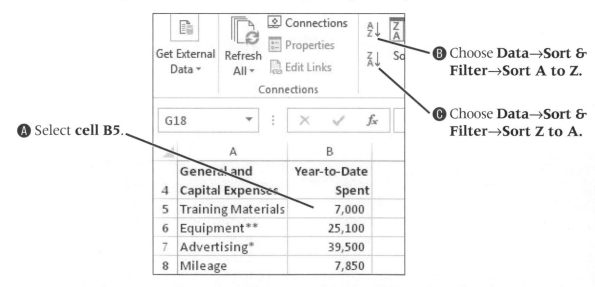

Ⓐ Select **cell B5**.

Ⓑ Choose **Data→Sort & Filter→Sort A to Z.**

Ⓒ Choose **Data→Sort & Filter→Sort Z to A.**

After sorting from A to Z you saw that the figures were presented from smallest to largest. Since this data will look better with the largest expenses on top, you decided to change the appearance and sort from Z to A.

4. Follow these steps to sort the Advertising Breakdown from largest to smallest:

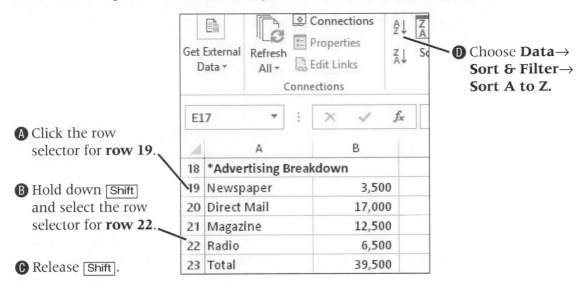

Ⓓ Choose **Data→ Sort & Filter→ Sort A to Z.**

Ⓐ Click the row selector for **row 19**.

Ⓑ Hold down ⎡Shift⎤ and select the row selector for **row 22**.

Ⓒ Release ⎡Shift⎤.

	A	B
18	*Advertising Breakdown	
19	Newspaper	3,500
20	Direct Mail	17,000
21	Magazine	12,500
22	Radio	6,500
23	Total	39,500

Only the selected data rows are sorted. You did not include the total in your selection.

5. Select any cell in the **range A11:C16**.

6. Choose **Data→Sort & Filter→Sort** 🔽.
The Sort dialog box appears.

7. Choose the options as shown to set the Sort By (first sort) settings.

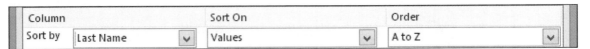

Column		Sort On		Order	
Sort by	Last Name	Values		A to Z	

8. Follow these steps to finish setting the sort criteria:

Ⓐ Click **Add Level** to add a second sort category.

Ⓑ Choose **Labor Expenses** for the second sort and make sure **Values** and **Largest to Smallest** are set as shown.

Ⓒ Make certain the **My Data Has Headers** option box is checked.

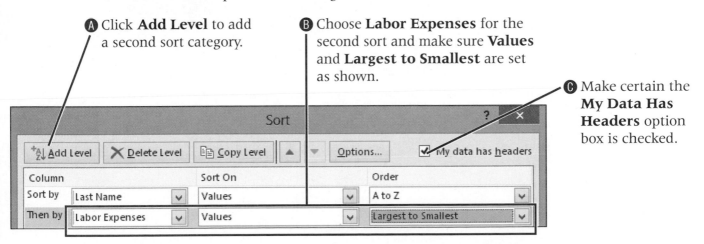

The sort will be performed on last names and then on labor expenses.

9. Click **OK**.
Notice that Adam Carter has higher labor expenses, and therefore appears above Aaron Carter.

10. Choose **Data**→**Sort & Filter**→**Sort** [Z↓A].

11. Change the second sort criteria to **First Name** (sorted A to Z) and then click **OK**.
    Now that First Name is the second sort category, Aaron Carter appears above Adam Carter.

12. Save the file and leave it open. You will modify it throughout this lesson.

Using Flexible Worksheet Views

Video Library   http://labyrinthelab.com/videos   Video Number: EX13-V0802

Excel allows you to view two areas of a large worksheet that normally could not be displayed together. When you are finished viewing this way, you can restore the worksheet to its original view. Two or more worksheets in the same workbook or different workbooks can also be viewed at once.

Freezing Rows or Columns

When you select the Freeze Panes command, Excel freezes all rows above the selected cell and all columns to the left of the selected cell. This "locks" the frozen rows and columns in place so they remain visible on the screen. This can be particularly useful for viewing headings while you scroll through a worksheet.

FROM THE RIBBON
View→Window→
Freeze Panes

Splitting the Worksheet Window

At times, you will want to split the window to scroll within two areas of a worksheet. For example, you may want to compare data in rows 3–15 with rows 203–215. You can use the Split command for this purpose. This type of command is called a toggle, as you click it once to switch it on and again to switch it off.

Splitting Compared to Freezing

Freezing is useful for keeping headings consistently visible. However, you may not easily view two nonadjacent groups of data by freezing rows and/or columns. Splitting the window allows you to view two or four nonadjacent groups. Each pane has its own set of scroll bars. You may drag the split bar to adjust the number of rows or columns displayed in each pane.

In this split window, each pane may be scrolled to view nonadjacent areas of the worksheet.

	A	B
10	Last Name	First Name
11	Alejo	Carmen
12	Carter	Aaron
15	Martin	Michael
16	Wintz	Siobhan

— Split bar

In this frozen window, headings remain visible regardless of where you scroll.

	A	B	C	D
1	Green Clean Website Usage			
2		Year 1		
3				
4	Last Name	Jan	Feb	Mar
18	Company N	18.5	36.0	15.5
19	Company O	7.0	2.0	16.0
20	Company P	1.5	0.0	0.0

TIP Use either Split or Freeze, but not both together. One does not operate correctly when the other is in effect.

QUICK REFERENCE	CONTROLLING WORKSHEET VIEWS
Task	**Procedure**
Freeze columns and rows	■ Select the cell below and to the right of the area to be frozen. ■ Choose View→Window→Freeze Panes ▦ menu ▼→Freeze Panes.
Freeze columns	■ Select the cell in row 1 of the column to the right of the column(s) to be frozen. ■ Choose View→Window→Freeze Panes ▦ menu ▼→Freeze Panes.
Freeze rows	■ Select the cell in column A of the row below the row(s) to be frozen. ■ Choose View→Window→Freeze Panes ▦ menu ▼→Freeze Panes.
Unfreeze all	■ Choose View→Window→Freeze Panes ▦ menu ▼→Unfreeze Panes.
Split a window between columns or rows	■ Select the first cell in the column to the right of (or row below) where the split is to occur. ■ Choose View→Window→Split ▦.
Adjust a split	■ Drag the split bar that divides the window panes.
Remove a split	■ Choose View→Window→Split ▦.

DEVELOP YOUR SKILLS EX08-D02

Freeze and Split Worksheets

In this exercise, you will freeze both rows and columns, and you will split a worksheet window into two panes to scroll and compare data in two areas.

1. Save your file as **EX08-D02-ProjectBudget-[FirstInitialLastName]**.

2. Choose the **Website Usage** worksheet and select **cell B5**.

3. Choose **View→Window→Freeze Panes ▦→Freeze Panes**.

   The area above and to the left of cell B5 is frozen, indicated by a horizontal and a vertical separation line.

4. Scroll to the right until the company totals are visible, and then scroll down to view the monthly totals.

The frozen column A and rows 1-4 remain visible, as you have frozen those areas of the worksheet.

5. Choose **File→Print** and view the preview in Backstage view.

The frozen panes do not affect printing, therefore the entire worksheet would print.

6. Tap ⟦Esc⟧ to exit the view without printing.

7. Press ⟦Ctrl⟧+⟦Home⟧ to jump back to the home cell.

Cell B5 is now the home cell because you froze the window panes at that location.

8. Choose **View→Window→Freeze Panes** ⊞**→Unfreeze Panes**.

Since you cannot both freeze and split a worksheet simultaneously, you unfreeze the worksheet here so you may next split it.

Display Split Bars

9. Follow these steps to split the window between columns:

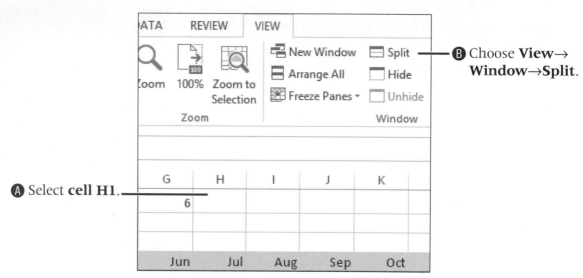

The window displays two panes with a gray split bar between them.

10. Drag the scroll bars within each pane and note that the panes move independently of one another.

11. Follow these steps to move the split bar:

Ⓐ Point to the split bar until the mouse pointer changes to a two-headed arrow.

Ⓑ Drag to the right until the split bar is to the right of **column M**.

Ensure that the split bar is positioned to the right of Column M in the window on the left.

12. Choose **View→Window→Split** 🔲 to remove the split.

Unlike Freeze Panes, the Split command toggles on and off when you click the same button.

13. Select **cell N5** and choose **View→Window→ Split**.

This time, the window splits into four panes because the pointer was not in the first cell of a row or column. The row 4 labels are in the upper panes because you selected a cell in row 5.

	L	M	N	O
1				
2			Year 2	
3				
4	Nov	Dec	Jan	Feb
5	13.0	7.0	2.0	7.5
6	18.0	17.5	10.0	8.5
7	0.0	0.0	0.0	4.0

14. Drag the scroll bars within each pane, and note that the panes move independently of one another.

15. Choose **View→Window→Split** 🔲 to remove the split.

16. Save the file and leave it open.

Viewing Worksheets in Multiple Windows

Video Library   http://labyrinthelab.com/videos   Video Number: EX13-V0803

As an alternative to splitting the worksheet window, you can display two areas of a large worksheet at once in separate windows. You can even display two or more worksheets in this way. The worksheets may be from the same workbook or different workbooks. This method allows you to compare, copy, or move data between worksheet areas more easily. Each window is numbered, and only one window can be active at one time.

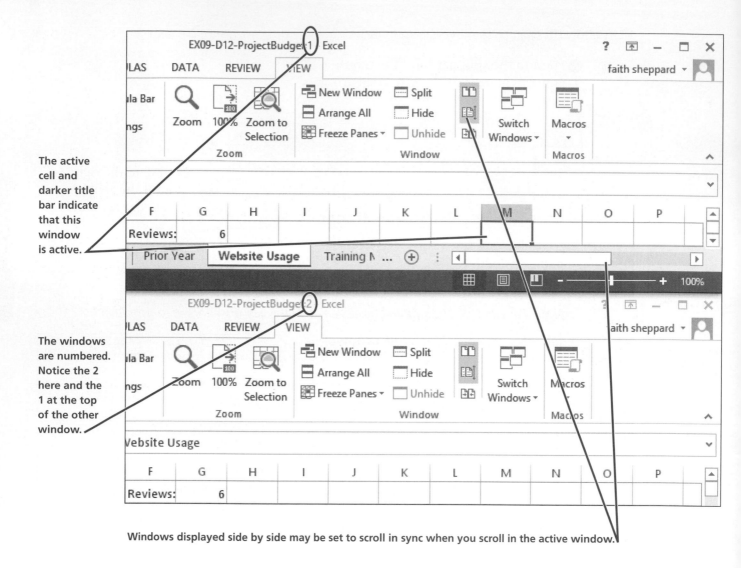

The active cell and darker title bar indicate that this window is active.

The windows are numbered. Notice the 2 here and the 1 at the top of the other window.

Windows displayed side by side may be set to scroll in sync when you scroll in the active window.

Synchronous Scrolling

Once windows are arranged, they may be scrolled independently with the scroll bars in each window. However, you may want to use synchronous scrolling so that the view in both windows moves simultaneously in the same direction as you scroll in the active window. This feature can keep the rows or columns aligned in the windows to help you compare data. To use synchronous scrolling, the windows must be set to be viewed side by side.

Creating Custom Worksheet Views

You can save certain display settings and print settings as custom views to redisplay later. You can create multiple custom views in a worksheet. A custom view, however, can be applied only to the worksheet for which you created the custom view.

To manage custom views, include the worksheet name when creating a custom view name.

Task	Procedure
View two areas of the same worksheet	■ Choose View→Window→New Window ▣. ■ Choose View→Window→Switch Windows ▣ menu ▼ and select the desired active window. ■ Choose View→Window→View Side by Side ▣. If necessary, select the second window and click OK. The active window will appear on top or to the left.
View two worksheets from the same workbook	■ Display the first worksheet, and choose View→Window→New Window ▣. ■ Click the tab of the second worksheet in the new window and arrange the windows as desired.
View two worksheets from different workbooks	■ Display the first worksheet. ■ Choose File→Open, navigate to the desired workbook, display the second worksheet, and arrange the windows as desired.
Scroll windows synchronously	■ Use one of the previous procedures to set up two or more windows and choose View→Window→View Side by Side ▣. ■ If Synchronous Scrolling does not turn on automatically, choose View→Window→Synchronous Scrolling.
Arrange windows	■ Choose View→Window→Arrange All ▤ and select a display option from the list.
Create a custom view	■ Change the worksheet display and print settings as desired. ■ Choose View→Workbook Views→Custom Views and click Add. ■ Enter a view name, and select the desired options.
Display a custom view	■ Choose View→Workbook Views→Custom Views. ■ Double-click the desired view in the Custom Views dialog box.

Excel 2013

DEVELOP YOUR SKILLS EX08-D03

Arrange Multiple Worksheet Windows

In this exercise, you will view nonadjacent areas of a worksheet in separate windows and scroll them synchronously. You will also arrange two worksheets from a workbook to view them simultaneously.

1. Save your file as **EX08-D03-ProjectBudget-[FirstInitialLastName]**.

2. Display the **Website Usage** worksheet.

3. Choose **View→Window→New Window** ▣.

   The Excel title bar displays EX08-D03-ProjectBudget-FirstInitialLastName:2 to indicate the window you just created.

4. Choose **View→Window→Switch Windows** ▣ and select **EX08-D03-ProjectBudget-FirstInitialLastName:1**.

   The EX08-D03-ProjectBudget-FirstInitialLastName:1 window is now the active window.

5. Choose **View→Window→View Side by Side** ▣.

   The EX08-D03-ProjectBudget-FirstInitialLastName:1 window appears to the left of the other window because it was active when you chose the side-by-side view. If you have other workbooks open, a dialog box will appear from which you can choose the desired workbook. If the windows do not appear side-by-side, this will be remedied in the next step.

6. Choose **View→Window→Arrange All** 🗗, choose **Horizontal**, and click **OK**.

   The windows are arranged top to bottom.

7. Choose **View→Window→Synchronous Scrolling** 📖 from either window to toggle off synchronous scrolling.

   The Synchronous Scrolling toggle button now should not appear highlighted when the window is active.

8. Follow these steps to compare data between the two worksheets:

Ⓐ Select **cell B5** in the EX08-D03-ProjectBudget-FirstInitialLastName:1 worksheet.

Ⓑ Choose **View→Window→Freeze Panes→Freeze Panes**.

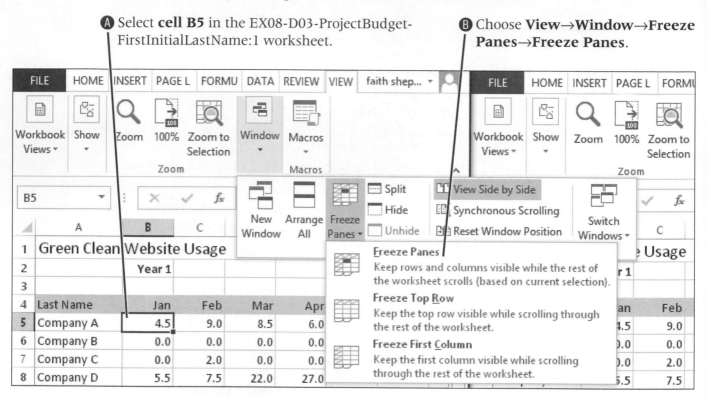

Ⓒ Repeat the prior two steps for the second worksheet.

Ⓓ Scroll to the right in the second worksheet until **column N** appears.

Since you turned off synchronous scrolling, only the active worksheet scrolled here.

9. Choose **View→Window→Synchronous Scrolling** 📖 to toggle on synchronous scrolling.

10. Click in the **EX08-D03-ProjectBudget-FirstInitialLastName:1** window, scroll to the right, and watch the other window scroll as well.

11. Click in the **EX08-D03-ProjectBudget-FirstInitialLastName:2** window and close it.

View Worksheets in the Same Workbook

12. Choose **View→Window→New Window** ⊞.

13. Click the **Summary** sheet tab in the **EX08-D03-ProjectBudget-FirstInitialLastName:2** window.

14. Choose **View→Window→Arrange All**, select **Tiled**, and click **OK**.

    The Summary sheet and Website Usage sheet display side by side. Since synchronous scrolling is off, you could scroll one sheet without impacting the other.

15. Close the **Summary** sheet window, maximize the **Website Usage** sheet window, and **Unfreeze** the panes.

16. Save the file and leave it open.

Printing Multipage Worksheets

| Video Library | http://labyrinthelab.com/videos | Video Number: EX13-V0804 |

Excel offers a variety of options that can improve the appearance of multipage worksheets when they are printed.

Sizing Options

The Page Setup and Scale to Fit command groups on the Page Layout tab contain options to help fit large worksheets on printed pages.

 You can use the orientation, margin presets, paper size, and scaling presets available in the Print tab of Backstage view to correct the worksheet size just before printing.

Margins

Margins determine the space between the edge of the paper and the worksheet. You may choose from three preset margin layouts—Normal, Wide, and Narrow—as well as a Custom Margins option. Choose Narrow to fit more columns and rows on the printed page. Choose Custom Margins to launch the Page Setup dialog box with the Margins tab displayed. On this tab you may set specific worksheet margins and center the worksheet horizontally and/or vertically on the paper.

Excel 2013

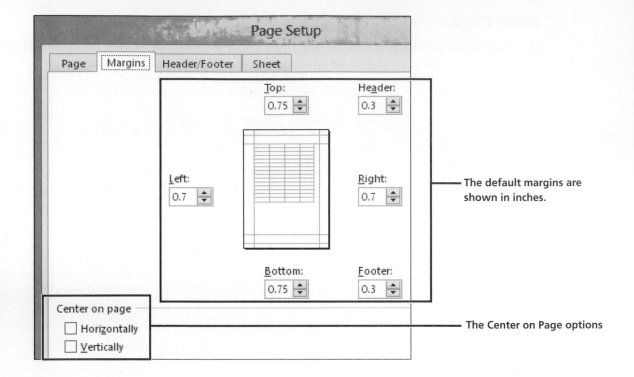

The default margins are shown in inches.

The Center on Page options

Orientation

Orientation indicates the direction of printing. Portrait is the default and prints across the narrow edge of the paper. Landscape orientation prints across the wide edge of the paper.

Portrait orientation   Landscape orientation

Size

The Size option refers to the paper size. The default is Letter 8.5″ x 11″ paper, while alternatives include Legal 8.5″ x 14″ paper.

Print Area

To print only a specific portion of your worksheet, you may set any range of cells as the print area. The Set Print Area command makes the range permanent until you set a different range or choose Clear Print Area to restore the entire worksheet for printing.

Scale to Fit

The Scale to Fit command group on the Page Layout tab provides automated scaling options to adjust the worksheet size for printing.

- **Width:** You may reduce the size of a worksheet containing many columns to fit its width on one, two, or more pages, as appropriate.

- **Height:** You may reduce the size of a worksheet containing many rows to fit its height on one, two, or more pages, as appropriate.

- **Scale:** To adjust the width and height in the same proportion, change the Scale, which is set to 100 percent by default. To use Scale, the Width and Height must be set to Automatic.

To reset the Height and Width to normal size, choose Automatic from each drop-down list. Make certain to change Scale to 100%, as the percentage does not reset automatically. The Undo command cannot reverse any Scale to Fit settings.

QUICK REFERENCE	SETTING PRINT OPTIONS
Task	**Procedure**
Display Page Layout View	■ Choose View→Workbook Views→Page Layout View 🗔 or click the Page Layout View button.
Change to preset margins	■ Choose Page Layout→Page Setup→Adjust Margins 🗔 menu ▼ and choose Normal, Wide, or Narrow.
Change specific margins	■ Choose Page Layout→Page Setup→Adjust Margins 🗔 menu ▼ and choose Custom Margins. ■ Change the Top, Bottom, Left, or Right margins.
Center the worksheet on printed page(s)	■ Choose Page Layout→Page Setup→dialog box launcher 🗔; click the Margins tab. ■ Under Center on Page, place a checkmark next to Horizontally and Vertically.
Change the orientation	■ Choose Page Layout→Page Setup→Change Page Orientation 🗔 menu ▼ and choose Portrait or Landscape.
Change paper size	■ Choose Page Layout→Page Setup→Choose Page Size 🗔 menu ▼ and choose a paper size.
Scale the worksheet to fit on fewer pages	■ Choose Page Layout→Scale to Fit, select 100% in the Scale box, type the desired percentage, and tap Enter.
Scale the worksheet width or height	■ Choose Page Layout→Scale to Fit→Width menu ▼ or Height menu ▼ and set the desired number of pages.
Set a print range	■ Select the desired cells, and choose Page Layout→Page Setup→Print Area ▼→ Set Print Area.
Remove the print range	■ Choose Page Layout→Page Setup→Print Area 🗔 menu ▼→Clear Print Area.

Use Orientation, Margin, and Sizing Options

In this exercise, you will change the orientation and margins. You also will scale a worksheet to print on fewer pages. You will use commands on the Ribbon as well as in the Page Setup dialog box.

1. Save your file as **EX08-D04-ProjectBudget-[FirstInitialLastName]**.

2. Display the **Website Usage** worksheet in **Page Layout View** at **40%** zoom.

   When you change sizing options you can see those changes within Page Layout view, but not within Normal view.

   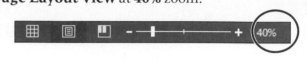

3. Choose **Page Layout→Page Setup→Change Page Orientation** →**Landscape**.

   Note that the entire worksheet will not fit on one page in Landscape orientation.

4. Choose **Page Layout→Page Setup→Adjust Margins** →**Narrow**.

   Decreasing the margins allows more columns and rows to fit on a page.

5. Go to **Page Layout→Scale to Fit→Scale**, change the scale to **42**, and tap Enter.

   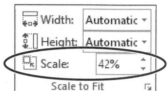

   The data now fits on one page, but would be too small to read if it were printed.

6. Change 42% in the Scale box to **100** and tap Enter.

   You manually changed the scale back to 100 because the Undo button wouldn't have worked in this instance.

7. Choose **Page Layout→Scale to Fit→Height menu** ▼→**1 page**.

   Now that the height is set to one page, the entire worksheet fits on two pages across.

Set the Print Area and Adjust Margins

8. Display the **Website Usage** worksheet in **Page Layout** view at **100%** zoom.

9. Follow these steps to set the print area for a portion of the year 1 data:

Ⓐ Choose **View→Workbook Views→Normal View**.

Ⓑ Select the range **A1:G14**.

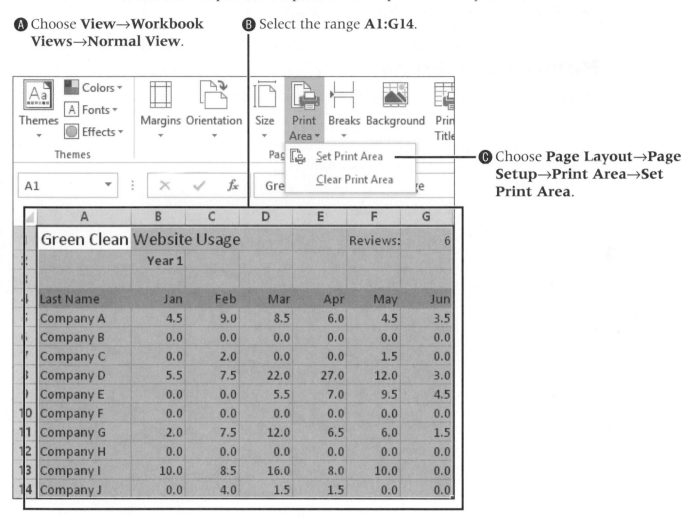

Ⓒ Choose **Page Layout→Page Setup→Print Area→Set Print Area**.

The print area appears surrounded by a border when you click any cell within the worksheet.

10. Choose **File→Print**.

   Notice that Excel would print only the cells that you set as the print area.

11. Exit Backstage view and choose **Page Layout→Page Setup→Print Area**⬚**→Clear Print Area**.

   The border disappears because the print area has now been reset.

12. Display the **Summary** worksheet in Page Layout view.

13. Choose **Page Layout→Page Setup→Adjust Margins** ⬚**→Custom Margins**.

   If multiple custom margins options appear, select the last one within the menu.

14. In the Center on Page area, place a checkmark next to **Horizontally** and **Vertically**, and click **OK**.

The worksheet would now be centered on the page if it were printed.

15. Save the file and leave it open.

Headers and Footers

Video Library   http://labyrinthelab.com/videos   Video Number: EX13-V0805

Headers print at the top of every page and footers print at the bottom of every page. Excel provides a variety of predesigned headers and footers. You may even create customized headers and footers to suit your needs and create a different header and footer on odd and even pages for double-sided printing.

Summary			1 of 1			11/14/2012	
Green Clean					Reviews:		
Budget and Expenses			11/13/2012				

A header displayed in Page Layout view

Use Page Layout view or the Print Preview in Backstage view to see headers and footers. They do not display in Normal view.

Creating and Formatting Headers and Footers

Headers and footers are created most conveniently in Page Layout view. Excel divides headers and footers into left, center, and right sections of the page. You need not fill in all three sections. To activate a section, just click in it to display the Design tab filled with header and footer options. When you choose an option from the Header & Footer Elements command group, Excel displays a code to represent the item. When you click outside the header section, Excel converts the code to properly display the selected option.

&[Time]	Excel's Current Time code		11:33 AM	Appearance of Current Time when printed

You may format headers and footers by changing elements such as the font, size, and color.

Task	Procedure
Display Page Layout view	■ Choose View→Workbook Views→Page Layout View 📄 or click Page Layout on the Status Bar.
Select a predesigned page header or footer	■ Display Page Layout 📄 view. ■ Select Click to Add Header above or Click to Add Footer below the worksheet. ■ Choose Header & Footer Tools→Design→Header & Footer→Header (or Footer) menu ▼ and choose a predesigned item.
Create a custom page header or footer	■ Display Page Layout 📄 view. ■ Select the left, center, or right header section above, or footer section below, the worksheet. ■ Type text and set options from the Header & Footer Elements command group.
Set header and footer margins	■ Choose Page Layout→Page Setup→dialog box launcher 🔲. ■ Click the Margins tab and change the Header or Footer margin.
Create a different header and/or footer to print on page 1	■ Choose Page Layout→Page Setup→dialog box launcher. ■ Click the Header/Footer tab, place a checkmark next to Different First Page, and click OK. ■ Display the worksheet in Page Layout view, and create the desired header/footer on pages 1 and 2.
Create different headers and/or footers to print on odd and even pages	■ Choose Page Layout→Page Setup→dialog box launcher. ■ Click the Header/Footer tab, place a checkmark next to Different Odd and Even Pages, and click OK. ■ Display the worksheet in Page Layout view, create the desired header/footer on an odd page, and then create the desired header/footer on an even page.
Remove a header or footer	■ Select any section of the header or footer, choose Header & Footer Tools→Design→Header & Footer→Header (or Footer) menu ▼, and choose (None).

Excel 2013

DEVELOP YOUR SKILLS EX08-D05

Set the Header and Footer

In this exercise, you will select predefined headers and footers, remove a footer, create custom headers and footers, and change the margins for these items.

1. Save your file as **EX08-D05-ProjectBudget-[FirstInitialLastName]**.

2. Select the **Website Usage** worksheet.

3. Choose **Page Layout view** and change the zoom level to **75%**.

4. Scroll up to the top of the page, if necessary, and choose **Click to Add Header**.

					Click to add header
Green Clean Website Usage			Reviews:	6	
	Year 1				

The center header section is activated, and the Design tab displays.

5. Choose **Header & Footer Tools→Design→Header & Footer→Header** and select **Page 1 of ?**.

   The "?" will update within the header to show the total number of pages.

6. Scroll to the bottom of the page.

7. Select **Click to Add Footer** in the center footer section.

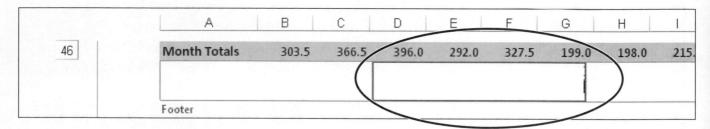

8. Choose **Header & Footer Tools→Design→Header & Footer→Footer→Website Usage**.

   The sheet name now displays within the footer of each page.

9. Select the footer, choose **Header & Footer Tools→Design→Header & Footer→Footer**, and select **(None)** to remove the footer.

10. Select the left header section, choose **Header & Footer Tools→Design→Header & Footer Elements→Sheet Name**.

    The Sheet Name code is displayed.

11. To complete the header, type a comma, tap [Spacebar], and choose **Header & Footer Tools→Design→Header & Footer Elements→File Name**.

    Although the header presently displays the codes for Sheet Name and File Name, the actual names will appear.

12. Select the right header section, type your name, and click outside the header.

13. Click any cell within the spreadsheet and select **Page Layout→Page Setup→dialog box launcher**.

14. Follow these steps to change the header and footer margins:

Ⓐ Display the **Margins** tab.

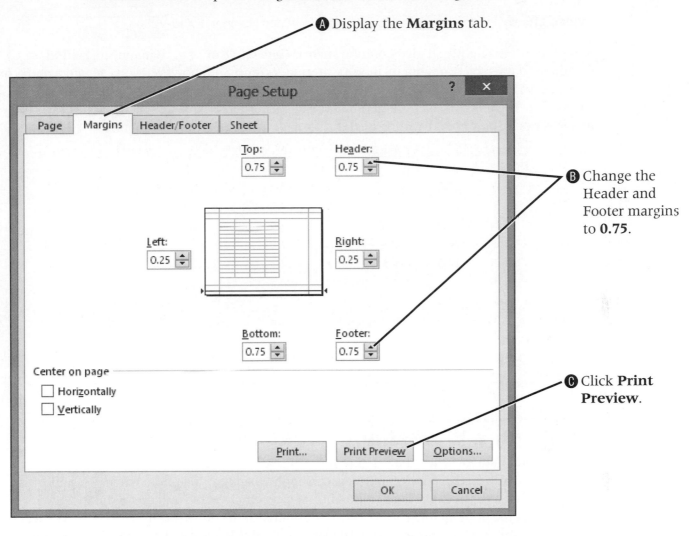

Ⓑ Change the Header and Footer margins to **0.75**.

Ⓒ Click **Print Preview**.

Note that the header and footer now overlap the data within the worksheet.

15. Click the **Page Setup** link at the bottom of the list of print options.

16. Under the Margins tab, change the **Header and Footer** margins to **0.3**, click **OK** and exit backstage view.

17. Save the file and leave it open.

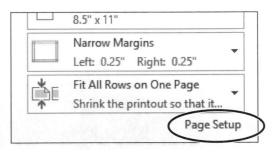

Excel 2013

Adding a Watermark Image

Video Library   http://labyrinthelab.com/videos   Video Number: EX13-V0806

A watermark is a lightly shaded notation such as *Confidential* or *Draft* that appears behind document data. Excel does not include a watermark command; however, you can add a photo or transparent image to a header or footer to achieve a watermark effect on each page of the worksheet. The image must be larger than the header or footer area in which you place it. The image is not displayed in the worksheet until you deselect the header or footer.

0.0	8.5	16.0	8.0	10.0	0.0	2.5	8.5	12.5	17.0	9.5	4.5	0
8.5	36.0	15.5	25.5	16.0	10.0	2.5	1.5	17.0	24.5	16.0	13.5	2
7.0	2.0	16.0	4.5	13.0	8.0	4.0	2.0	14.0	3.5	9.0	3.0	16
4.5	9.0	8.5	6.0	4.5	3.5	0.0	2.0	4.5	11.5	13.0	7.0	0
0.0	0.0	0.0	0.0	14.0	17.5	17.5	12.5	0.0	24.0	35.0	19.5	18
5.5	25.5	16.0	10.0	2.5	1.5	17.0	24.5	16.0	13.5	5.5	7.5	2
6.0	4.5	13.0	8.0	4.0	2.0	14.0	3.5	9.0	3.0	0.0	0.0	16
5.0	19.5	22.0	0.0	0.0	0.0	0.0	0.0	0.0	0.0	0.0	0.0	1
3.5	366.5	396.0	292.0	327.5	199.0	198.0	215.5	282.0	379.5	378.0	310.5	256

A logo watermark

Applying a Worksheet Background

You can use a photo or other image to fill the background and then turn off the gridlines to better display the image. For example, you can apply a background photo when you publish a workbook as a web page. The background image is repeated across and down the sheet, which requires that the original image be scaled appropriately and contrast well with the worksheet text colors. The image cannot be adjusted in Excel. The background image will not be included on a printed worksheet.

Green Clean Website Usage			
	Year 1		
Last Name	Jan	Feb	Mar
Company A	4.5	9.0	8.5
Company B	0.0	0.0	0.0
Company C	0.0	2.0	0.0
Company D	5.5	7.5	22.0

A photo background should contrast well with worksheet text.

Task	Procedure
Add a watermark image to a worksheet	■ Select the left, center, or right section of the header or footer. ■ Choose Header & Footer Tools→Design→Header & Footer Elements→Picture, navigate to the desired image, and double-click the image. ■ Choose Header & Footer Tools→Design→Header & Footer Elements→Format Picture and adjust the size, cropping, and image control as desired.
Remove a watermark image	■ Click in the appropriate header or footer section, which selects &[Picture], and tap Delete.
Apply a repeating background to a worksheet	■ Choose Page Layout→Page Setup→Background, navigate to the desired image file, and double-click the image.
Remove a background	■ Choose Page Layout→Page Setup→Delete Background.

Excel 2013

DEVELOP YOUR SKILLS EX08-D06

Apply a Watermark and Background to Sheets

In this exercise, you will add both a watermark effect and a "Draft" background image to a worksheet.

1. Save your file as **EX08-D06-ProjectBudget-[FirstInitialLastName]**.

2. Display the **Website Usage** sheet in **Page Layout** view and select the center header section.

   The page numbering within the header should now be selected.

3. Choose **Header & Footer Tools→Design→Header & Footer Elements→Picture** .

4. Navigate to your **EX2013 Lesson 08** folder through the From a File section, select **EX08-D06-GreenWater**, and click **Insert**.

   The header section displays the code &[Picture] in place of the page numbering, but the image is not displayed while the header is selected.

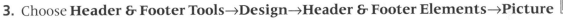

Website Usage				Reviews:		6
Year 1						
Jan	Feb	Mar	Apr	May	Jun	Jul
4.5	9.0	8.5	6.0	4.5	3.5	0.0
0.0	0.0	0.0	0.0	0.0	0.0	0.0
0.0	2.0	0.0	0.0	1.5	0.0	0.0
5.5	7.5	22.0	27.0	12.0	3.0	4.5
0.0	0.0	5.5	7.0	9.5	4.5	13.0
0.0	0.0	0.0	0.0	0.0	0.0	0.0
2.0	7.5	12.0	6.5	6.0	1.5	0.5

5. Click any cell in the worksheet to deselect the header.

   The image now displays on every page of the worksheet and would appear if it were printed.

6. Display the **Summary** sheet in Normal view.

7. Choose **Page Layout→Page Setup→Background** ⊞.

8. Navigate to your **EX2013 Lesson 08** folder through the From a File section, select **EX08-D06-DraftBack**, and click **Insert**.

   Excel now repeats as many copies of the word "Draft" as will fit based on the image size.

9. Press Ctrl + P to display the Print tab of Backstage view

   Notice in the preview that the background would not *print.*

10. Exit **Backstage view** without printing; save the file and leave it open.

Setting Title Rows and Columns

Video Library   http://labyrinthelab.com/videos   Video Number: EX13-V0807

You may specify one or more rows as title rows and one or more columns as title columns. Title rows and columns are printed on every page of a worksheet. This can be beneficial when worksheet data extends to multiple pages and requires headers to be fully understood.

The Title Rows and Title Columns options are not available if you display the Page Setup dialog box from within the Print tab of Backstage view. To use these options, you must launch the Page Setup dialog box from the Page Layout tab.

Sheet Options

The Sheet Options command group of the Page Layout tab contains options that affect the worksheet view and all printed pages of the worksheet. You may choose some options separately for viewing the worksheet and for printing.

Gridlines

By default, light gray gridlines surround every cell in the worksheet view. However, these gridlines do not print by default. In large worksheets, you may find it useful to print with gridlines to help track data across rows and down columns.

Company J	0.0	4.0	1.5
Company K	7.0	2.0	16.0
Company L	0.0	24.0	35.0

The printed worksheet without gridlines (the default setting)

Company J	0.0	4.0	1.5
Company K	7.0	2.0	16.0
Company L	0.0	24.0	35.0

The printed worksheet with gridlines

Headings

By default, column headings (letters A, B, C, etc.) and row headings (numbers 1, 2, 3, etc.) do not print. Similar to gridlines, these can also be included on the printed worksheet, if desired.

Task	Procedure
Print title rows on every page	■ Choose Page Layout→Page Setup→Print Titles 🖶. ■ Click in the Rows to Repeat at Top box. ■ Drag to select the desired rows in the worksheet; click Print Preview or OK.
Print title columns on every page	■ Choose Page Layout→Page Setup→Print Titles 🖶. ■ Click in the Columns to Repeat at Left box. ■ Drag to select the desired columns in the worksheet; click Print Preview or OK.
Print gridlines	■ Choose Page Layout→Sheet Options→Gridlines→Print Gridlines.
Print column and row headings	■ Choose Page Layout→Sheet Options→Headings→Print Headings.

QUICK REFERENCE: **SETTING TITLES, GRIDLINES, AND HEADINGS**

DEVELOP YOUR SKILLS EX08-D07
Set Sheet Options

In this exercise, you will set options to print repeating title rows and title columns, gridlines, and row and column headings on a multipage worksheet.

1. Save your file as **EX08-D07-ProjectBudget-[FirstInitialLastName]**.

2. Display the **Website Usage** worksheet in **Page Layout** view; click **cell A1**.

3. Choose **Page Layout→Page Setup→Print Titles** 🖶.

4. Follow these steps to set title rows and title columns:

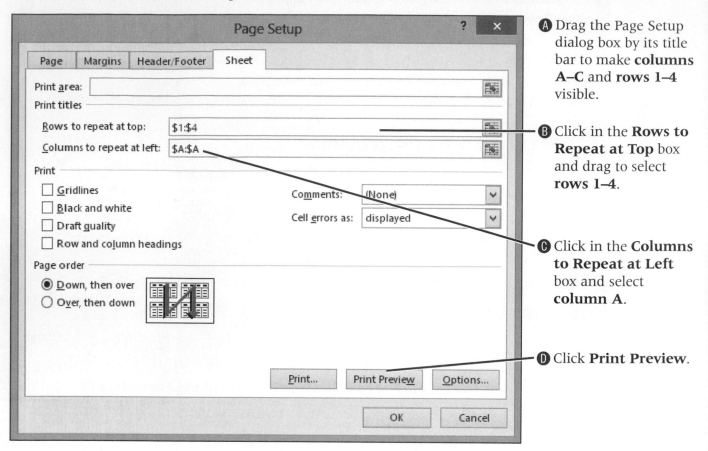

A Drag the Page Setup dialog box by its title bar to make **columns A–C** and **rows 1–4** visible.

B Click in the **Rows to Repeat at Top** box and drag to select **rows 1–4**.

C Click in the **Columns to Repeat at Left** box and select **column A**.

D Click **Print Preview**.

5. Click the **Next Page** button below the print preview in Backstage view.

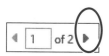

Note that the title rows and column repeat on the second page of the printed worksheet.

6. Exit Backstage view without printing; then display **Normal** view.

Turn Gridlines and Headings On and Off

7. Choose **Page Layout→Sheet Options→Gridlines→View Gridlines** to turn gridlines off.

8. Follow these steps to turn gridlines back on and to display gridlines and headings when you print:

A Choose **Page Layout→Sheet Options→Gridlines→View Gridlines**.

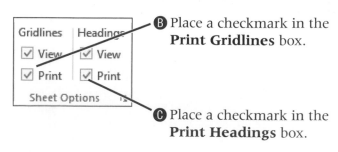

B Place a checkmark in the **Print Gridlines** box.

C Place a checkmark in the **Print Headings** box.

9. Choose **File→Print** and click the **Zoom to Page** ⊡ in the lower-right corner of Backstage view to zoom in.

   Gridlines appear as dotted lines but will print as solid lines. The column headings and row headings display as well.

10. Exit **Backstage view** without printing; save the file and leave it open.

Working with Page Breaks

Video Library   http://labyrinthelab.com/videos   Video Number: EX13-V0808

You can use Page Break Preview to see where Excel's automatic page breaks occur in a worksheet and which part of the worksheet will be printed. This view also allows you to insert additional page breaks manually when they are needed. In Page Break Preview, the print area appears in white. Nonprinting areas appear in gray.

Adjusting Automatic Page Breaks

Excel formats most printed worksheets by inserting automatic page breaks when pages are full. An automatic page break appears as a dashed line. You may adjust the location of a page break by clicking and dragging it in Page Break Preview. The page break then displays as a solid line, indicating that it is a manual page break.

	M	N	O	P	Q	R	S	T	U
1									
2		Year 2							
3									
4	Dec	Jan	Feb	Mar	Apr	May	Jun	Jul	Aug
5	7.0	2.0	7.5	12.0	6.5	6.0	1.5	0.5	9.0
6	17.5	10.0	8.5	16.0	8.0	10.0	0.0	2.5	8.5
7	0.0	0.0	4.0	1.5	1.5	0.0	0.0	3.5	0.0
8	27.0	18.5	36.0	15.5	25.5	21.⟷	10.0	2.5	6.5
9	12.0	7.0	2.0	16.0	4.5	13.0	8.0	14.0	16.0

This page break is being dragged to the left.

When adjusting page breaks, you cannot *increase* columns or rows on a full page without adjusting other print options.

Excel 2013

Inserting and Removing Page Breaks

You must select a cell in an appropriate column or row before inserting a manual page break. The page break appears as a solid line in the column to the left of or the row above the selected cell. You may remove any manual page break. If necessary, Excel inserts automatic page breaks after you remove manual page breaks.

QUICK REFERENCE	SETTING PAGE BREAKS
Task	**Procedure**
Adjust an automatic page break	■ Choose Page Break Preview ⊞ from the Status Bar. ■ Drag a vertical dashed automatic page break line to the left or a horizontal page break line up.
Add a manual page break	■ Choose Page Break Preview ⊞ from the Status Bar. ■ Select a cell below and/or to the right of the desired page break location. ■ Choose Page Layout→Page Setup→Breaks ⊟ menu ▼→Insert Page Break; or, right-click the cell and choose Insert Page Break.
Remove a manual page break	■ Choose Page Break Preview ⊞ from the Status Bar. ■ Select the cell to the right of the desired vertical page break line and/or below a horizontal page break line. ■ Choose Page Layout→Page Setup→Breaks ⊟ menu ▼→Remove Page Break; or, right-click the cell and choose Remove Page Break.

DEVELOP YOUR SKILLS EX08-D08

Work with Page Breaks

In this exercise, you will move, add, and remove a page break in Page Break Preview.

1. Save your file as **EX08-D08-ProjectBudget-[FirstInitialLastName]**.

2. On the **Website Usage** worksheet, press ⸢Ctrl⸣+⸢Home⸣ to display **cell A1**.

3. Click the **Page Break Preview** button from the Status Bar.

4. Click anywhere on the blue automatic page break line and drag to the left until it is to the left of **column N**.

5. Select a cell within **page 1** and choose **File→Print**.

6. Click the **Zoom to Page** ⊡ button at the lower-right corner of the print preview in Backstage view.

   Notice that page 1 ends with column M, which contains the December data for year 1.

7. Exit Backstage view without printing.

8. In **Page Break Preview**, select any cell in **column H**, which contains July data.

9. Choose **Page Layout→Page Setup→Breaks** ⊟→**Insert Page Break**.

   A solid blue, manual page break line now appears to the left of column H.

10. Point to any cell in **column T**, right-click, and choose **Insert Page Break**.

    Do not move the pointer off column T as you right-click.

11. Use either method you just learned to add a page break to the left of **column Z**.
   The worksheet would now print on five pages.

12. Select any cell in **column H**.

13. Choose **Page Layout→Page Setup→Breaks** 📑**→Remove Page Break**.

14. Point to any cell in **column T**, **right-click**, and choose **Remove Page Break**.

15. Use either method you just learned to remove the page break to the left of **column Z**.
   The worksheet now contains only one page break to the left of column N.

16. Save the file and leave it open.

Using Multiple Worksheets

Video Library   http://labyrinthelab.com/videos   Video Number: EX13-V0809

Like pages in a word-processing document, multiple worksheets are a convenient way to organize data logically into more manageable sections. Any worksheet can contain formulas that perform calculations on data contained in other worksheets. For example, you may set up a summary worksheet that totals data from multiple detail worksheets. You may also change the default number of sheets for new workbooks using the Excel Options dialog box.

Selecting Multiple Sheets

Cell entries and formatting may be created in the same cell or range of multiple sheets simultaneously. This action is recommended when the sheets have an identical structure. You can also perform other simultaneous actions to the selected sheets, such as inserting a row.

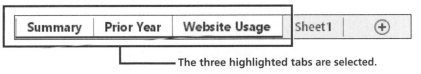

The three highlighted tabs are selected.

QUICK REFERENCE	USING MULTIPLE SHEETS
Task	**Procedure**
Change the default number of sheets for new workbooks	▪ Choose File→Options, and select the General category. ▪ In the When Creating New Workbooks section, indicate the desired number of sheets and click OK.
Select multiple worksheets	▪ Display the first sheet to be included in the selection. ▪ Hold down Ctrl and click each additional sheet tab desired; or, hold down Shift and click a sheet tab to include a consecutive range of sheets.
Remove sheets from the selection	▪ Hold down Ctrl and click a sheet tab to deselect it, click a sheet tab outside the selection to cancel a multiple selection; or, hold down Shift and click the first selected sheet tab to cancel an adjacent selection.

Select Multiple Sheets

In this exercise, you will change the number of sheets in new workbooks and select multiple worksheets.

1. Save your file as **EX08-D09-ProjectBudget-[FirstInitialLastName]**.

2. Choose **File→Options** to display the General options in the Excel Options dialog box.

3. Follow these steps to change the default number of sheets in a workbook:

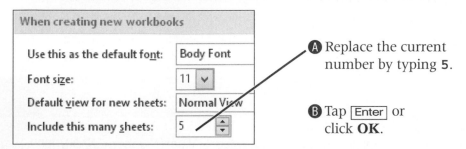

Ⓐ Replace the current number by typing **5**.

Ⓑ Tap Enter or click **OK**.

4. Press Ctrl + N to start a new workbook.
   Notice the five sheet tabs at the bottom of the worksheet window.

5. Close the new workbook without saving.

6. Display the **Excel Options** dialog box again, change the default number of sheets to **1**, and click **OK**.

7. With the **Summary** sheet active, hold down Ctrl and click the **Mileage** sheet tab.
   Both sheet tabs have a light background to indicate that they are selected.

8. Hold down Ctrl and click the **Mileage** sheet tab to remove it from the selection.

9. Follow these steps to select adjacent sheets:

Ⓐ Ensure that the **Summary** sheet is active.

Ⓑ Hold down Shift and click the **Mileage** sheet tab.

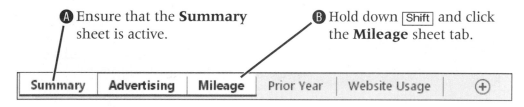

Ⓒ Notice that the three contiguous sheet tabs have a light background.

10. Select **cell A16**, choose **Home→Font→Bold B**, type **Total**, and tap Enter.

11. Hold down Shift and click the **Summary** sheet tab to cancel the multiple sheet selection.

12. Display the **Mileage** sheet and notice that the cell entry appears in **cell A16**.

13. Save the file and leave it open.

Linking Cells and Formulas

Video Library   http://labyrinthelab.com/videos   Video Number: EX13-V0810

Excel lets you link cells from different worksheets in the same workbook or in other workbooks. Linking places values from a source worksheet into a destination worksheet.

Why Link Cells?

Linking creates totals in summary worksheets from values in detail worksheets. This lets you keep detailed information in the detail sheets and see the totals in the summary worksheet. If the contents of the original cells are changed, the appropriate cell in the summary worksheet updates automatically.

Creating Linking Formulas

As with normal formulas, before you create a linking formula, you must select the cell in the summary worksheet where you want the result to appear. Also, as with all other formulas, a linking formula begins with the equals (=) sign.

You may type a linking formula, but using the mouse to select cells is more accurate and highly recommended.

Linking Cells from Other Worksheets in Formulas

The formulas shown will link the contents of one cell from a detail worksheet to a cell in the summary worksheet. The sheet name and cell reference are separated by an exclamation point (!). If the sheet name contains spaces or other non-alphabetic characters, the sheet name must be surrounded by single quotes ('), as in the second example.

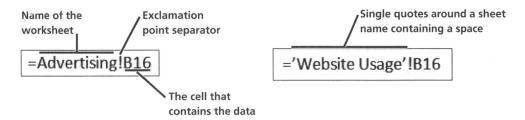

You may create calculation formulas on a summary worksheet using data from multiple detail worksheets. The following example sums the sales from four quarterly sheets to result in the yearly total. Notice that commas are used to separate the four cell references.

=SUM(Quarter1!D18, Quarter2!D18, Quarter3!D18, Quarter4!D18)

Linking Cells from Other Workbooks in Formulas

If the source cell is in a different workbook, you must include the full workbook name in square brackets. Because the example workbook name contains a space, single quotes (') are included before the workbook name and after the worksheet name. Selecting the cell with the mouse will add all of this syntax for you.

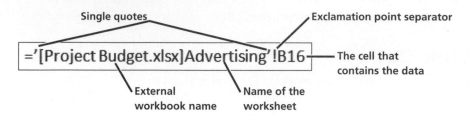

Create a Linking Formula

In this exercise, you will create a formula to link a cell in the Advertising worksheet to the Summary worksheet.

1. Save your file as **EX08-D10-ProjectBudget-[FirstInitialLastName]**.

2. Display the **Advertising** worksheet.

3. Select **cell B16**, choose **Home→Editing→AutoSum Σ**, and tap Enter.

   The total should equal 8,075. Notice that AutoSum summed the entire range B4:B15. This is desirable because AutoSum will keep a running total as you enter data throughout the year.

4. Display the **Summary** worksheet, select **cell C5**, and type an equals (=) sign.

5. Display the **Advertising** worksheet.

   Excel displays the Advertising worksheet. The sheet name Advertising appears in the Formula Bar followed by an exclamation point.

6. Select **cell B16**.

   The linking formula =Advertising!B16 displays in the Formula Bar.

7. Complete the formula by tapping Enter.

   Excel displays the Summary worksheet with the completed link in cell C5. The number 8,075 appears in cell C5.

8. Display the **Advertising** worksheet.

9. Select **cell B7**, type **1200**, and tap Enter.

   The total in cell B16 displays 9,275.

10. Repeat the **above steps** to link the total amount spent in the **Mileage** worksheet to the **Summary** Worksheet.

11. Copy the formula in **cell D5** of the **Summary** worksheet to the **range D6:D8** on that worksheet.

Cells C5 and C7 now display dynamic values, always reflecting the current value in the source cell. You will similarly fill in cells C6 and C8 later in this lesson.

12. Save the file and leave it open.

Using 3-D Cell References in Formulas

Video Library http://labyrinthelab.com/videos Video Number: EX13-V0811

Excel 2013

Excel also allows you to perform calculations using the contents of the same cell address in multiple worksheets. This is called a 3-D cell reference. Contrast the following linking formula and normal summing formula with a formula containing a 3-D cell reference.

Type of Formula	Example	What It Does
Linking	=Supplies!C6	Displays the contents from cell C6 in the Supplies worksheet
Normal	=Supplies!C6 + Utilities!C6	Sums cell C6 from the Supplies and Utilities worksheets only
3-D	=SUM(Supplies:Equipment!C6)	Sums cell C6 in all worksheets from Supplies through Equipment in the workbook

Why Use a 3-D Reference?

Using a 3-D reference provides two advantages over normal cell references in a multi-sheet formula. First, you do not have to click the cell in each worksheet to build the formula. Also, the formula automatically includes the specified cell from additional worksheets that you insert within the worksheet range.

Deleting a worksheet or moving a worksheet tab to outside the range in the 3-D reference removes that worksheet's values from the formula result.

Creating a 3-D Reference

Functions that you may use to create 3-D references include SUM, AVERAGE, COUNT, MAX, MIN, and some statistical functions. A formula may contain a single cell or a cell range as a 3D reference. The cell or range must also contain the same type of data, such as values.

Task	Procedure
Create a 3-D reference	■ Design all worksheets so that the cell contents to be calculated are in identical cell addresses.
	■ Select the cell to contain the formula in the summary worksheet, and type the function beginning, such as =SUM(.
	■ Click the first sheet tab and hold down Shift while clicking the last sheet tab to be referenced.
	■ In the sheet currently displayed, select the cell or range to be referenced, and complete the formula.

DEVELOP YOUR SKILLS EX08-D11

Create a 3-D Cell Reference

In this exercise, you will create 3-D cell references to one cell in several worksheets. You will also create a 3-D reference to a cell range.

1. Save your file as **EX08-D11-ProjectBudget-[FirstInitialLastName]**.

2. Display the **Summary** worksheet.

3. Follow these steps to create a formula that determines the total number of employee reviews of the data by adding the values in cell G1 in each worksheet:

Ⓐ Select **cell G1** in the **Summary** worksheet.

Ⓑ Type **=sum(** .

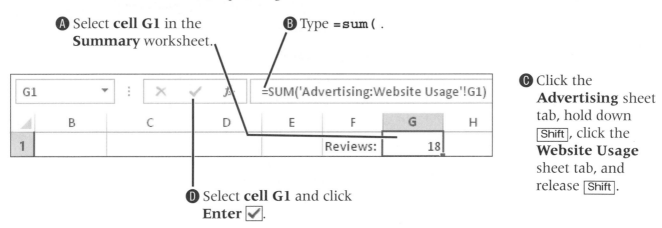

Ⓒ Click the **Advertising** sheet tab, hold down Shift, click the **Website Usage** sheet tab, and release Shift.

Ⓓ Select **cell G1** and click **Enter** ✓.

The formula result should be 18.

4. Save the file and leave it open.

Copying Worksheets

Video Library http://labyrinthelab.com/videos Video Number: EX13-V0812

Rather than inserting new blank sheets, you can use the Move or Copy Sheet command to copy an existing worksheet and then edit the duplicate.

The Move or Copy Dialog Box

A *copied* worksheet created with the Move or Copy Sheet command is an exact duplicate of the original. To move or copy a worksheet to another workbook, both workbooks must be open. Placing a checkmark in the Create a Copy box creates a *copy.* Leaving the box blank *moves* the selected worksheet. A worksheet moved to another workbook no longer exists in the original workbook.

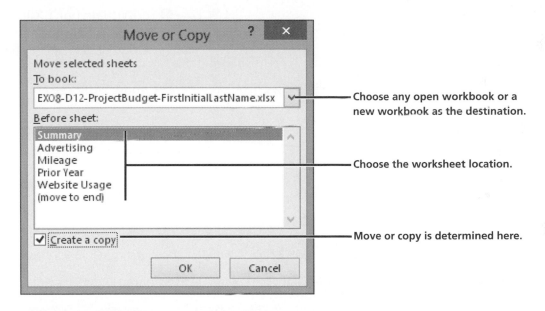

Choose any open workbook or a new workbook as the destination.

Choose the worksheet location.

Move or copy is determined here.

QUICK REFERENCE	COPYING AND MOVING WORKSHEETS
Task	**Procedure**
Copy or move a worksheet using a command	■ Select the desired sheet tab to be copied or moved. ■ Choose Home→Cells→Format ▦→Move or Copy Sheet; or, right-click the sheet tab and choose Move or Copy. ■ Choose the destination workbook or a new blank worksheet from the To Book list, and select the worksheet position. ■ To copy, place a checkmark in the Create a Copy box. To move, leave the box empty.
Copy or move a worksheet in the same workbook by dragging	■ To move, drag the sheet tab to the desired location within the tabs. ■ To copy, hold down ⎡Ctrl⎤ and drag the sheet tab.

Excel 2013

Create a Copy of a Worksheet

In this exercise, you will make two copies of the Advertising worksheet to create new sheets named Equipment and Training Materials.

1. Save your file as **EX08-D12-ProjectBudget-[FirstInitialLastName]**.

2. Display the **Advertising** worksheet.

3. Choose **Home→Cells→Format ▦→Move or Copy Sheet**.

4. Follow these steps to create a copy of the Advertising worksheet:

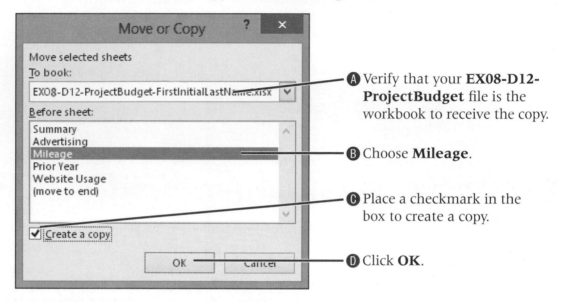

Ⓐ Verify that your **EX08-D12-ProjectBudget** file is the workbook to receive the copy.

Ⓑ Choose **Mileage**.

Ⓒ Place a checkmark in the box to create a copy.

Ⓓ Click **OK**.

Excel positions the duplicate worksheet before the Mileage sheet and names it Advertising (2).

5. Double-click the Advertising (2) sheet tab, type the new name **Equipment**, and tap Enter.

6. Change the entries in **cell A1** and the **range B4:B7**.

	A	B
1	Equipment Tracking Sheet	
2		
3		Amount Spent
4	September	8,547
5	October	3,640
6	November	5,072
7	December	1,211

7. Right-click the **Advertising** sheet tab and choose **Move or Copy**.

8. In the dialog box, choose **(Move to End)** from the Before Sheet list, place a checkmark in the **Create a Copy** box, and click **OK**.

9. Change the name of the new sheet to **Training Materials**.

Your sheet tabs should look like these. If necessary, drag a sheet tab to the correct position.

| Summary | Advertising | Equipment | Mileage | Prior Year | Website Usage | **Training Materials** |

10. Edit the title in **cell A1** of the **Training Materials** worksheet and change the numbers in the **range B4:B7**.

	A	B	C
1	Training Materials Tracking Sheet		
2			
3		Amount Spent	
4	September	145	
5	October	1,620	
6	November	(1,705)	
7	December	730	

11. Link the totals within the **Training Materials** worksheet and the **Equipment** worksheet to the **Summary worksheet**.

Copy the Salaries Worksheet from a Different Workbook

12. Open **EX08-D12-Salaries** from the **EX2013 Lesson 08** folder, right-click the **Salaries** sheet tab, and choose **Move or Copy**.

13. Follow these steps to copy the Salaries worksheet:

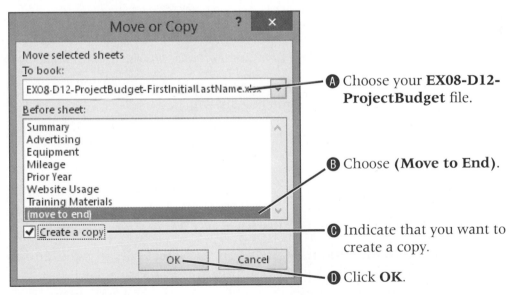

Ⓐ Choose your **EX08-D12-ProjectBudget** file.

Ⓑ Choose **(Move to End)**.

Ⓒ Indicate that you want to create a copy.

Ⓓ Click **OK**.

14. Close the **Salaries** workbook. Save the **Project Budget** workbook and leave it open.

Copying Formats between Worksheets

Video Library   http://labyrinthelab.com/videos   Video Number: EX13-V0813

Excel provides multiple ways to copy cell formatting from one worksheet to another without copying the text or numbers within the cells. The most basic of these methods is to use the Format Painter.

Use the Format Painter to copy formatting to cells in the target worksheet. You may select one or more cells, columns, or rows, or the entire worksheet before using the Format Painter button. The column width or row height is not applied unless you select an entire column or row before using the Format Painter.

Use the Select All ⬜ button above the top-left corner of the worksheet to select the entire worksheet.

DEVELOP YOUR SKILLS EX08-D13
Use the Format Painter to Copy Formats

In this exercise, you will copy formatting from one worksheet to another. You will also apply formatting from one worksheet to two other worksheets.

1. Save your file as **EX08-D13-ProjectBudget-[FirstInitialLastName]**.

2. Display the **Summary** worksheet.

3. Select **cell A2** and choose **Home→Clipboard→Format Painter** ✦.
   Cell A2 displays a marquee, and the mouse pointer changes to a block cross with a paintbrush.

4. Display the **Advertising** worksheet and select **cell A1** to copy the format to that cell.
   The font in cell A1 now has the same dark blue color and size as the subheading in the Summary worksheet.

5. Repeat **steps 3–4** to copy formats as shown.

From the Summary Worksheet	To the Advertising Worksheet
Cell D4	Cell B3
Range A16:B16	Range A16:B16

6. Click **Select All** ⬜ on the **Advertising** worksheet.

7. Double-click the **Format Painter** ✦, click **Select All** ⬜ in the **Equipment** worksheet, and click **Select All** ⬜ in the **Training Materials** worksheet.
   These two worksheets now have the same formatting as the Advertising worksheet.

8. Click the **Format Painter** ✦ to deactivate it. Click anywhere in the worksheet to deselect the cells.
   Deactivating the Format Painter ensures that you will not accidentally include formatting elsewhere, but does not undo the current formatting.

9. Display the **Mileage** worksheet and use the **Format Painter**  to copy the number and font formatting from **cell B4** to **cell C4**.

10. Use the **fill handle** to copy the formula and cell formatting in cell C4 down the column to **row 15**.

    Some of the cells will display zeros or dashes (depending on the default settings on your computer) because some values have not yet been entered into column B.

11. Deselect the highlighted cells.

12. Save the file and leave it open.

Paste Options

Video Library http://labyrinthelab.com/videos Video Number: EX13-V0814

You may use options on the Paste menu to control the type of formatting and content applied to the target cells. Options on the Paste menu vary depending on the attributes of the copied selection. Clicking the Paste drop-down menu button on the Ribbon displays the menu.

The Paste Options button appears at the lower-right corner of the destination cell(s) so you can customize after a copy-and-paste action is performed. When the button is clicked, the same options display as on the Paste menu on the Ribbon. The button disappears upon the next action you take.

The Paste menu on the Ribbon

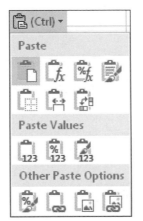

The Paste Options button

Pointing to an option in the Paste menu displays a preview of the result in the worksheet. The buttons and their actions are listed here.

PASTE MENU BUTTONS

Button	Name	Paste Action in the Destination Cell
	Paste	Pastes the source cell's contents and applies all its formatting
	Formulas	Pastes the source cell's contents and applies the destination cell's formatting
	Formulas & Number Formatting	Pastes the source cell's contents, applies the source cell's number format, and applies all other destination cell formatting
	Keep Source Formatting	Pastes the source cell's contents and applies all its formatting (used when pasting from an outside source)
	No Borders	Pastes the source contents and applies all its formatting except borders
	Keep Source Column Widths	Pastes the source cell's contents and applies the source cell's column width to the destination column
	Transpose	Pastes the source range's contents and formatting but reverses the row and column data
	Values	Pastes the value resulting from a formula (but not the formula) and applies the destination cell's formatting
	Values & Number Formatting	Pastes the value resulting from a formula (but not the formula), applies the source cell's number format, and applies all other destination cell formatting
	Values & Source Formatting	Pastes the value resulting from a formula (but not the formula) and applies the source cell's formatting
	Formatting	Applies the source cell's formatting but does not paste its contents
	Paste Link	Creates a linking formula to the source cell and applies the source cell's formatting
	Picture	Pastes a picture of the selected range as an object on top of the spreadsheet (or into other document, such as a Word document)
	Linked Picture	Pastes a picture of the selected range and creates a link to update the picture if any source cell is changed

Paste Special

The Paste Special command contains a dialog box with many of the same options that are on the Paste menu. The Operation options allow you to add a copied value to (or subtract it from) the existing value in the destination cell, multiply the values, or divide the destination values by their corresponding copied values. Certain other options are only available here as well.

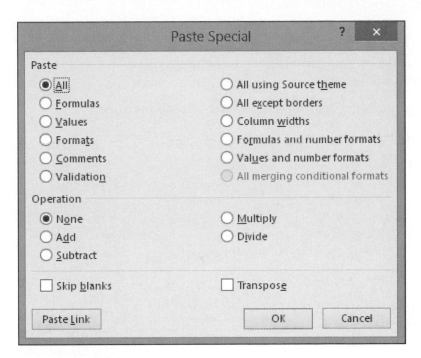

QUICK REFERENCE	USING THE FORMAT PAINTER, PASTE OPTIONS, AND PASTE SPECIAL
Task	**Procedure**
Copy formats to one other cell or range	■ Click the cell that has the format(s) you wish to copy. ■ Choose Home→Clipboard→Format Painter 🖌, and select the cell/range to which you wish to copy the format(s).
Copy formats to multiple locations	■ Click the cell that has the format(s) you wish to copy. ■ Double-click Home→Clipboard→Format Painter 🖌, and select the cell/range to which you wish to copy the format(s).
Apply an option while pasting using the Ribbon	■ Select a cell or range of cells and choose Home→Clipboard→Copy. ■ Choose Home→Clipboard→Paste menu ▼ and choose the desired option.
Apply an option after pasting	■ Copy and paste the desired cell or range of cells. ■ Click the Paste Options button at the lower-right corner of the destination cell(s) and choose an option.
Apply an option using Paste Special	■ Select and copy a cell or range of cells. ■ Select the destination cell or range of cells. ■ Choose Clipboard→Paste menu ▼→Paste Special, choose the desired option in the Paste Special dialog box, and click OK.

Use Paste Options and Paste Special

In this exercise, you will copy data from a column and paste it across a row, and you will add the values of copied cells to values in the corresponding destination cells. You will also copy only the column width formatting from one column to another column.

1. Save your file as **EX08-D14-ProjectBudget-[FirstInitialLastName]**.

2. Display the **Summary** worksheet, select the **range B4:B16**, and choose **Home→Clipboard→Copy**.

3. Select **cell H4** and choose **Home→Clipboard→Paste menu ▼**.

4. Follow these steps to view the result of various paste options:

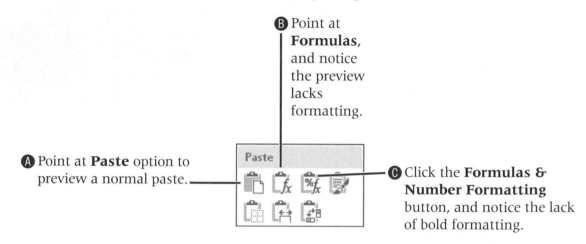

Ⓑ Point at **Formulas**, and notice the preview lacks formatting.

Ⓐ Point at **Paste** option to preview a normal paste.

Ⓒ Click the **Formulas & Number Formatting** button, and notice the lack of bold formatting.

5. **Undo** ⟲ the paste.

6. Follow these steps to copy cell values without formatting:

Ⓐ Copy the **range B4:B16**.　　　　　Ⓑ Select **cell H4**.

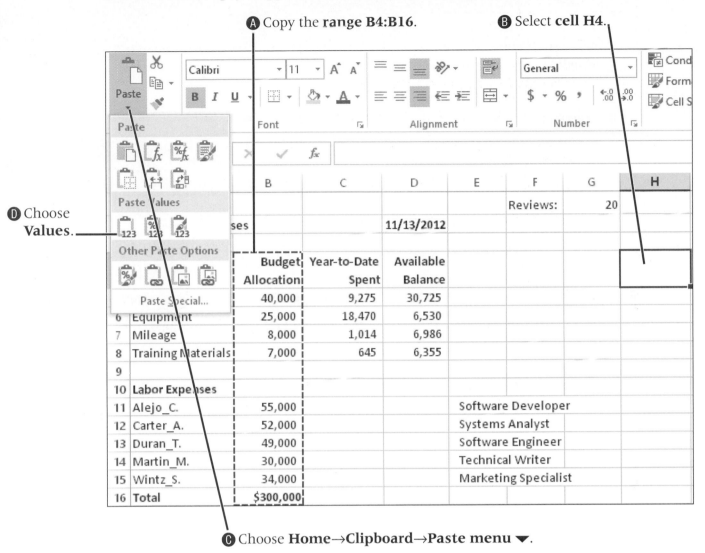

Ⓓ Choose **Values**.

Ⓒ Choose **Home→Clipboard→Paste menu ▼**.

7. Select the range **B4:B16** and choose **Home→Clipboard→Copy**.

8. Select **cell H4**, choose **Home→Clipboard→Paste Menu ▼→Formatting**, and widen **column H** to fit all entries.

   The formatting of column H is now consistent with the rest of the worksheet.

9. Select the **range A11:A15** and choose **Home→Clipboard→Copy**.

10. Display the **Salaries** worksheet, select **cell B3**, and choose **Home→Clipboard→Paste**.

   The employee names have replaced some values on the Salaries worksheet. You will now transpose these names in order to correct this issue.

11. Click the **Paste Options** button and choose **Transpose**.

	A	B	C
1	Salaries Tracking Sheet		
2			
3		Alejo_C.	
4	September	Carter_A.	4,333
5	October	Duran_T.	4,333
6	November	Martin_M.	4,333
7	December	Wintz_S.	4,333
8	January		📋 (Ctrl) ▾

	B	C	D	E	F
3	Alejo_C.	Carter_A.	Duran_T.	Martin_M.	Wintz_S.
4	4,583	4,333	4,083	2,500	-

The employee names are transposed across row 3 and the original values in the range B4:B7 are displayed.

12. Right-align the **range B3:F3** to align with the numbers below these employee names.

13. Display the **Advertising** worksheet, select **cell B3**, and choose **Copy**.

14. Display the **Salaries** worksheet.

15. Select **cell G16** and choose **Home→Clipboard→Paste menu ▾→Paste Special**.

16. Choose **Column Widths** and click **OK** in the Paste Special dialog box.
    Only the column width is applied from the source cell to all cells in column G.

17. Autofit the height of **row 3**, if necessary.

18. Calculate the monthly totals in the **range G4:G15** and link the totals in row 16 to the **range C11:C15** on the **Summary** worksheet. Format the range as necessary.

19. On the **Summary** worksheet, calculate the **Available Balances** in the range **D11:D15**. Copy the formula in **cell B16** to the range **C16:D16**.

Add Copied Values to Destination Cells
Next, you will use Paste Special to add the values from one range to another.

20. Display the **Summary** worksheet, select the **range B5:B8**, and press Ctrl + C.

21. Select **cell H5** and choose **Home→Clipboard→Paste menu ▾→Paste Special**.

22. In the Paste Special dialog box, choose **Add**, and click **OK.**
    The value in cell B5 was added to the value in cell H5. The result in cell H5 should be 80,000. Each of the other values in the range B6:B8 was added to its corresponding cell in column H.

23. Delete the contents of **column H**.

24. Save the file and leave it open.

Printing Multiple-Sheet Workbooks

Video Library   http://labyrinthelab.com/videos   Video Number: EX13-V0815

Excel prints the active worksheet when you choose the Quick Print command on the Quick Access toolbar. If you are working with a multiple-sheet workbook, you may use various techniques to set options and print multiple sheets simultaneously.

Applying Page Setup Options to Multiple Sheets

You may adjust the margins, page orientation, headers and footers, and a variety of other settings that affect the printed worksheet. Apply these settings to multiple worksheets by first using Ctrl to select nonadjacent sheet tabs or Shift to select adjacent sheet tabs.

Printing Multiple Sheets

You may print all sheets without selecting their tabs by choosing the Print Entire Workbook option in the Print tab of Backstage view. You may print only certain sheets by using Ctrl to select the desired sheet tabs and choosing Print or Quick Print.

DEVELOP YOUR SKILLS EX08-D15
Preview and Print Selected Sheets

In this exercise, you will select multiple sheets, change their orientation, and preview them all at once.

1. Save your file as **EX08-D15-ProjectBudget-[FirstInitialLastName]**.

2. With the **Summary** worksheet active, hold down Shift, and click the **Mileage** sheet tab.

Summary	Advertising	Equipment	Mileage	Prior Year	Website Usage	Training Materials	Salaries	⊕

3. Choose **Page Layout→Page Setup→Change Page Orientation→Landscape**.

4. Choose **File→Print**.

   Notice that the Print Active Sheets setting is selected. The bottom of the preview area displays "1 of 4," which indicates that four sheets are active and would print if you were to click Print.

5. Use the **Next Page** ▸ command to browse through the worksheets.

   Notice that the orientation of the four sheets is landscape.

6. Tap Esc to exit **Backstage view**; click any unselected sheet tab to deselect multiple sheet tabs.

Excel 2013

Select Multiple Nonadjacent Sheets

7. Display the **Advertising** worksheet.

8. Hold down Ctrl, click the **Mileage** sheet tab, click the **Salaries** sheet tab, and release Ctrl.
   Three sheets are selected.

9. Right-click any selected sheet tab and choose **Ungroup Sheets**.
   Now only one worksheet is active.

10. Choose **File→Print**.

11. In the Settings area of the Print tab, click **Print Active Sheets** and choose **Print Entire Workbook**.
    You may use this option to print the entire workbook without first selecting the sheets.

12. Press Esc to exit Backstage view without printing.

13. Save and close the file. Exit **Excel**.

Concepts Review

To check your knowledge of the key concepts introduced in this lesson, complete the Concepts Review quiz by choosing the appropriate access option below.

If you are...	Then access the quiz by...
Using the Labyrinth Video Library	Going to http://labyrinthelab.com/videos
Using eLab	Logging in, choosing Content, and navigating to the Concepts Review quiz for this lesson
Not using the Labyrinth Video Library or eLab	Going to the student resource center for this book

Reinforce Your Skills

Sort and Print Multiple Worksheets

In this exercise, you will use the Sort dialog box to sort worksheet rows. You will also arrange worksheets so you can view both open account balances and whether customers have defaulted in the past. Finally, you will print multiple worksheets.

Sort Worksheet Data

1. Start **Excel**. Open **EX08-R01-BalanceDue** from the **EX2013 Lesson 08** folder and save it as **EX08-R01-BalanceDue-[FirstInitialLastName]**.

2. On the **Balance Due** worksheet, select any account number below the **row 3 heading**.

3. Choose **Data→Sort & Filter→Sort A to Z** 🔽.

   The list is sorted by the Account Number column. Now you will sort on two sort keys.

4. Select any data cell below the **row 3** headings, choose **Data→Sort & Filter→Sort**, change the **Sort By** level to **Outstanding Balance**, and then set the **Order** to **Z to A**.

5. Click **Add Level**, change the **Then by** field to **Account Number**, and ensure **Order** is set to **Smallest to Largest**.

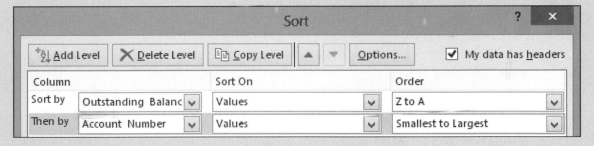

6. Click **OK** to perform the sort on two sort keys.

Use Flexible Worksheet Views

7. Choose **View→Window→New Window** 🗗 and select the tab of the **Previous Default** worksheet.

   Notice that the two Balance Due worksheets that are now open display :1 and :2 after the workbook name in the title bar.

8. Choose **View→Window→Arrange All** ▤, select **Vertical**, and click **OK**.

   Note how easily you can now compare the data within the two worksheets.

9. **Close** ⊠ the second Balance Due worksheet, and **maximize** ◻ the remaining window.

Print Multipage Worksheets

10. Choose **Page Layout→Scale to Fit→Scale** and change the scale to **200%**.

    In some instances, you will want to increase the size of your printed worksheet so it is easier to read.

11. Choose **File→Print** to view the print preview.

    Because of the scale increase, the worksheet does not fit on one page.

12. Exit **Backstage view** and choose **Page Layout→Page Setup→Adjust Margins→Narrow**.

    Reducing the margins allows for more of the worksheet to fit on the page.

13. Choose **File→Print** to view the print preview.

    The worksheet now fits on one page.

Use Multiple Worksheets

14. Choose **Options** to display the General options within the Excel Options dialog box.

    You intend to create more comparison workbooks with two worksheet tabs in the future, so you will change the default for new workbooks to include two worksheets.

15. Under **When Creating New Workbooks**, change the **Include This Many Sheets** option to **2**. Click **OK**.

16. Save and then close the file. Exit **Excel**.

17. Submit your final file based on the guidelines provided by your instructor.

    To view examples of how your file or files should look at the end of this exercise, go to the student resource center.

REINFORCE YOUR SKILLS EX08-R02

Copy and Link Worksheets

In this exercise, you will create formulas that link cells between worksheets, arrange worksheet tabs, and adjust print options.

Link Cells and Formulas

1. Start **Excel**. Open **EX08-R02-Marketing** from the **EX2013 Lesson 08** folder and save it as **EX08-R02-Marketing-[FirstInitialLastName]**.

2. On the **Summary** worksheet, select **cell B4** and type an equals sign.

3. On the **Eastern** worksheet, select **cell B4**, and type a plus sign.

    The formula now reads =Eastern!B4+. You will next add to this the figures within cell B4 on the other two worksheets.

4. Repeat the prior step for the **Western** and **Central** worksheets, remembering to type a plus sign between these two cell references. Press Enter .

    Excel displays the Summary worksheet, and shows a total of $32,000 in cell B4.

5. Drag the fill handle to copy this formula to the **range C4:E4**.

Use 3-D Cell References in Formulas

6. On the **Summary** worksheet, select **cell B5** and type =Sum(.

7. Select the **Eastern** sheet tab, press Shift, and select the **Central** sheet tab.

   All four sheet tabs are now highlighted, while the Eastern sheet remains active.

8. Select **cell B5** on the **Eastern** sheet (which is currently displayed), type a close parenthesis, and confirm the formula.

   This formula provides the same result as the formula in cell B4, but it was easier to construct. When data on multiple sheets line up in the same cells, as they do in this worksheet, 3-D cell references should always be used.

9. AutoFill with this formula the remaining quarters for **Area 2**, as well as all quarters for **Areas 3 and 4**.

Copying Worksheets

10. Click the **Eastern** sheet tab and click **Select All** ◢.

11. Choose **Home→Clipboard** then double-click the **Format Painter** button.

    Because you double-clicked, the Format Painter will remain active after you apply it in the next step.

12. Display the **Western** sheet tab and click **Select All** ◢.

    You were able to copy the formats in this manner because the sheets have an identical structure.

13. Repeat **step 12** to copy the formats to the **Central** and **Summary** worksheets.

14. Choose **Home→Clipboard→Format Painter** to deactivate the feature.

Print Multiple-Sheet Workbooks

15. Click the **Summary** sheet tab and choose **File→Print**.

16. In the **Settings** area, choose **Print Active Sheets→Print Entire Workbook**.

    If you were to now select print, all four worksheets would be printed.

17. Save and then close the file. Exit **Excel**.

18. Submit your final file based on the guidelines provided by your instructor.

    To view examples of how your file or files should look at the end of this exercise, go to the student resource center.

Sort, Link, and Organize Multiple Worksheets

In this exercise, you will sort expense data related to two monthly events hosted by Kids for Change. You will create linking formulas within a summary worksheet, and will organize the worksheets prior to printing.

Sort Worksheet Data

1. Start **Excel**. Open **EX08-R03-Events** from the **EX2013 Lesson 08** folder and save it as **EX08-R03-Events-[FirstInitialLastName]**.

2. On the **Fundraising** worksheet, select **cell N4** and highlight the **range N4:A7**.

3. Choose **Data→Sort & Filter→Sort Z to A** [icon].

   The expense data is now sorted from highest to lowest based on the total column.

4. Repeat the prior two steps on the **Awards** worksheet.

Use Flexible Worksheet Views

5. Choose **View→Window→New Window** [icon].

   Notice that the two Events worksheets that are now open display :1 and :2 after the workbook name in the title bar.

6. Choose **View→Window→Arrange All** [icon], select **Horizontal**, and click **OK**.

   Note how easily you can now compare the data within the two worksheets.

7. **Close** [icon] the second Events worksheet and **maximize** [icon] the remaining window.

Print Multipage Worksheets

8. On the **Fundraising** worksheet select **cell H1**.

9. Choose **Page Layout→Page Setup→Breaks** [icon] **→Insert Page Break**.

   Because the active cell was within row 1 when you inserted this page break, only a vertical break is applied to the worksheet.

10. Choose **Page Layout→Page Setup→Print Titles** [icon]; then click within the **Columns to Repeat at Left** box, select **column A,** and click **OK**.

    You will not see any change within the worksheet, however when you print you will see column A repeat on each printed page.

11. Repeat the prior two steps within the **Awards** worksheet.

Use Multiple Worksheets

12. Choose **File→Options** to display the General options within the Excel Options dialog box.

13. In the **When Creating New Workbooks** section, change the **Include This Many Sheets** option to **3**; click **OK**.

Link Cells and Formulas

14. Double-click the **Sheet3** worksheet tab and rename it **Summary**.

15. On the **Fundraising** worksheet, choose **Select All** ◢.

16. Choose **Home→Clipboard→Copy** 📋.

You can now paste all data and formatting into another worksheet.

17. Select the **Summary** worksheet, click **cell A1**, and choose **Home→Clipboard→Paste** 📋.

Next you will remove the Fundraising worksheet data and replace it with summary data.

18. Modify the title in **cell A1** to **Kids for Change - Summary**.

19. Select the **range B4:N7** and tap Delete.

20. Select **cell B4**, type **=**, choose the **Fundraising** worksheet tab, select **cell B4**, type **+**, choose the **Awards** worksheet tab, select **cell B4**, and tap Enter.

21. AutoFill the formula in **cell B4** to the **range B4:M7**.

The Summary worksheet now displays the total expenses for all events.

Use 3-D Cell References in Formulas

22. On the **Summary** sheet, select **cell N4** and type **=Sum(**.

23. Select the **Fundraising** sheet tab, hold Shift, and select the **Awards** sheet tab.

24. Select **cell N4** on the Fundraising sheet, type a close parenthesis, and confirm the formula.

25. Select **cell N4** and choose **Home→Clipboard→Copy** 📋.

26. Highlight the **range N5:N8** and choose **Home→Clipboard→Paste menu ▼→Formulas**.

Copy Worksheets

27. Drag the **Summary** worksheet tab prior to the **Fundraising** worksheet to rearrange the order of the worksheets.

Print Multiple-Sheet Workbooks

28. Choose **File→Print**.

29. In the **Settings** area, choose **Print Active Sheets→Print Entire Workbook**.

If you were to now select print, all three worksheets would be printed.

30. Save and then close the file. Exit **Excel**.

31. Submit your final file based on the guidelines provided by your instructor.

Apply Your Skills

Sort on Multiple Sort Keys

In this exercise, you will sort and adjust worksheets displaying customer orders.

Sort Worksheet Data and Use Flexible Worksheet Views

1. Start **Excel**. Open **EX08-A01-Orders** from the **EX2013 Lesson 08** folder and save it as **EX08-A01-Orders-[FirstInitialLastName]**.

2. Format the numbers in **column D** as **Comma style** with no decimal places.

3. AutoFit the width of **columns B–D**.

   Notice that the rows are currently sorted by Sales in column D.

4. Use the **Sort** dialog box to sort the rows using three sort keys:
   - Key 1: Area in smallest to largest order
   - Key 2: Customer in A to Z order
   - Key 3: Sales in largest to smallest order

   The rows for each area will be sorted within groups by customer according to their sales prices.

5. Freeze **rows 1–3** so the headers remain visible when you scroll down.

   Columns and rows cannot remain frozen when headers and footers are created, because Page Layout view must be used to do so. Therefore, you will unfreeze these rows so that you can create a header and footer in the upcoming steps.

6. Unfreeze **rows 1–3**.

Use Multiple Worksheets and Print Multipage Worksheets

7. Create a header that displays the filename at the top-right.

8. Create a footer that displays the current date at the bottom-right.

9. Use ⌈Ctrl⌉ to select **Sheet2** and **Sheet3**. Delete these sheets.

10. Save and then close the file. Exit **Excel**.

11. Submit your final file based on the guidelines provided by your instructor.

    To view examples of how your file or files should look at the end of this exercise, go to the student resource center.

Create a Linked Workbook

In this exercise, you will create a new workbook that contains three worksheets. You will also create linking formulas.

Link Cells and Formulas and Use 3-D Cell References

1. Start **Excel**. Open **EX08-A02-RegionSales** from the **EX2013 Lesson 08** folder and save it as **EX08-A02-RegionSales-[FirstInitialLastName]**.

2. Create defined names for each total in **row 7** of the region sheets. Name the totals in the **Eastern** worksheet **Eastern_January, Eastern_February**, and **Eastern_March**. Use similar names for the totals in the **Central** worksheet.

3. Use the defined names created in the prior step to include linking formulas in **rows 4–5** of the **Totals** worksheet to the totals in the detail sheets.

4. On the **Totals** worksheet, format the **range B4:D5** with **Accounting** number format displaying a $ sign and zero decimal places.

5. Create a **3-D cell reference** on the **Totals** worksheet in **cell B8** to add the number of accounts listed on the region worksheets.

   Notice that you are able to enter this formula in cell B8, even though the 3-D reference adds the contents of cell B9 on the other worksheets.

Copy Worksheets and Print Multiple-Sheet Workbooks

6. Move the **Totals** worksheet prior to the **Central** worksheet.

7. Copy the format of **cell A1** of the **Totals** worksheet to **cell A1** of the **Central** and **Eastern** worksheets.

8. Change the orientation to **Landscape** for all three worksheets by issuing one command.

9. Set the **Print Range** of the **Totals** worksheet to the **range A1:B6**.

10. Save and then close the file. Exit **Excel**.

11. Submit your final file based on the guidelines provided by your instructor.

    To view examples of how your file or files should look at the end of this exercise, go to the student resource center.

Sort, Link, and Organize Multiple Worksheets

In this exercise, you will sort expense data for two employees. You will create linking formulas within a summary worksheet, and will organize the worksheets prior to printing.

Sort Worksheet Data and Use Flexible Worksheet Views

1. Start **Excel**. Open **EX08-A03-Expenses** from the **EX2013 Lesson 08** folder and save it as **EX08-A03-Expenses-[FirstInitialLastName]**.

2. Sort the data within each worksheet, based on the total expenses, from smallest to largest.

3. View the worksheets in separate windows, and tile them horizontally.

Use Multiple Worksheets and Print Multipage Worksheets

4. Insert a page break within the worksheet so the last six months of the year display on a second page.

5. Set **column A** as a title column that will print on every page for each worksheet.

6. Adjust print options so **gridlines** display.

7. Increase the default number of worksheets to **3**, if necessary.

8. Close the second workbook; maximize the first workbook.

Link Cells and Formulas and Use 3-D Cell References in Formulas

9. Change the name of **Sheet3** to **Summary**. Create headers and a title for a summary worksheet that follows the format of the other two. Use the **Format Painter** to copy all formatting.

   Ensure that all components of the worksheet appear in the same cell as their counterparts in the other two worksheets.

10. Use **linking formulas** to create formulas throughout the monthly columns of the summary worksheet.

11. Create a **3-D cell reference** on the **Summary** worksheet to populate those **Total** cells for which this approach is appropriate. Use linking formulas for all other totals.

Copy Worksheets and Print Multiple-Sheet Workbooks

12. Move the **Summary** worksheet prior to the **David Sutton** worksheet.

13. Change the orientation to **Landscape** for all three worksheets by issuing one command.

14. Adjust the print options to print the **Entire Workbook**.

15. Save and then close the file. Exit **Excel**.

16. Submit your final file based on the guidelines provided by your instructor.

Extend Your Skills

In the course of working through the Extend Your Skills exercises, you will think critically as you use the skills taught in the lesson to complete the assigned projects. To evaluate your mastery and completion of the exercises, your instructor may use a rubric, with which more points are allotted according to performance characteristics. (The more you do, the more you earn!) Ask your instructor how your work will be evaluated.

EX08-E01 That's the Way I See It

You want to analyze your personal spending over the last three months. (If you do not wish to share your personal financial information, simply make up the figures.) Each monthly worksheet will list your personal expenses related to food, entertainment, and transportation. You will then create a summary worksheet that averages your expenses across the three months.

Open Excel and create a new, blank workbook named **EX08-E01-MyExpenses-[FirstInitialLastName]** in your **EX2013 Lesson 08** folder.

Create the first worksheet using appropriate headers and column titles. Fill in the necessary expense data, and use a formula to calculate the total expenses for the month. Use the Format Painter, where possible, to apply consistent formats to the second and third worksheets. Create a summary worksheet and use linking formulas to calculate your average expenses. Include a footer on the summary worksheet that displays the current date and your name. Change the page orientation to Landscape for all worksheets simultaneously, and ensure that each worksheet will print with gridlines displayed.

You will be evaluated based on the inclusion of all elements specified, your ability to follow directions, your ability to apply newly learned skills to a real-world situation, your creativity, and the relevance of your topic and/or data choice(s). Submit your final file based on the guidelines provided by your instructor.

EX08-E02 Be Your Own Boss

Blue Jean Landscaping has expanded to Draper, a small college town. In this exercise, you will sort and format a worksheet listing the hours worked for each client in the new location.

Open **EX08-E02-Draper** from your **EX2013 Lesson 08** folder and save it as **EX08-E02-Draper-[FirstInitialLastName]**.

Freeze the first three rows so you can view the headers as you scroll to the bottom of the worksheet. Find the last data row and create a new blank row to separate the data from the total row. Custom sort the users by category alphabetically and then by largest to smallest for the Totals column. Insert a page break that will display students on the second page, with all other client categories appearing on the first page. Lastly, increase the default number of worksheets within the workbook to five, as you will be creating extensive client listings in the future.

You will be evaluated based on the inclusion of all elements specified, your ability to follow directions, your ability to apply newly learned skills to a real-world situation, your creativity, and your demonstration of an entrepreneurial spirit. Submit your final file based on the guidelines provided by your instructor.

Transfer Your Skills

In the course of working through the Transfer Your Skills exercises, you will use critical-thinking and creativity skills to complete the assigned projects using skills taught in the lesson. To evaluate your mastery and completion of the exercises, your instructor may use a rubric, with which more points are allotted according to performance characteristics. (The more you do, the more you earn!) Ask your instructor how your work will be evaluated.

EX08-T01 WebQuest: Use the Web as a Learning Tool

Throughout this book, you will be provided with an opportunity to use the Internet as a learning tool by completing WebQuests. According to the original creators of WebQuests, as described on their website (WebQuest.org), a WebQuest is "an inquiry-oriented activity in which most or all of the information used by learners is drawn from the web." To complete the WebQuest projects in this book, navigate to the student resource center and choose the WebQuest for the lesson on which you are currently working. The subject of each WebQuest will be relevant to the material found in the lesson.

WebQuest Subject: Linking worksheets effectively

Submit your final file based on the guidelines provided by your instructor.

EX08-T02 Demonstrate Proficiency

You have built a budget workbook for Stormy BBQ with two worksheets, one for salaries and one for other expenses. You would like to ensure consistency throughout the workbook.

Open **EX08-T02-BudgetSummary** from your **EX2013 Lesson 08** folder and save it as **EX08-T02-BudgetSummary-[FirstInitialLastName]**. Use the Format Painter to copy the formatting from the Salaries worksheet to the Expenses sheet. Create a Summary worksheet containing identical formatting. Use 3-D cell references within this worksheet to summarize the total expenses for each month. Freeze columns A and B within each worksheet, name each of the sheet tabs (use your best judgment to create relevant names), and include a header within each worksheet that will display these names. Move the summary worksheet to the front of the workbook. When finished, use a single command to print only the salaries worksheet and the expenses worksheet.

Submit your final file based on the guidelines provided by your instructor.

Creating and Delivering a Presentation

LEARNING OBJECTIVES

After studying this lesson, you will be able to:

- Apply a document theme to a new presentation
- Insert new slides
- Add text to a slide
- View a slide show
- Present a slide show

In this lesson, you will create a PowerPoint presentation for the iJams music distribution company. Throughout the lesson, you will be using many PowerPoint features to develop the presentation. You will be working with document themes, text layout styles, and Microsoft Word outlines. By the end of the lesson, your presentation will be ready for delivery. Equipped with the tips and techniques for a successful presentation, you will practice its delivery to the JamWorks trade show.

Always save 3 versions –
2013 (or most current)
'97-'03 compatible
PDF
- on thumbdrive if taking
  somewhere to present
or
- to OneNote or dropbox for backup
Make photos big, even off screen
Picture border - Use Drop Shadow Rect.
To see slide realistically
  shift + F5, or
  slideshow ribbon, from current slide
- esc to go back
Putting shadow on fonts is good

Creating a Presentation

iJams is an online music distribution company that sells physical CDs in addition to downloadable music. Unsigned musicians send in an existing CD or MP3 files of their original material, and then iJams duplicates the CDs on demand as orders come in and makes the MP3s available for immediate purchase or download. Musicians can also send in digital files of CD artwork, and iJams will print full-color CD inserts and other supporting materials. Additionally, iJams sells promotional items such as T-shirts, stickers, and mouse pads branded for artists.

As an employee of iJams, you have been asked to make a presentation representing the company to the JamWorks trade show. Your goal is to introduce iJams to trade show attendees and entice them with a promotional offer. You decide to use PowerPoint with a new netbook computer and video projection system to develop and deliver your presentation. You choose PowerPoint because it is easy to learn and seamlessly integrates with other Microsoft Office applications.

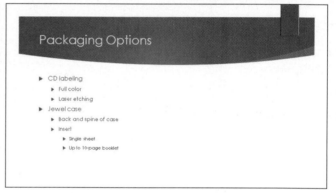

Slides from the iJams presentation

Presenting PowerPoint

Video Library   http://labyrinthelab.com/videos   Video Number: PP13-V0101

PowerPoint 2013 is an intuitive, powerful presentation graphics program that enables you to create dynamic, multimedia presentations for a variety of functions. Whether you are developing a one-on-one presentation for your manager or a sophisticated presentation for a large group, PowerPoint provides the tools to make your presentation a success. PowerPoint allows you to project your presentation in a variety of ways. Most presentations are delivered via a computer projection display attached to a notebook computer. There are also other ways to deliver presentations. For example, you can deliver a presentation as an online broadcast over the Internet or save it as a video to be emailed or distributed on CD.

PowerPoint provides easy-to-use tools that let you concentrate on the content of your presentation instead of focusing on the design details. Using PowerPoint's built-in document themes, you can rapidly create highly effective professional presentations.

Starting PowerPoint

To create a new presentation, use one of the following methods.

- In Windows 7, click the Start button then choose All Programs→Microsoft Office 2013→PowerPoint 2013.

- In Windows 8, scroll to the right of the Start screen then click the PowerPoint 2013 tile.

After the PowerPoint program has started, click Blank Presentation to create a new blank presentation. To open an existing presentation:

- Start PowerPoint, choose File→Open and click a recent presentation, or navigate to the presentation file and double-click it.

- In either version of Windows, navigate to the desired presentation by using Windows Explorer or Computer and double-click the presentation.

PowerPoint 2013

Start PowerPoint

In this exercise, you will start PowerPoint.

1. Follow these steps for the version of Windows you are running to open the PowerPoint 2013 program:

Windows 7

Ⓐ Click **Start**.

Ⓑ Point to **All Programs**.

Ⓒ Scroll down if necessary.

Ⓓ Click **Microsoft Office 2013**.

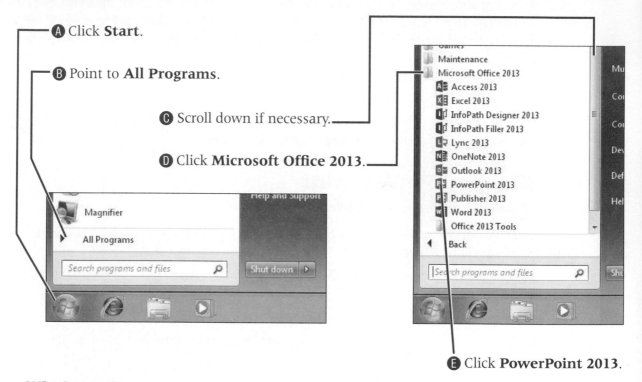

Ⓔ Click **PowerPoint 2013**.

Windows 8

Ⓐ Tap the [Windows] key, if necessary, to show the **Start screen**.

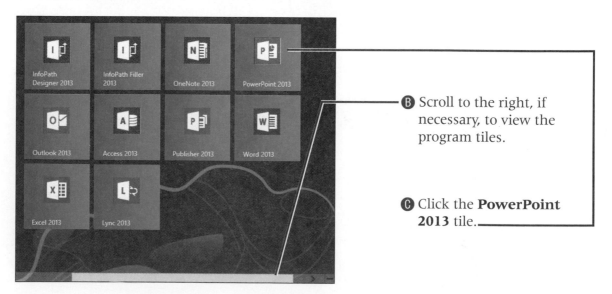

Ⓑ Scroll to the right, if necessary, to view the program tiles.

Ⓒ Click the **PowerPoint 2013** tile.

Creating a New Presentation

Video Library   http://labyrinthelab.com/videos   Video Number: PP13-V0102

When PowerPoint 2013 starts, it displays a Start screen that offers a variety of templates from which to choose. If your computer is connected to the Internet, PowerPoint will automatically display additional templates downloaded from the Microsoft web site. A template is a blank presentation that is preformatted with matching graphics, colors, and fonts. If you are not connected to the Internet, PowerPoint will display its default templates. A blank presentation option also is always available on the Start screen. Using the blank presentation template creates a blank, unformatted presentation to which you can add graphics, colors, and special fonts later.

Recently opened presentations are displayed here.

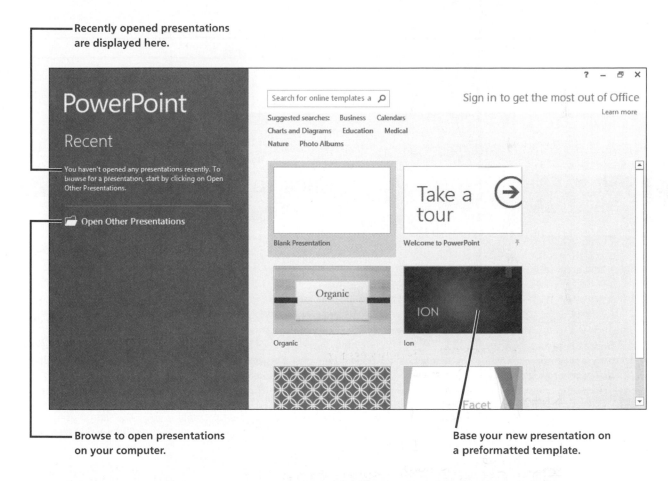

Browse to open presentations on your computer.

Base your new presentation on a preformatted template.

Create a Blank Presentation

In this exercise, you will create a new, blank presentation.

1. Click the **Blank Presentation** template on the PowerPoint Start screen.

A new, blank presentation appears. You will develop it throughout this lesson.

Navigating the PowerPoint Window

The PowerPoint 2013 program window, like other Microsoft Office programs, groups commands on the Ribbon. The following illustration provides an overview of the program window.

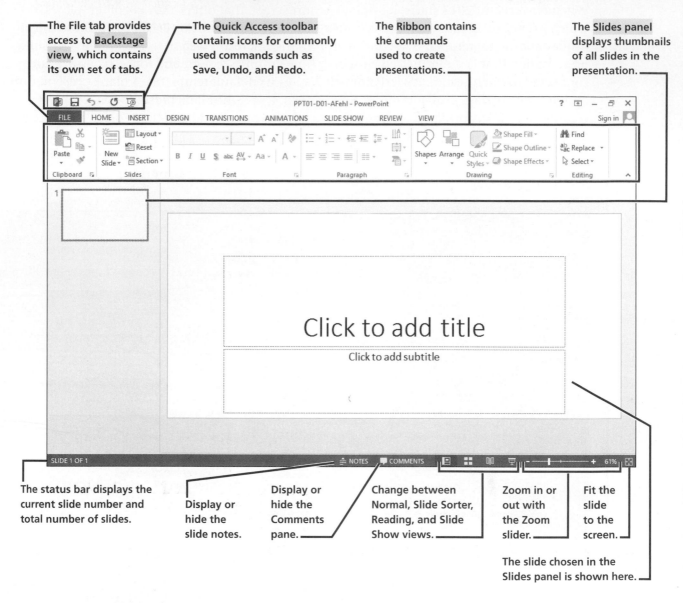

The File tab provides access to **Backstage** view, which contains its own set of tabs.

The Quick Access toolbar contains icons for commonly used commands such as Save, Undo, and Redo.

The Ribbon contains the commands used to create presentations.

The Slides panel displays thumbnails of all slides in the presentation.

The status bar displays the current slide number and total number of slides.

Display or hide the slide notes.

Display or hide the Comments pane.

Change between Normal, Slide Sorter, Reading, and Slide Show views.

Zoom in or out with the Zoom slider.

Fit the slide to the screen.

The slide chosen in the Slides panel is shown here.

Saving the Presentation

Video Library   http://labyrinthelab.com/videos   Video Number: PP13-V0103

The byword in PowerPoint is to save early and save often. You can use the Save button on the Quick Access toolbar or in Backstage view. If it's the first time a presentation has been saved, the Save As dialog box will appear because the file will need a name and location on your computer. You can also use the Save As dialog box to make a copy of a presentation by saving it under a new name or to a different location. If the file has already been saved, PowerPoint replaces the previous version with the new, edited version.

FROM THE KEYBOARD
Ctrl+S to save

FROM THE RIBBON
File→Save

Save the Presentation

In this exercise, you will save the presentation by giving it a name and a location on your computer.

Before You Begin: Navigate to the student resource center to download the student exercise files for this book.

1. Click the **Save** 🖫 button on the Quick Access toolbar.

   PowerPoint displays the Save As dialog box because this presentation has not yet been given a filename.

2. Follow these steps to save the presentation to your file storage location:

   🅐 Click **Computer**.   🅑 Click **Browse**.

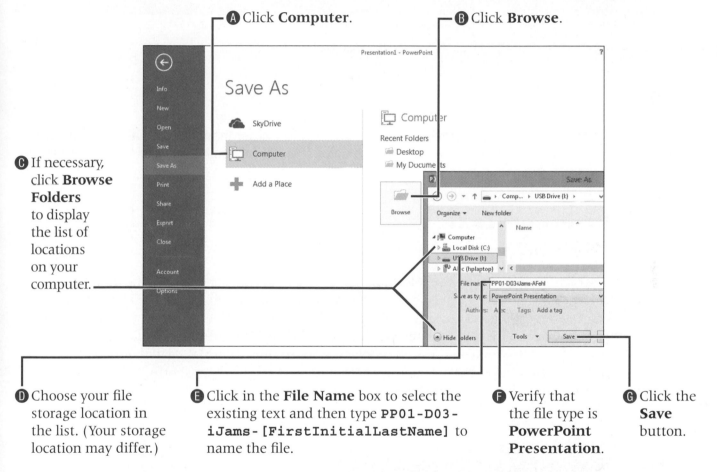

🅒 If necessary, click **Browse Folders** to display the list of locations on your computer.

🅓 Choose your file storage location in the list. (Your storage location may differ.)

🅔 Click in the **File Name** box to select the existing text and then type **PP01-D03-iJams-[FirstInitialLastName]** to name the file.

🅕 Verify that the file type is **PowerPoint Presentation**.

🅖 Click the **Save** button.

In the filename, replace the bracketed text with your first initial and last name. For example, the author's filename would look like this: PP01-D03-iJams-AFehl.

PowerPoint saves the presentation.

Save as Video

PowerPoint 2013 also allows you to save your presentation as a video. This is helpful if you want to distribute your presentation to others without requiring them to have PowerPoint or other special software. The video files are saved in the MPEG-4 (.mp4) format and are playable on any computer. When saving as a video, be patient as it takes some time to convert your presentation to the video format.

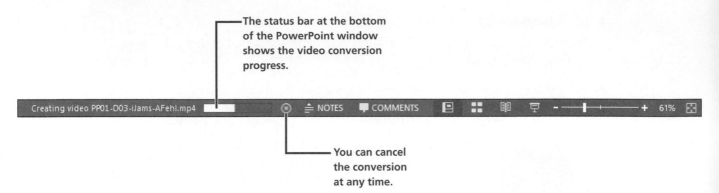

The status bar at the bottom of the PowerPoint window shows the video conversion progress.

You can cancel the conversion at any time.

The video version of a presentation can be 15 times larger than the original PowerPoint file. Be aware of the file size before you try to email a video to someone.

FROM THE RIBBON
File→Export→Create a Video

Inserting Text

Video Library   http://labyrinthelab.com/videos   Video Number: PP13-V0104

PowerPoint slides have placeholders set up for you to type in. For example, the title slide currently visible on the screen has placeholders for a title and subtitle. You click in the desired placeholder to enter text on a slide. For example, to enter the title on a slide, you click in the title placeholder and then type the text. Do not press the [Enter] key; the placeholders are already formatted with word wrap. The placeholders also are already formatted with font and paragraph settings to make a cohesive presentation. As you will see shortly, it's easy to make changes to the formatting of slides by applying a theme.

Type a Title Slide

In this exercise, you will enter a title and subtitle for the presentation.

1. Choose **File→Save As** and save your file as **PP01-D04-iJams-[FirstInitialLastName]**.

2. Follow these steps to add a title and subtitle:

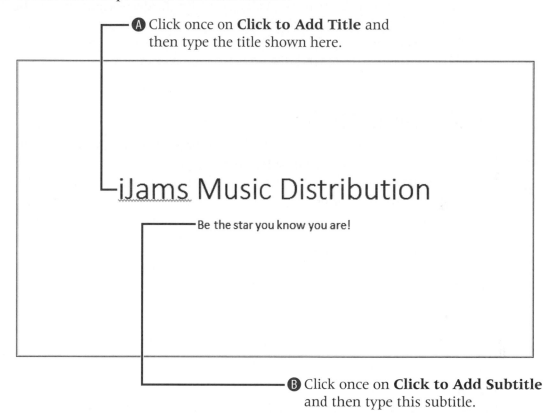

Ⓐ Click once on **Click to Add Title** and then type the title shown here.

iJams Music Distribution

Be the star you know you are!

Ⓑ Click once on **Click to Add Subtitle** and then type this subtitle.

PowerPoint enters the titles. At this point, you have a title slide, but it looks rather plain. This is about to change.

3. Save the presentation and leave it open; you will modify it throughout the lesson.

PowerPoint 2013

Using Document Themes

Video Library   http://labyrinthelab.com/videos   Video Number: PP13-V0105

You can use PowerPoint's built-in document themes, which provide a ready-made backdrop for your presentations, to easily format all slides in a presentation. When you use a document theme, your presentation automatically includes an attractive color scheme, consistent font style and size, and bulleted lists to synchronize with the design and style of the presentation. Document themes also position placeholders on slides for titles, text, bulleted lists, graphics, and other objects. By using document themes, you can focus on content by simply filling in the blanks as you create the presentation. You access document themes from the Themes group on the Design tab.

Choosing a Theme

Nine document themes are included with PowerPoint 2013. Additionally, each theme has four variations. A theme variation uses different colors and sometimes a different background. PowerPoint automatically downloads additional themes and adds them to the Themes gallery on the Ribbon if your computer is connected to the Internet. Match the theme to the type of presentation you are giving. Keep the design appropriate to the function and the audience.

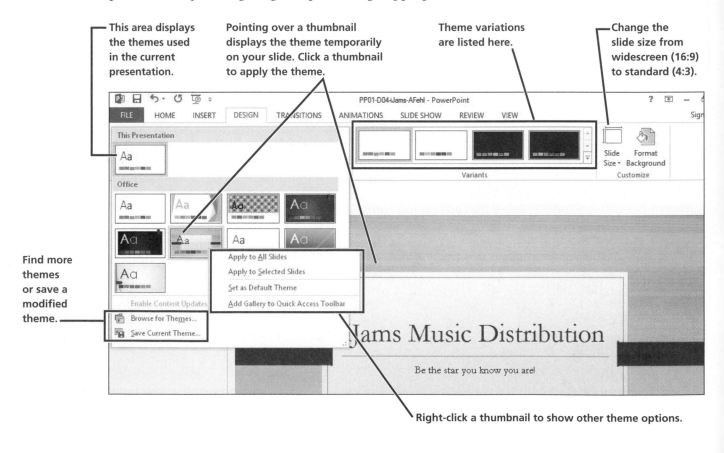

This area displays the themes used in the current presentation.

Pointing over a thumbnail displays the theme temporarily on your slide. Click a thumbnail to apply the theme.

Theme variations are listed here.

Change the slide size from widescreen (16:9) to standard (4:3).

Find more themes or save a modified theme.

Right-click a thumbnail to show other theme options.

Finding Additional Themes

New themes are sent to Microsoft daily, so if you just can't find the right one, browse the Microsoft Office Online website for new themes. You can also search for new themes from the PowerPoint Start screen.

Using the PowerPoint Ribbon

The PowerPoint Ribbon is organized into nine default tabs: File, Home, Insert, Design, Transitions, Animations, Slide Show, Review, and View. As in other Office 2013 applications, additional tabs appear when certain elements on a slide are selected. These additional tabs, called contextual tabs, offer commands specific to the selected element; for example, selecting a picture on a slide results in the Picture Tools Format tab being shown. Deselecting the picture returns the Ribbon to its original state with the nine default tabs.

FROM THE RIBBON
Design→Themes

Each tab contains many commands, which are organized in groups called command groups. Each group is labeled across the bottom and contains a variety of buttons or button menus.

The Home tab displays several groups of buttons.

Some groups contain a small icon in the bottom-right corner that, when clicked, displays a dialog box or a task pane.

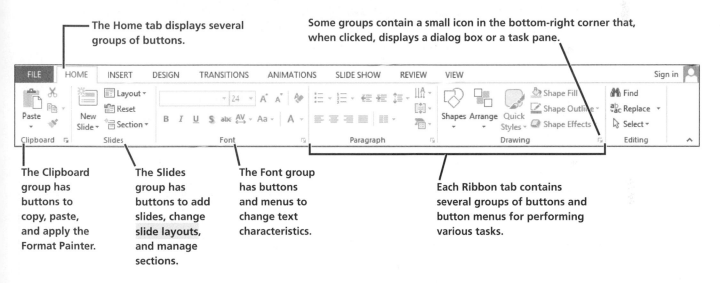

The Clipboard group has buttons to copy, paste, and apply the Format Painter.

The Slides group has buttons to add slides, change slide layouts, and manage sections.

The Font group has buttons and menus to change text characteristics.

Each Ribbon tab contains several groups of buttons and button menus for performing various tasks.

PowerPoint 2013

Apply a Document Theme

In this exercise, you will choose a document theme and apply it to the presentation.

1. Choose **File→Save As** and save your file as **PP01-D05-iJams-[FirstInitialLastName]**.

2. Follow these steps to choose a theme for the presentation:

   Depending on your monitor resolution, you may see a different number of thumbnails in the Themes group.

   Ⓐ Display the **Design** tab.

   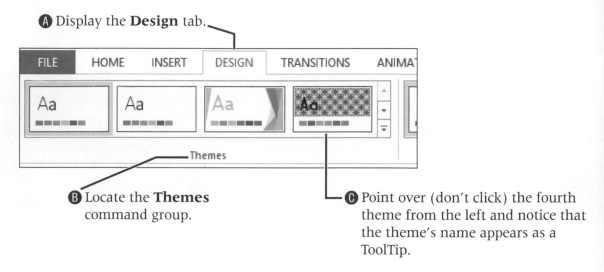

   Ⓑ Locate the **Themes** command group.

   Ⓒ Point over (don't click) the fourth theme from the left and notice that the theme's name appears as a ToolTip.

   PowerPoint displays a Live Preview of the theme on your title slide. This gives you a good idea of the overall design of the theme. Notice that the fonts and locations have changed for the title and subtitle. A different theme can radically redesign your presentation.

Throughout this book, the preceding command will be written as follows: Choose Design→Themes→[Theme command].

3. Point over (don't click) several more theme thumbnails.

   You see a Live Preview of each theme on the actual slide. The themes visible on the Ribbon are just a small portion of those available, however.

4. Follow these steps to choose a theme:

Ⓐ Choose **Design→Themes→More**.

Ⓑ Point to preview the **Organic** theme.

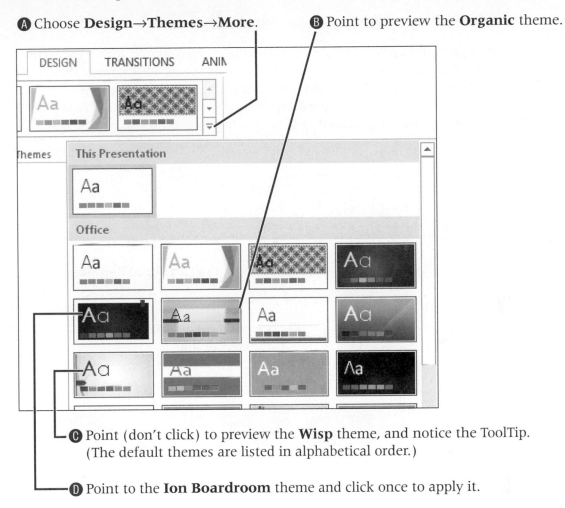

Ⓒ Point (don't click) to preview the **Wisp** theme, and notice the ToolTip. (The default themes are listed in alphabetical order.)

Ⓓ Point to the **Ion Boardroom** theme and click once to apply it.

PowerPoint applies the theme to your presentation.

5. Save the presentation and leave it open for the next exercise.

Choosing Slide Sizes

Video Library   http://labyrinthelab.com/videos   Video Number: PP13-V0106

By default, PowerPoint creates slides for widescreen format with a 16:9 ratio. This maximizes the use of space on the slide by taking advantage of the widescreen format on most modern computers. In fact, many of the new PowerPoint 2013 themes were designed specifically for widescreen use. You can easily switch to standard (4:3) format from the Ribbon if you need a narrower slide or have a non-widescreen computer monitor.

FROM THE RIBBON

Design→Customize →Slide Size to change the slide size

DEVELOP YOUR SKILLS PP01-D06
Apply a Theme Variation

In this exercise, you will experiment with slide sizes and choose a document theme variation.

1. Save your file as **PP01-D06-iJams-[FirstInitialLastName]**.

2. Follow these steps to change the slide size:

Ⓐ Display the **Design** tab.

Ⓑ Locate the **Customize** command group.

Ⓒ Click the **Slide Size** button.

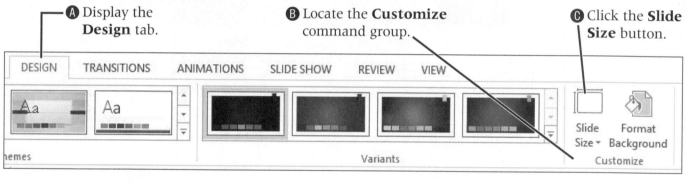

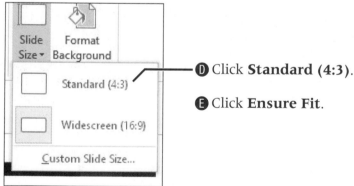

Ⓓ Click **Standard (4:3)**.

Ⓔ Click **Ensure Fit**.

The slide is resized, and the slide title shifts to wrap across two lines.

3. Choose **Design→Customize→Slide Size→Widescreen (16:9)** to return the slide to widescreen format.

4. Locate the **Design→Variants** group on the Ribbon.

5. Point to several theme variations to view the Live Preview on the slide.

6. Click the **second variation** (with the green background) to apply it.

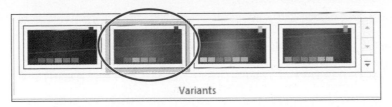

Variants

7. Save the presentation and leave it open for the next exercise.

Creating a Basic Presentation

Video Library   http://labyrinthelab.com/videos   Video Number: PP13-V0107

There is more to creating a presentation than placing one slide after another. Choosing the appropriate slide layout, just like choosing the appropriate design, will influence how well your audience understands your message. Use the following guidelines when choosing your slide design and layout:

- **Know your audience:** Will you be speaking to accountants or artists?
- **Know your purpose:** Are you introducing a product or giving a report?
- **Know your expectations:** When the last word of this presentation has been given, how do you want your audience to respond to your facts? Are you looking for approval for a project or customers for a product?

Adding Slides

You can add slides to a presentation from the Ribbon or by right-clicking with the mouse. PowerPoint always places the new slide after the currently selected slide.

The Slides panel displays thumbnails of your presentation while you work in the Normal view. The Slide Sorter view, like the Slides panel, also displays thumbnails of your slides. This view can be useful when there are more slides than can fit in the Slides panel display.

QUICK REFERENCE	ADDING SLIDES
Task	**Procedure**
Add a slide with the Ribbon	▪ Choose Home→Slides→New Slide 🖼.
Add a slide with the mouse	▪ Right-click a slide on the Slides panel.
	▪ Choose New Slide from the pop-up (context) menu.

Add a New Slide

In this exercise, you will add a new slide to the presentation and then enter content.

1. Save your file as **PP01-D07-iJams-[FirstInitialLastName]**.

2. Follow these steps to add a new slide:

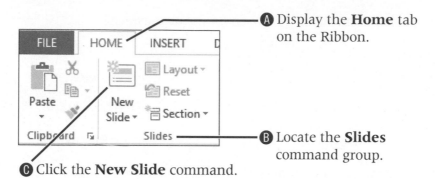

Ⓐ Display the **Home** tab on the Ribbon.

Ⓑ Locate the **Slides** command group.

Ⓒ Click the **New Slide** command.

PowerPoint adds a new slide to the presentation immediately after the title slide.

3. Click once in the title placeholder and then type **Our Services** as the title.

4. Click once on the **Click to Add Text** placeholder and then type the following list. Tap the Enter key after each list item except the last one.

   ■ **CD duplication on demand** Enter
   ■ **Jewel-case-insert printing** Enter
   ■ **Full-service online sales** Enter
   ■ **Downloadable MP3 distribution**

   PowerPoint adds a bullet in front of each line.

5. Save the presentation and leave it open for the next exercise.

Duplicating a Slide

Sometimes it is more efficient to duplicate a slide and then edit it rather than begin a new slide from scratch. Slides can be duplicated via the Slides panel.

QUICK REFERENCE	DUPLICATING A SLIDE
Task	**Procedure**
Duplicate a single slide	■ Right-click the slide you wish to duplicate in the Slides panel. ■ Choose Duplicate Slide. The new slide is inserted below the original.
Duplicate multiple slides	■ Use Ctrl+click or Shift+click to select the desired slides in the Slides panel. ■ Right-click any of the selected slides and choose Duplicate Slide. The new slides are inserted below the selected slides.

Indenting Bulleted Lists

Video Library　http://labyrinthelab.com/videos　Video Number: PP13-V0108

When using PowerPoint, you can effortlessly create bulleted lists to outline the thrust of your presentation. The bulleted list layout is an outline of nine levels. A different indentation is used for each level. The following illustration shows the Packaging Options slide you will create in the next exercise.

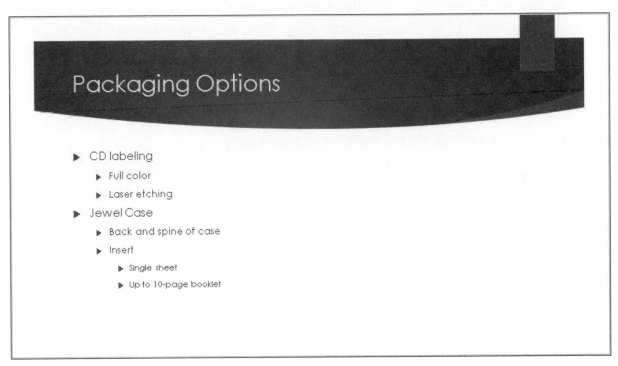

This bulleted list has three levels. Each level uses the same-shape character, but the text and bullet get smaller with each indentation.

Working with Bulleted Lists

When you use a document theme, each paragraph is automatically formatted as a bulleted list. The format includes a bullet style, indentation level, font type, and font size for each bulleted paragraph. This outline for the bulleted list is held within a placeholder or text box.

Working with List Levels

Indenting a bullet is referred to as demoting a bullet, or increasing the list level. Typically, a main bullet point has one or more sub-bullets. These sub-bullets, which are smaller than the main bullet, are created by increasing the list level. When a list level is increased, the bullets are indented toward the right. Conversely, decreasing a bullet's indent by moving it more toward the left and increasing the bullet size is referred to as promoting a bullet, or decreasing the list level. PowerPoint supports a main bullet and up to eight sub-bullets.

DEVELOP YOUR SKILLS PP01-D08

Create a Bulleted List

In this exercise, you will create a new slide and then enter information into a multilevel bulleted list.

1. Save your file as **PP01-D08-iJams-[FirstInitialLastName]**.

2. Choose **Home→Slides→New Slide** 🖿.

   PowerPoint creates a new slide after the current slide.

3. Click in the title placeholder and type **Packaging Options**.

4. Click once in the text placeholder.

5. Type **CD labeling** and then tap Enter.

   PowerPoint formats the new blank paragraph with the same large bullet. Paragraph formats are carried to new paragraphs when you tap the Enter key.

6. Tap Tab.

   PowerPoint indents the paragraph. It also introduces a new, slightly smaller style for the level-2 paragraph.

7. Type **Full color**.

   PowerPoint formats the paragraph in a smaller font too.

8. Tap Enter.

   PowerPoint maintains the same level-2 formatting for the next paragraph.

9. Type **Laser etching** and then tap Enter.

10. While holding down Shift, tap Tab once.

    PowerPoint promotes the new paragraph back to the level-1 style, which is the level of the first paragraph on the slide.

Manipulate Heading Levels

You can also adjust the level after you have typed a paragraph.

11. Type these lines:

- **Jewel case**
- **Back and spine of case**

12. Follow these steps to indent the last bullet:

Ⓐ Click once anywhere within the paragraph to be indented.

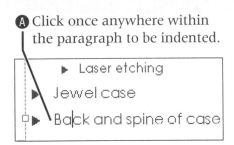

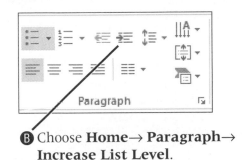

Ⓑ Choose **Home→ Paragraph→ Increase List Level**.

PowerPoint indents the paragraph and changes the bullet style. Demoting a paragraph makes it subordinate to the preceding paragraph.

13. Click the **Increase List Level** button three more times.

The bullet and font sizes change with each level increase. These formats are determined by the Ion Boardroom theme, on which the presentation is based.

14. Click **Home→Paragraph→Decrease List Level** three times until the bullet reaches the second indentation.

With each promotion, the bullet style changes.

Indent Multiple Bullets

15. Click once at the end of the last paragraph and then tap Enter.

16. Type these new lines:

- **Insert**
- **Single sheet**
- **Up to 10-page booklet**

17. Follow these steps to select the last two paragraphs for your next command:

Ⓐ Point at the beginning of *Single sheet*, taking care that a four-pointed arrow is not visible.

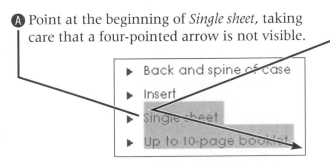

Ⓑ Drag down and right to select (highlight) to the end of the last paragraph; release the mouse button.

Ⓒ Ignore a Mini toolbar that appears. Take care not to click anywhere else on the slide before you perform the next step.

18. Choose **Home→Paragraph→Increase List Level**.

PowerPoint indents the two selected paragraphs.

19. Click anywhere outside the border to deselect the text. Your slide should match the following illustration.

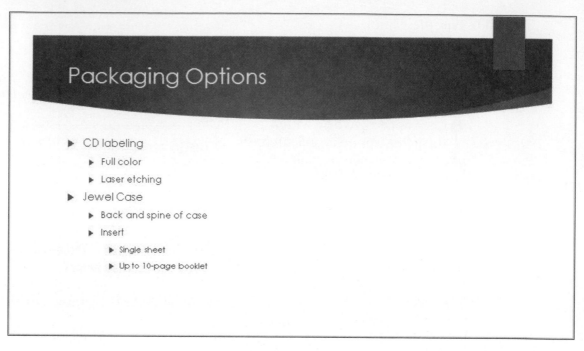

20. Save the presentation and leave it open for the next exercise.

Choosing the Slide Layout

Video Library http://labyrinthelab.com/videos Video Number: PP13-V0109

Slide layouts are named for the type of data they will contain. For example, the Title layout needs only a title and subtitle. The Content layout will hold other information on the slide, so it has a title and a bulleted list for points. Likewise, the Content with Caption layout is divided into three sections: title, text to one side, and an area for clip art or additional text. The slide layout organizes the information you put into the presentation by giving it a place on the slide. The new layout is applied to all selected slides. There are nine standard layouts, but many themes offer additional layouts.

FROM THE RIBBON
Home→Slides→
Layout ▼ menu

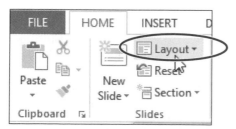

Clicking the Layout button in the Slides group on the Home tab allows you to apply a new layout to the selected slide(s).

Change the Slide Layout

In this exercise, you will add a new slide and then change its layout.

1. Save your file as **PP01-D09-iJams-[FirstInitialLastName]**.

2. If necessary, select the **Packaging Options** slide from the Slides panel on the left side of your screen.

3. Choose **Home→Slides→New Slide** ▦.

   PowerPoint adds another slide to the end of the presentation. Like the previous two slides, this one is set up to display a bulleted list.

4. Follow these steps to choose a new layout for the slide:

   A Choose **Home→Slides→Layout menu button.**▼

   B Choose the **Section Header** slide layout.

PowerPoint applies the new layout. Now there are two placeholders, for a title and subtext.

5. Enter the following text:

- Title: `Questions?`
- Text: `End of our brief presentation`

Your slide should resemble the following illustration.

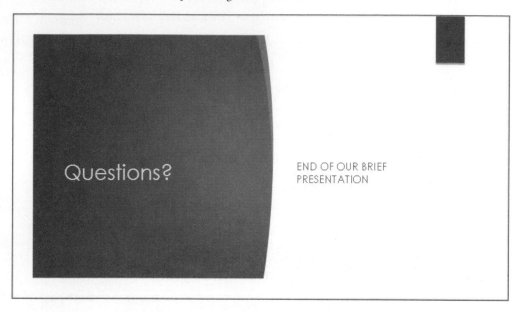

6. Save the presentation and leave it open for the next exercise.

Delivering the Slide Show

Video Library   http://labyrinthelab.com/videos   Video Number: PP13-V0110

The slides are created, and the presentation is complete. The first phase of the presentation development is over. The next phase, delivering the presentation, is just beginning. Before you stand before an audience, familiarize yourself with the following tips.

Delivery Tips

It is not only what you say, but how you say it that makes the difference between an engaging presentation and an unsuccessful one. Lead your audience. Help them to focus on the message of your presentation, not on you as the presenter. Use the following *PEER* guidelines to deliver an effective presentation:

- **Pace:** Maintain a moderate pace. Speaking too fast will exhaust your audience, and speaking too slowly may put them to sleep. Carry your audience with you as you talk.
- **Emphasis:** Pause for emphasis. As you present, use a brief pause to emphasize your point. This pause will give the audience time to absorb your message.

- **Eye contact:** Address your audience. Always face your audience while speaking. A common mistake is to speak while walking or facing the projection screen. Don't waste all of the work you have done in the presentation by losing the interest of your audience now. If you are speaking from a lectern or desk, resist the temptation to lean on it. Stand tall, make eye contact, and look directly at your audience.
- **Relax:** You are enthusiastic and want to convey that tone to the audience. However, when you speak, avoid fast movement, pacing, and rushed talking. Your audience will be drawn to your movements and miss the point. Remember that the audience is listening to you to learn; this material may be old hat to you, but it's new to them. So speak clearly, maintain a steady pace, and stay calm.

Navigating Through a Slide Show

You can use the mouse and/or simple keyboard commands to move through a slide show. These are the easiest ways to navigate from one slide to the next.

FROM THE KEYBOARD

Spacebar or → to advance a slide

Backspace or ← to back up a slide

PowerPoint 2013

The Slide Show Toolbar

The Slide Show toolbar is your navigator during the slide show. It is hidden when a slide show starts, but becomes visible when you move your mouse around or point to the lower-left area of the screen. The Slide Show toolbar can be used to navigate a slide show or to draw attention to a specific area on a slide. However, use of this toolbar is unnecessary when you present a simple slide show like this one.

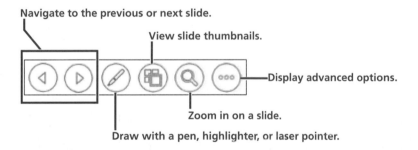

Navigate to the previous or next slide.

View slide thumbnails.

Display advanced options.

Zoom in on a slide.

Draw with a pen, highlighter, or laser pointer.

QUICK REFERENCE	USING BASIC SLIDE SHOW NAVIGATION
Task	**Procedure**
Advance a slide	■ Click once with the mouse, or tap Spacebar, →, Page Down, or Enter.
Back up a slide	■ Tap Backspace, Page Up, or ←.
Display the Slide Show toolbar	■ Move the mouse around on the screen for a moment.

Run the Slide Show

In this exercise, you will navigate through your slide show.

1. Follow these steps to start the slide show:

   Ⓐ Click the title slide in the Slides panel to select it.

   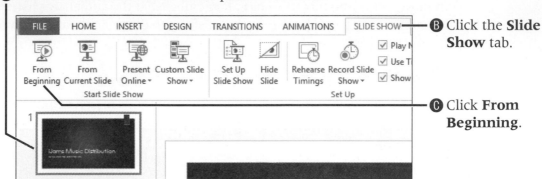

   Ⓑ Click the **Slide Show** tab.

   Ⓒ Click **From Beginning**.

2. Move the **mouse pointer** around the screen for a moment.

   Notice the Slide Show  toolbar that appears near the bottom-left corner of the screen when the slides are in full-screen view.

3. Click the **mouse pointer** anywhere on the screen to move to the next slide.

4. Tap ⎡Page Down⎤ twice and then tap ⎡Page Up⎤ twice by using the keys near the main keyboard (not the keys on the numeric keypad).

   PowerPoint displays the next or previous slide each time you tap these keys.

5. Follow these steps to use the Slide Show toolbar:

   Ⓐ Point to the lower-left area of the slide to display the Slide Show toolbar.

   Ⓑ Click **Show all Slides** to display thumbnails of all slides.

6. Click the **Packaging Options** slide.

   As you can see, there are many ways to navigate slides in an electronic slide show.

End the Slide Show

7. Continue to click anywhere on the screen until the last slide appears (the Questions slide).

8. Click once on the last slide.

   The screen turns to a black background, with a small note at the top.

9. Click anywhere on the black screen to exit the slide show and return to the main PowerPoint window.

10. Feel free to practice running your slide show again.

11. Choose **File→Close** to close the presentation.

Getting Help

Video Library   http://labyrinthelab.com/videos   Video Number: PP13-V0111

PowerPoint, like many other software programs, has so many features that it is unlikely you will learn and remember everything about it at once. That is where PowerPoint Help comes in. You can use the help system to learn to perform specific tasks or browse general information about a variety of categories.

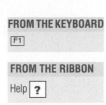

FROM THE KEYBOARD
F1

FROM THE RIBBON
Help ?

PowerPoint 2013

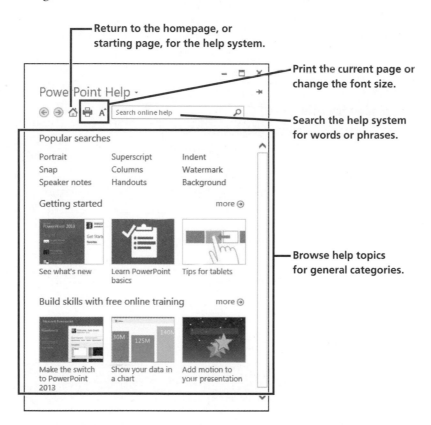

Return to the homepage, or starting page, for the help system.

Print the current page or change the font size.

Search the help system for words or phrases.

Browse help topics for general categories.

Using Online and Offline Help

If you are connected to the Internet when you open the PowerPoint Help window, PowerPoint connects to the Microsoft website and displays the most up-to-date help content. If you are not connected to the Internet, you can search for help topics in the offline help system that was installed on your computer when PowerPoint was installed.

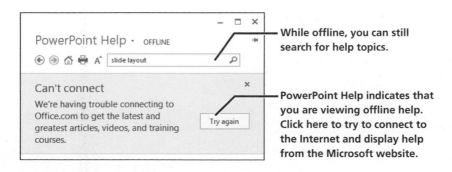

While offline, you can still search for help topics.

PowerPoint Help indicates that you are viewing offline help. Click here to try to connect to the Internet and display help from the Microsoft website.

Use PowerPoint Help

In this exercise, you will use the PowerPoint Help system.

1. Click the **Help** ? button on the right side of the Ribbon.

2. Follow these steps to search for help on a specific topic:

A Click in the search box, type
slide layout, and tap Enter.

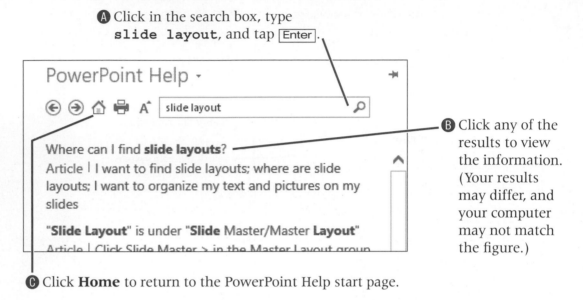

B Click any of the
results to view
the information.
(Your results
may differ, and
your computer
may not match
the figure.)

C Click **Home** to return to the PowerPoint Help start page.

3. **Close** ✕ the PowerPoint Help window.

4. Choose **File→Exit** to close PowerPoint.

Concepts Review

To check your knowledge of the key concepts introduced in this lesson, complete the Concepts Review quiz by choosing the appropriate access option below.

If you are...	Then access the quiz by...
Using the Labyrinth Video Library	Going to http://labyrinthelab.com/videos
Using eLab	Logging in, choosing Content, and navigating to the Concepts Review quiz for this lesson
Not using the Labyrinth Video Library or eLab	Going to the student resource center for this book

Reinforce Your Skills

Create a Presentation

In this exercise, you will begin to create a presentation for the Kids for Change organization—a community-based organization that helps socially aware youth plan and organize events that benefit their community. The presentation will be used to recruit new members and will be shown in high schools across the country.

Present PowerPoint

1. Start the **PowerPoint** program.

2. Click the **Blank Presentation** choice.

   A new presentation with a single slide is created.

3. **Save** 🖫 the file as **PP01-R01-Kids-[FirstInitialLastName]** in the **PP2013 Lesson 01** folder.

4. Click the **Design** tab and familiarize yourself with the various commands there.

5. Click the **Home** tab and familiarize yourself with the various commands there.

Apply a Document Theme

6. Choose **Design→Themes** and then choose the **Facet** theme.

   PowerPoint applies the theme to your presentation.

7. Locate **Design→Variants** and then choose the second (the blue) variation.

   PowerPoint applies the color variation to your presentation.

8. Click in the **Title** placeholder and type the title **Kids for Change**.

9. Click in the **Subtitle** placeholder and type the subtitle **I can make a difference**.

   As you type, the text is automatically colored because that is a design element of this particular document theme.

10. Save and then close the presentation. Submit your final file based on the guidelines provided by your instructor. Exit **PowerPoint**.

    To view examples of how your file or files should look at the end of this exercise, go to the student resource center.

Add Slides and Deliver a Presentation

In this exercise, you will complete the Kids for Change presentation by adding slides and text. Finally, you will deliver the presentation and learn how to find help in PowerPoint.

Create a Basic Presentation

1. Start **PowerPoint**; open **PP01-R02-Kids** from the **PP2013 Lesson 01** folder and save it as PP01-R02-Kids-[FirstInitialLastName].

2. Choose **Home→Slides→New Slide** 📄.

   A single-column, bulleted list slide is added to the presentation. Notice that the Facet document theme is applied to the new slide.

3. Choose **Home→Slides→** 📄 Layout ▾ **→Two Content**.

   A new, two-column layout is applied to the slide.

4. Click in the **Title** placeholder and type the title **Events**.

5. Add the following text to the bulleted list on the left:
   - iRecycling Day
   - Toy Collection
   - Shave and a Haircut
   - Diversity Festival

6. Add the following text to the bulleted list on the right:
   - Build-a-House
   - Bully No More
   - Adopt a Street
   - Tutoring

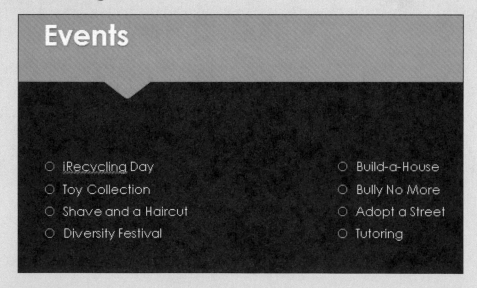

7. **Save** 💾 your presentation.

Create the Remaining Slides

8. Choose **Home→Slides→New Slide** ▤.

   A third slide is added to the presentation. The new slide has the same Two Content layout as the previous slide.

9. In the **Title** placeholder, enter the phrase **Program Benefits**.

10. In the first bullet of the left bulleted list, type **Personal** and tap Enter.

11. Choose **Home→Paragraph→Increase List Level** ▤.

    The bullet is indented, and a new smaller bullet character is applied by the design template.

12. Add the following text to the bulleted list on the left:

    ■ College application
    ■ Leadership skills
    ■ Sense of accomplishment

13. In the first bullet of the bulleted list on the right, type **Community** and tap Enter.

14. Choose **Home→Paragraph→Increase List Level** ▤.

    The bullet is indented, and a new smaller bullet character is applied by the design template.

15. Add the following text to the bulleted list on the right:

    ■ Crime reduction
    ■ Increased literacy
    ■ Improved health

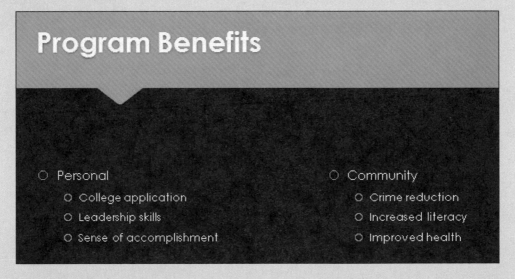

16. Choose **Home→Slides→New Slide** ▤.

17. Choose **Home→Slides→** ▤ Layout ▾ **→Title and Content**.

18. Type the title `Requirements`.

19. Type the following bullet points in the text box:
    - **You need**
    - **Positive attitude**
    - **Strong work ethic**
    - **Time commitment**
    - **One monthly event**
    - **One annual meeting**

20. Select the *Positive attitude* and *Strong work ethic* paragraphs and increase their list level.

21. Select the *One monthly event* and *One annual meeting* paragraphs and increase their list level.

22. Choose **Home→Slides→New Slide**.

23. Type `Regional Contact` for the title.

24. Type the following in the text box:
    - **Angelica Escobedo**
    - **(800) 555-1212**

25. Click the **dashed border** around the text box so it turns solid, and then choose **Home→Paragraph→Bullets** to remove the bullets. *The bullets are removed from all paragraphs in the text box.*

26. Choose **Home→Paragraph→Center** 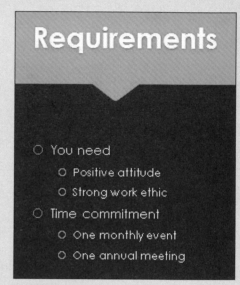 to center the text on the slide.

Deliver a Slide Show

27. Select the first slide from the **Slides** panel on the left side of your screen.

28. Choose **Slide Show→Start Slide Show→From Beginning** . *The title slide will occupy your whole screen as the slide show starts.*

29. Walk through the presentation by clicking each slide until the presentation is ended.

30. Click once more to return to the PowerPoint program window.

31. Choose **Slide Show→Start Slide Show→From Beginning**  to start the slide show again.

32. After the slide show begins, position the mouse pointer at the bottom-left corner of the screen to display the **Slide Show** toolbar.

33. Click the **Show all Slides** button on the Slide Show toolbar.

    You will see thumbnails of each slide.

34. Click the **Program Benefits** slide.

35. Position the mouse pointer at the bottom-left corner of the screen to display the Slide Show toolbar.

36. Click the **More** button on the Slide Show toolbar.

37. Click **End Show** on the pop-up menu to end the slide show.

38. Save the presentation.

Find Help in PowerPoint

39. Click the **Help** button at the top-right of the Ribbon.

40. Type `customize theme` in the search box and then tap Enter.

41. Click the first result shown in the Help window and then read the help topic.

42. Close the **Help window** and exit **PowerPoint**.

43. Submit your final file based on the guidelines provided by your instructor. Exit **PowerPoint**.

    To view examples of how your file or files should look at the end of this exercise, go to the student resource center.

REINFORCE YOUR SKILLS PP01-R03

Create and Deliver a Presentation

In this exercise, you will create a presentation for Kids for Change that promotes their special event of the month.

Present PowerPoint

1. Start the **PowerPoint** program.

2. Click the **Blank Presentation** choice.

    A new presentation with a single slide is created.

3. Save 🖫 your file as `PP01-R03-Kids-[FirstInitialLastName]` in the **PP2013 Lesson 01** folder.

Apply a Document Theme

4. Choose **Design→Themes→More** and then choose the **Slice** theme.
   PowerPoint applies the theme to your presentation.

5. Locate **Design→Variants** and then choose the fourth variation.
   PowerPoint applies the variation to your presentation.

6. Click in the **Title** placeholder and type the title `Kids for Change`.

7. Click in the **Subtitle** placeholder and type the subtitle `June Event`.
   As you type, the text is automatically colored because that is a design element of this particular document theme.

8. Save ⊞ your presentation.

Create a Basic Presentation

9. Choose **Home→Slides→New Slide** ▥.

10. Click in the **Title** placeholder and type the title `Shave and a Haircut`.

11. Add the following text to the bulleted list:
    - `Free haircuts`
    - `Free shaves`
    - `Free mustache and beard trimming`

12. Save your presentation.

Create the Remaining Slides

13. Choose **Home→Slides→New Slide** ▥.

14. Choose **Home→Slides→**▥ Layout ▾**→Two Content**.
    A new two-column layout is applied to the slide.

15. In the **Title** placeholder, type `Participating Locations`.

16. In the first bullet of the left bulleted list, type `Barbers` and tap [Enter].

17. Choose **Home→Paragraph→Increase List Level** ▤.

18. Add the following text to the bulleted list on the left:
    - `Sam the Barber`
    - `Hats Off`
    - `Clean Cuts`

19. In the first bullet of the bulleted list on the right, type `Shelters` and tap [Enter].

20. Choose **Home→Paragraph→Increase List Level** ▤.
    The bullet is indented, and a new smaller bullet character is applied by the design theme.

21. Add the following text to the bulleted list on the right:
    - `Shelter on Main`
    - `Helping Hand`
    - `Safe Night`

22. Choose **Home→Slides→New Slide** .

23. Choose **Home→Slides→** Layout **→Title and Content**.

24. Enter the title `Dates and Availability`.

25. Type the following bullet points in the text box:
    - `All Locations`
    - `Every Saturday in June`
    - `8:00am – 8:00pm`
    - `Availability`
    - `Free service to help our community's homeless`

26. Select the two paragraphs under **All Locations** and increase their list level.

27. Select the last paragraph and increase its list level.

28. Choose **Home→Slides→New Slide** to add the final slide to the presentation.

29. Type `Sponsored By` for the title.

30. Type the following in the text box:
    - `Kids for Change`

31. Click the dashed border around the text box so it turns solid, and then choose **Home→Paragraph→Bullets** to remove the bullets.
    The bullets are removed from all paragraphs in the text box.

32. Choose **Home→Paragraph→Center** from the Ribbon to center the text on the slide.

Deliver a Slide Show

33. Select the first slide from the **Slides** panel on the left side of your screen.

34. Choose **Slide Show→Start Slide Show→From Beginning** from the Ribbon.
    The Title slide will occupy your whole screen as the slide show starts.

35. Walk through the presentation by clicking each slide until the presentation is ended.

36. Click once more to return to the PowerPoint program window.

37. Choose **Slide Show→Start Slide Show→From Beginning** from the Ribbon to start the slide show again.

38. After the slide show begins, position the mouse pointer at the bottom-left corner of the screen to display the **Slide Show** toolbar.

39. Click the **Show all Slides** button on the **Slide Show toolbar**.

40. Click the **Participating Locations** slide.

41. Position the mouse pointer at the bottom-left corner of the screen to display the **Slide Show toolbar**.

42. Click the **More** button on the Slide Show toolbar.

43. Click **End Show** on the pop-up menu to end the slide show.

44. Save the presentation.

Find Help in PowerPoint

45. Click the **Help** button at the top-right of the Ribbon.

46. Type **save movie** in the search box and then tap Enter .

47. Click the first result shown in the Help window and then read the help topic.

48. Close the **Help window** and exit **PowerPoint**.

49. Submit your final file based on the guidelines provided by your instructor.

Apply Your Skills

Create a Presentation

In this exercise, you will begin to create a presentation for Universal Corporate Events, a meeting and event planning service that handles event planning for businesses.

Start PowerPoint and Apply a Theme to a New Presentation

1. Start **PowerPoint**; create a new, blank presentation named **PP01-A01-Events-[FirstInitialLastName]** in the **PP2013 Lesson 01** folder.

2. Apply the **Facet** design document theme.

3. Apply the fourth variation, as shown in the illustration at the end of the exercise.

4. Add the following text to the title slide:
   - Title: **Universal Corporate Events**
   - Subtitle: **Events made easy**

5. Save your presentation. Exit **PowerPoint**.

6. Submit your final file based on the guidelines provided by your instructor.

   To view examples of how your file or files should look at the end of this exercise, go to the student resource center.

Add Slides and Deliver a Slide Show

In this exercise, you will complete the Universal Corporate Events presentation and deliver a slide show. Finally, you will have an opportunity to find help in PowerPoint.

Add Slides to a Presentation

1. Start **PowerPoint**; open **PP01-A02-Events** from the **PP2013 Lesson 01** folder and save it as **PP01-A02-Events-[FirstInitialLastName]**.

2. Add a second slide with the following text:

Title	Event Types
Bulleted paragraphs	■ Celebrations
	■ Team building
	■ Tradeshows
	■ Ceremonies

3. Add a third slide with the following text:

Title	Services
Bulleted paragraphs	■ Venue scouting
	■ Catering
	■ Invitations
	■ Stage and sound equipment

4. Add a fourth slide and change its layout to a **Two Content** layout. Add the following text:

Title	Benefits
Left bulleted paragraphs	■ Our jobs
	■ Deal with paperwork
	■ Guarantee safety
	■ Scheduling
Right bulleted paragraphs	■ Your jobs
	■ Relax
	■ Enjoy your event

5. Select all but the first bullet in the left text box and increase the list level.

6. Select all but the first bullet in the right text box and increase the list level.

7. Add a final slide to the presentation and apply the **Section Header** layout.
   - ■ Title: **Universal Corporate Events**
   - ■ Text: **Events made easy**

Deliver a Slide Show

8. Select the first slide from the **Slides** panel on the left side of your screen.

9. Start the slide show from the beginning.

10. Advance to the second slide.

11. Use the Slide Show toolbar to display all the slides and then jump to the **Benefits** slide.

12. Continue navigating the slides until the slide show ends and you are returned to the main PowerPoint window.

13. Save the presentation.

Get Help in PowerPoint

14. Start **Help** and search for **clear text formatting**.

15. Read the first help topic and then close the Help window.

16. Exit **PowerPoint**.

17. Submit your final file based on the guidelines provided by your instructor.

To view examples of how your file or files should look at the end of this exercise, go to the student resource center.

Create and Deliver a Presentation

In this exercise, you will create a new presentation for Universal Corporate Events that outlines each of their services.

1. Start **PowerPoint**.

2. Click **Blank Presentation**.

   A new presentation with a single slide is created.

3. Save your file as **PP01-A03-Events-[FirstInitialLastName]** in the **PP2013 Lesson 01** folder.

Apply a Document Theme

4. Apply the **Retrospect** theme.

   PowerPoint applies the theme to your presentation.

5. Locate **Design→Variants** and then choose the third variation.

6. Click in the **Title** placeholder and type the title **Universal Corporate Events**.

7. Click in the **Subtitle** placeholder and type the subtitle **Services**.

8. Save your presentation.

Add Slides to a Presentation

9. Add a second slide with the following text:

Title	Venue Scouting
Bulleted paragraphs	▪ Locate three potential venues
	▪ Provide digital tour
	▪ Provide transportation for up to four

10. Add a third slide with the following text:

Title	Catering
Bulleted paragraphs	▪ Vegetarian and vegan options
	▪ Kosher options
	▪ Never frozen

11. Add a fourth slide and change its layout to a **Two Content** layout. Add the following text:

Title	Invitations
Left bulleted paragraphs	■ Creative
	■ Graphic design
	■ Matching envelopes
Right bulleted paragraphs	■ Business
	■ Create mailing labels
	■ Mail first class

12. Select all but the first bullet in the left text box and increase the list level.

13. Select all but the first bullet in the right text box and increase the list level.

14. Add a final slide to the presentation. Apply the **Title and Content** layout and add the following text:

Title	Stage and Sound Equipment
Bulleted paragraphs	■ Speaker podium and PA
	■ 1200 watt sound system for bands
	■ Portable dance floor

Deliver a Slide Show

15. Select the first slide from the **Slides** panel on the left side of your screen.

16. Start the slide show from the beginning.

17. Advance to the second slide.

18. Use the Slide Show toolbar to display all the slides and then jump to the **Catering** slide.

19. Continue navigating the slides until the slide show ends and you are returned to the main PowerPoint window.

20. Save the presentation.

Get Help in PowerPoint

21. Start **Help** and search for `insert YouTube video`.

22. Read the first help topic and then close the Help window.

23. Exit **PowerPoint**.

24. Submit your final file based on the guidelines provided by your instructor.

Extend Your Skills

In the course of working through the Extend Your Skills exercises, you will think critically as you use the skills taught in the lesson to complete the assigned projects. To evaluate your mastery and completion of the exercises, your instructor may use a rubric, with which more points are allotted according to performance characteristics. (The more you do, the more you earn!) Ask your instructor how your work will be evaluated.

PP01-E01 That's the Way I See It

You are creating a presentation for a charity that you feel strongly about in order to educate others about it. First, decide on a known charity you support or agree with. If you don't know of any charities, think of a few ideas for charities (such as saving animals or the environment, ensuring human rights, curing disease, etc.). Then, use the Internet to find a reputable charity that deals with one of those topics.

Create a new, blank presentation and save it as **PP01-E01-Charity-[FirstInitialLastName]** in the **PP2013 Lesson 01** folder. Apply the design theme and variation of your choice. Type the charity name as the slide title and type a short, descriptive phrase for the subtitle. Add a Title and Content slide that lists at least four actions the charity takes toward bettering their cause. Add a Two Content slide. On the left, list a few facts about the charity. On the right, list ways to donate to the charity. Create a final slide with the Section Header layout that duplicates the content shown on the title slide. View the presentation as a slide show and make a mental note of anything you want to change. When the slide show ends, make your changes and then save your presentation.

You will be evaluated based on the inclusion of all elements specified, your ability to follow directions, your ability to apply newly learned skills to a real-world situation, your creativity, and the relevance of your topic and/or data choice(s). Submit your final file based on the guidelines provided by your instructor.

PP01-E02 Be Your Own Boss

Your landscaping business, Blue Jean Landscaping, saves its customers money by having them share in the physical labor. In this exercise, you will create multiple slides with varying layouts and bulleted text to advertise your unique business to potential investors. To begin, create a new, blank presentation named **PP01-E02-BlueJean-[FirstInitialLastName]** and saved to the **PP2013 Lesson 01** folder.

Apply the desired design theme and variation. Use the company name as the slide title and create a catchy phrase for the subtitle. Add a Title and Content slide that lists four services your company provides. Add a Two Content slide that lists the mutual benefits to the company and the customer: the left column uses **Us** as the first bullet, and the right column uses **You** as the first bullet. Then list at least three benefits for the company (left) and at least three for the customer (right). Increase the list level of all bullets except the first in each column.

Create a final slide with the Section Header layout that duplicates the content on the title slide. Run the slide show. Use the Slide Show toolbar to navigate the slide show and experiment with the other buttons on the toolbar. When the presentation ends, close PowerPoint. You will be evaluated based on the inclusion of all elements specified, your ability to follow directions, your ability to apply newly learned skills to a real-world situation, your creativity, and your demonstration of an entrepreneurial spirit. Submit your final file based on the guidelines provided by your instructor.

Transfer Your Skills

In the course of working through the Transfer Your Skills exercises, you will use critical-thinking and creativity skills to complete the assigned projects using skills taught in the lesson. To evaluate your mastery and completion of the exercises, your instructor may use a rubric, with which more points are allotted according to performance characteristics. (The more you do, the more you earn!) Ask your instructor how your work will be evaluated.

PP01-T01 Use the Web as a Learning Tool

Throughout this book, you will be provided with an opportunity to use the Internet as a learning tool by completing WebQuests. According to the original creators of WebQuests, as described on their website (WebQuest.org), a WebQuest is "an inquiry-oriented activity in which most or all of the information used by learners is drawn from the web." To complete the WebQuest projects in this book, navigate to the student resource center and choose the WebQuest for the lesson on which you are currently working. The subject of each WebQuest will be relevant to the material found in the lesson.

WebQuest Subject: Compare Presentation Graphics Software.

Submit your final file(s) based on the guidelines provided by your instructor.

PP01-T02 Demonstrate Proficiency

Stormy BBQ, a restaurant featuring fresh, locally grown vegetables and local, farm-raised pork/beef, is considering expanding to new locations. Create a PowerPoint presentation to show at a local town hall meeting to convince the local residents and community leaders that Stormy BBQ would be a great fit for their community.

Use an appropriate theme for the business and its commitment to the community. Perhaps search for additional themes from the PowerPoint Start screen. Create at least five slides, including the title slide, with a different layout for each slide. At least one slide should include bullet points with varying list levels.

Save the file as **PP01-T02-Stormy-[FirstInitialLastName]** to the **PP2013 Lesson 01** folder. Submit your final file based on the guidelines provided by your instructor.

POWERPOINT 2013

Designing the Presentation

LEARNING OBJECTIVES

After studying this lesson, you will be able to:

- Use Outline view to create, move, and delete slides and edit text

- Create a presentation from a Microsoft Word outline

- Format and align text and adjust character spacing and line spacing

- Use Slide Sorter view and Sections

- Print a presentation

In this lesson, you will build on the fundamental design of the iJams presentation. To add professional credibility and make your presentation easier for an audience to follow, you will establish a consistent style throughout the presentation and format and organize the text. You will add from the Outline panel and organize your completed presentation by using Slide Sorter view and Sections. To quickly create a basic presentation, you will import a Microsoft Word outline. Finally, working with the printing function of PowerPoint 2013, you will examine page setup, print preview, print setup, and the output format options.

Designing a Presentation

Now that the initial slides of the iJams presentation are complete, you need to make sure that the style is consistent throughout the presentation. A consistent style appears more organized, is easier for an audience to follow, and adds professional credibility. You must also ensure that the slides are in a logical sequence so the presentation is clear.

Products and Promotional Items

▶ Audio CDs	▶ Pencils
▶ Downloadable MP3s	▶ Key chains
▶ T-shirts	▶ Posters
▶ Baseball caps	▶ Mugs
▶ Stickers	▶ Mouse pads

Sample of slide formatted with a layout Microsoft calls Two Content

Working with Slides

Video Library   http://labyrinthelab.com/videos   Video Number: PP13-V0201

As your presentation progresses and you insert additional slides, you may want to change the slide layout or order. For example, some slides may require two columns of bulleted text while others require only one. PowerPoint makes it easy to change the order of slides by using Slide Sorter view.

Copying Text and Objects

FROM THE RIBBON
Home→Clipboard→Cut
Home→Clipboard→Copy
Home→Clipboard→Paste

You can move and copy text and objects by using drag and drop or the Cut, Copy, and Paste commands. It is usually most efficient to use drag and drop if you are moving or copying text or objects within a slide. Drag and drop is also effective for rearranging slides. Cut, Copy, and Paste are most efficient when moving or copying to a location not visible on the current screen.

FROM THE KEYBOARD
Ctrl+X to cut
Ctrl+C to copy
Ctrl+V to paste

QUICK REFERENCE	MOVING AND COPYING TEXT AND OBJECTS
Task	**Procedure**
Drag and drop	■ Select the desired text or click an object (e.g., placeholder box).
	■ Drag the text/object to the desired location. Press Ctrl while dragging to copy.
Right-drag and drop	■ Select the desired text or click an object (e.g., placeholder box).
	■ Use the right mouse button to drag the text/object to the desired location.
	■ Release the mouse button at the desired location and choose Move, Copy, or Cancel.

DEVELOP YOUR SKILLS PP02-D01
Add a New Slide to a Presentation

In this exercise, you will add a new slide to a presentation, enter a bulleted list, and change the layout of the slide. You can always change the layout for a slide after the slide has been created.

1. Start **PowerPoint**. Open **PP02-D01-Design** from the **PP2013 Lesson 02** folder and save it as **PP02-D01-Design-[FirstInitialLastName]**.

   Replace the bracketed text with your first initial and last name. For example, if your name is Bethany Smith, your filename will look like this: PP02-D01-Design-BSmith.

2. Select the **Our Services** slide from the **Slides** panel on the left side of your screen.

   The Our Services slide appears. New slides are inserted after the selected slide.

3. Choose **Home→Slides→New Slide** 📄.

4. Click in the **Title placeholder** and type **Products and Promotional Items**.

5. Click in the **bulleted list placeholder** and type this list:

- Audio CDs
- Downloadable MP3s
- T-shirts
- Baseball caps
- Stickers
- Pencils
- Key chains
- Posters
- Mugs
- Mouse pads

When you begin typing Mugs, *PowerPoint reformats the bullets with a smaller font size so they all fit in the box. As you type the last bullet point, the font gets even smaller. A long list of bullets can be overwhelming, so strive for no more than six bullets. If there is more information, consider breaking the list into two columns. You will use this technique next by choosing a different layout for the slide.*

6. Follow these steps to change the slide layout:

Ⓐ Display the **Home** tab.

Ⓑ Click the **Layout** menu ▼.

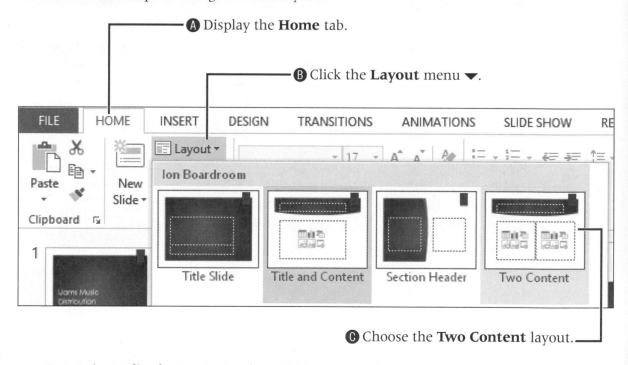

Ⓒ Choose the **Two Content** layout.

PowerPoint applies the Two Content layout to the current slide.

7. Follow these steps to move the last five bullets to the second box:

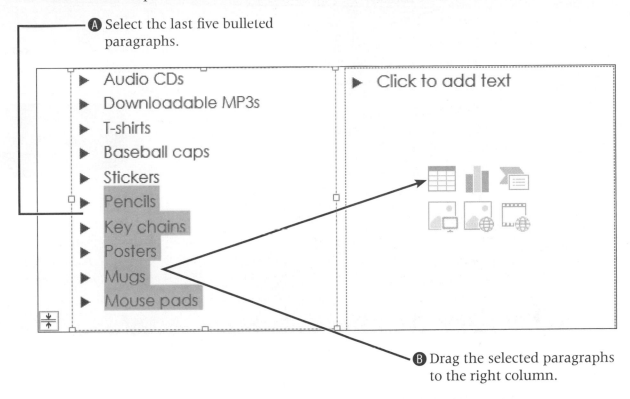

Ⓐ Select the last five bulleted paragraphs.

Ⓑ Drag the selected paragraphs to the right column.

This action moves the last five bulleted paragraphs into the right-side content area.

8. Save 🖫 the changes to your presentation.

Working with Outlines

Video Library   http://labyrinthelab.com/videos   Video Number: PP13-V0202

Although you have been working primarily in the slide to add or format text, the Outline panel is an alternative way to add, remove, and move text. The Outline panel is a useful interface to organize and structure your presentation.

Using the Outline Panel

The Outline panel helps you edit and reorganize slides. It's available on the left side of the screen in Outline view. You can type directly in the Outline panel to add or edit text on a slide. You can also select text from the Outline panel and format it with the standard Ribbon formatting commands. Any changes made in the Outline panel are immediately reflected in the actual slide.

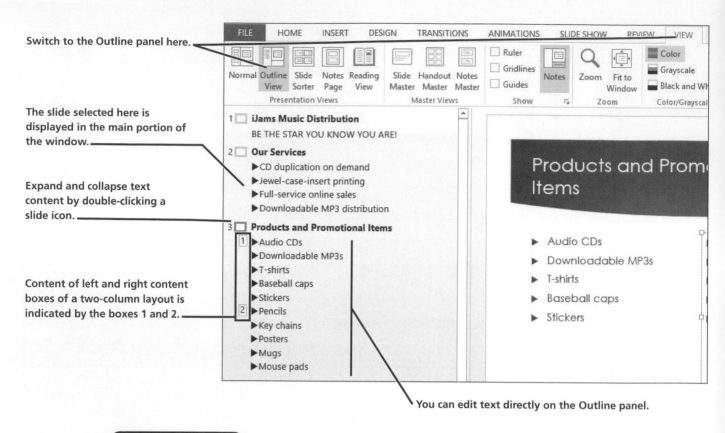

Switch to the Outline panel here.

The slide selected here is displayed in the main portion of the window.

Expand and collapse text content by double-clicking a slide icon.

Content of left and right content boxes of a two-column layout is indicated by the boxes 1 and 2.

You can edit text directly on the Outline panel.

QUICK REFERENCE	WORKING WITH OUTLINES
Task	**Procedure**
Select text in an outline	Drag over the desired text in the Outline panel.
Select an entire slide	Click the slide icon in the Outline panel.
Expand or collapse a slide	Double-click the slide icon in the Outline panel. Right-click the slide text in the Outline panel and choose Collapse (All) or Expand (All).
Add a new slide	Place the mouse pointer in the last group of bulleted paragraphs on a slide and press Ctrl+Enter.
Delete a slide	Right-click any text within a slide in the Outline panel and choose Delete Slide.

Add a Slide in the Outline Panel

In this exercise, you will work with the Outline panel to add text.

1. Save your file as **PP02-D02-Design-[FirstInitialLastName]**.

2. Follow these steps to select a slide while in the Outline panel:

Ⓐ Click the **View** tab.

Ⓑ Click **Outline View**.

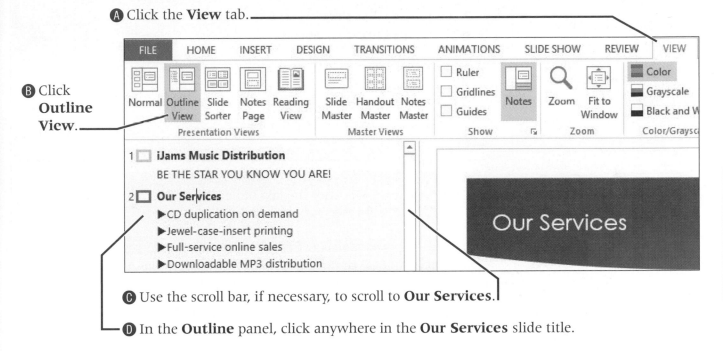

Ⓒ Use the scroll bar, if necessary, to scroll to **Our Services**.

Ⓓ In the **Outline** panel, click anywhere in the **Our Services** slide title.

3. Press Ctrl + Enter.
   The insertion point moves to the first bulleted paragraph in the slide.

4. Press Ctrl + Enter again.
   PowerPoint creates a new slide below the selected slide.

5. Follow these steps to add text to the new slide while in the Outline panel:

Ⓐ Type **Current Artists** here. Notice that the text also appears in the main portion of your window.

Ⓑ Press Ctrl + Enter to move to the first bulleted paragraph.

Ⓒ Type these bulleted paragraphs, tapping Enter after each.

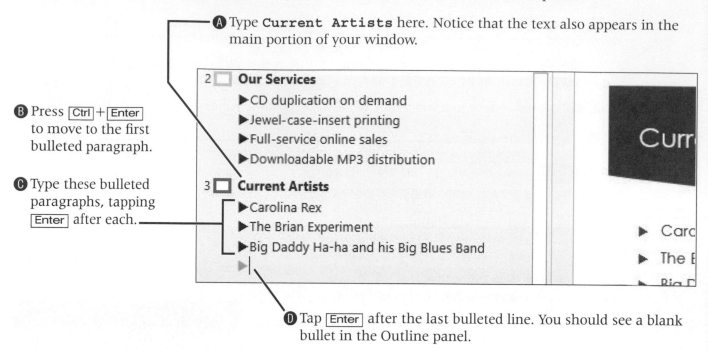

Ⓓ Tap Enter after the last bulleted line. You should see a blank bullet in the Outline panel.

PowerPoint adds a new slide to the presentation whenever the insertion point is positioned within the last box on a slide and the Ctrl + Enter *keystroke combination is issued. At this point, you should have a new, bulleted paragraph visible in the outline below the* Big Daddy Ha-ha *paragraph.*

6. Follow these steps to promote a paragraph to make a new slide:

Ⓐ Ensure that the insertion point is on the blank bulleted paragraph in the outline.

Ⓑ Choose **Home→Paragraph→ Decrease List Level**.

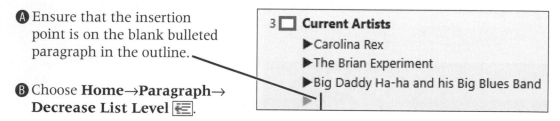

PowerPoint promotes the bulleted paragraph to create a new slide.

7. Type **New Artist Specials** and tap Enter.

Tapping Enter *created a new slide. You must use* Ctrl + Enter *to add a bulleted paragraph after a slide's title. However, you will fix this by demoting the new slide in the next step.*

8. Choose **Home→Paragraph→Increase List Level**.

The new slide created when you tapped Enter *in step 7 has been converted to a bullet under the New Artist Specials title.*

9. Complete the new slide in the outline as shown, tapping Enter after each paragraph (including the last one).

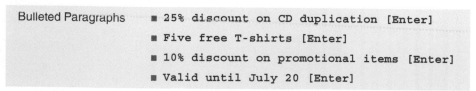

10. Choose **Home→Paragraph→Decrease List Level** 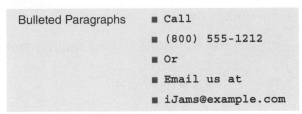 to promote the new paragraph that follows the *Valid until July 20* paragraph and convert it into a new slide.

11. Type `Contact Us` and then use Ctrl + Enter to create a bullet below the title.

12. Taking care not to tap Enter after the last bullet in this slide, complete the new slide as shown.

Bulleted Paragraphs	■ `Call`
	■ `(800) 555-1212`
	■ `Or`
	■ `Email us at`
	■ `iJams@example.com`

13. Save your presentation.

Collapsing and Expanding Slides

Video Library   http://labyrinthelab.com/videos   Video Number: PP13-V0203

As the Outline panel grows, it can be difficult to manage your slides when all the bulleted text is showing. PowerPoint lets you collapse slides so that only the title is visible. This makes it easier to manage your slides because more slides will be visible in the Outline panel.

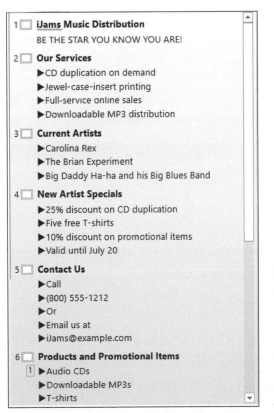

The same presentation in Outline view with all slides expanded and all slides collapsed

Use the Context Menu on the Outline Panel

In this exercise, you will use the context menu from the Outline panel.

1. Save your file as **PP02-D03-Design-[FirstInitialLastName]**.

2. Follow these steps to explore the Outline panel:

Ⓐ Scroll until **Products and Promotional Items** and **Packaging Options** are visible.

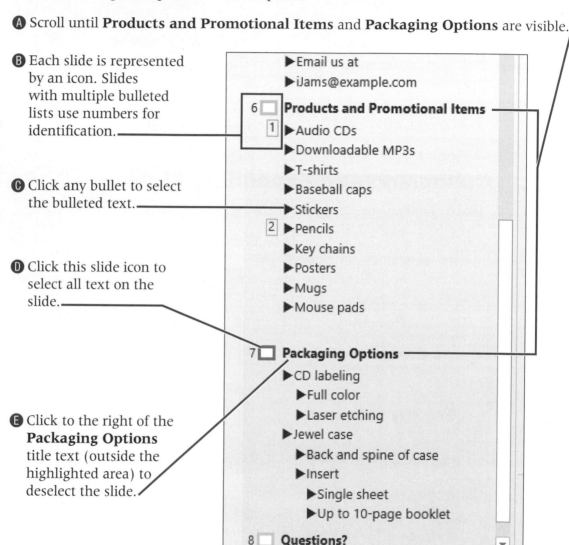

Ⓑ Each slide is represented by an icon. Slides with multiple bulleted lists use numbers for identification.

Ⓒ Click any bullet to select the bulleted text.

Ⓓ Click this slide icon to select all text on the slide.

Ⓔ Click to the right of the **Packaging Options** title text (outside the highlighted area) to deselect the slide.

3. Double-click the **slide icon** ▢ to the left of **Products and Promotional Items**.
   The bulleted paragraphs beneath the title are collapsed and hidden.

4. Double-click the **slide icon** ▢ to the left of **Products and Promotional Items** again.
   The bulleted paragraphs beneath the title are expanded and are once again visible.

5. Right-click anywhere in the **Outline panel** and choose **Collapse→Collapse All**.
   All bulleted paragraphs are collapsed and hidden. Only the slide titles remain visible.

6. Right-click anywhere in the **Outline panel** and choose **Expand→Expand All**.
   All bulleted paragraphs are expanded and are once again visible.

Move a Slide

The easiest way to move a slide in an outline is to first collapse all slides. Then you can click the desired slide title and drag it to its new position.

7. Right-click anywhere in the **Outline panel** and choose **Collapse→Collapse All**.

8. If necessary, scroll up until all slide icons and titles are visible in the **Outline panel**.

9. Follow these steps to move a slide:

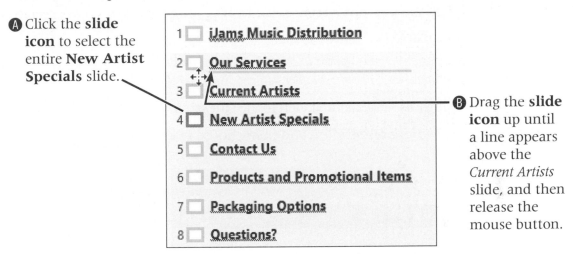

Ⓐ Click the **slide icon** to select the entire **New Artist Specials** slide.

Ⓑ Drag the **slide icon** up until a line appears above the *Current Artists* slide, and then release the mouse button.

The New Artists Specials slide appears above the Current Artists slide.

10. Using this same method, move the **Packaging Options** slide to the second position, just below the title slide.

11. Save your presentation.

Deleting Slides

Video Library   http://labyrinthelab.com/videos   Video Number: PP13-V0204

You can delete a slide from a presentation by clicking the slide icon in the Outline panel to select the entire slide and then tapping the ⎡Delete⎤ key. Likewise, slides can be deleted in Normal and Slide Sorter views by choosing the desired slide(s) and tapping ⎡Delete⎤. If you inadvertently delete a slide, you can use the Undo button on the Quick Access toolbar to undo the latest action and restore the deleted slide. If you later decide that you want to keep the change, click the Redo button on the Quick Access toolbar to go back to the previous action.

FROM THE KEYBOARD
⎡Delete⎤ to remove a slide

Delete a Slide from the Outline

In this exercise, you will delete slides using the Outline panel.

1. Save your file as **PP02-D04-Design-[FirstInitialLastName]**.

2. Right-click anywhere in the **Outline panel** and choose **Expand→Expand All**.

3. Click the **Current Artists slide icon** ☐ (not the title text) to select the entire slide.

4. Tap ⌈Delete⌋ to remove the slide.

   A faded bullet may appear at the end of the previous slide. This is PowerPoint readying itself for additional text. The ghost bullet will not display on the slide itself.

5. Using this same method, delete the **Questions** slide.

6. Save your presentation and then choose **File→Close** to close it.

Working with Word Integration

Video Library http://labyrinthelab.com/videos Video Number: PP13-V0205

Microsoft Word is an excellent word processing program that integrates with PowerPoint. Outlines created in Word can easily be converted to a PowerPoint presentation. You may need to create a presentation based on an outline someone else created in Word, or you may find it easier to plan a presentation using a Word outline rather than starting PowerPoint first and wondering what slides you will create.

Creating a Presentation Outline in Word

Word's powerful outlining tool makes setting up and modifying outlines easy. You can create an outline in Word and import it to PowerPoint. To use Word outlines in PowerPoint, you must apply the appropriate styles to the paragraphs in the Word document prior to importing the outline. PowerPoint converts the Word outline by using these rules:

- All level-1 paragraphs translate to Titles in a PowerPoint slide.
- All level-2 paragraphs translate to level-1 body bullets in a PowerPoint slide.
- All level-3 paragraphs translate to level-2 body bullets in a PowerPoint slide.

Once a Word outline is imported into PowerPoint, you can promote or demote the bullets, apply layouts and a design theme, and make other enhancements.

- ⊕ iJams Music Distribution
  - ⊖ A Year of Success
- ⊕ Online Downloads
  - ⊖ MP3 sales exceed $1M
  - ⊖ 350 thousand new user accounts
- ⊕ Promotional Items
  - ⊖ T-shirt sales exceed $500k
  - ⊖ Total promotional item sales exceed $1.5M
- ⊕ New Hires
  - ⊖ Jamal Lawrence – Web Master
  - ⊖ Malika Fayza – Search Engine Specialist
  - ⊖ Jin Chen – Marketing Analyst
- ⊕ Thank You!
  - ⊖ Our Success Is Your Success

1 ☐ **IJAMS MUSIC DISTRIBUTION**
   A Year of Success

2 ☐ **ONLINE DOWNLOADS**
   MP3 sales exceed $1M
   350 thousand new user accounts

3 ☐ **PROMOTIONAL ITEMS**
   T-shirt sales exceed $500k
   Total promotional item sales exceed
   $1.5M

4 ☐ **NEW HIRES**
   Jamal Lawrence – Web Master
   Malika Fayza – Search Engine Specialist
   Jin Chen – Marketing Analyst

5 ☐ **THANK YOU!**
   Our Success Is Your Success

SLIDE 1 OF 5

DEVELOP YOUR SKILLS PP02-D05

Create a Presentation and Import a Word Outline

In this exercise, you will create an outline in Word, use it to generate slides for a new presentation, and then modify the presentation.

1. Start **Word** and create a new, blank document.

2. Save your file as **PP02-D05-WordOutline-[FirstInitialLastName]** to the **PP2013 Lesson 02** folder.

   In the next few steps, you will type and apply Word styles to paragraphs.

3. With the blank document open, choose **View→Views→Outline**.

4. Type **iJams Music Distribution** and tap ⌈Enter⌉.

5. Tap ⌈Tab⌉. Then type **A Year of Success** and tap ⌈Enter⌉.

   Tapping ⌈Tab⌉ increases the list level and creates a level-2 style.

6. Press ⌈Shift⌉+⌈Tab⌉. Then type **Online Downloads** and tap ⌈Enter⌉.

   Pressing ⌈Shift⌉+⌈Tab⌉ decreases the list level and returns the text to a level-1 style.

   Next, you will create two level-2-styled paragraphs that will eventually be converted to text bullets in a PowerPoint slide.

7. Tap ⌈Tab⌉. Then type **MP3 sales exceed $1M** and tap ⌈Enter⌉.

8. Type **350 thousand new user accounts** and tap ⌈Enter⌉.

9. Now press ⌈Shift⌉+⌈Tab⌉ to return the indentation level to a level-1 style.

   You are now ready to continue typing the rest of the outline.

10. Complete the rest of the outline as shown, using [Enter] to create new paragraphs and [Tab] and [Shift]+[Tab] to adjust indent levels.

⊕ iJams Music Distribution
  ⊖ A Year of Success
⊕ Online Downloads
  ⊖ MP3 sales exceed $1M
  ⊖ 350 thousand new user accounts
⊕ Promotional Items
  ⊖ T-shirt sales exceed $500k
  ⊖ Total promotional item sales exceed $1.5M
⊕ New Hires
  ⊖ Jamal Lawrence – Web Master
  ⊖ Malika Fayza – Search Engine Specialist
  ⊖ Jin Chen – Marketing Analyst
⊕ Thank You!
  ⊖ Our Success Is Your Success

11. Save the file. Then close the outline and Word.

Word closes, and PowerPoint is visible.

Import the Outline

12. If necessary, restore **PowerPoint** from the **taskbar** (or start it, if necessary).

13. Choose **File→New** and click the **Blank Presentation** icon.

14. Save your file as `PP02-D05-WordOutline-[FirstInitialLastName]` to the **PP2013 Lesson 02** folder.

You can use the same filename as the Word document because the Word and PowerPoint files have different file extensions.

15. Choose **Design→Themes→More** ⤓→**Ion** to apply a document theme.

16. Locate the **Design→Variants** group on the Ribbon and click the **third variation** (the purple one) to apply it to all slides.

17. Choose **Home→Slides→New Slide menu** ▾→**Slides From Outline**.

18. Use the **Insert Outline** dialog box to navigate to the **PP2013 Lesson 02** folder.

19. Choose **PP02-D05-WordOutline-[FirstInitialLastName]** and click **Insert**.

PowerPoint will take a moment to import the outline. Note that the first slide is blank because PowerPoint inserted the slides from the outline after the existing blank title slide.

20. Choose **View→Presentation Views→Outline View** and examine the PowerPoint outline.

Each level-1 paragraph from the outline has become a slide title, and each level-2 paragraph has become a bulleted paragraph under the appropriate title.

21. Choose **View→Presentation Views→Normal** to view the slide thumbnails.

22. Choose the first slide (the blank one) and tap Delete.

The blank slide is deleted, and the iJams Music Distribution slide becomes selected.

Change a Layout

23. Choose **Home→Slides→Layout menu ▼→Title Slide**.

The layout of the selected slide changes.

24. Select the final slide, **Thank You**, and choose **Home→Slides→ Layout menu ▼→ Section Header**.

25. Choose the first slide, **iJams Music Distribution**.

Each slide is formatted with blue text because Word formatted the heading styles as blue.

Reset the Slide Formatting

26. With the first slide selected, choose **Home→Slides→Reset**.

The text formatting is removed and returns to the default setting for the current document theme. The slide subtitle is converted to uppercase because that is the formatting of the Ion theme.

27. Select the second slide, press Shift, select the last slide, and release Shift.

Slides 2–5 become selected.

28. Choose **Home→Slides→Reset** to reformat the text on the selected slides with the document theme formatting.

29. Save your presentation.

Formatting Your Presentation

Video Library   http://labyrinthelab.com/videos   Video Number: PP13-V0206

PowerPoint 2013 makes it so easy to create a presentation that the slides you create may not need any additional formatting. After all, the placeholders arrange the text, the bullets are automatic, and the color scheme is preformatted. However, in most cases, you will want to fine-tune your presentation. Formatting your presentation will make a good presentation even better.

Formatting Text

Formatting text is a common step in presentation development. For instance, when reviewing a slide, you might decide that the text could be emphasized by changing the font color. If you had the time, you could change the font color of each piece of text on the slide individually by using the Font group on the Home tab of the Ribbon. However, a more efficient way to change the font color is to first select the placeholder and then apply the color change. By selecting the placeholder, all text within the placeholder is changed in one swoop. The following illustration describes the buttons on the Home tab's Font group that assist you in formatting text.

FROM THE RIBBON

Home→Font→Bold
Home→Font→Underline
Home→Font→Italic

FROM THE KEYBOARD

Ctrl+B for bold
Ctrl+U for underline
Ctrl+I for italic

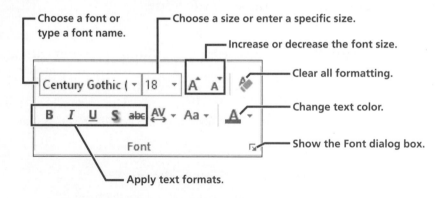

Setting Character Spacing

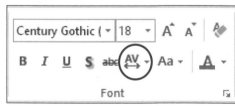

Character spacing refers to the horizontal space between characters. PowerPoint lets you adjust this spacing to give your text some breathing room. If none of the preset options fit your needs, you can enter a numerical value to specify the exact amount of spacing. In the professional world of print, this is referred to as *tracking* or *kerning*. You must first select characters before applying character spacing, or select the placeholder to apply spacing to all the text.

- MP3 sales exceed $1M
- 350 thousand new user accounts

- M P 3 s a l e s e x c e e d $ 1 M
- 3 5 0 t h o u s a n d n e w u s e r a c c o u n t s

The same slide with no character spacing (left) and a large amount of character spacing applied (right)

Setting the Text Case

A quick way to populate your slides with text is to copy text from an existing source, such as from an email message or Word document. However, the original text may not be formatted in the case appropriate for your slide. You can easily change the case of text, saving you from having to retype it.

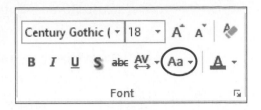

The following table illustrates the options available with the Change Case button.

TEXT CASE OPTIONS	
Menu Option	**How It Affects Text**
Sentence Case	Your text will look like this.
Lowercase	your text will look like this.
Uppercase	YOUR TEXT WILL LOOK LIKE THIS.
Capitalize Each Word	Your Text Will Look Like This.
Toggle Case	Wherever you typed an uppercase letter, it will become lowercase. Wherever you typed a lowercase letter, it will become uppercase. *Example:* If you type `Your Text Will Look Like This`, Toggle Case will change it to `yOUR tEXT wILL lOOK lIKE tHIS`.

DEVELOP YOUR SKILLS PP02-D06

Format Text

In this exercise, you will change the formatting of the fonts in the Title and Subtitle.

1. Save your file as **PP02-D06-WordOutline-[FirstInitialLastName]**.

2. Choose **View→Presentation Views→Normal** to return to Normal view, if necessary.

3. Display the **Home** tab so you can see the font settings as you work.

4. Click the title slide (the first one) to select it.

5. Follow these steps to select the subtitle placeholder box:

A Click anywhere on the text to position the insertion point inside the handles for this text box. The dashed line indicates the text box border.

B Click any edge of the dashed border to change it to a solid border (shown here).

The solid line indicates that the text box is selected. Any formatting change you make now will affect all text within the box. Notice also that the Font Size box on the Ribbon is currently set to 20. The Ion theme applied this font size to the subtitle.

6. Choose **Home→Font→Increase Font Size** A to increase the font size to **24**.

7. Choose **Home→Font→Bold** B.

PowerPoint makes the text bold.

8. Choose **Home→Font→Shadow** S.

The text stands out from the page a bit more because there is now a slight drop-shadow effect.

Format the Title

9. Click on the text of the title, **iJams Music Distribution**, and then click once on the dashed-line border to select the Title text box.

10. Choose **Home→Font→Font Size** ▼ and point to several different font sizes.

Notice how Live Preview displays the slide title size changes as you point to different settings on the Font Size menu.

11. Set the **font size** to **96**.

The text is not large enough. There is still some room to enlarge it so that the company name dominates the slide.

12. Click **96** in the **Home→Font→Font Size** menu.

13. Type **115** and tap Enter.

PowerPoint increases the size of the text to 115. You can select a font size from the menu or type in your own value.

14. Save the presentation.

Setting Line Spacing

Video Library   http://labyrinthelab.com/videos   Video Number: PP13-V0207

Sometimes, instead of changing the font size or adding many hard returns, you need to only increase or decrease the spacing between lines to have the proper effect. Line spacing determines the amount of space between lines of text.

This setting is useful if text appears cramped and you wish to open up some breathing room between lines.

The same slide before and after applying Line Spacing

Adjust the Line Spacing

In this exercise, you will adjust the line spacing to increase the amount of space between bullets.

1. Save your file as **PP02-D07-WordOutline-[FirstInitialLastName]**.

2. Display the **New Hires** slide.

3. Click any of the names to display a dashed border.

4. Click the dashed border to select the entire text box.

5. Choose **Home→Paragraph→Line Spacing ↕≡→2.0** to increase the spacing.

   PowerPoint redistributes the bulleted text vertically on the slide with more spacing between items.

6. Save and close your presentation.

Setting Paragraph Alignment

Video Library   http://labyrinthelab.com/videos   Video Number: PP13-V0208

In time, you will be able to "eye" a presentation and notice if the paragraph alignment is not balanced. You can select one or more paragraphs and then click an alignment button on the Ribbon to make the change. Use the following buttons from the Home→Paragraph group on the Ribbon to realign paragraphs.

PARAGRAPH ALIGNMENT BUTTONS		
Purpose	**Button**	**Example**
Left-align	☰	This text has been left aligned. Notice how the left edge is in a straight line, but the right edge appears jagged.
Center-align	☰	This text has been center aligned. Notice how the text is balanced and centered.
Right-align	☰	This text has been right aligned. Notice how the right edge is in a straight line.
Justify	☰	This text has been justify aligned. Notice how the text is spaced to maintain straight lines on the left and right.

It is often easiest to read left-aligned text because the eye can more easily find the starting point of subsequent lines.

PowerPoint 2013

Format the Contact Us Slide

In this exercise, you will reformat the Contact Us slide.

1. Open **PP02-D08-Contact** from your **PP2013 Lesson 02** folder and save it as **PP02-D08-Contact-[FirstInitialLastName]**.

2. If necessary, scroll down; select **slide 5, Contact Us**.

3. Click in the bulleted list and then click a border of the text box.

4. Choose **Home→Paragraph→Bullets** 📋 to remove the bullets.

5. Choose **Home→Paragraph→Center** 📄.

6. Select the entire telephone number.

    A faded formatting box appears. Pointing your mouse at it will cause it to become more visible. You may format the selected text from this formatting box, but we will use the Ribbon as in the next steps.

7. Choose **Home→Font→Font Size** ▼ and increase the size to **32**.

8. Using the same method, increase the size of the last line (the email address) to **32**.

9. Save your presentation.

Using the Format Painter

Video Library   http://labyrinthelab.com/videos   Video Number: PP13-V0209

Common to all Office programs, the Format Painter is a great tool that simplifies the formatting process. The Format Painter copies all text formats including the typeface, size, color, and attributes such as bold, italic, and underline. It also copies formatting applied to shapes or clip art. The Format Painter helps you easily maintain a standardized, uniform look in your presentation.

Loading the Format Painter

The key to using the Format Painter successfully is understanding when it is loaded. After formatting has been copied to the Format Painter, its Ribbon icon appears pressed in. This pressed-in icon indicates that the Format Painter is loaded and ready to use.

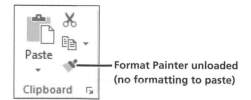
Format Painter unloaded (no formatting to paste)

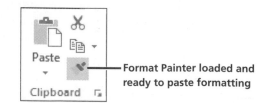
Format Painter loaded and ready to paste formatting

QUICK REFERENCE	COPYING FORMATS WITH THE FORMAT PAINTER
Task	**Procedure**
Copy formats with the Format Painter	■ Select the object (text, picture, drawn line, etc.) with the format you wish to copy. ■ Choose Home→Clipboard→Format Painter 🖌. ■ Select the object at the new location to which you wish to copy formatting.
Use the Format Painter repeatedly	■ Select the object with formatting to be copied. ■ Double-click Home→Clipboard→Format Painter 🖌. ■ Click with the Format Painter on all objects to which you wish the formatting copied. (The Format Painter will remain active until you switch it off.) ■ Click once on the Format Painter to switch it off again, or tap Esc.

When the Format Painter is loaded, the mouse pointer changes from an arrow ⬉ to a brush 🖌.

DEVELOP YOUR SKILLS PP02-D09
Copy Formatting with the Format Painter

In this exercise, you will copy and paste text formatting with the Format Painter.

1. Save your file as **PP02-D09-Contact-[FirstInitialLastName]**.

2. Select the fourth slide, **New Artist Specials**.

3. Double-click *free* in the second bullet to select it.

4. Choose **Home→Font→Font Size→32**.

5. Choose **Home→Font→Text Shadow** ⑤.

6. Follow these steps to choose a font color:

   Ⓐ Choose **Home→Font→Font Color menu ▼**.   Ⓑ Locate the **Theme Colors**.

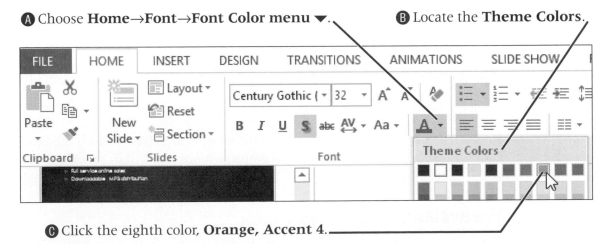

   Ⓒ Click the eighth color, **Orange, Accent 4**.

7. Choose **Home→Clipboard→Format Painter** 🖌.
   The Format Painter icon is pressed in and is now loaded.

8. Click once on *July* in the last bullet.

   The formatting is copied to the word July, *and the Format Painter icon on the Ribbon becomes unloaded.*

9. Choose **Home→Clipboard→Format Painter** 🖌️.

   The Format Painter has been reloaded with the formatting from the word July because that is where the insertion point is.

10. Click once on *20* in the last bullet.

    The formatting is copied to 20, and the Format Painter on the Ribbon becomes unloaded.

Use the Format Painter Repeatedly

11. Select the third slide, **Our Services**.

12. Drag across *on demand* in the first bullet to select it.

13. Choose **Home→Font→Bold** 🅑.

14. Choose **Home→Font→Italic** 🇮.

15. Choose **Home→Font→Font Color ▼→Theme Colors→Red Accent 2**.

16. Double-click **Home→Clipboard→Format Painter** 🖌️.

    Double-clicking the Format Painter will keep it loaded until you turn it off.

17. Click the word *online* in the third bullet.

    The formatting is copied to online, *and the Format Painter remains loaded.*

18. Click the word *sales* in the third bullet.

19. Click the words *MP3* and *distribution* in the last bullet.

20. Choose **Home→Clipboard→Format Painter** 🖌️.

    The Format Painter has been unloaded.

21. Save your presentation.

Using the Slide Sorter

| **Video Library** | http://labyrinthelab.com/videos | Video Number: PP13-V0210 |

Up until now, you've been working in Normal view, which is good for manipulating a handful of slides. However, as your presentation grows to more slides than are visible in Normal view, you will want to explore the function of Slide Sorter view.

Rearranging Slides

PowerPoint's Slide Sorter view is used to rearrange slides. In Slide Sorter view, each slide is a thumbnail image so the entire presentation is visible at a glance. As your presentation grows, often the order of the slides needs to be changed to create a logical concept flow. Using the Drag and Drop method in Slide Sorter view, you can quickly reorganize your slides by moving them to the correct spot.

Use the Slide Sorter View

In this exercise, you will practice using Slide Sorter view.

1. Save your file as `PP02-D10-Contact-[FirstInitialLastName]`.

2. Choose **View→Presentation Views→Slide Sorter** ▦.

3. Follow these steps to move a slide:

Ⓐ If necessary, drag the **Zoom** slider to change the zoom percentage until all six slides are shown. (Your slides may display differently.)

Ⓑ Drag the **Our Services** slide to the left of **Packaging Options**. (Your slides may display differently.)

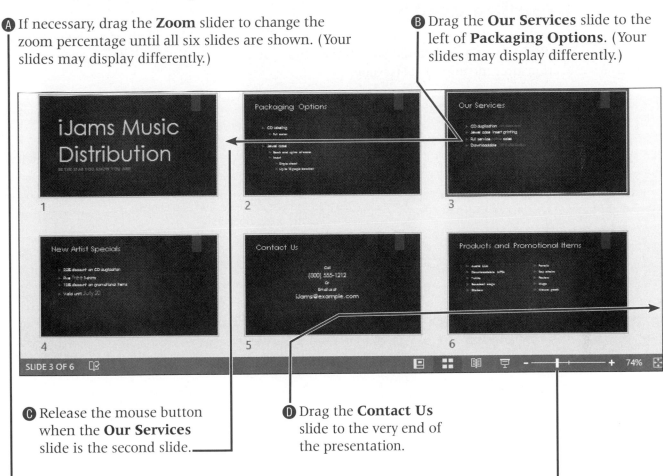

Ⓒ Release the mouse button when the **Our Services** slide is the second slide.

Ⓓ Drag the **Contact Us** slide to the very end of the presentation.

4. Choose **Views→Presentation Views→Normal** ▦.

5. Save and close the presentation.

Organizing with Sections

Video Library http://labyrinthelab.com/videos Video Number: PP13-V0211

Using the Slide Sorter with individual slides works well for small presentations. For presentations containing many slides, PowerPoint 2013's Sections feature helps you keep them organized.

Creating Sections

Sections are always created before the selected slide and include all following slides. This often results in a section containing more slides than intended. The fix is to simply create another section after the intended last slide.

QUICK REFERENCE	USING SECTIONS
Task	**Procedure**
Create a section	■ Select the first slide from the Slides panel for the section. ■ Choose Home→Slides→Section→Add Section. ■ Select the slide after the last in the section and choose Home→Slides→Section→Add Section.
Name a section	■ Right-click the section's title bar and choose Rename Section. ■ Type the new name for the section and click Rename.
Move a section	■ Drag a section's title bar above/below another section title bar.
Collapse or expand a section	■ Double-click the section's title bar.
Remove a section	■ Right-click the section's title bar and choose Remove Section (delete section and leave slides); choose Remove Section & Slides (delete section and its slides).

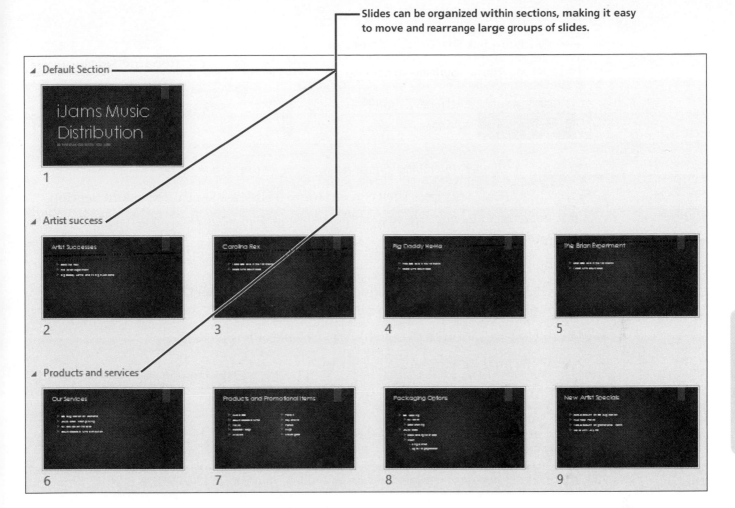

Slides can be organized within sections, making it easy to move and rearrange large groups of slides.

Default Section

Artist success

Products and services

Create Sections

In this exercise, you will create sections.

1. Open **PP02-D11-Sections** from your **PP2013 Lesson 02** folder and save it as `PP02-D11-Sections-[FirstInitialLastName]`.

   With so many slides, it may be easier to work in Slide Sorter view.

2. Choose **View→Presentation Views→Slide Sorter**.

3. Select slide 2, **Artist Successes**. Then choose **Home→Slides→Section ▼→Add Section**.

   A new section named Untitled Section is created before the selected slide. Every slide below it is included in the section.

4. Follow these steps to rename the section:

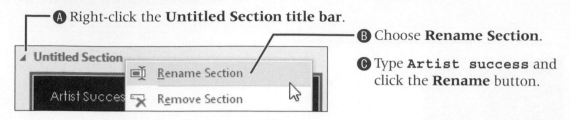

Ⓐ Right-click the **Untitled Section title bar**.

Ⓑ Choose **Rename Section**.

Ⓒ Type **Artist success** and click the **Rename** button.

The section is renamed, but contains slides not intended for this section.

5. Select slide 6, **Our Services**. Then choose **Home→Slides→Section ▼→Add Section**.

A new section is started before the selected slide, but PowerPoint scrolls the Slide Sorter window to the top of the presentation.

6. Scroll down until you see the new, untitled section.

7. Right-click the **Untitled Section** title bar, choose **Rename Section**, and rename the section to **Products and services**.

8. Click the last slide, **Contact Us**, and create a new section before it.

9. Rename the final section **Call to action**.

10. Save your presentation.

Managing Sections

Video Library   http://labyrinthelab.com/videos   Video Number: PP13-V0212

Once sections have been created, they can be dragged and rearranged in either the Slides panel or Slide Sorter view. Individual slides can even be dragged from one section to another. Additionally, sections can be collapsed, similar to slide titles in Outline view. Collapsed sections hide the slides, making it easy to drag and reorder the sections. However, the collapsed sections hide slides only when editing. The collapsed slides will display as normal when running the slide show.

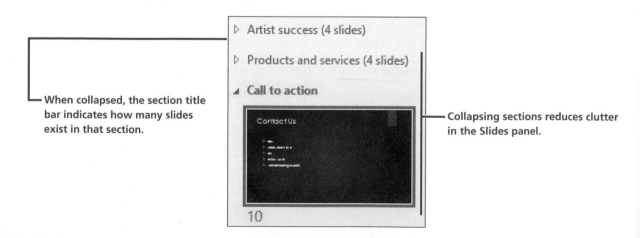

When collapsed, the section title bar indicates how many slides exist in that section.

Collapsing sections reduces clutter in the Slides panel.

Manage Sections

In this exercise, you will rearrange slides by using sections.

1. Save your presentation as **PP02-D12-Sections-[FirstInitialLastName]**.

2. With the presentation still displaying Slide Sorter view, scroll until you can see the **Artist success** section title bar, if necessary.

3. Double-click the **Artist success** section title bar to collapse it.

4. Double-click the **Products and services** section title bar.

5. Choose **View→Presentation Views→Normal**.

   The sections do not remain collapsed when you change views.

6. Follow these steps to rearrange the sections:

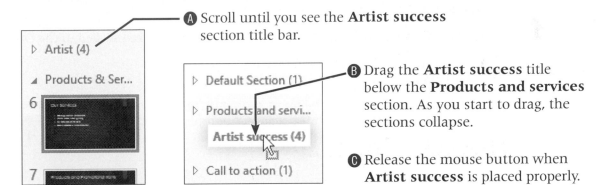

Ⓐ Scroll until you see the **Artist success** section title bar.

Ⓑ Drag the **Artist success** title below the **Products and services** section. As you start to drag, the sections collapse.

Ⓒ Release the mouse button when **Artist success** is placed properly.

7. Choose **View→Presentation Views→Slide Sorter**.

8. Click anywhere in the gray area outside the slide thumbnails to deselect any slides.

9. Scroll down, if necessary, until you see the entire **Call to Action** section with the **Contact Us** slide.

10. Use the **Zoom slider**, if necessary, to make the view smaller.

    You should see all slides in both the Products and Services and Call to Action sections.

11. Drag the last slide of the **Products and Services** section (New Artist Specials) to the left of the **Contact Us** slide to move it to the Call to Action section.

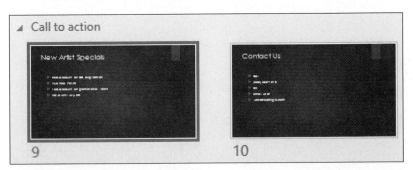

12. Save your presentation.

PowerPoint 2013

Printing Your Presentation

Video Library http://labyrinthelab.com/videos Video Number: PP13-V0213

Ninety percent of the time, you will be viewing or projecting the presentations you create from a PC or notebook computer. However, there may be times when a hard copy of the presentation is needed. In this lesson, you will simply explore the options of printing a presentation.

Knowing What You Can Print

PowerPoint can create the following types of printouts:

- **Slides:** Prints each slide of a presentation on a separate page
- **Handouts:** Prints one or more slides per page, leaving room for attendees to jot notes during the presentation
- **Speaker Notes:** Prints each slide on a separate page, with any speaker notes you created for the slide below
- **Outline:** Prints a text outline of each slide, similar to what is seen in the Outline panel

Previewing a Printout

The Print window, found in Backstage view, lets you see how each slide will be printed. You can then refine the appearance before printing.

FROM THE RIBBON
File→Print to display the Print tab in Backstage view

Using the Print Shortcut

If you have customized your Quick Access toolbar to display the Quick Print icon, you may find it tempting to just click it. However, before this becomes a habit, know that a click of this button sends the entire presentation to the current printer, whether or not you want to make adjustments. If you are working with a document theme that has a colored background, the printing process will not only be painstakingly slow, but may also waste your toner or ink!

FROM THE KEYBOARD
Ctrl+P to display the Print tab in Backstage view

The Quick Print button on the Quick Access toolbar sends your presentation directly to the printer.

Preview a Printout

In this exercise, you will use Backstage view to preview a printout.

1. Choose **File→Print**.

2. Follow these steps to examine the print options:

Ⓐ Use the **left arrow** or scroll bar to return to the first slide.

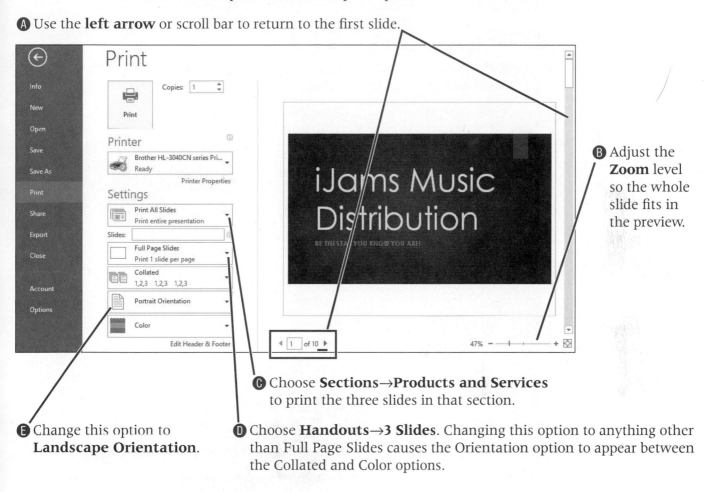

Ⓑ Adjust the **Zoom** level so the whole slide fits in the preview.

Ⓒ Choose **Sections→Products and Services** to print the three slides in that section.

Ⓔ Change this option to **Landscape Orientation**.

Ⓓ Choose **Handouts→3 Slides**. Changing this option to anything other than Full Page Slides causes the Orientation option to appear between the Collated and Color options.

3. Click the **Back** ⊖ button at the top of Backstage view to return to the main PowerPoint screen without printing. Close **PowerPoint**.

Concepts Review

To check your knowledge of the key concepts introduced in this lesson, complete the Concepts Review quiz by choosing the appropriate access option below.

If you are...	Then access the quiz by...
Using the Labyrinth Video Library	Going to http://labyrinthelab.com/videos
Using eLab	Logging in, choosing Content, and navigating to the Concepts Review quiz for this lesson
Not using the Labyrinth Video Library or eLab	Going to the student resource center for this book

PowerPoint 2013

Reinforce Your Skills

Work with Outlines and Formatting

In this exercise, you will format some slides in the Kids for Change presentation.

Work with Slides

1. Start **PowerPoint**. Open **PP02-R01-Design** from the **PP2013 Lesson 02** folder and save it as `PP02-R01-Design-[FirstInitialLastName]`.

2. Select the second slide, **Events**.

3. Choose **Home→Slides→Layout→Two Content** to change the slide layout to a two-column layout.

4. Select the last four paragraphs in the left column and drag them to the right column.

Work with Outlines

5. Choose **View→Presentation Views→Outline View**.

6. Locate the **Program Benefits** slide in the Outline panel.

7. Click to the right of the word *health* in the last paragraph of the **Program Benefits** slide in the Outline panel.

8. Tap [Ctrl]+[Enter] to create a slide.

9. Type `Requirements` in the Outline panel as the slide title.

10. Tap [Enter] and then tap [Tab] to create a new, bulleted paragraph.

11. Type `You need` in the Outline panel.

12. Tap [Enter] and then tap [Tab] to create a new, bulleted paragraph.

13. Type `Positive attitude`, tap [Enter], and type `Strong work ethic` to create another indented paragraph.

14. Tap [Enter] and then tap [Shift]+[Tab] to create and demote the next bullet.

15. Type `Time commitment`.

16. Tap [Enter] and then tap [Tab].

17. Type `One monthly event`, tap [Enter], and type `One annual meeting` to create the final two paragraphs.

18. Choose **Home→Slides→Layout→Title and Content**.

Format a Presentation

19. Choose **View→Presentation Views→Normal** and select the title slide from the **Slides** panel.

20. Click the **Title** box, and then click again on the edge of the box to select it.

21. Choose **Home→Font→Increase Font Size** once to increase the font size to **60**.

22. Choose **Home→Font→Bold**.

23. Display the **Requirements** slide on the Slides panel.

24. Choose **Home→Slides→New Slide**.

25. Type **Remember** as the title.

26. Type the following as bulleted paragraphs:

    - `Think globally, act locally.`
    - `Or think locally, act globally.`
    - `Just...`
    - `Think and act!`

27. Select the bulleted text box by clicking the border.

28. Choose **Home→Paragraph→Bullets** to remove the bullets from all paragraphs.

29. Choose **Home→Paragraph→Center** to center the text on the slide.

30. Choose **Home→Paragraph→Line Spacing→2.0** to increase the vertical spacing between bullets.

31. Select the text *think and act!*

32. Choose **Home→Font→Increase Font Size** four times to increase the size to 32.

Use Format Painter

33. With the *think and act!* text still selected, double-click the **Home→Clipboard→Format Painter** button to load it for multiple uses.

34. Click the words *Think* and *act* in the first line, and then click the words *think* and *act* in the second line to duplicate the formatting.

35. Choose **Home→Clipboard→Format Painter** to turn off the Format Painter.

36. Save the presentation; submit your final file based on the guidelines provided by your instructor. Exit **PowerPoint**.

    To view examples of how your file or files should look at the end of this exercise, go to the student resource center.

Import from Word; Organize and Print a Presentation

In this exercise, you will import an outline from Word, create sections, rearrange sections and slides, and print a slide.

Integrate with Word

1. Start **Microsoft Word**. Open **PP02-R02-Outline** from the **PP2013 Lesson 02** folder.

2. Choose **View→Views→Outline**.

3. Read over the outline. Then close **Word**.

4. Start **PowerPoint** and click **Blank Presentation**.

5. Save your file as `PP02-R02-Outline-[FirstInitialLastName]` in the **PP2013 Lesson 02** folder.

6. Choose **Design→Themes→Ion** to apply a design theme.

7. Choose **Home→Slides→New Slide ▼→Slides from Outline** to begin importing the Word outline.

8. Navigate to your **PP2013 Lesson 02** folder and double-click the **PP02-R02-Outline** Word document to import the outline and create the slides.

9. Select **slide 1** in the Slides panel and tap ⌞Delete⌟ to delete the blank slide.

10. Click **slide 1** in the Slides panel to ensure it is selected, scroll to the bottom of the Slides panel, and ⌞Shift⌟+click the final slide, **slide 7**, so all slides are selected.

11. Choose **Home→Slides→Reset** to reset the formatting of all slides.

Organize with Sections

12. Click slide 2, **College Application**, in the Slides panel to select it and deselect the others.

13. Choose **Home→Slides→Section→Add Section** to add a new section starting with the **College Application** slide.

14. Choose **Home→Slides→Section→Rename Section**.

15. Type `Personal Benefits` and then click **Rename**.

16. Click slide 4, **Crime Reduction**, in the Slides panel to select it and deselect the others.

17. Choose **Home→Slides→Section→Add Section** to add a new section starting with the **College Application** slide.

18. Choose **Home→Slides→Section→Rename Section**.

19. Type `Community Benefits` and then click **Rename**.

Use the Slide Sorter

20. Choose **View→Presentation Views→Slide Sorter**.

21. Drag the **Zoom** slider in the lower-right area of the PowerPoint window until all seven slides are visible.

22. Drag the **Leadership Skills** slide so it is between the College Application and Sense of Accomplishment slides.

23. Drag the **Community Benefits** section header up so that it is before the Personal Benefits section.

24. Save the presentation.

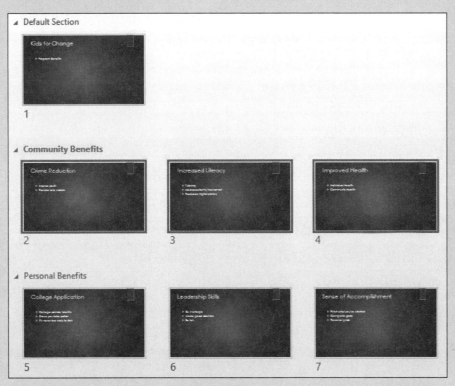

Print Your Presentation

25. Choose **File→Print** to display the Print tab in Backstage view.

26. Use the scroll bar at the right of the PowerPoint window to navigate the slides until slide 3, **Increased Literacy,** displays.

27. Choose your printer from the **Printer** option. Your instructor may prefer you to choose the PDF option.

28. Opt to print only the current slide; opt to print full-page slides, one slide per page.

29. Set the color option to **Grayscale**; print one copy.

30. Submit your final file based on guidelines provided by your instructor. Exit **PowerPoint**.
To view examples of how your file or files should look at the end of this exercise, go to the student resource center.

Create a Presentation from a Word Outline

In this exercise, you will import a Word outline to create the initial slides. You will then reset the formatting of the slides and arrange the slides into sections. Finally, you will print a slide.

Import an Outline and Reset Formatting

1. Start **PowerPoint** and click **Blank Presentation**.

2. Save your file as **PP02-R03-Outline-[FirstInitialLastName]** in the **PP2013 Lesson 02** folder.

3. Choose **Design→Themes→Retrospect** to apply a design theme.

4. Choose **Home→Slides→New Slide ▼→Slides from Outline** to begin importing a Word outline.

5. Navigate to your **PP2013 Lesson 02** folder and double-click the **PPT02-R03-Outline** Word document to import the outline and create the slides.

6. Select **slide 1** in the Slides panel and tap [Delete] to delete the blank slide.

7. Click **slide 1** in the Slides panel to ensure it is selected, scroll to the bottom of the Slides panel, and [Shift]+click the final slide, **slide 6**, so that all slides are selected.

8. Choose **Home→Slides→Reset** to reset the formatting of all slides.

Create Additional Slides

9. Choose **Views→Presentation Views→Outline View**.

10. Locate the **Bully No More** slide in the Outline panel.

11. Click to the right of the word *programs* in the last paragraph of the Bully No More slide in the Outline panel.

12. Tap [Ctrl]+[Enter] to create a slide.

13. Type **Kids for Change** in the Outline panel as the slide title, tap [Enter], and then tap [Tab] to create a new, bulleted paragraph.

14. Type **Part of the Solution** in the Outline panel.

15. Choose **Home→Slides→Layout→Section Header**.

16. Scroll to the top of the Outline panel and click anywhere in the text of the first slide to select the slide.

17. Choose **Home→Slides→Layout→Title Slide**.

Copy Formatting

18. Choose **Views→Presentation Views→Normal**.

19. Display slide 4, **Toy Collection**.

20. Select the text *foster homes*.

21. Choose **Home→Font→Bold**.

22. Double-click the **Home→Clipboard→Format Painter** button to load the Format Painter for multiple uses.

23. Click each of the words *emergency, responders, Child,* and *Services* to copy the bold formatting.

24. Choose **Home→Clipboard→Format Painter** to unload the Format Painter.

Organize with Sections

25. Choose **View→Presentation Views→Slide Sorter**.

26. Slide the **Zoom** slider at the bottom-right of the PowerPoint window until all seven slides are visible.

27. Click the **iRecycling Day** slide to select it.

28. Choose **Home→Slides→Section→Add Section** to create a new section.

29. Right-click the untitled section heading and choose **Rename Section**.

30. Type `Community` and then click **Rename**.

31. Click the **Bully No More** slide.

32. Choose **Home→Slides→Section→Add Section**.

33. Right-click the untitled section heading and choose **Rename Section**.

34. Type `School` and then click **Rename**.

35. Drag the **Tutoring** slide to the right of the **Bully No More** slide to move it to the **School** section.

36. Save the presentation.

Print Slides

37. Choose **File→Print** to display the Print tab in Backstage view.

38. Use the scroll bar at the right of the PowerPoint window to navigate the slides until **slide 1** displays.

39. Choose your printer from the **Printer** option. Use the PDF option if specified by your instructor.

40. Specify to print a **Custom Range** of **slides 1–3**; specify **3 slides per page**.

41. Set the color option to **Black and White**; print one copy.

42. Submit your final file based on guidelines provided by your instructor. Exit **PowerPoint**.

Apply Your Skills

Reformat a Presentation

In this exercise, you will create a presentation for Universal Corporate Events based on a Microsoft Word outline. You will then add a slide and format text.

Create a Word Outline

1. Start **Word** and click **Blank Document**.

2. Save the file as **PP02-A01-Outline-[FirstInitialLastName]** in your **PP2013 Lesson 02** folder.

3. Choose **View→Views→Outline**.

4. Type the following text, using Enter, Tab, and Shift + Tab as needed to create an outline in Word.

⊕ Universal Corporate Events
   ⊖ Events made easy
⊕ Event Types
   ⊖ Celebrations
   ⊖ Ceremonies
   ⊖ Team building
   ⊖ Trade shows
⊕ Services
   ⊖ Catering
   ⊖ Invitations
   ⊖ Stage and sound equipment
   ⊖ Venue scouting
⊕ Benefits
   ⊕ Our Jobs
      ⊖ Deal with paperwork
      ⊖ Guarantee safety
      ⊖ Scheduling
   ⊕ Your Jobs
      ⊖ Relax
      ⊖ Enjoy your event
⊕ Universal Corporate Events
   ⊖ Events made easy
—

5. Save and then close your file. Exit **Word**.

Import a Word Outline

6. Start **PowerPoint** and click **Blank Presentation**.

7. Save your file as `PP02-A01-Outline-[FirstInitialLastName]` to your **PP2013 Lesson 02** folder.

8. Choose **Home→Slides→New Slide→Slides from Outline**.

9. Browse to the **PP2013 Lesson 02** folder and double-click the **PP02-A01-Outline-[FirstInitialLastName]** Word outline.

10. Delete the blank first slide.

Work with an Outline

11. Display the presentation in **Outline View**.

12. Click at the end of the last paragraph of the **Benefits** slide in the Outline panel.

13. Press Ctrl + Enter to create a new slide.

14. Type `Specialties`, tap Enter, and then tap Tab.

15. Type the following paragraphs, tapping Enter after each except the last one.

    `Custom catering`
    `Individual transportation`
    `Group transportation`
    `Line dancing`
    `Graphic design`
    `Radio promotion`
    `Emergency medical`
    `Large-item printing`

Formatting a Presentation

16. Apply the **Facet** design document theme.

17. Display the presentation in **Normal** view.

18. Ensure that the Specialties slide is displayed and then apply the **Two Content** layout.

19. Select the last four paragraphs on the **Specialties** slide and move them to the new right-column placeholder.

20. Click **slide 1** in the Slides panel and then choose **Home→Slides→Layout→Title Slide**.

21. Click **slide 1** in the Slides panel and then Shift + click **slide 6** to select all slides.

22. Choose **Home→Slides→Reset**.

23. Display slide 4, **Benefits**.

24. Select the **Our Jobs** paragraph; bold the text.

25. Choose **Home→Font→Character Spacing→Loose** to spread the text out horizontally.

Using the Format Painter

26. Load the **Format Painter** with the formatting.

27. Drag across the *Your Jobs* paragraph to copy the formatting to the paragraph.

28. Save your presentation. Submit your final file based on the guidelines provided by your instructor. Exit **PowerPoint**.

    To view examples of how your file or files should look at the end of this exercise, go to the student resource center.

Organize and Print a Presentation

In this exercise, you will use Slide Sorter view to create sections and organize the slides within a presentation. You will then print a portion of the presentation.

Using the Slide Sorter

1. Start **PowerPoint**. Open **PP02-A02-Outline** from the **PP2013 Lesson 02** folder and save it as `PP02-A02-Outline-[FirstInitialLastName]`.

2. Display the presentation in **Slide Sorter** view.

3. Drag the **Zoom** slider in the lower-right area of the PowerPoint window until you can see all six slides.

Rearranging Slides

4. Drag the **Benefits** slide so that it is after the **Specialties** slide.

5. Drag the **Services** slide so that it is before the **Event Types** slide.

Sections

6. Click the **Services** slide and then add a section.

7. Rename the new section `Services`.

8. Click the **Benefits** slide and then add a section.

9. Rename the new section `Closing`.

10. Save the presentation.

Print a Presentation

11. Choose **File→Print**.

12. Select the **Specialties** slide.

13. Using the **Grayscale** option, print the single slide. Print the slide as a PDF file if directed to do so by your instructor.

14. Close the presentation and exit **PowerPoint**.

15. Submit your final file based on the guidelines provided by your instructor.

    To view examples of how your file or files should look at the end of this exercise, go to the student resource center.

Create, Format, and Organize a Presentation

In this exercise, you will create and import an outline from Word and then design and format a presentation.

Outline in Word

1. Start **Word** and use **Outline View** to create an outline that will produce the following slides:

SLIDES	
Title	**Bullets**
Universal Corporate Events	Specialized
Specialties	■ Custom catering
	■ Individual transportation
	■ Group transportation
	■ Line dancing
	■ Graphic design
	■ Radio promotion
	■ Emergency medical
	■ Large-item printing
Catering	■ Vegan dishes
	■ Kosher dishes
	■ Meat-lovers dishes
	■ Desserts
Transportation	■ Individual limos
	■ Group buses for 6-50
Line Dancing	■ Experienced dance leaders
	■ Country, pop, and hip-hop
Graphic Design	■ Invitation graphics
	■ Signs
	■ Banners
Radio Promotion	■ Script writing
	■ Voice talent
	■ High-definition recording
Emergency Medical	■ CPR-certified staff
	■ Onsite portable defibrillators
Large-Item Printing	■ Canvas, polyester, or vinyl
	■ Up to 64 square feet

2. Save the outline to your **PP2013 Lesson 02** folder as **PP02-A03-Outline-[FirstInitialLastName]** and close Word.

3. Start **PowerPoint** and create a new, blank presentation in the **PP2013 Lesson 02** folder named **PP02-A03-Outline-[FirstInitialLastName]**.

4. Import the **PP02-A03-Outline-[FirstInitialLastName]** Word outline.

5. Delete the blank first slide.

PowerPoint 2013

Work with Slides and Formatting

6. Select all slides in the Slides panel and use the **Reset** command to reset the formatting.

7. Apply the **Ion Boardroom** theme with the **orange variation**.

8. Change the layout of the first slide to **Title Slide**.

9. Change the layout of the second slide to **Two Content**.

10. Move the last four paragraphs of the second slide into the new right-column placeholder.

11. Increase the line spacing of both columns on **slide 2** to **2.0**.

Work with an Outline

12. Display the presentation in **Outline View**.

13. Collapse all the slides on the Outline panel.

14. Select the **Specialties** slide in the Outline panel and then expand only that one slide.

15. In the Outline panel, move the *Large-item printing* paragraph below the *Graphic design* paragraph.

16. In the Outline panel, move the *Large-Item Printing* slide below the **Graphic Design** slide.

17. Display the presentation in **Normal** view.

Formatting a Presentation

18. Display the **Catering** slide.

19. Make the word *Vegan* bold and italic and then use the **Format Painter** to copy the formatting to the words *Kosher* and *Meat-lovers*.

20. Change the case of all eight paragraphs on the **Specialties** slide to **Capitalize Each Word**.

Using the Slide Sorter

21. Display the presentation in **Slide Sorter** view.

22. Create a new section starting with **slide 1** named `Intro`.

23. Create a new section starting with the **Catering** slide named `Food and Entertainment`.

24. Create a new section starting with the **Transportation** slide named `Logistics and Emergency`.

25. Create a new section starting with the **Graphic Design** slide named `Promotion`.

26. Move the **Line Dancing** slide to the end of the **Food and Entertainment** section.

27. Move the **Emergency Medical** slide to the end of the **Logistics and Emergency** section.

28. Move the entire **Promotion** section so that it is before the **Logistics and Emergency** section.

29. Save the presentation.

Print a Presentation

30. Print the slides in the **Promotion** section in the **Handouts (3 slides per page)** format so that only a single page prints. Print in **Grayscale** to save on color ink. (Or print to PDF if instructed to by your instructor.)

31. Submit your final file based on the instructions provided by your instructor. Exit **PowerPoint**.

Extend Your Skills

In the course of working through the Extend Your Skills exercises, you will think critically as you use the skills taught in the lesson to complete the assigned projects. To evaluate your mastery and completion of the exercises, your instructor may use a rubric, with which more points are allotted according to performance characteristics. (The more you do, the more you earn!) Ask your instructor how your work will be evaluated.

PP02-E01 ## That's the Way I See It

You're teaching a cooking class and need a presentation to show others how to make your signature dish. Choose a recipe that you know well, or find one online. When you're ready, create a new presentation named **PP02-E01-Recipe-[FirstInitialLastName]** in your **PP2013 Lesson 02** folder.

Apply the design theme and variation of your choice. If you can't find a design theme you like, use PowerPoint's Start screen to search for others. Type the recipe name as the slide title and create an engaging subtitle. Add a Title and Content slide that lists the ingredients. Create at least three more slides, each of which describes a few fun facts about one of the ingredients (look it up or make it up).

Add a slide that lists a brief description of each step. Each paragraph should contain no more than four words. Create an additional slide for each step, using the brief description as the slide title and bulleted paragraphs to further explain the step. Copy the brief descriptions one by one and paste them onto the additional slides. Create an **Ingredients** section that contains all the ingredient slides and a **Steps** section that includes all the step slides.

Run the slide show and make note of anything you want to change. When the slide show ends, make the necessary changes and then save your presentation. You will be evaluated based on the inclusion of all elements specified, your ability to follow directions, your ability to apply newly learned skills to a real-world situation, your creativity, and the relevance of your topic and/or data choice(s). Submit your final file based on the guidelines provided by your instructor.

PP02-E02 ## Be Your Own Boss

Open **PP02-E02-BlueJean** from the **PP2013 Lesson 02** folder and save it as **PP02-E02-BlueJean-[FirstInitialLastName]**. View the presentation as a slide show and ask yourself if the slides are easy to read and in the best order. Based on your evaluation, use the skills taught in this lesson to make the necessary changes, ensuring that you cover these edits.

- Change the document theme.
- Adjust the text layout.
- Rearrange the order of slides.
- Edit text.

Be sure the design and formatting are consistent from slide to slide. Use the Format Painter to quickly duplicate formatting changes. Add at least three more slides, such as those to describe Blue Jean Landscaping products, a brief company history, or a price list. Rearrange the slides and create at least two sections to group slides in a logical order.

You will be evaluated based on the inclusion of all elements specified, your ability to follow directions, your ability to apply newly learned skills to a real-world situation, your creativity, and your demonstration of an entrepreneurial spirit. Submit your final file based on the guidelines provided by your instructor.

Transfer Your Skills

In the course of working through the Transfer Your Skills exercises, you will use critical-thinking and creativity skills to complete the assigned projects using skills taught in the lesson. To evaluate your mastery and completion of the exercises, your instructor may use a rubric, with which more points are allotted according to performance characteristics. (The more you do, the more you earn!) Ask your instructor how your work will be evaluated.

PP02-T01 Use the Web as a Learning Tool

Throughout this book, you will be provided with an opportunity to use the Internet as a learning tool by completing WebQuests. According to the original creators of WebQuests, as described on their website (WebQuest.org), a WebQuest is "an inquiry-oriented activity in which most or all of the information used by learners is drawn from the web." To complete the WebQuest projects in this book, navigate to the student resource center and choose the WebQuest for the lesson on which you are currently working. The subject of each WebQuest will be relevant to the material found in the lesson.

WebQuest Subject: Designing an Effective Presentation

Submit your final file(s) based on the guidelines provided by your instructor.

PP02-T02 Demonstrate Proficiency

Stormy BBQ is sponsoring a Father's Day picnic. Create a PowerPoint presentation to display on the widescreen monitors at Stormy's to play during business hours that gives details about the event.

Create an outline in Microsoft Word that will produce at least five slides when imported into PowerPoint. The slides should describe the picnic and various events and entertainment. Save the Word outline as **PP02-T02-FathersDay-[FirstInitialLastName]** to your **PP2013 Lesson 02** folder.

Import the outline into PowerPoint to create the initial slides. Use an appropriate theme and change the slide layouts as necessary. Format the text so important words stand out, but be careful not to overdo it! Experiment with character and line spacing, paragraph alignment, and other formatting. Use the Format Painter to quickly reuse preferred formatting. Create sections for different parts of the event, such as for food, games, and other activities.

Save your presentation as **PP02-T02-FathersDay-[FirstInitialLastName]** in your **PP2013 Lesson 02** folder.

Submit your final file based on the guidelines provided by your instructor.

Adding Graphics, Animation, and Sound

I n this lesson, you will enhance a presentation that currently includes only text. You will use online clip art to add interest to the presentation, a drawing object to add spark, and slide transitions and animation to "bring the presentation to life."

LESSON OUTLINE

Working with Online Pictures
Adding Other Graphics
Working with Slide Transitions
Using Slide Animation
Adding Sound Effects
Concepts Review
Reinforce Your Skills
Apply Your Skills
Extend Your Skills
Transfer Your Skills

LEARNING OBJECTIVES

After studying this lesson, you will be able to:

- Add clip art, photos, screenshots, and shapes to a presentation
- Remove backgrounds and apply artistic effects to slide images
- Add transition effects to a slide show
- Add animation to objects on a slide
- Add sound effects to transitions and animations

Adding Eye Candy

The iJams presentation is evolving nicely. However, you know you will have to add some pizzazz to it if iJams is to contend with competitors. Although you have created an error-free, technically perfect presentation, you can see that something is definitely missing! You decide that if used sparingly, clip art and animation will enhance the presentation.

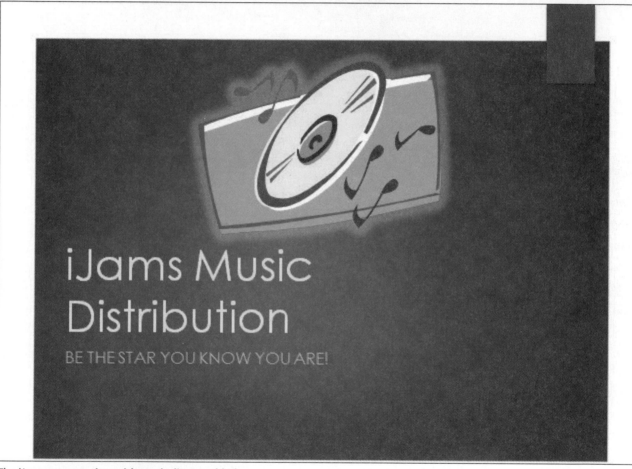

The iJams presentation with stock clip art added

Working with Online Pictures

Video Library http://labyrinthelab.com/videos Video Number: PP13-V0301

You can search for and insert clip art from the Internet directly from within PowerPoint. Adding clip art will help you emphasize key points and add polish to the presentation as a whole. The Microsoft Office website has a clip art collection of more than 130,000 pieces of art—and it grows daily. There is clip art available for any occasion.

While the term *clip art* is an industry-standard term referring to predrawn artwork that is added to computer documents, Microsoft uses the terms *clip art* and *online pictures* inconsistently to refer to the same thing. For example, PowerPoint's Online Pictures button opens the Insert Pictures dialog box, which allows you to search the Office.com website for clip art.

Using Text and Object Layouts

PowerPoint creates slides with different layouts, such as slides with titles only and slides with titles and text. These slide layouts allow you to easily create slides with a standardized title and bulleted text. Many of PowerPoint's layouts, including the Title and Content layout and the Two Content layout, provide placeholders for titles, text, and various types of content including tables, charts, clip art from the Internet, pictures from your computer, organizational charts, and movies.

PowerPoint 2013

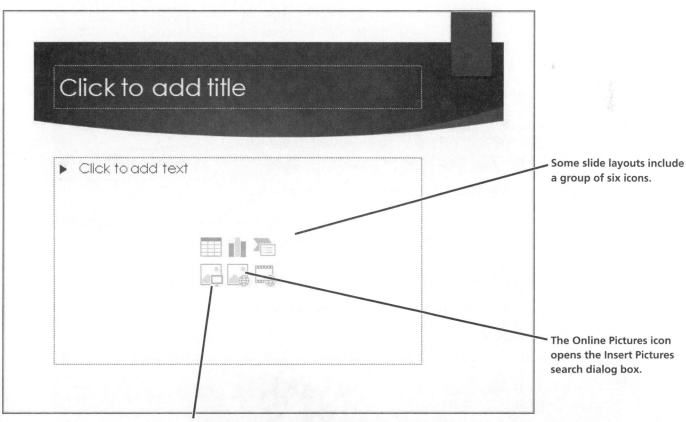

Some slide layouts include a group of six icons.

The Online Pictures icon opens the Insert Pictures search dialog box.

The Pictures icon inserts an image from your computer.

Slide Insert Shortcuts			
Icon	**What It Does**	**Icon**	**What It Does**
⊞	Inserts a table	🖼	Inserts an image
�	Inserts a chart or graph	📄	Inserts a SmartArt graphic
🖼	Opens the Online Pictures dialog box to insert clip art	🌐	Inserts a video clip

Deleting Placeholder Text

Sometimes you may decide to replace all text on a slide with a graphic. Deleting all text inside a placeholder results in the slide displaying its six default insert icons, making it easy to insert clip art or other objects.

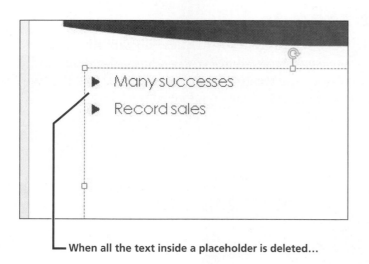

When all the text inside a placeholder is deleted...

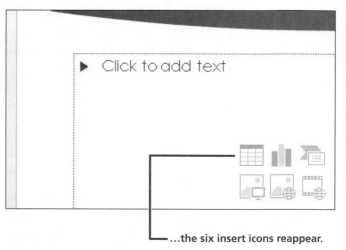

...the six insert icons reappear.

DEVELOP YOUR SKILLS PP03-D01
Get a Slide Ready for Clip Art

In this exercise, you will get a slide ready to accept clip art.

1. Start **PowerPoint**. Open **PP03-D01-Animation** from the **PP2013 Lesson 03** folder, and save it as **PP03-D01-Animation-[FirstInitialLastName]**.

   Replace the bracketed text with your first initial and last name. For example, if your name is Bethany Smith, your filename would look like this: PP03-D01-Animation-BSmith.

2. Select the **Our Services** slide from the **Slides panel**.

3. Choose **Home→Slides→New Slide** 📄.

   A new slide is inserted below Our Services. The new slide uses the same layout as the Our Services slide.

Choose a Layout and Format Text

4. Follow these steps to apply a slide layout suitable for clip art:

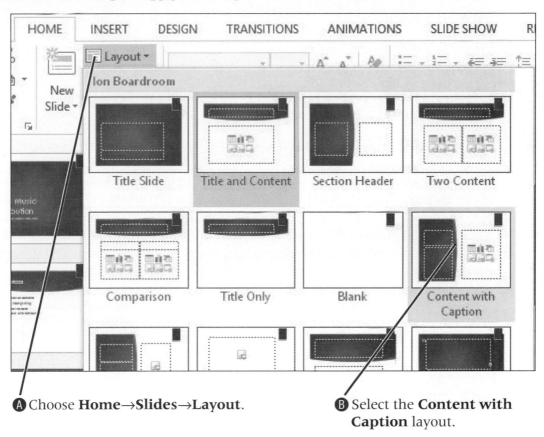

Ⓐ Choose **Home→Slides→Layout**.

Ⓑ Select the **Content with Caption** layout.

5. In the Title placeholder, type `Our Recent Success`.

6. In the text box beneath the title, type:

   `Top of the Rock` Enter `Excellence in Service to Musicians` Enter `League of Electronic Music Distributors.`

7. Select the text *Top of the Rock;* choose **Home→Font→Font Size menu** ▼ and then choose **24**.

8. Choose **Home→Font→Bold**.

9. Select the text *League of Electronic Music Distributors.*

10. Choose **Home→Font→Italic**.

    Your slide is ready for clip art.

11. Click in the large text placeholder at the right and type:

    `Many successes` Enter

    `Record-breaking sales`

    You decide instead to replace the bulleted text with clip art. You will delete all the text in the placeholder so the slide displays the six insert icons again.

12. Click inside the text box, if necessary, to display its dashed border.

13. Click the dashed border to select the text box.

14. Tap ⌊Delete⌋.

The text is deleted, and the six insert icons reappear.

15. Save your presentation.

Searching for Clip Art with the Insert Pictures Search Window

Video Library   http://labyrinthelab.com/videos   Video Number: PP13-V0302

The Insert Pictures search window replaces the Clip Art panel that existed in previous versions of PowerPoint. This new window lets you search for clip art on the Office.com Clip Art website or from the Bing™ search engine. Each piece of clip art is associated with keywords that describe its characteristics. The first illustration that follows describes the Insert Pictures search window. The second illustration shows the images that can be located by using the keyword *awards* or *prizes*.

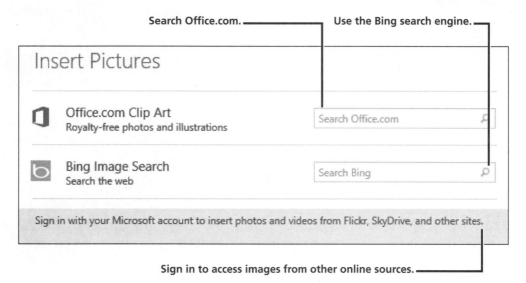

Begin a new search from a different search engine.   View a larger version of the image.

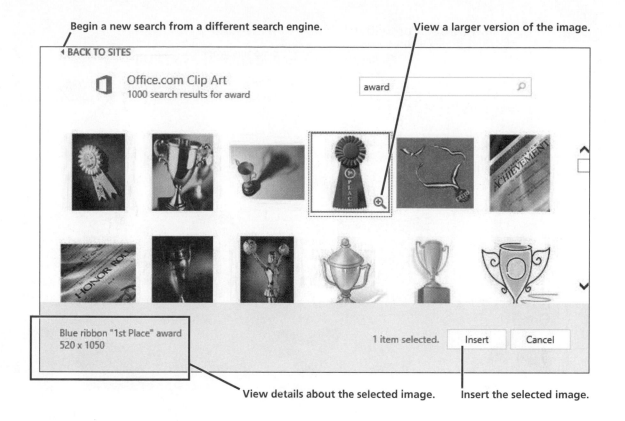

View details about the selected image.   Insert the selected image.

DEVELOP YOUR SKILLS PP03-D02

Insert Clip Art

In this exercise, you will insert clip art to add visual interest to a slide.

1. Save your file as **PP03-D02-Animation-[FirstInitialLastName]**.

2. On the **Our Recent Success** slide, click the **Online Pictures** ▣ icon to open the Insert Pictures search window.

3. Type **award** in the Office.com search box and then tap ⌷Enter⌷.

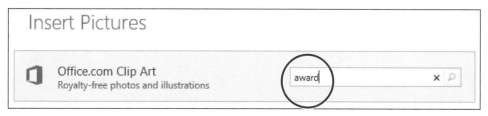

4. Follow these steps to insert a picture on the slide:

Ⓐ Scroll until you find an image you like.
Your results may differ from the figure.

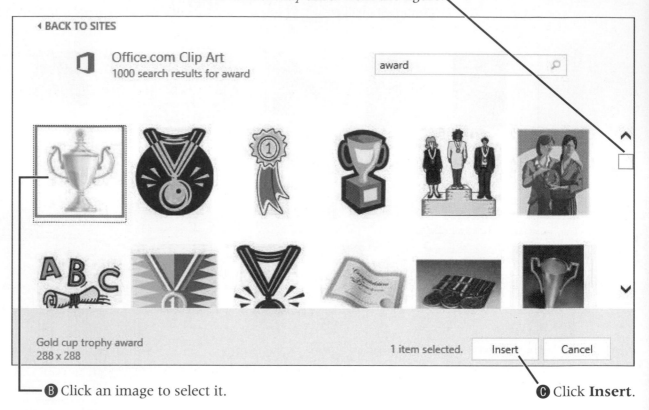

◀ BACK TO SITES

Office.com Clip Art
1000 search results for award

award

Gold cup trophy award
288 x 288

1 item selected.　Insert　Cancel

Ⓑ Click an image to select it.

Ⓒ Click **Insert**.

The clip art image is inserted on the slide and replaces the large text box.

5. Save the presentation.

Moving, Sizing, and Rotating Objects

Video Library   http://labyrinthelab.com/videos   Video Number: PP13-V0303

When you click an object (such as a clip art image), sizing handles and a rotate handle appear. You can easily move, size, and rotate the selected object.

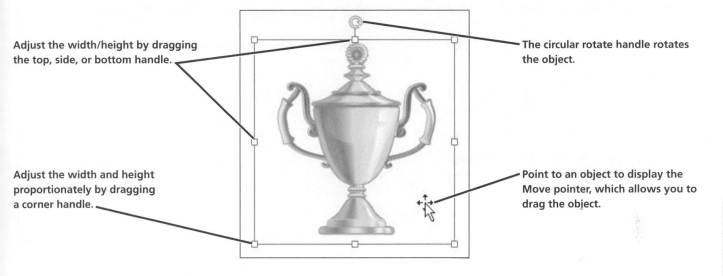

Adjust the width/height by dragging the top, side, or bottom handle.

The circular rotate handle rotates the object.

Adjust the width and height proportionately by dragging a corner handle.

Point to an object to display the Move pointer, which allows you to drag the object.

Stacking Objects

Sometimes when you insert a picture, it overlaps text or some other object. You can change the stacking order of objects, such as pictures and shapes, by moving them forward or backward.

If an object is covering text...

First Place!

...send it behind the text.

First Place!

Task	Procedure
Move an object back one object at a time	Select the object and then choose Picture Tools→Format→Arrange→Send Backward.
Move an object up one object at a time	Select the object and then choose Picture Tools→Format→Arrange→Bring Forward.
Move an object to the very back of a slide	Select the object and then choose Picture Tools→Format→Arrange→Send Backward ▼→Send to Back.
Move an object to the very front of a slide	Select the object and then choose Picture Tools→Format→Arrange→Bring Forward ▼→Bring to Front.

DEVELOP YOUR SKILLS PP03-D03
Move and Size Clip Art

In this exercise, you will manipulate clip art, sizing and moving it to place it on the slide.

1. Save your file as **PP03-D03-Animation-[FirstInitialLastName]**.

2. Follow these steps to rotate the clip art image:

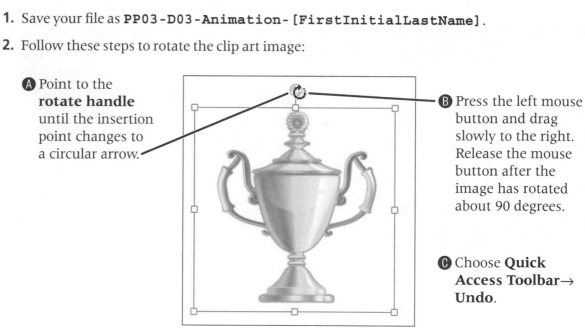

Ⓐ Point to the **rotate handle** until the insertion point changes to a circular arrow.

Ⓑ Press the left mouse button and drag slowly to the right. Release the mouse button after the image has rotated about 90 degrees.

Ⓒ Choose **Quick Access Toolbar→Undo**.

3. Follow these steps to resize the clip art image:

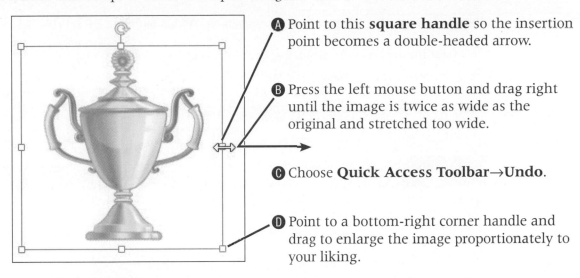

Ⓐ Point to this **square handle** so the insertion point becomes a double-headed arrow.

Ⓑ Press the left mouse button and drag right until the image is twice as wide as the original and stretched too wide.

Ⓒ Choose **Quick Access Toolbar→Undo**.

Ⓓ Point to a bottom-right corner handle and drag to enlarge the image proportionately to your liking.

4. Point to the image itself (not the border or a resize handle) until the pointer becomes a four-headed arrow. Drag so the image is centered next to the bar of text.

Compare your slide to the following illustration.

5. Save your presentation.

Formatting Clip Art

Video Library   http://labyrinthelab.com/videos   Video Number: PP13-V0304

After your image is on the slide, use the various groups on the contextual Format tab to add effects or align your image. You can add borders, drop-shadows, or bevels, or rotate your image in 3-D from the Picture Styles group on the Format tab. Other groups on this tab allow you to align, flip, crop, or perform basic image-editing tasks.

QUICK REFERENCE	PERFORMING CLIP ART TASKS
Task	**Procedure**
Insert a clip art image from an online source	■ Click the Online Pictures shortcut 🖼 or choose Insert→Images→Online Pictures. ■ Enter a search term and tap Enter . ■ Click the desired thumbnail and then click Insert.
Insert an image from your computer	■ Click the Pictures shortcut 🖼 or choose Insert→Images→Pictures. ■ Browse your computer's location for an image. ■ Click the desired image and then click Insert.
Resize a clip art image	■ Click the clip art image to display its border. ■ Drag any square handle along the top, bottom, or sides of the clip art's border to resize the image wider or taller. ■ Drag any handle in the clip art's corners to resize the image proportionately.
Move a clip art image	■ Point to the image until the mouse pointer becomes a four-headed arrow. ■ Drag the image to the desired location.
Rotate a clip art image	■ Click the clip art image to display its border. ■ Point to the rotate handle above the clip art's top border until the mouse pointer becomes a circular arrow. ■ Drag left or right to rotate the image.
Format a clip art image	■ Click the clip art image to display its border. ■ Choose Format→Picture Styles and then choose a command.

DEVELOP YOUR SKILLS PP03-D04
Insert and Format Clip Art

In this exercise, you will work with the Ribbon to insert and format an image on your slide.

1. Save your file as **PP03-D04-Animation-[FirstInitialLastName]**.
2. Display the **title slide**.
3. Choose **Insert→Images→Online Pictures** 🖼.

4. Follow these steps to insert clip art on the title slide:

Ⓐ Type **cd** in the Office.com search box and then tap Enter.

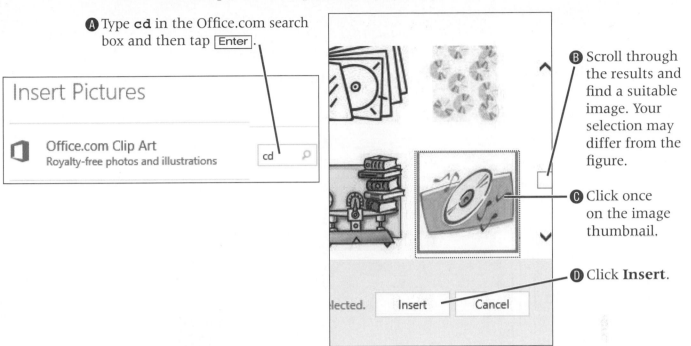

Insert Pictures

Office.com Clip Art
Royalty-free photos and illustrations

cd

Ⓑ Scroll through the results and find a suitable image. Your selection may differ from the figure.

Ⓒ Click once on the image thumbnail.

Ⓓ Click **Insert**.

Insert   Cancel

Size and Position the Image

Next, you will use the Format contextual tab to experiment with effect options.

5. Drag the image to the top of the slide so it no longer overlaps the text. Then drag the top-right corner handle toward the top-right corner of your slide to enlarge the image proportionately.

Be careful not to size it too large; the image should still fit on the slide.

iJams Music
Distribution

6. Choose **Format→Arrange→Align→Align Center**.

Selecting an image object forces the display of the contextual Format tab.

7. Make sure the image displays handles to indicate it is selected and then choose **Format→Picture Styles→Picture Effects**.

8. Roll your insertion point over several of the items in the **Picture Effects** gallery to view a Live Preview of each effect.

   As you have seen with other commands, Live Preview makes it easy to anticipate the effect of a command without the need to undo it if you don't like the effect.

9. Choose **Format→Picture Styles→Picture Effects→Glow→Gold, 18 pt glow, Accent color 3**.

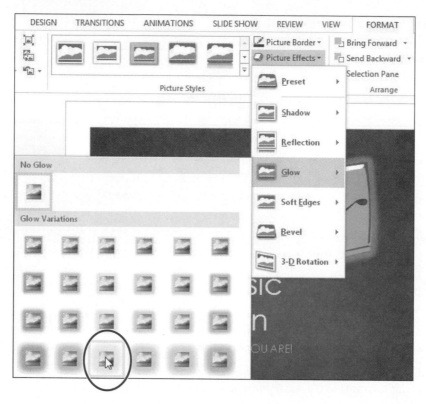

   PowerPoint applies a glowing effect to the edge of the image.

10. If necessary, resize and move your image so it doesn't overlap the text.

11. Save your presentation.

Adding Other Graphics

Video Library   http://labyrinthelab.com/videos   Video Number: PP13-V0305

Sometimes you just can't find that perfect image through clip art. Often you can incorporate more-unique and personal imagery if you take your own pictures or download professional photographs from a commercial website. PowerPoint 2013 includes tools and features to make the most of your images, including the ability to remove a background and add artistic effects.

Removing a Background

Many times a photograph contains more than what you need. In the past, it was necessary to use a graphics-editing program to remove the background or other unwanted elements. PowerPoint 2013 includes a feature that allows you to remove backgrounds with just a few clicks. When removing a background, the original picture is not harmed, because PowerPoint works on a copy of the picture embedded in the slide. Additionally, nothing is actually removed from the picture. PowerPoint just hides areas of the picture that you mark to be removed. The hidden areas can always be made visible again. You can adjust the settings of the removal tool at any time after the background's initial removal, so there is no need to worry about getting it perfect on your first try.

The Background Removal tool overlays in purple the areas to be removed.

With just a few clicks, the background can be removed.

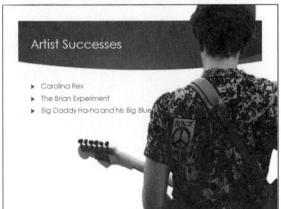

DEVELOP YOUR SKILLS PP03-D05
Remove a Background

In this exercise, you will insert a picture and remove the background.

1. Save your file as **PP03-D05-Animation-[FirstInitialLastName]**.

2. Scroll down the Slides pane, if necessary, and select the **Artist Successes** slide.

3. Choose **Insert→Images→Pictures**.

4. Navigate to your **PP2013 Lesson 03** folder, select the **PP03-D05-Guitarist** picture, and click **Insert**.

   The picture is inserted on the slide, but contains more imagery than we need.

Remove the Background

5. Drag the picture up so its top snaps to the top of the slide.

6. Drag the bottom handle down until the bottom of the picture snaps to the bottom of the slide.

   The picture now covers the whole slide.

7. Choose **Picture Tools→Format→Adjust→Remove Background**.

   PowerPoint places a rectangular border inside the picture and does its best to guess what you want to remove. A purple overlay indicates the content that will be removed. You will adjust this.

8. Drag the top-right handle of the rectangular box inside the picture so it snaps to the top-right corner of the picture.

9. Drag the bottom-left handle of the rectangular box down and right so the entire guitar is inside the box.

   Your slide should resemble the following figure, but it will not be exact.

   When you resize the box inside the picture, PowerPoint adjusts the purple overlay. The overlay still needs to be adjusted so you can see the whole guitarist.

10. Choose **Background Removal→Refine→Mark Areas to Keep**.

11. Follow these steps to adjust the overlay:

Ⓐ Point to the top of the left shoulder and drag down to the bottom of the elbow to tell PowerPoint not to remove this area.

Ⓑ Point to the left edge of the guitar and drag right to keep this area.

Ⓒ Drag over any other purple on the guitarist or the guitar.

12. Choose **Background Removal→Refine→Mark Areas to Remove**.

13. Follow these steps to define areas to be removed:

Ⓐ Drag over the background to tell PowerPoint to remove this area.

Ⓑ Drag over this section to remove it as well.

14. You will probably have to go back and forth with the **Mark Areas to Keep** and **Mark Areas to Remove** buttons as you continue to tweak the purple overlay.

15. Choose **Background Removal→Close→Keep Changes**.

16. Drag the image to the right so all three bulleted paragraphs are visible. If your slide doesn't resemble the following figure, choose **Picture Tools→Format→Adjust→Remove Background** to adjust the overlay.

Part of the image extends to the right beyond the slide. While it may look strange in Normal view, it will look fine as a slide show. The areas outside the slide will not display.

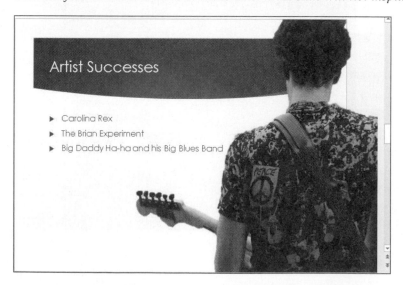

17. Save your presentation.

Applying Artistic Effects

Video Library   http://labyrinthelab.com/videos   Video Number: PP13-V0306

PowerPoint 2013 includes artistic effects that can be applied to pictures, making photographs look like pencil sketches, cement, or pastels. Additionally, pictures can be recolored to create a color cast that blends with your theme.

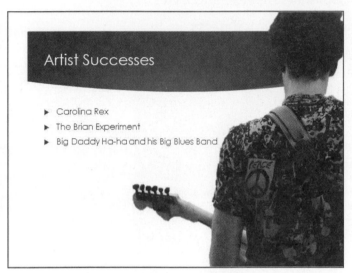

The picture before any effect has been applied

The picture after the Pencil Sketch and Recolor effects have been applied

QUICK REFERENCE	MODIFYING PICTURES
Task	**Procedure**
Remove a background	■ Select the picture and choose Picture Tools→Format→Adjust→Remove Background.
	■ Adjust the marquee to include the portion of the picture you want to keep.
	■ Choose Background Removal→Refine→Mark Areas to Keep and drag over additional areas to include.
	■ Choose Background Removal→Refine→Mark Areas to Remove and drag over additional areas to exclude.
	■ Choose Background Removal→Refine→Keep Changes.
	■ Choose Picture Tools→Format→Adjust→Remove Background to adjust the background removal at any time.
Apply artistic effects	■ Select the picture and choose Picture Tools→Format→Adjust→Artistic Effects.
	■ Choose an effect to apply the default settings, or choose Artistic Effects Options to customize the settings.
	■ If you choose to customize, choose an effect from the drop-down menu, adjust the settings, and click Close.

Apply Artistic Effects

In this exercise, you will apply artistic effects to a picture to enhance its visual appeal.

1. Save your file as **PP03-D06-Animation-[FirstInitialLastName]**.

2. If necessary, select the picture on the sixth slide, **Artistic Successes**.

3. Choose **Picture Tools→Format→Adjust→Artistic Effects**.

4. Point to several effects to see how they change the picture on the slide. Notice that a ToolTip appears when you point to an effect, indicating its name.

5. Select the **Pencil Grayscale** effect.

6. Choose **Picture Tools→Format→Adjust→Color**.

7. Point to several color adjustments to see how they change the picture on the slide. *Notice the ToolTip that appears.*

8. Select the **Teal, Accent Color 5 Light** adjustment.

9. Save your presentation.

Inserting a Screenshot

Video Library   http://labyrinthelab.com/videos   Video Number: PP13-V0307

Sometimes you may want to include a picture of something on your computer screen, such as a program window or web page, in a presentation. PowerPoint's Screenshot tool lets you insert a picture of any open window or program or drag on your screen to define an area to insert.

The Screenshot command is available on the Insert tab.

You can insert any open window as a picture.

You can drag on the screen to define an area to capture.

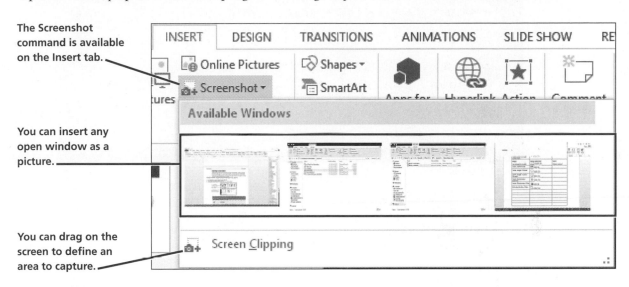

PowerPoint 2013

QUICK REFERENCE	INSERTING A SCREENSHOT
Task	**Procedure**
Insert a picture of an entire program window	▪ Start the program or open the window you want to capture. ▪ Return to PowerPoint and choose the desired slide. ▪ Choose Insert→Images→Screenshot menu ▼→desired screenshot.
Insert a picture of a portion of the screen	▪ Display the program or window you wish to insert. ▪ Return to PowerPoint and choose the desired slide. ▪ Choose Insert→Images→Screenshot menu ▼→Screen Clipping. ▪ Drag to define the area you wish to insert, or tap [Esc] to leave the Screen Clipping tool.

Working with Shapes

Video Library   http://labyrinthelab.com/videos   Video Number: PP13-V0308

PowerPoint offers more than 150 shapes that you can add to your slides. You can use these shapes to build your own custom flowcharts, mathematical equations, speech and thought bubbles, or other design. Shapes can even include text.

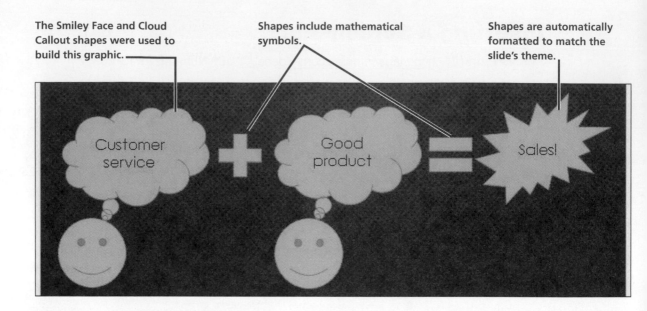

The Smiley Face and Cloud Callout shapes were used to build this graphic.

Shapes include mathematical symbols.

Shapes are automatically formatted to match the slide's theme.

Adding a Shape

When adding a shape to a slide, you can stretch it to make it wider/narrower or taller/shorter. All shapes are preformatted with a specific ratio of width to height, so stretching a shape can sometimes make it appear unbalanced. You can use the Shift key to maintain the original width-to-height ratio.

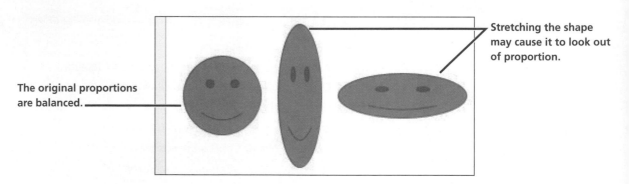

The original proportions are balanced.

Stretching the shape may cause it to look out of proportion.

Adding Text to a Shape

You can easily add text to a shape, but the text does not automatically resize itself to fit nicely. Text will, however, automatically wrap to the next line so there is no need to tap Enter as you type.

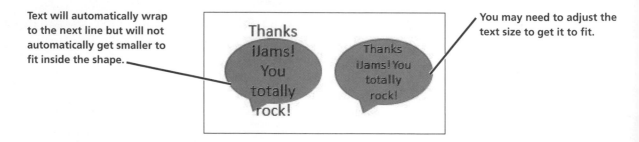

Text will automatically wrap to the next line but will not automatically get smaller to fit inside the shape.

You may need to adjust the text size to get it to fit.

Task	Procedure
Add a shape	■ Choose Insert→Illustrations→Shapes ▼.
	■ Select the desired shape and then drag on the slide to draw the shape.
	■ Hold Shift as you drag the shape to maintain the original proportions.
Add text to a shape	■ Add a shape to a slide.
	■ With the shape selected and displaying a solid border, start typing.

Resizing a Shape

Shapes can be resized and rotated just like clip art. Additionally, some shapes include a yellow square that you can use to change the shape's properties. For example, you can change the Smiley Face shape to a frown or you can change the head and body of an arrow shape.

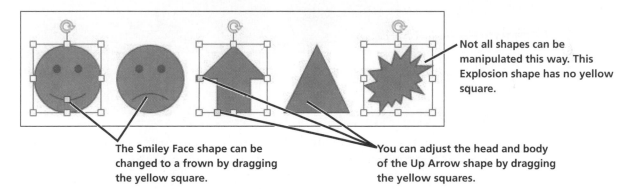

Not all shapes can be manipulated this way. This Explosion shape has no yellow square.

The Smiley Face shape can be changed to a frown by dragging the yellow square.

You can adjust the head and body of the Up Arrow shape by dragging the yellow squares.

Merging Shapes

New in PowerPoint is the ability to merge shapes. This feature allows you to create your own custom shape by combining existing shapes into a single one. The benefit of this is that your new custom shape has a single outline and truly looks like a single shape rather than several overlapped shapes.

The Merge Shapes command is available from the Drawing Tools→Format tab.

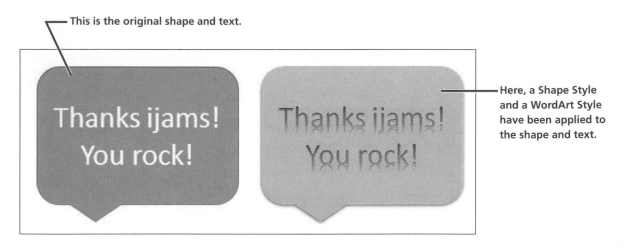

Non-merged shapes look like they are overlapped.

Merged shapes have a single outline.

Formatting Shapes and Shape Text

While shapes and the text they contain are automatically formatted to match the slide's theme, you may want a more exciting look such as a drop-shadow or three-dimensional effect. Adding a Shape Style or WordArt Style can make your shape graphics really pop.

This is the original shape and text.

Thanks ijams!
You rock!

Thanks ijams!
You rock!

Here, a Shape Style and a WordArt Style have been applied to the shape and text.

Task	Procedure
Format a shape	■ Select the desired shape.
	■ Choose a command from Drawing Tools→Format→Shape Styles.
Format shape text	■ Select the desired shape.
	■ Choose a command from Drawing Tools→Format→WordArt Styles.

DEVELOP YOUR SKILLS PP03-D07

Add and Format a Shape with Text

In this exercise, you will add and format a shape with text.

1. Save your file as **PP03-D07-Animation-[FirstInitialLastName]**.

2. Display the seventh slide, **Carolina Rex**.

3. Choose **Insert→Illustrations→Shapes ▼→Stars and Banners→5-Point Star**.

4. Hold ⌈Shift⌉ as you drag on the slide to create a star shape.

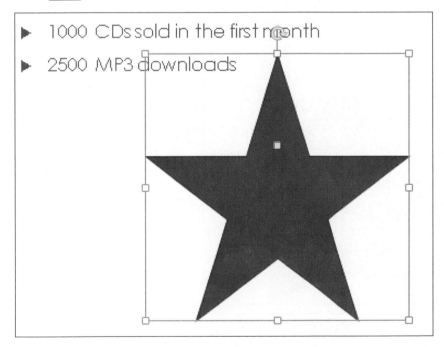

PowerPoint 2013

5. Type the following: `Top Seller!`

Your star shape should resemble this figure, though your text may fit on a single line.

6. Click the dashed border of the shape so it turns solid.

When the shape is selected, you can format its text.

7. Choose **Home→Font→Font Size ▼→44**.

The font size increases, but the text no longer fits nicely inside the shape. You will fix this in the next few steps.

Customize the Shape

8. Follow these steps to change the shape of the star and make the text fit nicely:

Ⓐ Drag the **yellow square** up a little bit to change the shape of the star.

Ⓑ Try to match your star shape to the figure. You may have to drag the yellow diamond up or down.

Format the Shape and Text

9. Choose **Drawing Tools→Format→Shape Styles→More→Intense Effect – Purple, Accent 6**.

The shape changes color and appears three-dimensional. However, the text remains the same.

10. Choose **Drawing Tools→Format→WordArt Styles→More→Fill – White, Outline – Accent 1, Shadow**.

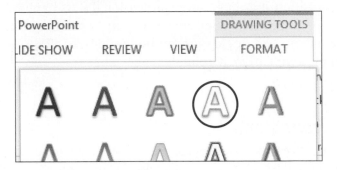

The text within the shape changes.

11. If necessary, change the size of the star shape so the text fits on two lines.

12. Save your presentation.

Working with Slide Transitions

Video Library   http://labyrinthelab.com/videos   Video Number: PP13-V0309

A slide transition is the animation between slides. Used properly, these transitions can add zest and excitement to your presentation and provide a distinct breaking point between slides. PowerPoint 2013 includes many transitions that are often used in video production, such as 3-D rotations and other animated effects.

The Vortex transition occurring between two slides

Consistency within a presentation helps keep the audience focused. Avoid using different transitions within a single presentation.

Creating Transitions in Slide Sorter View

Most of the time, you will want to apply the same transition to the entire presentation. Maintaining a consistent transition style looks more professional (less haphazard) and is less distracting for the audience. Using the Slide Sorter view is a quick and easy way to accomplish this task. You can apply transitions to a single slide, multiple slides, or all slides in a presentation. When you apply a transition, it animates the change from one slide to another, not individual elements of the slide.

Selecting Slides for Transitions

To easily select all slides in a presentation from Slide Sorter view, click to select any slide and then press ⌴Ctrl⌴+⌴A⌴. All slides will be selected. Then, choose Transitions→Transitions to This Slide and select a transition effect. The transition will be applied to all selected slides. You can also use this method from the Normal view's Slides panel to select all slides in a presentation.

To apply a transition to a single slide, select a single slide in either Normal or Slide Sorter view and then choose a slide transition. The transition will be applied to the selected slide.

The Transitions Tab

The Transitions tab contains the Transitions to This Slide group, which you use to implement your slide transitions. The Transitions tab contains commands to apply transitions, sound, and other transition options.

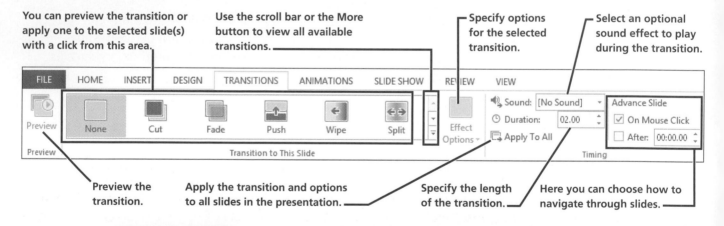

You can preview the transition or apply one to the selected slide(s) with a click from this area.

Use the scroll bar or the More button to view all available transitions.

Specify options for the selected transition.

Select an optional sound effect to play during the transition.

Preview the transition.

Apply the transition and options to all slides in the presentation.

Specify the length of the transition.

Here you can choose how to navigate through slides.

QUICK REFERENCE	ADDING TRANSITIONS TO A PRESENTATION
Task	**Procedure**
Add transitions to an entire presentation	■ From Slide Sorter view, press ⌴Ctrl⌴+⌴A⌴. ■ Choose Transitions→Transition to This Slide and select the desired transition.
Set a transition for individual slides	■ Select the desired slide(s). (Remember that transitions are seen when navigating to a slide when a slide loads.) ■ Choose Transitions→Transition to This Slide and select the desired transition.

Apply Transition Effects

In this exercise, you will apply a transition to all slides except the title slide to make the slide show more interesting.

Choose Transition Effects

1. Save your file as **PP03-D08-Animation-[FirstInitialLastName]**.

2. Choose **View→Presentation Views→Slide Sorter** ⊞.

3. Choose the **Transitions** tab.

4. Click the **Our Services** slide to select it.

5. Use [Shift]+click on the **Contact Us** slide.
   Slides 2–11 are selected.

6. Follow these steps to apply a transition effect to the selected slides:

B Choose **Vortex**. A preview of the transition appears on each slide.

A Click the **More** button and locate the Exciting category.

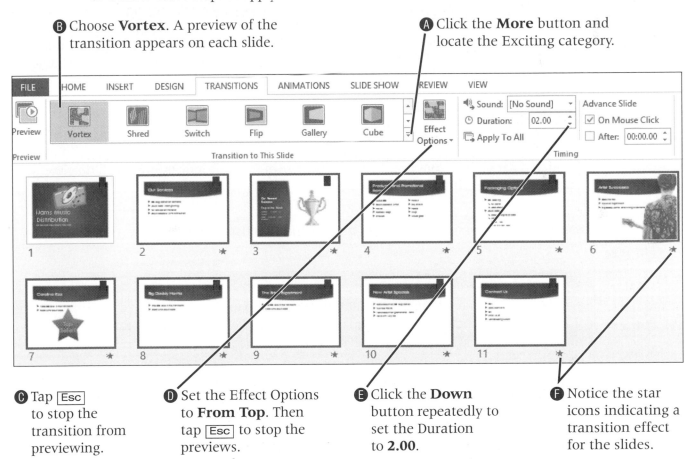

C Tap [Esc] to stop the transition from previewing.

D Set the Effect Options to **From Top**. Then tap [Esc] to stop the previews.

E Click the **Down** button repeatedly to set the Duration to **2.00**.

F Notice the star icons indicating a transition effect for the slides.

The title slide does not have the star icon because there is no transition applied to it.

PowerPoint 2013

Run the Presentation

7. Choose **Slide Show→Start Slide Show→From Beginning** 📽️.

   The title slide appears without a transition. The title slide would have opened with the Vortex transition if you had applied the transition to it.

8. Click the mouse button to advance to the next slide.

   The Vortex transition effect displays as the slides advance.

9. Continue to click the mouse button until you reach the end of the presentation and the Slide Sorter window reappears.

10. Save your presentation.

Using Slide Animation

Video Library   http://labyrinthelab.com/videos   Video Number: PP13-V0310

Whereas transitions are applied to slides as a whole, animations are applied to individual objects *within* a slide. Animations begin only after any transition effect is completed. Some examples of animation include the following:

- A clip art image that moves across the slide to its final location
- A slide that starts out empty, and then has a title and other elements that fade into view with a mouse click
- Bulleted paragraphs that fly in from the bottom of the slide, one by one, each time the presenter clicks with the mouse

Less is more. Animation can distract an audience, so use it sparingly.

Adding Animations

PowerPoint offers more than 40 animations you can add to objects on a slide by using a single command. For example, the Fade animation tells PowerPoint to gradually make objects on a slide fade into view after any transition effect is completed.

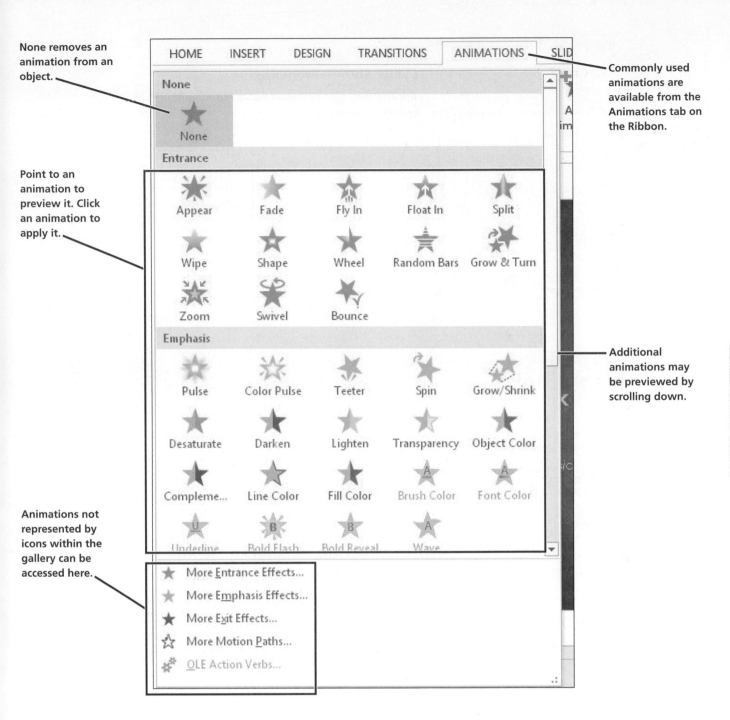

None removes an animation from an object.

Point to an animation to preview it. Click an animation to apply it.

Animations not represented by icons within the gallery can be accessed here.

Commonly used animations are available from the Animations tab on the Ribbon.

Additional animations may be previewed by scrolling down.

Setting Animation Options

After applying an animation to an object, you will likely want to set the animation options to control exactly how the animation effect works. The available options differ based on whether the animation was applied to text or an image. The options also differ based on the animation itself. Additionally, you can set timing options to control the speed of the animation.

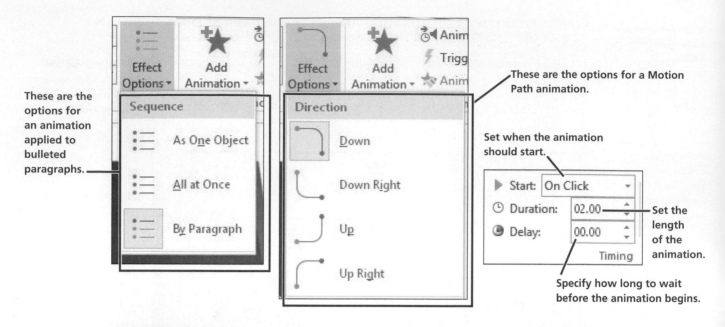

These are the options for an animation applied to bulleted paragraphs.

These are the options for a Motion Path animation.

Set when the animation should start.

Set the length of the animation.

Specify how long to wait before the animation begins.

QUICK REFERENCE	ADDING ANIMATION TO SLIDES
Task	**Procedure**
Apply a common animation to an object on a slide	■ Display the slide containing the object(s) to be animated. ■ Select the object (text object, picture, etc.) on the slide you wish to animate. ■ Choose Animations→Animation; choose the desired animation.
Set animation options	■ Select the object containing the animation. ■ Choose Animation→Animation→Effect Options menu ▼ and then choose the desired option. ■ Set the options in the Animation→Timing group if desired.
Remove an animation	■ Select the object containing the animation. ■ Choose Animation→Animation→None.

DEVELOP YOUR SKILLS PP03-D09

Apply Animation to Bulleted Paragraphs

In this exercise, you will apply an animation to text objects on a slide to draw attention to them.

1. Save your file as **PP03-D09-Animation-[FirstInitialLastName]**.

2. Choose **View→Presentation Views→Normal** 🖳.

3. Display the **Our Services** slide.

4. Click once in the **bulleted text** so a dashed border appears around the text box.

5. Choose **Animations→Animation→More→Entrance→Float In**.

   The animation previews, and you see each first-level paragraph animate across the slide.

6. Choose **Animations**→**Animation**→**Effect Option**→**Float Down** to have the paragraphs animate from the top of the slide down.

   The numbers next to each bulleted paragraph indicate the order in which the animation is applied. By default, each paragraph will animate after a mouse click.

7. Choose **Slide Show**→**Start Slide Show**→**From Beginning** to start the slide show.

8. Click anywhere with the mouse to advance to the second slide.

   The transition effect animates, but no bulleted paragraph appears yet.

9. Click anywhere with the mouse.

   The first bulleted paragraph animates into view.

10. Continue clicking until all four bulleted paragraphs are visible and the slide show advances to the third slide, Our Recent Success.

11. Tap ⌷Esc⌷ to end the slide show and return to Normal view.

12. Save your presentation.

Using the Animation Pane

Video Library   http://labyrinthelab.com/videos   Video Number: PP13-V0311

By using the Animation pane, you have many more choices for effects than you have in the animation menu you used previously. You can also individually set the animation for each element on a slide. When using the Animation pane, you can control the visual effects, timing, and sequencing of the animation process. For example, rather than having to click each time to display the next animated bulleted paragraph, you can set it so that the animation starts automatically after the slide transition and continues until all objects on the slide have been animated.

Budgeting Your Time

Using the Animation pane to customize each animation is a time-consuming process. Be prepared to spend a significant amount of time selecting each animated object individually and then setting its options. The following figure describes the options on the Animation pane.

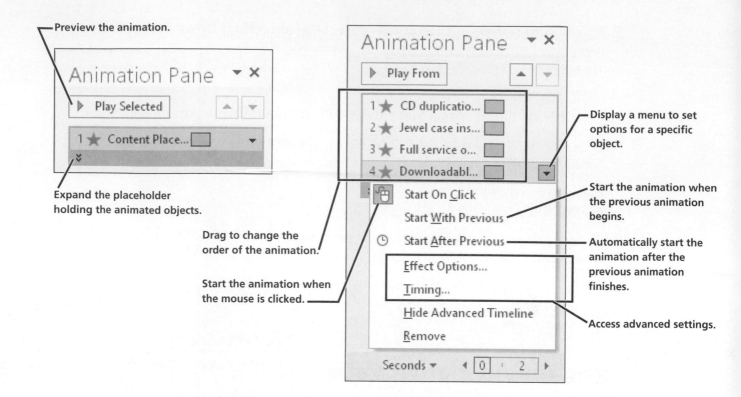

Preview the animation.

Expand the placeholder holding the animated objects.

Drag to change the order of the animation.

Start the animation when the mouse is clicked.

Display a menu to set options for a specific object.

Start the animation when the previous animation begins.

Automatically start the animation after the previous animation finishes.

Access advanced settings.

DEVELOP YOUR SKILLS PP03-D10

Use the Animation Pane

In this exercise, you will use the Animation pane to configure the bulleted paragraphs to animate automatically after the slide transition completes. This reduces the need for you to click constantly during a slide show.

1. Save your file as **PP03-D10-Animation-[FirstInitialLastName]**.

2. Display the second slide, **Our Services**.

3. Click once in the bulleted text so a dashed border appears around the text box.

4. Choose **Animations→Advanced Animation→Animation Pane**.

   The Animation pane displays on the right side of the screen.

5. Follow these steps to begin to configure the advanced animation settings:

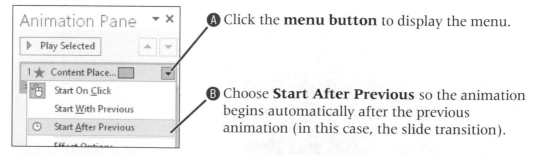

Ⓐ Click the **menu button** to display the menu.

Ⓑ Choose **Start After Previous** so the animation begins automatically after the previous animation (in this case, the slide transition).

Notice that the numbers next to each bulleted paragraph in the Animation panel have changed to zeros, indicating their animations all happen at the same time, automatically, after the slide transition.

6. Click the **Click to Expand Contents** bar to show each individual paragraph.

7. Follow these steps to customize the animation for the last paragraph:

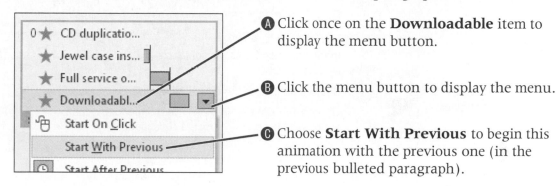

Ⓐ Click once on the **Downloadable** item to display the menu button.

Ⓑ Click the menu button to display the menu.

Ⓒ Choose **Start With Previous** to begin this animation with the previous one (in the previous bulleted paragraph).

8. Choose **Slide Show→Start Slide Show→From Beginning**.

9. Click anywhere with the mouse to advance to the second slide.

The bulleted paragraphs animate automatically after the slide transition ends. Each animation happens sequentially, except for the last bulleted paragraph, which animates with the previous item.

10. Tap ⎡Esc⎤ to end the slide show and return to Normal view.

11. Save your presentation.

Adding Sound Effects

Video Library   http://labyrinthelab.com/videos   Video Number: PP13-V0312

PowerPoint 2013 provides audio clips and sound effects to accompany or accentuate your slide elements. For example, you may attach sound effects to slide transitions or animations. You can use the Transitions tab to add a sound to a slide transition or the Animation pane to add a sound to an animation.

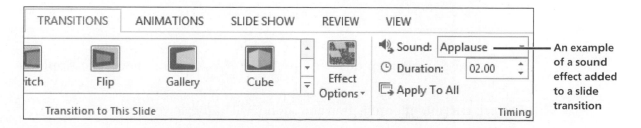

An example of a sound effect added to a slide transition

Adding a Sound Effect to an Animation

Sometimes you don't want a sound effect to play during a slide transition, but rather when an animation causes an object to move across the slide. The following table describes the steps used to apply sound effects to animations.

QUICK REFERENCE	ADDING SOUND TO SLIDES
Task	**Procedure**
Add sound to an animation	■ Display the slide with the animation to which you wish to add sound (or add an animation to the slide object). ■ Choose Animations→Advanced Animation→Animation Pane. ■ Click the menu button for the object to receive sound and choose Effect Options. ■ In the Enhancements section of the dialog box, choose the sound you wish to apply; click OK.
Add sound to a transition	■ Select a slide from the Slides panel or Slide Sorter view. ■ Choose Transitions→Timing→Sound menu and then select a sound effect. The sound will play as the selected slide loads.

DEVELOP YOUR SKILLS PP03-D11

Apply Sound Effects

In this exercise, you will apply two sounds to the presentation to enhance an animation.

1. Save your file as **PP03-D11-Animation-[FirstInitialLastName]**.

2. Choose the **Our Recent Success** slide and then select the clip art object.

3. Choose **Animations→Animation→More→Entrance→Bounce**.

4. Click the drop-down menu for the clip art animation in the Animation pane and choose **Effect Options**.

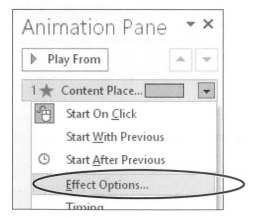

5. Click the **Sound drop-down menu** in the Effect tab and choose the **Applause** sound effect.

6. Click **OK**, and the animation and sound will be previewed.

Apply a Transition Sound Effect

7. Display the **Our Services** slide.

8. Follow these steps to add a transition sound effect:

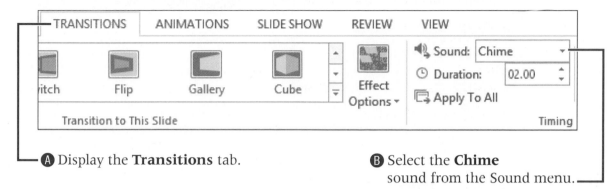

A Display the **Transitions** tab.

B Select the **Chime** sound from the Sound menu.

PowerPoint applies the Chime sound to the transition effect for this slide.

9. Choose **Slide Show→Start Slide Show→From Beginning** .

10. Navigate through the presentation until you hear the applause and see the Bounce animation on the Our Recent Success slide.

You may not be able to hear the sound effect if your computer does not have speakers.

11. Press the Esc key to end the slide show early and return to Normal view.

12. Close the **Animation pane**.

13. Save your presentation and exit **PowerPoint**.

Concepts Review

To check your knowledge of the key concepts introduced in this lesson, complete the Concepts Review quiz by choosing the appropriate access option below.

If you are...	Then access the quiz by...
Using the Labyrinth Video Library	Going to http://labyrinthelab.com/videos
Using eLab	Logging in, choosing Content, and navigating to the Concepts Review quiz for this lesson
Not using the Labyrinth Video Library or eLab	Going to the student resource center for this book

Reinforce Your Skills

Work with Images

In this exercise, you will add clip art to the Kids for Change animation presentation to add visual interest.

Prepare a Slide for ClipArt

1. Start **PowerPoint**. Open **PP03-R01-KidsClipArt** from the **PP2013 Lesson 03** folder and save it as **PP03-R01-KidsClipArt-[FirstInitialLastName]**.

2. Choose the **Events** slide (the second slide).

3. Choose **Home→Slides→Layout→Two Content**.

Insert ClipArt

4. Click the **Online Pictures** icon on the slide to display the Insert Pictures search window.

5. Type **calendar** in the Office.com search box and tap Enter.

6. Scroll through the results until you find an appropriate image.

7. Choose a clip art image that appeals to you and click **Insert**.

Move and Size Clip Art

8. Drag any of the image's corner handles to resize it so it fills the right half of the slide.

9. Drag from the center of the image to move and position it so it does not overlap any text.

10. Drag the rotate handle above the top edge of the image to rotate it slightly for visual interest.

Format Clip Art

11. Locate the **Picture Tools→Format→Picture Styles** group of commands.

12. Point to several of the thumbnail samples in the **Picture Styles gallery** to preview them and then click one to apply it. Choose a style that works well with your image. The following figure shows the **Reflected Rounded Rectangle** style applied.

Remove a Background

13. Display the **Contact Us** slide.

14. Choose **Insert→Images→Pictures**.

15. Browse to your **PP2013 Lesson 03** folder and insert the **PP03-R01-Phone** image.

16. With the phone image selected on the slide, choose **Picture Tools→Format→ Adjust→Remove Background**.

17. Drag the handles of the Background Removal border so the phone and wire are inside the border and then choose **Background Removal→Close→Keep Changes**.

Apply Artistic Effects

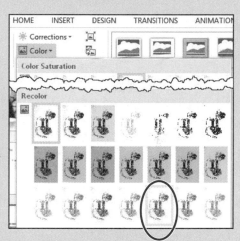

18. With the phone image selected on the slide, choose **Picture Tools→Format→Adjust→ Artistic Effects→Pencil Sketch**.

19. Choose **Picture Tools→Format→Adjust→Color →Recolor→Dark Green, Accent Color 4 Light**.

20. Move the phone, if necessary, so it is roughly centered below the phone number.

21. Save the changes and then exit **PowerPoint**. Submit your final file based on the guidelines provided by your instructor.

    To view examples of how your file or files should look at the end of this exercise, go to the student resource center.

REINFORCE YOUR SKILLS PP03-R02

Add Shapes and Animations

In this exercise, you will create a custom shape of a house and incorporate animation to add visual appeal to the presentation.

Add and Resize a Shape

1. Start **PowerPoint**. Open **PP03-R02-KidsAnimated** from the **PP2013 Lesson 03** folder and save it as PP03-R02-KidsAnimated-[FirstInitialLastName].

2. Display the second slide, **This Month**.

3. Choose **Insert→Illustrations→Shapes→Rectangles→Rectangle**.

4. Drag on the slide to draw a rectangle. Resize and move it so it roughly matches this figure.

5. Choose **Insert→Illustrations→Shapes→Basic Shapes→Isosceles Triangle**.

6. Drag on the slide to draw a triangle to act as the roof of the house. Resize and move it so it roughly matches the figure in step 8.

7. Choose **Insert→Illustrations→Shapes→Rectangles→Rectangle**.

8. Drag on the slide to draw a small rectangle to act as a chimney. Resize and move it so it roughly matches this figure.

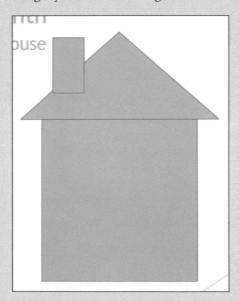

Merge Shapes

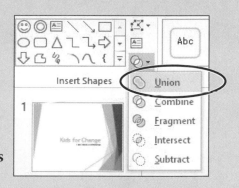

9. Click the large rectangle on the slide to select it, ⎡Shift⎤+click the triangular roof, and ⎡Shift⎤+click the small chimney so that all three shapes are selected.

10. Choose **Drawing Tools→Format→Insert Shapes→Merge Shapes→Union**.

11. Choose **Insert→Illustrations→Shapes→Rectangles →Rectangle**.

12. Drag on the slide to draw a rectangle to act as the door. Resize and move it so it roughly matches this figure.

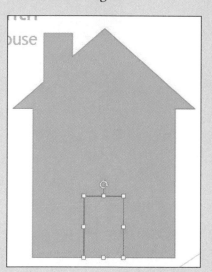

13. Click the door shape to select it, if necessary, and then ⎡Shift⎤+click the house so both shapes are selected.

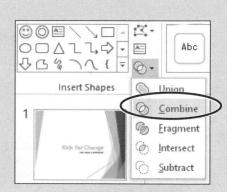

14. Choose **Drawing Tools→Format→Insert Shapes→Merge Shapes→Combine**.

Format and Add Text to a Shape

15. Click the dashed border of the shape to select it.

16. Type **Home** ⎡Enter⎤ **Sweet** ⎡Enter⎤ **Home** ⎡Enter⎤.

17. Click the dashed border of the shape to select it.

18. Choose **Home→Font→Font Size→36**. If your text no longer fits in the shape, choose a smaller font size or adjust the size of the house shape.

19. Choose **Drawing Tools→Format→Shape Styles→More→Intense Effect – Blue, Accent 2** (the bottom thumbnail in the third column).

20. Resize and move the shape so it fits in the upper-right area of the slide. You may have to adjust the font size.

Apply Transition Effects

21. Select slide 2, **This Month**, in the Slides panel.

22. ⎡Shift⎤+click the last slide in the Slides panel so all but the title slide are selected.

23. Choose **Transitions→Transition to This Slide→More→Random Bars**.

Add Animation

24. Display the second slide, **This Month**, if necessary.

25. Click the house shape to select it.

26. Choose **Animations→Animation→More→Entrance→Bounce**.

27. Choose **Animations→Timing→Start→After Previous**.

28. Click the up arrow on the **Animations→Timing→Delay** box four times to set the delay to 1 second.

29. Display the third slide, **Event Benefits**.

30. Click in any text in the left column so a dashed border appears around the text box.

31. Choose **Animations→Animation→More→Entrance→Float In**.

32. Click in any of the text in the right column so a dashed border appears around the text box.

33. Choose **Animations→Animation→More→Entrance→Float In**.

34. Choose **Animations→Advanced Animation→Animation Pane**.

35. Click the arrows to expand the top group of content in the Animation pane.

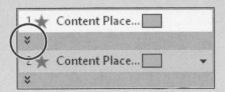

36. Click the second item, **Homeless families**, to display its menu button.

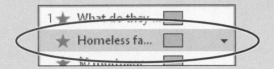

37. Click the item's menu button and then choose **Start After Previous**.

38. Click the third item, **$0 mortgage**, to display its menu button.

39. Click the item's menu button and then choose **Start After Previous**.

40. Click the fourth item, **A fresh start**, to display its menu button.

41. Click the item's menu button and then choose **Start After Previous**.

42. Expand the contents of the second group of content and set each item in the second group to **Start After Previous**.

Add a Sound Effect to an Animation

43. Display the second slide, **This Month**.

44. Click the house shape to select it.

45. Click the single item in the Animation pane, click its menu button, and choose **Effect Options** to view the effect's options.

46. Set the **Sound** menu to **Whoosh** and then click **OK**.

47. Close the **Animation pane**.

48. Choose **Slide Show→Start Slide Show→From Beginning** and click each slide until the slide show ends and you return to Normal view.

49. Save the changes and then exit **PowerPoint**. Submit your final file based on the guidelines provided by your instructor.

To view examples of how your file or files should look at the end of this exercise, go to the student resource center.

Add Visual Interest

In this exercise, you will add images and animation to a presentation.

Prepare a Slide for ClipArt

1. Start **PowerPoint**. Open **PP03-R03-KidsVisual** from the **PP2013 Lesson 03** folder and save it as `PP03-R03-KidsVisual-[FirstInitialLastName]`.

2. Display the third slide.

3. Choose **Home→Slides→Layout→Two Content**.

Insert ClipArt

4. Click the **Pictures** icon on the slide to insert a picture from your computer.

5. Browse to your **PP2013 Lesson 03** folder and insert the **PP03-R03-Girl** picture.

6. Drag the picture to roughly fill the right side of the slide.

7. Display the fourth slide.

8. Choose **Home→Slides→Layout→Two Content**.

9. Click the **Pictures** icon on the slide to insert a picture from your computer.

10. Browse to your **PP2013 Lesson 03** folder and insert the **PP03-R03-Truck** picture.

11. Drag the truck picture to roughly center it on the slide.

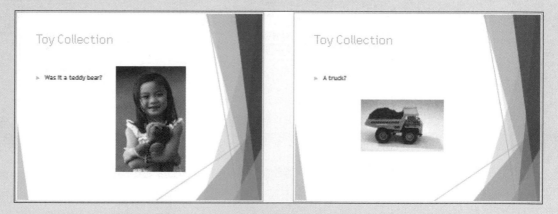

12. Display the fifth slide.

13. Choose **Insert→Images→Online Pictures**.

14. Type **toy** in the Office.com search box and tap Enter.

15. Scroll through the results until you find a toy you like, and then click the toy to select it.

16. Continue to scroll and look for more toys. Ctrl + click additional toys to add them to your selection. After you have selected a total of six toys, click **Insert**.

Move, Size, and Rotate ClipArt

17. Click an empty area of the slide to deselect the inserted pictures.

18. Click one of the toys on the slide to select it.

19. Drag a corner handle on the picture's border to make the picture smaller.

20. Drag the rotate handle above the top edge of the picture to slightly rotate it.

21. Drag the picture to move it to a position of your liking.

22. Resize, rotate, and move the remaining toys so your slide roughly matches the following figure. *Do not be concerned if the picture backgrounds overlap each other at this point.*

Format Clip Art

23. Display the third slide and click the picture of the girl and her teddy bear.

24. Choose **Picture Tools→Format→Picture Styles→More→Rotated, White**.

25. Drag the picture to reposition it, if necessary.

Remove a Background

26. Display slide 4 and click the truck picture.

27. Choose **Picture Tools→Format→Adjust→Remove Background**.

28. Drag the handles of the background removal border until the truck fits inside it.

29. Choose **Background Removal→Refine→Mark Areas to Remove**.

30. Drag on the light colored areas on the ground near the tires to remove them.

31. Choose **Background Removal→Close→Keep Changes**.

32. Drag a corner handle of the truck's border to resize it and then drag the truck into position so it roughly matches the following figure.

33. Display slide 5 and remove the background of the pictures so they can be overlapped.

Apply Artistic Effects

34. Display slide 3 and click the picture of the girl.

35. Choose **Picture Tools→Format→Adjust→Artistic Effects→Glow, Diffused**.

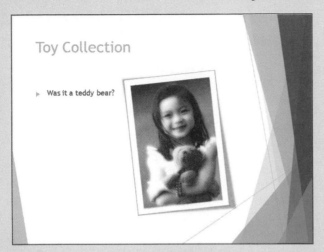

Add and Format a Shape with Text

36. Choose **Insert→Illustrations→Shapes→Stars and Banners→Up Ribbon**.

37. ⎡Shift⎤+drag to create a proportional ribbon that fills the left side of the slide under the text.

38. Type **My 1st toy**.

39. Click the blue ribbon shape to select it.

40. Tap ⎡Ctrl⎤+⎡C⎤ to copy the shape.

41. Display the fourth slide with the truck.

42. Tap ⎡Ctrl⎤+⎡V⎤ to paste the shape.

43. Drag the truck picture so the blue ribbon doesn't overlap it.

44. Click the blue ribbon shape to select it.

45. Choose **Drawing Tools→Format→Shape Styles→Shape Effects→Reflection→Reflection Variations→Half Reflection, Touching**.

46. Choose **Home→Clipboard→Format Painter** to copy the formatting.

47. Display the third slide and click the blue ribbon to duplicate the shape's effect.

Apply Transition Effects

48. Choose **View→Presentation Views→Slide Sorter**.

49. Click slide 2 and then [Shift]+click slide 5 so that all but the title slide are selected.

50. Choose **Transitions→Transition to This Slide→More→Exciting→Vortex**.

51. Choose **Transitions→Transition to This Slide→Effect Options→From Top**.

52. Click the down arrow of the **Transitions→Timing→Duration** box until the Duration is set to **02.00**.

Apply Animation

53. Double-click slide 5 to display it in **Normal** view.

54. Click one of the toys on the slide to select it.

55. Choose **Animations→Animation→More→Entrance→Grow & Turn**.

56. Click a second toy on the slide to select it.

57. Choose **Animations→Animation→More→Entrance→Grow & Turn**.

58. One at a time, click each remaining toy and apply the **Grow & Turn** animation.

Use the Animation Pane

59. Choose **Animations→Advanced Animation→Animation Pane**.

60. Click the first animated item in the Animation pane to display its menu button.

61. Click the menu button and choose **Start After Previous**.

62. One at a time, click each remaining item and set them to **Start After Previous**.

Add a Sound Effect to an Animation

63. Click the last item in the Animation pane, click its menu button, and choose **Effect Options**.

64. Set the sound effect to **Applause** and then click **OK**.

65. Close the **Animation** pane.

66. Choose **Slide Show→Start Slide Show→From Beginning** and click each slide to view the presentation, returning to **Normal** view when you are finished.

67. Save the changes and then exit **PowerPoint**. Submit your final file based on the guidelines provided by your instructor.

Apply Your Skills

Work with Images

In this exercise, you will add pictures and remove the backgrounds for the Universal Corporate Events presentation. You will also format the pictures to enhance the visual appeal of the slides.

Prepare a Slide for and Insert Clip Art

1. Start **PowerPoint**. Open **PP03-A01-UniversalClipArt** from the **PP2013 Lesson 03** folder and save it as **PP03-A01-UniversalClipArt-[FirstInitialLastName]**.

2. Choose the **Catering** slide (the third slide).

3. Apply the **Two Content** layout.

4. Apply the **Two Content** layout to slides 4–9.

5. Display slide 3.

6. Click the **Online Pictures** icon on the slide to display the Insert Pictures search window.

7. Search for and insert a photo appropriate for a catering slide.

8. Search for and insert an appropriate photograph on slides 4–9. The photograph should represent the slide's text content.

Move, Size, and Rotate Objects

9. Resize and reposition the photographs on each slide so they fill the right half of the slide.

Format Clip Art

10. Add a **Picture Style** or **Picture Effect** to each photograph. Use a maximum of two styles of effects.

Remove a Background and Apply Artistic Effects

11. Remove the backgrounds of each photo. You may want to resize or move the photos after removing the background.

12. Display slide 5, **Graphic Design**, and apply an **Artistic Effect** to the photo.

13. Save the changes and then exit **PowerPoint**. Submit your final file based on the guidelines provided by your instructor.

    To view examples of how your file or files should look at the end of this exercise, go to the student resource center.

Add Shapes and Animations

In this exercise, you will add shapes and animation to a presentation.

Add and Resize a Shape with Text

1. Start **PowerPoint**. Open **PP03-A02-UniversalAnimated** from the **PP2013 Lesson 03** folder and save it as `PP03-A02-UniversalAnimated-[FirstInitialLastName]`.

2. Display the third slide, **Vegan**.

3. Insert the **Explosion 1** shape.

4. Type `Certified Vegan!`

5. Resize and reposition the shape so it fills the area below the text.

6. Enlarge the font size of the shape's text to be as large as possible while remaining inside the shape.

7. Add the **Explosion 2** shape to slide 4 with the text `Certified Kosher!`

8. Resize and reposition the **shape** so it fills the area below the text.

9. Enlarge the font size of the shape's text to be as large as possible while remaining inside the shape.

10. Add the **Up Ribbon** shape to slide 5 with the text `Certified Organic!`

11. Resize and reposition the shape so it fills the area below the text.

12. Enlarge the font size of the shape's text to be as large as possible while remaining inside the shape.

Merge and Format Shapes

13. Display the last slide.

14. Insert a **Rectangle** shape and resize it so it is tall and thin.

15. Insert a **Teardrop** shape and adjust the size and shape so it looks like a candle flame. Position it on top of the thin rectangle.

16. Merge the **Rectangle** and **Teardrop** shapes into a single candle shape.

17. Copy the new candle shape and paste three copies on the slide, arranging them similarly to the following figure.

18. Apply the **Intense Effect – Blue-Gray, Accent 2** Shape Style to the shapes on slides 3–6.

Apply Transition Effects and Animations

19. Select all slides but the title slide.

20. Apply the **Checkerboard** transition and set the **Effect Options** to **From Top**.

21. Display the second slide, **Catering**.

22. Apply the **Fade** animation to the bulleted paragraphs.

23. Use the Animation pane to select the Kosher Dishes item and set it to **Start With Previous**.

24. Set *Meat-lovers dishes* and *Desserts* to **Start With Previous** so that all four paragraphs will fade in at the same time after a click.

Add a Sound Effect to an Animation

25. Select the *Vegan dishes* item in the Animation pane and apply the **Applause** sound effect.

26. Close the **Animation pane**.

27. Choose **Slide Show→Start Slide Show→From Beginning** and click each slide until the slide show ends and you return to Normal view.

28. Save the changes and then exit **PowerPoint**. Submit your final file based on the guidelines provided by your instructor.

To view examples of how your file or files should look at the end of this exercise, go to the student resource center.

Add Visual Interest

In this exercise, you will add images and animation to a presentation.

Prepare a Slide for and Insert Clip Art

1. Start **PowerPoint**. Open **PP03-A03-UniversalVisual** from the **PP2013 Lesson 03** folder and save it as `PP03-A03-UniversalVisual-[FirstInitialLastName]`.

2. Display the second slide and change its layout to **Two Content**.

3. Use the **Online Pictures** icon on the slide to search **Office.com** and insert a photo of a bus.

4. Use the **Ribbon** to search **Office.com** for a photo of a limousine and another photo of a ferry boat, and then insert them.

Move, Size, Rotate, and Format Clip Art

5. Resize and position the three images on the slide to your liking.

6. Apply a **Picture Style** to each of the pictures. Use the same style on all three pictures to maintain consistency.

Remove a Background and Apply Artistic Effects

7. Display the title slide.

8. Insert the **PPT03-A03-Hand** picture from the **PP2013 Lesson 03** folder.

9. Use the **Background Removal** tool to remove the white background of the picture.

10. Move the picture to the lower-right corner of the slide.

11. Apply the **Photocopy** artistic effect to the picture.

12. Adjust the **Color** of the picture to a **Color Tone** of **Temperature: 7200k**.

Add, Merge, and Format Shapes

13. On the third slide, draw a wide **Rounded Rectangle**, a small **Rounded Rectangle**, and two **Circles** and then arrange them into the shape of a bus.

14. Merge the shapes into a single bus shape.

15. On the fourth slide, use the **Rectangle**, **Oval**, **Right Triangle**, and **Manual Operation** shapes to create a limousine. (The Manual Operation shape is in the Flowchart category.)

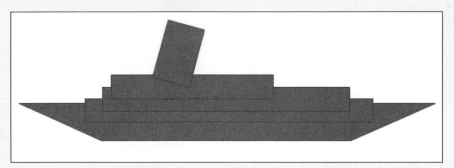

16. Merge the shapes into a single shape.

17. On the fifth slide, use the **Rectangle** and **Manual Operation** shapes to create a ferry boat.

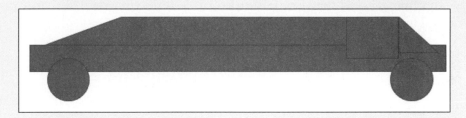

18. Merge the shapes into a single shape.

19. Apply the **Intense Effect – Olive Green, Accent 3** Shape Style to each of the shapes on slides 3–5.

20. Resize and position the shapes so they fill the maximum area of their slides without overlapping the text.

Apply Transition Effects and Add Animation

21. Apply the **Reveal** transition to all but the title slide.

22. Set the **Effect Option** on all slides to **Through Black from Right**.

23. Set the **Duration** on all slides to **3 seconds**.

24. Apply the **Fly In** animation to the hand picture on the title slide.

25. Set the **Effect Option** to **From Right**.

Use the Animation Pane to Add Sound

26. Use the **Animation Pane** to add the **Whoosh** sound effect to the hand's animation.

27. Close the **Animation** pane.

28. Choose **Slide Show→Start Slide Show→From Beginning** and click each slide to view the presentation, returning to **Normal** view when you are finished.

29. Save the changes and then exit **PowerPoint**. Submit your final file based on the guidelines provided by your instructor.

Extend Your Skills

In the course of working through the Extend Your Skills exercises, you will think critically as you use the skills taught in the lesson to complete the assigned projects. To evaluate your mastery and completion of the exercises, your instructor may use a rubric, with which more points are allotted according to performance characteristics. (The more you do, the more you earn!) Ask your instructor how your work will be evaluated.

PP03-E01 That's the Way I See It

New PowerPoint users often overuse transitions, animation, and sound effects. In this exercise, you will see how sometimes less is more. Create a presentation with at least six slides. Every slide except the title slide should include a title, text, and an image. Apply any design theme and variation. Make sure the presentation focuses on a single idea (for example, a classic car collection, your favorite movies, or inspirational people). Apply a different transition to each slide. Apply a different animation to each text block and each image. Add a different sound effect to each slide. In other words—overdo it! Save your file as **PP03-E01-AnimationOverkill-[FirstInitialLastName]** in the **PP2013 Lesson 03** folder. View the presentation as a slide show.

Save a copy of the presentation as **PP03-E01-AnimationAppropriate-[FirstInitialLastName]**. Edit the presentation so that each slide uses the same subtle transition. Remove the animation from each image, and standardize the animation on the text blocks. Choose a subtle Entrance animation. Remove all sound effects. Save your changes. View the revised presentation as a slide show and compare it to your "overkill" version.

You will be evaluated based on the inclusion of all elements specified, your ability to follow directions, your ability to apply newly learned skills to a real-world situation, your creativity, and the relevance of your topic and/or data choice(s). Submit your final files based on the guidelines provided by your instructor.

PP03-E02 Be Your Own Boss

In this exercise, you will edit the animation on the Blue Jean Landscaping presentation. Open **PP03-E02-BlueJeanAnimated** from the **PP2013 Lesson 03** folder and save it as **PP03-E02-BlueJeanAnimated-[FirstInitialLastName]**. View the presentation as a slide show and notice where the animations occur. Edit the presentation so the animations occur when a slide is clicked rather than automatically. Also, make sure the bulleted text animates one line at a time. Add a final slide using the Section Header layout. Use the title **Get Outside More** and the subtitle **It'll do you good!**. Insert **PPT03-E02-Flowers** from the **PP2013 Lesson 03** folder. Make these changes:

- Remove the photo background.
- Move the image to appear behind the text.
- Apply an adjustment to make it less distracting.
- Apply the same slide transition used by the other slides.
- Add a sound effect that you feel is appropriate.

You will be evaluated based on the inclusion of all elements specified, your ability to follow directions, your ability to apply newly learned skills to a real-world situation, your creativity, and your demonstration of an entrepreneurial spirit. Submit your final file based on the guidelines provided by your instructor.

Transfer Your Skills

In the course of working through the Transfer Your Skills exercises, you will use critical-thinking and creativity skills to complete the assigned projects using skills taught in the lesson. To evaluate your mastery and completion of the exercises, your instructor may use a rubric, with which more points are allotted according to performance characteristics. (The more you do, the more you earn!) Ask your instructor how your work will be evaluated.

PP03-T01 Use the Web as a Learning Tool

Throughout this book, you will be provided with an opportunity to use the Internet as a learning tool by completing WebQuests. According to the original creators of WebQuests, as described on their website (WebQuest.org), a WebQuest is "an inquiry-oriented activity in which most or all of the information used by learners is drawn from the web." To complete the WebQuest projects in this book, navigate to the student resource center and choose the WebQuest for the lesson on which you are currently working. The subject of each WebQuest will be relevant to the material found in the lesson.

WebQuest Subject: Licensing Media Usage

Submit your final file(s) based on the guidelines provided by your instructor.

PP03-T02 Demonstrate Proficiency

Stormy BBQ needs a slideshow to play on television screens throughout their seating area. It should feature images of mouth-watering barbeque. Create a PowerPoint presentation with at least five slides. Each slide should display a single photo of delicious barbeque. Remove the backgrounds from the images you use, as necessary. Use slide transitions to fade one slide into the next. Include an animated title on each slide that names the dish.

Choose one slide on which to add a shape. Add a shape from the Stars and Banners category with the text **Blue Ribbon Winner**. Format the shape and its text to add visual interest while keeping the text easy to read.

Save the presentation as **PP03-T02-BBQSlideShow-[FirstInitialLastName]** in your **PP2013 Lesson 03** folder.

Submit your final file based on the guidelines provided by your instructor.

POWERPOINT 2013

Inserting Charts

LESSON OUTLINE

Inserting Charts
Working with External Excel Documents
Creating SmartArt Diagrams
Concepts Review
Reinforce Your Skills
Apply Your Skills
Extend Your Skills
Transfer Your Skills

LEARNING OBJECTIVES

After studying this lesson, you will be able to:

- Insert charts to display numerical data
- Link to and use data in an Excel spreadsheet to create a chart
- Format charts and change chart types
- Repair broken links to external documents
- Create SmartArt diagrams

A cornerstone of the Microsoft Office suite of programs is the seamless way programs join, or integrate with each other. For example, in this lesson, you will learn how to place an Excel workbook into a PowerPoint presentation to harness the strength of Excel features in PowerPoint. You will also take advantage of the Microsoft Graph charting program to create dynamic and precise charts in your presentation. Finally, you will use SmartArt to add a beautifully arranged organization chart that is clear, concise, and stylish.

Adding Charts to Presentations

You continue to develop PowerPoint presentations for iJams, deciding it is time to expand iJams by opening a recording studio that local musicians can rent to record their original music. You schedule a meeting with the loan committee at Twilight Hollow Bank. You are concerned that you will have to re-create your best Excel workbook of financial projections until you remember that you can simply link the Excel file to the PowerPoint presentation.

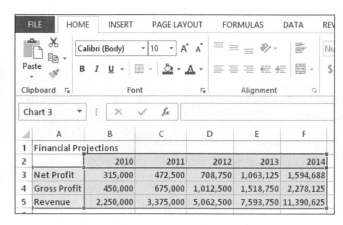

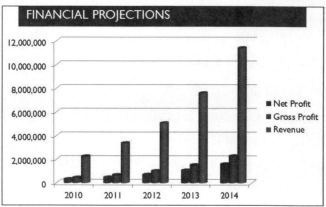

Inserting Charts

Video Library   http://labyrinthelab.com/videos   Video Number: PP13-V0401

PowerPoint is an intensely visual application. Although it is often the case that you will be creating presentations that represent concepts or goals, you may also present financial statistics or numerical data. PowerPoint allows you to create charts based on numerical data in a spreadsheet. If Microsoft Excel is installed, PowerPoint and Excel will work together to provide you with advanced options to design the chart layout and edit chart data. Without Excel installed, PowerPoint will use Microsoft Graph to create a new chart. Excel offers the more intuitive Ribbon interface, provides more formatting options, and creates more visually appealing charts than Microsoft Graph. Therefore, it is recommended that you use Excel to create charts for your PowerPoint presentations. In fact, if Excel is installed, PowerPoint launches it automatically whenever you insert a new chart.

Creating Embedded Charts

PowerPoint has four layouts (Title and Content, Two Content, Comparison, and Content with Caption) that make inserting new charts simple. Each of these common layouts includes an Insert Chart icon that you can click to insert a new chart. What if your slide doesn't use one of these layouts? You can always insert a chart manually from the Ribbon, no matter what layout your slide uses.

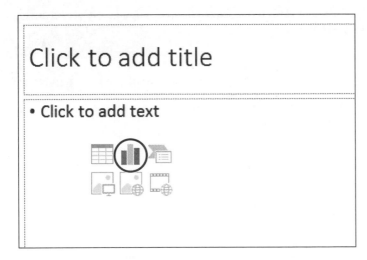

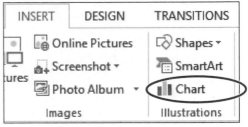

You can insert a chart via the Insert Chart slide icon or from the Ribbon.

Microsoft Graph

If Excel is not installed, PowerPoint launches a Microsoft Graph datasheet when you insert a new chart. (Microsoft Graph is a small program installed with many Office applications.) Charts created in Microsoft Graph lack the Chart Tools contextual Ribbon tabs and commands that are available with an Excel-generated chart for advanced formatting and easy editing (these tabs are discussed later in this lesson). A Microsoft Graph chart can be converted to Office 2013 format, which results in the contextual Ribbon tabs being made available and chart data editing handled by Excel. However, without Excel installed, a converted chart is not editable. The rest of this lesson assumes that you have Excel installed.

To convert a Microsoft Graph chart to Office 2013 format, double-click the chart on the slide and choose Convert. However, remember that Excel must be installed to edit numeric data in a converted chart.

Microsoft Graph datasheet

		A	B	C	D	E
		1st Qtr	2nd Qtr	3rd Qtr	4th Qtr	
1	East	20.4	27.4	90	20.4	
2	West	30.6	38.6	34.6	31.6	
3	North	45.9	46.9	45	43.9	
4						

Presentation1 - Datasheet

Excel spreadsheet

	A	B	C	D
1		Series 1	Series 2	Series 3
2	Category 1	4.3	2.4	2
3	Category 2	2.5	4.4	2
4	Category 3	3.5	1.8	3
5	Category 4	4.5	2.8	5

When you insert a new chart, PowerPoint starts you out with generic data labels and numbers that you replace with your own.

Choosing a Chart Type

Certain chart types are best suited to display specific types of data. Some of the most commonly used chart types are described in the following table.

Chart Type	Icon	Best Used to...
Column	Column	Show one-time (nonadjacent) results, such as those of a survey, depicted as vertical bars
Bar	Bar	Show the same type of results as a column chart, but with horizontal bars
Line	Line	Show continual change over time, such as profit / loss over several months
Pie	Pie	Compare a portion or portions to a whole, such as hours spent on various tasks in a single day

Editing Chart Data

When you create a new chart, PowerPoint launches a minimal version of Excel called Chart. A button at the top of the Chart window opens the full version of Excel. This way, you can edit data in a simple interface (Chart), or edit the data directly in Excel and take advantage of Excel's powerful tools for working with numeric data. Don't be confused when you insert a new chart and see data already entered in the spreadsheet window. This is sample data that PowerPoint inserts to get you started; simply replace it with your headings and numbers.

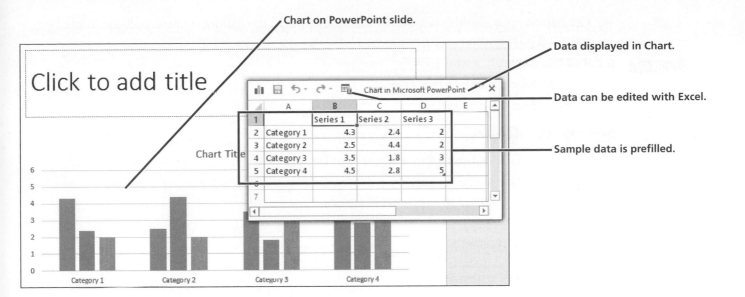

Chart on PowerPoint slide.

Data displayed in Chart.

Data can be edited with Excel.

Sample data is prefilled.

Formatting Charts

After a chart has been inserted, simply click the chart to select it. PowerPoint's Chart tools are displayed in the Ribbon as the Design and Format contextual tabs. You can use these tabs to create, modify, and format your chart without leaving the PowerPoint window.

DEVELOP YOUR SKILLS PP04-D01

Insert a Chart

In this exercise, you will create a chart inside your PowerPoint presentation and revise the default datasheet with your own custom data.

The instructions for this and other charting exercises assume that Excel 2013 is installed on your computer.

1. Start **PowerPoint**. Open **PP04-D01-Chart** from the **PP2013 Lesson 04** folder and save it as **PP04-D01-Chart-[FirstInitialLastName]**.

   Replace the bracketed text with your first initial and last name. For example, if your name is Bethany Smith, your filename would look like this: PP04-D01-Chart-BSmith.

2. Display slide 3, **Our Expansion Plan**.

   In the next few steps, you will add a new slide after Our Expansion Plan.

3. Choose **Home→Slides→New Slide** .

4. Choose **Home→Slides→ Layout ▾ →Two Content**.

   PowerPoint will apply the new layout, which includes a placeholder box on the left that you will use for your text, and a placeholder box on the right that you will use for your chart.

5. Type **Year-To-Date Results** as the title.

   The title is automatically formatted with all capitals because that is defined by the theme.

PowerPoint 2013

6. Click in the placeholder box on the left side and add the following bulleted text items, pressing Enter after each one except the last:

- **25% growth rate** Enter
- **Positive cash flow** Enter
- **Margins increasing**

Set Up the Chart

7. Click the **Insert Chart** 📊 icon in the middle of the placeholder box on the right side.

   The Insert Chart dialog box appears. Knowing the type of data you are charting will make it easier to select the appropriate type of chart. You are charting one-time results, so a column or bar graph is appropriate.

8. Follow these steps to insert a chart from the Insert Chart dialog box:

   A Choose the **Column** category.

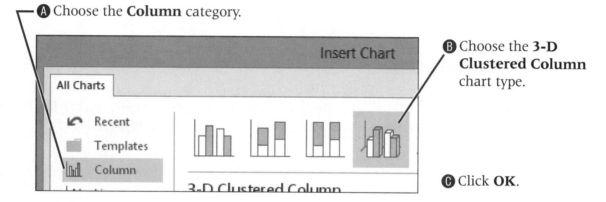

   B Choose the **3-D Clustered Column** chart type.

   C Click **OK**.

   The chart opens with sample data. You will replace the sample data with your own headings and numbers.

9. Follow these steps to set up the chart datasheet:

   A Click the cell with the text **Category 1**, type **Q1**, and tap Enter.

   B Enter the **remaining data** shown here. Click a cell, type the cell data, and then click another cell.

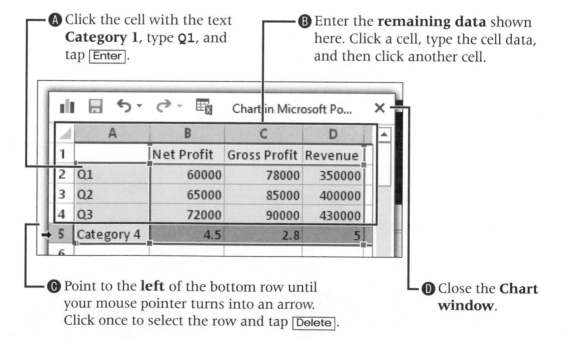

   C Point to the **left** of the bottom row until your mouse pointer turns into an arrow. Click once to select the row and tap Delete.

   D Close the **Chart window**.

Your slide should now resemble the following illustration. Notice how tightly squeezed the chart appears. In the next topic, you will learn how to modify a chart to aid readability and make it visually attractive.

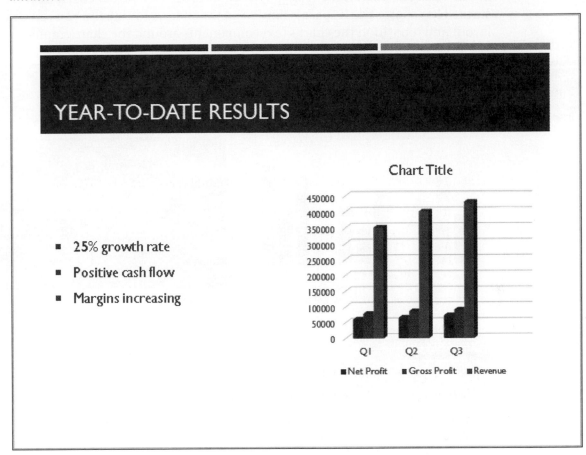

10. Save your presentation.

Modifying Charts

Video Library   http://labyrinthelab.com/videos   Video Number: PP13-V0402

After you insert a chart, you can make changes to it as necessary. For example, you can edit the chart data, change the color scheme, and even change to a different chart type. As you would expect, the two Chart Tools contextual tabs on the Ribbon give access to these modification commands.

If you don't see the Chart Tools contextual tabs, make sure that the chart is selected (displays sizing handles).

Changing the Chart Size and Layout

You can size the chart by dragging the sizing handles, and you can position the chart by dragging it to a different location. These handles work just as they do on clip art and other figures on slides. You can also choose a different layout for the chart from the Design tab under Chart Tools.

Changing the Chart Type

Sometimes you may want to change the chart type to better display the data. For example, you might want to switch from a normal bar chart to a 3-D-style bar chart. Or you may want to use a stacked bar chart style if space is limited on the slide. Additionally, you can change the chart's layout and reposition the chart's text components around the chart graphic.

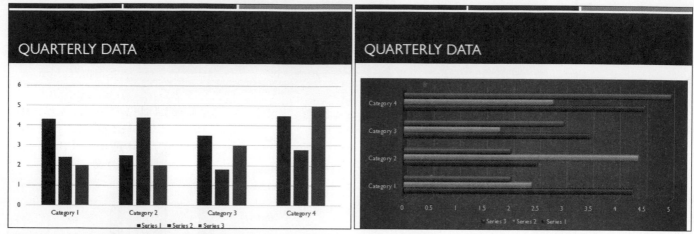

The same chart data first displayed as a Clustered Column, then as a 3-D Clustered Bar

QUICK REFERENCE	CHARTING IN POWERPOINT
Task	**Procedure**
Insert a chart	Click the Insert Chart icon on the slide or choose Insert→Illustrations→Chart.
Change the size of a chart	Point to a sizing handle around the chart's border. When the double-headed arrow appears, click and then drag the border.
Change the chart type	Select the chart and then choose Chart Tools→Design→Type→Change Chart Type.
Modify chart data	Select the chart and then choose Chart Tools→Design→Data→Edit Data.
Change the chart layout	Select the chart and then choose a layout from the Chart Tools→Design→Quick Layout gallery.

Modify a Chart

In this exercise, you will modify the chart slide by adjusting its size and editing the chart data.

1. Save your file as **PP04-D02-Chart-[FirstInitialLastName]**.

2. Follow these steps to resize the chart:

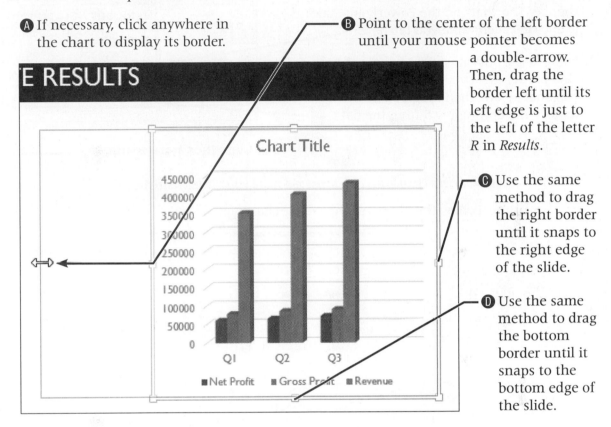

Ⓐ If necessary, click anywhere in the chart to display its border.

Ⓑ Point to the center of the left border until your mouse pointer becomes a double-arrow. Then, drag the border left until its left edge is just to the left of the letter *R* in *Results*.

Ⓒ Use the same method to drag the right border until it snaps to the right edge of the slide.

Ⓓ Use the same method to drag the bottom border until it snaps to the bottom edge of the slide.

You have resized the chart but have maintained some breathing room (white space) between the left border of the chart and the bulleted text. You have also maintained some white space between the right edge of the chart and the slide's right edge.

3. Make sure the chart is still selected and the Chart Tools contextual tabs are visible.

4. Choose **Chart Tools→Design→Data→Edit Data**.

This is an embedded chart. You can always edit the data in an embedded chart by selecting this command.

5. Follow these steps to edit the chart:

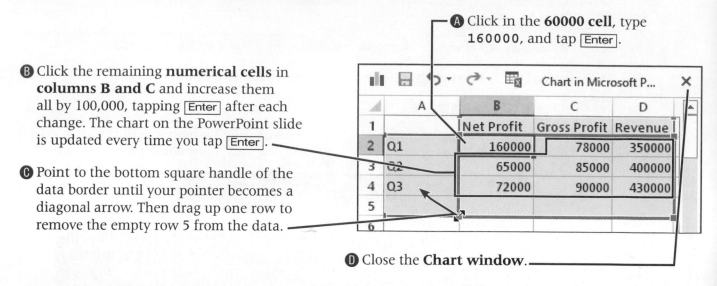

A Click in the **60000 cell**, type **160000**, and tap Enter.

B Click the remaining **numerical cells** in **columns B and C** and increase them all by 100,000, tapping Enter after each change. The chart on the PowerPoint slide is updated every time you tap Enter.

C Point to the bottom square handle of the data border until your pointer becomes a diagonal arrow. Then drag up one row to remove the empty row 5 from the data.

D Close the **Chart window**.

Now let's change the chart type to a more visually interesting style.

6. Follow these steps to change the chart type:

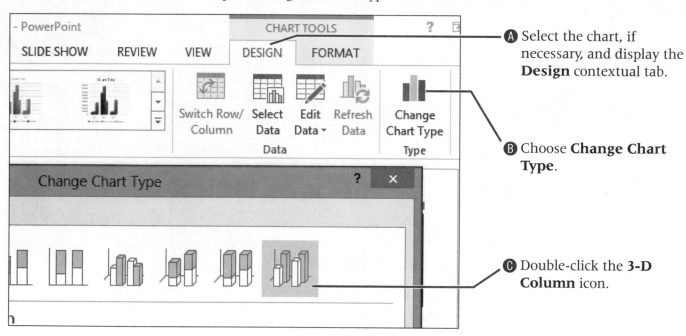

A Select the chart, if necessary, and display the **Design** contextual tab.

B Choose **Change Chart Type**.

C Double-click the **3-D Column** icon.

The chart type changes. However, the bars in the graph are too congested, and the text is difficult to read.

7. Choose **Chart Tools→Design→Chart Layouts→ Quick Layout→Layout 3**.

PowerPoint rearranges the slide layout to remove the text on the right side of the chart. The slide itself has a title, so we will delete the additional title inside the chart.

8. Click once on the **Chart Title** so it displays handles and then tap Delete .

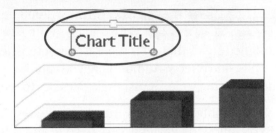

The chart title disappears. Your slide should resemble the following illustration.

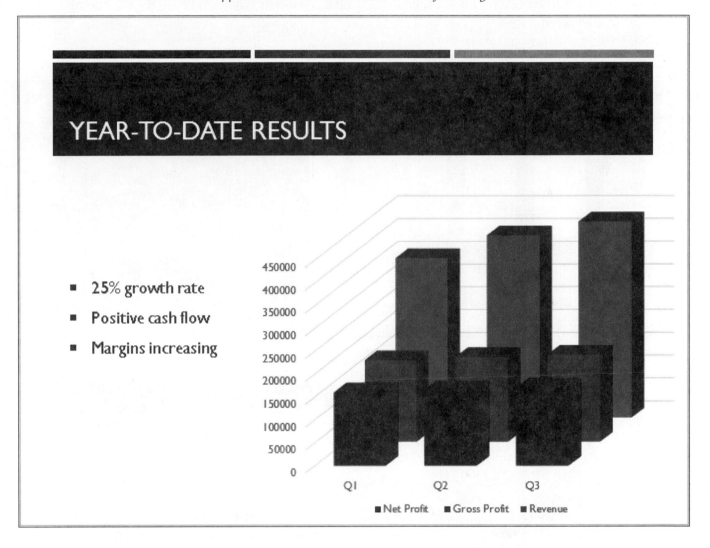

9. Save your presentation.

Changing Chart Style and Color Scheme

Video Library   http://labyrinthelab.com/videos   Video Number: PP13-V0403

You can format your charts with predesigned styles that alter several characteristics of the charts, including text used as labels, chart color fills, and effects. Additionally, you can change the colors used in a chart to make it stand out from the rest of the slide, or just make it easier to see from a distance.

While these changes can be made from the Ribbon, PowerPoint 2013 includes new chart buttons, which are also available in Excel, allowing easier access to style and color changes. PowerPoint charts now display three small buttons to the right of a selected chart, allowing you to quickly preview and apply changes to chart elements, style, and even the data being displayed.

Styles and colors can be changed here.

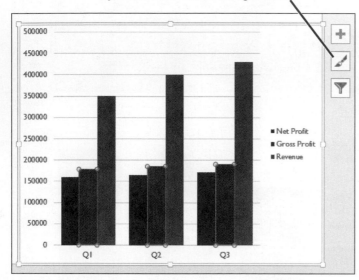

The default chart.

Chart after style and color are changed.

CHART BUTTONS		
Button Name	**Icon**	**What It Does**
Chart Elements	+	■ Show or hide chart title, axis labels, gridlines, and other chart elements. ■ The same options are available from Chart Tools→Design→Chart Layouts→Add Chart Element.
Chart Styles	✎	■ Change a chart style or color scheme. ■ The same options are available from Chart Tools→Design→Chart Styles.
Chart Filter	▼	■ Filter chart data to display only desired data.

Style and Color a Chart

In this exercise, you will modify the chart elements, style, and color scheme by using the new chart buttons.

1. Save your file as **PP04-D03-Chart-[FirstInitialLastName]**.

2. Follow these steps to change the chart's style:

Ⓐ Select the chart, if necessary, to display the **chart buttons**.   Ⓑ Click the **Chart Styles** button.

Ⓒ Click **Style**.

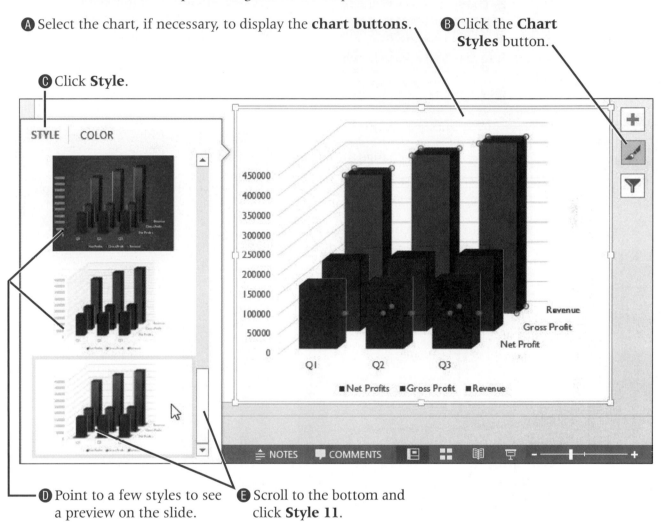

Ⓓ Point to a few styles to see a preview on the slide.   Ⓔ Scroll to the bottom and click **Style 11**.

The new style added back text to the right of the chart. You will delete it later in this exercise.

3. Follow these steps to change the chart's color scheme:

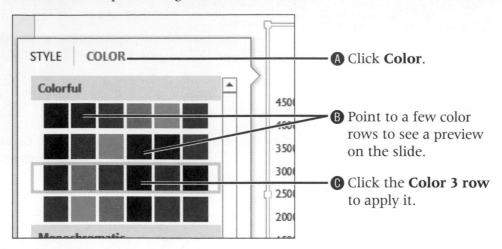

Ⓐ Click **Color**.

Ⓑ Point to a few color rows to see a preview on the slide.

Ⓒ Click the **Color 3 row** to apply it.

4. Follow these steps to change the chart's elements:

Ⓐ Click the **Chart Elements** button.

Ⓑ Point to each unchecked item to see a preview of the item on the chart. Do not click!

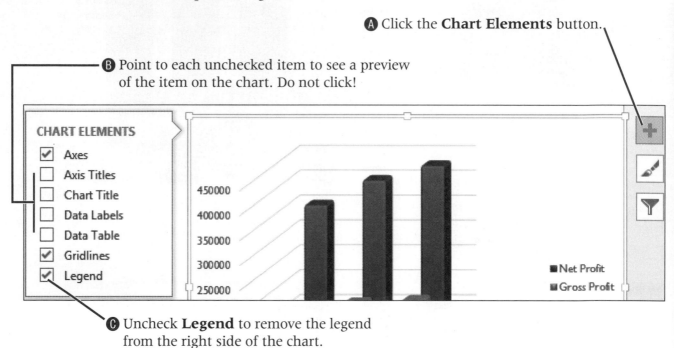

Ⓒ Uncheck **Legend** to remove the legend from the right side of the chart.

5. Click on the slide, but off the chart, to deselect it.

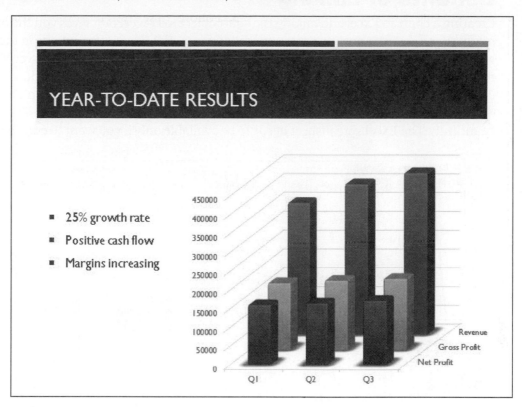

6. Save your presentation.

Working with External Excel Documents

Video Library   http://labyrinthelab.com/videos   Video Number: PP13-V0404

Office 2013 provides a variety of tools and techniques to let you exchange data between applications. Object Linking and Embedding (OLE) allows you to create links between source documents and destination documents. For example, you may want a chart in an existing Excel document to appear in a PowerPoint presentation. This makes it possible for another individual or department to maintain the Excel spreadsheet and its numerical data while you simply link to it and display an attractive chart based on its contents.

Benefits of Linking

Creating a chart in Excel and linking the chart object to PowerPoint gives you the opportunity to maintain modularity over presentation components. The Excel data remains in the Excel spreadsheet, which can be maintained by the financial wizards, while the PowerPoint presentation remains totally under your control as a separate document. Any changes made to the Excel document can be reflected in the chart displayed on the PowerPoint slide. Don't be worried if, during your actual presentation, the Excel spreadsheet is not available. The chart will still display beautifully. The Excel spreadsheet needs to be available only if you want to edit the chart data.

Changes to the Excel spreadsheet data here...

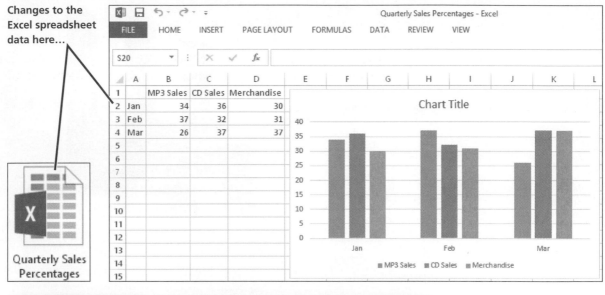

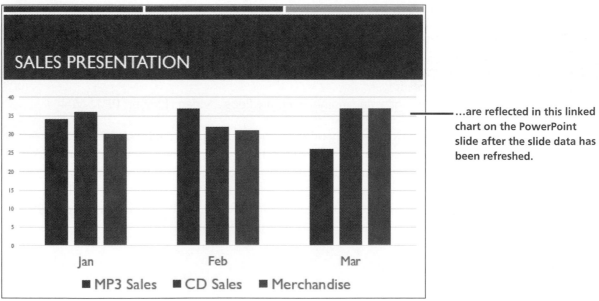

...are reflected in this linked chart on the PowerPoint slide after the slide data has been refreshed.

TIP

Changes to a linked Excel document *do not* result in automatic updating of the PowerPoint chart; you must manually refresh the PowerPoint chart's data to see the updated content.

Only Data Is Linked

A linked chart on a PowerPoint slide is linked to the Excel *data*, not to the Excel chart. The chart on the Excel spreadsheet simply establishes the initial link to its data. So, deleting or changing the format of the Excel chart has no effect on the PowerPoint chart. In the preceding illustration, notice that the formatting on the Excel chart is quite different from that on the PowerPoint slide. This independence allows PowerPoint to format the chart so it is consistent with the presentation theme's colors and fonts.

Linking Excel Charts

Your first step in linking to an Excel spreadsheet is to create the Excel spreadsheet that contains numerical data and an Excel chart. You simply copy and paste the chart (not the spreadsheet cells containing numerical data) from the Excel spreadsheet into your slide. The chart on the PowerPoint slide will be linked to the Excel spreadsheet's numerical data by default.

QUICK REFERENCE	LINKING CHARTS ON SLIDES
Task	**Procedure**
Link a chart	■ Select the Excel chart and choose Home→Clipboard→Copy.
	■ Select the desired PowerPoint slide and choose Home→Clipboard→Paste.
Edit linked data	■ Select the PowerPoint chart and choose Chart Tools→Design→Data→Edit Data.
	■ If available, the linked document will open. Edit the data in the Excel spreadsheet (not on the Excel chart), and save your changes.
Refresh chart data linked to an external file	■ Select the PowerPoint chart and choose Chart Tools→Design→Data→Refresh Data.
Repair a broken link	■ Select the chart, choose File→Info, and click the Edit Links to Files link.
	■ Click the Change Source button.
	■ Navigate to the source file, select it, and click Open.
	■ Click Close.

PowerPoint 2013

Paste Options

After you paste a chart from Excel, PowerPoint displays a set of three Paste Options buttons that allow you to control formatting of the pasted chart. The following table shows the function of each button.

PASTE OPTIONS		
Option	**Icon**	**What It Does**
Use Destination Theme & Embed Workbook		■ Changes the formatting of the chart to match the slide theme. ■ This is the default setting.
Keep Source Formatting & Embed Workbook		■ Keeps the formatting of the Excel chart.
Picture		■ Pastes the chart as a picture. The data is no longer editable.

DEVELOP YOUR SKILLS PP04-D04
Link to an Excel Chart

In this exercise, you will link to an existing Excel chart. You will then edit the Excel data to update the chart in PowerPoint.

1. Start **Microsoft Office Excel 2013**.

   The Excel program loads, and the Excel window appears.

2. Choose **Open Other Workbooks** from the bottom of the left column of Excel's Start screen.

3. Click **Computer→Browse**, navigate to the **PP2013 Lesson 04** folder, and open **PP04-D04-FinancialProjections**.

4. Click anywhere on the **Excel** chart to select it.

   A border appears around the chart to indicate that it has been selected.

5. Choose **Home→Clipboard→Copy**.

6. Close **Excel**.

   Excel closes, and you are returned to the PowerPoint window.

Link the Chart to PowerPoint

7. Save your PowerPoint presentation as `PP04-D04-Chart-[FirstInitialLastName]`.

8. Choose the **Year-To-Date Results** slide.

9. Choose **Home→Slides→New Slide** .

10. Choose **Home→Slides→ Layout →Title Only**.

    The new slide's layout is converted to the Title Only layout.

11. Click the title box of the new slide, type **Financial Projections**, and click below the title in a blank area of the slide.

The title box becomes deselected.

12. Choose **Home→Clipboard→Paste** 📋.

PowerPoint pastes the chart into the slide.

13. Tap Esc twice to dismiss the Paste Options buttons and accept the default setting.

Resize and Format the Chart

14. Follow these steps to resize the chart:

Ⓐ Point to the **bottom-left** sizing handle on the chart border until your mouse pointer becomes a white double-arrow, and then drag the border to the bottom-left corner of the slide.

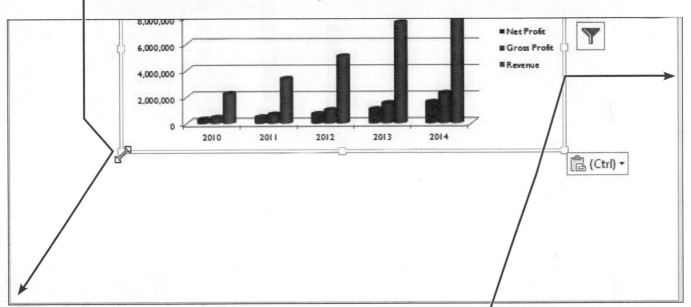

Ⓑ Using this same method, drag the **right edge** of the chart border until it snaps to the right edge of the slide.

The chart's text is too small to read comfortably. You will fix that in the next step.

15. Make sure the chart is selected and its border is displayed. Then choose **Home→ Font→Font Size menu ▼→20**.

All text on the chart is enlarged to size 20 and is easier to read. Your slide should resemble the following illustration.

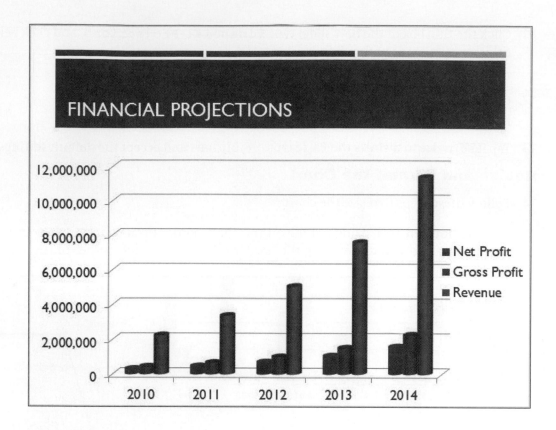

16. Save your presentation.

Effects of Linking

Video Library http://labyrinthelab.com/videos   Video Number: PP13-V0405

When working with a linked chart, any changes made to the Excel spreadsheet are reflected in the PowerPoint chart, but not necessarily immediately. If the data is edited from within PowerPoint, the slide's chart is updated automatically. However, if the data is edited by opening Excel outside PowerPoint, the chart data must be refreshed in PowerPoint before the changes are visible on the slide. If you choose to paste unlinked, changes to the Excel spreadsheet will have no effect on the chart in the PowerPoint slide. If you attempt to edit linked chart data from within PowerPoint, a Linked Data window will open and present the linked spreadsheet, ready for editing. The Linked Data window will also give you the option to open the spreadsheet in Excel. If the linked spreadsheet cannot be found, you will not be able to edit the chart data until the link is repaired.

Edit Data in a Linked Spreadsheet

In this exercise, you will edit the data in a linked Excel spreadsheet.

1. Save your file as **PP04-D05-Chart-[FirstInitialLastName]**.

2. Select the **Financial Projections** slide. If necessary, click the chart to select it; choose **Chart Tools→Design→Data→Edit Data**.

   The Linked Data window opens the data source for the chart.

3. Follow these steps to edit the chart data:

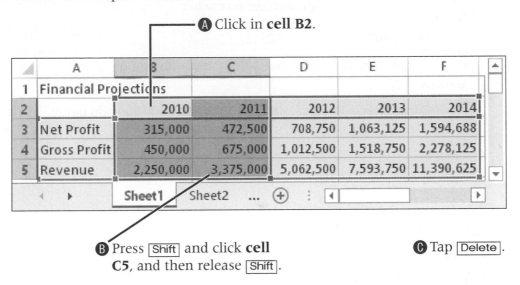

Ⓐ Click in **cell B2**.

Ⓑ Press ⎙Shift⎙ and click **cell C5**, and then release ⎙Shift⎙.

Ⓒ Tap ⎙Delete⎙.

   The selected data is deleted, and the change shows immediately on the slide, but there is a large gap on the chart where the data used to display. You will fix this in the next step.

4. Follow these steps to remove the empty cells:

   Ⓐ Point to the **square handle** in the bottom-right corner of **cell A1** until your pointer is a **diagonal double-arrow**.

   Ⓑ Drag the **handle** to the right, to the **bottom-right corner** of **cell C2**.

   Ⓒ Close the **Linked Data** window and click **Save** when prompted to save changes to the Excel spreadsheet.

   The blank cells are removed from the chart on the slide.

5. Save the presentation.

Editing the Source (Linked) Document

Video Library   http://labyrinthelab.com/videos   Video Number: PP13-V0406

If you make a change to the source document outside PowerPoint, you must manually refresh the data to see the changes on the slide. Refreshing data is possible only if you have healthy links (PowerPoint can locate the source document).

DEVELOP YOUR SKILLS PP04-D06

Edit and Refresh the Data Source

In this exercise, you will edit and refresh the data source.

1. Start **Microsoft Office Excel 2013**.

2. Choose **Open Other Workbooks** from the bottom of the left column of Excel's Start screen.

3. Click **Computer→Browse**, navigate to the **PP2013 Lesson 04** folder, and open **PP04-D04-FinancialProjections**.

4. Click in **cell A5** and type **Big Money**.

   Excel replaces the word Revenue *with* Big Money.

5. Save the worksheet and exit **Excel**.

Refresh the Data Source

6. In **PowerPoint**, display the last slide, **Financial Projections**, if necessary.

   Notice that the chart legend to the right of the chart still shows the word Revenue. *It must be refreshed to reflect the changes in the data source.*

7. Save your presentation as **PP04-D06-Chart-[FirstInitialLastName]**.

8. Select the chart so the **Chart Tools** contextual tabs appear.

9. Choose **Chart Tools→Design→Data→Refresh Data** ▥.

   PowerPoint refreshes the chart legend and now shows the phrase Big Money.

10. Save your presentation.

Maintaining Healthy Links

Video Library   http://labyrinthelab.com/videos   Video Number: PP13-V0407

Linked objects can reflect changes in the source document only if the link is maintained. Moving files to other locations on your file system or renaming files can lead to broken links, and your linked objects (like charts) will no longer reflect changes made to the source document.

If you try to edit chart data in PowerPoint and the Excel spreadsheet fails to open, you probably have a broken link.

Example

If you copied a chart from an Excel spreadsheet named Chart Data that was stored in a folder named My Excel Documents, PowerPoint would be looking for a file with that name in that location. If you moved the Excel file (or the containing folder) to another folder or changed its name, PowerPoint would no longer be able to find it; therefore, any changes made to the spreadsheet would have no effect on the chart in PowerPoint. And if you tried to edit the data from within PowerPoint, PowerPoint would not be able to find the Excel spreadsheet and thus would not be able to edit the data.

The following figure illustrates the prompt that PowerPoint displays if you break a link to an external file—for example, if you move or rename the data source file, and then try to edit a chart from PowerPoint.

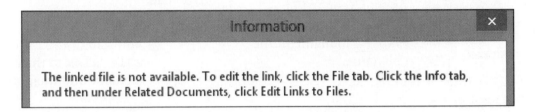

The linked file is not available. To edit the link, click the File tab. Click the Info tab, and then under Related Documents, click Edit Links to Files.

Break and Repair a Link

In this exercise, you will break a link by renaming the linked data file, and then you will repair the link from within PowerPoint.

1. Save your file as **PP04-D07-Chart-[FirstInitialLastName]**.

2. **Minimize** ▭ the PowerPoint window to the taskbar.

3. Follow the instructions for your version of Windows to open a window for your file storage location:

   - **Windows 7:** Use **Start→Computer** and open your file storage location.
   - **Windows 8:** Use the **File Explorer icon** on the **taskbar** to open a folder window and then open your file storage location.

4. Open the **PP2013 Lesson 04** folder.

In the next step, you will rename a file. Most windows systems hide the ends of filenames (called extensions). If they are visible, take care not to change them.

5. Follow these steps to rename the Excel worksheet file:

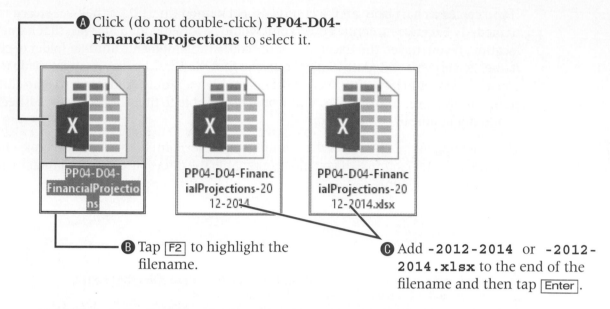

Ⓐ Click (do not double-click) **PP04-D04-FinancialProjections** to select it.

Ⓑ Tap F2 to highlight the filename.

Ⓒ Add **-2012-2014** or **-2012-2014.xlsx** to the end of the filename and then tap Enter.

If the filename displayed the .xlsx file extension, be sure your new filename looks like PP04-D04-FinancialProjections-2012-2014.xlsx. Otherwise, your filename should simply be PP04-D04-FinancialProjections-2012-2014. By renaming the source document, you have broken its link to PowerPoint.

6. Close the folder window and then click the **PowerPoint** button on the Windows taskbar to restore PowerPoint to the screen.

7. Click the chart to select it, if necessary.

8. Choose **Chart Tools→Design→Data→Edit Data** .

   You receive an error. PowerPoint is looking for a source document named PP04-D04-FinancialProjections, but you changed the name of the file.

9. Click **OK** in the error box.

Fix the Broken Link

10. Choose **File→Info** and then click **Edit Links to Files** at the bottom-right of the right column.

    The Links dialog box appears, listing all links to external files from the presentation. In this case, there is just one linked item, the Excel spreadsheet.

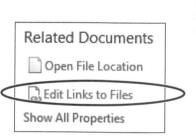

11. Click **Change Source**.

12. In the **Change Source** dialog box, navigate to the **PP2013 Lesson 04** folder, select **PP04-D04-FinancialProjections-2012-2014**, and click **Open**.

    PowerPoint updates the link. There may not be enough space in the dialog box to make the new name visible.

13. Click [Close] to close the **Links** dialog box.

    You have reestablished the link between the PowerPoint chart and the Excel source document.

Test the Repaired Link

14. Click **Back** ⊖ to close Backstage view; click the chart to select it, if necessary.

The chart must be selected in order to display the Chart Tools contextual tabs.

15. Choose **Chart Tools→Design→Data→Edit Data** ⊞.

The source document opens, ready to edit.

16. Click in **cell A5**. Then type **Revenue** and tap Enter.

Excel replaces Big Money *with the new word, and the change is immediately visible on the slide.*

17. Close the **Linked Data** window and click **Save** when prompted.

18. Save your presentation.

Creating SmartArt Diagrams

Video Library   http://labyrinthelab.com/videos   Video Number: PP13-V0408

SmartArt graphics are diagrams that automatically resize to accommodate the text within and allow the average user to enhance slides with visually appealing figures without having to learn advanced graphics software. With SmartArt, you simply select the type of diagram you'd like to create and type your text. The SmartArt diagram automatically sizes and flows your text. It also inherits colors and 3-D effects from your document theme. The resulting diagrams can help crystallize concepts in your presentation so that the audience will clearly understand your ideas. Using SmartArt, you can add graphics to your presentations, such as the following:

- Organization charts
- Flowcharts
- Colorful lists
- And many other sophisticated graphics

Inserting and Formatting SmartArt Graphics

Most slide layouts include an Insert SmartArt Graphic icon. Alternatively, SmartArt can be inserted at any time via the Ribbon. When you click the Insert SmartArt Graphic icon, the Choose a SmartArt Graphic dialog box appears. You can choose a diagram type from the gallery and then construct the diagram directly on the slide. PowerPoint displays examples and descriptions of the various SmartArt graphics as you select them in the gallery.

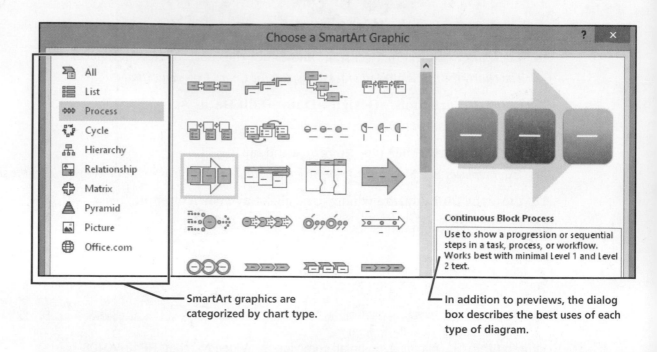

SmartArt graphics are categorized by chart type.

In addition to previews, the dialog box describes the best uses of each type of diagram.

SMARTART GRAPHIC CHART TYPES	
Graphic Category	**Usage**
List	Show nonsequential or grouped blocks of information
Process	Show a progression or sequential flow of data
Cycle	Show a continuing sequence of stages
Hierarchy	Show hierarchal relationships
Relationship	Show ideas, show interlocking or overlapping information, or show relationships to a central idea
Matrix	Show the relationships of components to a whole
Pyramid	Show proportional, interconnected, hierarchical, or containment relationships
Picture	Show a variety of information by using a central picture or several accent pictures
Office.com	Includes graphics from a variety of categories that can be downloaded from the Office.com website

Example

As you create your presentation, you need to include an organization chart that features the key players in your project or the leadership team of your organization. You give the command to insert a SmartArt graphic, browse through the Hierarchy list, and then choose an organization chart. You type the various organizational units in the SmartArt's text box. Three minutes later, you're finished!

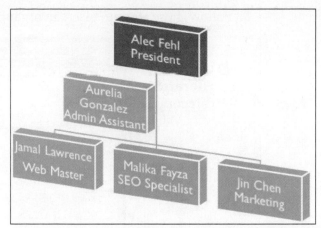

SmartArt organization charts automatically create and align boxes and lines as you type the names of the persons and departments.

PowerPoint 2013

QUICK REFERENCE	INSERTING SMARTART
Task	**Procedure**
Insert a new SmartArt graphic	■ Click the Insert SmartArt Graphic 🖼 icon in the center of a slide, or choose Insert→Illustrations→SmartArt.
	■ In the Choose a SmartArt Graphic dialog box, select a category of graphics to view the thumbnails and samples.
	■ Select a thumbnail and click OK.
Edit and format SmartArt	■ Select the SmartArt graphic (or any shape that is part of the graphic).
	■ Drag the handles on the shape's border to resize the shape.
	■ Make changes to the graphic's color, effects, or layout by choosing the commands from SmartArt Tools→Design or SmartArt Tools→Format.
	■ Reset a SmartArt graphic to its default settings by choosing SmartArt Tools→Design→Reset→Reset Graphic.
Add a new element to a SmartArt graphic	■ Select one of the shapes in the SmartArt graphic.
	■ Choose SmartArt Tools→Design→Create Graphic→Add Shape menu ▼ and select where you want the new shape to appear relative to the selected shape.

DEVELOP YOUR SKILLS PP04-D08
Set Up an Organization Chart

In this exercise, you will create an organization chart in PowerPoint, adding text to the various levels of the chart.

1. Save your file as **PP04-D08-Chart-[FirstInitialLastName]**.

2. Select the **Financial Projections** slide and choose **Home→Slides→New Slide**.

3. Choose **Home→Slides→** 🖼 Layout ▼ **→Title and Content**.

4. Type **Our Management Team** in the Title placeholder.

5. Click the **Insert SmartArt Graphic** 🖼 icon in the middle of the slide.
   The Choose a SmartArt Graphic dialog box appears.

6. Follow these steps to insert an organization chart:

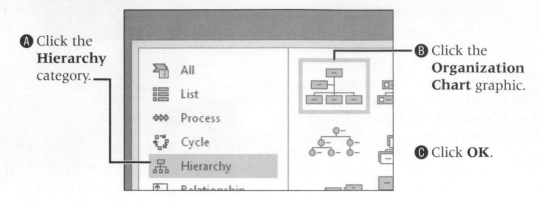

Ⓐ Click the **Hierarchy** category.

Ⓑ Click the **Organization Chart** graphic.

Ⓒ Click **OK**.

A sample organization chart is inserted. The contextual SmartArt Tools tabs appear on the right side of the Ribbon, including Design and Format.

Add Text

7. Follow these steps to add text to the organization chart:

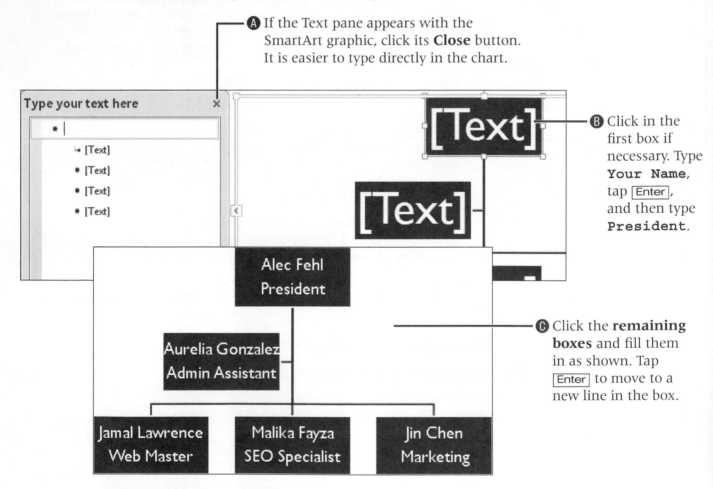

Ⓐ If the Text pane appears with the SmartArt graphic, click its **Close** button. It is easier to type directly in the chart.

Ⓑ Click in the first box if necessary. Type **Your Name**, tap Enter, and then type **President**.

Ⓒ Click the **remaining boxes** and fill them in as shown. Tap Enter to move to a new line in the box.

8. Save your presentation.

Formatting SmartArt

Video Library   http://labyrinthelab.com/videos   Video Number: PP-13-V0409

After a SmartArt graphic has been added to a slide, you can format its colors and other effects. For example, you can customize the graphic's text formatting, color scheme, and other features. Many SmartArt graphics have 3-D schemes and other cool effects that you can experiment with to add visual impact to a slide.

Adding Elements to SmartArt

You can also add elements to an original SmartArt graphic. For example, an organization chart might need a new branch for adding a department or lateral relationship. You may insert additional shapes above, below, or next to an existing shape. The SmartArt graphic will automatically resize itself and scale its text to accommodate the extra shapes.

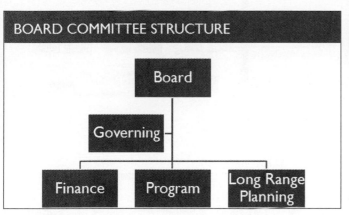
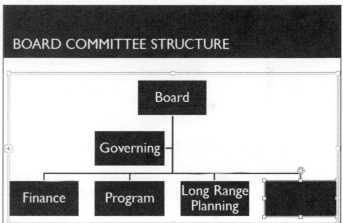

When a shape was inserted next to the Long Range Planning box, PowerPoint automatically resized the SmartArt to make room for the new, blank shape.

DEVELOP YOUR SKILLS PP04-D09
Add Shapes and Format SmartArt

In this exercise, you will add a new position in the organization chart and enhance its appearance with a different formatting effect.

1. Save your file as **PP04-D09-Chart-[FirstInitialLastName]**.

2. Click in the **Malika Fayza** box in the organization chart.

   This selects the appropriate box so you can add another shape beside it.

3. Choose **SmartArt Tools→Design→Create Graphic→Add Shape menu ▼→Add Shape After**.

   A new box is added to the right of the Malika Fayza box and is ready to accept text.

4. Type **Brett Schneider** in the new box, tap Enter to move to a second line in the box, and type **Fulfillment**.

Format the Chart

5. Follow these steps to format the chart:

Ⓐ Choose **SmartArt Tools→Design→ SmartArt Styles→More**.

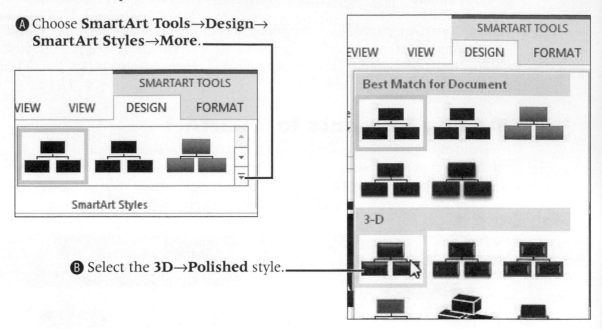

Ⓑ Select the **3D→Polished** style.

The Polished style is applied to every box in the chart.

6. Follow these steps to change the chart's colors:

Ⓐ Choose **SmartArt Tools→Design→ SmartArt Styles→Change Colors**.

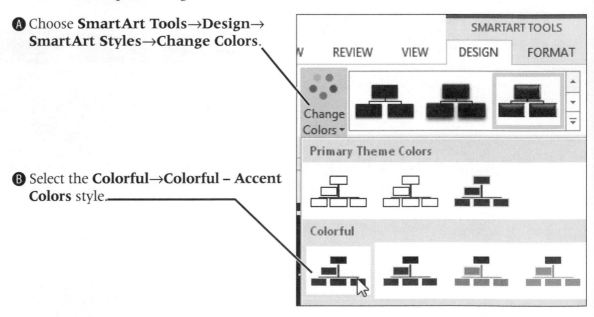

Ⓑ Select the **Colorful→Colorful – Accent Colors** style.

The organization chart should resemble the following illustration.

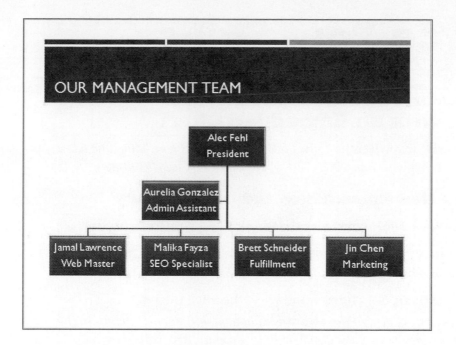

7. Save the presentation and then exit **PowerPoint**.

Concepts Review

To check your knowledge of the key concepts introduced in this lesson, complete the Concepts Review quiz by choosing the appropriate access option below.

If you are...	Then access the quiz by...
Using the Labyrinth Video Library	Going to http://labyrinthelab.com/videos
Using eLab	Logging in, choosing Content, and navigating to the Concepts Review quiz for this lesson
Not using the Labyrinth Video Library or eLab	Going to the student resource center for this book

Reinforce Your Skills

Work with an Embedded Chart

In this exercise, you will create a new presentation for Kids for Change and add a chart slide to the presentation. You will change the chart type to a pie chart to better display the data.

Begin a New Presentation and Insert a Chart

1. Start **PowerPoint** and click the **Blank Presentation** icon.

2. Save your file as `PP04-R01-Members-[FirstInitialLastName]` in the **PP2013 Lesson 04** folder.

3. Choose **Design→Themes** and select the **Slice** theme.

   Remember, the default themes are listed in alphabetical order. Point to a theme thumbnail and pause for a moment to view the theme name in a pop-up ToolTip.

4. In the **Title** box, type `Kids for Change`.

5. Click in the **Subtitle** box and type `New Members`.

6. Choose **Home→Slides→New Slide** and type `2013 New Members` in the title box.

7. Click the **Insert Chart** icon in the content placeholder box.

Modify a Chart

8. Choose the **3-D Clustered Bar** chart type and click **OK**.

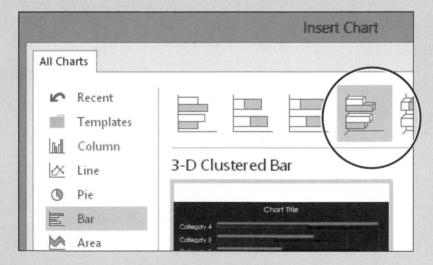

You will now enter the chart data.

9. Enter the data in **columns A and B** as shown and then delete the data in **columns C and D**. (The column headings will default to Column 1 and Column 2.)

	A	B	C	D
1		2013	Column1	Column2
2	9 and under	21		
3	10 to 12	36		
4	13 to 15	36		
5	16 to 17	47		
6				

10. Drag the bottom-right handle of cell D5 to the bottom-right corner of **cell B5** to remove the empty columns from the chart.

	A	B	C	D
1		2013	Column1	Column2
2	9 and under	21		
3	10 to 12	36		
4	13 to 15	36		
5	16 to 17	47		
6				

11. Close the **Chart** window.

   In the next steps, you will edit the chart data.

12. Click the chart on the slide to select it, if necessary, and choose **Chart Tools→Design→ Data→Edit Data**.

13. Click in **cell B4**, type **34**, and tap ⌊Enter⌋ to change the value.

14. Click the chart to display its border, and then click the chart border.

15. Close the **Chart** window.

   The chart bars are updated, and the 13 to 15 bar is now shorter than the 10 to 12 bar.

   Because the chart shows pieces of a whole (total new members broken down by age), a pie chart is a better choice, so you will change the chart type.

16. Choose **Chart Tools→Design→Type→Change Chart Type**.

17. Choose **3-D Pie** as the chart type and click **OK**.

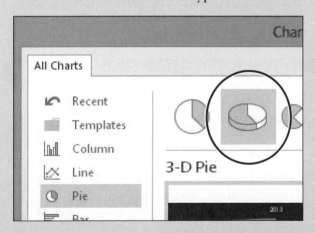

Change Chart Layout and Size

18. Choose **Chart Tools→Design→Chart Layouts→Quick Layout→Layout 1**.

The chart layout is changed, and percentages now display on each pie slice.

Change Chart Style

19. Choose **Chart Tools→Design→Chart Styles→Style 2**.

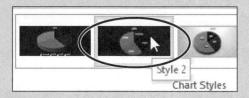

Change Chart Size

20. Drag the **bottom-right handle** of the chart's border to the **bottom-right corner** of the slide.

21. Drag the **left-center handle** of the chart's border to the right until the chart no longer overlaps the slide title.

22. Click the chart's title, **2013**, and tap ⌈Delete⌋.

23. Choose **Home→Font→Font Size menu ▾→20**.

24. Save the changes and then exit **PowerPoint**. Submit your final file based on the guidelines provided by your instructor.

    To view examples of how your file or files should look at the end of this exercise, go to the student resource center.

REINFORCE YOUR SKILLS PP04-R02

Work with a Linked Chart and SmartArt

In this exercise, you will link to an external data source, repair a broken link to a linked chart, and add SmartArt to display member and participant numbers.

Link to and Format an Excel Chart

1. Start **PowerPoint**. Open **PP04-R02-Projections** from the **PP2013 Lesson 04** folder and save it as **PP04-R02-Projections-[FirstInitialLastName]**.

2. Display slide 2 and choose **Home→Slides→New Slide**.

3. Type **Participant Projections** as the slide title.

4. Start **Excel**. Open **PP04-R02-Projections** from the **PP2013 Lesson 04** folder.

5. Click the chart on the Excel spreadsheet to select it.

6. Choose **Home→Clipboard→Copy**.

7. Exit **Excel**.

8. Click the **PowerPoint slide** so that the slide title is deselected.

9. Choose **Home→Clipboard→Paste**.

10. Drag the **top-left handle** of the chart's border to the **top-left corner** of the slide.

11. Drag the **center-right handle** of the chart's border toward the right until the chart is as wide as possible but the chart buttons are still visible.

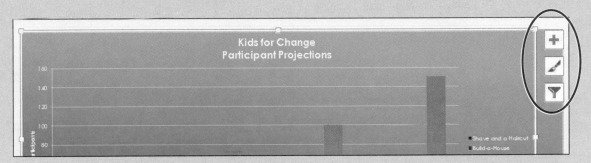

12. Click the **Chart Elements** button to the right of the chart.

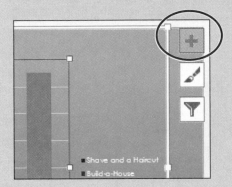

13. Choose to not display the **Chart Title** and remove the checkmark from **Primary Horizontal**.

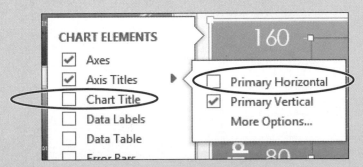

14. Tap [Esc] to close the **Chart Elements** menu.

15. Click the chart to display its border, and then click the chart border.

16. Choose **Home→Font→Font Size menu ▼→28**.

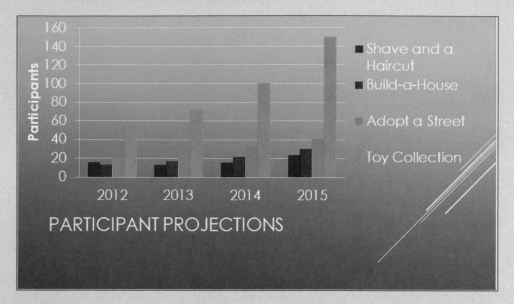

Edit a Linked Data Source and Repair a Broken Link

17. Display slide 2, **2013 New Members**.

18. Click the chart to select it.

19. Choose **Chart Tools→Design→Data→Edit Data**.
    A message appears, informing you that PowerPoint cannot find the linked Excel spreadsheet.

20. Click **OK** to close the Information box.

21. Choose **File→Info** and then click the **Edit Links to Files** link at the bottom of the right column.
    You will now perform the steps necessary to repair the link.

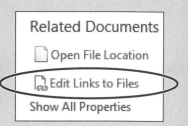

22. Click the entry that ends with **2013members.xlsx** and then click **Change Source**.

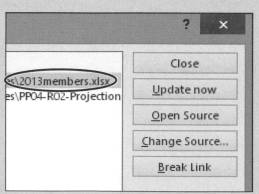

23. Browse to the **PP2013 Lesson 04** folder, if necessary. Select the **PP04-R02-Members** file and click **Open**.

24. Click **Close** to close the **Links** dialog box.

25. Click **Back** ⬅ to exit Backstage view.
    Now that the link is fixed, you will edit the data.

26. Choose **Chart Tools→Design→Data→Edit Data**.

27. Click **cell B5**, type **53**, and tap Enter.
    The chart on the slide is immediately updated.

28. Close the **Linked Data** window and click **Save** when prompted.

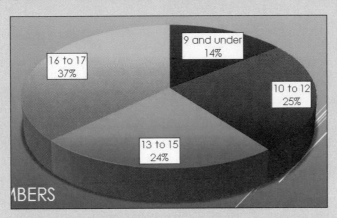

Insert SmartArt

29. Display slide 3, **Participant Projections**.

30. Choose **Home→Slides→New Slide**.

31. Choose **Home→Slides→Layout→Title and Content**.

32. Type **Current Members** as the slide title.

33. Click the **SmartArt** 📊 icon on the slide.

34. Click the **Process** category, choose **Step Up Process**, and then click **OK**.

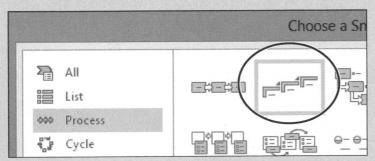

Although the Process category is typically used to show sequential steps, you will use this graphic to show age groups of members, from least members to the most members.

35. If the text box appears next to the SmartArt graphic, close it.

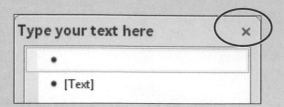

36. Type the text in each section of the SmartArt graphic as shown:

Format and Add Elements to SmartArt

37. With the SmartArt graphic selected, choose **SmartArt Tools→Design→SmartArt Styles→More→Best Match for Document→Intense Effect**.

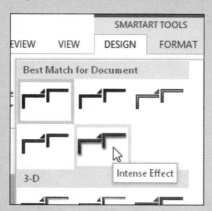

38. Click the text **Teens** to select that SmartArt text box.

39. Chose **SmartArt Tools→Design→Create Graphic→Add Shape menu ▼→Add Shape Before**.

40. Type **Under 10** in the new text box.

41. Save the changes and then exit **PowerPoint**. Submit your final file based on the guidelines provided by your instructor.

To view examples of how your file or files should look at the end of this exercise, go to the student resource center.

Work with Charts and SmartArt

In this exercise, you will use charts and SmartArt to compare Kids for Change events from several communities.

Begin a New Presentation and Create an Embedded Chart

1. Start **PowerPoint** and click the **Blank Presentation** icon.

2. Save your file as `PP04-R03-Events-[FirstInitialLastName]` in your **PP2013 Lesson 04** folder.

3. Choose **Design→Themes** and select the **Integral** theme.

4. In the **Title** box, type `Kids for Change`.

5. Click in the **Subtitle** box and type `2013 Events`.

6. Choose **Home→Slides→New Slide**.

7. Type `Event Totals` as the title.

8. Click the **Insert Chart** icon on the slide.

Modify a Chart Type

9. Click the **Bar** category, click the **Clustered Bar** chart type, and click **OK**.

10. Type the following data in rows 1 and 2 of the Chart spreadsheet:

	A	B	C	D	E	F
1		Westville	North Haven	Sunny Downs	Goodview	Echo Falls
2	2013	8	12	2	6	8

11. Drag the **bottom-right handle of cell F5** up to the **bottom-right corner of cell F2** to exclude rows 3 through 5.

12. Close the **Chart** window.

    You will now work to format the chart.

13. Choose **Chart Tools→Design→Chart Styles→More→Style 4**.

14. Choose **Chart Tools→Design→Quick Layout→Layout 2**.

15. Click the **Chart Elements** button to the right of the chart.

16. Uncheck **Axes** and then tap Esc to close the **Chart Elements** menu.

17. Click the **chart title** and type `2013 Events`.

18. Drag the right edge of the chart until it snaps to the right edge of the slide to widen it.

19. Choose **Home→Font→Font Size menu ▼→28**.

Edit Chart Data and Change a Chart Type

20. Choose **Chart Tools→Design→Data→Edit Data** 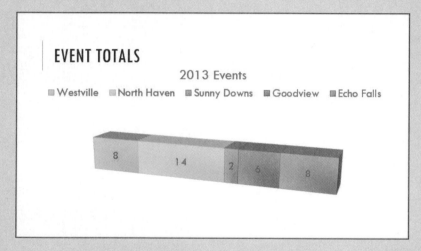.

21. Click **cell C2**, type **14**, and tap ⌷Enter⌷.

22. Close the **Chart** window.

23. Choose **Chart Tools→Design→Type→Change Chart Type**.

24. Choose the last chart type in the **Bar** category, **3-D 100% Stacked Bar**, and click **OK**.

25. Drag the **bottom-left handle** of the chart's border to the **bottom-left corner** of the slide.

26. Drag the **top-middle handle** of the chart's border up until the **top edge** of the chart touches the bottom of the slide's title text.

Change Chart Colors

27. Choose **Chart Tools→Design→Chart Styles→Change Colors→Color 2**.

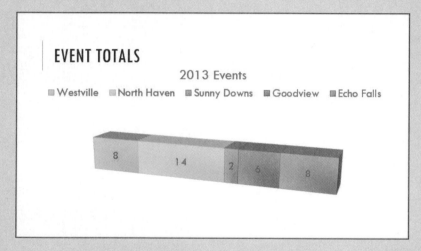

Link to an Excel Chart

28. Start **Excel** and choose **Open Other Workbooks**.

29. Browse to your **PP2013 Lesson 04** folder and double-click the **PP04-R03-Events** workbook file.

30. Click the **chart** to select it and then choose **Home→Clipboard→Copy**.

31. Exit **Excel**.

32. In PowerPoint, choose **Home→Slides→New Slide**.

33. Type **Event Popularity** as the slide title.

34. Choose **Home→Slides→Layout→Title Only**.

35. Choose **Home→Clipboard→Paste**.

36. Drag the **bottom-left handle** of the chart's border to the **bottom-left corner** of the slide.

37. Drag the **top-right handle** of the chart's border up and to the right, until the top edge of the chart touches the bottom of the title text and the chart is as wide as possible while keeping the chart buttons visible, as in the following figure.

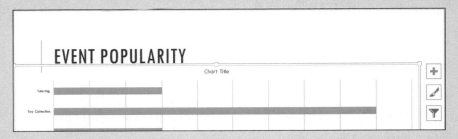

38. Click the **chart title** and tap [Delete].

39. Choose **Home→Font→Font Size menu ▼→24**.

Break a Link

40. Minimize **PowerPoint**.

41. Use **Computer** or **File Explorer** to navigate to the **PP2013 Lesson 04** folder and locate the **PP04-R03-Events** workbook.

42. Click the **PP04-R03-Events** workbook to select it and tap [F2] to highlight the filename.

43. Type `PP04-R03-Events2013` and tap [Enter] to rename the file.

Fix a Broken Link and Edit a Linked Data Source

44. Click the **PowerPoint** button on the **Windows taskbar** to restore PowerPoint.

45. Click the chart to select it, if necessary.

46. Choose **Chart Tools→Design→Data→Edit Data**.

47. Click **OK** to dismiss the **Information** dialog box.

48. Choose **File→Info→Edit Links to Files**.

49. Click **Change Source**, navigate to the **PP2013 Lesson 04** folder, and double-click the **PP04-R03-Events2013** workbook.

50. Click the **Close** button.

51. Click the **Back** button at the top of the left column to exit Backstage view.

At the time of this writing, a bug in PowerPoint causes the chart to no longer display even though the data is still linked. It may be necessary to delete and copy/paste the chart again if Microsoft hasn't released an update yet.

52. Choose **Chart Tools→Design→Data→Edit Data**.

53. Click **cell E2** and type **0**.

54. Click **cell E3** and type **1**.

55. Click **cell E5** and type **1**.

56. Close the **Linked Data** window and click **Save** when prompted.

Edit and Refresh External Data

57. Start **Excel** and choose **Open Other Workbooks**.

58. Browse to your **PP2013 Lesson 04** folder and double-click **PP04-R03-Events2013**.

59. Click **cell C9** and type **0**, and then click **cell C8** and type **4**.

60. Click **cell E9** and type **0**, and then click **cell E8** and type **3**.

61. Save the **Excel** workbook and exit **Excel**.

62. In **PowerPoint**, choose **Chart Tools→Design→Data→Refresh Data**.

Insert SmartArt

63. Choose **Home→Slides→New Slide**.

64. Choose **Home→Slides→Layout→Title and Content**.

65. Type `Most Popular` as the **slide title**.

66. Click the **Insert SmartArt** icon on the slide.

67. Choose the **Pyramid** category, the **Basic Pyramid** graphic, and then click **OK**.

68. Click the **bottom text box** of the pyramid and type `Bully No More`.

69. Click the **middle text box** of the pyramid and type `Adopt a Street`.

70. Click the **top text box** of the pyramid and type `Toy Collection`.

Format SmartArt

71. Choose **SmartArt Tools→Design→SmartArt Styles→More→3-D→Brick Scene**.

72. Choose **SmartArt Tools→Design→SmartArt Styles→Change Colors→Colorful→Colorful – Accent Colors**.

73. Drag the **top-center handle** of the SmartArt border to the **top** of the slide.

74. Drag the **bottom-right handle** of the SmartArt border to the **bottom-right corner** of the slide.

Add Elements to SmartArt

75. Click in the **bottom text box** of the pyramid.

76. Choose **SmartArt Tools→Design→Create Graphic→Add Shape menu ▼→Add Shape After**.

77. Type **Diversity Festival** in the bottom text box.

78. Save the changes and then exit **PowerPoint**. Submit your final file based on the guidelines provided by your instructor.

Apply Your Skills

Insert and Format an Embedded Chart

In this exercise, you will create a new presentation for Universal Corporate Events and add a nicely formatted, embedded chart to the presentation.

Begin a New Presentation and Create an Embedded Chart

1. Start **PowerPoint** and create a new, blank presentation.

2. Save the file as **PP04-A01-Review-[FirstInitialLastName]** in your **PP2013 Lesson 04** folder.

3. Apply the **Retrospect** theme.

4. Type the title **Universal Corporate Events** and the subtitle **Quarterly Review**.

5. Add a new slide with the title **Quarterly Breakdown**.

6. Insert a **Clustered Column** chart.

7. Enter this data:

◢	A	B	C	D	E
1		Jan-Mar	Apr-Jun	Jul-Sep	Oct-Dec
2	Total Events	22	72	34	115

8. Drag the data's border so that only **rows 1 and 2** are included and then close the **Chart window**.

Edit Chart Data and Change Chart Type, Layout, and Style

9. Edit the chart's data so that **cell B2** has a value of **18** and **cell E2** has a value of **132**.

10. Change the chart type to **3-D Clustered Column**.

11. Change the chart layout to **Layout 2**.

12. Change the chart style to **Style 11**.

Select Chart Elements and Change Chart Size and Text

13. Remove the chart's **Title, Gridlines, and Primary Vertical Axis label**.

14. Resize the chart so it fills the maximum area of the slide without overlapping the slide title.

15. Set the font size of the chart to **24**.

16. Click the number **18** above the first bar, locate the **Chart Tools→Format→Shape Styles gallery**, and choose the first style, **Colored Outline – Black, Dark 1**.

17. Apply the same **Shape Style** to the numbers on top of the remaining bars.

18. Save the changes and then exit **PowerPoint**. Submit your final file based on the guidelines provided by your instructor.

To view examples of how your file or files should look at the end of this exercise, go to the student resource center.

Work with Linked Charts and SmartArt

In this exercise, you will add a chart linked to an external data source. You will also add and format SmartArt.

Link and Format a Chart

1. Start **PowerPoint**. Open **PP04-A02-Projections** from the **PP2013 Lesson 04** folder and save it as **PP04-A02-Projections-[FirstInitialLastName]**.

2. Add a new third slide with the title **Event Projections**.

3. Start **Excel**. Open **PP04-A02-Projections** from the **PP2013 Lesson 04** folder.

4. Copy the chart from the **Excel spreadsheet** and paste it onto the **Event Projections PowerPoint slide**. Then exit **Excel**.

5. Resize the chart so it fills the maximum area of the slide without overlapping the slide title.

6. Use the **Chart Elements** button to display **Data Labels**.

7. Set the font size of the chart to **28**.

8. Change the colors of the chart to **Color 2**.

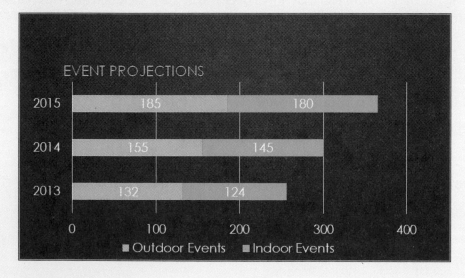

Fix a Broken Link and Edit a Linked Data Source

9. Select the chart on **slide 2** and attempt to edit the data.

   You must repair the broken link before you can edit the data.

10. Edit the link to the chart so that instead of pointing to the **Events2013.xlsx** workbook, the chart points to **PP04-A02-Events**.

11. Edit the chart data so that **cell B2** (Award Ceremonies value) is **67** instead of 7.

Insert and Modify SmartArt

12. Add a new fourth slide with the **Title and Content** layout.

13. Use `Growth` as the slide title.

14. Add the **Process→Upward Arrow** SmartArt graphic to the slide.

15. Type `Improved Catering` in the **left text box**, `Economic Transportation` in the **middle text box**, and `Building Ownership` in the **right text box**.

16. Add a shape **after** the right-most text box with the text `Growth in 2014`.

17. Use the **SmartArt Tools→Design** tab to apply the **Colorful→Colorful Range – Accent Colors 3-4** colors to the SmartArt.

18. Use the **SmartArt Tools→Design** tab to apply the **3-D→Polished** SmartArt Style.

19. Select each text box in the SmartArt graphic and use the Font Color menu on the **Home** tab to change all the SmartArt text colors to **Green, Accent 3**.

20. Enlarge the graphic and make the text **bold**.

21. Save the changes and then exit **PowerPoint**. Submit your final file based on the guidelines provided by your instructor.

   To view examples of how your file or files should look at the end of this exercise, go to the student resource center.

APPLY YOUR SKILLS PP04-A03
Work with Charts and SmartArt

In this exercise, you will add and format charts and SmartArt to the Universal Corporate Events presentation.

Begin a New Presentation and Create an Embedded Chart

1. Start **PowerPoint**. Create a new, blank presentation and save it to your **PP2013 Lesson 04** folder as `PP04-A03-Supplies-[FirstInitialLastName]`.

2. Apply the **Ion** theme with the **fourth (orange) variant**.

3. Give the slide a title of `Universal Corporate Events` and a subtitle of `Supplies`.

4. Change the font size of the slide title to **40**.

5. Add a second slide with the title `Projected Catering Supplies for 2014` and use the icon on the slide to insert a **Clustered Column** chart.

6. Type the following data in the spreadsheet and remove **row 5** from the chart data.

	A	B	C	D
1		2012	2013	2014
2	Bamboo Skewers	1250	1300	1500
3	Foil Pans	251	372	475
4	Foil Trays	175	310	400
5	Category 4	4.5	2.8	5

Format a Chart and Edit Chart Data

7. Resize the chart so it fills the maximum area of the slide without overlapping the slide title.

8. Delete the **chart title**.

9. Apply **Chart Style 6**.

10. Use the **Chart Elements** button to display the **Data Labels** and hide the **Gridlines** and **Primary Vertical axis**.

11. Apply the **Color 3** colors to the chart and increase the **font size** to **24**.

12. Edit the chart data to include the following data in **row 5**. Be sure to extend the data's border so row 5 is included in the chart.

	A	B	C	D
3	Foil Pans	251	372	475
4	Foil Trays	175	310	400
5	Sterno Cans	200	250	290

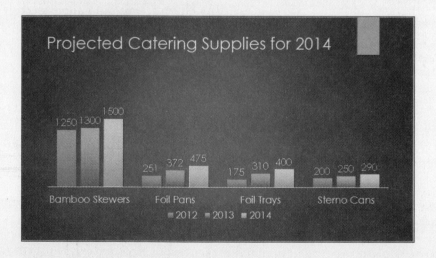

Link a Chart and Change and Format a Linked Chart

13. Create a new third slide with the title **Popular Dishes** and set the slide layout to **Title Only**.

14. Start **Excel**. Open **PP04-A03-Favorites** from the **PP2013 Lesson 04** folder.

15. Copy the chart from the **Excel spreadsheet** and paste it onto the **Popular Dishes PowerPoint slide**. Exit **Excel**.

16. Resize the chart so it fills the maximum area of the slide without overlapping the slide title.

17. Change the chart type to **3-D Pie**.

18. Apply a **Chart Style** of **Style 1** to the chart.

19. Change the layout of the chart to **Layout 1**.

20. Use the **Chart Elements button** next to the chart to hide the **Chart Title** and show **Data Labels→Data Callout**.

21. Set the font size of the chart to **24**.

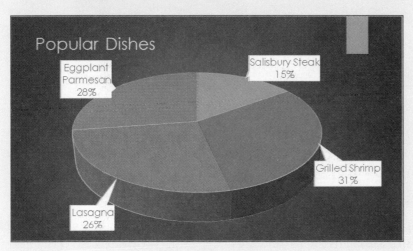

Break and Fix a Link and Edit a Linked Data Source

22. Minimize **PowerPoint** and use **Computer** or **File Explorer** to navigate to the **PP2013 Lesson 04** folder and locate the **PP04-A03-Favorites** workbook.

23. Rename the file `PP04-A03-Favorites2013`.

24. Restore **PowerPoint**, click the chart, and attempt to edit the data.

25. Dismiss the **Information** dialog box.

26. Edit the link to the spreadsheet so PowerPoint can find the newly named **PP04-A03-Favorites2013** file.

    At the time of this writing, a bug in PowerPoint causes the chart to no longer display even though the data is still linked. It may be necessary to delete and copy/paste the chart again if Microsoft hasn't released an update yet.

27. Edit the chart data to show `1938` servings of **Grilled Shrimp**.

28. Save the presentation and exit **PowerPoint**.

Edit and Refresh External Data

29. Start **Excel** and open **PP04-A03-Favorites2013**.

30. Change the **Lasagna** servings to `1164` and the **Eggplant** servings to `1223`.

31. Save the **Excel** workbook and exit **Excel**.

32. Start **PowerPoint** and open **PP04-A03-Supplies-[FirstInitialLastName]**.

33. Refresh the data on **slide 3**.

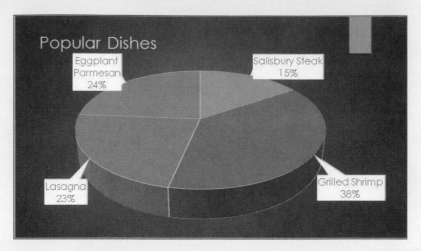

Insert and Format SmartArt

34. Create a **new fourth slide** with the **Title and Content** layout and a **slide title** of `Catering Goals`.

35. Insert a **Relationship→Radial Cycle** graphic.

36. In the **top circle**, type `Flavorful`. In the **right circle**, type `Healthy`. In the **left circle**, type `Economical`. In the **inner circle**, type `Respected and Desired`.

37. Click in the **bottom circle**, click the **text box's border**, and tap ⌈Delete⌉.

38. Apply the **3-D→Polished** SmartArt Style to the graphic.

39. Apply the **Primary Theme Colors→Dark 2 Fill** color.

40. Resize the SmartArt so it fills the maximum area of the slide without overlapping the slide title.

41. **Bold** the text and add a **text shadow**.

42. Save the changes and then exit **PowerPoint**. Submit your final file based on the guidelines provided by your instructor.

Extend Your Skills

In the course of working through the Extend Your Skills exercises, you will think critically as you use the skills taught in the lesson to complete the assigned projects. To evaluate your mastery and completion of the exercises, your instructor may use a rubric, with which more points are allotted according to performance characteristics. (The more you do, the more you earn!) Ask your instructor how your work will be evaluated.

PP04-E01 That's the Way I See It

Charts are often used in advertising to exaggerate results. Interview ten people and ask them to choose their favorite item from a list of three things (such as ice-cream flavors, cell-phone brands, or musical genres). Create a new presentation with an appropriate title and subtitle on the first slide. Apply an appropriate design theme. On a second slide, add a title and insert a pie chart that displays your survey results. Label each pie slice with a percentage to exaggerate the results. (Showing 60 percent prefer chocolate is more impressive than showing only six people!) Use the Chart Elements button to experiment with showing/hiding chart elements. Ensure that all information displays without looking too busy, and that the chart and labels are large enough for an audience to see when the slide show is presented. Add a third slide that displays the survey results as a visually appealing SmartArt graphic. Save the file as **PP04-E01-Survey-[FirstInitialLastName]** in the **PP2013 Lesson 04** folder.

You will be evaluated based on the inclusion of all elements specified, your ability to follow directions, your ability to apply newly learned skills to a real-world situation, your creativity, and the relevance of your topic and/or data choice(s). Submit your final file based on the guidelines provided by your instructor.

PP04-E02 Be Your Own Boss

In this exercise, you will create a presentation to show the flowers planted by your company, Blue Jean Landscaping, as well as a graphic to explain the basics of garden health for your clients. Create a new, blank presentation named **PP04-E02-BlueJeanChart-[FirstInitialLastName]** in the **PP2013 Lesson 04** folder. Apply the Wisp theme, the title **Blue Jean Landscaping**, and the subtitle **Flowers Planted**. Create a second slide with the Title Only layout and the title **Flowers Planted**. In Excel, create a new, blank spreadsheet that lists flowers down column A and numbers down column B. The spreadsheet should show **Roses – 972**, **Daisies – 473**, **Tulips – 554**, **Sunflowers – 576**, and **Asters – 327**. Select the cells containing data and insert a chart on the Excel spreadsheet. Save the spreadsheet as **PP04-E02-FlowerData-[FirstInitialLastName]**. Copy the chart and paste it onto the PowerPoint slide. Change the chart type in PowerPoint to best display the data. Apply chart elements, chart style, chart layout, and color to maintain a high level of readability.

Create a third slide with the title **Garden Health** and insert a SmartArt graphic appropriate for displaying these sequential steps: **Repel Bugs**, **Replenish Soil**, **Eliminate Weeds**, **Provide Water**, **Check Daily**. Format the SmartArt so it is attractive and easy to read.

You will be evaluated based on the inclusion of all elements specified, your ability to follow directions, your ability to apply newly learned skills to a real-world situation, your creativity, and your demonstration of an entrepreneurial spirit. Submit your final file based on the guidelines provided by your instructor.

Transfer Your Skills

In the course of working through the Transfer Your Skills exercises, you will use critical-thinking and creativity skills to complete the assigned projects using skills taught in the lesson. To evaluate your mastery and completion of the exercises, your instructor may use a rubric, with which more points are allotted according to performance characteristics. (The more you do, the more you earn!) Ask your instructor how your work will be evaluated.

PP04-T01 Use the Web as a Learning Tool

Throughout this book, you will be provided with an opportunity to use the Internet as a learning tool by completing WebQuests. According to the original creators of WebQuests, as described on their website (WebQuest.org), a WebQuest is "an inquiry-oriented activity in which most or all of the information used by learners is drawn from the web." To complete the WebQuest projects in this book, navigate to the student resource center and choose the WebQuest for the lesson on which you are currently working. The subject of each WebQuest will be relevant to the material found in the lesson.

WebQuest Subject: Using Different Chart Types

Submit your final file(s) based on the guidelines provided by your instructor.

PP04-T02 Demonstrate Proficiency

Stormy BBQ is displaying the results of a customer survey on their in-house television screens. New surveys have come in, and the data must be updated. Additionally, many customers report that the current survey results are hard to read.

Open **PP04-T02-BBQ** from the **PP2013 Lesson 04** folder and save it as **PP04-T02-BBQ-[FirstInitialLastName]**. Edit the chart data, after repairing the link, to indicate that 2 kids like the prices, 3 kids like the service, 115 kids like the ribs, 110 adults like the ribs, and 80 adults like the prices.

Apply an appropriate design theme to the presentation. Enlarge and format the chart, hiding/showing chart elements as necessary. Ensure that the chart is attractive and easy to read. On a third slide, create a SmartArt graphic that displays the top three reasons why people love Stormy's.

Submit your final file based on the guidelines provided by your instructor.

Exploring Access 2013

LEARNING OBJECTIVES

After studying this lesson, you will be able to:

- Start Access and identify elements of the application window
- Open and explore an existing database
- Identify database objects and explain how they are used
- Add data to an Access table
- Close a database and exit Access 2013

Have you ever wondered how sportscasters come up with fun and interesting facts about teams and players in a flash? Have you been taken by surprise when a customer service agent suddenly begins to recite your name, address, and a detailed purchase history? In most cases, these people have access to a powerful database from which they obtain the information.

In this lesson, you will explore the main elements of the Microsoft Access 2013 application window and its graphical user interface. You will discover how and when databases are used, learn about different kinds of databases, and explore database management software.

Updating Raritan Clinic East

Raritan Clinic East

Pediatric Diagnostic Specialists

Raritan Clinic East is an incorporated medical practice staffed by the finest clinical diagnosticians in the pediatric fields of neonatal care, general medicine, and emergency care. The practice serves a patient community ranging in ages from newborn to 18 years. Recently, the clinic moved to a brand new 21,000-square-foot state-of-the-art facility located in the center of a vast medical professional complex.

You work in the human resources department at the clinic and have been asked to review the records management system and develop a new database that will allow users to locate, retrieve, analyze, and report information more efficiently. You must determine how best to organize the data into a new database created with Access 2013.

In the old database file, the Employee Name field includes first name, last name, and specialty/position.

Employees

Employee Name	Address	Date Hired	Telephone
Judith Storm, Neonatal	234 McIntosh Dr., Sarasota, FL 34032	4/14/2010	(941)555-1235
John Ottome, GeneralMed	49 Osprey Ave., Sarasota, FL 34034	8/30/2010	(941) 555-8547
David Nealle, Emergency	100 Bee Ridge Rd., Sarasota, FL 34032	9/1/2010	(941)555-4327
Ruthann Good, GeneralMed	55 Lutz St., Tampa, FL 33172	9/11/2010	(941)555-4865
Mikayla Mansee-Emergency	19 Fruitville Rd., Sarasota FL 34201	9/14/2011	(941)555-9931
Anthony Adams, RN	53 Wildwood Terr., Bradenton, FL 34210	7/10/2011	(941)555-3648
Beverly Gauthier, RN	2552 Lime Ave., Sarasota, FL 34032	8/29/2010	(941)555-8162

Including several pieces of data in one field makes it difficult to find the right information quickly.

In the new database file, doctors' data is stored in one table and nurses' data is stored in another table.

The new database stores each category in a separate field.

Raritan Clinic East Doctors

DocID	Last Name	First Name	Street Address	City	ST	Zip	Telephone	Date Hired	Specialty
114	Storm	Judith	234 McIntosh Dr.	Sarasota	FL	34032	(941) 555-2309	4/14/2012	Neonatal
130	Ottome	John	49 Osprey Ave.	Sarasota	FL	34034	(941) 555-1304	8/30/2010	General Med
142	Nealle	David	100 Bee Ridge Rd.	Sarasota	FL	34032	(941) 555-1230	9/1/2010	Emergency
155	Good	Ruthann	55 Lutz St.	Tampa	FL	33172	(941) 555-2091	9/11/2010	General Med
200	Lawrence	Robert	32 Magellan Dr.	Sarasota	FL	34033	(941) 555-5926	2/9/2011	General Med

Raritan Clinic East Nurses

Nurse ID	Last Name	First Name	Street Address	City	ST	Zip	Telephone	Date Hired	Position
108162	Gauthier	Beverly	2552 Lime Ave.	Sarasota	FL	34032	(941)555-8162	8/9/2010	RN
111098	Kennerly	John	333 Tuttle	Sarasota	FL	34022	(941)555-1098	2/13/2011	LPN
111763	Ramirez	Maria	680 Main St.	Sarasota	FL	34032	(941)555-1763	1/15/2011	LPN
112963	Kristoff	Michael	1001 Pineapple St.	Sarasota	FL	34042	(941)555-2963	10/8/2011	RN
113648	Adams	Anthony	53 Wildwood Terr.	Bradenton	FL	34210	(941)555-3648	3/20/2011	RN

Defining Access Databases

Video Library   http://labyrinthelab.com/videos   Video Number: AC13-V0101

If you have ever pulled a file from a file cabinet; used your phone to store friends' names, phone numbers, and addresses; or purchased an item from an online retailer, you have used a database. For most of recorded history, databases were paper based. Today, databases are often stored electronically, allowing users to retrieve detailed information with amazing speed and accuracy. However, in each case, these filing systems consist of individual pieces of related data that, when combined, make up a database.

What Is a Database?

A database is an organized collection of related data files or tables. For example, a medical clinic might have a filing system that includes doctors' files, nurses' files, and files containing the records for nurses aides. These files are related to the same business and may be linked to each other, and when taken together compose a database. Data are pieces of information such as names, numbers, dates, descriptions, and other information organized for reference or analysis. The data stored in the Raritan Clinic East database might be the names, addresses, salaries, and hire dates of the medical clinic employees.

Purpose of Databases

Databases are used for many reasons. Doctors use them to track patient visits, maladies, and medications. Teachers use them to track students' grades and attendance. Business owners use them to keep a record of inventory and sales, while analyzing expenses, calculating profits, and printing reports. And you may have a database on your cell phone or iPad to organize the music, photo, and video files that you own.

Database Management Software

Database management software allows users to store, manipulate, and retrieve database information. Command-line driven database management can be performed by Structured Query Language (SQL), which is a database management programming language used by MySQL, the most popular Open Source database management system. Other successful data management software systems include DB2, which is IBM's relational database management system, and Oracle, which supports some of the largest business enterprises in the world.

```
mysql> insert into employees (EmpID, Name, Hours, Rate) values (101, "Allen", 40, 10);
Query OK, 1 row affected (0.04 sec)

mysql> select * from employees;
+-------+-------+-------+------+
| EmpID | Name  | Hours | Rate |
+-------+-------+-------+------+
|   101 | Allen |    40 |   10 |
+-------+-------+-------+------+
1 row in set (0.00 sec)
```

The process of inserting a single record into a MySQL file using command line can be challenging.

Access 2013

Microsoft Access 2013 and FileMaker Pro are examples of graphical user interface (GUI) database applications used by small- to medium-sized businesses. The graphical interface provides convenient tools and actions that are available by clicking icons (images, representing commands), text boxes, checkboxes, and many other items, combined with easy-to-use menus. Microsoft Access is far more user friendly than the more challenging command-line code.

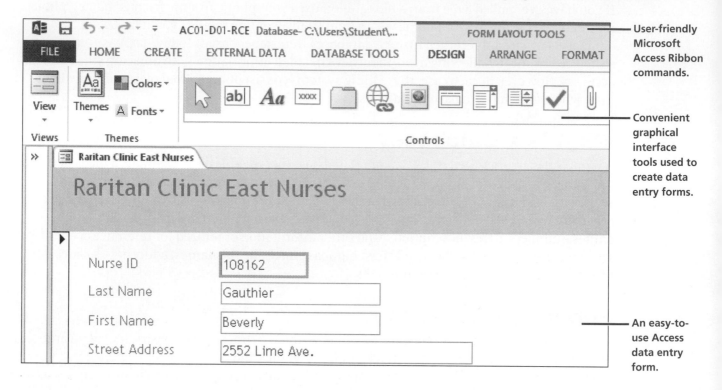

User-friendly Microsoft Access Ribbon commands.

Convenient graphical interface tools used to create data entry forms.

An easy-to-use Access data entry form.

Exploring the Access Environment

Video Library   http://labyrinthelab.com/videos   Video Number: AC13-V0102

Each time you start Access 2013, it opens in *Backstage view*, which offers a variety of file options. From this view, you can open an existing file, create a new blank database, or select from a number of predesigned templates for various business and personal applications.

Starting Access

The process for starting Access 2013 is the same process used for starting other Microsoft Office applications. After you start Access, you are prompted to take action to create or open a database. Depending on the version of Windows installed on your computer, and whether Access has been used on the computer before, the starting procedures may vary.

Start Access 2013

In this exercise, you will launch Access 2013 from the Start screen (Windows 8) or Start menu (Windows 7).

Before You Begin: *Navigate to the student resource center to download the student exercise files for this book.*

Follow the step(s) for your version of Windows.

Windows 7

1. Follow these steps to start Access 2013:

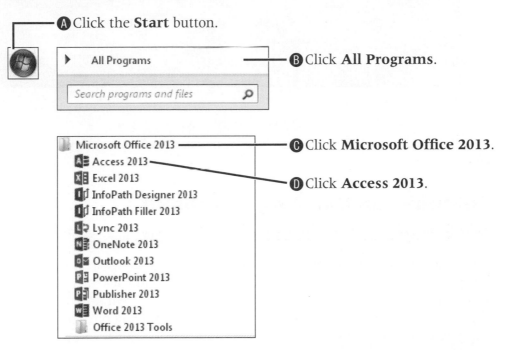

Ⓐ Click the **Start** button.

Ⓑ Click **All Programs**.

Ⓒ Click **Microsoft Office 2013**.

Ⓓ Click **Access 2013**.

After you launch Access for the first time, the program may appear on the Start menu. You can launch Access directly from the Start menu or from the All Programs list.

Continue with step 2 below.

Windows 8

1. Locate and click the **Access 2013** tile.

2. Leave **Access** open for the next exercise.

   Unless directed otherwise, keep Access and any databases being used open.

Opening an Existing Database

| Video Library | http://labyrinthelab.com/videos   Video Number: AC13-V0103 |

There are several methods available to open an existing database. If you want to open a file you recently worked on, it will be shown in the Recent area in Backstage view. You can also click the Open Other Files link, which takes you to the Access Open window. From the Open window, you can retrieve a recent database file stored on your computer or on a network. You can also retrieve a database stored on Microsoft's SkyDrive, a cloud-based file hosting service that offers at least seven gigabytes of free storage over the Internet.

Open a Database and Save It with a New Name

In this exercise, you will open a database and save it to your file storage location with a different name. Access should be open in Backstage view.

1. Click **Open Other Files** to search for database files.

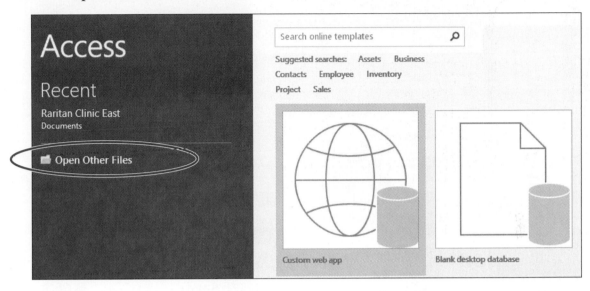

2. Follow these steps to open the Raritan Clinic East database file:

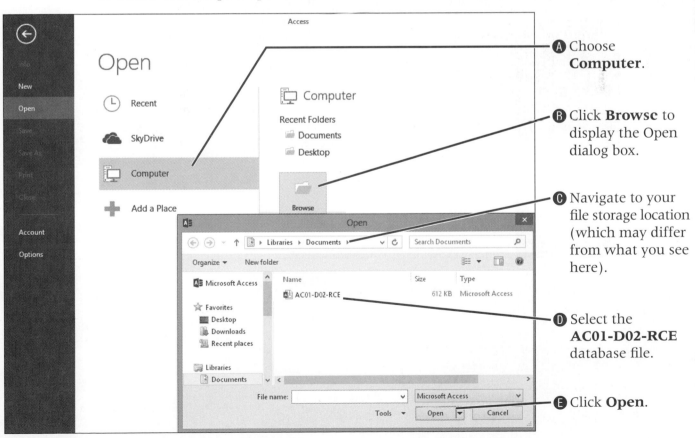

Ⓐ Choose **Computer**.

Ⓑ Click **Browse** to display the Open dialog box.

Ⓒ Navigate to your file storage location (which may differ from what you see here).

Ⓓ Select the **AC01-D02-RCE** database file.

Ⓔ Click **Open**.

Access 2013

Access opens the Raritan Clinic East database.

3. If a Security Warning bar displays, click **Enable Content**.

4. Click the **File** tab.

5. Follow these steps to rename and save the database:

Ⓐ Click the **Save As** option here.　　Ⓑ Choose **Save Database As→Access Database**.　　Ⓒ Click the **Save As** button at the bottom of the screen.

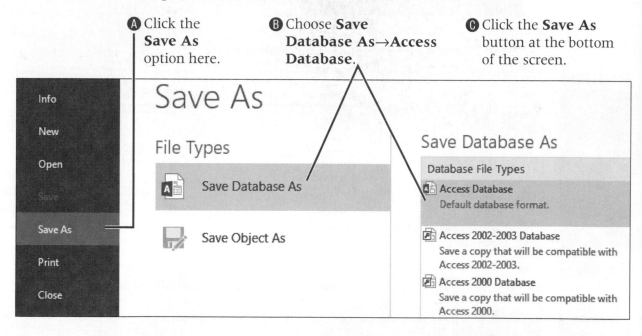

Access opens the Save As dialog box.

6. Navigate to your file storage location, type `AC01-D02-RCE-[FirstInitialLastName]` in the File Name box, and click **Save**.

Replace the bracketed text with your first initial and last name. For example, if your name is Bethany Smith, your filename would look like this: AC01-D02-RCE-BSmith.

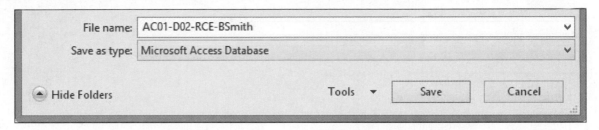

7. If a Security Warning bar displays, click **Enable Content**.

Identifying Features of the Database Window

Video Library http://labyrinthelab.com/videos Video Number: AC13-V0104

Now that you have opened the database file, explore the layout of the Database window. Compare the visual elements and features to those you have seen in other Microsoft Office applications. Acccss 2013 provides a Ribbon at the top of the window that contains tabs for groups of commands and toolbars, a Navigation Pane on the left side of the window that lists the objects in the database, and a Work Area for modifying database objects.

 If you don't see the Ribbon, it might be unpinned. Just choose Home→Pin the Ribbon ⊞ at the right end of the Ribbon. Or, press Ctrl+F1 to toggle the Ribbon.

The Work Area

The Work Area, or largest part of the screcn, is where you work with your main database objects. This is where you design tables, queries, forms, and reports, and where you enter actual data into your tables and forms. If you have multiple objects open at once, Access places a tab for each at the top of the Work Area. You can switch between objects by clicking on the tabs.

The Navigation Pane

The Navigation Pane, or Objects Panel, lists existing database objects, specifically, tables, queries, forms and reports.

 If you do not see the Navigation Pane, click the Shutter Bar Open/Close Button ⠶ or press F11 to toggle the pane.

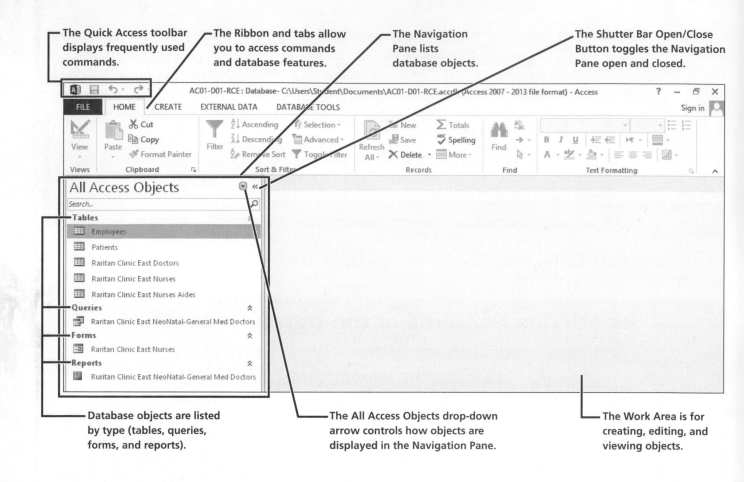

The Quick Access toolbar displays frequently used commands.

The Ribbon and tabs allow you to access commands and database features.

The Navigation Pane lists database objects.

The Shutter Bar Open/Close Button toggles the Navigation Pane open and closed.

Database objects are listed by type (tables, queries, forms, and reports).

The All Access Objects drop-down arrow controls how objects are displayed in the Navigation Pane.

The Work Area is for creating, editing, and viewing objects.

Introducing Access Objects

Video Library http://labyrinthelab.com/videos Video Number: AC13-V0105

A database object is a structure used to either store or reference data, such as a table, query, form or report.

ACCESS DATABASE OBJECT TYPES	
Object	Description
Table	A file or collection of related records. Tables contain the data used in all other database objects. A table allows you to view many or all of the records in a file at the same time.
Form	A database screen used to enter, edit, or view the data for an individual record in a layout that is more convenient and attractive than a table layout. Because a form primarily displays only one record at a time it is a safer way to enter data.
Query	A database object or module used to request, search, select, and sort data contained in tables based on specific criteria and conditions.
Report	A database page that presents processed and summarized data from tables and queries as meaningful information in a format that is easy to read and designed to be printed.

Tables

A table contains the database data. Tables allow you to enter, edit, delete, or view the data in a row and column layout, similar to an Excel spreadsheet. A business might use a database table to list inventory items, such as an item's part number, description, vendor, and price. Two other examples of tables are the Raritan Clinic list of doctors' records and the list of nurses' records. A table stores multiple related records.

A record is a collection of details about an individual person, place or thing, such as a doctor's record or a nurse's record in the Raritan Clinic East database. In a Microsoft Access table, each record is displayed in a row. A record is made up of multiple fields.

A field is a single named piece of information about each person, place or thing, such as a doctor's ID, telephone number, or specialty. In a Microsoft Access table each field is displayed in a column.

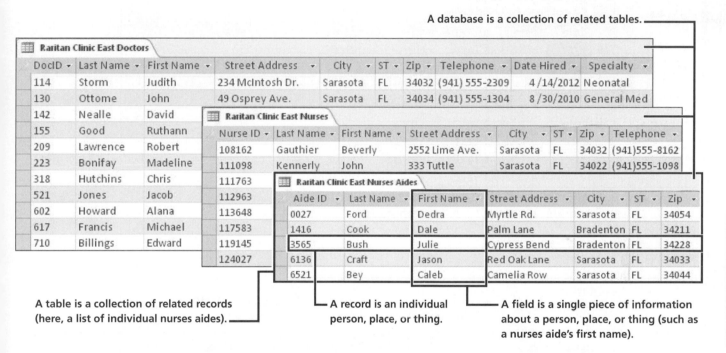

A database is a collection of related tables.

A table is a collection of related records (here, a list of individual nurses aides).

A record is an individual person, place, or thing.

A field is a single piece of information about a person, place, or thing (such as a nurses aide's first name).

Tables can be opened in Design View, which shows the properties or descriptions of fields in the table, and Datasheet View, which displays actual data values.

QUICK REFERENCE	OPENING TABLES IN DATASHEET VIEW AND IN DESIGN VIEW
Task	**Procedure**
Open a table in Datasheet View	▪ Double-click the table's name in the Navigation Pane. ▪ Right-click the table and choose Open. ▪ If the table is open in Design View, click the View menu ▼ and choose Datasheet View. ▪ If the table is open in Design View, right-click the table's object tab in the Work Area and choose Datasheet View.
Open a table in Design View	▪ Right-click the table's name and choose Design View. ▪ If the table is open in Datasheet View, choose Home→Views→View menu ▼→ Design View. ▪ If the table is open in Datasheet View, right-click the object tab in the Work Area and choose Design View.

Access 2013

Table Datasheet View and Design View are shown below.

The Object tab shows an identifying object icon and the name of the object.

Nurse ID ▾	Last Name ▾	First Name ▾	Street Address ▾	City ▾	ST ▾	Zip ▾	Telephone ▾	Date Hired ▾	Position ▾
108162	Gauthier	Beverly	2552 Lime Ave.	Sarasota	FL	34032	(941)555-8162	8/9/2010	RN
111098	Kennerly	John	333 Tuttle	Sarasota	FL	34022	(941)555-1098	2/13/2011	LPN
111763	Ramirez	Maria	680 Main St.	Sarasota	FL	34032	(941)555-1763	1/15/2011	LPN
112963	Kristoff	Michael	1001 Pineapple St.	Sarasota	FL	34042	(941)555-2963	10/8/2011	RN
113648	Adams	Anthony	53 Wildwood Terr.	Bradenton	FL	34210	(941)555-3648	3/20/2011	RN

Raritan Clinic East Nurses

Datasheet View displays actual data, or field values for records, and lets you add, delete, and edit records.

The Object tab shows an identifying object icon and the name of the object.

Raritan Clinic East Nurses   ×

Field Name	Data Type	Description (Optional)
NurseID	Short Text	Nurse Identification Number
Last Name	Short Text	Last Name
First Name	Short Text	First Name
Street	Short Text	Street Address
City	Short Text	City
State	Short Text	State
Zip	Short Text	Zipcode
Telephone	Short Text	Telephone Number
DateHired	Date/Time	Date Hired by Raritan
Position	Short Text	Staff Position

Field Properties

General | Lookup

Field Size	6
Format	
Input Mask	
Caption	Nurse ID
Default Value	
Validation Rule	
Validation Text	
Required	Yes
Allow Zero Length	Yes
Indexed	Yes (No Duplicates)
Unicode Compression	No
IME Mode	No Control
IME Sentence Mode	None
Text Align	General

A field name can be up to 64 characters long, including spaces. Press F1 for help on field names.

Design View lets you create or edit a table, enter field names, and set field properties.

Navigating through Access tables and forms is very similar.

Task	Procedure
Move to next field	■ Tap Tab or Enter; or click in the next field text box.
Move to previous field	■ Press Shift+Tab; or click in the previous text box.
Save entered data values	■ Tap Tab or Enter; or press Shift+Tab; or click in the next field text box.
Add new record	■ Click New (Blank) Record ▶*; or click Next Record ▶ until you reach an empty form.
Go to next record	■ Click Next Record ▶; or click to move with mouse.
Go to previous record	■ Click Previous Record ◀; or click to move with mouse.
Go to first record	■ Click First Record ◀◀; or press Ctrl+Home.
Go to last record	■ Click Last Record ▶▶; or press Ctrl+End.
Delete a record	■ Right-click record/row selector ➡ and select Delete Record or tap Delete. ■ Choose Yes to confirm.

DEVELOP YOUR SKILLS AC01-D03

Open a Table, Add a Record, and Edit a Record

In this exercise, you will explore a table in both Datasheet View and Design View. Then, you will add a new record and edit a field in another record.

1. Follow these steps to open a table in Datasheet View:

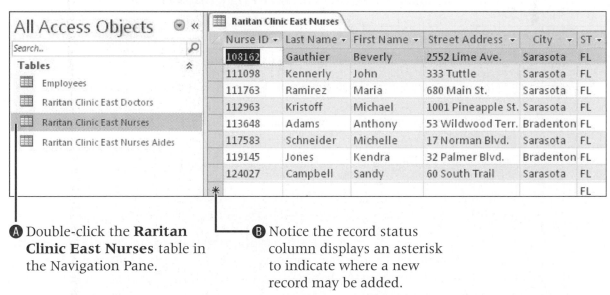

Ⓐ Double-click the **Raritan Clinic East Nurses** table in the Navigation Pane.

Ⓑ Notice the record status column displays an asterisk to indicate where a new record may be added.

If the table is not listed, click the All Access Objects drop-down arrow and select both Object Type and All Access Objects.

Access 2013

2. Follow these steps to add a new record and edit another record:

As you enter data, notice that you don't need to type the formatting characters in the Telephone, Date Hired, and Salary fields. Access automatically adds the formatting for you. Access will not allow you to move on to another record if the Nurse ID field is left blank.

A Enter the new record for **Janice Lombardo**, tapping Tab after each new field.

B Tap Tab after entering the salary to save the record.

Raritan Clinic East Nurses										
Nurse ID ▾	Last Name ▾	First Name ▾	Street Address ▾	City ▾	ST ▾	Zip ▾	Telephone ▾	Date Hired ▾	Position ▾	Salary ▾
108162	Gauthier	Beverly	2552 Lime Ave.	Sarasota	FL	34032	(941)555-8162	8/9/2010	RN	32,450.00
111098	Kennerly	John	333 Tuttle	Sarasota	FL	34022	(941)555-1098	2/13/2011	LPN	23,500.00
111763	Ramirez	Maria	680 Main St.	Sarasota	FL	34032	(941)555-1763	1/15/2011	LPN	25,750.00
112963	Kristoff	Michael	1001 Pineapple St.	Sarasota	FL	34042	(941)555-2963	10/8/2011	RN	30,250.00
113648	Adams	Anthony	53 Wildwood Terr.	Bradenton	FL	34210	(941)555-3648	3/20/2011	RN	28,000.00
117583	Schneider	Michelle	17 Norman Blvd.	Bradenton	FL	34212	(941)555-7583	2/24/2011	RN	31,700.00
119145	Jones	Kendra	32 Palmer Blvd.	Bradenton	FL	34212	(941)555-9145	11/7/2011	LPN	24,350.00
124027	Campbell	Sandy	60 South Trail	Sarasota	FL	34032	(941) 555-4027	2/15/2012	LPN	21,500.00
129022	Lombardo	Janice	5217 Palma Sola	Bradenton	FL	34209	(941) 555-9022	10/15/2012	RN	45,500.00
*				FL						0.00

C Tap ↑ and Tab to navigate to the **City** field in **Michelle Schneider's** record. Change *Bradenton* to **Sarasota** and tap Tab to save.

D Click the **Close** button when you are done.

TIP If you make a mistake while entering data, tap Esc to back out of an unwanted entry, if you have not yet tapped Tab to move to the next field. Press Esc twice to back out of an unwanted record if you have not moved on to the next record.

3. Click the **Close** ✕ button in the upper-right corner of the table.

Access saves your data whenever you press Tab or Enter in a table or a form. There is no need to save your data as long as you have entered a valid value for the ID field. If you modify the design of any table, query, form or report, Access will prompt you to save the changes made to any unsaved objects.

Forms

Video Library   http://labyrinthelab.com/videos   Video Number: AC13-V0106

Forms provide a quick, accurate, and user-friendly way to display individual records and enter data into tables. Forms may be opened in Design View, Layout View, and Form View.

In Design View, you can create a form, assign formatting to data fields, and edit the layout and content of the form. Layout View combines the editing ability of Design View with the layout look of Form View so you can better visualize and modify the form's appearance, but you cannot add, change, or delete records. Form View provides a user-friendly way to add, edit, and delete table records, but you cannot modify the form's layout.

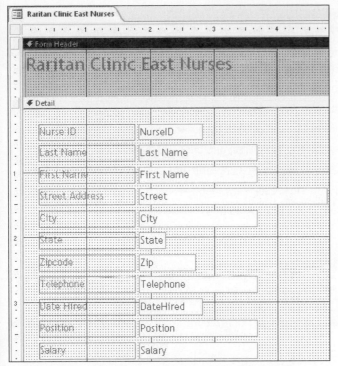

Design View enables you to create, customize, and modify a form. Fields can be added, deleted, or repositioned; colors, fonts, and sizes can be modified.

Layout View enables you to rearrange fields on the form while viewing actual data.

Form View enables you to enter new data and edit existing data.

The techniques for moving from field to field in Form View are the same as moving from field to field in a table in Datasheet View.

Task	Procedure
Open a form in Form View	▪ Double-click the form name in the Navigation Pane. ▪ Right-click the form and choose Open.
Open a form in Layout View	▪ Right-click the form name in the Navigation Pane and choose Layout View. ▪ If the form is open in Form View, click View menu ▼ and choose Layout View. ▪ Right-click the object tab in the Work Area and choose Layout View.
Open a form in Design View	▪ Right-click the form name in the Navigation Pane and choose Design View. ▪ If the form is open in Form View, click View menu ▼ and choose Design View. ▪ Right-click the object tab in the Work Area and choose Design View.

DEVELOP YOUR SKILLS AC01-D04

Add a Record Using an Existing Form

In this exercise, you will use an existing form to add a record to the table that you opened in the previous exercise.

1. Double-click the **Raritan Clinic East Nurses** form.

   Be sure to double-click the form, not the table.

2. Click the **Next Record** ▸ button a few times to page through the records.

3. Click the **Previous Record** ◂ button to go back to the first record.

4. Click the **New (Blank) Record** ▸* button.

5. Enter these data values, tapping Tab after entering a value in each field.

You do not have to enter the parenthesis or dash in the phone number, or enter the forward slashes between the numbers in dates. Access will add these for you.

You can use Shift + Tab to move to a previous field. Note the pencil icon 𝄃 that appears on the left side of the form as you begin typing. It indicates that you are currently working in this record.

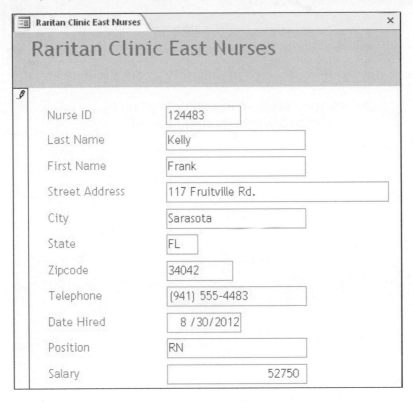

6. After entering the salary, tap Tab to save the record.

When you tap Tab after the last field in a form, Access will move to the next record or to a new blank record if you were working on the last record.

Deleting Records Using a Form

Video Library http://labyrinthelab.com/videos Video Number: AC13-V0107

There will come a time when a record in a table is no longer needed or relevant. You can delete records using a table in Datasheet View, using a query, and using an open form. When you delete a record that has a record number, Access will not renumber the records. Consequently, if the last record number is 20, there may not be 20 records in the table since some records may have been deleted.

QUICK REFERENCE	DELETING RECORDS USING A FORM
Task	**Procedure**
Delete a record using a form	Choose Home→Records→Delete→Delete Record. Or, click the Record Selection bar and click Delete.

Delete a Record Using a Form

In this exercise, you will delete a table record using a form. The Raritan Clinic East Nurses form should be open.

1. Follow these steps to delete a record from the nurses table using a form:

Ⓐ If necessary, click the **Home** tab.

Ⓑ Click the **Previous Record** ◀ button to navigate to Michael Kristoff's record.

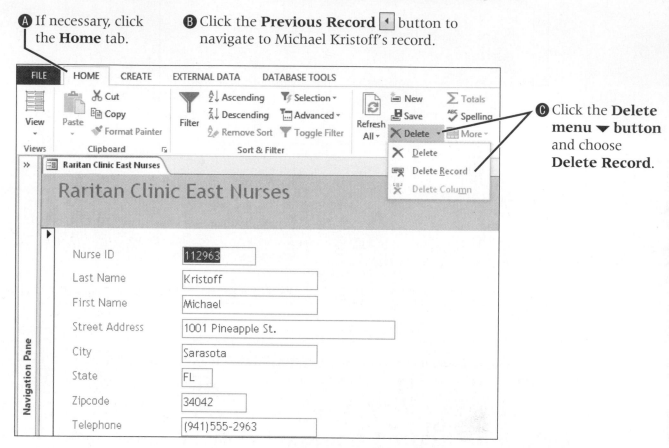

Ⓒ Click the **Delete menu ▾ button** and choose **Delete Record**.

2. Click **Yes** in the Microsoft Access warning box.

3. Close the form.

Queries

Video Library　http://labyrinthelab.com/videos　Video Number: AC13-V0108

Queries allow you to extract data from database tables based on specific criteria and display those results in a row and column format. They allow you to find specific records, select specific fields, and sort, organize, and perform calculations on the table data. Queries can be created and modified in Design View or in the more advanced Structured Query Language (SQL) View.

Task	Procedure
Open or run a query in Datasheet/Open View	■ Double-click the query name in the Navigation Pane. ■ Right-click the query and choose Open. ■ Open the query in Design View and choose Design→Results→Run.
Open a query in Design View	■ Right-click the query name and choose Design View. ■ If the query is open in Datasheet View, click View menu ▼ and choose Design View. ■ Right-click the object tab in the Work Area and choose Design View.
Open a query in SQL View	■ Open the query in Datasheet or Design View, click View menu ▼ and choose SQL View. ■ If the query is open in Design or Datasheet View, right-click the object tab in the Work Area and choose SQL View.

DEVELOP YOUR SKILLS AC01-D06

Open an Existing Simple Query

In this exercise, you will open a Select query in Design View, and then run it to select the doctors who specialize in Neonatal care or General Medicine.

1. Right-click the **Raritan Clinic East NeoNatal-General Med Doctors** query and choose **Design View**.

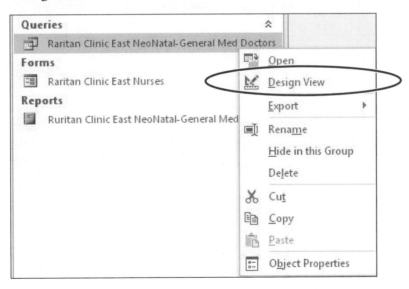

Access 2013

2. Follow these steps to run the query:

Ⓐ Note that the query will use the Raritan Clinic East Doctors table as input.

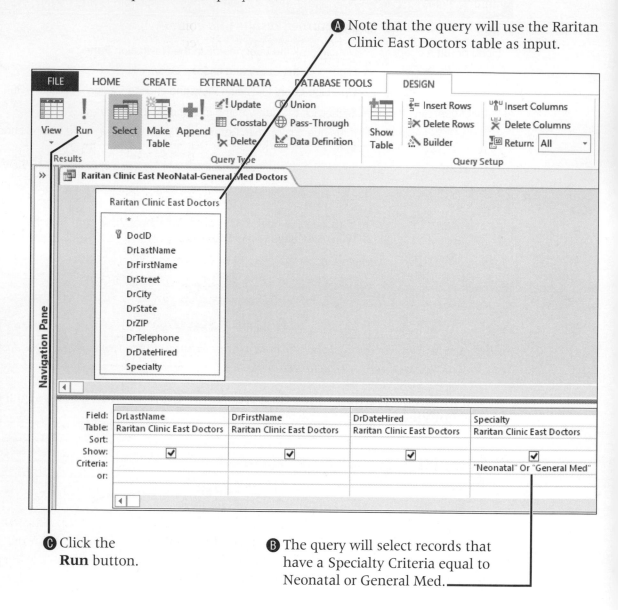

Ⓒ Click the **Run** button.

Ⓑ The query will select records that have a Specialty Criteria equal to Neonatal or General Med.

3. Follow these steps to analyze the query results:

Ⓐ The query returned results that contain the same fields that were displayed in Query Design View.

Last Name ▾	First Name ▾	Date Hired ▾	Specialty ▾
Storm	Judith	4/14/2012	Neonatal
Ottome	John	8/30/2010	General Med
Good	Ruthann	9/11/2010	General Med
Lawrence	Robert	2/9/2011	General Med
Bonifay	Madeline	12/3/2010	Neonatal
Hutchins	Chris	3/18/2012	General Med
Jones	Jacob	5/21/2012	General Med
Howard	Alana	6/2/2011	Neonatal
Billings	Edward	7/10/2011	Neonatal
Manford	Ryan	12/4/2011	General Med

Raritan Clinic East NeoNatal-General Med Doctors

Ⓑ The Specialty field identifies doctors who specialize in Neonatal care or General Med.

4. Click **Close** ✕ at the top-right corner of the query window.

Reports

Video Library   http://labyrinthelab.com/videos   Video Number: AC13-V0109

Reports display information retrieved from a table or query in an organized and formatted layout, providing detailed or summary information that can be useful for documenting, reporting, and making decisions. Reports are designed to be printed. Reports can be opened in Design View, Layout View, Report View, and Print Preview.

Task	Procedure
Open a report in Report View	■ Double-click the report name in the Navigation Pane. ■ Right-click the report and choose Open.
Open a report in Print Preview	■ Right-click the report name and choose Print Preview. ■ If the report is open in Report, Design, or Layout View, click View menu ▼ and choose Print Preview. ■ Right-click the object tab in the Work Area and choose Print Preview.
Open a report in Layout View	■ Right-click the report name and choose Layout View. ■ If the report is open in Report View, click View menu ▼ and choose Layout View. ■ Right-click the object tab in the Work Area and choose Layout View.
Open a report in Design View	■ Right-click the report name and choose Design View. ■ If the report is open in Report View, click View menu ▼ and choose Design View. ■ Right-click the object tab in the Work Area and choose Design View.
Print a report	■ Right-click the report name and choose Print. ■ Open the report in Print Preview and click the Print button on the Ribbon.

DEVELOP YOUR SKILLS AC01-D07

View an Existing Database Report

In this exercise, you will view an existing report in Design View and Print Preview.

1. Follow these steps to open a report in Design View:

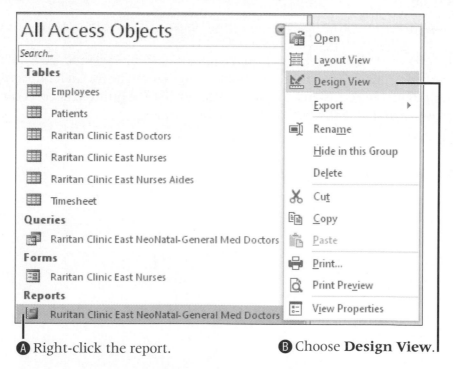

Ⓐ Right-click the report.　　　Ⓑ Choose **Design View**.

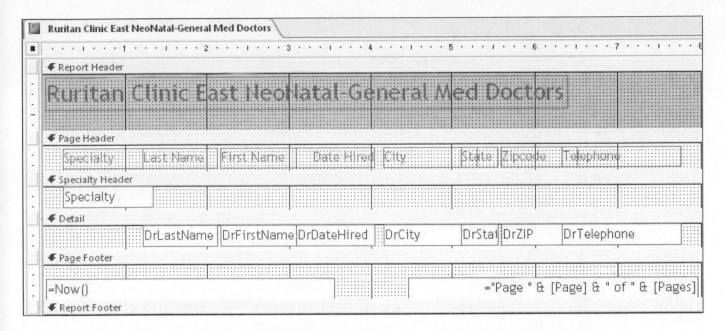

The report opens in Design View. In Design View you can add, delete, and reposition fields, and change font sizes and colors.

2. Follow these steps to switch to Print Preview:

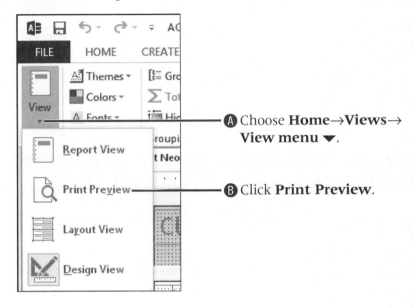

Ⓐ Choose **Home→Views→ View menu ▼**.

Ⓑ Click **Print Preview**.

Raritan Clinic East NeoNatal-General Med Doctors

Specialty	Last Name	First Name	Date Hired	City	State	Zipcode	Telephone
General Med							
	Good	Ruthann	9/11/2010	Tampa	FL	33172	(941) 555-2091
	Hutchins	Chris	3/18/2012	Sarasota	FL	34042	(941) 555-3809
	Jones	Jacob	5/21/2012	Bradenton	FL	34212	(941) 555-4613
	Lawrence	Robert	2/9/2011	Sarasota	FL	34033	(941) 555-5926
	Manford	Ryan	12/4/2011	Bradenton	FL	34212	(941) 555-8422
	Ottome	John	8/30/2010	Sarasota	FL	34034	(941) 555-1304
Neonatal							
	Billings	Edward	7/10/2011	Bradenton	FL	34205	(941) 555-2237
	Bonifay	Madeline	12/3/2010	Bradenton	FL	34205	(941) 555-1902
	Howard	Alana	6/2/2011	Sarasota	FL	34032	(941) 555-9910
	Storm	Judith	4/14/2012	Sarasota	FL	34032	(941) 555-2309

A typical report might include a title, heading, detail lines showing individual records, and a footer that displays the date and page number.

3. Click the **Print** button to print the report based on the guidelines provided by your instructor.

4. Click the **Close Print Preview** button.

5. Click **Close** ☒ to close the report.

Closing a Database and Exiting Access

Video Library   http://labyrinthelab.com/videos   Video Number: AC13-V0110

Remember that as long as a valid ID has been entered, Access automatically saves your data when you press Tab or Enter in a table or in a form. You don't have to repeatedly save your data.

If you modify the design of any table, query, form or report, Access will automatically prompt you to save any changes made to unsaved objects.

After all modified objects have been saved, you can close the database and exit Access. The procedures used to perform these tasks are the same as those used to close files and exit other Microsoft Office applications. Choose the File tab and select Close to close the database.

Because Access databases contain numerous objects, it is always a good idea to close each database object properly before exiting Access. This ensures that all objects in the database are put away carefully.

DEVELOP YOUR SKILLS AC01-D08

Close a Database and Exit Access

In this exercise, you will close the Raritan Clinic East database and exit Access.

1. Choose **File→Close** to close the database

2. Click the **Close** ⊠ button to exit **Access 2013**.

Concepts Review

To check your knowledge of the key concepts introduced in this lesson, complete the Concepts Review quiz by choosing the appropriate access option below.

If you are...	Then access the quiz by...
Using the Labyrinth Video Library	Going to http://labyrinthelab.com/videos
Using eLab	Logging in, choosing Content, and navigating to the Concepts Review quiz for this lesson
Not using the Labyrinth Video Library or eLab	Going to the student resource center for this book

Access 2013

Reinforce Your Skills

Add, Edit, and Delete Records

Kids for Change is a non-profit organization that helps young adults organize social/community service within the mindset of "think globally, act locally." In this exercise, you will explore the Access environment, open the Kids for Change database, and add a record to a table. You will also edit a table and use a form to delete a record.

Explore the Access Environment

1. To start Access, follow the step for your version of Windows:
   - **Windows 7:** Choose **Start→All Programs→Microsoft Office 2013→Access 2013**.
   - **Windows 8:** Locate and click the **Access 2013 tile**.

2. Click the **Open Other Files** link in Backstage view, click **Computer**, and click **Browse**.

3. Navigate to your file storage location, choose **AC01-R01-K4C**, and click **Open**.

4. Use the **Save As** command and name the file `AC01-R01-K4C-[FirstInitialLastName]`.

5. Click the **Collapse** ⏶ and **Expand** ⏷ buttons in the Navigation Pane to show/hide the different database objects.

6. Click the **Create**, **External Data**, and **Database Tools** tabs to see the commands available in each one; then, return to the **Home** tab.

   At this point you are just exploring Access. Note that the Create tab has commands that allow you to create your own tables, queries, forms, and reports.

Add a Record and Edit Data Using a Table

7. Double-click the **Activities** table in the Navigation Pane/Objects Panel.
   Be sure to double-click the table, not the form.

8. Enter the data values for the record indicated, tapping Tab after each field.

Activity ID ▾	Activity ▾	Location ▾	Day of Week ▾	Meet Time ▾
BCSat	Beach Cleanup	Coquina Beach	Saturday	9:00 AM
CCThu	Can Collection	Seabreeze School	Thursday	6:00 PM
ESSun	Eco-Bake Sale	Downtown Flea Market	Sunday	8:00 AM
GWWed	Garden Work	All Angels Church	Wednesday	5:00 PM
NCMon	Newspaper Collection	Seabreeze School	Monday	6:00 PM
RDTue	Recycling Drive	Seabreeze School	Tuesday	6:00 PM
SWFri	Sign Waving	Cortez Rd. & Tamiami Tr.	Friday	5:00 PM
PSSun	Petition Signing	Hernando Mall	Sunday	3:00 PM
*				

Be sure to tap Tab after entering the Meet Time. Remember that you cannot save your data if you have not entered a valid value for the unique key field, or ID, for a record.

9. Navigate to the **Location** field for **Newspaper Collection** and change the Location value from *Seabreeze School* to **Bayshore School**.

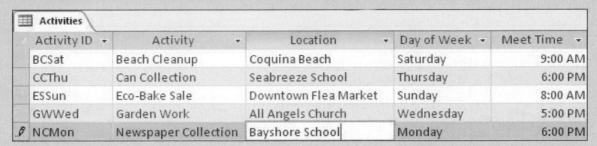

Be sure to tap Tab *after entering the school name.*

10. **Close** × the Activities table.

Add a Record and Delete a Record Using a Form

11. Double-click the **Activities** form in the Navigation Pane/Objects Panel.

Be sure to double-click the form, not the table.

12. Click the **New (Blank) Record** ▶ button then enter the data values shown.

13. Tap Tab or Enter after entering the Meet Time value to save your new record.

You will not be able to move to a new record or save the data if you have not entered an ID.

Access 2013

14. Using the **Previous Record** ◀ and **Next Record** ▶ buttons at the bottom of the form, navigate to the **Garden Work** record.

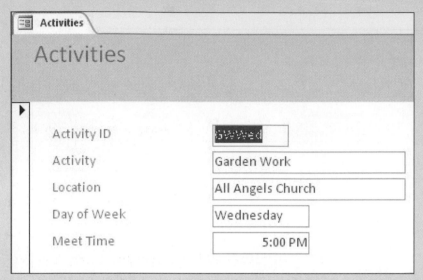

15. Click the **Record Selection** bar, then choose **Home→Records→Delete menu ▼→ Delete Record**.

The record is removed from Form View and deleted from the underlying table.

16. Click **Yes** in the warning box.

17. Close the **Activities** form and display the Activities table in Datasheet View.

The Garden Work record has been deleted and the new location for Newspaper Collection is Bayshore School.

18. Close the **Activities** table; exit **Access**.

19. Submit your final file based on the guidelines provided by your instructor.

To view examples of how your file or files should look at the end of this exercise, go to the student resource center.

Run a Query and View a Report

In this exercise, you will run a query in the Kids for Change database to gather and display the activities scheduled from Monday through Friday. You will also run and print a report that lists staff members available on weekdays.

Run a Query

1. Start **Access**.

2. Click **Open Other Files** in Backstage view, click **Computer**, and click **Browse**.

3. Navigate to your file storage location, choose **AC01-R02-K4C**, and click **Open**.

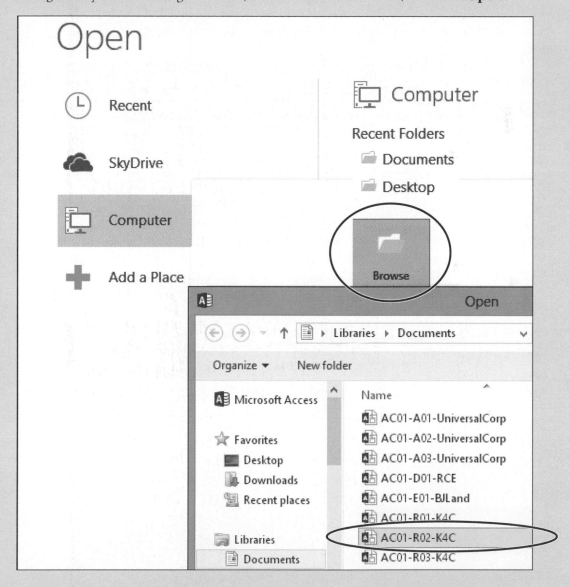

The database opens with the database objects displayed in the Navigation Pane.

4. Using the **Save As** command, name the file **AC01-R02-K4C-[FirstInitialLastName]**.

5. In the Navigation Pane, right-click **Weekday Activities Query** and choose **Design View**.

6. Hover the mouse pointer over the right edge of each grid column heading until the pointer becomes a resize pointer, then double-click to auto size each column.

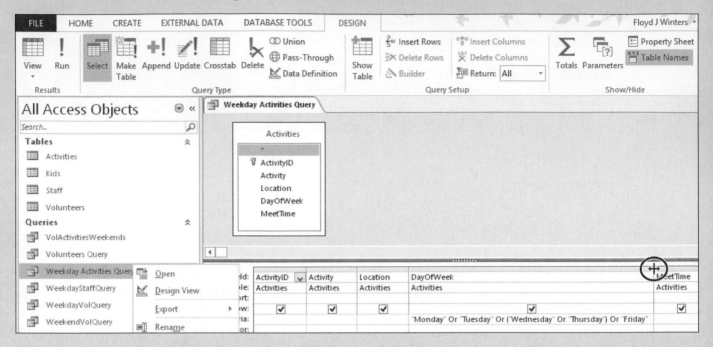

7. Choose **Design→Results→Run** to see the query results.

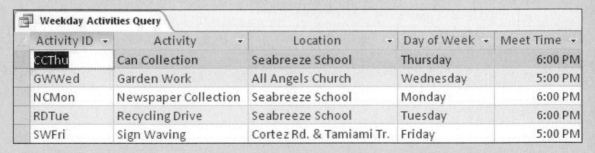

The query selects only the records in which DayOfWeek is a weekday (Monday through Friday).

8. **Close** ⊠ the Weekday Activities Query results.

View and Print a Report

9. Double-click **WeekdayStaffReport** to open it in Report View.

10. Click **View menu** ▼ and choose **Print Preview**.

Use the Print Preview Zoom tool to adjust the zoom level of the report.

Kids for Change
Weekday Staff Report

Day of Week	Activity	Location	Meet Time	Staff Last Name	Staff First Name	Staff Phone
Friday						
	Sign Waving	Cortez Rd. & Tami	5:00 PM	Kendall	Lonnie	941-555-2356
Monday						
	Newspaper Collection	Bayshore School	6:00 PM	Earle	Kevin	941-555-1368
Tuesday						
	Recycling Drive	Seabreeze School	6:00 PM	Jacoby	Jane	941-555-5050
Wednesday						
	Garden Work	All Angels Church	5:00 PM	Montagne	Francis	941-555-9032

11. Click the **Print** button.

12. Based on the guidelines provided by your instructor, send the **WeekdayStaffReport** to a printer, save it as a new database object, or publish it as a PDF or an XPS file.

13. Click the **Close Print Preview** button.

14. Close the **WeekdayStaffReport**, and any other open objects; exit **Access**.

15. Submit your final file based on the guidelines provided by your instructor.

To view examples of how your file or files should look at the end of this exercise, go to the student resource center.

REINFORCE YOUR SKILLS AC01-R03

Add a Record, Run a Query, and Generate a Report

In this exercise, you will explore the Access environment, open the Kids for Change database, and change the scheduled day of an activity. You will use a form to delete a record and add a new record. Then, you will run a query that generates a list of staff members who are available on weekends. Finally, you open a report that displays a list of all Kids for Change volunteers.

Explore the Access Environment

1. Start **Access**.

2. Click the **Open Other Files** link in Backstage view, click **Computer**, and click **Browse**.

3. Navigate to your file storage location, choose **AC01-R03-K4C**, and click **Open**.

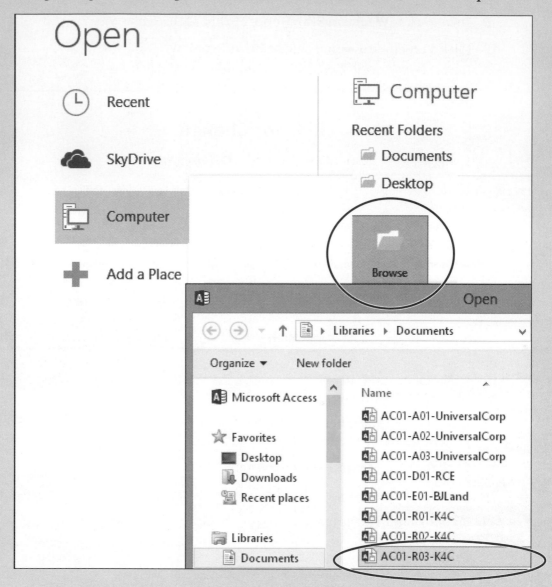

The database opens with the database objects displayed in the Navigation Pane.

4. Using the **Save As** command, name the file **AC01-R03-K4C-[FirstInitialLastName]**.

5. Click the **Collapse** ⊼ and **Expand** ⊻ buttons in the Navigation Pane to hide/show the different objects in the database.

6. Click the **Create**, **External Data**, and **Database Tools** tabs to see the commands available in each one; then, return to the **Home** tab.

At this point you are just exploring Access. Note that the Create tab has commands that allow you to create your own tables, queries, forms, and reports.

Edit and Enter Data with a Table and a Form

7. In the **Kids for Change** database, double-click the **Activities** table in the Navigation Pane.

8. Using ↓ and Tab, navigate to the **Day of Week** field for **Can Collection**.

9. Change the **Day of Week** value from *Thursday* to **Wednesday**.

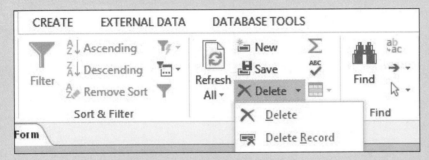

10. **Close** × the Activities table.

Remember that Access automatically saves your data once you tap Tab as long as you have entered a valid ID for the record.

11. Double-click **VolunteersForm**.

12. Using the **Previous Record** ◄ and **Next Record** ► buttons at the bottom of the form, navigate to the record for **Beverly Frith**.

13. Click the **Record Selection bar** and choose **Home→Records→Delete→Delete Record**.

The record will be removed from Form View and deleted in the underlying table.

14. Click **Yes** in the Microsoft Access warning box.

15. Click the **New (blank) Record** ►* button at the bottom of the form, if necessary.

If you have just deleted the last record in the form, a new, blank record will already be displayed.

16. Tap Tab to move to the **Last Name** field. Type **Harris**.

Because the Autonumber Data Type is selected for the ID for the Volunteers table, you cannot enter a value; Access automatically assigns consecutive numbers to the ID.

17. Add a new record using the data shown.

Volunteer ID	6
Last Name	Harris
First Name	Annie
Street Address	5140 Pine Ave.
City	Sarasota
State	FL
ZIP	34022
Telephone	941-555-5273
Available Day	Sunday

Tap Tab *after entering the Available Day field to save the new record. When you tap* Tab *after the last field in a form, Access will move to the next record or to a new blank record if you were working in the last record.*

18. Close the form.

Open and Run a Query

19. Right-click **WeekendVolQuery** and choose **Design View**.

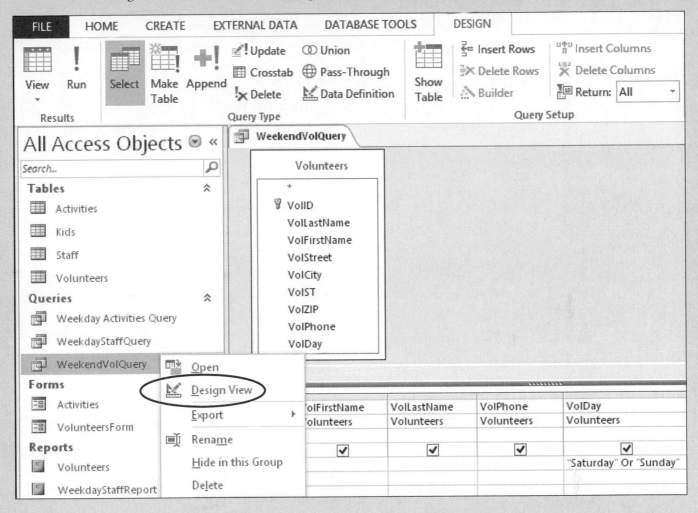

The query returns only the records in which DayOfWeek is a Saturday or Sunday.

20. Click the **Run** button on the Design tab to see the query results.

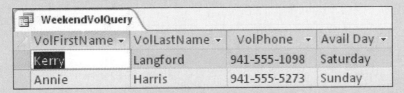

Only two volunteers are available on weekends.

21. Close ⨯ the WeekendVolQuery.

View and Print a Report

22. Double-click the **Volunteers** report to open it in Report View.

23. Click the **View ▼ menu** and choose **Print Preview**.

Kids for Change
Volunteers Report

Avail Day	Last Name	First Name	Street Address	City	ST	ZIP	Telephone
Monday	Simpson	Lance	59 Bahia Vista	Sarasota	FL	34032	941-555-3431
Saturday	Langford	Kerry	43 Wisteria Way	Bradenton	FL	34209	941-555-1098
Sunday	Harris	Annie	5140 Pine Ave.	Sarasota	FL	34022	941-555-5273
Tuesday	Jones	Stan	892 Southern Pkwy.	Sarasota	FL	34024	941-555-8929
Wednesday	Creger	Cindy	503 Hillview	Sarasota	FL	34022	941-555-0245

24. Click the **Print** button.

25. Based on the guidelines provided by your instructor, send the **Volunteers** report to a printer, save it as a new database object, or publish it as a PDF or an XPS file.

26. Click the **Close Print Preview** button.

27. Close the **Volunteers** report and any other open objects; exit **Access**.

28. Submit your final file based on the guidelines provided by your instructor.

Apply Your Skills

Add Data, Change Data Values, and Delete a Record

Universal Corporate Events is a meeting and event planning service. In this exercise, you will explore the Access environment, open the Universal Corporate Events database, open an existing form, and schedule a new event. Then, you will open a table, change a field, and delete a record.

Explore the Access Environment

1. Start **Access**. Open **AC01-A01-UniversalCorp** from the **AC2013 Lesson 01** folder in your file storage location and save it as **AC01-A01-UniversalCorp-[FirstInitialLastName]**.

2. Explore the Ribbon tabs to see the commands that are available in each one; then, return to the **Home** tab.

Work with Forms and Tables

3. Open the **Event Schedules** form in **Form View** and add this record.

Field Name	Data
Schedule ID	BRDMiller
Location	Meadows Clubhouse
Contact	Gail Miller
Event ID	Holiday
Menu Code	DessSel
Event Date	7/2/2014
Guests	25

In this case, you can enter the primary key (Schedule ID) value because it is the Short Text data type, not AutoNumber. Remember to tap Tab *or* Enter *after the Guests value to save the new record.*

4. Close the **Event Schedules** form.

5. Open the **Menus** table in **Datasheet View**.

6. Change the **Chg/PP** for the **Dinner-Buffet** (Menu Code = DinBuff) to **23.00**.

7. Delete the **Continental Breakfast** (Menu Code = ContBrk) record.

Menu Code	Menu Plan	Chg/PP
⊞ BoxLunch	Box Sandwich Lunch	10.00
⊞ BrkBuff	Buffet Breakfast	12.00
⊞ DessSel	Dessert Selections	7.50
⊞ DinBuff	Dinner-Buffet	23.00
⊞ DinSitDn	Dinner-Sit Down	35.00
⊞ HorsDvr	Hors d'oeuvre	8.00
⊞ LunchBuff	Buffet Luncheon	15.00
⊞ Thnksg	Thanksgiving Dinner	30.00

8. Close the table and the database; exit **Access**.

9. Submit your final file based on the guidelines provided by your instructor.

   To view examples of how your file or files should look at the end of this exercise, go to the student resource center.

Run a Query and View a Report

In this exercise, you will run a query to select events located at the Meadows Clubhouse. Then you will run a report that uses the results of the query as input for a printout of those events.

Explore and Run a Query

1. Start **Access**. Open **AC01-A02-UniversalCorp** from the **AC2013 Lesson 01** folder in your file storage location and save it as `AC01-A02-UniversalCorp-[FirstInitialLastName]`.

2. Run the **LocationSchedQuery** to select events by their location, in this case the **Meadows Clubhouse**.

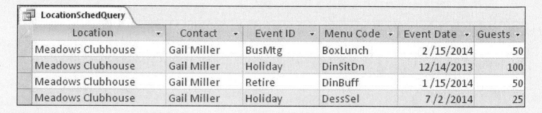

Location	Contact	Event ID	Menu Code	Event Date	Guests
Meadows Clubhouse	Gail Miller	BusMtg	BoxLunch	2/15/2014	50
Meadows Clubhouse	Gail Miller	Holiday	DinSitDn	12/14/2013	100
Meadows Clubhouse	Gail Miller	Retire	DinBuff	1/15/2014	50
Meadows Clubhouse	Gail Miller	Holiday	DessSel	7/2/2014	25

3. Close the query results.

View and Print a Report

4. Open the **Location Scheduling** report in **Print Preview**.

Universal Corporate Events
Location Scheduling

Event Name	Menu Plan	Guests	Location	Contact	Event Date	Attending
Business Meeting						
	Box Sandwich Lunch	50	Meadows Clubhouse	Gail Miller	2/15/2014	50
Holiday Party						
	Dessert Selections	25	Meadows Clubhouse	Gail Miller	7/2/2014	25
	Dinner-Sit Down	100	Meadows Clubhouse	Gail Miller	12/14/2013	100
Retirement Party						
	Dinner-Buffet	50	Meadows Clubhouse	Gail Miller	1/15/2014	50

5. Based on the guidelines provided by your instructor, send the **Location Scheduling** report to a printer, save it as a new database object, or publish it as a PDF or XPS file.

6. Close the report and the database. Exit **Access**.

7. Submit your final file based on the guidelines provided by your instructor.

   To view examples of how your file or files should look at the end of this exercise, go to the student resource center.

Add a Record, Run a Query, and Generate a Report

In this exercise, you will use a form to add a record to a table. You will then run a query to select the events that will use the Meadows Clubhouse as a venue. Finally, you will run a report using the query results and create a printout for the Meadows Clubhouse management so they can reserve the clubhouse for each event.

Explore the Access Environment

1. Start **Access**. Open **AC01-A03-UniversalCorp** from the **AC2013 Lesson 01** folder in your file storage location and save it as **AC01-A03-UniversalCorp-[FirstInitialLastName]**.

2. Explore the Ribbon tabs to see the commands that are available in each one; then, return to the **Home** tab.

Enter Data with a Form and Table

3. Open the **Event Schedules** form in the Navigation Pane.

4. Add this record.

Field Name	Data
Schedule ID	BRDMiller
Location	Meadows Clubhouse
Contact	Gail Miller
Event ID	BusMtg
Menu Code	HorsDvr
Event Date	2/28/2014
Guests	35

5. Close the form.

View Changes to a Query After Edits to a Table

6. Run the **EventsSchedQuery** to calculate the total cost of each event.

Event Name	Menu Plan	Chg/PP	Location	Contact	Event Date	Guests	Total Cost	Menu Code
Business Meeting	Box Sandwich Lunch	10.00	Meadows Clubhouse	Gail Miller	2/15/2014	50	$500.00	BoxLunch
Holiday Party	Hors d'oeuvre	8.00	Drake Country Club	Sue Croft	12/6/2013	150	$1,200.00	HorsDvr
Holiday Party	Dinner-Sit Down	35.00	Meadows Clubhouse	Gail Miller	12/14/2013	100	$3,500.00	DinSitDn
Retirement Party	Dinner-Buffet	23.00	Meadows Clubhouse	Gail Miller	1/15/2014	50	$1,150.00	DinBuff
Group Retreat	Dinner-Buffet	23.00	Brooksville Campgrounds	Lisa Luna	5/29/2014	80	$1,840.00	DinBuff

Note that the fourth event listed in the query, Retirement Party, currently has 50 guests expected and the Total Cost is $1,150.00.

Access 2013

7. Close the query.

8. Open the **Scheduling** table and increase the number of guests for the **Retirement Party** (Schedule ID = RTRMiller) to **60**.

9. Rerun the **EventsSchedQuery** to see the difference in Total Cost.

Event Name	Menu Plan	Chg/PP	Location	Contact	Event Date	Guests	Total Cost	Menu Code
Business Meeting	Box Sandwich Lunch	10.00	Meadows Clubhouse	Gail Miller	2/15/2014	50	$500.00	BoxLunch
Holiday Party	Hors d'oeuvre	8.00	Drake Country Club	Sue Croft	12/6/2013	150	$1,200.00	HorsDvr
Holiday Party	Dinner-Sit Down	35.00	Meadows Clubhouse	Gail Miller	12/14/2013	100	$3,500.00	DinSitDn
Retirement Party	Dinner-Buffet	23.00	Meadows Clubhouse	Gail Miller	1/15/2014	60	$1,380.00	DinBuff
Group Retreat	Dinner-Buffet	23.00	Brooksville Campgrounds	Lisa Luna	5/29/2014	80	$1,840.00	DinBuff

The Retirement Party now has a Total Cost of $1,380.00.

10. Close the **EventsSchedQuery** and the **Scheduling** table.

Produce and Print a Report

11. Open and preview the **Location Scheduling** report.

Universal Corporate Events
Location Scheduling

Event Name	Menu Plan	Guests	Location	Contact	Event Date	Attending
Business Meeting						
	Hors d'oeuvre	35	Meadows Clubhouse	Gail Miller	2/28/2014	35
	Box Sandwich Lunch	50	Meadows Clubhouse	Gail Miller	2/15/2014	50
Holiday Party						
	Dessert Selections	25	Meadows Clubhouse	Gail Miller	7/2/2014	25
	Dinner-Sit Down	100	Meadows Clubhouse	Gail Miller	12/14/2013	100
Retirement Party						
	Dinner-Buffet	60	Meadows Clubhouse	Gail Miller	1/15/2014	60

12. Based on the guidelines provided by your instructor, send the **Location Scheduling** report to a printer, save it as a new database object, or publish it as a PDF or XPS file.

13. Close the report and any other open objects; close the database. Exit **Access**.

14. Submit your final file based on the guidelines provided by your instructor.

Extend Your Skills

In the course of working through the Extend Your Skills exercises, you will think critically as you use the skills taught in the lesson to complete the assigned projects. To evaluate your mastery and completion of the exercises, your instructor may use a rubric, with which more points are allotted according to performance characteristics. (The more you do, the more you earn!) Ask your instructor how your work will be evaluated.

AC01-E01 That's the Way I See It

You will design and create a business database as you progress through the Access lessons. To begin, identify a business or a type of business for which you will create a database in the remaining lessons. Once you have identified your specific business or a business type, start Word and save a new document as **AC01-E01-MyCompany-[FirstInitialLastName]** in your **AC2013 Lesson 01** folder. Create a list of tables your database will need, as well as the fields that these tables will contain. Make sure your database design includes both text and numeric fields, which may be used for future calculations.

You will be evaluated based on the inclusion of all elements, your ability to follow directions, your ability to apply newly learned skills to a real-world situation, your creativity, and your accuracy in creating objects and/or entering data. Submit your final files based on the guidelines provided by your instructor.

AC01-E02 Be Your Own Boss

Your company, Blue Jean Landscaping, is a landscaping service that saves the customer money by employing the customer as a laborer. The company provides all plans and direction while the customer helps with the physical labor to cut costs and gain a sense of ownership of their new landscaping. In this exercise, you will take some time to analyze a business database and verify that the data is correct.

Open **AC01-E02-BJLand** from the **AC2013 Lesson 01** folder and save it as **AC01-E02-BJLand-[FirstInitialLastName]**.

- Ensure that the Large Equipment Query selects only equipment weighing more than 100 pounds.
- Using the Equipment Services Form, add **Spreader** to the Equip ID field for Pesticide Treatment.
- Add a new record for another landscape service and the corresponding tool/equipment of your choice.
- Remove Sprinkler Installation from the Services table.

You will be evaluated based on the inclusion of all elements, your ability to follow directions, your ability to apply newly learned skills to a real-world situation, your creativity, and your accuracy in creating objects and/or entering data. Submit your final files based on the guidelines provided by your instructor.

Transfer Your Skills

In the course of working through the Transfer Your Skills exercises, you will use critical-thinking and creativity skills to complete the assigned projects using skills taught in the lesson. To evaluate your mastery and completion of the exercises, your instructor may use a rubric, with which more points are allotted according to performance characteristics. (The more you do, the more you earn!) Ask your instructor how your work will be evaluated.

AC01-T01 Use the Web as a Learning Tool

Throughout this book, you will be provided with an opportunity to use the Internet as a learning tool by completing WebQuests. According to the original creators of WebQuests, as described on their website (WebQuest.org), a WebQuest is "an inquiry-oriented activity in which most or all of the information used by learners is drawn from the web." To complete the WebQuest projects in this book, navigate to the student resource center and choose the WebQuest for the lesson on which you are currently working. The subject of each WebQuest will be relevant to the material found in the lesson.

WebQuest Subject: Explore what Access databases are used for in industry.

Submit your final file(s) based on the guidelines provided by your instructor.

AC01-T02 Demonstrate Proficiency

Your employer, Stormy BBQ, bought out Grills R Us last year. You have discovered that Stormy BBQ's database tables still include the other company's obsolete merchandise, along with the new line of items. You need to remove the obsolete merchandise from the tables.

Stormy BBQ's signature line is staying on the books along with the new lines: Burner Grills and Fire Fly. The obsolete lines are Torchy Nites and Char-Cookery.

Open **AC01-T02-StormyBBQ** from the **AC2013 Lesson 01** folder and save it as **AC01-T02-StormyBBQ-[FirstInitialLastName]**. Update the company records using the Merchandise Form. Send the Merchandise Price report to a printer, save it as a new database object, or save it as a PDF or XPS file. Close the database and exit Access.

Submit your final file based on the guidelines provided by your instructor.

Designing a Database and Creating Tables

LEARNING OBJECTIVES

After studying this lesson, you will be able to:

- Plan, design, and create a relational database and associated tables
- Define and implement database normalization
- Define data relationships and primary and foreign keys
- Define and create an Entity Relationship Diagram
- Sort and filter records

Whether you are creating a new database to organize a soccer team or run a small business, it is essential to begin with careful planning. Successful projects often begin by examining existing business procedures and compiling a list of tasks to accomplish, designing an outline of how to accomplish those tasks, and making preparations to develop the final product. In short—analyze, design, and develop.

In this lesson, you will plan and design a database. You will gather information as needed to make a complete list of the required tables, records, and fields. You will define the data type for each field and assign ID fields so you can create relationships to link your tables. You will create several tables and enter records. Then, you will apply record sorts and filters.

Creating a Database

Winchester Web Design is a small website development company. The company specializes in websites for small businesses. The main deliverables are homepages (site navigation, overall website design, and cascading styles), secondary pages, blogs, and small business shopping carts.

Website designers must analyze a client's needs and desires before creating a website that includes the site homepage layout, navigation structure, and site styles. Once the homepage layout is determined, secondary pages can be developed. You have been asked to build a database for Winchester Web Design. As you begin your work, notice how the web design and development process has many similarities to designing a useful and efficient database: analyze, design, and develop.

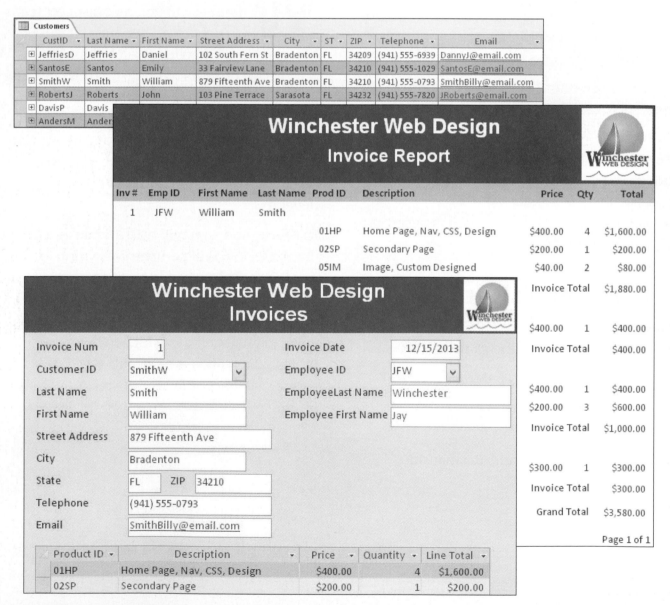

The Winchester Web Design database will contain tables from which forms, reports, and queries will be created.

Designing a Relational Database

Video Library   http://labyrinthelab.com/videos   Video Number: AC13-V0201

Early database programs stored data in one large, flat file similar to a spreadsheet. If a company sold merchandise and the same product was sold many times, these databases required a person to enter and store the same product description and product price for each transaction. Such repetitive data entry is time consuming and requires voluminous storage space.

Flat files also increase the chance of typos and are prone to inconsistent data. For example, just think of how many ways one might enter William into various tables: Will, Bill, Willy, Billy, or William. If you searched for all sales records for *William Smith*, you probably would not find the listing for *Bill Smith*.

InvNum	InvDate	EmpID	CustID	First Name	Last Name	ProdID	ProdDescription	Qty	Price	InvTotal
1	12/15/2013	JMM	SmithW	William	Smith	HP	Home Page	1	$400.00	$400.00
1	12/15/2013	JFW	SmithW	William	Smith	SC	Shopping Cart	2	$400.00	$800.00
1	12/15/2013	JFW	SmithW	William	Smith	BL	Blog	1	$300.00	$300.00
2	1/7/2014	MJW	SantosE	Emily	Santos	HP	Home Page	1	$400.00	$400.00

Flat file databases repeat data for each record. *Smith* is physically entered and stored three times in this table; the description and price are manually entered for each record.

The Employees table is related to the Invoices table via the EmpID field.

The Customers table is related to the Invoices table via the CustID field.

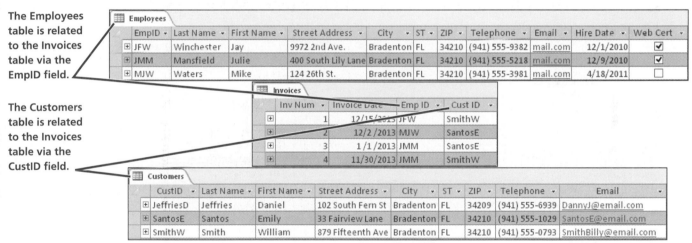

Well-designed relational databases separate data into linked tables to reduce storage space, data repetition, and potential errors.

What Is a Relational Database?

A relational database contains two or more tables that are linked (related) to each other by unique and identifying key fields, such as ProductID or Invoice Number. For instance, if you are adding a record to the Invoice table, you could select the ProductID from the linked Products table and also display the product description and product price. The product information is only stored once in the Products table, but it is available to all the tables, queries, forms, and reports that are linked in the database.

Access 2013

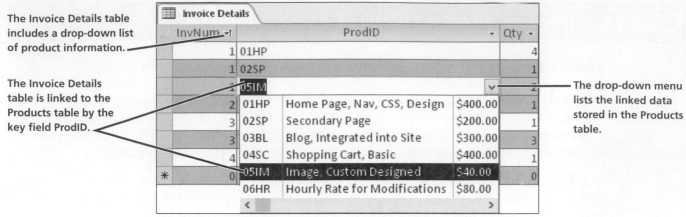

The Invoice Details table includes a drop-down list of product information.

The Invoice Details table is linked to the Products table by the key field ProdID.

The drop-down menu lists the linked data stored in the Products table.

You can select the key field ProdID to access the Product Description and Product Price from the Products table, without storing those two fields in the Invoice Details table.

Gathering Data

Before you create a database, you must analyze the needs of the business and the requirements of the database. You will need sample copies of employee records, customer records, product or service records, and any other pertinent documents or forms. You will need copies of every existing report, ranging from individual invoices to yearly sales summaries. You will also need a sketch, or mockup, of the complete layout for any new forms and reports that the business desires to add.

Samples of forms and reports collected at the start of a project. There may be handwritten forms as well.

This data gathering process must take place before you begin to design the objects in a database.

Collect Information for a New Database

In this exercise, you will use Microsoft Excel to create a list of the reports and forms needed to fully analyze the needs of your database. Of course, as a student, you will not have real documents; this is a brainstorming exercise. With this in mind, you will create a worksheet that represents the typical design process.

1. Start **Microsoft Excel 2013** and click **Blank workbook** in the Backstage view.

    If you do not have Excel 2013, you can use an older version of Excel.

2. Follow these steps to create a list of Winchester Web Design reports, records, forms, and relevant documents:

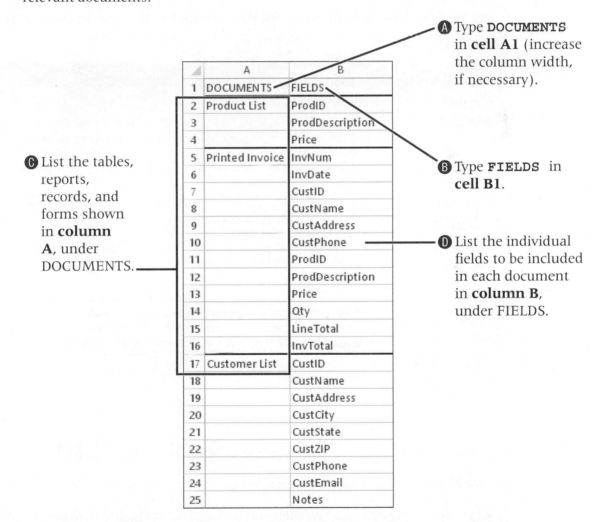

Ⓐ Type **DOCUMENTS** in **cell A1** (increase the column width, if necessary).

Ⓑ Type **FIELDS** in **cell B1**.

Ⓒ List the tables, reports, records, and forms shown in **column A**, under DOCUMENTS.

Ⓓ List the individual fields to be included in each document in **column B**, under FIELDS.

This figure shows only part of the data gathering process. Some fields may be included on more than one document, such as ProdID, ProdDescription, and Price.

3. Following the template above, after the last field in the Customer List, add a table named **Employees** that contains **Name** and **Address, Telephone, Email**, and **Hire Date** fields, and a **Yes/No Web Certification** field.

Access 2013

4. Click **Save** 🖫, navigate to your **AC2013 Lesson 02** folder, and save the workbook as
   `AC02-D01-WinWebDesign-[FirstInitialLastName]`.

   Replace the bracketed text with your first initial and last name. For example, if your name is Bethany Smith, your filename would look like this: AC02-D01-WinWebDesign-BSmith.

5. Keep the workbook open for the next exercise.

   Unless directed otherwise, always keep your working file open at the end of each exercise.

Importance of Good Database Design

Video Library   http://labyrinthelab.com/videos   Video Number: AC13-V0202

There are a few basic principles to guide you through the database design process. Follow the steps outlined here to create a database that will perform efficiently.

PRINCIPLES FOR GOOD DATABASE DESIGN	
Objective	**Description**
Separate Tables	Organize and separate data fields into tables with specific subjects (e.g., person, place, or product) so you can easily locate records and reduce redundant data and inconsistencies. Example: A small business may have an Employees table, a Products table, and an Invoices table.
Assign Keys	Set a unique key field for each main table to link to data in other tables. This is done so data are only entered and stored one time, saving time and disk space, and reducing data entry errors. Example: If the ProductID key field is entered into the Invoices table, the ProductDescription and ProductPrice can be linked from the Products table and displayed in an invoice.
Atomize Fields	Break fields into the smallest single values, called atomization. Example: Instead of a Name field that contains the value of Jay Winchester, create two fields—FirstName (Jay) and LastName (Winchester). This allows you to sort/search by LastName and, if desired, print a report without including FirstName.

Normalizing Databases

Video Library   http://labyrinthelab.com/videos   Video Number: AC13-V0203

Organizing tables and fields into their smallest distinct parts, and then efficiently linking the data together through the relationships of key fields, is called normalization. Normalization eliminates data duplication, decreases data entry errors and inconsistencies, reduces file size, and streamlines the search for necessary information.

As you add table fields, be aware that Access has reserved words, which have special meanings and cannot be used as field names. Examples of reserved words are *Name* and *Date*. If you need to use such fields, name them FirstName, LastName and BirthDate or HireDate, which are more descriptive.

When assigning field names, it is common practice to avoid using spaces, which you have no doubt noticed already. This is especially helpful when performing calculations on a field. For instance, a field named Hours Worked, almost looks like two fields (one named Hours and one named Worked). Consequently, most professionals would use the field name HoursWorked or Hours_Worked. Space can be easily added for readability when designing your forms and reports.

As you work through the activities in this lesson, you will begin to shape the relationships among database objects toward normalization.

DEVELOP YOUR SKILLS AC02-D02

Separate Data into Tables and Assign Key Fields

In this exercise, you will divide your gathered document data into tables, each of which describes a single category. You will break down each field into its smallest components, then name each field and assign them to the most appropriate table. Finally, you will add a unique identifying key field to each table.

1. In the **WinWebDesign** workbook, click the **New Sheet** ⊕ button.

2. Follow these steps to create a list of database tables and the fields that each table will contain:

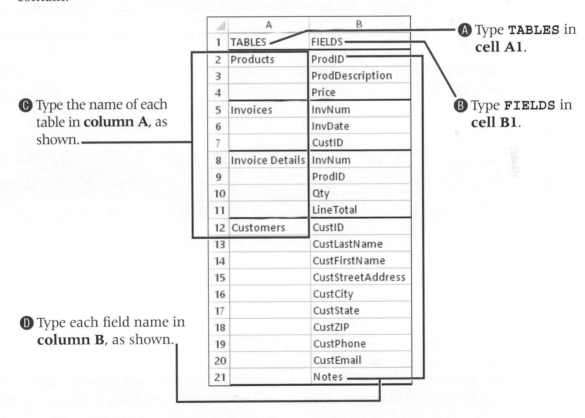

Ⓐ Type **TABLES** in cell **A1**.

Ⓑ Type **FIELDS** in cell **B1**.

Ⓒ Type the name of each table in **column A**, as shown.

Ⓓ Type each field name in **column B**, as shown.

	A	B
1	TABLES	FIELDS
2	Products	ProdID
3		ProdDescription
4		Price
5	Invoices	InvNum
6		InvDate
7		CustID
8	Invoice Details	InvNum
9		ProdID
10		Qty
11		LineTotal
12	Customers	CustID
13		CustLastName
14		CustFirstName
15		CustStreetAddress
16		CustCity
17		CustState
18		CustZIP
19		CustPhone
20		CustEmail
21		Notes

This figure shows only part of the normalization and data assigning process. With the exception of key ID fields, no field is listed more than once.

3. Enter the following fields for the **Employees** table:

- EmpID
- EmpLastName
- EmpFirstName
- EmpAddr
- EmpCity
- EmpST
- EmpZIP
- EmpPhone
- EmpEmail
- EmpHireDate
- EmpWebCert

4. Save ⊟ the workbook.

Planning Related Tables

Video Library   http://labyrinthelab.com/videos   Video Number: AC13-V0204

In most cases, determining the tables required for a database and identifying the data or fields each table should contain is relatively simple. After analyzing the business reports and forms for Winchester Web Design, you have determined that you will need an Employees table and a Customers table, in addition to a Products and an Invoices table. You have also identified which fields are required for each table. At this point you should examine each table and confirm that any unassociated data has been moved into a different but appropriate table.

Now you will link the tables with key ID fields so you don't have to enter the same names and products over and over. By establishing relationships between database tables, you prevent repeated data and redundant fields (except those key identifying fields that establish relationships between tables).

Linking Tables with Primary and Foreign Keys

Almost every database table should have a primary key field with a unique ID that will not be the same for any two database records. Your social security number and a student ID are examples of unique primary keys.

Primary Keys

Not everyone has a spouse or an email address, so some fields may remain null or empty. However, if a table contains a primary key, then a value must be entered for that key field every time a new record is added. Without a value, that record cannot be linked to any other table in the database. All taxpayers have a social security number; all students have a student ID.

Each time you create a new table in Datasheet View, Access automatically creates an ID field and marks it as the primary key field. When you manually create a table in Design View and do not assign a primary key field, Access asks if you want to create one before you save the table. By default, this primary key is the first field listed in a table and is assigned the AutoNumber data type. AutoNumber values start at 1 and are automatically increased by 1 for each subsequent record. You can also rename this field, change its data type, remove the primary key designation from the field, or assign the key to another field. The primary key field must contain data; the field cannot be empty.

Foreign Keys

As you review your Excel workbook, notice that most key fields (ProdID, EmpID, and CustID) are used in more than one table. In the Customers table, the CustID field is its unique primary key. However, individual customers will also need to be displayed in the Invoice table to show their purchases. A foreign key is a field in a secondary table that corresponds and links to the primary key field in the main table, where the specific information for a particular item is stored. The foreign key must be the same data type as the primary key, except in the case of AutoNumber. If the primary key is set to AutoNumber then the foreign key should be set to a Number data type with its Field Size property set to Long Integer.

Here, the CustID field in the Invoices table is a foreign key that links to the primary key in the Customers table to obtain the customer name, address, and customer contact information stored in the main table.

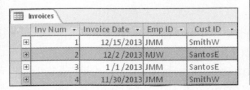

Inv Num	Invoice Date	Emp ID	Cust ID
1	12/15/2013	JMM	SmithW
2	12/2/2013	MJW	SantosE
3	1/1/2013	JMM	SantosE
4	11/30/2013	JMM	SmithW

Customers

CustID	Last Name	First Name	Street Address	City	ST	ZIP
JeffriesD	Jeffries	Daniel	102 South Fern St	Bradenton	FL	34209
SantosE	Santos	Emily	33 Fairview Lane	Bradenton	FL	34210
SmithW	Smith	William	879 Fifteenth Ave	Bradenton	FL	34210

If the primary key is a number, then the foreign key must also be a number; if the primary key is text, then the foreign key must also be text.

DEVELOP YOUR SKILLS AC02-D03

Assign Key Types to Key Fields

In this exercise, you will assign primary and foreign keys in the Winchester Web Design workbook.

1. Follow these steps to label the keys as primary or foreign:

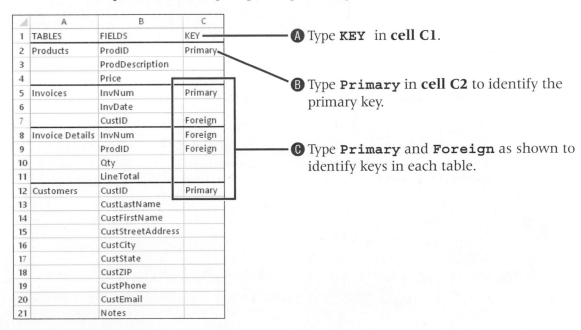

A Type **KEY** in **cell C1**.

B Type **Primary** in **cell C2** to identify the primary key.

C Type **Primary** and **Foreign** as shown to identify keys in each table.

2. Assign the primary key designation to the **EmpID** field in the **Employees** table.

3. **Save** 💾 the workbook.

Identifying Relationship Types

Video Library   http://labyrinthelab.com/videos   Video Number: AC13-V0205

Individuals and teams within organizations establish relationships to effectively interact and cooperate with other teams. The same is true of tables within an Access database—relationships must exist. Relationships in databases connect data in one table to data stored in other tables. Access supports three different types of relationships:

- One-to-one
- One-to-many
- Many-to-many

One-to-One Relationships

A one-to-one relationship means that each record in Table A can have only one matching record in Table B, and each record in Table B can have only one matching record in Table A. This is the least frequently used relationship. A one-to-one relationship requires both of the related fields to be primary keys. This relationship is generally used for storing information that applies only to one small portion of the main table, such as to isolate part of the table for security purposes. A good example of this is a main Customers table linked to a CustPassword table.

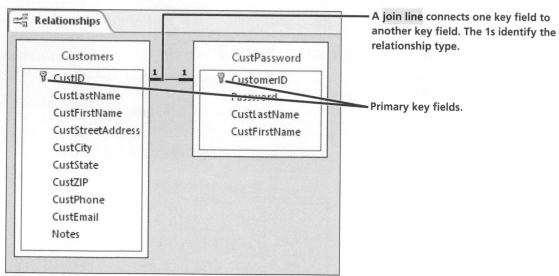

In this one-to-one relationship, each employee customer is only linked to one password.

One-to-Many Relationships

A one-to-many relationship means that each record in Table A can have multiple matching records in Table B, but a record in Table B can have only one matching record in Table A. For instance, one employee will have many sales, and a product will be sold many times. This is the most common type of relationship.

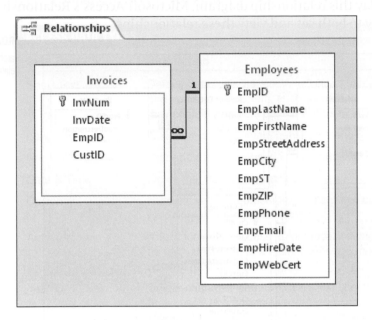

One employee may have many sales or invoices. The 1 on the join line for EmpID indicates *one* employee; the infinity (∞) symbol indicates *many* sales.

Many-to-Many Relationships

A many-to-many relationship occurs when two tables each have many matching records in the other table, but they do not share key fields, so they use a third *junction table* to tie other tables and complete the relationship. The junction table generally has a one-to-many relationship to each table. An example is a vendors table and a products table, where one vendor provides many different products and one product is available from many vendors.

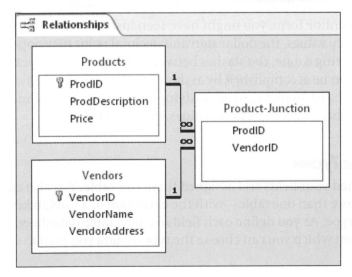

In this many-to-many relationship, items in the Products and Vendors tables each have a one-to-many relationship with the Product-Junction table. As a result, the business could buy the same products from multiple suppliers.

Access 2013

Define Data Types

In this exercise, you will assign data types and sizes to the fields in your Winchester Web Design workbook.

1. In your workbook, enter the data type of each field in **column D** as shown. Then, specify field sizes in **column E** (on the right).

	A	B	C	D	E
1	TABLES	FIELDS	KEY	DATA TYPE	SIZE
2	Products	ProdID	Primary	Short Text	4
3		ProdDescription		Short Text	25
4		Price		Currency	10
5	Invoices	InvNum	Primary	AutoNumber	6
6		InvDate		Date	8
7		CustID	Foreign	Lookup>Customers	15
8	Invoice Details	InvNum	Foreign	Integer	6
9		ProdID	Foreign	Lookup>Products	4
10		Qty		Decimal	auto
11		LineTotal		Calculated (Price*Qty)	10
12	Customers	CustID	Primary	Short Text	15
13		CustLastName		Short Text	25
14		CustFirstName		Short Text	25
15		CustStreetAddress		Short Text	25
16		CustCity		Short Text	25
17		CustState		Lookup>States	2
18		CustZIP		Short Text	5
19		CustPhone		Short Text	15
20		CustEmail		Hyperlink	40
21		Notes		Long Text	

The Notes field is a Long Text memo/comment field and has no entered size limit.

2. Assign the **Short Text** data type to these fields in the **Employees** table: EmpID, EmpLastName, EmpFirstName, EmpAddr, EmpCity, EmpST, EmpZIP, and EmpPhone.

3. Assign the **Hyperlink** data type to EmpEmail.

4. Assign the **Date & Time** data type to EmpHireDate.

5. Assign the **Yes/No** data type to EmpWebCert.

When in Datasheet View, tap [Spacebar] to check or uncheck a checkbox.

6. Assign the same field sizes you assigned to similar fields in the Customers table.

7. Save the workbook.

Creating Access Tables in a New Database

Video Library   http://labyrinthelab.com/videos   Video Number: AC13-V0207

Now that you have analyzed the needs of your new database and designed the structure for the tables, fields, and primary keys, you are now ready to create your database in Microsoft Access.

Creating a New Database

An Access database serves as a container that holds all the tools, data, and various database objects that help users enter and organize data and obtain meaningful information from that data. As a result, you must name and save the database when you create it. After you create a new database, Access automatically creates and opens an empty table, named Table1, in Datasheet View. When a table is created in Datasheet View, the first field, by default, is the AutoNumber data type.

DEVELOP YOUR SKILLS AC02-D05
Create a New Table in Datasheet View

In this exercise, you will create a new blank database and add an Invoices table in Datasheet View.

1. Start **Access 2013**.

2. Follow these steps to create and name the new database:

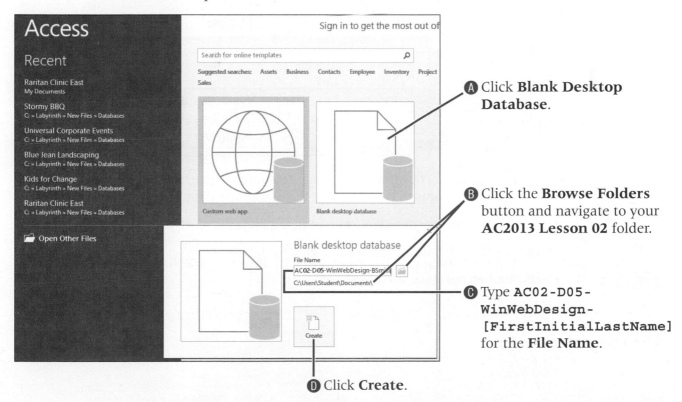

Ⓐ Click **Blank Desktop Database**.

Ⓑ Click the **Browse Folders** button and navigate to your **AC2013 Lesson 02** folder.

Ⓒ Type **AC02-D05-WinWebDesign-[FirstInitialLastName]** for the **File Name**.

Ⓓ Click **Create**.

In step c, remember to replace the bracketed text with your first initial and last name.

Access creates the new database, shows the database name in the application title bar, and creates a new table named Table1 in the Access window.

3. Follow these steps to add field names and set data type:

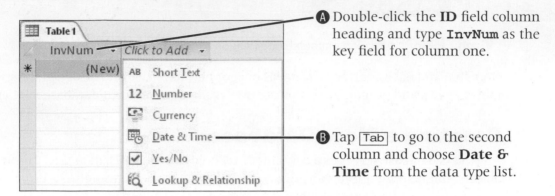

Ⓐ Double-click the **ID** field column heading and type **InvNum** as the key field for column one.

Ⓑ Tap Tab to go to the second column and choose **Date & Time** from the data type list.

Once the data type is selected, the heading Click to Add a new field is automatically named Field1.

4. Type **InvDate** as the new name for **Field1** in the second column and tap Tab to complete the name and move to a new field in the third column.

5. Choose the data type **Short Text** for the third field and change the field name to **EmpID**.

6. Tap Tab, choose **Short Text** for the fourth field and change the field name to **CustID**.
Full field names/column headings may not appear if the columns are narrower than the field name. Drag the right edge of the column heading to adjust column size.

7. Follow these steps to enter data in your new table:

Ⓐ Click in the first row under **InvDate** and type **12/15/2013**.

Ⓑ Tap Tab and type **JFW**.

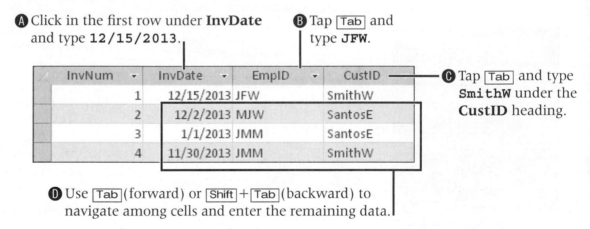

Ⓒ Tap Tab and type **SmithW** under the **CustID** heading.

Ⓓ Use Tab (forward) or Shift + Tab (backward) to navigate among cells and enter the remaining data.

When you create a table in Datasheet View, Access sets the first field as the Primary Key with an AutoNumber data type. Because InvNum uses the AutoNumber data type, Access fills in consecutive numbers automatically.

8. Follow these steps to save the table using a new table name:

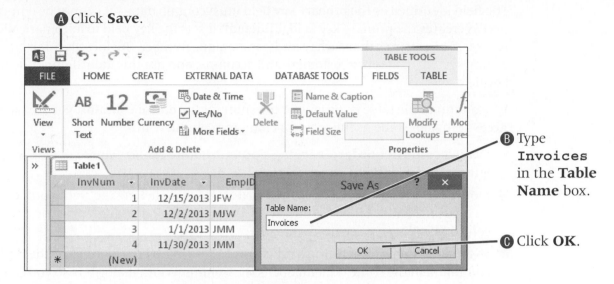

Ⓐ Click **Save**.

Ⓑ Type **Invoices** in the **Table Name** box.

Ⓒ Click **OK**.

The name in the object tab changes from **Table 1** *to* **Invoices**.

9. Click **Close** ☒ to close the table. Leave the database open.

Creating Tables in Design View

Video Library   http://labyrinthelab.com/videos   Video Number: AC13-V0208

Many people believe that it's easier to create a new table in Design View because it offers a straightforward layout and provides intuitive options for entering field descriptions, setting field properties, and easily setting or removing primary keys.

Entering Optional Descriptions

In Design View, descriptions may be added to each field in a table to help identify special information about a field. For example, in the Customers table, the customer ID consists of the customer last name plus the customer first initial. So you might enter the following description for the CustID field: ID = Last name and customer first initial.

Setting Field Properties

Once you assign a data type, you can modify the field's properties further. As you define each field in a database table, Access sets properties for the field that control the number of characters the field can contain as well as the format of the data and the type of characters that are valid for the field. You can accept Access default properties or modify the properties. Properties available depend on the data type selected for the field.

Access 2013

Requiring Data in Key Fields

The field identified as the primary key field must contain data—it cannot be empty. When Access creates the primary key field, by default it sets the key field to automatically number the records. This ensures that each record has a unique number. Businesses often create their own coding system to identify customers and accounts, and use this identifying code for the key field.

If a column in the table is too long or too short for the data it contains, you can adjust its width. Access provides some useful tools for changing column width.

- **Drag a column border:** Dragging a column border enables you to make the column on the left of the border wider or narrower.
- **Double-click a column heading border:** Double-clicking the right border of a column changes the width of the column on the left to fit the longest data entry in the column or column heading, whichever is wider.
- **Right-click a field heading and choose Field Width:** Selecting the Field Width command in the context menu opens the Column Width dialog box so you can type the desired column width, reset the standard column width, or select Best Fit to automatically size the field width to the longest entry.

DEVELOP YOUR SKILLS AC02-D06

Create a New Table in Design View

In this exercise, you will create a new table using Table Design View. Then, you will adjust the width of the columns in the table.

1. Choose **Create→Table Design**.

   Access opens an empty table in Design View.

2. Follow these steps to create the first table field, which will be the primary key:

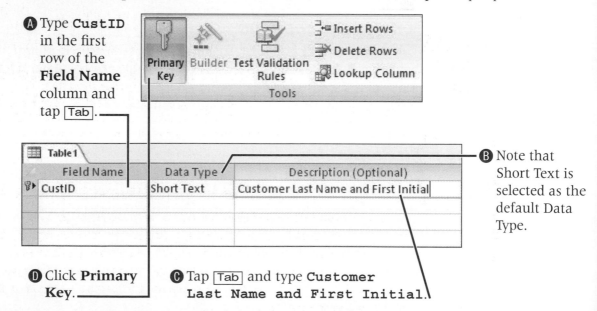

Ⓐ Type **CustID** in the first row of the **Field Name** column and tap Tab.

Ⓑ Note that Short Text is selected as the default Data Type.

Ⓓ Click **Primary Key**.

Ⓒ Tap Tab and type **Customer Last Name and First Initial.**

3. Tap ⎡Tab⎤ and repeat **step 2** to add the additional fields and field information shown here.

Field Name	Data Type	Description (Optional)
⚷ CustID	Short Text	Customer Last Name and First Initial
CustLastName	Short Text	
CustFirstName	Short Text	
CustStreetAddress	Short Text	
CustCity	Short Text	
CustState	Short Text	2 character state abbreviation
CustZIP	Short Text	5 digit ZIP code
CustPhone	Short Text	Area code and number
CustEmail	Hyperlink	
Notes	Long Text	Special comments

4. Click the CustLastName field and enter the values shown:

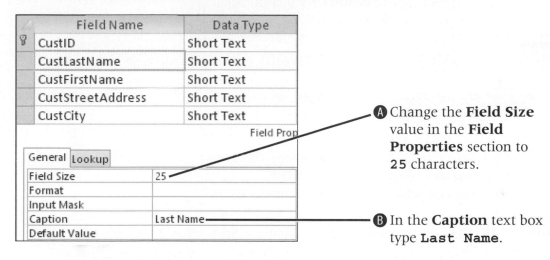

Ⓐ Change the **Field Size** value in the **Field Properties** section to **25** characters.

Ⓑ In the **Caption** text box type **Last Name**.

5. Repeat the procedure shown in **step 4** to change the caption properties of the following fields:

Field	Size	Caption
CustLastName	25	Last Name
CustFirstName	25	First Name
CustStreetAddress	25	Street Address
CustCity	15	City
CustState	2	ST
CustZIP	5	ZIP Code
CustPhone	15	Telephone
CustEmail		Email

6. **Save** 🖫 the table as **Customers**.

If you forget to save, Access will prompt you to save when you close the table.

7. Click the **View** drop-down arrow and choose **Datasheet View**.

8. Enter these records:

	CustID	Last Name	First Name	Street Address	City	ST	ZIP	Telephone	Email
⊞	AndersM	Anders	Mark	205 Montana St	Bradenton	FL	34211	(941) 555-2309	AndersM@email.com
⊞	DavisP	Davis	Peter	65 Terracotta Way	Sarasota	FL	34228	(941) 555-1792	DavisAngie@email.com
⊞	JeffriesD	Jeffries	Daniel	102 South Fern St	Bradenton	FL	34209	(941) 555-6939	DannyJ@email.com

Notice that the street address for DavisP is slightly cut off (the "y" in "Way" is difficult to make out). You will adjust column width next.

Change the Column Width

9. Follow these steps to change the width of two columns:

Ⓐ Double-click the column header between **Street Address** and **City** to auto size it.

	CustID	Last Name	First Name	Street Address	City	ST		ZIP	Telephone	Email
⊞	AndersM	Anders	Mark	205 Montana St	Bradenton	FL		34211	(941) 555-2309	AndersM@email.com
⊞	DavisP	Davis	Peter	65 Terracotta Way	Sarasota	FL		34228	(941) 555-1792	DavisAngie@email.com
⊞	JeffriesD	Jeffries	Daniel	102 South Fern St	Bradenton	FL		34209	(941) 555-6939	DannyJ@email.com

Ⓑ Click between the **ST** and **ZIP** header. The mouse pointer changes into a double-headed arrow. Drag the **ST** column header to the left to manually resize it.

10. Close the **Access** table and database. **Save** 💾 and close the **Excel** workbook.

Retrieving Data

Video Library http://labyrinthelab.com/videos Video Number: AC13-V0209

Whether you're processing an order, announcing statistics, or updating records, the primary purpose of any database is to be able to locate and retrieve data quickly and efficiently. Access provides three main tools and features for helping to locate and retrieve data.

- Sorting features
- Filtering tools
- Find and Replace commands

Sorting Records

Access automatically sorts records according to the primary key field identified when a table is created and fields are set up. You can also automatically sort tables by an AutoNumber as you enter records. The database sort feature enables you to rearrange table records based on data found in other table columns as well. Two main sort orders are available in Access.

■ **Sort Ascending:** Arranges data in alphabetical order from A to Z, in numeric order from lowest to highest, or in chronological order from first to last.

■ **Sort Descending:** Arranges data in reverse alphabetical order from Z to A, in numeric order from highest to lowest, or in reverse chronological order from last to first.

Sorting Records Using Tables and Forms

Regardless of whether you are working with a table or a form, the primary procedures for sorting records are the same.

Because the Winchester Web Design company is a small business with only a few employees, customers, and products, in the remainder of this lesson we will use the Raritan Clinic East database to get a better feel for the power of databases.

For the rest of this exercise, you will work with a Raritan Clinic East database.

DEVELOP YOUR SKILLS AC02-D07
Sort Records in a Table

In this exercise, you will sort records in the Raritan Clinic East database.

1. Open **AC02-D07-RCE** from the **AC2013 Lesson 02** folder and save it as **AC02-D07-RCE-[FirstInitialLastName]**.

2. Double-click the **Patients** table in the Navigation Pane to open it in Datasheet View.

3. Follow these steps to sort records alphabetically by last name:

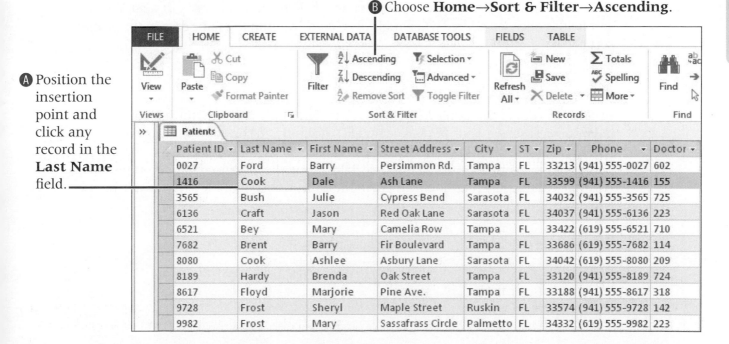

4. Follow these steps to set a descending sort order and then remove the sort:

A Click any record in the **Doctor** column.

B Choose **Home→ Sort & Filter→ Descending**.

C Click **Remove Sort**.

Records are rearranged in Patient ID order again—the default sort order.

Sorting Records Using Multiple Fields

Video Library   http://labyrinthelab.com/videos   Video Number: AC13-V0210

Data can be sorted in more than one table field at the same time. This can be useful, say, when more than one person in a family visits the same medical clinic. When this happens, selecting the first name field as a second sort field within a last name sort is appropriate. The last name field is the primary sort field and the first name field is the secondary sort field. The secondary sort field is only considered when multiple records contain the same data in the primary sort field.

How Multiple Column Sorts Work

Access sorts data in multiple fields from left to right. Consequently, the left column must be the one you want sorted first (primary sort field). Access then considers the second column (secondary sort field) only when it finds identical values in the primary sort field. You can perform more complex sorts on multiple fields using the Advanced Filter/Sort options, or sort multiple columns by rearranging them in the datasheet so that they appear side by side.

Task	Procedure
Sort ascending	Click in the desired field and choose Home→Sort & Filter→Ascending.
Sort descending	Click in the desired field and choose Home→Sort & Filter→Descending.
Clear sorts	Choose Home→Sort & Filter→Remove Sort.
Sort in multiple fields	Arrange the desired fields with the primary field left of the secondary field then select both field column headings and click the desired sort button.

DEVELOP YOUR SKILLS AC02-D08
Sort Records Using Multiple Fields

In this exercise, you will sort data in a table based on the values found in two columns.

1. Follow these steps to sort table records based on the values in multiple fields:

Ⓐ Click the **Last Name** column heading and drag the mouse to select the **First Name** column heading. Notice the downward pointing arrow as you drag the mouse.

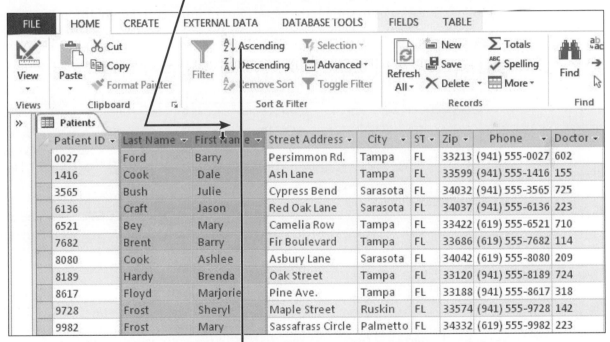

Ⓑ Choose **Home→Sort & Filter→Ascending**.

2. Review the record sort results to see the effect of sorting on two columns.

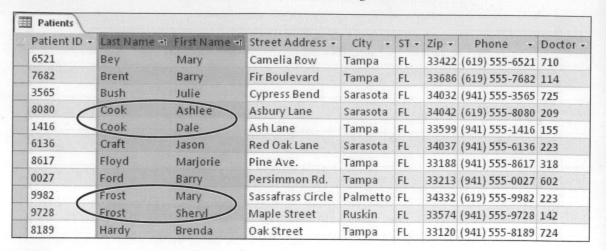

There are two patients named Cook and two named Frost. The patients with the same last names are also sorted alphabetically by first name.

3. Choose **Home→Sort & Filter→Remove Sort**. Click any value in the **Street Address** column to deselect both name columns.

4. Follow these steps to sort on the same two columns and obtain different results:

A Click the **First Name** column heading to select the column; then click and drag the column. left so that it appears to the left of the **Last Name** column. Click any other field to clear the selected column.

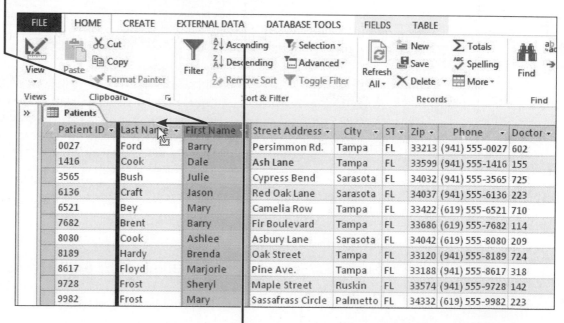

B Select both name columns and choose **Home→Sort & Filter→Ascending**.

The records appear in alphabetical order by first name—the Barrys are together and the Marys are together.

5. Click **Close** ☒ to close the Patients table.

Because you have changed the sort order a couple of times and then cleared the sorts, Access recognizes that you have changed the layout of the table and prompts you to save. If you click Yes, the changes will become part of the table design. You want to discard the changes.

6. Choose **No** in response to the prompt to save changes.

Filtering Records

Video Library   http://labyrinthelab.com/videos   Video Number: AC13-V0211

So far, you have sorted all the records contained in a table. When you work with large volumes of table data, there will be times when you want to locate a group of records that contain specific values in specific fields. Filtering enables you to select and work with a subset of records contained in a table.

Using the Filter Tools

The Filter tool lets you identify a value in a table field and tell Access to select only those records in the datasheet that contain the same value in the selected field. This process applies a filter to the table that hides (filters out) records whose active field contains data that does not match. For example, if you work with a database that contains thousands of records for consumers across the country, you could apply a filter to identify people who live in a specific state.

Access provides two types of methods for filtering records: Filter by Selection and Filter by Form.

■ Filter by Selection: Selects records based on the value contained in the active field in the table.

■ Filter by Form: Selects records based on values or conditions (criteria) you type into form fields. Access searches only the fields you specify.

Filtering Records by Selection

There are two basic ways to filter by selection. You can tell Access to select all records containing data that matches the value or selected text in the active field of the selected record. Or you can select all records containing any value *other than* the one selected. Access searches only the selected field to find matches.

Removing a Filter

If you close the table after you have applied a filter, Access prompts you to save changes to the table. You will often want to save changes, especially in cases where you widen or hide columns. However, filtering data in a table is typically a temporary view while you work with the data, so you do not want to save a filtered table. To remove a filter, choose Home, and in the Sort & Filter section, click the Advanced menu drop-down, then choose Clear All Filters.

Access 2013

Using the Toggle Filter Tool

The Toggle Filter tool in the Sort & Filter section of the Ribbon serves two purposes:

■ After you apply a filter, clicking the Toggle Filter button removes the filter and displays all records.

■ After removing a filter, clicking the Toggle Filter button reapplies the last filter applied.

In addition, when you point to the Toggle Filter button, a ToolTip displays to let you know what action you are performing. For example, when you point to the Toggle Filter button after applying a filter, the ToolTip displays *Remove Filter*. When you point to the Toggle Filter button after removing a filter, the ToolTip displays *Apply Filter*.

Filter Records by Selection

Two records in the Raritan Clinic East Doctors table contain an invalid zip code. In this exercise, you will filter table records, correct the zip code, and then remove the filter.

1. Open the **Raritan Clinic East Doctors** table.

2. Follow these steps to set a filter:

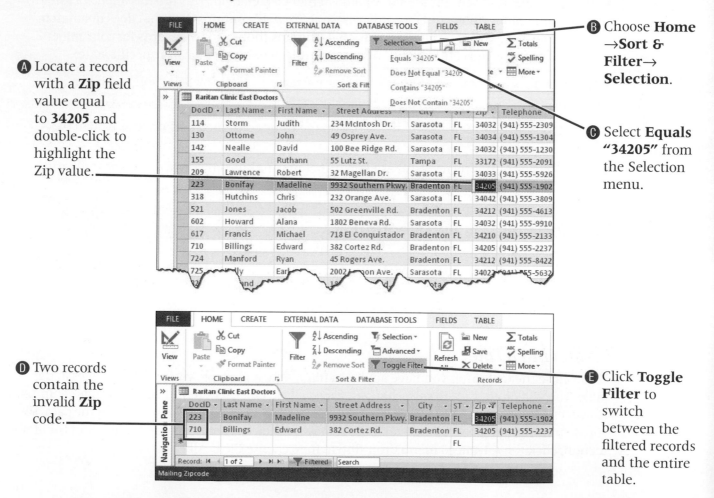

Ⓐ Locate a record with a **Zip** field value equal to **34205** and double-click to highlight the Zip value.

Ⓑ Choose **Home →Sort & Filter→ Selection**.

Ⓒ Select **Equals "34205"** from the Selection menu.

Ⓓ Two records contain the invalid **Zip** code.

Ⓔ Click **Toggle Filter** to switch between the filtered records and the entire table.

Access applies the filter immediately and displays two records that contain the value. The navigation bar indicates that the results are filtered.

3. Click the **Zip** field for each of the errant records and type **34207**.

4. Choose **Home→Sort & Filter→Advanced→Clear All Filters** ⟨icon⟩ to remove the filter and display all table records.

Filtering Records by Form

Video Library   http://labyrinthelab.com/videos   Video Number: AC13-V0212

Filter by Form allows you to select records based on values in multiple fields without rearranging the layout of table fields. When you filter by form, Access remembers the sort criteria. As a result, it is important to clear all filters after you apply this filter.

Identifying Comparison Operators

When you use the Filter by Form feature, you will often apply comparison operators so Access can locate the exact records or the range of records that contain the data you want to find.

COMPARISON INDICATORS AND SYMBOLS	
Comparison Symbol	**Description**
=	*Equal*: Records in the table must contain a value that equals the value you set for the field.
<	*Less than*: Records in the table must contain a value less than the value you set for the field.
>	*Greater than*: Records in the table must contain a value greater than the value you set for the field.
<>	*Unequal*: Records in the table must contain a value different from the value you set for the field.
<=	*Less than or equal*: Records in the table must contain a value less than or equal to the value you set for the field.
>=	*Greater than or equal*: Records in the table must contain a value greater than or equal to the value you set for the field.

The format of the Filter by Form entry palette depends on whether you are filtering from a table or from a form. If you are filtering from a table, a datasheet palette opens. If you are filtering from a form, a blank form opens.

Using Wildcards

Database users often want to locate records that contain data in a specific field which may contain additional text or data. To accommodate this, Access accepts the use of wildcards, such as the asterisk (*), which can be used to represent multiple characters, or the question mark (?), where each question mark represents a single character.

USING WILDCARDS TO LOCATE DATA

Example	Description
Will*	Finds all records with the search string text *will* at the beginning of the field value regardless of how many other characters follow it. This search string will find Will, Willy, and William.
*ill	Finds all records with the search string text *ill* at the end of the field value regardless of how many characters precede it. This search string will find Will, Bill, and Jill, but not Willy or William.
ill	Finds all records with the search string text *ill* anywhere in the field value, whether or not other characters appear before or after the search text. This search string will find Bill, Jill, Will, Willy, and William.
Will?	Finds all records with the search string text *will* at the beginning of the field value and with only one character after. This search string will find Willy but not Willie.
Will??	Finds all records with the search string text *will* at the beginning of the field value followed by exactly two additional characters. This search string will find Willie but not Willy or William.

DEVELOP YOUR SKILLS AC02-D10

Filter Records by Form

In this exercise, you will use a table to filter records by form.

1. If necessary, open the **Raritan Clinic East Doctors** table in Datasheet View.

2. Follow these steps to open the Filter by Form tool:

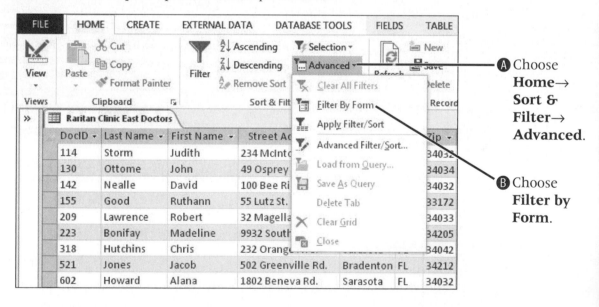

Ⓐ Choose **Home→ Sort & Filter→ Advanced**.

Ⓑ Choose **Filter by Form**.

A blank record opens.

AC02.28   Access 2013   Lesson 2: Designing a Database and Creating Tables

3. Follow these steps to filter and select records in which the City value is Sarasota:

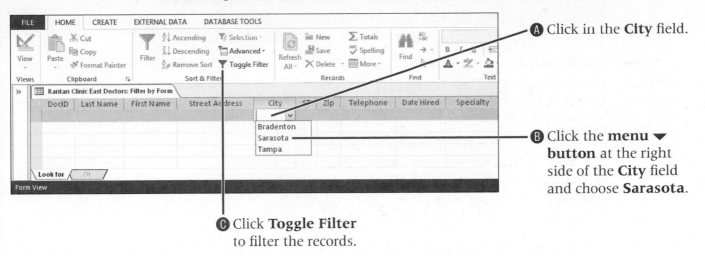

Ⓐ Click in the **City** field.

Ⓑ Click the **menu** ▼ **button** at the right side of the **City** field and choose **Sarasota**.

Ⓒ Click **Toggle Filter** to filter the records.

Access finds the records that meet the criteria and places a filter icon beside the field name.

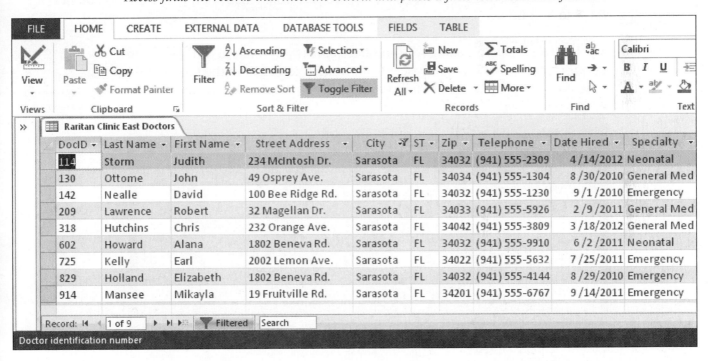

Only records with the City field value of Sarasota are displayed. Notice the Filter icon in the City heading to indicate that it is a filtered field.

4. Review the results then choose **Home→Sort & Filter→Advanced→Clear All Filters** 🖫.

Toggling the filter off does not remove the filter from the table; it just toggles between showing all the records and the filtered records. To remove a filter, choose Clear All Filters from the Advanced menu.

5. Click **Close** ✕ to close the table. Choose **No** when prompted to save.

Update Records with Find and Replace

Access' Find and Replace tool improves the efficiency of maintaining a database that constantly changes. Using this tool, you can easily locate, delete, and edit records.

When you have specific edits to make to individual records, finding the records and making the edits works well. There are also times when you need to update the data in one field for multiple records with the identical replacement data. For example, if the area code for a city changed, multiple records would need to be updated with the same value. The Replace command allows you to update these records by replacing existing data with new data. Use the Replace command to:

- **Replace:** Replace text for each occurrence of the search text, one at a time.
- **Replace All:** Replace all occurrences of the search text with the new text, all at the same time.

Use Replace All with caution to avoid unexpected results. For example, if you wanted to replace the area code 813 with 941, Replace All would also change the phone number 555-6813 to 555-6941.

FROM THE KEYBOARD

Ctrl + F to open the Find command page of Find and Replace

Ctrl + H to open the Find and Replace dialog box

The Find and Replace dialog box is probably already familiar to you. However, because data stored in a database is somewhat different from the text stored in other files, you will find some fields that are unique to the Access application.

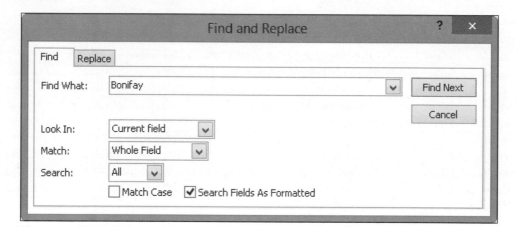

FIND AND REPLACE COMMANDS

Feature	Description
Find What	Enter the text, numbers, dates, and other values to locate.
Replace With	Finds a value and replaces it with a value you specify.
Look In	Search only in the active field or in the entire document.
Match	Search for only data matching the whole field, any part of the field, or at the start of the field.
Search	Search up or down from the active cursor (to the end of the table or to the beginning of the table) or the whole table.
Match Case	Matches the exact capitalization pattern you type.
Search Fields As Formatted	Search for data as it is displayed in the datasheet rather than as you type it. If you uncheck the box, you would find March 5, 2013, even if it Is formatted in the datasheet as 3/5/2013.

Update Records Using Find and Replace

After a long career, Dr. Bonifay (DocID 223) is retiring. In this exercise, you will use Find and Replace to transfer her patients to Dr. Lawrence (DocID 209).

1. Open the **Patients** table.

2. Click the **Doctor** column heading to select the field to search.
   You must select the field to search first.

3. Choose **Home→Find→** ab͓ac Replace

4. Follow these steps to locate and replace text with new values:

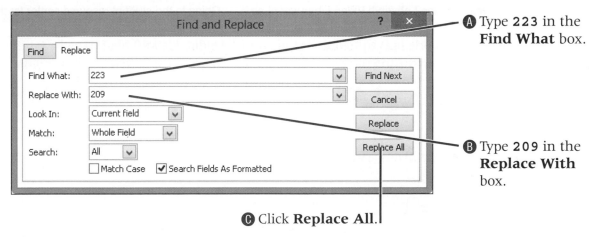

Ⓐ Type **223** in the **Find What** box.

Ⓑ Type **209** in the **Replace With** box.

Ⓒ Click **Replace All**.

Create a New Database and Add Tables

In this exercise, you will create a new database and add tables.

Before You Begin: You must complete Reinforce Your Skills AC02-R01 before beginning this exercise. If necessary, open your AC02-R01-K4C-[FirstInitialLastName] file in Excel.

Create a Database and a Table in Datasheet View

1. Start **Access**. Start a **Blank Desktop Database**, saving it as **AC02-R02-K4C-[FirstInitialLastName]** in your **AC2013 Lesson 02** folder.

   The new database opens and a new empty table named Table1 is open in Datasheet View.

2. Double-click **ID** in the first field heading of Table1 and type **StaffID**.

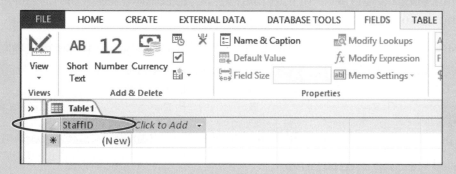

3. Press ⌈Tab⌉, keep the default data type **Short Text** in the next field and change the **Field1** heading to **StaffLastName**.

4. Press ⌈Tab⌉ and repeat the above steps to enter the remaining fields from the Staff table you created in your **AC02-R01-K4C** spreadsheet. (Possible field names that you might choose are shown below in step 6.)

   All the remaining fields in this table are the Short Text data type.

Remember to tap ⌈Tab⌉ after each field entry.

5. **Save** 🖫 the table as **Staff**.

6. Add the following records to the Staff table:

StaffID	StaffLastName	StaffFirstName	StaffAddress	StaffCity	StaffST	StaffZIP	StaffPhone	StaffAvail
1	Bryant	Matthew	12 E. MacIntosh	Sarasota	FL	34022	941-555-7523	Thursday
2	Earle	Kevin	77 Kingfisher	Sarasota	FL	34024	941-555-1368	Monday
3	Jacoby	Jane	4323 NW 63rd	Venice	FL	34222	941-555-5050	Tuesday
4	Pauly	Gerry	891 Waylon Lane	Bradenton	FL	34205	941-555-1988	Sunday

   Because StaffID is an AutoNumber data type, Access fills in consecutive numbers automatically. The StaffPhone field has not been formatted, so you must add the hyphens.

7. If necessary, double-click the line between the column headings to automatically resize the columns to display all the data.

8. Save and close ☒ the **Staff** table.

Create a Table in Design View

9. Choose **Create→Table Design**.

10. Enter **ChildID** in the first row of the Field Name column.

11. Tap [Tab] and leave the Data Type for ChildID as **Short Text**.

12. Tap [Tab] and in the Description field, type **ID = Last Name and First Initial**.

13. Click Primary Key to designate **ChildID** as the primary key field.

14. Enter the remaining fields, data types, and descriptions shown, choosing the **Date/Time** data type for **ChildBirthday**.

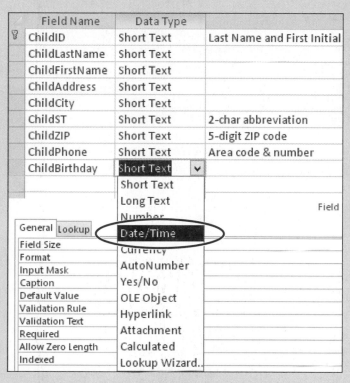

15. Click **Save** 🖫 and name the table **Children**.

16. Open the **Children** table in Datasheet View.

17. Enter these field values.

ChildID ▾	ChildLastName ▾	ChildFirstName ▾	ChildAddress ▾	ChildCity ▾	ChildST ▾	ChildZIP ▾	ChildPhone ▾	ChildBirthday ▾
CregerK	Creger	Kurt	503 Hillview	Sarasota	FL	34022	941-555-0245	10/12/2001
JonesP	Jones	Paul	892 Southern Pkwy	Sarasota	FL	34024	941-555-8929	09/03/1998
LangfordJ	Langford	James	43 Wisteria Way	Bradenton	FL	34209	941-555-1098	08/13/2000
PrestonW	Preston	Willy	162 Hamlet Lane	Sarasota	FL	34021	941-555-9372	03/11/2003

The ChildPhone and ChildBirthday fields have not been formatted, so you must add the hyphens and slashes.

18. Click **Close** ✕ to close the **Children** table. Exit both **Excel** and **Access**.

19. Submit your final file based on the guidelines provided by your instructor.

   To view examples of how your file or files should look at the end of this exercise, go to the student resource center.

Access 2013

Create New Tables and Enter Data

The staff director of Kids for Change would like you to add two new tables to the database, one that stores various community activities and one that stores parent volunteers. In this exercise, you will collect and organize the data needed for the lists, break down the data to its basic fields, and divide the fields into related tables. Then, you will create the tables.

Design and Normalize Database Tables

1. Start **Excel**. In a new blank worksheet, type a list of information to be included in a new **Volunteers** and a new **Activities** table. Break each piece of information into its smallest parts.

2. Type the **Volunteers** and **Activities** table names in **column A**.

3. Enter fields for each of the tables in **column B**. With the exception of key fields used to link tables, make sure no field appears in more than one table.

Relate Tables with Keys

4. Enter a key ID field for each table to show the relationships that should exist between tables. Indicate which fields are primary or foreign keys in **column C**.

5. Save the spreadsheet to your **AC2013 Lesson 02** folder as `AC02-R03-K4C-Excel-[FirstInitialLastName]`.

	A	B	C
1	Table	Field	Key
2	Volunteers	Vol ID	Primary
3		Vol Last name	
4		Vol First Name	
5		Vol Address	
6		Vol City	
7		Vol ST	
8		Vol ZIP	
9		Vol Phone	
10		Vol Avail	Foreign
11	Activities	Act ID	Primary
12		Act Name	
13		Act Day	Foreign
14		Act Time	
15		Act Address	
16		Act City	
17		Act Contact	

Your Excel worksheet should look similar to the figure above, though you may have different names.

Create a Table in Datasheet View

6. Start **Access**. Open **AC02-R03-K4C** from your **AC2013 Lesson 02** folder and save it as `AC02-R03-K4C-[FirstInitialLastName]`.

7. Choose **Create→Tables→Table** to create a new table in Datasheet View.

8. Double-click **ID** in the first field heading and type `VolID`.

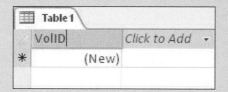

9. Press ⌷Tab⌷, choose the **Short Text** data type, and change the **Field1** heading to `VolLastName`.

10. Press ⌷Tab⌷ and repeat enter the remaining fields from the **Volunteers** table that you entered in **Excel**.

11. Save the table as `Volunteers`.

12. Add these records to the Volunteers table.

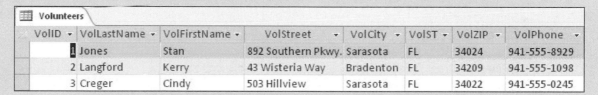

The VolPhone field has not been formatted, so you must add the hyphens.

13. Close the **Volunteers** table.

Create a Table in Design View

14. Choose **Create→Tables→Table Design** to create a new table in Design View.

15. Enter `ActivityID` in the first row of the **Field Name** column.

16. Tap ⌷Tab⌷ and leave the Data Type as **Short Text**.

17. Tap ⌷Tab⌷. In the **Description** field, type `Activity Initials + Activity Day`.

18. Set **ActID** as the primary key.

19. Enter the remaining **Short Text** fields from your **Excel** worksheet.

Field Name	Data Type	
⚷ ActID	Short Text	Activity Initials + Activity Day
ActName	Short Text	Name of Activity
ActLocation	Short Text	Where activity takes place
ActAddress	Short Text	**Street Address**
ActCity	Short Text	
ActDay	Short Text	Day of Week
ActTime	Date/Time	

Table 1

20. Choose **Date/Time** from the drop-down menu for **ActTime**.

21. Save the table as **Activities**.

22. Open the table in **Datasheet View** and enter these records.

Activities

ActID	ActName	ActLocation	ActAddress	ActCity	ActDay	ActTime
BCSat	Beach Cleanup	Coquina Beach	Gulf Drive	Bradenton	Saturday	9:00:00 AM
CCThu	Can Collection	Seabreeze School	72nd Street	Bradenton	Thursday	6:00:00 PM
ESSun	Eco-Bake Sale	DownTown Flea Market	Main Street	Sarasota	Sunday	8:00:00 AM
GWWed	Garden Work	All Angels Church	MacIntosh	Sarasota	Wednesday	5:00:00 PM

23. Close the table, saving changes if prompted. Then, exit **Excel** and **Access**.

24. Submit your final file based on the guidelines provided by your instructor.

Apply Your Skills

Plan and Design a Database

Universal Corporate Events is a corporate meeting and event planning service. They have hired you to build a new database to automate the company. In this exercise, you will create a new database and add a table that organizes the types of events that Universal Corporate Events plans.

Design and Normalize a Database

1. In **Excel**, create a list of all fields and information that you want to include in the database, such as event types, locations, a calendar or schedule, menu plans, and other relevant subjects.

2. Divide the data into four tables: **Staff**, **Events**, **Scheduling**, and **Menus**.

3. Determine the common key ID fields you will use to relate the tables to each other.

4. Assign a data type to each field.

5. Save the spreadsheet to your **AC2013 Lesson 02** folder as **AC02-A01-UniversalCorp-[FirstInitialLastName]**.

6. Exit **Excel**.

7. Submit your final file based on the guidelines provided by your instructor.

   To view examples of how your file or files should look at the end of this exercise, go to the student resource center.

Add Tables to a New Database

Now that you have collected and organized the data fields, you can create the database for Universal Corporate Events. In this exercise, you will create the new database, add an EventStaff table in Datasheet View, and then add a Menus table in Design View.

Before You Begin: You must complete Apply Your Skills AC02-A01 before beginning this exercise. If necessary, open yourAC02-A01-UniversalCorp-[FirstInitialLastName] file in Excel.

Create a Database and a Table in Datasheet View

1. Start **Access**. Open a **Blank Desktop Database** and save it as **AC02-A02-UniversalCorp-[FirstInitialLastName]** in your **AC2013 Lesson 02** folder.

2. Referring to your **AC02-A01-UniversalCorp** Excel workbook, enter the **Staff** table field names.

3. Save the table as **EventStaff**.

4. Enter these records in the **EventStaff** table.

StaffID	StaffLastName	StaffFirstName	StaffAddress	StaffCity	StaffST	StaffZIP	StaffPhone	StaffDay
1	Parker	Wesley	894 Second Ave	Ellenton	FL	34213	941-555-3009	Monday
2	Swenson	Tommy	10 Beacon Place	Palmetto	FL	34091	941-555-0915	Tuesday
3	Faulkner	Karen	458 Western Run	Bradenton	FL	34207	941-555-9723	Saturday
4	Trilman	Peter	72 Davison Way	Sarasota	FL	34222	941-555-1396	Wednesday
5	Dauntin	Rahim	442 Beneva Rd	Sarasota	FL	34901	941-555-9992	Tuesday
6	Blare	Trina	2921 Fruitville	Sarasota	FL	33218	941-555-4263	Monday

5. Close the **EventStaff** table, saving if prompted.

Create a Table in Design View

6. Choose **Create→Tables→Table Design**.

7. Enter the fields and data types for the Menus table from your **AC02-A01-UniversalCorp** workbook.

8. Designate **MenuCode** as the primary key field.

9. Save the table as **Menus**.

10. Open the table in **Datasheet View** and enter this data.

MenuCode	MenuPlan	Chg/PP
BRKBUF	Buffet Breakfast	17.00
DESSRT	Dessert Selections	14.00
DINBUF	Dinner-Buffet	45.00
LUNSIT	Luncheon w/Servers	34.00

11. Close the **Menus** table, saving it if prompted. Then, Exit **Excel** and **Access**.

12. Submit your final file based on the guidelines provided by your instructor.

To view examples of how your file or files should look at the end of this exercise, go to the student resource center.

Create a New Database and Add Related Tables

Every university and school has a giant database that stores data for students, faculty, classes, grades, and so forth. In this exercise, you will identify fields needed to store student data for such a database and group these fields into appropriate tables.

Design and Normalize a Database

1. Start **Excel**. In a new workbook, list the reports commonly generated by schools and universities, such as course schedules, grades, prerequisites, degree requirements, student aid, etc.

2. List data fields that would be required to generate the reports.

3. Determine the common key ID fields that can be used to relate the tables to each other.

4. Assign a data type to each field.

Create a Database and a Table in Datasheet View

5. Start **Access**. Create a new database named **A02-A03-SunStateU-[FirstInitialLastName]** and save it to your **AC2013 Lesson 02** folder.
    Access creates the new database, and opens a new table in Datasheet View.

6. In the new table, enter these fields and data types for university classes.

Field	Data Type
Department	Short Text
Class Number	Short Text
Section Number	Short Text
Building	Short Text
Room Number	Short Text
Start Time	Date/Time
End Time	Date/Time
Credit Hours	Number

7. Set **Department** as the primary key field.

8. Brainstorm and add at least four new records to the table.

9. Save the table as **Classes**.

10. Create a table in **Design View** containing these fields and data types, adding your own descriptions.

Field Name	Data Type	Description
ProfID	Short Text	
ProfLastName	Short Text	
ProfFirstName	Short Text	
ProfDept	Short Text	
ProfRank	Short Text	

11. Set **ProfID** as the primary key.

12. Save the table as **Professors**.

13. Close the **Classes** and **Professors** tables. Then, exit **Excel** and **Access**.

14. Submit your final file based on the guidelines provided by your instructor.

Extend Your Skills

In the course of working through the Extend Your Skills exercises, you will think critically as you use the skills taught in the lesson to complete the assigned projects. To evaluate your mastery and completion of the exercises, your instructor may use a rubric, with which more points are allotted according to performance characteristics. (The more you do, the more you earn!) Ask your instructor how your work will be evaluated.

AC02-E01 That's the Way I See It

Winchester Website Design is exploring expanding the number of items they currently recycle (cans, bottles, Styrofoam, paper, old electronics). To determine if there are additional ways to recycle, the company president has asked you to do some research. Go online and locate information about recycling in your state (recycling locations, contact persons, etc.). Plan the fields to include in a recycling information database. In Excel, create a spreadsheet that organizes your data into tables, along with key fields and data types. Save the spreadsheet as **AC02-E01-ExcelRecycle-[FirstInitialLastName]** in your **AC2013 Lesson 02** folder.

In Access, create a new database named **A02-E01-Recycling-[FirstInitialLastName]**. Create a table that includes fields for recycling locations throughout the state and a contact name for the person in charge of the recycling facility. Enter data for at least three sites/companies. Finally, add a record containing your school as a site/company and your name as the contact.

You will be evaluated based on the inclusion of all elements, your ability to follow directions, your ability to apply newly learned skills to a real-world situation, your creativity, and your accuracy in creating objects and/or entering data. Submit your final files based on the guidelines provided by your instructor.

AC02-E02 Be Your Own Boss

You are the owner of Blue Jean Landscaping and have decided to sponsor the Sarasota Service Guild, a nonprofit organization created to raise money to help adults with disabilities. The guild has successfully raised more than $60,000 annually through sponsoring an historic home tour. They would like a database that will enable them to track memberships, donations from businesses, ticket sales, etc. You can help them plan their database by identifying fields, such as donor names and tour schedules, and tables, such as Members and Tour Home Addresses. Using Excel, identify sample tables that need to be included in the database and the fields that you would place in each table, assign primary and foreign keys to relate the tables, and select data types for each field. Save the Excel spreadsheet as **AC02-E02-BJLandscaping-[FirstInitialLastName]** in your **AC2013 Lesson 02** folder. Once you have designed the database in Excel, start Access and create a new database named **AC02-E02-BJLandscaping-[FirstInitialLastName]**. Add the tables that you included in your Excel spreadsheet.

You will be evaluated based on the inclusion of all elements, your ability to follow directions, your ability to apply newly learned skills to a real-world situation, your creativity, and your accuracy in creating objects and/or entering data. Submit your final files based on the guidelines provided by your instructor.

Transfer Your Skills

In the course of working through the Transfer Your Skills exercises, you will use critical-thinking and creativity skills to complete the assigned projects using skills taught in the lesson. To evaluate your mastery and completion of the exercises, your instructor may use a rubric, with which more points are allotted according to performance characteristics. (The more you do, the more you earn!) Ask your instructor how your work will be evaluated.

AC02-T01 Use the Web as a Learning Tool

Throughout this book, you will be provided with an opportunity to use the Internet as a learning tool by completing WebQuests. According to the original creators of WebQuests, as described on their website (WebQuest.org), a WebQuest is "an inquiry-oriented activity in which most or all of the information used by learners is drawn from the web." To complete the WebQuest projects in this book, navigate to the student resource center and choose the WebQuest for the lesson on which you are currently working. The subject of each WebQuest will be relevant to the material found in the lesson.

WebQuest Subject: Design elements of a high-quality Access database.

Submit your final file(s) based on the guidelines provided by your instructor.

AC02-T02 Demonstrate Proficiency

Stormy BBQ wants to modernize its business. They have hired you to design and create a database for their BBQ restaurant. Using Excel, plan the new database. Then, in Access, create three tables: one for staff/employees, one for the menu, and one for customer information. Brainstorm and add at least six records to each table (make it up). Relate the menu and customer tables using a customer favorite ID.

Save the database to your **AC2013 Lesson 02** folder as **AC02-T02-StormyBBQ-[FirstInitialLastName]**. Submit your final file based on the guidelines provided by your instructor.

Working with Forms

LEARNING OBJECTIVES

After studying this lesson, you will be able to:

- Identify form design elements
- Create and print forms
- Modify form controls and layout
- Create a multiple item form and a split form
- Use Microsoft Access Help

Forms are part of our everyday lives. If you have ever entered your personal information on a college application, filled out a loan application, or purchased an item from an online retailer, you have used a form. You also use forms to sign up for Facebook, Flickr, and Gmail accounts. A form ideally provides an attractive and easy-to-use interface, which allows a user to enter one record at a time into a table.

In this lesson, you will create an Access form from scratch based upon an existing table. You will use the Form tools to modify the font, color, and size of the text, text boxes, and other objects on the form. Then you will create forms using the different methods provided in Access.

Designing Forms at Winchester Web Design

As the information technology (IT) director at Winchester Web Design, you are responsible for designing and formatting the forms and reports in the company database to make them more attractive, consistent, and user-friendly. Part of your job is to customize forms so that they better identify the company. To accomplish this, you plan to create a consistent color scheme and add the corporate name and logo to all the company's forms.

Drafts of some of the sample forms that you plan to create are shown below.

Exploring Form Design

Video Library   http://labyrinthelab.com/videos   Video Number: AC13-V0301

A form is a database object used to enter, edit, or view the data for an individual record. Focusing on one record at a time allows you to design a layout that is more convenient and attractive than the row and column arrangement of a table in Datasheet View.

Examining Form Views

Both Form Design View and Layout View provide tools for designing and modifying new forms. You cannot edit or enter data in either view.

When you open an existing form in Design View, Access displays a palette that contains the text and the fields used on the form. By default, the palette background contains dots that you can use to align fields neatly. A Field List showing all the fields in all the database tables can be opened while in Design View so you can drag and position fields on the form.

Layout View displays actual sample data values in the form fields as you are editing. This makes it easier to adjust the placement and size of controls so data displays correctly and attractively.

DEVELOP YOUR SKILLS AC03-D01
Display Form Views

In this exercise, you will open an existing form in Design View, in Layout View, and in Form View. You will examine controls on the form and explore the available tools in each view.

1. Open **AC03-D01-WinWebDesign** from the **AC2013 Lesson 03** folder and save it as **AC03-D01-WinWebDesign-[FirstInitialLastName]**.

   Replace the bracketed text with your first initial and last name. For example, if your name is Bethany Smith, your filename would look like this: AC03-D01-WinWebDesign-BSmith.

2. If a Security Warning appears, click **Enable Content**.

3. Right-click the **Employees Form** in the Navigation Pane and choose **Design View**.

Access 2013

4. Follow these steps to view the Form Design tools:

ⓐ Click the **Form Selector** button to select the entire form.

ⓑ Click the **Form Header** selector button to make the header section active.

ⓒ Click the **Detail selector button** to make the detail section active.

ⓓ Click the **Design** tab, if necessary.

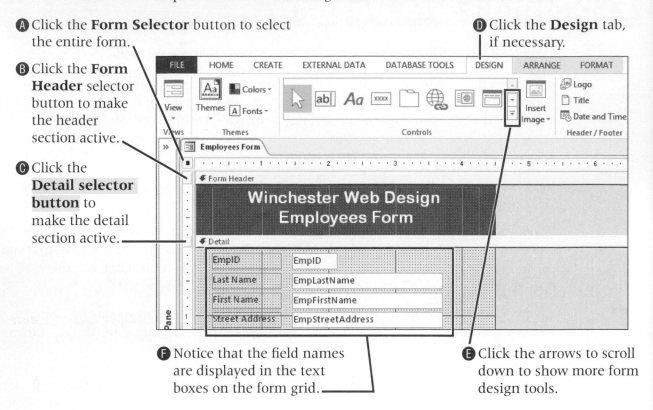

ⓕ Notice that the field names are displayed in the text boxes on the form grid.

ⓔ Click the arrows to scroll down to show more form design tools.

5. Follow these steps to open the form in Layout View:

ⓐ Click the **View menu** ▼ button and choose **Layout View**.

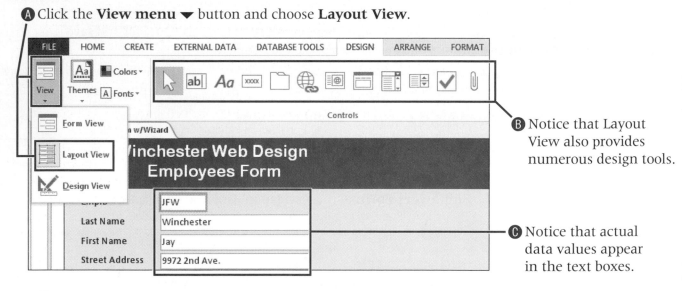

ⓑ Notice that Layout View also provides numerous design tools.

ⓒ Notice that actual data values appear in the text boxes.

From this point forward, instructions for switching views will simply direct you to switch to the appropriate view. For example, "Switch to Design View" or "Switch to Layout View."

6. Choose **Views→View→Form View**.

7. Keep the **Employees Form** open for the next exercise.

Unless directed otherwise, keep Access and any databases or database objects being used open at the end of each exercise.

The Property Sheet

Video Library   http://labyrinthelab.com/videos   Video Number: AC13-V0302

In Design View, Access provides a Property Sheet that contains attributes that control the appearance of different components of a form, each of its sections, and all controls on it. You can adjust colors, fonts, sizes, and other features on a form through the Property Sheet.

As you work on a form in Design View, it is important to know the key elements associated with form design. Each form in an Access database organizes data by sections and contains controls to display data and other items on the form.

BASIC FORM ELEMENTS

Element	Description
Sections	The main parts of a form, such as the Form Header, Form Footer, Detail, Page Header, and Page Footer. Section bars separate form sections.
Form Header	The top section with constant information, such as a title. It may also contain a logo, decorative line, or color scheme.
Form Footer	The bottom section that appears on the last page (or the first page of a one-page form). It might contain a summary or grand total. Unlike report footers, form footers are seldom used.
Page Header	The section that contains text and fields that repeat at the top of every *printed* page of an individual record displayed in the form, such as page number and perhaps the date. Page headers are not frequently used on forms.
Page Footer	The section contains text and fields that repeat at the bottom of every *printed* page of an individual record displayed in the form, such as page number and date. Unlike reports, page footers are seldom used in forms.
Detail section	The main section of a form that contains the text boxes that display data from database tables. Content values vary from record to record.
Controls	Items that display data, text, checkboxes, lines, images, and buttons.
Label	The part of a control that contains a caption identifying the data displayed in a text box or checkbox. By default, the label is either the field name or caption from the source table. For example, the caption *Last Name* (with a space) is a good label for the *LastName* field (no space). Label text cannot be edited in Form View.
Text Box	The control that displays the actual data from a table. The record source for a text box is a corresponding field in an underlying table. For example, *Smith* might be the data displayed in the *LastName* text box. Data can only be entered into a text box in Form View.
Bound control	A control that ties, or binds, form data to table data so the data appears on the form (i.e., the *LastName* text box is bound to the *LastName* field in the source table). Bound controls normally appear in the Detail section.
Unbound control	An item that is independent of any table data. Unbound controls can be text, shapes, and images, and may appear in any form section.
Calculated control	A control that is tied to a calculated field or expression built in a query (i.e., *Total= [Price]*[Quantity]* where *Total* is a text box and *Price* and *Quantity* are bound controls). Calculated controls normally appear in the Detail or Form Footer section of the form.

Access 2013

Examine Form Elements

In this exercise, you will open the Property Sheet for a form in Design View. You will select different sections and controls on the form and examine their properties.

1. Open the **Employees Form** in **Design View**.

2. If the Properties Sheet is not displayed, choose **Design→Tools→Property Sheet**.

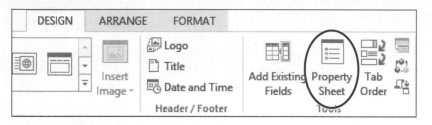

3. Follow these steps to examine the properties of the form:

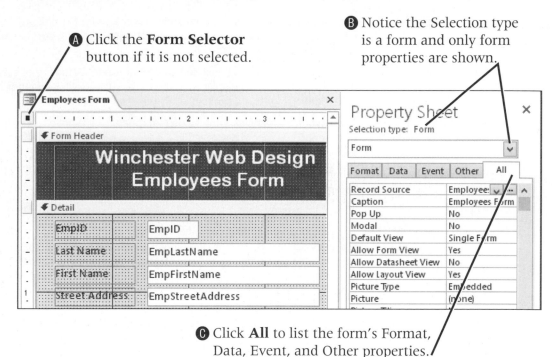

Ⓐ Click the **Form Selector** button if it is not selected.

Ⓑ Notice the Selection type is a form and only form properties are shown.

Ⓒ Click **All** to list the form's Format, Data, Event, and Other properties.

4. Click the **Last Name** label on the form grid.

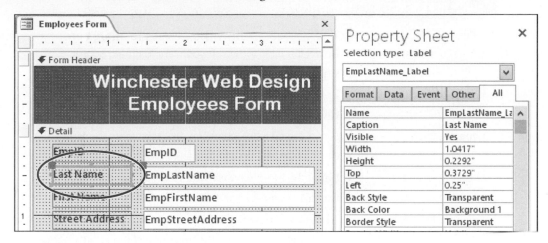

The Property Sheet now lists information about the selected control.

5. Close ⌧ the Employees form.

Creating Forms

Video Library　http://labyrinthelab.com/videos　Video Number: AC13-V0303

Access provides a number of ways to create forms. A quick and simple form can be created by clicking the record source name in the Navigation Pane and choosing Create→Form. Access then generates a basic form, which contains all the fields from the record source listed in order and in a uniform layout. For those who prefer a more hands-on approach, you can create a form in Design View, Layout View, or with the help of a Form Wizard.

FROM THE RIBBON

Create→Forms→Form to create a simple form

Another way to create a form is to right-click an existing form in the Navigation Pane and then use the Copy and Paste commands. To rename an existing form, right-click on the form in the Navigation Pane, select Rename, and then type the new name.

Identifying a Record Source

Every form in an Access database obtains its data from the primary source—one or more tables. The field property that contains and displays the fields and data in a form is called the record source. Normally a form contains fields from one table or one query. However, when a relationship exists between two database tables, you can access fields in the related tables. An example is an Invoice form that displays data from the Invoice, Products, Customers, and Employees tables.

Task	Procedure
Create a simple form	▪ Select the table for which you want to create a form. ▪ Choose Create→Forms→Form ▣.
Create a form using the Form Wizard	▪ Select the table for which you want to create the form. ▪ Choose Create→Forms→Form Wizard ▣.
Create a form in Layout View	▪ Select the table for which you want to create the form. ▪ Choose Create→Forms→Blank Form ▣.
Create a form in Design View	▪ Select the table for which you want to create a form. ▪ Choose Create→Forms→Form Design ▣.
Create a form from an existing form	▪ Right-click an existing form in the Navigation Pane and choose Copy. ▪ Use Paste to create another instance of the form; rename it as desired.
Create a multiple item form	▪ Choose Create→Forms→More Forms→Multiple Items ▣.
Create a split form	▪ Select the table for which you want to create the form. ▪ Choose Create→Forms→More Forms→Split Form ▣.

DEVELOP YOUR SKILLS AC03-D03

Create a Simple Form

In this exercise, you will use the quickest and easiest method to create a simple form using the Employee Spouses table.

1. Select the **Employee Spouses** table in the Navigation Pane.

2. Choose **Create→Forms→Form**.

   Access creates a simple, basic form and opens it in Layout View.

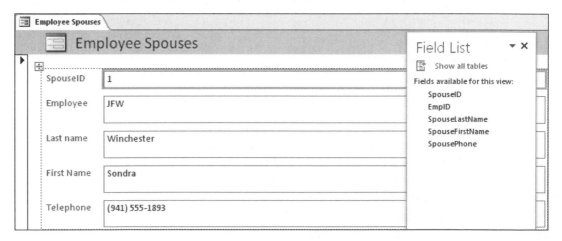

   Depending on your last Access session, the Field List may or may not show.

3. **Save** ▣ the new form as **SpousesSimpleForm**.

4. Close the form.

   You will modify form layouts later in this lesson.

Using the Form Wizard

Video Library   http://labyrinthelab.com/videos   Video Number: AC13-V0304

When you use the Form Wizard to create a form, the wizard walks you through the process of selecting the table or query that contains the specific fields and data you want to include on the form. Then Access places all the fields that you select from the source table or query onto the form.

Although you have complete freedom in field selection and placement when you create a form in Design View, many people prefer the ease of using the Form Wizard to initially select and place all the fields, and later use Form Design View to modify the layout and elements on the form. Regardless of which procedure you prefer, the techniques for building and designing the form—working with controls, setting properties, adding pictures, and so forth—are the same.

DEVELOP YOUR SKILLS AC03-D04
Create a Form Using the Form Wizard

In this exercise, you will create a form with the Form Wizard that displays all the fields from the Customers table.

1. Follow these steps to open the Form Wizard and add table fields:

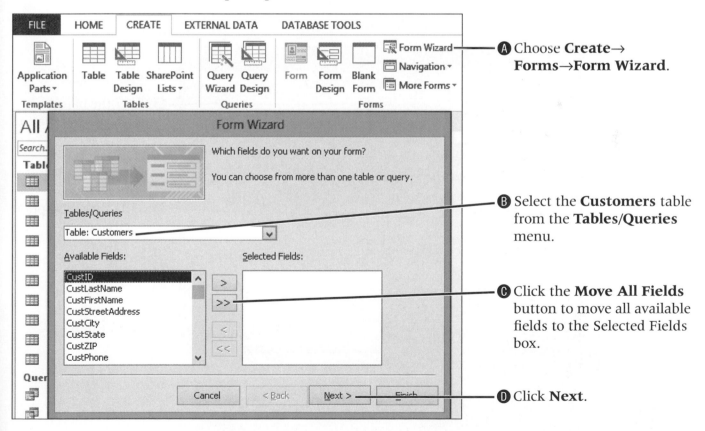

Ⓐ Choose **Create→ Forms→Form Wizard**.

Ⓑ Select the **Customers** table from the **Tables/Queries** menu.

Ⓒ Click the **Move All Fields** button to move all available fields to the Selected Fields box.

Ⓓ Click **Next**.

2. Leave the **Columnar** option selected and click **Next**.

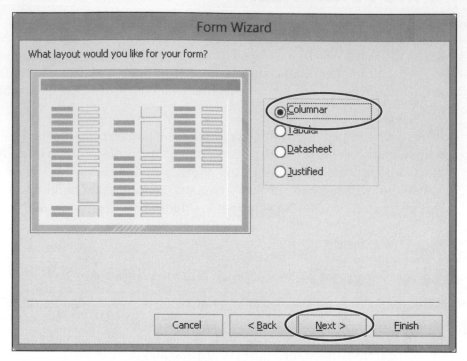

3. Follow these steps to name the form and open it in Form View:

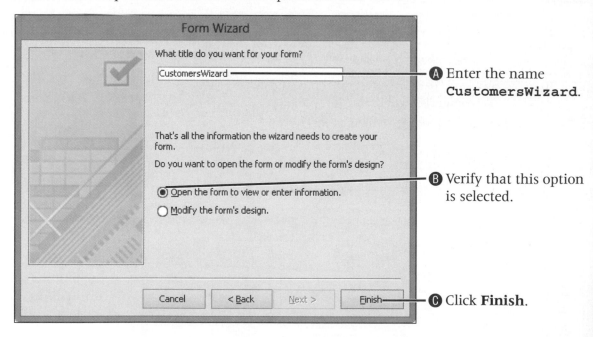

Ⓐ Enter the name **CustomersWizard**.

Ⓑ Verify that this option is selected.

Ⓒ Click **Finish**.

The form opens in Form View.

Customers

CustomersWizard

CustID	AndersM
Last Name	Anders
First Name	Mark
Street Address	205 Montana St
City	Bradenton
ST	FL
ZIP	34211
Telephone	(941) 555-2309
Email	AndersM@email.com
Notes	

4. **Close** ⊠ the CustomersWizard form.

Working with Form Controls

Video Library   http://labyrinthelab.com/videos   Video Number: AC13-V0305

Access provides three basic types of controls that you can add to forms: bound controls, unbound controls, and calculated controls. Bound controls tie form data to the source table data so that the data appears on the form. Unbound controls are independent of table data. Unbound controls can be text, shapes, and images, and may appear in any form section. A calculated control uses data from other fields to perform a calculation (i.e., Total=[Price]*[Quantity] where Total is a text box for the calculated control, and Price and Quantity are bound controls linked to fields in a table). Calculated controls normally appear in the Detail or Form Footer section of the form.

Adding Bound Controls to Forms

If you create a blank form, you will have to add all the controls to the form yourself—building the form from scratch. If you want to customize an existing form, you may also need to add controls to the form. These controls might be extra fields required to display additional data or they might be descriptive text and graphics. The fields used with bound controls appear in the Field List pane that opens when you create a new form and display it in Design View. To add a field to the form, you click it in the Field List panel, drag it onto the palette, and position it where you want it on the form.

Moving and Sizing Controls

When you create a form using the Form Design, Blank Form, or Form Wizard commands, you can easily move and resize text boxes and labels. Sizing controls in Access is similar to sizing drawn objects in other programs. You select the control and Access displays handles on the corners and sides of the control. You can drag the handle to resize the control. Because each bound control contains two parts by default—the label and the text box—you can size each part separately. You can also resize an object by selecting it, then resetting the Width and Height properties for the field in the Property Sheet.

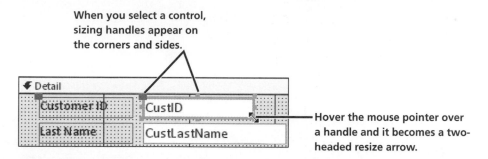

When you select a control, sizing handles appear on the corners and sides.

Hover the mouse pointer over a handle and it becomes a two-headed resize arrow.

It is a bit trickier to move and resize text boxes and labels if you create a simple form by choosing the Form command, instead of using the Form Design, Blank Form, or Form Wizard commands. Quick forms tie all the automatically inserted text boxes and corresponding labels into one group. You can move the entire group but not the individual controls. In order to move or resize an individual control you must ungroup these controls using the Remove Layout command.

Moving and positioning controls on a form is similar to resizing a control. The main difference is that the mouse pointer appears as a white select arrow on a black move arrow when it is positioned to move a control. This permits you to move both the text box and its associated label together.

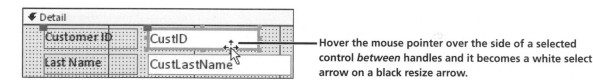

Hover the mouse pointer over the side of a selected control *between* handles and it becomes a white select arrow on a black resize arrow.

Selected controls are identified by the thick, usually orange border and the handles on their sides and corners. You may have noticed that the top-left handle is larger than other handles on the selected control and is usually gray. This larger handle enables you to separate the label from the text box, moving each part of the control individually to position it where you want it.

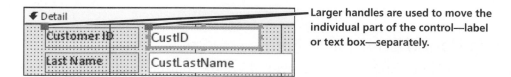

Larger handles are used to move the individual part of the control—label or text box—separately.

When you create a form in Design View, Access opens an empty form palette and the Field List pane. Design View enables you to drag fields from the Field List onto the form, modify existing fields, arrange fields, and build the form manually. If you click the Show All Tables option at the top of the Field List, Access displays a list of related tables at the bottom of the list of fields.

Although you have more control in Design View, it can be far more time consuming than using the Form Wizard.

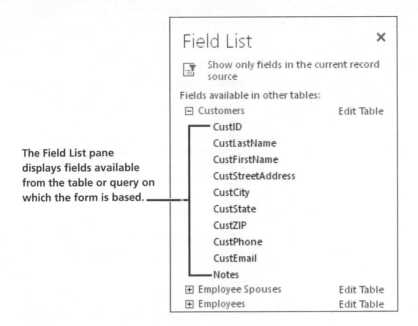

The Field List pane displays fields available from the table or query on which the form is based.

Create a Form Using Form Design

In this exercise, you will create a form in Design View for the Customers table. Then you will move and size the controls on the form.

1. Choose **Create→Forms→Form Design** .

   Access opens a new form in Design View.

2. Follow these steps to open the Field List pane and select the Customers table:

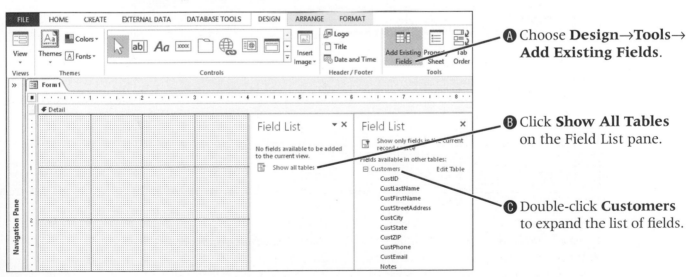

Ⓐ Choose **Design→Tools→ Add Existing Fields**.

Ⓑ Click **Show All Tables** on the Field List pane.

Ⓒ Double-click **Customers** to expand the list of fields.

Access 2013

3. Follow these steps to add a field to the blank form:

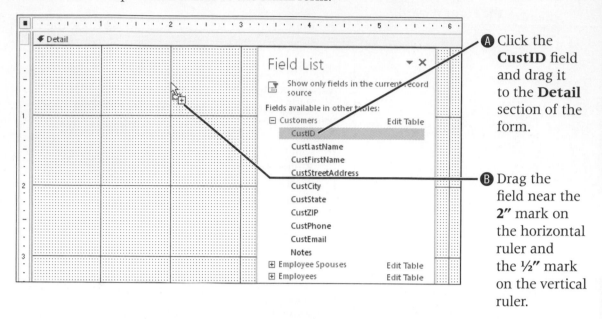

Ⓐ Click the **CustID** field and drag it to the **Detail** section of the form.

Ⓑ Drag the field near the **2″** mark on the horizontal ruler and the **½″** mark on the vertical ruler.

A plus symbol or crosshair appears just below the mouse pointer indicating it is copying the field. Each field you drag to the form grid includes a label control.

4. Repeat the procedures outlined in **step 3** to add the remaining fields as shown here and close the **Field List** pane.

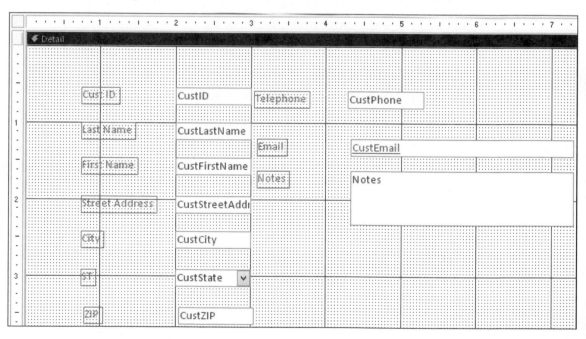

Don't worry about the alignment at this point. Next, you will move and arrange the Cust ID label and CustID text box to a location that makes them distinctively stand out on the form.

5. Follow these steps to move the label control separately from the text box control:

Ⓐ Click the **Cust ID** label control to select it.

Ⓑ Use the ruler as a guide.

Ⓒ Drag the label by the top-left corner handle to the approximate position on the form.

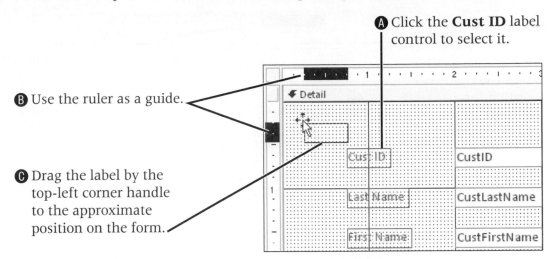

6. Repeat the procedures outlined in **step 5** to move the **CustID** text box under the **Cust ID** label.

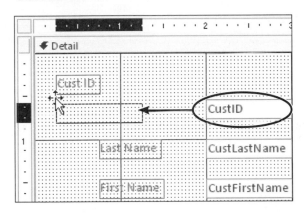

7. Hold the ⎡Ctrl⎤ key down while you click the **Telephone**, **Email**, and **Notes** labels to select all three objects; then tap →| several times to move the labels and associated text boxes to the right.

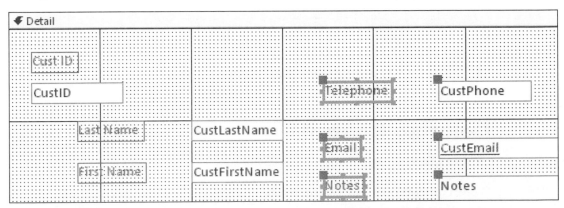

8. Follow these steps to size the CustID text box for its contents:

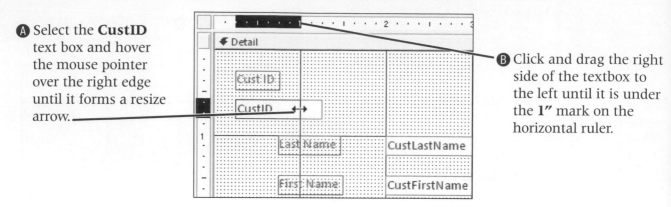

A Select the **CustID** text box and hover the mouse pointer over the right edge until it forms a resize arrow.

B Click and drag the right side of the textbox to the left until it is under the **1″** mark on the horizontal ruler.

9. Save the form as **CustomersDesign**.

10. Click the **View menu** ▼ button to open the form in **Form View**.

If you don't see the View button, right-click the form's tab and choose Form View.

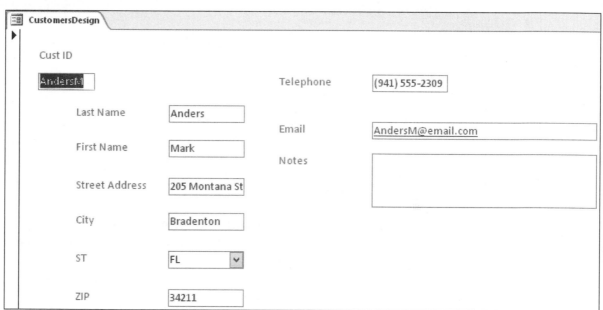

11. Leave the **CustomersDesign** form open.

Deleting Controls

Video Library   http://labyrinthelab.com/videos   Video Number: AC13-V0306

Some controls on a form stand by themselves without the need for a label. You can delete unnecessary labels to allow better arrangement and format on forms and also remove controls completely. Because each bound control contains two parts, removing labels and controls depends on the part of the control selected.

QUICK REFERENCE	DELETING CONTROLS AND LABELS
Task	**Procedure**
Delete an entire control (text box and label)	Select the text box part of the control then press Delete .
Delete label only	Select the label part of the control then press Delete .

Delete Labels and Edit Label Text

In this exercise, you will delete a label control and edit the text in another label on your CustomersDesign form.

1. Open the **CustomersDesign** form in **Design View**.

2. Follow these steps to delete a label:

Ⓐ Click the **Notes** label to select it.

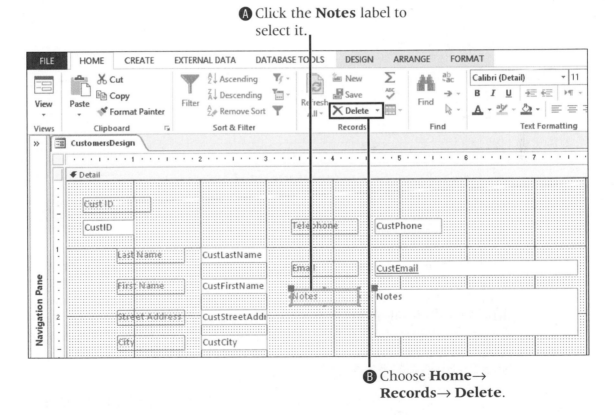

Ⓑ Choose **Home→ Records→ Delete**.

If you accidentally delete the wrong control, click Undo ↺ on the Quick Access toolbar to reverse the action and then try again.

Access removes just the label and leaves the text box.

Edit Control Labels

3. Click the **ST** label, highlight the text, and type `State`.

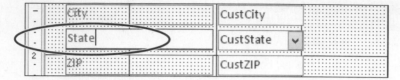

4. Repeat the procedures from **step 3** to change the **Cust ID** label to `Customer ID`, and the **ZIP** label to `ZIP Code`.

5. Switch to **Form View**.

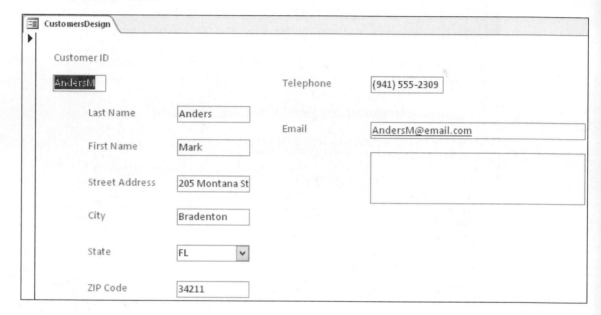

6. Save and close the **CustomersDesign** form.

Arranging Controls

Video Library   http://labyrinthelab.com/videos   Video Number: AC13-V0307

Now that you have positioned form controls where you want them to appear, you can arrange the controls more precisely and evenly to provide a more attractive, functional, and easy-to-read form. Tools for aligning, grouping, and distributing controls appear on the Arrange tab of the Ribbon.

Selecting Multiple Controls

Selecting, moving, positioning, and aligning each form control individually can be tedious and time-consuming. By selecting multiple controls and then moving or sizing them, you reduce the amount of time needed to position and format them. You may also select multiple controls in order to group them on a form.

QUICK REFERENCE	SELECTING MULTIPLE CONTROLS
Task	**Procedure**
Select controls individually	■ Click the first control on the form. ■ Press and hold [Shift] and click each additional control.
Select controls in a horizontal or vertical line	■ Click the vertical ruler to the left of the desired controls to select them all. ■ Click the horizontal ruler above the desired controls to select them all.
Select controls in one general area	■ Click above or to the left of the top left control and drag the pointer down and to the right to select the desired controls (aka *lassoing*.)

Aligning Controls

As you move and position controls on forms, it is sometimes challenging to position them so that they align properly. Access alignment tools help with aligning multiple controls.

FROM THE KEYBOARD
[Ctrl]+[←][↑][→] and [↓]
to *nudge* a control into place

QUICK REFERENCE	ALIGNING SELECTED CONTROLS
Task	**Procedure**
Align controls using the Ribbon	■ Select multiple controls. ■ Choose Arrange→Sizing & Ordering→Align and click the desired alignment.
Align controls using the shortcut menu	■ Select multiple controls. ■ Right-click one of the selected controls and click Align. ■ Choose the desired alignment.

Anchoring Controls

You can also anchor controls—tie them to a section or to other controls so that moving or sizing a section adjusts the size and position of the anchored controls as well. Access provides nine different anchor positions that range from top left to bottom right. Although you anchor controls in Design View and Layout View, the results of the anchor display only in Layout View and Form View.

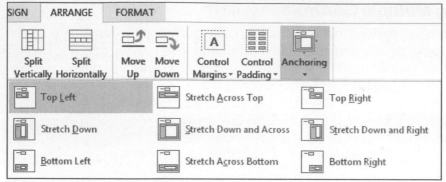

Access offers several different Anchor positions.

Arrange, Size, Group, and Anchor Form Controls

In this exercise, you will select multiple controls and arrange, resize, align, group, and anchor controls on the CustomersDesign form.

1. Open the **CustomersDesign** form in **Design View**.

2. Follow these steps to select and resize a group of form controls:

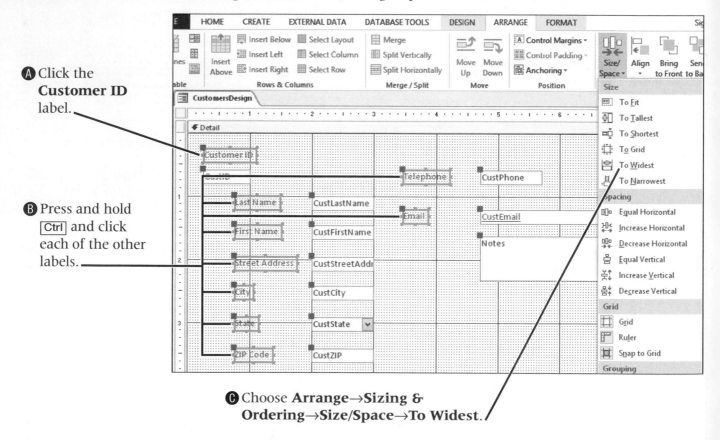

A Click the **Customer ID** label.

B Press and hold [Ctrl] and click each of the other labels.

C Choose **Arrange→Sizing & Ordering→Size/Space→To Widest**.

Don't worry if your form spacing isn't exactly as shown. You can move the controls to match the figures more precisely, if desired.

3. Click an unoccupied area of the form grid to deselect all controls.

4. Follow these steps to select and align controls:

Ⓐ Click the **Last Name** label.

Ⓑ Press and hold Ctrl and click the **CustLastName** text box, **Telephone** label, and **CustPhone** text box.

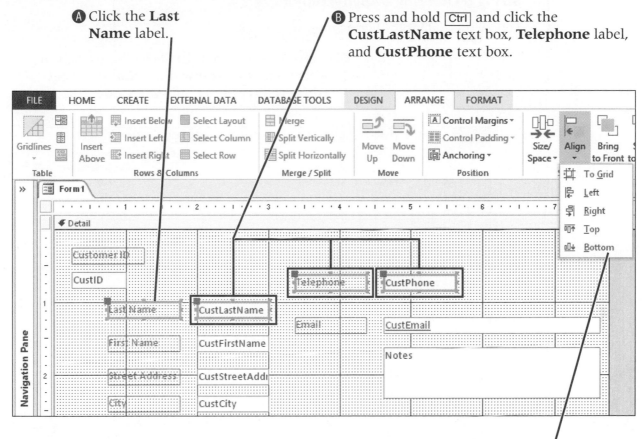

Ⓒ Choose **Arrange→Sizing & Ordering→Align→Bottom** to align the controls.

If the wrong control is selected, click a neutral area of the form and try again.

5. Select the **Email** label, **CustEmail** text box, and **Notes** text box, and tap ↓ until the **Email** controls are in line with the **FirstName** controls.

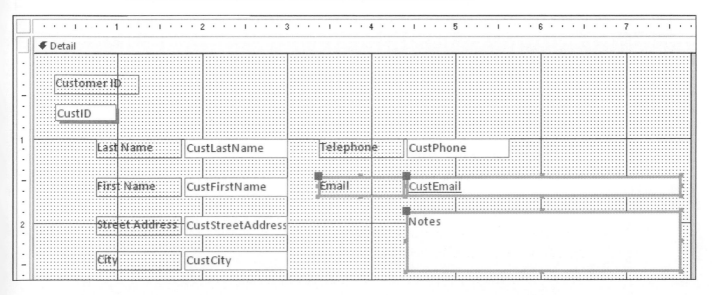

Access 2013

6. Click the vertical ruler to the left of the First Name controls and choose **Arrange→Sizing & Ordering→Align→Top** ⬆.

7. Follow these steps to align a group of controls:

A Click the horizontal ruler above these labels to select them: **LastName**, **FirstName**, **Street Address**, **City**, **State**, and **ZIP Code**.

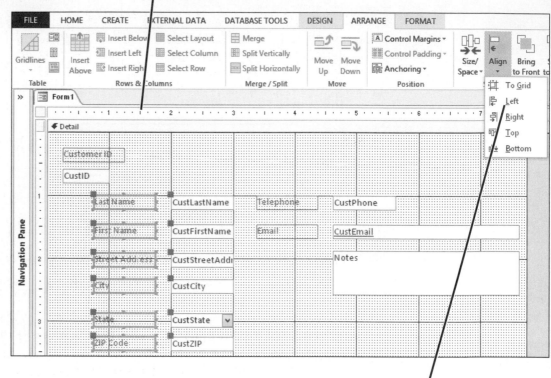

B Choose **Arrange→Sizing & Ordering→Align→Left.**

If you select more objects than you intended, press and hold ⬚Shift⬚ as you click the undesired controls to deselect them without deselecting the desired controls.

8. Follow **step 7** to align the associated text boxes to the left.

9. Align the **Telephone** and **Email** labels to the left.

10. Align the **CustPhone**, **CustEmail**, and **Notes** text boxes to the left.

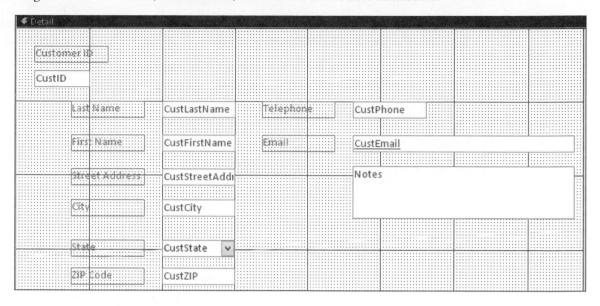

Size Multiple Controls

11. Follow these steps to size multiple text boxes at the same time:

A Click the **horizontal ruler** above the CustLastName text box to select the column of text boxes.

B Press and hold Ctrl and click the **horizontal border** above the CustPhone text box to also select this column of text boxes.

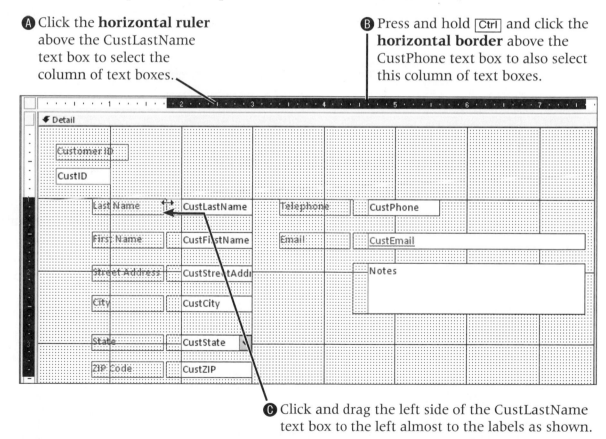

C Click and drag the left side of the CustLastName text box to the left almost to the labels as shown.

When you have multiple controls selected, you only have to drag the edge of one of them to resize them all.

Group Controls

12. Select the following controls using the technique you prefer: **Telephone** and **Email** labels, and **CustPhone** and **CustEmail** text boxes.

13. Choose **Arrange→Sizing & Ordering→Size/Space→Group**.

Now whenever you click one of the grouped controls, you select them all.

Anchor Controls

14. Select the **Notes** text box.

15. Choose **Arrange→Position→Anchoring** 📼.

16. Choose **Stretch Across Bottom** 📼.

17. Switch to **Form View** to display the form as users will see it.

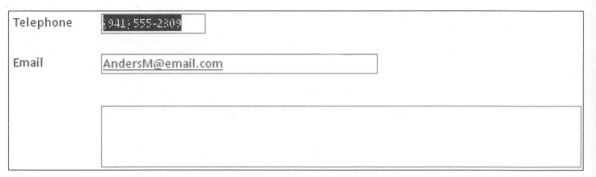

In Form View, the Notes text box is stretched and anchored across the bottom-right of the form.

18. Save the form.

Applying Themes to Forms

Video Library   http://labyrinthelab.com/videos   Video Number: AC13-V0308

Themes are designs that were developed by a group of professional design specialists and are similar to templates in Word and PowerPoint. When you apply a Theme to a database object, it applies the Theme to *every* object in the database. Themes contain colors, fonts, and control settings that enhance the form. You can use Themes to quickly and efficiently format all form sections and form controls. Rest the mouse pointer over a Theme icon to identify the Theme name in a ScreenTip.

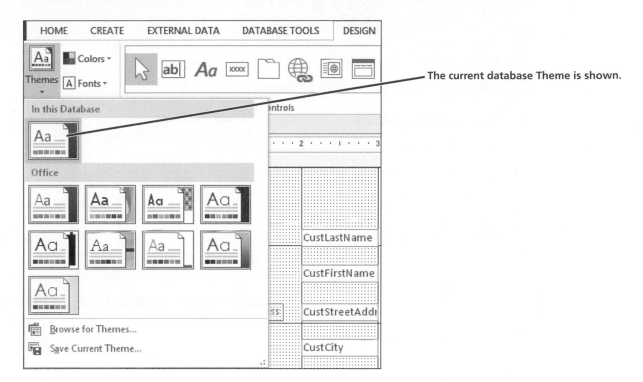

The current database Theme is shown.

QUICK REFERENCE	APPLYING THEMES TO A FORM
Task	**Procedure**
Apply Themes to a form	■ Open the desired form in Design View. ■ Choose Design→Themes→Themes ⬛ and select a Theme design.

Apply a Theme to a Form

In this exercise, you will apply Themes to the CustomersDesign form.

1. Display the **CustomersDesign** form in Design View.

2. Follow these steps to apply a new Theme to the form:

Ⓐ Choose **Design→Themes→Themes menu** ▼ and experiment by choosing various themes.

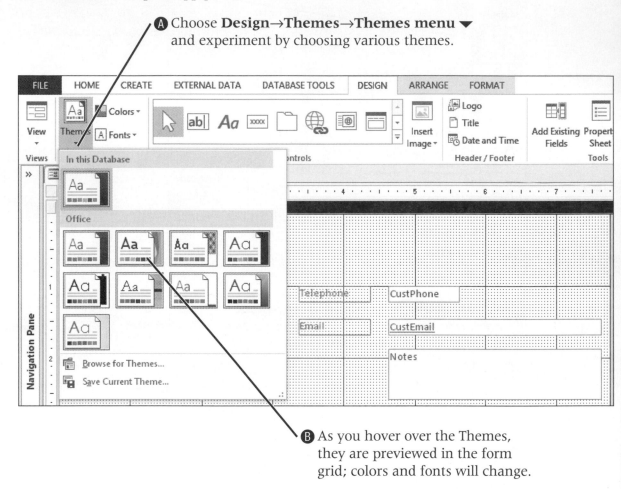

Ⓑ As you hover over the Themes, they are previewed in the form grid; colors and fonts will change.

Themes are arranged alphabetically and may vary depending on screen size and resolution.

3. Repeat the procedures in **step 2** to return to the Office default Theme. Do not save the form.

Modifying Form Controls

Video Library   http://labyrinthelab.com/videos   Video Number: AC13-V0309

As you design and work with forms, there will be times when you want to edit the appearance of controls or remove them from the form. Access offers tools that enable you to change the properties of form labels, change the format of the text box data to display as currency, for example, and to format the font and background color of controls.

Editing Labels

Label controls identify the values contained in the associated text boxes. As a result, they need to be as descriptive as possible and yet also be concise. You have already learned how to set field captions to change the column headings when field names contain text that runs together. When you add field controls to forms, you can edit the label text directly in the label control box.

Using Design Font Tools

Tools for formatting controls appear on the Design tab when Form Design and Layout views are active. Using these tools, you can change the font format, design, size, color, and alignment as well as the fill color of the control box.

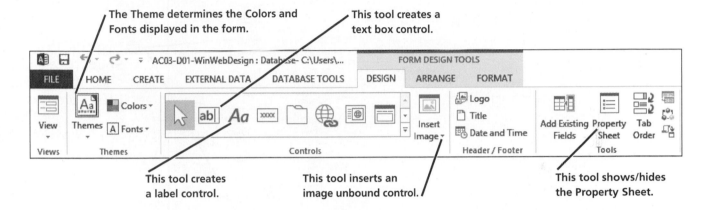

The Theme determines the Colors and Fonts displayed in the form.

This tool creates a text box control.

This tool creates a label control.

This tool inserts an image unbound control.

This tool shows/hides the Property Sheet.

Using the Property Sheet

The Property Sheet provides a full range of formatting properties for form controls, such as, font name, size, and color, field alignment, background colors, numeric field formats (general number, currency, etc.), and many others. The properties displayed vary depending on the type of control selected and whether the label or the text box part of a control is selected.

FROM THE KEYBOARD

F4 to open/close the Property Sheet

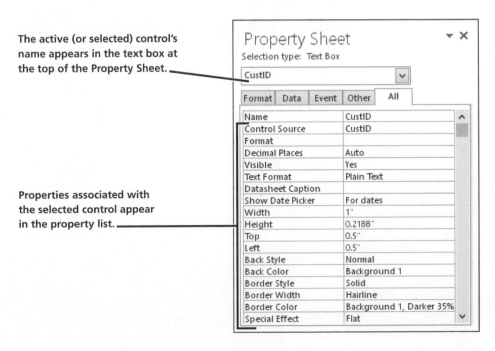

The active (or selected) control's name appears in the text box at the top of the Property Sheet.

Properties associated with the selected control appear in the property list.

Access 2013

Use the Property Sheet to Format a Form Control

In this exercise, you will use the Property Sheet to apply a special effect to a control on the CustomersDesign form.

1. Display the **CustomersDesign** form in **Design View**.

2. Follow these steps to add a special effect to a form control:

Ⓐ Click the **CustID** text box to select it.

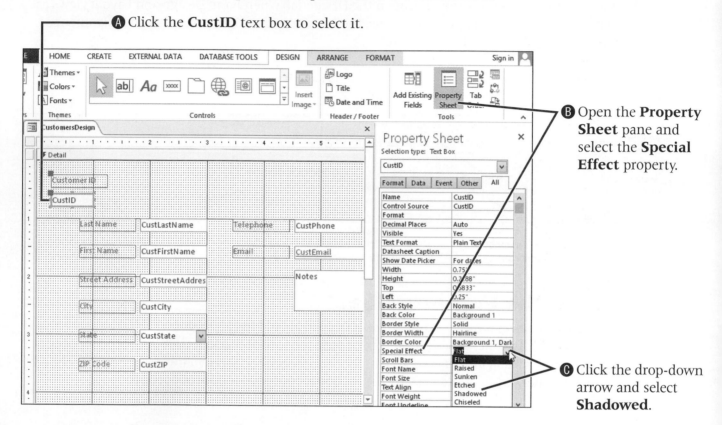

Ⓑ Open the **Property Sheet** pane and select the **Special Effect** property.

Ⓒ Click the drop-down arrow and select **Shadowed**.

Don't worry if your form spacing isn't exactly as shown here. You can move the controls to match the figures more precisely, if desired.

3. Save the form.

Using the Fill Color Palette

Video Library   http://labyrinthelab.com/videos   Video Number: AC13-V0310

Whether you are formatting text color or adding a background fill color, the techniques for using the color palette are the same. Access identifies the color names in three parts: Color Name, Color Type, Percent Light or Dark. So if you are formatting text or fill and the instructions say Dark Red, Accent 4, 20% Darker, you will be able to locate the appropriate color.

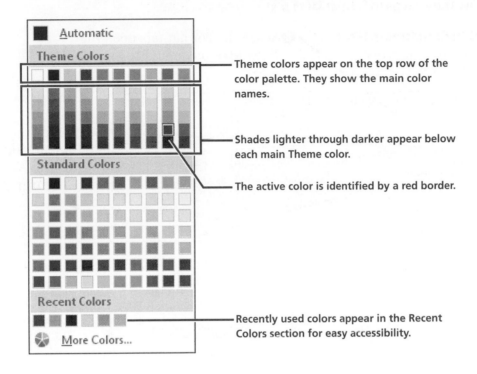

Theme colors appear on the top row of the color palette. They show the main color names.

Shades lighter through darker appear below each main Theme color.

The active color is identified by a red border.

Recently used colors appear in the Recent Colors section for easy accessibility.

Apply Formatting to Controls

In this exercise, you will format labels, set formatting, and use properties to format controls on the CustomersDesign form.

1. Open the **CustomersDesign** form in **Design View**.

2. Follow these steps to format label text:

Ⓐ Click the **Customer ID** label to make it active.

Ⓑ Select the Format tab, open the **Font Size** menu and choose **12**.

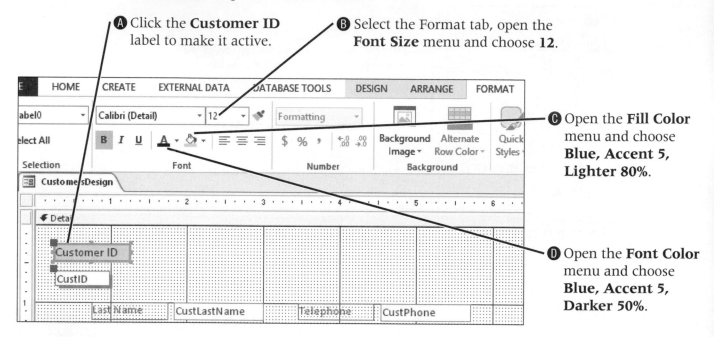

Ⓒ Open the **Fill Color** menu and choose **Blue, Accent 5, Lighter 80%**.

Ⓓ Open the **Font Color** menu and choose **Blue, Accent 5, Darker 50%**.

If you chose a different Theme, your color selections will be different. Choose good contrasting colors from your palette.

Use the Property Sheet

3. Click the **Notes** text box to make it active.

4. If necessary, choose **Design→Tools→Property Sheet** ▤ to open the Property Sheet.

5. Follow these steps to set the Fore Color property for the Notes field:

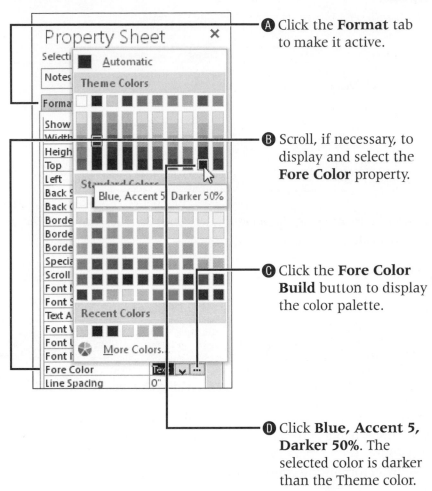

Ⓐ Click the **Format** tab to make it active.

Ⓑ Scroll, if necessary, to display and select the **Fore Color** property.

Ⓒ Click the **Fore Color Build** button to display the color palette.

Ⓓ Click **Blue, Accent 5, Darker 50%**. The selected color is darker than the Theme color.

Use Format Painter

6. Click the **Customer ID** label to make it active.

7. Choose **Format→Font** and double-click **Format Painter** 🖌 to copy the formats applied to the **Customer ID** label.

If you only single-click the Format Painter then it will only work one time and you will have to single-click it again to apply the formatting to the next object.

Access picks up the format of the label, and the mouse pointer changes to a paint brush ⯈ so you can "paint" the format onto other labels.

8. Click each of the other labels on the form, one at a time, to apply the format to them.

9. Press Esc to drop the paint brush.

10. Adjust the size of each label to show all the text.

11. Switch to **Form View**.

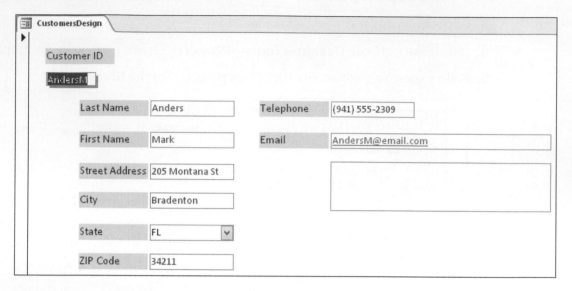

Don't worry if your form spacing isn't exactly as shown here. You can move the controls to match the figures more precisely, if desired.

12. Save and close the form.

Modifying Form Layout

Video Library   http://labyrinthelab.com/videos   Video Number: AC13-V0311

So far, you have added, edited, arranged, and formatted controls on a new form and saved the form. These changes had no effect on the form's layout and design. For example, the form palette is still white and the Detail section is the only section displayed. Formatting a form, as distinguished from formatting controls, involves such additional tasks as:

- Displaying and editing Form Header and Form Footer sections.
- Formatting section backgrounds.
- Adding design elements to sections.

Displaying Form Header and Form Footer

Controls such as page number, page title, logos, and lines that you choose to place in the header or footer sections of the form repeat on form pages just as they do on a Word document. By default, Access hides the Form Header and Form Footer sections of a new form until you are ready to display them. To display the Form Header and Footer, right-click the Detail section bar and choose Form Header/Footer. Then, select the control that you want to add to the sections on the Design tab.

Form Headers may contain controls you want repeated at the top of each form.

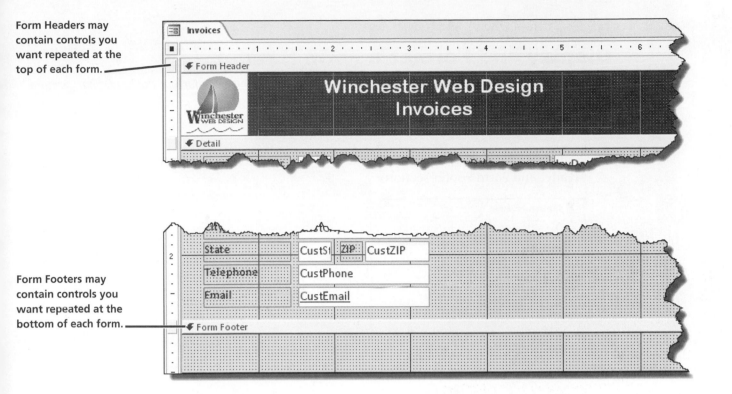

Form Footers may contain controls you want repeated at the bottom of each form.

Sizing Form Sections

To resize form sections, drag the bottom of the section up or down, or drag the bar for the section that appears below the section you want to resize. For example, to make the Form Header section larger, drag the Detail section bar down. To make the Form Header section smaller, drag the Detail section bar up.

The mouse pointer appears as a two-headed arrow with a bar ✛ when positioned appropriately for sizing a section.

Display and Format a Form Header

In this exercise, you will display the Form Header and Footer sections and format the header background on the CustomersDesign form.

1. Open the **CustomersDesign** form in **Design View**.

2. Right-click the **Detail** section bar and choose **Form Header/Footer** to display the Form Header and Form Footer sections.

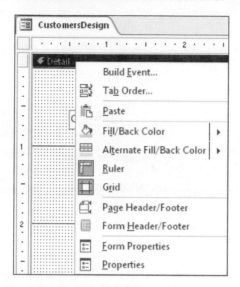

3. Follow these steps to make the Form Header section larger to accommodate a title and logo:

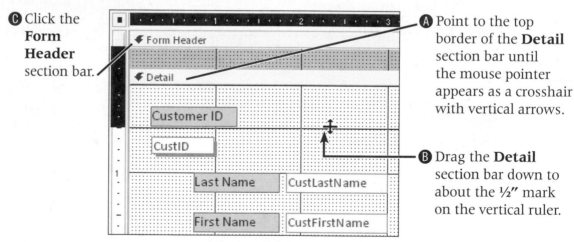

C Click the **Form Header** section bar.

A Point to the top border of the **Detail** section bar until the mouse pointer appears as a crosshair with vertical arrows.

B Drag the **Detail** section bar down to about the ½" mark on the vertical ruler.

4. Choose **Format→Font→Fill Color** 🎨 ▾ menu, and then choose **Blue, Accent 5, 60% lighter**.

5. Save the changes to the form.

Adding Unbound Controls to a Form

Video Library   http://labyrinthelab.com/videos   Video Number: AC13-V0312

Design elements (drawn shapes, logos, graphics, and titles) improve the appearance of a form. Because these elements do not require access to data in database tables, they are considered unbound controls and are not bound to data. Tools for adding unbound controls appear on the Design tab of Ribbon. You can point to a control and use the ToolTip to identify the control.

Titles and logos can be added to a form in more than one way. To add a title, you can drag a Label control to the Form Header section and then type in the caption. To add a logo, you can use the Image tool and drag the image where you want it, or click Logo on the Ribbon and Access will place the logo on the left-hand side of the Page Header section. If the Page Header section is not open and you use the Title or Logo tool, Access opens the Page Header section for you.

To add a subtitle to a form that already has a title, click at the end of the title, tap Ctrl + Enter , and add the subtitle text under the existing title.

The expanded Controls group on the Design tab displays controls you can add to a form.

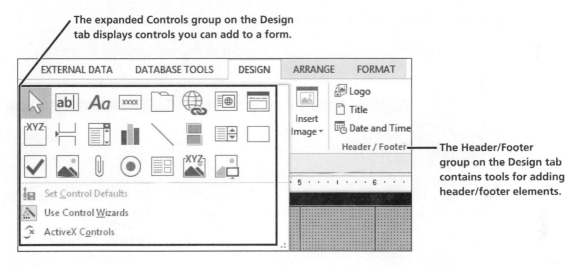

The Header/Footer group on the Design tab contains tools for adding header/footer elements.

When you use most of the unbound controls to add design elements to a database object, the mouse pointer becomes a plus symbol called a *crosshair*. Sometimes the character, or symbol, on the control icon appears with the mouse pointer crosshair to identify the control you are adding to the form.

Crosshair mouse appears above the symbol.

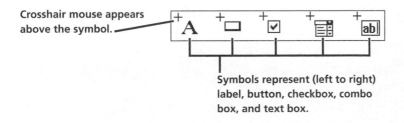

Symbols represent (left to right) label, button, checkbox, combo box, and text box.

Access 2013

Add Unbound Controls to Forms

In this exercise, you will add a title and image to the Form Header section of the CustomersDesign form using unbound controls.

Add a Title

1. Display the **CustomersDesign** form in **Design View**.

2. Choose **Design→Header/Footer→Title** 📄.

   Access adds the title section to the Form Header section and selects the CustomersDesign text so you can edit it.

3. Type **Winchester Customers** and press **Enter**.

   When you add a title control, Access automatically places an empty Auto-Logo object immediately to the left of the title control. You will not be using the Auto-Logo on this form.

4. Follow these steps to delete the Auto-Logo and size the new title:

   Ⓐ Click the **faint dotted border** of the logo control shown here to the left of the title and tap **Delete**.

   Ⓑ Drag the **lower-right corner handle** of the title control to the position shown.

5. Press **F4** to display the Property Sheet and set the following properties for the label control to format the label text:

Property	Setting
Back Color	Blue, Accent 5, Darker 50%
Border Color	Blue, Accent 5, Lighter 80%
Special Effect	Raised
Font Name	Lucida Calligraphy
Font Size	30
Text Align	Center
Fore Color	Blue, Accent 5, Lighter 80%

6. Adjust the size of the title, if necessary, by dragging the borders of the control.

7. Center the title using the left, right, up, and down arrows.

Add an Image

8. Click an unoccupied area of the form and choose **Design→Controls→Insert Image** and click **Browse**.

9. Navigate to the **AC2013 Lesson 03** folder, select **WWD-Logo.bmp**, and click **OK**.
   If you do not see WWD-Logo.bmp, click the file type arrow and select All Files.

10. Click to the left of the title and drag the mouse down and to the right.

11. Select the new image and the title.

12. Choose **Arrange→Sizing & Ordering→Align→Top**.

13. Choose **Design→Views→View→Form View**.

14. Save the changes to the form.

Setting Additional Form Properties

Video Library   http://labyrinthelab.com/videos   Video Number: AC13-V0313

You have already used the Property Sheet to format controls and sections on the form. Now that you have the visual elements of the form set, you can focus on the functional elements of the form. Additional form properties include those form items that affect the whole form, such as the record selector bar, scroll bars, and navigation buttons.

Choosing Items to Show on Forms

The navigation buttons at the bottom of most form windows are important to display different form records. Scroll bars can be useful when the form and data extend beyond the monitor boundaries. When the form is sized to display the complete form, there is no need for scroll bars; they can be removed from view. However, just because the entire form appears onscreen on one computer does not necessarily mean the entire form will appear onscreen on every computer. Allowances must be made for individual screen size and resolution.

The record selector bar can also be useful. However, many businesses find that their employees inadvertently click the record selector bar and delete records when they really want to delete data in a form field. As a result, many businesses remove the record selector bar from their forms to prevent accidental data loss.

Record selector bar appears on the left side of the form.

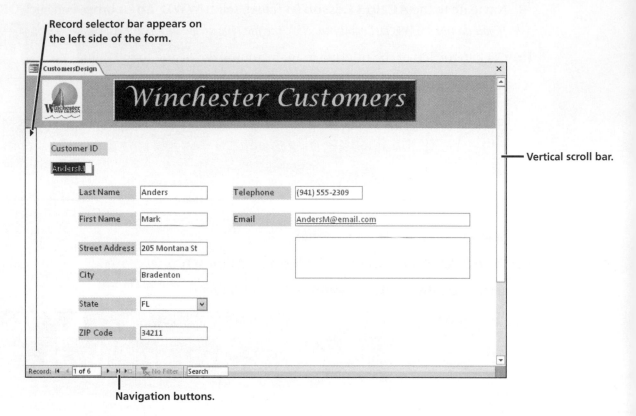

Vertical scroll bar.

Navigation buttons.

Displaying the Form Property Sheet

Properties displayed in the Property Sheet vary, depending on the item that is selected or active on the form. To access properties that affect the whole form, no other controls or sections on the form can be selected, other than the Form Selector button. You can click a blank area of the form outside of the entire form grid/palette to display Form properties or select Form from the Property Sheet Selection Type list, or right-click the Form Selector button and choose Properties. The Property Sheet is available in both Design and Layout Views.

The Property Sheet contains numerous properties, some familiar—such as caption—and some unfamiliar—such as Allow PivotTable View. To learn more about properties, use Access Help.

Set Form Properties

In this exercise, you will use the Property Sheet to set properties for the CustomersDesign form to remove the record selector bar and scroll bars, and to ensure that you will be able to use navigation buttons, the Close button, and Min and Max buttons.

1. Display the **CustomersDesign** form in **Design View**.

2. Press F4 to display the Property Sheet.

3. Follow these steps to set Form properties:

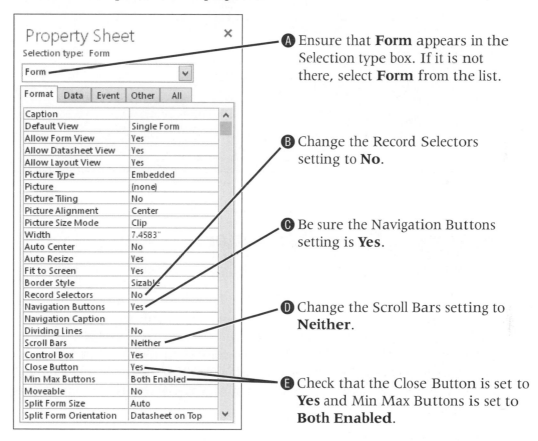

Ⓐ Ensure that **Form** appears in the Selection type box. If it is not there, select **Form** from the list.

Ⓑ Change the Record Selectors setting to **No**.

Ⓒ Be sure the Navigation Buttons setting is **Yes**.

Ⓓ Change the Scroll Bars setting to **Neither**.

Ⓔ Check that the Close Button is set to **Yes** and Min Max Buttons is set to **Both Enabled**.

Access 2013

4. Save changes and switch to **Form View** to display the form.

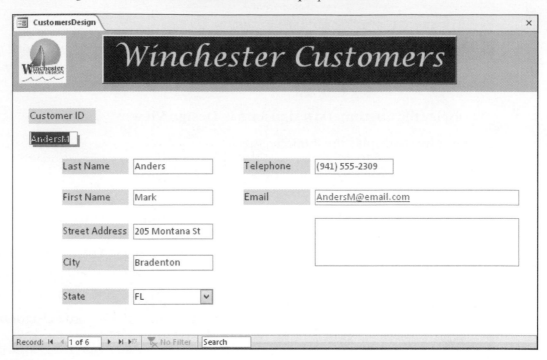

Setting a Form Tab Order

Video Library   http://labyrinthelab.com/videos   Video Number: AC13-V0314

Regardless of the arrangement of bound and unbound controls, when you use a form to enter records, Access moves from one field to the next each time you press Tab or Enter. Access moves among form fields in the order in which the fields appear in the table datasheet or query grid on which you base the form. When you design custom forms, how you position controls may be significantly different from the order in which they appear in a table datasheet. As a result, tapping Tab sometimes makes it appear as if Access is randomly hopping from control to control.

You can control the order in which Access moves by changing the tab order. This enables you to view data on the form and access each field in the order it appears onscreen. If you rearrange the field order or insert a new field in between two existing fields you often will alter the traditional tab order of top-down, left-right. If that is the case, you should reset the tab order. In addition, you may want to modify the tab order to skip fields containing data that should not be changed, move onscreen to fields in the order in which fields appear on a printed form, or move to fields in a more logical order.

The Detail section contains bound
controls used to enter data.

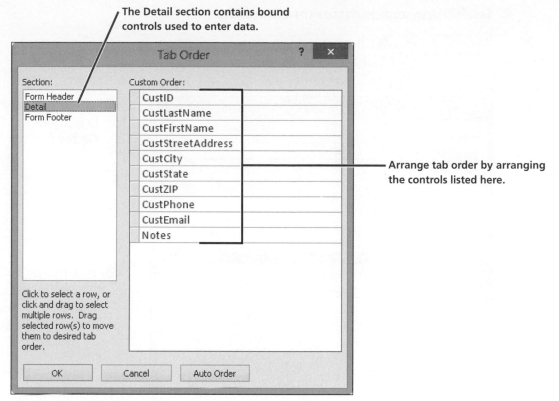

Arrange tab order by arranging
the controls listed here.

The Tab Order dialog box contains the setting to control tab order.

Set Tab Order

In this exercise, you will set the tab order for the CustomersDesign form.

1. Display the **CustomersDesign** form in **Form View** and press ⎡Tab⎤ to advance through all fields on the form.

2. Switch to **Design View**.

3. Choose **Design→Tools→Tab Order** ▦.

4. Follow these steps to change the tab order:

Ⓐ Click the selector button in front of the **CustPhone** field.

Ⓑ Drag the **CustPhone** field up in the **Custom Order** list.

Ⓒ Release the field when the black bar appears just below the **CustID** field.

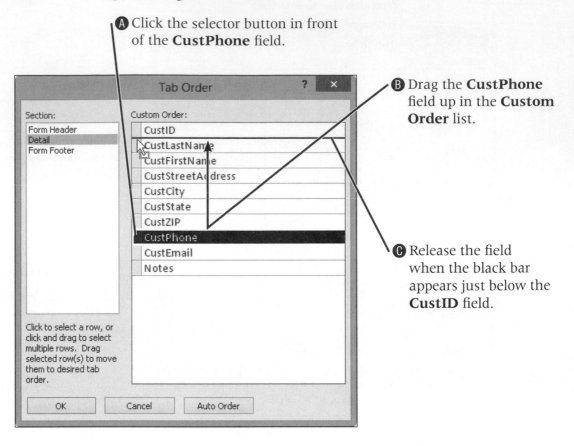

5. Click **OK**.

Test the Tab Order

6. Switch to **Form View** and press ⸢Tab⸥ to move through all fields.

Access moves from field to field, starting in CustID, then moving to Telephone, stopping at each field, and finishing in the Notes field.

7. Save and close the form.

Creating Multiple Items Forms

Video Library   http://labyrinthelab.com/videos   Video Number: AC13-V0315

Custom designing a form and creating simple forms are good ways to format forms when you want to display or print each record individually. Sometimes, however, you will want to print multiple items in a table using a layout that is more appropriate for printing and distributing than a table datasheet. The Multiple Items form is used for those occasions.

When you create a Multiple Items form, Access creates a form that resembles a datasheet because data appears in rows and columns. However, you can customize a Multiple Items form. For example, you can adjust the size of text boxes, add graphic elements to the form, and enhance the form with color.

Create a Multiple Items Form

In this exercise, you will create a new form for the Customers table.

1. Follow these steps to create a Multiple Items form for the Customers table:

Ⓐ Select the **Customers** table.

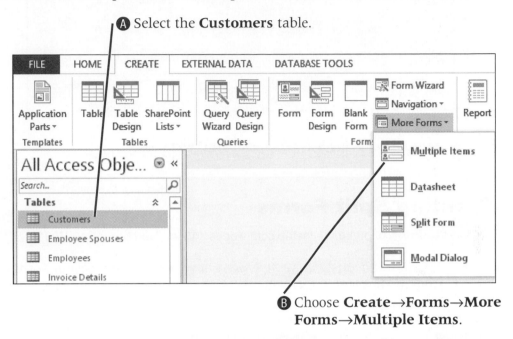

Ⓑ Choose **Create→Forms→More Forms→Multiple Items**.

Access creates a new multiple item form and displays it in Layout View.

2. Drag the **right border** of each column heading to resize the data fields.

3. Select the graphic to the left of the **Form Header** section and press ⎣Delete⎤.

4. Switch back to **Form View**.

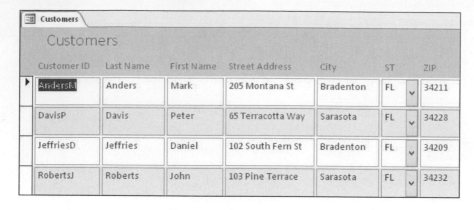

5. Close the form, saving it as `CustomersMultiItem`.

Creating Split Forms

Video Library   http://labyrinthelab.com/videos   Video Number: AC13-V0316

A split form simultaneously shows two views of your table data: Layout/Form View and Datasheet View. The views are synchronized so that a selected record in one view is also selected in the other view.

DEVELOP YOUR SKILLS AC03-D16
Create a Split Form

In this exercise, you will examine the Split Form feature using the Customers table.

1. Select the **Customers** table.

2. Choose **Create→Forms→More Forms→Split Form** .

Access opens the new split form in Form Layout View on the top and Datasheet View on the bottom.

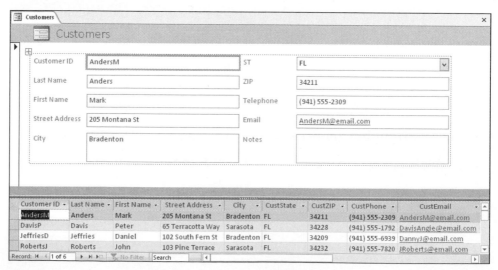

3. Save the form as `CustomersSplitForm` and close it.

Printing Forms

Video Library   http://labyrinthelab.com/videos   Video Number: AC13-V0317

Procedures for printing forms are basically the same procedures you would use to print in other programs, such as Word, Excel, and PowerPoint. As with each different program, print options in Access vary with different objects. For example, you can print individual forms—one for each record—or print forms so that they print continuously, one after another, on standard sheets of paper.

FROM THE RIBBON

File→Print→Print Preview to open Print Preview

File→Print→Print to open the Print dialog box

Printing All Record Forms

The default setting in Access for printing forms is to print as many individual records that can fit on one page. The easiest way to determine how forms will look when you print them is to view them in Print Preview before printing.

FROM THE KEYBOARD

Ctrl + P to print

The Quick Print command sends all records directly to the printer without opening the Print dialog box. When dealing with large files, this option should be used with caution.

Printing Selected Record Forms

When you want to print selected records, you would first select the record and then display it in Print Preview. When you click the Print button on the Ribbon in Print Preview, the Print dialog box opens so that you can choose to print all records, print specific record numbers, or print the selected records.

QUICK REFERENCE	PRINTING RECORD FORMS
Task	**Procedure**
Open Print Preview	■ Choose File→Print→Print Preview.
Print all records	■ Choose File→Print→Quick Print.
Print specific records	■ Choose File→Print→Print and set the print options for the records to print, or press Ctrl+P and set the print options for the records to print.

DEVELOP YOUR SKILLS AC03-D17
Print Form Information

In this exercise, you will print the third record of the CustomersDesign form.

1. Display the **CustomersDesign** form in Form View.

2. Choose **File→Print→Print** to open the **Print** dialog box.

Access 2013

3. Follow these steps to print only record/page 3:

Ⓐ Choose the **Pages** option.

Ⓑ Type **3** in both the **From** box and the **To** box.

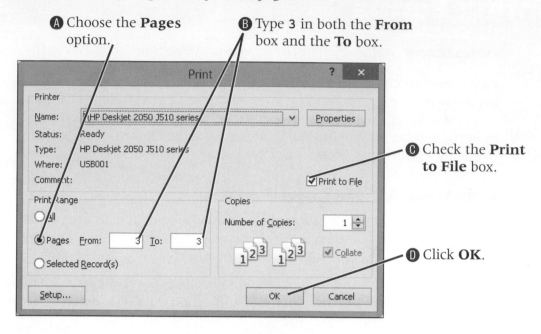

Ⓒ Check the **Print to File** box.

Ⓓ Click **OK**.

Access prints the third form record to your file.

4. Type CustomersDesign-[FirstInitialLastName] in the Print to File dialog box and click OK.

5. Close the form and save if prompted.

Using Help

Video Library   http://labyrinthelab.com/videos   Video Number: AC13-V0318

As you begin using Help in Access 2013, you will soon realize that the Help system is a massive database file comprised of numerous records, each of which is related to an Access feature. If you use the search tools available on most Web sites, you can also quickly and efficiently locate help for any Access feature.

FROM THE KEYBOARD
F1 to launch Help

Use Help in Access 2013

In this exercise, you will use the Help tool to learn more about creating controls in Access.

1. Click the **Help ?** button on the title bar.

2. Follow these steps to search for help on creating controls:

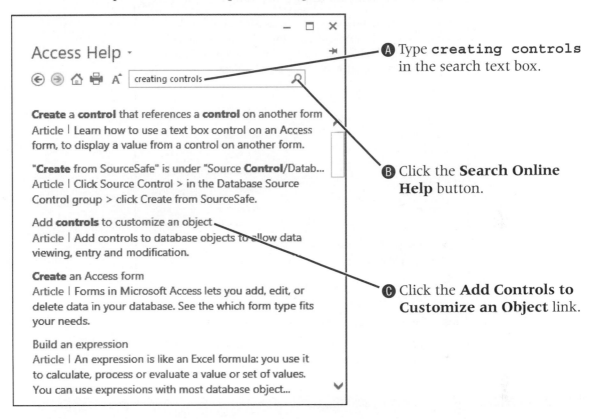

The topics listed in the Help window are constantly updated. As such, the topics listed when you do your search may differ from those shown here.

3. Review the article.

4. Close the article; exit **Access**.

Closing the article also closes the Access Help dialog box.

Concepts Review

To check your knowledge of the key concepts introduced in this lesson, complete the Concepts Review quiz by choosing the appropriate access option below.

If you are...	Then access the quiz by...
Using the Labyrinth Video Library	Going to http://labyrinthelab.com/videos
Using eLab	Logging in, choosing Content, and navigating to the Concepts Review quiz for this lesson
Not using the Labyrinth Video Library or eLab	Going to the student resource center for this book

Reinforce Your Skills

Create a Form Using the Form Wizard and Customize It

Kids for Change has hired you to create a new form and customize it with a new design. In this exercise, you will use the Form Wizard to create a form, add an image, and set several formatting properties.

Create a Form Using the Form Wizard

1. Start **Access**. Open **AC03-R01-K4C** from the **AC2013 Lesson 03** folder and save it as **AC03-R01-K4C-[FirstInitialLastName]**.

2. If a Security Warning appears, click **Enable Content**.

3. Click the **Children** table in the Navigation Pane.

4. Choose **Create→Forms→Form Wizard**.

5. Choose **Table: Children** from the Tables/Queries list.

6. Click **Move All** `>>` to add all fields to the Selected Fields box; click **Next**.

7. Keep the **Columnar** default layout selected; click **Next**.

8. Name the form **Kids for Change Children Volunteers** and click **Finish**.
   The form opens in Form View.

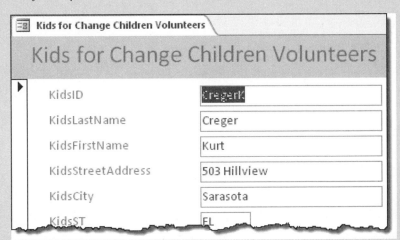

Edit Label Text

9. Choose **Home→Views→View menu ▼→Design View**.

10. Double-click the **Title** label to select it.

11. Click in front of the word **Children**, press ⌈Shift⌉, and tap ⌈Enter⌉ to bump the last two words down under the name of the organization.

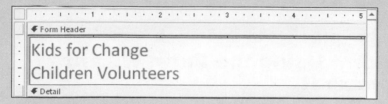

12. Click outside of the title control to make the **Insert Image** command available for the next step.

Add and Adjust an Image (Control)

13. Choose **Design→Controls→Insert Image** and click **Browse**.

14. Navigate to your **AC2013 Lesson 03** folder, select **K4C-logo.bmp**, and click **OK**.

If the K4C-logo.bmp file does not display, choose All Files (*.*) from the File type drop-down in the Browse dialog box.

15. Click to the right of the title and drag the mouse down and to the right.

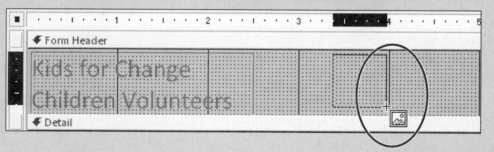

16. Release the mouse to insert the image.

Use the Property Sheet to Format Objects

17. Click the **All** tab on the Property Sheet, and set these properties for the new image.

Property	New Value
Name	K4C-Logo
Width	.7
Height	.7
Border Style	Solid
Border Width	1 pt
Border Color	Green, Accent 6, Darker 25%

18. Select and then set the following properties for the **Title** control.

Property	New Value
Name	K4C-Title
Width	3
Height	.7
Font Name	Arial
Font Size	18
Text Align	Center
Font Weight	Semi-bold
Fore Color	Green, Accent 6, Darker 50%

Modify a Form Layout

19. Click the vertical ruler to the left of the title and image to select the two controls.

20. Choose **Arrange→Sizing & Ordering→Align→Top**.

21. Click the **Form Header** section bar and change the Back Color property to **Green, Accent 6, Lighter 80%**.

22. Using any method, select all labels in the Detail section and change these properties.

Be sure not to include the title in your selection.

Property	New Value
Width	1.5
Height	.25
Back Color	Green, Accent 6, Lighter 80%
Special Effect	Raised
Font Name	Arial
Font Weight	Semi-bold
Fore Color	Green, Accent 6, Darker 50%

23. Select all text boxes in the Detail section and change these properties.

Property	New Value
Height	.25
Special Effect	Sunken
Font Name	Arial
Font Weight	Semi-bold
Fore Color	Green, Accent 6, Darker 50%

24. Switch to **Form View**.

25. Save and close the form. Exit **Access**.

26. Submit your final file based on the guidelines provided by your instructor.

To view examples of how your file or files should look at the end of this exercise, go to the student resource center.

REINFORCE YOUR SKILLS AC03-R02

Create a Multiple Item Form and Apply a Theme

Kids for Change has hired you to redesign their database forms and apply a consistent and attractive Theme to both new and existing forms. In this exercise, you will create a multiple item form for entering and managing staff information. Then you will apply a Theme to the new form and print it for the next staff meeting.

Create a Multiple Item Form

1. Start **Access**. Open **AC03-R02-K4C** from the **AC2013 Lesson 03** folder and save it as `AC03-R02-K4C-[FirstInitialLastName]`.

2. If a Security Warning appears, click **Enable Content**.

3. Select the **Staff** table in the Navigation Pane and choose **Create**→**Forms**→**More Forms**→**Multiple Items**.

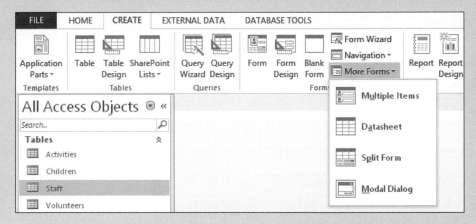

A new multiple item form displaying the staff information opens in Layout View.

4. Drag up the lower edge of the **Staff ID** text box to better fit the height of the data.

5. Resize each column by clicking in a text box and dragging the right border to the left to better fit the width of the data.

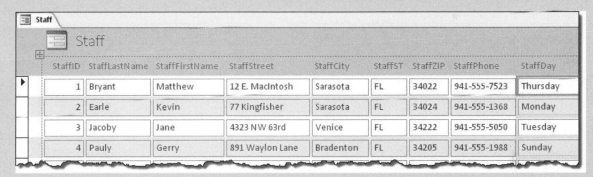

If the Property Sheet is in the way, you may close it.

Apply a Theme to a Form

6. On the Design tab, choose any Theme from the Themes menu.

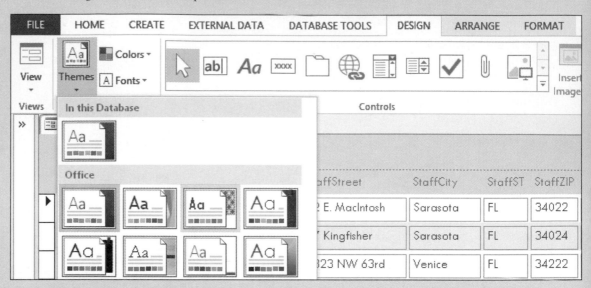

7. Resize the text boxes, as needed.

8. Switch to **Form View**.

Print a Form Page

9. Choose **File→Print→Print**.

10. Choose the **Pages** option.

11. Type **1** in both the **From** box and the **To** box.

12. Check the **Print to File** box, and click **OK**.

13. Save the file as `AC03-R02-K4CForm-[FirstInitialLastName]` in your **AC2013 Lesson 03** folder.

14. Save the form as `Staff-MultiItem`, and then close all open objects and exit **Access**.

15. Submit your final files based on the guidelines provided by your instructor.

    To view examples of how your file or files should look at the end of this exercise, go to the student resource center.

Create a Form and Add a Title and an Image

Kids for Change, an organization that gets children involved in community activities, has hired you to help redesign their forms. In this exercise, you will create a form in Design View to facilitate management of the Activities table. Then you will add an image to the Form Header and print one page of the form. Finally, you will use Access Help to learn about the Image Gallery.

Create a Form in Design View

1. Start **Access**. Open **AC03-R03-K4C** from the **AC2013 Lesson 03** folder and save it as **AC03-R03-K4C-[FirstInitialLastName]**.

2. If a Security Warning appears, click **Enable Content**.

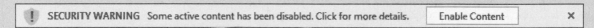

3. Choose **Create→Forms→Form Design**.

   A blank form design grid opens. The Property Sheet may also be open.

4. Choose **Design→Tools→Add Existing Fields**.

5. Click **Show All Tables** to display the available tables.

6. Double-click the **Activities** table to show the fields in the table.

7. Click and drag each field to the form design grid, then close the **Field List**.

Arrange Controls on a Form

8. Click in the **horizontal ruler** above the left column of labels to select the three controls (Activity ID, Activity, Location) and choose **Arrange→Sizing & Ordering→Align Left**.

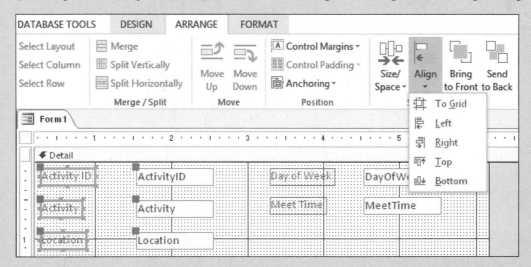

9. Left-align the three columns of the remaining controls (text boxes, labels, and text boxes).

10. Click the **vertical ruler** to the left of the top row of controls and choose **Arrange→ Sizing & Ordering→Align Top**.

11. Top-align the second row of controls.

Modify Form Controls

12. Select all the label controls.

    Hint: Lasso the left column of labels, press Shift *and lasso the right column of labels.*

13. Choose **Design→Tools→Property Sheet** and click the **Format** tab.

14. Enter **1** in the **Width** property and **.25** in the **Height** property.

15. Select *all* the controls in the Detail section.

16. Make these settings.

Font Name	Arial Narrow
Font Size	14
Fore Color	Black (Text 1)

17. Select the **ActivityID** and **MeetTime** text boxes and type **.8** for the **Width** property.

18. Select the **Activity** and **Location** text boxes and type **1.8** for the **Width** property.

19. Select just the first column of labels and type **.1** for the **Left** property.

20. Select the first column of text boxes and type **1.2** for the **Left** property.

21. Type **3.1** for the **Left** property of the second column of labels, and type **4.2** for the **Left** property of the second column of text boxes.

Modify Form Layout

22. Choose **Design→Header/Footer→Title**.

    Access opens the Form Header to accommodate the new title.

23. Type **Kids for Change** as the new **Title** label and tap Enter.

24. Click the **Auto-Logo box** to the left of the new Title label and tap Delete.

25. Click the Title control; press Ctrl and tap C to copy the title.

26. Press ⌈Ctrl⌉ and tap ⌈V⌉ to paste the copy below the title.

If Access does not automatically enlarge the Form Header section to accommodate the subtitle, you can resize the section manually.

Your form now includes a title and a subtitle in the Form Header section.

27. Highlight the existing text in the subtitle control; type **Activities** in the subtitle control, and tap ⌈Enter⌉.

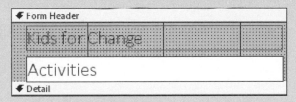

28. Save the form as **Activities Form**.

Apply a Theme and Add an Image

29. Choose **Design→Themes→Themes** and choose a Theme for the form.

30. Choose **Design→Controls→Insert Image** and click **Browse**.

31. Choose **All Files** (*.*) in the Browse dialog box and navigate to the **AC2013 Lesson 03** folder, select **K4C-logo.bmp**, and click **OK**.

32. Click to the right of the title, drag the mouse down and to the right, and release it to insert the image.

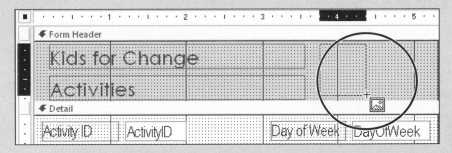

33. Change the **Width** and **Height** properties to **.7** for the image.

34. Switch to **Form View**.

If some of your data values do not fit in the text boxes, you can switch to Layout View and resize the controls using the techniques you learned in this lesson.

Print a Form Page

35. Choose **File→Print→Print**.

36. Choose the **Pages** option.

37. Type **1** in both the **From** box and the **To** box.

38. Check the **Print to File** box, and click **OK**.

39. Save the file as **AC03-R03-K4CForm-[FirstInitialLastName]**, in your **AC2013 Lesson 03** folder.

40. Save and close the form.

Use Access Help

41. Click **Microsoft Access Help** [?].

42. Type **image gallery** in the Search box.

43. Find and read an article or video that teaches how to add images to the Image Gallery.

44. Exit **Access**. Submit your final files based on the guidelines provided by your instructor.

Apply Your Skills

Create a Form in Design View

Universal Corporate Events is a planner of corporate, professional, and high-end private events. UCE has been purchased by retired New York banker J. G. Buckley. As the head of in-house development for the newly-acquired company, you have been tasked with revamping the image of Universal Corp, including everything from reports to forms. In this exercise, you will create a new Personnel form in Design View.

Create a Form in Design View

1. Start **Access**. Open **AC03-A01-UniversalCorp** from the **AC2013 Lesson 03** folder and save it as **AC03-A01-UniversalCorp-[FirstInitialLastName]**.

2. If a Security Warning appears, click **Enable Content**.

3. Choose **Create→Forms→Form Design** and open the Field List.

4. Click **Show All Tables** in the Field List, and double-click the **Personnel** table.

5. Drag each field to the form design grid.

6. Select the left-most column of **labels**, and choose **Arrange→Sizing & Ordering→Align→Left**.

7. Neatly align the remaining controls.

8. Open the **Property Sheet** and resize all the Labels to **1** width.

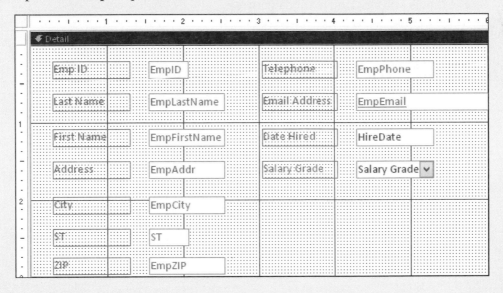

All the fields should be placed in the Detail section on the form grid.

Add a Logo and Apply a Theme

9. Display the **Form Header** section and choose **Design→Header/Footer→Title**.

10. Type **Universal Corporate Events Ltd.**, press ⌨Ctrl and tap ⌨Enter to move to the next line, and type **Personnel**.

11. Delete the **Auto_Logo** box to the left of the title then drag the left edge of the title to the right to make room for the logo.

12. Choose Insert Image, then navigate to the **AC2013 Lesson 03** folder and select **UCE-logo.bmp**.

13. Click to the left of the title, drag the mouse down and to the right, and release it to insert the image.

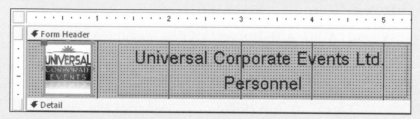

14. Open the **Property Sheet**, if necessary. Set the logo Width and Height to **.7** each.

15. Make the **Top** property **.05**.

16. Choose **Solid** for the Border Style property and **1 pt** for the Border Width.

17. Choose **Blue, Accent 5, Darker 50%** for the Border Color.

18. Make any desired cosmetic changes to the form, such as changing formatting properties of the labels and resizing text box controls.

19. Choose **Design→Tools→Tab Order** and change the tab order so the control passes from Emp ID to Telephone and then to Last Name.

20. Save the form as **Personnel Mgmt** and open it in **Form View**.

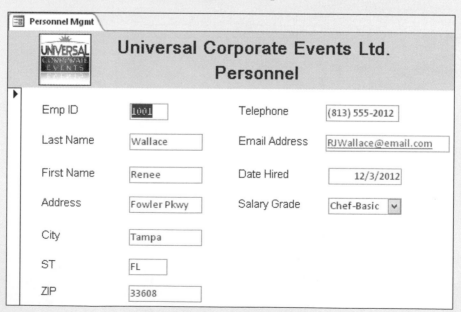

21. Close the **Personnel Mgmt** form and the database. Exit **Access**.

22. Submit your final file based on the guidelines provided by your instructor.

    To view examples of how your file or files should look at the end of this exercise, go to the student resource center.

Edit Labels, Format Controls, and Set Properties

J.G. Buckley's son, Hubert, new CEO of Universal Corporate Events, has asked you to revamp the image of Universal Corp. In this exercise, you will redesign a company form, editing the labels, formatting the controls, and setting its properties. Then, you will use Access Help to explore how to add a command button. You will finish by printing a sample page of the form for the CEO's approval.

Open a Form and Edit Label Text

1. Start **Access**. Open **AC03-A02-UniversalCorp** from the **AC2013 Lesson 03** folder and save it as **AC03-A02-UniversalCorp-[FirstInitialLastName]**.

2. If the Security Warning appears, click **Enable Content**.

3. Open the **Event Schedules** form in **Design View**.

4. Change the **Location** label to **Venue**.

5. Change the **Event ID** label to **Event Code**.

Modify Form Control Properties

6. If the Property Sheet is not shown, choose **Design→Tools→Property Sheet**.

7. Select the **Title** control (Universal Corporate Event) and set these properties.

Property	New Value
Caption	Universal Corporate Events Ltd.
Width	4.5
Height	.3
Left	.02
Font Name	Georgia
Fore Color	Blue, Accent 5, Darker 50%

8. Select the subtitle (Scheduling) and set these properties.

Property	New Value
Width	4.5
Height	.3
Left	.02
Font Weight	Light
Fore Color	Blue, Accent 5, Darker 50%

Access 2013

9. Select all the labels in the Detail section and change these properties.

Property	New Value
Width	1.3
Height	.3
Left	1
Special Effect	Raised
Font Name	Arial
Font Size	12
Font Weight	Semi-bold
Fore Color	Blue, Accent 5, Darker 50%

10. Select all the text boxes in the Detail section and change these properties.

Property	New Value
Height	.3
Left	2.75
Special Effect	Sunken
Font Name	Arial
Font Size	14

Modify Form Layout

11. Click the Form Header section bar and change the Back Color property to **White, Background 1**.

12. Click the Detail section bar and change the Back Color to **Blue, Accent 5, Lighter 80%**.

13. Open the form in **Form View**.

Print a Form Page

14. Check the **Print to File** box and print one page of the form (as a PDF file or a print file) to your **AC2013 Lesson 03** folder, naming the file `AC03-A02-UCEForm-[FirstInitialLastName]`.

15. Save and close the form.

16. Submit your final file based on the guidelines provided by your instructor.

Use Access Help

17. Click **Help** ⍰ and type `command button` in the Search Help box.

18. Find an article or video that instructs how to create a form command button.

19. As directed by your instructor, create and submit a write-up on what you found.

20. Close the database and exit **Access**.

To view examples of how your file or files should look at the end of this exercise, go to the student resource center.

APPLY YOUR SKILLS AC03-A03

Create a Form, Work with Form Headers, and Add a Logo

In this exercise, you will create a new form for managing UCE's event venue information, add and format a form header and title, and add an original company logo.

Create a Form Using the Form Wizard

1. Start **Access**. Open **AC03-A03-UniversalCorp** from the **AC2013 Lesson 03** folder and save it as `AC03-A03-UniversalCorp-[FirstInitialLastName]`.

2. If a Security Warning appears, click **Enable Content**.

3. Use the Form Wizard to create a form that uses the **Venues** table as the record source. Include all the fields from the table, use the **Columnar** layout, and name the form **Event Venues Form**.

Add a Title and Logo (Controls) to a Form

4. Switch to **Design View**.

5. Select the default title, open the Property Sheet, and set these properties.

Property	New Value
Width	3.5
Top	.4
Left	.75
Font Name	Georgia
Text Align	Center
Fore Color	Blue, Accent 5, Darker 50%

Now you have room for a company name title and company logo.

6. Choose **Design→Header/Footer→Title**.

7. Delete the **Auto_Logo** control.

8. Click the new **Title** control and set the following properties:

Property	New Value
Caption	Universal Corporate Events
Width	3.5
Height	.35
Left	.75
Font Name	Georgia
Text Align	Center
Font Weight	Semi-bold
Fore Color	Blue, Accent 5, Darker 50%

9. Click the **Form Header** bar and choose **Design→Controls→Insert Image**.

10. Navigate to your **AC2013 Lesson 03** folder and select **UCE-logo.bmp**.

11. Click near the top-left corner of the **Form Header**, to the left of the title, and drag the mouse down and to the right.

Modify Form Controls

12. Type **.7** as the **Width** and **Height** properties for the image.

13. Select all the labels in the Detail section and change these properties.

Property	New Value
Width	1.5
Height	.25
Left	.25
Special Effect	Raised
Font Name	Arial
Font Size	12
Font Weight	Semi-bold
Fore Color	Blue, Accent 5, Darker 50%

14. Select all the text boxes in the Detail section and change these properties.

Property	New Value
Height	.25
Left	2
Special Effect	Sunken
Font Name	Arial
Font Size	12

15. Press Shift, deselect the **VenueWebSite** text box, and change the Fore Color property to **Black, Text 1** for all the other text box controls.

Modify Form Layout

16. Click the **Form Header** section bar and change the Back Color property to **White, Background 1**.

17. Click the **Detail** section bar and change the Back Color to **Blue, Accent 5, Lighter 80%**.

18. Switch to **Form View**.

Print a Form Page

19. Check the **Print to File** box and print one page of the form (as a PDF file or to a print file) to your **AC2013 Lesson 03** folder, naming the file `AC03-A03-UCEForm-[FirstInitialLastName]`.

20. Save and close the form. Close the database and exit **Access**.

21. Submit your final files based on the guidelines provided by your instructor.

Extend Your Skills

In the course of working through the Extend Your Skills exercises, you will think critically as you use the skills taught in the lesson to complete the assigned projects. To evaluate your mastery and completion of the exercises, your instructor may use a rubric, with which more points are allotted according to performance characteristics. (The more you do, the more you earn!) Ask your instructor how your work will be evaluated.

AC03-E01 That's the Way I See It

In this exercise, you will design and format a new form. In the **AC2013 Lesson 03** folder, open **AC03-E01-BJL** and save it as **AC03-E01-BJL-[FirstInitialLastName]**.

Use Access Help to learn about Navigation Forms; then create a navigation/switchboard form and save it as **AC03-E01-Navigation-[FirstInitialLastName]**. Use the Sales Invoices query as the source (include all the query fields on the form) for the form. Use the skills you learned in this lesson to customize the form and its controls, and add a title and image.

As directed, send one page of the form to a printer, save the form as a database object, or publish it as a PDF or an XPS file named **AC03-E01-NavigationForm-[FirstInitialLastName]**.

You will be evaluated based on the inclusion of all elements, your ability to follow directions, your ability to apply newly learned skills to a real-world situation, your creativity, and your accuracy in creating objects and/or entering data. Submit your final files based on the guidelines provided by your instructor.

AC03-E02 Be Your Own Boss

In this exercise, you will create and format a split form for Blue Jean Landscaping. You will use Access Help to learn how to change an existing form into a split form and then change a database form into a split form.

Open **AC03-E02-BJL** from the **AC2013 Lesson 03** folder and save it as **AC03-E02-BJL-[FirstInitialLastName]**. Search Access Help for information about creating split forms from existing forms, and then convert the Equipment Services form into a split form named **ESF-SplitForm**. Apply a Theme and resize the labels and text boxes to best fit the data. Brainstorm and enter ten new records. As directed, send one page of the form (that contains a new record) to a printer, save the form as a database object, or publish it as a PDF or an XPS file named **AC03-E02-SplitForm-[FirstInitialLastName]**.

You will be evaluated based on the inclusion of all elements, your ability to follow directions, your ability to apply newly learned skills to a real-world situation, your creativity, and your accuracy in creating objects and/or entering data. Submit your final files based on the guidelines provided by your instructor.

Transfer Your Skills

In the course of working through the Transfer Your Skills exercises, you will use critical-thinking and creativity skills to complete the assigned projects using skills taught in the lesson. To evaluate your mastery and completion of the exercises, your instructor may use a rubric, with which more points are allotted according to performance characteristics. (The more you do, the more you earn!) Ask your instructor how your work will be evaluated.

AC03-T01 Use the Web as a Learning Tool

Throughout this book, you will be provided with an opportunity to use the Internet as a learning tool by completing WebQuests. According to the original creators of WebQuests, as described on their website (WebQuest.org), a WebQuest is "an inquiry-oriented activity in which most or all of the information used by learners is drawn from the web." To complete the WebQuest projects in this book, navigate to the student resource center and choose the WebQuest for the lesson on which you are currently working. The subject of each WebQuest will be relevant to the material found in the lesson.

WebQuest Subject: Investigate designing and creating custom, original images for Access forms.

Submit your final file(s) based on the guidelines provided by your instructor.

AC03-T02 Demonstrate Proficiency

Stormy BBQ, a local BBQ restaurant featuring fresh locally grown vegetables and local farm raised pork and beef is opening a new restaurant on Main Street. The owner would like to change the look of their forms and reports to appeal to the downtown clientele.

Open **AC03-T02-StormyBBQ** from the **AC2013 Lesson 03** folder and save it as **AC03-T02-StormyBBQ-[FirstInitialLastName]**. Use the formatting tools and techniques you learned in this lesson to modify the Restaurant Form to reflect a more sophisticated, elegant look. Change the colors and styles of the form sections and the controls. Add the Stormy BBQ name to the title and a subtitle that describes the form. Select appropriate fonts. Be sure to add a Form Header to the Restaurant Form that maintains the same style as the Form Header in the Merchandise Form. Use Access Help to learn about background images and add the background image **SBQ-logo.bmp** to the Merchandise Form. Create a form using the Staff table as the record source, format it in the style you prefer, and save it as **Staff List**. Enter at least five more records using the Staff List form. Print one page from each form (Restaurant Form, Merchandise Form, and Staff List) and then save the database in your **AC2013 Lesson 03** folder.

Submit your final files based on the guidelines provided by your instructor.

Querying a Database

LEARNING OBJECTIVES

After studying this lesson, you will be able to:

- Create, save, and run select queries
- Set query criteria and sort order
- Create and format a calculated field
- Use functions in query expressions
- Create special types of queries

One of the main goals of a database is to organize data so that information can be located and retrieved quickly. People in all types of businesses retrieve stored data and information daily, often at a moment's notice. When data is stored in tables in a relational database, you can search that information and extract records that meet specific criteria using a query, a database object used to locate records based on the conditions you set.

In this lesson, you will create select and crosstab queries and set query criteria. You will also create and format a calculated field, set a query sort order, and set multiple query conditions. Finally, you will create special queries designed to find unmatched records between tables and find duplicate entries in a database table.

Using Queries to Get Answers

As technology evolves, a smart business person will take advantage of the new opportunities that arise. An example of one such technology is *Quick Response* (QR) code. QR code is a square-shaped barcode that can be scanned by smartphones to quickly provide additional information about a product, open a website, send an email, or transfer contact information.

You have been asked to query the Winchester Web Design database and compile two separate customer lists. The lists will be used to notify all past clients of the QR code upgrade that can be added to their website contact forms. The first list will include only the first and last name of the clients and their email address. The second list will include the first and last name of the clients and their mailing addresses, sorted by ZIP code. Additionally, you have been asked to build queries that instantly calculate the total income from all the Winchester Web Design services, and from specific areas such as blogs or shopping carts.

Winchester Web Design Invoices

Inv Num	Inv Date	Description	Price	Qty	Line Total
1	3/15/2012	Home Page, Nav, CSS, Design	$400.00	1	$400.00
1	3/15/2012	Secondary Page	$200.00	3	$600.00
1	3/15/2012	Image, Custom Designed	$40.00	3	$120.00
2					
3					
3					
4					
5					
5					
6					
6					
6					
7					
7					
7					
7					
8					
8					
9					
9		Image, Custo			
9	7/20/2012	Hourly Rate f			
10	7/30/2012	Secondary Pa			

Customer Mailing List

Last Name	First Name	Street Address	City	ST	ZIP
Blaser	Helen	600 Fowler	Sarasota	FL	33802
Mansur	Jo	985 Del Prado	Bradenton	FL	33850
Roberts	John	103 Pine Terrace	Tampa	FL	34022
Fleetwood	Candace	92 Highland St	Northport	FL	34023
Davis	Peter	65 Terracotta Way	Sarasota	FL	34024
Klein	Joyce				
Thibeaux	Pierre				
Hassan	Ahmed				
Jeffries	Daniel				
Santos	Emily				
Anders	Mark				
Abrams	John				
Winkler	Samuel				
Smith	William				

Customer Email List

Last Name	First Name	Email
Abrams	John	JPAbrams@email.com
Anders	Mark	AndersM@email.com
Blaser	Helen	BlasingHel@email.com
Davis	Peter	DavisAngie@email.com
Fleetwood	Candace	CandyWin@email.com
Hassan	Ahmed	HansAnge@email.com
Jeffries	Daniel	DannyJ@email.com
Klein	Joyce	KleinBrian@email.com
Mansur	Jo	Mansur@email.com

Creating Select Queries

Video Library   http://labyrinthelab.com/videos   Video Number: AC13-V0401

Some tables, such as a Customers table, may contain ten or more fields. Once you exceed seven or eight fields, it may be difficult to display the entire record on one line of a printout or screen. However, when you create a select query to display or select only certain fields, such as customer names and addresses, the resulting product will be small enough to attractively display each record on a single line. Consequently, the address list will be easier to look at in Datasheet View or on a printed report. You can create and save a query to use each time you need to print an updated list.

A select query allows you to select records based upon certain criteria that you set. A query asks a question, such as *What are the customer addresses?* Or, *How much money did the company make last month?* The answer to the question is a set of records. A select query is basically a database inquiry that selects only the requested records.

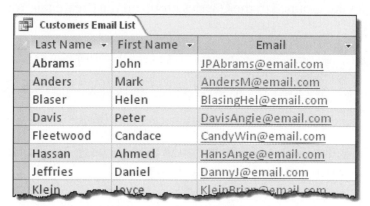

A select query displays only the requested fields from the Customers table.

Reviewing Query Features

Some important points about queries to keep in mind:

- A query acts as a saved question you ask a database.
- A query is a subset of data from one or more tables.
- Data displayed in query results remain stored in the original table rather than in the query.
- When you edit data in query results, you are actually editing the data stored in the source table.
- Queries are dynamic objects that display up-to-date data stored in database tables.
- Queries can be used to create forms and reports, which may contain fields from multiple tables.

Query results datasheets enable you to filter or selectively organize data using the same techniques you may use to filter and organize table datasheets.

Identifying Tools for Creating Select Queries

The most common type of query is the select query. A select query retrieves data from one or more tables and displays the results in a datasheet. You can update records that appear in the query results datasheet, group records, and calculate sums, counts, averages, and other types of equations using query results.

The Query Wizard walks you through the query creation process. —

Query Design enables you to create a query from scratch.

Access provides two distinct tools for creating queries:

■ Query Wizard

■ Query Design

Buttons for creating queries are grouped in the Queries group on the Create tab. You will use both tools to create queries.

DEVELOP YOUR SKILLS AC04-D01

Create a Select Query Using the Query Wizard

In this exercise, you will create a select query using the Query Wizard to create a customer email list.

1. Open **AC04-D01-WinWebDesign** from the **AC2013 Lesson 04** folder and save it as **AC04-D01-WinWebDesign-[FirstInitialLastName]**.

   Replace the bracketed text with your first initial and last name. For example, if your name is Bethany Smith, your filename would look like this: AC04-D01-WinWebDesign-BSmith.

2. Follow these steps to activate the Query Wizard:

Ⓑ Choose **Create →
Queries→Query
Wizard**.

Ⓐ Select the **Customers** table in the Navigation Pane. —

3. Follow these steps to select the query type:

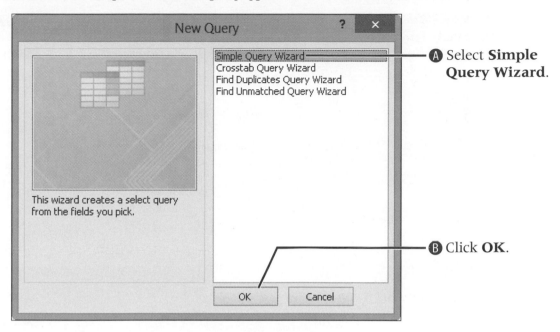

Ⓐ Select **Simple Query Wizard**.

Ⓑ Click **OK**.

4. Follow these steps to move selected fields to the query:

Ⓐ Select the **Customers table** in the Tables/Queries box.

Ⓑ Select the **CustLastName** field in the Available Fields list.

Ⓒ Click the **Move** button to move the field to the Selected Fields list.

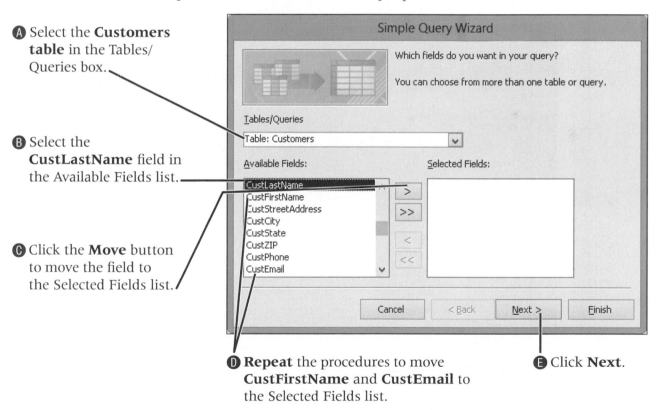

Ⓓ **Repeat** the procedures to move **CustFirstName** and **CustEmail** to the Selected Fields list.

Ⓔ Click **Next**.

If you add the wrong field by accident, double-click the name to move it back to the Available Fields list or select it and click Move Back.

5. Follow these steps to complete the query:

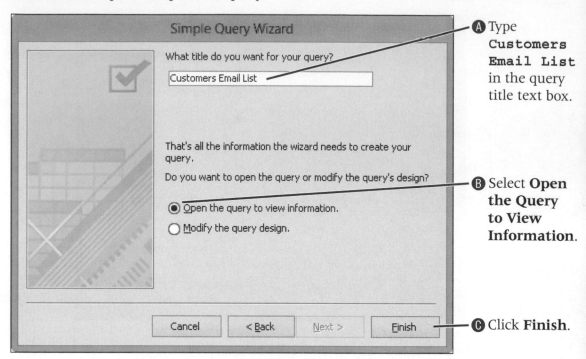

ⓐ Type **Customers Email List** in the query title text box.

ⓑ Select **Open the Query to View Information.**

ⓒ Click **Finish.**

The query results datasheet only includes the three selected fields from all the records.

6. Review the query results datasheet then **close** ☒ the query.

Unless directed otherwise, keep Access and any databases or database objects being used open at the end of each exercise.

Creating a Select Query Using Query Design

Video Library http://labyrinthelab.com/videos Video Number: AC13-V0402

The query you created in the previous exercise only displayed a few fields, but it reported every single record in the table. That may not be a problem for a small table, but when thousands of records and multiple tables are involved, it is often necessary to select only specific records by setting precise criteria. Using Query Design View, Access allows you to:

■ Select fields from multiple tables.

■ Set criteria to locate records based on data contained in one or more fields.

■ Calculate totals.

■ Show or hide fields containing criteria that are in the query results datasheet.

Identifying Features of the Query Design Grid

When in Query Design View, you are able to add fields from one or more tables into the display grid. You can place the fields in the order in which you want them to appear in the query results datasheet. In addition, the query design grid contains elements that enable you to set specific search criteria or sort the data.

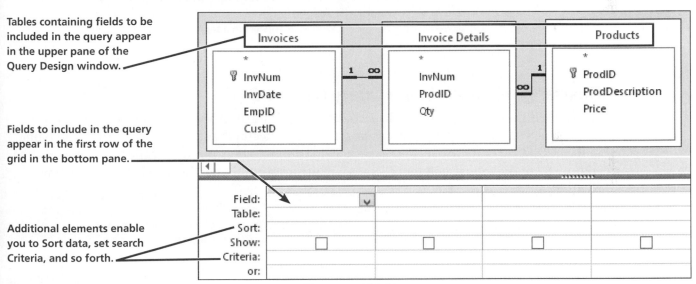

The query design grid lets you add fields to a query.

Adding Fields to the Query Design Grid

Access offers a variety of techniques for adding fields to the query grid.

■ Double-click a field name to add the field to the next available column of the query design grid.

■ Drag a field to the next column in the grid.

■ Click the Field row of a column in the query grid and select the field from the drop-down list.

■ Double-click the asterisk (*) that appears at the top of the field list to add all fields to the grid.

When you use the asterisk to add all table fields to the grid, Access only places the table name in the Field row followed by a .* (dot asterisk). But when you run the query, each field appears in a separate column of the query results datasheet.

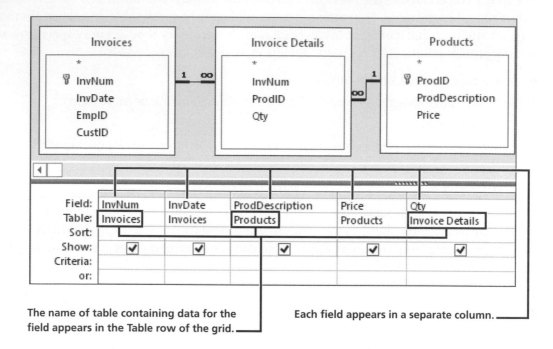

The name of table containing data for the field appears in the Table row of the grid.

Each field appears in a separate column.

Rearranging Fields in the Query Design Grid

You can rearrange query columns in Design View or Datasheet View by dragging and dropping them into position. Click the gray Column Heading selector that appears above the Field name in the query grid or datasheet to select the field column. Then, hover over the top of the selected column until the mouse pointer becomes a white arrow and drag the field column to a new position.

The gray Column Heading selector is used to select the field column.

You can click and move a field column when the mouse pointer becomes a white move arrow.

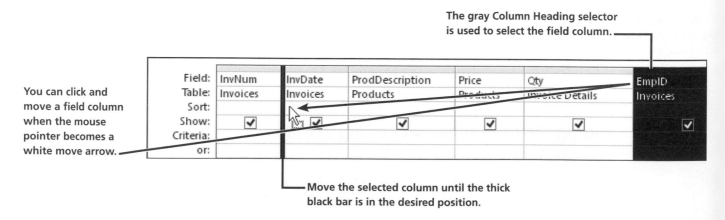

Move the selected column until the thick black bar is in the desired position.

Task	Procedure
Create a query using Query Design	Choose Create→Queries→Query Design 🗒.
Display query design from the query Datasheet View	Choose Home→Views→View to toggle between Design and Datasheet View; or, right-click the query tab and choose Design View.
Add fields to a query grid	Double-click a field name in the table field list; drag a field from the table field list to a query grid column; or, double-click the asterisk in the table field list to add all fields.
Add criteria to a query grid	Type the desired criteria into the Criteria row for the field that should contain the value. For instance, if you want all customers from Sarasota, type *Sarasota* in the Criteria row of the City field column.
Save a query	Click Save, name the query, and click OK; or close the query and name it when prompted.
Run a query	Double-click a query name in the Navigation Pane, or choose Design→Results→Run.

Create a Query Using Query Design

You have already created an email list for the Winchester Web Design customers and now need one for the company's employees. In this exercise, you will create a query to select fields from the Employees table in the Winchester Web Design database and then rearrange the columns in the query grid.

1. Choose **Create→Queries→Query Design** to display the Query Design Grid.

   Access displays a list of tables and existing queries in the database so you can choose the sources you want to include in the new query.

2. Follow these steps to add a table to the query:

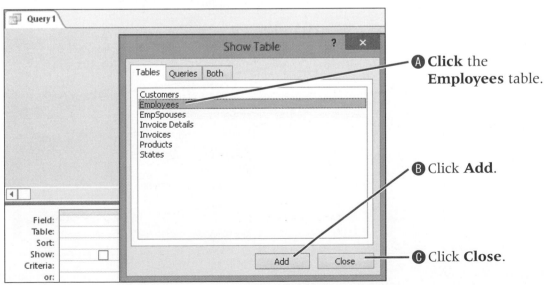

Ⓐ **Click** the **Employees** table.

Ⓑ Click **Add**.

Ⓒ Click **Close**.

Access 2013

3. Follow these steps to add fields (in a different order than they are in the underlying table) to the query grid:

Ⓐ Double-click **EmpFirstName** to add it to the query grid's first column.

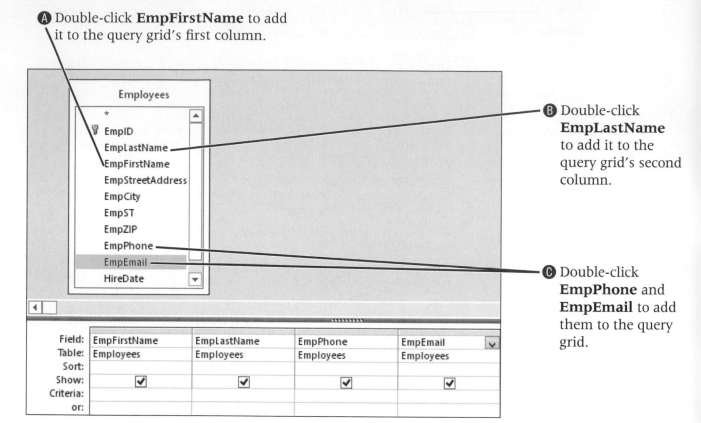

Ⓑ Double-click **EmpLastName** to add it to the query grid's second column.

Ⓒ Double-click **EmpPhone** and **EmpEmail** to add them to the query grid.

You can also click and drag fields to the query grid.

4. Follow these steps to save and then run the query:

Ⓐ Click **Save**.

Ⓑ Type **Employee Contact Info** in the **Query Name** text box and click **OK**.

Ⓒ Click **Run**.

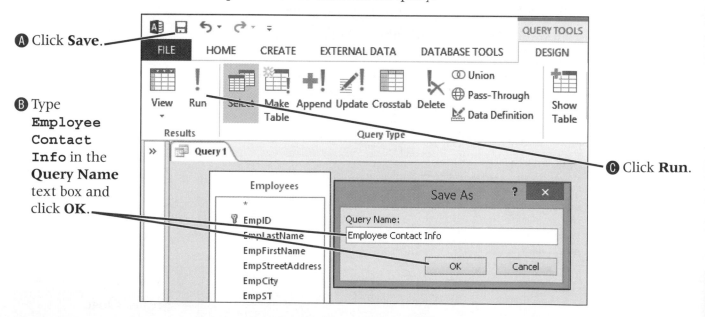

Access runs the query and displays four columns of data (First Name, Last Name, Telephone, and Email) for all Employee records.

First Name	Last Name	Telephone	Email
Jay	Winchester	(941) 555-9382	WinchesterJay@email.com
John	Kramer	(941) 555-3490	KramerJ@email.com
Julie	Mansfield	(941) 555-5218	JulieMansfield@email.com
Mike	Waters	(941) 555-3981	MikeWaters@email.com

5. Switch to **Design View**.

6. Follow these steps to rearrange fields in the query grid:

Ⓐ Hover the mouse pointer over the **Column Heading selector** for the EmpLastName column until the mouse pointer becomes a solid down-pointing arrow ↓, and click to select the field.

Ⓑ Click the **Column Heading selector** for EmpLastName again and use the new white move arrow to drag the selected field column to the left of the EmpFirstName column.

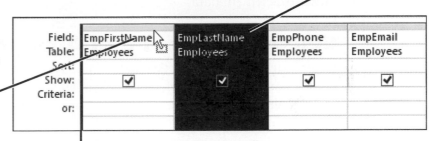

Ⓒ **Release** the **EmpLastName** field column when the thick black bar appears.

7. Choose **Design→Results→Run** to run the query again.

Last Name	First Name	Telephone	Email
Winchester	Jay	(941) 555-9382	WinchesterJay@email.com
Kramer	John	(941) 555-3490	KramerJ@email.com
Mansfield	Julie	(941) 555-5218	JulieMansfield@email.com
Waters	Mike	(941) 555-3981	MikeWaters@email.com

The Last Name field is now the first field displayed in the query.

8. Close the query, saving changes when prompted.

Designing a Query Using Multiple Tables

Video Library   http://labyrinthelab.com/videos   Video Number: AC13-V0403

Until now, the datasheets you have worked with have displayed data from only one table. There will be times when you need to view data contained in different tables within the same database. Queries allow you to do this.

Choosing Fields to Include in a Query

When you build a query, you select only those tables and fields that you want to display in the query results datasheet and leave out those fields that have no impact on the data you want to view or that are confidential. For example, if you were responsible for maintaining a list of FBI agents, would you want everyone with access to the database to know the addresses and phone numbers of all agents? By specifying only certain tables and fields in a database and displaying only the desired fields in a query, you can create a report or a form that only presents pertinent data.

Selecting a Field that Appears in Multiple Tables

When you work with table field lists, you may see multiple tables that contain the same ID field names. You may wonder which ID field to add to a query. The best practice is to identify the table for which the ID field is the *primary* key. This table will best allow you to retrieve other related data contained in that table.

Note that when you add fields from multiple tables, these tables must be related in order for the intended results to be displayed.

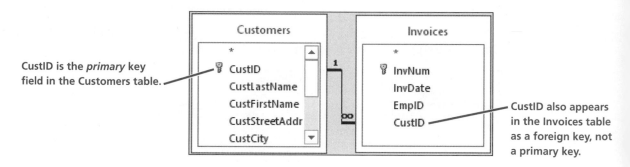

CustID is the *primary* key field in the Customers table.

CustID also appears in the Invoices table as a foreign key, not a primary key.

DEVELOP YOUR SKILLS AC04-D03
Create a Multi-Table Query

In this exercise, you will create a multi-table query to track the Winchester Web Design invoices by invoice number using Query Design View.

1. Choose **Create→Queries→Query Design** .

   An empty query grid and the Show Table dialog box open.

2. Double-click the following table names in the Show Table dialog box to add the table field lists to the upper pane of the query: **Invoices**, **Invoice Details**, and **Products**.

   If the Show Table dialog box does not appear, choose Design→Query Setup→Show Table.

3. Close the Show Table dialog box, then follow these steps to add fields to the query grid:

Ⓐ Double-click fields from the **Invoices** table in this order: **InvNum, InvDate, EmpID**.

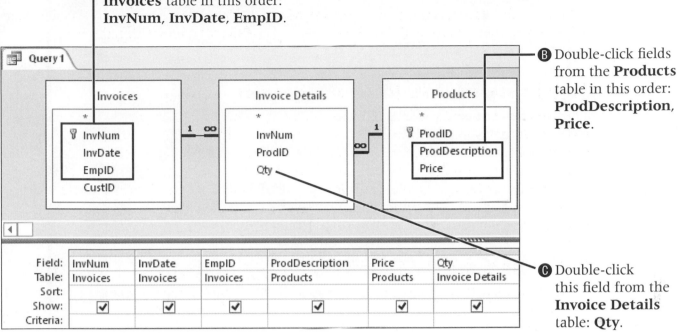

Ⓑ Double-click fields from the **Products** table in this order: **ProdDescription, Price**.

Ⓒ Double-click this field from the **Invoice Details** table: **Qty**.

Your tables may be aligned differently, but the fields should appear in the query grid in the order shown.

If your tables do not line up neatly, click and drag the table title bar to the left or to the right as desired.

4. Click in the **Sort** row for the InvNum field in the query grid and choose **Ascending**.

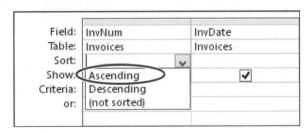

5. Save the query as **InvoicesList** and click **OK**.

Access 2013

6. Choose **Design→Results→Run** to display the query results.

InvNum	Invoice Date	Emp ID	Description	Price	Qty
1	3/15/2012	JFW	Secondary Page	$200.00	6
1	3/15/2012	JFW	Image, Custom Designed	$40.00	11
1	3/15/2012	JFW	Home Page, Nav, CSS, Design	$400.00	1
2	4/2/2012	MJW	Image, Custom Designed	$40.00	14
2	4/2/2012	MJW	Home Page, Nav, CSS, Design	$400.00	1
2	4/2/2012	MJW	Secondary Page	$200.00	7
2	4/2/2012	MJW	Hourly Rate for Modifications	$80.00	5
3	5/11/2012	JMM	Image, Custom Designed	$40.00	6
3	5/11/2012	JMM	Secondary Page	$200.00	2
4	5/30/2012	JMM	Blog, Integrated into Site	$300.00	1
4	5/30/2012	JMM	Hourly Rate for Modifications	$80.00	2
4	5/30/2012	JMM	Image, Custom Designed	$40.00	2
5	6/19/2012	JFW	Image, Custom Designed	$40.00	9
5	6/19/2012	JFW	Secondary Page	$200.00	11
5	6/19/2012	JFW	Home Page, Nav, CSS, Design	$400.00	1
6	6/23/2012	MJW	Hourly Rate for Modifications	$80.00	3
6	6/23/2012	MJW	Blog, Integrated into Site	$300.00	1
6	6/23/2012	MJW	Home Page, Nav, CSS, Design	$400.00	1
6	6/23/2012	MJW	Secondary Page	$200.00	6
7	7/11/2012	JMM	Image, Custom Designed	$40.00	14

Setting Query Criteria

Video Library   http://labyrinthelab.com/videos   Video Number: AC13-V0404

As you begin working with large databases that contain thousands or even hundreds of thousands of records, you will experience the power behind queries that enables you to specify criteria, or conditions that data must meet. When you run the query, Access lists only those records containing data that meet the criteria. This is the feature used by sportscasters, live chat specialists working for an online retailer, and others who need data and questions answered right away.

Adding Criteria to a Query

You can filter and sort records while working in Table Design View, Form Design View, and to a limited degree in Report Design View. However, the best way to sort and filter data is through a query, because you can save each individual query with a meaningful name. Access uses standard comparison operators ($<$, $>$, $=$, $>=$, $<=$, $<>$) to set validation rules to help define a query's criteria. Setting query criteria limits the number of records displayed in query results to only those records with values in the selected field columns that meet the criteria. In addition, the following comparison and logical criteria can be used to limit data returned in queries.

Criteria Expression	Criteria Description and Sample
> 123	*Greater than*: For a numeric data field; returns records for all values greater than 123
< 100.45	*Less than*: For a currency data field; returns all values less than 100.45
>= Smith	*Greater than or equal*: For a text data field—all values from Smith through the end of the alphabet
<> 2	*Unequal*: For a numeric data field—all values unequal to 2. You could also use Not
Not Smith	For a text data field—all records for values except Smith
Not T*	For text data field—all values that don't start with the letter T
"London" Or "Hedge End"	For a text data field—orders shipped to London or Hedge End
In("Canada", "UK")	For a text data field—records containing the values Canada or UK in the criteria field
Between #1/1/2013# And #12/31/2013#	For date data field—dates from January 1, 2013 through December 31, 2013 (Access inserts the # signs after you type: Between 1/1/2013 and 12/31/2013)
Between Date( ) And DateAdd ("M", 3, Date( ))	For a date data field—values required between today's date and three months from today's date
Date()	For a date data field—values for today's date
< Date( ) – 30	For a date data field—values 30 days prior to the current date

Hiding Columns in the Query Results Datasheet

Suppose your company determines the price of a product by marking up the cost by 50%. So if your company bought a widget for $100, they would sell it for $150. As a salesperson, you need to show your customers the price of your products, but it would not be wise to disclose the amount of markup. Consequently, you include the Cost field in your query, but hide it when you run the query. This is easily accomplished by unchecking the Show checkbox for the Cost field in the query grid.

Access 2013

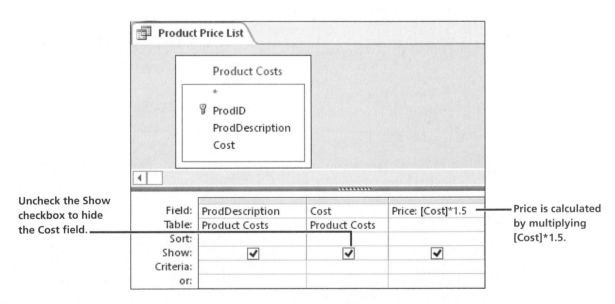

Uncheck the Show checkbox to hide the Cost field.

Price is calculated by multiplying [Cost]*1.5.

Building Queries with Criteria

When building a query you often add criteria to locate specific records in the database. Access recognizes any added or modified criteria as a change in the query design. As a result, when you close the query, Access prompts you to save it. Saving the query saves the criteria as part of the query. However, you may be just running what-if scenarios or you want to set different criteria each time you run the query. In those cases, you would choose *No* when Access prompts you to save the file.

DEVELOP YOUR SKILLS AC04-D04
Add Criteria and Run a Query

In this exercise, you will add criteria to the query grid and run the query.

1. Open the **InvoicesList** query, if necessary, and choose **Home→Views→View** ![icon].

2. Follow these steps to add criteria to the query grid:

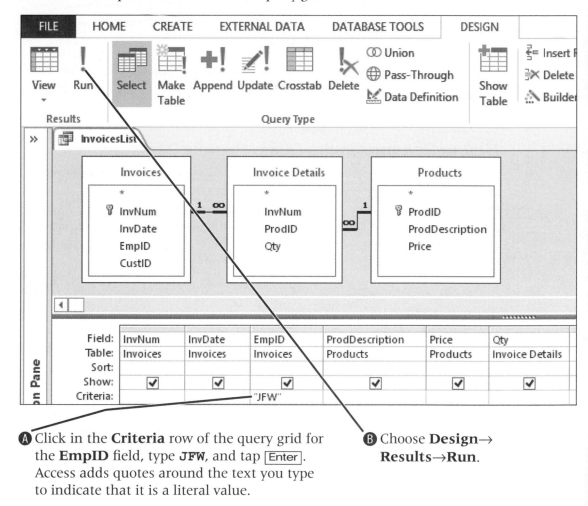

Ⓐ Click in the **Criteria** row of the query grid for the **EmpID** field, type **JFW**, and tap Enter. Access adds quotes around the text you type to indicate that it is a literal value.

Ⓑ Choose **Design→ Results→Run**.

Access runs the query and only returns the invoices associated with EmpID JFW.

InvNum	Invoice Date	Emp ID	Description	Price	Qty
1	3/15/2012	JFW	Secondary Page	$200.00	6
1	3/15/2012	JFW	Image, Custom Designed	$40.00	11
1	3/15/2012	JFW	Home Page, Nav, CSS, Design	$400.00	1
5	6/19/2012	JFW	Image, Custom Designed	$40.00	9
5	6/19/2012	JFW	Home Page, Nav, CSS, Design	$400.00	1
5	6/19/2012	JFW	Secondary Page	$200.00	11
8	7/11/2012	JFW	Home Page, Nav, CSS, Design	$400.00	1
8	7/11/2012	JFW	Secondary Page	$200.00	9
8	7/11/2012	JFW	Shopping Cart, Basic	$400.00	1
8	7/11/2012	JFW	Image, Custom Designed	$40.00	21
8	7/11/2012	JFW	Hourly Rate for Modifications	$80.00	7
10	7/30/2012	JFW	Secondary Page	$200.00	4
10	7/30/2012	JFW	Image, Custom Designed	$40.00	9
10	7/30/2012	JFW	Blog, Integrated into Site	$300.00	1
19	12/10/2012	JFW	Hourly Rate for Modifications	$80.00	4

3. Close the query. Choose **No** when prompted to save the changes.

Saving changes to the query at this time would save the JFW criteria as part of the query. However, you plan to use the query for all employees in the future.

Using Wildcards

Video Library   http://labyrinthelab.com/videos   Video Number: AC13-V0405

The two most frequent wildcards with which you may be familiar are the asterisk (*) and the question mark (?). There are four additional wildcards. Each wildcard is described in the following table.

WILDCARD SYMBOLS	
Symbol	**Description of Use**
An asterisk (*)	Substitutes for a group of characters that appear at the position of the asterisk **Example**: If you type R* in the last name column of a query grid, Access will locate all last names beginning with *R* regardless of how many characters make up the name. In this case, *Rogers, Rich,* and *Rodriquez* would all appear in the results datasheet.
A question mark (?)	Substitutes for a single character that might appear at the position of the question mark **Example**: If you type m?s in the criteria row for a column, Access will locate records containing values such as *mrs, ms, mbs.*
Open/close brackets [ ]	Matches text or individual characters placed within the brackets individually **Example:** If you type ca[rt], Access will find cat and car but not cab or cad.
Exclamation point (!)	Matches any character within the brackets *except* those characters that follow the ! **Example:** If you type ca[!rt], Access will find cab, cad, cam, etc., but not cat or car.
Hyphen (-)	Matches characters at the wildcard position that fall within a range of ascending values **Example:** If you type ca[a-r], Access finds cab, cad, cam, car, etc., but not cat or cay.
Number sign (#)	Locates any numeric digit at the position of the # **Example:** If you type #10, Access locates 010, 110, 210, etc.

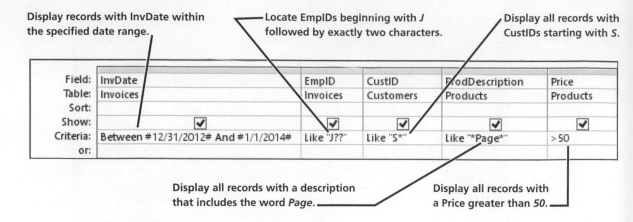

Display records with InvDate within the specified date range.

Locate EmpIDs beginning with *J* followed by exactly two characters.

Display all records with CustIDs starting with *S*.

Display all records with a description that includes the word *Page*.

Display all records with a Price greater than *50*.

Setting AND and OR Criteria

In some cases, you may need to select records that meet multiple criteria. Access uses two basic criteria conditions that apply to setting multiple criteria for a query: AND and OR. The basic principles for determining whether to use AND criteria or OR criteria in queries are as follows.

AND AND *OR* CRITERIA	
Criterion Type	**Description**
AND operator	Use to select records that meet *all* criteria set in all query grid fields. **Example:** Set an AND criteria to locate employees who are from Sarasota *and* who are web-certified by using *Sarasota* in the City field and *Yes* in the Web Certification field on the query grid.
OR operator	Use to select records meeting *one* condition *or another* condition whether the criteria are set for the same field or different fields. **Example:** Set OR criteria to locate customers from *either* Sarasota *or* Bradenton.

Positioning Multiple Criteria in the Query Grid

In the query grid, the AND criteria all appear on the same Criteria row even when criteria are set for different fields. When you set OR criteria, the first criterion is entered on the Criteria row in the grid while other criteria appear on the Or row in the grid.

Example of an AND Criteria

Setting criteria for two different fields on the same Criteria row creates an AND condition. With this type of criterion, Access locates only those records for employees who live in Sarasota *and* are web certified.

Field:	EmpLastName	EmpFirstName	EmpCity	HireDate	WebCert
Table:	Employees	Employees	Employees	Employees	Employees
Sort:					
Show:	☑	☑	☑	☑	☑
Criteria:			"Sarasota"		Yes
or:					

The AND criteria are on the same row.

Example of an OR Criteria

Setting criteria on both the Criteria row and the Or row creates an OR condition. With this type of criterion, Access locates those records for employees who live in Sarasota *or* in Bradenton.

The OR criteria are on different rows.

Setting OR criteria sometimes seems to operate backwards. In this example, you wanted to locate all records for employees from Sarasota *and* Bradenton, yet you use an OR condition. If you consider that there are no records that contain both Sarasota and Bradenton in the City field, it begins to make sense.

DEVELOP YOUR SKILLS AC04-D05

Use Wildcards and Multiple Criteria in Queries

In this exercise, you will use wildcards to locate variable data and set multiple criteria in a query to find out which customers have gotten blogs and which customers have added more than ten images at a time to their websites.

1. Right-click **Invoices Query** in the Navigation Pane and choose **Design View**.

2. Follow these steps to set multiple criteria in a query grid:

Ⓐ Click the **Criteria** row for **ProdDescription**, type **Blog***, and tap Enter. *Blog** converts to *Like "Blog*"*.

Ⓑ Click in the **Or** row for **ProdDescription** and type **Image***.

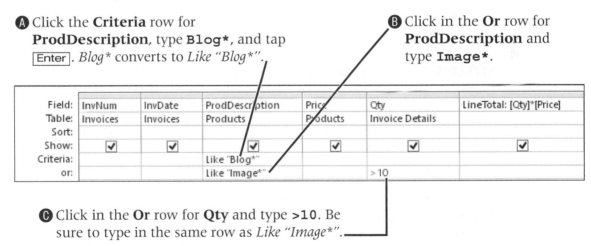

Ⓒ Click in the **Or** row for **Qty** and type **>10**. Be sure to type in the same row as *Like "Image*"*.

These criteria will select all records for Blogs and all records for Images with a Qty greater than 10.

3. Switch to **Datasheet View**.

Inv Num	Inv Date	Description	Price	Qty	LineTotal
4	5/30/2012	Blog, Integrated into Site	$300.00	1	$300.00
6	6/23/2012	Blog, Integrated into Site	$300.00	1	$300.00
10	7/30/2012	Blog, Integrated into Site	$300.00	1	$300.00
15	10/30/2012	Blog, Integrated into Site	$300.00	1	$300.00
34	8/5/2013	Blog, Integrated into Site	$300.00	1	$300.00
13	9/3/2012	Blog, Integrated into Site	$300.00	1	$300.00
16	11/5/2012	Blog, Integrated into Site	$300.00	1	$300.00
24	2/7/2013	Blog, Integrated into Site	$300.00	1	$300.00
29	3/12/2013	Blog, Integrated into Site	$300.00	1	$300.00
1	3/15/2012	Image, Custom Designed	$40.00	11	$440.00
7	7/11/2012	Image, Custom Designed	$40.00	14	$560.00
20	1/5/2013	Image, Custom Designed	$40.00	14	$560.00
21	1/12/2013	Image, Custom Designed	$40.00	18	$720.00
2	4/2/2012	Image, Custom Designed	$40.00	14	$560.00
8	7/11/2012	Image, Custom Designed	$40.00	21	$840.00
17	11/20/2012	Image, Custom Designed	$40.00	12	$480.00
24	2/7/2013	Image, Custom Designed	$40.00	19	$760.00
26	2/12/2013	Image, Custom Designed	$40.00	14	$560.00

Access displays the records that meet the specified criteria: either a blog or a transaction with more than ten images.

4. Close the query. Choose **No** when prompted to save the changes.

Saving changes at this point would store the temporary criteria with the query.

Entering Date Criteria

Video Library http://labyrinthelab.com/videos Video Number: AC13-V0406

You can set date criteria to determine age, hired date, invoice date, and so forth. Access acknowledges the same comparison criteria for performing date comparisons that it does for locating other types of data—regardless of the format used to enter dates.

SAMPLES OF DATE CRITERIA	
Criterion	**Locates**
06/22/2013	Finds records containing a specific date
<22-Oct-2013	Finds records containing dates that occur before a specific date—regardless of how the date is typed
>01/01/13	Finds records containing dates that occur after a specific date
<=#06/01/13#	Finds records containing dates on or before a specific date; the # signs that appear before and after the date help Access identify the data between them as a date
Between 01/01/13 and 06/30/13	Finds records containing dates after the first date and before the second date

Use Date Criteria in Queries

Winchester Web Design needs to track all invoices issued in 2012. In this exercise, you will create a query to set criteria using date values for locating customers with invoices dated from Jan 1, 2012 through December 31, 2012.

1. Choose **Create→Queries→Query Design** .

2. Follow these steps to add table field lists to the query:

Ⓐ Double-click the **Customers** table.

Ⓑ Double-click the **Invoices** table.

Ⓒ Double-click the **Invoice Details** table.

Ⓓ Double-click the **Products** table.

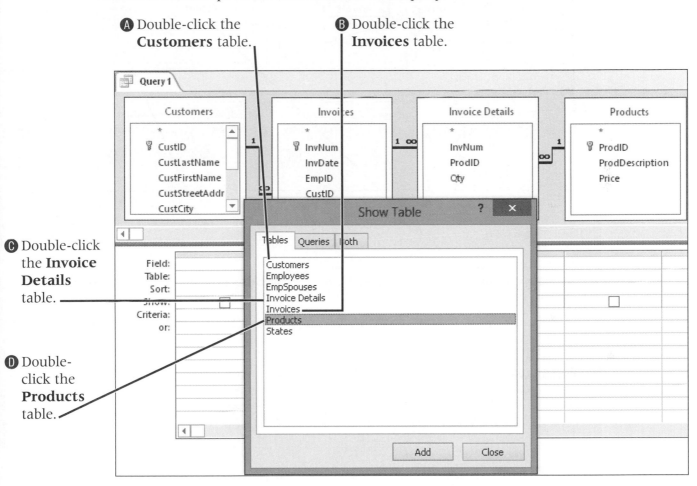

If the Show Table box does not appear, choose Design→Query Setup→Show Table.

3. Close the **Show Table** dialog box.

4. Follow these steps to add fields to the query grid:

Ⓐ Double-click **InvNum** and **InvDate** in the **Invoices** table to add the fields to the query grid.

Ⓑ Double-click **CustID** in the **Customers** table.

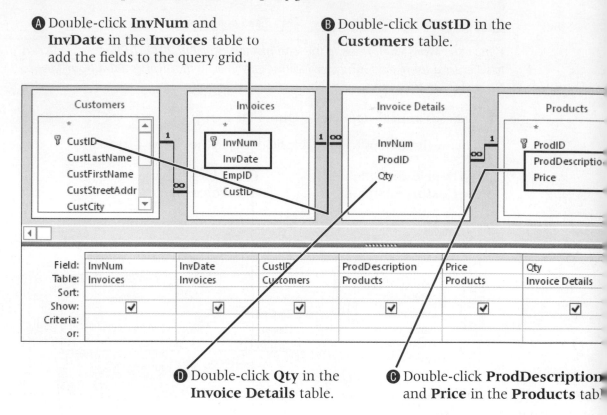

Ⓓ Double-click **Qty** in the **Invoice Details** table.

Ⓒ Double-click **ProdDescription** and **Price** in the **Products** tab

5. Type **Between January 1, 2012 and December 31, 2012** in the **Criteria** row for the **InvDate** field and tap Enter.

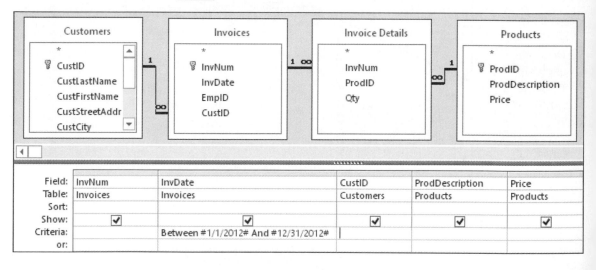

Regardless of how you type the dates, whether January 1, 2012, 01/01/12, or 1-1-2012, Access formats the date after you enter it so that it appears as #1/1/2012#.

6. Choose **Design→Results→Run**.

InvNum	Invoice Date	CustID	Description	Price	Qty
1	3/15/2012	SmithW	Home Page, Nav, CSS, Design	$400.00	1
1	3/15/2012	SmithW	Secondary Page	$200.00	6
1	3/15/2012	SmithW	Image, Custom Designed	$40.00	11
2	4/2/2012	SantosE	Home Page, Nav, CSS, Design	$400.00	1
2	4/2/2012	SantosE	Secondary Page	$200.00	7
2	4/2/2012	SantosE	Image, Custom Designed	$40.00	14
2	4/2/2012	SantosE	Hourly Rate for Modifications	$80.00	5
3	5/11/2012	SantosE	Secondary Page	$200.00	2
3	5/11/2012	SantosE	Image, Custom Designed	$40.00	6
4	5/30/2012	SmithW	Blog, Integrated into Site	$300.00	1
4	5/30/2012	SmithW	Hourly Rate for Modifications	$80.00	2
4	5/30/2012	SmithW	Image, Custom Designed	$40.00	2
5	6/19/2012	AndersM	Home Page, Nav, CSS, Design	$400.00	1
5	6/19/2012	AndersM	Secondary Page	$200.00	11
5	6/19/2012	AndersM	Image, Custom Designed	$40.00	9
6	6/23/2012	JeffriesD	Home Page, Nav, CSS, Design	$400.00	1
6	6/23/2012	JeffriesD	Secondary Page	$200.00	6
6	6/23/2012	JeffriesD	Blog, Integrated into Site	$300.00	1
6	6/23/2012	JeffriesD	Hourly Rate for Modifications	$80.00	3

Access locates the records for invoices from January 1, 2012 through December 31, 2012.

7. Save the query as **Invoices2012** then click **OK**.

8. Close the query.

Sorting a Query and Limiting Results

| Video Library | http://labyrinthelab.com/videos | Video Number: AC13-V0407 |

The query grid contains a Sort row that you can use to sort data in ascending or descending order. Sorting queried data helps ensure consistency and makes locating data in the query results more efficient.

Setting a Query Sort Order

There may be times when you need to sort data based upon two fields. For instance, if there are duplicate last names, you have to do a secondary sort on first name. When two fields are set as sort fields, Access sorts the fields left to right as they appear in the query grid. The first sort field is identified as the *primary* sort field; the next sort field is the *secondary* sort field. Multiple sorted fields do not need to be side by side in the query grid.

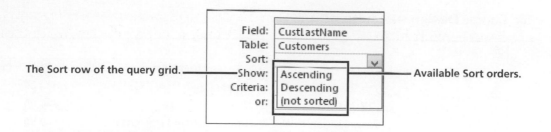

The Sort row of the query grid. ——————————— Available Sort orders.

Field:	CustLastName
Table:	Customers
Sort:	
Show:	Ascending
Criteria:	Descending
or:	(not sorted)

Limiting Number of Results Displayed

Running queries on large databases that contain hundreds of thousands of records often return such a large number of results that it can be challenging to find what you are looking for. So limiting the number of records displayed when you run a query can be beneficial, especially when these records are sorted.

For example, if you set up a query to sort in descending order and then limit the number of items displayed to ten, you would, in effect, have a list of the top ten items in the table being queried.

— This query datasheet includes all the records in the database.

Notice the item totals are in random order. ——

InvoiceTotalQuery

Inv Num ▾	Invoice Date ▾	Description ▾	Price ▾	Qty ▾	LineTotal ▾
41	12/7/2013	Shopping Cart, Basic	$400.00	1	$400.00
41	12/7/2013	Secondary Page	$200.00	2	$400.00
41	12/7/2013	Image, Custom Designed	$40.00	6	$240.00
40	11/14/2013	Home Page, Nav, CSS, Design	$400.00	1	$400.00
40	11/14/2013	Secondary Page	$200.00	7	$1,400.00
40	11/14/2013	Image, Custom Designed	$40.00	3	$120.00
39	11/4/2013	Secondary Page	$200.00	3	$600.00

InvoiceTotalQuery

Inv Num ▾	Invoice Date ▾	Description ▾	Price ▾	Qty ▾	LineTotal ▾
24	2/7/2013	Secondary Page	$200.00	13	$2,600.00
13	9/3/2012	Secondary Page	$200.00	12	$2,400.00
21	1/12/2013	Secondary Page	$200.00	12	$2,400.00
5	6/19/2012	Secondary Page	$200.00	11	$2,200.00
29	3/12/2013	Secondary Page	$200.00	9	$1,800.00
8	7/11/2012	Secondary Page	$200.00	9	$1,800.00
2	4/2/2012	Secondary Page	$200.00	7	$1,400.00
40	11/14/2013	Secondary Page	$200.00	7	$1,400.00
26	2/12/2013	Secondary Page	$200.00	6	$1,200.00

After sorting with the results limited, only the largest item totals are shown, and in descending order.

 Depending on the content of your tables and specified criteria, this feature may not always return the *exact* number of records that you specify.

The Return feature on the Query Design tab enables you to set the number of records to be displayed, or returned, in the query results. The default setting for the Return feature is All.

The Return menu allows you to set the number of records to display in the query results datasheet.

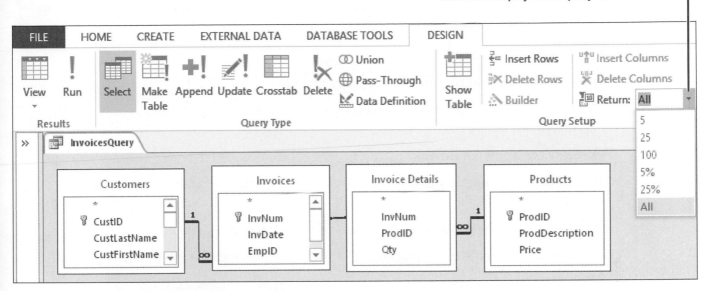

QUICK REFERENCE	SETTING A QUERY SORT ORDER
Task	**Procedure**
Set a sort order	■ Display the query in Query Design View.
	■ Click the Sort row of the query grid for the desired sort field and select the appropriate field sort order.
Set sort orders for multiple fields	■ Display the query in Query Design View
	■ Arrange the fields left to right in the order to sort.
	■ Click the Sort row of the query grid for the desired sort field and select the appropriate field sort order.
	■ Repeat steps for each additional field that you want to sort.
Limit the number of records returned	■ Display the query in Query Design View.
	■ Choose Design→Query Setup→Return menu and select the number of records you want to view.

Set a Query Sort Order and Limit Records

The art department at Winchester Web Design wants to know which customers are using its services the most. In this exercise, you will create a query that sets a sort order in the query grid and limits the number of records in the query results to display the invoices with the most images from the art department.

Apply a Query Sort

1. Choose **Create→Queries→Query Design**.

2. Double-click the **Customers, Invoices, Invoice Details**, and **Products** tables in the Show Table dialog box.

3. Close the **Show Table box**.

4. Double-click **CustID** and **CustLastName** in the **Customers** table to add the fields to the query grid.

5. Double-click **InvDate** in the **Invoices** table to add it to the query grid.

6. Double-click **ProdDescription** in the **Products** table and **Qty** in the **Invoice Details** table.

7. Follow these steps to set criteria and a sort order:

 Ⓐ Type **Image*** in the Criteria row under **ProdDescription** and tap Tab .

 Ⓑ Click the arrow in the **Sort** row for the **Qty** field.

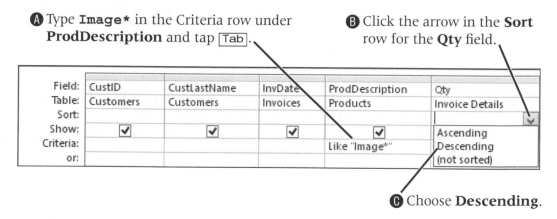

 Ⓒ Choose **Descending**.

Limit the Number of Records to Display

8. Follow these steps to limit the number of records displayed in the results:

 Ⓐ Choose **Design→Query Setup→Return**.

 Ⓑ Choose **5**.

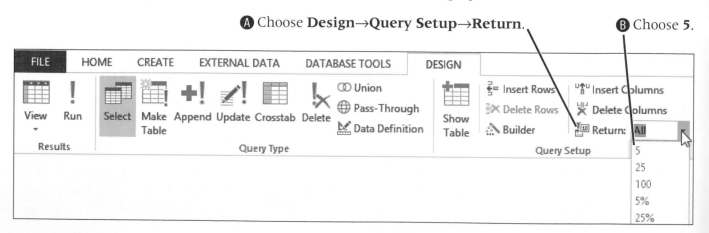

9. Choose **Design→Results→Run** ![Run] .

Access returns only the records with the largest quantities.

CustID	Last Name	Invoice Date	Description	Qty
DavisP	Davis	7/11/2012	Image, Custom Designed	21
ThibeauxP	Thibeaux	2/7/2013	Image, Custom Designed	19
JeffriesD	Jeffries	1/12/2013	Image, Custom Designed	18
SantosE	Santos	4/2/2012	Image, Custom Designed	15
RobertsJ	Roberts	7/11/2012	Image, Custom Designed	14
BlaserH	Blaser	2/23/2013	Image, Custom Designed	14
DavisP	Davis	2/12/2013	Image, Custom Designed	14

The number of records returned is not always the exact number you have specified in Design View. The seven highest records are returned here because Access includes all records with a Qty value of 14.

10. Close the query, saving it as **Most Images**.

Performing Calculations in Queries

Video Library   http://labyrinthelab.com/videos   Video Number: AC13-V0408

So far, the activities in this lesson have introduced the basics of creating, running, sorting, and selecting records based on criteria. As you developed the queries, you used fields already available in database tables. Access also contains features that enable you to use the query grid to create a *calculated field*, which contains no data in a table but uses data in other fields to obtain its value.

A calculated field:

- Creates a new field in the query that can be used in a form or report.
- Can be used to perform mathematical operations such as add, multiply, etc.
- Has a name and can be formatted with properties just like a regular field.
- Enables you to combine values in two text fields into one field, such as LastName and FirstInitial.
- Updates and recalculates each time you run the query.

Queries, forms, tables, and reports can contain calculated fields. It is helpful to identify calculated fields as Calculated data types as you design a database.

Identifying Parts of a Calculated Field

The structure of a calculated field includes a field name and expression elements that tell Access which fields, operators, and punctuation marks to use to create the field. Two examples of calculated fields in an Access query would be Wage: Hours * Rate and Total: Price * Quantity.

Each calculated field contains the following elements.

ELEMENTS OF CALCULATED FIELDS	
Element	**Description**
Calculated field name	■ The unique name you assign to the field, followed by a colon (:) to separate the field name from the expression
Field names from existing tables	■ The field containing the data used in the calculation. Access will add brackets [ ] around field names.
Arithmetic or comparison operators	■ +, -, *, /, ( ), ^, <, =,> to perform mathematical operations or compare values
Concatenation	■ Combining fields and expressions by using the ampersand (&) to join text values from multiple fields For example, FirstName&LastName
	■ Required spaces appear within quotation marks (" ") For example, FirstName& " " &LastName

Existing field names.

Price	Qty	ItemTotal: [Price]*[Qty]
Products	Invoice Details	
		Descending
☑	☑	☑

This is an example of elements that compose a simple query calculation.

Newly assigned field names must have a colon followed by the operands in brackets.

Identifying Order of Calculations

Time for a little math. What is the answer to 6 + 6 / 2? Keep your answer in mind as you continue to read. As with Excel, Access calculates mathematical operations in a formula from left to right as it applies the order of calculations rules. The standard order for performing mathematical operations is often abbreviated *PEMDAS* (you may have learned the phrase *Please Excuse My Dear Aunt Sally*, a phrase often taught in middle schools to teach order of operations). The initials represent the order of mathematical operations Excel and Access use, as described in the following table.

ORDER OF MATHEMATICAL CALCULATIONS	
Calculation	**Description**
Parentheses ( )	Calculations enclosed in parentheses are performed first. In the calculation (6 + 6) / 2, the answer is 6 because what is in parentheses is always performed first. However, in the calculation 6 + 6 / 2 the answer is 9, because without the parentheses, multiplication and division occur before addition and subtraction.
Exponentials ^	Calculations "raised to the power of," such as squared or cubed, are performed next. Because superscripts are not on the keyboard, the caret (^) is used to represent exponentials. For example, $5\char`\^2$ is 5 squared or 5^2 and equals 25.
Multiplication * **D**ivision /	Multiplication and division are equal in calculation order and are calculated left to right, after calculations on parentheses and exponentials.
Addition + **S**ubtraction -	Addition and subtraction are equal in calculation order and are calculated last, left to right across a formula after calculations on parentheses, exponentials, and multiplication and division.

Calculating Dates

In addition to performing simple calculations, Access provides alternative ways to use dates in calculated fields. You can use these expressions to calculate age, number of years in business, and so forth.

CALCULATED DATES IN EXPRESSIONS	
Sample Field	**Returns**
CurrentDate: =Date()	Displays the current date in the *mm/dd/yyyy* format, where *mm* is the month, *dd* is the day, and *yyyy* is the year. For example: 10/25/2013
CurrentDT: =Now()	Displays the current date and time, for example: 10/25/2013 1:02:41 PM
OrderProcessing: DateDiff("d", [OrderDate], [ShippedDate])	Displays the number of days (d) between the value in the OrderDate field and the ShippedDate field.
(Now()-[DOB])/365	Subtracts the value in the DOB (date of birth) field from the current date and divides the difference by 365 to display the calculated value in years.

Creating and Formatting a Calculated Field

Each calculated field stored in a query appears in a separate column in the query grid. You can type the calculated field expression directly into the Field row of the column. You can also create a calculated field by using the tools in Query Design View to access the expression builder.

Setting Calculated Field Properties

When you create tables in Access, you can set field properties, such as field size, format, caption, and default values. With the exception of small whole numbers, calculated fields almost always need to be formatted using field properties to indicate decimal places, commas, and currency formats. To assign field properties to calculated fields, you use the Query Property Sheet.

FROM THE RIBBON

Design→Show/ Hide→Property Sheet to open the Property Sheet

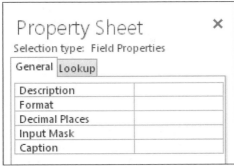

The Property Sheet for formatting query fields.

Access 2013

Create and Format a Calculated Field

In this exercise, you will add and format a calculated field for a query in the Winchester Web Design database.

1. Right-click the **InvoicesList** query in the Navigation Pane and choose **Design View**.

2. Follow these steps to create a calculated field:

Ⓐ Type `LineTotal:Price * Qty` in the top of the first blank column and tap Enter.

Ⓑ Notice that Access automatically adds brackets [ ] around existing fields.

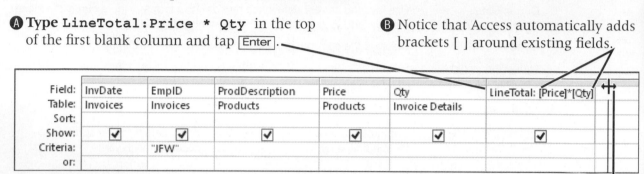

Field:	InvDate	EmpID	ProdDescription	Price	Qty	LineTotal: [Price]*[Qty]	
Table:	Invoices	Invoices	Products	Products	Invoice Details		
Sort:							
Show:	☑	☑	☑	☑	☑	☑	
Criteria:		"JFW"					
or:							

Ⓒ Drag the column border to widen the query grid column so you can view the entire entry.

3. Right-click in the **LineTotal** column and choose **Properties** to open the Property Sheet, if necessary.

4. Follow these steps to format the field:

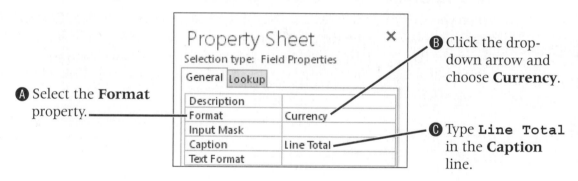

Ⓐ Select the **Format** property.

Ⓑ Click the drop-down arrow and choose **Currency**.

Ⓒ Type **Line Total** in the **Caption** line.

Property Sheet

Selection type: Field Properties

General | Lookup

Description	
Format	Currency
Input Mask	
Caption	Line Total
Text Format	

5. Run the query.

InvNum	Invoice Date	Emp ID	Description	Price	Qty	Line Total
1	3/15/2012	JFW	Secondary Page	$200.00	6	$1,200.00
1	3/15/2012	JFW	Image, Custom Designed	$40.00	11	$440.00
1	3/15/2012	JFW	Home Page, Nav, CSS, Design	$400.00	1	$400.00
2	4/2/2012	MJW	Image, Custom Designed	$40.00	14	$560.00
2	4/2/2012	MJW	Home Page, Nav, CSS, Design	$400.00	1	$400.00
2	4/2/2012	MJW	Secondary Page	$200.00	7	$1,400.00
2	4/2/2012	MJW	Hourly Rate for Modifications	$80.00	5	$400.00
3	5/11/2012	JMM	Image, Custom Designed	$40.00	6	$240.00
3	5/11/2012	JMM	Secondary Page	$200.00	2	$400.00
4	5/30/2012	JMM	Blog, Integrated into Site	$300.00	1	$300.00
4	5/30/2012	JMM	Hourly Rate for Modifications	$80.00	2	$160.00
4	5/30/2012	JMM	Image, Custom Designed	$40.00	2	$80.00
5	6/19/2012	JFW	Image, Custom Designed	$40.00	9	$360.00
5	6/19/2012	JFW	Secondary Page	$200.00	11	$2,200.00
5	6/19/2012	JFW	Home Page, Nav, CSS, Design	$400.00	1	$400.00
6	6/23/2012	MJW	Hourly Rate for Modifications	$80.00	3	$240.00
6	6/23/2012	MJW	Blog, Integrated into Site	$300.00	1	$300.00
6	6/23/2012	MJW	Home Page, Nav, CSS, Design	$400.00	1	$400.00
6	6/23/2012	MJW	Secondary Page	$200.00	6	$1,200.00
7	7/11/2012	JMM	Image, Custom Designed	$40.00	14	$560.00

6. Save then close the query.

Using a Function in a Query Expression

Video Library   http://labyrinthelab.com/videos   Video Number: AC13-V0409

If you have worked with Microsoft Excel, you are most likely familiar with the types of functions that provide Excel with its calculating power. In Access, you have many of the same functions for performing specific calculations, such as finding the minimum, maximum, and average values, and counting and summing the entries in a datasheet. These are known as aggregate functions and are built into Access. You can use these functions in queries, forms, and reports to aid in database reporting.

Adding Functions to the Query Grid

When you want to add aggregate functions to total, average, or find minimum and maximum values you must first display the Total row on the query grid. From the Total row, you choose the function(s) you want to use for the specified field. You use a separate column for each additional function. For example, if you want to find the minimum, maximum, and average of the same field, you would add three new fields to the query grid—one for each function.

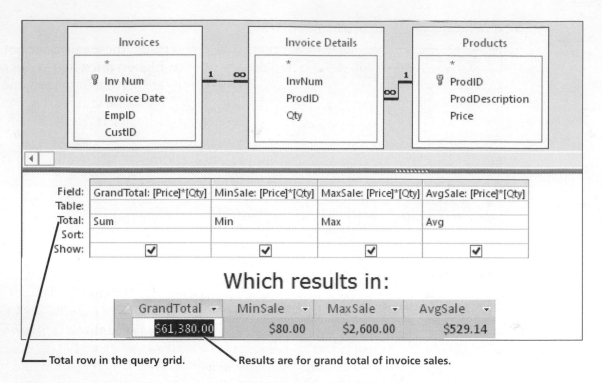

Total row in the query grid.

Results are for grand total of invoice sales.

When you first display the Total row in the query grid, Access places the Group By command in the Total row of every occupied column. The Group By function allows you to calculate, among other things, the running total, minimum, maximum, and average for each group. This is handy if you need totals and averages for each employee, customer, or product.

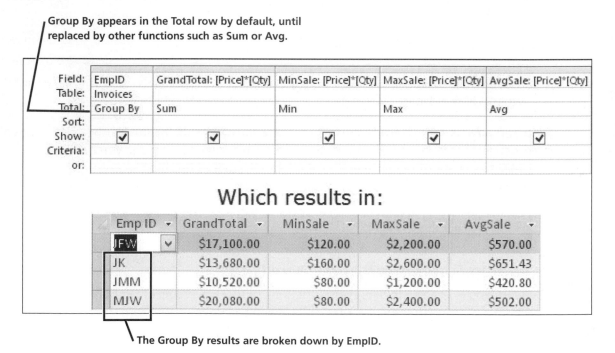

Group By appears in the Total row by default, until replaced by other functions such as Sum or Avg.

The Group By results are broken down by EmpID.

Creating Aliases in Query Fields

Aggregate functions are designed to summarize data. As a result, these values are not stored in database tables. Suppose you want to find the lowest price, highest price, and average price of the products in your inventory. Although all three columns are derived from the same Price field, you need a unique name for each calculated column. When the same expression or field is assigned to several different field names, each additional field name is referred to as an alias.

Price is the original field name.

Field:	MinPrice: Price	MaxPrice: Price	AvgPrice: Price
Table:	Products	Products	Products
Total:	Min	Max	Avg
Sort:			

MinPrice, MaxPrice, and AvgPrice are the calculated field name aliases.

Identifying Function Types

Simple aggregate functions allow you to count the number of entries in a field, locate the maximum or minimum values in a field, total the values of a group of records, and find the average value from a group of values. Access contains numerous additional functions that enable you to calculate the standard deviation and variance of values, and so forth. It is also important to know that Access limits or restricts the use of these functions to specific data field types. Some of the more commonly used aggregate functions are identified here.

AGGREGATE FUNCTION TYPES

Function	Description	Valid Field Data Types
Sum	Totals values in a field.	Number, Currency
Avg	Averages values in a field.	Number, Date/Time, Currency
Min	Identifies lowest value in a field.	Text, Number, Date/Time, Currency
Max	Identifies highest value in a field.	Text, Number, Date/Time, Currency
Count	Counts the number of values in a field, not counting blank values.	All types except multi-value lists
StDev	Calculates standard deviation of the values in a field.	Number, Currency
Var	Calculates variance of the values in a field.	Number, Currency
First	Locates the first record in the group on which you are performing calculations in chronological order without sorting.	All data types
Last	Locates the last record in the group on which you are performing calculations in chronological order without sorting.	All data types

Access 2013

Use Functions in Queries

In this exercise, you will create a query that uses functions to identify minimum, maximum, and average invoice amounts for customers of Winchester Web Design.

1. Choose **Create→Queries→Query Design**.

2. Double-click the **Employees, Invoices, Invoice Details**, and **Products** tables in the Show Table dialog box.

3. Close the **Show Table** dialog box.

4. Follow these steps to add the Group By field to the query:

Ⓐ Choose **Design→Show/Hide→Totals** to display the Totals row.

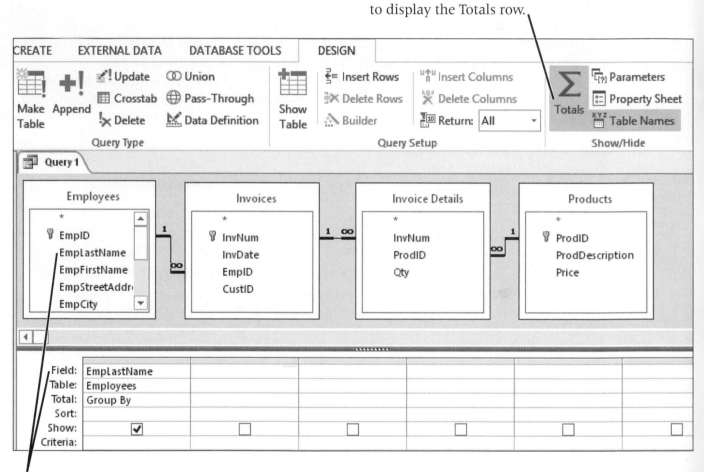

Ⓑ Double-click **EmpLastName** in the **Employees** table to add it to the grid.

5. Follow these steps to add functions to the query:

A Type **MinTotal:Price*Qty**
for the second column field
name and expression.

B Click in the **Total** row,
click the drop-down arrow,
and choose **Min**.

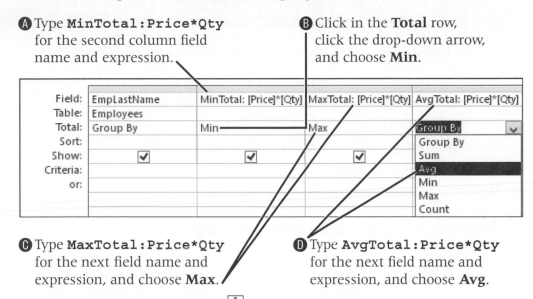

C Type **MaxTotal:Price*Qty**
for the next field name and
expression, and choose **Max**.

D Type **AvgTotal:Price*Qty**
for the next field name and
expression, and choose **Avg**.

6. Choose **Design→Results→Run** ⓘRun. Adjust the datasheet column widths to display all
data and field names.

Access displays the aggregate minimum, maximum, and average totals.

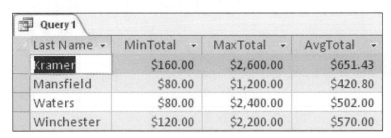

Last Name ▾	MinTotal ▾	MaxTotal ▾	AvgTotal ▾
Kramer	$160.00	$2,600.00	$651.43
Mansfield	$80.00	$1,200.00	$420.80
Waters	$80.00	$2,400.00	$502.00
Winchester	$120.00	$2,200.00	$570.00

*Each Last Name is listed only one time. And, each calculated field column shows the column heading
that identifies what the value represents.*

7. Save the query as **InvoiceFunctions** and close it.

Access 2013

Creating Special Types of Queries

Video Library   http://labyrinthelab.com/videos   Video Number: AC13-V0410

The queries you have created so far are select queries where Access selects records according to the fields you add to the query grid and the criteria you set. Access also contains tools for creating special types of queries. In this lesson, you will explore three of these special queries:

- Crosstab query
- Find Unmatched query
- Find Duplicates query

Creating a Crosstab Query

Crosstab queries allow you to easily analyze data. A crosstab query lists the fields to be grouped on the left side of the datasheet. It arranges the fields to be summarized across the top so you can calculate sums, averages, counts, or totals by group and subgroup. For example, if you have a database that contains sales records for your employees, the description of each product they sell, and their total sales for each product, you could create a crosstab query to display the total sales by product for each employee. Such a grouping and summarization might appear as shown in the following illustrations.

Original Data		
Employee	**Product Description**	**Line Total**
JFW	Secondary Page	$1,200.00
JFW	Image, Custom Designed	$440.00
JFW	Home Page, Nav, CSS, Design	$400.00
MJW	Image, Custom Designed	$560.00
MJW	Home Page, Nav, CSS, Design	$400.00
MJW	Secondary Page	$1,400.00
MJW	Hourly Rate for Modifications	$400.00
JMM	Image, Custom Designed	$240.00
JMM	Secondary Page	$400.00
JMM	Blog, Integrated into Site	$300.00
JMM	Hourly Rate for Modifications	$160.00
JMM	Image, Custom Designed	$80.00
JFW	Image, Custom Designed	$360.00
JFW	Secondary Page	$2,200.00
JFW	Home Page, Nav, CSS, Design	$400.00
MJW	Hourly Rate for Modifications	$240.00
MJW	Blog, Integrated into Site	$300.00

Original data format is arranged by record.

Reorganized by Crosstab Query							
Emp Name	Tot Sales	Home Pg	2nd Page	Blogs	Carts	Images	Hourly
Kramer	$13,680.00	$800.00	$7,600.00	$600.00		$2,520.00	$2,160.00
Mansfield	$10,520.00	$400.00	$4,800.00	$600.00	$1,200.00	$1,680.00	$1,840.00
Waters	$20,080.00	$1,600.00	$10,000.00	$1,200.00	$1,200.00	$2,080.00	$4,000.00
Winchester	$17,100.00	$2,000.00	$8,800.00	$300.00	$800.00	$3,040.00	$2,160.00

Using a crosstab query, you can display the data grouped by employee and product.

Using the Crosstab Query Wizard

As you work with crosstab queries, you will discover a vast difference between the query grid you have used to create select queries and the crosstab query palette. You can, of course, use the palette to manually construct a crosstab query. Until you become better acquainted with the queries, using the Crosstab Query Wizard is more helpful. Crosstab queries can use both tables and queries as the basis of the query.

Fields to group appear in the left column and across the top.

Summarized values appear in the TOTAL area.

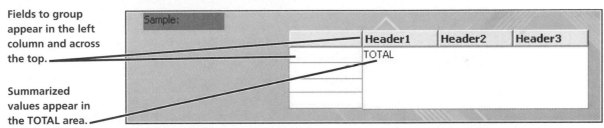

The crosstab query palette organizes data so that it is easier to summarize.

QUICK REFERENCE	CREATING CROSSTAB, UNMATCHED, AND DUPLICATES QUERIES USING WIZARDS
Task	**Procedure**
Create a crosstab query	■ Choose Create→Queries→Query Wizard 🔲. ■ Double-click Crosstab Query Wizard. ■ Follow the prompts to select objects and fields for the query.
Create a find duplicates query	■ Choose Create→Queries→Query Wizard 🔲. ■ Double-click Find Duplicates Query Wizard. ■ Follow the prompts to select objects and fields for the query.
Create a find unmatched query	■ Choose Create→Queries→Query Wizard 🔲. ■ Double-click Find Unmatched Query Wizard. ■ Follow the prompts to select objects and fields for the query.

Create a Crosstab Query

In this exercise, you will create a crosstab query that lists each employee and their total invoice amount generated by product.

1. Choose **Create→Queries→Query Wizard** 🔳 to open the New Query dialog box.

2. Double-click the **Crosstab Query Wizard** to launch the Crosstab Query Wizard.

3. Follow these steps to select the query to use for the crosstab query:

Ⓐ Select the **Queries** option to display a list of queries.

Ⓑ Select **Query: EmployeeSales**.

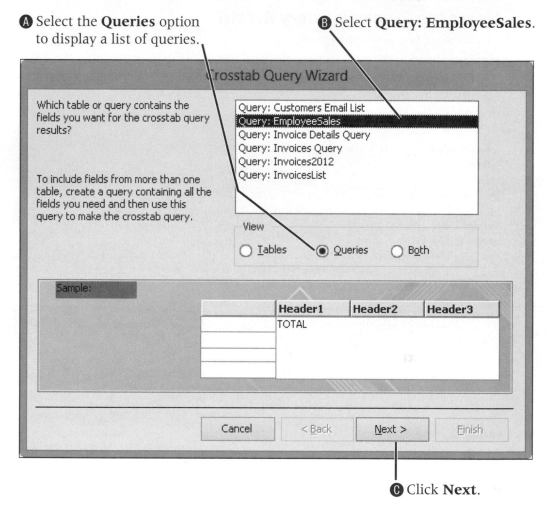

Ⓒ Click **Next**.

In the next wizard screen, Access asks what data you want to display down the left side of the query. In this query, you want the employee last name to appear down the left column.

4. Double-click **EmpLastName** in the Available Fields list to move it to the **Selected Fields** list.

5. Click **Next**, and then double-click **ProdDescription** as the field to appear in the column headings, and advance to the next wizard screen.

6. Select **LineTotal** in the Fields list and **Sum** in the Functions list to identify the field that contains values and the function you want to calculate.

Your crosstab query grid should look similar to the following illustration, with the EmpLastName fields as row headings, the ProdDescription as column headings, and the Sum function applied to the LineTotal field.

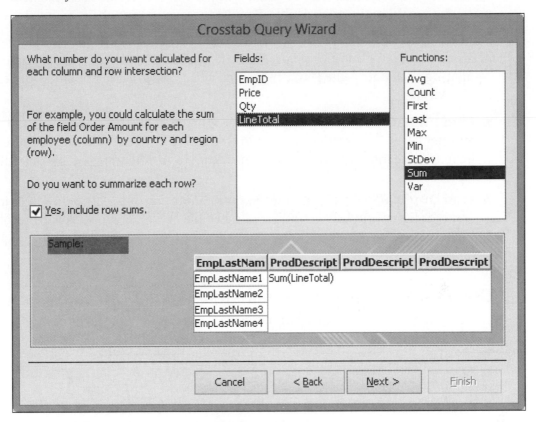

7. Click **Next** to display the final page of the Crosstab Query Wizard.

8. Name the query **EmployeeCrosstab** and click **Finish**.

Access runs and displays the query results, which show each employee and their total invoice amount generated by product. Adjust the columns as needed.

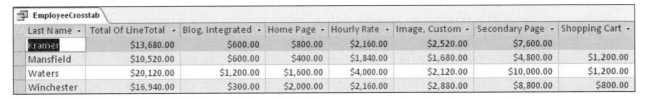

Last Name ▾	Total Of LineTotal ▾	Blog, Integrated ▾	Home Page ▾	Hourly Rate ▾	Image, Custom ▾	Secondary Page ▾	Shopping Cart ▾
Kramer	$13,680.00	$600.00	$800.00	$2,160.00	$2,520.00	$7,600.00	
Mansfield	$10,520.00	$600.00	$400.00	$1,840.00	$1,680.00	$4,800.00	$1,200.00
Waters	$20,120.00	$1,200.00	$1,600.00	$4,000.00	$2,120.00	$10,000.00	$1,200.00
Winchester	$16,940.00	$300.00	$2,000.00	$2,160.00	$2,880.00	$8,800.00	$800.00

9. Save and close the query.

Creating Unmatched and Duplicates Queries

Video Library   http://labyrinthelab.com/videos   Video Number: AC13-V0411

Data contained in database tables often shares key fields so that you can include data from multiple tables in queries. As a result, it is important that records entered in one table have a matching record in the related table. For instance, you cannot have an invoice without a matching record in the products table.

Access contains two additional query wizards that enable you to create specialized queries for comparing such data—the Find Unmatched Query Wizard and the Find Duplicates Query Wizard.

- **Find Unmatched Query:** Locates records in one table that have no related records in another table. For example, you could create an Unmatched Query to ensure that each record in an Invoice table has a corresponding record in the Customers table or in the Products table.

- **Find Duplicates Query:** Locates records containing duplicate field values in a single table or query. For example, you could create a Duplicates Query to locate any records in the Customers table that were unintentionally entered twice, or to find customers from the same city.

Creating Queries to Find Unmatched and Duplicate Records

Creating and running the Find Unmatched Query Wizard and the Find Duplicates Query Wizard help maintain the integrity of the database.

DEVELOP YOUR SKILLS AC04-D11

Find Unmatched and Duplicate Records

In this exercise, you will create a query to locate customers in the Customers table who have no matching CustomerID in the Invoices table. You will then create a query to identify records with duplicate customer last names.

Create a Query to Find Unmatched Records

1. Choose **Create→Queries→Query Wizard** 📄 and double-click **Find Unmatched Query Wizard**.

   The Find Unmatched Query Wizard opens. From this screen, you select the table you want to check against another table.

2. Double-click **Table: Customers** to identify the table and automatically advance to the next screen.

3. Double-click **Table: Invoices** to identify the table to compare to the **Customers** table entries and automatically advance to the next screen.

   The next screen displays a list of fields in both selected tables. From the lists, you will identify the field in the Customers table that must have a matching record in the Invoices table.

4. Follow these steps to identify the fields that should match:

The next screen asks you to identify the field(s) you want to view in the query results.

Ⓐ Ensure that the **CustID** field is selected in the Fields in 'Customers' list.

Ⓑ Ensure that the matching **CustID** is the selected field in the Fields in 'Invoices' list.

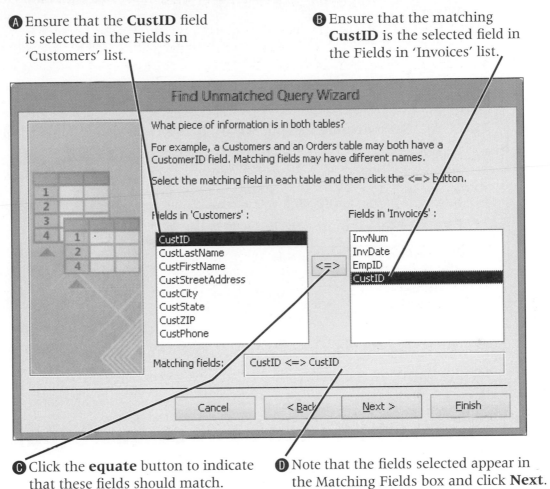

Ⓒ Click the **equate** button to indicate that these fields should match.

Ⓓ Note that the fields selected appear in the Matching Fields box and click **Next**.

5. Click **Move** > to add the following fields to the Selected Fields list: **CustLastName**, **CustFirstName**, **CustPhone**, and **CustEmail**.

6. Click **Next**, and then click **Finish** to accept the default query name Access assigns.

Your query results should resemble the figure. You can use the results to find and delete the unmatched or contact those customers to offer your services.

7. Close the query.

Create a Query to Find Duplicate Records

8. Choose **Create→Queries→Query Wizard** ⊞ and double-click **Find Duplicates Query Wizard**.

9. Double-click **Table: Customers** as the table you want to check for duplicates and to automatically advance to the next screen.

10. Select the **CustLastName** field, click **Move** `>` to move the field to the Duplicate-Value Fields box, and click **Next**.

11. Click **CustFirstName** and click **Move** `>` to move it to the Additional Query Fields box.

12. Click **CustPhone** and click **Move** `>` to move it to the Additional Query Fields box, and click **Next**.

13. Name the query `Customers with the Same Last Name` and click **Finish**.

    The query results show two customers with the last name Roberts.

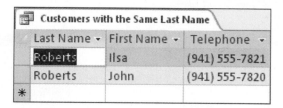

14. Save then close the query, close the database, and exit **Access**.

Viewing Structured Query Language (SQL)

Video Library   http://labyrinthelab.com/videos   Video Number: AC13-V0412

When you create queries, Access generates code that contains instructions for the query according to the criteria you set. For skilled users, viewing the coded instructions that Access creates may help identify reasons why a query might display inaccurate or unexpected results.

In Access, viewing the code is as simple as changing the query view to SQL View. SQL View for the Invoices Details Query is shown here.

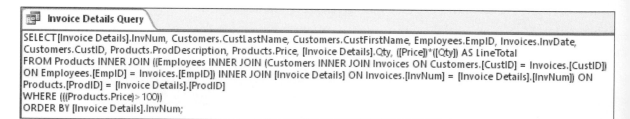

SQL CODE FOR QUERIES

SQL command	Purpose
SELECT	Identify the fields to be selected or used in the query
FROM	Identify the tables that the query fields will come from
ORDER BY	Sort
WHERE	Find
GROUP BY	Arrange fields according to categories determined by key fields, such as EmpID
AS	Assign an alias or perform a calculation
AND	All fields in the query must match
OR	Only one field in the query must match
JOIN...ON	Combine tables that are linked by key fields

Concepts Review

To check your knowledge of the key concepts introduced in this lesson, complete the Concepts Review quiz by choosing the appropriate access option below.

If you are...	Then access the quiz by...
Using the Labyrinth Video Library	Going to http://labyrinthelab.com/videos
Using eLab	Logging in, choosing Content, and navigating to the Concepts Review quiz for this lesson
Not using the Labyrinth Video Library or eLab	Going to the student resource center for this book

Reinforce Your Skills

Create Queries and Use Criteria and Wildcards

Kids for Change is planning to fine-tune their database by adding queries that enable them to track activities as well as staff/volunteer availability. In this exercise, you will create various queries that will yield the desired information.

Create a Query Using the Query Wizard

1. Start **Access**. Open **AC04-R01-K4C** from the **AC2013 Lesson 04** folder and save it as `AC04-R01-K4C-[FirstInitialLastName]`.

2. Choose **Create→Queries→Query Wizard**.

3. Double-click **Simple Query Wizard**.

4. Select the **Activities** table from the Tables/Queries list.

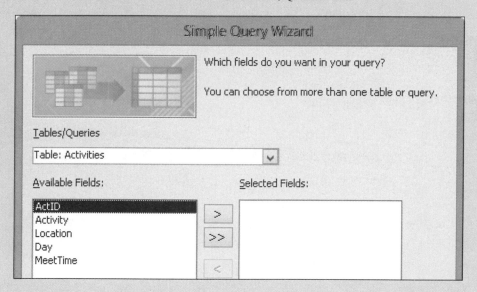

5. Click the **Activity** field in the Available Fields list then click **Move**.

6. Move the **Location**, **Day**, and **MeetTime** fields to the Selected Fields list.

7. Click **Next**.

8. Type `Activities List` in the query title text box.

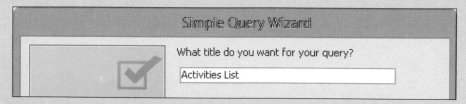

9. Click **Finish**. Then, close the query.

Activity	Location	Day	Meet Time
Beach Cleanup	Coquina Beach	Saturday	9:00 AM
Can Collection	Seabreeze School	Thursday	6:00 PM
Car Wash	Sarasota Fairgrounds	Saturday	12:00 PM
Eco-Bake Sale	Downtown Flea Market	Sunday	8:00 AM
Eco-Tag Sale	River Village Market	Saturday	9:00 AM
Foodbank Collection	Community Center	Sunday	7:00 PM
Garden Work	All Angels Church	Wednesday	5:00 PM
Newspaper Collection	Seabreeze School	Monday	6:00 PM
Petition Signing	Hernando Mall	Sunday	2:00 PM
Recycling Drive	Seabreeze School	Tuesday	6:00 PM
Sign Waving	Cortez Rd. & Tamiami Tr.	Friday	5:00 PM

The query results datasheet includes just the four selected fields from all the records.

Create a Query in Design View

10. Choose **Create→Queries→Query Design**.

    Access displays a new query grid and a list of tables and existing queries contained in the database so that you can choose the sources you want to include in the new query.

11. Double-click the **Volunteers** table in the Show Table dialog box, then click **Close**.

    If the Show Table dialog box does not appear, choose Design→Query Setup→Show Table.

12. To add fields to the query grid, double-click **VolLastName**, **VolFirstName**, **VolPhone**, and **VolDay** (in that order).

13. Save the query as **Volunteer List**.

14. Click **Run**.

    Access runs the query and displays four columns of data (Last Name, First Name, Telephone, and Avail Day) for all the Volunteer records.

Last Name	First Name	Telephone	Avail Day
Jones	Stan	941-555-8929	Tuesday
Langford	Kerry	941-555-1098	Thursday
Creger	Cindy	941-555-0245	Wednesday
Simpson	Lance	941-555-3431	Monday
Frith	Beverly	941-555-7489	Sunday

15. Switch to **Design View**.

Access 2013

16. To rearrange the field order, hover the mouse pointer over the top of the **VolDay** column until you see the black arrow. Click the column to select it.

17. When the pointer becomes a white move arrow, click the selected column and drag it to the left of the **Last Name** field.

The VolDay field should now be the first field in the query grid.

18. Choose **Design→Results→Run**.

19. Close the query, saving the changes when prompted.

Avail Day	Last Name	First Name	Telephone
Tuesday	Jones	Stan	941-555-8929
Thursday	Langford	Kerry	941-555-1098
Wednesday	Creger	Cindy	941-555-0245
Monday	Simpson	Lance	941-555-3431
Sunday	Frith	Beverly	941-555-7489

Volunteer List

Create a Multi-Table Query

20. Choose **Create→Queries→Query Design** .

21. Double-click the following table names in the **Show Table** dialog box to add the table field lists to the top pane of the query: **Activities** and **Staff**.

22. Close the **Show Table** dialog box.

23. Double-click these fields from the **Activities** table in the order presented: **Activity**, **Day**, **MeetTime**.

24. Double-click these fields from the **Staff** table in the order presented: **StaffLastName**, **StaffFirstName**, **StaffPhone**.

25. Click in the **Sort** row for Activity, click the list arrow, and choose **Ascending**.

Field:	Activity	Day	MeetTime	StaffLastName	StaffFirstName	StaffPhone
Table:	Activities	Activities	Activities	Staff	Staff	Staff
Sort:	⌄					
Show:	Ascending	✔	✔	✔	✔	✔
Criteria:	Descendin~~gs~~					
or:	(not sorted)					

26. Save the query as `Activity Staffing List`.

27. Choose **Design→Results→Run**. Then, close the query.

Activity	Day	Meet Time	Last Name	First Name	Telephone
Beach Cleanup	Saturday	9:00 AM	Lockwood	Bill	941-555-6531
Can Collection	Thursday	6:00 PM	Bryant	Matthew	941-555-7523
Car Wash	Saturday	12:00 PM	Lockwood	Bill	941-555-6531
Eco-Bake Sale	Sunday	8:00 AM	Yellen	George	941-555-1205
Eco-Bake Sale	Sunday	8:00 AM	Pauly	Gerry	941-555-1988
Eco-Tag Sale	Saturday	9:00 AM	Lockwood	Bill	941-555-6531
Foodbank Collection	Sunday	7:00 PM	Yellen	George	941-555-1205
Foodbank Collection	Sunday	7:00 PM	Pauly	Gerry	941-555-1988
Garden Work	Wednesday	5:00 PM	Montagne	Francis	941-555-9032

Add Wildcard and AND/OR Criteria to a Query

28. Display the **Activities Staffing List** query in Design View.

29. Type `Saturday` in the Criteria row of the Day field.

30. Type `Sunday` in the Or row of the Day field, and tap [Tab].

31. Click **Run**.

Activity	Day	Meet Time	Last Name	First Name	Telephone
Beach Cleanup	Saturday	9:00 AM	Lockwood	Bill	941-555-6531
Car Wash	Saturday	12:00 PM	Lockwood	Bill	941-555-6531
Eco-Bake Sale	Sunday	8:00 AM	Yellen	George	941-555-1205
Eco-Bake Sale	Sunday	8:00 AM	Pauly	Gerry	941-555-1988
Eco-Tag Sale	Saturday	9:00 AM	Lockwood	Bill	941-555-6531
Foodbank Collection	Sunday	7:00 PM	Yellen	George	941-555-1205
Foodbank Collection	Sunday	7:00 PM	Pauly	Gerry	941-555-1988
Petition Signing	Sunday	2:00 PM	Yellen	George	941-555-1205
Petition Signing	Sunday	2:00 PM	Pauly	Gerry	941-555-1988

This is an OR condition: Activities for either Saturday or Sunday are returned.

32. Switch to **Design View**.

33. Delete **Sunday** from the Day Or row.

34. Type **12:00** in the Criteria row for the **MeetTime** field and tap Tab.

35. Run the query.

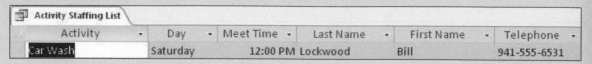

This is an AND condition: only the activities on Saturday and at 12:00 are returned.

36. Switch to **Design View**.

37. Remove all criteria.

38. Type **S*** in the criteria row for the **Day** field and tap Tab.

Access changes the criteria to Like "S*":

39. Run the query.

The results are the same as when you typed Saturday in the Criteria row and Sunday in the Or row.

40. Close the query. Choose **No** when prompted to save the changes.

Saving changes to the query at this time would save the criteria as part of the query.

Add Date Criteria to a New Query

Now you will create a query that returns the records of the very youngest children so you can determine which children may need more supervision.

41. Choose **Create→Queries→Query Design**.

42. Add the **Children** table to the query work area; close the **Show Table** dialog box.

43. Add **ChildLastName**, **ChildFirstName**, and **BirthDate** to the query design grid.

44. Choose **Design→Results→Run**.

Last Name	First Name	BirthDate
Abbot	Sami	2/15/2005
Creger	Kurt	9/12/2003
Driver	Sally	7/22/2005
Finkel	Evelyn	2/26/2003
Frith	Hermy	10/14/2005
Georgia	Pete	6/6/2004
Jones	Paul	1/10/2005
Kendall	Olivia	4/21/2004
Langford	James	3/9/2003
Lockwood	Timmy	8/10/2005
Preston	Willy	12/4/2004
Riggs	Dina	11/2/2004
Shamik	Ravi	6/28/2003
Simpson	Belinda	7/17/2004

45. Switch to **Design View**.

46. Type **>January 1, 2005** in the **Criteria** row for the **BirthDate** field and tap Enter.

Regardless of how you type the dates (January 1, 2005 or 01/01/05 or 1-1-2005) Access formats the date after you enter it so that it appears as #1/1/2005# in the Criteria row.

47. Run the query.

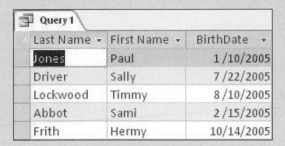

Your query returns only the records of children who were born after January 1, 2005.

48. Save the query as **Younger Children** and click **OK**.

Your Queries Objects list now contains the names of the queries you created.

49. Save and close the query, then close the database; exit **Access**.

50. Submit your final file based on the guidelines provided by your instructor.

To view examples of how your file or files should look at the end of this exercise, go to the student resource center.

Access 2013

Use Queries to Ensure Data Integrity

Kids for Change is planning to fine-tune their database by adding queries that will produce calculated results and also confirm and maintain data integrity. You are in charge of their IT department, and it is your responsibility to generate the desired query results.

Limit and Sort Query Results

1. Start **Access**. Open **AC04-R02-K4C** from the **AC2013 Lesson 04** folder and save it as **AC04-R02-K4C-[FirstInitialLastName]**.

2. Double-click the **Children List** query in the Navigation Pane to run it.

Last Name	First Name	Birth Date
Abbot	Sami	2/15/2005
Creger	Kurt	9/12/2003
Driver	Sally	7/22/2005
Finkel	Evelyn	2/26/2003
Frith	Hermy	10/14/2005
Georgia	Pete	6/6/2004
Jones	Paul	1/10/2005
Kendall	Olivia	4/21/2004
Langford	James	3/9/2003
Lockwood	Timmy	8/10/2005
Preston	Willy	12/4/2004
Riggs	Dina	11/2/2004
Shamik	Ravi	6/28/2003
Simpson	Belinda	7/17/2004

The query returns the records of all children in the table in alphabetical order by last name.

3. Switch to **Design View**.

4. Choose **Design→Query Setup→Return** and type **10** in the Return box.

   Access may add another zero to the 10 you enter. If Access displays 100 in the Return box, delete the last 0.

5. Click in the **Sort** row of the BirthDate field and choose **Descending**.

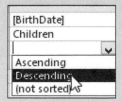

6. Click **Run**.

Children List		
Last Name ▾	First Name ▾	Birth Date ▾
Frith	Hermy	10/14/2005
Lockwood	Timmy	8/10/2005
Driver	Sally	7/22/2005
Abbot	Sami	2/15/2005
Jones	Paul	1/10/2005
Preston	Willy	12/4/2004
Riggs	Dina	11/2/2004
Simpson	Belinda	7/17/2004
Georgia	Pete	6/6/2004
Kendall	Olivia	4/21/2004

Your query should display the records of the ten youngest children.

7. Close the query without saving it.

Add a Calculated Field to a Query and Format the Field

As part of their community-give-back policy, Kids for Change puts 10 percent of all donations into a scholarship fund. Now you will add a field that calculates 10 percent of each donation.

8. Double-click the **Donations Query** in the Navigation Pane to run it.

Donor ▾	Last Name ▾	First Name ▾	Address ▾	City ▾	State ▾	ZIP ▾	Telephone ▾	Tribute ▾	Date ▾	Amo
1	Bloodworth	Timothy	50th Street South	Tampa	FL	33605	(813) 555-6666	Tim and Joan Bloodworth	4/4/2013	$
1	Bloodworth	Timothy	50th Street South	Tampa	FL	33605	(813) 555-6666	Tim and Joan Bloodworth	1/5/2013	$1,
2	Boltwood	Nancy	Casey Key Rd.	Tampa	FL	33607	(813) 555-9486	In loving memory of Miriam Miller.	3/6/2013	$
2	Boltwood	Nancy	Casey Key Rd.	Tampa	FL	33607	(813) 555-9486	In loving memory of Miriam Miller.	1/6/2013	$
2	Boltwood	Nancy	Casey Key Rd.	Tampa	FL	33607	(813) 555-9486	In loving memory of Miriam Miller.	2/1/2013	$
3	McGovern	Elton		Atlanta	GA	30314	(470) 555-4958		3/12/2013	$
3	McGovern	Elton		Atlanta	GA	30314	(470) 555-4958		4/6/2013	$
3	McGovern	Elton		Atlanta	GA	30314	(470) 555-4958		2/15/2013	$1,
4	Franklin	Joseph		Miami	FL	33184	(800) 555-0928		3/31/2013	$1,
5	Shelton	Adelle	Alexander Drive	Las Vegas	NV	89119	(800) 555-9040	For Shelley	4/5/2013	$
5	Shelton	Adelle	Alexander Drive	Las Vegas	NV	89119	(800) 555-9040	For Shelley	4/9/2013	$
6	Simpson	Lance	59 Bahia Vista	Sarasota	FL	34234	(941) 555-5522	Grateful for the Love	4/10/2013	$1,
7	Frith	Herman	Bay to Gulf Terr	Sarasota	FL	34228	(941) 555-1400		4/12/2013	$
8	Boltwood	Clay	Bayfront Blvd.	Sarasota	FL	34228	(800) 555-3821	To Miriam	4/12/2013	$1,
10	Blumenthal	Joyce	298 West Biscayne	Miami Beach	FL	33139	(305) 555-2909	My Dear Abbie Blumenthal	4/13/2013	$

9. Switch to **Design View**.

10. Type **ScholarFund:Amount*.1** in the first empty query grid line and tap ↓.

11. If the Property Sheet is not shown, right-click in the **ScholarFund** column and choose **Properties**.

12. Click in the **Format** line, open the drop-down list, and choose **Currency**.

13. Type **Scholar Fund** in the **Caption** line.

Access 2013

14. Run the query.

City	State	ZIP	Telephone	Tribute	Date	Amount	Scholar Fund
Tampa	FL	33605	(813) 555-6666	Tim and Joan Bloodworth	4/4/2013	$500.00	$50.00
Tampa	FL	33605	(813) 555-6666	Tim and Joan Bloodworth	1/5/2013	$1,000.00	$100.00
Tampa	FL	33607	(813) 555-9486	In loving memory of Miriam Miller.	3/6/2013	$500.00	$50.00
Tampa	FL	33607	(813) 555-9486	In loving memory of Miriam Miller.	1/6/2013	$500.00	$50.00
Tampa	FL	33607	(813) 555-9486	In loving memory of Miriam Miller.	2/1/2013	$500.00	$50.00
Atlanta	GA	30314	(470) 555-4958		3/12/2013	$250.00	$25.00
Atlanta	GA	30314	(470) 555-4958		4/6/2013	$400.00	$40.00
Atlanta	GA	30314	(470) 555-4958		2/15/2013	$1,000.00	$100.00
Miami	FL	33184	(800) 555-0928		3/31/2013	$1,500.00	$150.00
Las Vegas	NV	89119	(800) 555-9040	For Shelley	4/5/2013	$500.00	$50.00
Las Vegas	NV	89119	(800) 555-9040	For Shelley	4/9/2013	$250.00	$25.00
Sarasota	FL	34234	(941) 555-5522	Grateful for the Love	4/10/2013	$1,000.00	$100.00
Sarasota	FL	34228	(941) 555-1400		4/12/2013	$500.00	$50.00
Sarasota	FL	34228	(800) 555-3821	To Miriam	4/12/2013	$1,000.00	$100.00
Miami Beach	FL	33139	(305) 555-2909	My Dear Abbie Blumenthal	4/13/2013	$750.00	$75.00

15. Save and close the query.

Create a Query Containing Functions

Now you will create a query that returns the total amount of donations received and the minimum, maximum, and average amount of donations.

16. Choose **Create→Queries→Query Design**.

17. Click the **Queries tab** in the Show Table dialog box to list the queries in the database.

18. Double-click **Donations Query** to add it to the query work area, and **close** the Show Table box.

19. Choose **Design→Show/Hide→Totals** to show the Total line in the query grid.

20. Type **TotalDonations: Amount** in the first line of the grid.

21. Click in the **Total** line and choose **Sum**.

22. Type **MinDonation: Amount** in the second Field line of the query grid.

23. Click in the **Total** line and choose **Min**.

24. Type **MaxDonation: Amount** in the third Field line of the query grid.

25. Click in the *Total* line and choose **Max**.

26. Type **AvgDonation: Amount** in the third Field line of the query grid.

27. Click in the **Total** line and choose **Avg**.

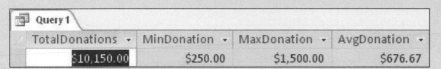

Field:	TotalDonations: Amount	MinDonation: Amount	MaxDonation: Amount	AvgDonation: Amount
Table:	Donations Query	Donations Query	Donations Query	Donations Query
Total:	Sum	Min	Max	Avg
Sort:				
Show:	✓	✓	✓	✓

28. Run the query.

Access displays the aggregate total, minimum, maximum, and average donation amounts.

Query 1			
TotalDonations ▾	MinDonation ▾	MaxDonation ▾	AvgDonation ▾
$10,150.00	$250.00	$1,500.00	$676.67

29. Save the query as **Donation Functions** and then close it.

Create a Crosstab Query

30. Choose **Create→Queries→Query Wizard** 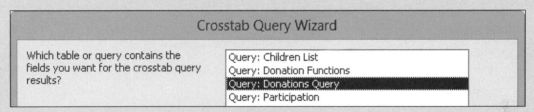 to open the New Query dialog box.

31. Double-click **Crosstab Query Wizard**.

32. Select the **Queries** option button and choose **Query: Donations Query**.

Crosstab Query Wizard

Which table or query contains the fields you want for the crosstab query results?

Query: Children List
Query: Donation Functions
Query: Donations Query
Query: Participation

33. Click **Next** to display the next wizard screen.

Access wants to know what data you want to display down the left side of the query. In this query, you want the employee last name to appear down the left column.

34. Double-click **DonorLName** in the Available Fields list to move it to the Selected Fields list.

35. Click **Next**, double-click **DonationDate** as the field to appear in the column headings, and advance to the next wizard screen.

36. Click **Month** as the interval by which you want to group your Date/Time column information and click **Next**.

37. Select **Amount** in the Fields list and **Sum** in the Functions list to identify the field that contains values and the function you want to calculate.

Your crosstab query grid should show DonorLName fields as row headings, DonationDate as column headings, and Sum being applied to the Amount field.

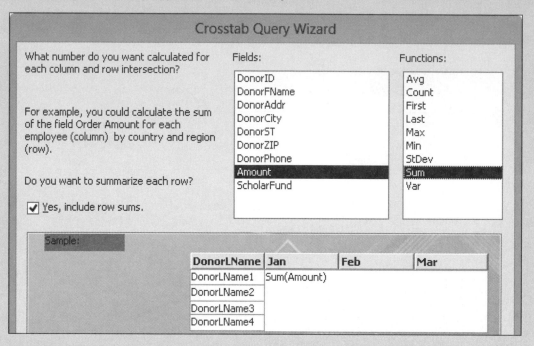

38. Click **Next** to display the final page of the Crosstab Query Wizard.

39. Name the query **DonationsCrosstab**, click the **Modify the Design** option button, and click **Finish**.

Access displays the query in Design View.

40. Click in the **Total of Amount** column.

41. Open the Property Sheet, if necessary, and type **Donor Total** in the Caption property line.

42. Save, run, and then close the query.

Last Name	Donor Total	Jan	Feb	Mar	Apr
Bloodworth	$1,500.00	$1,000.00			$500.00
Blumenthal	$750.00				$750.00
Boltwood	$2,500.00	$500.00	$500.00	$500.00	$1,000.00
Franklin	$1,500.00			$1,500.00	
Frith	$500.00				$500.00
McGovern	$1,650.00		$1,000.00	$250.00	$400.00
Shelton	$750.00				$750.00
Simpson	$1,000.00				$1,000.00

Create an Unmatched Records and a Find Duplicate Records Query

43. Choose **Create→Queries→Query Wizard** 🔲 and double-click **Find Unmatched Query Wizard**.

    Access opens the Find Unmatched Query Wizard. From this screen, you select the table you want to check against another table.

44. Double-click **Table: Activities** to identify the table and automatically advance to the next screen.

45. Double-click **Table: Volunteers** to identify the table to compare to the **Activities** table entries and automatically advance to the next screen.

    The next screen displays a list of fields in both selected tables. From the lists, you will identify the fields in the Activities and Volunteers tables to compare for matching values.

46. Click the **Day** field in the Fields in 'Activities' list.

47. Scroll down the Fields in 'Volunteers' list and click **VolDay**.

48. Click **Equate** <=> to locate any days without a matching volunteer record.

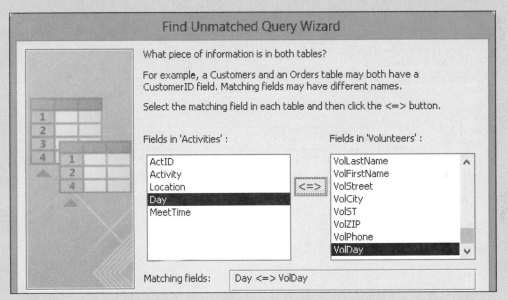

49. Click **Next** and **Move** > to move the following fields to the Selected Fields list: **Activity**, **Day**, and **MeetTime**.

50. Click **Next** and then click **Finish**.

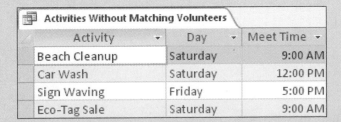

You can use such results to find and delete unmatched activities from the schedule or to assign the unmatched activities to paid Staffers.

51. Close the query.

52. Choose **Create→Queries→Query Wizard** 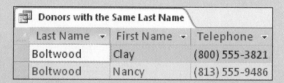 and double-click **Find Duplicates Query Wizard**.

53. Double-click **Table: Donors** as the table you want to check for duplicates and to automatically advance to the next screen.

54. Select the **DonorLName** field, click **Move** ▶ to move the field to the Duplicate-Value Fields box, and click **Next**.

55. Move **DonorFName** to the Additional Query Fields box.

56. Move **DonorPhone** to the Additional Query Fields box, and click **Next**.

57. Type the name `Donors with the Same Last Name` for the query name, and click **Finish**.

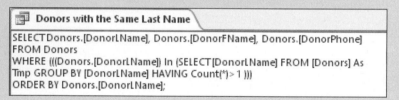

The query results datasheet shows that there are two donors with the last name Boltwood.

View a Query in SQL View

58. Open the query in **SQL View**.

```
SELECT Donors.[DonorLName], Donors.[DonorFName], Donors.[DonorPhone]
FROM Donors
WHERE (((Donors.[DonorLName]) In (SELECT [DonorLName] FROM [Donors] As
Tmp GROUP BY [DonorLName] HAVING Count(*) > 1 )))
ORDER BY Donors.[DonorLName];
```

59. Notice the SQL commands and reserved words are in uppercase lettering.

Your Queries Objects list now contains the names of the queries you created.

60. Save and close the query and the database, then exit **Access**.

61. Submit your final file based on the guidelines provided by your instructor.

    To view examples of how your file or files should look at the end of this exercise, go to the student resource center.

Create and Customize Queries

Kids for Change is planning to fine-tune their database by adding queries that will produce calculated and formatted results based on specific search criteria. In this exercise, you will use tables to create various queries.

Create a Query Using the Query Wizard

1. Start **Access**. Open **AC04-R03-K4C** from the **AC2013 Lesson 04** folder and save it as **AC04-R03-K4C-[FirstInitialLastName]**.

2. Choose **Create→Queries→Query Wizard**.

3. Double-click **Simple Query Wizard**.

4. Select the **Donors** table from the Tables/Queries list.

5. Click the **DonorLName** field in the Available Fields list and click the **Move** button.

6. Move the **DonorFName**, **DonorPhone**, and **DonorEmail** fields to the Selected Fields list.

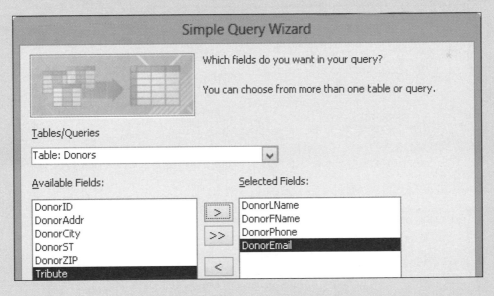

7. Click **Next**.

8. Type **Donor Contact List** in the query title box and click **Finish**.

Last Name ▾	First Name ▾	Telephone ▾	DonorEmail ▾
Bloodworth	Timothy	(813) 555-6666	BloodworthTim@email.com
Boltwood	Nancy	(813) 555-9486	NancyMB@email.com
McGovern	Elton	(470) 555-4958	McGovern4958@email.com
Franklin	Joseph	(800) 555-0928	JoeyTFranklin@email.com
Shelton	Adelle	(800) 555-9040	ShelleyAddie@email.com
Simpson	Lance	(941) 555-5522	SimpsonLanceJ@email.com
Frith	Herman	(941) 555-1400	BevAndHerman@email.com
Boltwood	Clay	(800) 555-3821	PowerPlayerInc@email.com
Blumenthal	Joyce	(305) 555-2909	JoyceBBlum@email.com

The query results datasheet should include the four selected fields from every Donor record.

9. Review the query results datasheet then close the query.

Create a Query in Design View

10. Choose **Create→Queries→QueryDesign**.

11. Click the **Staff** table, click **Add**, then close the Show Table dialog box.

12. Double-click the **StaffLastName** field name to add it to the query grid.

13. Double-click **StaffFirstName**, **StaffStreet**, **StaffCity**, **StaffST**, and **StateZIP** to the query grid in the order shown.

Field:	StaffLastName	StaffFirstName	StaffStreet	StaffCity	StaffST	StaffZIP
Table:	Staff	Staff	Staff	Staff	Staff	Staff
Sort:						
Show:	☑	☑	☑	☑	☑	☑

You can also click and drag fields to the query grid.

14. Click **Save**, name the query **Staff Mailing List**, and click **OK**.

15. Choose **Design→Results→Run**.

Last Name ▾	First Name ▾	Street Address ▾	City ▾	ST ▾	ZIP ▾
Bryant	Matthew	12 E. MacIntosh	Sarasota	FL	34022
Earle	Kevin	77 Kingfisher	Sarasota	FL	34234
Jacoby	Jane	4323 NW 63rd	Venice	FL	34285
Pauly	Gerry	891 Waylon Lane	Bradenton	FL	34205
Lockwood	Bill	32 Cortez Rd	Bradenton	FL	34207
Kendall	Lonnie	803 Magellan Dr	Sarasota	FL	34232
Montagne	Francis	3102 Beneva	Sarasota	FL	34222
Yellen	George	105 Landfall Rd	Palmetto	FL	34221

Access runs the query and displays four columns of data for all Employee records. Resize the columns as desired by double-clicking the column heading borders.

16. Close the query, saving the changes if prompted.

Create a Multi-Table Query

17. Choose **Create→Queries→Query Design**.

An empty query grid opens.

18. Double-click the following table names in the **Show Table** dialog box to add the table field lists to the upper pane of the query: **Activities**, **ActivityParticipation**, and **Children**.

19. Close the **Show Table** box.

20. In the Activities table, double-click **Activity** to move it to the query grid.

21. Double-click **Day** and **MeetTime**.

22. In the Children table, double-click **ChildLastName**, **ChildFirstName**, and **ChildPhone**.

Field:	Activity	Day	MeetTime	ChildLastName	ChildFirstName	ChildPhone
Table:	Activities	Activities	Activities	Children	Children	Children
Sort:						
Show:	✔	✔	✔	✔	✔	✔
Criteria:						

Your tables may be aligned differently, however the fields should appear in the query grid in the order shown in the figure above.

23. Save the query as `Participant List`.

24. Choose **Design→Results→Run**.

Participant List

Activity	Day	Meet Time	Last Name	First Name	Telephone
Beach Cleanup	Saturday	9:00 AM	Creger	Kurt	(941) 555-0245
Beach Cleanup	Saturday	9:00 AM	Driver	Sally	(941) 555-2272
Beach Cleanup	Saturday	9:00 AM	Finkel	Evelyn	(941) 555-2324
Beach Cleanup	Saturday	9:00 AM	Georgia	Pete	(941) 555-6121
Beach Cleanup	Saturday	9:00 AM	Kendall	Olivia	(941) 555-2356
Beach Cleanup	Saturday	9:00 AM	Langford	James	(941) 555-1098
Beach Cleanup	Saturday	9:00 AM	Preston	Willy	(941) 555-9372
Beach Cleanup	Saturday	9:00 AM	Riggs	Dina	(941) 555-2190
Beach Cleanup	Saturday	9:00 AM	Simpson	Belinda	(941) 555-0944
Can Collection	Thursday	6:00 PM	Abbot	Sami	(941) 555-2890
Can Collection	Thursday	6:00 PM	Creger	Kurt	(941) 555-0245
Can Collection	Thursday	6:00 PM	Frith	Hermy	(941) 555-7485
Can Collection	Thursday	6:00 PM	Lockwood	Timmy	(941) 555-6531
Car Wash	Saturday	12:00 PM	Abbot	Sami	(941) 555-2890

Add Criteria to a Query

Now you will add criteria to the Participant List query to list the children signed up for 9:00 AM Saturday activities.

25. Switch to **Design View**.

26. Type `Saturday` in the Criteria row of **Day**.

27. Type `9:00` in the Criteria row of **MeetTime**.

    This creates an AND condition. Only records with a Day value of Saturday AND a MeetTime value of 9:00 will be returned.

28. Run the query.

Activity	Day	Meet Time	Last Name	First Name	Telephone
Beach Cleanup	Saturday	9:00 AM	Creger	Kurt	(941) 555-0245
Beach Cleanup	Saturday	9:00 AM	Driver	Sally	(941) 555-2272
Beach Cleanup	Saturday	9:00 AM	Finkel	Evelyn	(941) 555-2324
Beach Cleanup	Saturday	9:00 AM	Georgia	Pete	(941) 555-6121
Beach Cleanup	Saturday	9:00 AM	Kendall	Olivia	(941) 555-2356
Beach Cleanup	Saturday	9:00 AM	Langford	James	(941) 555-1098
Beach Cleanup	Saturday	9:00 AM	Preston	Willy	(941) 555-9372
Beach Cleanup	Saturday	9:00 AM	Riggs	Dina	(941) 555-2190
Beach Cleanup	Saturday	9:00 AM	Simpson	Belinda	(941) 555-0944
Eco-Tag Sale	Saturday	9:00 AM	Frith	Hermy	(941) 555-7485
Eco-Tag Sale	Saturday	9:00 AM	Jones	Paul	(941) 555-8929
Eco-Tag Sale	Saturday	9:00 AM	Langford	James	(941) 555-1098
Eco-Tag Sale	Saturday	9:00 AM	Shamik	Ravi	(941) 555-1092

Access runs the query and returns the records with both Saturday and 9:00 AM.

29. Save and close the query.

Use Wildcard Criteria

Now you will use a wildcard to select nearby donors so they can be invited to local activities.

30. Right-click **Donations Query** in the Navigation Pane and choose **Design View**.

31. Type `34*` in the Criteria row of DonorZIP and tap Tab.

Field:	DonorLName	DonorFName	DonorAddr	DonorCity	DonorST	DonorZIP
Table:	Donors	Donors	Donors	Donors	Donors	Donors
Sort:						
Show:	✓	✓	✓	✓	✓	✓
Criteria:						Like "34*"
or:						

Access changes the 34* to Like "34*".

32. Run the query.

Donor	Last Name	First Name	Address	City	State	ZIP
6	Simpson	Lance	59 Bahia Vista	Sarasota	FL	34234
7	Frith	Herman	Bay to Gulf Terr	Sarasota	FL	34228
8	Boltwood	Clay	Bayfront Blvd.	Sarasota	FL	34228

Add Date Criteria to a Query

33. Switch to **Design View**.

34. Remove the criteria from the **DonorZIP** field.

35. Type >**01/01/2013** in the Criteria row of the DonationDate field and tap ⌨Tab.

36. Run the query.

Donor	Last Name	First Name	Address	City	State	ZIP	Telephone	Tribute	Date
3	McGovern	Elton		Atlanta	GA	30314	(470) 555-4958		3/12/2013
3	McGovern	Elton		Atlanta	GA	30314	(470) 555-4958		4/6/2013
10	Blumenthal	Joyce	298 West Biscayne	Miami Bea	FL	33139	(305) 555-2909	My Dear Abbie Blumenthal	4/13/2013
3	McGovern	Elton		Atlanta	GA	30314	(470) 555-4958		2/15/2013
4	Franklin	Joseph		Miami	FL	33184	(800) 555-0928		3/31/2013
5	Shelton	Adelle	Alexander Drive	Las Vegas	NV	89119	(800) 555-9040	For Shelley	4/5/2013
6	Simpson	Lance	59 Bahia Vista	Sarasota	FL	34234	(941) 555-5522	Grateful for the Love	4/10/2013
7	Frith	Herman	Bay to Gulf Terr	Sarasota	FL	34228	(941) 555-1400		4/12/2013
2	Boltwood	Nancy	Casey Key Rd.	Tampa	FL	33607	(813) 555-9486	In loving memory of Miriam Miller.	2/1/2013
5	Shelton	Adelle	Alexander Drive	Las Vegas	NV	89119	(800) 555-9040	For Shelley	4/9/2013
8	Boltwood	Clay	Bayfront Blvd.	Sarasota	FL	34228	(800) 555-3821	To Miriam	4/12/2013

Sort and Limit Query Results

37. Switch to **Design View**.

38. Click in the Sort row of the DonationDate field; click the list arrow, and choose **Descending**.

39. Choose **Design→Query Setup→Return**.

40. Click the list arrow and choose **5**.

41. Run the query.

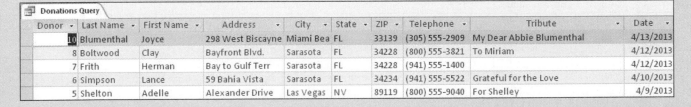

Donor	Last Name	First Name	Address	City	State	ZIP	Telephone	Tribute	Date
10	Blumenthal	Joyce	298 West Biscayne	Miami Bea	FL	33139	(305) 555-2909	My Dear Abbie Blumenthal	4/13/2013
8	Boltwood	Clay	Bayfront Blvd.	Sarasota	FL	34228	(800) 555-3821	To Miriam	4/12/2013
7	Frith	Herman	Bay to Gulf Terr	Sarasota	FL	34228	(941) 555-1400		4/12/2013
6	Simpson	Lance	59 Bahia Vista	Sarasota	FL	34234	(941) 555-5522	Grateful for the Love	4/10/2013
5	Shelton	Adelle	Alexander Drive	Las Vegas	NV	89119	(800) 555-9040	For Shelley	4/9/2013

Access returns only the five most recent donor records.

Add a Calculated Field to a Query and Format the Field

42. Switch to **Design View**.

43. Choose **Design→Query Setup→Return** and choose **All**.

44. Type `NetAmt:Amount-ScholarFund` in the first empty **Field** row.

45. Open the **Property Sheet**.

46. Click in the **Format** line, open the drop-down list, and choose **Currency**.

47. Type `Net Donation` in the **Caption** line.

48. Run the query.

State	ZIP	Telephone	Tribute	Date	Amount	Scholar Fund	Net Donation
FL	33139	(305) 555-2909	My Dear Abbie Blumenthal	4/13/2013	$750.00	$75.00	$675.00
FL	34228	(800) 555-3821	To Miriam	4/12/2013	$1,000.00	$100.00	$900.00
FL	34228	(941) 555-1400		4/12/2013	$500.00	$50.00	$450.00
FL	34234	(941) 555-5522	Grateful for the Love	4/10/2013	$1,000.00	$100.00	$900.00
NV	89119	(800) 555-9040	For Shelley	4/9/2013	$250.00	$25.00	$225.00
GA	30314	(470) 555-4958		4/6/2013	$400.00	$40.00	$360.00
NV	89119	(800) 555-9040	For Shelley	4/5/2013	$500.00	$50.00	$450.00
FL	33184	(800) 555-0928		3/31/2013	$1,500.00	$150.00	$1,350.00
GA	30314	(470) 555-4958		3/12/2013	$250.00	$25.00	$225.00
GA	30314	(470) 555-4958		2/15/2013	$1,000.00	$100.00	$900.00
FL	33607	(813) 555-9486	In loving memory of Miriam Miller.	2/1/2013	$500.00	$50.00	$450.00

49. Save and close the query.

Create a Duplicate Records Query

50. Choose **Create→Queries→Query Wizard** and double-click **Find Duplicates Query Wizard**.

51. Double-click **Table: Children** as the table you want to check for duplicates.

52. Double-click **ChildLastName** to move it to the Duplicate-Value Fields box. Click **Next**.

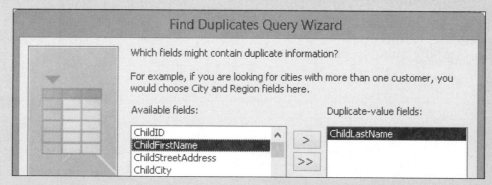

53. In the next wizard screen, move **ChildFirstName**, **ChildStreetAddress**, **ChildCity**, **ChildST**, **ChildZIP**, and **ChildPhone** to the Additional Query Fields box.

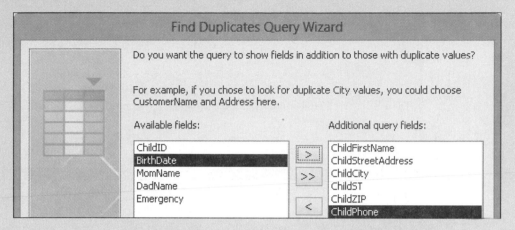

54. Click **Next**, type `Children with the Same Last Name` for the query name, and click **Finish**.

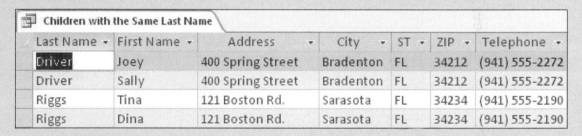

55. Close the query.

Create an Unmatched Record Query

56. Start the **Query Wizard** and double-click **Find Unmatched Query Wizard**.

57. Double-click **Table: Children** to identify the table that contains the values for which you are searching.

58. Double-click **Table: Volunteers** to identify the table to compare to the **Children** table entries.

59. Click **ChildLastName** in the Children list and **VolLastName** in the Volunteers list. Click **Equate**.

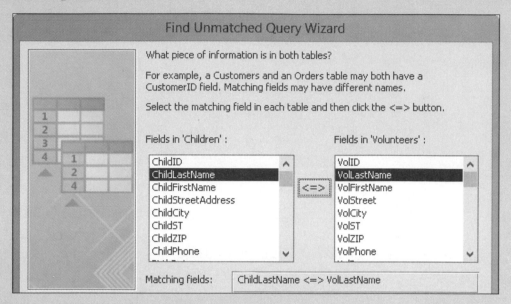

The Matching Fields box contains the selected fields to compare.

60. Click **Next**.

61. Move the following fields to the Selected Fields list: **ChildLastName**, **ChildFirstName**, **ChildPhone**, **MomName**, and **DadName**.

62. Click **Next** and then **Finish**.

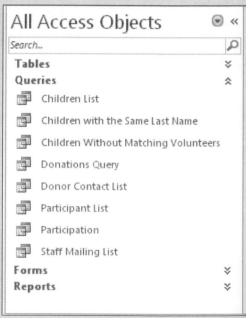

The Queries Objects list contains the names of the queries you created.

63. Close the query and the database, then exit **Access**.

64. Submit your final file based on the guidelines provided by your instructor.

Apply Your Skills

APPLY YOUR SKILLS AC04-A01

Create Queries Containing Criteria

Hubert Buckley, new CEO of Universal Corporate Events, has asked you to refine a number of queries to be more selective in data output. In this exercise, you will create queries; add criteria, wildcards, and AND/OR conditions to a query; and add date criteria to a query.

Create a Query Using the Query Wizard

1. Start **Access**. Open **AC04-A01-UCE** from the **AC2013 Lesson 04** folder and save it as **AC04-A01-UCE-[FirstInitialLastName]**.

2. Use the **Query Wizard** to create a simple select query from the **Personnel** table that includes the **PerLastName**, **PerFirstName**, **PerPhone**, and **PerEmail** fields.

3. Save the query as **Personnel Contact List** and then run it.

Query 1			
Last Name	First Name	Telephone	Email Address
Wallace	Renee	(813) 555-2012	RJWallace@email.com
Dhana	Nazrene	(941) 555-6924	NazzJazz@email.com
Phattal	Rasha	(941) 555-6925	RashaP@email.com
Franks	Jade	(941) 555-9392	BobFranks@email.com
Montero	Jaime	(941) 555-2890	GourmetCiao@email.com
Winstead	Thomas	(941) 555-1921	TKWinstead@email.com
Buckley	Hubert	(813) 555-2000	BuckleyHJ@email.com
Buckley	J.G.	(813) 555-1000	BuckleyJG@email.com
Buckley	Connie	(813) 555-8811	BuckleyConnie@email.com
Goldstein	Marv	(941) 555-4603	MarvinGoldstein52@email.com

4. Close the query.

Create a Multi-Table Query in Design View

5. Create a query in **Design View** that uses the **Events**, **Schedules**, and **Menus** tables.

6. From the **Events** table, add **EventName** to the grid.

7. From the **Schedules** table, add **VenueID**, **ContactID**, **EventDate**, and **Guests**.

8. From the **Menus** table, add **MenuPlan** and **Chg/PP**.

9. Run the query.

Event Name	VenueID	Contact ID	Event Date	Guests	Menu Plan
Business Meeting	Meadow	LunaL	2/15/2014	50	Luncheon Sit Down
Holiday Party	Drake	CroftS	12/6/2013	150	Hors d'oeuvre
Holiday Party	Meadow	Miller	12/14/2013	100	Dinner Sit Down
Retirement Party	Meadow	Miller	1/15/2014	50	Dinner Buffet
Business Meeting	HyattS	LunaL	5/29/2014	80	Dinner Buffet
Course Training	Manate	Benson	6/8/2014	75	Dinner Sit Down
Holiday Party	Meadow	Miller	7/2/2014	25	Dessert Selections
Business Meeting	HyattS	LunaL	1/20/2014	55	Dinner Buffet
Business Seminar	HyattS	LunaL	1/30/2014	70	Dinner Sit Down
Business Seminar	Meadow	Miller	1/25/2014	45	Dinner Buffet
Group Retreat	Brooks	Benson	2/22/2014	50	Dinner Buffet
Group Retreat	Brooks	Benson	2/1/2014	40	Buffet Luncheon

10. Save the query as **Event List** and then close it.

Use Wildcards and AND/OR Criteria in a Query

UCE, Ltd. is planning a recruiting event in Sarasota and would like to contact employees from greater Sarasota (area code 941) to involve them in planning the event. You will modify a query to return the records of personnel who live in the Sarasota area.

11. Open the **Personnel Contact List** in Design View.

12. Type ***941*** in the Criteria row for **PerPhone**.

13. Run the query.

Last Name	First Name	Telephone	Email Address
Dhana	Nazrene	(941) 555-6924	NazzJazz@email.com
Phattal	Rasha	(941) 555-6925	RashaP@email.com
Franks	Jade	(941) 555-9392	BobFranks@email.com
Montero	Jaime	(941) 555-2890	GourmetCiao@email.com
Winstead	Thomas	(941) 555-1921	TKWinstead@email.com
Goldstein	Marv	(941) 555-4603	MarvinGoldstein52@email.com
Chauncy	Dina	(941) 555-3481	DinaWChauncy

*If the source table included records with the telephone numbers (813) 555-0**941** and (800) 555-**941**7, they would also be included in the results based on the criteria *941*.*

14. Close the query, but do not save it.

15. Create a query in Design View from the **Venues** table that includes the **VenueName**, **VenueCity**, **VenuePhone**, and **VenueWebSite**.

16. In the **VenueCity**, type **Sarasota** in the Criteria row and **Tampa** in the Or row.

17. Click **Run**.

18. Save the query as `Tampa-Sarasota Venues`. Close the query.

Add Date Criteria to a Query

19. Run the **Event List** query and examine the results.

20. Switch to **Design View**.

21. Type `>June 1, 2013` in the Criteria row of the **EventDate** field.

22. Click the **Sort** row and choose **Ascending** for the **EventDate** field.

23. Run the query.

Your results should include 31 records.

24. Close the query, clicking **No** when prompted to save it. Close the database and then exit **Access**.

25. Submit your finals file based on the guidelines provided by your instructor.

To view examples of how your file or files should look at the end of this exercise, go to the student resource center.

Create Queries Using Comparison Criteria

Hubert Buckley has asked you to improve UCE data retrieval and formatting. In this exercise, you will sort and limit records returned in query results, add and format a calculated field, create a query that uses functions, create a crosstab query, and create a query that find records without matching fields between tables. You will also create a query that finds duplicate values within a table.

Limit and Sort Query Results

UCE wants to know which events and venues bring in the best revenue.

1. Start **Access**. Open **AC04-A02-UCE** from the **AC2013 Lesson 04** folder and save it as **AC04-A02-UCE-[FirstInitialLastName]**.

2. Run the **Event Revenue** query and examine the results.

Event Name	VenueID	Contact ID	Event Date	Menu Plan	Guests	Chg/PP	Customer Total
Business Meeting	Meadow	LunaL	2/15/2014	Luncheon w/Servers	50	$34.00	$1,700.00
Holiday Party	Drake	CroftS	12/6/2013	Hors d'oeuvre	150	$20.00	$3,000.00
Holiday Party	Meadow	Miller	12/14/2013	Dinner-Sit Down	100	$65.00	$6,500.00
Retirement Party	Meadow	Miller	1/15/2014	Dinner-Buffet	50	$45.00	$2,250.00
Business Meeting	HyattS	LunaL	5/29/2014	Dinner-Buffet	80	$45.00	$3,600.00
Course Training	Manate	Benson	6/8/2014	Dinner-Sit Down	75	$65.00	$4,875.00
Holiday Party	Meadow	Miller	7/2/2014	Dessert Selections	25	$14.00	$350.00
Business Meeting	HyattS	LunaL	1/20/2014	Dinner-Buffet	55	$45.00	$2,475.00
Business Seminar	HyattS	LunaL	1/30/2014	Hors d'oeuvre-Deluxe	70	$35.00	$2,450.00
Business Seminar	Meadow	Miller	1/25/2014	Dinner-Buffet	45	$45.00	$2,025.00
Group Retreat	Brooks	Benson	2/22/2014	Dinner-Buffet	50	$45.00	$2,250.00
Group Retreat	Brooks	Benson	2/4/2014	Buffet Luncheon	40	$25.00	$1,000.00

3. Switch to **Design View**. Then, choose **Descending** for the sort order of the **TotalRev** calculated field.

4. Choose **Design→Query Setup→Return**; choose **5** in the **Return** box.

5. Run the query.

Event Name	VenueID	Contact ID	Event Date	Menu Plan	Guests	Chg/PP	Customer Total
Business Seminar	TBForm	CroftS	1/26/2014	Hors d'oeuvre-Deluxe	300	$35.00	$10,500.00
Holiday Party	Meadow	Miller	12/14/2013	Dinner-Sit Down	100	$65.00	$6,500.00
Business Meeting	HyattS	LunaL	2/20/2014	Dinner-Sit Down	75	$65.00	$4,875.00
Course Training	Manate	Benson	6/8/2014	Dinner-Sit Down	75	$65.00	$4,875.00
Business Seminar	HyattS	LunaL	3/14/2014	Dinner-Sit Down	65	$65.00	$4,225.00
Group Retreat	Brooks	Benson	4/12/2014	Dinner-Sit Down	65	$65.00	$4,225.00

The query returns the records of the five highest-grossing scheduled events, however six records are displayed due to the tie of $4,875.

6. Switch to **Design View** and change the Return value to **All**.

Add a Calculated Field to a Query and Format the Field

7. With the **Event Revenue** query in Design View, type `Comm:TotalRev*.08` in the first empty query grid line and tap Enter.

8. Open the **Property Sheet**; choose **Currency** for the Format and type `Commission` for the **Caption**.

9. Run the query.

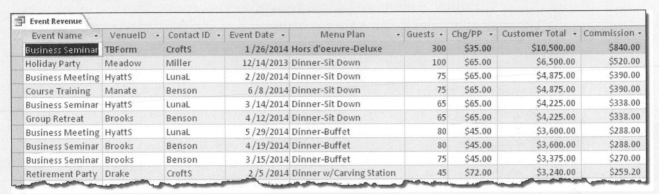

Event Name	VenueID	Contact ID	Event Date	Menu Plan	Guests	Chg/PP	Customer Total	Commission
Business Seminar	TBForm	CroftS	1/26/2014	Hors d'oeuvre-Deluxe	300	$35.00	$10,500.00	$840.00
Holiday Party	Meadow	Miller	12/14/2013	Dinner-Sit Down	100	$65.00	$6,500.00	$520.00
Business Meeting	HyattS	LunaL	2/20/2014	Dinner-Sit Down	75	$65.00	$4,875.00	$390.00
Course Training	Manate	Benson	6/8/2014	Dinner-Sit Down	75	$65.00	$4,875.00	$390.00
Business Seminar	HyattS	LunaL	3/14/2014	Dinner-Sit Down	65	$65.00	$4,225.00	$338.00
Group Retreat	Brooks	Benson	4/12/2014	Dinner-Sit Down	65	$65.00	$4,225.00	$338.00
Business Meeting	HyattS	LunaL	5/29/2014	Dinner-Buffet	80	$45.00	$3,600.00	$288.00
Business Seminar	Brooks	Benson	4/19/2014	Dinner-Buffet	80	$45.00	$3,600.00	$288.00
Business Seminar	Brooks	Benson	3/15/2014	Dinner-Buffet	75	$45.00	$3,375.00	$270.00
Retirement Party	Drake	CroftS	2/5/2014	Dinner w/Carving Station	45	$72.00	$3,240.00	$259.20

10. Save and close the query.

Create a Query Containing Functions

11. Choose **Create→Queries→Query Design**, click the Queries tab, and add the **Event Revenue** query to the query work area.

12. Add the **ContactID** field to the grid.

13. Show the Total Σ line in the query grid.

14. Type `MinEvent:TotalRev` in the second Field line of the query grid, click in the **Total** line, and choose **Min**.

15. Type `MaxEvent:TotalRev` in the third Field line, click in the **Total** line, and choose **Max**.

16. Type `AvgEvent:TotalRev` in the third Field line, click in the **Total** line, and choose **Avg**.

17. Run the query.

Contact ID	MinEvent	MaxEvent	AvgEvent
Miller	$350.00	$6,500.00	$2,781.25
Benson	$1,000.00	$4,875.00	$2,371.82
LunaL	$1,250.00	$4,875.00	$2,822.50
CroftS	$3,000.00	$10,500.00	$4,935.00

Your query datasheet should show the minimum event revenue, maximum event revenue, and average event revenue for each venue contact person.

18. Save the query as `Contact Functions` and close it.

Create a Crosstab Query

19. Start the **Query Wizard** and double-click **Crosstab Query Wizard**.

20. Select the **Queries** option button and double-click **Query: Event Revenue**.

21. Choose **VenueID** as the field for the query results row headings and click **Next**.

22. Choose **ContactID** as the field to appear in the column headings and click **Next**.

23. Select **TotalRev** in the Fields list and **Sum** in the Functions list to identify the field that contains values and the function you want to calculate.

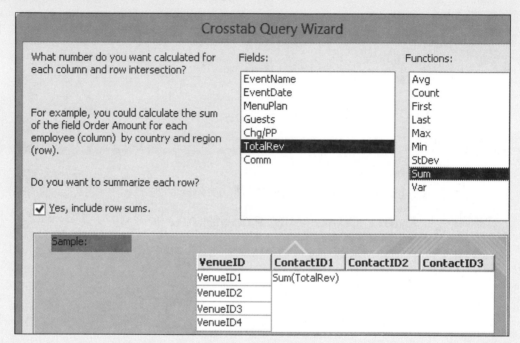

24. Click **Next**, name the query `Contact Revenue by Venue`, and click **Finish**.

Total Revenue	Total Of TotalRev	Gail	Harold	Lisa	Suzy
Brooks	$21,215.00		$21,215.00		
Drake	$6,240.00				$6,240.00
HyattS	$26,525.00			$26,525.00	
Manate	$4,875.00		$4,875.00		
Meadow	$12,825.00	$11,125.00		$1,700.00	
TBForm	$10,500.00				$10,500.00
TmpCon	$3,000.00				$3,000.00

25. Close the query, saving changes if prompted.

Create an Unmatched Records and a Find Duplicate Records Query

26. Start the **Query Wizard** and double-click **Find Unmatched Query Wizard**.

27. Choose **Venues** as the table with the field value for which you are seeking a match and **Schedules** as the table to compare values.

28. Verify that **VenueID** is selected in both lists; click **Equate**.

29. In the next wizard screen, move **VenueName**, **VenueStreet**, **VenueCity**, **VenueST**, **VenueZIP**, **VenuePhone**, and **VenueWebSite** to the Selected Fields list.

30. Name the query `Venues Without Events Scheduled` and click **Finish**.

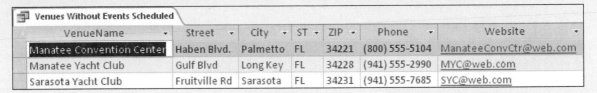

You can use such results to find and delete unscheduled venues or to call your venue contact and ask why no events have been scheduled at the location.

31. Close the query.

32. Start the **Query Wizard** and double-click **Find Duplicates Query Wizard**.

33. Choose **Query: Event List** as the query to search for duplicate values and **EventDate** as the Duplicate-Value Fields box. Click **Next**.

34. Include **VenueID**, **ContactID**, **MenuPlan**, and **Guests** in the query results.

35. Name the query `Find Double-Booked Dates`; click **Finish**.

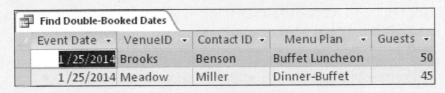

The query results show two events scheduled for January 25, 2014. This kind of information can help you plan for extra personnel or scheduling conflicts.

View a Query in SQL View

36. Right-click the query name tab and choose **SQL View**.

> **Find Double-Booked Dates**
>
> SELECT [Event List].[EventDate], [Event List].[VenueID], [Event List].[ContactID], [Event List].[MenuPlan], [Event List].[Guests]
> FROM [Event List]
> WHERE (((([Event List].[EventDate]) In (SELECT [EventDate] FROM [Event List] As Tmp
> GROUP BY [EventDate] HAVING Count(*)> 1)))
> ORDER BY [Event List].[EventDate];

Commands/reserved words are uppercase and field names are preceded by the name of the table or query in which they are stored.

37. Close the query and the database, saving it if prompted. Exit **Access**.

38. Submit your final file based on the guidelines provided by your instructor.

To view examples of how your file or files should look at the end of this exercise, go to the student resource center.

Create Queries

In this exercise, you will create and modify a number of queries for more precise, targeted data selection for Universal Corporate Events.

Create Queries and Add Criteria

To begin, you will create a query to list contact information for the event venues that have an 800 telephone number so they can be reached by phone from anywhere at any time and at no charge to the caller.

1. Start **Access**. Open **AC04-A03-UCE** from the **AC2013 Lesson 04** folder and save it as **AC04-A03-UCE-[FirstInitialLastName]**.

2. Create a simple select query that uses the **Venues** table to generate a list of Venue names and their corresponding telephone numbers and websites.

3. Name the query **TollFreeVenues**.

4. In **Design View**, add criteria and wildcards to select only the venues that have an *800 phone number* by typing ***800*** in the Criteria row of the **VenuePhone** field.

5. Run the query to view the results; resize the columns, as necessary.

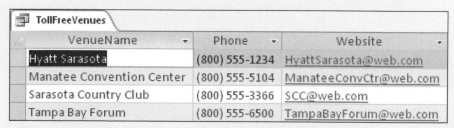

VenueName	Phone	Website
Hyatt Sarasota	(800) 555-1234	HyattSarasota@web.com
Manatee Convention Center	(800) 555-5104	ManateeConvCtr@web.com
Sarasota Country Club	(800) 555-3366	SCC@web.com
Tampa Bay Forum	(800) 555-6500	TampaBayForum@web.com

6. Save and close the query.

Add Wildcard and Date Criteria to a Query and Sort the Query

Because June is the most popular month for weddings, UCE wants to pay special attention to weddings scheduled for June so they can hire extra part-time workers.

7. Create a new query that uses the **Event List** query as a record source.

8. Include all of the fields in Event List in the new query, leave the default Detail query option, name it **June Weddings**, and display it in Design View.

9. Add the wildcard criteria **Wed*** (for Weddings) to the EventName field.

10. Choose **Ascending** for the Sort order of EventDate, and type **Between June 1, 2014 and June 30, 2014** in the EventDate criteria row.

11. Run the query.

12. Close the query, saving it if prompted.

Limit the Number of Records in Query Results

Now you will sort the Location Scheduling query by the largest number of guests, and return the ten highest values so the company can focus extra personnel and resources to those events if the guests are scheduled for a full menu plan.

13. Display the **Location Scheduling** query in Design View.

14. Sort the query in **Descending** order by **Guests**, and type **10** as the number of records to be returned.

If Access changes the 10 to 100, delete the extra zero (0).

15. Run the query. Then, save and close it.

Add and Format Calculated Fields to a Query

Now you will add a calculated field that subtracts the venue contact's commission from the total revenue to result in a net revenue amount.

16. Display the **Event Revenue** query in Design View.

17. Add a calculated field named **NetRev** that subtracts Comm from TotalRev; format the new field as **Currency**, and give it the Caption **Net Revenue**.

18. Add criteria to return only records with a **Total Revenue** greater than **5000**.

Do not include a comma in the 5000 as you will get an error message.

19. Run the query.

20. Switch to **Design View**.

21. Delete the > **5000** criteria.

22. Save and close the query.

Create Special Queries

Now you will create a crosstab query that displays the full revenue generated from each venue broken down by month.

23. Open the **Query Wizard** and choose **Crosstab Query Wizard**.

24. Click the **Queries** option to list the queries, and select the **Event Revenue** query.

25. Choose **VenueID** for the Row Headings.

26. Choose **EventDate** for the Column Heading, and choose the **Month** interval.

27. Choose the **TotalRev** field and the **Sum** function.

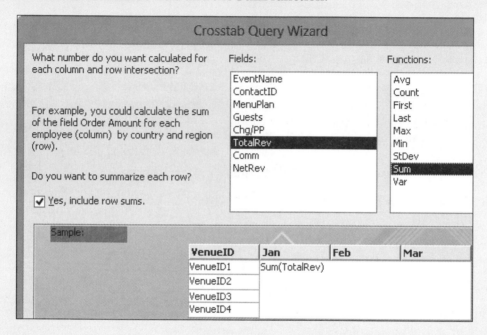

28. Name the query `Venue Revenue by Month` and open it to view the results. Save the query.

View Query SQL

29. Right-click the query name tab and choose **SQL View**.

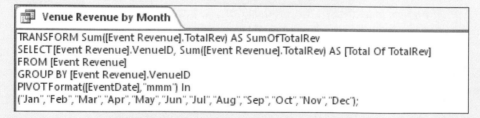

30. Examine the SQL, then close the query and exit **Access**.

31. Submit your final file based on the guidelines provided by your instructor.

Extend Your Skills

In the course of working through the Extend Your Skills exercises, you will think critically as you use the skills taught in the lesson to complete the assigned projects. To evaluate your mastery and completion of the exercises, your instructor may use a rubric, with which more points are allotted according to performance characteristics. (The more you do, the more you earn!) Ask your instructor how your work will be evaluated.

AC04-E01 That's the Way I See It

In this exercise, you will create several queries for either your own business or for Blue Jean Landscaping. Open **AC04-E01-BJL** from your **AC2013 Lesson 04** folder, and save the file as **AC04-E01-BJL-[FirstInitialLastName]**.

Using the skills you learned in this lesson, create queries to help your company better assess its needs in the areas of sales, recruitment, inventory, personnel, and any other aspects that you would find beneficial to managing a business. Use wildcards and other criteria—such as date ranges—to select records containing specified field values; sort query datasheet results; add at least one calculated field, format it, and give it a caption.

You will be evaluated based on the inclusion of all elements, your ability to follow directions, your ability to apply newly learned skills to a real-world situation, your creativity, and your accuracy in creating objects and/or entering data. Submit your final file based on the guidelines provided by your instructor.

AC04-E02 Be Your Own Boss

Blue Jean Landscaping wants to devise more targeted data retrieval. In this exercise, you will create several queries. Open **AC04-E02-BJL** from the **AC2013 Lesson 04** folder and save the file as **AC04-E02-BJL-[FirstInitialLastName]**. Create a query that will return a contact list for BJL's customers and sort it by last name. Create a mailing list sorted by ZIP code. Use wildcards to select records by area code. Add a calculated field to the Sales Invoices query that multiplies Cost by Qty Sold to produce a line total. Format the new field and assign it a caption; then limit the number of records returned to the largest five invoice totals, so those customers can be targeted for preferred customer offers.

You will be evaluated based on the inclusion of all elements, your ability to follow directions, your ability to apply newly learned skills to a real-world situation, your creativity, and your accuracy in creating objects and/or entering data. Submit your final file based on the guidelines provided by your instructor.

Transfer Your Skills

In the course of working through the Transfer Your Skills exercises, you will use critical-thinking and creativity skills to complete the assigned projects using skills taught in the lesson. To evaluate your mastery and completion of the exercises, your instructor may use a rubric, with which more points are allotted according to performance characteristics. (The more you do, the more you earn!) Ask your instructor how your work will be evaluated.

AC04-T01 Use the Web as a Learning Tool

Throughout this book, you will be provided with an opportunity to use the Internet as a learning tool by completing WebQuests. According to the original creators of WebQuests, as described on their website (WebQuest.org), a WebQuest is "an inquiry-oriented activity in which most or all of the information used by learners is drawn from the web." To complete the WebQuest projects in this book, navigate to the student resource center and choose the WebQuest for the lesson on which you are currently working. The subject of each WebQuest will be relevant to the material found in the lesson.

WebQuest Subject: Research the most effective ways to use queries for your business.

Submit your final file(s) based on the guidelines provided by your instructor.

AC04-T02 Demonstrate Proficiency

Business is booming for Stormy BBQ! They have opened a number of restaurants in Georgia and Florida, including their new flagship location in Key West. They would like to focus on what menu items sell best and use only the best vendors. They have hired you as lead tech to create a pilot program for the Key West store to track item receipts. The database includes a form written by a former employee, but no record source exists. Open **AC04-T02-StormyBBQ** from your **AC2013 Lesson 04** folder and save it as **AC04-T02-StormyBBQ-[FirstInitialLastName]**. Display the Daily Receipts form in Design View to see what fields are required for it. Use the DailyReceipts and MenuItems tables to create a query that will be the record source for the Daily Receipts form.

Examine the existing form in Design View to determine what fields you need in the query. Within the query, create a formatted, calculated field to generate gross profit. Name the new query **Daily Receipts Query**. (The form looks for Daily Receipts Query.) Stormy also wants a contact list for employees at each store that includes telephone numbers and email addresses, sorted by area code, and a mailing list for employees, as well, sorted by ZIP code. Use the skills you learned in this lesson to add the queries necessary to meet Stormy BBQ's needs.

Submit your final file based on the guidelines provided by your instructor.

ACCESS 2013

Using Reports to Display Information

LESSON OUTLINE

Designing Reports

Creating Reports Based on Multiple Tables

Modifying a Report

Exploring Other Report Tools

Printing Reports

Concepts Review

Reinforce Your Skills

Apply Your Skills

Extend Your Skills

Transfer Your Skills

LEARNING OBJECTIVES

After studying this lesson, you will be able to:

■ Design a report

■ Create a report

■ Modify a report

■ Use report tools

■ Print reports

Reports organize and summarize data into meaningful information for display. Although reports can summarize data from a single database table, they often present specific data from multiple tables or from queries based on multiple tables. Both forms and reports use many of the same tools and techniques to change layout and better organize and present information in a readable format. You may decide that you want to reposition fields, modify fonts, or add a title and images. You may also decide that you want to add calculated controls to generate subtotals and grand totals. In this lesson, you will create a report and modify the design and layout of a report. You will also format and align controls, create calculated and total controls, and print a report.

Turning Data into Information with Reports

Forms are great for entering data and displaying single records. Most businesses, however, want to filter and summarize data, as well as display specific data, such as running totals, in a readable format. Winchester Web Design needs a new report to summarize the sales for each employee and display sales totals. As their database manager, you have agreed to create a report to meet these needs. The draft of the report design is shown here.

Winchester Website Design
Invoice Details Report

Inv #	Emp ID	Inv Date	First Name	Last Name	Description	Price	Qty	Total
1	JFW	3/15/2012	William	Smith				
					Home Page, Nav, CSS, Design	$400.00	1	$400.00
					Secondary Page	$200.00	6	$1,200.00
					Image, Custom Designed	$40.00	11	$440.00
					Invoice Total			$2,040.00
2	MJW	4/2/2012	Emily	Santos				
					Home Page, Nav, CSS, Design	$400.00	1	$400.00
					Secondary Page	$200.00	7	$1,400.00
					Image, Custom Designed	$40.00	14	$560.00
					Hourly Rate for Modifications	$80.00	5	$400.00
					Invoice Total			$2,760.00
41	JMM	12/7/2013	Jo	Mansur				
					Secondary Page	$200.00	2	$400.00
					Shopping Cart, Basic	$400.00	1	$400.00
					Image, Custom Designed	$40.00	6	$240.00
					Invoice Total			$1,040.00
					Grand Total			$61,380.00

Sunday, December 30, 2012

Page 1 of 1

Designing Reports

Video Library   http://labyrinthelab.com/videos   Video Number: AC13-V0501

Access provides several ways for you to create a report. You can create a simple report based on a single record source. Or, you can create a new report using the Report Wizard, which permits you to select specific fields from multiple sources, set up grouping, add sort orders and totals, and choose a basic layout. Access also allows you to create a blank report from scratch in either Design View or Layout View, adding all the fields and controls yourself.

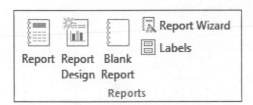

Report Essentials

Because reports are often presented in a readable format and end up as a printout, there are some basics that every report should include. Of course it should be well organized, look professional, and be visually appealing. Imagine finding a report on your desk without a date, without page numbers, or without a title that states what it is for. How might this affect the usability and readability of the data?

Most reports should have both a title and a subtitle. The title may simply be the company name. The subtitle should state specifically what the report is for, such as *Monthly Income* or *Product List*. Every report page requires a date and should include the page number; even if the report is only one page.

Once you have a good handle on the who, what, and when, you will be ready to create your first report.

Create a Quick Report

In this exercise, you will create a simple report.

1. Open **AC05-D01-WinWebDesign** from your **AC2013 Lesson 05** folder and save it as **AC05-D01-WinWebDesign-[FirstInitialLastName]**.

   Replace the bracketed text with your first initial and last name. For example, if your name is Bethany Smith, your filename would look like this: AC05-D01-WinWebDesign-BSmith.

2. Click the **Products** table in the Navigation Pane.

Access 2013

3. Choose **Create→Reports→Report** 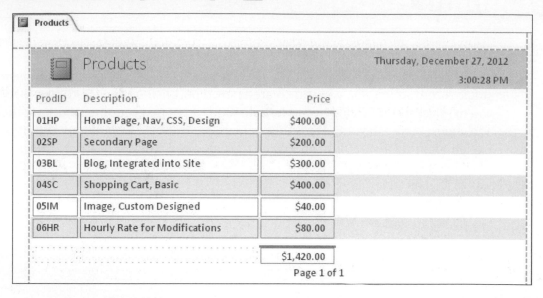.

Products		
Products		Thursday, December 27, 2012
		3:00:28 PM
ProdID	Description	Price
01HP	Home Page, Nav, CSS, Design	$400.00
02SP	Secondary Page	$200.00
03BL	Blog, Integrated into Site	$300.00
04SC	Shopping Cart, Basic	$400.00
05IM	Image, Custom Designed	$40.00
06HR	Hourly Rate for Modifications	$80.00
		$1,420.00
		Page 1 of 1

A simple report is displayed in Layout View. It may need additional formatting, but the basic layout is ready in just a few seconds.

4. Leave the **Products** report open.

Unless directed otherwise, keep Access and any databases or database objects being used open at the end of each exercise.

Identifying Report Design Tools

Video Library http://labyrinthelab.com/videos   Video Number: AC13-V0502

If you have created and customized forms you will find that many of the same tools are available in Report Design View and Report Layout View.

Displaying Report Views

There are three views available for designing, creating, and editing reports: Report View, Layout View, and Design View. Working with these views is similar to working with views in Form design. Each view has its own distinct purpose.

REPORT VIEWS		
View	**Description**	**Procedure**
Report View	Previews a report as it will print out. Displays when you open a report. Does not permit control modification or formatting.	Open a report or choose Home→Views→View→Report View.
Layout View	Previews a report layout with actual data displayed so you can format, resize, and position controls appropriately.	Right-click a report name in the Navigation Pane and choose Layout View.
Design View	Displays the design palette containing controls, labels, and other report design elements that you can add to a report.	Right-click a report name in the Navigation Pane and choose Design View.

Display Report Views

In this exercise, you will display a report in different views and examine the tools available and layout differences between the views.

1. If necessary, choose **Home→Views→View ▼ menu** and choose **Layout View** to display the **Products** report in Layout View.

2. Choose the **Design** tab.

3. Follow these steps to examine the tools and commands available in Layout View:

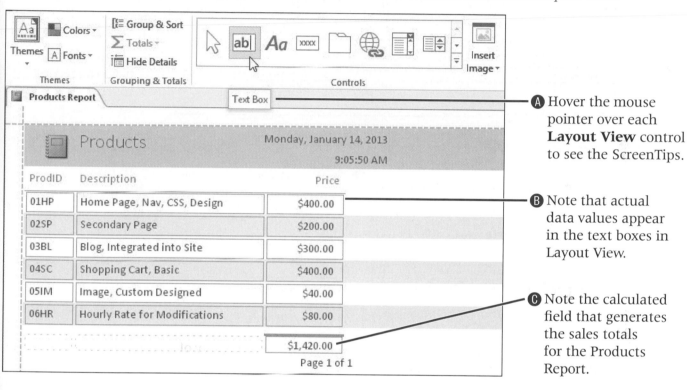

Ⓐ Hover the mouse pointer over each **Layout View** control to see the ScreenTips.

Ⓑ Note that actual data values appear in the text boxes in Layout View.

Ⓒ Note the calculated field that generates the sales totals for the Products Report.

4. Choose **Home→Views→View ▼ menu** and choose **Design View**.

5. Follow these steps to examine the report in Design View:

Ⓐ Section bars identify report sections.

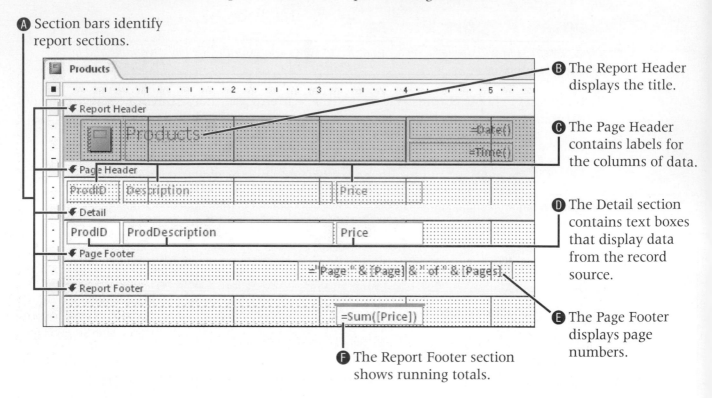

Ⓑ The Report Header displays the title.

Ⓒ The Page Header contains labels for the columns of data.

Ⓓ The Detail section contains text boxes that display data from the record source.

Ⓔ The Page Footer displays page numbers.

Ⓕ The Report Footer section shows running totals.

6. Choose **Design→Controls→Controls**.

The available controls are displayed.

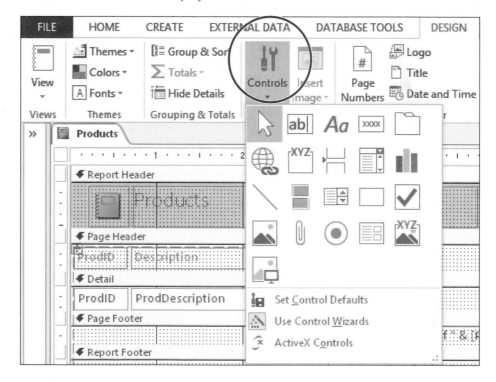

The Access report design tools.

7. Tap ⌜Esc⌝ to close the **Controls** menu.

8. Follow these steps to examine the properties of an unbound label control:

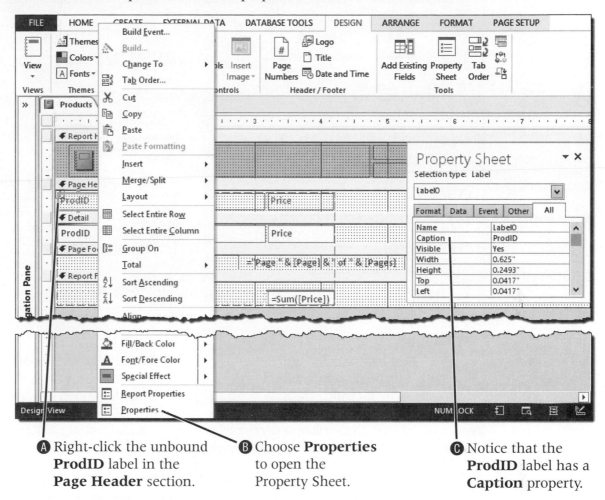

Ⓐ Right-click the unbound **ProdID** label in the **Page Header** section.

Ⓑ Choose **Properties** to open the Property Sheet.

Ⓒ Notice that the **ProdID** label has a **Caption** property.

Due to differences in screen settings, your property values may vary from those shown here.

Labels have a caption, or text, used to identify objects. Labels are unbound controls and do not have a Control Source property.

Access 2013

9. Follow these steps to examine the properties of a bound control:

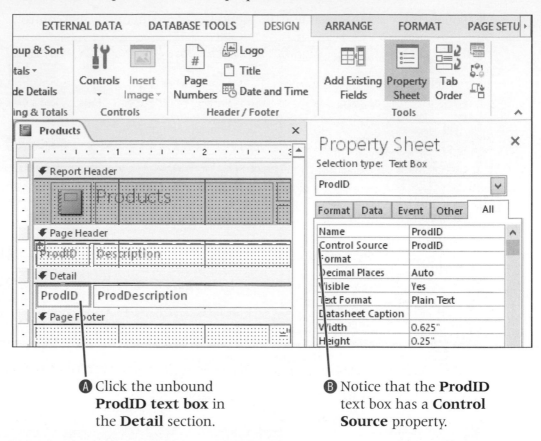

Ⓐ Click the unbound **ProdID text box** in the **Detail** section.

Ⓑ Notice that the **ProdID** text box has a **Control Source** property.

The ProdID text box does not have a Caption property. It is a bound control and has a Control Source property that binds or links it to the record source to display data from the ProdID field.

10. Switch to **Report View** to see how the report would look if it were printed.

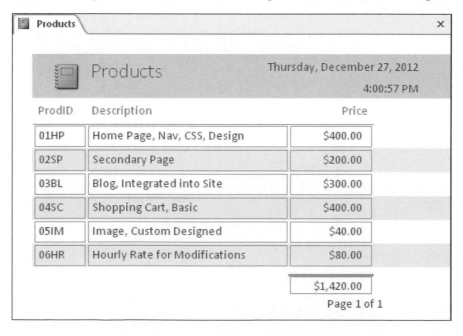

11. Save the report as **Products Report** and close it.

Creating Reports Based on Multiple Tables

Video Library   http://labyrinthelab.com/videos   Video Number: AC13-V0503

You can easily create a quick report based on a single table, but there are often times when you need to view data gathered from multiple tables. The Report Wizard allows you to do this.

Creating a Report Using the Report Wizard

You can create a report using the Report Wizard that uses one or more tables as the record source, or you can use a query based on multiple tables as the record source. You can create calculations in queries, whereas you cannot in tables. Therefore, it is usually easier to create the report from an existing query that already includes all the required tables, desired fields, and necessary calculations.

DEVELOP YOUR SKILLS AC05-D03
Create a Report Using the Report Wizard

In this exercise, you will create a detailed Invoice report using the Report Wizard.

1. Click the **Invoice Details Query Q1 2013** in the Navigation Pane to select it.

2. Choose **Create→Reports→Report Wizard**.

3. Double-click the **EmpID** field in the Available Fields box to move it to the Selected Fields box.

4. Double-click **InvNum**, **InvDate**, **CustLastName**, **ProdID**, **Price**, **Qty**, and **LineTotal**, in the order shown.

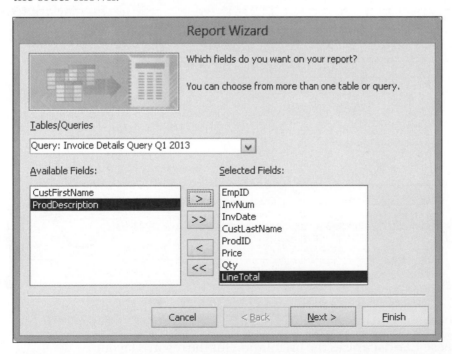

Do not select CustFirstName and ProdDescription. If you add every field to the report there will not be enough room to display all of the information. Be sure that EmpID is the first field in the row.

5. Click **Next**.

   The next wizard screen asks about grouping levels.

6. With **EmpID** selected, click **Move** $\boxed{>}$ to set EmpID as the primary grouping level.

7. With **InvNum** selected, click **Move** $\boxed{>}$ to set the secondary grouping level.

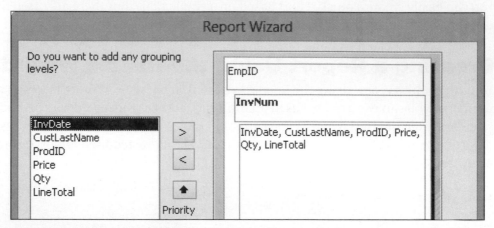

The grouping order should be set with EmpID at the first level and InvNum at the secondary level.

8. Click **Next**.

9. Follow these steps to set the Summary Options:

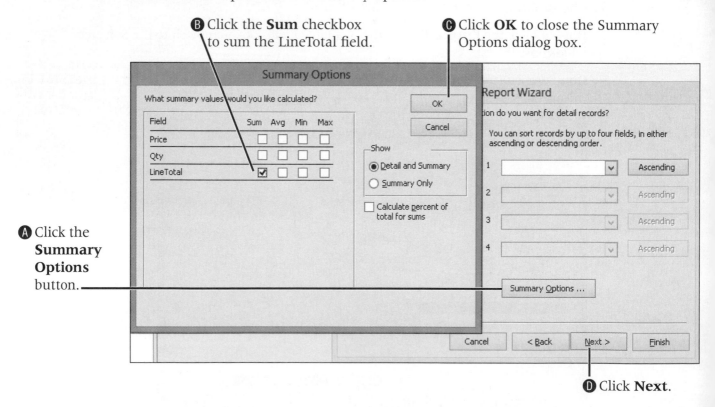

10. Choose the **Outline** layout.

11. Choose **Landscape** as the orientation for the report's layout.

12. Confirm that the **Adjust the Field Width So All Fields Fit on a Page** box is checked.

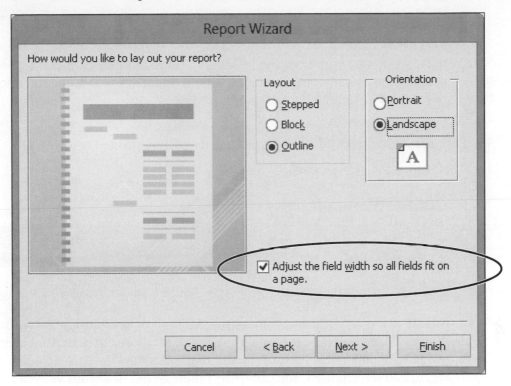

13. Click **Next**. Name the report `Invoice Details Report Q1 2013`.

14. Click **Finish**.

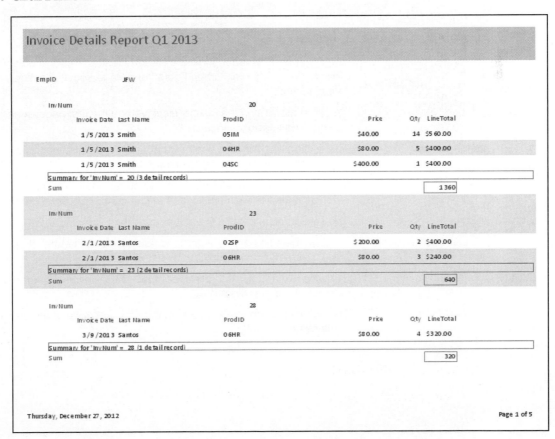

Your report displays in Print Preview, showing invoice totals and summary totals for each employee. The report needs formatting and layout work, which must be done in Design View. However, almost all of the controls and calculations are now in place.

Your report layout may vary from the figure. The page number control may be much wider than necessary and positioned so far to the right that it spills to a second page. You will learn how to resolve these issues throughout this lesson.

15. Page through the report to see how it will look when printed.

16. Click **Close Print Preview**.

Modifying a Report

Video Library   http://labyrinthelab.com/videos   Video Number: AC13-V0504

You can create a new report from scratch using Ribbon tools, but many professionals prefer to use the Report Wizard because it is much easier and far more efficient. However, when you finish using the Report Wizard you often find that fields may have to be added, deleted, resized, repositioned, and reformatted. You can correct these issues in Layout View or in Design View, if necessary. Design View has the same controls, functionality, and section layout that you have when you create a blank report.

REPORT SECTIONS	
Section	**Description**
Sections	The major parts of the report—the Report Header, Report Footer, Detail, Page Header, Group Header, Group Footer, and Page Footer. Section bars divide report sections.
Report Header	Contains information that is only displayed on the first page, such as the title, subtitle, and possibly a logo.
Page Header	The section that contains controls that are repeated at the top of every printed page—mainly labels displaying column headings.
Group Header	Identifies a field (such as EmpID) by which report data is grouped, so a summary (such as a total of each employee's sales) can be displayed for the grouped field.
Detail	The section that contains the actual table data in the report.
Group Footer	Displays the summary for a grouped field, such as the total of each employee's sales, grouped by the EmpID.
Page Footer	Contains text and fields that are repeated at the bottom of every printed page, such as page number and date.
Report Footer	The bottom section that appears on the very last page of a report. It typically contains grand totals.

Working with Report Controls

If you create or modify a report in Design View, you can select the table that contains any new fields you want to add to the report and drag those fields to the appropriate sections. You can also add controls to create titles or subtitles, add graphics, and insert footer controls.

Access has three basic types of controls that you can add to reports.

- **Bound controls:** Controls that tie, or bind, the field value (data) displayed on a report to a field in a database table. Bound controls normally appear in the Detail section of a report.

- **Unbound controls:** Lines and other drawn objects, text for titles, graphics, etc., that can enhance a report's appearance or present additional text.

- **Calculated controls:** Controls that are tied to an expression, aggregate function, or calculated field constructed in a query or built directly on the report. These controls normally appear in the Detail or report Footer section.

REPORT CONTROLS

Control	Description
Controls	Items that display data, text, checkboxes, lines, and images.
Bound control	A control that ties data to be displayed to a field in a table. Bound controls normally appear in the Detail section (e.g., ProductID or ProdPrice).
Unbound control	An item that is independent of data and fields in a database table, such as text, lines, and images. Unbound controls may appear in any report section.
Calculated control	A control tied to a calculated field or an expression constructed in a query or in the report itself. Calculated controls normally appear in the Detail or Report Footer.
Control label	The part of a control that contains text that identifies the data in the associated text box. (e.g., Last Name).
Control text box	A control that displays the field value from an associated table (e.g., a textbox named LastName containing the value Smith).

Adding and Deleting Controls

Video Library   http://labyrinthelab.com/videos   Video Number: AC13-V0505

When you create a report with the Report Wizard you may want to add a company logo to the report header; or you may want to delete a field, such as the Summary for InvNum control that was added to the Invoice Details Report Q1 2013 that you just created. Fortunately, these controls can be added or deleted using the same techniques that you use in Form Design.

Adding Controls from the Ribbon

When you display a report in Design View, you can use the tools on the Ribbon to add bound and unbound controls to reports. A limited number of design tools are also available in Layout View, but it is often necessary to work in Design View to set and modify properties for controls.

QUICK REFERENCE	ADDING CONTROLS TO A REPORT
Task	**Procedure**
Drag bound controls	■ Display the report in Layout or Design View.
	■ Choose Design→Tools→Add Existing Fields 🔳.
	■ Expand the table containing the field you want to add.
	■ Drag the field into position on the report.
Add unbound controls from a Ribbon	■ Display the report in Design View.
	■ Choose Design→Controls and click the desired control.
	■ Click or drag a control into the position and size you want.

Adding Controls from Field Lists

The Field List contains a list of all the tables that appear in the database. You can expand each table in the list to display all the fields the table contains.

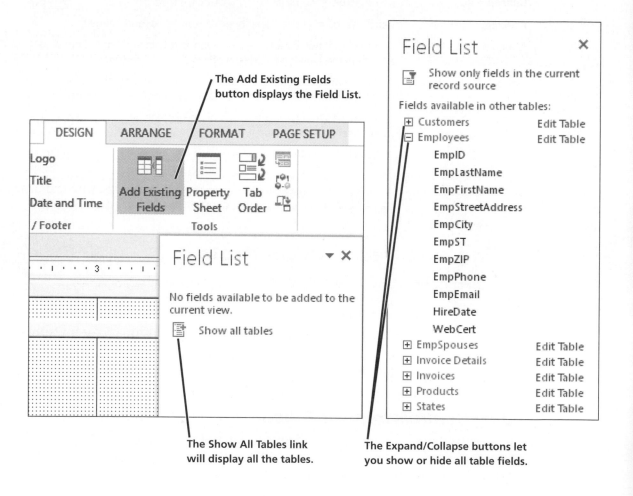

The Add Existing Fields button displays the Field List.

The Show All Tables link will display all the tables.

The Expand/Collapse buttons let you show or hide all table fields.

Dragging Controls from the Field List

To add bound controls from the available field list, click and drag the field name onto the appropriate report section. When you add a bound control from the Field List to the Detail section of the report page, Access places both the text box and label for the bound control on the report. Because most reports display the control label in the Page Header section, you will have to cut the label from the Detail section and paste it into the Page Header section.

Add, Delete, and Edit Controls on a Report

In this exercise, you will delete unneeded controls, add controls, and rearrange and resize controls to produce a more attractive, well-balanced report.

Delete a Report Control

1. Display the **Invoice Details Report Q1 2013** in Layout View.

2. Follow these steps to delete and rearrange report controls:

Ⓐ Click the first **Summary for 'InvNum'** control and tap Delete.

Invoice Details Report Q1 2013

Invoice Details Report Q1 2013					
EmpID	JFW				
InvNum		20			
Invoice Date	Last Name	ProdID	Price	Qty	LineTotal
1/5/2013	Smith	05IM	$40.00	14	$560.00
1/5/2013	Smith	06HR	$80.00	5	$400.00
1/5/2013	Smith	04SC	$400.00	1	$400.00

Summary for 'InvNum' = 20 (3 detail records)
Sum   1360

Ⓑ Select the **Sum** label and tap → to move the label so it is lined up under the **Qty** label.

Ⓒ With the **Sum** label still selected, press Shift and click the corresponding **Sum** text box. Tap ↑ three times to move both Sum controls up.

The right side of the page should look similar to this figure. More records appear on the page.

3. Scroll down to the end of the first employee's records.

Price	Qty	LineTotal
$40.00	14	$560.00
$80.00	5	$400.00
$400.00	1	$400.00
	Sum	1360

Access 2013

4. Follow the procedure outlined in **step 2** to delete the **Summary for 'EmpID'** control and move the **Sum** label.

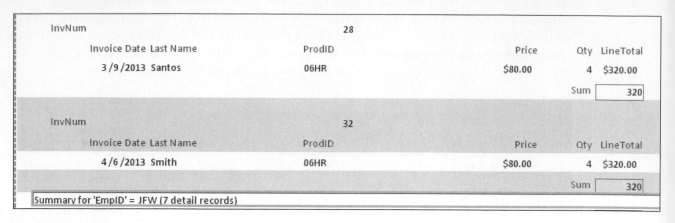

5. Click the **Price** label in the InvNumHeader section. Press ⌈Ctrl⌉ and click the **Price** text box in the Detail section.

6. If the Property Sheet is not shown, choose **Design→Tools→Property Sheet**.

7. Follow these steps to resize and align controls:

Ⓐ Set the Width property for both controls to **.8"**.

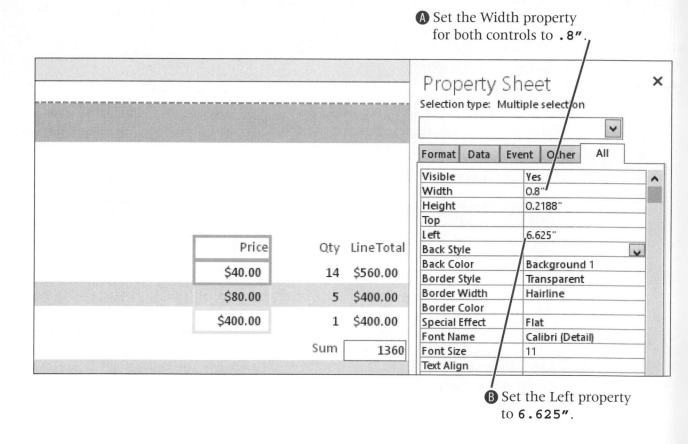

Ⓑ Set the Left property to **6.625"**.

Add a Report Control

8. Switch to **Design View**.

9. Click the **="Page"** control in the Page Footer section to select it.

10. Type **2″** for **Width** property.

11. Click in the **Selection Type** drop-down list box at the top of the Property Sheet and choose **Report**.

12. Type **9″** for the **Width** property.

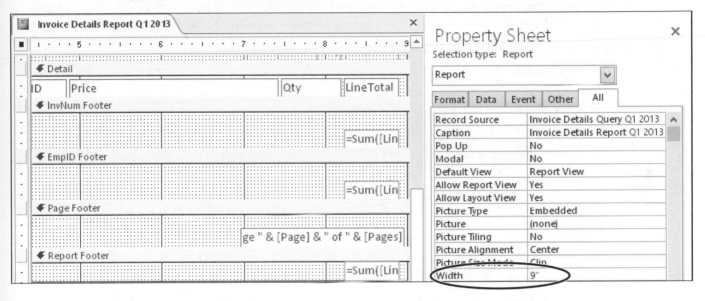

13. Choose **Design→Tools→Add Existing Fields** [icon] to open the Field List and click **Show All Tables**.

14. Double-click the **Products** table name in the Field List to show the table fields.

15. Follow these steps to add the ProdDescription controls to the report:

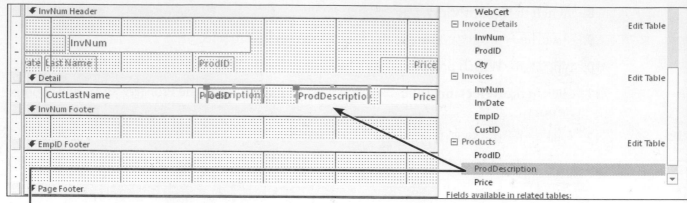

Ⓐ Drag **ProdDescription** from the
Field List into the Detail section
between **ProdID** and **Price**.

Ⓑ Right-click the Description
label and choose **Cut**.

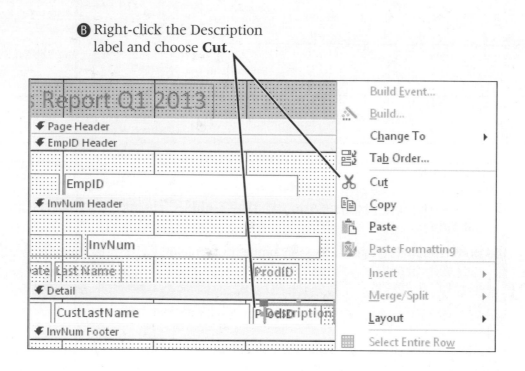

Ⓒ Right-click the InvNum Header
section bar and choose **Paste**.

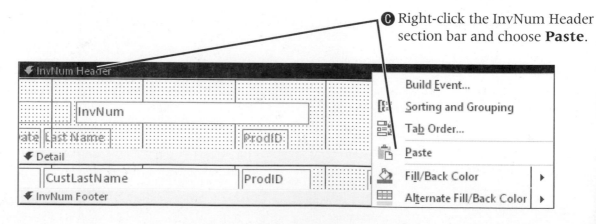

16. Drag the **Description** label in the Header section so that it is lined up above the ProdDescription text box in the Detail section.

17. Close the **Field List**.

18. Switch to **Layout View**.

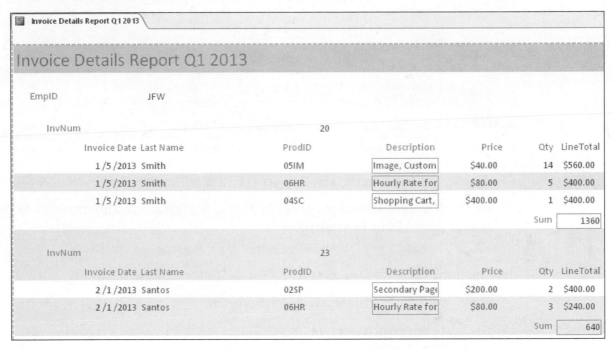

At this point, your report begs for alignment and resizing. However, you still have controls to add, so you will wait until all items are on the report before making alignment and size adjustments.

Adding a Logo to the Report

Video Library   http://labyrinthelab.com/videos   Video Number: AC13-V0506

Adding a visual element or image is especially useful when creating forms and reports. A graphic that identifies the business, such as a corporate logo, can make forms and reports look more professional and visually appealing. Access provides two basic tools for adding graphics to a report or a form:

- **Image or Insert Image control:** Enables you to add and position a graphic on any report section
- **Logo control:** Places a logo in the Report Header section of a report

An inserted image is saved in the Image Gallery, which will make it easy to find it again later. Simply click Insert Image and the Image Gallery is displayed.

When you add a logo using the Logo control from the Ribbon, Access automatically adds a Title control. You can then type in your new report title. If you want to move the logo and title to separate locations, choose Arrange→Table→Remove Layout to detach and unlink the controls.

DEVELOP YOUR SKILLS AC05-D05
Add a Logo to the Page Header

In this exercise you will add a logo to your report's page header.

1. Display the **Invoice Details Report Q1 2013** in Design View.
2. Choose **Design→Header/Footer→ 🖼 Logo** . Navigate to and double-click **WWD-Logo. bmp** in the **AC2013 Lesson 05** folder.

   Access places the logo in the upper-left corner of the Report Header section.

3. Open the Property Sheet and type **4** for the **Left** property.
4. Type **.8** for the **Width** and **Height** properties.
5. Click the **Report Header** bar.

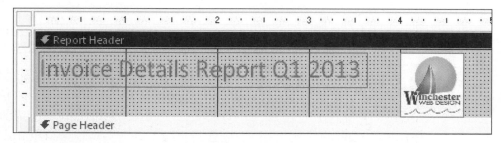

The new logo added to the report header.

6. Save the report.

Adding a Title or Subtitle to a Report

Video Library	http://labyrinthelab.com/videos	Video Number: AC13-V0507

Titles identify the purpose of forms and reports and often contain only the name of the company. However, a more effective report also includes a subtitle that explains what the report is about, such as Invoice Summary or Customer Addresses. You can use Design View or Layout View to add a Label control containing the title or subtitle. If you create a report from scratch, you can use the Title tool to add a formatted title to the appropriate section of a form or report. You can then change the text and formatting using tools on the Ribbon and Property Sheet.

Using the Property Sheet

The Property Sheet contains property settings that control the way database objects look and function, such as font family, font size, font color, border style, and so on. You have probably used the Property Sheet to format data in tables and forms. Many of these same properties are available for controlling data display in reports.

Add a Report Title/Subtitle and Format Text

In this exercise, you will use Layout View to add a report title and subtitle. Then, you will format text using the Property Sheet and the Ribbon.

1. Display the **Invoice Details Report Q1 2013** in Design View.

2. If necessary, choose **Design→Tools→Property Sheet** 📋 to open the Property Sheet.

3. Select the **title** control (Invoice Details Report Q1 2013) in the Report Header and type **Winchester Web Design** as the *Caption* in the Property Sheet.

4. Click the **Report Header** section bar and type **.9** as the Height property to expand the section for a subtitle and logo.

5. Choose **Design→Controls→Label** 🄰. Click and drag to draw a new label for the subtitle (under the report title).

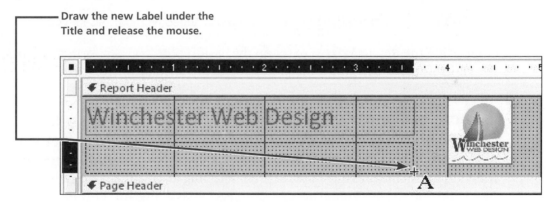

6. Type **Invoices for Q1 2013** as the subtitle; tap `Enter`.

7. Set the following properties for the new subtitle:

PROPERTY	SETTING
Width	3.5
Height	.35
Special Effect	Shadowed
Font Size	18
Text Align	Center
Font Weight	Bold

8. Select the **Winchester Web Design** title.

9. Set the following properties for the title:

PROPERTY	SETTING
Width	3.5
Font Size	22
Text Align	Center
Font Weight	Bold

10. Select the logo and type **.8** for both the **Width** and **Height** properties.

11. Save your changes.

Formatting Controls

Video Library   http://labyrinthelab.com/videos   Video Number: AC13-V0508

After using the Report Wizard to set up the basic report, you can format, align, size, and position the controls using the same procedures you use to format controls on forms.

Selecting Controls

Just as with forms, each report control contains two parts: the control label and the control text box. To select multiple controls at the same time, you have several options: Clicking each control individually, while pressing Shift or Ctrl; selecting all controls along a horizontal or vertical line by clicking on the horizontal or vertical rulers; or lassoing—or outlining—an area of the report to select all controls within the area.

Sizing Controls

It is important to ensure that the data values are fully displayed in a report, while at the same time taking care not to leave unsightly and unnecessary blank space between columns. To accomplish this, you must resize controls on the report. It is best to size controls in Layout View because you can see the actual field values for multiple records.

In Layout View, active—or selected—controls display a thicker border than inactive controls. Use these borders to size the control. As you drag the border to resize the active record, the controls for that field in all other records also resize.

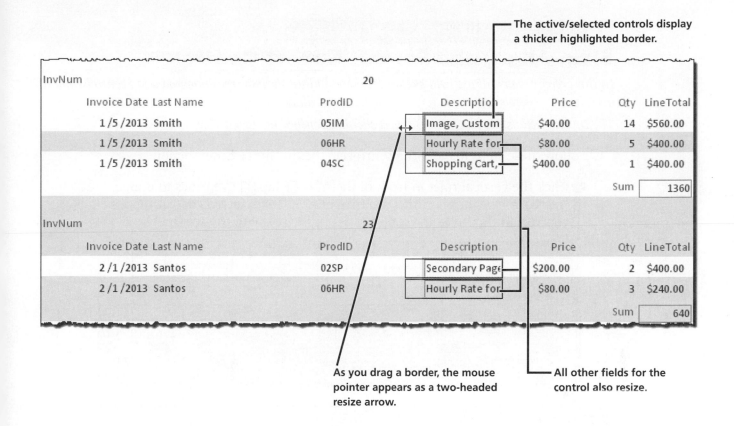

The active/selected controls display a thicker highlighted border.

As you drag a border, the mouse pointer appears as a two-headed resize arrow.

All other fields for the control also resize.

Identifying Mouse Shapes

The mouse pointer shape is important when working in Design View and Layout View.

REPORT MOUSE POINTERS	
Field Property	**Description**
‡	Section resize pointer
↔	Resize a control
⬚	Select control to drag to desired location
⬚	Select and move a control
⬇	Select a column
➡	Select a row

Size, Align, and Format Report Controls

In this exercise, you will use both Design View and Layout View to reposition and align controls. You will also size the controls to better accommodate the data values.

The Invoice Details Report Q1 2013 report should be opened in Design View.

1. Follow these steps to move the controls in the InvNum Header section:

Ⓐ Click the vertical ruler in front of the **InvNum** label to select the two InvNum controls in the InvNum Header.

Ⓑ Tap ↑ five times to nudge the selected controls up close to the section bar.

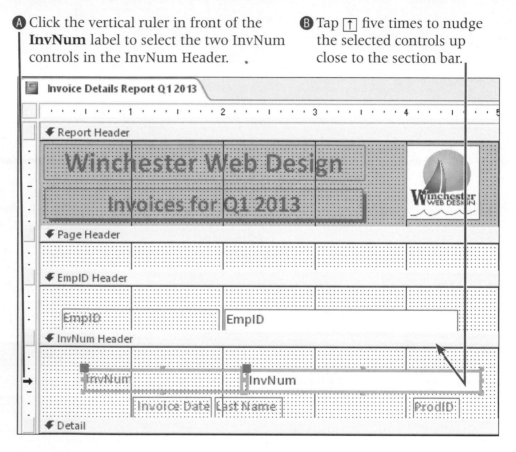

Ⓒ Click the vertical ruler in front of the **Invoice Date** label to select the lower row of controls in the InvNum Header. Tap ↑ five times to nudge the selected controls up.

Ⓓ Hover the mouse pointer over the top of the **Detail** section bar until it becomes a Section Resize Pointer and drag the bar up to just under the lower row of controls.

2. If the Property Sheet is not open, choose **Design→Tools→Property Sheet**.

3. Follow these steps to move controls in a report section:

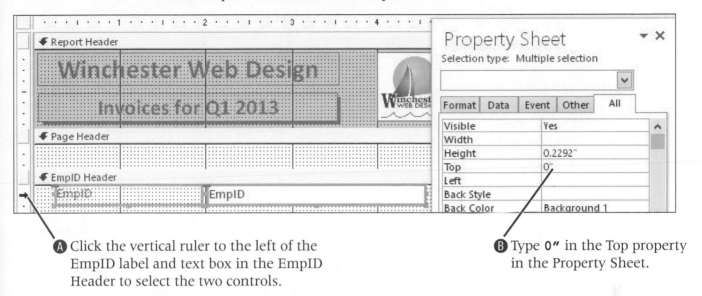

Ⓐ Click the vertical ruler to the left of the EmpID label and text box in the EmpID Header to select the two controls.

Ⓑ Type **0″** in the Top property in the Property Sheet.

4. Follow these steps to resize the EmpID Header section:

Ⓐ Click the **EmpID Header** section bar to select the section (*GroupHeader0*).

Ⓑ Type **.33** in the Height property to shorten the section and tap Enter.

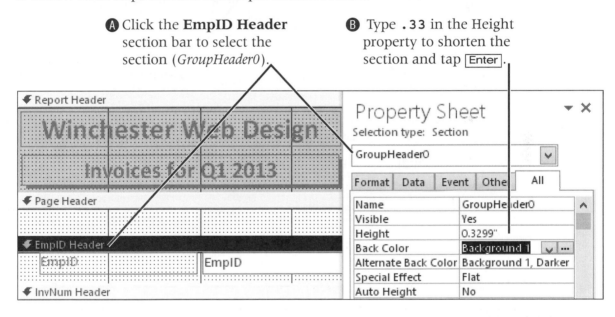

Access sometimes changes a precise property value that you type, so don't worry if your Height property differs slightly from the figure.

5. Switch to **Layout View**.

6. Follow these steps to size the controls:

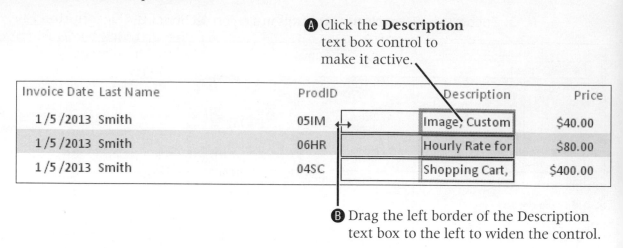

Ⓐ Click the **Description** text box control to make it active.

Ⓑ Drag the left border of the Description text box to the left to widen the control.

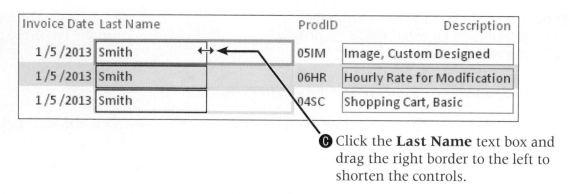

Ⓒ Click the **Last Name** text box and drag the right border to the left to shorten the controls.

Leave the Last Name text boxes wide enough to display longer last names.

7. Select the **Last Name** label, press ⎡Shift⎤ and click a **Last Name** text box.

8. Tap ⎡→⎤ to nudge the selected controls to the right.

Sometimes while moving a group of controls in Layout View, the screen scrolls down to the end. If this occurs, scroll back up and continue moving the controls.

9. Select the **ProdID** labels and text boxes and nudge them to the left.

10. Select the **InvNum** text box and use the resizing arrow to make it narrower.

11. Follow these steps to align the InvNum text box and Description label:

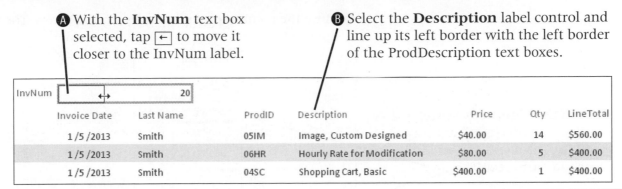

Ⓐ With the **InvNum** text box selected, tap ⬅ to move it closer to the InvNum label.

Ⓑ Select the **Description** label control and line up its left border with the left border of the ProdDescription text boxes.

12. Scroll to the end of the report. Click the **Sum** calculated control for the InvNum group; press Shift, click the **Sum** text box for the EmpID group and click the calculated control text box for the grand total at the end of the report.

13. Choose **Format→Number→** [▾] **→Currency**.

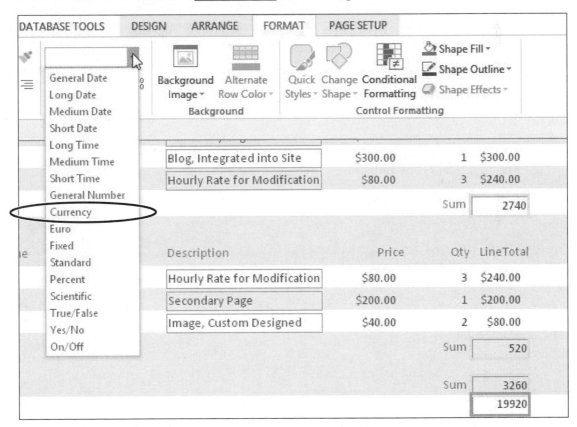

When you apply formatting, the fields may no longer fit in the text box. When a value is too large for the text box, it fills the box with the # symbol.

14. Follow these steps to resize the Currency controls:

B Move the pointer until it becomes a resize arrow. Then, click and drag one of the borders to the right as shown.

A With the **Sum** controls still selected, press Shift and click a **LineTotal** text box and the **grand total** text box.

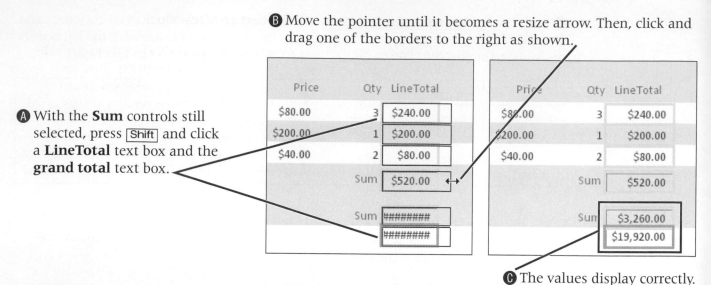

C The values display correctly.

15. Select the calculated controls. Choose **Transparent** for the Border Style property for the selected Sum controls.

16. Select the **Description** text box and set its Border Style property to **Transparent**.

17. Switch to **Print Preview**. Use the navigation buttons to page through the report.

Winchester Web Design

Invoices for Q1 2013

EmpID   JFW

InvNum   20

Invoice Date	Last Name	ProdID	Description	Price	Qty	LineTotal
1/5/2013	Smith	051M	Image, Custom Designed	$40.00	14	$560.00
1/5/2013	Smith	06HR	Hourly Rate for Modification	$80.00	5	$400.00
1/5/2013	Smith	04SC	Shopping Cart, Basic	$400.00	1	$400.00
					Sum	$1,360.00

InvNum   23

Invoice Date	Last Name	ProdID	Description	Price	Qty	LineTotal
2/1/2013	Santos	02SP	Secondary Page	$200.00	2	$400.00
2/1/2013	Santos	06HR	Hourly Rate for Modification	$80.00	3	$240.00
					Sum	$640.00

InvNum   28

Invoice Date	Last Name	ProdID	Description	Price	Qty	LineTotal
3/9/2013	Santos	06HR	Hourly Rate for Modification	$80.00	4	$320.00
					Sum	$320.00

InvNum   32

Invoice Date	Last Name	ProdID	Description	Price	Qty	LineTotal
4/6/2013	Smith	06HR	Hourly Rate for Modification	$80.00	4	$320.00
					Sum	$320.00
					Sum	$2,640.00

Tuesday, April 2, 2013   Page 1 of 4

---

18. Close **Print Preview**. Then, save and close the report.

Applying Themes

Video Library   http://labyrinthelab.com/videos   Video Number: AC13-V0509

Formatting a report using the Themes, or existing style schemes, available in Access can help make a report more readable and attractive. Themes contain design elements such as background color, font family and font size, and other properties to quickly format an entire report without the tedious formatting of each individual control. Because reports are designed for printing, the report Themes are much more subtle than for forms.

Caution should be used when applying Themes. Applying a Theme reformats all objects in the active database with the color scheme defined in the Theme.

QUICK REFERENCE	APPLYING THEMES TO FORMS AND REPORTS
Task	**Procedure**
Apply a Theme	■ Prepare the desired report or form.
	■ Display the report or form in Design View or Layout View.
	■ Choose Design→Themes→Themes Aa.
	■ Select the desired Theme.

DEVELOP YOUR SKILLS AC05-D08
Apply Themes to a Report

In this exercise, you will apply a Theme to the Invoice Details Report Q1 2013 report.

1. Open and display the **Invoice Details Report Q1 2013** report in Design View.

2. Choose **Design→Themes→Themes** Aa and hover over each Theme's thumbnail to see how the report changes.

3. Choose your favorite **Theme** from the palette.

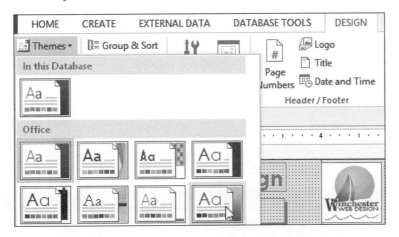

Depending on the Theme you select, you may see little or no difference until you display the report in Layout or Report View. You may also have to readjust control sizes because of font changes.

4. Save changes to the report.

Access 2013

Exploring Other Report Tools

Video Library http://labyrinthelab.com/videos Video Number: AC13-V0510

One important difference between customizing forms and reports is the general layout of the objects. Reports normally display control labels in the Report Header section to serve as column headings. Control text boxes appear in the Detail section. In addition, when you add group summary data in a report, Access displays Group sections that hold group titles, group field control labels, and group summary data.

Adding Report Sorting and Grouping Levels

A group is a collection of records that has at least one data element or key field in common. For example, if you group the data using the Employee ID field, you create a report that shows the total sales for each employee. If you want to display all vendors with offices in the same state, you could group by the State field. Or, you could group by the Vendor field to see all transactions with a particular vendor. A group consists of a Group Header, records, and a Group Footer. Grouping records enables you to separate records visually on a report and display introductory and summary data for each group. Access allows you to include totals by group level.

Most novices and professionals sort through queries and add grouping levels using the Report Wizard, which is far easier and more efficient. However, you can also sort and add grouping levels—with or without totals—in Design View.

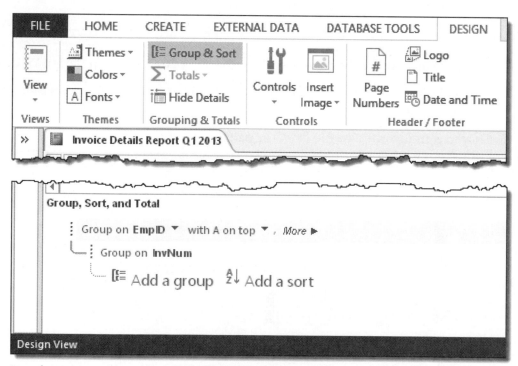

Records are grouped by each employee, then by invoice number.

Using the Group, Sort, and Total Pane

The Group, Sort, and Total pane allows you to add groups and sort settings or review them after you set them. You can also add groups using commands on the shortcut menus and then review them in the Group, Sort, and Total pane. You can set properties in the Group, Sort, and Total pane to display or hide group headers and footers. Additional properties enable you to tell Access how to group data, set a grouping interval, and set group properties for keeping items in a group together on a page.

FROM THE RIBBON

Design→Grouping & Totals→Group & Sort to add group/sort settings

Working with Group Sections

Manually setting a group and sort order on a report in Design View does not automatically place a control in the Group column heading. It simply sets the grouping and sorting order and creates a header section on the report to hold the controls. After manually setting the group, you must move the group field (i.e., the EmpID text box when you group by employees) from the Detail section to the Group Header section (i.e., the EmpID Header which is created when you group by EmpID). By placing the field text box control in the Group Header section, Access attractively arranges all entries by the group field you choose and the Group Header section prints only at the start of a new group value.

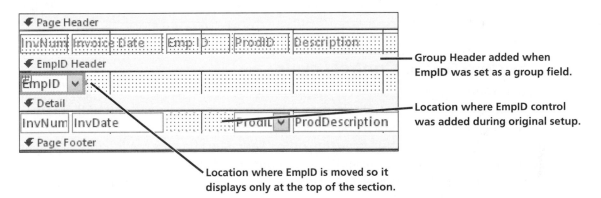

Group Header added when EmpID was set as a group field.

Location where EmpID control was added during original setup.

Location where EmpID is moved so it displays only at the top of the section.

Creating Multi-Level Groupings

Access provides multi-level grouping for records on a report. If, for example, you want to print invoices that group items ordered by invoice for each employee, you would use two-level grouping. You can set multiple groups using the Sort, Group, and Total pane or you can right-click an empty area of the report design grid or a section bar and choose Sorting and Grouping from the shortcut menu.

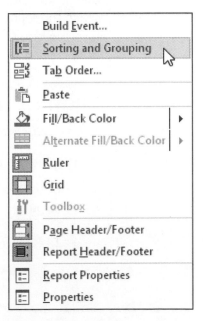

The properties you see when you right-click a field name to group or sort by depends on the data type of the field.

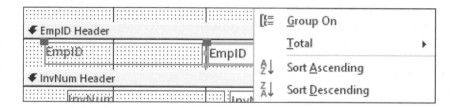

Sorting Group Control Levels

If a group control level, such as EmpID, is not sorted, it will not group properly. For example, assume Anderson was the salesperson for the first two invoices, and Williams was the salesperson for the third invoice, and Anderson was the salesperson for the fourth invoice. As soon as Access sees a different employee (Anderson changes to Williams) it will assume that it has arrived at a new group and will total the records for the preceding group—Anderson's first two sales, but it will not include Anderson's sales for the fourth invoice in the current group.

There are a couple ways to resolve this. The data could be presorted in the table or the query on which the report was based. Alternately, the data could be sorted by adding a Sort Level Control in the report.

Display the Group and Sort Pane

In this exercise, you will display the group and sort pane for the Invoice Details Report Q1 2013 report.

1. Display the **Invoice Details Report Q1 2013** in Design View.

2. Choose **Design→Grouping & Totals→Group & Sort** to open the Group, Sort, and Total pane.

3. Follow these steps to explore the Group, Sort, and Total pane.

Ⓐ Click **Add a Sort** to display the list of fields and a link to the expression builder.

Ⓑ Notice that this report is grouped on InvNum within EmpID.

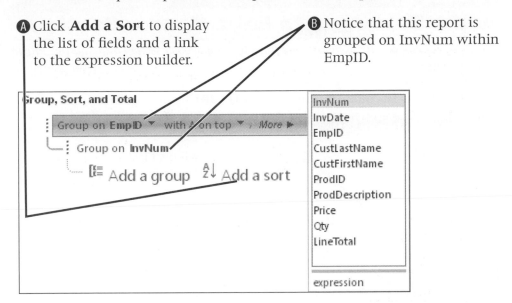

4. Tap [Esc] to exit without saving any changes. Close the **Group, Sort, and Total** pane.

5. Close the **Invoice Details Report Q1 2013** report. *Do not* save the file.

Adding Date and Time Data to a Report

Video Library   http://labyrinthelab.com/videos   Video Number: AC13-V0511

Keeping track of the most current report can be a challenge. Adding a date and/or time to the footer section of a report can help you track reports. When you add the date and time controls to an existing report, Access places the controls in the Report Header section by default. You can either move them or leave them in the Report Header.

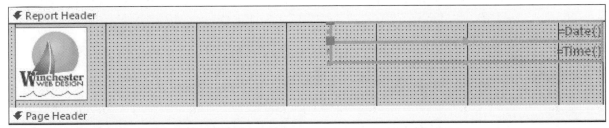

The Date and Time controls in the Report Header section.

QUICK REFERENCE	ADDING DATE AND TIME FIELDS TO A REPORT
Task	**Procedure**
Add a date field	■ Choose Design→Header/Footer→📅 Date and Time.
	■ Check the Include Date checkbox, select the format option, and click OK.
Add a time field	■ Choose Design→Header/Footer→📅 Date and Time.
	■ Check the Include Time checkbox, select the format option and click OK.

Add a Date Field to Page Header Section

In this exercise, you will delete the date from the Page Footer section and add the date to the Page Header section of your report.

1. Display the **Invoice Details Report Q1 2013** in Design View.

2. Follow these steps to delete the date from the Page Footer section:

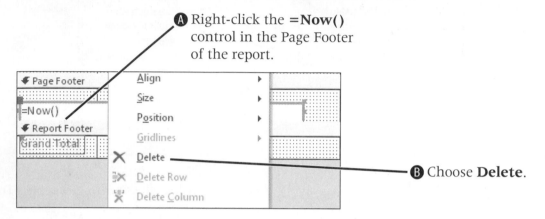

Ⓐ Right-click the **=Now()** control in the Page Footer of the report.

Ⓑ Choose **Delete**.

3. Follow these steps to add date and time controls to the Report Header:

Ⓐ Choose **Design→Header/Footer→Date and Time**.

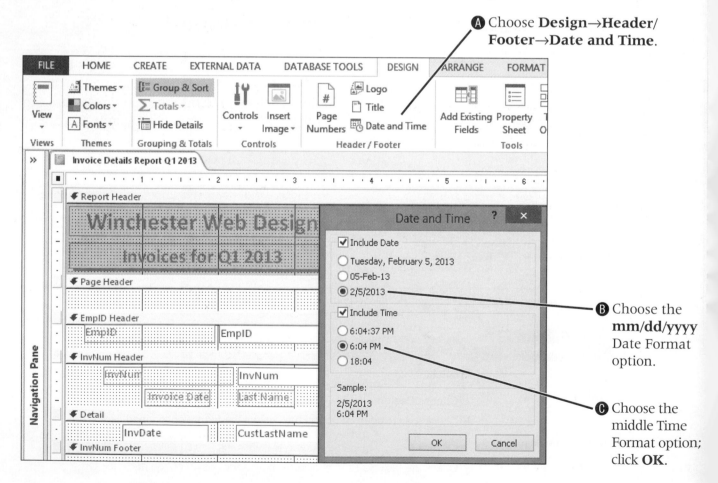

Ⓑ Choose the **mm/dd/yyyy** Date Format option.

Ⓒ Choose the middle Time Format option; click **OK**.

The date and time you see onscreen will vary from the figure.

4. Switch to **Report View** to see the new date and time controls.

5. Save your changes to the report.

Adding Page Breaks to a Report

Video Library   http://labyrinthelab.com/videos   Video Number: AC13-V0512

When you have a report with grouped data, such as EmpID, you may want to start a new page when the EmpID changes so each employee is shown on its own page or set of pages.

DEVELOP YOUR SKILLS AC05-D11

Add Page Break Controls to a Report

In this exercise, you will set page breaks to print each employee's summary records on a separate page or set of pages.

1. Display the **Invoice Details Report Q1 2013** in Design View.

2. Follow these steps to insert a page break after each EmpID group:

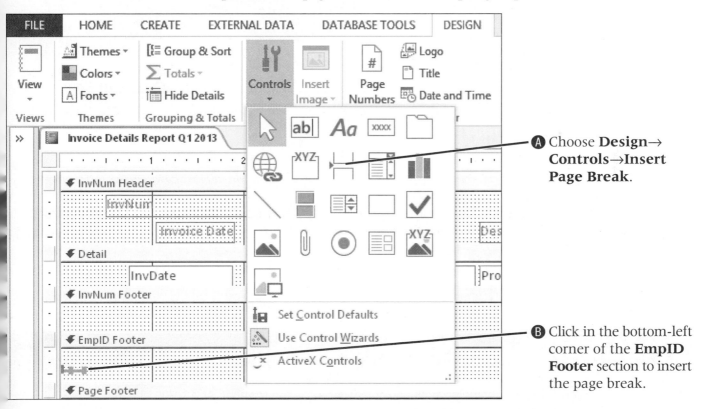

Ⓐ Choose **Design→ Controls→Insert Page Break**.

Ⓑ Click in the bottom-left corner of the **EmpID Footer** section to insert the page break.

Access 2013

3. Switch to **Print Preview**.

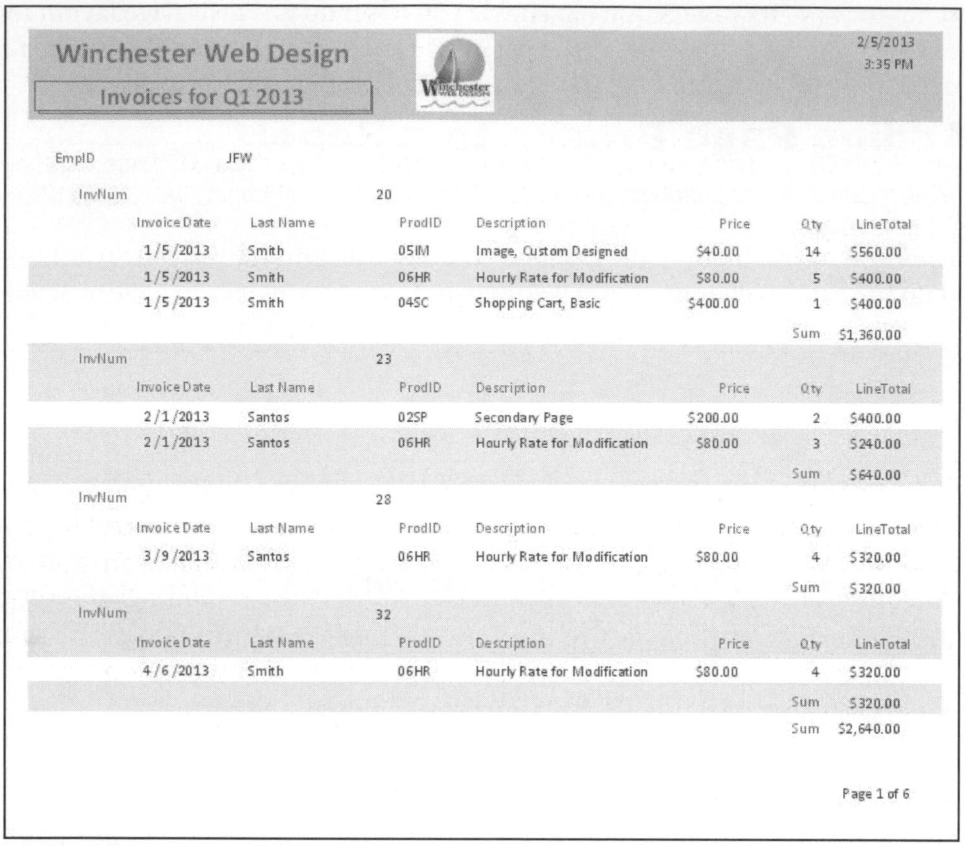

Winchester Web Design

Invoices for Q1 2013

2/5/2013
3:35 PM

EmpID JFW

InvNum	20					
Invoice Date	Last Name	ProdID	Description	Price	Qty	LineTotal
1/5/2013	Smith	05IM	Image, Custom Designed	$40.00	14	$560.00
1/5/2013	Smith	06HR	Hourly Rate for Modification	$80.00	5	$400.00
1/5/2013	Smith	04SC	Shopping Cart, Basic	$400.00	1	$400.00
					Sum	$1,360.00
InvNum	23					
Invoice Date	Last Name	ProdID	Description	Price	Qty	LineTotal
2/1/2013	Santos	02SP	Secondary Page	$200.00	2	$400.00
2/1/2013	Santos	06HR	Hourly Rate for Modification	$80.00	3	$240.00
					Sum	$640.00
InvNum	28					
Invoice Date	Last Name	ProdID	Description	Price	Qty	LineTotal
3/9/2013	Santos	06HR	Hourly Rate for Modification	$80.00	4	$320.00
					Sum	$320.00
InvNum	32					
Invoice Date	Last Name	ProdID	Description	Price	Qty	LineTotal
4/6/2013	Smith	06HR	Hourly Rate for Modification	$80.00	4	$320.00
					Sum	$320.00
					Sum	$2,640.00

Page 1 of 6

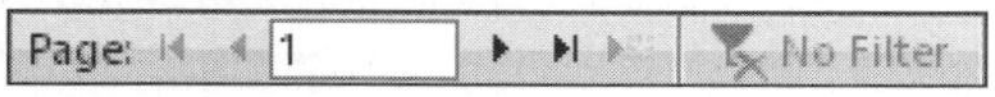

4. Click **Next Page** in the navigation bar to page through the report.
   No two employee's records appear on the same page. The grand total is shown on the last page.

NOTE

If you want a report header to appear on every page, select all the report header controls, and cut and paste them into the page header section.

5. Save the report.

Printing Reports

Video Library http://labyrinthelab.com/videos Video Number: AC13-V0513

After you create and format a report, set grouping and sorting levels, and add summary controls, you are ready to print the report. Procedures for printing in Access are similar to those in other Microsoft applications (e.g., Word, Excel, and PowerPoint). For example, you can print individual pages, all pages, or a set range of pages. Print options in Access may vary slightly with different database objects.

Setting Report Print Layout

Commands on the Page Setup tab enable you to set up the basic page layout for a report. You can use these commands to change the paper size and orientation, to set margins and columns, or to print data only—leaving off the design elements and header controls.

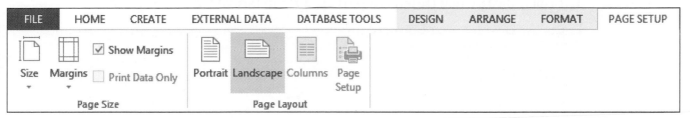

The Page Layout tools on the Page Setup tab.

Controlling Page Breaks

If you have used Word to create long documents, you know that controlling page breaks is important to prevent an individual line of a paragraph (often called an orphan) from appearing on a page by itself. The same is true for printing reports. You want to adjust settings so that a group header section stays with the first record in the report, or to prevent an individual record or line from appearing on a page by itself. Access offers tools to help you control what is contained in report sections and produce a better organized report.

Setting Page Breaks

Setting a page break for a report is different from setting a hard page break in a Word document or Excel worksheet. Because your report design contains controls for defining the report layout, it can be challenging to determine how many records will appear for each group—each employee will have a different number of sales. As a result, setting a page break is an uncertain way to try to control page printouts.

Setting Group Controls

Instead of setting page breaks for printing reports, Access lets you control how you want to keep groups together on report pages. Setting these controls prevents lone headers on report pages and enables you to keep each group on a single page. Setting these controls also reduces excessive pages.

QUICK REFERENCE	PRINTING REPORTS
Task	**Procedure**
Display Print Preview	■ Choose File→Print→Print Preview.
Print specific pages	■ Choose File→Print→Print to display the Print dialog box.
	■ Select the Pages option and enter the page numbers you want to print.
Print all report pages	■ Choose File→Print→Print to display the Print dialog box.
	■ Click OK.

Access 2013

Set Print Options

In this exercise, you will set up group controls for printing and view a report in Print Preview.

1. Display the **Invoice Details Report Q1 2013** in Design View.

2. Choose **Design→Grouping & Totals→** 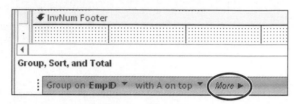 to open the Group, Sort, and Total pane.

3. Click **More**.

4. Follow these steps to set up group controls for printing:

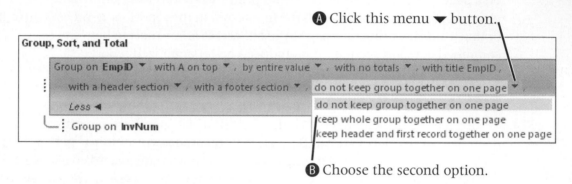

Ⓐ Click this menu ▼ button.

Ⓑ Choose the second option.

5. Switch to **Print Preview**.

   This option ensures that the headings will always be printed on the same page as the first detail section line (record).

6. Close **Print Preview**.

7. Save your report and close the database. Exit **Access**.

Concepts Review

To check your knowledge of the key concepts introduced in this lesson, complete the Concepts Review quiz by choosing the appropriate access option below.

If you are...	Then access the quiz by...
Using the Labyrinth Video Library	Going to http://labyrinthelab.com/videos
Using eLab	Logging in, choosing Content, and navigating to the Concepts Review quiz for this lesson
Not using the Labyrinth Video Library or eLab	Going to the student resource center for this book

Reinforce Your Skills

Create and Modify Reports

The president of Kids for Change wants a report that lists financial donations the organization has received since its inception, grouped by donor. He also wants to list the amount that K4C is depositing into its scholarship fund for local high school students. In this exercise, you will create a simple donations report and create a more customized report. Then, you will rearrange, resize, and format controls, and add a logo and title.

Create a Quick Report and Examine Report Views

1. Start **Access**. Open **AC05-R01-K4C** from your **AC2013 Lesson 05** folder and save it as
   AC05-R01-K4C-[FirstInitialLastName].

2. Click the **Donations** table in the Navigation Pane.

3. Choose **Create→Reports→Report** 📄.

Access creates a report of all donations to K4C and displays it in Layout View. The report needs some formatting, but the basic layout is complete.

4. Hover the mouse pointer over the controls, tools, and features in **Layout View** to see the ScreenTip descriptions.

5. Choose **Home**→**Views**→**View menu** ▾ and choose **Design View**.

6. Choose **Design**→**Controls**→**More** ⯆.
   You can see all the tools available in Design View.

7. Tap Esc.

8. Open the **Property Sheet**, if necessary.

9. Click the unbound **DonorID** label in the **Page Header** section.
   Notice that the DonorID label has a Caption property.

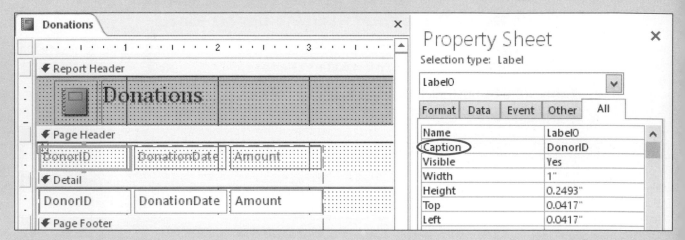

10. Click the bound **DonorID** text box in the **Detail** section.
    Notice that the DonorID text box has a Control Source property.

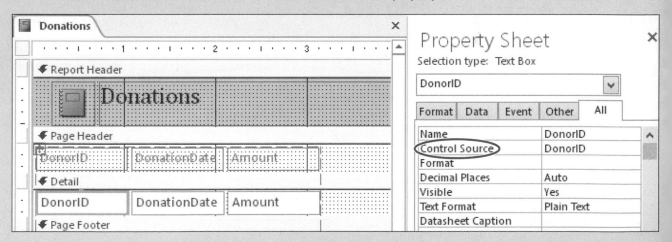

11. Switch to **Report View** and review its layout.
    Report View is similar to Layout View, but there are fewer tools and you cannot modify the formatting of the report or its controls.

12. Save the report as **Quick Donations List** and close it.

Create a Report Using the Report Wizard

Now you will create a donations report that is grouped by donor IDs and includes donation totals.

13. Click **Donations Query** in the Navigation Pane.

14. Choose **Create→Reports→Report Wizard**.

15. Double-click the **DonorID** field in the Available Fields box to move it to the Selected Fields box.

16. Double-click **DonorLName**, **DonorFName**, **DonationDate**, and **Amount** in the order shown.

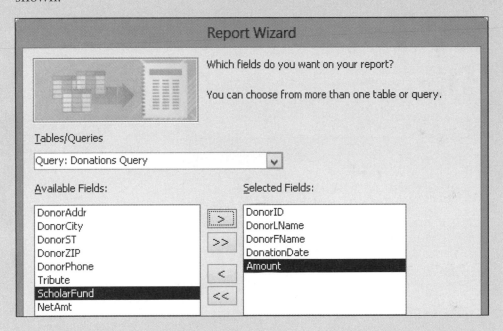

Many fields were not selected. If you select every field in a single report there won't be enough room to display all the information.

17. Click **Next**.

The next wizard screen asks how you want to view the data.

18. Select **By Donations**.

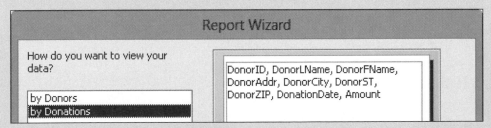

19. Click **Next**.

20. Select **DonorID** as the grouping field and click **Move** > .

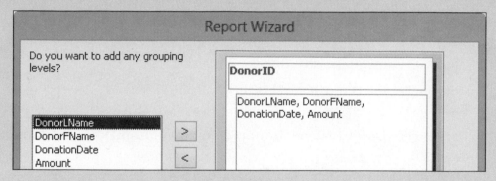

Be sure that your screen shows the grouping in the figure.

21. Click **Next**.

22. Click the **Summary Options** button and check the box for **Sum**. Leave the remaining options as they are.

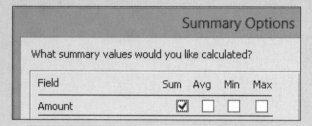

23. Click **OK** to close the Summary Options dialog box. Click **Next**.

24. Choose the **Block** Layout and **Landscape** Orientation.

25. Confirm that the **Adjust the Field Widths So All Fields Fit** box is checked.

26. Click **Next** and name the report **Donations Report 2013-2014**.

27. Click **Finish**.

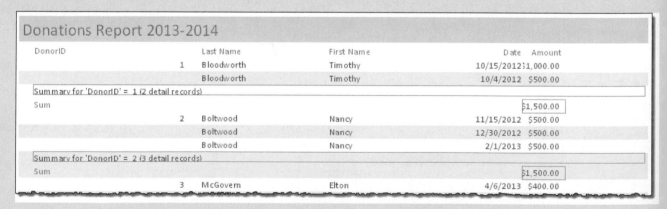

Your report displays in Print Preview, showing donation totals and summary totals for each donor. The report needs formatting and layout work, which must be done in Design View.

28. Navigate through the pages of the report. Then, click the ![Close Print Preview] button but leave the report open.

    The report is in Design View.

Add, Delete, and Edit Report Controls

29. In Design View, open the **Property Sheet**, if necessary.

30. Click the **DonorID** text box and type **.5** in the **Width** property line.

31. Click the **DonorLName** text box, press Ctrl and click the **DonorFName** text box to select both controls.

32. Type **1″** in the **Width** property to set the width for both controls.

33. Click the **Last Name** label, press Ctrl, and click the **DonorLName** text box.

34. Type **1.5** for their **Left** Property.

35. Select the **First Name** label and the **DonorFName** text box and type **3** for their **Left** property.

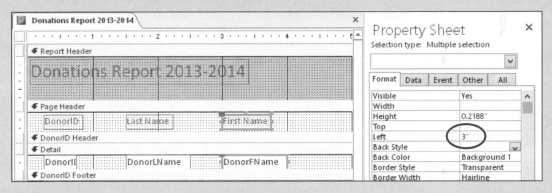

36. Scroll to the right of the report grid to see the other controls.

37. Click the **Date** label and type **5** for its **Left** property.

38. Click the **DonationDate** text box and type **4.5** for its **Left** property.

39. Click the **Amount** label and type **6.2** for its **Left** property.

40. Click the **Amount** text box, press Ctrl, and click the two **=Sum(Amount)** controls.

41. Type **1** for their **Width** property and **6** for their **Left** property.

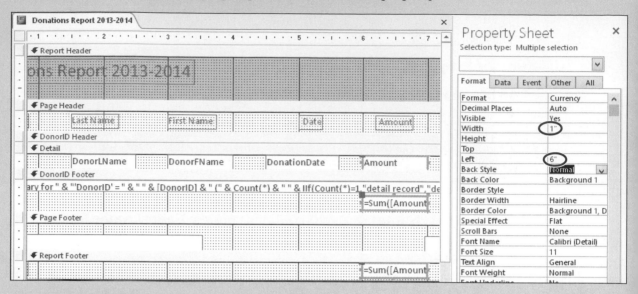

42. Choose **Design→Tools→Add Existing Fields** to open the **Field List**.

43. Drag **ScholarFund** from the Field List and drop it to the right of the **Amount** text box in the **Detail** section.

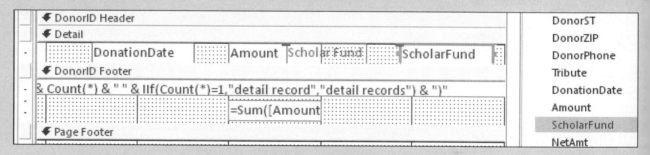

Access places a ScholarFund text box in the Detail section; the corresponding Scholar Fund label is partly on top of the Amount text box. If you recall, 10% of the donations are set aside for the scholarship fund.

44. Click the **Scholar Fund** label and tap ⌫Delete.

45. Choose **Design→Controls→Label** *Aa*.

46. Draw a label control in the **Page Header** section above the **ScholarFund** text box.

47. Type **Scholarship** into the new label.

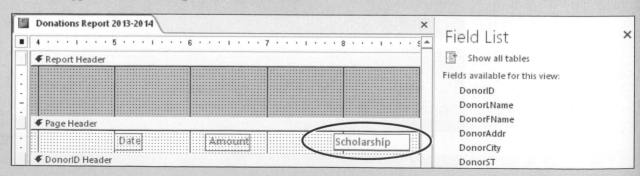

48. Close the Field List.

49. Click the **Summary for " & "'DonorID'...** control in the **DonorID Footer** section.

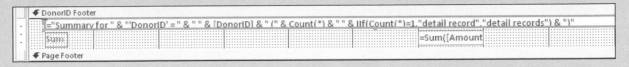

50. Tap [Delete].

51. Click the **Sum** label in the **DonorID Footer**. Click in the label and type `Donor ID Total`.

52. Select the title in the **Report Header** section, highlight the existing header text and type `Kids for Change`. Click an open area of the report grid to deselect all controls.

Add a Logo and a New Title to a Report

53. Drag the **Page Header** section bar down to about the .75" mark on the vertical ruler to make room for the logo and subtitle.

54. Choose **Design→Controls→Insert Image**.

55. Choose **Browse**, navigate to the **AC2013 Lesson 05** folder, choose All Files (*.*) from the file type drop-down list in the Insert Image dialog box, if necessary, and double-click **K4C-Logo.bmp**.

Once you have inserted an image, it is saved in the Image Gallery so you can find it quickly and easily.

56. Draw the logo as shown.

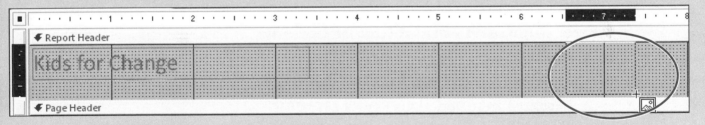

57. Choose **Design→Header/Footer→Title**.

The new title control sits in the Report Header section on top of the Kids for Change title.

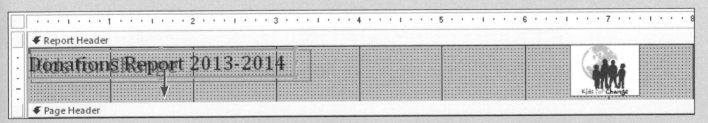

58. With the new title selected, tap [↓] until you can see the entire Kids for Change title.

59. Switch to **Report View**.

Kids for Change

Donations Report 2013-2014

DonorID	Last Name	First Name	Date	Amount	Scholarship
1	Bloodworth	Timothy	10/15/2012	$1,000.00	$100.00
	Bloodworth	Timothy	10/4/2012	$500.00	$50.00
Donor ID Total				$1,500.00	
2	Boltwood	Nancy	11/15/2012	$500.00	$50.00
	Boltwood	Nancy	12/30/2012	$500.00	$50.00
	Boltwood	Nancy	2/1/2013	$500.00	$50.00

60. Save and close **Donations Report 2013-2014**. Exit **Access**.

61. Submit your final file based on the guidelines provided by your instructor.

To view examples of how your file or files should look at the end of the exercise, go to the student resource center.

Use Controls, Apply Themes, Sort and Print Reports

In this exercise, you will size, align, and format report controls, apply a Theme to a report, add the date to the page header, display the Sort and Group pane, add page break controls, and set print options.

Size, Align, and Format Report Controls

1. Start **Access**. Open **AC05-R02-K4C** from the **AC2013 Lesson 05** folder and save it as **AC05-R02-K4C-[FirstInitialLastName]**.

2. Double-click the **Donations Report 2013-2014**.

The report has alignment problems, and the formatting of controls is inconsistent.

3. Switch to **Design View** and open the **Property Sheet**, if necessary.

4. Select the two title controls in the **Report Header** section and add these property values:

Property	Value
Width	4
Height	.4
Left	2
Text Align	Center
Font Name	Cambria (Header)
Fore Color	Blue, Accent 1, Darker 25%

5. Press Ctrl and click the **Donations Report** subtitle to deselect it.

6. With just the *Kids for Change* title selected, choose **22** for the **Font Size** property.

7. Click the **Kids for Change** logo.

8. Type **.8** for both the **Width** property and the **Height** property.

9. Type **.05** for the logo's **Top** property.
   Be sure to type .05 and not .5.

10. Click the **vertical ruler** to the left of the controls in the **Detail** section to select all the controls in the section.

11. Choose **Arrange→Sizing & Ordering→Size/Space→Equal Horizontal**.
    The Detail section controls are evenly spaced across the section.

12. Click the **Last Name** label, press Shift, and click the **DonorLName** text box.

13. Choose **Arrange→Sizing & Ordering→Align→Left**.
    Access lines up the Last Name controls.

14. Follow the procedures in **steps 12–13** to left align the **First Name** controls.

15. Click the **Date** label in the Page header and drag it so it is centered above the **DonationDate** text box.

16. Select the **Donor ID Total** and **Grand Total** labels, and the **DonationDate** text box.

17. Choose **Arrange→Sizing & Ordering→Align→Right**.

18. Select the **ScholarFund** text box, press Ctrl, and then click the two calculated field controls.
    You should have three selected controls.

19. Click **Border Style** in the Property Sheet and choose **Transparent**.

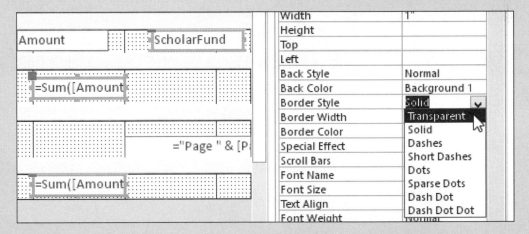

20. Right-align the **Amount** text box and the two **=Sum(Amount)** calculated fields.

21. Switch to **Print Preview**.

22. Save and close **Donations Report 2013-2014**.

Apply Themes to a Report

23. Display the **Quick Donations List** report in Design View.

24. Choose **Design→Themes→Themes** [Aa] and hover over each theme to see how the report style changes.

25. Select a **Theme** from the palette.

26. Save and close the report.

Add Date to the Page Header Section

Now you will add a date control to the Page Header section so when viewing the report on a computer, readers don't have to scroll to the very end of the report to check the date.

27. Open the **Donations Report 2013-2014** file in Design View.

28. Click the **=Now()** text box in the Page Footer section and tap [Delete].

29. Choose **Design→Header/Footer→Date and Time**.

30. Choose **mm/dd/yyyy**.

31. Uncheck the **Include Time** check box.

32. Click **OK**.

The new date control is inserted on the right-hand side of the Page Header.

33. Click the new **=Date()** control and enter the following property values:

Property	Value
Width	1
Top	.875
Left	3.5
Text Align	Center

34. Switch to **Print Preview** to see the new date control centered under the titles.

35. Close **Print Preview** and save **Donations Report 2013-2014**.

Display the Group and Sort Pane

36. Display **Donations Report 2013-2014** in Design View.

The report colors might have changed to the Theme you applied to the Quick Donations List.

37. Choose **Design→Grouping & Totals→Group & Sort** to open the Group, Sort, and Total pane.

The report is grouped by DonorID.

38. Click **Add a Sort** to display the list of fields.

39. Tap [Esc] to exit without making any changes.

40. Close the **Group, Sort, and Total** pane.

Add Page Break Controls to a Report

You will now set page breaks so each donor's summary records on a separate page or separate set of pages.

41. Display the **Donations Report 2013-2014** in Design View.

42. Choose **Design→Controls→Insert Page Break** ⊟.

43. Click in the bottom-left corner of the **DonorID Footer** section. Then, click to add the page break.

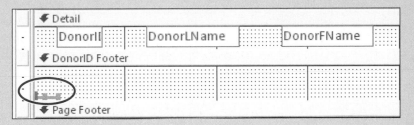

An orange marker indicates a page break.

44. Switch to **Print Preview**. Click **Next Page** ▸ to see that no two donor's records appear on the same page.

If you want the report header to appear on every page, you can select all the report header controls, cut them, and paste them into the page header section.

45. Close **Print Preview** and close the report *without* saving it.

Set Print Options

46. Display the **Donations Report 2013-2014** in Design View.

47. Choose **Design→Grouping & Totals→Group & Sort** [⧉ Group & Sort] to open the Group, Sort, and Total pane.

48. Click **More** in Group On DonorID.

49. Click the **menu** ▾ button for Do Not Keep Group Together on One Page, and choose **Keep Header and First Record Together on One Page**.

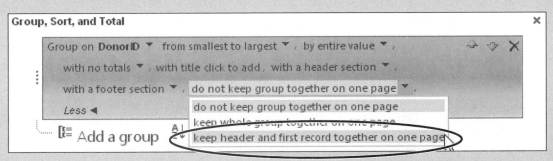

50. Switch to **Print Preview**.

Kids for Change
Donations Report 2013-2014

1/17/2013

DonorID	Last Name	First Name	Date	Amount	Scholarship
1	Bloodworth	Timothy	10/15/2012	$1,000.00	$100.00
	Bloodworth	Timothy	10/4/2012	$500.00	$50.00
			Donor ID Total	$1,500.00	
2	Boltwood	Nancy	11/15/2012	$500.00	$50.00
	Boltwood	Nancy	12/30/2012	$500.00	$50.00
	Boltwood	Nancy	2/1/2013	$500.00	$50.00
			Donor ID Total	$1,500.00	

51. Click the **Close Print Preview** button then close the **Group, Sort, and Total** pane.

52. Save and close the report. Exit **Access**.

53. Submit your final file based on the guidelines provided by your instructor.

To view examples of how your file or files should look at the end of the exercise, go to the student resource center.

Create Reports, Modify Controls, Add a Title and Logo, and Print

Kids for Change (K4C) is rapidly expanding, adding new activities and staff members almost daily. To meet the organization's need to match staffers with the new activities, you will create two new reports for them.

Create a Quick Report and Display Different Report Views

First, you will create a simple report that lists all activities organized by K4C.

1. Start **Access**. Open **AC05-R03-K4C** from the **AC2013 Lesson 05** folder and save it as
   AC05-R03-K4C-[FirstInitialLastName].

2. Click the **Activities** table in the Navigation Pane then choose **Create→Reports→Report**.

Access generates a report of K4C's activities in Layout View. Notice that the report extends beyond a standard 8.5" x 11" printed page (the vertical dotted line).

3. Click an **Activity** text box to select the Activity column of text boxes.

4. Hover the mouse pointer over the right border of the text box until it is a resize arrow. Click and drag its border to the left to resize the text boxes.

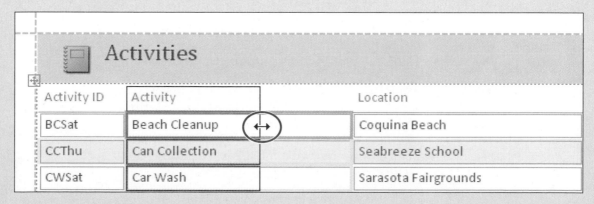

Access 2013

5. Resize the remaining text boxes, including the Date and Time controls.

6. Scroll to the bottom of the report and click the **Page** text box control to select it.

7. Switch to **Design View** and choose **Design→Tools→Property Sheet**.

8. Type **1″** for the Page control's **Width** property and type **6″** for the **Left** property.

9. Click in the upper-left corner of the report to select the entire report.

10. Type **7″** for the **Width** property.

11. Select the **=Count(*)** control in the **Report Footer** and type **.175** for the **Height** property.

12. Switch to **Print Preview**.

    The report fits a standard printed page.

13. Click the ![Close Print Preview] button then open the **Property Sheet**, if necessary.

14. Click the unbound **Activity ID label** in the Page Header section.

    Notice that the Activity ID label has a Caption property.

15. Click the bound **ActID** text box in the **Detail** section.

    Notice that the ActIDtext box has a Control Source property.

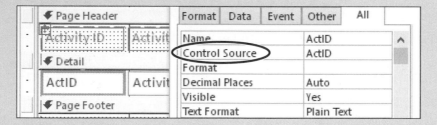

16. Save the report as **Activities Report** and close it.

Create a Report Using the Report Wizard

Now you will use the Report Wizard to create a staff availability report to match staffers with specific activities. The report will be grouped by activity.

17. Click the **Staff Schedule** query in the Navigation Pane then choose **Create→Reports→Report Wizard**.

18. Double-click the **Activity** field in the Available Fields box to move it to the Selected Fields box.

19. Double-click **Day, MeetTime, StaffLastName, StaffFirstName, StaffPhone,** and **Hours,** in the order shown.

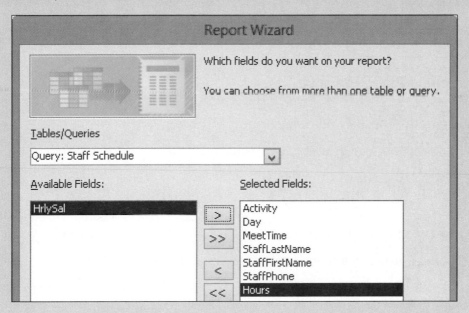

20. Click **Next**.

The next screen asks if you want to add grouping.

21. Select **Activity** and click **Next**.

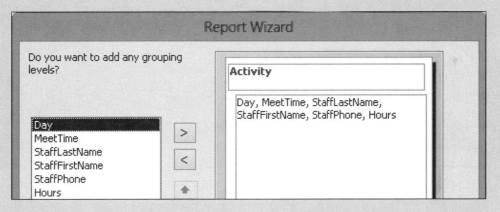

Activity appears in a header.

22. In the Sort Order and Summary Information screen, click **Next**.

23. Leave the default Layout options selected (**Stepped** and **Portrait**).

24. Confirm that the **Adjust the Field Widths so All Fields Fit** box is checked.

25. Click **Next** and name the report `Staff Availability Report`. Click **Finish**.

    Your report displays in Print Preview. It needs formatting and layout work, which will be done in Design View and Layout View. However, most of the controls are now in place.

26. Close **Print Preview**.

Size, Add, Delete, and Edit Report Controls

27. Display the **Staff Availability Report** in Layout View.

28. Open the **Property Sheet**, if necessary.

29. Click the **Activity** label, press Ctrl, and click an **Activity** text box.

30. Type `1.2` for the **Width** property.

31. Click the **Day** label to select it, press Ctrl, and click a **Day** textbox.

32. Type `.9` for the **Width** property and `1.5` for the **Left** property.

33. Select the **Meet Time** label and text boxes. Type `.75` for the **Width** property and `2.5` for the **Left** property.

34. Select the **Last Name** label and text boxes. Type `.8` for the **Width** property and `3.3` for the **Left** property.

35. Select the **First Name** label and text boxes. Type `.8` for the **Width** property and `4.2` for the **Left** property.

36. Select the **Telephone** label and text boxes. Type `1.1` for the **Width** property and `5.1` for the **Left** property.

37. Switch to **Design View**.

38. Choose **Design→Tools→Add Existing Fields** 🔢.

39. Drag **HrlySal** to the right of the **StaffPhone** text box in the Detail section.

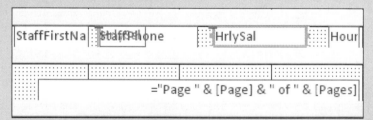

Access includes a label control with the text box. You will add a new label in the Page Header section rather than using the default label.

40. Click the **Hrly Sal** label control and tap Del.

If you delete the wrong control, tap Ctrl+Z to undo the last task.

41. Close the **Field List** and open the **Property Sheet**.

42. Select the **HrlySal** text box. Type **.55** for the **Width** property and **6.3** for the **Left** property.

43. Click the **Label**  button and drag a new label between the Telephone and Hrs labels in the Page Header section.

44. Type **Hrly Sal** in the new label and tap ⟨Enter⟩.

45. Type **.55** for the **Width** property and **6.3** for the **Left** property.

46. Select the **Hrs** label and the **Hours** text box. Type **.4** for the **Width** property and **7** for the **Left** property.

47. Choose Report from the Selection Type list at the top of the Property Sheet, and type **7.875″** for the report **Width** property.

48. Switch to **Print Preview**.

Staff Availability Report

Activity	Day	Meet Time	Last Name	First Name	Telephone	Hrly Sal	Hrs
Animal Shelter							
	Wednesday	5:00 PM	Kline	Victor	(941)555-6893	$18.50	10
	Friday	5:00 PM	Sanchez	Cokie	(941)555-0008	$23.50	4
	Monday	5:00 PM	Earle	Kevin	(941)555-1368	$18.00	9
	Tuesday	5:00 PM	Jacoby	Jane	(941)555-5050	$17.75	8
	Thursday	5:00 PM	Bryant	Matthew	(941)555-7523	$20.25	4
	Friday	5:00 PM	Kendall	Lonnie	(941)555-2356	$18.50	4
Beach Cleanup							

If an error message appears saying that the width is greater than the page width, make sure that you followed all the steps precisely. If the report does not display correctly, you may have to adjust the report width, depending on your settings.

49. Save the report and close **Print Preview**.

Add a New Title and a Logo to a Report

50. Display **Staff Availability Report** in Design View and, if necessary, open the **Property Sheet**.

51. Select the title control in the **Report Header**, type the caption **Kids for Change**, and tap ⌈Enter⌋.

52. Choose **Design→Header/Footer→Title** and tap ⌈Enter⌋.

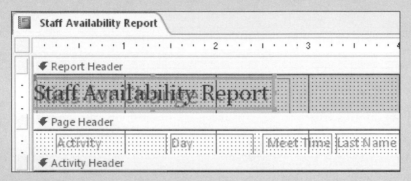

Access adds a new title control in the Page Header section on top of the Kids for Change title.

53. Type **.46″** for the **Top** property of the new title.

Access automatically resizes the Report Header section when you move the control.

54. Select the *Kids for Change* title and enter the following property values:

Property	New Value
Width	4
Left	2
Font Name	Georgia
Font Size	22
Text Align	Center
Fore Color	Blue, Accent 1, Darker 25%

55. Choose **Home→Clipboard→Format Painter**, and then click the *Staff Availability Report* subtitle to format the report, and type 20 for the Font Size property.

Your Report Header should look similar to this header.

56. Choose **Design→Header/Footer→ Logo**.

57. Navigate to your **AC2013 Lesson 05** folder, select **K4C-Logo.bmp**, and click **OK**.

Access places the logo to the left of the title and subtitle in the Report Header.

58. Type **.8** for the **Width** and **Height** properties.

59. Save the **Staff Availability Report**.

Align and Format Report Controls

The Staff Availability Report is slightly too wide to fit on a standard printed page, so you will format and arrange the controls to make it fit.

60. Display the **Staff Availability Report** in **Design View**.

61. Click the **=“Page”** control in the **Page Footer** to select it.

62. Type **1** for the **Width** property and **6.5** for the **Left** property.

63. Hover the mouse pointer over the right border of the report grid until it becomes a resize arrow and drag the report border left as shown.

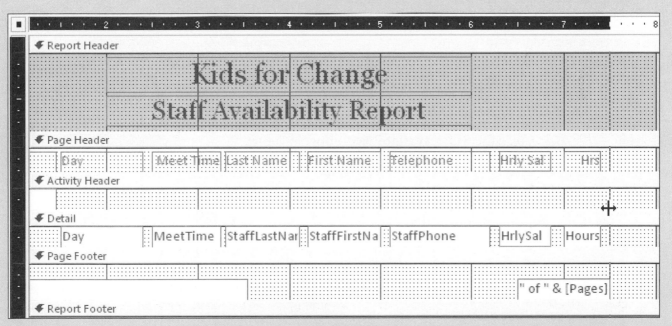

The report now fits on a standard sheet of paper.

64. Click the **HrlySal** text box and change the **Border Style** property to **Transparent**.

65. Switch to **Report View**.

Kids for Change
Staff Availability Report

Activity	Day	Meet Time	Last Name	First Name	Telephone	Hrly Sal	Hrs
Animal Shelter							
	Wednesday	5:00 PM	Kline	Victor	(941) 555-6893	$18.50	10
	Friday	5:00 PM	Sanchez	Cokie	(941) 555-0008	$23.50	4
	Monday	5:00 PM	Earle	Kevin	(941) 555-1368	$18.00	9
	Tuesday	5:00 PM	Jacoby	Jane	(941) 555-5050	$17.75	8
	Thursday	5:00 PM	Bryant	Matthew	(941) 555-7523	$20.25	4
	Friday	5:00 PM	Kendall	Lonnie	(941) 555-2356	$18.50	4
Beach Cleanup							

66. Save and close the **Staff Availability Report**.

Apply Themes to a Report

67. Display the **Activities Report** in Design View.

68. Choose **Design→Themes→Themes** and select a Theme for the report.

You may have to readjust control sizes because of font changes.

69. Save and close the report.

Add Date to the Page Header Section

Now you will add a date control to the Page Header section so when viewing the report on a computer, readers do not have to scroll to the very end to check the date.

70. Display the **Staff Availability Report** in Design View.

71. Right-click the **=Now( )** date text box in the Page Footer and choose **Delete**.

72. Choose **Design→Header/Footer→Date and Time**.

73. Choose the **mm/dd/yyyy** option, uncheck the **Include Time** checkbox, and click **OK**.

Access places the new date control on the right-hand side of the Page Header section.

74. Click the new date control and tap ⬆ repeatedly to move it to the top of the **Page Header** section.

75. Drag the left border to the right to the **6.5″ mark** on the horizontal ruler.

76. Save the report.

Display the Group and Sort Pane

77. Choose **Design→Grouping & Totals→Group & Sort**.

78. Click **Add a Sort** to display the list of fields.

Notice that this report is grouped by Activity.

79. Tap `Esc` to exit without making any changes. Then, close the **Group, Sort, and Total** pane and the **Staff Availability Report**.

Add Page Break Controls to a Report

Now you will set page breaks so each donor's summary records on a separate page or separate set of pages.

80. Display the **Donations Report** in **Design View**.

81. Choose **Design→Controls→Insert Page Break** ⊞.

82. Click in the bottom-left corner of the **DonorID Footer** section and click to add the page break.

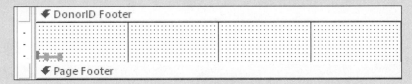

The orange marker indicates a page break.

83. Switch to **Print Preview** and click **Next Page** ▶ to view each page of the report. Each donor's records appear on a separate page.

If you want the report header to appear on every page, select the report header controls, cut them, and paste them into the page header section.

84. Click the **Close Print Preview** button then close **Donations Report** *without saving* it.

Set Print Options

85. Display the **Donations Report** in **Design View**.

86. Choose **Design→Grouping & Totals→Group & Sort** ⧉ Group & Sort.

87. Click **More** in **Group on DonorID**.

88. Click the **menu** ▼ button for Do Not Keep Group Together on One Page, and choose **Keep Header and First Record Together on One Page**.

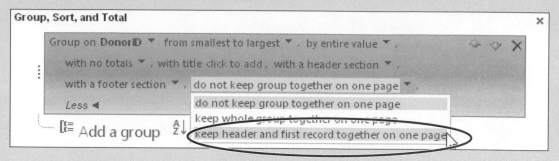

89. Save the report and display it in **Print Preview**.

90. Close your report. Close the database, and exit **Access**.

91. Submit your final file based on the guidelines provided by your instructor.

Apply Your Skills

Create and Modify Reports

Universal Corporate Events, Ltd. is ready to add several reports to its database. In this exercise, you will create two reports: the first is a simple report that lists contacts' telephone numbers; the second lists the event venues and their contact information (address, telephone number, and website), grouped by the contact person. Then you will add, delete, and edit the venue report controls, and add a logo and title.

Create a Quick Report and Examine Report Views

1. Start **Access**. Open **AC05-A01-UCE** from the **AC2013 Lesson 05** folder and save it as `AC05-A01-UCE-[FirstInitialLastName]`.

2. Click the **Contacts** table, and choose **Create→Reports→Report**.

   Access generates a quick report using the Contacts table and displays it in Layout View.

3. Hover the mouse pointer over each of the control tools on the Ribbon and features in Report **Layout View** to see the ScreenTip descriptions.

4. Switch to **Design View**.

   The Report Header section contains an auto-logo, a title, an auto-date control, and an auto-time control. The Detail section contains text box controls that display the data values.

5. Choose **Design→Controls→More** to see all the control tools available in Design View; then tap ⎋Esc.

6. Select the unbound **ContactID** label in the Page Header section, open the **Property Sheet**, and notice that the label has a Caption property.

7. Select the bound **ContactID text box** in the Detail section and notice that it has a Control Source property.

8. Switch to **Report View**.

9. Save the report as `Contacts List` and close it.

Use the Report Wizard and Delete and Edit Report Controls

Now you will use the Report Wizard to create a list the event venues, their addresses, phone number, and website, grouped by the contact person.

10. Click the **Venues** table and start the Report Wizard.

11. Select all the fields *except* VenueID.

12. Leave **VenueContact** as the only grouping level.

13. Do not add a sort, leave the layout default values, and name the report `Venues List`. Click **Finish**.

    Access opens the report in Print Preview.

    Now you will delete the Page control from the Page Footer section in the Venues List and modify label captions to improve readability.

14. Close **Print Preview** and switch to **Design View**.

15. Select the **=Now( )** control in the Page Footer and tap `Delete`.

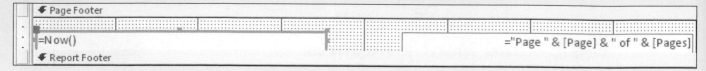

16. Change the caption of the **VenueContact** label in the Page Header to `Contact`.

17. Change the caption of the **VenueName** label in the Page Header to `Name of Venue`.

18. Save your changes.

Add a Logo and a New Title to a Report

19. If necessary, open the **Property Sheet**.

20. Choose **Design→Header/Footer→Logo**. Choose **UCE-Logo.bmp** from the **AC2013 Lesson 05** folder.

    Access adds the logo to the left side of the Page Header.

21. Type **.8** for the **Width** and **Height** properties.

22. Click the **Venues List** title control and enter the following property values:

Property	New Value
Caption	Universal Corporate Events, Ltd.
Width	4
Height	.4
Left	2
Font Name	Arial Narrow
Font Size	22
Text Align	Center
Fore Color	Blue, Accent 5, Darker 50%

23. Choose **Design→Header/Footer→Title**.

24. Use the **Format Painter** to paint the new title with the same format as the title.

25. Switch to **Report View**.

Universal Corporate Events, Ltd.

Venues List

Contact	Name of Venue	Street	City	ST	ZIP	Phone	Website
Benson							
	Manatee Yacht Clu	Gulf Blvd	Long Key	FL	3422	(941) 555-2990	MYC@web.c
	Manatee Conventi	Haben Blvd.	Palmetto	FL	3422	(800) 555-5104	ManateeCon
	Brooksville Campg	John Brown Rd	Brooksville	FL	3322	(813) 555-3298	BrksCamping
CroftS							
	Tampa Convention	Tampa Dr	Tampa	FL	3360	(813) 555-1100	TampaCente
	Tampa Bay Forum	Channelside Dr	Tampa	FL	3360	(800) 555-6500	TampaBayFo
	Drake Country Clu	DeWinters Ln	Tampa	FL	3360	(813) 555-1700	DrakeCC@w

Page 1 of 1

26. Save and close the report. Close the database and exit **Access**.

27. Submit your final file based on the guidelines provided by your instructor.

To view examples of how your file or files should look at the end of the exercise, go to the student resource center.

APPLY YOUR SKILLS AC05-A02

Fine-Tune Reports

Universal Corporate Events, Ltd. CEO Hugh Buckley has sent back the first draft of the Contacts List and Venues List with a list of modifications he would like you to make. In this exercise, you will resize, align, and format controls on the Venues List, examine the sorting and grouping settings, and prepare it for printing. You will also apply a Theme to the Contacts List, and print the modified report.

Size, Align, and Format Report Controls and Apply a Theme

1. Start **Access**. Open **AC05-A02-UCE** from the **AC2013 Lesson 05** folder and save it as **AC05-A02-UCE-[FirstInitialLastName]**.

2. Display the **Venues List** report in **Layout View**.

The report controls must be resized.

3. In either Layout View or Design View, modify the **Width** and **Left** properties of the labels and text boxes so that all the information displays.

4. Save and close the **Venues List** report.

5. Display the **Contacts List** report in **Design View**.

6. Apply a **Theme** to the report, and keep in mind that it will be applied to *every* object in the database.

7. Switch to **Layout View**. Resize the controls to display the full contents.

8. Save and close the **Contacts List**.

Add the Date to the Page Header and Display the Group, Sort, and Total Pane

9. Display the **Venues List** report in **Design View**.

10. Click ⏲ Date and Time. Choose the **mm/dd/yyyy** format and do not include the time.

11. Move the new **Date** control to the top of the **Report Header**, and shorten its width so it doesn't overlay the title.

12. Switch to **Report View**.

Contact	Name of Venue	Street	City	ST	ZIP	Phone	Website
							1/14/2013

Universal Corporate Events, Ltd.
Venues List

Contact	Name of Venue	Street	City	ST	ZIP	Phone	Website
Benson							
	Manatee Yacht Club	Gulf Blvd	Long Key	FL	34228	(941) 555-2990	MYC@web.com
	Manatee Convention Center	Haben Blvd.	Palmetto	FL	34221	(800) 555-5104	NorthCC@web.com
	Brooksville Campgrounds	John Brown Rd	Brooksville	FL	33222	(813) 555-3298	BrksCamp@web.com
CroftS							
	Tampa Convention Ctr	Tampa Dr	Tampa	FL	33608	(813) 555-1100	TampaCtr@web.com
	Tampa Bay Forum	Channelside Dr	Tampa	FL	33602	(800) 555-6500	TBForum@web.com
	Drake Country Club	DeWinters Ln	Tampa	FL	33608	(813) 555-1700	DrakeCC@web.com
LunaL							
	Hyatt Sarasota	Tamiami Tr	Sarasota	FL	34236	(800) 555-1234	HyattSara@web.com
Miller							
	Sarasota Yacht Club	Fruitville Rd	Sarasota	FL	34231	(941) 555-7685	SYC@web.com
	Sarasota Country Club	Tamiami Tr	Sarasota	FL	34231	(800) 555-3366	SCC@web.com
	Meadows Clubhouse	Meadows Pkwy	Lakewood	FL	33505	(813) 555-5050	Meadows@web.com

Page 1 of 1

Your report should include the new date control in the Page Header section.

13. Switch to **Design View** and open the **Group, Sort, and Totals** pane.
The report is sorted and grouped by Venue Contact.

14. Investigate the various settings, but make no changes.

15. Close the **Group, Sort, and Totals** pane. Then, close the **Venues List** report, but do not save it.

Add a Page Break Control and Set Print Options

16. Display the **Event Revenue Report** in **Design View**.

17. Click the **Page Break** control tool and click in the bottom-left corner of the **EventDate Footer** section to insert the page break.

18. Switch to **Print Preview** and page through the report.

Each month's records are on a separate page.

19. Close the report *without saving* it.

20. Display the **Event Revenue Report** in **Design View**.

21. Open the **Group, Sort, and Totals** pane and click More ►.

22. Click the **menu** ▼ button for Do Not Keep Group Together on One Page and choose **Keep Header and First Record Together on One Page**.

23. Switch to **Print Preview**, and navigate to the second page.

The second page of the report begins with the EventDate Header because you instructed Access to keep the group header together with the first detail record.

Universal Corporate Events, Ltd.
Event Revenue Report
1/20/2013

Month	Event Date	Menu Plan	Guests	Chg/PP	Total Revenue	Taxes	Net Revenue
December 2013							
	12/6/2013	Hors d'oeuvre	150	$35.00	$5,250.00	$525.00	$4,725.00
	12/14/2013	Dinner Sitdown	100	$65.00	$6,500.00	$650.00	$5,850.00
	12/28/2013	Wedding Cake-Level 2	75	$82.00	$6,150.00	$615.00	$5,535.00
		Subtotals			$17,900.00	$1,790.00	$16,110.00
January 2014							

Month	Event Date	Menu Plan	Guests	Chg/PP	Total Revenue	Taxes	Net Revenue
May 2014							
	5/3/2014	Buffet Luncheon	50	$25.00	$1,250.00	$125.00	$1,125.00
	5/10/2014	Luncheon Sitdown	35	$34.00	$1,190.00	$119.00	$1,071.00
	5/29/2014	Dinner Buffet	80	$45.00	$3,600.00	$360.00	$3,240.00
		Subtotals			$6,040.00	$604.00	$5,436.00

24. Click the **Close Print Preview** button then close the **Group, Sort, and Total** pane.

25. Save and close the **Event Revenue Report**. Close the database and exit **Access**.

26. Submit your final file based on the guidelines provided by your instructor.

To view examples of how your file or files should look at the end of the exercise, go to the student resource center.

Create Customized Reports

Universal Corporate Events, Ltd. is ready to add more reports to its database. In this exercise, you will create two reports: a quick, simple report using the Menus table as the record source and a report that lists Personnel contact information grouped by last name. Then, you will add, delete, and edit report controls, modify captions of several labels to make them more readable, and add a logo, title, and subtitle to the venue report.

Create Reports

1. Start **Access**. Open **AC05-A03-UCE** from the **AC2013 Lesson 05** folder and save it as **AC05-A03-UCE-[FirstInitialLastName]**.

2. Click the **Menus** table, and choose **Create→Reports→Report**.

   Access opens the new report in Layout View.

3. Save the report as **Menus List** and close it.

   Now you will use the Report Wizard to create a list of the company personnel, their addresses, phone numbers, and email addresses. The report will be grouped by last name.

4. Click the **Personnel** table and start the **Report Wizard**.

5. Include last and first name, address, city, state, ZIP, phone number, and email.

6. Group by last name.

7. Do not add a sort, and leave the layout default values. Name the report **Personnel List** and click **Finish**.

   Access opens the report in Print Preview.

Delete and Edit Report Controls; and Add a Logo and a New Title to a Report

8. Switch to **Design View**.

9. Select the **=Now()** control in the Page Footer and tap ⎡Delete⎤.

10. Delete the **="Page"** control in the Page Footer.

11. Change the caption of the **PerLastName** label in the Page Header to **Last Name**.

12. Save your changes.

13. Using either the **Logo** control or the **Insert Image** control, add **UCE-Logo.bmp** from the **AC2013 Lesson 05** folder to the Report Header.

14. Type **.8** for the Logo's **Width** and **Height** properties.

15. Click the **Personnel List** title control and enter the following property values:

Property	New Value
Caption	Universal Corporate Events, Ltd.
Width	4
Height	.4
Left	2
Font Name	Arial Narrow
Font Size	22
Text Align	Center
Fore Color	Blue, Accent 5, Darker 50%

16. Choose **Design→Header/Footer→Title**.

17. Enter the following property values for the new title:

Property	New Value
Width	4
Height	.4
Top	.5
Left	2
Font Name	Arial Narrow
Font Size	20
Text Align	Center
Fore Color	Blue, Accent 5, Darker 50%

18. Switch to **Report View** to determine what controls need realigning and resizing.

19. Save and close the report.

Size and Rearrange Report Controls and Apply a Theme

20. Display the **Personnel List** report in **Layout View**.

Several report controls need resizing.

21. Click and drag the controls to space them out across the report.

22. Resize the controls to display their contents fully, but do not extend the report beyond the vertical dotted line.

23. Save the **Personnel List** Report.

24. Display the **Menus List** report in **Design View**.

25. Choose a *Theme* that you like for the report, keeping in mind that it will be applied to *every* object in the database.

26. Switch to **Layout View**, and resize controls to display the full contents, as necessary.

27. Save and close the **Menus List** report.

Add the Date to the Page Header and Display the Group, Sort, and Total Pane

28. Display the **Personnel List** report in **Design View**.

29. Click ⊞ Date and Time.

30. Choose the **Short Date** format (1/13/2013) and uncheck the **Include Time** box.

31. Move the new **Date** control to the top of the **Report Header**, and shorten it so it doesn't overlay the title.

32. Switch to **Report View** to see the new date control in the Report Header.

33. Save and close the **Personnel List** report.

34. Display the **Event Revenue Report** in **Design View**.

35. Open the **Group, Sort, and Totals** pane.

    The report is sorted and grouped by EventDate.

36. Investigate the various settings, but make no changes. Then close the **Group, Sort, and Totals** pane.

Set Print Options

37. Display **Event Revenue Report** in **Design View**.

38. Open the **Group, Sort, and Totals** pane. Choose to keep the header and first record together on one page.

39. View the results in **Print Preview**. Then, switch to **Design View**.

40. Now choose to keep the group together on one page.

41. View the results in **Print Preview** to see if there are any changes.

42. Click the **Close Print Preview** button then close the **Group, Sort, and Total** pane.

43. Save and close the report. Close the database and exit **Access**.

44. Submit your final file based on the guidelines provided by your instructor.

Extend Your Skills

In the course of working through the Extend Your Skills exercises, you will think critically as you use the skills taught in the lesson to complete the assigned projects. To evaluate your mastery and completion of the exercises, your instructor may use a rubric, with which more points are allotted according to performance characteristics. (The more you do, the more you earn!) Ask your instructor how your work will be evaluated.

AC05-E01 That's the Way I See It

In this exercise, you will create several reports for either your own business or for Blue Jean Landscaping. Open **AC05-E01-BJL** from your **AC2013 Lesson 05 folder** and save the file as **AC05-E01-BJL-[FirstInitialLastName]**.

Using the skills you learned in this lesson, create reports and lists to help your company track customers, sales, invoices, inventory, and any other aspects that you would find beneficial to managing your business. Include a title and a logo or other image in the Report Header. Remember that when you use the Logo control from the Ribbon, Access includes a Title control with the logo. You can use the auto-title or, if you want to edit the logo or title separately, choose Arrange→Table→Remove Layout to unlink the controls.

You will be evaluated based on the inclusion of all elements, your ability to follow directions, your ability to apply newly learned skills to a real-world situation, your creativity, and your accuracy in creating objects and/or entering data. Submit your final file based on the guidelines provided by your instructor.

AC05-E02 Be Your Own Boss

Blue Jean Landscaping wants to add several reports to the company database that will provide a listing of its equipment, services, and customer tables in an attractive and useful manner. In this exercise, you will create these reports. Open **AC05-E02-BJL** from the **AC2013 Lesson 05** folder and save the file as **AC05-E02-BJL-[FirstInitialLastName]**. Using the Store Inventory query as a record source, create a report using the Report Wizard that is grouped by manufacturer and includes item name, price, quantity in stock, and inventory amount, and a sum of the InvTot field. Use the default layout settings. Name the report **Store Inventory Report**. Use the skills you learned in this lesson to size, rearrange, and format the report controls. Add the **BJL-Logo** from your **AC2013 Lesson 05** folder, along with a title and subtitle using the existing Available Equipment as a guide. Then, create a report with the wizard using the Service Invoices Query that includes all the fields except InvNum. Group the results by InvDate, sum the LineTotal field, choose the Stepped and Landscape layout options, and name the report **Service Invoices Report**. Format the report controls and add the logo, title, and subtitle as directed above.

You will be evaluated based on the inclusion of all elements, your ability to follow directions, your ability to apply newly learned skills to a real-world situation, your creativity, and your accuracy in creating objects and/or entering data. Submit your final file based on the guidelines provided by your instructor.

Transfer Your Skills

In the course of working through the Transfer Your Skills exercises, you will use critical-thinking and creativity skills to complete the assigned projects using skills taught in the lesson. To evaluate your mastery and completion of the exercises, your instructor may use a rubric, with which more points are allotted according to performance characteristics. (The more you do, the more you earn!) Ask your instructor how your work will be evaluated.

AC05-T01 Use the Web as a Learning Tool

Throughout this book, you will be provided with an opportunity to use the Internet as a learning tool by completing WebQuests. According to the original creators of WebQuests, as described on their website (WebQuest.org), a WebQuest is "an inquiry-oriented activity in which most or all of the information used by learners is drawn from the web." To complete the WebQuest projects in this book, navigate to the student resource center and choose the WebQuest for the lesson on which you are currently working. The subject of each WebQuest will be relevant to the material found in the lesson.

WebQuest Subject: Using parameter values in reports.

Submit your final file(s) based on the guidelines provided by your instructor.

AC05-T02 Demonstrate Proficiency

Stormy BBQ wants a new, attractive, and exciting menu for their flagship Key West restaurant. The menu will have a tropical theme, include item names and prices, and use the new company logo, SBQ-Logo. You will also create a fun take-out menu for the store that will include their food as well as their off-the-shelf merchandise. Use the MenuItems and Merchandise tables for ideas on how to display what Stormy BBQ offers. Open **AC05-T02-StormyBBQ** from the **AC2013 Lesson 05** folder and save it as `AC05-T02-StormyBBQ-[FirstInitialLastName]`. Use the report design and formatting tools you learned in this lesson to create the two fun, tropical-themed menus described.

Submit your final file based on the guidelines provided by your instructor.

Multitasking with Office 2013

LEARNING OBJECTIVES

After studying this lesson, you will be able to:

- Create a chart in Excel from data in an Access database

- Integrate data from an Excel document into a Word document

- Integrate an Excel chart into a Word document

- Create a PowerPoint presentation from a Word document

- Integrate Excel charts into a PowerPoint presentation

The Office 2013 applications are designed to work together seamlessly, allowing you to use the most suitable program for each part of a complex task. For example, you can place Excel charts into Word documents and PowerPoint presentations, or use Word to draft the outline of a PowerPoint presentation. In this lesson, you will undertake a project in which each Office 2013 program performs the tasks they do best.

Preparing for a Meeting

You are an administrative assistant at the Help for the Homeless shelter in your community. The shelter provides year-round support and lodging for homeless persons. In addition to aiding the homeless, the shelter also helps families find permanent housing and coordinates the donation of automobiles and furniture to help these families get established. On a Monday morning, the following message is in your inbox.

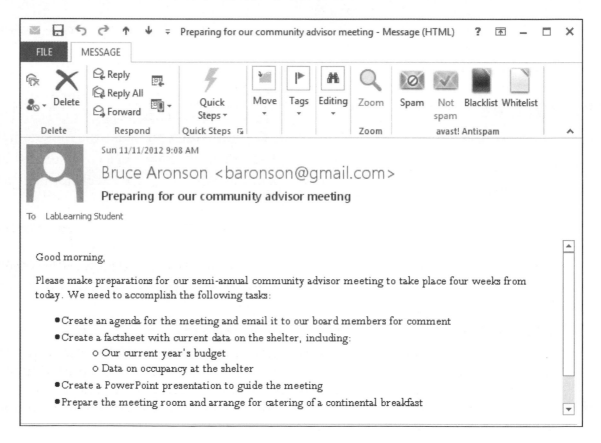

Twice a year, the shelter organizes a meeting of its community advisory committee. Committee members review the shelter's operations and make recommendations to enhance its role. They are also an important facet of community outreach, helping to recruit support in local government and corporate donations.

You must play a key role bringing this meeting together. To accomplish this complex task, you will use several programs in the Office 2013 suite.

Task 1: Outlining the Project

To make preparations for the meeting, you will use several programs. The following table lists the tasks you will undertake and the programs you will use.

Task		Brief Description	Programs
2.	Type and email a meeting agenda.	Create a new folder to hold all the project files. Type and email an agenda to board members for review and comment.	Word/Outlook
3.	Check board member replies.	Review board member replies and revise the agenda as advised.	Outlook/Word
4.	Create a budget workbook.	Create a worksheet with the current shelter budget and create a pie chart to display it.	Excel
5.	Query a database.	Determine how many beds were occupied in the shelter during the past three years and determine the average number of beds occupied per week.	Access/Excel
6.	Create a column chart.	Chart the occupancy data discovered in task 4.	Excel
7.	Create a factsheet document.	Create a summary of facts about the shelter, its operating budget, and its occupancy rates.	Word/Excel
8.	Create a presentation.	Create a presentation to guide the meeting.	PowerPoint/Word/Excel
9.	Review and print handouts.	Review all handouts for accuracy and errors, and then print originals for copying.	Word/PowerPoint

Multitasking

Notice that some programs are used several times. This mirrors how most people work with programs on a project such as this. You don't necessarily foresee every need you will have for a particular program; instead, you start programs and open files as your needs dictate. You may leave a program open and switch back and forth between it and other programs. Or you may exit a program and then launch it again later.

Integrating 2013

Task 2: Emailing a Meeting Agenda (Word/Outlook)

In this task, you will type a draft meeting agenda and email it to the three board members. Before you create the new document, you will create a folder in your file storage location to organize all the files you will use on this project. It is a common practice to make new folders for specific projects. Otherwise, the list of files in your storage location may become quite long.

DEVELOP YOUR SKILLS IN01-D01

Type and Email a Meeting Agenda

In this exercise, you will begin by setting up project files. Then you will create a draft of the meeting agenda in Word. Finally, you will draft an email message to the three board members.

Before You Begin: Navigate to the student resource center to download the student exercise files for this book.

Copy Project Files

1. Use Ctrl + A to select all items in the **IN2013 Lesson 01** folder and then use Ctrl + C to copy them.

   Windows copies the file information. In a few minutes, you will paste these files.

Create the Folder

Now you will create a project folder to hold the files that will be created and used in the course of planning for the meeting.

2. Follow the step for your version of Windows to create a new folder:
   - **Windows 8:** Choose **File→New→New Folder button**.
   - **Windows 7:** Click the **New Folder button** on the toolbar.

   The new folder appears with the name selected, ready for you to type a new name.

3. Name the new folder **Advisory Committee Meeting** and tap Enter.

4. Open the newly created folder.

5. Paste the files you copied by pressing Ctrl + V.

6. **Minimize** ▬ / – the folder window.

Type the Meeting Agenda

7. Start **Word 2013**; create a new document and type the following agenda. Use styles to make the document appear consistent and professional.

Read these bulleted notes below before you begin typing.

- Use **Design→Themes** to select a theme for the document.
- Use the **Title**, **Heading 1**, and **Heading 2 Quick Styles** to format the various major headings.
- Use bullets as appropriate.

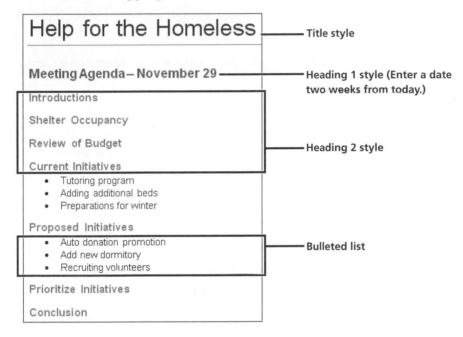

8. Save the document to the **Advisory Committee Meeting** folder as `IN01-D01-MeetingAgenda-[FirstInitialLastName]`.

Replace the bracketed text with your first initial and last name. For example, if your name is Bethany Smith, your filename would look like this: IN01-D01-MeetingAgenda-BSmith.

9. Close ☒ the Word window.

Email the Agenda to Board Members

Because most computer labs are not set up for Outlook email, you will open a message that is already created.

10. Use Alt + Tab to flip to the **Advisory Committee Meeting** folder.

11. Double-click to open **Message to Board Members**.

An Outlook 2013 Startup window may appear if Outlook has not been set up to work with your login ID.

12. Follow these steps if the **Outlook 2013 Startup** window appears; otherwise, skip to step 13.

- Click **Next**.
- **(Win 8 only)** Choose **No** and then click **Next**.
- Place a **checkmark** to use Outlook without an email account.
- Click **Finish**.

A blank message appears, in which you can create your email message.

13. Taking care to place a semicolon between addresses, enter the following recipients in the To box:

```
josie.anime@hfh.org
owen.hugo@hfh.org
chas.vigil@hfh.org
jaemi.lee@hfh.org
```

14. Carbon copy (CC) the message to your own email address. (Make up an email address if you don't have one.)

15. Type this text as the email subject: `Draft advisory committee meeting agenda`

16. Type this text as the email body:

```
Dear Board Members,
Attached is a draft version of the agenda for next month's
Community Advisory Committee meeting. Please review it and let me
know of any revisions you wish to recommend.
Regards,
[Your Name]
```

17. Click the [📎 Attach File] button, navigate to your **Advisory Committee Meeting** folder, and attach your **IN01-D01-MeetingAgenda** file.

The file appears in the Attached box just below the Subject line. Normally, you would send the message at this point. Instead, you will save it with a new name.

18. Choose **File→Save As**.

Outlook prepares to save the message to the Documents library. Notice that the Subject line is proposed as the filename.

19. Navigate to the **Advisory Committee Meeting** folder and click **Save**.

20. Choose **File→Close**. Choose **Yes** if you are asked to save changes.

The message window closes. The Advisory Committee Meeting folder is visible again.

Task 3: Checking Email Replies (Outlook/Word)

After the board members review the draft agenda, they may have some comments and recommend revisions. In this task, you will check for replies and any necessary revisions.

DEVELOP YOUR SKILLS IN01-D02
Edit the Meeting Agenda

In this exercise, you will open email messages from board members to review their recommendations. You will edit the draft agenda as necessary.

1. Open the **Replies to Email Message** folder.

   Four replies appear as individual messages in the folder.

2. Open the email message from Chas, read it, and then close it.

3. Open the email message from Jaemi.

   He has comments; they are attached to the message.

4. Double-click to open the attached **Word document**.

   Notice the Protected View bar at the top of the document area. It's warning you that the file came from an email attachment and might not be safe. In this case, you know the attachment is from a reliable source.

5. Click the **Enable Editing** button on the right side of the Protected View bar.

6. Scan down the document. Then select and copy the highlighted revision.

   You will paste his revision into the draft agenda.

7. **Close** ☒ the Word document and then close the email message.

Edit the Agenda

8. Go back ◉ / ◉ to the **Advisory Committee Meeting** folder.

9. Open your **IN01-D01-MeetingAgenda** file and paste Jaemi's revision as a new bulleted item in the Proposed Initiatives section of the agenda.

10. Click the **Paste Options** SmartTag, and then choose **Keep Text Only** to make the new text match the agenda formatting.

    The yellow highlight disappears from the newly pasted revision.

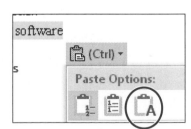

11. **Save** ⊟ the revision and then **minimize** ⊟ the Word window.

12. Go **forward** ◉ / ◉ to the **Replies to Email Message** folder.

13. Open the email message from Josie.

    Josie has marked two revisions in red in a partial copy of the agenda in her message.

14. Using any method you like, delete one line and insert a new line in the Proposed Initiatives list. (You might want to put the Word and message windows side by side on the screen.)

15. Choose **File→Save As** and then choose the **Advisory Committee Meeting** folder.

16. Rename the document `IN01-D02-FinalAgenda-[FirstInitialLastName]` and then **close** ⊠ the Word window.

17. **Close** ⊠ the message window.

18. Go back ⬅/⬅ to the **Advisory Committee Meeting** folder.

Task 4: Creating a Budget Workbook (Excel)

In this task, you will use Excel to produce a summary of the shelter's operating expenses. You will use this budget data later to create a factsheet about the shelter. You will also use it to create charts for the factsheet and a PowerPoint presentation.

DEVELOP YOUR SKILLS IN01-D03
Create a Budget Workbook

In this exercise, you will create a budget workbook in Excel and use its data to create a chart of the shelter's operating expenses.

1. Start **Excel 2013** and then create a **Blank Workbook**.

2. Double-click the **Sheet1** tab and rename it **Budget Summary Data**.

3. Choose **Page Layout→Themes** and apply the same theme you used for the agenda document.

4. Use the following notes to enter the budget information for the previous year:
   - Format the title, subtitle, and headings to appear similar to the first two rows of the example.
   - Format number cells to display commas and no decimals, as shown.
   - Create and copy formulas to calculate totals for the rows and columns.

	A	B	C	D	E	F
1	Help for the Homeless					
2	2014 Budget Summary					
3		Q1	Q2	Q3	Q4	Totals
4	Mortgage & Insurance	11,337	11,337	11,337	11,337	45,348
5	Utilities	2,021	1,464	1,504	1,809	6,798
6	Food	5,480	4,512	3,452	5,437	18,881
7	Staff Salaries	17,685	17,685	17,685	17,685	70,740
8	Maintenance & Repairs	2,188	3,113	3,928	3,392	12,621
9	Outreach & Fundraising	820	2,006	576	712	4,114
10	Grand Totals	39,531	40,117	38,482	40,372	158,502

5. Save the workbook in the **Advisory Committee Meeting** folder as `IN01-D03-CommitteeBudget-[FirstInitialLastName]`.

Create a Chart

6. Follow these steps to select the data for a pie chart that will summarize the year's budget allocation:

Take care *not* to select the Grand Totals row at the bottom.

🅐 Drag down from **cell A4** to **cell A9**.

🅑 Hold down ⌈Ctrl⌉ and drag down from **cell F4** to **cell F9**. Release ⌈Ctrl⌉.

	A	B	C	D	E	F
3		Q1	Q2	Q3	Q4	Totals
4	Mortgage & Insurance	11,337	11,337	11,337	11,337	45,348
5	Utilities	2,021	1,464	1,504	1,809	6,798
6	Food	5,480	4,512	3,452	5,437	18,881
7	Staff Salaries	17,685	17,685	17,685	17,685	70,740
8	Maintenance & Repairs	2,188	3,113	3,928	3,392	12,621
9	Outreach & Fundraising	820	2,006	576	712	4,114
10	Grand Totals	39,531	40,117	38,482	40,372	158,502

This technique allows you to select nonadjacent cells for the chart.

7. Follow these steps to select the chart type:

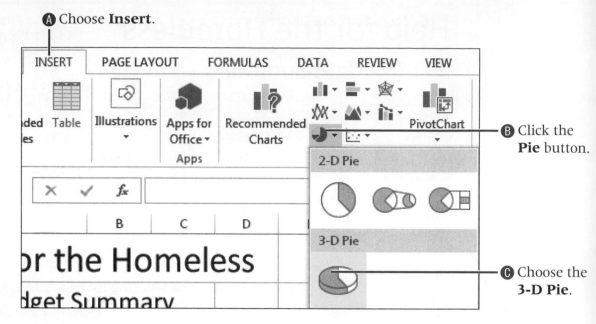

Ⓐ Choose **Insert**.

Ⓑ Click the **Pie** button.

Ⓒ Choose the **3-D Pie**.

The new chart appears on the worksheet. It may cover some of the data.

8. Follow these steps to add labels to the chart:

Ⓐ Click the **pie chart**.　　Ⓑ Choose **Chart Elements**.

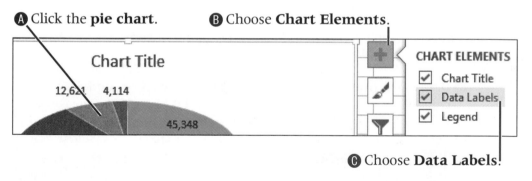

Ⓒ Choose **Data Labels**.

Dollar amounts appear for each pie slice. Notice that the Chart Elements menu remains open, ready for you to make additional adjustments.

9. Follow these steps to rearrange the chart legend:

Ⓐ If necessary, click inside the chart.

Ⓑ If necessary, choose **Chart Elements**.

Ⓒ Point at **Legend** and then click the **menu button**.

Ⓓ Choose **Right**.

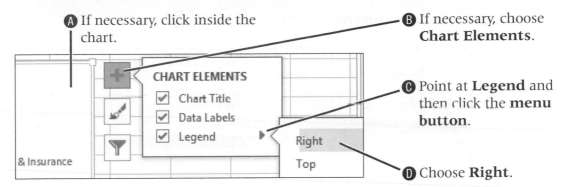

10. Drag the chart to the right of the data cells (so it doesn't cover them).

11. Follow these steps to change the title:

Ⓐ Click the **Chart Title** element.

Ⓑ Type **2014 Budget Summary** and then tap ⎡Enter⎤.

12. **Save** 🖫 the workbook and then minimize the **Excel window**.

Task 5: Querying a Database (Access/Excel)

One piece of information required for the meeting is data on occupancy at the shelter over the past three years. The shelter maintains a database with records of each week's occupancy.

DEVELOP YOUR SKILLS IN01-D04

Query a Database for Occupancy History

In this exercise, you will query the shelter database to summarize information on shelter occupancy. In the next exercise, you will create an occupancy chart in Excel.

1. Start **Access**. Open **IN01-D04-ShelterDatabase** from the **Advisory Committee Meeting** folder and save it as **IN01-D04-ShelterDatabase-[FirstInitialLastName]**.

   Choose Enable Content if Access displays a security warning.

2. If necessary, choose **Tables** on the Objects panel. Then, double-click to open the **Shelter Occupancy Data** table and briefly review the table data.

   The table contains week-to-week data on shelter occupants. It's always a good idea to familiarize yourself with data before you run a query. This way, you are more likely to spot a mistake if the query does not work as intended. In this table, notice that 300–500 shelter beds were occupied each week.

3. Taking care not to close the Access program window, **close** ☒ the table window.

4. Choose **Create→Queries→Query Wizard** .

5. Choose **Simple Query Wizard** and click **OK**.

6. Select the **Week** and **Occupants** fields for the query, and click **Next**.

Available Fields:		Selected Fields:
ID	>	Week
Male		Occupants
Female	>>	

7. Choose **Summary** and then click the **Summary Options** button.

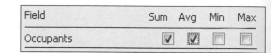

Field	Sum	Avg	Min	Max
Occupants	☑	☑	☐	☐

8. Place a checkmark in the **Sum** and **Avg** boxes, and click **OK**.

9. Click **Next** and then choose **Year**.

10. Click **Next** and then click **Finish**.

    The result of the query appears in a new window, similar to the following figure.

Week By Yea ▾	Sum Of Occu ▾	Avg Of Occu ▾
2011	21151	399.075471698
2012	17368	334
2013	19570	376.346153846

Copy the Query Results

11. Choose **Home→Find→Select→ Select All**.

    All the cells in the query are selected.

12. Choose **Home→Clipboard→Copy**.

13. **Close** ☒ the Access window.

    Even though you are exiting the program from which you have given the Copy command, the information is still on the Clipboard, ready for you to paste later.

Paste the Query Results into Excel

14. Restore the **Excel** window to the Desktop.

15. Click the **New Sheet** button beside the current worksheet.

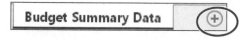

16. Double-click the **Sheet1** tab and rename it `Occupancy Data`.

17. Select **cell A2** and paste the data you copied in step 12.

    Excel pastes the results of the query you copied in step 12 onto the new worksheet.

18. Select **cell A1** and type `Annual Occupancy Data` as a heading for the worksheet.

Format the Data

The data could use some formatting to make it easier to read.

19. Select the **range B3:C5**; apply the **Comma format** and decrease the decimal places to none.

20. **Save** 🖫 the workbook.

Task 6: Creating a Column Chart (Excel)

Now that you have the data from the Access database, you can use Excel to create a new chart of this data.

DEVELOP YOUR SKILLS IN01-D05
Create a Column Chart

In this exercise, you will use Excel to create a column chart of the shelter occupancy data queried in the previous exercise.

1. Select the **range A2:C5** and then choose **Home→Cells→Format→AutoFit Column Width**.

   Notice the small green triangles at the top-left corner of each year cell in column A. This alerts you to a possible problem with the data.

2. Select the **range A3:A5** and then click the **Trace Error** ◈ SmartTag button.

   Excel displays Number Stored as Text as the error. This is not a problem in this case, since you will not be performing calculations on the years.

3. Choose **Ignore Error** from the Trace Error menu.

   The green triangles disappear.

Create the Column Chart

4. Select the **range A3:B5** (the Week by Year and Sum of Occupants data).

5. Choose **Insert→Charts→Column→3-D Clustered Column**.

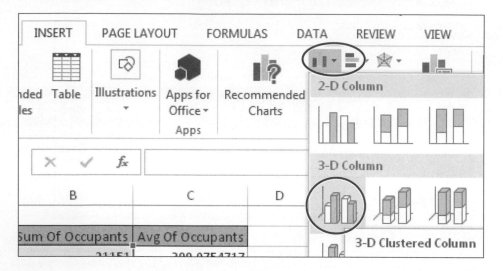

6. Rename the chart title to **Total Occupants, By Year**.

7. Drag the chart by its border to reposition it below the data.

8. **Save** 🖫 the workbook. Then **minimize** ⬜ the Excel window.

Task 7: Creating a Factsheet Document (Word/Excel)

Now that the Excel data is complete, you will create a factsheet in Word. You will also bring some of the Excel data into the factsheet.

Import Excel Data into a Word Document

In this exercise, you will paste data from Excel into a Word document for use as a factsheet about the shelter.

1. Start **Word** and begin typing the following factsheet. Consider these points as you work.

   - Use font and paragraph formatting as desired to make the document appear readable and professional. (See the sample figure below.)

   - Use tab settings to neatly align the factsheet data items.

   - Choose **Home→Paragraph→Bottom Border** to place a line below the Factsheet and Current Budget subheadings. (You may need to choose the command from the arrow portion of the button.)

Help for the Homeless Factsheet

Location:	2525 Center Street, Espanola
Founded in:	1983
Staff:	1 full-time manager
	2 part-time evening coordinators
	1 part-time counselor
	1 part-time legal advocate
	24 volunteers
Capacity:	80 beds
Current Budget:	

2. Save the document in the **Advisory Committee Meeting** folder as `IN01-D06-Factsheet-[FirstInitialLastName]`.

Import the Excel Budget Data

Now you will copy and paste budget data from the Excel workbook into the factsheet.

3. Activate the **Excel** window and display the **Budget Summary Data** worksheet.

4. Select the **range A3:F10** (all data and column headings, but not the worksheet title and subtitle).

5. Choose **Home→Clipboard→Copy**.

6. Activate the **Word** window and place the insertion point on the line below the **Current Budget** subheading (tap ⌑Enter⌑ if necessary).

7. Choose **Home→Clipboard→Paste**.

Word pastes the table, keeping the Excel font formatting.

8. Follow these steps to make the pasted data match the Word document style:

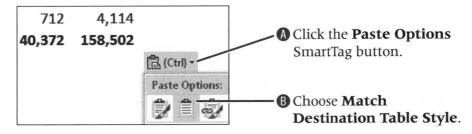

Ⓐ Click the **Paste Options** SmartTag button.

Ⓑ Choose **Match Destination Table Style**.

Now the table fonts match the fonts used in the factsheet. It has a pretty ugly grid of borders, however. Let's change that.

9. Click anywhere within the table in **Word**, choose **Table Tools→Design→Table Styles**, and choose any **table style**.

Word formats the table to the style you chose.

Import the Occupancy Column Chart

10. Activate the **Excel** window and display the **Occupancy Data** worksheet.

11. Select and copy the column chart.

12. Make **Word** the active window.

13. Use [Ctrl]+[End] to jump to the bottom of the Word document and tap [Enter].

14. Type the new subheading **Shelter Occupancy** and tap [Enter].

15. Paste the column chart below the new subheading.

The chart appears at the insertion point. Depending on the theme you've chosen, the chart might end up on a separate page. If necessary, you can scale it so everything fits.

Scale and Format the Chart

16. If the chart fits the bottom of the page, skip to step 18. Otherwise, click once to select the chart.

A selection border appears around the chart.

17. Point at the **bottom-right corner** of the chart and then hold down the mouse button and drag the border up and left until it jumps up to the first page.

18. Choose **Chart Tools→Design→Chart Styles** and choose a **Quick Style** you think goes well with the rest of the factsheet.

19. **Save** ⊟ the document and **minimize** ⊟ the **Word** window.

20. **Minimize** ⊟ the **Excel** window, if it is still visible.

Task 8: Creating a Presentation (PowerPoint/Word)

Now that you have created the handouts for the meeting (Agenda and Factsheet), you are ready to create a PowerPoint presentation to help guide the meeting. A computer projection display can show the slides from a notebook computer during the meeting. The slides can also be printed for handing out. You will use content from the Agenda document to create the presentation. You will also place the two Excel charts on slides.

Importing Slides from a Word Outline

PowerPoint can use a Word outline to create new slides in a presentation. You simply insert the Word document with your outline into the PowerPoint presentation. PowerPoint lays out the information onto slides with titles and bullets according to the organization of the outline.

Styles

In order for PowerPoint to interpret the outline properly, the Word outline *must* be formatted with specific heading styles. (A *style* is a method used to apply formatting to paragraphs and text characters.) You applied styles (Heading 1, Heading 2, etc.) to your meeting agenda. When you import the agenda into PowerPoint, those styles help it create new slides.

In-place Editing of Office Program Objects

When you paste an object such as an Excel chart into PowerPoint, you can edit the object by using standard Excel commands. For example, you can edit the fonts used for the chart or change the chart type after the chart has been pasted. To activate this in-place editing, simply double-click the chart on the PowerPoint slide, and then use normal editing commands to revise the chart.

DEVELOP YOUR SKILLS IN01-D07
Create a Presentation

In this exercise, you will use PowerPoint to create a presentation to guide the advisory panel meeting.

1. Start **PowerPoint** and create a new presentation using any theme you wish. Your theme doesn't have to match the one used in the Word documents.

2. On the title slide, enter the following:
   - Title: `Advisory Committee Meeting`
   - Subtitle: `Help for the Homeless`

3. Save the presentation in the **Advisory Committee Meeting** folder as `IN01-D07-Presentation-[FirstInitialLastName]`.

Prepare the Agenda for Importing

To import smoothly into PowerPoint, you need to make some modifications to the original agenda outline.

4. If necessary, start **Word** and open your **IN01-D02-FinalAgenda** document.

5. Choose **File→Save As** and rename the file `IN01-D07-FinalAgendaOutline-[FirstInitialLastName]`.

   This renaming keeps the original agenda document intact for printing later.

6. Follow these steps to begin revising the agenda:

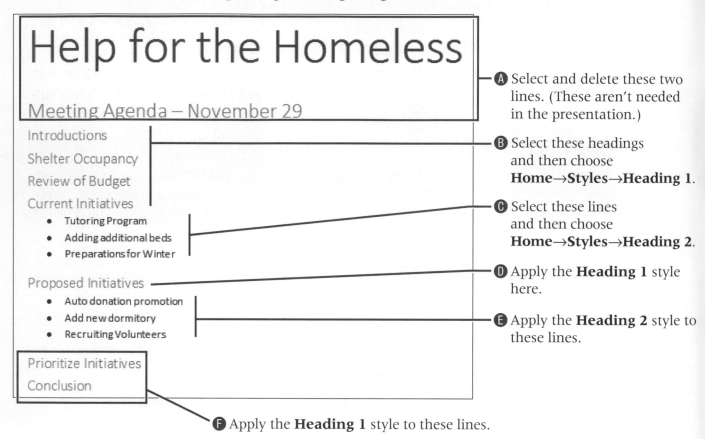

Help for the Homeless

Meeting Agenda – November 29

Introductions
Shelter Occupancy
Review of Budget
Current Initiatives
- Tutoring Program
- Adding additional beds
- Preparations for Winter

Proposed Initiatives
- Auto donation promotion
- Add new dormitory
- Recruiting Volunteers

Prioritize Initiatives
Conclusion

Ⓐ Select and delete these two lines. (These aren't needed in the presentation.)

Ⓑ Select these headings and then choose **Home→Styles→Heading 1**.

Ⓒ Select these lines and then choose **Home→Styles→Heading 2**.

Ⓓ Apply the **Heading 1** style here.

Ⓔ Apply the **Heading 2** style to these lines.

Ⓕ Apply the **Heading 1** style to these lines.

7. **Save** 🖫 and then close the document.

   PowerPoint won't import an outline from an open document.

Import the Outline into the Presentation

8. Choose **Home→Slides→New Slide menu ▼→Slides From Outline**. (The command is near the bottom of the menu list.)

9. Navigate to the **Advisory Committee Meeting** folder, choose your **IN01-D07-FinalAgendaOutline** document, and click **Insert**.

   The outline flows into your presentation. Notice that each Level 1 item has created a new slide automatically. The Level 2 lines are now bulleted items on slides.

Reset the Slides to Use Default Theme Elements

One potential problem with the import is that the document formatting also went into the presentation. This font and color scheme probably doesn't match well with your PowerPoint theme, so you will reset the new slides to use the theme fonts and colors.

10. Click the **title slide** in the Slides panel on the left. Then use [Ctrl] + [A] to select all slides in the Slides panel.

11. Choose **Home→Slides→Reset**.

PowerPoint sets the formatting for all imported text to the default font and color settings of the theme. This ensures that all of the text and its formatting are easy to read and consistent with the presentation theme.

Import an Excel Chart to a Slide

12. Display the **Shelter Occupancy** slide and then choose **Home→Slides→Layout→Title and Content**.

13. If necessary, start **Excel** and open the **Committee Budget** workbook.

14. Select the **Column** chart on the **Occupancy Data** worksheet and then choose **Home→Clipboard→Copy**.

15. Activate the **PowerPoint** window and click once to select the content (lower) section of the slide (not the heading).

16. Choose **Home→Clipboard→Paste**.

The chart enlarges to fill the content area of the slide automatically. Notice that the color scheme of the bar chart has changed to conform to the PowerPoint theme.

Perform In-place Editing on the Excel Chart

The numbers along the left and bottom axes of the chart are too small to read. You will adjust the font setting to make these numbers larger.

In the next step, take care that the mouse pointer is shaped like a pointer and not like move arrows, as shown below.

 Correct (pointer)   **Incorrect (move arrows)**

17. Follow these steps to adjust the font size:

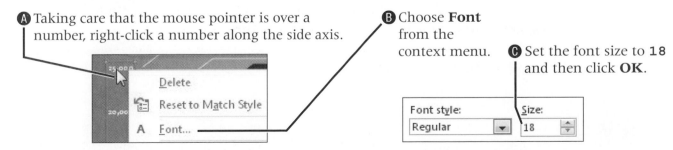

Ⓐ Taking care that the mouse pointer is over a number, right-click a number along the side axis.

Ⓑ Choose **Font** from the context menu.

Ⓒ Set the font size to **18** and then click **OK**.

18. Resize the Years along the bottom of the chart to **18 points**.

Notice that PowerPoint resizes the bar chart to accommodate the larger numbers.

19. Click anywhere outside the chart border to view the result.

20. Save 🖫 the presentation.

It's always a good idea to save when you've just finished a significant chunk of work.

Import and Edit Another Excel Chart

21. Activate the **Excel** window and display the **Budget Summary Data** worksheet. Select and copy the pie chart.

22. Activate the **PowerPoint** window and select the **Review of Budget** slide. Then choose **Home→Slides→Layout→Title and Content**.

23. Click once on the content area of the slide and paste the pie chart.

Notice that the text labels are too small to read. You must again adjust their size.

24. Set the font size for the numbers found on or near each pie slice of the chart to **18 points** and then click anywhere outside the chart boundary.

25. Set the font size for the legend text to **18 points** and then click anywhere outside the chart boundary.

26. Select the chart title and then tap ⎡Delete⎤.

27. Save 🖫 the presentation.

Finish the Presentation

28. Display **slide 2** and add the following bulleted items to the slide:

- ■ Shelter Staff
- ■ Shelter Board of Directors
- ■ Civic and Business Leaders

29. Display **slide 7** and then choose **Home→Slides→Layout→Title Only**.

30. Display **slide 8** and choose **Home→Slides→Layout→Title Slide**.

Now this slide matches the style of the first slide.

31. Save 🖫 the presentation.

32. Choose **Slide Show→Start Slide Show→From Beginning**.

PowerPoint starts the slide show at slide 1.

33. Navigate through all of the slides and verify that they display properly. Then return to the **Normal** slide view.

34. Close ⎡×⎤ PowerPoint and any other open program windows.

Task 9: Printing Handouts (Word/PowerPoint)

Now that the files you will use as handouts in the meeting are complete, you are ready to review and print them. You will want to scan the files before printing and then examine the printouts. Sometimes a mistake you overlook on the computer screen can be spotted on a printout.

DEVELOP YOUR SKILLS IN01-D08
Review and Print Handouts

In this exercise, you will use PowerPoint to print handouts for the meeting.

1. Start **Word** and open your **IN01-D02-FinalAgenda** (not the outline) and **IN01-D06-Factsheet** documents from the **Advisory Committee Meeting** folder.

2. Review each document for spelling and other types of errors. Is the formatting consistent within each document?

3. Save each document if you make any revisions and then print them.

4. Review each printout for neatness and typographical errors. Revise and reprint the documents if necessary. Close the documents and Word when you are finished.

Save PowerPoint Handouts in PDF Format
Rather than print copies of the PowerPoint slides, you will create a PDF document ready to attach to an email message.

5. Start **PowerPoint** and open your **IN01-D07-Presentation** file.

6. Review the presentation one last time and make any necessary revisions.

7. Save the file when you are finished.

8. Choose **File→Save As**, choose the **current folder**, and then follow these steps to save handouts in PDF format:

Ⓐ Rename the file **IN01-PresentationPDF-D08-[FirstInitialLastName]**. Choose **PDF** as the file type.

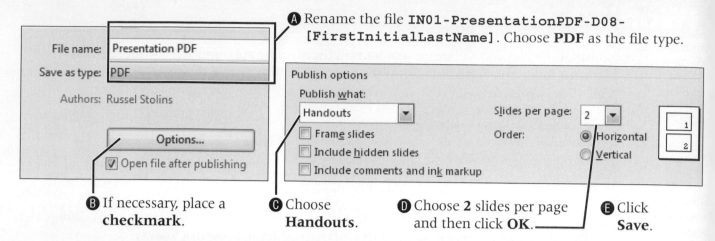

Ⓑ If necessary, place a **checkmark**.

Ⓒ Choose **Handouts**.

Ⓓ Choose **2** slides per page and then click **OK**.

Ⓔ Click **Save**.

PowerPoint opens the PDF file. If you are running Windows 8, the PDF may open in the Reader app (and you will no longer be in the traditional desktop). Anyone with the free Adobe Reader program or the Microsoft Reader app in Windows 8 (or other third-party software) can open this file; they won't need PowerPoint to view the slides.

9. Scroll through the PDF file and review the conversion.

10. *(Windows 8 Only)* Use Alt + Tab from the keyboard to return to PowerPoint on the traditional desktop if the PDF opened in the Microsoft Reader app. Or tap the Windows ⊞ key, then click Desktop.

11. If necessary, make revisions, save the presentation, and repeat step 8 to save the revised handouts.

12. **Close** × the PowerPoint window.

Index

Notes

Notes

Notes